Windows® 10
IN DEPTH

Second Edition

Brian Knittel
Paul McFedries

800 East 96th Street
Indianapolis, Indiana 46240 USA

WINDOWS® 10 IN DEPTH

ISBN-13: 978-0-7897-5977-1

ISBN-10: 0-7897-5977-2

Library of Congress Control Number: 2017962807

1 18

Trademarks

Editor-in-Chief
Greg Wiegand

Senior Acquisitions Editor
Laura Norman

Development Editor
Rick Kughen

Managing Editor
Sandra Schroeder

Senior Project Editor
Tonya Simpson

Copy Editor
Rick Kughen

Indexer
Lisa Stumpf

Proofreader
Gill Editorial Services

Technical Editor
Karen Weinstein

Editorial Assistant
Cindy Teeters

Cover Designer
Chuti Prasertsith

Compositor
codemantra

Warning and Disclaimer

Every effort has been made to make this book as complete and as accurate as possible, but no warranty or fitness is implied. The information provided is on an "as is" basis. The authors and the publisher shall have neither liability nor responsibility to any person or entity with respect to any loss or damages arising from the information contained in this book.

Special Sales

For information about buying this title in bulk quantities, or for special sales opportunities (which may include electronic versions; custom cover designs; and content particular to your business, training goals, marketing focus, or branding interests), please contact our corporate sales department at

corpsales@pearsoned.com or (800) 382-3419.

For government sales inquiries, please contact

governmentsales@pearsoned.com.

For questions about sales outside the U.S., please contact

intlcs@pearson.com.

CONTENTS AT A GLANCE

CONTENTS

III Multimedia and Imaging

10 Windows Media Player   243

11 Windows and Imaging Devices   257

12 Scanning and Faxing   271

ABOUT THE AUTHORS

Brian Knittel is a software developer, consultant, and writer. He has authored or coauthored many of Que's best-selling Windows books, including Que's leading Windows books, *Windows 10 In Depth*, *Windows 8.1 In Depth*, *Windows 8 In Depth*, *Windows 7 In Depth*, and *Special Edition Using Microsoft Windows* for Windows 2000 and XP. Brian is also the author of *Windows 7 and Vista Guide to Scripting, Automation, and Command Line Tools* and *Windows XP Under the Hood*. In addition, Brian coauthored *Upgrading and Repairing Microsoft Windows* with Scott Mueller.

Paul McFedries is the author of more than 90 computer books that have sold more than 4 million copies worldwide. His recent titles include the Microsoft Press book *MOS 2016 Study Guide for Microsoft Excel Expert* and the Que Publishing books *PCs for Grownups*, *Formulas and Functions for Excel 2016*, *Fixing Your Computer Absolute Beginner's Guide*, and *My Office 2016*. Paul also is the proprietor of Word Spy (www.wordspy.com), a website devoted to tracking new words and phrases as they enter the English language.

Dedication

To my parents, who supported every odd interest and hobby that led to this topsy-turvy career. —Brian

To Karen, who gives new meaning to the phrase "better half." —Paul

ACKNOWLEDGMENTS

It's an honor to work with a highly respected publisher like Que. We are grateful to our editor-in-chief, Greg Wiegand, and executive editor, Laura Norman, who played matchmaker and shepherd and brought together a great team to write and produce this book. We are ever so pleased that Rick Kughen was back on our team as development editor with his incisive edits and insightful suggestions, and we extend a big thank you to Tonya Simpson and Dhayanidhi Karunanidhi for keeping everyone on track and making the production process seem effortless. Don't let those job descriptions fool you—at Que at least, titles such as "development editor" and "copy editor" don't begin to describe the breadth of the contributions that each team member makes to each book.

We'd also like to acknowledge the support of our technical editor, Karen Weinstein, who meticulously checked every detail and tried every procedure. Then, there is an entire army of people who labor largely unseen and unthanked—the people who do the real work—the editorial, indexing, layout, art, proofing, and other production staff at Que. And finally, thanks to everyone from the marketing and sales folks at Que to the booksellers who ensured that this book made it from the printing press to your hands.

We also thank Maureen Maloney at Waterside Productions for great work in taking care of the legal mumbo-jumbo part of the book business.

WE WANT TO HEAR FROM YOU!

As the reader of this book, *you* are our most important critic and commentator. We value your opinion and want to know what we're doing right, what we could do better, what areas you'd like to see us publish in, and any other words of wisdom you're willing to pass our way.

We welcome your comments. You can email or write to let us know what you did or didn't like about this book—as well as what we can do to make our books better.

Please note that we cannot help you with technical problems related to the topic of this book.

When you write, please be sure to include this book's title and author as well as your name and email address. We will carefully review your comments and share them with the author and editors who worked on the book.

Email: feedback@quepublishing.com

Mail: Que Publishing
ATTN: Reader Feedback
800 East 96th Street
Indianapolis, IN 46240 USA

READER SERVICES

Register your copy of *Windows 10 In Depth*, Second Edition at quepublishing.com for convenient access to downloads, updates, and corrections as they become available. To start the registration process, go to quepublishing.com/register and log in or create an account*. Enter the product ISBN, 9780789759771, and click Submit. Once the process is complete, you will find any available bonus content under Registered Products.

*Be sure to check the box that you would like to hear from us in order to receive exclusive discounts on future editions of this product.

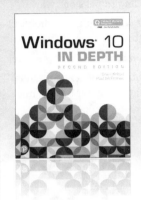

Introduction

Welcome

We shall not cease from exploration

And the end of all our exploring

Will be to arrive where we started

And know the place for the first time.

—T. S. Eliot

Thank you for purchasing or considering the purchase of *Windows 10 In Depth*, 2nd Edition.

To get right to the point, Windows 10 is a bold, thoughtful, and well-executed step forward in Microsoft's quest to create a single operating system that looks and acts the same across all devices, from desktop PCs to tablets, notebooks to telephones, and eventually even vending machines and gaming consoles. Rather than taking Apple's approach of having one OS for computers (OS X) and a second OS for phones and tablets (iOS), Microsoft has committed itself to the "One Ring to Rule Them All" principle and has engineered Windows 10 to efficiently manage both types of devices.

If this sounds familiar, it's because Microsoft attempted to do this in 2013 with Windows 8, which was, not to put too fine a point on it, universally reviled. If there was one positive thing that you could say about it, it was that in comparison it made Windows Vista look like a spectacular success. There were two main problems: first, a lack of flexibility, especially on desktop computers. While a full-screen, one-application-at-a-time interface is sensible on a phone or tablet, on a desktop computer, it was a productivity drain of black hole proportions. The second and worse problem was that Microsoft could have made it work well but refused to. The company's attitude at the time was essentially, "This is what you're going to get, and it doesn't matter if you don't like it. You're stuck with it, so get used to it."

It turns out that this wasn't a spectacularly effective business strategy.

So, after firing the CEO and the Windows Division president, eating nearly $2 billion in losses on the first generation of its Surface Tablet product line, and skipping an entire version number just to show that it really moved on, a much humbler, much more responsive Microsoft released a new operating system. It kept what was good about Windows 8 and either tossed out or fixed the rest. The folks at Microsoft listened...really listened; in fact, they let the public vote on how Windows 10 would work. The result is very, very good. And, in the two-plus years since it was initially released, it's only gotten better.

After the Windows 8 debacle, Microsoft backtracked on two key points:

- On traditional desktop, laptop, and tablet computers, "Modern" apps no longer have to run full screen, one at a time. They can now run in normal windows, which you can move around and open and close. ("Modern" apps are the tablet-style apps that debuted in Windows 8. We talk about this in Chapter 1.)

- The Start menu is back. It's modernized, but it's recognizable as the Windows Start menu that we've had since 1995.

And still, Windows 10 has enough of the new to be interesting. There's an online personal digital assistant named Cortana. There are Modern apps and the Windows Store from which to find and install them. And, according to Microsoft, this is the last version of Windows you'll ever have to install. The plan is to incrementally improve and polish it bit by bit over the years, through frequent automatic updates.

If you're upgrading from Windows 8.1, you'll find that this version of Windows is easier to use. There are fewer "secrets." You know what we mean: those invisible places you had to click or bizarre gestures you had to make with your finger to perform even basic tasks.

And, despite all the new features, if you skipped Windows 8 and are moving up, or you are considering moving up, from Windows 7 or XP, you'll find that almost everything you know about Windows still applies to Windows 10—you just have to learn some new routes to reach old places. In this book, we show you not only how to use all the new features, but also how to quickly and easily navigate to the parts of Windows that you're already familiar with.

This book covers the main desktop, notebook, and tablet versions of Windows 10: Windows 10 Home, Windows 10 Pro (which includes advanced features such as virtualization, encryption, Remote Desktop hosting, and group policy), and Windows 10 Enterprise (which includes additional features for enterprise IT support and security). Windows 10 Education version is Windows 10 Enterprise licensed for educational institutions. We cover how to use Enterprise and Education, although we don't cover the server-side management tools that are supplied with Windows Server operating systems. This book will also help you work with some of the newer, more arcane editions of Windows 10, with a few caveats:

- **Windows 10 Pro Education**—This is Windows 10 with special sales and licensing arrangements for academic institutions. It has mostly the same feature set as Windows 10 Pro but displays fewer "suggestions" (advertising). Administrators who manage Windows 10 in an educational setting should visit docs.microsoft.com and search for "Windows 10 configuration recommendations for education customers" for configuration tips.

- **Windows 10 S**—This is Windows 10 Pro with two restrictions: It can only install apps downloaded from the Windows Store, not traditional desktop applications, and it can't be joined to an enterprise domain network. The tips and management procedures in this book will work for Windows 10 S; you just won't be able to install some of the third-party programs we discuss.

- **Windows 10 Pro for Workstations**—This is Windows 10 Pro licensed for beefy computers with up to four separate processors, very large amounts of RAM, and high-end networking adapters. This book covers management of this Windows version, but we don't describe how to format secondary hard disks with the new Resilient File System (ReFS).

Although some of what we cover here also applies to the small-device version called Windows Mobile, we don't explicitly cover that version in this book.

Why This Book?

Windows has been evolving, mostly incrementally, since 1985. Each new version has new features. Some you can figure out on your own, but some require explanation. Some features, such as networking, are easy enough to use but are very complex underneath, and setting them up can involve making complex technical decisions. In some cases, years might go by between the times that you use some management tool, and your human random access memory might need refreshing. Computer books come to the rescue for all of these needs, giving step-by-step instructions, helpful advice, and detailed reference material for the future.

Although usually the path from one version of Windows to the next is smooth and straight, every so often there is a big bump in the road. The first was with Windows 95, where the Start button appeared and the right mouse button suddenly became very important. The next bump was Windows XP, which marked the move from MS-DOS to the Windows NT operating system kernel, to a security system for files, and to a whole new way of managing Windows. It happened again with Windows 8. The Start button disappeared, and you had to use arcane "gestures" and tools to get anywhere.

Windows 10 fixes most of those problems, but there are still a bunch of shortcuts and tricks that you'll want to know about. We found these out for ourselves as we worked with Windows 10 daily, for months, as we wrote this book. We didn't have anyone's guidance then, but you do now. In this book, we'll show you how to manage the Windows 10 interface without a struggle. We've also tracked the changes made to Windows 10 since it was initially released, and we have updated our procedures and tips in this book to use the new ways of doing old things.

In addition to getting you through the steeper parts of the Windows 10 learning curve, we'll give you the benefit of our combined 50-plus years of experience working with, writing about, and even writing software for Microsoft Windows. We know what parts of using and managing Windows are confusing. We know the easy ways to do things. We've seen just about every bug and glitch, have been through just about every ugly scenario one can come up with, and have made just about every mistake one can make. Therefore, we can spare you from having to repeat some of them.

You might also appreciate that, in this book, we can be honest with you. We don't work for Microsoft, so we can tell you what we really feel about the product: the good, the bad, and the downright ugly. If we say something's great, it's because we think it is; and if we hate something, we'll tell you, and we'll try to show you how to avoid it.

And finally, as Windows 10 evolves over time, so does this book. If you're reading this paragraph (which wasn't in the first edition), it's because we are tracking Windows 10's evolution and updating this book through Que's Content Update Program. Your purchase gives you access to the most up-to-date, online version of the book.

Refer to the Content Update Program page in the front section of this book for more information.

Our book addresses both home and business computer users. As we wrote, we imagined that you, our reader, are a friend or coworker who is familiar enough with your computer to know what it's capable of but might not know the details of how to make it all happen. So we show you, in a helpful, friendly, professional tone. We make an effort to tell you not just what to do, but why you're doing it. If you understand how Windows and its component parts work, you can get through rough patches: diagnosing problems, fixing things that the built-in wizards can't fix, and otherwise solving problems creatively.

And if you're looking for power-user tips and some nitty-gritty details, we make sure you get those, too. We try to make clear what information is essential for you to understand and what is optional for just those of you who are especially interested.

However, no one book can do it all. As the title says, this book is about the versions of Windows 10 that run on desktop computers, notebooks, and mobile devices (tablets) that have an Intel-compatible processor. Our coverage of the new Modern interface, Start menu, apps, management tools, and setup panels, for the most part, apply to tablets that run Windows 10 Mobile; however, a few parts of this book won't apply to those devices, and if you have one, you might want to get a book that specifically addresses that operating system.

And, as we mentioned earlier in this introduction, we also don't have room to cover how to set up or manage the various Microsoft Server operating systems, such as Windows Server 2016, or how to deploy or manage Windows 10 using enterprise tools that are provided only with those operating systems. For these topics, you'll need to consult a Windows Server book.

Because of space limitations, only one chapter is devoted to coverage of the numerous Windows 10 command-line utilities, its batch file language, Windows Script Host, and Windows PowerShell. For that (in spades!), you might want to check out Brian's book *Windows 7 and Vista Guide to Scripting, Automation, and Command Line Tools*, which is equally applicable to Windows 10.

Even when you've become a Windows 10 pro, we think you'll find this book to be a valuable source of reference information in the future. Both the table of contents and the very complete index provide an easy means for locating information when you need it quickly.

How Our Book Is Organized

Although this book advances logically from beginning to end, it's written so that you can jump in at any location, quickly get the information you need, and get out. You don't have to read it from start to finish. (Remember, the index at the back of the book is your best friend.)

If you're new to Windows 10, however, we do recommend that you read Chapter 3, "Your First Hour with Windows 10," and Chapter 4, "Using the Windows 10 Interface," in their entirety. Windows 10 has new ways of doing things that aren't always entirely intuitive or obvious. Reading these two chapters might save you hours of frustration.

This book is broken down into six major parts. Here's the scoop on each one:

Part I, "Starting Out with Windows 10," introduces the new Windows 10 user interface and shows you how to install Windows 10 on a new computer or upgrade an older version of Windows to Windows 10. In addition, we take you on a one-hour guided tour that shows you the best of the new Windows 10 features, and we walk you through making essential settings and adjustments that will help you get the most out of your computer. Consider this the Windows 10 version of "freshman orientation."

In Part II, "Using Windows 10," we cover the new Modern user interface and apps, managing documents and files, starting and stopping applications, searching for files and media, printing, and using the included desktop accessories and accessibility tools. In other words, this section covers all the routine, day-to-day stuff. However, it's very important material: Windows 10 does many things differently, and using it can be frustrating and confusing, especially if you don't know the basic tricks and techniques.

Part III, "Multimedia and Imaging," covers the Windows 10 bells and whistles, including Windows Media Player, imaging devices, using a document scanner, faxing, and all the other media tools that ship with Windows.

In Part IV, "Windows 10 and the Internet," we help you set up an Internet connection and then move on to cover the Windows 10 Internet tools. The final chapter in this part shows you how to diagnose Internet connection problems.

Any home or office with two or more computers needs a local area network (LAN) to easily transfer and back up files, share printers, and use a shared high-speed Internet connection. In Part V, "Networking," we walk you through setting up a network in your home or office, and show you how to take advantage of it in day-to-day use. We also show you how easy it is to share a DSL or cable Internet connection with all your computers at once, show you how to network with other operating systems, and, finally, help you fix it when it all stops working.

Part VI, "Maintaining Windows 10," covers system configuration, maintenance, and troubleshooting. We tell you how to work with the huge assortment of Windows 10 management tools, show you various useful tweaks and customizations, take you through some hard disk management techniques, give you advice on troubleshooting and repairing problems, show you how to manage software and hardware, and give you the details on editing the Windows Registry. And for real power users, we show how to use and tweak the command-line interface.

When Windows was introduced more than two decades ago, computer viruses, online fraud, and hacking were only starting to emerge as threats. Today (thanks in great part to gaping security holes in previous versions of Windows), computer threats are a worldwide problem, online and offline. In Part VII, "Security," we provide a 360-degree view of the ways in which Windows protects you and your data. Here, you'll find out both what Windows 10 will do to help you and what you must do for yourself. We cover protection against viruses and spyware, data loss and theft, hackers and snoops, and fraud and spam—in that order.

Part VIII, "Windows On the Move," shows you how to get the most out of Windows 10 when either you or your computer, or both, are on the go. We show you how to use a touch or pen interface on a Windows tablet or some other mobile PC, how to use wireless networking safely, how to get the most out of your laptop or tablet PC when traveling, and how to connect to remote networks. We also show you how to remotely connect to and use your Windows 10 computer from anywhere in the world.

Appendix A, "Virtualization," explains how to use Microsoft's Hyper-V virtualization technology to run other operating systems side by side with Windows 10, or to run Windows 10 within some other operating system. This can be an excellent alternative to setting up a dual-boot system. Finally, Appendix B, "Command-Line Utilities," takes you through a tour of various Windows command-line utilities.

Conventions Used in This Book

Special conventions are used throughout this book to help you get the most from the book and from Windows 10.

Text Conventions

Various typefaces in this book identify terms and other special objects. These special typefaces include the following:

Type	Meaning
Italic	New terms or phrases when initially defined
`Monospace`	Information that appears in code or onscreen in command-line tools

All Windows book publishers struggle with how to represent command sequences when menus and dialog boxes are involved. In this book, we separate commands using a comma. Yeah, we know it's confusing, but this is traditionally how Que's books do it, and traditions die hard. So, for example, the instruction "Choose Edit, Cut" means that you should open the Edit menu and choose Cut. Another, more complex example is "Select Control Panel, System and Security, Change Battery Settings."

Key combinations are represented with a plus sign. For example, if the text calls for you to press Ctrl+Alt+Delete, you would press the Ctrl, Alt, and Delete keys at the same time. The letterless "Windows Logo" key is very useful in Windows 10. In key combinations, it appears as, for example, "Windows Logo+X."

Special Elements

Throughout this book, you'll find Notes, Tips, Cautions, Sidebars, Cross-References, and Troubleshooting Notes. Hopefully, they'll give you just the tidbit you need to get through a tough problem or the one trick that will make you the office hero. You'll also find little nuggets of wisdom, humor, and lingo that you can use to amaze your friends and family or that might come in handy as cocktail-party conversation starters.

 tip

We specially designed these tips to showcase the best of the best. Just because you get your work done doesn't mean you're doing it in the fastest, easiest way possible. We show you how to maximize your Windows experience. Don't miss these tips!

 note

Notes point out items that you should be aware of, but you can skip them if you're in a hurry. Generally, we've added notes as a way to give you some extra information on a topic without weighing you down.

 caution

Pay attention to cautions! They could save you precious hours in lost work.

 Something Isn't Working

Throughout the book, we describe some common trouble symptoms and tell you how to diagnose and fix problems with Windows, hardware, and software. We designed these elements to call attention to common pitfalls that you're likely to encounter.

We Had More to Say

We use sidebars to dig a little deeper into the more esoteric features, settings, or peculiarities of Windows. Some sidebars are used to explain something in more detail when doing so in the main body text would've been intrusive or distracting. Sometimes, we just needed to get something off our chests and rant a bit. Don't skip the sidebars, because you'll find nuggets of pure gold in them (if we do say so ourselves).

Finally, cross-references are designed to point you to other locations in this book (or other books in the Que family) that provide supplemental or supporting information. Cross-references appear as follows:

> ➡️ *To learn more about sharing account preference between devices,* **see** *"Synchronizing Your Settings Between Devices," **p. 236.***

Let's get started!

MEET WINDOWS 10

An Overview of Windows 10

In the first paragraph of a book about Windows, it's traditional to describe how this newest version is a straightforward evolutionary advance over the previous version, with some nifty new features that we can't wait to tell you about; otherwise, Windows *N* is basically Windows (*N*-1), plus 1.

Microsoft certainly went out of its way to make that impossible the last two times. Windows 8 was definitely not just a simple enhancement of Windows 7; it was a radical change, and, if we can choose only one description from the many possibilities, such as "a disaster," "an affront," "a half-baked mess designed by a committee," let's say it was "a difficult transition." But that was more than five years ago. Now we have Windows 10, for which Microsoft has decided to jump ahead by *two* version numbers, just to put some extra distance between this version and its unfortunate predecessor.

Is Windows 10 just an incremental improvement over Windows 8? Happily, the answer is no. It's much more than that. There *is* a lot of Windows 8 in it—you can certainly see the family resemblance—but it is so significantly overhauled and rethought that it really deserves to be evaluated for itself, and not what came before. In this respect, Microsoft is keeping true to form. Versions of Windows are like the old *Star Trek* movies: They alternate. The first one was terrible, the next one was good, then terrible, then good, and so on. Here we have a good one.

We'll go through things in detail, of course, but if you are looking for the capsule summary, here it is: Windows 10 is a fast, effective operating system that works really well and looks great on everything from high-end desktops to small tablets and phones. And this matters because the majority of users have more than one computing device now: a phone and a desktop or laptop and/or a tablet. The theory is that having one operating system for all devices gives you not only visual and functional continuity across all of them, but also an effortless ubiquity. Your documents, photos, music, apps, and even your sign-in and password are all there, in the same place and the same format, on whatever device you happen to pick up.

Internally, Windows 10 has all the accumulated improvements in speed and reliability that Microsoft developed as it built Windows 7, 8, and 8.1. You'll notice this right away when you start it up. Startup and shutdown times have been significantly improved, device drivers are ever more reliable thanks to the automatic crash report data that Microsoft has been collecting for years now, tools such as File Explorer (renamed from Windows Explorer starting in Windows 8) have been revamped and extended, there's built-in support for Internet connections through cellular data providers, and so on.

On the surface, there is a new look. The familiar Start button, Start menu, and desktop are back (having taken an unfortunate forced vacation for the three years of the Windows 8 era), and all graphics elements have been simplified, as shown in Figure 1.1. Window borders are rectangular, and their colors are plain and uniform. Icon graphics are simpler than they were in Windows 8. The Start menu is a toned-down version of the Windows 8 screen with *tile* icons for each program. It's easily customizable so that the stuff you use most is the easiest to find.

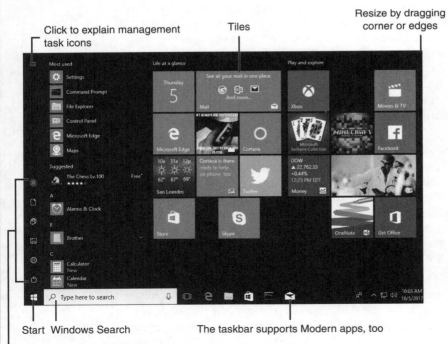

Click to explain management task icons

Tiles

Resize by dragging corner or edges

Figure 1.1
The Start menu features tiles that represent either Modern apps or traditional Windows Desktop applications. You can reorganize and resize it, too.

Start   Windows Search

The taskbar supports Modern apps, too

Switch Users, Settings, Power, and other management tasks

Windows 10 runs two types of application programs: *Modern* and *Desktop*, which are illustrated in Figure 1.2. Desktop applications are the familiar Windows programs of the last three decades, with a menu bar that runs across the top—either the traditional pull-down menu or a ribbon interface like the one that first appeared in Microsoft Office 2007. You install them by downloading or purchasing setup programs on disc.

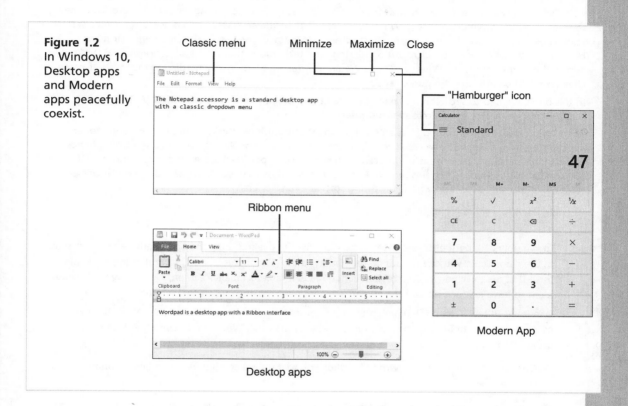

Figure 1.2 In Windows 10, Desktop apps and Modern apps peacefully coexist.

Classic menu · Minimize · Maximize · Close

"Hamburger" icon

Ribbon menu

Modern App

Desktop apps

Modern apps, on the other hand, tend to fill their entire window with content and have controls that remain hidden until you open them up using the "hamburger" menu icon, shown in the Calculator app in Figure 1.2. (Depending on your sensibilities, you could also call this the "tofu sandwich" icon. But I digress.) In Modern apps, this symbol always opens a menu of some sort, just as a gear-shaped icon lets you change settings. We talk more about the term *Modern* in the accompanying Note.

The idea of the Modern design is that you can look *through* the computer screen at pictures and text and movies, and not so much *at* the screen with its buttons and sliders and text entry fields and dialog boxes and window title bars and so on. Modern apps are found and installed through the Windows Store app.

> ### 🔍 note
>
> *Modern* in this case doesn't mean "new" but is meant to name and evoke a style, like the term *Art Deco*. The new interface design scheme was called Metro when Microsoft first discussed it. It has since had its name changed more often than Zsa Zsa Gabor. Due to trademark infringement issues just before Windows 8 was released, Microsoft had to replace the name in a hurry, and in a creative fit it came up with "Windows 8–style app," which was true but not durable. (How confusing would it have been to have to call something a Windows 8–style Windows 10 app?) Then the apps were called, variously, Universal apps, Modern apps, Windows apps, and most recently, Windows Store apps. This one might turn out to be temporary as well because Microsoft is working on a technology that might allow traditional Desktop apps to be sold through the Windows Store. We are not taking a big risk by predicting that further name changes could be in store. (No pun intended.)
>
> In this book, we had to settle on one name. We call them Modern apps, with a capital M. This seems sensible and clean, like the style to which it refers.
>
> There are underlying technical differences in the way that traditional Desktop applications and Modern apps are programmed, with the result that Modern apps can run equally well on anything from phones to desktop computers, on dozens of different microprocessor types. Desktop apps can run only on x86 or x64 compatible processors. For this reason, Microsoft (somewhat inconsistently) uses the term Universal Windows Platform (UWP) app when addressing software developers.

In Windows 10, both of these styles coexist nicely: On desktop PCs, they can both be on the screen at the same time, you can rearrange them, and so on. (The incredibly irritating flipping back and forth that made Windows 8 so reviled is gone.) On a tablet's smaller screen, it's usually more convenient to have just one app on the screen at a time, but again, you can control this.

Windows 10 has a deep relationship with the Internet and online cloud services. Now that most computers have an Internet connection virtually all the time, Windows 10 can provide some really great features:

- One sign-in name and password identifies you to multiple computers and a host of online services.

- Your preferences—screen backgrounds, application settings, bookmarked websites, memorized passwords for other systems, Wi-Fi network keys, and so on—can follow you to any computer you use.

- You can have access to your documents, photographs, and other media on any computer you use.

- Apps, music, movies, and other items you've purchased or rented online can be automatically available on any computer you use if the app's license permits this.

- "Any computer you use" can really be *any* computer: laptops, desktops, tablets, and phones, at your home, at your office, or in other people's homes and offices.

On the Cloud

The term *cloud* comes from early engineering drawings of computer networks in which straight lines and boxes represented one's own network cables and server computers, and a cloud, drawn as a child might draw one, represented a network that was owned and managed by someone else whose details were unknown and unimportant. Data went into the cloud, data came out of the cloud somewhere else, and how that was accomplished wasn't a big concern. A cloud thus represented something opaque but useful.

Now, *the cloud* refers to disk storage services and data processing services reachable over the Internet. They exist physically somewhere, but international and domestic spying concerns aside, we don't really care where they are. We just want to be able to see our Instagram pictures. And that's the fundamental shift: We no longer think about where our data is; we just expect it to be where *we* are.

Windows 10 really shines on a device whose screen is touch-sensitive. Finger-pointing is more than just a major preoccupation of politicians; it turns out to make a very intuitive and natural way of communicating your intentions to a computer. Pointing, poking, and dragging with a fingertip come naturally and become second nature almost instantly; and once you experience this technique, it's very hard to go back (as witnessed by all the fingerprints on my old computer's standard monitor from the futile poking I give it). Still, if you don't have a touch screen, Windows 10 works just fine with only a traditional mouse or touchpad.

One major crime of Windows 8 was that many of the necessary icons, menus, and command buttons were hidden and exposed themselves only if you clicked or touched secret, invisible places or made odd gestures on the screen that you had to be shown and would never have guessed to try. Thankfully, Windows 10 has fixed this, and there are now visual cues for almost every control element, and right-clicking things exposes everything else you need.

Should I Get Windows 10?

In a previous book, when we posed the same question about Windows 7, the answer was absolutely clear, for virtually everyone: "Yes! Run, don't walk." For Windows 8 and 8.1, we had to mumble "Um, er... no, yes, maybe." Now, with Windows 10, we can give you an enthusiastic "Almost surely!" Here's how it breaks down:

- If you're getting a new computer or tablet, the answer is yes, by all means, buy one with Windows 10 on it. (You won't have much choice, really.) And if you're getting a laptop or desktop, it's worth spending a little more to get one with a touchscreen.

- If you have Windows 8 or 8.1 now, you'll want to upgrade to Windows 10. Yesterday, if not sooner. You'll find that Windows 10 is a big improvement.

- If you have a computer with 7 on it now, an upgrade may be worthwhile. The hardware and software requirements are virtually the same. But before you buy an upgrade, be sure that all your hardware and software will continue to work. It's very likely that all of it (except maybe third-party antivirus programs and VPN networking clients) will work, but you should check. We show you how in Chapter 2, "Installing or Upgrading to Windows 10." If there are no compatibility issues, upgrading is probably a wise choice because you'll have an operating system that Microsoft will be updating for many years after it stops supporting Windows 7. Windows 10 will feel familiar, although, for setup and management, you'll still need to learn several tricks. This book will get you up to speed.

- For Windows 7 and 8 users, the offer for a free upgrade has expired. An upgrade to Windows 10 Home costs $119, and an upgrade to Windows 10 Pro costs $199. (Although, as we discuss in Chapter 2, a free upgrade is still available if you use accessibility software or devices.)

- If you have a computer with Windows XP or Vista on it now, your computer is probably pretty old! If so, we recommend leaving it alone and getting a new computer. You could *possibly* install Windows 10 on it, but you'd have to reinstall all of your application software, and not all of its hardware might work. The upgrade advisor discussed in Chapter 2 will tell you. (As a point of reference, I have a 2007 vintage Toshiba laptop that is working well with 32-bit Windows 10 Pro, although I did decide to add more RAM, at a cost of $30.) As far as figuring out how to use Windows 10, XP or Vista users will have some catching up to do. We show you the ways that Windows 10 helps make routine tasks much easier than before.

Why would you want to upgrade to Windows 10 if you're happy with your current version of Windows? Here are some reasons:

- You get access to the Windows Store, a software marketplace that makes finding and adding new programs to your computer almost effortless. And most apps you install through the Store are yours to use on all of your devices, if the app's developer permits this.

- Startup and shutdown are *really fast*.

- Windows 10 is a much more secure operating system due to advances in its programming and thanks to its Windows Defender Security Center providing real-time protection. Windows 10 is where Microsoft is going to be focusing its efforts at improvements, bug fixes, and security fixes. Windows 8, 8.1, 7, or Vista? Not so much.

- Updates will come more frequently and fluidly than for other versions of Windows. Microsoft's stated intent is that this is the last version of Windows; it'll just continue to improve Windows 10 indefinitely. (Let's come back in five years and check on that, OK?)

- Many of the apps that come with Windows 10 have been given much-needed makeovers, especially Mail, Calendar, and People. These are now decent, useful apps that are easy to sync with other Windows 10 devices.

- Windows 10 is designed to run on all devices, from smartphones to tablets and from notebooks to desktop PCs. The interface senses the device it's running on and adapts automatically. For example, one of the nicest features is Continuum; if you're using Windows 10 on a smartphone or tablet and you connect the device to a monitor, Windows changes to the desktop interface.

We think it adds up to a compelling argument for upgrading. Now, let's go into a little more detail.

Windows 10 Editions

For a long time, we got one new version of Windows every three years or so. It was called Windows *Some Number*: Windows 1, Windows 2, Windows 3, Windows 3.1, Windows 95, Windows 98, and

Windows 666 (well, technically, it was called Windows Me, but Windows 666 was more apt). There was just one one-size-fits-all version: Windows.

In parallel, the New Technology (NT) product line—written from scratch without MS-DOS underneath it—spawned Windows NT Workstation and Windows 2000 Professional. NT was stable and much more secure than Windows 3 and 9x, although its improvements to its user interface always trailed behind the consumer versions by about three years. That was due mostly to the difficulty and expense of developing and maintaining two completely separate versions of Windows. Still, it was revered in the business world, where reliability matters more than appearance.

Microsoft finally, thankfully, closed the book on the original Windows code when it released Windows XP, so ever since then, everyone's been using some flavor of Windows NT. However, it kept the home/business split. We got Windows XP Home Edition and Windows XP Professional. They were really the same product, but Home Edition lacked a few features found in Professional. There was also Windows XP Media Center Edition, which was XP Professional sold to home users, with an additional application that let Windows record TV shows and drive a TV as its monitor. And, a Starter Edition with stripped-down features was sold in some countries.

Now, the Windows 10 family has the following breakdown, from the simplest to the most complex:

- **Windows 10 IoT Core** is an ultra-miniature version of Windows for the *Internet of Things*, tiny microcomputers that control home appliances, vending machines, robots, and so on. These are called "embedded" applications where a computer and its software are built in to the fabric of some device. Windows 10 IoT Core runs on small, inexpensive devices, and it's free to hobbyists. (You can read more about it at https://dev.windows.com/en-us/iot, if you're curious.)

- **Windows 10 Mobile** is for smartphones, tablets, and other devices with screens smaller than 8 inches diagonal. Versions are available for several different microprocessor families, including ARM and Intel-compatible CPUs. It's sold only to equipment manufacturers for inclusion in their products. It replaces and merges the Windows Phone and Windows RT product lines. However, at the time this was written, Microsoft appears to have given up on the Mobile platform, ceding the smart phone operating system market to Apple (iOS) and Google (Android). Existing phones will be supported (at least for a while), but ongoing development and new generations of phones now seem unlikely.

- **Windows 10 Mobile Enterprise** adds management support to phones and tablets so that they can safely and securely be connected to corporate networks and managed by corporate IT staff.

- **Windows 10 Home** is available to consumers, either preinstalled or as a downloaded upgrade, or for purchase to be installed on home-built computers. This and the rest of the listed versions can be used on tablets with screens 8 inches diagonal or larger, or desktops, but in either case, require an Intel-compatible 32-bit or 64-bit processor. Windows Updates are installed automatically, without consent, in this edition.

- **Windows 10 Pro** has everything that Home has, and it adds support for business use. It's intended for devices that are to be connected to a business network that is managed by Windows Server, supports encryption of the files on its drives, and has some other advanced features, as listed in Table 1.1. It's available for direct purchase or as an upgrade for comparable versions of Windows Vista, 7, or 8.

- **Windows 10 Pro for Workstations** adds support for faster networking hardware, the Resilient File System (ReFS) that supports large hard disk arrays and makes disk storage more reliable, supports up to four CPUs, and can handle up to 6TB of RAM, among other features. It's meant for advanced applications such as engineering simulation, visualization, and large-scale data analysis. At the time this was written, its pricing and retail availability were not yet known.

- **Windows 10 S** is essentially Windows 10 Pro, but it's restricted to running only apps installed from the Windows Store, as well as the programs pre-installed with Windows. It won't, for example, let you install or run software from DVDs or downloads. If you can live with this restriction, it *might* turn out to be more resistant to viruses and other malware than other versions of Windows. At the time this was written, it's too early to tell.

- **Windows 10 Enterprise** adds additional corporate management features to Pro. The primary difference between Pro and Enterprise is how it's licensed for use on desktops, in virtual machines, and on Terminal Services (remote desktop) servers. Network managers also have a great deal of control over how, when, and if Windows Update patches are delivered to computers running the Enterprise edition. It's only available to business customers, through volume licensing agreements.

- **Windows 10 Pro Education and Windows 10 Education** are essentially Windows 10 Pro and Windows 10 Enterprise with licensing arrangements attractive to schools and other educational institutions, and a few changes to default advertising and management settings.

Table 1.1 Primary Differences in the Feature Sets of Windows 10 Home, Windows 10 Pro, and Windows 10 Enterprise

Feature	Windows 10 Home	Windows 10 Pro, S	Windows 10 Enterprise
Presentation Settings		✓	✓
Remote Desktop Host		✓	✓
Boot from VHD file		✓	✓
Hyper-V Virtual Machine Manager		✓ +	✓ +
BitLocker and BitLocker To Go (whole-drive encryption of storage)		✓	✓
Encrypted File System (file-level encryption)		✓	✓
Domain network member		✓	✓
Manageable by Group Policy		*	*
AppLocker (restriction of runnable apps by IT managers)			*
Boot from USB drive (Windows To Go)			✓
DirectAccess (automatic VPN to the office)			*

+ Available only on 64-bit versions.

* Only when joined to a Windows Domain network. Feature is not user configurable but is controlled entirely by network managers.

Besides these various editions, versions suffixed with the letters *N*, *E*, *K*, or *KN* are sold in specific geographic markets. They are missing a few of the usual preinstalled multimedia and web browser applications, as a way of resolving antitrust troubles. (For example, Microsoft had to remove Windows Media Player and fork over $784 million to buy the letter *N* from the European Commission.) If you have one of these flavors, you need only download the missing application(s) from www.microsoft.com to get rid of the distinction.

Just to be clear, this book covers Windows 10 Home, Pro, S, Enterprise, and Pro Education and Education. And although Windows Pro for Workstations wasn't yet released at the time this was written, this book applies to it as well, with the exception of coverage of the Resilient File System (ReFS) option. If you have Windows 10 Mobile (and apparently very few of you do), most of our coverage is applicable to you, but we also talk about some features that your edition of Windows doesn't have, and we don't cover phone components. And we focus on the features that you can use and manage yourself as an end user. We don't cover features that are controlled entirely by network managers from the Windows Server operating system, so we don't cover the server side of management for Windows 10 Enterprise or Windows 10 Education.

 tip

Administrators who manage Windows 10 in an educational setting should visit docs.microsoft.com and search for "Windows 10 configuration recommendations for education customers" for some important advice.

There appear to be a lot of versions to choose from, but thankfully you can usually narrow down the choice to one or two. In a corporate setting, your IT department will select the Pro, S, or Enterprise edition for you. In Europe or South Korea, the N and KN flavors will be the only ones available. If you do have a choice to make, it will be between Windows 10 Home and Windows 10 Pro. Now, if you're interested enough in Windows versions to be reading this section, you've probably done plenty of research online already, so we'll keep this brief. Table 1.1 lists the *primary* feature differences between the editions.

Windows Media Center, a television digital video recorder application, has been eliminated from all Windows 10 versions and is not available as an add-on like it was with Windows 8.

Windows 10 comes in both 32-bit and 64-bit versions. This is a significant decision to make because you can't change back and forth between 32-bit and 64-bit versions; you'll be stuck with the choice and will have to do a complete, clean install to change. If you're not sure which to choose, here are some pointers:

- Some ultra-portable notebook PCs and low-end tablets have 32-bit CPUs, so you can't install the 64-bit version on them. (I don't mean to knock them; I have seen devices that cost as little as $150, with a 32-bit processor and only 2GB of RAM, that work perfectly well for basic web browsing, reading, email, and so on, primarily because they have solid state disks.)

- The 32-bit versions can use only up to 3GB of RAM (program memory) in your computer, even if you have more installed. (This is a technical limitation). This can seriously slow you down, especially if you edit video or use image-editing programs such as Adobe Photoshop. The 64-bit versions can take advantage of as much RAM as you can stuff in. This is the main reason that 64-bit computing has taken over. Windows can certainly run in 2GB of RAM, but it's a lot faster with 4GB or more.

- The 32-bit versions can run antique MS-DOS and 16-bit Windows 3.1 applications directly; the 64-bit versions can't. If you need to use MS-DOS or 16-bit applications on a computer that runs 64-bit Windows, you'll have to run them in a virtual machine that runs a 16- or 32-bit version of Windows or MS-DOS. We discuss this in Appendix A, "Virtualization."

- The 64-bit versions of Windows 10 Pro and Enterprise include Microsoft's Hyper-V virtual machine manager (VMM). If you don't want to use Hyper-V, or if you want to run virtual machines on 32-bit Windows 10 Pro or Enterprise, or any variety of Windows 10 Home, you'll have to install VMware, VirtualBox, or another VMM. Microsoft Virtual PC, the VM tool in earlier Windows versions, is not available for any edition of Windows 10.

- You'll need the 64-bit version if you want to run 64-bit versions of applications like Microsoft Office. The 64-bit versions of applications take advantage of the full 64-bit CPU capability and the additional memory, so they tend to run faster than their 32-bit counterparts.

- If you have devices in or connected to your computer that were manufactured before 2008, you might not be able to find 64-bit device drivers for them. Most equipment made since then has both 32- and 64-bit support.

When Windows Vista was released in January 2007, 64-bit versions of Windows were still considered exotic, and device driver support lagged. Now, virtually all new computers ship with 64-bit Windows preinstalled.

Upgrading Windows

As we mentioned previously, if you have Windows 8 or 8.1 already, or if you purchase a new computer, tablet, or laptop that has Windows 8 or 8.1 on it but not 10, you can easily upgrade to the comparable (Home or Pro) edition of Windows 10. We talk about this in Chapter 2.

For earlier versions of Windows, upgrading is a bit more complicated. You can upgrade an existing installation of Windows 7 to Windows 10, with applications, settings, and personal data (user accounts and files), subject to the restrictions listed in Table 1.2. If you're updating from Vista, you'll have to reinstall all of your desktop applications. If you're moving up from Windows XP (and if your old Windows XP computer is capable of running Windows 10), you can buy an upgrade Windows 10 license, but you'll have to do a clean install. This means your files and documents will be available, but your settings will be lost and you'll have to reinstall your application programs if you want to use them in Windows 10. It's probably not worth doing; in the long run, it's usually better to get a new computer. (A 10-year-old hard disk is not likely to last that much longer, anyway.)

Table 1.2 lists the upgrade paths that Microsoft supports.

Table 1.2 Windows Upgrade Paths

From...	To... 10 Home	10 Pro	Keeping... Users/Files	Settings	Applications
XP Home	✓		+		
XP Professional	—	✓	+		
Vista Home Basic	✓		✓	*	
Vista Home Premium	✓				
Vista Business	—	✓	✓	*	

From...	To... 10 Home	10 Pro	Keeping... Users/Files	Settings	Applications
Vista Ultimate	—	✓	✓	*	
7 Home Basic	✓	✓	✓	✓	✓
7 Home Premium	✓	✓	✓	✓	✓
7 Professional	—	✓	✓	✓	✓
7 Ultimate	—	✓	✓	✓	✓
8 (8.0)	○				
8 (8.0) Pro	○	○			
8.1	✓		✓	✓	✓
8.1 Pro	—	✓	✓	✓	✓

+ Upgrade allowed only if XP SP3 is installed.

* Settings copied only if Vista SP1 or SP2 is installed.

○ Windows 8 must first be updated to Windows 8.1; then the Windows 8.1 upgrade options apply.

— Allowed, but it would be a downgrade. Windows 10 Pro is the comparable version. In a downgrade, user files are retained but applications and settings are not.

Microsoft intends to permit the update of Windows Phone 8.1 devices to Windows 10 Mobile, but the update depends on cooperation from phone carriers.

There is no path to update Microsoft Surface tablets that run Windows RT to the full version of Windows 10, but Windows 8.1 RT Update 3, which was released through Windows Update, at least updated the Start Menu to more closely match Windows 10's.

When you're upgrading, although you can choose which edition of Windows you want to install, you can't change between 32-bit and 64-bit versions. Doing so requires a clean install.

➡ *To learn more about upgrading, **see** "Upgrading to Windows 10," p. 43.*

What's New in Windows 10?

In the following sections, we review the ways in which Windows 10 differs from its predecessors both on the screen and under the covers. First, we discuss how Windows 10 differs from Windows 7 and earlier versions. Then we list ways in which Windows 10 differs from Windows 8 and 8.1. If you used Windows 8 or 8.1, you could just skip ahead to "What Changed Between Windows 10 and Windows 8 and 8.1."

And you should know that this list of changes is going to be changing itself, as Windows 10 evolves. Between its initial release in 2015 and the time this was written, Windows 10 has had four significant updates and many small changes. From time to time, Windows 10 features will be changed, added, and in some cases, removed via Windows Update. This is one of the reasons that this book comes with the Content Update Program, as described in the inside back cover, so that we can adjust our descriptions and procedures as Windows itself changes.

The New Start Menu

The most obvious new feature in Windows 10 is the new Start menu (refer to Figure 1.1), which melds concepts from both Windows 7 and 8, yielding a slick design that's easy to use. Applications (apps) are represented with various-sized tiles. Touching or clicking a tile opens the app. Tiles don't necessarily display just static images and text: *Live tiles* can display dynamic information, such as the latest news, date, time, weather forecast, and arrival of new email messages.

➡ *To learn more about the Start menu and Modern apps, **see** "Taking a Tour of the Windows 10 Interface," **p. 109**.*

Touch-a Touch-a Touch-a Touch Me!

Our apologies to *The Rocky Horror Picture Show*, but Windows 10 just begs to be touched, prodded, and poked. The interface for Modern apps only truly makes sense the first time you interact with Windows on a tablet or on a computer with a multitouch monitor. Scrolling, selecting, and manipulating objects on the screen feels completely natural and intuitive, even pleasurable.

This isn't to say that Windows 10 is difficult to use without a touchscreen. You can definitely get by quite well with just a keyboard and mouse or touchpad. In fact, if you're a good typist, you might actually prefer to keep your fingers on the keyboard most of the time. The trick here is that it's not always immediately apparent just what you should *do* with the mouse or touchpad and keyboard to get Windows 10 to do what you want. On Modern apps, the pull-down menu is gone, replaced in most cases with just a hamburger icon, which we show in Figure 1.2 and explain in Chapters 3 and 4. You'll master hamburgers in no time.

Modern Apps

As discussed previously, apps are divided into two completely separate categories. There are still traditional Windows Desktop applications, such as Windows Notepad, Microsoft Word (if purchased separately), and the Control Panel. Unless you have Windows 10 S, you can install your favorite traditional Windows desktop applications from downloads or setup discs, just as you did in the past, and some desktop apps can be installed via the Store.

Then there are Modern apps, which you can obtain only by visiting the Windows Store (which is itself an app).*

Modern apps use a very simplified user interface. These apps emphasize "content over chrome," meaning the apps show users what they want to see, not a bunch of graphical gimmickry. The new look is simple and clean, with large type, not many words, and plain interface objects that don't try to look like real-world materials. Refer to Figure 1.2 for an example. The days of the etched 3D dialog box pushbutton that looks like brushed stainless steel are numbered.

➡ *To learn more about using Modern apps, **see** "Working with Running Apps," **p. 116**.*

---

* This is true for home users anyway. In a corporate environment, system managers can install locally developed Modern apps—so-called Line of Business apps—on managed and employee-owned computers.

Hey, Cortana

Windows 10 includes Microsoft's Cortana natural-language digital assistant, which you can enable so that it's available at all times right in the taskbar. Cortana can perform web searches, schedule and remind you of appointments, look up directions, and so on, and "she" can do it with typed or spoken commands in English and in some other languages (with more coming, presumably).

In fact, if your computer has a microphone, and if you want to, you can leave Cortana turned on all the time, and all you have to do is say "Hey, Cortana" to have the software respond to your spoken commands. This is cool and creepy at the same time.

Online User Accounts

One very useful feature in Windows 10 is the capability to use your online Microsoft account name as your Windows sign-in name. This could be something like yourname@live.com or whatever email address you use to create the Microsoft account.

If you elect to use your Microsoft account on Windows 10, Windows will automatically sync your Windows preferences over the Internet, including

- Your chosen background screens, colors, and pictures

- Account password and passwords you use to connect to shared network and Internet resources

- Ease of Access and language settings

- Apps and app settings

- Passwords to the Wi-Fi networks you use

- Preferences you set in File Explorer (discussed in the next section) and some other tools

This information is stored on Microsoft's servers and will follow you to any Windows 10 computer you sign in on, provided it has an Internet connection.

(By the way, if it bothers you that your Wi-Fi network keys get uploaded to Microsoft's servers, where, say, the National Security Agency (NSA) might gain access to them, consider these two points: First, you can tell Windows not to sync passwords and keys. Second, if it wanted to, the NSA could easily break into your Wi-Fi network without bothering to squeeze the key out of Microsoft. So, personally, I'm happy to use the syncing feature. It's very convenient to have all of your devices "just work" on a given Wi-Fi network after having set up just one.)

> **note**
> You can't just walk up to any Windows 10 computer and sign in using your Microsoft account sign-in name; the computer's owner must set up an account for you by entering your Windows account name. This person doesn't, however, need to know your password.

➡ *To learn more about creating a Microsoft account,* **see** *"Setting Up User Accounts," **p. 75.***

Virtual Desktops

Now that the desktop has returned to its former prominence in the Windows interface, Microsoft has decided to go all-in with the desktop idea. In Windows 10, you can have not just one desktop, but as many as you like, each with its own set of running apps. So you could have one desktop with just your productivity apps, another with just social networking tools, a third with media apps, and so on. You can easily switch from one to another, with each organized as you wish.

Expanded Settings App

Veteran Windows power users will have an intimate relationship with Control Panel, the venerable tool for configuring many different aspects of Windows and your PC's hardware and software. Windows 8 introduced the PC Settings app, which was, like so much of Windows 8, a dumbed-down version of an existing tool—Control Panel, in this case. Veteran Windows power users stuck with Control Panel, thank you very much.

In Windows 10, PC Settings has been rechristened Settings and has been greatly expanded to assume more configuration responsibilities. And, more are added with every Windows 10 update. Starting with the 2017 Creators Update, for instance, Settings now covers most—though not all—networking functions.

It's now very much a worthwhile app to get to know. Control Panel is still around and still has lots of useful features, so power users need to know both programs. But it's hard to know which program to use for which configuration task. *That* is now a big problem and remains one of the few areas where Windows 10 falls down on the job. We hope our coverage of both tools throughout this book will help.

File Explorer Ribbon

Beginning in Windows 8, the venerable, aged Windows Explorer was renamed File Explorer (a sensible change, if you ask us). It also was given a whole new look, including a ribbon interface to replace the traditional File/Edit/View drop-down menu.

In place of a menu, you have a graphical toolbar whose contents change depending on what you've selected below it. It takes some getting used to. Gone are the days when you could just look through all of a program's menus to see what's possible. Microsoft says its research shows that people actually do "discover" more functions and features with a ribbon interface than with a traditional menu system. I'm not so sure. There are probably things in there that nobody will ever discover because they appear only if you happen to select three different files in three different folders, on a Saturday afternoon, about teatime.

➡ To learn more about the new File Explorer, *see* "Navigating Folder Windows," **p. 160.**

The Windows Store

Modern apps can be purchased only from the Windows Store, Microsoft's online marketplace for free and paid apps from both Microsoft and other vendors. There, presumably, apps are vetted for viruses and malicious intent before they're released to the public. This marketplace is relatively new, but still, the number of available apps is growing much more slowly than Microsoft had hoped.

Angry Birds was an early arrival, and although Games is clearly going to be one of the biggest sections of the Store, we hope that the range and quantity of apps will eventually match those of the iPhone/iPad world. These apps can be used on the purchaser's desktop computers as well as on tablets and phones, thus adding to their appeal (and market base).

➡️ *To learn more about the Windows Store, see "Store," p. 152.*

 note

During the initial development period of Windows 8, there was a persistent rumor that you would not be able to install older software that you already owned, and you would have to buy everything from the Store. This was false. Except for people stuck with the short-lived Windows 8 RT tablets and the relatively new Windows 10 S edition, you can install any *desktop* software you want, from any source, past, present, or future, on Windows 8, 8.1, and 10 computers that have Intel-compatible x86 or x64 processors. Only Modern apps *must* be acquired through Microsoft.

And even this restriction has some loopholes. Software developers can build, test, and use Modern apps of their own devising to their heart's content, although only on their own computers. And enterprise IT departments can install locally developed Modern "line of business" apps on computers that they deploy in their organizations and on employee-owned devices.

Management Tools

Managing Windows has always been somewhat of a challenge because it's complex, and it's not something most of us do every day. When the management tools are switched around, it can be pretty taxing. This is an area where Windows 10 can be frustrating if you are moving up from Windows 7 or XP. Although the old Control Panel and Computer Management tools still exist, with each incremental release of Windows, Microsoft is moving more settings to new Modern apps. The job of moving Control Panel functions to the Settings app (shown in Figure 1.3) is only partly done, even within individual areas of management, such as networking. It doesn't help that the location of items within the Settings app—and even the wording used to find them—gets changed once or twice a year as Windows 10 gets updated.

Chapter 3 takes you on a quick tour of the new Windows 10 management tools. We cover the new and old-style management tools in detail throughout the book. If a particular topic interests you, the index should lead you straight to it. And as things change over time, our online Content Update Program editions will let you keep up to date.

Improved Antivirus Protection

Built-in antivirus protection has been improving with each successive version of Windows. Windows 10's offering is called Windows Defender Security Center, and it includes several components: antivirus and antispyware protection, a network firewall (Windows Firewall is now considered part of Windows Defender), and a brand new feature called Controlled Folder Access. If you enable Controlled Folder Access, only the application programs you authorize can access the contents of a designated list of folders. For example, you might specify that only Microsoft Office and Excel are allowed to modify files in your Documents folder. This feature is meant to help protect against ransomware attacks, where a virus program encrypts and holds hostage your documents and data.

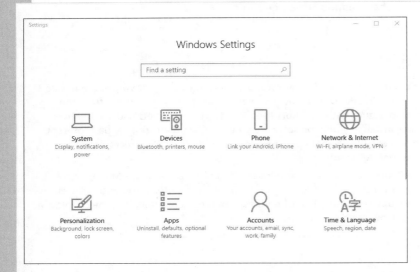

Figure 1.3
The new Settings panel takes over most, but not all, of what the Control Panel did.

For more information about antivirus protection using Windows Defender Security Center and third-party options, see Chapter 31, "Protecting Windows from Viruses and Spyware."

Installation and Setup

The Windows 10 installation and setup process is much like that in Windows 7 and 8. The install process is smooth and fast due to a deployment technology that copies an "image" of a fully installed Windows system onto your hard disk rather than copying and configuring files piecemeal. (One downside for hard-core operating system geeks, though, is that you can't select the drive letter that will be assigned to the new copy of Windows. It's going to be drive C: no matter what. If you have other hard disks in your system, they will be assigned letters other than C: when Windows boots.)

Windows 8 did one thing that Windows 10 doesn't do: The first time you signed in, you were taken on a quick tour of the Windows 8 user interface, including touch gestures if your computer had a touchscreen. This was necessary because Windows 8 was essentially unusable unless you'd been shown the secret touching and clicking gestures. This isn't the case with Windows 10; its interface is mostly "discoverable" just by poking around at it. Still, a guided tour is very helpful, which is why we wrote Chapter 3.

➡ *To learn more about installing Windows 10,* **see** *"Windows 10 System Requirements," p. 31.*

Storage Spaces

Storage Spaces was first introduced in Windows 8 and offers a sensible approach to adding disk space to a personal computer. Instead of having to deal with separate disk drives and having to move files around between them, you can choose to simply "pool" their collective capacity. If your first disk fills up, you add another, and Windows combines the added free space with your existing disk volume. You don't have to keep track of what data is stored on which drive; Windows does that. You see just one big drive. Makes sense, yes?

You can have Storage Spaces present the entire combined storage space of your disks, or you can dedicate some space to storing redundant information to help recover from a physical disk failure. If you want, you can choose to use added disks the old way, separately.

➡ *To learn more about growing your hard disk storage,* **see** *"Working with Storage Spaces," p. 563.*

Improved Web Browsing with Microsoft Edge and Internet Explorer 11

Windows 10 ships with two web browsers installed: Microsoft Edge and Internet Explorer 11, with Microsoft Edge being the default browser. Both offer much better HTML5 support than previous versions, have much faster JavaScript engines to make interactive websites snappier, and take advantage of your computer's graphics processor to significantly speed up the rendering (drawing) of complex web pages. They're more secure as well, due to features such as High Entropy Address Space Layout Randomization, which randomizes the location of sensitive system code modules. This makes them moving targets for malicious code that tries to exploit bugs in known program locations.

Microsoft Edge (formerly known as Project Spartan) is a newly written browser that was designed to be extremely fast and responsive. It includes new features that, for example, let you annotate (write on) and share comments about websites. And it eliminates the ActiveX software plug-in system that let software developers add features to the browser and let hackers take over hundreds of millions of computers. Support for plug-ins (are now called *extensions*) came to Edge with the Windows 10 Anniversary update, and they contain only HTML markup and JavaScript programming. This should keep Edge *much* more secure than Internet Explorer.

Still, Windows 10 also includes Internet Explorer 11, because some sites and some web applications in particular require IE's particular quirks and capabilities and/or special plug-ins to operate correctly.

➡ *To learn more about IE 11,* **see** *Chapter 15, "Web Browsing with Microsoft Edge."*

Wi-Fi Sense

Windows 10 has a feature called Wi-Fi Sense that, when enabled, lets your computer or device connect automatically to open (unsecured) Wi-Fi hotspots as you travel around, and it's especially useful if you also use a cellular data service because it can help you reduce your data plan usage. This feature allows you to get online faster than if you had to manually search for a Wi-Fi hotspot.

Data about available public, unsecured networks comes from Microsoft partners and other Windows Phone and Windows 10 users who have connected to them. In hotspots such as airports or cafes where a Terms of Usage Agreement is presented before access is granted, Wi-Fi Sense might even be able to bypass that by automatically agreeing to the terms on your behalf.

(In the original Windows 10 release, WiFi Sense also let you use password-secured networks shared by friends, but this feature was removed from Windows 10 in the summer of 2016, with the Anniversary Update.)

➡ *To see how to take advantage of Wi-Fi Sense, **see** "Connecting with Wi-Fi Sense," p. 823.*

Faster Startup

One thing you're sure to notice about Windows 10 is that it starts up and shuts down much faster than previous versions. If you have it installed on a solid state disk (SSD), bootup is *amazingly* fast, usually just a few seconds.

Microsoft has tuned up the techniques it used to speed up Windows' boot time. It keeps a list of which operating files get read in during startup, in which order, and uses at least one core of a multicore CPU to read those files into memory as quickly as possible, so they're loaded even before they're needed. And it defers the loading of nonessential services and subsystems until after the sign-in screen is up so that you can start signing in while Windows is still putting itself together.

Windows 7 did this, too, but Windows 10 and 8 have another trick up their sleeves: kernel hibernation. As you may know, hibernation is a way of putting the computer to sleep by writing the contents of memory to disk before shutting off the power entirely. When you power it back up, the computer reads the stored data back into memory and takes up where it left off. When you do a normal, power-off shutdown, Windows 10 ignores all the memory used by applications but hibernates the Windows kernel—just a few hundred megabytes, so the saving process takes almost no time at all. When you power on the next time, the kernel is restored intact, saving the time it would take to load and configure it from scratch. The sign-in screen follows in short order, and then the rest of Windows loads in the normal manner. This shaves several seconds off the startup time. It's remarkably helpful.

One consequence of this is that the loaded copy of the Windows kernel can stick around for a long time—months perhaps. It's stable enough to do that, but performing a shutdown and startup won't always clear up a software glitch like it used to. You now have to use the Start Menu power icon's Restart option to do a full reboot, discarding everything in memory and reloading everything from scratch.

Secure Boot

Secure Boot is a feature that protects your computer from malware that takes control of your computer at the moment it boots up before the Windows security system can kick in. This kind of malware can sneak in on a USB thumb drive or appear in a virus that infects the disk's Master Boot Record, the first code that's executed after the BIOS self-test has finished.

When Windows 10 is installed on a computer that has a Unified Extensible Firmware Interface (UEFI) BIOS on its motherboard, you (or your organization's IT department or your computer's manufacturer) can lock down the system so that only an authorized, unmodified, digitally signed operating system can boot.

In fact, to earn a Windows 10–family logo sticker, computer vendors are required to ship computers with Secure Boot enabled. To install an alternative operating system such as a version of Linux, you might need to disable Secure Boot in the computer's BIOS settings. Alternatively, your OS vendor might be able to supply a digitally signed copy that is recognized by the BIOS in your computer.

Integrated Cellular Data Connections

Windows 10 includes built-in support for Internet connectivity using 3G, 4G, and 4G LTE mobile broadband (cellular) networks. This support is an obvious feature for tablets, letting Windows tablets compete with Android tablets and Apple's iPad, but it's also available for laptop computers that have a SIM card and a cellular data modem either built-in or added on. In past versions of Windows, mobile connectivity required third-party software, but this is built in to Windows 10. Windows can determine from the SIM card which mobile carrier you use and can help you get additional broadband accessories from your carrier through the Windows Store.

Also, Windows can help meter your Internet usage through a mobile broadband connection so that you don't exceed your data plan's cap.

Tools for Creators

In the Windows 10 Creators Update, released in the fall of 2017, Microsoft added several tools aimed specifically at people who want to create with Windows 10. These include an update to the venerable Paint program—there is a new app called Paint 3D—that lets you build cubes, spheres, and other three-dimensional models; an app called View 3D that enables you to open and interact with several 3D model file types; and an app called Mixed Reality Portal, where you can set up your mixed reality-compatible headset and access your mixed reality apps. (In Microsoft-speak, *mixed reality* refers to a hardware platform that combines virtual reality, augmented reality, and holography.)

Changes Since the Initial Release of Windows 10

Most of the changes made to Windows 10 since its initial release are gradual but significant, across-the-board improvements to the pre-installed apps. Here are just a few of the things that you might want to look for if you're already familiar with Windows 10:

- The Edge browser is much more capable now than when it was initially released.

- The Settings app has much more depth than it did initially. You'll find that if you search for settings by name in the taskbar, many of the search results now lead to Settings app panels rather than to the Control Panel.

- The onscreen touch keyboard now supports Swype-style writing, in which you can spell out words by dragging your finger from one letter to another without lifting your finger from the keyboard.

- OneDrive now supports download-on-demand. You can choose to have the contents of OneDrive folders appear in your computer's local folders without waiting for the files to actually be downloaded. Files will be downloaded when you attempt to open or view them. (This is an option; you can still have folders downloaded in their entirety, or not at all.)

- The Windows My People app lets you easily communicate with select people through Skype, messaging, email, and other apps. A new People icon appears in the taskbar.

- For more technical users and software developers, there are new features such as the Windows Subsystem for Linux and support for Windows Containers. The Network File System (NFS) Client has been restored to Windows Pro and Enterprise editions.

If you've already used Windows 10, you might also want to run through the guided tour in Chapter 3 to see if you notice any changes.

What Changed Between Windows 10 and Windows 8 and 8.1

If you're familiar with Windows 8 and 8.1, here is a brief list of the changes and enhancements in Windows 10:

- The Start menu is *back*. 'Nuff said.

- Modern and Desktop apps live together. There is no more flipping back and forth, which, if you ask me, is flippin' wonderful.

- The charms are gone, and there are no more secret gestures. There are now visual indicators of where to click and navigate, and they remain visible all the time. The gestures you used in Windows 8 are mostly still available; for example, you can still swipe in from the right side of the screen. This now displays the Notifications panel and Action Center, a truly wonderful new tool. You can still right-click the bottom-left corner of the screen to get the Power User's menu. (Actually, you can right-click anywhere on the Start button.) But you don't *have* to use these tricks. They're just there to use if they feel natural.

- You can close, move, and resize Modern apps. They act more like familiar Desktop applications than they did in Windows 8 and 8.1.

- The default location to save files from apps is Microsoft's OneDrive cloud storage solution. Having a default location makes it very easy to save things in a way that makes them available on all of your devices. (This change occurred in Windows 8.1, but we wanted to remind you.)

- Almost all of the preinstalled Modern apps, such as Mail and Maps, have been improved. Improvements are something that you can expect on an ongoing basis. Microsoft says that it will continue to adjust and improve Windows 10 apps.

- On Windows 10 Home, updates will be delivered and installed automatically and can't be turned off. On Windows 10 Pro, you can defer but not permanently ignore updates. This change is a bit heavy-handed, but it should significantly improve security and reduce virus infections. It also will tend to make Windows 10 more uniform—your copy and my copy will pretty much be the same.

- More Control Panel settings have been moved to the Modern Settings app, which you can reach from the Settings link on the Start menu. Some of the changes are annoying and confusing. (We show you how to deal with them throughout the book.)

- On a corporate domain network, the Workplace Join feature lets you connect your personal tablet or computer to the corporate network without actually becoming a domain member. This strikes a balance, leaving you in control of your device but giving network managers control over what resources you can use. There are also improvements in ways to connect to network printers. Virtual private networking features include more built-in support for more VPN vendors and an autoconnect feature that lets an app initiate a VPN connection when necessary.

Beyond Windows 10

The previous sections described what changed getting *to* Windows 10. What comes after it? That, it turns out, is an interesting question. Microsoft has said that Windows 10 is the last version it'll make. And Microsoft now officially calls Windows a *service* rather than a product. Instead of coming out with a major new version every three years, as it has for the past two decades, Microsoft's stated intention is to release incremental changes to Windows 10 indefinitely, and frequently, through Windows Update. Since its initial release in 2015, that has indeed been the case, with frequent minor fixes, and major updates at least once a year.

And the Windows Update mechanism, which in previous versions of Windows gave you control over which individual updates were installed and when, and could be even be turned off entirely, is no longer so flexible. On Windows 10 Home, it can't even be turned off, and you can't control which updates are installed. From the standpoint of security, this is probably a very good thing, as out-of-date operating systems and applications are fodder for hackers and criminals. On Windows 10 Pro and Enterprise, you can delay, but not prevent updates from being installed.

So, change is in your future, like it or not. It should be at least some comfort that Microsoft has promised that changes will be rolled out in small groups of users with careful monitoring and gathering of feedback so that if a future change causes problems, it can be pulled back and corrected before it causes widespread difficulties. (This may be of small consolation if you happen to be randomly placed in the first group of guinea pigs. An update in 2016 made a lot of Windows 10 tablets unbootable until their owners or repair shops performed a manual repair operation).

And there will be widespread testing before changes are sent out to the public at large. If you're hot to see the latest and greatest Microsoft has to offer, you can sign up to be a Windows Insider at insider.windows.com, and ask to participate in testing new features. Choose to be in the "fast ring" if you want to get changes right away, or choose the "slow ring" if you want to get changes in a few months. You can evaluate, vote on, and give feedback about the changes, and your input will help determine what other Windows 10 users will eventually see—all one billion of them—if Microsoft succeeds in its intention to make Windows 10 the universal Windows platform worldwide.

 note

Because Microsoft is promising to update Windows 10 gradually, on an ongoing basis, you might be wondering what it means to have a printed book that can't update with it. Good news! If you check out the information on the inside cover, you'll find information about Que's online Content Update Program and how it lets us keep this information up to date.

In the Modern Age

A lot of good engineering and usability research has been applied to Windows 10. Computer interfaces are evolving toward more natural physical interactions with us mortals, meeting us closer to a middle ground where they figure out what we want, rather than our having to figure out what *they* want.

And that leads us to a final comment about a way to look at your interactions with Windows 10: Let it work for *you* rather than the other way around. If you find yourself struggling to remember how to get to some setting or activate some feature, remember that Windows 10 is all about *searching* and *prioritizing*.

You might find that you miss the hierarchy of programs in the Start menu, which lets you dig down through sensible categories to find what you were looking for. (Well, they started out as sensible categories. After a few years when your Start menu had 50 or 100 items in it, they weren't so sensible.)

But you don't need to dig anymore. Instead, *search* for what you want by typing the first few letters of a word or title into the search box that appears in the taskbar, the Settings app, or the Control Panel. Don't try to *navigate* the Control Panel; instead, search it. This takes just a fraction of a second. It's much quicker than poking around with the mouse.

Then, *prioritize* the Start menu by moving tiles for your most-used apps to the top of the first page. This way, you can start up a favorite application with just one poke of your finger or one click.

The same holds for the desktop. Pin your favorite programs to the taskbar so that you don't need to locate them more than once. This is so easy, once you remember to do it.

If you remember to search, organize, and pin, you'll find that Windows 10's Start menu and desktop are more efficient than any previous version of Windows, bar none.

Also, remember that there are keyboard and mouse shortcuts for almost everything important. Searching, File Explorer, Cortana, and almost all Windows management tools are always just *two keystrokes*, or *one mouse click* away *if* you know the right keys to press or the right place to click. This book will help you learn them quickly.

2

INSTALLING OR UPGRADING TO WINDOWS 10

Windows 10 System Requirements

Personal computing is governed by two inexorable, and not unrelated, "laws":

- **Moore's Law**—Processing power doubles every 18 months (from Gordon Moore, co-founder of Intel),

- **Parkinson's Law of Data**—Data expands to fill the space available for storage (from the original Parkinson's Law: Work expands to fill the time available). Oh, and

- **Murphy's Law**—So it's three inexorable laws: Whatever can go wrong, will. Never forget that.

The latter we discuss later in this chapter when we show how to make a system backup. The first two observations help explain why, when the computers we use are becoming increasingly powerful, our day-to-day tasks never really seem all that much faster. The leaps in processing power and memory are being matched by the increasing complexity and resource requirements of the latest programs. Therefore, the computer you're using today might be twice as muscular as the one you were using a year and a half ago, but the applications you're using are twice the size and require twice as many resources.

Windows fits neatly into this scenario. With each new release of Microsoft's flagship operating system, the hardware requirements become more stringent, and our computers' processing power is taxed a little more. Even though Microsoft spent an enormous amount of time and effort trying to shoehorn Windows 10 into a minimal system configuration, you need a reasonably powerful computer if you don't want to spend most of your day waiting, thumbs a-twiddle. The good news is that in Windows 10, just like Windows 8/8.1, the hardware requirements are nowhere near as onerous as many people believed they would be. In fact, most midrange or better systems purchased in the past year or two should run Windows 10 without a problem.

The next few sections present a rundown of the system requirements you need to meet to install and work with Windows 10. Note that we give the minimum requirements, as stipulated by Microsoft, as well as a set of reasonable requirements that we believe you need to make working with Windows 10 more or less pleasurable.

 note

Although we said that each new Windows release requires more PC horsepower, that's actually not the case with Windows 10, which, for upgrade scenarios, has the same system requirements as Windows 8/8.1. Basically, if your system does a good job of running Windows 8/8.1, it will perform just as well running Windows 10.

Processor Requirements

Windows 10 desktop minimum: 1GHz modern processor

This is a true minimum requirement because these days you'd be hard-pressed to even find a PC with a processor as slow as 1GHz. There are plenty of cheap PCs available running old Intel Core 2 Duo CPUs at 1.8GHz and AMD Athlon processors at 2.0GHz. But for adequate Windows 10 performance, you want at least a midrange processor, which means an Intel Core i3 or i5, or an AMD Phenom II X3 or X4, running at 2.5GHz–3.0GHz. Faster is better, of course, but only if money is no object. Moving up to an Intel i9 or AMD Ryzen- or APU-series chip running at 3.2GHz or even 3.8GHz might set you back a few hundred more dollars, but the performance improvement won't be all that noticeable. You'd be much better off investing those funds either in extra memory (discussed later) or in a quad-core (or better) processor.

 note

What does quad-core mean? It describes a CPU that combines four separate processors, each with its own cache memory, on a single chip. (The cache memory is an onboard storage area that the processor uses to store commonly used bits of data. The bigger the cache, the better the performance.) This enables the operating system to perform four tasks at once without a performance hit. For example, you could work in your word processor or spreadsheet program in the foreground using one processor, while the other processors take care of a background File History backup, virus check, and print operation. Current examples of quad-core processors are the Intel Core i5, i7, and i9 and the AMD Ryzen-, APU-, and FX-series. Note, as well, that you can get systems with 6-core and even 8-core processors, although they tend to be quite expensive.

Memory Requirements

Windows 10 minimum: 32-bit Windows: 1GB for upgrading, 2GB for new devices
64-bit Windows: 2GB

You can run 32-bit Windows 10 on a system with 1GB of RAM, and Microsoft will permit you to upgrade an older version of Windows to Windows 10 with this little RAM, but the performance will be quite slow. Microsoft has raised the minimum spec for new devices to 2GB, and this is a more realistic minimum for day-to-day work on 32-bit systems. If you regularly have many programs running at the same time, if you use programs that manipulate digital photos or videos, or if you do extensive work with large files such as databases, 3GB should be your RAM goal on a 32-bit system. And 32-bit desktop versions of Windows can't use any more than 3GB of RAM. (See the accompanying note that discusses this.)

If you're running a 64-bit version of Windows 10, you should seriously consider upgrading your system RAM far above the 2GB minimum. The conventional wisdom is that because 64-bit machines deal with data in chunks that are twice the size of those in 32-bit machines, you need twice the memory to see the full benefit of the 64-bit advantage. Therefore, if you'd need 1GB of RAM in a 32-bit machine, it makes sense that you'd want at least 2GB in a 64-bit computer. However, the real reason 64-bit versions of Windows are superior to 32-bit versions for most people is that 64-bit systems can utilize much more memory than the 3GB practical maximum of 32-bit systems. These days, 64-bit machines installed with 8GB, 16GB, or even 32GB of RAM are commonplace, with 64GB systems not hard to find. It's unlikely you need triple-digit gigabytes of RAM, but you won't regret getting a 32GB system, which offers plenty of room for your programs and data to roam.

Finally, consider the speed of the memory. Older DDR2 (double data rate) memory chips typically operate between 200MHz and 533MHz. DDR3 chips operate between 1066MHz and 2800MHz, and the latest DDR4 chips range from 2133MHz to 3400MHz, which is a substantial speed boost that improves Windows 10 performance noticeably (as long as your PC's motherboard supports the faster memory and all of your RAM is high speed. Most motherboards run all memory at the speed of the slowest module).

 note

That "32-bitness" of 32-bit Windows means that these systems can address a maximum of 4GB RAM (because 2 raised to the power of 32 is 4,294,967,296 bytes, which is essentially 4GB). However, if you install 4GB on your motherboard and then check the amount of system memory, you might see only 3,198MB (3.12GB). What's going on here? The problem is that some devices require a chunk of system memory to operate. For example, the memory on the video card must be mapped to an area in system memory. To allow for this, 32-bit versions of Windows set aside a chunk of the 4GB address space for devices. On these systems, the amount of RAM available to your programs will always be 3.12GB or less.

Storage Requirements

Windows 10 hard disk free space minimum: 16GB (32-bit Windows) or 20GB (64-bit Windows)

The disk space requirements depend on which version of Windows 10 you're installing, but you should count on the new OS requiring at least 16GB free space to install. The OS will use perhaps another few gigabytes for storing items such as the paging file, System Restore checkpoints, web browser temporary files, and the Recycle Bin, so 32-bit Windows 10 will require at least 20GB of storage, and 64-bit Windows at least 24GB.

These days, of course, it's not the operating system that usurps the most space on our hard drives; it's the massive multimedia files that now seem to be routine for most of us. Multi-megabyte digital photos and spreadsheets, and even multi-gigabyte database files and digital video files, are not unusual. Fortunately, hard disk storage is dirt cheap these days, with most disks costing less—often much less—than a dime a gigabyte.

Note, too, that the type of hard drive can affect performance. For desktop systems, an older drive that spins at 5,400RPM will be a significant performance bottleneck. Moving up to a 7,200RPM drive will help immeasurably, and a 10,000RPM (or even 15,000RPM) drive is even better if you don't mind the extra expense. You should also look for Serial Advanced Technology Attachment (SATA) drives that boast throughput rates of 6GBps. Look for a SATA drive with a 32MB or 64MB cache.

If having a ton of storage space isn't a priority for you, consider opting for a solid-state hard drive (SSD). These 2.5-inch drives are made from solid-state semiconductors, which means they have no moving parts. As a result, SSDs are much faster than regular hard drives, last longer, use less power, weigh less, and are completely silent. The downside is price. This technology is still newish (although no longer bleeding-edge), so expect to pay from 50 to 70 cents a gigabyte.

Finally, you should also bear in mind that one longstanding feature of Windows is the capability to burn data to recordable optical discs (CDs, DVDs, and Blu-ray discs). To take advantage of this feature, your system requires an optical disc burner, at the very least one that supports both the DVD-RW and DVD+RW disc formats (that is, a DVD±RW drive).

Graphics Requirements

Windows 10 graphics memory minimum: DirectX 9 video card with WDDM 1.0 driver; 1024×768 resolution for Modern apps

Windows 10's interface is graphics intensive, but it will be smart enough to adopt a less intensive interface based on what your PC can handle. Whether Windows 10 holds back on the visual bells and whistles depends on whether you have a separate graphics card (as opposed to an integrated motherboard graphics chip), the capability of the card's graphics processing unit (GPU), and how much graphics memory the card has onboard.

To get the beautiful Windows theme look as well as the animated effects offered by many Modern apps, your system should have a graphics processor that supports DirectX 9, Pixel Shader 2.0 (in hardware, not as a software emulation), and 32 bits per pixel. The graphics processor must also come with a device driver that supports the Windows Display Driver Model (WDDM). (If you purchase a new video card, look for the Windows 10 Capable or Windows 10 Pro Ready logo on the box. If you just need to upgrade the driver for an existing graphics card, look for "WDDM" in the driver name or description.)

Note that for best performance, some games and programs might require a graphics card compatible with DirectX 10 or higher.

The amount of onboard graphics memory you need does not depend on the resolution you plan to use. For example, even a card running at HD (1920×1080) resolution requires only a bare minimum of 8MB of graphics memory to display an image, whereas a card running at a whopping 2560×1600 resolution really needs only 16MB. However, factor in features such as triple buffering (rendering images while the current image is displayed) and high-end game features (such as rendering textures), and the more graphics memory you can afford, the better.

Hardware Requirements for Various Windows 10 Features

Windows 10 is a big, sprawling program that can do many things, so it's not surprising that you might need a long list of miscellaneous equipment, depending on what you plan to do with your system. Table 2.1 provides a rundown.

Table 2.1 Equipment Required for Various Windows 10 Tasks

Task	Required Equipment
Using the Internet	For a broadband connection: A cable or DSL modem and a router for security.
	For a dial-up connection: A dial-up modem.
Networking	For a wired connection: A network adapter, preferably one that supports Gigabit Ethernet (1Gbps) connections, a network switch or hub, and network cables.
	For a wireless connection: A wireless adapter and wireless access point that support IEEE 802.11n. Ideally, the access point will double as a router to provide wireless Internet access.
Multitouch	A tablet PC or a PC with a touchpad or touch-sensitive screen that recognizes multiple points of touch simultaneously.
Photo editing	A USB or HDMI slot for connecting the digital camera. If you want to transfer the images from a memory card, you need the appropriate memory card reader. Memory card readers are built in to most newer desktop and laptop computers, but if yours doesn't have one, you can purchase an external memory card reader. For serious Photoshop editing, you probably want at least 8GB of RAM, too.
Document scanning	A document scanner or an all-in-one printer that includes scanning capabilities.
Faxing	A dial-up modem that includes fax capabilities.
Ripping and burning CDs	For ripping: A CD or DVD drive.
	For burning: A recordable CD or DVD drive.
Burning DVDs	A recordable DVD drive.
Video editing	An internal or external video-capture device, or a USB or IEEE 1394 (FireWire) port. And again, lots of RAM—8GB or more.
Videoconferencing	A webcam or a digital camera that has a webcam mode.
BitLocker	A PC with Trusted Platform Module (TPM) 1.2.
Listening to digital audio files	A sound card or integrated audio, as well as speakers or headphones. For the best sound, use a subwoofer with the speakers.
Watching TV	A TV tuner card (preferably one that supports video capture). A remote control is useful if you are watching the screen from a distance.

Preparing Your System: A Checklist

Installing a new operating system—especially one that makes relatively radical changes to your system, as Windows 10 does (assuming you're upgrading from Windows 7 or earlier)—is definitely a "look before you leap" operation. Your computer's operating system is just too important, so you shouldn't dive blindly into the installation process. To make sure that things go well, and to prevent any permanent damage in case disaster strikes, you need to practice "safe" installing. This means taking some time beforehand to run through a few precautionary measures and to make sure your system is ready to welcome Windows 10. To that end, the next few sections run through a checklist of items you should take care of before firing up the Setup program.

Check Your System Requirements

Before getting too involved in the Setup process, you need to make sure your computer can run Windows 10. Go back over the system requirements we outlined earlier to make sure your machine is Windows 10 ready.

This would also be a good time to get yourself a Microsoft account, if you don't have one already. Much of Windows 10 works better—particularly across multiple devices—if you log in to Windows 10 with a Microsoft account.

➡ *To find out more about Microsoft accounts, **see** "Microsoft Versus Local Accounts," **p. 75**.*

Back Up Your Files

Although the vast majority of Windows 10 installations make it through without a hitch, there's that pesky third law—Murphy's Law—that we mentioned at the beginning of this chapter. Software (particularly complex operating system software) always seems to follow Murphy's Law, which means if anything can go wrong, it will. Windows 10 Setup has a feature that will reverse its changes and (theoretically) restore your system to its original state, getting you out of most jams. However, you should still make backup copies of important files, in case Setup's restore option fails. At the very least, you should back up your data files, which are both precious and irreplaceable.

Clean Up Your Hard Disk

To maximize the amount of free space on your hard disk (and just for the sake of doing some spring cleaning), you should go through your hard disk with a fine-toothed comb, looking for unnecessary files you can delete.

The easiest route here is to use the Disk Cleanup utility. In most recent versions of Windows, open Windows Explorer or File Explorer, display the Computer folder or This PC folder, right-click drive C (or whatever drive contains the Windows system files), click Properties, and then in the General tab, click Disk Cleanup. Chapter 25, "Managing Hard Disks and Storage Spaces," offers more details about the Disk Cleanup utility.

➡ *To learn more about Disk Cleanup, **see** "Deleting Unnecessary Files," **p. 556**.*

Check and Defragment Your Hard Disk

Windows 10 Setup uses CHKDSK to give your hard disk a quick once-over before settling down to the serious business of installation. Sure, a "quick once-over" is better than nothing, but you should be more thorough. Specifically, use your version of the Windows Check Disk program to give your hard disk a "surface" scan. The surface scan checks your hard disk for physical imperfections that could lead to trouble down the road. In most recent versions of Windows, open Windows Explorer or File Explorer, display the Computer folder or This PC folder, right-click drive C (or whatever drive contains the Windows system files), click Properties, click the Tools tab, and then click Check Disk or Check. If you're running the Windows 7 version, check the Scan For and Attempt Recovery of Bad Sectors check box. Click Start.

Don't forget to do a virus check if you have antivirus software. Viruses have been known to wreak havoc on the Windows 10 Setup program (in addition to their other less-endearing qualities, such as locking up your system and trashing your hard drive).

When that's done, you should next defragment the files on your hard drive. This action ensures that Setup will store the Windows 10 files with optimal efficiency, which will improve performance and lessen the risk of corrupted data. In most recent versions of Windows, open Windows Explorer or File Explorer, display the Computer folder or This PC folder, right-click drive C (or whatever drive contains the Windows system files), click Properties, click the Tools tab, and then click Defragment Now or Optimize.

Create a System Image Backup and a System Repair Disc

If you're upgrading to Windows 10 from Windows 7, you should prepare for the worst by creating both a system image backup and a system repair disc.

The worst-case scenario for an operating system upgrade is a system crash that renders your hard disk or system files unusable. Your only recourse in such a case is to start from scratch with either a reformatted hard disk or a new hard disk. This usually means that you have to reinstall Windows 7 and then reinstall and reconfigure all your applications. In other words, you're looking at the better part of a day or, more likely, a few days, to recover your system. However, Windows 7 has a feature that takes most of the pain out of recovering your system. It's called a system image backup, and it's actually a complete backup of your Windows 7 installation. Creating a system image takes a long time (at least several hours, depending on how much stuff you have), but it's worth doing for the peace of mind. Here are the steps to follow to create the system image:

1. On your Windows 7 PC, select Start, type **backup**, and then click Backup and Restore in the search results.

2. Click Create an Image. The Create a System Image Wizard appears.

3. The wizard asks you to specify a backup destination. You have three choices. (Click Next when you're ready to continue.)

   ■ **On a Hard Disk**—Select this option if you want to use a disk drive on your computer. If you have multiple drives, use the list to select the one you want to use.

- **On One or More DVDs**—Select this option if you want to use DVDs to hold the backup.

- **On a Network Location**—Select this option if you want to use a shared network folder. Either type the UNC address of the share or click Select, and then either type the UNC address of the share or click Browse to use the Browse for Folder dialog box to select the shared network folder. Type a username and password for accessing the share, and then click OK.

4. The system image backup automatically includes your internal hard disk in the system image, and you can't change that. However, if you also have external hard drives, you can add them to the backup by activating their check boxes. Click Next. Windows Backup asks you to confirm your backup settings.

5. Click Start Backup. Windows Backup creates the system image.

6. When the backup is complete, click Close.

The second half of your Windows 7 recovery system is the system repair disc, which is a CD or DVD that enables you to boot to the disc and then restore your system using the system image backup you just created. Here's how you go about creating a system repair disc:

1. On your Windows 7 PC, select Start, type **system repair**, and then click Create a System Repair Disc in the search results. The Create a System Repair Disc dialog box appears.

2. Insert a blank recordable CD or DVD into your burner. If the AutoPlay dialog box shows up, close it.

3. If you have multiple burners, use the Drive list to select the one you want to use.

4. Click Create Disc. Windows 7 creates the disc (it takes a minute or two) and then displays a particularly unhelpful dialog box.

5. Click Close, and then click OK.

Eject the disc, label it, and then put it someplace where you'll be able to find it later.

Installing Windows 10

This section tells how to install a clean (no apps, no users) copy of Windows 10, even though the term "upgrade" appears in the text that follows. To upgrade or update Windows 7, 8, or 10 so that your users and apps are preserved, see the next section, "Upgrading to Windows 10." And if you want to retain your previous copy of Windows (or another operating system) *and* have the choice of which OS to boot up when you start your computer, see "Dual- (and Multi-)Booting Windows 10."

To begin the standard installation process, boot up your computer from Windows 10 installation media, such as a DVD disc or a USB flash drive containing the USB installation system. If you don't already have installation media, you can download

 note

Installing always starts by booting up your computer from installation media, such as a DVD or a USB flash drive. We discuss this in this section. *Upgrading* is performed by running the Windows setup program from within your existing, running copy of Windows. We discuss that in the next section.

the files needed to create a set from microsoft.com. Just search for "Download Windows 10." You will also need a valid Windows 10 product key—a long string of digits and letters—as discussed shortly.

The installation process for Windows 10 is probably the easiest—and, certainly, the least interactive—Windows install to date. Upgrading takes just a few mouse clicks, and even a clean install is a simple affair, although it does come with some welcome tools for managing partitions.

After the Setup program boots from the install media, it copies a file named boot.wim (located in the \sources subfolder on the Windows 10 install media) into RAM. This file is a scaled-down OS called the Windows Preinstallation Environment (Windows PE) that boots after a few seconds, so the rest of the install takes place in GUI mode. Windows PE begins by displaying the Windows Setup dialog box shown in Figure 2.1, which acts as kind of a Welcome screen for Windows PE.

Figure 2.1
This dialog box is the first stop in the Windows 10 installation process, which uses a GUI for all user interaction.

Click Next, and then click Install Now to get the install underway. At this point, you are running in the Windows PE OS. The next major screen asks for your Windows 10 product key. You can enter any of the following:

- A Windows 10 product key that you purchased or that came with your computer,

- Your Windows 7, 8, or 8.1 product key, if you had a licensed copy of one these operating systems previously running on this computer and you upgraded it to Windows 10 during the one-year free upgrade offer, or

- You can skip entering a key and can activate Windows after installation. If your product key was linked to your Microsoft account, this can be quite easy to accomplish later.

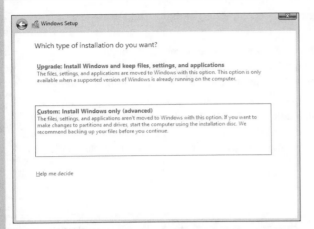

Figure 2.2
You can install Windows 10 either as an upgrade or as a clean (or custom) version.

Then, the installer displays the license agreement and asks whether you accept its terms. The install program next asks you what type of installation you want to perform. You have two choices, as shown in Figure 2.2:

- **Upgrade**—Click this choice to upgrade Windows 10 over your existing operating system. Note, however, that this option does not preserve data such as your user accounts, apps, and Windows settings. You will have to create new user accounts, install apps again, and dig around for your old data. (There are third-party tools that can help with this, as discussed in the Tip in the next section.) If you want to preserve your accounts and apps, you must run the upgrade from within your current Windows installation. See the next section for more details.

- **Custom**—Click this choice to install a clean version of Windows 10. This is the install that we cover in this section.

If you choose the Custom option, you come to the most interesting part of the setup process. The installer begins by showing you a list of your system's available partitions, and you click the one on which you want to install Windows 10. The real install fun begins if you click the Drive Options (Advanced) link, which appears for only unformatted partitions. It displays a few extra commands, as you can see in Figure 2.3.

Depending on the partition, one or more of the following commands become available:

- **Delete**—Click this command to delete the selected partition.

- **Format**—Click this command to format the selected partition. Note that the installer formats the partition using NTFS.

 tip
When Windows PE is running, you can display the command prompt at any time by pressing Shift+F10.

 caution
If you're going the clean install route and you have an existing product key for Windows 7, 8, 8.1, or 10, make sure you install a compatible version of Windows 10. For example, if you have a product key for Windows 7 Home, then you must install Windows 10 Home; your product key won't work for Windows 10 Pro.

Figure 2.3
The installer gives you some options for manipulating the partition on which you want to install Windows 10.

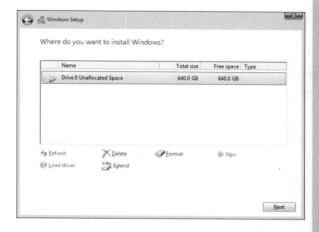

- **New**—Click this command to create a new partition out of the selected unallocated disk space, which displays a spin box that you can use to set the partition size. Click Apply to create the new partition.

- **Extend**—Click this command to increase the size of the selected partition by extending it into adjoining unallocated disk space.

- **Load Driver**—Click this command to load a third-party device driver for the selected partition. Note that Windows 10 can install the drivers from a CD, DVD, or USB Flash drive.

Clicking Next ends the interactive portion of the installation. From here on, the installer handles everything from copying files to rebooting the machine without prompting you.

When the installation is complete, you're asked whether you want to use Express settings, which set up Windows 10 with defaults chosen by Microsoft. Going this route is, in our opinion, a really bad idea. For example, one of the defaults is to connect to any unsecured wireless network within range. Other defaults also send private information (such as your location) to Microsoft and "trusted partners." No thanks.

Click Customize Settings to run through a set of screens that cover the following:

- Selecting the type of Personalization and Location information you want to send to Microsoft (and those trusted partners), as shown in Figure 2.4.

- Selecting browsing options, such as using SmartScreen (the Windows 10 antiphishing tool), and page prediction, which helps preload pages but has the downside of sending your browsing history to Microsoft. (We always turn off the latter, as shown in Figure 2.5.)

- Deciding how Windows 10 connects to networks (for example, you can turn off automatic connections to open networks; see Figure 2.5) and whether you want to send problem reports to Microsoft.

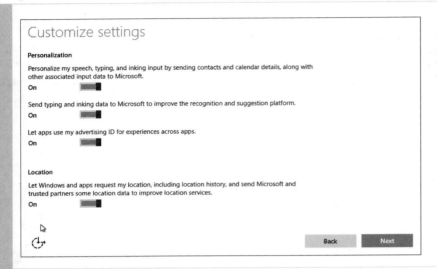

Figure 2.4
Customize install settings to control the information sent to Microsoft and its partners.

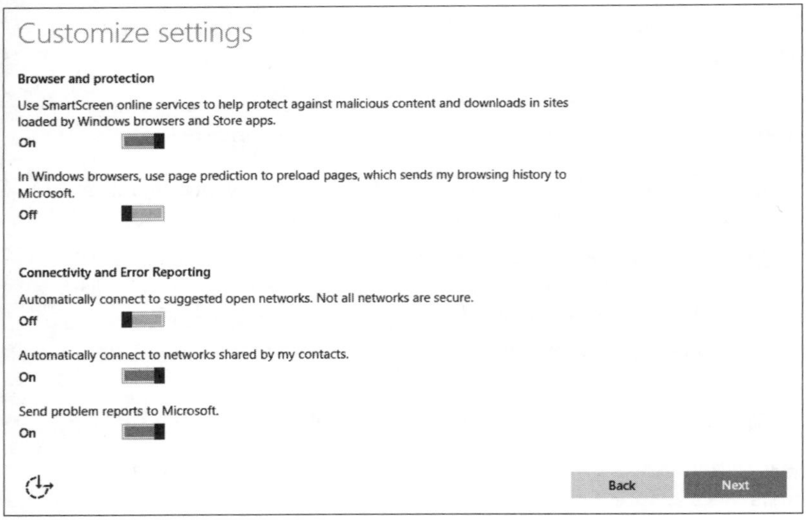

Figure 2.5
Take the customize settings route to override some of the Windows 10 installer's less welcome defaults.

After the customized settings section is done, you're taken through a few screens to configure Windows 10. Configuration chores include the following:

- Specifying whether your PC is owned by you or your company

- Signing in to an existing Microsoft account or creating a new Microsoft account

- An introduction to Cortana, the voice-activated Windows 10 assistant

- Deciding whether you want to activate network discovery and file and printer sharing (a good idea on your home network) ·

If you performed a clean install and haven't already entered your product key, you'll be prompted to do this now, to activate Windows 10. If you have previously run Windows 10 on this computer and used a Microsoft (online) account on this computer, the product key might be recovered automatically.

Upgrading to Windows 10

If you're currently running either Windows 7 with Service Pack 1 (all versions except Enterprise) or Windows 8/8.1, you were most likely pestered incessantly for the first year after Windows 10's release by Microsoft's aggressive attempts to get you to accept a free upgrade, through notifications and pop-up windows that appeared several times a day. Many people woke up one morning to find that they had Windows 10 anyway, despite having done everything they could think of to say "No, thanks. Really."

If you somehow managed to avoid the free upgrade, you probably had good reasons why you didn't accept it. Perhaps you had hardware, applications, or networking tools that were known not to work with Windows 10. Maybe you just didn't want to risk losing your stable computer setup, or maybe you didn't trust that free meant free.

In any event, if you're reading this, you are now thinking about updating. Maybe you don't need that pesky old hardware or software anymore, or, you're just feeling lucky. Or left out. Sadly, though, the free offer has expired, and the update no longer comes effortlessly through Windows Update. (A free upgrade is still available to Windows 7 and 8.1 users if you have a disability that requires you to use assistive technologies such as the Narrator, Magnifier, or Sticky Keys, or comparable third-party tools. For more information, visit support.microsoft.com/accessibility/disability-answer-desk or do a web search for "Microsoft Disability Answer Desk.")

To upgrade, you need to acquire a Windows 10 license key—a long string of digits and letters. You can purchase one online from microsoft.com or from other online vendors. The cost for an upgrade is the same as for a fresh copy of Windows: $119 for Windows 10 Home, or $199 for Windows 10 Pro. (If you are a student or teacher, you might be eligible for a discounted price. Also, you can find "OEM" licenses online for less than this, but, technically these are licensed for clean installs on new computers only. Also, the license is tied to the one computer on which you install it, and using it to upgrade is not licensed, or supported, and might not even work.)

 tip

Microsoft doesn't offer an easy upgrade path to Windows 10 for Windows XP or Vista, but there are third-party tools that will do the job. For example, Zinstall Migration Kit Pro (zinstall.com/products/zinstall-migration-kit-pro) and Laplink PCmover (laplink.com/pcmover) can transfer your old user account files, settings, and more. The idea is that you run a clean install of Windows 10 as discussed in the previous section and then run the utility, which uses the Windows.old folder (where the Windows 10 Setup saved your old system files) to extract your user data and settings.

You can either buy an installation DVD with the license key attached to a label or purchase just the key and then download the Windows 10 Media Creation Tool. To get this tool, search microsoft.com for "Download Windows 10," and then follow the prompts to download and run the tool. You'll need either a blank recordable DVD or a removable USB flash drive that you can allow to be completely erased. You can only use a USB flash drive if your computer supports booting from removable media. The procedure for doing so varies from PC to PC, so in most cases burning a DVD is the easiest route.

Once you have the install media ready and your license key in hand, sign in to Windows, insert the DVD or plug the USB drive into your computer, and run the setup.exe program it contains. (This is the difference between *installing* and *upgrading*. For a clean install, you boot up from the installation media. For an upgrade, you run setup.exe from within your current version of Windows.)

After a minute of preparation or so, you will be prompted to download updates to the installation process. If you have an unmetered Internet connection, click Next; otherwise, select Not Right Now, and then Next. Click Accept to accept the license agreement. If you chose to download updates, setup might now take several minutes to check for and download updates.

 note

You can upgrade Windows 7 or 8/8.1 Pro to Windows 10 Pro, and you can upgrade Windows 7 or 8/8.1 Home to either Windows 10 Home or Pro. You can't, however, use the upgrade process to move "down" from Windows 7 or 8/8.1 Pro to Windows 10 Home. Your only option, if you want to move from Pro to Home is to do a clean install, in which case you will have to reinstall your applications, re-create your user accounts, and dig your old files out of the Windows.old folder that will remain after the new copy of Windows is installed. As mentioned in the previous Tip, there are third-party tools that can help with this process.

You will next be asked to confirm what you wish to keep. If you are upgrading from Windows 7 or 8/8.1, your application programs, user accounts, and documents will be retained intact by default, unless you select Change What to Keep and make one of the following choices:

- **Keep Personal Files and Apps**—Your user accounts, applications, documents, and other files will be available in Windows 10. This is the default setting.

- **Keep Personal Files Only**—Your user accounts and documents will be kept, but applications, application setup data, and other Windows settings will be wiped clean and reset to all default settings.

- **Nothing**—This will perform a clean install of Windows, with your applications, user accounts, and all files wiped out.

If desired, click Change What to Keep and make an alternative selection. Then click Next. Windows may check for more updates. Finally, click Install to begin the upgrade process. Up until the first restart, you can click Cancel to stop the upgrade process.

The update process may take up to an hour. During that time, it will restart one or more times. If during these restarts you see a prompt along the lines of "Press any key to boot from the DVD or CD," do *not* press a key; let Windows boot up from the hard disk.

If you retained your user accounts, the first time you sign in there will still be a per-user setup process that takes up to several minutes, while Windows sorts through your retained or reset user account settings.

Dual- (and Multi-) Booting Windows 10

The last thing you need to mull over before getting down to the nitty-gritty of the Setup program is whether you want to run Windows 10 exclusively or dual-boot with another operating system. Dual-booting means that when you start your computer, you have the option of running Windows 10 or some other operating system, such as Windows 7 or XP. It's even possible to multiboot, which means having the choice of three or more operating systems at startup.

Windows 10 keeps track of which operating systems are installed on your PC by using a data store called the Boot Configuration Data (BCD). Earlier Windows versions that are compatible with the BCD are Windows 8/8.1, Windows 7, and Windows Vista. This means that if you have a system currently running any of these versions of Windows, when you install Windows 10, the BCD will automatically set up a dual-boot configuration. Actually, we should say that Windows 10 sets up the automatic dual-boot provided you do two things:

- Install Windows 10 to a separate partition on your hard disk or to a separate hard disk connected to your PC.

- Install Windows 10 after you install the earlier OS.

For versions of Windows prior to Vista that aren't compatible with the BCD store, the BCD lumps everything together under the rubric "Earlier Version of Windows," and it uses the legacy BOOT.INI file to store the boot data from these older operating systems.

You might be surprised to hear that the BCD is actually quite configurable. We show you the details a bit later in this chapter. (See "Customizing the Boot Configuration Data [BCD].")

The next two sections show you how to dual- and multiboot Windows 10 with various other systems.

Dual-Booting Windows 10

Assuming your PC has the earlier version of Windows already installed, follow these steps to install Windows 10 for dual-booting with the other OS:

1. Boot to the Windows 10 install media, and then follow the initial prompts to launch the installation, enter your product key, and accept the license agreement.

2. When you get to the Which Type of Installation Do You Want? dialog box (see Figure 2.2, earlier in this chapter), be sure to click the Custom option.

3. Click the partition you want to use to install Windows 10. Be sure to choose a partition other than the one where your current version of Windows is installed. This will be the partition with System shown in the Type column, as you can see in Figure 2.6.

4. Follow the install steps we outlined earlier to complete the Windows 10 installation (see "Installing Windows 10").

 caution

You must boot to the install media to set up a dual-boot. Otherwise, the Windows 10 installer will upgrade your existing version of the Windows instead of creating a separate version.

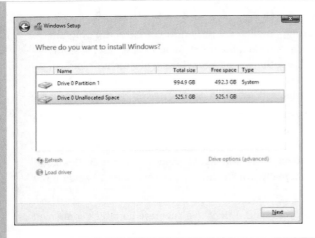

Figure 2.6
When installing Windows 10, be sure to select a partition other than the one where your current version of Windows is loaded.

Multibooting with Three or More Operating Systems

For maximum OS flexibility, you want to have three or more systems available on your machine so that you can multiboot among them. Depending on the operating systems you want to use, this isn't all that much more work than setting up a dual-boot system.

If you're installing only Windows operating systems, you need only keep the following two points in mind for foolproof multibooting:

- Install each operating system to its own partition on your hard disk or to its own hard disk connected to your PC.

- Install the operating systems in release date order, with the oldest operating first and Windows 10 last. For example, if you want to multiboot Windows XP, Windows 7, and Windows 10, you should install Windows XP, then Windows 7, and then Windows 10.

If you want to multiboot other operating systems, such as Linux, your best bet is a third-party boot manager program or the boot manager that comes with the OS (such as any of the boot managers that come with Linux distributions).

Using Windows Boot Manager

Now that your system can boot to one or more operating systems other than Windows 10, you need to know how to control your OSs. You do this using the Windows Boot Manager, which is a menu of the operating systems installed on your PC.

By default, Windows Boot Manager appears automatically when you start your PC. However, you can also invoke Windows Boot Manager from within Windows 10 itself by following these steps:

1. Click Start and then click Settings to launch the Settings app.

2. Click Update & Security and then click the Recovery tab.

3. Under the Advanced Startup heading, click Restart Now. The Choose an Option screen appears.

4. Click Use Another Operating System. The Choose an Operating System screen appears, which is the Windows 10 version of Windows Boot Manager.

The screen you see depends on your dual-boot setup. For example, if you're dual-booting with Windows 8/8.1, Windows 7, or Windows Vista, you see a screen similar to the one shown in Figure 2.7.

Figure 2.7
If you're dual-booting Windows 10 with Windows 8/8.1, Windows 7, or Windows Vista, you use this startup screen to choose which operating system you want to load.

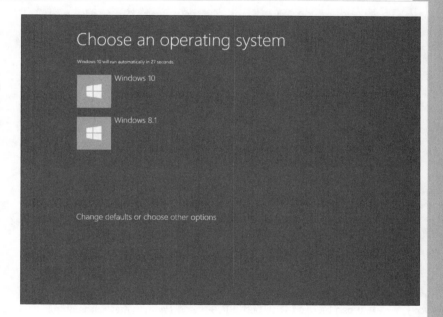

If you're dual-booting with Windows XP or earlier, you see a screen similar to the one shown in Figure 2.8. Again, notice that the BCD simply refers to the legacy OS as "Earlier Version of Windows."

If you invoke Windows Boot Manager at startup and you do nothing at this point, Windows Boot Manager will automatically boot the default OS—usually Windows 10—after 30 seconds. Otherwise, you click the operating system you want to boot. To change the default operating system or the default wait time before bootup proceeds, see the next section.

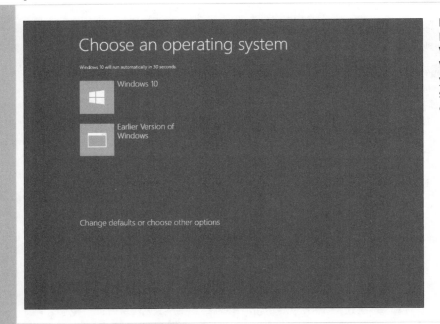

Figure 2.8
If you're dual-booting Windows 10 with Windows XP or earlier, you use this startup screen to select an operating system to boot.

Customizing the Boot Configuration Data (BCD)

As we mentioned earlier, the specifics of the Windows Boot Manager menu are determined by the BCD, which offers the following features:

- It can be used with both BIOS-based systems and Extensible Firmware Interface (EFI)-based systems. BCD creates a common store for both types.

- It supports boot applications, which refers to any process that runs in the boot environment that the Windows Boot Manager creates. The main types of boot applications are Windows 10 partitions, legacy installations of Windows, and startup tools. In this sense, Windows Boot Manager is a kind of miniature operating system that displays an interface (the Windows Boot Manager menu) that lets you select which application you want to run.

 note
We don't discuss the BCD WMI provider in this book. To get more information, see the following page: https://msdn.microsoft.com/en-us/library/windows/desktop/aa362639(v=vs.85).aspx.

- Boot options are scriptable. The BCD exposes a scripting interface via a Windows Management Instrumentation (WMI) provider. This interface enables you to create scripts that modify all aspects of the BCD.

Windows 10 gives you five methods to modify some or all the data in the BCD store:

- Windows Boot Manager
- The Startup and Recovery feature
- The System Configuration Utility
- The BCDEDIT command-line utility
- The BCD WMI provider

Using Windows Boot Manager to Modify the BCD

You can use the Windows Boot Manager to modify just a couple of BCD options: the default operating system and the maximum time the Windows Boot Manager menu is displayed. Here are the steps to follow:

1. Display the Windows Boot Manager, either at startup or from within Windows 10.

2. Click Change Defaults or Choose Other Options. (If you invoked Windows Boot Manager from within Windows 10, this command is called Change Defaults.)

3. To change the time that elapses before Windows Boot Manager selects the default OS, click Change the Timer and click the time you want to use (5 Minutes, 30 Seconds, or 5 Seconds).

4. To change the default OS, click Choose a Default Operating System, and then click the OS you want to use as the default.

5. Click the Back arrow to return to the Choose an Operating System screen.

6. Click the operating system you want to boot.

Using Startup and Recovery to Modify the BCD

You can modify a limited set of BCD options using the Startup and Recovery dialog box: the default operating system, the maximum time the Windows Boot Manager menu is displayed, and the maximum time the Windows 10 startup recovery options are displayed. Here are the steps to follow:

1. In the taskbar's Search box or the Run dialog box (press Windows Logo+R), type **systempropertiesadvanced** and then press Enter. The System Properties dialog box appears.

2. In the Advanced tab, click the Settings button in the Startup and Recovery group. Windows 10 displays the Startup and Recovery dialog box, shown in Figure 2.9.

3. In the Default Operating System list, click the operating system that Windows Boot Manager highlights by default at startup. (In other words, this is the operating system that runs automatically if you do not make a choice in the Windows Boot Manager screen.)

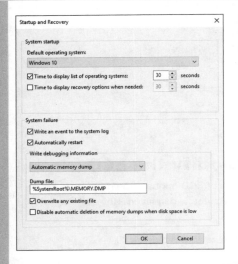

Figure 2.9
Use the Startup and Recovery dialog box to modify some aspects of the Boot Configuration Data.

4. Use the Time to Display List of Operating Systems spin box to set the interval after which Windows Boot Manager launches the default operating system. If you don't want Windows Boot Manager to select an operating system automatically, uncheck the Time to Display List of Operating Systems check box.

5. If Windows 10 is not shut down properly, Windows Boot Manager displays a menu of recovery options at startup. If you want the default options selected automatically after a time interval, check the Time to Display Recovery Options When Needed check box and use the associated spin box to set the interval.

6. Click OK in all open dialog boxes to put the new settings into effect.

Using the System Configuration Utility to Modify the BCD

For more detailed control over the BCD store, you can modify the data by using the System Configuration Utility. To start this program, follow these steps:

1. In the taskbar's Search box or in the Run dialog box (press Windows Logo+R), type **msconfig** and then press Enter.

2. If you see the User Account Control dialog box, either click Continue or type an administrator password and click Submit. The System Configuration window appears.

3. Select the Boot tab, shown in Figure 2.10.

Figure 2.10
In the System Configuration Utility, use the Boot tab to modify the BCD store.

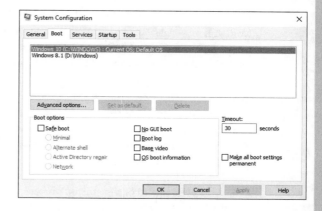

The large box near the top of the tab displays the operating systems on the current computer. You see "Current OS" beside the operating system you're running now; you see "Default OS" beside the operating system that's set up as the default. (Note, however, that the Boot tab does not include an entry for any legacy OS—that is, Windows XP or earlier—that you have installed.) There are four main tasks you can perform:

- Click the Set as Default button to set the highlighted operating system as the default for the Windows Boot Manager menu.

- Use the Timeout text box to set the maximum time that Windows Boot Manager waits before selecting the default OS.

- Use the check boxes in the Boot Options group to set the following startup options for the currently highlighted Windows 10 install:

  Safe Boot: Minimal—Boots Windows 10 in Safe mode, which uses only a minimal set of device drivers. Use this switch if Windows 10 won't start, if a device or program is causing Windows 10 to crash, or if you can't uninstall a program while Windows 10 is running normally.

  Safe Boot: Alternate Shell—Boots Windows 10 in Safe mode but also bypasses the Windows 10 GUI and boots to the command prompt instead. Use this switch if the programs you need to repair a problem can be run from the command prompt or if you can't load the Windows 10 GUI.

  Safe Boot: Active Directory Repair—Boots Windows 10 in Safe mode and restores a backup of the Active Directory service. (This option applies only to domain controllers.)

  Safe Boot: Network—Boots Windows 10 in Safe mode but also includes networking drivers. Use this switch if the drivers or programs you need to repair a problem exist on a

 note
The shell loaded by the /safeboot:minimal (alternateshell) switch is determined by the value in the following Registry key: HKEY_LOCAL_MACHINE\SYSTEM\ CurrentControlSet\SafeBoot\ AlternateShell. The default value is CMD.EXE (the command prompt).

shared network resource, if you need access to email or other network-based communications for technical support, or if your computer is running a shared Windows 10 installation.

No GUI Boot—Tells Windows 10 not to load the VGA display driver that is normally used to display the progress bar during startup. Use this switch if Windows 10 hangs while switching video modes for the progress bar or if the display of the progress bar is garbled.

Boot Log—Boots Windows 10 and logs the boot process to a text file named `ntbtlog.txt` that resides in the `%SystemRoot%` folder. Move to the end of the file, and you might see a message telling you which device driver failed. You probably need to reinstall or roll back the driver. (See Chapter 26, "Troubleshooting and Repairing Problems.") Use this switch if the Windows 10 startup hangs, if you need a detailed record of the startup process, or if you

note

`%SystemRoot%` refers to the folder into which Windows 10 was installed. This is usually `C:\Windows`.

suspect (after using one of the other Startup menu options) that a driver is causing Windows 10 startup to fail.

Base Video—Boots Windows 10 using the standard VGA mode: 640×480 with 256 colors. This is useful for troubleshooting video display driver problems. Use this switch if Windows 10 fails to start using any of the Safe mode options, if you recently installed a new video card device driver and the screen is garbled, if the driver is balking at a resolution or color depth setting that's too high, or if you can't load the Windows 10 GUI. After Windows 10 has loaded, you can reinstall or roll back the driver, or you can adjust the display settings to values that the driver can handle.

OS Boot Information—Displays the path and location of each device driver as it loads, as well as the operating system version and build number, the number of processors, the system memory, and the process type.

- Click the Advanced Options button to display the BOOT Advanced Options dialog box shown in Figure 2.11:

Figure 2.11
In the Boot tab, click Advanced Options to display the dialog box shown here.

Number of Processors—In a multiprocessor system, specifies the maximum number of processors or cores Windows 10 can use. Check this check box if you suspect that using multiple processors is causing a program to hang.

Maximum Memory—Specifies the maximum amount of memory, in megabytes, that Windows 10 can use. Use this value when you suspect a faulty memory chip might be causing problems.

PCI Lock—Check this check box to tell Windows 10 not to dynamically assign hardware resources for PCI devices during startup. The resources assigned by the BIOS during the POST are locked in place. Use this switch if installing a PCI device causes the system to hang during startup.

Debug—Enables remote debugging of the Windows 10 kernel. This sends debugging information to a remote computer via one of your computer's ports. If you use this switch, you can use the Debug Port list to specify a serial port, IEEE 1394 port, or USB port. If you use a serial port, you can specify the transmission speed of the debugging information using the Baud Rate list; if you use an IEEE 1394 connection, activate Channel and specify a channel value; if you use a USB port, type the device name in the USB Target Name text box.

 note

In the System Configuration window, if you check the Make All Boot Settings Permanent check box and then click Apply, you see a scary message saying that "you will not be able to undo the changes at a later time." This is misleading. What it should say is, "you will not be able to undo the changes at a later time simply by selecting the Normal Startup option in the General tab." Instead, you must manually reverse the individual changes you made. (For example, if you checked the Safe Book check box, then you must manually uncheck that check box.)

Using BCDEDIT to Customize the Startup Options

The System Configuration Utility makes it easy to modify BCD store items, but it doesn't give you access to the entire BCD store. For example, the Boot tab doesn't list any legacy boot items on your system, and there are no options for renaming boot items or changing the order in which the boot items are displayed in the Windows Boot Manager menu. For these tasks, and indeed for every possible BCD task, you need to use the BCDEDIT command-line tool.

Note that BCDEDIT is an Administrator-only tool, so you must run it under the Administrator account (not just any account in the Administrators group). The easiest way to do this is to run a Command Prompt session with elevated privileges, as described in the following steps:

1. Press Windows Logo+X (or right-click the Start button). A menu of power user commands appears.

2. Click Command Prompt (Admin). The User Account Control dialog box appears.

3. Either click Yes or type an administrator password and click Yes. The Command Prompt window appears.

➡️ *To learn how to add Command Prompt (Admin) to the Start Menu's shortcut menu, see "Adding Command Prompt to the Shortcut Menu," p. 129.*

Table 2.2 summarizes the switches you can use with BCDEDIT.

Table 2.2 Switches Available for the BCDEDIT Command-Line Tool

Switch	Description
/bootdebug	Toggles boot debugging for a boot application on and off
/bootems	Toggles Emergency Management Services for a boot application on and off
/bootsequence	Sets the one-time boot sequence for the boot manager
/copy	Makes a copy of an entry
/create	Creates a new entry
/createstore	Creates a new and empty BCD store
/dbgsettings	Sets the global debugger settings
/debug	Toggles kernel debugging for an operating system entry
/default	Sets the default entry
/delete	Deletes an entry
/deletevalue	Deletes an entry value
/displayorder	Sets the order in which Boot Manager displays the operating system entries
/ems	Enables or disables Emergency Management Services for an operating system entry
/emssettings	Sets the global Emergency Management Services settings
/enum	Lists the entries in the BCD store
/export	Exports the contents of the BCD store to a file
/event	Sets remote event logging for an entry to ON or OFF
/eventsettings	Is an alias for /dbgsettings
/hypervisorsettings	Sets or displays the hypervisor debugger settings, which are similar to the Debug options described in the previous section
/import	Restores the BCD store from a backup file created with the /export switch
/mirror	Creates a mirror (that is, a clone on a separate physical disk) for an entry
/set	Sets an option value for an entry
/store	Specifies the BCD store to use
/sysstore	Specifies the BCD store device on an Extensible Firmware Interface (EFI) PC
/timeout	Sets the Boot Manager timeout value
/toolsdisplayorder	Sets the order in which Boot Manager displays the Tools menu
/types	Displays the data types required by the /set and /deletevalue commands
/v	Displays all entry identifiers in full, instead of using well-known identifiers

To help you understand how BCDEDIT works, let's examine the output that appears when you run BCDEDIT with the /enum switch on a system that dual-boots Windows 10 and Windows 8.1:

```
Windows Boot Manager
--------------------
identifier{bootmgr}
devicepartition=\Device\HarddiskVolume1
description Windows Boot Manager
localeen-US
inherit {globalsettings}
integrityservices Enable
default {current}
resumeobject{14d214f2-caf4-11e1-b73a-83d46d071b71}
displayorder{current}
{14d214ef-caf4-11e1-b73a-83d46d071b71}
toolsdisplayorder {memdiag}
timeout 30

Windows Boot Loader
-------------------
identifier{current}
devicepartition=C:
path\Windows\system32\winload.exe
description Windows 10
localeen-US
inherit {bootloadersettings}
recoverysequence{14d214f4-caf4-11e1-b73a-83d46d071b71}
integrityservices Enable
recoveryenabled Yes
allowedinmemorysettings 0x15000075
osdevicepartition=C:
systemroot\Windows
resumeobject{14d214f2-caf4-11e1-b73a-83d46d071b71}
nxOptIn
bootmenupolicyStandard

Windows Boot Loader
-------------------
identifier{14d214ef-caf4-11e1-b73a-83d46d071b71}
devicepartition=D:
path\Windows\system32\winload.exe
description Windows 8.1
localeen-US
inherit {bootloadersettings}
recoverysequence{14d214f0-caf4-11e1-b73a-83d46d071b71}
recoveryenabled Yes
osdevicepartition=D:
systemroot\Windows
resumeobject{14d214ee-caf4-11e1-b73a-83d46d071b71}
nxOptIn
```

Here's another example from a system that dual-boots with Windows 10 and Windows XP:

```
Windows Boot Manager
--------------------
identifier{bootmgr}
devicepartition=D:
description Windows Boot Manager
localeen-US
inherit {globalsettings}
integrityservices Enable
default {current}
resumeobject{bdf44e81-cad5-11e1-b38b-cbbdd9e7fb08}
displayorder{ntldr}
{current}
toolsdisplayorder {memdiag}
timeout 30

Windows Legacy OS Loader
------------------------
identifier{ntldr}
devicepartition=D:
path\ntldr
description Earlier Version of Windows

Windows Boot Loader
-------------------
identifier{current}
devicepartition=C:
path\Windows\system32\winload.exe
description Windows 10
localeen-US
inherit {bootloadersettings}
recoverysequence{bdf44e83-cad5-11e1-b38b-cbbdd9e7fb08}
integrityservices Enable
recoveryenabled Yes
allowedinmemorysettings 0x15000075
osdevicepartition=C:
systemroot\Windows
resumeobject{bdf44e81-cad5-11e1-b38b-cbbdd9e7fb08}
nxOptIn
bootmenupolicyStandard
```

As you can see, this BCD store has four entries: one for Windows Boot Manager, one for a legacy Windows install (on partition C:), and two for Windows 10 installs (on our test machine, partitions D: and G:). Notice that each entry has an Identifier setting, and these IDs are unique to each entry. All IDs are actually 32-digit globally unique identifiers (GUIDs), such as the one shown earlier for the first Windows Boot Loader item:

```
14d214f4-caf4-11e1-b73a-83d46d071b71
```

The other entries have GUIDs as well, but by default BCDEDIT works with a collection of well-known identifiers, including the following. (Type **bcdedit id /?** to see the complete list.)

- bootmgr—The Windows Boot Manager entry

- ntldr—An entry that uses a legacy operating system loader (NTLDR) to boot previous versions of Windows

- current—The entry that corresponds to the operating system that is currently running

- default—The entry that corresponds to the Windows Boot Manager default operating system

- memdiag—The Windows Memory Diagnostics entry (deprecated in Windows 10)

If you want to see the full GUIDs for every entry, add the /v (verbose) switch:

```
bcdedit /enum /v
```

Running through all the BCDEDIT switches would take dozens of pages, so we'll just give you a few examples so you can get a taste of how this powerful utility operates.

Making a Backup Copy of the BCD Store

Before you do any work on the BCD store, you should make a backup copy. That way, if you make an error when you change something in the BCD, you can always restore the backup copy to get your system back to its original state.

You create a backup copy using the /export switch. For example, the following command backs up the BCD store to a file named bcd_backup in the root folder of drive C:

```
bcdedit /export c:\bcd_backup
```

If you need to restore the backup, use the /import switch, as in this example:

```
bcdedit /import c:\bcd_backup
```

Renaming an Entry

The names that Windows Boot Manager assigns to the boot applications leave a lot to be desired. For a legacy operating system entry, for example, the default Legacy (pre-Longhorn) Microsoft Windows Operating System name is overly long and not particularly descriptive. A simpler name, such as Windows XP Pro or Windows 2000, would be much more useful. Similarly,

 tip

GUIDs are 32-character values, so typing them by hand is both time-consuming and error-prone. To avoid this, first run the bcdedit /enum command to enumerate the BCD entries, and then scroll up until you see the GUID of the entry with which you want to work. Pull down the system menu (click the upper-left corner of the window or press Alt+Spacebar), select Edit, Mark, click-and-drag over the GUID to select it, and then press the Enter key to copy it. Begin typing your BCDEDIT command, and when you get to the part where the identifier is required, pull down the system menu again and select Edit, Paste.

all Windows 10 installs get the same name: Microsoft Windows, which can be quite confusing. Names such as Windows 10 Home Premium and Windows 10 Ultimate would be much more understandable.

To rename an entry using BCDEDIT, use the following syntax:

```
bcdedit /set {id} description "name"
```

Here, replace *id* with the entry identifier (the GUID or the well-known identifier, if applicable) and replace *name* with the new name you want to use. For example, the following command replaces the current name of the legacy operating system entry (`ntldr`) with Windows XP Pro:

```
bcdedit /set {ntldr} description "Windows XP Pro"
```

Changing the Order of the Entries

If you'd prefer that the Boot Manager menu entries appear in a different order, you can use the BCDEDIT tool's /displayorder switch to change the order. In the simplest case, you might want to move an entry to either the beginning or the end of the menu. To send an entry to the beginning, include the /addfirst switch. Here's an example:

```
bcdedit /displayorder {a8ef3a39-a0a4-11da-bedf-97d9bf80e36c} /addfirst
```

To send an entry to the end of the menu, include the /addlast switch instead, as in this example:

```
bcdedit /displayorder {current} /addlast
```

To set the overall order, include each identifier in the order you want, separated by spaces:

```
bcdedit /displayorder {current} {a8ef3a39-a0a4-
11da-bedf-97d9bf80e36c} {ntldr}
```

Installing Windows 10 Components

Like a hostess who refuses to put out the good china for just anybody, Windows 10 doesn't install all of its components automatically. Don't feel insulted; Windows is just trying to go easy on your hard disk. The problem, you see, is that some of the components that come with Windows 10 are software behemoths that will happily usurp acres of your precious hard-disk land. In a rare act of digital politeness, Windows bypasses these programs (as well as a few other nonessential tidbits) during a typical installation. If you want any of these knickknacks on your system, you have to tell Windows 10 to install them for you.

Many of the not-installed components are only useful in specific business networking environments or for software developers. (Developers should know that Windows has a

 note

There's a very good reason that many Windows components are not installed by default. The more software that's installed, the more likely that one of the components has a bug that could someday be exploited by hackers. Minimizing the amount of installed software is called "reducing the attack surface." This is why we suggest that you uninstall much of the unneeded junk software that comes preinstalled on most new computers these days. To learn more about getting rid of third-party programs, see the "Uninstalling Software" section in Chapter 27.

"Developer Mode" setting that, when enabled, makes several additional choices appear in the Turn Windows Features On or Off list. To turn on Developers Mode, click Start, Settings, Update & Security, For Developers. Select Developer Mode, and then scroll down for some more tools that let you tweak the Windows user interface.)

The good news about installing features is that Windows 10 makes it easy to add any of those missing pieces to your system without having to dig out the installation media (wherever it may be) or (shudder) trudge through the entire Windows installation routine. The reason is that when Windows 10 was foisting itself upon your PC, it was thoughtful enough to also deposit the files necessary to install the features on your hard drive. They reside in a special folder in a compressed format, so they don't take up much room. You must tell Windows 10 to decompress them, which sounds hard, but it's not. You just have to follow these steps:

1. In the taskbar's Search box, type **features**, and then click Turn Windows Features On or Off. The Windows Features dialog box appears, as shown in Figure 2.12.

Figure 2.12
The Windows Features dialog box helps you add the bits and pieces that come with Windows 10.

2. If a component has a plus sign (+), it means it has multiple subcomponents. Click the plus sign to see those subcomponents.

3. Check the box beside the component you want to install. (We should also mention that if there's a Windows feature you no longer need, you can uncheck its box to uninstall it.)

4. Click OK. Windows 10 installs the feature.

3

YOUR FIRST HOUR WITH WINDOWS 10

The First Things to Do After Starting Windows 10

If you just installed Windows 10 or have just purchased a new computer that came with Windows 10 already installed, you're probably itching to use it. This chapter is designed to help get you off to a good start. We're going to take you and your computer on a guided tour of the new and unusual features of Windows 10 and walk you through making some important and useful settings. Here's our itinerary:

- A quick tour of the important Windows 10 features

- Setting up user accounts

- Personalizing system settings to make using Windows more comfortable and effective

- Transferring information from your old computer

- Logging off and shutting down

Our hope is that an hour or so invested in front of your computer following us through these topics will make you a happier Windows 10 user in the long run.

At the end of the chapter, we have some additional reference material. If you're one of the last holdouts just now moving to Windows 10 from Windows XP, you will almost certainly want to read the final sections. If you have previously used Windows Vista, 7, 8, or 8.1, you might want to quickly scan the last sections just to know what's there. The information might come in handy at some point in the future.

A Quick Tour of the Important Windows 10 Features

This section discusses some of the most important features and the most significant differences between Windows 10 and its predecessors. It is best if you read this while seated in front of your computer and follow along. That way, when you run into these features and topics later in this book and in your work with Windows, you'll already have "been there, done that" at least once. We'll start with the Lock screen, which you'll see after you finish installing Windows 10 or when you turn on a new Windows 10 computer for the first time.

If you used Windows 8 or 8.1 previously and have purchased a new device or upgraded to Windows 10, you might also want to refer to "What Changed Between Windows 10 and Windows 8 and 8.1" on page 28.

 note

If you're using Windows in a corporate setting and your computer was set up for you, some of the steps in this chapter won't be necessary, and they might not even be available to you. Don't worry—you can skip over any parts of this chapter that have already been taken care of, don't work, or don't interest you.

The Lock and Sign In Screens

When Windows starts, you see the Lock screen, which displays just a picture, the time, and the date. Type any key, click anywhere on the screen with your mouse or, if you have a touchscreen, touch it and slide your finger upward. (This gesture is called a *swipe*.) The Lock screen slides up and out of view to reveal the Sign In screen, shown in Figure 3.1, which has an icon (*tile*) in the lower-left side of the screen for each person (*user*, in computer parlance) who has been authorized to use the computer.

At the bottom-right corner of the screen are icons that let you enable the computer's Internet connection, activate accessibility aids, and power off the computer without having to sign in first. There might also be an icon that lets you switch languages and keyboard layouts if your computer was set up for multilingual input.

 tip

If your device has a touch screen, here's something you'll want to remember: If you touch something on the screen and hold your finger on it without moving it for a second or two, until the circle around your finger turns into a square, this does the same thing as right-clicking with a mouse. When you release your finger, the right-click action will occur; for example, a menu will pop up. This works anywhere a right-click would work.

Touch or click your account's tile to sign in. The last account used is preselected.

If your account has a password associated with it, by default, Windows will prompt you for a password, as in previous versions. There are other ways to sign in, using setup options we describe shortly. They are as listed here:

- **Password**—Enter your password and press Enter, or click or touch the right-arrow button to complete the sign-in process.

- **Picture Password**—Make your preset three gestures on the sign-in picture. To make a gesture, touch a point on the picture, drag your finger or the mouse pointer to another point, and release.

Figure 3.1
The Sign In screen is the starting point for logging on.

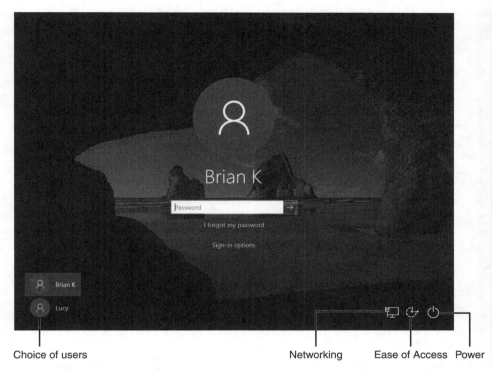

Choice of users   Networking   Ease of Access Power

 note

If you just purchased a new computer, the first screen you see might be from the tail end of the installation process described in Chapter 2, "Installing or Upgrading to Windows 10." Your computer's manufacturer set it up this way so that you could choose settings such as your local time zone and keyboard type. If you do see something other than the Lock or Sign In screens, scan back through Chapter 2. If you recognize the screen you see in one of that chapter's illustrations, carry on from there.

If Windows jumps right up to the desktop and skips the Sign In screen, your computer's manufacturer set up Windows not to require a username or password. In this case, skip to the following section in this chapter, where we show you how to set up a user account.

- **PIN**—Type your PIN code using your keyboard or the touchscreen keyboard.

- **Biometric**—If your device includes a fingerprint scanner or a camera that has infrared capabilities, you can use these as sign-in devices. The device's manufacturer will provide instructions for these methods.

The first time you sign in (and only the first time), it might take a few minutes for Windows to prepare your *user profile*, the set of folders and files that hold your personal documents, email, pictures, preference settings, and so on.

If you have difficulty hearing or seeing the Windows screen, use the Ease of Access icon at the lower-right corner of the Sign In screen to display a list of accessibility options. These include Narrator, which reads the screen aloud; Magnifier, which enlarges the display; and High Contrast, which makes menu and icon text stand out more clearly from the background. You can select any of these items that will make Windows easier for you to use. You can press the left Alt key, the left Shift key, and the PrtScr key together to toggle High Contrast. After you're signed in, you can use the Windows Logo+U keyboard shortcut to open the Ease of Access Center anytime.

➡ *For more information about Windows' accessibility aids, **see** "Accessibility Tools," p. 212.*

The Start Menu

When you've signed in, Windows displays a familiar Windows desktop. If you click or touch the Start button (the Windows logo button) in the lower-left corner, you'll see the new style Start menu, shown in Figure 3.2. We talk more about the Start menu in Chapter 4, "Using the Windows 10 Interface." Here, we just want to point out a few things, and you might want to follow along with your copy of Windows as we go:

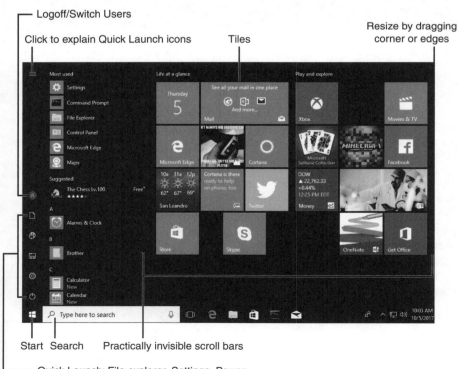

Logoff/Switch Users

Click to explain Quick Launch icons   Tiles

Resize by dragging corner or edges

Start   Search   Practically invisible scroll bars

Quick Launch: File explorer, Settings, Power

Figure 3.2
The new style of the Start menu. You can resize it and scroll through it.

- You can bring up the Start menu at any time by pressing the Windows Logo key or by touching or clicking the Start button.

- The large icons on the Start menu are called *tiles*. Some of them, such as the Calendar, News, and Finance apps, display live, updated data from the Internet.

- You can scroll the app list section and the tile section up and down. You can move them by using the mouse (there is a scrollbar at the right edge of each section) or your finger if you have a touchscreen. The scrollbars are practically invisible until you touch them or point the mouse at them. Annoyingly, the PgUp and PgDn keys don't work.

- **Best Tip Ever:** Personalizing the Start menu is the key to making Windows 10 easy to use. Pin your favorite applications (*apps*) and folders to the Start menu. Drag tiles around so that the apps you use most often appear on the first page of the menu. Right-click or touch and hold tiles to make them larger or smaller. You can even create groups of apps and assign names to the groups. And, as in previous versions of Windows, you can pin apps to the taskbar. It's your choice.

- The left part of the menu lists frequently used and "quick launch" apps. If there is a > symbol, touch or click it to display a *jump list*, which lets you instantly open frequently or recently used files.

- Below the list of Most Used apps, all apps are listed alphabetically. Click or touch one of the alphabet letter headings to get a pop-up menu that lets you instantly jump to any letters. Still, it's tiring to have to scroll to find apps all the time. This is why we suggest you pin your most-used apps to the Start menu or the taskbar.

➡ *For more information, see "Customizing the Start Menu," p. 124.*

Modern Apps

The Start menu holds icons for standard Windows desktop applications, such as Microsoft Word and the old familiar Notepad, and new Modern apps, which have a simplified, clean graphical user interface without the traditional menu. This new graphical style has also been referred to as Metro and Windows-8 Style, but the official name is now *Modern*. In this book, when we refer to a Modern app, we're referring to this new, simplified full-screen graphical look.

To see how this looks, open the Start menu and touch or click the Weather tile. If a prompt asks whether it's okay to use your location, click Yes. You might also be asked to choose between Fahrenheit and Celsius temperatures and to enter your city name. You should end up with a window like that shown in Figure 3.3. (It might not be *exactly* the same. Microsoft changes these apps all the time. Sometimes subtly, sometimes in a major way.)

Notice that Modern apps have a normal Windows title bar across the top, with the usual Minimize, Maximize, and Close buttons at the far right. In Windows 10, they are not distinct square buttons, just symbols, but they work just as they have in all previous versions of Windows.

"Hamburger" menu

Minimize — Maximize

Close

Search

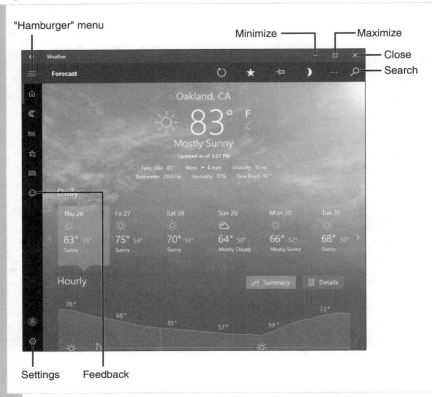

Settings   Feedback

Figure 3.3
Modern apps have a standard Windows title bar. Apps vary in their design, but they usually have common graphics elements such as the "hamburger" menu icon and the "gear" settings icon.

Modern apps have no standard menu bar (File, Print, Edit) under the title bar, but most Modern apps have one or more icons that perform these functions. The most common icon is the "hamburger" icon, which displays a menu of commands and options. It's typically in the upper-left corner of the app's window. There might be a gear-shaped icon that lets you change settings and sometimes a magnifying glass icon that performs a search function. You can find out what these icons do by hovering your mouse over them or just clicking or touching them. Some apps might have a feedback icon that lets you tell Microsoft or the app's developers what you like or don't like about the app's design and function. This icon is usually a smiley face.

To get to an app's commands, touch or click its hamburger icon. For apps that were designed for Windows 8, the hamburger icon appears in the title bar. In these Windows 8-style apps, you can press Windows Logo+Z as a shortcut to the App Commands menu panel, which slides into the top and/or bottom part of the window.

➡ *To learn more about using and managing Modern apps, **see** "Working with Running Apps," p. 116.*

Close the Weather app by touching or clicking the X in its upper-right corner.

The Touch Tour

If your computer has a touch interface, you can make several gestures with one or two fingers to make quick work of navigating through Windows. (Yes, we've all been making certain finger gestures at our computers for years, but this is different.)

In "Navigating Windows 10 with a Touch Interface" in Chapter 4, we list the touch gestures in detail. Here, we just want to show you some basic navigation moves. Follow these steps:

1. Open the Start menu, touch the Calendar tile, and keep your finger on it. Drag it to another location on the menu and release it. This is *dragging*. Drag the icon back where it came from.

2. Tap the Maps tile. This is the same as a mouse click. (If you don't see the Maps tile, touch anywhere in the tile area and slide your finger up; this will scroll through tiles. Still can't find it? Touch in the taskbar's search box, at the bottom the screen, and type **map**. Maps will appear under Best Match as a "trusted Windows Store app." Touch Maps there.)

3. You may need to touch Lets Go. If the app says it needs to access your location, touch Yes.

4. When a map is displayed, touch one finger to the screen and drag the map side to side. Touch two fingers to the map, say, your thumb and forefinger, a few inches apart. Then squeeze them together. The map should zoom out. Slide your fingers apart, and the map should zoom in.

5. Touch one finger just outside the far-right edge of the screen and quickly drag it back toward the middle about an inch or two, like you were trying to flip the page of a book. This is a *swipe*, and it should bring up the Action Center, a very useful panel that contains notifications and a bunch of handy control buttons. You can swipe it away using the reverse of that gesture: swipe from the middle of the App Center window to the right edge of the screen.

6. Go back to the Start menu and touch the Calendar app.

7. Swipe your finger from the left edge of the screen toward the center (just an inch or two), again as if you were flipping the pages of a book. This should let you easily select an app to bring up to the foreground.

8. Touch your finger to the Start button and hold it a couple of seconds, until the touch indicator circle under your finger changes to a square. Release your finger, and a menu will pop up. The touch-and-hold gesture is the same as right-clicking with a mouse. (Take a quick look at this menu while you're here. It's called the Power User menu and leads to almost every Windows management tool.)

If you practice these gestures a few times, you'll quickly get a feel for using the touch interface.

Throughout this book, if we use the terms "click" or "right-click," and you are using a touchscreen without a keyboard, remember that a touch is the same as a click, and a touch-and-hold is the same as a right-click.

➡ *To read more about using a touchscreen,* **see** *"Navigating Windows 10 with a Touch Interface," p. 113.*

In current versions of Windows 10, a nifty new touchscreen toolkit called Windows Ink Workspace is parked in the notification area of the taskbar, as shown in Figure 3.4. Windows Ink Workspace gives you the ability to sketch on the screen, and you can draw or type on-screen sticky notes that feed directly into Cortana calendar and reminders. It's most useful with touch devices that include a pen or stylus, but you can use it with your finger or even just a mouse. If you don't have a touchscreen, you can still enable it with just a couple of clicks.

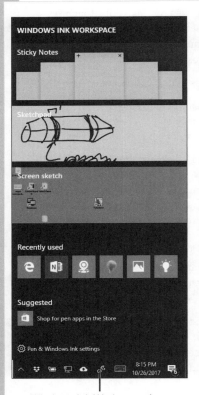

To learn more, **see** *"Windows Ink Workspace," **p. 813.***

Figure 3.4
The new Windows Ink Workspace tool adds a pen- or touch-centric tool panel to your taskbar.

Windows Ink Workspace icon

Important Keyboard Shortcuts

If you're not using a touchscreen, you'll find it *much* easier to use Windows 10 if you memorize at least a few keyboard shortcuts. The ones in the following table are the most important to learn.

Keyboard	Displays
Windows Logo	Start menu
Windows Logo+Q	Search
Windows Logo+Tab	Tiles for all running apps
Windows Logo+X	Pop-up Power User menu of Windows management tools; equivalent to right-clicking the Start button
Windows Logo+Z	App Command bar, for Modern apps that were designed for Windows 8 rather than Windows 10
Windows Logo+O	On tablets, turns orientation lock on or off

If you memorize just these shortcuts, you'll be way ahead of the game!

➡ *For more useful keyboard shortcuts,* **see** *"Navigating Windows 10 with a Keyboard,"* *p. 112.*

There are also useful keyboard shortcuts to switch between apps. Alt+Tab cycles through traditional desktop applications and Modern apps.

Tablet Mode

The biggest criticism of Windows 8 was that the Start menu (called the Start Screen in Windows 8) and Modern apps occupied the entire screen. The Windows desktop and desktop applications lived in another world, and the way that Windows 8 flipped back and forth between was jarring.

On tablets, this behavior wasn't quite so annoying, because on a device with a smaller screen, you usually want an app to fill as much of the screen as possible.

In Windows 10, you get to choose how you want Windows 10 to behave, on both desktops and tablets, by enabling or disabling Tablet mode.

When Tablet mode is off, both Modern and desktop apps can be resized and moved around as on older versions of Windows.

If you have a Windows 10 computer in a tablet format device, review this section carefully, following along on your device as you read. When Tablet mode is turned on, the following changes take effect to get the most out of limited screen real estate:

- The Start menu displays either tiles or the list of apps, not both at once. Use the icons at the upper left of the Start menu, below the Hamburger icon, to switch between Pinned Tiles and the All Apps list. Tablet mode can be frustrating until you learn this! You can scroll the menu using your finger to drag it up or down. Alternatively, touch or point your mouse at the far right edge, and a hidden scrollbar appears as shown in Figure 3.5.

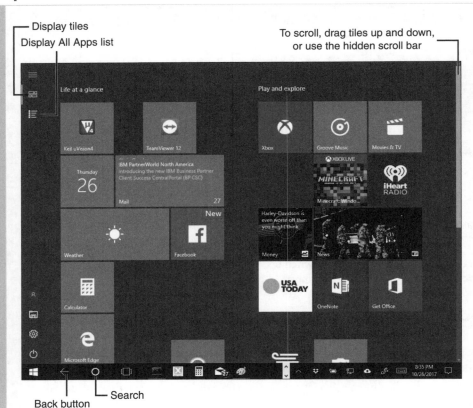

Display tiles
Display All Apps list
To scroll, drag tiles up and down, or use the hidden scroll bar

Back button — Search

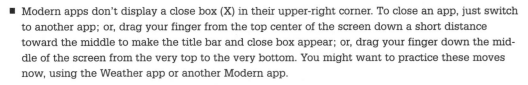

Figure 3.5
In Tablet mode, the Start menu fills the screen. Use the icons at the upper left to view tiles or the apps list.

- The Start menu and all open apps are automatically maximized to fill the screen.

- By default, the taskbar doesn't show icons for running apps. Instead, you switch between apps by swiping in from the left edge of the screen. We prefer to have the taskbar icons appear. We'll tell you to have them show up shortly.

- The taskbar's search box collapses to a circle icon just to the right of the Start button. Touch it to perform a search.

- Modern apps don't display a close box (X) in their upper-right corner. To close an app, just switch to another app; or, drag your finger from the top center of the screen down a short distance toward the middle to make the title bar and close box appear; or, drag your finger down the middle of the screen from the very top to the very bottom. You might want to practice these moves now, using the Weather app or another Modern app.

> ## 🎙 tip
> Throughout this book, we frequently tell you to click Start, then Settings. Remember that the Settings icon is the gear-shaped icon. The word *Settings* doesn't appear unless you select the hamburger menu.

If you connect or remove a keyboard and mouse from a tablet, or you dock or undock a hybrid tablet/laptop, Windows can automatically switch Tablet mode on or off for you. This is called the Continuum feature.

To configure Tablet mode, touch or click the Start button. Select Settings (the gear icon), System, Tablet Mode. You might want to go there now and turn *off* the setting Hide App Icons on the Taskbar in Tablet Mode. This lets the taskbar show icons for active Modern apps.

To have Windows switch automatically between Desktop mode and Tablet mode when you attach or detach a keyboard, under When This Device Automatically Switches..., select Don't Ask Me and Always Switch, or Always Ask Me Before Switching, as you prefer. Choose Don't Ask Me and Don't Switch to prevent automatic switching.

There are two ways to turn Tablet mode on or off manually: You can select Start, Settings, Tablet Mode and use the On/Off switch. But this is quicker: Swipe your finger in from the right edge of the screen toward the middle to display the Action Center, and then use the Tablet Mode button at the bottom-right part of the screen. The Action Center panel also has a handy Rotation Lock button to prevent your screen from flipping around as you turn your tablet.

Windows Explorer Is Now Called File Explorer

To continue our tour, let's take a quick look at Windows Explorer... oops, we mean File Explorer. It has a new name (as of Windows 8) and a ribbon bar in place of a menu. By default, File Explorer is pinned to the taskbar. To open File Explorer, touch or click the taskbar icon that looks like a manila file folder. If there is no File Explorer icon in the taskbar, touch or click Start, touch the hamburger menu at the top, and then find the File Explorer icon farther down the left edge. Right-click it, or touch and hold your finger on it until a pop-up menu appears. Select Pin to Taskbar. Now you can open File Explorer from the taskbar.

File Explorer will open in the Quick Access view, which shows your most recently used files and folders, and files and folders that you've pinned for Quick Access.

Click or touch This PC in the left pane to see the view shown in Figure 3.6.

In the left pane, which is called the Navigation pane, you can select the major categories Quick Access, This PC, Homegroup (if one is set up on your network—more on that in Chapter 18, "Creating a Windows Network"), and Network. If you are signed in using a Microsoft account, OneDrive will also appear; it's the folder that is synced with your account's online storage.

Collectively, all of these various categories display what the old separate Favorites, My Documents, [My] Computer, and other links displayed in earlier versions of Windows.

As you select items in the *right* pane, which we call the Content pane, the ribbon bar changes to show actions that you can perform on the selected object(s). Be aware of this: The ribbon does not respond to or act on items you select in the *left* (Navigation) pane; the ribbon only responds to the right (Content) pane.

Did you like the old Windows 7 and 8 Libraries feature, which collected the files in several folders and displayed them together? Libraries still exist in Windows 10, but they're turned off by default. To show them, select View (along the top of the window), Options, Change Folder and Search Options. Then select the View tab, scroll the list of Advanced Settings past Navigation Pane, check Show Libraries, and then click OK.

Tabs   Ribbon

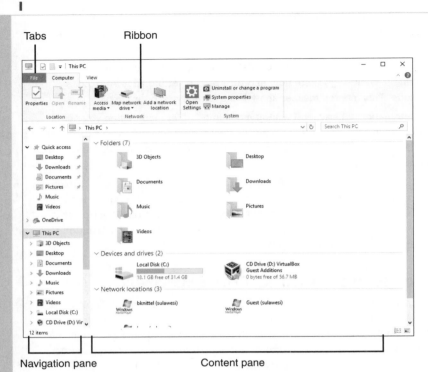

Navigation pane   Content pane

Figure 3.6
File Explorer sports a new name and a new ribbon interface. The list of actions shown in the ribbon changes when you select a tab and when you select items in the Content pane.

Cortana

The desktop's taskbar has a full-time resident search tool. It appears either as a circle icon or as a rectangular box just to the right of the Start button. When Windows 10 was originally released, this search tool looked only within your computer to find Settings and Control Panel entries, the names of files in local (internal and external drive) and online (OneDrive) storage, and used Bing to search the Web, presenting the combined results from all of these locations.

➡ *To customize the search tool, **see** "Customizing the Start Menu," p. 124.*

Microsoft now more or less forces the use of Cortana, a much more (helpful? invasive?) search tool that performs something like Apple's Siri. It still searches, based on whatever text you type, for your files, apps and settings, and so on, but it also can understand questions and commands in human language, such as "What will the weather be in Boise, Idaho

🔍 **note**
We say Microsoft "more or less forces the use of Cortana," but there are exceptions. On Windows 10 Education and Pro Education, and on a corporate domain network, your network administrator may, in fact, disable Cortana, in which case the search tool will just search your computer and do basic web searches. And if you have Windows 10 Pro, there is a cumbersome way to disable Cortana using the policy editor. But, it's better to leave Cortana on and just decide what it can see.

tomorrow?" or "Set an alarm for 8:30 tomorrow morning." It not only searches the Web but also interacts with your calendar, contacts list, email, and other information it learns about you, such as the places you frequently visit, so that it can provide much more personally tailored answers and service. If you have a microphone attached, you can speak your commands and questions. You can even tell Cortana to "listen" all the time, so all you have to do is say "Hey, Cortana" and ask your question without touching a thing.

To give Cortana a try, follow these steps:

1. Click in the taskbar's Search box (or, on a tablet, touch the circle icon.)

2. The first time you activate Cortana, a panel may appear asking what you'd like to be called. You can enter your first name or a nickname here if you want. ("Oh Master" is especially nice.)

3. In the search box, type **what time is it in Boise?**, or, if your device or PC has a microphone, click the microphone icon and just ask the question. Cortana should give you a quick response.

4. Click the X at the upper right of the search box to dismiss the search results.

As you set up apps such as Mail on your device, Cortana's ability to gather information for you will grow exponentially. But, as we discuss in Chapter 4, there are privacy issues that you need to consider. You have to weigh convenience against having a big corporation recording a lot about what you are doing and what interests you.

 To learn more about searching your computer with Cortana, and to see how to control what it learns about you, *see "Searching Windows 10," p. 120.*

Search Before You Look

Here's one of the most important tips we can give you for Windows 10: Although there are usually many different ways to get to the same thing in Windows, the *fastest way is to let Windows find it for you.*

Click in the taskbar's Search box and just type away. If your computer doesn't have a keyboard, touch the Search box in the taskbar, and then type using the screen's Touch keyboard. Simply type the first few letters or words associated with the Control Panel item, app, setting, or file that you're looking for. If your device has a microphone and you have enabled Hey Cortana, you can just say "Hey, Cortana" and say what you're looking for.

Windows can find apps, files, settings, or Control Panel items much faster than you could ever get to them by poking around with the mouse or by scrolling through the Start menu.

The same applies to the search boxes at the upper-right corner of Settings, Control Panel, and any File Explorer screens. It's usually *much* faster and easier to type a few letters of the name of what you're looking for than to hunt, click, and dig using the mouse. Don't remember what the Control Panel app is called? No worries. Just type a related word or words. Chances are that the item you want will appear in the search results under Settings.

> 🔍 **note**
>
> As I was writing this, from somewhere on my cluttered desk a disembodied computer voice said, "Sorry, I missed that." Surprised, I exclaimed, "Who just said that? Siri? Cortana?" But nobody fessed up.
>
> I think the future is going to be a lot like that.

Getting to the Management Tools

It might seem difficult at first to get to the tools you need to use to manage Windows. Remember, you can simply search for any desired management tool or setting by typing its name or a word that describes it in the taskbar's Search box. This will usually do the trick.

The best thing to know is that you can pop up a menu of management tools by right-clicking the Start button or by pressing Windows Logo+X. Without a keyboard, touch and hold the Start button until the circle under your finger changes to a square, and then release. A pop-up Power User menu appears.

From there, you can instantly open Settings, Device Manager, Computer Management, the Command Prompt, Task Manager, and more. Try it now: Right-click or touch and hold the Start button, and see what's there.

 tip

On Windows XP through 7, you right-clicked My Computer to get to the Windows management tools. On Windows 10, right-click or touch and hold the Start button. This displays a big list of tools. Settings is one of the choices, but to get to the Settings panels, it's faster to just touch the Start button, then the Settings (gear) icon.

Memorize these two paths, and you'll save yourself hours of poking around looking for things!

Table 3.1 lists quick ways to get to many management tools using keyboard shortcuts. If your device doesn't have a keyboard, where the instructions say press Windows Logo+X, instead touch and hold the Start button, and then release it.

Table 3.1 Shortcuts to Management Tools

To Get To	Follow These Steps
Administrative Tools	Many of the administrative tools appear individually on the Start button's right-click menu (Windows Logo+X). If the desired tool is not listed there, open the Start menu, select All Apps, scroll down and select Windows Administrative Tools, and then continue to scroll down to the desired item.
Command Prompt	Press Windows Logo+X, and then select Command Prompt. (You can choose to have either Command Prompt or Windows PowerShell on this menu. We show you how to change this later in the chapter under "Important Adjustments and Tweaks.")
Computer Management	Press Windows Logo+X, and then select Computer Management.
System Properties	Press Windows Logo+X, and then select System.
Control Panel	Microsoft has made it harder to get to the old (and now less-used) Control Panel system. The fastest way is to click in the taskbar's search box, type the word **control**, and then select Control Panel. You can also use the Start menu: view All Apps (if in Tablet mode), scroll down to Windows System, Control Panel.
Devices and Printers	Click Start, Settings (gear icon), Devices, Printers & Scanners. To get to the old Devices and Printers screen, go through the old Control Panel.

To Get To	Follow These Steps
Elevated Command Prompt	Press Windows Logo+X, and then select Command Prompt (Admin). If Command Prompt (Admin) isn't listed, but Windows PowerShell is, see the steps for Command Prompt earlier in this table.
Networking	Click the network icon in the notification area (right end of the taskbar), and select Network & Internet Settings. You can select Change Adapter Options or Network and Sharing Center from there.
System Tools	At the Start menu, select All Apps (if in tablet mode), scroll down and select Windows System, and then scroll down to the desired tool.

If you need to run a tool with elevated privileges, right-click or touch and hold the item in the menu or search results, and then select Run as Administrator.

By the way, in the Control Panel, the View By drop-down item lets you instantly switch back and forth between the Category view and an icon view that resembles the Windows 9x Control Panel. In this book, our instructions refer to the Category view unless we state otherwise.

 note

The Back button is located all over the place in Windows 10. It can come in handy, so make a mental note to look for it as you use various Control Panel options, File Explorer, setup wizards, and so on.

Setting Up User Accounts

On a computer that's joined to a corporate Windows domain network, the network servers take care of authorizing each user, and accounts are created by network managers.

On home and small office computers, this job is up to you. It's best to set up a separate account for each person who will use the computer. Having separate user accounts keeps everyone's stuff separate: email, online purchasing, preferences and settings, documents, search history, stored passwords, and so on. Although it's certainly possible for everyone to share one account, having separate accounts often turns out to be much more convenient than sharing.

 tip

If you have trouble finding a setting, check this book's index, which should lead you to instructions for finding the correct links in the Control Panel or elsewhere. You can also use the Search box at the top of the Control Panel window.

Microsoft Versus Local Accounts

On a computer that has Internet access, you can create two types of user accounts: *Microsoft accounts* and *local accounts*. A local account is what we had in previous versions of Windows. You can specify an account (sign in) name and password. Information about each account stays on the computer. If you set up accounts for yourself on two different computers, your password on the two machines would not necessarily be the same; your individual preferences would have to be set up separately on both computers, and so on.

If you use a Microsoft account (formerly called a Windows Live account) to sign in to Windows 8, 8.1, or 10, Windows uses Microsoft's online services to securely back up certain information from your account to Microsoft's servers "in the cloud," which means "in some big data center somewhere—you won't really know where, but it works." You use an email address and password to sign in to Windows. If you use the same Microsoft account to sign in to another Windows 8, 8.1, or 10 computer, your information follows you—your password, preferences, purchased apps, and so on. It's pretty spiffy. (Documents, music, and so on don't follow you automatically, but you can use OneDrive or other online data services for that.)

For the online account scheme to work, the computer must have a working Internet connection when you sign in for the first time so that Windows can check your password. Also, it's best if the computer has an always-on Internet connection so that your information can be backed up as you work. If the Internet connection goes down later, you can still sign in. Windows remembers your last-used password.

This is important: The first time you sign in to any given computer with your Microsoft account, you must verify to Microsoft that you are who you say you are. You must perform the verification step before any of your files, apps, or other content will be pulled in from your Microsoft account's online storage to the computer. If Windows doesn't prompt you to verify your account shortly after you sign in for the first time, click the Action Center icon at the far-right end of the taskbar. The icon looks like a square cartoon "voice balloon." In the Action Center panel, click or touch Verify Your Identity on this PC; then follow the instructions to receive a code by text message or email. Enter the code when you're asked for it, and then your computer's account will be fully linked up with your online account.

You can change from using a Microsoft account to a local account, and vice versa. If you switch to a local account, settings you change and purchases you make from that point forward won't follow you from computer to computer. You can switch back to an online account anytime.

 tip

If you purchased a computer with Windows 10 preinstalled, the manufacturer might have set up Windows to skip the sign-in process entirely. There actually is a user account set up for you, and when you start Windows, it automatically signs in to that one account.

If you expect to have other people use your computer, go ahead and create more user accounts now. We show you how to make the Sign In screen work later in the chapter, in the section "Just One User?"

Also, you can choose between Administrator and Standard User types. An Administrator can change any setting as well as view any file on the computer (even someone else's). A Standard User can't change Windows settings that involve networking or security and can view other people's files only if they've chosen to share them.

The first account set up on your computer during installation and finalization is always an Administrator account. At this point on our tour, let's add user accounts for other people who will be using your computer.

Create New Accounts

Open the Start menu by clicking or touching the Start button in the bottom-left corner of the screen. Then, starting at the bottom-left side of the Start menu, select Settings (the gear icon), then Accounts. You should see information about your own account in the right pane, as shown in Figure 3.7. You can scroll the window down to get to other items that let you use your device's camera to take your picture, link to additional Microsoft accounts, and so on.

Figure 3.7
The Accounts section in Settings lets you manage your and other users' accounts.

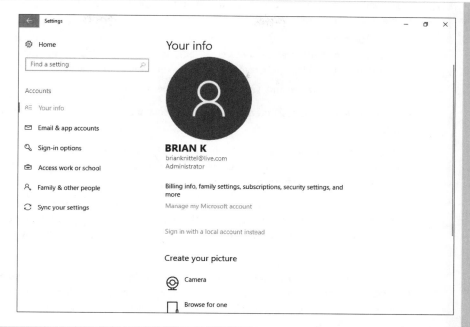

If you want to create a new Microsoft account so that someone else can use your computer, either she must have already set up her account online at login.live.com, or she should be present to set up a new account while you're adding her to your computer, because she will have to create a password and enter personal information.

Windows 10 includes a family-computing feature that lets a family's adults manage, limit, and supervise their children's computer use. This feature works only with Microsoft online accounts so that the managing (parent) accounts can restrict and monitor the use of the managed (child) accounts on any devices they have. This feature includes receiving activity reports that show what the managed (child) accounts were looking up on various search engines, websites they visited, how long they were on the computer, and which games and apps they used.

 tip

If you want maximum protection against viruses and other malware, reserve that first Administrator account for management work only, and then create a standard user account for yourself for day-to-day use. This makes it harder to get tricked into letting bad software run without noticing.

If you don't need to use this supervisory feature, you can set up regular Microsoft or local accounts for other users.

To set up family-centered user accounts with restricted and monitored access for children, select Family & Other People (on the left side), Add a Family Member, and then select Add a Child or Add an Adult.

Otherwise, to add another user without making him part of a family group, select Family & Other People (on the left side), and choose Add Someone Else to This PC.

Then you must choose to create a Microsoft (online) or local (offline) account. Remember, a local account gives less information about your computer use to Microsoft but will not automatically sync up preferences and settings between the user's different computers.

To set up a Microsoft account, use one of the following options:

- If the person has already created a Microsoft account online, enter his Microsoft Account email address.

- If the person has an email address already but hasn't set up a Microsoft account yet, type in his email address and click Next. Follow the series of prompts as they appear. At the end, select Finish to create the Microsoft account.

- If the person doesn't have an email address, you can create one by clicking I Don't Have This Person's Sign-In Information and then following the prompts. This will let you create a new email address on one of Microsoft's free online email services at the same time you set up the online account.

When setting up a Microsoft account, be sure to provide at least one alternative email address, and if possible a mobile phone number that can receive text messages. Microsoft needs at least one of these to validate that the user really wants an account on your computer, and it helps recover from a forgotten password.

The first time the new user signs in on your computer, he or she should immediately perform the validation step discussed previously under "Microsoft Versus Local Accounts."

If you want to create a local account and not use Microsoft's online account system, on the Family & Other People panel select Add Someone Else To This PC, I Don't Have This Person's Sign-In Information, Add a User Without a Microsoft Account. Enter a username consisting of letters and, if desired, numbers. Choose a password and enter it twice as indicated. Enter a hint that will remind the user what his password is but won't give a clue to anyone else. (This can be hard to come up with!) Click Next and then Finish.

If you've elected to set up accounts using the Family structure—if you designated users as adults or children—the adult users can manage and monitor what the child users can do and have done by visiting account.microsoft.com/family. Alternatively, click Start, Settings, Accounts, Family & Other People, Manage Family Settings Online.

Initially, all new users are created as Standard Users. If you want them to be Administrators, under Add Someone Else To This PC, select the icon for the newly created account, select Change Account Type, in the drop-down list change the Account Type to Administrator, and then click OK.

 tip

A Microsoft account user actually has a local user account on the computer, and Windows checks online to update the password and settings. The account is given a goofy name along the lines of brian_000. If you want your computer's local accounts and user profile folders to have predictable, useful names, create accounts as local accounts first. Then have the users sign in and change them to Microsoft accounts. This is especially helpful if you want to share files and printers with Macs and other types of computers, as discussed in Chapter 20.

Change Account Settings

To change the settings shown in Figure 3.7 for your own account, use the Accounts panel described in the preceding section. You can do the following:

- To switch your account from a local account to a Microsoft account or vice versa, select Your Info in the left column, and then select Sign In with a Local Account Instead or Sign In with a Microsoft Account Instead. You can only do this for your own account. To change the type of another account, you must sign in using that account.

- Select Sign-In Options in the left column to change your password, create a picture password, or set a PIN.

    A picture password lets you select a picture instead of a password to sign in. You draw three lines on the picture with your mouse or fingertip, gestures that only you know.

    A PIN lets you use a four (or more)-digit number instead of a password to sign in. This PIN works only at the Sign In screen, not over the network.

    And, while a password follows a Microsoft account from device to device, PINs and Picture Passwords work only on the device on which you set them up.

- Select Access Work or School to access resources, apps, settings, and network connections provided by your organization's network managers. If your organization uses this feature, it will provide you with detailed instructions for connecting to and using its resources.

- Select Sync Your Settings to change what kind of information gets uploaded and associated with your Microsoft account.

Two settings on the Sync Your Settings panel that have significant privacy implications are Internet Explorer Settings and Passwords. If Internet Explorer Settings and Passwords are turned on, Windows may upload to Microsoft's servers the names of websites you visit and the passwords you use to sign in to them. You can be assured that in the United States at the very least, this information is available to government agencies upon subpoena without any notification to you and maybe even without a judge's warrant. You also might wonder what happens if Microsoft's servers get hacked by criminals or governments.

At this point on our tour of Windows 10, we recommend that you take a moment to add a user account for each person who will be using your computer. Definitely set a password on each Administrator account. We recommend that you set a password on each standard user account as well.

After you add your user accounts, continue to the next section.

 note

Passwords to Wi-Fi networks to which you connect are also saved online, so be aware that government agencies are probably getting the key to your Wi-Fi networks, too. It's only somewhat comforting to know that if they wanted to, they could just as easily get into your Wi-Fi networks *without* your handing them this information, so letting Microsoft sync it isn't really making things any worse.

 tip

If you are in a home or small office environment, have more than one computer, and plan on setting up a local area network, we suggest you read about the Homegroup feature in Chapter 18. It really simplifies file sharing on Windows. If you don't want to use it, though, but you do want to share files and printers, create local accounts for every one of your users on each of your computers using the *same name and same password* for each person on each computer. This makes it possible for anyone to use any computer, and it makes it easier for you to manage security on your network.

Enable Controlled Folder Access

Windows has a new feature that can help protect you from ransomware and viruses. It's called Controlled Folder Access, and it prevents unknown applications from making changes in the folders that contain your personal data: your documents, spreadsheets, and so on. If an unexpected application tries to modify data in a protected folder, you'll be asked whether you want to allow the change. Once Windows learns that you trust an application, it won't ask again, so even though this feature might start out a *little* bit annoying, it will quickly fade into the background and just do its job.

Controlled Folder Access is turned off by default. We suggest you turn it on now, using these steps:

1. Right-click the small shield-shaped icon at the right end of the taskbar and select Open, or click Start, Settings, Update & Security, Windows Defender, Open Windows Defender Security Center.

2. Select Virus & Threat Protection, Virus & Threat Protection Settings.

3. Scroll down to Controlled Folder Access, and slide the switch on. Approve the User Account Control prompt.

4. By default, your users' desktops, Documents, Music, Pictures, Videos, and Favorites folders will be protected. You can click the + icon to add any other folders in other locations that you've created that hold valuable data.

➡ *For more information about Controlled Folder Access,* **see** *"Controlled Folder Access," p. 705.*

Before You Forget Your Password

If you use a Microsoft (online) account, as discussed in the preceding section, and you forget your password, you can go online to reset your password and regain access to your computer accounts—as long as you can get to your mobile phone or one of the email accounts you linked to your Microsoft account, and as long as your computer has Internet access.

If you use a *local* account and forget your account's password, you could be in serious trouble. On a corporate domain network, you can ask your network administrator to save you. However, on a home computer or in a small office, forgetting your password is very serious: You can use another Administrator account to change the password on your own account, but you will lose access to any files that you encrypted and to passwords stored for automatic use on websites. (Do you even remember them all?) And if you can't remember the password to any Administrator account, you'll really be stuck. You'll most likely have to reinstall Windows and all your applications, and you'll be *very* unhappy.

There is something you can do to prevent this disaster from happening to you. You can create a password reset disk *right now* and put it away in a safe place. A password reset disk is a removable thumb drive or other type of removable, writable disk linked to your account that lets you sign in using data physically stored on the disk. It's like a physical key to your computer. Even if you later change your account's password between making the disk and forgetting the password, the reset disk will still work to unlock your account.

So, if you use a local (offline) account, make a password reset disk now! Here's how. You need a removable USB thumb drive or some other such removable medium, and some determination, as Microsoft doesn't make it easy. Follow these steps:

 caution

A password reset disk, or rather the file userkey.psw that's on it, is as good as your password for gaining access to your computer, so store the reset disk in a safe, secure place. By "secure," we mean something like a locked drawer, filing cabinet, or safe deposit box.

1. Connect the removable storage device to your computer.

2. Press Ctrl+Alt+Del, and release the keys. Select Change a Password, Create a Password Reset Disk. (If nothing happens, sign out, sign back in, and try again. My experience has been that the wizard opens reliably only if you insert the removable drive while signed in, and then sign out, sign back in, and try this step again.)

3. When the wizard appears, click Next.

4. If necessary, select a removable drive from the list and click Next.

5. Enter your current password and click Next.

6. Follow the wizard's instructions. When the wizard finishes writing data, click Next and then click Finish.

7. In the taskbar, click the Safely Remove Hardware and Eject Media icon, and eject the removable media you used.

 note

Each local user should create her own password reset disk. In theory, an Administrator user could always reset any other user's password, but that user would then lose her encrypted files and stored passwords. It's better to have a separate password reset disk for *every* local user account. But if you don't do it for every local account on your computer, at least do it for one Administrator account.

The disk will now contain a file called userkey.psw, which is the key to your account. (You can copy this file to another medium if you want.) Remove the disk, label it so that you'll remember what it is, and store it in a safe place.

You don't have to re-create the disk if you change your password in the future. The disk will still work regardless of your password at the time. However, a password disk works only to get into the account that created it, so each user should create one.

If you forget your password and can't sign in, see "After You Forget Your Password," toward the end of this chapter.

Just One User?

If you are the only person who is going to use your computer, there is a setting you can use so that Windows starts up and goes directly to your desktop without asking you to sign in. You might find that your computer does this anyway; some computer manufacturers turn on this setting before they ship the computer to you. Technically, a password is still used; it's just entered for you automatically.

We recommend that you don't use this automatic sign-in option. Without a password, your computer or your Internet connection could be abused by someone without your even knowing it. Still, in some situations, it's reasonable to change this setting. For example, if your computer manufacturer set up your computer this way, you can disable it. Or you might want to use the feature in a computer that's used in a public place or in an industrial control setting. To change the startup setting, follow these steps:

1. Press Windows Logo+R, type **control userpasswords2**, and press Enter.

2. To require a sign-in, check Users Must Enter a User Name and Password to Use This Computer, and then click OK.

Alternatively, to make Windows sign in automatically, uncheck Users Must Enter a User Name and Password to Use This Computer, and click OK. Then type the username and password of the account you want to have signed in automatically, and click OK.

The change takes effect the next time Windows starts.

 tip

Setting up an automatic logon on a workplace domain member computer is more difficult. If this is permitted in your organization, you can do it using the autologon tool, which you can download from live.sysinternals.com. (This is a Microsoft-owned website, and it's safe.)

Downloading Critical Updates

The next thing to do is update Windows with the latest and greatest updates from Microsoft. Open the Start menu and select the Settings (gear) icon. Select Update & Security, Windows Update. Before we check for updates, there are some one-time changes to make, using these steps:

1. Select Advanced Options, and check Give Me Updates for Other Microsoft Products when I Update Windows.

2. Select Delivery Optimization, and be sure Allow Downloads from Other PCs is set on, and below that, PCs On My Local Network is selected. (This makes sure that your Internet bandwidth isn't used up delivering updates to random other peoples' computers).

3. Click the back arrow (at the top-left corner of the Settings window, or in tablet mode, just to the right of the Start button) and select Sign-in Options. Scroll down to Privacy, and turn on Use My Sign-In Info to Automatically Finish Setting Up My Device after an Update or Restart, so Windows can complete an update without intervention.

4. Click Back twice.

Now, select Check for Updates.

If updates are available, wait for the download, install, and restart process to complete before continuing our tour of Windows 10. If updates have already been downloaded, the button might already say Install Now or Restart Now. Click this.

When the process has completed, sign in and immediately return to Windows Update to see whether any *additional* updates are available. You might have to repeat this process several times with a brand-new computer or installation. It's essential that you get all security fixes installed before proceeding.

You should know that installing updates from Windows Update is no longer optional. On Windows 10 Home, they're installed automatically. On Windows 10 Pro and Enterprise, you can delay them for a while but not indefinitely. There is, however, an option to prevent installation of specific updated device drivers.

 To read about the (limited) ways you can control updates, see "Configuring Automatic Updates," p. 611.

Be sure to check out the inside front cover of this book to see how we'll track Windows as it evolves.

Personalizing Windows 10

For the next part of your first hour with Windows 10, we want to help you make changes to some settings that make Windows easier and faster to use and understand. With a little touching up, you can then spend more time looking *through* the computer's screen at what you're working on, and less time looking *at* the screen trying to make the computer do what you want it to do. So, in this section, we'll tear through some tweaks and adjustments.

To start with, if you are using a tablet, laptop, or smartphone, you might enable a helpful service that lets you find your device if you lose it.

Enable Find My Device

If you are using a Microsoft (online) account, as we discussed earlier in this chapter, and you are using a portable device you can to turn on the Find My Device feature so that you might have better luck recovering it if it it's ever lost or stolen. To enable it, open Settings, Update & Security, Find My Device. If it's not enabled, click Change, and then slide the switch to On. Later, if you lose the device, visit account.microsoft.com/devices to see if it can be located.

Find My Device does have privacy implications, as it gives Microsoft permission to track and record your device's whereabouts at all times. Your location is being tracked by all sorts of websites and other apps all the time anyway, so, personally, I don't see this as much of an additional concern. (I've given in, and I understand that I have a radio dog collar on all the time.)

Personalize Screen Settings

Now we're ready to make a couple of quick selections to the settings that control the Windows appearance. To do this, click Start, Settings (the gear icon), and then select Personalization. There are several subcategories under Personalization that you might want to examine.

You can select a *theme*, which is a collection of desktop and sound settings, or you can customize individual settings, such as the desktop background, by selecting the categories at the left side of the window. To change the theme, select Themes, Theme Settings or click to Get more themes in the Store.

> **🔍 note**
>
> If you have a desktop computer, you can put its unused computer processor cycles to better use than making the Windows logo swim around your screen. Several worthy screensaver alternatives actually might help find a cure for cancer or eavesdrop on ET phoning home. You can find our favorites at http://boinc.berkeley.edu.

If you are annoyed by Windows 10's overall design preference for bright white screens throughout, select Colors, scroll down, and change Choose Your Default App Mode from Light to Dark. Not all apps respect this setting, but many respond by changing the overall background color from white to black. Whether this is actually easier on your eyes or not is your call. Try it and see.

To choose what your computer screen shows when you're not actively signed in, select Lock Screen. The default is to display random lovely images downloaded from Microsoft, which is called the Windows Spotlight background. You can select a different background picture, though, and enable apps such as Weather and Calendar to display notifications on the screen. To designate a screen saver program, select Screen Saver Settings.

➡ *For more information on personalizing the user interface, **see** "Customizing the Start Menu" and "Customizing the Lock Screen," **p. 124 and 133.***

Resolution

In addition to changing the appearance of the display, you can change its physical characteristics, such as its resolution (that is, how many pixels make up the display).

Windows should automatically use the highest resolution (smallest pixels) your monitor can display, but you can change the resolution manually. Using a lower resolution than the monitor's maximum can result in a somewhat blurry display image on LCD monitors.

To change the display settings, right-click the desktop and select Display Settings. (Or, select Start, Settings, System, Display). From here, you can drag a slider to change the size of text, apps, and other items. Making them larger makes the display easier to read without changing the resolution. (See the "Font Size" section later in this chapter for details.) You can also adjust the screen orientation (portrait or landscape) and adjust the display brightness (if it's a portable PC or device).

To change the resolution, open the Resolution drop-down list and select the desired dimensions. If the screen goes black and doesn't come back, don't touch anything; just wait a bit, and it will revert to the previous setting. If the display does work and you want to keep it, select Keep Changes.

Multiple Monitors

If you have two or more monitors attached to your computer, Windows should have offered you the option of extending your desktop onto all of them. If not, follow these steps:

1. Under Multiple Displays, select Extend These Displays and then click Apply.

2. Select Identify, and then drag the numbered icons in the top pane so that they are in the same arrangement as your monitors. Click Apply again.

You can select the numbered icons in the top pane and adjust the corresponding monitors' resolution independently.

Font Size

The problem with using the default (highest) resolution on a screen is that the text and icons appear very small. If you have trouble seeing what's going on, select the Display settings panel again. Adjust the slider under Change the Size of Text, Apps and Other Items from 100 to 125 percent, and then click Apply.

This setting changes the general size of text and graphical elements used on the desktop, Start menu, and apps.

ClearType Tuner

Finally, use the nifty ClearType Tuner tool to ensure that the text displayed on your monitor is sharp and easy to read. Each pixel on an LCD screen is actually composed of three smaller pixels: one red, one green, and one blue. By finely adjusting the color displayed in the pixels around the edges of each letter, ClearType ekes out a bit of extra resolution from the screen. Because different screens have different arrangements of the colors within each pixel, to get the most out of the technology you must do a one-time adjustment (well, once for each different monitor you use). Here's what to do:

1. In the taskbar's search box, type the word `cleartype`. From the results, select Adjust ClearType Text. This starts the ClearType Text Tuner.

2. Be sure that Turn On ClearType is checked, and then click Next. Follow the wizard's instructions to select the text layout that looks best to you. (It's like getting an eye exam: The doctor keeps asking "Which looks better?" but they look just the same to you. Don't worry; just look at the selections and choose the one that seems easiest on your eyes.) Click Finish when you're done.

3. If you have multiple monitors, scroll up, select the next monitor icon, and repeat the process.

 note

If you're interested in seeing how ClearType works, check out www.grc.com/cleartype.htm for the geeky details. The "Free & Clear" demo program you can download from the site is fun to play with.

You will want to repeat this process if you get a replacement monitor or if you connect to a video projector to make a presentation and want to project the best possible image.

Now, we'll make some other adjustments to the desktop.

Tune Up the Taskbar, Action Center, and Start Menu

You might want to take a moment now to add taskbar icons for the programs you use frequently. These shortcuts can let you get to work using your favorite tools with just a single click or touch of the screen.

Personally, I always add taskbar icons for the Command Prompt, File Explorer, and Microsoft Word because I use these frequently, but you might have other favorites. To add an application's icon, search for the app using the taskbar's search function, and then right-click it or touch and hold it. Then select Pin to Taskbar.

 note

The old Show Desktop icon that parks all applications in the taskbar is now the unlabeled, wafer-thin rectangle at the far right end of the taskbar.

The Action Center shows you important notifications from Windows and gives you Quick Action buttons to open commonly used tools. You'll be using this often, and as you might guess, there are several ways to get to it:

- Click or touch the Action Center icon at the far-right end of the taskbar, just to the right of the time of day.

- Press Windows Logo+A.

- Or, on a touchscreen, swipe your finger from just outside the right edge of the screen in toward the center.

At the bottom of the Action Center, notice that there are rectangular buttons, as shown in Figure 3.8, which are called the Quick Action buttons. These provide a fast way to get to frequently changed settings.

Figure 3.8
The bottom of the Action Center has Quick Action buttons, which you can customize.

To customize the Quick Action buttons that appear, open the Action Center as just described and click the Settings (gear) icon at its top. (This is yet another way to get to Settings.) Select System, and then in the left column, Notifications & Actions. Under Quick Actions, select Add or Remove Quick Actions to determine which buttons appear. Choose the items that make the most sense to you: certainly All Settings; Airplane Mode for tablets, laptops, and phones; Tablet Mode if you have a tablet or a touchscreen computer with a small screen; VPN if you connect to a network at work. Click the Back arrow. Then you can rearrange the icons if you want. Drag the icons with your mouse, or touch-and-hold an icon until the others change color, and then drag it to the position you desire.

I also suggest that you put some commonly used tools and folders right on the Start menu, for even faster access. You'll use them all the time. To customize the Start menu, click Start, Settings, Personalization, Start (in the left column), and then Choose Which Folders Appear on Start.

From the list of items that appear, you might want to select File Explorer, Settings, and Documents, at least. I recommend always leaving the Settings icon turned on. Click X to close the settings panel.

Store to OneDrive or This PC

If you are using a Microsoft account to sign in, you have the option of saving new documents, music, pictures, and videos and other content to either your regular user account folders (Documents, Music, and so on) or to a matching set of folders in your OneDrive folder. If you save files in OneDrive, they're also stored online, so they will be copied to any other devices you use with the same Microsoft account.

Having online access from anywhere in the world can be a great thing, but only you can decide whether you want your files copied to a big corporation's data centers, which could be anywhere in the world and where they could conceivably eventually be read by friendly or unfriendly governments or criminals. This might be unlikely, but it's certainly not out of the realm of possibility, and you might never even know whether it happens.

By default, Modern and Desktop apps will try to save new files into a folder inside your OneDrive folder. Thus, the saved files will make their way up to Microsoft's servers and then to other devices you use. If you don't want this to happen, you can manually select a folder outside your OneDrive folder each time you save a new file; or, you can change the Auto Save setting in the OneDrive app.

Changing the default save location from OneDrive to your normal Documents folder, or vice versa, is a bit cumbersome: locate the small cloud-shaped OneDrive icon at the right end of the taskbar. (You may need to click the ∧ symbol to see it.) Right-click the OneDrive icon and select Settings. On the Auto Save tab, you can set the default save locations for Documents and Pictures to either This PC Only or OneDrive.

You can also choose to set the default save location to another drive entirely (such as a second disk drive or a removable SD card or Flash drive). To do this, click Start, Settings, System, Storage. Under More Storage Settings click Change Where New Content is Saved, you can set any or all of the entries to This PC (C:), which defaults the new file save location to a folder your user account profile or another separate disk drive. This just sets the *default* file save location, which is the easiest to use. Later, you can always choose the folder into which an app saves any individual file, on a file-by-file basis.

By the way, at the time this was written, OneDrive had just received a major update and has several new features such as download-on-demand, where you can wait to download files from your online storage until the moment you want to use them. This can save a lot of local storage space.

➡ *To learn how to set up OneDrive so you can access your files from all of your devices and from anywhere else in the world,* **see** *"OneDrive,"* **p. 836.**

Privacy Settings

The preceding discussion of OneDrive brings us to the general topic of privacy. Windows 10, more than any previous version of Windows, is set up to send lots of information to Microsoft—not only your documents and other files, but your Internet shortcuts, online and local hard disk search topics, physical location, email and phone contacts and calendar appointments, the Wi-Fi networks and apps you use, what you were doing when Windows ran into trouble, and more. Much of this data collection is done, reasonably, to give you seamless and ubiquitous access to your data and content and to help Microsoft provide a constantly improving, quality experience. (And to help select which advertisements to show you.)

Still, you must understand that everything that goes into and out of your computer, and everything you look at and do with your computer and where and when you do it, is being analyzed, and possibly recorded and stored somewhere. Microsoft has access to it, and if you've been following the news lately, you have to expect that criminals and agencies of various governments currently have or could eventually get explicit or covert access to it. You can imagine the news flash, I'm sure: "Data breach reveals personal information of 1 billion Windows users; researchers believe it was the work of the <fill in name of a random country> Army." So, you must decide whether this data sharing is agreeable to you. If not, you can control it to some extent, if not totally. Here are some ways that you could limit the amount of information that Windows shares with Microsoft and other online services. You'll pay the price in limited functionality, but this should be your choice to make:

- Use a local account rather than a Microsoft account.

- Do not set up cloud file storage services like OneDrive, Dropbox, and so on.

- Use web-based email or a trusted Desktop-style mail program rather than a Modern app, whose privacy policies might not be disclosed.

- Be wary of Modern apps in general, because many record your usage and track your location.

- Review and change Windows privacy settings to restrict the types of information that Windows can share.

- Limit the sources of information Cortana can access and what it can store.

To review privacy settings, click or touch Start, Settings, Privacy. There are a large number of categories of settings, and many settings within each. In many cases, you can choose which specific apps have access to various information such as your contacts, location, name, and so on. Personally, I prefer to turn access off except when I am sure that the app needs to know; but it can be tedious and frustrating to do this for dozens of apps times dozens of settings.

There are more privacy-related settings under Accounts, Sync Your Settings. In addition, the Smart-Screen filter sends URLs you visit and which your apps use to Microsoft to verify that they don't lead to known criminally hacked sites. This has privacy implications but is a huge security boon, and we recommend you leave it turned on. If you want to, though, you can control it from the Windows Defender Security Center's App & Browser Control settings page. (You can get there by typing **smartscreen** into the taskbar's search box.)

Important Adjustments and Tweaks

With the major adjustments discussed in the previous sections out of the way, you are down to just a few minor adjustments. These are items that aren't absolutely required, but I've found over years of working with Windows to be important enough that I go through them on every computer I use.

Command Prompt or Windows PowerShell

Are you a command-line guru? If you're not, skip this one. If you are, adjust the Windows Logo+X management menu to show your preferred environment: Command Prompt or Windows PowerShell. To change this, right-click the taskbar in an empty space, select Taskbar Settings, and turn on or off Replace Command Prompt with Windows PowerShell.

Enable Libraries

As we mentioned previously, if you want to use the Libraries feature in File Explorer, open File Explorer from the taskbar or Start menu, and then select View (along the top of the window), and then Options in the ribbon. Select the View tab, scroll to the bottom of the list of Advanced Settings and check Show Libraries, and then click OK.

Show Extensions for Known File Types

By default, File Explorer hides the file extension at the end of most filenames. This is the .doc at the end of a Word document, the .xls at the end of an Excel spreadsheet, or the .exe at the end of an application program. Hiding the extension makes it more difficult for you to accidentally delete it when renaming the file, but we think it also makes it more difficult to tell what a given file is. It can also make it easier to fall for ruses, as when someone sends you a virus program in a file named payroll.xls.exe. If Explorer hides the .exe part, you might fall for the trick and think the file is just an Excel spreadsheet.

To make File Explorer show filenames in all their glory, follow these steps:

1. Open File Explorer from the taskbar or Start menu.

2. At the top, select View, and in the Show/Hide section, check File Name Extensions.

3. Make a mental note that you can use this same settings section to let you see hidden files and folders, which Window normally doesn't display. (Files are marked hidden when they're useful to software but not generally interesting to humans.) Just check Hidden Items to make them visible.

4. This one is optional: If you're curious about the Windows internal files and folders and plan on investigating them, you can tell File Explorer to display "super-hidden" files and folders. These are items that Windows has marked as, in effect, uninteresting to users and of critical importance to Windows. To show them, at the right end of the View ribbon select Options, Change Folder and Search Options. Select the View tab, and scroll the list of Advanced Settings down. Uncheck Hide Protected Operating System Files (Recommended), click Yes, then OK.

Set Web Browser and Home Pages

With Windows 10, Microsoft is trying to move users to its new Edge web browser. In the long term, Edge should be more secure and more stable than Internet Explorer because it doesn't support the software plug-ins that extend Internet Explorer's capabilities. The plug-in mechanism has unfortunately also been a constant source of annoyance because spammers, criminals, and hackers have used it to hijack web searches and install advertising pop-ups, viruses, extortion software, and worse. But, in the near term, you might feel that Edge isn't quite ready for prime time. Many websites don't function properly with it, and some corporate tools require custom plug-ins.

Take a look at your taskbar and compare its icons to those shown in Figure 3.9. The Microsoft Edge icon has a break in it. The Internet Explorer icon has a sort of orbit around it.

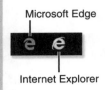

Microsoft Edge

Internet Explorer

Figure 3.9
Windows 10 comes with two web browsers: Internet Explorer and Microsoft Edge. Note the difference between the two icons. Internet Explorer may not be shown, until you add it.

By default, the Microsoft Edge icon should appear in the taskbar. If you want Internet Explorer as well, and its icon doesn't also appear, in the taskbar's search box type the word **internet**. In the search results, right-click or touch and hold Internet Explorer, and select Pin to Taskbar. You might also want to repeat the process and select Pin to Start.

As initially installed, whenever you open either Microsoft Edge or Internet Explorer, it immediately displays a Microsoft website or a website specified by your computer manufacturer. Personally, I prefer to have my web browser open to a blank page because I don't want to see advertising, and I rarely start my browsing in the same place twice. You also might want to select a different home page, one that *you* want to visit rather than one selected by some company's marketing department.

To take control of Internet Explorer's startup page, follow the steps under "Changing the Home Page" in Chapter 15.

To configure the startup page in Microsoft Edge, select the ... icon at the upper right, and then select Settings. Under Open Microsoft Edge With, select A Specific Page or Pages. In the box that appears underneath, type **about:blank** or a URL of your own choosing. Then click the small icon to the right of the box to save your selection. To open multiple tabs at startup, click + Add New Page and add additional URLs.

You might also want to download and install a different web browser entirely. Safari, Chrome, Firefox, Opera, and Tor are popular alternatives.

Search Providers

Microsoft Edge and Internet Explorer have a search tool built right in to the URL address box. If you type something that doesn't look like a URL and press Enter, the browser sends the text to an Internet search engine and displays the results. This saves you from having to open the search engine page first, type the search text, and then wait for the results.

By default, Microsoft sets up its browsers to send you to Microsoft's own search engine, called Bing. (Or your computer manufacturer might have specified a different default search engine.) Again, we suggest that you take control and tell Edge and IE which search engine *you* want to use. You can use Bing, of course, but you can also select a different default site.

➡ *To change the default search provider for Internet Explorer, **see** the instructions under "Searching the Web," Chapter 15*

To change the default search provider for Microsoft Edge, first view the site that you'd like to use for searching (for example, google.com). Then click the ... icon at the upper right, select Settings, scroll down, and select View Advanced Settings. Scroll the Advanced Settings down until you can see Search In the Address Bar With, and click Change Search Engine. If the name of your chosen site appears, select it, and then click Set As Default. (If your desired search provider's name doesn't appear, check their help information for an alternative procedure. It's up to them to make this function work.)

Enable System Restore

By default, System Restore, which lets you roll back system changes and updates that cause problems, is not enabled. To enable it, type the word **restore** in the taskbar's search box or the Settings panel's search box, and select Create a Restore Point from the results. In the Protection Settings list, select the C: drive and select Configure. Check Turn On System Protection, and set a Max Usage value of 10%. Click OK to save the changes.

Enable Metering for Cellular Data

If your device uses a cellular data service that has monthly limits, Windows can defer some downloads and uploads until you're hooked up to an unlimited Wi-Fi or Ethernet network. To change the setting, select Start, Settings, Network & Internet, and in the left column, select the category for your cellular data connection. Touch the icon near the top, just under the on/off switch, and be sure that Set as a Metered Connection is turned on.

If necessary, you can set other connection types, such as Wi-Fi, as metered also. When the list of potential connection names appears (as is usually the case on the Wi-Fi page), the Metered Connection setting applies only to the currently active connection.

That's the end of our list of "must do" Windows settings. You can, of course, change hundreds of other things, which is why we went on to write Chapters 4 through 39.

Transferring Information from Your Old Computer

If you have set up a new Windows 10 computer rather than upgrading an old one, you probably have files you want to bring over to your new computer.

If your old computer has Windows 7, 8, or 8.1, you might have noticed that it has a program called Windows Easy Transfer, which lets you package up your user accounts, files, and settings for transfer to a new computer. Unfortunately, Windows 10 does not have the "receiving" end of Windows Easy Transfer, so it's useless now.

Here are some options you might use instead, to move your stuff from an old computer to a new computer with Windows 10:

- On the old computer, you can copy files to cloud-based storage like OneDrive, Google Drive, Dropbox, or the like. If you install the same cloud file storage app on your new computer, the files will automatically be copied to your new computer. This option is easiest, and having your important files in cloud storage is great because you can then get to them from any device anywhere in the world. But it won't work if you have more files than will fit in your online storage quota, and it can be problematic if your Internet service is slow or limited in the amount of data you can transfer.

- You can manually copy your most important files and folders directly from your old computer to your new computer using a network. This option is fast, and if you set up a Homegroup network as we show you in Chapter 18, it's pretty easy, but it copies data only, not programs or settings.

- You can copy files from your old computer to a removable drive, take the removable drive to your new computer, and then copy the files onto the new computer. Like the network method, this copies data only, not settings or programs.

  We give you some tips for the network or external disk methods later in this section.

- You can use a paid third-party program to transfer data, settings, and possibly application programs. These products can copy your user accounts, files, preferences, app data (such as email, if you use an email reading program), and so on. You must pay for these, but they can do a very thorough job, and the vendors provide customer support if you need help. We discuss these options more in the next section.

- You could venture into some spooky territory. Microsoft has a free program called the User State Migration Tool, meant for use by corporate network managers. It's difficult to use. If you want to read more about it, go to technet.microsoft.com and search for "User State Migration Tool."

We don't have room to give you detailed instructions for all of these methods, but we can give you some pointers. We talk about LapLink PCmover Express first; then we discuss manual transfers using a network or external disk.

Third-Party User Transfer Programs

One fairly simple way to move your files and other data from an old computer to a new Windows 10 computer is to purchase a program to perform the job. Most of the available commercial products can move your user account, including documents, music, videos, and so on. Some versions can move application programs as well, so that you don't need to reinstall them. Some can move user data from any version of Windows to any other, 32-bit or 64-bit, on different computers, or even on the same computer as you change versions of Windows on it. (This is called an *in-place upgrade* and is particularly useful if you want to change your copy of Windows from a 32-bit version to a 64-bit version, as the Windows installer can't automatically migrate your user account in this case.)

- Laplink (www.laplink.com) makes several paid products. The PCmover Home version ($40) copies user accounts, files, and settings. The Professional version ($60) can also copy application programs and carry users, data, and applications across an upgrade or clean reinstall of Windows 10 from any prior Windows version, 32-bit or 64-bit.

- Zinstall (www.zinstall.com) makes several products with increasing capabilities. Easy Transfer ($59) copies user accounts, files, and settings over a network. WinWin ($119) moves application programs as well. Migration Kit Pro ($169) can carry users, data, and applications across an upgrade or clean reinstall of Windows 10 from any prior Windows version, and it can use an external hard disk instead of just a network.

Although you can use a program that copies application programs, we recommend that unless you've lost the installation discs or setup programs for your older programs, have the transfer program copy users, files, and data, but reinstall applications from scratch. This gives you a cleaner Windows 10 installation.

Copying Your Old Data Manually

If you have an external hard disk with a large free capacity, you can use it to copy data from your old computer to your new. (It's worth buying a disk with 2TB or 3TB capacity just for this. Afterward, you can use the hard disk so that Windows can back up your new computer, as discussed in Chapter 32, "Protecting Your Data from Loss and Theft.") You can also use a removable USB flash drive, although if you have lots of pictures, video, or music on your old computer, it might be difficult to fit all of it on a flash drive.

Alternatively, if you have a network that connects both your old computer and your new computer, you can transfer data through the network. Setting up a network is described in Chapter 18. If your old computer runs Windows 7, 8, 8.1, or 10, it's well worth making your new and old computers members of a homegroup right now, as discussed in Chapter 18.

We can't give detailed instructions for copying all of your files, but we can give you some pointers. (When you get to item 3 below, you might wonder what detailed instructions would look like. Seriously, this is the scaled-down version, and it's why one of those transfer assist programs can be a good deal.) You will be able to copy files, documents, pictures, and so on, but not user accounts, application settings, or application programs. Follow these steps:

1. You must be able to see hidden files and folders. Do the following on both your new *and* your old computers:

   - On Windows XP, Vista, or 7, open Windows Explorer. Press and release the Alt key. In the menu, select Tools, Folder Options, and then select the View tab. Select Show Hidden Files and Folders, uncheck Hide Protected Operating System Files, and then click OK. Leave Windows Explorer open.

   - On Windows 8, 8.1, or 10, open File Explorer. At the top, select View, Options, and then select the View tab. Select Show Hidden Files and Folders, uncheck Hide Protected Operating System Files, and then click OK. Leave File Explorer open.

   If you are going to use a network to transfer data, proceed to step 3.

2. If you are going to use an external disk, go to your *old* computer and attach the external disk. In the open Explorer window, select the removable drive in the left pane under My Computer, Computer, or This PC, depending on the version of Windows. In the right pane, right-click in an empty part and select New, Folder. Name the folder Old Stuff. Right-click it and select Open in New Window. This is where you will put files from the old computer. Proceed to step 4.

3. If you have your computers networked together, go to your *new* Windows 10 computer. In File Explorer's left pane, select this PC, and under that, select Local Disk (C:). In the right pane you should see folders Data, Program Files, Users, and so on. In the ribbon, select New Folder and name the folder Old Stuff.

If both the new and the old computers are members of a homegroup, lucky you. Right-click Old Stuff and select Give Access To, Homegroup (Read/Write). Right-click it again, and select Open in New Window. This is where you will put files from the old computer. Proceed to step 5.

If you don't have a homegroup, right-click Old Stuff and select Properties, Sharing, Advanced Sharing. Check Share This Folder, and then click Permissions. In the top part, select Everyone, and then in the bottom under Allow, check the box next to Change so that both Change and Read are checked. Click OK and then OK again. Select the Security tab. Click Edit, Add. Type the word **everyone**, and then click OK. In the bottom, check Modify. You should end up with settings that look similar to Figure 3.10, where Everyone has Modify privileges. Finally, click Close.

Figure 3.10
The Old Stuff folder needs to be modifiable by Everyone.

Phew! The folder Old Stuff is now shared on your network.

4. On your *old* computer, in the left pane of the open Explorer window, right-click My Computer, Computer, or This PC, depending on the version of Windows, and in the ribbon select Map Network Drive. Next to the Folder box, click Browse, and see if you can find the Old Stuff folder shared by the new computer. If you can, select it and then click OK. If you can't, you'll have to type *newcomputername*\Old Stuff into the Folder box, where *newcomputername* is the name of your new computer. (You can find that name by clicking its Start button and then selecting Settings, System, About. The computer name will be displayed above the button Rename This PC.)

Click Finish, and a new drive should appear in the left pane. If the process fails because of a username or password issue, go to your new Windows 10 computer, click the network icon in the taskbar and select Network & Internet Settings, Sharing Options. Scroll down, click the arrow to expand the All Networks section, and select Turn Off Password Protected Sharing. Click Save Changes. Now go back to the old computer and try step 4 again.

If the process succeeds, right-click the new mapped drive and select Open in New Folder. You should see an empty folder. This is where you will put files from your old computer.

5. On your *old* computer, move the empty Old Stuff window aside, and select the original Windows [File] Explorer window. In the left pane, select the icon for your computer, labeled My Computer, Computer, or This PC, depending on the version of Windows. Under that, select the C: drive. In the right pane, look for these folders, if they exist:

Documents and Settings
ProgramData
Users

Then drag them one at a time to the Old Stuff folder that you parked aside. Windows will copy these folders and their contents to the Old Stuff folder. This process can take quite awhile.

Repeat this step with any other folders with recognizable names, but *not* the following, which contain data and files you can't use:

> (Any folder name starting with $)
> Boot
> Config.MSI
> EFI
> MSOCache
> Program Files
> Program Files (x86)
> Recovery
> System Volume Information
> Windows
> WinNT

Folders with recognizable names other than these were probably ones you or other users on your computer created, and you probably want them.

If your computer has other hard drives installed, you might want to copy folders from them into Old Stuff as well.

If you are using a network, proceed to step 7.

6. If you are using a removable drive, in [Windows or File] Explorer's left pane, right-click the name of the removable drive and select Eject. Then unplug the drive and plug it into your new computer.

On your new computer, open File Explorer. In the left pane, under This PC, locate the icon for the removable drive. Select it, and in the right pane, you will see the Old Stuff folder. Double-click it, and you will see the folders you copied from your old computer. Proceed to step 8.

7. On your *new* computer, open File Explorer. In the left pane, under This PC, select the entry for your C: drive, and in the right pane, double-click Old Stuff. You should see the stuff copied from your old computer.

8. You can now dig in to these folders. All the users on your new computer can repeat this step to retrieve their own stuff from the removable drive.

Under Documents and Settings or Users, you will find folders for each user on your old computer. When you try to open them, Windows might prompt you saying that you will need permission to view them, and it will offer to give you access. This is normal.

Dig in to *your* old account folder, and you can drag the contents of the old folder to the correct places in the left pane on your new computer: My Documents into your Documents folder, Pictures into your Pictures folder, and so on. You can drag the ProgramData folder and the AppData folders into your personal Documents folder and then dig in to them when you need to locate something from the old computer. It's not safe to copy them to their corresponding places in your new computer.

If you're not familiar with these folders, you might want to read "Where's My Stuff? The User Profile Structure" on page 100 (this chapter) to see what these folders are for and how they're organized.

9. If you used your network to transfer files, and in step 4 you followed the instructions to turn off Password Protected Sharing on your new computer, repeat that part, but this time, select Turn On Password Protected Sharing.

10. Undo the changes you made in step 1 on your new computer at least, if not both the new and old.

As we said, that was a general overview. You might have to work harder to get to specific application data.

You can see why using OneDrive, or another cloud service, makes a lot of sense: You simply drag the files you care about on the old computer to the OneDrive, Google Drive, Dropbox, or other service folder, and the cloud service takes care of everything.

How the Heck Do I Shut This Thing Off?

We end our tour and setup marathon by showing you how to sign out and turn off your computer.

Remember the ribbing we Windows users got from Mac users because we had to click Start to stop? It's only a little better now.

Here are the sign-out and shutdown options:

- **To make the computer sleep, shut down, or restart**—Click or press the Start button, and select the power icon at the lower left. Select Sleep, Shutdown, or Restart. Also, if your device or laptop has a cover, closing the cover should automatically make it sleep. And if you have Cortana set up for voice activation, you may also be able to say, "Hey Cortana, put the computer to sleep."

- **To sign out**—Click or touch the Start button, and click or touch the user account picture or icon at the top of the column of icons at the left edge of the Start menu. Select Sign Out.

- **To switch users**—Click or touch the Start button, click or touch the user account picture or icon at the top of the column of icons at the left edge of the Start menu, and select another username.

Alternatively, right-click the Start button or press Windows Logo+X, select Shut Down or Sign Out, and then select one of the following choices: Sign Out, Sleep, Shutdown, or Restart.

Sleep is a great way to save energy if you're leaving your computer for more than 10 minutes or so and plan to come back. However, if the computer loses power, Windows might not have a chance to shut down properly, and you could lose data if you haven't saved your documents. You can tell Windows that if you leave the computer "asleep" for some time, it should automatically turn the computer back on, save its memory to disk, and then really power itself off. This is called *hibernation*. When you turn the computer back on, it'll take a bit longer to restart than it would from sleep, but it's still usually faster than a cold Windows startup.

To set up automatic hibernation, click in the taskbar's Search box and type `edit power`. Select Edit Power Plan, Change Advanced Power Settings. Scroll down to the Sleep entry and expand the list. If Allow Hybrid Sleep appears, expand it and change the value(s) under it to On. Expand Hibernate After, and change the time(s) from Never to, say, 120 minutes (2 hours), and then click OK. (If your computer has a battery or backup power, there might be two values to change: On Battery and Plugged In.)

This ends our tour. To close the book, so to speak, click the Start button, and then select Power, Shut Down. Watch Windows power off. When it's finished shutting down, press your computer's power button briefly and see how fast it powers back up.

 caution

Always use Shut Down before you unplug a desktop computer.

 note

When you shut down Windows 10, it closes all running applications and services, but it actually hibernates the Windows kernel. When you start up again, the kernel loads nearly instantly, speeding up the boot time by several seconds.

tip

On desktop computers, Hibernate isn't shown as an option on this Shut Down menu because the automatic hibernate-after-sleep mechanism, called *Hybrid Sleep*, is enabled by default. If you disable Hybrid Sleep in the Advanced Power Settings control panel, Hibernate will appear as an option on this Shut Down menu. On laptops, Hibernate should appear on the Shut Down menu because Hybrid Sleep is disabled by default.

More Than You Wanted to Know

In the rest of this chapter, we cover some more advanced topics that some of you might want to know about and some of you won't. Feel free to skim the rest of the chapter and read just what interests you. You're probably itching to start poking around with Windows 10 now anyway, and you can always come back to these items later if the need arises.

Now, let's go on to learn where Windows 10 stores your documents, music, and so on, and how this differs from Windows XP and earlier versions of Windows.

After You Forget Your Password

Forgetting the password to your computer account is an unpleasant experience. If this happens to you, take a deep breath. You might recover from this. Here are the steps to try, in order of preference:

1. If you are using a Microsoft account, use another computer and open a web browser to go to account.live.com/password/reset.

If you can't get this to work with your Microsoft account, you must deal with two separate steps. First, access your online Microsoft account, which we can't help you with here. Second, gain access to your information on your computer. For the latter, you can use a different Administrator–level account to disconnect your account from online and switch it to local. Then at least you'll be able to sign in.

The remaining steps are for users with local accounts.

2. If you created a password reset disk, as described earlier in the chapter in the section "Before You Forget Your Password," you're in good shape. Follow the instructions in the next section, "Using a Password Reset Disk."

3. If you are a member of a domain network, contact the network administrator to have her reset your password. Don't proceed to the remaining steps unless you absolutely have to. The administrator *might* be able to recover any encrypted files you created if you stop here.

4. Sign in using a different Administrator account and use the User Accounts control panel to change your primary account's password.

 caution

If you have to resort to step 4 (signing in as an administrator and changing your primary account's password), you will lose any stored website passwords linked to your account and, worse, any files that you encrypted using Windows file encryption (a feature found on Windows 10 Pro and Enterprise only). There will be absolutely *no way* to recover the encrypted files.

5. If you don't remember the password to any administrator account, or you can't find someone else who does, you're in big trouble. If you used BitLocker to encrypt your hard disk, you're done for. End of story.

If you have a Windows 8, 8.1, or 10 installation DVD handy, you can use a fairly easy but dirty trick to reset an account's password. I won't describe the procedure here, but you can find it online at http://pcsupport.about.com/od/windows-8/a/reset-password-windows-8.htm, or google Windows 8, 8.1, or 10 reset password ease of access for instructions. This technique works, and it's free.

Alternatively, programs are available that can break into Windows and reset one of the Administrator accounts' passwords. It's a gamble; there's a chance these programs might blow out your Windows installation. Still, if you're in this situation, you might want to risk it. Here are some programs you might look into:

- Passware Kit Basic (www.lostpassword.com) creates a Linux boot disk, which pokes through your NTFS disk volume, finds the Windows security Registry file, and replaces the administrator's password so that you can reboot and sign in.

- Active@ Password Changer (www.password-changer.com) works on a similar principle, booting up in Free-DOS from a DVD/CD or flash drive. The program finds the security Registry file on your Windows installation and deletes the password from selected accounts.

- There are some free password-reset programs that you might find by searching the Internet. The ones we tested did not work with Windows 10. We encourage you not to try unvetted downloads under any circumstances. You have no idea if they will do what they say or if they will install viruses or ransomware. We have two better options coming up next.

6. If you need to retrieve only files, you can remove the hard drive and install it in another Windows computer as a *secondary* drive. Boot it up, sign in as an administrator, and browse into the added drive. You probably need to take ownership of the drive's files to read them. (If the files are encrypted, or if the hard drive is encrypted with BitLocker, this technique won't work either.)

7. If you get this far and are still stuck, things are pretty grim. You'll need to reinstall Windows using the Clean Install option, which will erase all your user settings. Then, as an administrator, you can browse into the \Users folder to retrieve files from the old user account folders. Again, you'll need to take ownership of the files before you can give yourself permission to view or copy them.

 caution

The existence of techniques that enable you to reset passwords should raise your eyebrows. The fact is that with physical possession of your computer, people can get into it. However, these break-in tools won't work if your hard drive is encrypted with BitLocker, a feature available in the Pro and Enterprise editions.

If you are not a member of a domain network, you can avoid all this by creating a password reset disk ahead of time, as instructed earlier in this chapter.

Using a Password Reset Disk

If you have lost your password but have a password reset disk that you made earlier, you can use it to sign in. Just attempt to sign in using the Sign In screen. When the sign in fails, click Reset Password. Then follow the Password Reset Wizard's instructions to change your password, and store the password reset disk away for another rainy day. You don't need to remake the disk after using it.

Accessing the Real Administrator Account

In Windows NT, 2000, and XP, there was an account named Administrator that was, by definition, an Administrator-level account. You might have noticed that it's nowhere to be seen in Windows 10.

Actually, it's still there but hidden. There's a good reason for this. It's disabled by default and hidden on the Sign In screen and even in Safe Mode, and it requires no password to sign in. This was done to provide a way to recover if you somehow manage to delete the last (other) Administrator-level account from your computer. In this case, Windows will automatically enable the built-in Administrator named account so that you can sign in and re-create one or more personal Administrator-level accounts, or turn a Standard User into an Administrator. (You would then immediately sign out and use the repaired account.)

This is a good fail-safe scheme, and we recommend that you leave it set up this way. Still, if for some reason you want to set a password on the built-in Administrator account or use it directly, here's how. This method works even on Windows 10 Home.

1. Right-click the Start button and select Command Prompt (Admin) or Windows PowerShell (Admin), whichever appears. Approve the User Account Control prompt.

2. Type the following command, and then press Enter:

   net user administrator /active:yes

3. Sign out or switch users, and then sign in as Administrator, which now appears on the Sign In screen.

4. We strongly urge you to create a password reset disk for the Administrator account right now, using the steps described earlier in this chapter. Be sure to store it in a secure place.

5. Press Ctrl+Alt+Del, and then click Change a Password. Leave the old password field blank and enter a new password as requested. Press Enter when you finish.

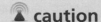

⚠ caution

When you are signed in using the real Administrator account, User Account Control is bypassed, and all privileged programs run with elevated privileges.

Now, the Administrator account is accessible and secured.

If you're worried that if by not making the changes we just described, having a disabled, password-less Administrator account is a security risk, remember that by default it can't be accessed unless all other Administrator accounts have been deleted, and only an administrator user could manage to do that. Therefore, a nonadministrator can't do anything personally to get to Administrator. (Not easily, anyway. As discussed previously, someone with physical access to your computer can work around anything but BitLocker encryption.) If you enable the Administrator account, then, yes, you really *must* set a password on the account.

If you enable the Administrator account and later want to set it up as it was before, log on as Administrator, change its password by leaving the new password blank, repeat step 1 above, and type the command **net user administrator /active:no**.

If You're Moving to Windows 10 from XP

If you somehow avoided using Windows Vista, 7, 8, and 8.1, and you're moving straight from Windows XP to Windows 10, you have about 15 years of catching up to do. In the following sections, we go through a few things that are going to be fairly big changes for you.

Setting and Control Panels

If you're used to the old Control Panel, the Settings panels and even the updated Control Panel are going to read like a Russian novel. There is so much text, and as you poke around, you see that many links lead to the same place. Why? We mentioned it earlier in the chapter: Search. You're meant to find things by searching now, not by poking around. So, use the taskbar, Settings and Control Panel search boxes to find what you want. If you get stuck, check the index of this book.

Where's My Stuff? The User Profile Structure

Windows 10, 8.1, 8, 7, and Vista store your documents, music, and pictures in a different folder layout than did Windows XP and earlier versions of Windows. Each user's personal files are stored in a folder with the same name as the user account name inside folder \Users. In some cases, Windows adds other letters or numbers to the username to create a unique folder name.

This folder is called a *user profile*, and it contains not only your personal documents but also some hidden files that contain your personal Windows Registry data (which contains information used by Windows and application programs), temporary files used by Internet Explorer, and so on. Another folder inside \Users is named Public, and this folder can be used by any of the computer's users. It's a place to put files that you want to share with everyone else.

In Windows 10, for security reasons you *can't* store your own files inside \Program Files, \Windows, or the root (top) folder of the drive on which Windows is installed, although you can create folders there and put files in the new folders.

The directory structure looks like this:

```
C:\
   Windows
   Program Data
   Program Files
   Program Files (x86)   (on 64-bit versions of Windows only)
   Users
    myname
    yourname
    :
    Default
    Public
```

Here's a brief tour:

- The Windows and Program Files folders have the same purpose as older versions of Windows: to hold Windows and application programs, respectively. On 64-bit versions of Windows, the Program Files (x86) folder holds 32-bit applications.

- The Program Data folder is hidden, so you won't see it unless you elected to show hidden files earlier in the chapter in the section "Show Extensions for Known File Types." In it, the Start Menu subfolder contains shortcuts to programs that end up on the Start menu. This was the folder \Documents and Settings\All Users\Start Menu on Windows XP.

- The Users folder contains user profiles, the Public folder (which contains the rest of what was \Documents and Settings\All Users in Windows XP), and the hidden Default user profile, which is copied when a new user account is created.

- A user profile folder for a given account is created only when the user signs in for the first time.

The user profile folder for the account named "myname" is c:\Users\myname, the folder for the account named "yourname" is c:\Users\yourname, and so on.

Inside each user's profile folder is a series of subfolders, which are listed in Table 3.2.

Table 3.2 User Profile Folders

Folder Name	Purpose
AppData (hidden folder)	Per-user application data. Subfolders Local, LocalLow, and Roaming are used to separate data that will never leave this computer from data that should be copied back to a central server if the account is on a corporate network with roaming profiles.
Contacts	Address book data.
Desktop	Files and shortcuts that appear on the desktop.
Documents	On Window 10, its name is displayed in File Explorer as My Documents or Username's Documents; but in reality, the folder is named just Documents.
Downloads	Files downloaded from the Internet.
Favorites	Favorites links for Internet Explorer.
Links	Shortcuts to important Windows folders.
OneDrive	Contains files and folders that are synced to your online storage and then to other devices you use. Inside the OneDrive folder are folders named Documents, Music, and so on. These are the default save locations for new documents and other content.
Music	Personal folder for music files.
Pictures	Personal folder for images.
Saved Games	Data saved by games.
Searches	Saved search queries.
Videos	Personal folder for multimedia files.

These folders are organized differently than in Windows XP, but correctly written application programs won't need to know about the differences; Windows has mechanisms to provide to programs the paths to these various folders based on their function rather than their location. Still, for those applications whose programmers "wired in" the old XP structure, Windows 10 has a mechanism to let them run without problems, as we show you in the next section.

Windows 10 setup creates *junction points* and *symbolic links* in the Windows drive that provide a measure of compatibility with applications that were hard-wired to expect the Windows XP user profile structure. Junction points and symbolic links are special "virtual" folders that point to other, real folders. When a program attempts to examine files in the virtual folder, Windows shows it the files in the real folder. If older applications attempt to read from folder \Documents and Settings, for example, Windows shows them the contents of \Users.

You should ignore these special link folders. Don't delete them, and to the extent possible, forget that they exist. They are hidden system files by default, so you only see them, in fact, when you instruct File Explorer or use the dir command-line tool to display both hidden and system files.

Compatibility and Virtualization

In previous versions of Windows, applications could store files inside the \Program Files and \Windows folders, and they often took advantage of this to store common data that was shared among all users. The same was true for the Registry, a database of user and setup information—programs frequently stored information in the HKEY_LOCAL_MACHINE Registry section.

To make Windows more secure, user programs are no longer allowed to store files or Registry data in these areas unless their setup programs explicitly change Registry security settings to permit it. (And this must happen while the program is being installed under elevated privileges.)

Most of the applications that ship with Windows are subject to these restrictions. Try it yourself: Open Notepad, type a few words, and try to save a file in \Program Files. You can't. Any application that Windows deems as new enough to know better is entirely blocked from saving information in these protected areas. (Technically, the presence of a *manifest file* in the program's folder or inside the program file itself is what tells Windows that the program is "new enough.")

Older programs, however, expect to write in these privileged directories and Registry areas. Therefore, to maintain compatibility, Windows 10 gives them an assist called *file and Registry virtualization*. If an older program attempts to create a file in one of the protected folders or Registry areas and access is blocked, and the program is not running with elevated permissions and the file doesn't have a manifest file, Windows stores the file or Registry data in an alternative, safer location. Whenever an older program tries to read a file or Registry data from a protected location, Windows first checks the alternative location to see whether it had been shunted there earlier and, if so, returns the data from that location.

Thus, the application doesn't actually store information in the secure locations but thinks it does.

Why are we explaining this to you? There are two reasons:

- One consequence of virtualization is that older programs that try to share data between users can't. Each user will see only his private copy of the files that should have been stored in a common place. For example, in the "high score" list in a game, each user might see only his own name and scores. This can also cause problems with programs that track licensing or registration.

- If you go searching for files in File Explorer or the command-line prompt, you won't see the files that got virtualized where you expected them to be because explorer.exe and cmd.exe have manifests. They don't get the virtualization treatment, so they see only the files stored in their intended locations.

 note

Some Registry keys are not virtualized in any case. For example, most keys under HKEY_LOCAL_MACHINE\Software\Microsoft\Windows will not be virtualized; attempts to write data in this key or most of its subkeys will simply fail. This prevents rogue applications from creating startup program Run entries.

The first problem can't be helped; the older programs just have to be redesigned and replaced. Knowing that virtualization occurs, you can work around the second problem by knowing where to look.

Files intended for \Windows or \Program Files (or any of their subfolders) will be placed into \Users\username\AppData\Local\VirtualStore\Windows or ...\Program Files, respectively.

Registry data intended for HKEY_LOCAL_MACHINE will be shunted to HKEY_CURRENT_USER\ Software\Classes\VirtualStore\Machine.

User Account Control

Windows NT, 2000, and XP had the necessary structure to secure the operating system against viruses and hackers. The way Windows security works, any program that a user runs gains the privileges associated with the user's account; this determines what folders the user can save files in, what settings the user can change, and so on. Administrator accounts can change any system setting, change any security setting, change any file, install any software, or modify Windows itself. In effect, software run by an Administrator account could do *anything*.

Unfortunately, in Windows XP, all user accounts were by default created as Administrator-level accounts, and it took a lot of effort and training to work with Windows any other way. So, for most home and small office users, Windows security was entirely bypassed. One consequence of this was that tens of millions of Windows computers became infected with spam-sending and otherwise malicious software, unbeknownst to their owners.

Windows Vista, 7, 8, 8.1, and now 10 have tightened up security through several means, including these:

- The disk on which Windows is installed *always* uses the NTFS disk formatting system so that access to files and folders can be tightly controlled.

- As initially installed, the security system is actually used and ensures that users cannot randomly create, delete, or modify files in the Windows program folders. This protects Windows not only from accidents but also from rogue software.

- Programs and system control panels that can make changes that have security implications use a special feature called *User Account Control (UAC)* to ensure that changes can't be made without your knowing it.

This latter part is what we want to talk about and show you now.

As mentioned earlier, Windows programs run with the permissions associated with a user account. Permissions include things such as the ability to create or modify files in each folder, change settings on features such as networking and hard disk management, install software and hardware device drivers, and so on. Administrator accounts can do any of these things.

What changed starting with Windows Vista is that programs run even by users with administrator accounts *don't* automatically get all those privileges. The potential is there, but by default, programs run with a reduced set of privileges that let them modify files in the user's own folders but *not* in the Windows folder or the Program Files folder. Likewise, by default, programs run even by an Administrator cannot change networking settings, install applications, install device drivers, or change system software services.

Instead, you must take a special step to run a program with *elevated privileges*—that is, with the full complement of Administrator privileges. On Windows Vista, when *any* privileged program was run, you had to respond to a dialog box to confirm that you did intend to run it. This behavior was fairly intrusive and annoying. On Windows 10, as we explain shortly, this mechanism is still there, but Windows requires this sort of confirmation in fewer circumstances.

What is important is that when this "go or no-go" dialog box is displayed, it's displayed by Windows in a secure way, from a deep, protected part of Windows, and there is no way for rogue software to bypass it, block it, or fake your approval. Thus, there is no way for rogue software to install itself *without your consent*. This is called User Account Control (UAC).

If you are signed in using an Administrator-level account, Windows just asks you to consent to running the program. However, if you signed in using a standard user account, Windows *can still run the administrative program*; the UAC prompt asks you to select the username and enter the password of an Administrator account.

All this makes Windows more secure *and* usable. It makes it safer to let people have and use Administrator accounts. And it is now reasonable to set up Standard User accounts for everyday use, for anyone, and especially for people whom you'd rather not be asked to judge which programs should run—for example, children or non-computer-literate employees. Should they actually need to change some setting that brings up a UAC prompt, you can simply reach over their shoulder, type in a privileged account name and password, let them make the one change, and poof!—they're back to being a limited-privilege user.

Of course, this type of intervention is required only for programs that involve security-related settings.

A program can be run with elevated privileges in three ways:

- Some applications are "marked" by their developers as *requiring* elevated privileges. These programs display the UAC prompt whenever you try to run them.

- You can right-click *any* program's icon and select Run as Administrator. Generally, you would do this only if you attempted some task and were told that you don't have permission. This can happen, for example, if you try to delete some other user's document from the printer's queue.

- If you have an old program that you find doesn't work correctly with UAC, right-click its icon and select Properties. On the Shortcut tab, click the Advanced button, check Run as Administrator, and then click OK. This will make the program run with elevated privileges every time you run it.

> ⚠ **caution**
>
> Don't get in the habit of just clicking Yes every time one of these dialog boxes appears. Read it and consider it every time.
>
> If you have any doubts about the program listed in the dialog box, especially if a UAC pop-up appears when you didn't expect it, click No.

> ⚠ **caution**
>
> User Account Control can be configured. The default setting makes Windows 10 much less annoying than Vista, without compromising security too much. We *strongly* urge you *not* to reduce the UAC warning level below the default setting. Doing so makes your computer much more vulnerable to being taken over by criminals. If you have specific programs that don't work well with UAC enabled, you can work around this *just for those specific programs*.

> ### 🔍 note
>
> If you're interested in reading the nitty-gritty details about how User Account Control works, go to technet. microsoft.com and search for "Inside Windows 7 User Account Control." Look for the article with this name written by Mark Russinovich, who is one of the Windows gurus behind sysinternals.com, and who is now employed by Microsoft. This article is applicable to Windows 10 as well.

The New Taskbar

The taskbar at the bottom of the desktop shows an icon for each running application. This much hasn't changed since Windows 95. You might also recall the Quick Launch bar from previous versions of Windows, which had little icons you could use to start commonly used programs with a single click.

In Windows 10, the Quick Launch bar and the taskbar have been combined and enhanced, and now there is just one set of icons; they represent applications that *are* running and those that represent programs you *could* run. This new arrangement might seem strange at first, but it's actually pretty handy, and we think you'll like it a lot. (And if it seems vaguely familiar, the reason might be that the Apple Mac has worked this way for more than a decade.)

Take these actions to see the taskbar in action:

1. In the taskbar, click the pale yellow File Explorer icon. (If it's not present on your computer, use another of the icons for these steps.) When you click the icon for an application that isn't running, Windows starts it.

2. Click the same taskbar icon two more times. When you click the icon for an application that's already running, Windows hides or brings up the application's window, in alternation.

3. Right-click the taskbar icon and select File Explorer. This opens another, separate instance of the application.

4. Click the taskbar icon. When you click the icon for an application that has more than one instance open, Windows displays thumbnail views of the various windows so you can select (click on) which one you want to use.

In practice, you won't have to think about it. When you want to use a program, you just click its icon, and you get it, whether it was already running or not.

You can also easily organize the icons on the taskbar:

- You can drag around the icons to reorder them any way you want.

- To put an application in the taskbar permanently, start it, right-click its taskbar icon, and then select Pin This Program to Taskbar. You can also right-click an icon on the Start menu and select Pin to Taskbar.

- To remove an icon, right-click and select Unpin This Program from Taskbar. Use this technique to get rid of icons that some application installers insist on putting on the taskbar whether you want them or not.

Jumplists

Another neat feature of the taskbar is the jumplist. Remember the old Recent Documents list from previous versions of Windows? This feature is now part of the taskbar, and recently used documents are automatically linked to the icons for the applications that opened them.

Right-click the taskbar's Internet Explorer icon, for example, and you'll see a list of frequently visited websites. Right-click Microsoft Word or WordPad or Notepad, and you'll see the last several documents you saved using those programs. It's all very intuitive and natural. (However, it works only with applications that know about this feature. Older applications might not create a jumplist.)

 tip

If you want to keep a website or document in a jumplist permanently, right-click it and select Pin to This List. If you no longer want it pinned, right-click it and select Remove from This List.

4

USING THE WINDOWS 10 INTERFACE

Taking a Tour of the Windows 10 Interface

"Ah, that's better." That was our first thought when we saw the Windows 10 interface, which does away with the much-maligned Windows 8/8.1 interface and its jarring and inefficient switching between the Start screen and the desktop. Instead, we're back to an interface that's more reminiscent of Windows 7, with a desktop front and center supplemented by a Start menu that implements some of the nicer features of the Windows 8/8.1 Start screen. The Windows 10 interface might look familiar, but there's lots that's new, so the goal of this chapter is to help you get comfortable with this new look. That is, you learn exactly how the Windows 10 interface works, what shortcuts you can use to make it easier, and what customizations you can apply to make it your own.

Let's begin with a tour of the Windows 10 interface. Figure 4.1 shows the Windows 10 desktop and Start menu. There, a lot to show you!

The Windows 10 screen offers the following main features:

- **Start button**—As with Windows 7 and most earlier versions of Windows, the Start button appears in the lower-left corner of the screen, and you click it to display the Start menu. Right-click the Start button for a pop-up menu of management tools.

- **Start menu**—The new Start menu is divided into two sections. On the left is a navigation section that gives you access to your installed apps (listed alphabetically), as well as icons for your user account, Settings, and Power. On the right is a scaled-down version of the Windows 8/8.1

Start screen that offers quick viewing and access to the tiles (see the next item) of a few apps. On desktop computers, the Start menu fills only part of the screen, and you can resize it. On tablets, by default, the Start menu fills the screen, and most apps run full screen, unless you resize them. This is called Tablet Mode, and you can easily turn it on and off. Try it both ways and see which you prefer.

note

If you have a touchscreen, remember that throughout this chapter, where we say "click," you can just touch. And where we say right-click, you can touch-and-hold until a square box appears. We talk more about the touch interface later in this section.

➡ *For more about using Tablet Mode with Windows 10, **see** "Tablet Mode," **p. 69.***

- **Tiles**—Each of the rectangles you see on the right side of the Start menu represents an item on your PC—most tiles represent apps, but you can also add tiles for folders and websites—and you click a tile to launch that item. Tiles can appear in one of four sizes. (See "Resizing a Tile," later in this chapter.) A key to making Windows 10 easy to use is to pin your favorite apps here and to rearrange the tiles to put your favorites near the top.

- **Live tiles**—Many of the Start menu tiles are "live" in the sense that they display often-updated information instead of the app icon. For example, the Weather tile shows the current weather for your default location. However, live tiles don't display any live content until you have used their app at least once.

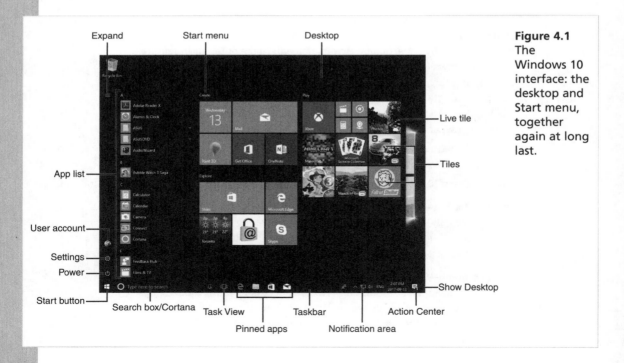

Figure 4.1
The Windows 10 interface: the desktop and Start menu, together again at long last.

- **App list**—At the left side of the Start Menu, all your installed apps are listed alphabetically. You can scroll through this listing using a scroll bar that's invisible until you hover the mouse over it or touch it. You can click on any of the letter headings to view the entire alphabet and then click on a letter to jump right to that section.

- **Power**—Click this button to sleep, shut down, or restart your PC.

- **System Icons**—Above the Power button, you see the system icons. By default, there are two: Settings and the icon for your user account. However, you can customize which system icons appear; see "Customizing the Start Menu's System Icons," later in this chapter.

- **User account**—Clicking this icon gives you access to several account-related tasks (see Figure 4.2):

  - Click Change Account Settings to open the Accounts section of the Settings app.

  - Click Lock to lock your PC.

  - Click Sign Out to log off your account.

  - If you have other user accounts on your PC, you can click one from the account list to switch to that user while your account remains signed in.

Figure 4.2
Click your user account icon for quick access to some account features and commands.

- **Desktop**—Relegated to a mere "app" in Windows 8/8.1, the desktop is back in Windows 10 and resumes its (rightful, in our opinion) place in the main interface as the default location for programs and documents.

- **Taskbar**—This strip along the bottom of the screen displays icons for each running app. You can also pin an app's icon so that a shortcut to it remains in the taskbar even when the app isn't running. This is another key to making Windows easy to use: Pin favorite apps to the taskbar, so they're always instantly available.

- **Search box/Cortana**—You use this box to search your PC. We've found that this feature is the easiest way to launch apps, settings, and documents in Windows 10. If your computer has a microphone, you can click the Voice Search icon to say what you want to find. (If you enable the Hey Cortana feature, Windows listens for questions all the time. More about this later.)

- **Task View**—Click this taskbar icon to display thumbnails of your running apps and to create virtual desktops. (See "Working with Virtual Desktops," later in this chapter.)

- **Pinned apps**—The Windows 10 taskbar comes with several pinned apps, which means those icons remain on the taskbar even when the apps are closed. To learn how to work with pinned apps, see "Pinning an App to the Taskbar," later in this chapter.

- **Notification area**—This part of the taskbar displays various system icons for features such as networking, sound, and power, as well as the notification issued by Windows.

- **Action Center**—Click the taskbar's Action Center icon to display a panel of notifications and "speed dial" access buttons for management tools.

- **Show Desktop**—Desktop too cluttered? Click the tiny sliver at the far right end of the taskbar to instantly minimize all apps down into the taskbar.

If you're new to Windows 10, it's worth spending a few minutes familiarizing yourself with all these features.

Navigating Windows 10 with a Keyboard

Windows 10 offers a huge number of Windows Logo key–based shortcuts that not only enable you to navigate the Windows 10 interface quickly but also let you easily invoke many Windows 10 features and programs. Table 4.1 provides the complete list. You certainly don't have to memorize them all. But do read through the list, as you'll probably find two or three that you'll find useful every day.

Table 4.1 Keyboard Shortcuts for Navigating Windows 10

Press This	To Do This
Windows Logo	Toggle the Start menu
Windows Logo+A	Open the Action Center
Windows Logo+D	Minimize all open windows to display the desktop
Windows Logo+E	Run File Explorer
Windows Logo+F	Open the Feedback Hub.
Windows Logo+I	Run the Settings app
Windows Logo+K	Display the Devices pane
Windows Logo+L	Lock your computer
Windows Logo+M	Minimize all windows
Windows Logo+O	Turn the tablet orientation lock on and off
Windows Logo+P	Display the Project pane to configure a second display
Windows Logo+Q	Open Cortana/search for text input.
Windows Logo+R	Open the Run dialog box
Windows Logo+S	Open Cortana for keyboard commands
Windows Logo+T	Activate the taskbar icons (use the arrow keys to navigate the icons)

Press This	To Do This
Windows Logo+U	Open the Ease of Access settings
Windows Logo+W	Activate the Windows Ink Workspace
Windows Logo+X	Display a menu of Windows tools and utilities
Windows Logo+Z	Display an app's commands (although this works only in some Modern apps)
Windows Logo+*n*	Launch or switch to the app that's in the *n*th pinned position on the taskbar (where *n* is a number from 1 to 9)
Windows Logo+=	Open Magnifier and zoom in
Windows Logo+-	Zoom out (if already zoomed in using Magnifier)
Windows Logo+,	Temporarily display the desktop
Windows Logo+Break	Open Control Panel's System window
Windows Logo+Enter	Open Narrator
Windows Logo+Left arrow	Snap the current app to the left side of the screen
Windows Logo+Right arrow	Snap the current app to the right side of the screen
Windows Logo+Up	Restore a minimized app; maximize a restored app
Windows Logo+Down	Restore a maximized app; minimize a restored app
Windows Logo+PgUp	Move the current app to the left monitor
Windows Logo+PgDn	Move the current app to the right monitor
Windows Logo+PrtScr	Capture the current screen and save it to the Pictures folder
Windows+Alt+D	Open the Date/Time/Calendar taskbar popup
Windows Logo+Spacebar	Display the available input languages
Windows Logo+Ctrl+D	Create a virtual desktop
Windows Logo+Ctrl+Right arrow	Switch to the next virtual desktop
Windows Logo+Ctrl+Left arrow	Switch to the previous virtual desktop
Windows Logo+Ctrl+F4	Close the current virtual desktop
Windows Logo+Tab	Open Task View, which displays thumbnails for each running app as well as the available virtual desktops
Ctrl+Shift+Esc	Open Task Manager

Navigating Windows 10 with a Touch Interface

We used to always say that Windows was built with the mouse in mind. After all, the easiest way to use screen elements such as the Start menu, the taskbar, toolbars, ribbons, and dialog boxes was via mouse manipulation. However, for tablet PCs that come with no input devices other than a touchscreen, it's now safe to say that Windows 10 was built with touch in mind. That is, instead of using a mouse or keyboard to manipulate Windows 10, you can use your fingers to touch the screen in specific ways called gestures. (Some tablet PCs also come with a small penlike device called a stylus, and you can use the stylus instead of your finger for some actions.) If your computer has touch, a keyboard, and a mouse or trackpad, you can use whichever input methods you wish—and if you're like us, you'll find yourself switching back and forth all the time. What are these gestures? Here's a list:

- **Tap**—Use your finger (or the stylus) to touch the screen and then immediately release it. This is the touch equivalent of a mouse click.

- **Double-tap**—Tap and release the screen twice, one tap right after the other. This is the touch equivalent of a mouse double-click.

- **Touch and hold**—Touch the screen and leave your finger (or the stylus) resting on the screen until a square box appears under your finger. When you release it, the shortcut menu appears. This is the touch equivalent of a mouse right-click.

- **Swipe**—Quickly and briefly run your finger along the screen. This usually causes the screen to scroll in the direction of the swipe, so it's roughly equivalent to scrolling with the mouse wheel. You also swipe to display some of the Windows 10 interface elements:

  - Swipe up from the bottom edge of the screen to display the taskbar.

  - Swipe from the left edge of the screen toward the middle to open Task View.

  - Swipe from the right edge toward the center to open the Action Center.

  - Some Modern elements (especially those designed for Windows 8) have a menu that appears if you swipe down from the top edge.

  - In Tablet mode, you can close a running app by swiping down all the way from the top edge of the screen to the bottom.

 note

There is nothing on the screen that shows you these swipe gestures exist; like keyboard shortcuts, you have to be told or be lucky enough to find them by accident. But they're just handy shortcuts. You can still use Windows 10 without knowing about them. What made Windows 8 so horrible is that it was unusable if you didn't know these invisible secrets.

- **Slide**—Place your finger on the screen, move your finger, and then release. This is the touch equivalent of a mouse click and drag, so you usually use this technique to move an object from one place to another. However, this is also ideal for scrolling, so you can scroll an app vertically by sliding your finger up and down on the screen, or horizontally by sliding your finger right and left on the screen, making this technique the touch equivalent of clicking and dragging the scroll box.

- **Pinch**—Place two fingers apart on the screen and bring them closer together. This gesture zooms out on whatever is displayed on the screen, such as a photo.

- **Spread**—Place two fingers close together on the screen and move them farther apart. This gesture zooms in on whatever is displayed on the screen, such as a photo.

- **Turn**—Place two fingers on the screen and turn them clockwise or counterclockwise. This gesture rotates whatever is displayed on the screen, such as a photo.

You can also use touch to enter text by using the onscreen touch keyboard, shown in Figure 4.3. To display the keyboard in an app, tap inside whatever box you'll be using to type the text; you can also tap the Touch Keyboard icon that appears in the taskbar's notification area.

As pointed out in Figure 4.3, you can tap the key in the bottom-right corner to see a selection of keyboard layouts, including

note

If you don't see the Touch Keyboard icon in the taskbar, tap and hold the taskbar to display the shortcut menu, and then tap Show Touch Keyboard Button.

Figure 4.3
To type on a touch PC, use the onscreen keyboard.

Tap here for more keyboard layouts.

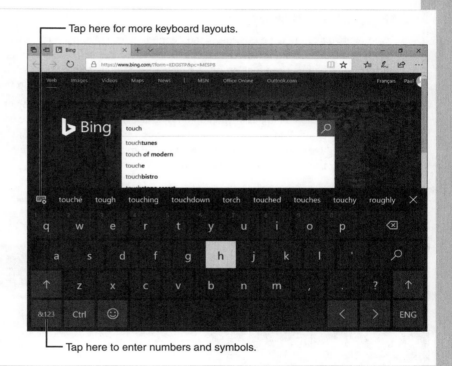

Tap here to enter numbers and symbols.

the one shown in Figure 4.3, a split keyboard, a full keyboard, and a writing pad for inputting hand-written text using a stylus (or, in a pinch, a finger).

➡ *To learn more about using the touch keyboard,* ***see*** *"Touch Keyboard," **p. 811.***

➡ *To learn about a handy new pen- and touch-centric toolkit,* ***see*** *"Windows Ink Workspace," **p. 813.***

Working with Running Apps

One of the ironies of Windows 8/8.1 "features" that we didn't like was that, at least as far as the interface went, there no longer seemed to be any windows. After all, when you launched an app, it didn't appear inside a box. Apps technically did appear in a window; it's just that by default those windows took up the entire screen. Fortunately, that window weirdness is behind us now, and in Windows 10 all apps appear within bona fide, readily recognizable windows. You'll see this for yourself over the next three sections as we take you through various techniques for manipulating running apps.

Snapping an App

One way you can take advantage of the "windowness" of apps, both Modern and Desktop, is to show more than one app onscreen at the same time. (This is why Windows was created after all.) So, for example, you can display what's playing in Groove Music while simultaneously surfing the Web, or watch what your Facebook friends are up to while also shopping in the Windows Store.

A convenient way to fit an app to exactly half of the screen is to snap the app to the left or right side of the screen. This means that the app automatically resizes itself and parks itself on the left or right side of the screen. You can then snap another app to the opposite side of the screen. For example, Figure 4.4 shows the Groove Music app snapped to the left side of the screen, while Microsoft Edge covers the rest, with no annoying overlap.

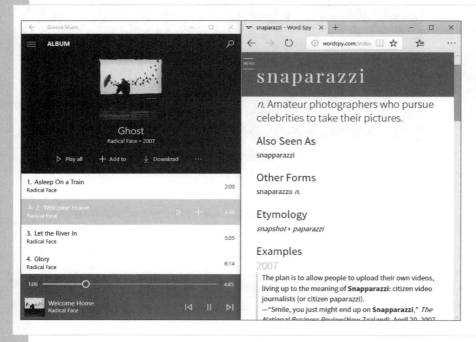

Figure 4.4
You can neatly display two apps at the same time by snapping an app to the left or right side of the screen.

To snap an app, use the mouse or your finger to drag the app's title bar to the left or right side of the screen and then release. If you have one or more other apps open, Windows 10 invokes the Snap Assist feature, which automatically displays those other windows as thumbnails on the open part of the desktop. Click an app thumbnail, and Windows 10 snaps that app to fill the rest of the screen.

 tip

Another way to snap the current app is to hold down the Windows Logo key and tap either the left- or right-arrow key repeatedly. Windows 10 cycles the app through snap left, snap right, and unsnapped.

That's a pretty good trick, but Windows 10 goes one better by enabling you to snap four apps at once. You do so by snapping apps to the corners of the screen instead of to the sides. For example, if you drag an app window to the upper-left corner of the screen, Windows 10 snaps the app into that corner and automatically resizes it so that it takes up half the screen width and half the screen height.

Note, too, that you can mix these snap techniques. For example, you could snap two apps to the left side of the screen—one in the upper-left corner and one in the lower-left corner—and then snap a third app to the right edge to fill the remainder of the screen.

 tip

You're not restricted to snapped apps taking up exactly one-half or one-quarter of the screen. After you snap an app, you can adjust the size of the window as needed. When you then snap an app to an adjacent area, Windows 10 is smart enough to resize that app's window to fit the space available. For example, suppose you snap an app to the right side and then adjust the width so that it takes up two-thirds of the screen. If you then snap an app to the left side, Windows 10 will resize that app's window to take up just the remaining one-third of the screen. You can also resize two snapped apps at once. Position the mouse or your finger on the border between the two snapped apps and then click and drag left or right.

Switching Between Running Apps

If you have multiple apps going, Windows 10 does away with the convoluted Windows 8/8.1 techniques for switching between them. Now you can switch to any running app either by clicking a visible portion of its window or by clicking its taskbar button. If an app isn't visible or you're not sure which taskbar icon to click, here are two other techniques you can use:

- Click the taskbar's Task View button to display thumbnails of your running apps, as shown in Figure 4.5; then click the app you want to use. From the keyboard, press Windows Logo+Tab to activate Task View, use the arrow keys to select the app, and then press Enter.

- Hold down Alt and press Tab until the app you want is selected; then release Alt to switch to that app.

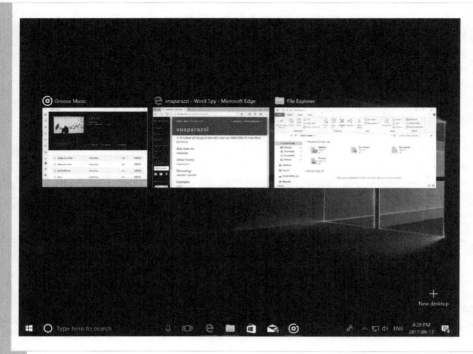

Figure 4.5
Use Windows 10's new Task View to view and switch between your running apps.

Pinning an App to the Taskbar

For our money, by far the easiest way to launch an app in Windows 10 is to pin your favorite programs to the taskbar, which puts the app just a click away.

You can pin a program to the taskbar either from the Start menu or the desktop. First, here's the Start menu method:

1. Click Start and then locate the app you want to pin.

2. Right-click the app.

3. Click Pin to Taskbar. Windows 10 displays an icon for the program in the taskbar, whether the app is running or not.

Here's how to pin a running desktop program to the taskbar:

1. Launch the program you want to pin.

2. Right-click the running program's taskbar icon.

3. Click Pin This Program to Taskbar. Windows 10 adds an icon for the program to the taskbar.

If you no longer want an app pinned to the taskbar, right-click the app's taskbar icon and then click Unpin from Taskbar.

 tip

You can also pin an app to the taskbar by dragging the app from the Start menu and dropping it on an empty section of the taskbar.

 tip

Windows 10 displays the taskbar icons left to right in the order in which you pinned them. To change the order, click and drag a taskbar icon to the left or right and then drop it in the new position.

Using Desktop Apps as the Defaults

It's an unfortunate fact of Windows 10 life that many of the so-called Modern apps are actually extremely simple programs that offer only minimal feature sets. We don't recommend using many of them, at least the ones that have good desktop alternatives, but Windows 10 often tries to force the issue by using many apps as the default programs for certain file types. For example, if you double-click a JPEG file in File Explorer, Windows 10 opens it in the Photos app. Similarly, double-click an MP3 file, and Windows 10 plays the song using the Groove Music app. Adobe PDF files open in the Edge browser.

Fortunately, with a bit of work, you can configure Windows 10 to open these and other file types using alternative apps or desktop programs. Here are the steps to follow:

1. In the taskbar's Search box, type **default app**, and then, in the search results, click Default App Settings. The Default Apps window appears.

2. For each app category—Email, Maps, Music Player, and so on—click the current default app and then click a desktop program that you want to use for opening one or more file types. For example, to change how Windows opens music files, click Groove Music under the Music Player category, and then click Windows Media Player.

3. To set the default app for a particular file type, scroll down to the bottom of the screen and click Choose Default Apps by File Type, click the current default app beside the file type's extension, and then click the new default app you want to use.

4. To set the default file types associated with a particular app, scroll down to the bottom of the screen, click Set Defaults by App, click the app you want to work with, and then click Manage. Windows 10 displays all the file types you can associate with the app.

5. Beside each file type that you want to associate with this program, click the current default app and then click the new default app. For example, in Figure 4.6 you can see that we're working with Windows Media Player and that we've associated it with the .mp3 file type.

 tip

If you make a mess of your defaults, or if you decide you want a fresh start, open the Default Apps window and click Reset to restore everything to Microsoft's preset defaults.

Figure 4.6
You can assign file types to desktop apps such as Windows Media Player.

Working with Notifications

If you're a Windows old-timer, you're certainly all too familiar with the notification area in the taskbar, which displays balloons whenever Windows or an application has information for you. Those notifications are still available, but that older style of notification appears only for desktop programs. Windows 10 and all apps use a different system in which the notifications appear as larger fly-out messages above the notification area. For example, you might add an appointment to the Calendar app and ask the app to remind you about it, and that reminder appears as a notification. Similarly, if you use the Alarms app to set an alarm, the alarm message and options appear as a notification.

These notifications appear briefly in the lower-right corner of the screen. For example, Figure 4.7 shows the notification that appears when you insert a USB flash drive. In this case, Windows 10 is wondering what you want to do with the drive.

 tip

Notifications appear for only a few seconds. To keep a notification onscreen indefinitely, move your mouse pointer over the notification.

Figure 4.7
Notifications appear in the lower-right corner of the screen.

To handle the notification, click it. Windows 10 then takes you to the app that generated the notification. If the notification was generated by Windows 10 itself, it displays more information. In the flash drive example, Windows 10 displays a list of options similar to the one shown in Figure 4.8.

Figure 4.8
Click a notification, and Windows 10 either displays more information, as shown here, or switches to the app that generated the notification.

Searching Windows 10

If you use your PC regularly, there's an excellent chance that its hard drive is crammed with thousands, perhaps even tens of thousands, of files that take up hundreds, perhaps even thousands, of gigabytes. That's a lot of data, but it leads to a huge and growing problem: finding things. We all want to have the proverbial information at our fingertips, but these days our fingertips tend to fumble around more often than not, trying to locate not only documents and other data we've created ourselves, but also apps, Windows settings, and that wealth of information that exists "out there" on the web, in databases, and so on.

And it's not just our content—documents and photos and the like—that can be difficult to find. There are hundreds if not thousands of settings in Windows. Trying to find some barely remembered feature in Settings or the Control Panel can be a nightmare. But, it's completely avoidable, if you let Windows do the work for you.

Searching via the Taskbar

Windows 10 attempts to solve this problem by combining all search operations into a single interface element called the Search box. Using this deceptively simple taskbar-based text box, Windows 10 lets you search for apps by name, for Windows 10 settings and features, for documents, for app data, for web content, and more.

As initially released, Windows 10 had two options for the taskbar search tool: a basic search function, and Cortana. Cortana is a much more powerful tool that uses (limited) artificial intelligence to try to gather relevant data from many sources, and which, to some, causes concerns about privacy because even searches within your own computer are transmitted to Microsoft, and presumably recorded. As of the Anniversary Update, Cortana is set up by default, and it's very difficult to disable it. Later in this section, we show you how to limit the amount of information it transmits to Microsoft.

Click in the search box and type any word or phrase that seems relevant to what you're interested in: a phrase from a document, a contact's name, and so on. As you type, Cortana tries to figure out what you're looking for, whether you're looking for an app you have installed, or text in some document you want to find, or the time and date of an appointment in your calendar, or, perhaps, the answer to life, the universe, and everything. As you type, results appear in various categories, as shown in Figure 4.9; Cortana displays what it thinks are the most likely results at the top (which you can select by clicking, or highlighting and pressing Enter), and then the rest of the top results are divided into categories such as Settings, Store, Documents, and Web.

Figure 4.9
The Search box displays as-you-type results.

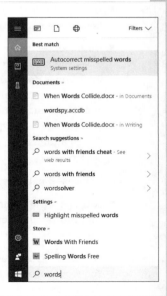

You can limit the results to apps, your own content and documents, or web searches, using the quick filtering icons at the top of the search box. Or, select Filters, and then select one of nine categories such as Folders, Music, and so on, as shown in Figure 4.10.

Figure 4.10
When you click Filters, Windows 10 displays a list of categories by which to filter the search results.

Down the left edge of the search box are icons that let you control Cortana. The hamburger menu expands their names:

- **Home**—Displays the basic search results page. If you don't type anything in the search box, the home page displays tips, tricks, and examples of things Cortana can do.

- **Notebook**—Despite the name, Notebook is a settings control panel. It includes over 20 tabs full of settings covering a wide arrange of topics, which is how you control how deeply Cortana intertwines itself with your life and the sources of information it can use. Here, you can tell Cortana what social networks you use, what packages you're tracking (it can pick them up from your email automatically!), which financial markets you're interested in, what kind of restaurants you like, and a plethora of other things. The more you define, the more Cortana watches out for things it thinks you need to hear about. You should spend a few minutes going through all the categories.

- **Devices**—Enables you to set up devices that Cortana can operate, such as a speaker.

- **Settings**—The Settings panel controls Cortana's access to your location, the microphone, and your browsing history. You can also configure Cortana so that you can use it from the Windows lock screen.

- **Feedback**—The Feedback icon lets you send feedback to Microsoft about Cortana's performance. You would use this to report examples of botched searches, and so on. It can include a screen-shot automatically.

Voice Search with Cortana

Software engineers, having grown up watching *Star Trek* characters interact with computers using voice commands, have been trying to get the rest of us to use voice to control our PCs for many years. The problem is that most people feel awkward "speaking" to a PC, and although voice would in some cases be a more efficient way to interact with the machine, the inaccuracies, glitches, and slow performance of early voice-recognition systems almost always made such systems less efficient in the long run.

Still, the engineers keep trying, and Microsoft is no different with its Cortana voice-activated personal assistant, debuted originally on the Windows Phone and now available on all Windows 10 computers and tablets.

At the right edge of the taskbar's search box, there is a microphone icon. Click it to interact with Cortana using voice commands.

You can also instruct Windows to monitor your device's microphone constantly, listening for the phrase "Hey, Cortana" followed by a query. It's a great feature (if a bit creepy, although Microsoft emphatically states that nothing that Cortana hears while waiting for this catchphrase is recorded or sent out of your computer). To enable Hey Cortana:

1. Click inside the taskbar's Search box.

2. Select the Settings (gear) icon.

3. Click the Let Cortana Respond to "Hey Cortana" switch to On.

4. Follow the prompts to train Cortana to recognize your voice. Only your voice will trigger the Hey Cortana mechanism.

Managing Search Privacy

Cortana's usefulness depends on its being able to see into your documents, schedule, email, and search history, and on learning (that is, recording) what kinds of results are the ones you end up choosing. To be ever more useful, it has to learn more and more about you.

But there is very definite trade-off here: to gain its insights, you have to give up the expectation that your information stays entirely inside your computer. When your information goes somewhere else, you have no way to prevent its getting loose due to hacking, or government subpoena, or who knows what. To be sure, as we have come to depend more and more on cloud services, we have become used to the idea that staggering amounts of information about us are being stored by people we'll never know. We use Dropbox and iCloud and OneDrive, and our data is stored, well, *somewhere*. We know, too, that our web browsing is monitored. Remember that time you looked up the price of foot fungus ointment? Google and Microsoft do. It's recorded somewhere. The information increases the likelihood that you'll be shown an ad for Lotrimin. This, precisely, is what pays for your free email account. We have accepted this as normal, and the services we get in return for our privacy are addictive and useful.

You do have some choice in the matter. Microsoft has made it exceedingly difficult to turn off Cortana entirely, but you can restrict what gets sent out of your computer:

- **Disconnect Cortana from your Microsoft account**—This will ensure that search information is not linked to your account. Click in the search box, and then click the Notebook icon. Under About Me, click your Microsoft account name, and then click Sign Out.

- **Clear the info Cortana knows about you**—This removes all the data that Cortana is storing about you in the cloud. Click in the search box, click Settings, and then click Permissions & History. Click Change What Cortana Knows About Me in the Cloud, scroll to the bottom of the screen that appears, and then click Clear.

- **Manage the info that Cortana can access about you**—This lets you control Cortana's access to information such as your location, contacts, and browsing history. Click in the search box, click Settings, and then click Permissions & History. Click Manage the Information Cortana Can Access From This Device, and then use the switches to give or withhold permission for each type of information.

- **Manage your search history**—This enables you to control whether Cortana saves your search history, and to clear your search history. Click in the search box, click Settings, and then click Permissions & History. Scroll down to the History section. To disable search history on this device, click the My Device History switch to Off. To remove your Cortana search history from this device, click Clear My Device History. To prevent Cortana from using your search history from your other signed-in devices, click the My Search History switch to Off.

Customizing the Start Menu

The Start menu, with its live tiles and easy access (just press the Windows Logo key), is meant to be kind of an automatically and frequently updated bulletin board that tells you what's going on in your life: your latest messages, your upcoming appointments, the music you're listening to, the weather, the latest news and financial data, and so on. The key phrase here is "your life," meaning that it's unlikely the default configuration of the Start menu will be a reflection of who you are, what you do, and how you use Windows 10. Fortunately, the default Start menu layout isn't set in stone, so you're free to customize it by resizing and moving tiles, adding new tiles, and much more. The next few sections provide the details.

Resizing a Tile

The Start menu tiles come in up to four sizes (we say "up to" because not all app tiles support all four sizes). Medium is the most common (see, for example, the default Music and Video tiles), and the other sizes are based on the Medium dimensions: Small is one-quarter the size of Medium; Wide is the equivalent of two Medium tiles side-by-side; and Large is the equivalent of four Medium tiles arranged in a square.

The Wide and Large sizes are useful for tiles that are live because the tile has more room to display information. However, if you've turned off the live tile for an app (see "Turning Off a Live Tile," later in this chapter), these bigger tile sizes now seem like a waste of menu real estate, so you might prefer to use the smaller size. Similarly, if you turn on the live tile for an app that's using the Medium tile size, you might see only limited information in the tile (or none at all if the tile is using the Small size). For example, when the Mail app tile is set to Medium, it shows only the number of new messages you have, compared to showing you a preview of the new messages when the tile is set to Wide.

Whatever the scenario, you can resize a tile by right-clicking it, clicking Resize, and then clicking the size you want (see Figure 4.11).

Figure 4.11
Right-click a tile, click Resize, and then click a tile size.

Moving a Tile

One of the problems many new users have with the Windows 10 Start menu is the slight delay that occurs when they try to find the app they want to launch. This is particularly true when you have many live tiles on the go, because you no longer see the app name in each tile, just the app icon. If this is the case with just the default Start menu tiles displayed, it's only going to get worse after you start adding more tiles (see "Pinning an App to the Start Menu," later in this chapter).

One way to reduce this problem is to rearrange the Start menu in such a way that it helps you locate the apps you use most often. For example, you could place your favorite apps on the left side of the screen, or you could arrange similar apps together (for example, all the media-related apps).

Here are the techniques to use to move an app tile:

- **Regular PC**—Use your mouse to click and drag the tile and then drop it on the new location.

- **Tablet PC**—Use your finger (or a stylus) to tap and drag the tile and then drop it on the new location.

Turning Off a Live Tile

As we mentioned earlier, the Start menu offers a kind of aerial view of what's happening in your life, and it does this by displaying live content—called tile notifications—on many of the tiles. That seems like a good idea in theory, but much of that live content is not static. For example, if you have multiple

> **tip**
> You can clear tile notifications automatically when you sign in or when you restart or shut down Windows 10. In the taskbar's Search box (or the Run dialog box; press Windows Logo+R), type **gpedit.msc** and then press Enter to open the Local Group Policy Editor (which is not available in Windows 10 Home Edition). Open the User Configuration, Administrative Templates, Start Menu and Taskbar branch, double-click the Clear Tile Notifications During Log On policy, select Enabled, and then click OK.

email messages waiting for you, the Mail tile continuously flips through previews of each unread message. Similarly, the News and Money tiles constantly flip through several screens of content.

This tile animation ensures that you see lots of information, but it can be distracting and hard on the eyes. If you find that the Start menu is making you less productive instead of more, you can tone down the Start menu by turning off one or more of the less useful live tiles. You do that by right-clicking a tile, clicking More, and then clicking Turn Live Tile Off.

Pinning an App to the Start Menu

One of the significant conveniences of the Start menu is that all the apps you see can be opened with just a couple of clicks or taps. Contrast this with the relatively laborious process required to launch just about any other app on your PC: Display the Start menu, scroll through the list to find the app you want to run, and then click it. Alternatively, you can use the taskbar's Search box to start typing the name of the app and then click it when it appears in the Search results.

Either way, this seems like a great deal of effort to launch an app, and it's that much worse for an app you use often. You can avoid all that extra work and make a frequently used program easier to launch by pinning that program to the Start menu.

Follow these steps to pin a program to the Start menu:

1. Use the Start menu or File Explorer to locate the app you want to pin.

2. Right-click the app.

3. Click Pin to Start. Windows 10 adds a tile for the program to the Start menu.

 tip

If you have a large number of apps, you can navigate them faster by clicking any of the headings that organize the apps alphabetically and then clicking the heading that contains the app you want to use.

Pinning a Web Page to the Start Menu

If you have a web page that you visit often, you can use the Internet Explorer app to pin the page to the Start menu. This means that you can surf to that page by clicking its Start menu tile.

Follow these steps to pin a web page to your Start menu using Microsoft Edge:

1. On the taskbar or Start menu, select Microsoft Edge.

2. Navigate to the web page you want to pin.

3. Click More Actions, which is the ellipsis icon near the upper-right corner of the window.

4. Click Pin This Page to Start. Click Yes when you are asked to confirm. Windows 10 adds a tile for the web page to the Start menu.

 tip

If you have a folder that you open frequently, you can pin that folder to the Start menu. Open File Explorer, and then open the location that contains the folder you want to pin. Right-click the folder and then click Pin to Start.

 note

To remove a tile from the Start menu, right-click it and then click Unpin from Start. Windows 10 removes the tile from the Start menu.

Creating an App Group

At first, the right side of the default Start menu appears like nothing so much as a random collection of tiles scattered willy-nilly. However, look closer, and you see that there are actually two collections of tiles: the one on the left is labeled Life at a Glance, while the one on the right is labeled Play and Explore. These are called app groups, and you can create your own to help organize the Start menu to suit the way you work and play.

Follow these steps to create an app group:

1. Pin to the Start menu an app, website, or Control Panel icon, as described earlier in this chapter. Alternatively, drag an existing tile to an empty section of the Start menu.

2. Add the other tiles you want to include in the group and drag each one to the same area of the Start menu as the first tile.

3. Move the mouse pointer just above the new group until you see an icon with two horizontal bars, and then click that icon. Windows 10 displays a text box above the group, as shown in Figure 4.12.

Figure 4.12
Move the mouse pointer above the group and click the icon to see the app group's Name text box.

4. Type the name you want to use for the group, as shown in Figure 4.12.

5. Press Enter. Windows 10 applies the name, and your new group is ready to use.

You can rename the group at any time (including the default Start menu app groups) by repeating steps 3, 4, and 5.

Displaying the Administrative Tools on the Start Menu

Windows 10 comes with a set of advanced programs and features called the administrative tools. We cover many of these tools in this book, including Performance Monitor, Resource Monitor, and Services (all covered in Chapter 23, "Windows Management Tools") as well as Disk Cleanup, Defragment and Optimize Drives, and Computer Management (all covered in Chapter 25, "Managing Hard Disks and Storage Spaces").

➡️ *For a rundown of all the administrative tools,* **see** *"Reviewing the Control Panel Icons,"* *p. 219.*

Some of these tools are relatively easy to launch. For example, you can press Windows Logo+X or right-click the Start button to display a menu that includes Event Viewer, Disk Management, Computer Management, and a few other administrative tools (see Figure 4.13). However, the remaining tools are difficult to access in Windows 10. For example, to run Defragment and Optimize Drives, you click in the taskbar's Search box, type **defrag**, and then click Defragment and Optimize Your Drives in the search results. Other administrative tools aren't even accessible via an apps or settings search, so instead you need to know the tool's filename. For example, to run the System Configuration utility, in the taskbar's Search box, type **msconfig** and then press Enter.

Figure 4.13
Press Windows Logo+X (or right-click the Start button) to display this handy menu of power user tools, which includes a few of the administrative tools.

This extra effort isn't that big of a deal if you use the administrative tools only once in a while. If you use them frequently, however, all those extra steps are real productivity killers. Instead, configure the Start menu with a tile for Control Panel's Administrative Tools icon by following these steps:

1. In the taskbar's Search box, type **control**, and then select Control Panel in the search results.

2. Use the View By list to select either Large Icons or Small Icons.

3. Right-click Administrative Tools.

4. Select Pin to Start. Windows 10 adds an Administrative Tools tile to the Start menu.

Adding Command Prompt to the Shortcut Menu

Pressing Windows Logo+X (or right-clicking the Start button) displays the power user's best friend: the shortcut menu shown in Figure 4.13. If you take a good look at this menu, you'll notice that it includes the following two commands: Windows PowerShell and Windows PowerShell (Admin). These commands launch the PowerShell command-line tool—the former with standard permissions and the latter with Administrator permissions.

These are handy if you're a PowerShell user, but if, like us, you still use the good old Command Prompt far more often, then these commands don't help your productivity.

Fortunately, you can fix that by configuring Windows 10 to replace the PowerShell commands with their Command Prompt equivalents. Here's how:

1. Click Start and then Settings.

2. Click Personalization.

3. Click Taskbar.

4. Click the Replace Command Prompt with Windows PowerShell... switch to Off.

Adding Shutdown and Restart Shortcuts

Although the Start menu does offer a few productivity improvements—at-a-glance info with live tiles, one-click app launching, as-you-type searching—a few tasks are maddeningly (and, in our view, unnecessarily) inefficient. We're thinking in particular of shutting down and restarting the PC. To perform these tasks using a mouse, you must click the Start button to open the Start menu, click Power, and then click either Shut Down or Restart. It's just inefficient, particularly if you regularly shut off or reboot your machine.

If you use Cortana and you have the "Hey Cortana" feature enabled, then things get a bit easier because you can use the following voice commands:

"Hey Cortana, restart PC."

"Hey Cortana, turn off PC."

When Cortana asks you to confirm, say "Yes."

If you want an even easier way of shutting down and restarting your PC, we show you how you can do just that. The basic idea is to create shortcut files that perform the shutdown and restart tasks and then pin those shortcuts to the Start menu or taskbar or leave them on the desktop.

So, let's begin with the steps required to create the shortcuts:

1. Right-click the desktop and then select New, Shortcut. The Create Shortcut dialog box appears.

2. Type **shutdown /s /t 0**. This command shuts down your PC. Note that the last character in the command is the number zero.

3. Click Next. Windows 10 prompts you to name the shortcut.

4. Type the name you want to use. The name you type is the name that will appear on the Start menu. I typically use Shut Down.

5. Click Finish.

6. For the restart shortcut, repeat steps 2–5, except in step 3, type **shutdown /r /t 0** (again, the last character is a zero).

To help differentiate between these two shortcut files, follow these steps to apply a different icon to each file:

1. Right-click a shortcut and then click Properties. The shortcut's Properties dialog box appears.

2. Click Change Icon. Windows 10 warns you that the shutdown command contains no icons.

3. Click OK. The Change Icon dialog box appears.

4. Click the icon you want to use, and then click OK to close the Change Icon dialog box.

5. Click OK to close the Properties dialog box.

6. Repeat steps 1–5 to apply a new icon to the other shortcut file.

> **tip**
>
> Although the `Shell32.dll` file contains plenty of shortcut icons, you can also try two other files:
>
> `%SystemRoot%\system32\`
> `pifmgr.dll`
> `%SystemRoot\explorer.exe`
>
> Press Enter after you type each location to see the icons.

Finally, you can now pin the shortcuts to either the Start menu or the taskbar by right-clicking each shortcut and then clicking Pin to Start or Pin to Taskbar.

Personalizing the Start Menu

As you work with the Start menu, you'll find it changes over time. One day, you'll see a recently added app at the top of the app list; another day, Windows 10 shows you a suggested app that you might like. Fortunately, these and other Start menu behaviors are fully controllable, enabling you to personalize the Start menu to your own liking. Here's how it's done:

1. Open the Start menu and select Settings to display the Settings app. (You can also press Windows Logo+I.)

2. Click Personalization. The Settings app displays the Personalization window.

3. Click the Start tab.

4. Enable or disable the following settings:

   - **Show More Tiles on Start**—By default, the Start menu is wide enough to display one Medium tile and one Large tile (or three Medium tiles) side by side. We've always thought that was too skinny because it requires vertical scrolling to see more Start menu tiles. One way to solve this problem is to click this switch to On.

> **tip**
>
> Another way to get a wider Start menu is to click and drag the right edge of the Start menu to expand it to the size you want.

- **Show App List in Start Menu**—To get even more room for Start Menu tiles, click this switch to Off to hide the app list. If you do this, you can display your apps by clicking the All Apps command that now appears in the navigation area.

- **Show Recently Added Apps**—When this switch is On, Windows 10 displays a Recently Added section in the Start Menu's navigation area, which includes icons for any apps that you've installed recently. If you prefer not to see this list, click this switch to Off.

- **Show Most Used Apps**—When this switch is On, Windows 10 displays a Most Used section in the Start Menu's navigation area, which includes icons for those apps you've launched most often.

- **Occasionally Show Suggestions in Start**—When this switch is On, the Start menu sometimes shows suggested apps. If you find these suggestions as annoying as we do, disable them by clicking this switch to Off.

- **Use Start Full Screen**—If you click this switch to On, Windows 10 expands the Start menu so that it takes up the entire screen. It also hides the app list, so you get the maximum screen area for the tiles.

- **Show Recently Opened Items in Jump Lists on Start of the Taskbar**—When this switch is On, Windows 10 shows your most recently opened documents (or whatever) in the app jump lists.

Customizing the Start Menu's System Icons

As mentioned earlier, the left side of the Start menu includes a collection of system icons just above the Power button. In a default install, there are two system icons: your user account and Settings. However, Windows offers 10 icons in all, including one for File Explorer, several that take you to the specific user account folders (such as Documents, Downloads, and Pictures), and a few system folders such as HomeGroup and Network. Follow these steps to add one or more of these icons to your Start menu:

1. Open the Start menu and select Settings to display the Settings app. (You can also press Windows Logo+I.)

2. Click Personalization. The Settings app displays the Personalization window.

3. Click the Start tab.

4. At the bottom of the screen, click Choose Which Folders Appear on Start. The Settings app displays a list of system icons that you can add to the Start menu.

5. For each icon you want to add to the Start menu, click its switch to On.

Customizing the Start Menu Background

If you're getting tired of the same old, same old on your Start menu, you can tweak the background and color scheme, as described here:

1. Open the Start menu and select Settings to display the Settings app. (You can also press Windows Logo+I.)

2. Click Personalization. The Settings app displays the Personalization window.

3. Click the Colors tab to display the controls shown in Figure 4.14.

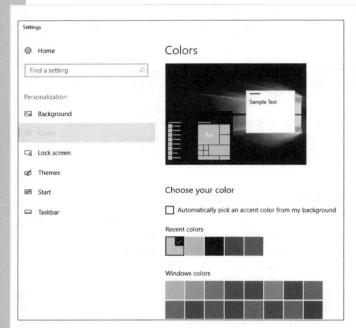

Figure 4.14
Use the Colors tab to customize the Start menu background and colors.

4. If you want Windows 10 to assign a color to the Start menu background automatically based on the desktop background, click the check box next to Automatically Pick an Accent Color from My Background. If this box is not checked, Settings displays a collection of color swatches, and you click a swatch to assign that color to the Start menu background.

 note

The color you select also applies to both the taskbar and the Action Center.

5. By default, the backgrounds of the Start menu, taskbar, and Action Center pane have a slight transparency effect. If you want to disable that effect, click the Transparency Effects switch to Off.

6. In the Show Accent Color on the Following Surfaces section, use the Start, Taskbar, and Action Center check box to toggle the color from step 4 on and off.

Customizing the Lock Screen

The Lock screen is the screen that appears before you sign in to Windows 10 (or, if your PC has multiple user accounts, it's the screen that appears before you select which account to sign in to). You have four ways to invoke the Lock screen:

- Turn on or restart your PC.

- Wake your device from sleep.

- Sign out of your user account (by clicking your user account tile and then clicking Sign Out).

- Lock your PC (by clicking your user account tile and then clicking Lock, or by pressing Windows Logo+L).

In other words, the Lock screen comes up relatively often when you use Windows 10, so you might as well get the most out of it by customizing it to suit how you work. The next three sections take you through these customizations.

➡ *To learn more about locking your computer, **see** "Locking Your Computer," **p. 700.***

Customizing the Lock Screen Background

If you use the Lock screen frequently, you might prefer to view a background image that's different from the default image. To choose a different Lock screen background, follow these steps:

1. Open the Start menu and select Settings to display the Settings app. (You can also press Windows Logo+I.)

2. Click Personalization. Windows 10 displays the Personalization window.

3. Click the Lock Screen tab. The Settings app displays the Lock Screen settings, as shown in Figure 4.15.

4. In the Background drop-down list, select Picture. If you want to see a random series of photos from Microsoft's Bing site as the Lock screen background, select Windows Spotlight instead. (They're quite lovely.)

5. Either select one of the supplied images or select Browse and then use the Open dialog box to choose an image from your Pictures folder.

note

Another way to apply one of your own images as the Lock screen background is to launch the Photos app, display the image you want to use, select See More (the three dots), select Set As, and then select Set as Lock Screen.

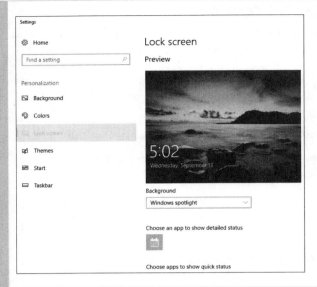

Figure 4.15
Use the Lock Screen settings to customize the background image displayed on the Lock screen.

Controlling the Apps Displayed on the Lock Screen

As you'll learn in Chapter 31, "Protecting Windows from Viruses and Spyware," locking your computer is a useful safety feature because it prevents unauthorized users from accessing your files and your network. When you lock your PC, Windows 10 displays the Lock screen, which includes the current date, an icon that shows the current network status, and an icon that shows the current power state of your computer (that is, either plugged in or on battery). By default, Windows 10 also includes Lock screen icons for apps that have had recent notifications. For example, the Mail app shows the number of unread messages, and the Calendar app shows upcoming appointments. The Lock screen also shows any new notifications that appear for these apps.

If you lock your computer frequently, you can make the Lock screen even more useful by adding icons for other apps that support notifications. Here are the steps to follow:

1. Open the Start menu and select Settings to display the Settings app. (You can also press Windows Logo+I.)

2. Click Personalization. Windows 10 displays the Personalization window.

3. Click the Lock Screen tab. The Settings app displays the Lock Screen window.

4. Under Choose an App to Show Detailed Status, click the icon (or click + if no app is currently selected).

5. Click the app for which you want to display detailed status updates (such as the name, location, and time of an upcoming event in the Calendar app).

6. Under Choose Apps to Show Quick Status, click +. Settings opens the Choose an App window.

7. Click the app you want to add to the Lock screen. Windows 10 puts the new settings into effect, and the apps appear on the Lock screen the next time you use it.

To control whether the Cortana taskbar search tool can display information on the Lock Screen, follow these steps:

1. Click in the taskbar's search box, and then select the Settings (gear icon) at the left of the search window.

2. Click the Use Cortana Even When My Device Is Locked switch to On. If you have also enabled Hey Cortana, Cortana will respond to your voice even if your device is locked.

3. If you want Cortana to look up and display calendar and other notification messages on the lock screen, activate the Let Cortana Access... check box under the Use Cortana switch. Be aware, though, that this may result in your device displaying private information when you're not expecting it (for example, if you boot your PC in a public place).

 *For more information about customizing Cortana and its privacy issues, **see** "Searching Windows 10," p. 120.*

Disabling the Lock Screen

The Lock screen is one of those innovations that seems like a good idea when you first start using it but then quickly loses its luster the more you come across it. In the case of the Lock screen, the problem is that it forces you to take the extra step of dismissing it before you can sign in:

- **Regular PC**—Press any key or click the screen.

- **Tablet PC**—Swipe up.

If you've had to perform this extra task one too many times, and if you don't find the Lock screen all that useful anyway, you can disable it. This means you don't see the Lock screen when you start or lock your PC. Instead, Windows 10 takes you directly to the sign-in screen.

Follow these steps to disable the Lock screen:

1. In the taskbar's Search box (or the Run dialog box; press Windows Logo+R), type **gpedit.msc** and then press Enter. The Local Group Policy Editor appears.

2. Open the Computer Configuration, Administrative Templates, Control Panel, Personalization branch. The Personalization policies appear.

3. Double-click the Do Not Display the Lock Screen policy. The policy details appear.

4. Click Enabled.

5. Click OK. Windows 10 puts the new policy into effect.

> **⚠ caution**
>
> In Chapter 31, we show you how to require that users press Ctrl+Alt+Delete before they log on, which is a helpful security precaution. However, if you configure your PC to require Ctrl+Alt+Delete, Windows 10 ignores the Do Not Display the Lock Screen policy setting.

If you're running a version of Windows 10 that doesn't have the Local Group Policy Editor, you can still disable the Lock screen using the Registry, as shown in the following steps:

1. In the taskbar's Search box (or the Run dialog box; press Windows Logo+R), type **regedit** and then press Enter. Click Yes in the User Account Control box. The Registry Editor appears.

2. Navigate to the following branch:

   `HKEY_LOCAL_MACHINE\SOFTWARE\Policies\Microsoft\Windows\`

3. If you do not see a key named `Personalization`, select Edit, New, Key, type **Personalization**, and then press Enter.

4. Select the Personalization key.

5. Select Edit, New, DWORD (32-bit) Value, type **NoLockScreen**, and then press Enter.

6. Double-click the NoLockScreen setting, set its value to **1**, and then click OK.

Working with Virtual Desktops

Now that the desktop is once again a first-class Windows citizen, we can all go back to cluttering our screens with umpteen app windows scattered around the desktop. Well, we could go back to that, or we could take advantage of a useful Windows 10 feature: virtual desktops. A virtual desktop is just like the regular Windows 10 desktop—that is, you can add icons to it, open apps on it, and so on—except that it resides offscreen until you summon it with your mouse or the keyboard. When you do that, Windows 10 moves the current desktop, as well as its icons and running apps, offscreen and replaces them with the second desktop, meaning you now see its icons and apps. So rather than having all your running apps on one desktop, you could create separate desktops for, say, productivity apps, media apps, Internet apps, and so on, and then cycle through them as needed.

Adding a Virtual Desktop

To add a new virtual desktop, you have two choices:

- In the taskbar, select the Task View button (or press Windows Logo+Tab) to display the Task View, and then select New Desktop. Windows 10 adds the new virtual desktop to the Task View, as shown in Figure 4.16. Select the desktop thumbnail to switch to it.

- Press Windows Logo+Ctrl+D. Windows 10 creates and switches to the new virtual desktop.

Figure 4.16
The Task View screen lets you add new desktops and manage how apps are displayed.

Working with Virtual Desktops

Once you have two or more desktops on the go, here's a rundown of the techniques you can use:

- **Switching desktops**—Click the Task View icon or press Windows Logo+Tab, and then select the icon of the desktop you want. You can also scroll through desktops using the keyboard, using Windows Logo+Ctrl+Right arrow or Windows Logo+Ctrl+Left arrow.

- **Viewing Desktop Contents**—When you open Task View, the current desktop is shown in the upper part of the window. Hover the mouse over the thumbnails in the lower part of the window to view a different desktop.

- **Moving an app to a different desktop**—Switch to the desktop that has the app you want to move, and then invoke Task View. Drag the app's thumbnail and drop it on the desktop to which you want it moved. Alternatively, open Task View, right-click the app, and select Move To.

- **Pinning an app to all desktops**—If there is an app (or apps) that you want to see no matter which desktop you're using, invoke Task View. Hover the mouse over the desktop that has the app you want to use. This displays the desktop's content. Right-click the app you want to pin, and then select Show This Window On All Desktops to make this instance of the app appear in every virtual desktop. If you have multiple copies of the same app open (for example, several Excel windows), you can select Show Windows From This App On All Desktops to show all copies in every virtual desktop.

- **Closing a virtual desktop**—Invoke Task View, move the mouse pointer over the desktop you want to remove, and then click Close (X). You can also close the current virtual desktop by pressing Windows Logo+Ctrl+F4.

Customizing Virtual Desktops

Windows 10 offers a couple of customization settings for virtual desktops. To see them, open the Settings app, select System, and then select the Multitasking tab. The Virtual Desktops section offers two lists:

- **On the Taskbar, Show Windows That Are Open On**—By default, Windows 10 shows a taskbar icon for only the current virtual desktop's apps. If you'd rather the taskbar show icons for all running apps, regardless of which virtual desktop is current, use this list to select All Desktops.

- **Pressing Alt+Tab Shows Windows That Are Open On**—By default, Windows 10 cycles through only the current virtual desktop's apps when you hold down Alt and press Tab. If you'd rather that pressing Alt+Tab cycle through every running app, regardless of which virtual desktop is current, use this list to select All Desktops.

5

WINDOWS APPS AND THE WINDOWS STORE

The Windows Apps

One of Microsoft's fundamental design principles for its so-called *Modern* apps (that is, apps created for Windows 8/8.1/10, in contrast to the so-called *Desktop* apps, which precede Windows 8) is "content before chrome." That is, the typical interface that these apps use is characterized by an overall style that places content front and center, and where chrome—including window borders, menus, scrollbars, and icons—is hidden or minimized, relegated to the edge, or eliminated altogether.

For the most part, Modern apps adhere to the following guidelines:

- **Clean layout**—App interfaces are characterized by a generous amount of open space, so you won't find lots of graphical knickknacks such as lines, boxes, and borders. These interfaces are also visually simple, so you won't find color tricks such as gradients and blurs. The result is that the content gets some room to breathe.

- **Uncluttered interface**—Apps have lots of white (or black or green or whatever) space surrounding the content. Most apps achieve this look by not leaving commands, navigational aids, and other features displayed full-time. Instead, apps "leverage the edge" by placing commands and features out of sight or minimized. One common interface feature is to display a menu of icons down the left side, or sometimes across the top, as shown in Figure 5.1. Clicking the Menu icon (the three-line "hamburger" icon in the top-left corner) expands the menu to show the command names, as shown in Figure 5.2. Many Modern apps also use the See More icon, the three dots at the upper right of Figure 5.1, to display extra commands or interface elements, and a gear-shaped Settings icon, as shown at the lower left of Figure 5.1.

Menu

See More

Settings

Figure 5.1
Many Modern apps have a minimal menu down the left side or across the top of the window.

Figure 5.2
Clicking the "hamburger" icon expands the menu to show the command names.

- **Typography conveys hierarchy**—Traditional programs use boxes and lines to separate sections and establish interface hierarchies. Modern apps use typographical indicators—particularly text size, weight, and color—to convey boundaries and hierarchies.

- **Direct content interaction**—In most apps, you manipulate the content itself by performing taps, drags, zooms, and swipes directly on an item. Wherever possible, an app doesn't offer separate controls for manipulating content.

These were Microsoft's design goals for Modern apps, at least. Over the past few years, we have noticed a trend toward more cluttered layouts as originally very simple apps such as Maps have been expanded with more and more features.

To see the list of apps on your computer, click Start, and then scroll down the Start menu. As of the Anniversary Update, there is no longer an icon labeled All Apps that you need to click before you can scroll through the full list. It's now always there just below your most-used apps.

In the following sections, we list the default apps that come with most freshly installed copies of Windows. You can easily add more free and paid apps from the Store app. Also, your PC manufacturer may have added apps we don't describe, and in a corporate environment, you may find more or fewer apps installed. There are some games and apps that are really just advertisements that we don't describe here. Finally, Microsoft fairly frequently adds and modifies apps via Windows Update, so, apps may well change over time (hopefully getting ever more useful, but, you never know). All this is to say: Read this list, but check your copy of Windows to see what you actually have.

To launch these apps, you can click Start, scroll down to find the app, and then click the app's icon. But that's the hard way! It's easier to type the app's name (or even just a few letters of the name) into the taskbar's search box and then select it from the results. Or, if you have a microphone on your computer and have enabled Hey Cortana, just say, "Hey Cortana, open the _____ app," and that should do it. And remember, if you use an app all the time, right-click its icon in the taskbar and select Pin to Taskbar/or Pin to Start so you'll have instant access to it in the future.

Alarms & Clock

The Alarms & Clock app (it's new in Windows 10) is the home of all things temporal. With this app, you can do the following:

- **Set alarms**—Select the Alarm tab to create alarms that ring at specified times and frequencies.

- **See times in other locations**—Select the World Clock tab to add one or more clocks that show the time in different locations around the world.

- **Count down a specified interval**—Select the Time tab to set a time in hours, minutes, and seconds and then count down to 0 from that time.

- **Time an event**—Select the Stopwatch tab to start a timer. You can also get split times along the way by clicking or touching the Laps/Splits icon (the flag).

Calculator

Many of the Modern apps offer only a minimal set of features, but that's not the case with the new Calculator app (which replaces the venerable Desktop version). It comes not only with very good Standard and Scientific calculators, but also a nice Programmer calculator that offers a bit-toggling keyboard and Boolean operations such as OR, XOR, NOT, and AND, and a new date calculator. You also get a full set of converters for things like volume, length, weight, and temperature.

You switch between these modes by selecting the Menu icon in the top-left corner, as shown in Figure 5.3. Widen the Calculator window to see the History "adding machine tape" and Memory panel.

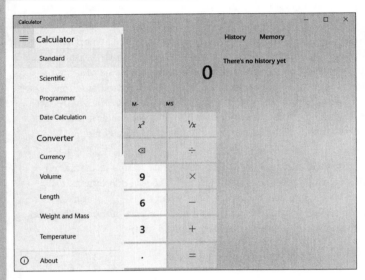

Figure 5.3
The new Calculator app offers four calculator types and some converters.

The Memory tab is worth looking at, too. Like most electronic calculators, the Calculator app can save numbers on a sort of scratch pad, using MS (memory save), M+ (memory add), M- (memory subtract), MR (memory recall), and MC (memory clear). If you expand the window and select the Memory tab, the MS button lets you save *multiple* values. Click any saved value to recall it into whatever calculation you're doing. This is a handy tool, as it lets you save multiple intermediate values as you work.

Calendar

Calendar (shown earlier in Figures 5.1 and 5.2) is the scheduling app for Windows 10, enabling you to create events for meetings, appointments, get-togethers, and all-day tasks such as conferences and vacations. By default, Calendar displays events from four calendars:

- Your personal calendar associated with your Microsoft account. These events use a green background.

- A Birthday calendar that displays birthdays from contacts associated with your Microsoft account. Birthdays appear with a red background.

- A Holidays calendar that shows prominent holidays from your location (for example, a U.S. Holidays calendar if you're located in the United States). Holidays use a pink background.

- A generic calendar for all other events. These items appear with a blue background.

note

You control the calendar display by clicking an account under the mini-calendar and then clicking a calendar to toggle its events on and off. If you don't see the mini-calendar, select the Menu icon in the upper-left corner.

You can also add other accounts to Calendar so you can, for example, view your Gmail calendar directly from the Calendar interface. Click the Settings icon (the gear) at the bottom of the screen, and then click Manage Accounts to open the Manage Accounts pane. Click Add Account, click the account type, and then fill in the details.

To change the calendar view, select one of the five views that appear along the top of the window: Day, Work Week, Week, Month, or Year. Whichever view you choose, note that you navigate by clicking the Next and Previous arrows, which are downward- and upward-pointing in Month view, and right- and left-pointing in the other views. (If you don't see these arrows, move your mouse pointer over the Calendar screen.) If you're using a touchscreen, you can also navigate the Calendar view by moving down and up in Month view, or right and left in the other views. The Today button scrolls today's date back into view.

To add an event, click the day of the event in Month view, or click the time the event occurs (on the day it occurs) in Week, Work Week, or Day view, or just click the + at the left side of the window. Then fill in the event information in the box that opens.

By the way, as of the Anniversary Update, the clock icon at the right end of the taskbar now includes a calendar. If you click the taskbar clock, you'll see the time, calendar, and your scheduled events. Click an event or the add event (+) icon to jump right into the Calendar app.

Camera

If your PC or tablet has a built-in or connected camera, you can use the Camera app to take a photo or record a video:

- **Take a photo**—Select the Camera app on the Start menu, and then either click or tap the screen or select the Camera icon to take the photo.

- **Record a video**—Select the Camera app on the Start menu, select the small video icon to switch to Video mode, and then select the large Video icon to start recording. When you're finished, select the Video icon again.

Photos and videos you shoot with the Camera app are stored in your user account's Pictures folder, in the Camera Roll folder.

Finally, you can also select the Settings icon (the gear) to configure various options, which vary depending on your camera. For example, you can choose a photo aspect ratio, a video resolution, and you can display a framing grid within the camera window.

Connect

The Connect app lets your PC, tablet, laptop, or other device act as a remote screen for another device, such as a Windows or Android phone, that supports Miracast technology. Both devices must have Wi-Fi adapters that support WiFi Direct but don't need to be connected to a wireless network or router. Run Connect on your PC, and then instruct your phone to cast to it. Now you can use the big PC screen (and keyboard) as a more convenient interface to your phone.

Cortana

Selecting the Cortana app is the same as clicking in the taskbar's Search box. This gives you an alternative way to access Search (or Cortana, if you use it) if you'd prefer to remove the Search box from the taskbar to gain more room for pinned apps. Here are the steps to follow to remove the Search feature from the taskbar:

1. Right-click an empty section of the taskbar.

2. Select Cortana or Search.

3. Select Hidden. If you want extra room on the taskbar but prefer to keep easy access to the Search feature, select Show Cortana Icon or Show Search Icon, which replaces the text box with a small Search icon.

Feedback Hub

This app lets you send feedback about Windows 10—comments, suggestions, and bug reports—directly to Microsoft. The app was originally provided only to Windows Insiders, people who have volunteered to test and evaluate new Windows features, but as of the Anniversary Update, the app is now installed on all copies of Windows.

If you decide to send feedback, we suggest that you first spend some time searching the Feedback Hub for the issue you want to report, using various different phrasings. If you find that someone else has already reported your issue, click Upvote. The more "me too" marks a feedback item gets, the more likely it will get attention from Microsoft. You can also add comments to the entry. But, creating a new, duplicate report just diffuses their attention. If you think an issue really does need a new feedback report, select the best matching categories you can, and to the extent possible provide exact steps for reproducing the problem.

 tip

if you're a Feedback fanatic, use Windows Logo+F to take a screenshot and open the Feedback Hub with one keystroke. If you create a new feedback item, the screenshot will be attached automatically.

Films & TV

You use the Movies Films & TV app (formerly titled Movies and TV) to play the digital videos that are on your PC, to purchase or rent movies, or to purchase TV show episodes. The main screen is divided into three tabs:

- **Explore**—This section lets you check out commercial video content in three categories: Trailers, Films, and TV.

- **Purchased**—This section displays movies and TV shows that you've purchased or rented.

- **Personal**—This section displays your videos. To view a video, select it, and the playback begins immediately. Move the mouse to display the playback controls (see Figure 5.4), which include the Pause/Play button, a scrubber to scroll through the video, a volume control, a full-screen control, a command to play the video on a connected device, and a zoom feature.

Figure 5.4
Move the mouse during video playback to see the controls.

Get Help

The Get Help app provides guidance and links for contacting Microsoft for support with Windows, Microsoft hardware and software products, and Microsoft online accounts. Be aware that in most cases, Microsoft support will cost you. Free support may be available under certain limited circumstances, such as support for assistive technologies for people with disabilities.

Groove Music

You use the Groove Music app to play the music that's on your PC. Note, however, that you can no longer use Groove Music to purchase new songs or albums. The Groove Music window is divided into three main sections that organize your music by Albums, Artists (see Figure 5.5), and Songs. You can also choose Now Playing to see your current music and New Playlist to create a playlist of songs.

> **caution**
>
> If you receive an unexpected phone call from someone claiming to be from Microsoft telling you that he has detected a problem with your computer, hang up! (Or, have some fun with the caller for a while, and then hang up.) It's a scam. Microsoft never calls customers out of the blue.

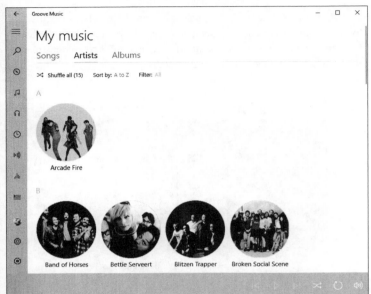

Figure 5.5
You can organize your music collection by artists, as shown here, or by albums or songs.

Mail

The Mail app is an extremely simple mail client that offers only the most basic functionality: sending messages, responding to messages (Reply, Reply to All, or Forward), moving messages to different folders, and deleting messages. We discuss this app in detail (such as it is) in Chapter 16, "Windows 10 Internet Communications."

➡ *For more coverage of the Mail app, see "Working with Email," p. 331.*

Maps

The Maps app is a simple mapping program. When you first start the app, it asks whether it can use your location, as shown in Figure 5.6. To get the most out of Maps, you'll want to select Yes.

Besides enabling you to peruse the map, the Maps app also offers the following features:

- **Search for a location**—Click the spyglass icon at the upper left, and then type the address or name of the location you want.

- **Display your current location**—Select Show My Location to have the map zero in on your present location. (If this doesn't work, see the steps that follow this list.)

- **Get directions to a location**—Select the diamond icon at the upper left, specify a starting point (the default is your current location) and a destination (you can include stops on the way to your destination), and specify the method of travel (car, transit, or walking).

Figure 5.6
The Maps App toolbar lets you zoom and orient the map.

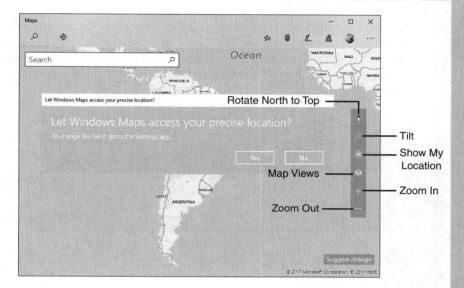

- **Change the map view**—Select Map Views and then click Aerial (that is, satellite) or Road (traditional map diagram) view. The Traffic switch lets you overlay traffic data onto the map. Routes shown in green have good traffic, routes shown in orange have some traffic, and routes shown in red have heavy traffic.

To get the most out of Maps, you should make sure your PC has the Windows Location platform turned on:

1. In the taskbar's Search box, type **location**.

2. In the search results, select Location Privacy Settings. The Settings app runs, opens the Privacy window, and selects the Location tab.

3. Make sure that Location for this Device and Location Service are on and that you've set your Default Location.

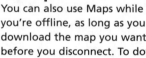

tip
You can also use Maps while you're offline, as long as you download the map you want before you disconnect. To download a map for offline use, click the Map app's See More icon, click Settings, and then click Choose Maps. (You can also open the Settings app, click Apps, and then click Offline Maps.) Click Download Maps and then select the map you want.

You also need to give Maps (and other apps) permission to use your location. In the Settings app's Location tab, scroll down to the Choose Apps That Can Use Your Precise Location section and set the switch to On for each app you want to access your location.

Messaging

This app, which was introduced in Windows 10 Version 1511, appears to be intended to let you send text messages to people on your contact list. As of the Creators Update, it's still not functional enough to bother using.

Microsoft Edge

The Microsoft Edge app is brand new. (It's not just a scaled-down version of desktop Internet Explorer.) Besides standard web browsing (that is, typing a new address, clicking links, and using the Back and Forward buttons to navigate your session history), you can save favorites, save a site to the reading list, annotate web pages (see Figure 5.7), and then share those annotations with friends. We discuss Microsoft Edge in Chapter 15.

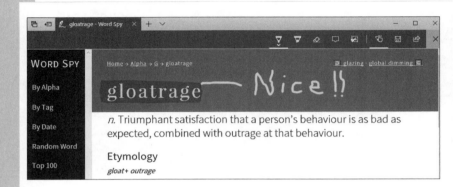

Figure 5.7
Microsoft Edge lets you annotate web pages.

Mixed Reality Portal

In Microsoft lingo, *mixed reality* refers to a hardware platform that combines virtual reality, augmented reality, and holography. Headsets that support mixed reality—such as the Microsoft HoloLens—will combine real and virtual worlds, virtual objects, and holograms to create immersive games and apps.

The control center for all this in Windows 10 Creators Update is the Mixed Reality Portal, where you can set up your mixed reality-compatible headset and access your mixed reality apps.

OneDrive

The OneDrive "app," reached from the Start menu, actually does nothing more than open File Explorer and display your Microsoft account's OneDrive folder, which you use to send files from your PC to your OneDrive. To manage OneDrive itself, use the OneDrive icon in the taskbar.

OneNote

One of the nice surprises in Windows 10 is the inclusion of a simplified but still useful version of the OneNote note-taking app. Many of us keep paper notebooks handy for jotting down these random bits of data, but we live in an electronic age, so wouldn't it be great to be able to jot down stray bits of information in a digital format?

We're happy to report that the answer to that question is, "You can!" The electronic version of your paper notebook is OneNote, which enables you to quickly and easily record just about anything that you'd normally scribble on a piece of paper. With OneNote (see Figure 5.8), you can do all that and also much more:

- Paste pictures, clip art, and text
- Insert links to websites
- Organize data into tables
- Share your notes with other people

Figure 5.8
Use the Windows 10 version of OneNote to write notes; create to-do lists; and save websites, photos, and much more.

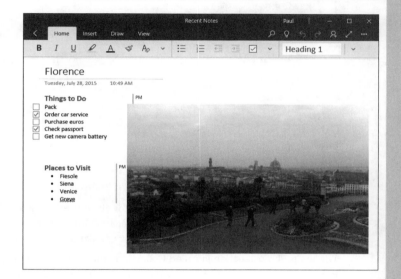

Paint 3D

Paint 3D is a major update to the venerable Paint program that has shipped with every version of Windows since Windows 1.0 was released way back in 1985. As the name implies, Paint 3D lets you build models in three dimensions instead of just two, as shown in Figure 5.9. You can build cubes and spheres, add text and effects, and much more. Have fun!

People

The Windows 8/8.1 version of the People app was arguably the most ambitious of the default apps because it acted as the social networking hub for your Windows PC by connecting to Facebook, Twitter, and other social networks. Alas, all that functionality has been removed from the Windows 10 version of People. Now the app is just a competent contacts manager that can store a wide variety of information about each person, including name, company name, email address, web address, street address, phone number, and job title. People gets significantly more useful when you add other accounts to it, such as your Gmail or iCloud contacts.

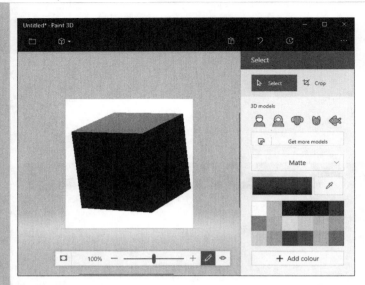

Figure 5.9
The new Paint 3D takes the old Paint program into the third dimension.

Photos

The Photos app is the Windows 10 home for all your PC's photos. The Photos app offers some useful editing tools that enable you to perform basic photo fixes, such as cropping and rotating, adjusting brightness and contrast, and fixing the tint and saturation.

The main Photos section is called Collection, and it organizes the photos from your user account's Pictures folder by month. You can scroll up and down through the images, or you can click an image to view it full-screen and then use the left- and right-arrow keys to navigate the rest of the photos.

Click the screen to display the photo tools: Zoom, Rotate, Draw, Edit, Share, and Print. (You can also click See More to access the following commands: Slideshow, Open With, Copy, Set As (which displays three subitems: Set as Lock Screen, Set as Background, and Set as Photos Tile), View Actual Size, and File Information.) When you click Edit, Photos displays its editing tools, as shown in Figure 5.10.

Settings

You use the Settings app to customize and configure many Windows 10 features and options. See Chapter 24, "Tweaking and Customizing Windows." We cover many individual Settings items throughout the book as we cover the features that they control. You can launch the Settings app from the Start menu's app list, though it's easier to use the Start menu's Settings (gear) icon,

Figure 5.10
Display a photo, click the screen, and then click Edit to see a decent collection of photo editing tools.

Skype

This app, which was added by the Anniversary Update, lets you make and receive Skype video calls. You can use the app to add contacts to your phonebook, accept or decline contact requests, search the Skype directory, invite people to a video call via email, and more. At present, this is just a preliminary version of what we expect to become a full-featured Skype app.

Sticky Notes

The Windows 10 Anniversary update brought a refresh of the old Sticky Notes app. It's now a Modern app. If you have a touchscreen, the easiest way to launch it is to touch or click the Windows Ink Workspace icon in the notification area of the taskbar and then select Sticky Notes. Without a touchscreen, to launch it from the Start menu you'd have to scroll down to Windows Accessories and then open that folder. It's easier to type **stick** in the taskbar's search box and select the app from the results. If you end up using Sticky Notes a lot, pin the app to your taskbar.

The Sticky Note app displays a yellow square onto your screen that you can type into and move around. It "sticks" around and comes back even if you sign off and back on, just like a real 3M Post-It Note would if it was were stuck to your monitor. Click + to add a new note. This is one of those apps that you can go ten years without ever using, but once you start, you can't imagine how you lived without it.

One of the interesting features of this refreshed Sticky Notes app is that, with your permission, Cortana can read the contents of your notes and can automatically assist you in completing the tasks that the sticky notes discuss. For example, if you type (or write with a pen), "Call Mom tomorrow," Cortana will recognize that the word tomorrow means you're scheduling something and will automatically offer to add "Call Mom" to tomorrow's calendar. This feature is called Insights, and it's enabled by default. To disable it, click the More (...) icon on the Sticky Notes app, then the Settings (gear) icon, and then switch Insights off.

Store

You use the Store app to access the online Windows Store and browse and purchase new apps and media for your Windows 10 PC. The main Store screen is divided into five tabs: Home, Apps, Games, Music, Films & TV, and Books (see Figure 5.11). On each tab, there are links for Top (selling) and Featured items, and a Collections link that gathers items into premade collections (such as sports apps). The user interface of the Store app changes fairly frequently.

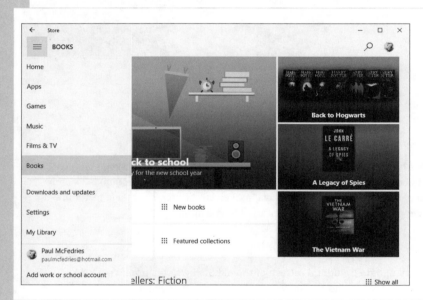

Figure 5.11
The Windows Store offers apps, games, music, movies, and TV shows.

Clicking an item displays its details, including its user rating, price, description and features, user reviews, permissions, and more. See also "Installing Apps from the Windows Store," later in this chapter.

Tips

This simple app just displays a collection of tips for using Windows 10. Click the Browse Tips tab to see the tips organized into various categories, including Get Connected, Microsoft Edge, and Ease of Access.

View 3D

You use the View 3D app to open and interact with 3D models. The app supports five 3D model file types: 3MF (3D Manufacturing Format), PLY (Polygon File Format), OBJ (3D Object Format), FBX (Filmbox), and STL (Stereolithography).

Voice Recorder

If you have a microphone connected to your PC, you can use the Voice Recorder app to create and save simple voice recordings.

Weather

The Weather app is a straightforward weather forecast program. When you first start the app, it asks you to specify a default location. If it's the local forecast you're after, start typing your city and then select it in the list that appears. You're pretty much done, but you can also add other places to the Weather app:

1. Select Menu in the upper-left corner, and then select Favorites. The Favorites screen appears.

2. Click Add (+). Weather prompts you to enter the city name.

3. Start typing the name of the city you want to add.

4. When you see the name of the city in the list that appears, click it. Weather adds the city to the Places screen.

 tip

To change the default location (that is, the city that appears on the Weather app's live tile and that appears first when you launch the Weather app), select Menu, then Settings, and be sure the General tab is displayed. Check the Default Location option and use the text box to type the location you want to use as the default. If you're traveling and you want Weather to always use your current location as the default, check the Always Detect My Location option instead.

Windows Defender Security Center

In Windows 10 Creators Update, Windows Defender has been revamped as a full-featured security tool. No longer confined to just squashing spyware, Windows Defender now targets all malware and also manages the firewall (now renamed Windows Defender Firewall).

The place to configure all things Windows Defender is the new Windows Defender Security Center. We take you through the various features and settings in this app in Chapter 31, "Protecting Windows from Viruses and Spyware."

➡ *To learn more about Windows Defender Security Center, **see** "Checking Your Computer's Security Settings," **p. 701.***

Xbox

The Xbox app lets you play compatible Xbox and PC games and connects you to your Xbox account. It can also mirror the display of your Xbox console, record, and edit game movies. The Xbox window is divided into several sections. If you click the Menu icon in the upper-left corner, the choices are as follows:

- **Home**—This section offers an overview of your account and your friends' activities.

- **My Games**—The list of your installed and purchased games.

- **Achievements**—Your and your friends' high scores.

- **Game DVR**—This section shows your recorded games. (You can record games on your computer by typing Windows Logo+G, if your video card is capable of it.)

- **Clubs**—Lets you access, search for, and create gaming clubs.

- **Trending**—Advertisements and recorded videos from social media.

- **Store**—You can guess where this leads you. Note that some games are linked to your Xbox account and are licensed so that they can be played on any of your PC or Xbox devices.

- **Search**—Searches for detailed information about any PC or Xbox game.

- **Connection**—Establishes a network connection with an Xbox console.

- **Settings**—Displays several categories of settings for your Xbox account, friends and linked accounts, notifications, recording, and network connections to an Xbox console.

At the right side of the screen is a panel used for social networking. Across its top are more icons:

- **Friends & Clubs**—Adds and displays connected gaming friends and your gaming clubs.

- **Parties**—This is a new feature that lets you create a group voice and text chat session with other Xbox users. Use the padlock icon to restrict the party to invited guests only.

- **Messages**—You use this section to exchange receive messages with your Xbox friends.

- **Activity Alerts**—This section shows alerts for all your recent activities, including likes, shares, comments, and friend requests.

Installing Apps from the Windows Store

Windows 10 comes with quite a few apps, but it doesn't cover every base, not by a long shot. If there's an app that you need, you can obtain the app yourself and then install it on your PC. Here are the steps to follow to install an app from the Windows Store:

1. On the taskbar or Start screen, tap Store. The Store appears.

2. Select the Apps tab.

3. Display the app that you want to install. See the "Store" section, earlier in this chapter, to learn how to navigate the Windows Store.

4. If it's a paid app, tap Buy; otherwise, tap Get. The Store app shows the progress of the install as well as buttons for pausing or canceling the install (see Figure 5.12).

 tip

When you install an app, it appears on the main Start menu under the Recently Added heading.

Figure 5.12
The Store app shows the progress of the app install and enables you to pause or cancel the install.

By default, Windows 10 stores all new apps on the system hard drive, usually drive C. If you prefer to use a different drive (say, if your system drive is getting low on disk space), you can follow these steps to specify a different app install default drive:

1. Click Start and then click Settings (the gear icon) to open the Settings app.

2. Click System.

3. Click the Storage tab.

4. Click Change Where New Content Is Saved.

5. In the New Apps Will Save To list, select the drive you want to use as the default for app installs.

Uninstalling Apps

If you have an app that you no longer use, you can free up some disk space and reduce clutter on the Start screen by uninstalling that app. Here's how it works for apps that allow an uninstall:

1. Use the Start menu to locate the app you want to uninstall.

2. Right-click the app tile.

3. Select Uninstall. Windows 10 asks you to confirm.

4. Select Uninstall. Windows 10 removes the app.

6

MANAGING FILES AND SEARCHING

Understanding File Types

To get the most out of this chapter, you need to understand some background about what a file type is and how Windows 10 determines and works with file types. The next couple of sections tell you everything you need to know to get you through the rest of the chapter.

File Types and File Extensions

One of the fictions that Microsoft has tried to foist on the computer-using public is that we live in a "document-centric" world. That means that people care only about the documents they create and not about the applications they use to create those documents. The reality is that applications are still too difficult to use, and the capability to share documents between applications is still too problematic. In other words, you can't create documents unless you learn the ins and outs of an application, and you can't share documents with others unless you use compatible applications.

Unfortunately, we're stuck with Microsoft's worship of the document and all the problems that this worship creates. A good example is the hiding of file extensions. As you'll learn in Chapter 24, "Tweaking and Customizing Windows," Windows 10 hides file extensions by default, and this creates a whole host of problems, including

- Confusion when trying to determine a file type based on a teensy icon

- Not being able to edit extensions

- Not being able to save a file under an extension of your choice

- The risk of opening a virus program masquerading as a safe document

You can overcome all these problems by turning on file extensions, which you can do by checking the View tab's File Name Extensions check box.

➡ *To learn more about file extensions,* **see** *"Turning On File Extensions," p. 537.*

The lack of file extensions causes such a fuss because file extensions determine the file type of a document. In other words, if Windows 10 sees that a file has a .txt extension, it concludes the file uses the Text Document file type. Similarly, a file with the extension .bmp uses the Bitmap Image file type.

The file type, in turn, determines the application that's associated with the extension. If a file has a .txt extension, Windows 10 associates that extension with Notepad, so the file will always open in Notepad. Nothing else inherent in the file determines the file type; therefore, at least from the point of view of the user, the entire Windows 10 file system rests on the scrawny shoulders of a dot and a few letters: the humble file extension.

This method of determining file types is, no doubt, a poor design decision. For example, there is some danger that a novice user could render a file useless by imprudently renaming its extension. Interestingly, Microsoft seems to have recognized this danger: Windows displays a warning dialog box when you try to change an extension. Microsoft has also programmed a subtle behavior into the file system: When "display file extensions" is turned on and you activate the Rename command (click the file and then press F2), Windows displays the usual text box around the entire filename, but it selects only the file's primary name (the part to the left of the dot), as shown in Figure 6.1. When you start typing, this obliterates the primary name but leaves the extension intact. This, at least, is very helpful.

Figure 6.1
When you activate the Rename command with file extensions turned on, Windows selects just the file's primary name.

Despite the drawbacks that come with file extensions, they lead to some powerful methods for manipulating and controlling the Windows 10 file system, as you see in the rest of this chapter.

File Types and the Registry

Now, we're going to get into the nitty-gritty here. If you want, you can skip this section. Still, knowing how things work can help you understand why things go awry in the ways they do. As you might expect, everything Windows 10 knows about file types is defined in the Registry. (See Chapter 29, "Editing the Windows Registry," for the details on understanding and using the Registry.) Open the Registry Editor (in the taskbar's Search box, type **regedit**, press

Enter, and enter your UAC credentials) and examine the HKEY_CLASSES_ROOT key. Notice that it's divided into two sections:

- The first part of HKEY_CLASSES_ROOT consists of dozens of file extension subkeys (such as .bmp and .txt). There are well over 400 such subkeys in a basic Windows 10 installation, and there could easily be two or three times that number on a system with many applications installed.

note

HKEY_CLASSES_ROOT also stores information on ActiveX controls in its CLSID subkey. Many of these controls also have corresponding subkeys in the second half of HKEY_CLASSES_ROOT.

- The second part of HKEY_CLASSES_ROOT lists the various file types associated with the registered extensions. When an extension is associated with a particular file type, the extension is said to be *registered* with Windows 10.

To see what this all means, take a look at Figure 6.2. Here, we've selected the .txt key, which has txtfile as its Default value.

Figure 6.2
The first part of the HKEY_CLASSES_ ROOT key contains subkeys for all the registered file extensions.

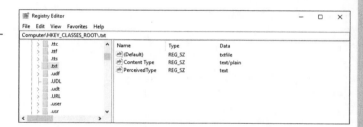

That Default value is a pointer to the extension's associated file type subkey in the second half of HKEY_CLASSES_ROOT. Figure 6.3 shows the txtfile subkey associated with the .txt extension. Here are some notes about this file type subkey:

Figure 6.3
The second part of HKEY_CLASSES_ ROOT contains the file type data associated with each extension.

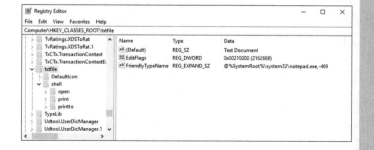

- The Default value is a description of the file type
  (Text Document, in this case).

- The DefaultIcon subkey defines the icon that's displayed
  with any file that uses this type.

- The shell subkey determines the actions that can be performed with this file type. These actions vary depending
  on the file type, but Open and Print are common. The Open
  action determines the application that's associated with
  the file type. For example, the Open action for a Text Document file type is the following:

  `%SystemRoot%\system32\NOTEPAD.EXE %1`

 note

The %1 at the end of the command is a placeholder that refers
to the document being opened
(if any). If you double-click a file
named memo.txt, for example,
the %1 placeholder is replaced by
memo.txt, which tells Windows
to run Notepad and open
that file.

Navigating Folder Windows

Let's take a quick tour of the interface features you'll find in folder windows. Figure 6.4 shows a
typical example of the species, the Documents folder.

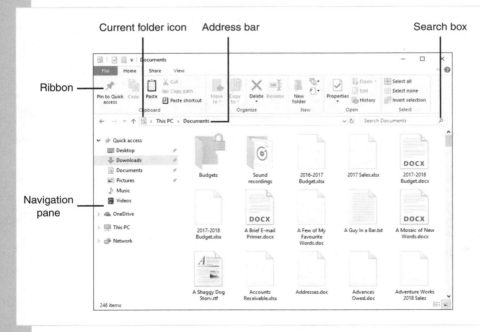

Figure 6.4
The main inter-
face elements in
a folder window.

Folder Navigation

Windows 10 implements drives and folders as hierarchies that you navigate up, down, and even across. As you can see in Figure 6.4, the Address bar doesn't show any drive letters or backslashes. Instead, you get a hierarchical path to the current folder. The path in Figure 6.4 has three items, separated by right-pointing arrows:

- **Current folder icon**—This icon represents the current folder. You'll see a bit later that you can use this icon to navigate to your computer drives, your network, the Control Panel, your user folder, and more.

- **This PC**—This represents the second level of the sample hierarchy. In the example, this level represents the contents of your PC, including its disk drives (both internal and external), the desktop, and your main user folders.

> **tip**
>
> To copy the full path name (drive, folders, and filename) of the selected file, select Home, Copy Path.

- **Documents**—This represents the third level of the sample hierarchy. In the example, this level represents all the subfolders and files that reside in the user's Documents folder.

This is a sensible and straightforward way to view the hierarchy. However, the real value here lies in the navigation features of the Address bar, and you can get a hint of these features from the nickname that many people have applied to the Address bar: the breadcrumb bar.

Breadcrumbing refers to a navigation feature that displays a list of the places a person has visited or the route a person has taken. The term comes from the fairy tale of Hansel and Gretel, who threw down bits of bread to help find their way out of the forest. This feature is common on websites where the content is organized as a hierarchy or as a sequence of pages.

Windows 10 implements breadcrumb navigation not only by using the Address bar to show you the hierarchical path you've taken to get to the current folder but also by adding interactivity to the breadcrumb path:

- You can navigate back to any part of the hierarchy by clicking the folder name in the Address bar. For example, in the path shown in Figure 6.4, you could jump immediately to the top-level hierarchy by clicking This PC in the path.

- You can navigate "sideways" to any part of any level by clicking the right-pointing arrow to the right of the level you want to work with. In Figure 6.5, for example, you see that clicking the arrow beside the current folder icon displays a list of the other navigable items, such as Homegroup, Network, and Control Panel. Clicking an item in this list opens that folder.

Instant Search

The next major element in the Windows 10 folder window interface is the Search box, which appears to the right of the Address bar in all folder windows. Search is everywhere in Windows 10, and we go into it in much more detail later in this chapter (see "Searching Your PC"). For folder windows,

Click the arrow to see the items in that level.

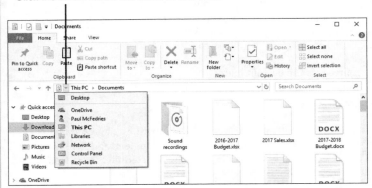

Figure 6.5
Breadcrumb navigation: In the Address bar, click a folder's arrow to see a list of the navigable items in that folder.

however, the Instant Search box gives you a quick way to search for files within the current folder. Most of us nowadays have folders that contain hundreds or even thousands of documents. To knock such folders down to size in Windows 10, you need only type all or part of a filename, and Windows 10 filters the folder contents to show just the matching files, as shown in Figure 6.6. Windows 10 also matches those files that have metadata—such as the author or tags—that match your text.

Type text in the Search box...

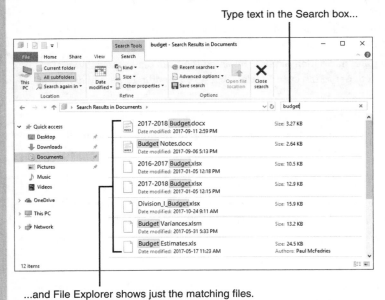

Figure 6.6
With Instant Search, Windows 10 displays just those files with names or metadata that match your search text.

...and File Explorer shows just the matching files.

This is one of the most important things to remember about Windows today: don't click around and try to look for things by hand; let Windows search for you.

The Ribbon

Windows 10's version of the venerable File Explorer file management program comes with a ribbon interface that replaces the menu bar and toolbar in versions prior to Windows 8. As with all ribbons, File Explorer's is divided into several tabs: File, Home, Share, and View. Also, when you open certain folders or activate certain features, the ribbon sprouts extra contextual tabs that display commands related to the folder or feature. For example, in Figure 6.6 you can see that when you run a search, File Explorer adds the Search Tools contextual tab to the ribbon.

The Navigation Pane

The Navigation pane appears on the left side of each folder window, and it offers quick links to the major sections of your system, including your OneDrive, This PC, Network, and Homegroup. The Quick Access section offers access to a few common folders, including Desktop and Downloads, and it displays folders that you've visited frequently.

 tip

The Quick Access section is fully customizable. For example, you can add a link to one of your own favorite folders by clicking and dragging that folder and dropping it inside the Quick Access section. (You can also right-click the item and then click Pin to Quick Access.) If a frequently used folder appears in Quick Access, you can keep it there by pinning it. (Right-click it and then click Pin to Quick Access.) You can also remove links you don't use. (Right-click a link under Quick Access and click Unpin from Quick Access.)

We use this ability all the time. When we start a project, we put the folder that contains all of its documents into the Quick Access list. When the project's done, we remove it so the list doesn't get cluttered.

Basic File and Folder Chores

Now that you're familiar with Windows 10's folders, it's time to put them through a workout. The next few sections take you through a few basic file and folder chores, including selecting, moving and copying, and renaming.

Selecting Files with Check Boxes

In this chapter, you learn about quite a few substantive elements in the Windows file system: metadata, searching, grouping, filtering, and more. All these are fairly sophisticated and useful technologies. However, sometimes it's the small, mundane elements that make your life with an operating system easier and more efficient. In this section, you learn about one of our favorites of Windows 10's many small but quite useful tweaks: a technique that affects the way you select files.

When you need to select multiple, noncontiguous objects, the easiest method is to hold down the Ctrl key and click each item you want to select. However, when we use this technique to select more than a few files, we always end up accidentally selecting one or more files that we don't want.

It's not a big deal to deselect these extra files, but it's one of those small drains on productivity that bugs us (and many other users).

Windows 10 offers a file-selection technique that promises to eliminate accidental selections. With this technique, you use a check box to select individual files and folders. To activate this feature, display File Explorer's View tab and then check the Item Check Boxes box.

> ### tip
> Bonus technique: You can also select all the items in the folder quickly by clicking the check box that appears at the top of the Name column.

As you can see in Figure 6.7, when you turn on this feature, Explorer creates a column to the left of the folder contents in Details view. When you point at a file or folder, a check box appears in this column, and you select an item by activating its check box. You don't need to hold down Ctrl or use the keyboard at all. Just check the boxes for the files and folders you want to select.

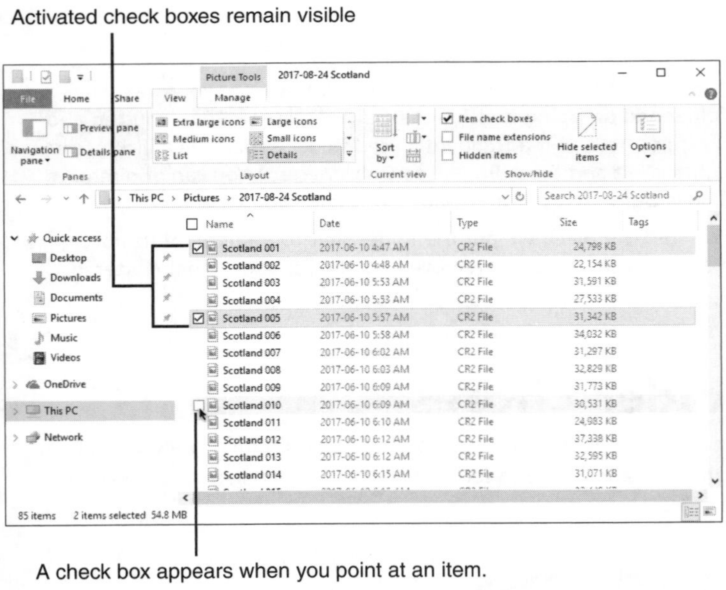

Activated check boxes remain visible

Figure 6.7
In Windows 10, you can select files and folders using check boxes.

A check box appears when you point at an item.

Resolving File Transfer Conflicts

When you move or copy a file into the destination folder, it sometimes happens that a file with the same name already resides in that folder. In earlier versions of Windows, you'd see a dialog box asking whether you want to replace the existing file, and you'd click Yes or No, as appropriate.

Understanding Size on Disk

To see the total size of the objects in the current selection, right-click the selection and then click Properties. Windows 10 counts all the files, calculates the total size as well as the total size on the disk, and then displays this data in the General tab on the property sheet that appears.

What's the difference between the Size and Size on Disk values? Windows 10 stores files in discrete chunks of hard disk space called *clusters*, which have a fixed size. This size depends on the file system and the size of the partition, but 4KB is typical. The important point to remember is that Windows 10 always uses full clusters to store all or part of a file. For example, suppose that you have two files: one that's 2KB and another that's 5KB. The 2KB file will be stored in an entire 4KB cluster. For the 5KB file, the first 4KB of the file will take up a whole cluster, and the remaining 1KB will be stored in its own 4KB cluster. Therefore, the total size of these files is 7KB, but they take up 12KB on the hard disk.

Unfortunately, Windows didn't give you much information to go on to help you make the choice. Windows 10 takes a step in the right direction by displaying the Replace or Skip Files dialog box instead. Figure 6.8 shows an example.

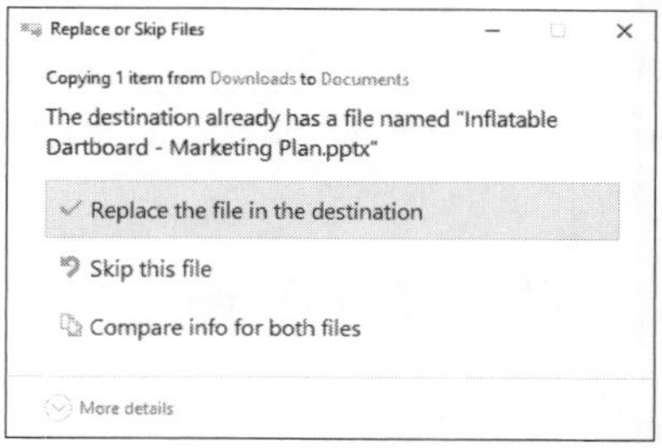

Figure 6.8
This dialog box appears if a file with the same name already exists inside the destination folder.

This dialog box gives you the following choices:

- **Replace the File in the Destination**—Click this option if you want the file you are copying (or moving) to replace the existing file.

- **Skip This File**—Click this option if you want Windows 10 to not copy (or move) the file, so the original remains in the destination folder.

- **Compare Info for Both Files**—Click this option to see more information about both files, including a thumbnail, the last modified date, and the size. Check the box for the version you want to keep, and then click Continue. Note, too, that you can keep both files by activating both check boxes and then clicking Continue. In this case, the existing file remains as is, and the file being copied or moved is placed in the folder with (2) appended to the filename.

Expert Drag-and-Drop Techniques

You'll use the drag-and-drop technique throughout your Windows career. To make drag-and-drop even easier and more powerful, here are a few pointers to bear in mind:

- **"Lassoing" multiple files**—If the objects you want to select are displayed in a block within the folder list, you can select them by dragging a box around the objects. This is known as *lassoing* the objects.

- **Drag-and-scroll**—Most drag-and-drop operations involve dragging an object from the contents area and dropping it on a folder in the Folders list. (Be sure to display the Folders list first.) If you can't see the destination in the Navigation pane, drag the pointer to the bottom of the pane. File Explorer will scroll the pane up. To scroll the pane down, drag the object to the top of the pane.

- **Drag-and-open**—If the destination is a subfolder within an unopened folder branch, drag the object and hover the pointer over the unopened folder. After a second or two, File Explorer opens the folder branch.

- **Inter-window dragging**—You can drag an object outside of the window and then drop it on a different location, such as the desktop.

- **Drag between Explorer windows**—Windows 10 lets you open two or more copies of File Explorer (select File, Open New Window). If you have to use several drag-and-drop operations to get some objects to a particular destination, open a second copy of File Explorer and display the destination in this new window. You can then drag from the first window and drop into the second window.

- **Canceling drag-and-drop**—To cancel a drag-and-drop operation, either press Esc or click the right mouse button. If you're right-dragging, click the left mouse button to cancel.

Taking Advantage of the Send To Command

For certain destinations, Windows 10 offers an easier method for copying or moving files or folders: the Send To command. To use this command, select the objects you want to work with, right-click the selection, and then click Send To in the shortcut menu. You see a submenu of potential destinations, as shown in Figure 6.9.

Figure 6.9
The Send To command offers a menu of possible destinations.

Note that the items in this menu (except the disk drives) are taken from the following folder that contains shortcut files for each item:

`%UserProfile%\appdata\roaming\Microsoft\Windows\SendTo`

This means that you can customize the Send To menu by adding, renaming, and deleting the shortcut files in your `SendTo` folder.

Click the destination you want, and Windows 10 sends the object there. What do we mean by *send*? We suppose that *drop* would be a better word because the Send To command acts like the drop part of drag-and-drop. Therefore, Send To follows the same rules as drag-and-drop:

- If the Send To destination is on a different disk drive, the object is copied.

- If the Send To destination is on the same disk drive, the object is moved.

 note

The user profile folder for a user is the following:

`%SystemDrive%\Users\User`

Here, `%SystemDrive%` is the drive on which Windows 10 is installed (such as C:), and *User* is the person's username. Windows 10 stores the user profile folder for the current user in the `%UserProfile%` environment variable.

Forcing a Move or Copy

With both Send To and drag-and-drop operations, you can force Windows to either *copy* or *move* the file(s) you've selected.

With drag-and-drop, before you release the mouse to drop the selected file(s), there is some visual feedback of what is going to happen: You will see a + appear on the icon(s) you're moving if you're about to do a copy rather than a move. If you remember to check for this before you release the mouse, you'll have the chance to change it before the wrong thing happens. Hold the Shift key down to turn a Copy into a Move, or hold the Ctrl key down to turn a Move into a Copy. Then, while you're holding the key down, release the icon(s).

With Send To, to force a move, hold down Shift when you select the Send To command. To force a copy, hold down Ctrl when you select the Send To command. To force a shortcut, hold down Shift and Ctrl when you select the Send To command.

The Recycle Bin: Deleting and Recovering Files and Folders

In our conversations with Windows users, we've noticed an interesting trend that has become more prominent in recent years: People don't delete files as often as they used to. We're sure that the reason for this is the absolutely huge hard disks that are offered these days. Even entry-level systems come equipped with 1TB disks, and multi-terabyte-sized drives are no longer a big deal. Unless someone's working with digital video files, even a power user isn't going to put a dent in these massive disks any time soon. So, why bother deleting anything?

Although it's always a good idea to remove files and folders you don't need (it makes your system easier to navigate, it speeds up defragmenting, and so on), avoiding deletions does have one advantage: You can never delete something important by accident.

Just in case you do, however, Windows 10's Recycle Bin can bail you out. The Recycle Bin icon on the Windows 10 desktop is actually a front end for a collection of hidden folders named Recycled that exist on each hard disk volume. The idea is that when you delete a file or folder, Windows 10 doesn't actually remove the object from your system. Instead, the object moves to the Recycled folder on the same drive. If you delete an object by accident, you can go to the Recycle Bin and return the object to its original spot. Note, however, that the Recycle Bin can hold only so much data. When it gets full, it permanently deletes its oldest objects to make room for newer ones.

It's important to note that Windows 10 bypasses the Recycle Bin and permanently deletes an object under the following circumstances:

- When you delete the object from a removable drive

- When you delete the object from the command line

- When you delete the object from a network drive

tip

If you're absolutely sure you don't need an object, you can permanently delete it from your system (that is, bypass the Recycle Bin) by selecting it and pressing Shift+Delete.

note

OneDrive has its own online Recycle Bin for your OneDrive folder, but it uses it only if you use the web interface for One-Drive; when you delete from the local cache of OneDrive, the deleted item goes to your local Recycle Bin.

Setting Some Recycle Bin Options

The Recycle Bin has a few properties you can set to control how it works. To view these properties, right-click the desktop's Recycle Bin icon and then click Properties. Windows 10 displays the Recycle Bin Properties dialog box shown in Figure 6.10.

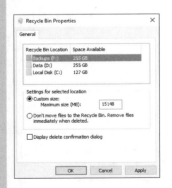

Figure 6.10
Use this dialog box to configure the Recycle Bin to your liking.

Here's a rundown of the various controls:

- **Recycle Bin Location**—Choose the Recycle Bin you want to configure: You see an icon for each of the hard drive partitions on your computer.

- **Custom Size**—Enter the size of the Recycle Bin. The larger the size, the more disk space the Recycle Bin takes up, but the more files it will save before permanently deleting them.

- **Don't Move Files to the Recycle Bin**—If you activate this option, all deletions are immediate and permanent.

- **Display Delete Confirmation Dialog**—For the first time in Windows history, Windows 10 does not ask for confirmation when you delete an object. If you miss the prompt, or if you just want to be super careful about deletions, check this box.

Click OK to put the new settings into effect.

 tip
You can clean out your Recycle Bin at any time by right-clicking the desktop's Recycle Bin icon and then clicking Empty Recycle Bin. The Recycle Bin contents can also be purged using Windows 10's Disk Cleanup utility.

Recovering a File or Folder

If you accidentally delete the wrong file or folder, you can return it to its rightful place by using the following method:

1. Open the desktop's Recycle Bin icon, or open any Recycled folder in File Explorer.

2. Select the object you want to restore.

3. Click the Manage tab and then click Restore the Selected Items. (You can also right-click the file and then click Restore.)

Undoing a File or Folder Action

If deleting the file or folder was the last action you performed in File Explorer, you can recover the object by selecting the Edit, Undo Delete command (or by pressing Ctrl+Z). Note, too, that Windows 10 enables you to undo the ten most recent actions.

File Maintenance Using the Open and Save As Dialog Boxes

One of the best-kept secrets of Windows 10 is the fact that you can perform many of these file maintenance operations within two of Windows 10's standard dialog boxes:

- **Open**—In most applications, you display this dialog box by selecting the File, Open command, or by pressing Ctrl+O.

- **Save As**—You usually display this dialog box by selecting File, Save As. Or, if you're working with a new, unsaved file, you select File, Save, or press Ctrl+S.

Most of the time, the dialog that appears for Open or Save operations is a full-scale File Explorer window, in which you can do anything that File Explorer can do before you finally choose a file to open or save. Here are several techniques you can use within these dialog boxes:

- To perform maintenance on a file or folder, right-click the object to display a shortcut menu like the one shown in Figure 6.11. In particular, note that you can click Cut to move an item, click Copy to copy an item, navigate to the destination folder, and then click Paste to complete the move or copy.

- You can click and drag files or folders and drop them on any local or OneDrive folder that appears in the Navigation pane.

- To create a new object, right-click an empty section of the file list and then click New to get the New menu.

- To create a new folder within the current folder, click the New Folder button.

Figure 6.11
You can perform most basic file and folder maintenance right from the Open and Save As dialog boxes.

Metadata and the File Explorer Property System

We mentioned earlier that Windows is gradually lessening the importance not only of drive letters but also specific file locations. If file location will become less important, what can you use to take its place as a basis for file organization? Content seems like a pretty good place to start. After all, it's what's inside the documents that really matters. For example, suppose you're working on the Penske account. It's a pretty good bet that all the Penske-related documents on your system actually have the word *Penske* inside them somewhere. If you want to find a Penske document, a file system that indexes document content sure helps because then you need only do a content search on the word *Penske*.

However, what if a memo or other document comes your way with an idea that would be perfect for the Penske account, but that document doesn't use the word *Penske* anywhere? This is where purely content-based file management fails because you have no way of relating this new document with your Penske documents. Of course, you could edit the new document to add the word *Penske* somewhere, but that's a bit kludgy and, in any case, you might not have write permission for the file. It would be far better if you could somehow identify all of your documents that have "Penske-ness"—that is, that are directly or indirectly related to the Penske account.

This sounds like a job for metadata, and that's fine because metadata is nothing new in the Windows world:

- Digital photo files often come with their own metadata for things such as the camera model and image dimensions, and some imaging software enables you to apply tags to pictures.

- In Windows Media Player, you can download album and track information that gets stored as various metadata properties: Artist, Album Title, Track Title, and Genre, to name just a few.

- The last few versions of Microsoft Office have supported metadata via the File, Properties command.

- For all file types, Windows displays in each file's property sheet a Summary tab that enables you to set metadata properties such as Author, Comments, and Tags.

In Windows 10, metadata is an integral part of the operating system. With the Windows Search engine, you can perform searches on some or all these properties (see "Searching Your PC," later in this chapter). You can also use them to group and filter files (see "Grouping and Filtering with Metadata," later in this chapter).

To edit a document's metadata, you can use two methods in Windows 10:

- In File Explorer, select View, Details Pane. In the Details pane that now appears on the right side of the window, click the property you want to edit. Windows 10 displays a text box in which you can type or edit the property value. For example, Figure 6.12 shows a photo's Title property being edited. Click Save when you're done.

- Right-click the document and click Properties to display the property sheet, and then click the Details tab. This tab displays a list of properties and their values. To edit a property, click inside the Value column to the right of the property.

 note

By default, in most folder windows, Windows 10 displays the Tags and Type properties in File Explorer's Details view. (Specialized folders such as Music, Pictures, and Videos display other properties in Details view.) To toggle a property's column on and off, right-click any column header and then click the property. Click More to see a complete list of the available properties.

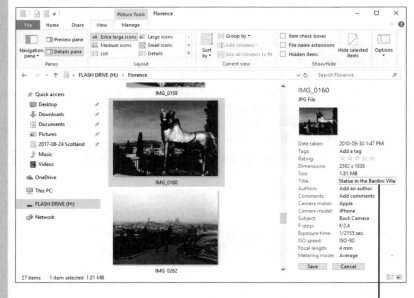

Figure 6.12
You can edit a document's configurable metadata directly in the Details pane.

Click the property you want to edit.

Searching Your PC

We mentioned earlier that one of the consequences of having massive hard drives is that people tend not to delete files as often as they used to. This means you always have access to your files, but first, you have to find them, and the more data you store on your PC, the harder it gets to locate the data you need.

The good news with Windows 10 is that desktop searching—which disappeared in Windows 8/8.1—is back. As you could in Windows 7, you can quickly search your system from the desktop, but instead of using the Start menu, you use the taskbar's Search box. When you type a search string, Windows 10 generates a list of matching items on your PC—including Modern apps, desktop programs, settings, and documents—as well as matching items from the Windows Store and the web (see Figure 6.13). For the web, you can view the search results without having to open Microsoft Edge by clicking the arrow to the right of the "See web results" text, as pointed out in Figure 6.13.

If too many items appear, or if you don't see the item you're looking for, you can filter the results quickly by clicking Apps, Documents, or Web at the top of the results. For more choices, click Filters at the top-right of the search window to choose a category within which to search. As you can see in Figure 6.14, you can narrow the results to various local and Internet categories: Apps, Documents (names and contents), Folders (that is, folder names), Music, and so on. Click a category to see that subset of the results. Note, too, that Documents, Photos, Videos, and Music show the matching items not only from your PC, but also from your OneDrive.

Figure 6.13
Use the taskbar's Search box to run quick desktop searches in Windows 10.

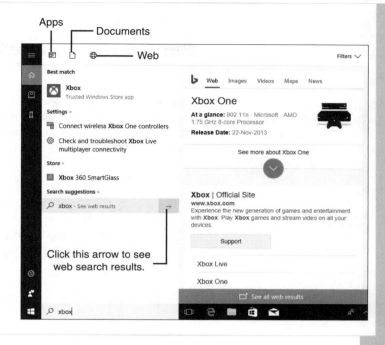

Apps

Documents

Web

Filters ∨

Best match

Xbox
Trusted Windows Store app

Settings

Connect wireless **Xbox** One controllers

Check and troubleshoot **Xbox** Live multiplayer connectivity

Store

Xbox 360 SmartGlass

Search suggestions

xbox - See web results

Click this arrow to see web search results.

Web Images Videos Maps News

Xbox One

At a glance: 802.11n · Microsoft · AMD · 1.75 GHz 8-core Processor
Release Date: 22-Nov-2013

See more about Xbox One

Xbox | Official Site
www.xbox.com
Experience the new generation of games and entertainment with **Xbox**. Play **Xbox** games and stream video on all your devices.

Support

Xbox Live

Xbox One

See all web results

Figure 6.14
Clicking Filters lets you restrict the search results to a specific category.

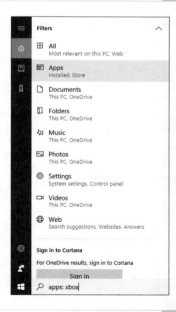

Filters   ∧

⊞ **All**
Most relevant on this PC, Web

▦ **Apps**
Installed, Store

▢ **Documents**
This PC, OneDrive

▨ **Folders**
This PC, OneDrive

♫ **Music**
This PC, OneDrive

▨ **Photos**
This PC, OneDrive

⚙ **Settings**
System settings, Control panel

▭ **Videos**
This PC, OneDrive

⊕ **Web**
Search suggestions, Websites, Answers

Sign in to Cortana

For OneDrive results, sign in to Cortana

Sign in

apps: xbox

Desktop searching is powerful in Windows 10 because it uses the Windows Search service, which starts automatically each time you load Windows 10. On the downside, it can still take Windows 10 a long time to search, say, all of drive C. However, that's because Windows Search does not index the entire drive. Instead, it just indexes your user account data, your offline files (local copies of network files), and your email messages. If you're searching for one of these indexed locations, Windows 10 searches are lightning quick.

Note that you can control what Windows Search indexes and force a rebuild of the index by opening File Explorer, clicking inside its Search box to display the Search pane in the ribbon, and then selecting Advanced Options, Change Indexed Locations. (You can also open Control Panel and click Indexing Options.) This displays the dialog box shown in Figure 6.15. To customize the search engine, you have two choices:

Figure 6.15
Use the Indexing Options dialog box to control the Windows Search engine.

- **Modify**—Click this button to display the Indexed Locations dialog box, which enables you to change the locations included in the index. Check the box for each drive or folder you want to include.

- **Advanced**—Click this button to display the Advanced Options dialog box, which enables you to index encrypted files, change the index location, specify the file types (extensions) you want to include in or exclude from the index. You can also click Rebuild to re-create the index.

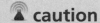 **caution**

Windows Search takes a long time to index even a relatively small amount of data. If you're asking Windows Search to index dozens of gigabytes of data, wait until you're done working for the day and let the indexer run all night.

As-You-Type Searches with Instant Search

You can also perform desktop-based as-you-type searches in any folder by using the Search box that appears in every File Explorer window.

What gets searched depends on several things:

- If you just want to search within a folder, display that folder before clicking inside the Search box. By default, Windows searches within subfolders as well. To turn that off, click All Subfolders in the ribbon's Search tab.

- If you want to search your entire computer, either display the This PC folder and then run the search or click inside the Search box and then click This PC in the ribbon's Search tab.

- If you want to search your user account, click the arrow next to the current folder icon in the Address bar (see Figure 6.5, earlier in this chapter), click your user account in the list, and then run the search.

 tip

In a folder window, you can access the Search box via the keyboard by pressing Ctrl+E.

Whatever location you choose, as you type, Explorer displays those files in the location with names or metadata that matches your search text, as shown earlier in Figure 6.6.

Using Advanced Query Syntax to Search Properties

When you run a standard text search from any File Explorer Search box, Windows looks for matches not only in the filename and the file contents, but also in the file metadata—the properties associated with each file. That's cool and all, but what if you want to match only a particular property? For example, if you're searching your music collection for albums that include the word *Rock* in the title, a basic search on *rock* will also return music in which the artist's name includes *rock* and the album genre is Rock. This is not good.

To fix this kind of thing, you can create powerful and targeted searches by using a special syntax—called Advanced Query Syntax (AQS)—in your search queries.

For file properties, you use the following syntax:

property:*value*

Here, *property* is the name of the file property you want to search on, and *value* is the criteria you want to use. The property can be any of the metadata categories used by Windows. For example, the categories in a music folder include Name, Track, Title, Artists, Album, and Rating. Right-click any column header in Details view to see more properties such as Genre and Length, and you can click More to see the complete list.

You can also access these properties using the controls in the Search tab's Refine group. (Click inside File Explorer's Search box to see the Search tab.) For example, you can use the Date Modified, Kind, and Size lists to construct query strings for those properties, and you can use the Other Properties list to access more properties. (The ones you see depend on the current folder.)

Here are a few things to bear in mind when constructing AQS strings:

- If the property name is a single word, use that word in your query. For example, the following code matches music where the Artists property is Coldplay:

```
artists:coldplay
```

- If the property name uses two or more words, remove the spaces between the words and use the resulting text in your query. For example, the following code matches pictures where the Date Taken property is August 23, 2018:

```
datetaken:8/23/2018
```

- If the value uses two or more words and you want to match the exact phrase, surround the phrase with quotation marks. For example, the following code matches music where the Genre property is Alternative & Punk:

```
genre:"alternative & punk"
```

- If the value uses two or more words and you want to match both words in any order, surround them with parentheses. For example, the following code matches music where the Album property contains the words *Head* and *Goats* in any order:

```
album:(head goats)
```

- If you want to match files where a particular property has no value, use empty braces, [], as the value. For example, the following code matches files where the Tags property is empty:

```
tags:[]
```

You can also refine your searches with the following operators and wildcards:

>	Matches files where the specified property is greater than the specified value. For example, the following code matches pictures where the Date Taken property is later than January 1, 2018: `datetaken:>1/1/2018`
>=	Matches files where the specified property is greater than or equal to the specified value. For example, the following code matches files where the Size property is greater than or equal to 10,000 bytes: `size:>=10000`
<	Matches files where the specified property is less than the specified value. For example, the following code matches music where the Bit Rate property is less than 128 (bits per second): `bitrate:<128`

<=	Matches files where the specified property is less than or equal to the specified value. For example, the following code matches files where the Size property is less than or equal to 1024 bytes: `size:<=1024`
..	Matches files where the specified property is between (and including) two values. For example, the following code matches files where the Date Modified property is between August 1, 2018 and August 31, 2018, inclusive: `datemodified:8/1/2018..8/31/2018`
*	Substitutes for multiple characters. For example, the following code matches music where the Album property includes the word Hits: `album:*hits`
?	Substitutes for a single character. For example, the following code matches music where the Artists property begins with Blu and includes any character in the fourth position: `artists:blu?`

For even more sophisticated searches, you can combine multiple criteria using Boolean operators:

AND (or +)	Use this operator to match files that meet all of your criteria. For example, the following code matches pictures where the Date Taken property is later than January 1, 2018 and the Size property is greater than 1,000,000 bytes: `datetaken:>1/1/2018 AND size:>1000000`
OR	Choose this option to match files that meet at least one of your criteria. For example, the following code matches music where the Genre property is either Rock or Blues: `genre:rock OR genre:blues`
NOT (or –)	Choose this option to match files that do not meet the criteria. For example, the following code matches pictures where the Type property is not JPEG: `type:NOT jpeg`

 note

The Boolean operators AND, OR, and NOT must appear in all-uppercase letters in your query.

Saving Searches

After taking all that time to get a search just right, it would be a real pain if you had to repeat the entire procedure to run the same search later. Fortunately, Windows 10 takes pity on searchers by enabling you to save your searches and rerun them anytime you like. After you run a File Explorer search, you save it by following these steps:

1. In the ribbon's Search tab, click the Save Search button. The Save As dialog box appears.

2. Type a name for the search.

3. By default, Windows 10 saves your searches in the Searches folder, appropriately enough. However, you're free to use the Save As dialog box to save your search anywhere that's most convenient, including the desktop.

4. Click Save.

Grouping and Filtering with Metadata

Metadata is a useful file system element, but people might not be motivated to apply metadata to their documents unless they can be convinced that metadata is worth the short-term hassle. The Windows programmers seem to understand this because they built two file-management techniques into File Explorer, both of which become more powerful and more useful the more metadata you've applied to your files. These techniques are grouping and filtering.

Grouping Files

Grouping files means organizing a folder's contents according to the values in a particular property. In the Windows 10 version of File Explorer, select the ribbon's View tab and then click Group By. This displays a list of the properties you can use for the grouping. Clicking one of these properties groups the files according to the values in that property. Figure 6.16 shows the Documents folder grouped by the values in the Type property.

As Figure 6.16 shows, Windows 10 enhances the grouping feature with two techniques:

- You can select all the files in a group by clicking the group title.

- You can collapse the group (that is, show just the group title) by clicking the arrow to the left of the group title. (You can collapse all the groups by right-clicking any group title and then clicking Collapse All Groups.)

Figure 6.16
Windows 10 enables you to group and work with files based on the values in a property.

Click here to select the group.

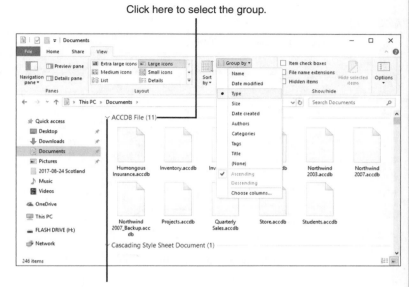

Click here to collapse the group.

Filtering Files

Filtering files means changing the folder view so that only files that have one or more specified property values are displayed. Returning to the Type property example, you could filter the folder's files to show only those where Type was, say, JPG File or File Folder.

In Details view, when you pull down the list associated with a property's header (hover the mouse over the property and a down arrow appears, which you click to display the associated list), you see an item for each discrete property value, along with a check box for each value. To filter the files, check the boxes for the property values you want to view. For example, in Figure 6.17 we've checked the boxes beside the Doc File, DOCM File, and Office Open XML Document values in the Type property, and only those three types appear in the folder.

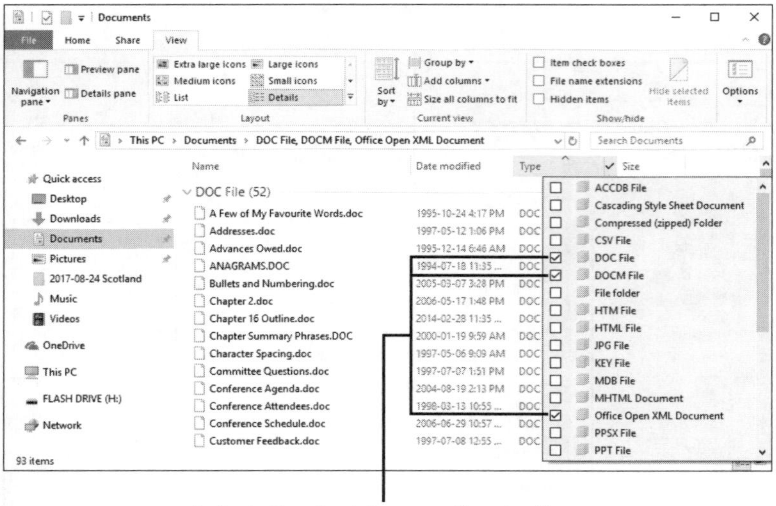

Figure 6.17
You can filter a folder to show only those files that have the property values you specify.

Activate the check boxes to filter the files.

7

DEVICES AND PRINTERS

Windows Printing Primer

In most cases, the process of installing and using a printer with Windows is nearly effortless. Just plugging in the printer to your computer is usually enough. Installation and setup are automatic and silent. Within a few seconds, you can start printing from whatever programs you use, without thinking any more about it. This process doesn't always go quite this smoothly, though, so we've devoted this chapter to the ins and outs of installing and using a printer in Windows 10.

Windows gives you control over the printing system through the new Devices settings page and through the Devices and Printers window in the old desktop-style Control Panel. Here are the easiest ways to get to these places:

- For the new settings page, click or touch Start, then the Settings (gear) icon, and Devices, Printers & Scanners. The new settings page is finally fully enough featured that you should be able to perform most printer maintenance tasks with it.

- If you'd prefer to start from the old Devices and Printers page, type the words `control panel` into the taskbar's search box. Then select Control Panel from the results, and under Hardware and Sound (in Category view), click View Devices and Printers.

Figure 7.1 shows the new Printers & Scanners settings panel. At the top, the window has a button titled Add a Printer or Scanner, which you can use if Windows does not automatically detect a new printer you've connected. We discuss this shortly.

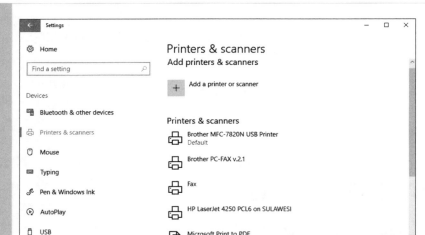

Figure 7.1
The Printers & Scanners settings page lists any printing devices known by your computer. It's the starting point for adding and managing printers.

Below that are icons for each print device on your computer. On my computer, you can see in Figure 7.1 that there are six. (Yours will be different.)

- The Brother MFC (multifunction) printer, which is installed directly on the computer. This is the default printer, where I want the output to go most of the time.

- The Brother PC-FAX printer. This is a second print device added by my multifunction printer. If I select this for printing, the printer sends its output as a fax from its own phone connection rather than printing it on paper.

- The Fax printer. My computer also has a dial-up modem with fax capability. This printer device is added by Windows. You might also see a Fax icon if your organization has a networked fax-sending server. Either way, the Fax printer lets you send faxes directly from your applications without having to first print a hard copy and then feed it through a fax machine or scanner. We show you how to use this feature in Chapter 12, "Scanning and Faxing."

- The HP Laserjet printer, which is connected to a different computer named Sulawesi. It is being used through the network. If you have set up a Homegroup network, as described in Chapter 18, all the printers on all of the computers in your homegroup will appear automatically, and you can use any of them from your computer.

- Microsoft Print to PDF, which lets you create the popular PDF file format from any app that can print. When you use this printer selection, whatever you "print" is saved as a PDF file, which you can then email, share, save, or print later. This built-in, free feature is new in Windows 10, and it's terrific, if long overdue.

- The Microsoft XPS Document Writer, like Microsoft Print to PDF, also isn't a printer in the physical sense. This printer selection lets any app that can print save its output as an XPS or Open XPS (.oxps) file. XPS was Microsoft's attempt to match the PDF file's popularity. Hardly anyone uses it.

If you click one of the printer icons, three items appear underneath it:

- Open Queue, which lets you cancel print jobs that have not yet completed
- Manage, which lets you print a test page or change printer settings
- Remove Device which, as you might expect, removes the printer from the list of installed devices when you know you will not use it again

If you're lucky, you will rarely need to use the Printers & Scanners settings page. However, there are two things you might want to do from time to time:

- **Cancel something that's printing**—On rare occasions, you might have printed something by mistake or find that the printer has the wrong paper inserted. Just click or touch the printer's icon, select Open Queue, right-click (or touch and hold) the item that you want to stop, and select Cancel. This just stops Windows from sending more output to the printer. It might keep going for a while unless it has a Cancel button of its own that you can push.

- **Print a test page**—Unsure whether your printer is working? Click or touch the printer's icon, and then select Manage, Print a Test Page. That should send a page demonstrating both text and graphics if the printer is working.

We discuss printing and maintenance tasks like these in more detail later in this chapter.

Below the list of printers are some other items you should know about. You might need to scroll down to see them:

- **Let Windows Manage My Default Printer**—If you check this box, whenever you select a different printer from within an app or desktop application, Windows will automatically make that printer your default printer. The printer will become the default selection from then on, until you change it again. Windows automatically associates your printer choice with the Wi-Fi or wired network you're currently using. This means the default printer at home can be different from the default printer at work.

    If you use your computer at different locations, this is probably a good setting to check. If you use it in just one place, it's probably best to leave it turned off.

- **Download Over Metered Connections**—If you have a device with a metered Internet connection (cellular or satellite, for example), Windows won't automatically update your printer's software over the metered connection, but waits until you're on an unlimited connection. You can check this box to force Windows to update over your metered connection, if you need it to.

- **Print Server Properties**—Further down is a choice that lets you manage settings common to all printers attached to your computer, such as special paper sizes or types. We discuss this later in the chapter. It's not commonly used.

If you're lucky, that's about all you'll ever need to do to manage printers in Windows 10. However, things can go awry. In the next section, we show you how to add new printers that don't appear automatically. The subsequent sections tell you how to manage your printers in more detail.

➡ *If you want to let other users on your network use an installed printer, see "Sharing Printers," p. 469.*

Installing and Configuring a Printer

The basic game plan for installing and configuring a printer is as follows:

caution

Some printer manufacturers ask you to install their driver software *before* you plug in and turn on the printer for the first time. *Heed their advice!* If you plug in the printer first, Windows might install incorrect drivers. (If this happens to you, unplug the printer, delete the printer icon, run the manufacturer's setup program, and try again.)

- Read your printer's installation manual and follow the instructions for Windows 10, 8.1, 8, or 7. If no instructions are included for these operating systems, look for instructions for Windows Vista or XP.

- Plug in the printer. Most printers are detected when you connect them to the computer. Your printer might be found and then configure itself automatically.

- If the printer doesn't configure itself, you can run the Add a Printer Wizard (or use a setup program, if one is supplied with your printer). We go over this procedure in detail in the next section.

- If you want, set print defaults pertaining to two-sided printing, scaling, paper source, halftone imaging, ink color, and paper orientation. These will be the default print settings that every Windows application starts with when you select this printer.

- Share the printer and specify its share name so that other network users can use your printer.

- If you are on a network and want to control who gets to use your printer, set custom access permissions.

- On the Printers & Scanners settings page, click the printer icon, select Manage, and then select Set as Default. This way, your printer will be preselected as the printer of choice when you use the Print function of Windows applications. If you transport your computer to different locations and use different printers there, go back to the main Printers & Scanners settings page, scroll down, and select Let Windows Manage My Default Printer. This lets Windows associate a different default printer with each network you use.

We discuss these topics in more detail in the following sections.

Adding a New Printer

How you go about adding a new printer depends on how you'll be connecting to it:

- If your printer is connected directly to your computer with a cable, you are installing a *local printer*. Installing a local printer is covered in the next section.

- If you want to use a printer that's shared by another computer on your network, you still need to set up a printer icon on your own computer. This is called installing a *network printer*.

     To see how to install a network printer, **see** *"Using Printers on the Network,"* **p. 455.**

- A printer that's physically connected to the network itself and not cabled to another computer is called a *local printer on a network port*, which is somewhat confusing, or a *network-attached printer*, which makes a little more sense. We cover the installation of these in Chapter 21, "Using a Windows Network," also. If you're in a hurry, try the standard Add Printer procedure we describe in the next section. Windows is pretty smart about finding and using network-attached printers.

Installing a Local Printer

In most cases, Windows will detect and set up a printer that's directly attached to your computer with no help at all. In some cases, though, you might have to lend a hand. This section can assist you in such instances. The procedures vary, depending on how the printer is connected to your computer:

- Parallel printer port

- USB

- Network, wireless, or Bluetooth

- Serial port. (Serial port printers are still used by point-of-sale systems and the occasional true retro-computing geek.)

Here's the basic game plan, which works with most printers. You must be signed in to Windows 10 using an Administrator account. Follow these steps:

> ### 🔍 note
>
> If you have an old printer that has a parallel connector and no USB connector, and your new computer has no parallel port, you can purchase a USB-to-Parallel (also called IEEE-1284) adapter cable. These cables cost about $20 at a local computer store (less online). Alternatively, you can get a network parallel print server device or add a parallel port to your computer, but the adapter cable is the easiest way to go.

1. Read the printer's installation instructions specific to Windows 10, 8.1, 8, or 7. If no instructions are included for these operating systems, look for Windows Vista or XP instructions. You might be instructed to install software *before* connecting the printer to your computer the first time. This is especially important if your printer connects via USB.

2. If the printer uses a cable, connect the printer to the appropriate port on your computer according to the printer manufacturer's instructions.

3. Locate the type of connection that your printer uses in the following list, as directed:

- **USB**—Install any driver programs provided by your manufacturer, and then connect the printer's USB cable to your computer. Windows will detect it and automatically start the Add a Device Wizard. Follow the instructions onscreen to finish installing the printer.

- **Network, wireless, or Bluetooth**—If your printer can be directly attached to your network, connect it and then click Add a Printer or Scanner in the Printers & Scanners window. If Windows finds the printer, select it and click Next. Otherwise, follow the printer manufacturer's specific instructions.If you are using a wireless network or Bluetooth, be sure that your computer's wireless or Bluetooth adapter is turned on and enabled. On some laptops, they are switched off by default to conserve power.

- **Parallel port**—Connect the printer to your computer's parallel port. Windows *should* detect and install the printer. If it doesn't, see the next section.

- **Serial port**—Many barcode, label, and point-of-sale receipt printers use a serial data connection. Serial printers must be set up manually. The next section describes how.

If Windows can't automatically detect the make and model of your printer, it will ask you to assist in selecting the appropriate type. If you can't find your printer's make and model in the list of choices, see "What to Do If Your Printer Isn't Listed," later in this chapter.

When your printer is installed and working, you might want to skip ahead to the section titled "Changing a Printer's Properties" to see ways that you can configure your printer to make it easier to use.

If the Printer Isn't Found

If your printer isn't found automatically using the options in the preceding section, you must fake out Plug and Play and go the manual route. To do so, follow these steps:

1. Open the Settings app and select Printers & Scanners, Add a Printer or Scanner.

2. If your printer does not appear within 20 seconds or so, click The Printer That I Want Isn't Listed. Select My Printer Is a Little Older... and click Next. If that locates the printer, click Next. Otherwise, click the back arrow and then select Add a Local Printer or Network Printer with Manual Settings, and then click Next.

   If you are connecting to a printer that's directly hooked up to your computer, select Use an Existing Port, and proceed to step 3.

   ➡️ *If you intend to send output directly to a computer that's attached to your network, use the Create a New Port option instead. For a discussion of this option, **see** "Using Unix and LPR Printers," **p. 458**. After the port information has been set up, continue with the following step.*

3. Select the port to which the printer is connected. The usable choices are as follows:

- **LPT1:, LPT2:, LPT3:**—These are parallel port connections. Most computers have only one parallel port connection, LPT1, if they have one at all. These ports will still appear in the list even if your computer doesn't have them—so be careful.

- **COM1: through COM4:**—If you know your printer is of the serial variety, it's probably connected to COM1 or COM2. If COM1 is tied up for use with some other device, such as a modem, use COM2.

- **File**—If you select this port, when you subsequently print a document, you will be prompted for the name of a file into which the printer commands will be stored. The main use for this option is with a PostScript printer driver, to create a file for submission to a print shop.

After selecting the correct port, click Next.

4. Select the manufacturer and model of your printer in the next dialog box, as shown in Figure 7.2. You can quickly jump to a manufacturer's name by pressing the first letter of the name, such as *H* for HP. Then use the up- and down-arrow keys to home in on the correct one.

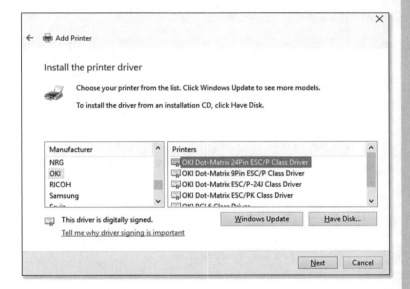

Figure 7.2
Choose the make and model of your printer here.

If you can't find the appropriate model, you have three choices:

- If you have an Internet connection, click Windows Update to see whether Microsoft has a driver available; this might work.

- Get the manufacturer's driver on a CD/DVD or download it via the Internet, open or run the downloaded file to expand its files, and then click Have Disk. Locate the driver (look for an INF file, which is an information file that points to the correct driver files), and click OK.

- Choose a similar, compatible model and risk getting less-than-perfect output. This option can often be successful with dot-matrix printers and *older* inkjet and laser printers, but it is less likely to work with modern cheap inkjet or laser printers that have no internal processing "smarts."

For more information on dealing with unlisted printers, **see** the next section, "What to Do If Your Printer Isn't Listed."

If the wizard finds that the appropriate driver is already installed on your machine, you can elect to keep it or replace it. The choice is up to you. If you think the replacement is newer and will be better, go for it. By contrast, if no driver is listed, you might be prompted to install it or insert a disk from the vendor. On the whole, drivers downloaded directly from the manufacturer's website tend to be better and more full-featured than the default ones provided with Windows, so your best bet is to download the most recent driver version. Avoid downloading from any site other than the original manufacturer's, though, because third-party sites often deliver software laden with viruses.

After you select a printer manufacturer and model, click Next.

5. By default, the printer is named using its full model name. You can change or shorten it if you like. Then click Next.

6. By default, the printer is not shared on your network. You can elect to share the printer, and you can adjust the sharing name if you like. It's best to keep the share name to no more than 31 characters if you want to share the printer with older computers or non-Windows devices. To help other users identify the printer, you can also type in a location and a comment.

> To read more about signed and unsigned drivers, **see** "Configuring Windows to Ignore Unsigned Device Drivers," **p. 642.**

If you do not want to share the printer, click Do Not Share This Printer. Then click Next.

note

If the driver software isn't signed with digital proof that it came from the manufacturer that it says it came from, Windows might warn you. Allow the software to be installed only if you *know* that it came directly from a reputable manufacturer. If it came from a website other than the manufacturer's, do not trust it. On a corporate network, you might be prevented from installing any unsigned drivers.

7. If you want this printer to be your default (primary) printer, check Set As the Default Printer.

If you want to be sure the printer is working, click Print a Test Page; otherwise, click Finish.

A User Account Control prompt may appear, confirming that you want to install the driver. Click Yes.

When you're finished, the icon for the printer appears in your Printers & Scanners settings window.

> If you later want to share the new printer with other users on your network, **see** "Sharing Printers," **p. 469.**

If you have just set up a printer that's connected to a serial (COM) port, click the printer's icon and select Manage, Printer Properties. Select the Ports tab, highlight the correct COM port line (which should be checked), and click Configure Port. Select the proper data transfer rate in bits per second (baud rate), data bits, parity, stop bits, and flow control. The settings must exactly match those used by the printer. For *most* serial printers, these settings will be 9600, 8, None, 1, and Xon/Xoff, respectively. Finally, click OK to save the changes.

If your printer is set up and working now, you can skip ahead to the section "Changing a Printer's Properties."

What to Do If Your Printer Isn't Listed

If your printer isn't detected with Plug and Play and isn't listed in the printer manufacturer and model selection list discussed in the previous section, you'll have to find a driver elsewhere.

First, your printer probably came with a disc containing driver software. In the Add Printer dialog box (refer to Figure 7.2), click Have Disk and then click Browse to find the Windows 10, 8.1, 8, 7, or Vista driver files for your printer. If you are running a 32-bit version of Windows 10, you might also be able to use a driver designed for Windows XP. If there are separate folders for 64-bit and 32-bit drivers, choose the one appropriate for your copy of Windows. Select the appropriate INF file and click OK.

The Windows Update button lets Windows download additional printer drivers from Microsoft, and this may well obtain the correct driver for you.

If Windows Update doesn't help, your next step should be to visit the printer manufacturer's website. Check out the Product Support section, and look for a way to locate and download drivers. If you can find an appropriate driver, follow the manufacturer's instructions for downloading it. It will probably come as a compressed or executable file that has to be expanded or run, and this will put the installation files into a folder on your hard drive. You can then use the Have Disk feature (discussed earlier) to point Windows to this folder. If you cannot locate a downloadable Windows 10, 8.1, 8, 7, or Vista driver set, you could try a Windows XP driver; however, doing so is a gamble and is unlikely to work on a 64-bit version of Windows.

 tip

Use the Internet to see whether other people have run in to the same problem and have found a solution. For instance, you might use Google to search for "Windows 7 8 10 printer driver *manufacturer model*," substituting the manufacturer's name and model number. However, do *not* download a driver from some random site: It could be infected with a virus. Download drivers *only* from the manufacturer's website or a credible corporate or institutional website (for example, the site of a major computer manufacturer like Dell).

If neither Microsoft nor the manufacturer provides a driver, hope is fading. Still, some off-brand printers or models are designed to be compatible with one of the popular printer types, such as the Apple LaserWriters, HP LaserJets, or one of the Epson series. Also, many printer models are very similar and can use the same driver (with mostly correct results). Check the product manual or manufacturer's website to see whether your printer supports an *emulation mode*. This workaround might help you identify an alternative printer model, and you can try its driver.

Assuming that you have obtained a printer driver, follow these instructions to install it:

1. If you obtained a driver by downloading it from the Internet, run the downloaded file. This either installs the driver directly or expands or unzips a set of files into a location on your hard disk. Take note of the location.

2. Follow steps 1 through 4 in the preceding section.

3. Click the Have Disk button.

4. You're now prompted to insert a disk. Click the Browse button. If you downloaded the driver, locate the folder in which the driver files were expanded or unzipped. If you have a CD, insert the CD, wait a few moments, and then browse to the driver files on the CD.

The wizard is looking for a file with an `.inf` extension, which is a file type that describes to Windows what components, files, and settings the driver installs and is provided with all drivers. You might have to hunt around a bit to find a folder with drivers for Windows 10, 8.1, 8, 7, Vista, or XP.

5. After you locate the folder with INF files, click OK. You might have to choose a printer model from a list if multiple options exist.

6. Continue through the wizard dialog boxes, as explained in the previous section.

Changing a Printer's Properties

Every printer has several sets of preference and properties dialog boxes, each with enough settings to choke a horse. Different printers have different features, and your particular printer's driver will dictate the particular set of options available to you. You should make yourself familiar with the options for your printer(s) so that you can know what kinds of adjustments and printing shortcuts are available to you.

If you click a printer's icon in the Printers & Scanners settings page and select Manage, you will see several choices. The different sets of printer properties and preferences each serve a different purpose.

- **Printing Preferences**—These are the default settings that each application will start with when you use an application's Print function. They include paper size, page orientation, and paper source. Although most applications let you make changes for an individual document, it's annoying to have to keep adjusting the same settings every time you print. You can save time if you change the printer's Printing Preferences. This way, each application starts with those selections as the default.

  Preferences are *per-user* settings. Each computer user can set his or her own printing preferences.

- **Printer Properties**—These are settings that apply to the printer itself, most of which tell Windows how to communicate with the printer, what capabilities and optional features it has, and so on. Printer properties also include settings that determine the initial Printing Preferences for each user before they customize them with their personal Printing Preferences. So, if you're setting up a computer that several other people will use, you might want to set up default Printer Properties before they log on.

- **Hardware Properties**—This one is fairly useless. It's just there because of the way that device settings are organized. (It *is* useful for other device types, however.)

On the Printers & Scanners settings page, well below the list of icons, is a final settings choice called Print Server Properties. This leads to settings that apply to all printers used by the computer, including paper size and form definitions.

We describe the most general and common options in the following sections. We cover settings related to network printer sharing in Chapter 21.

Printing Preferences

These settings are used as the defaults whenever you select a printer in one of your applications. If you find yourself having to change the same page setup settings nearly every time you start to print something, you can save yourself time by changing the settings in the Printing Preferences dialog box.

 tip

A given *physical* printer can have multiple icons, each with different Printing Preferences and other settings because each icon is just a pointer to the actual printer, much the way a shortcut on the Windows desktop represents a document or application. If you have different sets of printing options that you use frequently, you might want to use extra icons, each with its own Printing Preferences settings.

For example, you could set up one printer icon for plain paper, portrait orientation, and one-sided printing for reports, and another with landscape orientation, legal-sized paper, manual feed, and two-sided printing for booklet covers, if these were common tasks for you. Of course, you can always adjust these settings every time you start to print a document, but that can get tedious. With different icons, you can choose a complete setup just by selecting the appropriate printer icon.

To create extra printer icons, first install and configure your printer as described at the beginning of this chapter. Then follow these steps:

1. On the Printers & Scanners settings page, click the installed printer icon, select Manage, Printer Properties, and choose the Ports tab. Make note of which port is checked. Then close the Printer Properties dialog box.

2. Go back to the main Printers & Scanners page, and at the top select Add a Printer or Scanner; then select The Printer That I Want Isn't Listed. Choose Add a Local Printer or Network Printer with Manual Settings, and click Next.

3. From the drop-down list of existing ports, select the port you noted in step 1, and click Next. Select the manufacturer and model of your already installed printer, and then click Next. Choose Use the Driver That Is Currently Installed, and then click Next.

4. Edit the name to reflect the different settings you want to set up for the alternative icon. For example, I changed mine to read Brother Landscape Manual Feed. Then click Next. Be sure Set as Default Printer is not checked, and then click Finish.

5. Click the new icon and select Manage, Printing Preferences. Change the settings as described in this section (in my example, Landscape and Manual Feed), and then click OK.

Now, from any app that can print, you can choose this printer selection and get all the alternative settings you preset in step 5.

To change your personal printing preferences for a particular printer, open Printers & Scanners as described at the beginning of this chapter. Click the printer icon and select Manage, Printing Preferences. The number of tabs and the choices they offer vary widely from printer to printer. Table 7.1 describes them in general terms.

Table 7.1 Printing Preferences Tabs

Tab	What It Controls
Layout	Landscape or portrait paper orientation, the number of pages placed on each sheet, and so on
Paper/Quality	The bin or feed slot to use, paper size, type, and so on
Effects	Page resizing, watermarks, and so on
Finishing	Stapling, duplexing (two-sided printing), collating, binding, and so on
Advanced	Printer features, color management, and, in some cases, paper and layout choices
Services	Links to manufacturer web pages and online services

 tip

If the Layout tab is not present, you should be able to set the default page orientation on one of the other tabs: General, Basics, Paper/Quality, or perhaps Effects. The exact location of printer settings varies by manufacturer.

If your printer's preferences dialog box looks like the one shown in Figure 7.3, you must click the unlabeled icon to change the orientation. You might run in to this issue especially if you're using a Hewlett-Packard printer that is shared by a Windows 7 computer. We have no idea why HP made such an important setting so unobvious, but it appears to have done a better job with the drivers supplied with Windows 8 and 10.

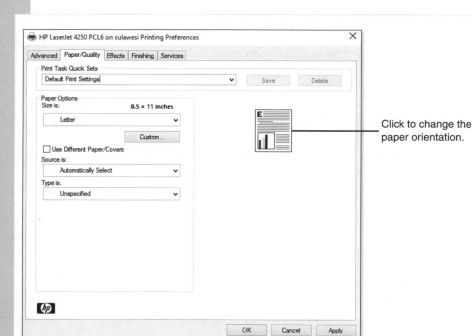

Click to change the paper orientation.

Figure 7.3
With some Hewlett-Packard printer drivers, to change the page orientation, you must click the unlabeled icon in the right side window.

If you want to change a printer's default preferences for all users, view its Printer Properties, as described in the next section, and click Printing Defaults on the Advanced tab. This brings up what looks like the Printing Preferences dialog box, but these settings will become the default settings for all users. Users can then customize their printing preferences from that starting point.

Printer Properties

To make changes to a printer driver or its physical connection to your computer, or to define some of the default settings that will be supplied to every user, you'll use Printers & Scanners as described at the beginning of this chapter. Click the printer icon and select Manage, Printer Properties. (That's *Printer Properties*, not Printing Preferences or Hardware Properties.) A dialog box like the one shown in Figure 7.4 opens.

Figure 7.4
A typical printer's Printer Properties dialog box. The settings available vary among printers. Some have more or fewer tabs.

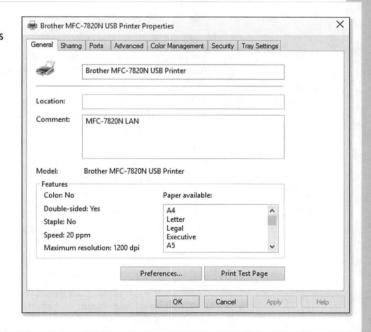

A printer's Properties dialog box can have any of several tabs. Table 7.2 shows the general breakdown. Again, the tabs you'll see and the choices they offer can vary depending on the capabilities of your printer.

Table 7.2 Printer Properties Tabs

Tab	What It Controls
General	This tab lists the name, location, model number, and features of the printer. From this tab, you can print a test page. You also can click the Preferences button to change your personal printing preferences (the same settings described in the previous section). Some color printers may have settings for paper quality and color control as well as buttons for maintenance functions on this tab.
Sharing	On this tab, you can alter whether the printer is shared with other network users and what the share name is.
Ports	On this tab, you can select the printer's connection port, add and delete ports, and in some cases configure the physical connection itself. This tab also lets you set up additional ports for network-connected printers.
Advanced	This tab controls time availability, printer priority, driver changes, spooling options, and advanced printing features such as booklet printing and page ordering. The first two settings are pertinent to larger networks and should be handled by a server administrator. Booklet printing is worth looking into if you do lots of desktop publishing. Using this option, you can print pages laid out for stapling together small pamphlets. The New Driver button on the Advanced tab lets you replace the current driver with a better one, should this be necessary. The Printing Defaults button lets you set the default printing properties supplied to each user.
Color Management	On this tab, you can set optional color profiles on color printers, if this capability is supported.
Security	This tab lets you control who has access to print, manage printers, or manage documents from this printer.
Device Settings	The settings on this tab vary greatly among printers. For example, you can set the paper size in each tray, tell Windows how much RAM is installed in the printer, and substitute fonts.
About	Lists the printer's driver components.
Utilities	This tab, if present, might contain options for inkjet nozzle cleaning, head cleaning, head alignment, and so on.
Bluetooth	This tab, if present, contains information about your Bluetooth printer and connection in case you need to troubleshoot connection problems.

➡ *For more details about printer sharing, printer pooling, and other server-related printing issues,* **see** *Chapter 21.*

Print Server Properties

To define paper sizes or forms, or to change the location of the spooling folder used to hold data being sent to the printer, open the Settings app, and select Devices, Printers & Scanners. Scroll down and select Print Server Properties under Related Settings.

The Print Server Properties dialog box is covered in Chapter 21 because it's mainly a networking topic.

Removing a Printer

You might want to remove a printer setup for several reasons:

- The physical printer has been removed from service.

- You don't want to use a particular network printer anymore.

- You have several definitions of a physical printer using different default settings, and you want to remove one of them.

- You have a nonfunctioning or improperly functioning printer setup and want to remove it and start over by running the Add a Printer Wizard.

---

 tip

The removal process removes only the printer icon in the Printers & Scanners window. The related driver files and font files are *not* deleted from your hard disk. Therefore, if you ever want to re-create the printer, you don't have to insert discs or respond to prompts for the location of driver files. On the other hand, if you are having problems with the driver, deleting the icon and then reinstalling the printer won't delete the bad driver. There are two ways to fix this. You can try the New Driver tool on the Advanced tab of the Printer Properties dialog box to solve the problem in this case. If that doesn't help, delete the printer icon, and use the Print Management tool mentioned at the end of this chapter to delete the bad printer driver package entirely.

In any of these cases, the approach is the same:

1. Be sure you are signed in with Administrator privileges.

2. Open the Settings app and select Devices, Printers & Scanners, as described at the beginning of this chapter. Locate the icon of the printer you want to remove.

3. Be sure nothing is in the printer's queue. If there are print jobs, you have to cancel all jobs in the printer's queue before deleting the printer. If you don't, Windows will try to delete all jobs in the queue for you, but it isn't always successful.

4. Select the printer icon you want to delete, and then choose Remove Device.

5. Windows will ask you to confirm that you want to delete the printer. Click Yes. The printer icon disappears from the window.

Printing from Your Applications

The steps for printing from applications is not universally standardized and can vary from app to app. We can give you some general guidance here and some tips for making the job easier.

The ability to print from Modern apps is not always available. Some apps can print, some can't, and some print only under certain circumstances. Sometimes, a small printer icon appears at the left edge of the app. However, in some apps, you must select an icon that offers hidden additional choices, usually an ellipsis (...) or as an icon that appears as three horizontal lines, one above the other, at the top-right or -left corner of the window. The setup is left up to each app's developer, and unfortunately, there is no consensus among developers to do it any one particular way, even within Microsoft. (I'm a little peeved about this. You will be, too.)

For desktop applications that use the ribbon interface, again, the Print function could be anywhere, either as a ribbon button or in a drop-down menu. The current trend is to provide a list of ribbon titles across the top of the app window, with the first entry named File. Typically, you can click on that and then select Print.

Desktop-style applications that use the traditional pull-down menu system almost universally have File as the first menu item and Print as a selection under that. (I'm sure I don't have to tell you that. That's what 30 years of design consistency does for you.)

If you're lucky enough to find it, the Print menu selection usually displays a Print dialog box that lets you select a printer. Usually, a button next to the printer selection list is labeled Preferences. This button lets you change the orientation of the printing on the page, the paper source, and so on. The settings are the same as discussed in "Printing Preferences" in this chapter, except, here, you're changing the settings just for one particular document in one application.

If an application doesn't provide a way to select a specific printer, your default printer is used. As mentioned at the beginning of this chapter, there are two ways to choose which printer you'd like to use as the default.

- One way is to let Windows manage it for you; Windows 10 will make the most recently selected printer be the default printer, and it changes the default every time you choose a different printer. And, it keeps track of which printer you prefer to use as you move from one Wi-Fi network another. To use this method, open Settings, Devices, Printers & Scanners, and scroll down to Let Windows Manage My Default Printer. Check this box.

- If you'd like your default printer selection to "stick," open the Settings app, select Devices, Printers & Scanners, and scroll down to Let Windows Manage My Default Printer. Uncheck this box. Then click a printer's icon and select Manage, Set As Default Printer.

 tip

You don't always have to print from an application. As a shortcut, in many cases, you can simply right-click a document's icon in File Explorer and select Print. You won't have the option of setting any print options; your Printing Preference settings are used. The document type must also have an association linking the filename extension (for example, .doc or .bmp) to an application that can open and print files this way. To set those associations, open Settings, Apps, Default Apps, Choose Default Apps By File Type.

When you print from a Windows application, it generates commands and data that tell the printer to form letters and images on a page. Applications generally produce these much faster than a printer can consume them, so the work is done in two separate steps. As an application generates print commands, the Windows Print Spooler service spools the output. Here, *spooling* refers to a process in which the output of an application is stored on disk or in RAM and then fed to an output device at the device's own pace. The application then turns its attention back to you while the Print Spooler plays back the list of commands to the printer. The Print Spooler can coordinate individual printouts (called *jobs*) from possibly several applications and users at once, and it feeds the output to the assigned printer(s) one at a time. We talk about managing queued print jobs in the next section.

No Output from Printer

If you try to print your application but nothing comes out of the printer, open the Printers & Scanners settings page, as described at the beginning of this chapter, and work through the following checklist:

- First, check that you printed to the correct printer. Check to see whether your default printer is the one from which you are expecting output. If you're on a LAN, you or Windows may have changed the default printer.

- Click the printer icon and select Open Queue. In the window that opens, select Printer, and if Pause Printing is checked, uncheck it. On the same menu, see whether the option Use Printer Offline appears. If it does and it's checked, uncheck it.

- Check to see whether the printer you've chosen is actually powered up, loaded with paper, and ready to roll. Be sure its "online" or "ready" light is lit up.

- If you're using a network printer, check whether the station serving the printer is powered up and ready to serve print jobs.

- Check the cabling (unless, of course, it is a wireless printer). Is it tight? You might also try using a different cable to see if the cable itself is defective.

- Does the printer need ink, toner, or paper? Are any error lights or other indicators on the printer itself flashing or otherwise indicating an error, such as a paper jam?

- Are you printing from an MS-DOS application? You might need to use the net use command to redirect an LPT port to your Windows printer. See "Printing from MS-DOS Applications" in Chapter 30, "Command-Line and Automation Tools."

- If none of these steps help, turn the printer off and back on. If that doesn't help, restart Windows. It's sad that we have to suggest this, but it often does bring a zombie printer back to life.

- Finally, see if you can print to a different printer. Printers have been known to fail!

Printer Produces Garbled Text

If your printed pages contain a lot of garbled text or weird symbols, check the following:

- You might have the wrong driver installed. Run the print test page and see whether it works. Open the Printers & Scanners settings page, click the printer's icon, select Manage, Printer Properties, and on the General tab, click Print Test Page. If that works, you're halfway home. If it doesn't, try removing the printer and reinstalling it. Click the printer icon in the Printers & Scanners window and choose Remove Device. Then add the printer again and try printing.

- Some printers have emulation modes that might conflict with one another. Check the manual. You might think you're printing to a PostScript printer, but the printer could be in a Hewlett-Packard emulation mode or vice versa.

PDF and XPS Print Output

Windows 10 is the first Windows version that includes built-in support for creating PDF files from any application that can print. Anyone can view or print a PDF file on any computer that has an appropriate viewer program, without having to have a copy of the application that created the original document. For example, you can view and print a PDF version of a Microsoft Word document without needing to have a copy of Word.

Windows 10 can also create an additional document file type called XPS, which stands for XML Paper Specification. XPS was Microsoft's attempt to create a free alternative to PDF, but it never gained much traction.

You can generate PDF or XPS documents by following these steps:

1. Edit and format a document in one of your applications. Be sure to save the document in the application's native format so that you can come back and change it later. You can't edit a PDF or XPS file. (Not easily, anyway, and not without losing a lot of the organizational structure in the original document.)

2. Use the application's Print function. Set the printer to Microsoft Print to PDF or Microsoft XPS Document Writer, as desired. Click Print.

3. When the Save Print Output As dialog box appears, select a location and name for the PDF or XPS document.

If you are using Microsoft XPS Document Writer, the default output format is actually Open XPS, a variation of XPS that uses the .oxps file extension. If you are going to share the resulting document with users running Windows XP, 7, or Vista, change the output format to Microsoft XPS, with extension .xps, because these operating systems can't display Open XPS documents.

You can now distribute the PDF, Microsoft XPS, or Open XPS document to others to view and print as desired.

Windows 10, 8.1, and 8 use the preinstalled Reader app to view PDF files, but it is rather limited. On most computers, regardless of operating system, you will probably want to download the Acrobat Viewer program from http://get.adobe.com/reader. (Alternatively, you might want to install a more full-featured PDF creating, viewing, and editing tool such as Adobe Acrobat.)

Also, Windows 10, 8.1, 8, 7, and Vista have a pre-installed XPS document viewer. On these versions of Windows, just double-click an XPS file to open and view it. You can download XPS support for Windows XP from Microsoft.com; search for "Microsoft XPS Essentials Pack." There are also XPS viewers for Apple's iOS and OS X, Android, Linux, and other Unix-like operating systems.

> **note**
>
> Both the PDF files and the XPS files created by Windows 10's built-in tools do the right thing and embed the fonts used in the published documents so that they can be viewed correctly even on computers that don't have your unique set of fonts installed.

Faxing

If your computer has a fax-capable modem installed, you can use it to send and receive faxes. All Windows 10 editions come with fax software built in.

To send a fax from Windows 10, set up the fax service as described in Chapter 12, "Scanning and Faxing." Then create a document using your favorite application, click Print, and select Fax as the printer. Windows will ask you for the fax phone number and make the call—no paper is involved. The fax service can even add a cover sheet to your document on the way out. You can attach additional documents to an outgoing fax, so you don't need to send a group of documents in several separate phone calls.

Printing Offline

You can print from applications even if your printer is turned off or disconnected. You might do this while traveling, for instance, if you don't want to drag a 50-pound laser printer along in your carry-on luggage or when you don't want to wake the baby.

If you try this, however, you'll quickly find that the Print Manager will beep, pop-up messages to tell you about the missing printer, and otherwise make your life miserable. To silence it, open the Printers & Scanners settings page, as described at the beginning of this chapter. Click your printer's icon and select Open Queue. Then, in the window that opens, click Printer, Use Printer Offline. The printer's icon will turn a light-gray color to show that it has been set for offline use, and Windows will now quietly and compliantly queue up anything you "print." It just won't try to send it to the printer.

Just don't forget that you've done this, or else nothing will print out even when you've reconnected your printer. You'll end up yelling at your unresponsive printer when it's only doing what it was told. When you've reconnected the printer, repeat the preceding steps and uncheck Use Printer Offline. This is a nifty feature, but it's available only for local printers, not printers shared by other computers.

Working with the Printer Queue

After you or other users on your computer or on the network have sent print jobs to a given printer, an entry appears in its print queue window until the printer has absorbed the last of the data for the printout. You can view a printer's queue window in several ways:

- Open Settings, Devices, Printers & Scanners, as described at the beginning of this chapter, click the printer's icon, and select Open Queue.

- For a local printer attached to your computer, when there are active jobs, an icon appears in the desktop's notification area, near the clock. Hover the mouse pointer over it to see the number of documents waiting to print. Right-click it and select the printer's name to display the queue.

tip

If you find yourself doing this a lot, you can put a printer's icon on your desktop for quick access. To get there, type **control panel** into the taskbar's search box. Select Control Panel from the result, and under Hardware and Sound (in the Category view), select View Devices and Printers. Drag the desired printer's icon to the desktop.

Figure 7.5 shows a sample printer's queue window. The window displays the status of the printer (in the title bar) and the documents that are queued up, including their size, status, owner, pages, date submitted, and so on.

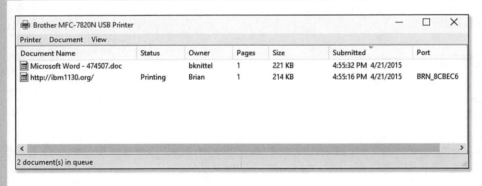

Figure 7.5
A printer's queue window showing one job printing and one pending.

If you're looking at the print queue for a printer that's shared by another computer on your network, the screen won't update itself very frequently. Press F5 or select View, Refresh to see the most up-to-date information.

Deleting a File from the Queue

After sending a document to the queue, you might change your mind about printing it, or you might want to reedit the file and print it again later. To remove a job from the queue, view the printer's queue window, right-click the document you want to delete, and choose Cancel. Alternatively, choose Document, Cancel from the menu. The document is then removed from the printer's queue window.

If you're trying to delete the job that's currently printing, it might take awhile to disappear from the list. And, the printer might have several pages in its own memory. You might need to press a cancel button on the printer itself to really stop it.

By default, all users can pause, resume, restart, and cancel the printing of their own documents. If you want to manage documents printed by other users, your user account must have the Manage Documents privilege for the printer. If Windows says you don't have permission to perform some function, such as deleting a document from the queue or changing printer settings, in most cases you can right-click the document or printer and select Run As Administrator to perform the operation with elevated privileges. From the pop-up menu, select the task you were trying to perform and then try again.

Alternatively, a Computer Administrator user can edit the printer's Security properties to give your account Manage Documents permission. We discuss this shortly.

Canceling All Pending Print Jobs on a Given Printer

To cancel all pending and active print jobs on a printer, open the Printers & Scanners settings page, click the printer icon, and choose Open Queue. From the queue window, select Printer, Cancel All Documents. A confirmation dialog box appears to confirm this action. Click Yes.

Pausing, Resuming, and Restarting the Printing Process

If you need to, you can pause the printing process for a particular printer or even just a single document print job. You can do this to give other jobs a chance to print first, or if you just want to adjust or quiet the printer for some reason.

To pause an individual print job, in the printer's queue window, right-click the document name and choose Pause. The word *Paused* then appears on the document's line under Status. The printer might not stop immediately. First, Windows won't stop sending data until it has reached the end of a page. Second, the printer might have one or more pages already in its memory, and it will finish printing them unless you take the printer offline. Third, Windows might go on and start sending pages for the next job in the print queue. When you're ready to resume printing, right-click the job in question and choose Resume.

 tip

Pausing an individual document lets other documents later in the queue proceed to print, essentially moving them ahead in line. To stop the printer entirely, you must pause the printer.

In some situations, you might need to pause *all* the jobs on your printer so that you can add paper to it, alter the printer settings, or just quiet the printer while you take a phone call. To pause all jobs, open the printer's queue window and choose Printer, Pause Printing. (Again, the printer might not stop immediately; it will continue to print any pages already in its memory.) To start up the printer again, uncheck Pause Printing.

If you need to (because of a paper jam or other botch), you can restart a printing document from the beginning. Just right-click the document and choose Restart.

Advanced Printer Management

In Chapter 21, we describe some advanced printer management topics that apply mostly to printers that you are sharing on a network.

➡ To control who has permission to use and/or manage a printer, **see** "Setting Printer Permissions," **p. 470.**

➡ To change the disk drive on which Windows stores (spools) printer data that's waiting to be sent to printers, **see** "Changing the Location of the Spool Directory," **p. 472.**

➡ To connect multiple printers to one queue in a high-print-volume environment, **see** "Printer Pooling," **p. 472.**

Also, Windows 10 comes with a printer management tool that's part of the Windows Management Console system. It's intended primarily for network administrators who sometimes have to manage dozens of printers spread around an office. We don't go into great detail on this tool here because it's fairly self-explanatory, but we show you how it works.

To run the tool, in the taskbar's search box type **admin**. From the results, select Administrative Tools. Then double-click Print Management. (Alternatively, at the command prompt, type **printmanagement.**) You might need to confirm the User Account Control prompt or enter an Administrator password because this tool requires elevated privileges.

The left pane lets you choose views that include lists of all the printers installed on the local computer (or on a domain network), all installed drivers, all printers that have documents pending, and so on. You can also create custom "filters" to select only printers with specific attributes.

Under the Print Servers section, the local computer is listed, and you can right-click the Print Servers title to add the names of other computers on your network (or named print server devices). You can use this feature to build a single panel that lists all your organization's printers. Print servers that you add to this list will remain in the list the next time you run the printer management tool.

 tip

You can use Print Management to delete a printer driver package from your computer if an incorrect driver is preventing Windows from getting the right driver installed on your computer or on a network computer that's using a printer you're sharing. Open the Print Management tool, select All Drivers, right-click the driver package you want to delete, and select Remove Driver Package. If the driver is reported as in use, restart Windows and try again.

ACCESSORIES AND ACCESSIBILITY

A Boatload of Useful Tools

Tools. Better yet, *power tools*. Do those words make you start to drool? Are you a tool freak, always looking for the latest gadget that will both (a) simplify your life and (b) prove that you truly are cooler than anyone else in the room? If that's you, you're probably an app junkie and spend more time scouring the Windows Store than actually working. (After all, your reasoning goes, if you find the right tool, you'll recover the time and money many times over.)

Or do you see tools as just the means to an end? Do you look *through* the computer screen at what you're working on rather than *at* it? If that's you, you seek simplicity, and you just want to get on with the job.

Whichever "type" you are, what if I told you that those simple, forgettable accessories and apps that come with Windows—some of which have been there since the late 1980s—are worth more than you think? We're going to give them a quick review, to remind you that they're there, to show you some interesting tips, and to show that they're actually more useful than you might remember. At the end of the chapter, we cover additional accessibility tools that can make Windows easier to use.

Of course, the Windows Store does have a fair stock of useful tools and gadgets. But it's still worth knowing about the basics—the ones that you can count on being there on every copy of Windows you encounter.

note
Personally, I find that I use some of these accessories all day, every day: Notepad for writing quick notes to myself and for editing scripts, batch files, and other types of programs; and Calculator for little math problems. I use Character Map at least once a week to find that odd little symbol that I *know* is in one of my fonts somewhere but can't remember where. You might have a few favorites of your own. If you scan through this chapter, you might find a new favorite, and you might find a few uses and capabilities that will surprise you.

Gadgets Are Gone

If you used Windows Vista or Windows 7, you might have used some of the desktop tools that Microsoft called "Gadgets" in Windows 7 and "Sidebar" in Windows Vista. These included a graphical clock, calendar, news headline feed, CPU tachometer, and more. There was also an online Windows Live Gallery where you could download other Gadgets. Starting with Windows 8, Start screen/menu tiles and apps replaced these Gadgets, and Windows Store replaced the Windows Live Gallery.

The Sidebar system was removed for two reasons. For one thing, as we mentioned, "live tiles" can do the same things that the Gadgets did. But the primary reason the Gadgets are gone is that security risks were discovered in the Sidebar system's design. (See the accompanying caution.)

> **⚠ caution**
> If you still have Windows 7 or Vista computers that you aren't going to update to Windows 10, Microsoft recommends that you disable the Sidebar and Gadget tools. For details, search Microsoft.com for Microsoft Knowledge Base article 2719662, or see and follow the instructions under "Disable the Sidebar in the System Registry."

Apps as Accessories

Windows 10 comes with a number of preinstalled Modern-style apps that you could consider to be part of the same family as the preinstalled desktop accessories. And the Store app is a gateway to potentially thousands of other downloadable apps, both free and paid. Perhaps as an incentive for you to start looking at the Windows Store, some apps that should really have been preinstalled require you to search for and download them. For example, the Remote Desktop app is a free Modern app that enables you to connect to and control other Windows computers. The Desktop version of this app is preinstalled; the Modern version you have to download.

The Modern apps that are standard on all copies of Windows 10 are covered in Chapter 5, "Windows Apps and the Windows Store." In this chapter, we cover the standard Desktop accessories. Later in the chapter, we cover the accessibility tools.

Desktop Accessories

A number of standard-issue accessories live in Windows 10's desktop world. Some of them might be familiar to you from previous versions of Windows, but as mentioned at the start of the chapter, it's worth browsing through the list so that you are reminded of what's available. They're actually pretty useful. You can start them in several ways:

- In the taskbar's search box, or while viewing the Start menu, type the first few letters of the accessory's name, wait a moment, and then select the accessory from the search results.

- Scroll the Start menu down to Windows Accessories and click the V-shaped mark to expand the list.

  (You might notice that other sets of tools are listed near Windows Accessories. We cover Windows Ease of Access later in this chapter. The entries under Windows Administrative Tools and Windows System are covered elsewhere in this book, under the relevant maintenance topics. You might want to take a quick look at them now to see what's available.)

- You can start some accessories quickly if you know the accessory's program filename. Just press Windows Logo+R followed by the name, or type the name into a Command Prompt window or the taskbar's search box. In the descriptions that follow, we list the filename for each command that can be run this way. (The technical scoop is this: The filename technique works only for those commands whose program file is in a folder that's listed in the PATH environment variable.)

We also try to offer an obscure, helpful tidbit about each accessory, just to prove that they're more interesting than they seem.

By the way, some of the accessories are covered in other chapters, as follows:

- **Calculator**—Now a Modern app, covered in Chapter 5. Program name: calc.

- **Quick Assist**—Formerly called Remote Assistance, covered in Chapter 39. Program name: quickassist.

- **Remote Desktop Connection**—Covered in Chapter 39. Program name: mstsc.

- **Sound Recorder**—Now a Modern app called Voice Recorder, covered in Chapter 13.

- **Sticky Notes**—Now a Modern app, covered in Chapter 5.

- **Windows Fax and Scan**—Covered in Chapter 12, "Scanning and Faxing." Program name: wfs.

Also, the Windows Journal accessory has been eliminated from all versions of Windows due to an unrepairable, severe security problem in the way it stored information in files.

Character Map

Character Map enables you to find obscure or interesting typographic symbols quickly. You can select any of your computer's installed fonts from the list at the top and then scroll through the font's characters. Highlight a symbol and click Select to add a character to the text box; then click Copy to put those symbol(s) onto the Clipboard. Then you can paste them into another application. If the application accepts Rich Text Format through the Clipboard, the pasted text will come through in the selected font; otherwise, you get the characters in the font active at the application's cursor's location.

Program name—charmap (works with Windows Logo+R, in the taskbar's search box or at the command prompt).

What you might not have known—By default, Character Map displays fonts by their Unicode (16-bit) numerical value, and *all* of the font's symbols are listed. But only some applications accept Unicode characters and values. Many applications accept only local (regional) Windows encodings, where just 8 bits (or 256 numbers) are used to represent a subset of the font's symbols. If you check Advanced View, you can display various encodings. When an 8-bit encoding is selected, the status bar at the bottom of Character Map shows the Unicode value followed by the 8-bit value. For example, when you've selected the Windows: Western character mapping used in the United States, you can see that the Em Dash symbol is 2014 (hexadecimal) in Unicode but 97 (hexadecimal) in the Windows encoding (see Figure 8.1). Character 97 might be something else in other encodings.

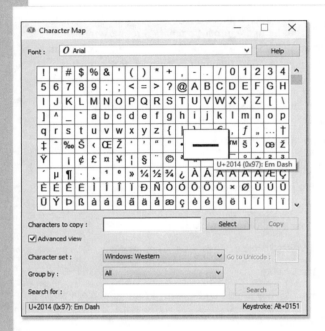

Figure 8.1
Character Map's advanced view.

If you get the wrong characters when you use Copy and Paste to move characters in Character Map into an application, check Advanced View, set the Character Set to Windows: Western, clear out Characters to Copy, and start over.

Alternatively, you can put symbols into an application by character number: hold down the Alt key and type the *decimal* representation of the number on the numeric keypad. The decimal representation is shown at the right side of Character Map's status bar.

Math Input Panel

Using the Math Input Panel (MIP), you can sketch out mathematical equations and then paste them into programs that support the Mathematical Markup Language (MathML). The accessory is useful if you have a program that accepts MathML, such as the built-in equation editor in Microsoft Word 2007 and later; math formatting add-ons such as MathType from Design Science (dessci.com); or symbolic math programs such as Mathematica, Maple, and MathCAD.

The MIP works better with a stylus and a touch-sensitive screen than with your fingers or a mouse, although you can make do with those. It takes some trial and error to train yourself to draw symbols the way the MIP expects them. It's quite a trial, actually.

To enter an equation, open the MIP, and then draw the letters and symbols in the large lower portion of the MIP window, just as you would on paper. As you write, Windows typesets and displays its interpretation in a second window. You can't edit anything in the result window. You have to edit your input. If Windows gets a symbol wrong (and it does, frequently), touch Select and Correct; then touch the symbol you drew. You might be able to select the correct symbol from the pop-up list. If that doesn't help, touch Erase and then rub out the symbol you drew. Touch Write, and try again. When you're satisfied with the result, touch Insert. If the cursor is in an application that can accept MathML, it will be pasted in automatically. Otherwise, you might have to paste in the equation manually. When you close the MIP window, it will minimize itself to the notification area of the taskbar.

Program Name—MIP (works with Windows Logo+R, or in the taskbar's search box.) At the command prompt, type `start mip`.

What you might not have known—As I wrote this chapter, I found that if your cat faces away from the computer's touchscreen and you scratch her head, her tail draws equations. Most of them are unsolvable. (Bonus question: Calculate how long it would take for Schrödinger's cat to come up with Schrödinger's equation by chance alone.)

Notepad

The simple Notepad accessory is surprisingly useful for typing quick notes to yourself as well as for editing scripts and batch files, web page HTML files, programs, configuration files, and so on.

I use Notepad so often myself that I always install a shortcut batch file named `n.bat` on my computers, so I don't have to type out `notepad` all the time; I can just type the letter `n`. You learn how to do this in Chapter 30, "Command-Line and Automation Tools," under "Batch File Tips."

Program name—notepad (works with Windows Logo+R, in the taskbar's search box or at the command prompt).

What you might not have known—If you turn off Word Wrap in the Format menu, you can use the Ctrl+G keyboard shortcut to jump to a specific line in the file, by number. This shortcut is really handy when you're editing programs or Windows Script Host scripts. Error messages usually tell you on which line the error occurred. Ctrl+G takes you right to the broken program statement.

Paint

Paint was revamped between Windows XP and Windows 7 and now sports a ribbon interface (see Figure 8.2). It's still a bitmap graphics tool, meaning that you can't grab and resize various elements in your drawing. Once they're placed on the screen, they stay where they are. However, Paint is still a useful tool for creating simple graphics and for touching up graphics made in other programs.

If you're new to ribbon interfaces, using this tool can take some getting used to. The trick is to notice the small downward arrows in each of the sections of the ribbon. They lead to more detailed choices. The other tricky thing is that, on the Home menu, usually Color 1 and Color 2 mean "foreground" and "background"—the colors laid down by drawing and erasing, respectively. When you're drawing shapes, Color 1 is used for the shape's edges, and Color 2 is used to fill in the middle of the shape. To control whether shapes have an outside line or a fill color, use the unlabeled icons at the right side of the Shapes ribbon section.

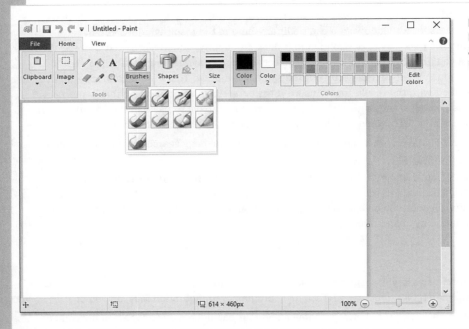

Figure 8.2
Paint comes with a snazzy ribbon interface.

You can set the image's desired dimensions using the familiar File, Properties menu item.

The new Paint can read and write files in Windows Bitmap (BMP), JPEG, GIF, TIFF, and PNG formats. If you don't know which to use, here's a short description of each format, along with some pros and cons:

- **BMP**—The Windows Bitmap format stores images with all details preserved. The three BMP formats are 16 Color, 256 Color, and 24-bit color. The 16 and 256 Color formats can record only that many distinct colors in the whole image. If an image has a larger variety of colors, Windows degrades the image. (You may see *dithering*, which looks like someone sprinkled salt or pepper on the image, or *posterizing*, where large swaths of the image are the same color—a sort of paint-by-numbers effect.)

- **TIFF**—TIFF format preserves all colors, and the saved file size can be much smaller than BMP due to lossless compression. The downside of TIFF is that not every application can display it. It's not used to store images for web pages but is great for pasting into Word documents or storing scanned images.

- **GIF**—This format uses lossless compression and is widely supported by web browsers and email clients. It's suitable mostly for drawings in color or black-and-white where there are relatively few distinct colors.

- **PNG**—This format is similar to GIF and is used primarily for web page and app graphics, when it's used at all. It was created to circumvent a patent on software used to create the GIF format (which is a rather funny, sad story, but I don't have room to digress). GIF is still the most widely used format for drawings and small graphics.

- **JPEG** (JPG)—JPEG is a highly compressed, lossy format that's appropriate only for photographic images of natural (real-world) scenes. *Lossy* means that the image degrades with each edit-and-save iteration. JPEG does a terrific job of reducing the amount of storage needed to hold pictures by eliminating fine detail that our brains tend to overlook, so to speak (for example, fine gradations in color in a section of an image where brightness and darkness are changing rapidly). It's a very poor format for drawings and text because the JPG format blurs sharp edges.

If you're editing and saving photographs, use JPG to get smaller file sizes. If you're editing a graphic to put on a web page, try GIF, and try PNG or JPEG if you end up with bad color dithering. If you're storing drawings or computer images that you'll later put into documents, use TIFF rather than BMP.

(By the way, Microsoft at some point in the future will stop installing Paint by default. You'll be able to download it from the Windows Store, though. Microsoft appears to be nudging us to a new Modern app called Paint 3D,which is installed along with Windows 10. Paint3D lets you manipulate drawing objects in 3D but has a much steeper learning curve.)

Program name—mspaint (works with Windows Logo+R, in the taskbar's search box or at the command prompt).

What you might not have known—When you drag or paste a selected part of a picture and drop it, you'll see that the background pixels in the selection get copied, too. On the Home panel, if you check Transparent Background under Select, when you paste or drop a selection on another part of the screen, Paint drops only those copied or dragged pixels that are *not* the background color (Color 2). If you set Color 2 before you paste, you'll be able to control which color gets ignored in the pasting process.

Snipping Tool

The Snipping Tool lets you grab a portion of the computer screen and paste it into a document. It's useful for taking notes while you're working with your computer, especially to extract information from websites that don't let you easily select text or graphics from the displayed pages. You can simply pick up the interesting part of the page and paste it into a Word or WordPad document as an image. It's also helpful if you create how-to manuals that involve computer programs. Note that this tool saves bitmap images, not editable or pasteable text, when you use it to snip text off the screen. Think of it as a type of scanner.

To use it, start the Snipping Tool and select the down arrow next to New. Then, before you select the portion of the screen you want to capture, choose the shape you'd like to snip. Here are your options:

- **Free-form**—Use the cursor to encircle the exact portion of the screen that you want.

- **Rectangular**—Drag the cursor to select a rectangular portion of the screen.

- **Window**—Click the cursor in an open window to capture the entire window (including its frame and menu).

- **Full-screen**—Use this to capture the entire screen. Using this option is like pressing Shift+PrintScrn, but you get to draw on the captured image before you save it.

When you've selected the snipping region, the Snipping Tool window expands to show the captured image. You can draw on it with the Pen Tool, shade sections with the Highlighter Tool, and erase portions with the—you guessed it—Eraser Tool. You can paste whatever the Snipping Tool shows directly into another program, or you can save the result as an image file in GIF, JPEG, PNG, or HTML format. (The HTML format is actually saved with an .mht extension and contains the image as a MIME enclosure. It's very strange.)

Program name—snippingtool (works with Windows Logo+R, in the taskbar's search box or at the command prompt).

Steps Recorder

The Steps Recorder records a movie of your entire computer screen (or screens, if you have more than one monitor) while you perform some task. It saves the recording of what happened on the screen so that you or anyone else can later play it back. The finished product isn't very elegant, but it can be useful if you want to create a tutorial of how to perform a computer task or to document a software bug. What it creates is a slideshow of the steps you take while you're recording—every mouse click, keyboard entry, and window movement is recorded.

To create a recording, start the Steps Recorder and then click Start Record. Perform the task you want to document. You can do the following:

- Click Pause Record if you have to stop to think about things, or if you need to, say, open another window to look up information that doesn't pertain to what you're recording. Close the window, and then click Resume Record.

- If you want the slideshow to explain something on the screen, click Add Comment. Use the mouse to drag a box around a part of the screen that you want to call attention to, and then type a message into the text box. Click OK to continue recording the slideshow.

Click Stop Record when you're finished. Save the recording using the Save menu item. This creates a ZIP file that contains the slideshow in MHTML format. You can send the ZIP file to someone else, who can open it and then open the MHTML file inside it to view the recording. The top of the recording contains links that let you view the recording step by step or view it as a slideshow. The best way to view a Steps Recorder slideshow is to click Pause and then use Next and Previous to step through the recording manually.

Program name—psr (works with Windows Logo+R, in the taskbar's search box, or at the command prompt).

What you might not have known—The Steps Recorder is really useful if you're having a problem with a software program. Record yourself performing the task that's vexing you, review the recording, and if it does a good job of illustrating the problem, send it to a tech support person. This person might be able to tell you whether you're doing something wrong or might see evidence of a bug that needs fixing.

- Each whole stroke of the stylus (or your finger or the mouse) is stored separately and can be selected, moved, or deleted independently.

- To convert handwriting to text, click the Selection tool button. It looks like a loop of rope. Draw completely around the writing you want to convert, and then click Actions, Convert Handwriting to Text.

- File, Save and File, Save As save files in the Journal application's file format. You can save a document as a Journal template, which makes it available as a starting point for future documents.

- File, Export lets you save pages as MHTML or TIF image files.

WordPad

WordPad looks like a stripped-down version of Microsoft Word, complete with a ribbon bar. It's a decent, if *very* basic, word processor that supports any variety of fonts, text coloring, and background shading as well as left, right, and hanging paragraph indents; paragraph alignment; bulleted and numbered lists; image embedding; and generic object embedding.

This tool actually provides a good introduction to ribbon bar applications, because in this rather singular case, it's simple, pretty intuitive, and well organized. About the only flaws are a couple of obscure symbols in the ribbon's Paragraph section. Just hover the mouse over them to see what they do. The program's options are set in the View menu (which is odd because, in Microsoft Office applications, options are set in the File menu; the best advice we can give on that score is to learn to enjoy playing hide-and-seek). You can set tab stops by dragging the mouse in the ruler at the top of the page.

Program name—wordpad (works with Windows Logo+R or in the taskbar's search box). At the command prompt, type **start wordpad**.

What you might not have known—WordPad saves files in formats that are compatible with most other word processing programs: Rich Text Format (.rtf) and Office Open XML (.docx) are both native formats for Microsoft Word. Use either of these formats if you want to trade documents with Office users. WordPad can read documents created by Microsoft Word, too; however, it just might not display all the document's fancy formatting. Tables and page headers and footers, for example, don't show up correctly. And if you edit and save a Word document with WordPad, the undisplayed formatting will be lost permanently. Most Apple programs and almost all Windows publishing programs can read .rtf files, too. OpenDocument Text (.odt) format is compatible with the Apache Open Office productivity suite (www.openoffice.org), a free alternative to Microsoft Office.

XPS Viewer

XPS is Microsoft's universally unpopular response to the universally popular Adobe PDF page description file format. You can print from any application using the Microsoft XPS Document Writer virtual printer, which creates a file that has all the text, graphics, and font information needed to display the "printed" page. The XPS Viewer can then display the file exactly as it would have looked on paper. An XPS Viewer program comes with Windows Vista and later and can be downloaded for Windows XP. Third-party viewers are available for Macintosh OS X, iOS, and Linux.

Windows 10 has built-in PDF creation software (which you will see as the Microsoft Print to PDF printer selection), so the handwriting is on the wall for XPS format.

Program name—xpsrchvw (works with Windows Logo+R, in the taskbar's search box or at the command prompt).

What you might not have known—Microsoft may also have chosen the Edge browser as the xps viewer. If you don't like Edge as a document viewer, and if you want to use the Desktop version of the XPS Reader, you must change a setting. Here's how: Click Start, Settings (gear icon), Apps, Default Apps. Scroll down and click Choose Default Apps By File Type. Scroll down to .oxps, and if it doesn't say XPS Reader next to it, click the icon and select XPS Reader. Scroll down and repeat this for the .xps entry.

Accessibility Tools

Windows can be made more accessible to people with varying hearing, movement, sight, and cognitive abilities. The following is a list of the various accessibility tools:

- **Ease of Access**—In the Settings app, Ease of Access lets you control a large number of settings and features that make Windows more accessible.

- **Ease of Access Center**—In the Control Panel, the Ease of Access Center provides the same settings as Ease of Access and has an additional wizard that helps you select appropriate accessibility aids.

- **Magnifier**—The Magnifier accessory lets you see an enlarged version of a portion of the screen.

- **Narrator**—The Narrator uses a synthesized voice to speak aloud the contents of the screen. Narrator's Scan Mode feature provides keyboard shortcuts to help you navigate to relevant content more quickly.

- **Speech Recognition**—Speech Recognition lets you use a computer without touching it. This topic is covered in Chapter 13, "More Windows 10 Media Tools."

- **On-Screen Keyboard**—The On-Screen Keyboard lets you type by clicking on the screen with a mouse, or if you have a touch-sensitive screen by touching the screen. The On-Screen Keyboard is similar to the Touch Keyboard, which is discussed in Chapter 4, "Using the Windows 10 Interface," but it uses much smaller on-screen buttons for the keys. Its layout exactly matches a standard PC keyboard.

- **Welcome (logon) screen**—The dashed-circle icon in the lower-right corner of the Welcome screen opens a panel that lets you turn on various accessibility settings. The Narrator starts reading the contents of this panel aloud when you open it. The Welcome screen is discussed in Chapter 3, "Your First Hour with Windows 10."

The last three tools are discussed in other chapters. The remaining tools are described in the following sections.

Ease of Access (in Settings)

In Windows 10, you can adjust all accessibility settings in the Settings app. The settings are described by category.

There are several ways to open the Ease of Access settings page:

- Open the Start menu and select Settings (the gear icon), Ease of Access.

- Press Windows Logo+U (hold down the Windows Logo key, and press U) to go right to the Ease of Access app.

- In the taskbar or Start menu search box, type the word **ease** and then select Other Ease of Access Settings.

- If you have enabled the Cortana voice search mechanism, you can just say, "Hey, Cortana, open Ease of Access."

 tip

If you're just starting to use the Windows accessibility aids, you might find it easier to start with the Ease of Access Center in the Control Panel, which is described in the next section, because it has a more task-oriented approach to discovering the right settings. When you know which adjustments you find useful, you can use the Ease of Access Settings page to turn them on and off.

The Ease of Access app lists several accessibility categories in the left pane. You can select any of the following categories:

- **Narrator**—Enables the Narrator tool, which reads the screen aloud.

- **Magnifier**—Enlarges a selected portion of the screen for better visibility.

- **Color & High Contrast**—Lets you select a visual theme that makes text more readable.

- **Closed Captioning**—Lets you change the color and other attributes of text displayed over TV shows and other CC-enabled media.

- **Keyboard**—Has options to make the keyboard easier to use if you have limited mobility.

- **Mouse**—Has settings to make the mouse pointer and cursor more visible.

- **Other Options**—Let you reduce the visual distraction of animated menus and background images. Touch Feedback gives enhanced visual feedback of touchscreen contacts.

Ease of Access Center (in Control Panel)

The Ease of Access Center in the Control Panel controls the same accessibility settings and tools as the Ease of Access page in the Settings app, but it has a more task-oriented approach to categorizing them. It also has a wizard tool that guides you through the process of making appropriate Accessibility settings.

To open the Ease of Access Center, type **ease** into the taskbar's search box, and then select Ease of Access Center.

To run the settings wizard, select Get Recommendations to Make Your Computer Easier to Use. This wizard lets you describe your limitations in eyesight, hearing, and so on. Windows adjusts itself in response. Alternatively, under Explore All Settings, you can select specific accessibility settings from a long list of tasks, such as the following:

tip

You can use the Make Touch and Tablets Easier to Use link to assign an accessibility tool to the Windows Logo+Volume Up keyboard shortcut.

- Make the computer easier to see

- Make the mouse easier to use

- Make the keyboard easier to use

- Use text or visual alternatives for sounds

- Make it easier to focus on tasks

- Make touch and tablets easier to use

Magnifier

The Magnifier tool enlarges the contents of the Windows screen, so you see an enlarged version of a small portion of it. You can move the display around to see the whole screen, a bit at a time.

To open the Magnifier, use the Settings Ease of Access app described in the previous sections and click the Turn On Magnifier switch to On, or just press the Windows Logo+= key combination. (Press the Windows logo key and the = key at the same time.)

The Magnifier's control box enables you to adjust the way the tool works. If you see just a magnifying glass icon (somewhere) on the screen, click it to restore the control box and then make one of the following choices:

- Click the + or – icon to zoom in or out, respectively.

- Click Views to change how the Magnifier works.

    - In the Full-Screen view, the screen is expanded, and the zoomed portion moves to follow the mouse pointer.

    - In the Lens view, you drag a box around, and it shows a zoomed view of what's underneath it.

    - In Docked view, the upper part of the screen shows a magnified version of the lower part of the screen. The zoomed part follows the mouse pointer.

- Click the gear-shaped icon to change Magnifier's settings. You can enable Color Inversion to make the magnified portion have higher contrast.

Whenever Magnifier is in operation, you can use the following hot keys:

- Windows Logo+= and Windows Logo++ (that is, the Windows logo key and either + or =) increases the magnification.

- Windows Logo+– (Windows logo key and –) decreases the magnification.

- Ctrl+Alt+Space temporarily zooms out so that you can see what part of the full screen you're looking at.

- Other shortcuts let you switch the view mode. The Views menu lists these.

Program name—magnify (works with Windows Logo+R; in the Start menu or at the command prompt, type `magnify`).

Narrator

Narrator is a screen reader application that describes the contents of the Windows screen in a synthesized voice. To activate it, use the Windows Logo+Enter keyboard shortcut, or on tablet devices, Windows Logo+the Volume Up button. Alternatively, search the Start menu for `narrator` and select it from the Apps list.

By default, Narrator reads the contents of any window when you activate it—that is, when it becomes the topmost window. It will also describe what's under the mouse pointer as you move it. As Narrator reads menus and dialog box controls, the input focus follows along so that you can press the spacebar to trigger the most recently described pushbutton, check box, or radio button, or you can type to enter text into the most recently described input field.

Be forewarned, though, that check boxes work as toggles. If you trigger a check box that's already checked, you will *uncheck* it. So, for example, if you press spacebar after Narrator says, "Always read this section aloud," and the box was already checked, you will turn off the option. Just press the spacebar again to toggle it back on.

When Narrator is active, its icon appears in the Desktop's taskbar. You can click that icon to open the Narrator's Settings window, where you can change the voice and navigation options as well as fine-tune what sorts of events Windows will describe, from pop-up warnings to keystrokes. Turn off Narrator by clicking Exit in the Narrator's Settings window.

Also, when Narrator is active, you can press the Caps Lock+Spacebar shortcut (that is, hold down Caps Lock and press the Spacebar) to enable Scan Mode. The Narrator will say "scan." With Scan Mode active, a long list of keyboard shortcuts becomes available to move quickly around any screen, web page, or document. (This also leaves the Caps Lock function active; tap Caps Lock by itself to turn off Caps Lock.) Some of the Scan Mode shortcuts include the following:

Up Arrow	Move to the previous line of text on the page
Down Arrow	Move to the next line of text on the page
Spacebar	Activate the current button or check box
p	Move to the next paragraph
Shift+P	Move to the previous paragraph
H	Move to the next heading

To see the whole list, open the Narrator settings page, and then scroll down and click Get More Info About Scan Mode.

Press Caps Lock+Spacebar again to turn Scan Mode off. This probably activated Caps Lock again, so you may have to tap Caps Lock again to turn it back off. This gets annoying.

The Narrator Settings page also includes a button to download accessory software for Braille output devices.

Program name—Narrator (Windows Logo+Enter; works with Windows Logo+R, in taskbar's search box, or at the command prompt).

9

CONFIGURING WINDOWS 10

Configuring Windows 10 with Control Panel

Control Panel is a folder that leads to a large number of dialog boxes and pages of settings that each control some aspect of Windows: hardware, system services, applications, fonts, printers, multimedia, and much more. On a default Windows 10 setup, there are about 45 separate dialogs or pages, but depending on your system configuration, even more could be available.

Opening a Control Panel item displays a window or dialog box containing various properties related to that area of Windows. For example, launching the Programs and Features icon enables you to uninstall third-party applications and to activate or deactivate Windows 10 components.

 note

The Windows 10 Settings panel covers many of the more commonly used Windows settings and is over time growing to cover more, but Control Panel is still where most of the nitty-gritty settings are managed.

Touring the Control Panel Window

You have two main ways to launch Control Panel:

- In the taskbar's Search box, type **control**, and then click Control Panel in the search results.

- Press Windows Logo+R to open the Run dialog box, type **control**, and then press Enter.

By default, Windows 10 displays the Control Panel in Category view, shown in Figure 9.1, which displays icons for eight different categories (System and Security, Network and Internet, and so on), as well as one or more links to common tasks under each category icon.

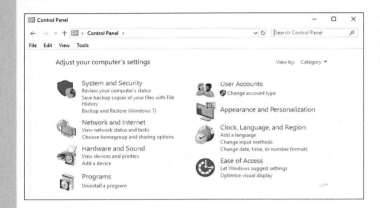

Figure 9.1
Control Panel's default home page Category view displays icons for eight categories.

Category view is designed to help novice users, but even power users quickly get used to its layout. There is a lot of duplication, with some control items listed several times with different wording, to make it more likely that you'll find what you're looking for by poking around, or even easier, using the search box. However, if you feel that the category view just delays you unnecessarily, you can switch to the classic Icon view by selecting Small Icons in the View By list, which opens the All Control Panel Items window, as shown in Figure 9.2.

 tip

If you prefer the All Control Panel Items window but you find that the Small Icons view makes the icons too small, you can make it a tad easier to manage by switching to the Large Icons view. This view still enables you to see every icon if you enlarge or maximize the Control Panel window. In the View By list, click Large Icons.

Figure 9.2
Switch Control Panel to the Small Icons view to see all the icons in one window.

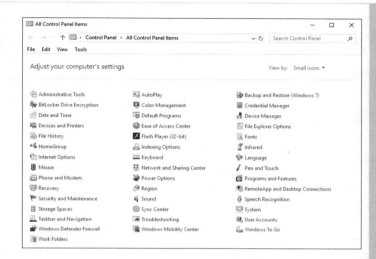

Reviewing the Control Panel Icons

To help you familiarize yourself with what's available in Control Panel, this section offers summary descriptions of the Control Panel icons found in a standard Windows 10 installation when using either the Large or the Small Icons view. Note that your system might have extra icons, depending on your computer's hardware, its configuration, and the programs you have installed.

- **Administrative Tools**—Displays a window with more icons, each of which enables you to administer a particular aspect of Windows 10:

  - **Component Services**—Displays the Component Services window, which you can use to investigate Component Object Model (COM) and Distributed COM (DCOM) applications and services.

  - **Computer Management**—Enables you to manage a local or remote computer. You can examine hidden and visible shared folders, set group policies, access Device Manager, manage hard disks, and much more.

  - **Defragment and Optimize Drives**—Enables you to defragment your hard drives and set a defragmentation schedule. See "Defragmenting Your Hard Disk" in Chapter 25, "Managing Hard Disks and Storage Spaces."

  - **Disk Cleanup**—Enables you to remove old and unneeded files from your system. See "Deleting Unnecessary Files" in Chapter 25 for more details on this tool.

  - **Event Viewer**—Enables you to examine Windows 10's list of *events*, which are unusual or noteworthy occurrences on your system, such as a service that doesn't start, the installation of a device, or an application error. See "Event Viewer" in Chapter 22, "Troubleshooting Your Network."

- **iSCSI Initiator**—Displays the iSCSI Initiator property sheet, which enables you to manage connections to iSCSI devices such as tape drives and disk arrays.

- **Local Security Policy**—Displays the Local Security Settings snap-in, which enables you to set up security policies on your system. See "Policing Windows 10 with Group Policies," in Chapter 23.

- **ODBC Data Sources**—Enables you to create and work with *data source names*, which are connection strings that you use to connect to local or remote databases. This tool comes in 32-bit and 64-bit versions.

- **Performance Monitor**—Runs the Performance Monitor, which enables you to monitor various aspects of your system. See "Using the Performance Monitor," later in this chapter.

- **Print Management**—Displays the Print Management console, which enables you to manage, share, and deploy printers and print servers.

- **Recovery Drive**—Enables you to create a recovery drive to get your PC back on its feet in the event of a crash. In Chapter 32, "Protecting Your Data from Loss and Theft," see the "Creating a Recovery Drive" section.

- **Resource Monitor**—Enables you to view real-time data related to your computer's CPU, memory, hard disk usage, and networking.

- **Services**—Displays a list of the system services available with Windows 10. System services are background routines that enable the system to perform tasks such as network logon, disk management, Plug and Play, Internet connection sharing, and much more. You can pause, stop, and start services, as well as configure how services load at startup.

- **System Configuration**—Opens the System Configuration utility. In Chapter 2, "Installing or Upgrading to Windows 10," see the "Using the System Configuration Utility to Modify the BCD" section, and in Chapter 26, "Troubleshooting and Repairing Problems," see the "Disabling Startup Services" section.

- **System Information**—Displays a summary of your computer's hardware and software resources.

- **Task Scheduler**—Runs the Task Scheduler console, which enables you to run programs or scripts on a schedule.

- **Windows Defender Firewall with Advanced Security**—Enables you to control every aspect of Windows 10's bidirectional firewall. See "Configuring Windows Firewall" in Chapter 33, "Protecting Your Network from Hackers and Snoops."

- **Windows Memory Diagnostic**—Runs the Windows Memory Diagnostics Tool, which checks your computer's memory chips for problems. See "Running the Memory Diagnostics Tool" in Chapter 26.

- **AutoPlay**—Opens the AutoPlay window, which enables you to configure AutoPlay defaults for various media.

- **Backup and Restore (Windows 7)**—Operates as a front end for the Windows 7 version of the Backup utility.

- **BitLocker Drive Encryption**—Turns on and configures BitLocker, which encrypts your Windows 10 system drive to protect it from unauthorized viewing. In Chapter 32, "Protecting Your Data from Loss and Theft," see "Encrypting a Disk with BitLocker."

- **Color Management**—Enables you to configure the colors of your monitor and printer to optimize color output.

- **Credential Manager**—This new tool enables you to store and work with usernames and passwords for servers, websites, network shares, and other secure resources.

- **Date and Time**—Enables you to set the current date and time, select your time zone, and set up an Internet time server to synchronize your system time. You can also display extra clocks to monitor other time zones.

- **Default Programs**—Displays the Default Programs window, which enables you to change the programs associated with Windows 10's file types.

- **Device Manager**—Launches Device Manager, which enables you to view and work with your system devices and their drivers. See "Troubleshooting Device Problems" in Chapter 26 for more information.

- **Devices and Printers**—Displays a list of the major devices connected to your computer.

- **Ease of Access Center**—Enables you to customize input (the keyboard and mouse) and output (sound and display for users with special mobility, hearing, or vision requirements).

- **File Explorer Options**—Enables you to customize the display of Windows 10's folders, set up whether Windows 10 uses single- or double-clicking, work with file types, and configure offline files. (This control panel icon was called "Folder Options" in earlier versions of Windows.)

- **File History**—Enables you to save previous versions of your personal files to an external hard drive or network share. See "Activating File History" in Chapter 32 for more details on this feature.

- **Flash Player**—Displays the Flash Player Settings Manager, which enables you to customize and configure Windows 10's built-in Flash player.

- **Fonts**—Displays the Fonts folder, from which you can view, install, and remove fonts.

- **HomeGroup**—Enables you to join a homegroup, which is Windows 10's user-account-free networking technology. In Chapter 18, "Creating a Windows Network," see "Setting Up a Homegroup."

- **Indexing Options**—Enables you to configure the index used by Windows 10's search engine.

- **Infrared**—In the unlikely event your device has infrared data (IrDA) hardware, this item lets you enable or disable it. Bluetooth and WiFi have largely supplanted IrDA, but it's still used by some DSLR cameras.

- **Internet Options**—Displays a large collection of settings for modifying Internet properties (how you connect, the Internet Explorer interface, and so on).

- **Keyboard**—Enables you to customize your keyboard, work with keyboard languages, and change the keyboard driver.

- **Language**—Enables you to add languages to Windows 10.

- **Mouse**—Enables you to set various mouse options and install a different mouse device driver.

- **Network and Sharing Center**—Displays general information about your network connections and sharing settings. See "The Network and Sharing Center" in Chapter 22.

- **Pen and Touch**—Displays the Pen and Input Devices dialog box, which enables you to configure your tablet PC's touch gestures and digital pen.

- **Phone and Modem**—Enables you to configure telephone dialing rules and to install and configure modems.

- **Power Options**—Enables you to configure power management properties for powering down system components (such as the monitor and hard drive), defining low-power alarms for note-book batteries, enabling sleep and hibernation modes, and configuring notebook power buttons.

- **Programs and Features**—Enables you to install and uninstall applications, add and remove Windows 10 components, and view installed updates.

- **Recovery**—Enables you to recover your system by restoring it to an earlier working configuration.

- **Region**—Enables you to configure international settings for country-dependent items such as numbers, currencies, times, and dates.

- **RemoteApp and Desktop Connections**—Enables you to create and work with remote programs and desktops.

- **Security and Maintenance**—Displays a list of your computer's current security issues and hard-ware and software problems. In earlier versions of Windows, this control panel was named Action Center.

- **Sound**—Enables you to control the system volume; map sounds to specific Windows 10 events (such as closing a program or minimizing a window); and specify settings for audio, voice, and other multimedia devices.

- **Speech Recognition**—Enables you to configure Windows 10's speech recognition feature.

- **Storage Spaces**—Enables you to pool multiple hard drives into a single storage area. In Chapter 25, see "Working with Storage Spaces."

- **Sync Center**—Enables you to set up and maintain synchronization with other devices and with offline files.

- **System**—Displays basic information about your system, including the Windows 10 edition, system rating, processor type, memory size, computer and workgroup names, and whether Windows 10 is activated. Also gives you access to Device Manager and settings related to perfor-mance, startup, System Protection, Remote Assistance and Quick Assist, and Remote Desktop.

- **Tablet PC Settings**—Displays settings for configuring handwriting and other aspects of your tablet PC.

- **Taskbar and Navigation**—Enables you to customize the taskbar. In Chapter 24, see "Customizing the Taskbar for Easier Program and Document Launching" for more information. (This Control Panel icon was called Taskbar in earlier versions of Windows.)

note

You'd think that with more than 40 icons in a default Control Panel, Microsoft wouldn't be in the business of *removing* icons. However, a few have been relegated to the dustbin of Windows history. The following Windows 7 icons are gone from the Windows 10 version of Control Panel:

- Windows PowerShell Modules
- Getting Started
- Location and Other Sensors (moved to Settings)
- Region and Language (replaced by separate icons for Region and for Language)
- Taskbar and Start Menu (replaced by Taskbar and Navigation)
- Windows CardSpace

Here are the Windows 8/8.1 icons removed in Windows 10:

- Family Safety
- Location Settings (now part of Settings)
- Notification Area icons (also moved to Settings)
- Windows Live Language Setting
- Windows Update (also to Settings)

Windows 10 Creators Update removes the following:

- Display and Personalization (both now in Settings)
- Windows Defender

The renamed Windows 10 icons are

- Action Center (renamed as Security and Maintenance)
- Folder Options (renamed as File Explorer Options)
- Taskbar (renamed as Taskbar and Navigation)

For the most part, though, even as the Settings app gains more capabilities, Microsoft seems to be leaving most of the old Control Panel items intact.

- **Troubleshooting**—Displays a collection of tasks related to troubleshooting various aspects of your system.

- **User Accounts**—Enables you to set up and configure user accounts.

- **Windows Defender Firewall**—Enables you to configure Windows Defender Firewall. See "Configuring Windows Firewall" in Chapter 33.

- **Windows Mobility Center**—Displays Windows 10's Mobility Center for notebooks.

- **Windows To Go**—Some editions of Windows support this feature, which lets you make a bootable copy of your Windows installation on a removable USB drive.

- **Work Folders**—Enables you to configure files to make them available on multiple devices.

Understanding Control Panel Files

Many of the Control Panel icons represent Control Panel extension files, which use the .cpl extension. These files reside in the %SystemRoot%\System32 folder. When you open Control Panel, Windows 10 scans the System32 folder looking for CPL files and then displays one or more icons for each one, depending on how many functions the .cpl file provides.

The CPL files offer an alternative method for launching individual Control Panel dialog boxes. The idea is that you run control.exe and specify the name of a CPL file as a parameter. This bypasses the Control Panel folder and opens the icon directly. Here's the syntax:

```
control CPLfile [,option1 [, option2]]
```

- CPLfile—The name of the file that corresponds to the Control Panel icon you want to open. (See Table 9.1, later in this chapter.)

- option1—This option is obsolete and is included only for backward compatibility with batch files and scripts that use Control.exe for opening Control Panel icons.

- option2—The tab number of a multitabbed dialog box. Many Control Panel icons open a dialog box that has two or more tabs. If you know the specific tab you want to work with, you can use the option2 parameter to specify an integer that corresponds to the tab's relative position from the left side of the dialog box. The first (leftmost) tab is 0, the next tab is 1, and so on.

For example, to open Control Panel's System icon with the Hardware tab displayed, run the following command (using the Run command or the Command Prompt accessed by pressing Windows Logo+X):

```
control sysdm.cpl,,2
```

 note

If the dialog box has multiple rows of tabs, count the tabs from left to right and from bottom to top. For example, if the dialog box has two rows of four tabs each, the tabs in the bottom row are numbered 0 to 3 from left to right, and the tabs in the top row are numbered 4 to 7 from left to right.

Also, note that even though you no longer use the option1 parameter, you must still display its comma in the command line.

➡ *To learn how to add Command Prompt (Admin) to the Start Menu's shortcut menu, see "Adding Command Prompt to the Shortcut Menu," **p. 129.***

Table 9.1 lists the various Control Panel icons and the appropriate command line to use as well as the number of tabs (although this number can vary depending on your system configuration). Note, also, that some Control Panel icons—such as Taskbar and Navigation—can't be accessed by running Control.exe.

(If you're really interested in the details of the packaging of control panel items, search msdn.microsoft.com for the phrase "Canonical Names of Control Panel Items.")

Table 9.1   Command Lines for Launching Individual Control Panel Icons

Control Panel Icon	Command	Dialog Box Tabs
Administrative Tools	control admintools	N/A
Date and Time	control timedate.cpl	Two
Ease of Access Center	control access.cpl	N/A
File Explorer Options	control folders	Two
Fonts	control fonts	N/A
Infrared	control irprops.cpl	Three
Internet Options	control inetcpl.cpl	Six
Keyboard	control keyboard	One
Mouse	control mouse	Five
Network Connections	control ncpa.cpl	N/A
Pen and Touch	control tabletpc.cpl	N/A
Phone and Modem	control telephon.cpl	Two
Power Options	control powercfg.cpl	N/A
Printers	control printers	N/A
Programs and Features	control appwiz.cpl	N/A
Region	control intl.cpl	Two
Scanners and Cameras	control scannercamera	N/A
Security and Maintenance	control wscui.cpl	N/A
Sound	control mmsys.cpl	Three
System	control sysdm.cpl	Four
Tablet PC Settings	control tabletpc.cpl	N/A
User Accounts	control nusrmgr.cpl	N/A
Windows Defender Firewall	control firewall.cpl	N/A

Gaining Easier Access to Control Panel

Control Panel is certainly a useful and important piece of the Windows 10 package. It's even more useful if you can get to it easily. In this section, we show you a few methods for gaining quick access to individual icons and the entire folder.

Access to many Control Panel icons is scattered throughout the Windows 10 interface, meaning that you can launch an icon in more than one way. Many of these alternative methods are faster and more direct than using the Control Panel folder. Here's a summary:

- **Administrative Tools**—You can display an icon for these tools on the main Start menu. To learn how, see "Displaying the Administrative Tools on the Start Menu" in Chapter 4, "Using the Windows 10 Interface."

- **Date and Time**—Right-click the clock in the notification area, and then click Adjust Date/Time.

- **Device Manager**—Press Windows Logo+X or right-click the Start button, and then click Device Manager.

- **Event Viewer**—Press Windows Logo+X or right-click the Start button, and then click Event Viewer.

- **Fonts**—In File Explorer, open the `%SystemRoot%\Fonts` folder.

- **Internet Options**—In Internet Explorer, select Tools, Internet Options.

note

If you find your Control Panel folder is bursting at the seams, you can trim it down to size by removing those icons you never use. You can do this in a number of ways in Windows 10, but the easiest is probably via group policies. See "Removing an Icon from Control Panel" in Chapter 23.

- **Network & Internet settings**—Right-click the Network icon in the notification area, and then click Open Network & Internet settings.

- **Power Options**—Click the Power icon in the notification area, and then click Power & Sleep Settings. Alternatively, press Windows Logo+X or right-click the Start button, and then click Power Options.

- **Sound**—Right-click the Volume icon in the notification area, and then click Sounds.

- **System**—Press Windows Logo+X or right-click the Start button, and then click System. Alternatively, in File Explorer, click This PC, click the Computer tab, and then click System Properties.

- **Taskbar and Navigation**—Right-click an empty section of the taskbar, and then click Properties.

- **Windows Mobility Center**—Press Windows Logo+X or right-click the Start button, and then click Mobility Center. Alternatively, right-click the Power (battery) icon in the notification area and then click Windows Mobility Center.

In Windows 10, you can also jump directly to some Control Panel tasks by searching the settings. If you know the task you want to run, use the taskbar's Search box to type a word or short phrase that exemplifies the task. As a demonstration, we typed **font** in the Search box and then selected Settings in the Filters list. (We could also have typed **settings: font** directly into the Search box.) For best results, click the See All link to see all the results. As you can see in Figure 9.3, the search results include items such as Change Font Settings and Preview, Delete, or Show and Hide Fonts. These just happen to be two of the task links that appear when you click the Appearance and Personalization heading in Control Panel's Category view (refer to Figure 9.1).

Figure 9.3
You can use the Settings search pane to search for and link directly to most Control Panel tasks.

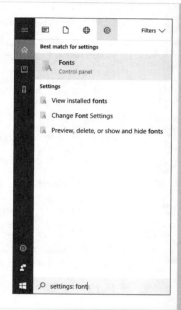

Configuring Windows 10 with the Settings App

As you've seen so far in this chapter, you still tweak many Windows settings using Control Panel (as well as advanced tools such as the Local Group Policy Editor and the Registry Editor), but the customizing tool of choice in the Windows 10 interface is the Settings app (see Figure 9.4). This app is more powerful than the one that shipped with Windows 8/8.1 (which was called PC Settings)

Figure 9.4
In the Windows 10 interface, the Settings app is the go-to customizing tool.

because Microsoft has added many options and features that were previously only in the Control Panel into the Settings app. And over time, Microsoft is adding more and more settings.

In this chapter, we give you an overview of just some of the settings. We discuss many more settings throughout this book, in the context of various topics such as networking, customization, security, and so on.

To get the Settings app running, use any of the following techniques:

- Click Start, and then click Settings (the gear-shaped icon).

- Press Windows Logo+I.

- Click the notification area's Action Center icon, and then click All Settings.

- In File Explorer, click This PC, click the Computer tab, and then click Open Settings.

The main Settings screen displays several icons, each of which represents a different customization category. Here's a summary:

- **System**—Configure the display resolution, customize notifications, toggle tablet mode, set the sleep options, set storage locations, and get info about your PC.

- **Devices**—View a list of your PC's connected devices, configure and connect Bluetooth devices, work with printers and scanners, configure the mouse and virtual keyboard, and configure AutoPlay.

- **Phone**—Link your Android phone or iPhone to Windows 10, which then enables you to start a task on one device and then continue on the other.

- **Network & Internet**—See a list of wireless devices connected to your PC, put your PC into Airplane mode (see Chapter 36, "Wireless Networking"), view your network data usage, and more.

- **Personalization**—Customize the Windows 10 desktop background, colors, lock screen, themes, and Start menu settings.

- **Apps**—Manage your installed Modern and desktop apps, set your default apps, work with offline maps, manage apps that open websites, and configure app video playback.

- **Accounts**—Work with your user account—for example, giving your account a new password (see "Changing a Password," later in this chapter), and setting up a picture password (see "Creating a Picture Password," later in this chapter). You also use this section to add other user accounts to your PC and to configure how Windows 10 syncs your data across your other devices.

- **Time & Language**—See and change the data and time, set the time zone, specify a date and time format, set your region, add languages, and configure your microphone and text-to-speech options.

- **Gaming**—Configure various gaming-related features, such as Game bar, game recording, and Game Mode.

- **Ease of Access**—Adjust the Windows 10 accessibility settings.

- **Cortana**—Configure Cortana's settings and permissions.

- **Privacy**—Set your Windows 10 privacy options, including toggling app access to your location, camera, microphone, contacts, and calendar.

- **Update & Security**—Check for new updates (see Chapter 27, "Managing Your Software"). You can also configure some Windows Defender settings (see Chapter 31, "Protecting Windows from Viruses and Spyware") and access the Reset This PC, Go Back to an Earlier Build, and Advanced Startup options (see Chapter 26, "Troubleshooting and Repairing Problems").

 tip

You don't have to spend time digging through all these categories. It's often far easier to just type a word related to the thing you want to change into the Find a Setting search box near the top left of the window.

When you navigate to a section of the Settings app, click the Back button in the upper-left corner to return to the previous screen. (If you're in tablet mode, click the Back button that appears in the taskbar.)

Changing Your User Account Picture

When you install Windows 10, the setup program takes you through several tasks, including choosing a username and password. However, it doesn't ask you to select a picture to go along with your user account. Instead, Windows 10 just supplies your account with a generic illustration. (If you're running Windows 10 under a Microsoft account, your Windows 10 user picture is whatever image your Microsoft account uses.) This picture appears in the top-left corner of the Start menu, the sign-in screen, and the Your Account section of the Settings app. So rather than using the default illustration, you might prefer to use a photo or other artwork. In that case, you can configure your user account to use another picture, which can either be an existing image or a new shot taken with your webcam.

For an existing image, you can use any picture you want, if it's in one of the four image file types that Windows 10 supports: BMP, JPEG, GIF, or PNG. Here are the steps to follow:

note

If you don't have the Settings app open, you can head directly to the Accounts screen from the Start menu by clicking your user account on the Start menu and then clicking Change Account Settings.

1. In the Settings app, click Accounts.

2. Select Your Info, if it's not already selected.

3. Under Create Your Picture, click Browse for One. The Open dialog box appears.

4. Open the folder that contains the image you want to use.

5. Click the image.

6. Click Choose Picture. Windows 10 applies the new picture to your user account.

Alternatively, if your computer comes with a webcam or you have a similar camera attached to your PC, you can use the camera to take your account picture. Follow these steps:

1. In the Settings app, click Accounts.

2. Select Your Info, if it's not already selected.

3. Click Camera to open the Camera app. If prompted to let Windows Camera access your location, click Yes or No as desired.

4. Compose your shot, and then click the screen to take the picture.

5. Click and drag the account picture box to set the image area, and then click Done. Alternatively, if you're not happy with the result, click Cancel to try again.

If you prefer to use a short video (up to 5 seconds) instead:

1. Follow steps 1–3, and then click the Video Mode button to switch to Video mode.

2. Click the screen to begin recording.

3. Click the screen again when the recording is complete.

4. Click OK to set the video as your account picture.

If you are using a Microsoft account, your selected picture (or video) will automatically be used on any device on which you use your account.

 tip

If you change your account picture again, the Your Account tab displays a thumbnail of your old picture, so you can revert to the previous image just by clicking it. If you change your account picture frequently, the tab maintains thumbnails of your last two account pictures. To control these thumbnails individually, use File Explorer to navigate to the following folder:

```
%UserProfile%\AppData\
Roaming\Microsoft\Windows\
AccountPictures
```

Changing a Password

Assigning a password to each user account is a necessary practice because otherwise someone who sits down at the PC can sign in using an unprotected account—and worse, can then gain access to any websites and online accounts for which there are stored passwords. However, it's not enough to just use any old password. You can improve the security of Windows by making each password robust enough that it's impossible to guess and is impervious to software programs designed to try different password combinations. Such a password is called a *strong* password. Ideally, you should build a password that provides maximum protection while still being easy to remember.

Lots of books will suggest absurdly fancy password schemes (we've written some of those books ourselves), but you really need to know only three things to create strong-like-a-bull passwords:

- **Use passwords that are at least eight characters long**—Shorter passwords are susceptible to programs that just try every letter combination. You can combine the 26 letters of the alphabet into about 12 million 5-letter word combinations, which is no big deal for a fast program. If you bump things up to 8-letter passwords, however, the total number of combinations rises to 200 *billion*, which would take even the fastest computer quite a while. If you use 12-letter passwords—as many experts recommend—the number of combinations goes beyond mind-boggling: 90 *quadrillion*, or 90,000 trillion!

- **Mix up your character types**—The secret to a strong password is to include characters from the following categories: lowercase letters, uppercase letters, punctuation marks, numbers, and symbols. If you include at least one character from three (or, even better, all five) of these categories, you're well on your way to a strong password.

- **Don't be too obvious**—Because forgetting a password is inconvenient, many people use meaningful words or numbers so that their passwords will be easier to remember. Unfortunately, this means that they often use extremely obvious things such as their name, the name of a family member or colleague, their birth dates, their Social Security numbers, or even their usernames. Being this obvious is just asking for trouble. Adding 123 or ! to the end of the password doesn't help much either. Password cracking programs try those.

Whether you want to assign a password to another user account or change an existing password to one that's stronger or easier to remember, you can use the Settings app to change an existing password.

First, here are the steps to follow to change the password of a Microsoft account, using the Windows 10 settings app. (You can change it using a web browser at https://microsoft.com/account/ as well.)

1. In the Settings app, click the Accounts icon and then click Sign-In Options.

2. Under the Password heading, click Change. Settings asks you to enter your current password.

3. Type your existing account password, and then click Sign In. The Change Your Password screen appears, as shown in Figure 9.5.

4. Use the Old Password text box to type your old password.

tip
How will you know whether the password you've come up with fits the definition of *strong*? One way to find out is to submit the password to an online password complexity checker. (If you're the least bit paranoid about these things, consider submitting a password that's only similar to the one you want to use.) You can try https://password.kaspersky.com. A Google search on "password complexity checker" leads to many others.

Figure 9.5
Use the Change Your Password screen to update the password for your main Windows user account.

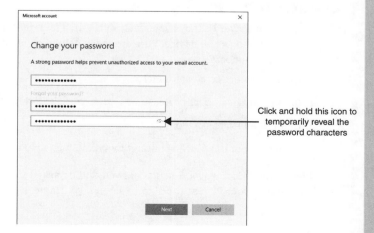

Click and hold this icon to temporarily reveal the password characters

5. Use the Create Password and Reenter Password text boxes to type and then retype the new password. If you're not sure whether you typed a password correctly (and you're sure no one can see your screen), click and hold the Display Characters icon (pointed out in Figure 9.5) to temporarily display the password.

6. Click Next.

7. Click Finish. Windows 10 updates the user account password.

Your new Microsoft account password will now work on all devices on which you use this account, as long as they have Internet connectivity. (If you sign on to another device with this account when it can't reach the Internet, it will still need the old password.)

Here are the steps to follow to add or change the password on a local or domain (corporate) Windows 10 user account:

1. Sign in as the user you want to work with.

2. In the Settings app, click the Accounts icon and then click Sign-In Options.

3. Under the Password heading, click Change to display the Change Your Password screen. If the account has no password, click Add instead and skip to step 5.

4. In the Current Password text box, type the old password and then click Next.

5. In the New Password and Reenter Password text boxes, type and then retype the new password.

6. Type a password hint. Make the hint useful enough to jog your (or the user's) memory but vague enough that it doesn't make the password easy to guess.

7. Click Next.

8. Click Finish. Windows 10 updates the local user account password.

If you are using a local account, this password change affects only this one device. If you are using a domain (corporate) account, the password change is good for all computers in the domain.

Creating a PIN Sign-In

If typing a password annoys you, you can set up a four-digit numeric PIN as a quick way to sign on to your Windows 10 device. PINs are really helpful on tablets and phones, where typing a text password is cumbersome.

Follow these steps to create a PIN:

1. In the Settings app, click Accounts and then click Sign-In Options.

2. Under the PIN, click Add.

3. Type in a four-digit PIN, confirm it by typing it again, and then click OK.

Now, at the Windows sign-in screen, you will be asked to enter your PIN rather than a password. If you forget your PIN, at the sign-in screen, you can click Sign-In Options to select another method of authenticating yourself: password, picture, or fingerprint, whichever methods(s) you have set up.

Setting a PIN only affects the device on which you set it. It doesn't automatically follow your Microsoft account.

Creating a Picture Password

As you learned in the "Changing a Password" section, if you're serious about your system's security, you should have configured your Windows 10 user account with a strong password. This means a password that is at least eight characters long and uses at least one character from at least three of the following five sets: lowercase letters, uppercase letters, punctuation marks, numbers, and symbols. However, the stronger the password you use, the more cumbersome it is to enter using a touch keyboard.

If you find that it's taking you an inordinate amount of time to sign in to Windows 10 using, for example, your tablet's touch keyboard, you can switch to a picture password instead. In this case, your "password" is a series of three gestures—any combination of a tap, a straight line, and a circle—that you apply to a photo. Windows 10 displays the photo at startup, and you repeat your gestures, in order, to sign in to Windows.

However, in the same way that you shouldn't choose a regular account password that is extremely obvious (such as the word *password* or your username), you should take care to avoid creating an obvious picture password. For example, if you're using a photo showing three faces, an obvious picture password would be a tap on each face. A good picture password not only uses all three available gestures, but also uses them in ways that aren't obvious.

Follow these steps to create a picture password on your Windows 10 tablet:

 caution

The biggest drawback to using a picture password is that it's possible for a malicious user to view and possibly even record your gestures using a camera. Unlike a regular text password where the characters appear as dots to prevent someone from seeing them, your gestures have no such protection.

1. In the Settings app, click Accounts and then click Sign-In Options.

2. Under the Picture Password heading, click Add. Windows 10 prompts you for your account password.

3. Type your password, and then tap OK. The Welcome to Picture Password screen appears.

4. Tap Choose Picture. The Open dialog box appears.

5. Select the picture you want to use, and then tap Open. The How's This Look? screen appears.

6. Drag the picture so that the image is positioned where you prefer.

7. Tap Use This Picture. The Set Up Your Gestures screen appears.

8. Use your finger or a stylus to draw three gestures. As you complete each gesture, Windows 10 replays it briefly on the screen, as shown in Figure 9.6.

Figure 9.6
After you draw each gesture, Windows 10 replays the gesture on the screen.

9. Repeat the gestures to confirm. After successfully repeating the gestures, the screen will say "Congratulations!"

10. Tap Finish. The next time you sign in to Windows 10, you'll be prompted to enter your picture password gestures.

A picture password affects only the device on which you set it up.

To ensure you've memorized your picture password, you should practice signing out from your account and then signing back in using the picture password a few times.

If you forget the gestures in your picture password, tap Switch to Password in the sign-in screen to sign in with your regular password. To get a reminder of your picture password gestures, open the Settings app, select Accounts, select Sign-In Options, tap Change under Picture Password, type your user account password, and tap OK. In the Change Your Picture Password screen, tap Replay and then tap the picture to see each gesture.

Creating a Fingerprint Sign-In

If your PC comes with a built-in fingerprint reader, or you have an external reader attached to your PC, you can teach Windows your fingerprint and use it to sign in. Since your fingerprint is unique, this ensures that only you can access your PC. Also, if you are in a public place, you do not have to enter a password or use picture password sign-in gestures that could be observed by a nearby snoop.

Follow these steps to set up a fingerprint sign-in:

1. In the Settings app, click Accounts and then click Sign-In Options.

2. If you don't yet have a PIN, click Add under the PIN heading and follow the prompts to assign a PIN to your account.

3. Under the Fingerprint heading, click Set Up. Windows 10 prompts you for your account PIN. If you don't see a Fingerprint heading, Windows doesn't see your fingerprint ID hardware.

4. Type your PIN. The Windows Hello Setup dialog box appears.

5. Click Get Started. Windows Hello prompts you to scan your fingerprint.

6. Swipe your finger across your PC's fingerprint reader.

7. Repeat the swipe until the scan is complete.

8. Click Close.

Customizing Notifications and Quick Actions

An app notification is a message that appears in the upper-right corner of the screen when an application has information to impart. This could be a new text message or email or a message letting you know some operation has completed.

App notifications can be useful if you want to know what's going on in another app without having to switch to that app. However, app notifications can also distract you from your current work by focusing your attention elsewhere. That is, not only do you take your eye off your current task to view the notification, but the notification message itself might cause you to begin thinking about the content of the message.

If you find that a certain app is particularly distracting (either in its frequency or its content), you can tell Windows 10 to no longer display notifications for that app. Similarly, you might prefer to turn off all app notifications for a while if you don't want to be disturbed.

Finally, you can customize the Quick Actions, which are the "Speed Dial" icons located at the bottom of the Notifications pane that appears when you click the Action Center icon at the right end of the taskbar (as indicated in Figure 9.7), or on a touch screen, swipe in from the right edge of the screen.

(To learn how to choose which icons appear in the taskbar and to control the notification area's system icons, which is a separate topic, see "Taking Control of the Notification Area" in Chapter 24.)

Follow these steps to customize notifications and Quick Actions:

1. In the Settings app, click System and then click Notifications & Actions. The Notifications & Actions settings appear, as shown in Figure 9.7.

2. Use the box under Quick Actions to select and arrange the items you want to have on your Quick Actions panel. Click Add or Remove Quick Actions to change which buttons appear. Drag and drop the buttons to rearrange them to your preference.

3. Under Notifications, if you don't want to see notifications, click Get Notifications from Apps and Other Senders to Off.

4. To prevent a particular app from showing notifications, scroll down to Get Notifications from These Senders, and set the app's switch to Off.

5. If you only want to prevent a particular app from displaying a banner, but still leaving the app's notifications in the Notifications pane, click the app's name and then set the Show Notification Banners switch to Off.

6. Repeat steps 4 and 5 for each app that you want to customize.

Figure 9.7
Use the Notifications & Actions settings to customize app notifications.

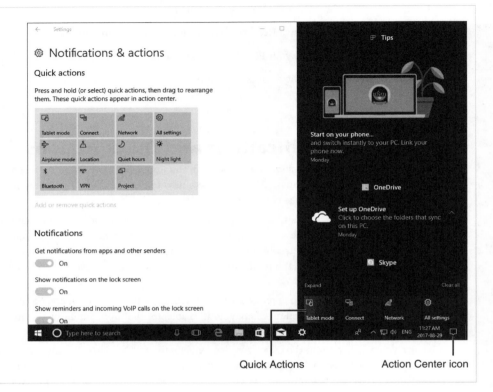

Quick Actions

Action Center icon

Synchronizing Your Settings Between Devices

You can run Windows 10 using either a local user account or a Microsoft account. Using the latter enables you to store data online, connect social networks such as Facebook and Twitter, and access services such as the Windows Store for purchasing apps.

However, arguably the most useful feature of using a Microsoft account is that you can use it to synchronize your settings across multiple devices. If besides your desktop computer you also have a notebook, tablet, and phone, all running Windows 8 or later and all using the same Microsoft account, you can synchronize data between them. You can sync customizations (such as the user account picture and screen backgrounds), system settings (such as languages and regional settings), Web browser data (such as favorites and history), app settings, and more. This gives you a consistent interface across your devices, and consistent data so you can be more productive.

Follow these steps to customize how Windows 10 synchronizes your settings across devices:

1. In the Settings app, click Accounts, and then click Sync Your Settings. The Sync Your Settings screen appears, as shown in Figure 9.8.

2. If you don't want your settings synced at all, click the Sync Settings switch to Off.

3. Under the Individual Sync Settings heading, click the switch to Off beside each type of setting you don't want to include in the sync.

Figure 9.8
Use the Sync Your Settings screen to customize Microsoft account syncing across your Windows 8/8.1/10 devices.

Creating a Shortcut to a Specific Settings Tab

If you have a particular Settings app tab that you access frequently, consider creating a shortcut that takes you directly to that tab. The secret here is that most of the tabs have a corresponding command that loads the tab directly. We list these commands in Table 9.2. Here are the steps to follow to create a desktop shortcut for a Settings app tab:

1. Right-click the desktop and select New, Shortcut. The Create Shortcut dialog box appears.

2. Enter the following in the Type the Location of the Item text box, where *tab* is the text that specifies the tab you want to display (again, see Table 9.2):

   ```
   ms-settings:tab
   ```

3. Click Next.

4. Type a name for the shortcut and click Finish.

5. Right-click the shortcut and click Properties.

6. Click Change Icon. Windows 10 displays the icons that come with the shell32.dll file. (If Windows 10 tells you the program contains no icons, just click OK.)

7. Select an icon, click OK, and then click OK to close the Properties dialog box.

Table 9.2   Commands for Displaying Individual Settings App Tabs

Settings App Tab	Command
System	
Display	`ms-settings:display`
Notifications & Actions	`ms-settings:notifications`
Power & Sleep	`ms-settings:powersleep`
Battery	`ms-settings:batterysaver`
Battery Usage By App	`ms-settings:batterysaver-usagedetails`
Storage	`ms-settings:storagesense`
Tablet Mode	`ms-settings:tabletmode`
Multitasking	`ms-settings:multitasking`
Projecting to This PC	`ms-settings:project`
Shared Experiences	`ms-settings:crossdevice`
Remote Desktop	`ms-settings:remotedesktop`
About	`ms-settings:about`
Devices	
Bluetooth & Other Devices	`ms-settings:bluetooth`
Printers & Scanners	`ms-settings:printers`
Connected Devices	`ms-settings:connecteddevices`
Mouse & Touchpad	`ms-settings:mousetouchpad`
Typing	`ms-settings:typing`
Pen & Windows Ink	`ms-settings:pen`
AutoPlay	`ms-settings:autoplay`
USB	`ms-settings:usb`
Phone	
Phone	Unknown
Network & Internet	
Status	`ms-settings:network-status`
Wi-Fi	`ms-settings:network-wifi`
Ethernet	`ms-settings:network-ethernet`
Dial-up	`ms-settings:network-dialup`
VPN	`ms-settings:network-vpn`
Airplane Mode	`ms-settings:network-airplanemode`
Mobile Hotspot	`ms-settings:network-mobilehotspot`
Data Usage	`ms-settings:datausage`
Proxy	`ms-settings:network-proxy`

Settings App Tab	Command
Personalization	
Background	`ms-settings:personalization-background`
Colors	`ms-settings:colors`
Lock Screen	`ms-settings:lockscreen`
Themes	`ms-settings:themes`
Start	`ms-settings:personalization-start`
Taskbar	`ms-settings:taskbar`
Apps	
Manage Optional Features	`ms-settings:optionalfeatures`
Default Apps	`ms-settings:defaultapps`
Offline Maps	`ms-settings:maps`
Apps for Websites	`ms-settings:maps`
Video Playback	`ms-settings:maps`
Accounts	
Your Info	`ms-settings:yourinfo`
Email and App Accounts	`ms-settings:emailandaccounts`
Sign-in Options	`ms-settings:signinoptions`
Access Work or School	`ms-settings:workplace`
Family & Other People	`ms-settings:otherusers`
Sync Your Settings	`ms-settings:sync`
Time & Language	
Date & Time	`ms-settings:dateandtime`
Region & Language	`ms-settings:regionlanguage`
Speech	`ms-settings:speech`
Gaming	
Game bar	`ms-settings:gaming-gamebar`
Game DVR	`ms-settings:gaming-gamedvr`
Broadcasting	`ms-settings:gaming-broadcasting`
Game Mode	`ms-settings:gaming-gamemode`
TruePlay	`ms-settings:gaming-trueplay`
Xbox Networking	`ms-settings:gaming-xboxnetworking`
Ease of Access	
Narrator	`ms-settings:easeofaccess-narrator`
Magnifier	`ms-settings:easeofaccess-magnifier`

Table 9.2 Continued

Settings App Tab	Command
Color & High Contrast	ms-settings:easeofaccess-highcontrast
Closed Captions	ms-settings:easeofaccess-closedcaptioning
Keyboard	ms-settings:easeofaccess-keyboard
Mouse	ms-settings:easeofaccess-mouse
Other Options	ms-settings:easeofaccess-otheroptions
Cortana	
Talk to Cortana	ms-settings:cortana
Permissions & History	ms-settings:cortana-permissions
Notifications	ms-settings:cortana-notifications
Privacy	
General	ms-settings:privacy
Location	ms-settings:privacy-location
Camera	ms-settings:privacy-webcam
Microphone	ms-settings:privacy-microphone
Notifications	ms-settings:privacy-notifications
Speech, Inking, & Typing	ms-settings:privacy-speechtyping
Account Info	ms-settings:privacy-accountinfo
Contacts	ms-settings:privacy-contacts
Calendar	ms-settings:privacy-calendar
Call History	ms-settings:callhistory
Email	ms-settings:privacy-email
Tasks	ms-settings:privacy-tasks
Messaging	ms-settings:privacy-messaging
Radios	ms-settings:privacy-radios
Other Devices	ms-settings:privacy-customdevices
Feedback & Diagnostics	ms-settings:privacy-feedback
Background Apps	ms-settings:privacy-backgroundapps
App Diagnostics	ms-settings:privacy-appdiagnostics
Automatic File Downloads	ms-settings:privacy-automaticfiledownloads
Update & Security	
Windows Update	ms-settings:windowsupdate
Windows Defender	ms-settings:windowsdefender
Troubleshoot	ms-settings:troubleshoot

Settings App Tab	Command
Backup	ms-settings:backup
Recovery	ms-settings:recovery
Activation	ms-settings:activation
Find My Device	ms-settings:findmydevice
For Developers	ms-settings:developers
Windows Insider Program	ms-settings:windowsinsider

WINDOWS MEDIA PLAYER

Getting to Know Media Player

Windows Media Player (WMP) is your computer's one-stop media shop, with support for playing digital music, audio CDs, digital videos, and recorded TV shows; ripping music from CDs; burning files to disc; synchronizing with external audio devices; and much more. (Actually "one-stop" isn't quite accurate. In Windows 10, you must use a third-party app to play DVD movies and listen to Internet radio.) Windows 10 ships with version 12 of this popular program (see Figure 10.1), which is essentially the same version as the one that came with Windows 7. That Microsoft has barely updated this software in more than eight years tells you that the company's priorities lie elsewhere.

Figure 10.1
As with Windows 7, 8, and 8.1, Windows 10 ships with Windows Media Player 12.

Navigation pane

To launch the program, open the Start menu, type **media**, and then click Windows Media Player in the search results.

Navigating the Library

WMP organizes its media library by category, and by default it displays the Music category at startup. However, you can change to a different category (Music, Videos, Pictures, Recorded TV, Other Media, or Playlists) using either of the following techniques:

- Use the Navigation pane (pointed out in Figure 10.1) to click the category you want, if it's displayed. (See "Customizing the Navigation Pane," later in this chapter, to learn how to add more views to the Navigation pane.)

- Drop down the Library tab list (see Figure 10.2), and then click the category you want.

The path information beside the Select a Category list tells you the name of the current category, folder, and view, as pointed out in Figure 10.2.

By default, WMP opens in the Music category's All Music view, which groups songs according to the values in the

 tip

If you're looking for a good third-party app for playing DVDs and other media, we recommend VLC, by VideoLAN. In the Store app, look for the app named VLC.

 note

If you're running Windows 10 on a small tablet or phone powered by an ARM processor, you can search high and low and you won't find Windows Media Player. The ARM version of Windows 10 doesn't include it.

Current category
Current folder
Current view

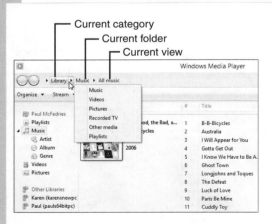

Figure 10.2
You navigate to a different category using either the Navigation pane or the Library list.

Album Artist property and then by the values in the Album property. WMP also offers several other Music views based on media metadata. Here's a sampling:

- **Artist**—Stacks the albums using the values in the Album Artist property.

- **Album**—Groups the albums alphabetically using the values in the Album property.

- **Genre**—Stacks the albums using the values in the Genre property.

- **Year**—Groups the albums by decade using the values in the Date Released property.

- **Rating**—Stacks the albums using the values in the Rating property.

Three of these views—Artist, Album, and Genre—are available in the Navigation pane. For the rest, drop down the Music list (see Figure 10.3) and then click the view you want.

Figure 10.3
Drop down the folder list to see all the views available in that folder.

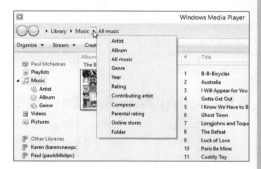

You get a different set of views for each category. For example, you can view items in the Videos category by actors, genre, and rating, and you can view items in the Recorded TV category by series, genre, actors, and rating. In each category, you can see even more views by clicking the folder list in the path.

Customizing the Navigation Pane

The Navigation pane is a handy way to get around the WMP interface, but by default, it includes only a few categories and even fewer views. If you have sections of the library that you use frequently, you can make WMP easier to use by adding those sections to the Navigation pane. Here's how it's done:

1. Select Organize, Customize Navigation Pane. WMP opens the Customize Navigation Pane dialog box, shown in Figure 10.4.

2. To add a category to the Navigation pane, check its box.

3. Use the check boxes within each category to control the views that appear in the Navigation pane.

4. Click OK.

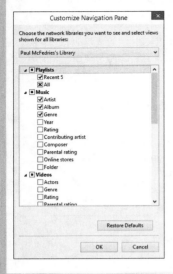

Figure 10.4
Use the Customize Navigation Pane dialog box to control which categories and views you see in the Navigation pane.

Syncing Media Devices

When you attach a WMP-compatible media device, WMP recognizes it and automatically displays the device, its total capacity, and its available space in the Sync tab's List pane, as shown in Figure 10.5.

To create a list of items to add to the device, display the album, song, or whatever in the Contents pane; click and drag the item; and then drop it inside the Sync List. WMP automatically updates the available storage space in the device as you drop items in the Sync List. You can also click and drag the items within the Sync List to control the order.

When you're ready to add the item, click Start Sync. WMP switches to the device's Sync Status folder to display the progress of the sync.

WMP supports two-way synchronizing, which means that you can not only sync files from your PC to a media device but also sync files from a media device to your PC. This capability is handy if you've purchased music directly to the device or uploaded media to the device using a different application.

To sync from a media device to your PC, you open a view on the media device, find the files you want to sync, and then click and drag them to the Sync List. Alternatively, just click Start Sync to synchronize everything on the device with WMP.

 tip
If you're not sure whether a device is compatible with Windows Media Player, see the Windows Compatibility Center at www.microsoft.com/ en-us/windows/compatibility/ CompatCenter/Home.

 tip
You can "preshuffle" the media files before starting the sync. Pull down the Sync List button and click Shuffle List.

Figure 10.5
When
you insert
a media
device,
information
about the
device
appears in
the Sync
tab's List
pane.

Device info

Sync List

The device appears in
the Navigation pane.

Playing Media Files

Windows 10 gives you many indirect ways to play media files via Windows Media Player. Here's a summary:

- Open File Explorer, find the media file you want to play and then double-click the file.

- Insert an audio CD in your computer's optical drive. The first time you do this, Windows 10 displays an AutoPlay notification that asks you what you want to do when you insert an audio CD (see Figure 10.6). Click the notification and then click Play Audio CD.

DVD RW Drive (H:) ASidesWinSingles
Select to choose what happens with
enhanced audio CDs.

Figure 10.6
You see this AutoPlay notification the first time you insert an audio CD.

- If you have a memory card reader, insert a memory card (such as a CompactFlash card or a Multi-Media Card). Click the drive when it appears in Media Player and then open a media folder from the drive.

- Download media from the Internet.

- Open files directly from Media Player by pressing Alt, pulling down the File menu, and selecting either Open (to launch a media file from your computer or from a network location) or Open URL (to launch a media file from the Internet).

tip

Many of today's keyboards are *media enhanced*, which means they come with extra keys that perform digital media functions such as playing, pausing, and stopping media, adjusting the volume, and changing the track. Also, here are a few Windows Media Player shortcut keys you might find useful while playing media files:

Ctrl+P—Play or pause the current media.

Ctrl+S—Stop the current media.

Ctrl+B—Go to the previous track.

Ctrl+Shift+B—Rewind to the beginning of the media.

Ctrl+F—Go to the next track.

Ctrl+Shift+F—Fast forward to the end of the media.

Ctrl+H—Toggle shuffle playback.

Ctrl+T—Toggle repeat playback.

Ctrl+1—Switch to the Library window.

Ctrl+2—Switch to the Skin window.

Ctrl+3—Switch to the Now Playing window.

Alt+1—Display video size at 50%.

Alt+2—Display video size at 100%.

Alt+3—Display video size at 200%.

F7—Mute sound.

F8—Decrease volume.

F9—Increase volume.

Setting Media Player's Playback Options

Windows Media Player comes with several options you can work with to control various aspects of the playback. To see these options, select Organize, Options. The Player tab, shown in Figure 10.7, contains the following settings:

- **Check for Updates**—Use these options to determine how often Windows Media Player checks for newer versions of the program.

- **Keep Now Playing on Top of Other Windows**—When this box is checked, WMP's Now Playing window stays on top of other windows. This is useful if you want to access Windows Media Player's playback controls while working in another program.

Figure 10.7
Use the Player tab to configure Windows Media Player's playback options.

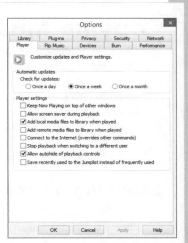

- **Allow Screen Saver During Playback**—When this box is checked, the Windows 10 screensaver is allowed to kick in after the system has been idle for the specified number of minutes. If you're watching streaming video content or a recorded TV show, leave this box unchecked to prevent the screensaver from activating.

- **Add Local Media Files to Library When Played**—When this box is checked, Windows Media Player adds files that you play to the library. For example, if you play a downloaded MP3 file, Windows Media Player adds it to the library. Note that, by default, Windows Media Player doesn't add media from removable media and network shares to the library. (See the next setting.)

- **Add Remote Media Files to Library When Played**—When this box is checked, Media Player adds music files to the library that you play from removable media, such as a CompactFlash card, as well as from shared network folders. Note that you won't be able to play these items unless the removable media is inserted or the network share is available.

- **Connect to the Internet**—When this box is checked, Windows Media Player always connects to the Internet when you select a feature that requires Internet access. This connection occurs even if you have activated the File menu's Work Offline command.

- **Stop Playback When Switching to a Different User**—When this box is checked, Media Player stops playing when you switch to a different user account.

- **Allow Autohide of Playback Controls**—When this option is checked, the Now Playing window hides the playback controls if you haven't done anything within the window after a few seconds. This makes it easier to view the Now Playing art or visualization, and you get the controls back by moving the mouse pointer into the window. If you find this a hassle, uncheck this option to display the playback control full time.

- **Save Recently Used to the Jumplist Instead of Frequently Used**—When this box is unchecked, Media Player populates its taskbar jumplist with a Frequent section that lists the media you've played the most. If you uncheck this option, Media Player replaces the jumplist's Frequent section with a Recent section, which shows the media you've played most recently.

Copying Music from an Audio CD

Windows Media Player comes with the capability to copy (*rip* in the vernacular) tracks from an audio CD to your computer's hard disk. Although this process is straightforward, as you'll see, you need to take several options into account before you start copying. These options include the location of the folder in which the ripped tracks will be stored, the structure of the track filenames, the file format to use, and the quality (bit rate) at which you want to copy the tracks. You control all these settings in the Rip Music tab of the Options dialog box. (Select Organize, Options to get there.)

➡ *To learn more about bit rates,* **see** *"Specifying the Quality of the Recording," p. 252.*

Selecting a Location and Filename Structure

The Rip Music to This Location group displays the name of the folder that will be used to store the copied tracks. By default, this location is %UserProfile%\Music. To specify a different folder (for example, a folder on a partition with lots of free space), click Change and use the Browse for Folder dialog box to choose the new folder.

The default filenames that Windows Media Player generates for each copied track use the following structure:

Track_Number Song_Title.ext

Here, *Track_Number* is the song's track number on the CD, *Song_Title* is the name of the song, and ext is the extension used by the recording format (such as WMA or MP3). Windows Media Player can also include additional data in the filename, such as the artist name, the album name, the music genre, and the recording bit rate. To control which of these details the name incorporates, click the File Name button in the Rip Music tab to display the File Name Options dialog box, shown in Figure 10.8. Check the boxes beside the details you want in the filenames, and use the Move Up and Move Down buttons to determine the order of the details. Finally, use the Separator list to choose which character to use to separate each detail.

Figure 10.8
Use the File Name Options dialog box to specify the details you want in the filename assigned to each copied audio CD track.

Choosing the Recording File Format

Windows Media Player's default file format is WMA (Windows Media Audio). This is an excellent music format that provides good quality recordings at high compression rates. If you plan to listen to the tracks only on your computer or on a custom CD, the WMA format is all you need. However, if you have an MP3 player or other device that might not recognize WMA files (although most do, unless you're one of the zillions with an iPod, iPhone, or iPad), you need to use the MP3 recording format. Windows Media Player 12 supports the following formats:

- **Windows Media Audio**—This is Windows Media Player's default audio file format. WMA compresses digital audio by removing extraneous sounds that are not normally detected by the human ear, which results in high-quality audio files that are a fraction of the size of uncompressed audio.

- **Windows Media Audio Pro**—This version of WMA can create music files that are smaller than regular WMA and therefore are easier to play on mobile devices that don't have much room.

- **Windows Media Audio (Variable Bit Rate)**—This version of WMA is a bit "smarter" in that it changes the amount of compression depending on the audio data. If the data is more complex, it uses less compression to keep the sound quality high; if the data is less complex, it cranks up the compression.

- **Windows Media Audio Lossless**—This version of WMA doesn't compress the audio tracks at all, which gives you the highest possible audio quality, but it takes up much more space (up to about 400MB per CD).

- **MP3**—This is a popular format on the Internet. Like WMA, MP3 compresses the audio files to make them smaller without sacrificing quality. MP3 files are generally about twice the size of WMA files, but more digital audio players support MP3 (although not many more, these days).

- **WAV**—This uncompressed audio file format is compatible with all versions of Windows, even going back to Windows 3.0.

tip

Another way to access the format list is to click the audio CD in Media Player's Navigation pane and select Rip Settings, Format.

Use the Format list in the Rip Music tab to choose the encoder (that is, the software that writes the music data to the specific format you chose) you want to use. Note that if you select any Windows Media Audio format, the Copy Protect Music check box becomes enabled. Here's how this check box affects your copying:

- If Copy Protect Music is activated, Media Player applies a license to each track that prevents you from copying the track to another computer or to any portable device that is SDMI compliant. (SDMI is the Secure Digital Music Initiative; see www.sdmi.org for more information.) Note, however, that you are allowed to copy the track to a writeable CD. So this is the route to take if you'll be lending out a music CD that you created, and you don't want the borrower to illegally copy any of the tracks.

- If Copy Protect Music is deactivated, there are no restrictions on where or how you can copy the track. As long as you're copying tracks for personal use, deactivating this check box is the most convenient route to take.

Specifying the Quality of the Recording

The tracks on an audio CD use the CD Audio Track file format (.cda extension), which represents the raw (uncompressed) audio data. You can't work with these files directly because Windows doesn't support the CDA format and because these files tend to be huge (usually double-digit megabytes, depending on the track). Instead, the tracks need to be converted into a Windows 10–supported format (such as WMA). This conversion usually involves compressing the tracks to a more manageable size. However, because the compression process operates by removing extraneous data from the file (that is, it's a *lossy* compression), there's a trade-off between file size and music quality. That is, the higher the compression, the smaller the resulting file, but the poorer the sound quality. Conversely, the lower the compression, the larger the file, but the better the sound quality. Generally, how you handle this trade-off depends on how much hard disk space you have to store the files and how sensitive your ear is to sound quality.

The recording quality is usually measured in kilobits per second (Kbps; this is called the bit rate), with higher values producing better quality and larger files, as shown in Table 10.1 for the Windows Media Audio format.

To specify the recording quality, use the Audio Quality slider in the Rip Music tab. Move the slider to the right for higher quality recordings (for example, 192Kbps is considered the minimum for CD-quality recordings), and to the left for lower quality (128Kbps is considered radio-quality, while 48Kbps is considered voice-quality).

Table 10.1   WMA Ripping Bit Rates and the Disk Space They Consume

Kbps	KB/Minute	MB/Hour
32	240	14
48	360	21
64	480	28
96	720	42
128	960	56
160	1,200	70
192	1,440	84
256	1,920	112
320	2,400	140

Copying Tracks from an Audio CD

After you've made your recording choices, you're ready to start ripping tracks. Here are the steps to follow:

1. Insert the audio CD. Windows Media Player displays a list of the available tracks.

2. Check the boxes beside the tracks you want to copy.

3. Click Rip CD.

 tip

Another way to select the recording quality is to click the audio CD in Media Player and then select Rip Settings, Audio Quality.

Copying Tracks to a Recordable CD or Device

In addition to copying music to your computer from a CD, Windows Media Player can perform the opposite task: copying media files from your computer to a recordable CD or portable device.

Creating a Playlist

Most people find recording is easiest if it's done from a *playlist*, a customized collection of music files. Here's how to create a new playlist:

1. Click Create Playlist. Windows Media Player adds the new playlist.

2. Type a name for the playlist and press Enter.

3. For each song you want to include in the new playlist, drag it from the library and drop it on the playlist in the Navigation pane. Alternatively, right-click the song, click Add To, and then click the playlist in the menu that appears.

After your playlist has been created, you can view, play, or edit the list by clicking it in the Navigation pane.

Recording to a CD

Here are the steps to follow to burn music files to a recordable CD:

1. Insert the recordable CD.

2. Click Burn in the Windows Media Player taskbar. The Burn List appears on the right side of the window.

3. For each playlist or song you want to burn, drag it from the library to the Burn List pane.

4. Click Start Burn.

Streaming Your Media Library

If you've spent a great deal of time ripping audio CDs, downloading music files, adding other media to your library, and organizing the library, you probably do not want to repeat all that work on another computer. If you have a wired or wireless network, however, you can take advantage of the library work you have done on one computer by sharing—or *streaming*—that library through your local homegroup. Streaming allows any other homegroup users to include your media in their Media Player library and to other user accounts on your computer. Those users can sign on and then access your shared library. Your shared library is also available to other media devices on the network, such as an Xbox or a networked digital media receiver.

➡ *To learn how to create and join a local homegroup,* **see** *"Setting Up a Homegroup," p. 396.*

To activate media streaming, select Stream, More Streaming Options. Windows 10 displays the Media Streaming Options window, shown in Figure 10.9. The large box in the middle lists the network computers and devices that Media Player has detected. In each case, click an icon and then either check or uncheck the Allowed box. If you allow an item, you can also click Customize to specify exactly what you want to share based on star ratings and parental ratings. When you're finished in the Media Streaming Options window, clicking Next displays the Share with Other Homegroup Members dialog box, shown in Figure 10.10. For Pictures, Videos, and Music, select Shared in the Permissions list. Click Next and then click Finish.

To return to the Media Streaming Options window in the future, open Media Player and select Stream, More Streaming Options.

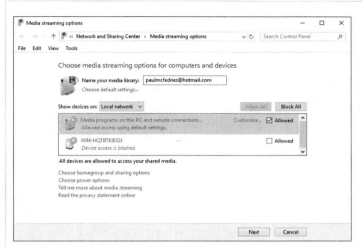

Figure 10.9
Use the Media Streaming Options window to allow or deny other network devices access to your Media Player library.

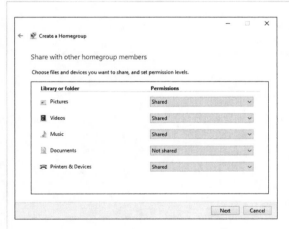

Figure 10.10
You can stream your Media Player library's pictures, videos, and music with your homegroup.

 note

You can also allow network devices to control your local Media Player, which enables those devices to add music and other media to your library. To set this up, click Stream and then click Allow Remote Control of My Player. In the Allow Remote Control dialog box, click Allow Remote Control on This Network.

WINDOWS AND IMAGING DEVICES

Connecting Imaging Devices

Windows 10 can work with both digital cameras and document scanners and often identifies them by a single generic name—*imaging devices*—because both produce image files. Windows 10 comes with support for a variety of cameras and scanners, so getting your images from out here to in there has never been easier, as you see in this chapter.

To install an imaging device, you have three choices:

- If the device is Plug and Play–compatible (as the vast majority are these days), just connect the device and turn it on. Windows 10 should recognize the device and install the appropriate drivers. Note, however, that for multifunction printers that include a scanner, Windows often installs just the printer driver, not the scanner driver, so you'll need to use one of the following two options to install the scanner manually.

- If Windows 10 doesn't recognize your imaging device, type **scanners** into the taskbar Search box, and then click Printers & Scanners. The Settings app launches and opens the Printers & Scanners tab. Click Add a Printer or Scanner to see a list of the available devices.

- If you still can't access your imaging device, install the device software. Any scanner or digital camera worth its salt comes with software for setting up the device. If the first two options don't work, try installing the software.

After you connect the imaging device, you might see a notification like the one shown in Figure 11.1. To set the AutoPlay default for the device, select the notification and, in the option list that then appears, select the action you want Windows 10 to take whenever you connect the device (see Figure 11.2).

Figure 11.1
You might see a notification similar to this when you connect your imaging device.

Figure 11.2
Click the notification, and then click the AutoPlay default action you want Windows 10 to take each time you insert the device.

Testing an Installed Scanner

If you installed a scanner, you can test it using these steps:

1. In the taskbar Search box, type **scanners**.

2. Click Printers & Scanners to open the Settings app's Printers & Scanners tab.

3. Click the device, and then click Manage. The Manage Your Device window appears.

4. If the device has multiple functions, select the scanner function, and then click Scanner Properties to open the Scanners and Cameras dialog box.

5. Double-click the device. User Account Control asks you to confirm.

6. Click Yes or enter your PC's administrative credentials. Windows 10 opens the device's property sheet.

7. Display the General tab.

8. Click the Test Scanner button. Ideally, you then see the Test Successful dialog box, which tells you that your scanner successfully completed the diagnostic text. If the scanner fails the test, double-check the scanner–PC connection. If that seems fine, try reinstalling the scanner's device driver or see whether an updated driver is available from the manufacturer.

9. Click OK.

Configuring Device Events

The imaging device might support one or more *events*, which are actions taken on the device. For example, most scanners support "push" scanning, in which you press a button on the scanner to initiate the scanning process. Windows 10 recognizes the pressing of the scan button as an event, and you can configure Windows 10 to specify which scanning program loads and scans the current image. If your scanner supports this and other events, you can tell Windows how you want these events handled by following these steps:

1. In the taskbar Search box, type **scanners**.

2. Click Printers & Scanners to open the Settings app's Printers & Scanners tab.

3. Click the device, and then click Manage. The Manage Your Device window appears.

4. Click Scanner Properties to open the Scanners and Cameras dialog box.

5. Double-click the device. User Account Control asks you to confirm.

6. Click Yes or enter your administrative credentials. Windows 10 opens the device's property sheet.

7. Display the Events tab, shown in Figure 11.3.

Figure 11.3
Open the image device's property sheets, and then use the Events tab to configure events such as pressing the scan button.

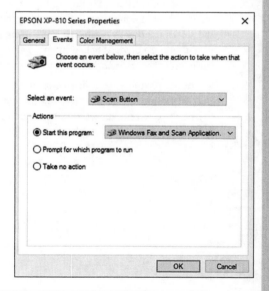

8. Use the Select an Event list to choose which event you want to configure.

9. Use the Actions group to choose the action you want Windows 10 to take whenever the event occurs:

- **Start This Program**—Select this option to have Windows 10 automatically launch a program whenever it detects the event. Use the list to choose the program you want to use. For example, if you're configuring the scan event for a scanner, you can choose to run Windows Fax and Scan.

- **Prompt for Which Program to Run**—Select this option to have Windows 10 ask you what to do each time it detects the event.

- **Take No Action**—Select this option to have Windows 10 ignore the event.

10. Repeat steps 8 and 9 to configure other events as needed.

11. Click OK.

Accessing Media on a Memory Card

Most digital cameras store images using a storage device called a *memory card*. These miniature memory modules come in many different shapes and sizes, including CompactFlash cards, MultiMedia cards, Memory Sticks, SecureDigital cards, and more. They're handy because after you transfer your images to your computer, you can wipe the card and start all over again. Although you usually get at the card's images by connecting the camera directly to your computer, as described in the next section, there are devices called memory card readers into which you can insert one or more memory cards and then connect the unit to the computer.

Windows 10 treats each filled slot in a memory card reader as a disk drive, and they show up in the Disk Management snap-in (diskmgmt.msc) as Removable drives. You're then free to browse a memory card's contents directly, as described in the next section. In Figure 11.4, you see three Removable drives created by a card reader—F:, G:, and I:.

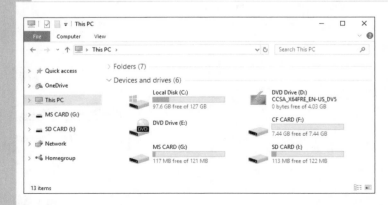

Figure 11.4
When you insert a memory card reader, Windows 10 creates a temporary removable disk drive for each card inserted into the reader's slots.

Importing Photos from a Digital Camera

Although you can certainly leave your photos on your digital camera, at least until space becomes an issue, you can get more out of them if you transfer some or all of them to your computer hard drive. The reason is that after they're on your computer, you can edit the photos, print them, email them to friends or family, put them on a social media site such as Facebook or Instagram, or simply store them for safekeeping.

Viewing Digital Camera Images

One of Windows 10's nicer features is the capability to interface directly with a digital camera—whether it's a standalone camera or a smartphone camera—using File Explorer. This is possible because Windows 10 treats whatever the camera uses to store the digital photos as an honest-to-goodness folder. This means you can open the folder and work with the images yourself.

To do this, launch File Explorer (pressing Windows Logo+E is one way) and then click This PC. As shown in Figure 11.5, you see a Devices and Drives section that includes an icon for your digital camera.

Figure 11.5
Connect your digital camera, and an icon appears for it in This PC's Devices and Drives section. In this case, the digital camera is a Canon EOS 60D.

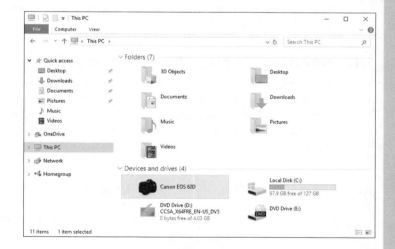

Now double-click the camera icon (although bear in mind that this technique also applies to memory cards). Windows 10 connects to the camera and displays the folders the camera uses for storage. Open the folders to get to your pictures (you might have to wade through a few levels of subfolders). Windows 10 displays the images thumbnail style, as shown in Figure 11.6. To copy an image from the camera to your hard disk, click and drag the image and drop it onto the Pictures folder.

Figure 11.6
Drill down into your camera storage to show the camera's digital photos in a folder window.

Note, too, that you can clear out the camera's photos by selecting all the images (press Ctrl+A) and then pressing Delete. You will be asked if you are sure you want to permanently delete the images. Click Yes to confirm.

Importing Digital Camera Photos

Rather than wading through the seemingly endless hierarchy of digital camera storage to copy your photos by hand, you might prefer to let Windows do most of the work. You do that by using Windows 10's built-in importing features. To start, open File Explorer and then click This PC. Right-click the camera and then click Import Pictures and Videos. Windows 10 offers up the Import Pictures and Videos dialog box, shown in Figure 11.7.

Figure 11.7
Use this dialog box to get your Windows 10 digital camera import underway.

The next few sections take you through the details of the import process.

Configuring the Import Settings

When you need to import images from a device such as a digital camera, you can always connect the camera and then open the camera using the icon that appears in the This PC window, as described earlier. You can then move or copy the image from the camera to your PC using the standard cut (or copy) and paste techniques.

The only problem with that approach is that you end up with photos that use the existing filenames of the images. This is a problem because most cameras supply images with cryptic filenames, such as IMG_1083. These nondescriptive names can make finding and working with images difficult, particularly if you use the Details view in the Pictures folder.

To work around this problem, the Import Pictures and Videos dialog box asks you to enter an import name for your photos, which can be a word or a short phrase. Windows 10 uses the import name as follows:

- It creates a subfolder in the Pictures folder, and the name of the new subfolder is today's date followed by the import name. For example, if today is August 23, 2018, and the import name is Scotland Vacation, then the new subfolder will have the following name:

  2018-08-23 Scotland Vacation

- It gives the file the same name as the import name, with the number 001 after it, like so:

  Scotland Vacation 001.jpg

  If you're importing several images from your digital camera, the number gets incremented for each image: 002, 003, and so on.

Even better, Windows lets you customize the folder name using any of the following variations (where in each case *Name* is the import name that you supply):

- **Date Imported + Name**—This is the default folder name.

- **Date Taken + Name**—This folder name combines the date the photos were taken with the import name.

- **Date Taken Range + Name**—This folder name combines the date the first photo was taken, the date the last photo was taken, and the import name. Here's an example:

  2018-08-09 - 2018-08-23 Scotland Vacation

- **Name + Date Imported**—This folder name combines the import name followed by the import date.

- **Name + Date Taken**—This folder name combines the import name followed by the photo date.

- **Name + Date Taken Range**—This folder name combines the import name followed by the photo date range.

- **Name**—This folder name uses just the import name.

- **None**—This option bypasses the subfolder altogether and imports the photos directly to the Pictures folder.

You can also customize the filename using these variations (where, again, *Name* is your import word or phrase):

- **Name**—This filename uses just the import name followed by 001, 002, and so on.

- **Original File Name**—The filename is the internal name supplied by the camera.

- **Original File Name (Preserve Folders)**—The filename is the internal name supplied by the camera. If the camera storage uses subfolders, those subfolders are included in the import.

- **Name + Date Taken**—The filename combines the import name followed by the date the photo was taken.

- **Date Taken + Name**—The filename combines the date the photo was taken with the import name.

To configure these and other import settings, click More Options in the Import Pictures and Videos dialog box. Windows 10 opens the Import Settings dialog box, shown in Figure 11.8.

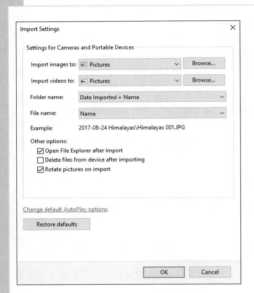

Figure 11.8
Use the Import Settings dialog box to configure custom import folder and filenames and other import tweaks.

Follow these steps to configure custom photo import names and set a few other useful importing options:

1. Accept the default import location for Import Images To, or click Browse and choose a different one.

2. If you'll also be importing videos from your camera, accept the default import location for Import Videos To, or click Browse and choose a different location.

3. In the Folder Name list, choose the format you want to use for the destination folder name.

4. In the File Name list, choose the format you want to use for the imported filenames.

5. (Optional) If you do not want Windows to open the destination folder once the import is complete, uncheck the Open File Explorer After Import box.

6. (Optional) If you want the files deleted from the camera after the import, mark the Delete Files from Device after Importing check box.

7. By default, Windows 10 rotates photos automatically during the import. If you would prefer to handle this chore by hand, uncheck the Rotate Pictures on Import box.

8. Click OK to put the new settings into effect and return to the Import Pictures and Videos dialog box.

From here, you must decide whether you want to import all the pictures from the camera or import only selected groups of photos. The next two sections explain the difference.

Importing Everything from the Camera

By far, the easiest way to handle the import is to import everything at once. We should mention here that "everything" doesn't necessarily mean all the photos on your camera. This is certainly true the first time you import from the camera, but subsequent runs of the Import Pictures and Videos tool will detect and import only those images you haven't imported previously.

To import everything, follow these steps:

1. In the Import Pictures and Videos dialog box, select the Import All New Items Now option.

2. Use the text box to type a name for the import.

3. If you want to add tag metadata to your photos, click Add Tags and then type your tags, separating each with a semicolon (;).

4. Click Import. Windows 10 imports all the new photos to your hard drive.

5. During the import, if you want Windows 10 to delete the photos from the camera when the import is complete, check the Erase After Importing box.

Importing Selected Groups of Photos

Rather than importing all new photos from your camera, you might prefer to be a bit more selective and import only a subset of the photos. For example, if you have photos of a wedding and the groom's earlier bachelor party, you might want to import those separately! By default, Windows 10 organizes camera photos into groups based on the photo dates, so you can use this fact to import photos into different folders by giving each group you want to import its own import name.

Follow these steps to import selected groups of photos:

1. In the Import Pictures and Videos dialog box, select the Review, Organize, and Group Items to Import option.

2. Click Next. Windows 10 presents your photos in groups by date.

3. Use the Adjust Groups slider to set the interval Windows 10 uses to separate the groups based on the time each photo was taken. The default is 4 hours, meaning that Windows 10 creates groups at 4-hour intervals. You can choose an interval in hours (between 0.5 hours and 23 hours) or days (between 1 day and 30 days), or you can choose to have all the photos in one group rather than separate groups.

4. If you want to import only a group or two, uncheck the Select All box to deactivate all the group check boxes.

5. For each group you want to import, check the group's box, and type a name for the group. You can also click Add Tags to import the group with tag metadata.

 tip

If you want two different groups to import to the same folder, give them the same import name.

6. Click Import. Windows 10 starts importing the selected photos.

7. During the import, if you want Windows 10 to delete the photos from the camera when the import is done, check the Erase After Importing box.

Burning Photos to an Optical Disc

Although it carries with it the faint scent of the old fashioned, you can copy a selection of photos to a recordable optical (CD or DVD) disc—a process called *burning*. You can then send the disc to a friend or relative to share your photos.

If you have a CD or DVD burner—that is, a CD or DVD drive capable of recording data to a disc—attached to your computer (almost all new computers come with one), Windows should recognize it and be ready to burn at will.

Selecting an Optical Disc Format

Before getting to the burning steps, you need to decide which disc format you want to use. You have two choices:

- **Mastered**—This format requires that you burn photos to the disc in a single operation. That is, you first gather all the photos you want to copy to the disc, and then you run the burn. Mastered optical discs are compatible with most optical drives and CD or DVD players. For discs that can be rewritten with new data (such as CD-R, CD-RW, DVD-R, and DVD-RW), you can burn a new set of photos to the disc in each session. Keep in mind that you can't delete individual photos from a mastered CD-R or DVD-R disc, but you can delete individual photos from a mastered CD-RW or DVD-RW disc.

- **Live File System**—This is a Universal Disk Format (UDF) that treats the optical disc just like a USB flash drive. This means you can copy files to the disc anytime you like, delete one or more files, and use the disc just like a removable drive. While a recording session is open, you can only use the disc on your PC. To use the disc on another PC, you must close the session. Live File System discs are compatible only with optical drives on computers that are running Windows XP or later.

 note

Optical discs that can be rewritten in multiple recording sessions—such as CD-R, CD-RW, DVD-R, and DVD-RW discs—are known as *multisession discs*. Optical discs that can be written to only once—such as CD-ROM and DVD-ROM discs—are known as *single-session discs*.

Burning a Mastered Disc

If you want to use the optical disc in a CD or DVD player, or on an older computer, you should burn a mastered disc. Here are the steps to follow:

1. Insert a blank optical disc into your optical drive. Windows 10 reads the disc and then displays a notification asking what you want to do with blank discs.

2. Click the notification, and then click Burn Files to Disc. Windows 10 displays the Burn a Disc dialog box, shown in Figure 11.9.

Figure 11.9
Use the Burn a Disc dialog box to initialize the optical disc.

3. Type a disc title.

4. Select the With a CD/DVD Player option.

5. Click Next. Windows opens the drive.

6. In File Explorer, open a folder that contains one or more of the photos you want to burn.

7. Select the photos you want to burn and then drag them to the disc. You can also select the photos, right-click any selected item, click Send To, and then click the optical drive.

8. Repeat steps 6 and 7 until you've selected all the photos you want to burn.

9. Click This PC, and then right-click the disc.

10. Click Burn to Disc. The Burn to Disc Wizard appears.

11. Adjust the title, select a recording speed, and then click Next. Windows burns the files to the disc and then ejects the disc.

12. Click Finish.

 tip

If you don't want Windows 10 to automatically eject the disc after the mastered burn is complete, you can turn off this setting. In File Explorer, click This PC, right-click the optical drive, and then click Properties. Click the Recording tab, uncheck the Automatically Eject the Disc After a Mastered Burn box, and then click OK.

Closing a UDF Session

As we mentioned earlier, if you use the Live File System format, Windows 10 sets up a UDF recording session that enables you to leave the disc in the drive and add or delete files at will, just like a USB flash drive. However, while the session is open, you cannot use the disc on another computer, so you must close the session when you are done with the disc.

By default, Windows 10 automatically closes the current session when you eject a disc. If you prefer to control when the session is closed by hand (for example, if you prefer to leave the disc inserted so you can view or access its files), follow these steps to turn off automatic session closing:

1. In File Explorer, click This PC.

2. Right-click the optical drive and then click Properties. The drive's Properties dialog box appears.

3. Click the Recording tab.

4. Click Global Settings. Windows 10 displays the Global Settings dialog box shown in Figure 11.10.

Figure 11.10
Use the Global Settings dialog box to control automatic UDF session closing.

5. If you don't want Windows 10 to automatically close the current session when you eject a single-session disc, uncheck the Single Session-Only Discs Are Ejected box.

6. If you don't want Windows 10 to automatically close the current session when you eject a multi-session disc, uncheck the Multi Session-Capable Discs Are Ejected box.

7. Click OK to put the new settings into effect and return to the optical drive's Properties dialog box.

8. Click OK.

Burning a Live File System Disc

If you want to burn the disc using the Live File System, you first must initialize the disc by following these steps:

1. Insert a blank optical disc into your optical drive. Windows 10 reads the disc and then displays a notification asking what you want to do with blank discs. If you see the Burn a Disc dialog box instead, skip to step 3.

2. Click the notification, and then click Burn Files to Disc. Windows 10 displays the Burn a Disc dialog box, shown earlier in Figure 11.9.

3. Type a disc title.

4. Select the Like a USB Flash Drive option.

5. Click Next. Windows formats the disc to make it ready to receive files, which may take awhile, depending on the disc and the speed of your burner. You know the task is complete when you see an AutoPlay notification asking what you want to do with removable drives.

With that done, you're ready to burn your photos by following these steps:

1. In File Explorer, open a folder that contains one or more of the photos you want to burn.

2. Select the photos you want to burn to the disc.

3. Click the Share tab.

4. Click Burn to Disc. Windows copies the files to the disc.

5. Click This PC, and then examine the disc to see how much free space you have left.

6. Repeat steps 1 to 5 until you've sent all the files you want to the disc.

7. Click This PC.

8. Right-click the disc.

9. Click Close Session. Windows 10 closes the recording session.

10. When you see the Disk Ready message, click Eject. Windows 10 spits out the disc.

SCANNING AND FAXING

Introducing Windows Fax and Scan

Windows Fax and Scan (WFS) is a built-in tool that lets you do the following:

- Send and receive faxes using a fax modem connected to a telephone line. On a corporate network, WFS can also let you send faxes through a shared Fax Server.

- Scan images, drawings, and documents using a scanner or a multifunction (all-in-one) printer that has scanning capability.

You don't need to have both a scanner and a fax modem to take advantage of WFS. The program does let you use both together, but it can be useful even if you have just one or the other. Truth be told, fax machines have become like tail fins on Cadillacs: interesting maybe but unnecessary. Still, it's handy to be able to send and receive faxes on occasion. And the scanning part of WFS is eminently useful for scanning documents that you can then send as email attachments.

Installing Fax and Scanner Hardware

If your scanner or fax device is not already installed, follow the manufacturer's recommendations to install the fax or scanner hardware before you use Windows Fax and Scan. Use Windows 10 drivers and software, if available, but Windows 8.1, 8, 7, or Vista drivers

 note

If your computer doesn't already have a modem with fax capability, you can easily buy and install an inexpensive internal or USB external fax modem. If you have Internet-based telephone service, contact your phone service provider to see whether your line can carry fax signals. In a corporate setting, check to see whether your organization uses digital telephone wiring before you try to hook up a dial-up modem. Digital phone lines can damage your modem.

should work, too. You might want to visit the manufacturer's website to download the most current version of its software rather than relying on a disc included in the package, which could be months or years old. (And, to repeat a warning we make all over this book: Don't download drivers or software from any site other than the original manufacturer's! Sites that offer collections of drivers and software are often—intentionally or not—actually in the business of distributing viruses and other malware.)

Installing a Fax Modem

Many modems require you to install the manufacturer's driver software before you attach the modem for the first time, so be sure to read the instructions before you connect the device. Internal and USB external modems will then self-install when you plug them in. For an external serial-port modem (if you somehow have dug up one of these), you might need to give Windows a nudge. Type `control panel` into the taskbar's search box, select Control Panel from the results, and then click Add a Device under Hardware and Sound (in Category view).

Once the modem is installed, follow the instructions in the next section to configure the fax service.

Installing a Scanner

A scanner or multifunction printer that is connected via USB or FireWire should self-install when you connect it. However, your manufacturer might suggest that you install its software *before* you plug in the device for the first time. Heed this advice.

For network-attached scanners and all-in-one printers, install the manufacturer's software first. It will then find the device on your network.

If you are given a choice between installing either TWAIN or WIA (Windows Imaging Architecture) drivers for your scanner, choose to use the WIA drivers. TWAIN drivers may support more advanced scanner features, such as transparency adapters and dust/scratch removal, found on some models, but they are not compatible with Windows Fax and Scan. Some scanners install both types of drivers; that's fine.

 tip

If you try to install driver software and you get a message saying that it won't work on your version of Windows, be sure that you are using the right 32-bit or 64-bit version to match Windows. If that's not the problem, right-click the installer program, select Properties, select the Compatibility tab, and then set the compatibility mode to Windows 7. If the installer first unzips files and then runs a second installer, you'll have to locate and then perform this compatibility trick on the second installer program.

note

If you have an all-in-one printer, it most likely will *not* appear as a fax modem device for Windows Fax and Scan. Instead, its software will likely set up two printer devices: one for printing and one for faxing. A multifunction device should be able to scan, though, using Windows Fax and Scan.

 note

Windows Fax and Scan doesn't help you scan slides or transparencies. For that, you must use third-party software or software provided with your scanner. You likely also need to install TWAIN drivers for that software to run the transparency adapter hardware.

Configuring the Fax Service

To set up your system to send or receive faxes with a fax modem, go to the Start menu. If you see no tile for Windows Fax and Scan, just type **fax** and then select Windows Fax and Scan.

🅦 tip

If you'll be using WFS frequently, pin it to your Start menu. Here's how: In the taskbar's search box, type **fax**. Right-click Windows **Fax** and Scan and select Pin to Start. Then move the new tile to a convenient location. You can also pin it to the desktop's taskbar: Open the app, right-click its icon in the taskbar, and select Pin to Taskbar.

Click Fax at the bottom of the left pane. Next, click the New Fax button on the toolbar (see Figure 12.1). The Fax Setup dialog box appears. The first time you do this, Windows will walk you through the process of setting up the faxing software, using these steps:

Figure 12.1
Windows Fax and Scan lets you scan or fax documents. (You probably guessed that.)

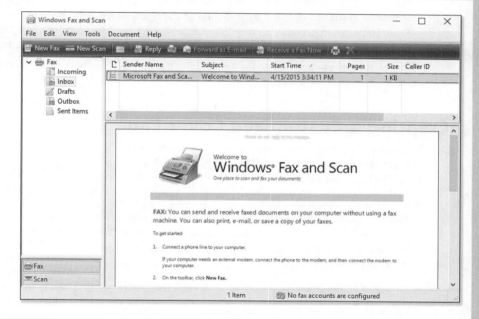

1. Select Connect to a Fax Modem. On the next screen, enter a name for the modem or keep the default name, Fax Modem. Click Next to continue.

2. Choose how you want to receive faxes from the following choices:

   ■ **Answer Automatically**—Choose this option if you have a dedicated fax line and want the fax modem to pick up every incoming call.

- **Notify Me**—Choose this option if you share the telephone line with voice calls. Windows will pop up a notification when there is an incoming call, and you can tell Windows whether or not to answer it and receive an incoming fax.

- **I'll Choose Later**—Choose this option if you don't want the computer to answer incoming calls.

3. A New Fax window appears. Close it.

4. A blinking icon might appear in the taskbar. If it does, open it. The message will start with "Windows Firewall has blocked some features of Microsoft Windows Fax and Scan...." Be sure that Private Networks is checked and Public Networks is unchecked. Click Allow Access.

5. Back in Windows Fax and Scan, click Tools, Sender Information. Enter your name, address, and telephone number information. This info will later be used in fax cover sheets. Click OK when you're done.

6. Click Tools, Fax Settings, and then click the More Options button. Enter your preferred incoming fax number or company name in the TSID (Transmitting Subscriber Identification) box. This text is printed at the top of every fax you send and appears on the recipient's fax machine's screen. Enter the same information in the CSID (Called Subscriber Identification) box. This info will be displayed on the screen and transmit log of fax machines that call you. Click OK.

Now that you've set up the basic fax service, you can go on to create customized cover pages if you like.

Creating a Customized Cover Page

To create a customized cover page, click Tools, Cover Pages. Existing personalized cover pages (if any) are listed. Then take one of the following actions:

- To customize one of the standard cover pages provided by Microsoft, click Copy, select a cover page template, and select Open. Then highlight the copied entry and click Rename. Give it a new name, but be sure that the name still ends with .cov. Press Enter and then click Open to personalize the cover page.

- To create a new cover page from scratch, click New.

- To modify one of your existing cover pages, select it and click Open.

In each case, this opens the Fax Cover Page Editor, shown in Figure 12.2.

Use the Insert menu to place text, fields, and simple shapes. Fields are automatically replaced with information from the sending document and sending user, whereas literal text is fixed for all time. Use the Format menu to align objects, adjust

 tip

When you insert a field name and associated field, they are selected as a group and will move as a group. If you want to move one of the components separately, click somewhere in the cover page away from any items. Then move the desired item.

To move several items at once, hold down the Shift key and click each of them and then drag them. You can also click the Select icon (leftmost on the toolbar) and drag a box around the items you want to move.

spacing, center the page, or change the order of overlapping objects. Use the View menu to show or hide menus and gridlines. (Gridlines are hidden by default but can be useful in aligning design elements.) Use the File menu to print or save your cover page. Cover pages are saved with the `.cov` file extension and are saved in your `Documents\Fax\Personal CoverPages` folder by default.

Figure 12.2
Creating a cover page with the Fax Cover Page Editor.

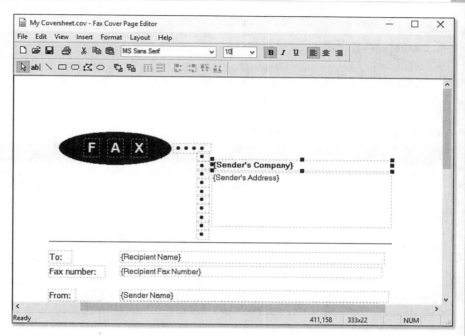

To make your personalized cover page available to all users, you must copy the cover page file to `\ProgramData\Microsoft\Windows NT\MSFax\Common CoverPages\xx-xx`, where `xx-xx` is a code that specifies your geographic region and language. Moving the file to that location is a bit tricky. Follow these steps:

1. Create a cover page and save the cover page file in the default location (your `Personal CoverPages` folder). Test it by sending it in a fax, to be sure that it looks the way you want it to. After you're sure that it's correct, proceed to the next step.

2. From the Desktop, click the File Explorer icon in the taskbar. (If it's not there, press Windows Logo+X and select File Explorer.) Browse into This PC, Documents, Fax, Personal CoverPages. Locate the cover page file, right-click it, and select Cut.

3. Click in File Explorer's address bar. Type `c:\programdata` and press Enter. Then double-click, in turn, Microsoft, Windows NT, MSFax. Windows will notify you that you don't have permission to view MSFax. Click Continue to grant yourself permission and continue into Common Coverpages and then into the regional folder, which is `en-US` for U.S. English (but might be different on your computer).

(Programdata is a hidden folder, and you normally can't navigate to it by clicking. That's why we have you type in its name.)

4. Right-click in the folder's contents pane and select Paste. In the Destination Folder Access Denied dialog box, click Continue to paste the file into this folder.

Creating a cover page is a painful process, but now it will be available to all users on your computer.

Changing Fax Settings

To change your computer's fax settings after the initial setup described in the previous sections, open Windows Fax and Scan and select Fax in the left pane. Then use the menu options listed in Table 12.1 to change fax settings.

Table 12.1 Fax Service Settings

Setting	Menu Selection
Autoanswer	Tools, Fax Settings, General tab. To answer automatically, check Allow...to Receive fax calls, select Automatically Answer After, and set to 1 ring. To be prompted to answer, check Allow...to Receive and select Manually Answer. To block incoming faxes, uncheck Check Allow...to Receive.
Cover page data	Tools, Sender Information.
Fax arrival/complete sounds	Tools, Fax Settings, Tracking tab, Sound Options button.
Fax complete/failed pop-ups	Tools, Fax Settings, Tracking tab.
Fax send progress pop-up	Tools, Fax Settings, Tracking tab.
Multiple fax devices	Tools, Fax Accounts.
Personal cover pages	Tools, Cover Pages. To share a customized cover page with other users on your computer, see the previous section.
Redialing on busy/no answer	Tools, Fax Settings, Advanced tab.
TSID/CSID strings	Tools, Fax Settings, General tab, More Options button.
TSID/Page # on header	Tools, Fax Settings, Advanced tab. When Include Banner in Sent Faxes is checked, Windows puts your TSID and the page number at the top of every sent fax page.

Sending Faxes from Windows Fax and Scan

To send a fax, in most cases you start by creating a document using a word processing application such as Microsoft Word or the built-in WordPad application. You can fax from any application that can print. To send a document as a fax, open the application's Print menu and select the printer named Fax. When you click Print, Windows will pop up a dialog box in which you specify the recipients for the fax, as shown in Figure 12.3. A printed version of your document will appear as the first attachment of this new fax.

Figure 12.3
You can send a fax by printing to the Fax printer, but you can also create one from scratch by clicking New Fax.

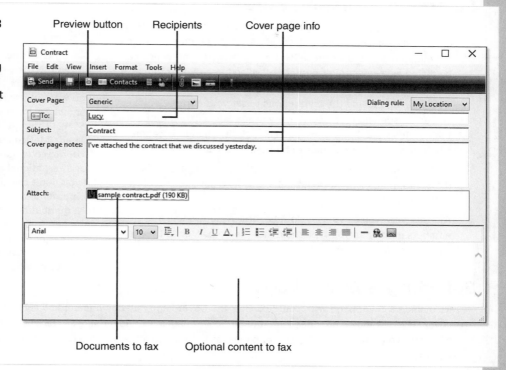

Preview button   Recipients   Cover page info

Documents to fax   Optional content to fax

If you want to send more than one document in the same fax call, use the Print menu to print the first document and then add the other documents as attachments, as we describe shortly.

You can also open Windows Fax and Scan, click New Fax, and manually construct an entire fax.

Selecting Recipients

To send a fax to a recipient not on your Contacts list, enter the fax number in the To field. If you want to enter numbers for more than one recipient, use a semicolon to separate multiple fax numbers.

To send a fax to someone in your Contacts list, or to create and save a new contact, click the To: button. Then select one or more entries from the list of contacts, and click the To-> button to add them to the recipient list. Click OK.

If a contact has a fax number listed, you might need to add the area code or country code to the number to enable Windows Fax and Scan to make the call correctly. Use the same information as you would provide for a standalone fax machine.

If you have selected contacts that have no associated fax number, the name will appear in red in the fax recipient list. Double-click these names and enter their fax numbers on the Home or Work tab. Click OK. The names will no longer appear in red.

Selecting a Dialing Rule

In many cases, you will send faxes to recipients outside your own area code. You can have Windows automatically figure out which fax numbers need to be preceded by an area code and which can be dialed as a seven-digit number by selecting a dialing rule at the right side of the New Fax window. If no rule is listed, select New Rule and follow the instructions to set your current location and area code and click OK. When you see My Location in the Dialing Rules list, highlight it and select Edit. Change Location name to your actual city name and then click OK.

If you travel to a different area code with your computer, select the appropriate location from the Dialing Rule list or select New Rule to create a new one.

Alternatively, you can select No Rule, and Windows will dial numbers exactly as you type them into the To box, or as they're entered in your contacts list.

 tip

Dialing works best if you *always* use the Dialing Rule system, or *never* use it. If you want to use it, enter all contact fax numbers in (333) 555-1212 format for U.S./ Canada/Mexico numbers and *+countrycode number* format for international numbers. If you don't travel with your computer and don't want to use numbering rules, enter numbers in 555-1212 format for local numbers and 1-333-555-1212 format for long-distance numbers.

Selecting a Cover Page

To include a cover page with your fax, click the Cover Page pull-down menu and select the desired cover page. Windows provides four standard cover pages: Confidential, FYI, Generic, and Urgent. To create your own customized cover pages, see "Creating a Customized Cover Page" earlier in this chapter.

Entering Subject and Comment Text

If you're using a cover page that displays a subject line, enter the subject of your fax into the Subject field. If your cover page has a Notes field, you can add a paragraph or two of comments in the Cover Page Notes box. These text fields don't support complex formatting.

At the bottom of the New Fax dialog box is a large text entry box that includes a text-formatting toolbar (refer to Figure 12.3). You can use this box to create a document for your fax, with full formatting, and any number of pages. You can use the menu item Insert, Picture to add images, which will get scaled down to fit the faxed page, even if they look too large in this window.

You aren't able to save whatever you create here, however. Once it's faxed, it's gone. I recommend that rather than use this input area, you create a document in a word processor or WordPad, save it, and then attach it to the fax using the steps in the next section.

If you leave the large input area blank, the fax will consist just of the optional cover page and any attachment documents you add in the next step.

Adding Other Documents to the Fax

To send a previously scanned document, a word processing file, a PDF file, or other printable file in the fax, click Insert, File Attachment. Navigate to the file and click Open. The file will be converted to fax pages when the fax is sent. You must have an installed application capable of printing this file.

You can insert any number of attachments here, to construct a single fax from multiple components.

tip

You can use your scanner like a standard fax machine using this technique. Open Windows Scan and Fax, select New Fax, fill in the recipient list, and then click Insert, Pages from Scanner. What makes this beat a standard fax machine is that Windows keeps a copy of every fax it sends. This capability can come in really handy.

Adding Scanned Pages

You can scan pages and directly add them to your fax. Place the pages you want to scan into your scanner's automatic document feeder (ADF) or place one sheet on its platen. Click Insert, Pages from Scanner. The pages are scanned automatically and show as an attachment. If your scanner does not have an automatic feeder, remove the first page after scanning it, insert the next page, and repeat the process until all pages have been scanned. Each scanned page is inserted as a TIFF file.

Previewing the Fax

After typing and inserting all the information needed into the fax, click View, Preview to see a preview of the fax. Alternatively, click the Preview icon, which is just to the right of the Save icon on the toolbar. Attachments are converted into text or graphics, as appropriate. Use the Zoom Level pull-down menu to select a magnification for review.

Uncheck View, Preview (or click the Preview icon again) to return to the normal fax-editing mode.

Sending the Fax

To send the fax, click Send. The fax is placed in the Windows Fax and Scan program's Outbox folder until transmission is complete. After the fax is transmitted, the fax is placed in the Sent Items folder.

You can view any previously sent fax by viewing this folder in Windows Fax and Scan. To print a copy of a sent fax, right-click it in the fax list and select Print. To resend, right-click it and select Forward As Fax.

Monitoring Outgoing Faxes

After you click Send, a pop-up window appears, displaying the status of the current fax and previous fax events. At the end of the fax transmission, a notification is also displayed over the system tray. You can turn off these notifications if you find them annoying; see "Changing Fax Settings," earlier in this chapter.

Can't Detect a Dial Tone

If the fax modem doesn't detect a dial tone, Windows won't send the fax. Make sure the RJ-11 telephone cable is properly connected to the fax modem and to the phone jack. Some fax modems use a pair of RJ-11 ports: one for the phone line and one to permit a telephone to share the line when the modem is not in use. Make sure you connect your telephone cables to the correct ports. A good way to start troubleshooting is to unplug the phone cable from your modem and plug it into a regular telephone. Be sure the phone gets a dial tone.

Receiving Faxes

To configure Windows Fax and Scan to receive a fax automatically, select Tools, Fax Settings, and then make sure that the option Allow the Device to Receive Fax Calls is enabled, the Automatically Answer After option is selected, and the number of rings is set to 1. The computer will now answer incoming calls on the telephone line connected to its modem, just like a standard fax machine. If you configure Windows Fax and Scan to receive faxes manually, a notification appears when an incoming call is detected. If you are expecting a fax, click the notification balloon to have the modem pick up the call.

Incoming faxes are received and saved to the Inbox.

During the reception, the Review Fax Status window displays the status of the incoming fax. Click Close to close the window after receiving the fax.

Printing Received Faxes Automatically

If you want received faxes to print automatically, click Tools, Fax Settings. On the General tab, click More Options. In the When a Fax Is Received section, open the Print a Copy To pull-down menu and select a printer. When you receive a fax, the fax will automatically print on the specified printer.

Scanning Documents with Windows Fax and Scan

To start Windows Fax and Scan, go to the Start menu. If you see no tile for Windows Fax and Scan, right-click the Start menu and select All Apps, or you can just type **fax** into the Search box. Then select Windows Fax and Scan.

Click the Scan button in the bottom of the left pane to switch to the Scan view.

You can later change the scanner's settings for any individual photo or document, but it helps to predefine the settings you use most frequently as the defaults. We discuss this in the next section.

 tip

If you'll be using WFS frequently, pin it to your Start screen. Here's how: At the Start screen, type **fax**. Right-click Windows Fax and Scan and select Pin to Start. You can also pin it to the desktop's taskbar.

Editing Scan Profile Defaults

Before you scan your first documents, take a moment to configure the program's scan settings. Click Tools, Scan Settings. The dialog box lists the default settings, known as scan profiles, for different types of scans. As initially installed, there will be two: Photo (color) and Documents (grayscale, like old movies).

The Photo setting is the default scan profile. If you plan to scan printed documents more often than color photos, click the Documents profile name and then click the Set as Default button. This will make this profile the one to be used with your scanner's "one-button scanning" feature, if it has one.

To edit the default scan resolution or other settings for a profile, select the profile and then click Edit. Figure 12.4 illustrates the settings for a typical Documents profile.

Figure 12.4
Editing the Documents scan profile.

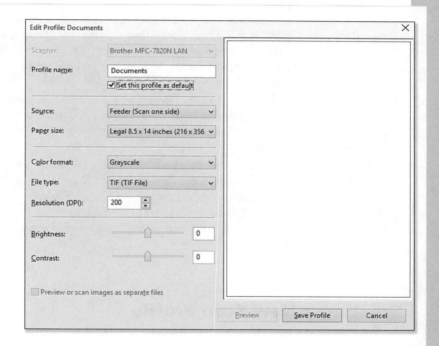

From this dialog box, you can select the following:

- Scanner (if you have more than one installed)

- Profile name

- Paper source (such as flatbed or automatic document feeder [ADF])

- Paper size

- Color format (black and white, grayscale, or color)

- File type (JPEG, BMP, TIFF, or PNG)

- Scan resolution

- Scan brightness

- Scan contrast

Make the changes you want to the profile and click Save Profile to replace the current settings with your changes.

Choosing the Right Settings

What resolution should you use? If you're going to send the scan as a fax, 300dpi matches the Very Fine (best quality) black-and-white document resolution setting supported by standard fax machines. However, for most faxing applications, 200dpi is adequate. Use a higher resolution, such as 600dpi, if you are scanning a photo for printing on a high-quality color inkjet or laser printer or for publishing in print form. For images that you plan to email or use on a web page, try 75dpi to 96dpi. This resolution will produce a smaller image that is better suited for displaying on a computer screen. Set the File Type to TIF.

For color photographs, set the Color Format to Color. For black-and-white pictures or faded documents, set the Color Format to Grayscale. For typed documents and for pencil or pen-and-ink line drawings, try Black and White. This option produces the smallest scan file, but thin lines might drop out...try it and see.

Under File Type, the TIFF format produces the best quality but can produce rather large files (often too large to email). If you are scanning photographs and want to save disk space, use JPEG. Applications that do not support other file types can use BMP, but BMP files are very large. For black-and-white scans of documents or line drawings, use the TIFF format. JPEG is *not* a good choice; it can cause blurriness and weird image distortions in black-and-white scans.

Creating a New Scan Profile

You can create a new profile to give yourself an additional set of default settings to choose from. To create a new scan profile, click Tools, Scan Settings, Add. Enter the profile name, select the paper source, and make other changes as needed. Click Save Profile to save the new scan profile.

---

 tip

The preset resolution for a new scan profile is 200dpi. To match the dpi of current Windows desktops, we recommend 96dpi for viewing or emailing. Use a resolution of at least 200dpi or more for profiles intended for printing or faxing. See the sidebar "Choosing the Right Settings" for specific resolution recommendations for different types of documents and destinations.

Scanning Images

Window Fax and Scan has no functions for color correction, image restoration, or photo editing, and only primitive ways to let you organize and label groups of pictures, so it's not the best of all possible tools for converting your old photo albums to a digital archive. For that, professional image scanning and processing applications as Adobe Photoshop or GIMP would probably be better. Still, if you can accept these limitations, Fax and Scan can scan photos as easily as it scans line drawings and black-and-white documents.

 tip

Windows Fax and Scan doesn't let you drag and drop files, which is sort of annoying. It's sometimes easier to work with scanned files using File Explorer. You can find the files under Documents, inside the Scanned Documents folder.

To scan a photo with Windows Fax and Scan, insert the photo into your scanner. If the scanner is a flatbed design, insert the photo face down (photo against the cover glass). If the scanner includes a feeder (ADF) or uses a sheet-fed design, see the documentation or markings on the scanner to determine whether photos are inserted face up or face down.

Click New Scan. If you have more than one scanner installed, select a scanner. Select the profile desired and then click Preview to see a preview scan. If you want, click and drag the bounding boxes to the edges of the photo, or crop the photo as desired. If the photo is too bright or too dark, adjust the Brightness slider. Adjust the Contrast slider if the photo is too flat (contrast too low) or too harsh (contrast too high). To see the results of the changes, click Preview again. When you are satisfied with the scan quality, click Scan.

A scanning progress bar appears, and the scanned image is displayed in the workspace after being saved to disk.

You can select items in the Fax and Scan workspace list and right-click to choose various actions such as View, Print, Send To (for faxing), Rename, and Move to Folder.

 ## Slow Scanning Speed

If you have a USB-connected scanner and scans seem slow, make sure you have connected the scanner to a USB 3.0 or 2.0 port. On some computers, some of the USB ports run only at slower USB 1.1 speeds. If you inadvertently plug in to a slow USB port, Windows will usually pop up a notification telling you. If this happens, unplug the scanner and try a USB port elsewhere on the computer. If you have connected the scanner to an external USB hub, try connecting the scanner directly to a USB port on the computer.

Emailing and Faxing Scans

To fax a scanned document or photo without switching to the Fax view, select the item you want to fax and click Document, Forward as Fax. The New Fax dialog box appears. If you want to fax more than one scanned image (or set of images), click Insert, File Attachment and then locate the additional image(s). You can find them under Documents inside the folder Scanned Documents.

➡ *For more information,* **see** *"Sending Faxes from Windows Fax and Scan,"* **p. 276.**

If you have a standalone email program installed (such as Outlook), you can easily email a scanned document or photo. Just open Windows Fax and Scan, click Scan, and locate the image file. Select the item you want to email, and click Document, Forward as Email. Enter the recipient(s), message, and other information, and click Send to send the scan. Be aware, though, that really large scanned image files might get rejected as too large by the email system. You may need to reduce the size of images before you can email them. (You can use any number of image editing programs to create reduced-resolution copies of your pictures. The free Windows Photo Gallery program can do it. You can download this program from www.microsoft.com.)

If you use a web-based email service, this approach won't work. You'll have to compose an email and use your email system's Add Attachment feature to upload the image files. You can find them under Documents inside the folder Scanned Documents.

13

MORE WINDOWS 10 MEDIA TOOLS

Controlling the Volume

Controlling the volume of your audio is crucial. During playback, you might want to turn down the volume if you're in a public place where you don't want to disturb others nearby. If you have no such worries, you might want to crank up a particularly good audio CD. During recording, setting the right input levels can make the difference between recording high-quality audio and distorted noise. Windows 10 gives you the tools to set these volume levels, equalize the volume, and more.

Controlling the Overall System Volume

The *system volume* is the volume that Windows uses for all things audio on your computer: the sounds that Windows itself makes (warning beeps, the sign-in and sign-out tones, and so on) and the sounds that waft from your applications (such as music from Media Player and the mail notification from Microsoft Outlook).

To control the system volume, click the Volume icon in the taskbar's notification area to open the volume control, shown in Figure 13.1. Drag the slider to the volume level you prefer, or click Mute Speakers to get the sounds of silence.

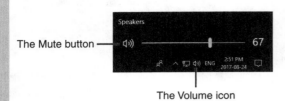

The Mute button

The Volume icon

Figure 13.1
Click the Volume icon, and then drag the slider to set the system volume.

Controlling an Application's Volume

Controlling the system volume is the easiest way to get the sound level you need, but in many cases, it's not the best way. For example, suppose you're waiting for an important email message, so you set up Windows Live Mail to play a sound when an email message comes in. Suppose further that you're also using Windows Media Player to play music in the background. If you get a phone call, you want to turn down or mute the music. If you mute the system volume, you mute the music playback but you also mute other system sounds, including Windows Live Mail's audio alerts. So, while you're on the phone, there's a good chance that you'll miss that important message you've been waiting for.

 note

The volume you hear depends not only on where you set the Volume slider, but also on where you set the volume on the speakers themselves, assuming they come with a volume knob or similar control. We'd be embarrassed to tell you how many times we've wondered why our PC had no sound despite having the Volume slider cranked to its maximum, only to realize that the speakers themselves were turned down.

Many programs that produce sound also come with options for controlling or muting those sounds, so you could always control application sounds individually. However, that's a hassle. The Windows 10 solution to this kind of problem is called *per-application volume control*. This means that Windows 10 gives you a volume control slider for every running program and process that is a dedicated sound application (such as Windows Media Player) or is currently producing audio output. In our example, you would have separate volume controls for Windows Media Player and Windows Live Mail. When that phone call comes in, you can turn down or mute Windows Media Player while leaving the Windows Live Mail volume as is, so there's much less chance that you'll miss that incoming message. Note, however, that many newer applications don't support per-application volume control, particularly any of the so-called Modern apps that come with Windows 10.

Figure 13.2 shows the Volume Mixer window that appears when you right-click the Volume icon in the taskbar notification area and then click Open Volume Mixer. The Device section on the left has a slider that controls the speaker volume, so you can use it as a systemwide volume control. The rest of the window contains the *application mixer*, which includes sliders and mute buttons for individual programs.

note

How long an application's slider remains in the Volume Mixer window depends on how often the application accesses the audio stack. If a program just makes the occasional peep, it will appear only briefly in the Volume Mixer and then disappear. If a program makes noise fairly often, it remains in the Volume Mixer for much longer. So, for example, if you use Windows Media Player, it will remain in the Volume Mixer as long as you have it open.

Figure 13.2
Windows 10 uses per-application volume control to enable you to set the volume level for each program that outputs audio.

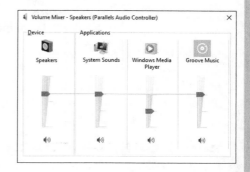

Note, too, that when you move the speaker volume slider, the program sliders move along with it. That's a nice touch, but what's even nicer is that the speaker volume slider preserves the relative volume levels of each program. So, if you adjust the speaker volume to about half its current level, the sliders in the application mixer also adjust to about half of their current level.

The volume control also remembers application settings between sessions. So, if you mute *Solitaire*, for example, it will remain muted the next time you start the program.

Balancing Your Speakers or Headphones

Many of us have computer speakers that are placed in odd positions (say, one on top of a book and the other behind a cat), so music can sound a bit off; or we have one ear that doesn't hear as well as the other. In this situation, adjusting the system volume or an application's volume is problematic because turning up the sound enough to hear things clearly in your bad ear can make those sounds too loud in your good ear.

Windows can help by enabling you to balance the sound in each ear. That is, you will perceive sounds equally from both speakers. Here's what you do:

1. Right-click the Volume icon in the taskbar notification area and then click Playback Devices. Windows 10 displays the Sound dialog box with the Playback tab selected.

2. In the list of playback devices, click your headphones.

3. Click Properties.

4. Click the Levels tab.

5. Click Balance. Windows displays the Balance dialog box shown in Figure 13.3. If you have a headphone attached, you will probably see only L (left) and R (right) sliders. For desktop speaker systems, you may see additional sliders for the center, subwoofer, and rear channels, even if you don't have those speakers attached.

6. Drag the L (left) and R (right) sliders to the volume levels you prefer. (In some cases, instead of L you see the number 1, and instead of R you see the number 2.) If you're not sure whether the balance is correct, run Windows Media Player and start playing some music; then try balancing the headphones.

7. Click OK in each of the open dialog boxes to put the new levels into effect.

III

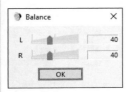

Figure 13.3
Use the Balance dialog box to adjust the headphone volume for each ear.

Equalizing the Volume

You might find that wide fluctuations in volume can make sounds—particularly speech—much harder to perceive. You can compensate by turning on the Loudness Equalization enhancement for your computer's speakers or your headphones, which makes all sounds that emanate from your computer equally loud.

Follow these steps to turn on Loudness Equalization:

1. Right-click the Volume icon in the taskbar notification area and then click Playback Devices. Windows 10 displays the Sound dialog box with the Playback tab selected.

2. In the list of playback devices, click the sound device you want to adjust.

3. Click Properties. Windows 10 opens the Properties dialog box for the device.

4. Click the Enhancements tab.

5. Check the Loudness Equalization box, as shown in Figure 13.4.

6. Click OK in each of the open dialog boxes to put the new levels into effect.

Figure 13.4
With the Loudness Equalization feature on the job, sounds such as speech will be easier to discern.

Setting the Default Output Device

Windows 10 is happy to let you have more than one audio playback device installed on your system. For example, you might have your PC connected to desktop speakers, headphones, and a home theater receiver. Fortunately, Windows doesn't play audio through all the connected devices! Instead, it sets one device as the default and uses that device for the playback. If you'd prefer that Windows use a different device, you must set up that device as the default. To do this, in the taskbar notification area, right-click the Volume icon, and then click Playback Devices to open the Sound dialog box with the Playback tab selected. Click the device you want to use, and then click Set Default.

Assigning Sounds to Events

As you work with Windows 10, you hear various sounds emanating from your speakers, corresponding to particular system events. There's the odd two-note beat when you connect a device; there's the short, sharp shock of a sound when a warning dialog box pops up; and there's the nice and perhaps all-too-familiar chime when a new email message arrives.

If you're getting tired of the same old sounds, however, Windows 10 lets you customize what you hear by assigning different WAV files to these events. You can also assign sounds to a couple of dozen other events. The sounds assigned to various Windows 10 events comprise a sound scheme. To view the current scheme, type **sounds** in the taskbar's Search box, and then click Change System Sounds in the search results. (You can also right-click the Volume icon and then click Sounds.) Windows 10 opens the Sound dialog box with the Sounds tab displayed, as shown in Figure 13.5.

Figure 13.5
Use the Sounds tab in the Sound dialog box to change the current Windows 10 sound scheme.

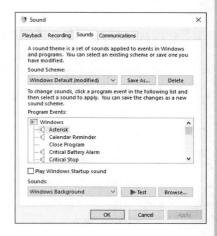

Here's a rundown of the various controls on the Sounds tab:

- **Sound Scheme**—This drop-down list displays the currently selected sound scheme. (Windows 10 ships with just two schemes: Windows Default and No Sounds.)

- **Program Events**—This list displays a number of Windows 10 events, including four that apply to the various types of dialog boxes displayed by Windows 10 and Windows applications: Asterisk, Critical Stop, Exclamation, and Question. If an event has a sound icon beside it, this means a WAV file is currently assigned to that event.

- **Sounds**—This drop-down list shows you the name of the WAV file assigned to the currently highlighted event. You can use the Browse button to select a different WAV file (or just use the Name drop-down list to select a WAV file from Windows 10's Media subfolder).

- **Test**—Click this button to try out the WAV file shown in the Sounds list.

You can use three methods to work with sound schemes:

- To change the current sound scheme, select items in the Program Events list and use the Sounds list to change the associated WAV file.

- To use a different sound scheme, select it from the Sound Scheme drop-down list.

- To create your own sound scheme, first associate WAV files with the various system events you want to hear. Then click Save As, enter a name for the new scheme, and click OK.

Recording Sounds with Voice Recorder

If you have a system capable of recording sounds from a microphone (most desktops or laptops are), you can have hours of fun creating your own Windows Media Audio (WMA) files. Preserving silly sounds for posterity is the most fun, of course, but you can also create serious messages and embed them in business documents or for use as a Windows Live Movie Maker narration track.

Setting Up the Microphone

Before you start recording, you need to set up your microphone, particularly the volume levels for recording. Follow these steps:

1. In the taskbar's Search box, type **sound**, and then click Sound. Windows 10 displays the Sound dialog box.

2. Click the Recording tab.

3. Click your microphone and then click Configure to open the Speech Recognition control panel.

4. Click Set Up Microphone. Windows 10 displays the Microphone Setup Wizard.

5. Click the radio button for the type of microphone you're using, and then click Next. The wizard shows you how to set up your microphone properly.

6. Click Next. The wizard displays some text for you to read, as shown in Figure 13.6.

7. Read the text into the microphone using your normal speaking voice, and then click Next when you're finished.

8. Click Finish. The wizard completes the configuration of your microphone.

Figure 13.6
The Microphone Setup wizard takes you step-by-step through the microphone configuration.

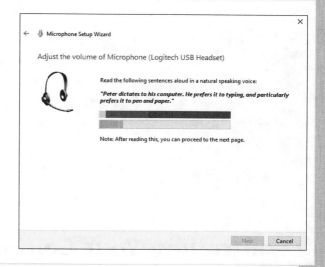

Making a Voice Recording

To get started with Voice Recorder, type **voice** in the taskbar's Search box, and then click the Voice Recorder app in the search results. When you're ready to begin recording, here are the steps to follow:

1. With your microphone ready, click the Record button (the white microphone in the blue circle).

2. Speak (yell, sing, whatever) into the microphone. Sound Recorder shows you the length of the file as you record.

3. When you're finished, click the Stop Recording button. Voice Recorder adds the recording to the list.

4. Click the new recording, click Rename (the pencil icon), type a name for the recording, and then click Rename.

5. If you want to trim excess or unwanted audio from the beginning or the end (or both), click Trim to open the Trim tool (see Figure 13.7), click and drag the start point and end point to the positions you want, and then click Accept (the check mark).

 note
Voice Recorder creates MPEG 4 Audio (.m4a) files. The default save location is %UserProfile%\ Documents\Sound recordings, which you can open directly from Voice Recorder by right-clicking a recording and clicking Open File Location.

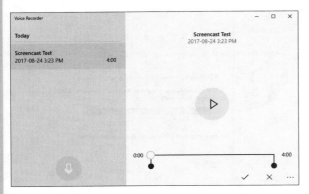

Figure 13.7
When your recording is finished, you can use the Trim tool to remove unwanted audio from the beginning and end of the recording.

Controlling Your Computer with Speech Recognition

If due to injury, age, or for various other reasons you find that using a mouse and keyboard is too time-consuming, too difficult, or too frustrating, you might think you're out of luck—because how else are you supposed to control your computer? Fortunately, there *is* another way: voice commands. Using the Speech Recognition feature, you can speak commands into a microphone, and Windows will do your bidding.

Does it really work? Actually, most of the time, yes—it really does. Windows 10 has very good voice-recognition technology, and as long as you're in a relatively quiet room and speak clearly, Windows will recognize actions such as click, double-click, and select; commands such as Save, Copy, and Close; keystrokes such as Backspace, Delete, and Enter; and screen features such as Minimize, Scroll, and Back.

To get started, you need a system with a built-in mic or the ability to attach a microphone to your computer. A microphone that's part of a headset is easiest to use, but you can also use a standalone microphone that sits on your desk.

With your microphone attached to your computer, your next task is to configure the Speech Recognition feature (if you configured your microphone earlier, you can skip through steps 2 to 6):

1. In the taskbar's Search box, type **speech**, and then click Windows Speech Recognition. The Welcome to Speech Recognition Wizard appears.

 tip
One of Speech Recognition's handiest tricks you can use is to say, "Show numbers," which then places a number over everything in the current window that can be clicked. You can then state the number of the item you want and then say, "OK," and Speech Recognition will "click" that item for you *and* tell you the correct command name.

2. Click Next. The wizard asks what type of microphone you have.

3. Make your selection (Headset Microphone, Desktop Microphone, or Other) and then click Next. The wizard displays a screen that tells you about the proper placement of your microphone.

4. After you've made any necessary adjustments, click Next. The wizard now displays some text for you to read aloud.

5. Read the text in your normal voice, and then click Next. The wizard lets you know that your microphone is set up and ready for use.

6. Click Next. The wizard asks whether it can examine your documents to look for words that it should learn.

7. This is a good idea, so select Enable Document Review and click Next. The wizard wants to know how you want to activate speech recognition.

8. The easiest route here is to select Use Voice Activation Mode, which means you can start Speech Recognition by saying, "Start listening" and stop Speech Recognition by saying, "Stop listening." (If you choose Use Manual Activation Mode instead, you must manually activate Speech Recognition each time by pressing Windows Logo+Ctrl or by clicking the microphone icon in the Speech Recognition window.) Click Next. The wizard suggests that you print the Speech Reference Card, which contains a list of useful commands.

9. If you want to print the card, click View Reference Sheet and then click the Print button in the Help window that appears.

10. Return to the Set Up Speech Recognition Wizard (if you printed the card in the previous step) and then click Next. The wizard wonders whether you want to start Speech Recognition automatically each time you start your computer.

11. This is a good way to go, so leave the Run Speech Recognition at Startup box checked and click Next. The wizard now offers to take you through a Speech Recognition tutorial, which enables you to practice the voice commands.

12. The tutorial is definitely worthwhile, so click Start Tutorial.

13. When you're done, click Finish.

> **tip**
>
> If you no longer want Speech Recognition to run at startup, type **speech** in the Search box and then, under Settings, select Speech Recognition. In the Speech Recognition window, select Advanced Speech Options, and then deselect the Run Speech Recognition at Startup check box.

With all that out of the way, you can start using Speech Recognition, which appears as a small window at the top of the desktop. You speak your commands, and Speech Recognition will either carry them out or will say, "What was that?" if it doesn't recognize what you said. In Figure 13.8, I've just said "Open Run," and Speech Recognition not only has opened the Run dialog box but has also echoed the command in its window.

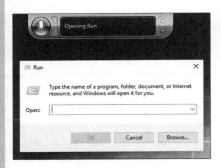

Figure 13.8
Speech Recognition at work: say, "Open Run" to open the Run dialog box.

GETTING CONNECTED

Going Worldwide

In this chapter, you find information about choosing an Internet service provider (ISP), making the connection through a modem or other link, installing and configuring your system, and making your system safe and secure. This chapter tells how to select an Internet connection technology and connect a single computer to the Internet. However, this isn't your only option. You can take any one of several routes:

- If your computer is part of an existing local area network (LAN) with Internet access, you can skip this chapter entirely because Internet access comes as part and parcel of your LAN connection. In fact, if you are part of a corporate LAN, it is most likely a violation of your company's security policy to establish your own independent connection.

- If you have or are willing to set up a LAN for your home or office, you can provide Internet access to all your computers through one connection. You should read Chapter 19, "Connecting Your Network to the Internet," and decide whether you want to connect to the Internet through a LAN. This is the case for almost all homes and offices now. Your Internet service provider might have installed a wired or wireless router, in which case you already have the makings of a LAN. Use the instructions in this chapter to set up the initial connection, and Chapter 19 tells you how to share it with the rest of your workgroup.

  (If you don't already have a network, and you have two or more computers, you should seriously consider creating one. Chapter 18, "Creating a Windows Network," tells you how.)

- If you have already selected your ISP and connection technology, you can skip the introductory sections of this chapter and go right to "Installing a Network Adapter for Broadband Service," later in this chapter.

- If you need to make a clean start with the Internet, read on!

By the way, we don't have room to describe using dial-up Internet service in great detail, but, if you have to use it, we do give you some pointers.

➡ *For information on using dial-up Internet service,* **see** *"Dial-Up Internet," p. 307.*

Understanding Connection Technologies

Not long ago, you had but one choice to make for your Internet connection: which brand of modem to buy. Now options abound, and you can choose among several technologies, speeds, and ISP types. In the past decade, high-speed (broadband) DSL and cable digital service have largely replaced dial-up modem service, but in some regions, dial-up and satellite services remain the only options.

Let's take a look at the basic Internet connection technologies that are appropriate for an individual user or workgroup, in increasing order of performance and usability. After describing each one, we show you roughly what each costs to set up and use.

DSL

Digital Subscriber Line (DSL) service sends a high-speed digital data signal over regular telephone wires. In most cases, DSL signals can be sent over the same telephone wire that serves your telephone, at the same time. This means that you can usually get DSL service installed without needing an extra telephone line. The most common DSL service is called *asymmetric*, or *ADSL*, because it receives data at 128Kbps to 6000Kbps but sends at a lower rate. (This is fine because most web surfing involves sending a very small request out and receiving a large amount of data back.) With the VDSL, VDSL2, and G.Fast technologies (where data travels by fiber optic cable to your immediate neighborhood), you can get speeds of 20Mbps to 200Mbps or more, depending on your budget and your distance from the provider's data cabinets.

DSL has at least one Achilles heel: its availability and speed are restricted by your distance from the telephone company's equipment in your neighborhood or in their central office, and it isn't available when the distance is more than a couple of miles (as the wires run, not as the crow flies). DSL's reach can be extended by optical fiber lines and special equipment, but this is expensive for the telephone companies to install. DSL might never make it into rural areas.

DSL modems come in two varieties: external units connect to your computer through a network adapter or a USB cable, whereas internal units plug right into your computer. If your ISP uses external adapters, before you buy a network

note

DSL varieties include asymmetric, symmetric, high-speed, very high speed, and DSL over ISDN, so you might run into the acronyms SDSL, ADSL, HDSL, ADSL2+, VDSL, VDSL2, G.Fast, and IDSL, or the collective xDSL. For this chapter, these distinctions are unimportant, so we just call it DSL.

adapter, check with your DSL provider because often one is included in the installation kit. Also, before you decide to pay extra to get service for multiple computers, read Chapter 19 to see how all your computers can share a single connection.

Some external DSL modems include a built-in connecting-sharing router that lets you share the Internet connection with several computers over a wired or wireless network. If your modem includes a router, you just need to connect your computers to the router, and you don't really need this chapter at all. Instead, see Chapter 19.

 note

If you consider DSL service, shop around before you buy. The signal has to come over your local phone company's wiring, but you can usually select among several Internet service providers that have a presence in the phone company central office or equipment cabinets that serve your neighborhood. The availability of different speeds and different pricing options can vary from neighborhood to neighborhood, so you have to check with the different ISPs by giving them your street address to find out what's available. You might also want to check out broadband availability at dslbyzip.com and read user reviews at dslreports.com.

Cable Modem

Your local television cable company might provide cable modem Internet service, which sends high-speed data signals through the same distribution system it uses to carry high-quality TV signals.

Cable modem service has none of the distance limitations of DSL. One early criticism of cable service was that data speeds could drop during high-use times, such as the early evening, because everyone in a given neighborhood shares a single network "pipe." That may have been true when cable service was introduced, but cable vendors seem to have built up their networks considerably, and this seems to happen less frequently now. Surveys show that cable subscribers usually get several times the download speed of standard DSL subscribers. In a few locations, DSL can now match its speed, but cable is still a good option.

Cable modems generally are external devices that connect to your computer through a network adapter or a USB cable. Before you buy a network adapter, though, check with your ISP; one might be included in the installation kit. Some ISPs charge extra to lease the modem. The price of a cable modem is $30–$120 new and can be $1 on eBay, so leasing one from your cable company isn't such a great deal. Also, if you have more than one computer and your cable ISP wants to charge you for extra connections, read Chapter 19 to see how all your computers can use a router to share a single connection.

Some cable companies now provide a cable modem that includes a built-in connection-sharing router that lets you share the Internet connection with several computers over a wired or wireless network. If your modem includes a router, you just need to connect your computers to the router, and you don't really need this chapter at all. Instead, see Chapter 19.

Satellite Service

Satellite Internet service uses microwave signals and small (roughly 2-foot-diameter) dish antennas to connect to an orbiting communication satellite. Whereas satellite TV works in a single direction—from the satellite to your dish—satellite Internet service is bidirectional, meaning the dish has both a transmitter and a receiver.

Satellite's one advantage is that it's available where DSL and cable haven't yet reached, wherever there's a good view of either the southern sky in the Northern Hemisphere or the northern sky in the Southern Hemisphere. The disadvantages are numerous:

- The equipment and service plans can be expensive.

- You'll have to sign a long-term contract to get discounts on installation and equipment.

- The system slows when many people are using it.

- You can lose the signal entirely when it's raining or snowing.

- If you download more than your monthly quota allows, you'll be punished by having your download speed cut to a crawl for the remainder of the month.

Despite all this, many people beyond the reach of cable and DSL say that satellite service beats dial-up, and it's worth the hassle.

Satellite service requires you to purchase a dish antenna, a transmitter/receiver, and a satellite modem. Your ISP should furnish these devices and will provide professional installation service. Professional installation is an FCC requirement because of the transmitter.

After the dish is installed and its connecting cable has been run in to your home or office, installing the satellite modem is not terribly tricky, but the procedure is specific to the type of hardware you're using. Therefore, unfortunately, we have to leave you at the mercy of the manufacturer's instruction manual and can't provide specific instructions in this book.

Wireless and Cellular Service

Wireless Internet service is available in most major metropolitan areas, and even in some remote areas, through cellular telephone providers and other vendors. These services transfer high-speed data without using physical cabling. It's a great option for mobile devices like tablets and phones, but in some cases it's also a feasible type of service to use for a home or office network when other options are not available.

Several types of service are available:

- **3G, 4G, and 4G LTE cellular data**—Wireless phone providers sell data service as a standalone service or as part of a bundled service package that includes voice and text messaging, for devices such as tablets and phones with built-in cellular data modems. Download speeds vary from place to place depending on the type of cellular network you are able to reach, but 40Mbps is not unheard of, which is as good or better than home DSL or cable Internet service. However, coverage of the higher-speed 4G and LTE networks is patchy: it's available in some cities and some parts of the country, and not at all in large swaths of it.

The hardware to support this type of service is usually built in to a phone or tablet. You can also purchase cellular modems for laptops to give them Internet connectivity where Wi-Fi isn't available.

- **WiMax**—WiMax is a cellular service with speeds that can range from tens of Mbps for mobile devices to 1Gbps for fixed modems. WiMax service is not widely available, but its use is growing in some parts of the world. On the other hand, in the U.S., Sprint shut down its 6,000 WiMax service sites in favor of 4G LTE.

- **Hotspots**—Some cellular data providers sell or lease small "hot-spot" devices, which contain both a cellular data modem and a Wi-Fi networking adapter. The hot-spot takes care of the cellular part, and you can connect one or more computers to the hotspot via standard Wi-Fi networking.

- **Tethered data service**—Windows 10 devices with cellular data service, and many cell phones and cellular-enabled tablets, can share their Internet data service by serving as a mobile Wi-Fi hotspot for nearby computers. Some phone providers charge an extra monthly fee for using this feature, and you do have to be careful not to exceed your phone's monthly limit if you are on a limited plan. (Be sure to tell your Windows 10 devices that they are using a metered connection.)

➡ *To learn how you can share your Windows 10 device's cellular data connection with nearby computers,* **see** *"Mobile Hotspot,"* **p. 829.**

The primary limitation of wireless service is that many data plans are metered—you pay for a maximum amount of data transferred per month, and if you exceed the limit, it can get very expensive. Unlimited data plans are becoming increasingly popular, but you might find in the fine print that after a certain amount of data has been transferred in any given month, the data rate will be cut way back. So even with an unlimited plan, it's a good idea to connect to WiFi wherever you can so you don't end up getting throttled back. You also tend to have to sign up for long-term contracts. You might be able to find data plans that let you buy service on a day-by-day basis rather than committing to a long-term service contract. This can be very cost effective when you travel. Microsoft is attempting to provide a pay-as-you-go service called Microsoft Wi-Fi and is pre-installing its Microsoft WiFi app on Windows 10 computers, but at the time this was written, the pricing and geographic availability of the service were not yet determined. Its success presumably will depend on how widely Microsoft is able to recruit WiFi service providers.

Because the setup and usage steps are specific to each provider, we can't provide instructions in this chapter.

 note

Wireless Internet is a strange business. Promising technologies appear and then disappear. Wildly optimistic business plans crumble seemingly overnight. Sprint invested heavily in WiMax service in the U.S., only to dismantle the network it built only a few years later. A startup called Starry Internet is promising 200 Mbps wireless Internet for $50 a month, but at the time this was written, it was available only in Boston. All we can say is, keep your eyes and ears open, and perhaps think twice before signing a long-term service contract!

Analog Modem

Standard, tried-and-true dial-up modem service might seem like the horse and buggy of Internet connectivity, but it's the only option available in some areas and requires only a standard telephone line and a modem in your computer. The data transfer speed provided by dial-up service is just barely adequate for email and limited web surfing—that is, reading text and viewing pictures. (That is, as long as the websites you visit were designed by people who understand the technology and made them usable at dial-up speeds.) Dial-up is completely unsuitable for viewing or streaming video. In other words, forget about YouTube or Netflix.

To use standard dial-up Internet service, you need a modem and a telephone cable. Modems are no longer standard equipment on modern computers. Your best bet today is most likely using an external USB modem from a reliable manufacturer, such as USRobotics, although internal, external serial, and PC card models are available from a number of vendors. Due to space limitations, we don't have room to describe how to set up dial-up Internet service in much detail. We can tell you that the procedures for setting up and using a modem connection are essentially the same as they were in Windows 7 and 8. Your ISP will be able to provide additional assistance. The process is described at the end of this chapter, under the heading "Dial-Up Internet."

Choosing a Technology

With all the options potentially available to Windows users for Internet access, making a choice that fits your needs and limitations can become a bit confusing. Research the options that local and national ISPs provide, and then start narrowing them. Table 14.1 summarizes the costs and speeds of several ways for a single computer user to access the Internet (excluding ISDN and wireless service). The prices shown are typical costs for the service in question after applying the usual discounts and special offers.

Table 14.1 Internet Connection Options for the Individual User

Method	Approximate Cost (per Month)	Approximate Setup and Equipment Cost	Data Limits?	Availability	Download Speed
Analog modem	$10–$25	$50	Unlimited	Worldwide	33Kbps–56Kbps
DSL	$30 and up	$100	Unlimited	Widely available	312Kbps–50Mbps
Cable modem	$30–$60	$100	Unlimited	Widely available	1Mbps–100Mbps
Cellular	$30–$100	$100 and up	Limited and "Unlimited"*	Patchy	1Mbps–50Mbps
Satellite	$50–$150	$150–$800	Limited	Almost worldwide	400Kbps–15Mbps

*exede.com offers an "unlimited" data plan but, as you might guess, if you have to use quote marks and an asterisk, there are limitations on what and when data is unlimited.

Remember that you have several costs to factor in:

- The cost of hardware required to make the connection

- The cost of installation and setup

- The cost of a standard wired telephone line, which may be required for some DSL services

- The cost of canceling service if you terminate it before a long-term contract has expired

- The savings you'll get if you can bundle several separate data plans into a family or group plan

Also, if you travel frequently, ask prospective ISPs to tell you whether they provide free WiFi hotspot service when you're on the road. These costs can add up quickly if you select an ISP that makes you pay extra for this service.

For more information on selecting an Internet technology and to help choose an ISP, check out these sites:

- For information on DSL and cable, see www.dslreports.com. The site includes customer reviews of ISPs.

- For information on satellite service in North and Central America, check out www.dish.com, www.hughesnet.com, and www.exede.com. I don't have direct experience with these providers, but Exede advertises download speeds up to 12 Mbps, and up to 25 Mbps in some areas. If that is true, it's terrific. Satellite services are often resold through regional companies. For example, companies like wildblue.com and sonic.net resell satellite service. You might get better customer support if you buy through a regional ISP.

- For information on wireless service, check with the cellular service providers that cover your geographical area.

Choosing Equipment

You must purchase equipment that is compatible with the particular type of Internet service you'll be using. If you will be buying new connection hardware, here are some points to consider:

- Broadband service requires a modem that your ISP will either provide, sell, or lease (rent) to you. DSL modems were originally sold to you as part of the setup price in many cases, but the trend is to encourage or force you to rent them. They want to ding you every month—and it adds up! You can get a new or used DSL or cable modem independently, and very cheaply, but be sure it will be compatible with the equipment your ISP uses. (A used cable modem is more likely to be usable than a used DSL modem, as DSL requires complex configuration settings that the ISP might not even provide to you.) Broadband modems connect to your computers and other devices via Wi-Fi, USB, or through an Ethernet network adapter.

- If you want to share your Internet connection with other computers via a LAN, read Chapter 19 before making any hardware purchases; you'll find information on some special hardware setups.

Installing a Network Adapter for Broadband Service

Most DSL and cable service providers now provide devices that combine a modem and a wired-plus-wireless router, giving you the ability to connect your computer wirelessly, or with a network cable. If you get just a modem, you will need to supply your own router, or your computer will require an Ethernet network adapter to connect to the modem. Any computer capable of running Windows 10 should have a Wi-Fi or Ethernet adapter built in, ready to use. If not, your ISP might supply and install one for you, or you can install one yourself.

If you want to purchase or install a network adapter yourself, the process will go something like this:

- For an internal adapter in a desktop computer, shut down Windows, unplug the computer, and install the card. Then power up the computer and log on.

- For a USB adapter, install any software provided by the adapter's manufacturer first; then plug in the USB networking adapter.

The Plug and Play system should take care of the rest for you. The driver software will in all likelihood install itself automatically.

After installation, confirm that the network adapter is installed and functioning by following these steps:

1. Press Windows Logo+X, and then select Device Manager. (Alternatively, from the taskbar's search box, search for **manager**, and in the results, select Device Manager.)

2. The list should show only "first-level" items. Under Network Adapters, you should see no items listed with an exclamation mark icon superimposed.

 caution

When your network adapter is working and connected to your DSL or cable modem, Windows will pop up a box asking you, "Do you want your computer to be discoverable by other PCs and devices on this network?" If you connected directly to the cable or DSL modem that does not have a built-in router, you must select No. This way, Windows knows to block network services that let hackers break into your computer. If you are connecting to a connection-sharing router, either standalone or built in to your broadband modem, it's okay to select Yes. We talk about this in detail in Chapter 19.

 note

Installing a network adapter to connect to a broadband modem doesn't give you a LAN; it's just a way of connecting to the modem. If you want to set up a LAN in addition to an Internet connection, see Chapters 18 and 19.

If the network adapter appears and is marked with a yellow icon with an exclamation point, follow the network card troubleshooting instructions in Chapter 22, "Troubleshooting Your Network."

If you're using cable Internet service, skip ahead to the "Configuring a High-Speed Connection" section not far ahead.

Installing Filters for DSL Service

For standard DSL service with self-installation, you will be provided with filters, which are small boxes that plug in to your home's or office's telephone jacks. Then the cord from your phone plugs into the filter. The filters block the DSL signal from reaching your telephones and answering machines. You must locate every phone jack that has something plugged in to it, and that is connected to the line your DSL service uses, and install a filter on every jack except the one that plugs in to your DSL modem. If you need to plug in a phone to the same jack that the DSL modem uses, use a filter that has two sockets clearly labeled "Phone" and "DSL."

 tip

If a jack is unused, you don't need to plug a filter in it, but it's a good idea to put a label over the jack indicating that it carries the DSL signal. This way, you'll remember to add a filter if you ever do plug in a phone or other device to this jack.

Alternatively, and virtually always for VDSL service, the service installer might connect your telephone line to a device called a *splitter* inside or outside the house and will install a separate cable to bring the DSL signal to your modem or router. These devices separate the high-frequency DSL carrier signal from the normal telephone signal before it reaches your house's internal phone wiring.

Configuring a High-Speed Connection

Your ISP's installer might set up your computer for you. "Self-install" providers give you a set of instructions specific to your service. We can give you a general idea of what's required.

---

 tip

If professional installers come to configure your computer for your new Internet service and want to add software to it, you should know that Windows has all the software it needs to use virtually all cable or DSL services. There is no need for them to install additional software on your computer. I initially try to refuse to let them. What they're after is installing a modified version of Internet Explorer that carries their brand name and steers you toward their websites; however, they also sometimes want to install customer support and antivirus software. You can decide whether you want this. They might say it's up to you to set everything up for yourself if you refuse it. You can always uninstall their stuff after they've left.

In any case, take thorough notes of what any installer does. Don't hesitate to ask questions; you have a right to know exactly what the installer is doing to your computer. And be sure to thoroughly test the setup before the installer leaves—especially any Wi-Fi and Ethernet connections to other computers.

If your broadband service uses a network adapter (that is, an Ethernet adapter) to connect directly to a cable or DSL modem that has no built-in router, you *must* start by taking the following steps to secure your computer against hackers.

1. Click the network icon in the notification area of the taskbar, and then click Network and Internet Settings.

    Under Network Status, be sure that the label under the network name reads Public Network, as shown in Figure 14.1, *not* Private Network. Because the connection hooks up directly to the Internet, it *must* be designated as a public network.

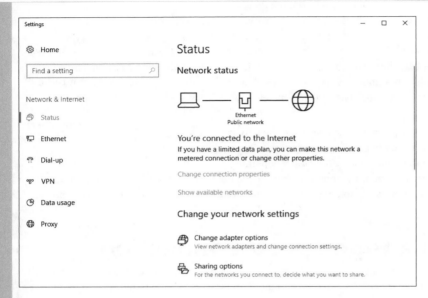

If the label says Private Network, click Change Connection Properties, or click the connection type (Ethernet) at the left, and then click the Network icon just above the Related Settings label. Select Public, and then click the back arrow in the upper-left corner of the window to get back to the screen shown in Figure 14.1. The label should now read Public.

2. Now, for additional insurance, click Ethernet again, and select Change Adapter Options. Locate the icon for the Ethernet adapter that goes to your DSL or cable modem, right-click it, and select Properties.

3. Under This Connection Uses the Following Items, uncheck File and Printer Sharing for Microsoft Networks and then uncheck Client for Microsoft Networks.

4. If your ISP requires you to set a specific IP address for the network adapter, highlight Internet Protocol Version 4 (TCP/IPv4) and click Properties. Check Use the Following IP Address and then enter the IP address, subnet mask, and default gateway provided by your ISP. You may also be instructed to enter DNS server addresses. Most of this step is not necessary.

5. Click OK.

After the adapter has been configured and attached to the DSL or cable modem with a network cable, you configure the connection. The procedure you should use depends on whether your ISP uses PPPoE or an always-on connection. The following sections describe these procedures.

Configuring a PPPoE Broadband Connection

Some DSL and a very few cable Internet providers use a connection scheme called *Point-to-Point Protocol over Ethernet (PPPoE)*. This technology uses a login name and password to establish the link from your broadband modem to your ISP. It works a lot like an old dial-up modem connection did, but the "call" takes place through the DSL or cable data service instead of over a voice connection, and it's nearly instantaneous. You might never see this happen if you have a modem/router that performs this step automatically.

If you have a simple modem with no router and your provider uses PPPoE to establish its connection, you might have to set up the connection manually. If this is necessary, your provider should give you clear instructions. We can give you the general procedure here, though.

After you connect your computer's network adapter to the broadband modem, follow these steps:

1. Click the network icon in the taskbar and select Network and Internet Settings. Scroll down and select Network and Sharing Center.

2. Click Set Up a New Connection or Network. Select Connect to the Internet and click Next. If Windows says you are already connected to the Internet, click Set Up a New Connection Anyway. If Windows asks, "Do you want to use a connection that you already have?" click No, Create a New Connection and then click Next.

3. Select Broadband (PPPoE).

4. Enter the username and password assigned by your ISP. You might want to check Show Characters before you enter the password, to make sure you enter it correctly.

5. Check both Remember This Password and Allow Other People to Use This Connection.

6. Click Connect.

At this point, you're prompted to sign in.

From now on, you can just click the Network icon in the taskbar whenever you want to connect or disconnect from the Internet.

 note

If you are going to install your own router to share the broadband connection with a network, you'll set up the router to perform the login process for you automatically. Read Chapter 19, "Connecting Your Network to the Internet," for the considerations and steps for doing this. We recommend that you start by connecting the modem directly to your computer, following the steps described here, and verifying that your service works. Then disconnect the modem and set up the router and your network.

 note

Some ISPs give you a disc with installation software that does the next setup procedure for you. I intensely dislike this practice: Who knows what other software—including adware and "customer support" spyware—they're installing? Personally, I lie to them, tell them I'm installing the connection on a Macintosh or Linux computer that can't use their software, and ask for the information needed to perform the setup manually. Sometimes this works, and sometimes it makes life difficult. For instance, one major ISP I worked with required you to set up the service account through a special website, so if you wanted to shun its software, you needed Internet access to set up your Internet access.

Configuring an Always On Connection

For some DSL service and most cable Internet service, you need to make no further settings to get your computer online.

Some ISPs require you to give them the media access control (MAC) address of your broadband router or your computer's network adapter. This is an identification number built in to the hardware that uniquely identifies your particular device. To find this number on a router, look for a label on it with a number like 00-03-FF-B9-0E-14. For a computer, follow these steps:

1. Click the network icon in the taskbar and select Network and Internet Settings. Scroll down and select Change Adapter Options.

2. Locate the icon for the network adapter that leads to your cable or DSL modem. This might be named Ethernet or Local Area Connection (or Ethernet 2 if you've installed an extra adapter). If you have multiple adapters and can't tell which is which, unplug the network cable from all but the one that goes to the modem and then look for the one that doesn't say "Disconnected."

3. Right-click the icon and select Status, Details. Find the line titled Physical Address. It will be followed by six pairs of numbers and letters, as in 00-03-FF-B9-0E-14. This is the information to give to your ISP.

Your ISP can then configure its equipment to communicate with your device.

Setting Up a Fixed IP Address

In rare cases, your ISP will require you to set your network adapter to a fixed IP address. This might be required with either PPPoE or "always-on" service. To set the address, follow these steps:

1. Click the network icon on the right side of the taskbar, and then click Network and Internet Settings. Scroll down and select Change Adapter Options.

2. Locate the icon for the network adapter you're using for your broadband connection. This might be named Ethernet or Local Area Connection (or Ethernet 2 if you've installed an extra adapter). Right-click it and select Properties.

3. Select the Networking tab, select the Internet Protocol (either Version 6 or Version 4, depending on the IP provided by your ISP), and click the Properties button.

4. Select Use the Following IP Address and then enter the IP address, subnet mask, and default gateway information provided by your ISP, as shown in Figure 14.2.

5. Select Use the Following DNS Server Addresses, and enter the two DNS addresses provided by your ISP.

6. Click OK to return to the Local Area Connection Properties dialog box.

When you have completed this procedure, return to the PPPoE setup steps. Alternatively, if you have always-on service, open Internet Explorer to test-drive your new connection.

Figure 14.2
Here, you can add the network address, subnet mask, and DNS information supplied by your ISP.

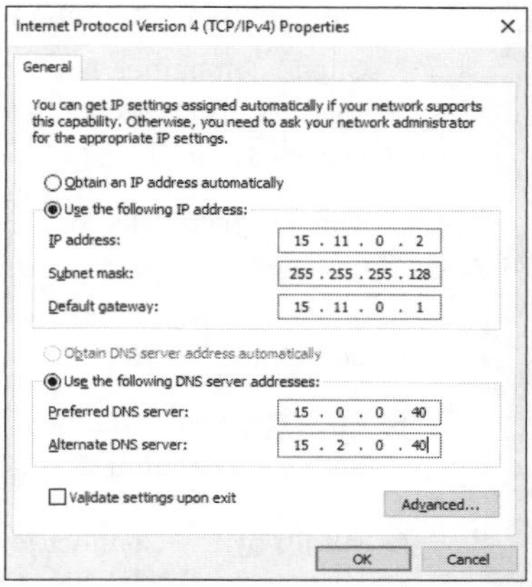

Dial-Up Internet

Dial-up Internet service, which uses audible signals sent over a standard telephone call to send data, is rarely used today. But in some locations, it's the only Internet service available. We can't devote much space in this book to it, but we do want to make sure that if you have to use it with Windows 10, you can perform the necessary setup and connection steps.

Your computer will need an analog modem. With modern computers, about the only option is to use an external USB modem plugged in to a USB port on your computer. When you buy one, it will typically come with a disc containing required software. We suggest that you install the software first, before plugging in the modem for the first time.

When it's installed, press Windows Logo+R, type **telephon.cpl**, and then press Enter. (You can also get here through the Control Panel by searching for the phrase *Phone and Modem*.) The first time you open this, you will be prompted to enter your current location and telephone area code information. Enter the required information, and then click OK to close the dialog box.

Creating a New Dial-Up Connection

To set up a connection to your dial-up Internet service, follow these steps:

1. Click the network icon at the bottom-right corner of the taskbar, and select Network and Internet Settings. (You can also get there from the Settings icon on the Start menu.)

2. At the left, select Dial-Up; then select Set Up a New Connection, Connect to the Internet, Next, Dial-Up.

3. Fill in the information provided by your ISP. The first field asks for the local access telephone number for your ISP. Enter the local number, optionally preceded by any other codes needed to dial the call. For example, in the United States, if you enter an area code, you must first enter a 1 and then the area code, as shown in Figure 14.2. You can enter parentheses or dashes (-) between the parts of the number; the modem ignores them.

The next fields record your username and password. You can check Show Characters to verify whether you are typing the password correctly.

Check Remember This Password unless you want Windows to prompt you for it every time you connect. If other people who use your computer use the same ISP account, check Allow Other People to Use This Connection.

4. The last field asks for a connection name. Type in a name that will help you identify what the connection is used for. The name of your ISP is always good. If you will be traveling, you'll probably accumulate several of these dial-up connections, one for each location you visit, so it would be helpful to add the location to the name, as in "Sonic-Oakland."

5. Click Connect. Windows immediately dials your ISP. Check to be sure that the connection works before proceeding. If it doesn't, click Skip and continue anyway.

As set up by the Connect to the Internet Wizard, your dial-up connection will not correctly handle area codes in the number it dials. If you entered just a seven-digit number and you never intend to travel with your computer, you don't have to worry about this. However, if the number has an area code or you travel, you'll have to fix this.

Click the network icon in the taskbar, and select Network and Internet Settings. At the left, click Dial-Up; then, under Related Settings, click Change Adapter Options. Right-click the icon for the dial-up connection you just created and select Properties.

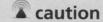

caution

Be sure to use a local number. Your ISP will not help pay your phone bill if you choose a toll number by mistake!

The General tab lists modem properties and the ISP telephone number. If you travel with your computer, or the dial-up number has an area code, check Use Dialing Rules and be sure that the ISP's area code appears correctly in its own box and is not entered in the same box as the phone number. Then click the Dialing Rules button to be sure that your local area code is set correctly.

If your telephone line has call waiting service, click Dialing Rules. Check To Disable Call Waiting, Dial; then select the code used by your telephone company. In most parts of the U.S., this is *70. Click OK twice to return to the connection properties dialog box.

Click OK to save your changes.

Making and Ending a Dial-Up Connection

After you've set up an icon for your ISP, making the connection is a snap.

1. Click the Network icon in your taskbar.

2. Click the desired connection name near the top of the panel. This opens the Settings app. Click the telephone-shaped Dial-up Connection icon in the settings panel, shown in Figure 14.3, and then click Connect.

Figure 14.3
To establish a dial-up connection, click the telephone-shaped icon in the Dial-Up settings page.

3. Windows displays a connection dialog box. If you previously let Windows remember the password, you can simply skip ahead to step 4. Otherwise, enter the password assigned by your ISP. You can check Save This User Name if you want to use this information the next time you dial, and you can select Anyone Who Uses This Computer if it's OK for other people on this computer to use your dial-up account.

4. For a dial-up connection only, Windows shows you exactly how it's going to dial the number. Double-check that the prefix and area code are correct. You might need to click Properties to correct your current location (Dialing From) and/or Dialing Rules if the prefix or area code isn't correct.

5. Click Dial to make the connection.

Windows then dials your ISP and establishes the connection.

Some external USB modems give no audible feedback that they're dialing. Even if you don't hear anything, wait a bit and watch the connection dialog box to see whether it succeeds.

When you finish using your Internet connection, click the Network icon in the taskbar to view the Networks panel. Click the name of your Internet connection to bring up the Dial-Up Settings page. Click the telephone-shaped icon, and then click Disconnect. Windows will hang up the connection.

WEB BROWSING WITH MICROSOFT EDGE

Taking a Tour of the Edge Window

Let's begin with a tour of the Microsoft Edge interface. Figure 15.1 shows the Edge window and points out the most important features.

Although we discuss most of these interface elements in more detail later in this chapter, for now, let's take a quick look at what each element does:

- **Back**—Takes you back to the previous page in the current tab session.

- **Forward**—Takes you to the next page in the current tab session.

- **Refresh**—Reloads the current web page.

- **Tabs You've Set Aside**—Displays a list of the tabs that you've set aside.

- **Set These Tabs Aside**—Sets a tab aside.

- **Tab**—Represents a single web page session and shows the title of the web page that is currently open in the session.

- **Close Tab**—Closes the tab.

- **New Tab**—Creates a new tab.

- **Show Tab Previews**—Displays thumbnail versions of your open tabs.

- **Address/Search Bar**—Displays the address of the current web page and enables you to type the address of another page or a search term.

- **Reading View**—Displays the current page without distractions such as ads, images, and navigation.

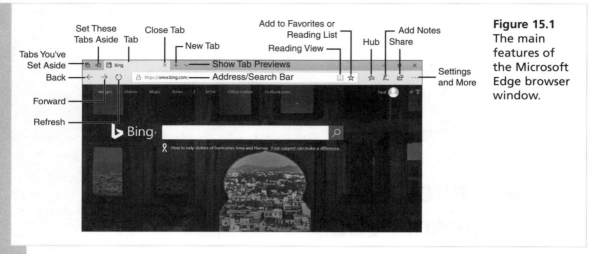

Figure 15.1
The main features of the Microsoft Edge browser window.

- **Add to Favorites or Reading List**—Saves the current page to the Favorites list or to the Reading list.

- **Hub**—Displays your saved Edge content, including your Favorites list, Reading list, eBooks purchased from the Windows Store, browsing history, and downloads.

- **Add Notes**—Displays the Edge tools for annotating a web page.

- **Share**—Enables you to share a link to the current web page with a contact or with an app such as Mail or OneNote.

- **Settings and More**—Displays a pane that enables you to access the Edge settings as well as other program commands.

What About Internet Explorer?

We'll admit that we hated Edge when it was first released because it was a mere toy browser. Of course, we also hated Internet Explorer because of its long history of non-compliance with web standards and its litany of security issues, but it was still better than Edge. But now Edge is a mature browser—the latest version even has Developer Tools!—that is secure, fast, and standards-friendly. Internet Explorer's time has passed, so we no longer cover it in this book. However, it's still hidden away in the attic of Windows 10, so if you want to run it, use the taskbar's Search box to type **explorer** and then click Internet Explorer in the search results. You can then pin it to the Start menu or taskbar or even change it to the default browser (all of which is described in Chapter 4, "Using the Windows 10 Interface").

Tips and Techniques for Better Web Surfing

Surfing web pages with Microsoft Edge is familiar, straightforward, and easy, but even experienced users might not be aware of all the ways they can open and navigate pages. Here's a review of all the techniques you can use to open a web page in Edge:

- **Type a URL in any Address bar**—In the Edge Address bar, in the Address bar of any File Explorer window, or in the taskbar's Address toolbar, type the URL and press Enter.

 tip

You can activate the Address bar by pressing Ctrl+O.

- **Type a URL in the Run dialog box**—Press Windows Logo+R, type the URL you want in the Run dialog box, and click OK.

Fixing Run URL Problems

When you type a URL in the Run dialog box, you must include the "www" portion of the address. For example, typing **microsoft.com** won't work, but typing **www.microsoft.com** will. If the URL doesn't have a "www" component—for example, support.microsoft.com—you must add **http://** to the front of the address.

- **Select a URL from the Address bar**—Edge's Address bar remembers sites you've previously visited, so you can type the first few letters of the URL and then select the full URL in the drop-down list of matching addresses that appears.

- **Select a pinned page**—If you've pinned a web page to the Start Menu, click the pinned tile; if you've pinned a page to the taskbar, click the pinned taskbar button.

  ➡ *To learn how to pin web pages,* **see** *"Pinning a Web Page to the Start Menu," **p. 126.***

- **Select a favorite**—Press Ctrl+I to open the Favorites list, and then click the site you want to open.

- **Click a Favorites bar button**—If you've displayed the Favorites bar (right-click an empty section of the title bar and then click to activate the Favorites Bar command), click a button to navigate to that site.

- **Click a web address in a Mail message**—When Mail recognizes a web address in an email message (that is, an address that begins with http://, https://, ftp://, www., and so on), it converts the address into a link. Clicking the link opens the address in Edge. Note, too, that many other programs are "URL aware," including the Microsoft Office suite of programs.

After you've opened a page, you usually move to another page by clicking a link: either a text link or an image. However, there are more techniques you can use to navigate to other pages:

- **Open a link in another window**—If you don't want to leave the current page, you can force a link to open in another Edge window by right-clicking the link and then clicking Open in

New Window. You can open a new Edge window by selecting Settings and More and then selecting New Window or by pressing Ctrl+N.

- **Retrace the pages you've visited**—To return to a page you visited previously in this session, either click Edge's Back button or press Alt+Left arrow. After you go back to a page, you move ahead through the visited pages by clicking the Forward button or pressing Alt+Right arrow.

- **Display the start page**—The Start page is an MSN-powered local page that offers a search box and a feed that includes the latest news, weather, sports, and financial information. You can display this page at any time by pressing Alt+Home.

- **Use the History list**—Press Ctrl+H to open the Hub with the History tab displayed to see a list of the sites you've visited over the past three weeks. Then click a URL to go to the desired page. The items you see in the History list are based on the contents of the %UserProfile%\AppData\Local\Microsoft\Windows\History folder. See "Using the Handy History List," later in this chapter, for more details on the History list.

 tip

You can also hold down the Shift key and click a link to open that link in a new browser window.

 tip

If you find yourself using the Start page quite often, do yourself a favor and add the Home button to the Edge toolbar for quick access. Select Settings and More, select Settings, select View Advanced Settings, and then click the Show the Home Button switch to On.

Taking Advantage of the Address Bar

Edge's Address bar (and the Address bars that appear in all Windows 10 folder windows) appears to be nothing more than a simple type-and-click mechanism. However, it's useful for many things and comes with its own bag of tricks for making it even easier to use. Here's a rundown:

- To edit the Address bar text, press Ctrl+O, Alt+D, or F4 to select it.

- The Address bar's AutoComplete feature monitors the address as you type. If any previously entered addresses match your typing, they appear in a list. To choose one of those addresses, use the down-arrow key to select it and then press Enter. The quickest way to use AutoComplete is to begin typing the site's domain name. For example, if you want to bring up http://www.microsoft.com/, start typing the **microsoft** part. If you start with the full address, you must type **http://www.** or just **www.** and then one other character.

- Edge assumes that any address you enter is for a website. Therefore, you don't need to type the **http://** prefix because Edge adds it for you automatically.

- Edge also assumes that most web addresses are in the form http://www.*something*.com. Therefore, if you simply *type* the *something* part and press Ctrl+Enter, Edge will automatically add the http://www. prefix and the .com suffix. For example, you can get to the Microsoft homepage (http://www.microsoft.com) by typing **microsoft** and pressing Ctrl+Enter.

- The Edge Address bar also doubles as a Search box, which means you can type your search text and then press Enter. To ensure Edge runs a search rather than trying to load a URL, type a question mark (**?**) and a space before your search text (you can press Ctrl+E to add the question mark and space automatically), and then press Enter.

Working with Tabs

Edge supports *tabbed browsing*, in which each open page appears in its own tab within a single Edge window. You can open dozens of tabs in each window, which makes surfing multiple sites easy. One of the nicest features of tabs is that Edge supplies each tab with its own execution thread, which means that you can start a page loading in one tab while reading downloaded page text in another tab. You can also specify multiple home pages that load in their own tabs when you start Edge (see "Changing the Home Page," later in this chapter).

Opening a Page in a New Tab

Tabs are only as useful as they are easy to use, and Edge does a good job of making tabs simple. One way that it does this is by giving you a satisfyingly wide variety of methods to use for opening a page in a new tab. There are six in all:

- **Hold down Ctrl and click a link in a web page**—This creates a new tab and loads the linked page in the background.

- **Hold down Ctrl+Shift and click a link in a web page**—This creates a new tab and loads the linked page in the foreground.

- **Use the middle mouse button (if you have one) to click a link in a web page**—This creates a new tab and loads the linked page in the background.

- **Type the page URL in the Address bar and then press Alt+Enter**—This creates a new tab and loads the page in the foreground.

- **Click the New Tab button (or press Ctrl+T) to add another tab**—Then type the page URL in the Address bar and press Enter. This loads the page in the foreground.

- **Click a link in another program**—This creates a new tab and loads the linked page in the foreground.

 tip

If you have a site that you use frequently, create a shortcut for it on the taskbar. This is called *pinning* the site to the taskbar. The easiest way to do this is to navigate to the site, select Settings and More, and then select Pin This Page to the Taskbar.

 tip

By default, in each new tab that you add, Edge displays the Top Sites page, which shows icons for the pages you've visited most often. That's handy, but if you don't want other people to see these sites, you should load a blank page instead. Click Settings and More, click Settings, and then use the Open New Tabs With list to select A Blank Page.

Navigating Tabs

When you have two or more tabs open, navigating them is straightforward:

- With your mouse, click the tab of the page you want to use.

- With your keyboard, press Ctrl+Tab to navigate the tabs from left to right (and from the last tab to the first tab); press Ctrl+Shift+Tab to navigate the tabs from right to left (and from the first tab to the last tab).

Unfortunately, Edge has only so much room to display tabs. Edge does reduce the tab width as you add more tabs, but the width can shrink only so far if the tabs are to remain usable. On a 1024×768 screen, Edge can display a maximum of ten tabs. If you open more tabs than Edge can display, Edge adds two new buttons to the tab strip, as shown in Figure 15.2. Click Scroll Tab List Backward to display the previous unseen tab, and click Scroll Tab List Forward to display the next unseen tab.

Scroll Tab List Backward   Scroll Tab List Forward

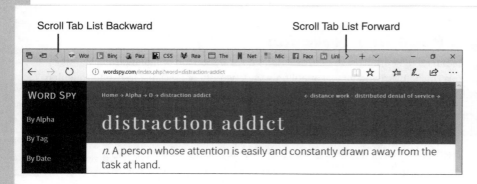

Figure 15.2
If you have more tabs open than Edge can display, use the arrow buttons to display the unseen tabs.

Setting Tabs Aside

If you end up with a ton of tabs open (and don't we all, these days?), it can be a hassle to scroll the tab list back and forward, particularly if you're temporarily not using all or most of the tabs. Instead, you can get a fresh start without having to shut down all those tabs by "setting the tabs aside." This means that Edge removes the tabs from the tab list and places them in a special area of the Edge window. You can then recall one or all of the tabs when you need them again.

To set the tabs aside, click the Set These Tabs Aside button, pointed out earlier in Figure 15.1. Edge keeps the tabs open but shuffles them off to the side and out of sight.

To restore those tabs, click the Tabs You've Set Aside button (again, refer to Figure 15.1). Edge displays the set-aside tabs as shown in Figure 15.3. You can then either click one or more tabs to restore them or click the Restore Tabs link to put them all back where they were.

Figure 15.3
Click Tabs You've Set Aside to see and restore your set-aside tabs.

Click this arrow to see more of your set-aside tabs.

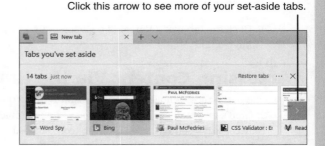

Pinning a Tab

If you have a web page that you visit often, you can save that page to Edge's Favorites list, as described later in this chapter. (See "Saving Your Favorite Pages.") That's a useful way to store oft-surfed pages, but for your *most*-surfed pages, it would be better just to have Edge open that page in its own tab every time you launch the program.

That's easy enough to do by *pinning* a tab for that page, which tells Edge to create a permanent tab for the page. You do this by right-clicking the page tab and then clicking Pin. (see Figure 15.4).

If you no longer need a pinned tab, right-click it and then click Unpin.

Figure 15.4
Pinned tabs get loaded each time you start Microsoft Edge.

Pinned tabs

Closing Tabs

To close a tab, Edge gives you up to six choices:

- Hover the mouse pointer over the tab and then click the tab's Close Tab (X) button.

- Select the tab and then press Ctrl+W.

- Right-click the tab and then click Close Tab.

- To close every tab except one, right-click the tab you want to keep open and then click Close Other Tabs.

- To close all the tabs you opened after a particular tab, right-click that tab and then click Close Tabs to the Right.

- Click the tab using the middle mouse button (if you have one).

Accessing Content Via the Hub

One of the nicer innovations in Microsoft Edge is the Hub, the app's one-stop shop for all your saved and stored content. To access this content, click the Hub icon, pointed out earlier in Figure 15.1. The pane that appears contains five icons, as shown in Figure 15.5. Here's a summary:

- **Favorites**—Your favorite web pages. (See "Saving Your Favorite Pages," later in this chapter.)

- **Reading List**—Pages you've saved to read later. (See "Saving Pages to Read Later," later in this chapter.)

- **Books**—eBooks that you've purchased from the Windows Store.

- **History**—Web pages you've visited in the recent past. (See "Using the Handy History List," later in this chapter.)

- **Downloads**—Files you've downloaded from the web.

 tip

If you close a tab accidentally, you can get it back by right-clicking any open tab and then clicking Reopen Closed Tab. You can repeat this command as needed to reopen multiple tabs.

 tip

By default, Edge stores downloaded files in your user account's Downloads folder. To change that, click Settings and More, click Settings, and then click View Advanced Settings. In the Downloads section, click Change, choose the folder where you prefer to have your downloads saved, and then click Select Folder.

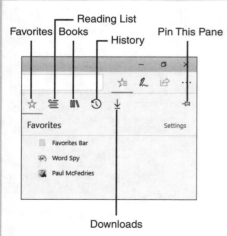

Favorites | Books
— Reading List
— History
Pin This Pane

Downloads

Figure 15.5
The Hub is where Edge keeps your saved and stored content.

Using the Handy History List

You saw earlier (in "Tips and Techniques for Better Web Surfing") how you can click the Back and Forward buttons to follow your own footsteps on the web. However, Edge wipes those lists clean when you exit the program. What do you do when you want to revisit a site from a previous session? Happily, Edge keeps track of the addresses of all the pages you perused recently in the History list.

 tip

If you use the Hub frequently, you can leave it on-screen full-time by displaying it and then clicking the Pin This Pane icon (see Figure 15.5).

To bring a site into view using the History list, follow these steps:

1. Click the Hub icon (pointed out in Figure 15.1).

2. Click History (pointed out in Figure 15.5).

3. Click the day or week you want to work with. Edge displays a list of the pages you visited on that day or during that week.

tip

You can jump directly to the History list by pressing Ctrl+H.

4. Click the name of the page you want to visit.

Changing the Startup Page

In Edge, the *startup page* is what the browser opens when you start a new session. The default startup page is usually Bing.com, but most computer manufacturers substitute their own pages.

You can take control over your startup page by configuring your own page or pages to load when Edge is launched. Here are the steps to follow:

1. Click Settings and More.

2. Click Settings.

3. In the Open Microsoft Edge With list, choose one of the following:

   - **Start Page**—Choose this option to show a local page that displays a search box and an MSN news feed.

   - **New Tab Page**—Choose this option to display the same page that you see when you start a new tab.

   - **Previous Pages**—Choose this item to tell Edge to start with all the tabs that were open at the end of your previous web browsing session.

   - **A Specific Page or Pages**—Choose this item to specify which pages you want Edge to open at startup. Click the Add New Page link, type or paste a URL, and then press Enter.

Changing the Edge Search Engine

Veteran surfers, having seen a wide range of what the web has to offer, usually prefer to tackle it using a targeted approach that enables them to find information quickly. This means using one or more of the Web's many search engines. It's usually best to deal with a search engine site directly, but Edge offers some default searching options. For example, you saw earlier in this chapter (in "Taking Advantage of the Address Bar") that Edge lets you run searches directly from the Address bar.

Enter your search terms in the Address bar, and then press Enter or click Search. (You can also press Alt+Enter to open the results in a new tab.)

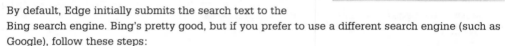 **tip**

In some cases, you might want to search for text only within the currently displayed web page. To do that, press Ctrl+F (or click Settings and More and then click Find on Page) to open the Find on Page bar, and then type your search text. Edge highlights each instance on the page, and you can navigate these by clicking the Next Result (>) and Previous Result (<) arrows.

By default, Edge initially submits the search text to the Bing search engine. Bing's pretty good, but if you prefer to use a different search engine (such as Google), follow these steps:

1. Navigate to the search engine you want to use. This step in necessary because, bizarrely, Edge requires it to "discover" the search engine. Don't ask us why.

2. Click Settings and More.

3. Click Settings.

4. Click View Advanced Settings.

5. Click Change Search Engine. Edge displays a list of search engines that it has discovered.

6. Click the search engine you prefer to use.

7. Click Set as Default. Edge sets the search engine as the new default for all searches.

Saving Your Favorite Pages

The sad truth is that much of what you'll see on the web will be utterly forgettable and not worth a second look. However, there are all kinds of gems out there waiting to be uncovered—sites you'll want to visit regularly. Instead of memorizing the appropriate URLs, jotting them down on sticky notes, or plastering your desktop with shortcuts, you can use the Hub's Favorites list to keep track of your choice sites.

Adding a Page to the Favorites List

When you find a page you'd like to declare as a favorite, follow these steps:

1. Click the Add to Favorites or Reading List icon (pointed out earlier in Figure 15.1), and then click the Favorites tab (or press Ctrl+D).

 tip

You can add all your open tabs as favorites by right-clicking any tab and then clicking Add Tabs to Favorites.

2. The Name text box displays the title of the page. The title is the text that will appear when you view the list of your favorites later. Feel free to edit this text if you like.

3. Edge enables you to set up subfolders to hold related favorites. If you don't want to bother with this, skip to step 4. Otherwise, click the Save In list. Click Create New Folder, type a folder name, and then press Enter.

4. Use the Save In list to select the folder in which you want to store the favorite.

5. Click Add.

 tip

If you have another browser installed on your PC, you can import its favorites (or bookmarks) into Edge. Click Settings and More, click Settings, and then click Import from Another Browser. Click to activate the option for the browser you want to import from, and then click Import.

Displaying the Favorites Bar

In the previous section, you might have noticed that in the Favorites tab, the Save In list includes a folder named Favorites Bar. This is a useful bar that appears just below the Edge toolbar, thus giving you one-click access to favorites. Alas, this bar is hidden by default, but you can fix that by following these steps:

1. Click Settings and More.

2. Click Settings.

3. Click the Show the Favorites Bar switch to On.

 tip

Because the Favorites bar offers one-click access to pages, you'll probably load it up with lots of favorites. Alas, you can only fit so many in the bar thanks to the page titles. To fix this, click Settings and More, click Settings, and then click the Show Only Icons on the Favorites Bar switch to On.

Opening a Page from the Favorites List

The purpose of the Favorites list, of course, is to give you quick access to the pages you visit regularly. To open one of the pages from your Favorites list, you have two choices:

- Click the Hub (pointed out in Figure 15.1), click Favorites (pointed out in Figure 15.5), and then select the favorite you want.

- If you added a site to the Favorites bar (pointed out in Figure 15.6), click the favorite you want.

 tip

You can quickly display the Favorites list by pressing Ctrl+I.

Figure 15.6
You can open your favorite pages using either the Hub's Favorites list or the Favorites bar.

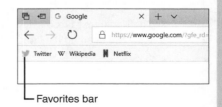

Favorites bar

Maintaining Favorites

When you have lots of favorites, you need to do some regular maintenance to keep things organized. This involves creating new subfolders, moving favorites between folders, changing URLs, deleting unused favorites, and more. Here's a summary of a few maintenance techniques you'll use most often:

- **Change a favorite's URL**—Display the Favorites list or the Favorites bar, and right-click the item you want to work with. Click Edit URL, and then use the text box to adjust the URL.

- **Rename a favorite**—Display the Favorites list or the Favorites bar, and right-click the item you want to work with. Click Rename and then use the text box to adjust the URL.

- **Move a favorite**—Display the Favorites list or the Favorites bar, and then drag the item to another spot in the list or bar.

- **Create a subfolder**—Display the Favorites list, and right-click anywhere within the list. Click Create New Folder, and then use the text box to type the folder name.

- **Sort the favorites**—Display the Favorites list, right-click anywhere within the list, and then click Sort By Name.

- **Delete a favorite**—Display the Favorites list or the Favorites bar, right-click the item you want to work with, and then click Delete.

Saving Pages to Read Later

One of the most common experiences on the web is to come across a page that looks like a fun or fascinating read but lack the time right then to dive in. What most of us do is leave the tab open and go on with our lives, with the assumption being that we'll return to the page when we have time. Of course, what usually happens is that we forget and end up closing the tab a few days or weeks later.

If you're tired of missing out on all those great reads, a better way to manage them is to use Edge's Reading list feature, which saves read-worthy pages for you in a single place for easy (and unforgotten) access.

Saving a Page to the Reading List

When you come across a page you want to read later, follow these steps to save it to the Reading list:

1. Click the Add to Favorites or Reading List icon (pointed out earlier in Figure 15.1), and then click the Reading List tab.

2. The Name text box displays the title of the page. The title is the text that will appear when you view the Reading list later. Edit this text if you like.

3. Click Add.

Opening a Page from the Reading List

When you finally get a bit of time and are ready to catch up on your reading, follow these steps to open a page from your Reading list:

1. Click the Hub (pointed out in Figure 15.1).

2. Click Reading List (pointed out in Figure 15.5).

3. Click the page you want to read. If you prefer to load the page into a new tab, right-click the page and then click Open in New Tab.

> **tip**
> You can also display the Reading list by pressing Ctrl+M.

Deleting Pages from Your Reading List

Unless you want to read a page again (in which case, you might consider adding it as a favorite), you can reduce clutter in your Reading list by deleting pages you've already read or that you no longer want to read. Here's how:

> **note**
> When reading a web page, you can scroll down one screen by pressing the spacebar. To scroll up one screen, press Shift+Spacebar.

1. Click the Hub (pointed out in Figure 15.1).

2. Click Reading List (pointed out in Figure 15.5).

3. Right-click the page you want to remove and then click Delete.

Configuring Edge Privacy Settings

One of the reasons we now consider Edge a serious web browser is that it comes with a decent collection of tools for safeguarding and managing your online privacy. Sure, we might all "have zero privacy anyway," as Sun Microsystem's then-CEO Scott McNeally famously said (way back in 1999!), but that doesn't mean you should just give up. You still have passwords and other personal data that needs to be kept out of other people's hands. The following sections show you how to do just that using Edge's built-in privacy tools.

Preventing Passwords from Being Saved

Many websites require registration to access certain pages and content. In almost all cases, before you can navigate to any of these restricted pages, you must first enter a password, along with your username or email address. When you fill in this information and log on to the site, Edge offers to save the password so that you don't have to type it again when you visit the same page in the future (see Figure 15.7).

Figure 15.7
When you enter a password into a web page form, Edge offers to save it for you.

Would you like to save your password for twitter.com?
More info

Yes   No   ×

If you click Yes and then access the site's login page later, Edge fills in the password for you automatically.

This is convenient, to be sure, but it has a downside: Anyone who uses your computer can also access the password-protected content. If you don't want this to happen, one solution is to click No when Edge asks to remember the password. Alternatively, you can tell Edge not to offer to save your passwords:

1. Click Settings and More.

2. Click Settings.

3. Click View Advanced Settings.

4. Under the Privacy and Services heading, click the Offers to Save Passwords switch to Off.

Instead of preventing all passwords from being saved, you might prefer a more targeted approach where you remove a saved password from a particular site, as shown in the following steps:

1. Click Settings and More.

2. Click Settings.

3. Click View Advanced Settings.

4. Under the Privacy and Services heading, click Manage Passwords to see a list of your saved website passwords.

5. Right-click the password you want to remove, and then click Delete Credential. (Alternatively, move the mouse pointer over password and then click the Delete (X) icon that appears.)

 caution

Many websites offer to "remember" your login information. They do this by placing your username and password in a small file called a *cookie* that's stored on your computer. Although convenient, it might lead to a problem: Other people who use your computer can access the password-protected content. To avoid this, be sure to deactivate the check box that asks if you want to save your login data.

Preventing Form Data from Being Saved

Filling in web forms is no one's idea of fun, particularly data that comes up repeatedly, such as your email address, telephone number, and home or work address. Edge makes this drudgery a tad easier to take by saving the data you enter into forms and then enabling you to quickly re-enter the data the next time you're filling in a similar form.

That's awfully nice, but it can be a privacy headache if someone else has (or gains) access to your PC because that person can now easily see your saved form data.

If you don't want to take that chance, you can follow these steps to tell Edge not to save your form info:

1. Click Settings and More.

2. Click Settings.

3. Click View Advanced Settings.

4. Under the Privacy and Services heading, click the Save Form Entries switch to Off.

Clearing Browsing Data

As you surf the web, Edge maintains what it calls your *browsing data*, which consists of the following nine data types:

- **Browsing history**—This is a list of addresses of the sites you've visited, as well as each of the pages you visited within those sites. This is a major privacy accident just waiting to happen because anyone sitting at your computer can see exactly where you've been online recently.

- **Cookies and saved website data**—*Cookies* are small text files that sites store on your computer. We discuss cookies in more detail later in this chapter, but for now, it's enough to know that although most cookies are benign, they can be used to track your activities online. Some websites also save data on your PC, which might be site customizations you've applied or information you've entered into forms. Because much of this information would be available to someone sitting at your computer, it represents a potential privacy hazard.

- **Cached data and files**—This consists of copies of text, images, media, and other content from the pages you've visited recently. Edge stores all this data so that the next time you view one of those pages, it can retrieve data from the cache and display the site much more quickly. This is clearly a big-time privacy problem because it means that anyone can examine the cache to learn where you've been surfing.

- **Set-aside and closed tabs**—Set-aside tabs are always available when Edge starts, so a snoop at your keyboard can easily see these sites. Similarly, your most recently closed tabs can be easily restored by that same snoop by right-clicking any tab and then clicking Reopen Closed Tab.

- **Download history**—This refers to the Hub's Downloads list, which shows the files you've downloaded using Edge. An intruder can click any file in this list to access that file.

- **Form data**—This refers to the AutoComplete feature, which stores the data you type in forms and then uses that saved data to suggest possible matches when you use a similar form in the future. For example, if you use a site's Search box frequently, Edge remembers your search strings and displays strings that match what you've typed. This is definitely handy, but it also means that anyone else who uses your computer can see your previously entered form text.

- **Passwords**—This is another aspect of AutoComplete, and Edge uses it to save form passwords. For example, if you enter a username and a password on a form, Edge asks if you want to save the password. If you click Yes, Edge stores the password and enters it automatically the next time you fill in the form (provided you enter the same username). Again, this is nice and convenient, but it's really just asking for trouble because it means that someone sitting down at your computer can log on to a site, a job made all the easier if you activated the site option to save your username.

- **Media licenses**—This refers to digital rights management (DRM) licenses that websites have granted you to download or stream music, video, or other content. Permission to use this content is therefore also granted to a system intruder.

- **Website permissions**—This refers to the permissions you've granted to websites to use PC features such as your location, camera, or microphone. If you've granted those permissions, then an unauthorized user of your PC also grants those same permissions.

Fortunately, you can plug any and all of these privacy holes by deleting the data. Here's how it's done in Edge:

1. Click Settings and More.

2. Click Settings.

3. Under the Clear Browsing Data heading, click Choose What to Clear. The Clear Browsing Data pane appears, as shown in Figure 15.8.

Figure 15.8
Use the Clear Browsing Data pane to choose what types of saved browsing data you want to remove.

4. Activate the check box beside each type of browsing data you want to get rid of.

5. Click Clear.

 tip
You can configure Edge to remove the browsing data you selected in step 4 each time you exit the program, which is an easy way to improves the privacy of your Windows 10 system. In the Clear Browsing Data pane, click the Always Clear This When I Close the Browser switch to On.

Deleting Specific Browsing History

Rather than deleting your entire browsing history, you might prefer to delete history only for a certain page, site, or date. Click Hub and click History (or click Ctrl+H) to display the History list.

To clear a single page from the History list, right-click the page and then click Delete, or hover the mouse pointer over the page and then click the Delete (X) icon.

To clear all your visits to a particular domain from the History list, right-click any page from that domain and then click Delete All Visits to Domain, where Domain is the domain name of the site you want to clear.

To clear a particular date from the History list, hover the mouse pointer over the date and then click the Delete (X) icon.

Blocking Third-Party Cookies

A *cookie* is a small text file that's stored on your computer. Websites use them to "remember" information about your session at that site: shopping cart data, page customizations, usernames, passwords, and so on.

No other site can access your cookies, so they're generally safe and private under most—but definitely not all—circumstances. To understand why cookies can sometimes compromise your privacy, you have to understand the different cookie types that exist:

- **Temporary cookie**—This type of cookie lives just as long as you have Edge running. Edge deletes all temporary cookies when you shut down the program.

- **Persistent cookie**—This type of cookie remains on your hard disk through multiple Edge sessions. The cookie's duration depends on how it's set up, but it can be anything from a few seconds to a few years.

- **First-party cookie**—This is a cookie set by the website you're viewing.

- **Third-party cookie**—This is a cookie set by a site other than the one you're viewing. Advertisers that have placed an ad on the site you're viewing create and store most third-party cookies.

These cookie types can compromise your privacy in two ways:

- A site might store *personally identifiable information*—your name, email address, home address, phone number, and so on—in a persistent first- or third-party cookie and then use that information in some way (such as filling in a form) without your consent.

- A site might store information about you in a persistent third-party cookie and then use that cookie to track your online movements and activities. The advertiser can do this because it might have (for example) an ad on dozens or hundreds of websites, and that ad is the mechanism that enables the site to set and read their cookies. Such sites are supposed to come up with *privacy policies* stating that they won't engage in surreptitious monitoring of users, they won't sell user data, and so on.

To help you handle these scenarios, Edge implements a privacy feature that gives you extra control over whether sites can store cookies on your machine. To check out this feature, follow these steps:

1. Click Settings and More.

2. Click Settings.

3. Click View Advanced Settings.

4. In the Cookies list, select one of the following:

   ■ **Block All Cookies**—This setting tells Edge to reject all requests to set and read cookies.

   ■ **Block Only Third Party Cookies**—This setting tells Edge to allow first-party cookies but to prevent third-party cookies. This is the optimum setting for online privacy.

   ■ **Don't Block Cookies**—This setting tells Edge to accept all requests to set and read cookies.

Opening a Private Browsing Session

The privacy techniques you've seen so far suffer from a complete set of glaring problems:

■ **They work after the fact**—For example, if you've visited a site with sensitive data, you delete your browsing history after you leave the site. This is a problem because you might forget to delete your history.

■ **They're all or nothing**—When you delete form data, passwords, browsing history, cookies, or the cache files, you delete *all* of them. This is a problem because you often want to remove the data for only a single site or a few sites.

Fortunately, Edge implements a single feature that solves both problems: InPrivate browsing. When you activate this feature, Edge stops storing private data when you visit websites. It no longer caches files or saves websites, and it no longer stores browsing data such as cookies, browsing history, form data, and passwords. Here's how this solves the privacy problems I mentioned earlier:

■ **It works before the fact**—By turning on InPrivate browsing before you visit a site, you don't have to worry about deleting data afterward because no data is saved.

 note

You can request that sites not track you online by using Edge to send a Do Not Track request. Few sites honor such requests these days, but if you want to try, click Settings and More, click Settings, click View Advanced Settings, and then click the Send Do Not Track Requests switch to On.

 caution

Blocking all cookies might sound like the easiest way to maximize your online privacy. However, many sites rely on cookies to operate properly, so if you block all cookies, you might find that your web surfing isn't as convenient or as smooth as it used to be. Some sites will display a message letting you know that cookies are needed for the site to run smoothly and will offer to enable them for that site, which is usually a good idea.

- **It works only while it's on**—When you activate InPrivate browsing and surf some private sites, no data is stored, but all your other privacy data remains intact. When you then deactivate InPrivate browsing, Edge resumes saving privacy data.

To use InPrivate browsing, click Settings and More and then click New InPrivate window (or press Ctrl+Shift+P). Edge opens a new browser window as shown in Figure 15.9. The InPrivate logo in the upper-left corner of the window tells you InPrivate browsing is activated.

Figure 15.9
When you activate InPrivate browsing, Edge opens a new window and displays the InPrivate logo in the upper-left corner of the window.

InPrivate logo

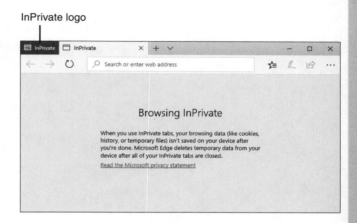

WINDOWS 10 INTERNET COMMUNICATIONS

Working with Email

The short history of the Modern-style Mail app that comes pre installed with Windows is not a particularly happy tale. Debuting with Windows 8, you can safely say that, despite its prominence on the Windows 8 Start screen, Mail might have been the most underwhelming email client ever created. You could literally use the fingers of one hand to count the tasks you could perform with the original version of Mail: send new messages, read incoming messages, reply to a message, forward a message, and move a message to a different folder. Yes, that's the complete list.

The Windows 8.1 version of Mail was an improvement, to be sure, with new features for easier folder management, designating favorite people, and selecting multiple messages.

In Windows 10, the Mail app has had a complete makeover to give it a clean, modern look and to make its interface consistent with other updated Windows 10 apps, particularly Calendar and People. You can also flag messages, easily switch between Mail and Calendar, and format your messages with several new font, paragraph, and style options.

In previous editions, we concluded that the Mail app was not a serious email tool, and that judgment still stands. If you're a heavy email user, you're still better off using Outlook or a strong web-based client such as Outlook.com or Gmail. However, this chapter is about Windows 10 Internet communications, so it's high time we dealt with the details of the native Mail app, if for no other reason than you can see what it's capable of doing.

 note

Microsoft pushes out updates of the Mail app fairly frequently. To read about what's changed, open the Mail app, select Settings (the gear icon at the lower left), and then select What's New.

Setting Up Mail Accounts

If you haven't yet started Mail—and therefore haven't yet defined your first mail account—or if you have multiple accounts and need to set up the others, this section shows you how to do it within Mail.

Specifying Basic Account Settings

Here are the steps to follow to set up an email account with just the basic settings (which should be enough to get most accounts up and running):

1. Start the process using one of the following techniques:

   ■ Start Mail for the first time. Select Add Account.

   ■ In Mail, select Settings (the gear icon), select Manage Accounts, and then select Add Account.

2. In the Choose an Account dialog box, select the type of account you're adding: Outlook.com, Exchange, Google, Yahoo!, iCloud, or Other Account (see Figure 16.1). Note that although the dialog box lists POP (Post Office Protocol) under Other Account, in our experience most POP accounts don't get set up properly if you go that route. Instead, you need to select Advanced Setup and enter your account details manually, as described in the next section. This also applies if Mail has trouble identifying your IMAP (Internet Message Access Protocol) account settings.

3. In the dialog box that appears, type the email address, click Next, and then enter the password for the account. Click Next.

4. Click Sign In. Mail connects to the server and obtains the settings to configure the account automatically.

5. Follow any further instructions that appear. For example, in some cases, you might need to specify your name (iCloud) or that you accept a connection to the account (Gmail). You may need to scroll down through a list of settings to find a final OK or Allow button.

6. Click Done.

Figure 16.1
The Mail app's supported account types.

Specifying Advanced Internet Account Settings

If Mail can't configure your account automatically (which is the case with most POP-based accounts, as well as some IMAP accounts), or if you want complete control over the settings used in your account configuration, you must perform an advanced Internet account setup. Here are the steps to follow:

1. Start the process using one of the following techniques:

   - Start Mail for the first time. Select Add Account.

   - In Mail, select Settings (the gear icon), select Manage Accounts, and then select Add Account.

2. In the Choose an Account dialog box, scroll down and select Advanced Setup. The Advanced Setup dialog box appears.

3. Select Internet Email; the Internet Email Account dialog box appears, as shown in Figure 16.2.

4. Specify your account data:

   - **Email address**—Your email address on the service to which you're connecting.

   - **Username**—The username assigned to your account by your mail provider. (In some cases, this is the same as your email address.)

   - **Password**—The password assigned to your account by your mail provider.

   - **Account Name**—The name you'd like to give this email account. This will be the title in the Mail app under which your emails will be listed.

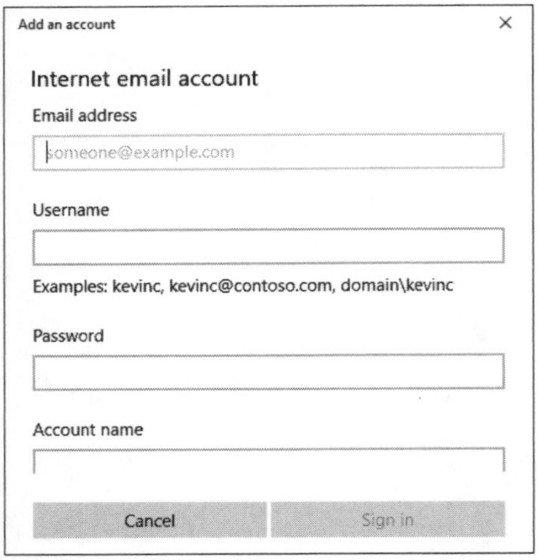

Add an account   ✕

Internet email account

Email address

someone@example.com

Username

Examples: kevinc, kevinc@contoso.com, domain\kevinc

Password

Account name

Cancel   Sign in

Figure 16.2
Use the Internet Email Account dialog box to fill in your POP or IMAP account details.

- **Send Your Messages Using This Name**—Your name. This will appear in the From heading line of messages you send from this account.

- **Incoming Email Server**—The full name for your incoming mail server (such as pop.provider.com).

- **Account Type**—Use this list to select the incoming mail server type: POP3 or IMAP4.

- **Outgoing (SMTP) Email Server**—Type the domain name for your outgoing mail server (such as **smtp.provider.com**).

- **Outgoing Server Requires Authentication**—Leave this box checked if your mail provider requires authentication before it will send your messages. (See the sidebar "SMTP Authentication" for more details.)

 note

The data for your incoming and outgoing mail servers should have been supplied to you by your ISP when you set up your account. If not, or if you can't find the data, contact the ISP's tech support department.

SMTP Authentication

With spam such a never-ending problem, many ISPs now require *SMTP authentication* for outgoing mail, which means that your email program must log on to the SMTP server to confirm that it really is you sending the mail (as opposed to some spammer spoofing your address). If your ISP uses authentication, be sure to leave the Outgoing Server Requires Authentication box checked. By default, Mail logs you on using the same username and password as your incoming mail server. If your ISP has given you separate logon data, uncheck the Use the Same User Name and Password for Sending Email box, and then type your account name and password in the text boxes that appear.

- **Use the Same User Name and Password for Sending Email**—Leave this box checked if your provider's outgoing server uses the same logon as the incoming server.

- **Require SSL for Incoming Email**—Leave this box checked if your provider requires that incoming mail be sent over a Secure Sockets Layer (SSL) connection.

- **Require SSL for Outgoing Email**—Leave this box checked if your provider requires that outgoing mail be sent over an SSL connection.

5. Click Sign-In. Mail adds your Internet account.

Specifying Advanced Exchange Account Settings

If you're setting up an Exchange ActiveSync account and Mail can't configure your account directly from the server, or if your Exchange server requires special settings, you must perform an advanced Exchange account setup. Follow these steps:

1. Begin by using one of the following techniques:

   - Start Mail for the first time. Select Add Account.

   - In Mail, select Settings, select Manage Accounts, and then select Add Account.

2. In the Choose an Account dialog box, select Advanced Setup. The Advanced Setup dialog box appears.

3. Select Exchange ActiveSync. The Exchange dialog box appears, as shown in Figure 16.3.

Figure 16.3
Use the Exchange dialog box to fill in the details for your Exchange ActiveSync account.

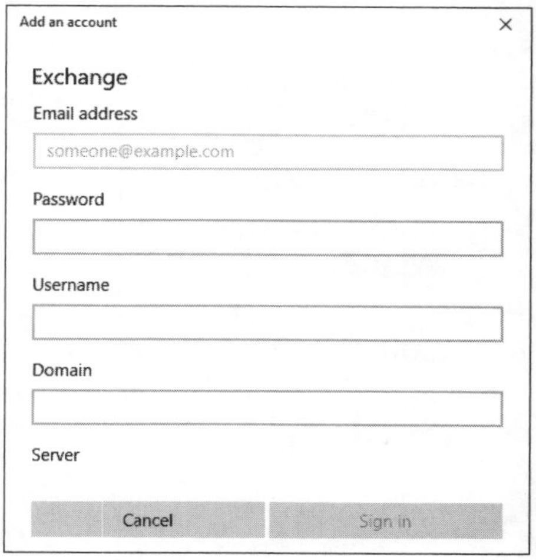

4. Specify your account data:

- **Email Address**—Type the address assigned to your Exchange account.

- **Password**—Type the password assigned to your account.

- **User Name**—Type the username assigned to your account.

- **Domain**—Type the internal domain address used by your Exchange server.

- **Server**—Type the Internet domain name for your Exchange server.

- **Server Requires Encrypted (SSL) Connection**—Leave this box checked if your Exchange server requires that mail be sent and received over a secure connection.

- **Account Name**—Type the name you want Mail to use for the account.

5. Click Sign-In. Mail adds your Exchange account.

 note

The data for your account and servers should have been supplied to you by your Exchange administrator when you set up your account. If not, or if you can't find the data, contact your support department.

Maintaining Accounts

Your accounts appear in the Accounts pane (select Settings and then Manage Accounts), as shown in Figure 16.4. To make changes to an account's settings, click it in the Manage Accounts pane and use the dialog box that appears. Depending on the account, this dialog box enables you to change the password, edit the name associated with the account, specify what gets synced, and delete the account.

Figure 16.4
Your email accounts are listed in the Manage Accounts pane.

Handling Incoming Messages

Incoming email messages are stored in your mailbox on your ISP's server until you use an email client such as Mail to retrieve them. The easiest way to do that is to let Mail check for and download new messages automatically. However, if you want to check for messages manually, click the Sync icon (the two arrows forming a circle) at the top of the message list.

Controlling Sync Settings for an Account

For IMAP accounts, Mail downloads incoming messages as soon as the server sends the notification that new items are available. (Only a copy is downloaded; emails stay on an IMAP server, unless you delete them.) Mail uses a dynamic process to determine the optimal frequency for syncing. For example, if you receive new messages only sporadically, Mail will eventually start checking for new messages less often to save battery power. If your incoming message count rises, Mail will adapt by increasing its syncing frequency.

To control the sync settings yourself, follow these steps:

1. In Mail, select Settings (the gear icon) and then select Manage Accounts to open the Manage Accounts pane.

2. Select the account you want to configure. Mail opens the Account Settings pane for that account.

3. Select Change Mailbox Sync Settings. Mail opens the Sync Settings pane for that account type. For example, Figure 16.5 shows the Sync Settings pane for an Outlook account.

Figure 16.5
Use an account's Sync Settings pane to control when Mail downloads new items.

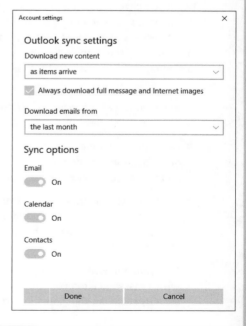

4. In the Download New Content (or Download New Email) list, select the frequency with which you want Mail to sync new messages to your PC: As Items Arrive, Based On My Usage (this is the default dynamic option), Manually (no automatic syncing), or a specific interval (such as Every 15 Minutes).

5. For web-based accounts (such as Outlook and Gmail), use the Download Email From list to specify how far back Mail should sync your older messages: The Last 7 Days, The Last 2 Weeks, The Last Month, The Last 3 Months, or Any Time (to download all available messages).

6. If you don't want Mail to sync email automatically, under Sync Options click the Email switch to Off.

7. Select Done to close the Sync Settings pane.

8. Select Save to put the new settings into effect.

Processing Messages

Each new message that arrives is stored in the Inbox folder's message list and appears in a bold font. To view the contents of any message, select it in the message list; Mail displays the message text in the reading pane.

When you have a message selected, you can do plenty of things with it (in addition to reading it, of course). You can flag it, move it to another folder, reply to it, delete it, and more. Most of these operations are straightforward, so we'll just summarize the basic techniques here:

- **Dealing with attachments**—If a message has an attachment, you'll see a paper clip icon to the right of the sender's name. You have two choices:

- **Open the attachment**—In the reading pane, click the attachment icon to download the file; then click the thumbnail that appears once the download is complete.

- **Save the attachment**—In the reading pane, click the attachment icon to download the file. When the download is done, right-click the attachment thumbnail and then click Save.

- **Flagging a message**—If you want to remember to deal with a message later, you can add a flag icon to the message by selecting the message and then selecting Flag.

 tip

It's possible to change the sound that indicates the arrival of a new message. Right-click the Volume icon in the notification area and then select Sounds. In the Program Events list, select New Mail Notification and then click Browse to choose the sound file you want Mail to play when it delivers new messages.

 tip

By default, Mail "organizes" incoming messages into two categories: Focused and Other. If you find this as annoying as we do, turn off this feature by clicking Settings (the gear icon) and then Reading, From the Reading pane, click the Sort Messages into Focused and Other switch to Off.

 caution

Open an attachment only if you are certain—absolutely, positively, dead-to-rights *certain*—not only that the attachment came from someone you know, but that it was either expected or not an unusual occurrence from that person. Email attachments are a distressingly common way to infect PCs with malware, so always think twice—thrice, even—before opening an attachment.

- **Moving a message to a different folder**—Later in this chapter, we show you how to create new folders you can use for storing related messages. To move a message to another folder, if you are viewing the list of emails, drag the message from the email list toward the left and then drop it onto one of the folder names at the left. If the desired folder name doesn't appear, drag it to the left anyway. A full list of folder names will appear in the middle of the app window. Alternatively, right-click the message (or click the message and then click ... in the reading pane), select Move, and then select the destination folder.

tip

On a touch PC, you can toggle a message flag by swiping right on the message.

tip

In the latest version of Mail, you can now set up automatic replies, which are useful if you're out of the office, on vacation, or otherwise indisposed and don't want your correspondents to think you're ignoring them. Select Settings and then select Automatic Replies to open the Automatic Replies pane. Click the Send Automatic Replies switch to On, and then enter your message in the text box.

- **Replying to a message**—Mail gives you two reply options:

  - **Reply**—This option sends the reply to only the person who sent the original message. Mail ignores any names in the Cc line. To use this option, select the message and then select Reply (or press Ctrl+R).

  - **Reply all**—This option sends the reply not only to the original author but also to anyone else mentioned in the Cc line. To use this option, select the message and then select Reply to All (or press Ctrl+Shift+R).

- **Forwarding a message**—You can forward a message to another address by selecting the message and then selecting Forward (or pressing Ctrl+F). Mail inserts the full text of the original message into the body of the new message and appends a greater than sign (>) to the beginning of each line.

tip

On a touchscreen, you can delete a message by swiping left on the message.

- **Deleting a message**—To get rid of a message, select it in the folder and then either select the Delete icon (the trash can) or press Delete (or Ctrl+D). Note that Mail doesn't really delete the message. Instead, it just moves it to the Trash folder. If you change your mind and decide to keep the message, open the Trash folder (select the More Folders icon and then select Trash) and move the message back to the folder it came from. To remove a message permanently, open the Deleted Items folder and delete the message from there.

Setting Swipe Options

Mail is configured to respond to touchscreen swipes by initiating so-called *quick actions*: By default, swiping right on a message toggles the message flag, whereas swiping left on a message deletes it. You can configure these quick actions by following these steps:

1. In Mail, select Settings (the gear icon) to open the Settings pane.

2. Select Quick Actions to open the Quick Actions pane.

3. If you have multiple accounts and you only want to use the quick actions with a particular account, choose it using the Select an Account list. Otherwise, activate the Apply to All Accounts check box.

4. Tap the Swipe Actions switch to Off if you don't want to use any quick actions.

5. Use the Swipe Right/Hover list to select the quick action that Mail performs when you swipe right on a message.

6. Use the Swipe Left/Hover list to select the quick action that Mail performs when you swipe left on a message.

7. Tap outside the Quick Actions pane to close it and put the new settings into effect.

Sending Messages

Composing a basic message in Mail is straightforward, and it isn't all that much different from composing a letter or memo in WordPad.

Initiating a New Message

There are several ways to get a new message started, not all of them in the Mail app, and not all of them well known. Here's a summary:

- In Mail, select the New Mail (+) icon or press Ctrl+N.

- In Microsoft Edge, to email a link to the current page, select the Share icon to open the Share pane, and then select Mail. The Share icon works similarly in some other apps as well.

- In a web page, click a mailto link. This creates a new message addressed to the recipient specified by the link.

From here, use the To field to enter the address of the recipient. Click Cc & Bcc, and then use the Cc field to enter the address of a recipient that you want to receive a copy of the message. Use the Bcc field to enter the addresses of any recipients you want to receive blind copies of the message. Note that in each field you can specify multiple recipients by separating the addresses with a semicolon (;).

Use the Subject field to enter a brief description of the message, and then use the box below the Subject field to enter your message. After you click or tap inside the message body, the ribbon comes alive, as shown in Figure 16.6. Use the Format tab to apply font formatting, paragraph formatting, and styles; use the Insert tab to attach a file, build a table, insert a picture, or add a link; use the Options tab to check the message spelling and to mark the message as either High Importance or Low Importance. When you're done, select Send (or press Alt+S).

 note

If you have multiple email accounts configured, it's not all that obvious how you specify which account to use to send a message. Ideally, the From field would be a drop-down list of your accounts, but alas that's not the case. Instead, you must first select the Mail app's Menu button (the hamburger icon in the upper-left corner), select the account you want to use, and then initiate the New Mail command.

Figure 16.6
Use the ribbon's Format, Insert, and Options tabs to craft your message.

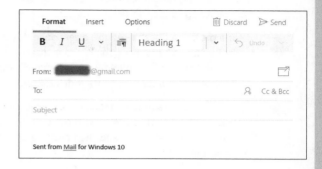

If you don't want each of the emails you send to advertise Windows, see the next section.

Creating a Signature

A *signature* is (usually) a few lines of text that are automatically added to the end of each sent email to provide contact information and other data. Mail provides a default signature—Sent from Mail for Windows 10—that redefines the word *lame*. To craft your own signature (or to control whether Mail uses a signature at all), follow these steps:

1. In Mail, select the Settings (gear) icon to open the Settings pane.

2. Select Signature to open the Signature pane.

3. If you have multiple accounts and you only want to use the signature with a particular account, choose it using the Select an Account list. Otherwise, activate the Apply to All Accounts check box.

4. Tap the Use an Email Signature switch to Off if you don't want to use a signature (including that insipid default signature) and skip to step 6.

5. Use the text box to type the signature you want to use, deleting Sent from Mail for Windows 10.

6. Tap outside the Signature pane to close it and put the new settings into effect.

Maintaining Mail

For the most part, Mail is a set-it-and-forget-it application. After the program and your accounts have been set up, you can go about your email business without worrying about Mail itself. However, to ensure trouble- and worry-free operation, here are two maintenance chores you should perform from time to time:

■ **Remove clutter from your Inbox**—Few things in business life are more daunting and frustrating than an Inbox bursting at the seams with a huge list of new or unprocessed messages. To prevent this from happening, you should regard the Inbox folder as a temporary holding area for all your incoming messages. Periodically, you should perform the following routine to keep your Inbox clean:

> If a message doesn't require a response, file it or delete it. By "file it," we mean move the message to another folder. You can set up folders for all major recipients, projects, customers, and categories that you deal with.
>
> If a message requires a response and you can answer it without further research or without taking a lot of time, answer it immediately and then either delete or file the message.

tip

Before moving the message to whatever you've designated as your "action items" folder, be sure to mark the message as unread. That way you'll be able to see at a glance whether you have items in that folder and how many there are.

> If a message requires a response but you can't send a reply right away, move the message to a folder designated for messages that require further action. You can then handle those messages later in the day when you have some time.

- **Clean out your Trash folder**—This folder is a good safeguard to help you recover accidentally deleted messages. However, after a while, it's extremely unlikely that you'll need to recover a message from this folder. Therefore, you should regularly delete messages from the Trash folder. We recommend leaving the last month's worth of deleted messages and deleting everything older.

TROUBLESHOOTING AN INTERNET CONNECTION

It's Great When It Works, But...

Browsing the Internet is great fun and very useful. Just watch as I instantly transfer millions of dollars from my secret Swiss bank account to...wait a minute, what's a "404 Server Not Found Error"? What's going on? Did the DSL go out? Is the NSA closing in on me? Help! Where's my money?

If you've used the Internet for any length of time, this scene might seem all too familiar (give or take a Swiss bank account). Using the Web on a modern computer is an experience that would have astounded people just 20 years ago, yet we can't escape that it's a staggeringly complex system. If something goes wrong at any step along the way between your finger-tips and a server in cyberspace, the whole system comes to a crashing halt. Where do you begin to find and fix the problem?

In this chapter, we show you the basic strategies to use when tracking down Internet problems, and we briefly discuss some of the diagnostic tools available to help you pinpoint the trouble.

Troubleshooting Step by Step

A functioning Internet connection depends on an entire chain of hardware and software components that reaches all the way from the tips of your fingers to a computer that might be halfway around the world. Trouble-shooting is a real detective's art, and it's based more on methodical track-ing down of potential suspect problems than intuition. If something goes wrong, you have to go through each component, asking "Is this the one that's causing the problem?"

Windows 10 comes with network-troubleshooting capabilities that, in some cases, can identify and repair problems automatically. If you encounter Internet connection problems—especially problems using high-speed broadband Internet service—try these steps:

1. If you have other computers or devices sharing the same Internet connection, can they reach any Internet sites? If they can't reach any websites, then you know that the problem is with your network, your Internet connection hardware, or your ISP. Reset your Internet hardware as described in step 4 in this procedure.

   If you are using Microsoft's Internet Connection Sharing, and the computer that is sharing its connection can reach websites but other computers can't, you have a network problem. See Chapter 22, "Troubleshooting Your Network." If the computer that's sharing its connection can't reach websites either, follow these steps on that computer.

2. If you're using a wireless Internet connection, try moving your computer or device closer to your wireless router. If signal strength is a problem in your home or office, you might need to add additional wireless access points.

   → *For more information on devices that can extend wireless networking range, **see** "801.11ac, 802.11n, and 802.11g Wireless (Wi-Fi) Networking," **p. 366.***

3. If your Internet connection was working previously but stopped working right after you installed a new hardware device, new software, or after a Windows Update was installed, a software change might be responsible for the problem. You might try using System Restore to bring Windows back to its configuration before the change.

   → *For instructions on using System Restore, **see** "Recovering Using System Restore," **p. 607.***

4. If you are using high-speed Internet, power off your Internet modem and router, wait five seconds, and then power them back on. Wait about a minute, and then see whether the problem has gone away. (If this works but you find yourself having to do it more than, say, once a month, contact your ISP and tell them.)

5. Click the network icon at the right end of the taskbar and select Open Network & Internet Settings. If there is a problem with your Internet connection, it will say so under Network Status. Windows also displays a yellow exclamation point icon in the taskbar, as shown in Figure 17.1.

6. Click the Troubleshoot button. If Windows displays a message indicating that it might be able to repair the problem, click Apply This Fix.

7. If the wizard's diagnosis is "Your broadband modem is experiencing connectivity issues" or "The DNS server isn't responding," and if you connect to the Internet through a shared connection using a router, this most likely means that your connection sharing router can't connect to the Internet. The problem is either with the router, your cable or DSL modem, or its connection to the Internet. Use your preferred web browser to connect to your sharing router, as described later in the chapter under "Identifying Network Hardware Problems." If you can bring up the router's setup web page, the router itself is working, so your best bet is to contact your ISP for further assistance.

If the problem occurred because your computer failed to obtain its network settings from a router, this procedure will often work. In many cases, though, you'll need to locate the problem yourself, using good, old-fashioned Sherlock Holmes–style deductive reasoning. For example, let's assume you are having trouble using a certain website. Here are some scenarios:

- You can view some of its pages, but not others, or you see text displayed but not the streaming video or sound. In this case, you know that your Internet connection itself is working because sometimes something *does* appear. The problem, then, is that the video or sound application isn't working. You might want to check the index to see whether we discuss the application in this book. You might also check the application's built-in help pages. If the application was one that you downloaded or purchased, check the manufacturer's website for support information or an updated software version.

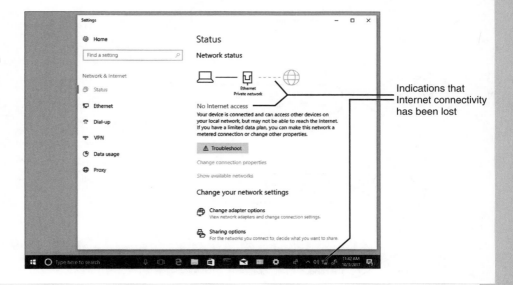

Figure 17.1 Windows displays a notification on the network icon in the taskbar, showing that your Internet connection is not working.

Indications that Internet connectivity has been lost

- Nothing on this particular site is responding. In this case, see if you can view any other website. Try www.google.com, www.quepublishing.com, your ISP's website, or your local newspaper's website.

  If you get a response from even one other website, again, your Internet connection is fine. The problem is most likely with the site you're trying to use or with your ISP. Check to be sure that your web browser isn't set up to block access to the site you're interested in. (See Chapter 15, "Web Browsing with Microsoft Edge," for more help on this topic.)

  You also might try using a different web browser. In some cases, it's not a bad Internet connection but a compatibility issue that makes a website show just a blank screen. If you're using Microsoft Edge, try Internet Explorer, or vice versa. Google Chrome, Opera, and Firefox are other good alternatives.

  Finally, Windows 10 can help with troubleshooting issues related to contacting specific websites. To use it, click Start, Settings, Update & Security, Troubleshoot, Internet Connections, Run the Troubleshooter, and Help Me Connect to a Specific Web Page. Paste in the address of the website you were having trouble reaching. Click Next, and you'll see whether the tool can help diagnose the problem.

- You can't view web pages on any site. If this is the case, you know that your Internet connection itself is at fault. This chapter can help you find out what's wrong.

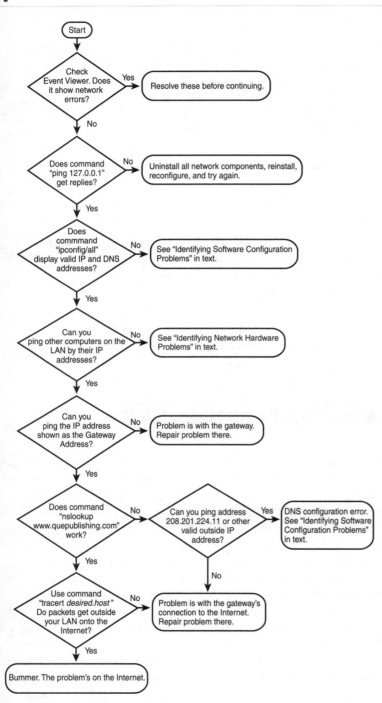

Figure 17.2
Flowchart for diagnosing broadband or LAN-based Internet connection problems.

Figure 17.3
Flowchart for diagnosing
dial-up Internet
connection problems.

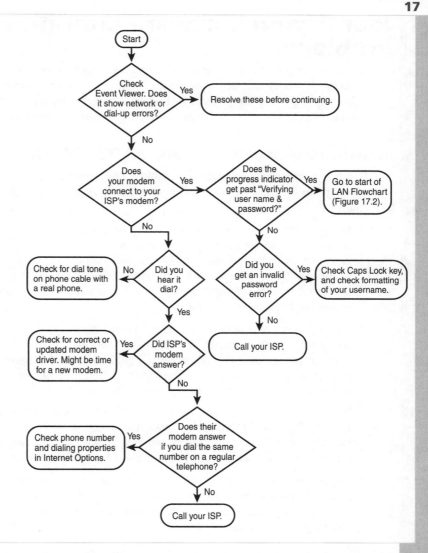

To that end, Figures 17.2 and 17.3 show flowcharts to help direct you to the source of the problem.
The first chart is for broadband or LAN Internet connections; the second is for those who still have
to use a dial-up modem connection to an ISP. If you're having Internet connection trouble, follow the
appropriate flowchart for your type of connection. The endpoints in each flowchart suggest places to
look for trouble. We discuss these in the sections that follow.

Identifying Software Configuration Problems

Software configuration problems can easily be the cause of Internet connection problems. It's fairly simple to determine that this is the problem: You can't make any Internet connection whatsoever, although the Device Manager says your network card or modem seems to be working correctly. The potential problems depend on the type of Internet connection you use.

Troubleshooting a Cable or DSL Modem Connection

If your computer connects directly to a cable or DSL modem, via an Ethernet cable between the modem and your computer, follow these steps:

note

If you have DSL or cable service, but your computer connects to a router and the router connects to the DSL or cable modem, don't follow these instructions. Instead, see "Identifying Network Hardware Problems," later in this chapter.

1. To open a Command Prompt window, press Windows Logo+R, type **cmd**, and press Enter. Type **ipconfig /all** and press Enter. Be sure that the IP address and DNS information for the network card that connects to your broadband modem are accurate. Your ISP's tech support people can help you confirm this.

2. If your provider requires you to "sign on" before using the Internet, you'll be using a sort of "dial-up" connection, except that the connection is made digitally over the DSL network. This is called Point-to-Point Protocol over Ethernet, or PPPoE. You set up this connection using the Broadband (PPPoE) option, as described in Chapter 14, "Getting Connected."

    If this is the case, and if you use a network adapter to connect to your DSL modem, the IP address displayed for the network adapter is used to communicate with your DSL modem. Be sure to check with your ISP to be certain that this computer-to-modem connection is configured correctly; if it's not, you won't be able to make the connection to your ISP.

3. Establishing the DSL connection whenever you need it is just a bit awkward. Click the Network icon in the taskbar (see Figure 17.4), and at the top of the pop-up panel click the name of the DSL connection. This brings up the Network Settings window. Touch the name of the DSL connection again here, and then click Connect.

When the logon process has completed, typing **ipconfig /all** should show a "dial-up" connection with a different IP address. This is your real, public Internet address for the duration of the connection.

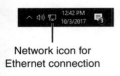

Network icon for
Ethernet connection

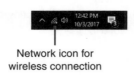

Network icon for
wireless connection

Figure 17.4
The Network icon on the taskbar, for wired and wireless connection types. Click to display a connection list. One more click lets you open Network & Internet Settings.

Troubleshooting a LAN Connection

If you connect to the Internet via a wired or wireless connection on your LAN, the first question is, can you communicate with other computers on your LAN? To test this, you should use the `ping` command.

To open a Command Prompt window, right-click the Start button and select Command Prompt or Windows PowerShell, whichever appears. Type the command **ipconfig** and press Enter. The output of `ipconfig` lists a number called a gateway address, as shown in the following example:

```
Ethernet adapter Ethernet:
   Connection-specific DNS Suffix  . :
   Link-local IPv6 Address . . . . . : fe80::d8c:b88b:dfa2:87bc%3
   IPv4 Address. . . . . . . . . . . : 192.168.0.130
   Subnet Mask . . . . . . . . . . . : 255.255.255.0
   Default Gateway . . . . . . . . . : 192.168.0.1
```

To test the connection to your gateway, type **ping** followed by whatever number is listed as the gateway address on your computer, and then press Enter. For example:

```
ping 192.168.0.1
```

This tests the connection to the computer or router that is sharing its Internet connection. If `ping` says "Request timed out" or "Transmit failed" instead of listing four successful replies, you have a LAN problem that you need to fix first.

If you are using a wireless network connection, be sure your wireless connection is working correctly, that you are connected to the correct wireless network, and that you have the correct network key entered. Chapter 22, "Troubleshooting Your Network," is devoted to LAN troubleshooting.

If you can communicate with other computers on the LAN but not the Internet, can anyone else on your LAN access the Internet? If no one can, the problem is in your LAN's connection to the Internet. Follow these steps to see what's wrong:

1. Open a Command Prompt window and type **ipconfig /all** to view your TCP/IP settings. The output appears similar to that shown in Listing 17.1. (The Tunnel Adapter entries are not important here and are not shown.)

Listing 17.1 Output from the **ipconfig /all** Command

```
Windows IP Configuration
   Host Name . . . . . . . . . . . . .: MyComputer
Primary Dns Suffix . . . . . . . .:
Node Type . . . . . . . . . . . . .: Hybrid
IP Routing Enabled. . . . . . . . .: No
```

 tip

Windows has a diagnostic and repair function that resets all the software components of a LAN connection, including the DHCP address assignment. This often solves LAN problems. To use it, first power off your Internet modem and router for a few seconds, and then turn them back on. Wait about a minute. Click Start, Settings, Update & Security, Troubleshoot. Scroll down and click Network Adapter, Run the Troubleshooter. If a problem is identified, follow the instructions to fix it.

 note

If you have a laptop, see if yours has a little slide or pushbutton switch that turns the internal wireless adapter on and off. It's easy for that switch to get turned off. If you have a tablet or laptop that has a software switch (often labeled Airplane Mode), be sure that you haven't inadvertently turned on Airplane Mode or turned off WiFi. Doing either shuts down your network and Internet connections.

```
WINS Proxy Enabled. . . . . . . . .: No
Ethernet adapter Local Area Connection:
Connection-specific DNS Suffix . .:
Description . . . . . . . . . . . .: Intel PCI Fast Ethernet Adapter
Physical Address. . . . . . . . . .: 00-03-FF-D0-CA-5F
DHCP Enabled. . . . . . . . . . . .: Yes
Autoconfiguration Enabled . . . . .: Yes
Link-local IPv6 Address . . . . . .: fe80::8014:cfc7:9a98:cdfe%10(Preferred)
IPv4 Address. . . . . . . . . . . .: 192.168.1.106(Preferred)
Subnet Mask . . . . . . . . . . . .: 255.255.255.0
Lease Obtained. . . . . . . . . . .: Thursday, August 21, 2015 3:13:14 PM
Lease Expires . . . . . . . . . . .: Friday, August 22, 2015 3:13:26 PM
Default Gateway . . . . . . . . . .: 192.168.1.1
DHCP Server . . . . . . . . . . . .: 192.168.1.1
DHCPv6 IAID . . . . . . . . . . . .: 252182567
DHCPv6 Client DUID. . . . . . . . .: 00-01-03-01-37-F2-EB-C2-38-3C-40-F3-02-38
DNS Servers . . . . . . . . . . . .: 192.168.1.1
NetBIOS over Tcpip. . . . . . . . .: Enabled
```

Within the output, check the following:

- The DNS suffix search list and the connection-specific DNS suffix should be set correctly for your ISP's domain name or your company's domain name. (This is helpful but not crucial.) It can also be left blank.

- The IP address should be appropriate for your LAN. The address might be 192.168.0.*xxx* or something similar, possibly with a different number in place of the 0.

- If your IP address starts with the numbers 169.254, your router or the sharing computer was not running when you booted up your computer, or it is no longer set up to share its connection. It is not doing its job of passing out network IP addresses to other computers. Get the sharing computer or router restarted, and then skip to step 2.

- The default gateway address should be the IP address of your router or sharing computer—usually something similar to 192.168.0.1 or 192.168.1.1.

- The default gateway address and your IP address should be identical for the first few sets of numbers, corresponding to those parts of the subnet mask that are set to 255. That is, both might start with 192.168.0 or 192.168.1.

- If your computer gets its IP address information automatically, DHCP Enabled should be set to Yes. If your computer has its IP address information entered manually, no DHCP server should be listed.

- If you're using connection sharing, the DNS server address will be 192.168.0.1. Otherwise, the DNS server numbers should be those provided by your ISP or network administrator. Some routers substitute their own address as the DNS server address and do DNS lookups themselves, as in the example shown here. The DNS address will match the default gateway address in this case.

- If your computer gets its settings automatically or uses a shared connection, continue with the next two steps.

2. Be sure the router or sharing computer is running. Then click Start, Settings, Update & Security, Troubleshoot. Scroll down and click Network Adapter, Run the Troubleshooter. Follow the steps it suggests.

3. Repeat the `ipconfig` command and see whether the correct information appears now. If it does, you're all set. If not, the master computer or the router is not supplying the information described previously and needs to be set correctly before you can proceed.

These steps should take care of any software configuration problems. If not one of these steps indicates or solves the problem, check that your network or modem hardware is functioning correctly.

Identifying Network Hardware Problems

If you suspect hardware as the source of your Internet connection problems, check the following:

- Log on using an account with Administrator privileges. Right-click the Start button and select Device Manager. Look for any yellow exclamation point (!) icons in the device list. If your network adapter is marked with this trouble indicator, you must solve the hardware problem before continuing. If the device needs an updated driver, see "Updating a Device Driver" in Chapter 28, "Managing Your Hardware," for more information.

- Right-click the Start button, select Event Viewer, and look in the Administrative Events section under Custom Views for any potentially informative error messages that might indicate a hardware problem.

- Use `ipconfig` on each of your computers to check that all the computers on your LAN have the same gateway and network mask values, and similar but distinct IP addresses.

- If your LAN has indicator lights on the network cards and switches, open a Command Prompt window and type

  ```
  ping -t x.x.x.x
  ```

  where *x.x.x.x* is your network's default gateway address. (This might be something similar to 192.168.0.1.) This forces your computer to transmit data once per second. Confirm that the indicator lights blink on your network adapter and the switch, if you have one. This test might point out a cabling problem.

- If your switch or network adapter's indicator doesn't flash, you might have a bad network adapter, the wrong driver might be installed, or you might have configured the card incorrectly. You can stop the `ping` test by pressing Ctrl+C when you're finished checking.

If you use a router for a broadband (DSL or cable) connection, your router might provide further assistance. To access the router, follow these steps:

1. Right-click the Start button and select Command Prompt or Windows PowerShell, whichever appears.

2. Type the command **ipconfig** and press Enter.

3. Note the gateway address. It will be something along the lines of 192.168.*x*.*x*, such as 192.168.0.1.

4. Open your preferred web browser. In the Address bar, type **http://** followed by the gateway address. This will look something like http://192.168.0.1.

5. You are prompted to enter the administrative username and password for your router. Each manufacturer has a default name and password, which you can find in the router's user manual. You might also have changed it when you installed it. (You might try username admin and password admin or password.)

6. Most routers have a Status menu item that displays the status of the router's Internet connection. If it says that it can't connect, you might have an incorrect PPPoE username or password entered. Or it might have dropped the connection. In this case, there might be a Connect button you can click, or you might want to just power off and then power on the router.

If you use a dial-up Internet connection, the next section can help you diagnose modem problems.

Troubleshooting Internet Problems with Windows TCP/IP Utilities

If you think you are connected to your ISP but you still can't communicate, you can use some of the command-line tools provided with Windows to trace TCP/IP problems. (TCP/IP is the network language or protocol used by the Internet.)

To run the command-line utilities, first open a Command Prompt window. (Right-click the Start button and select Command Prompt or Windows PowerShell, whichever appears.) Then type in the commands as we describe them later. If you're not familiar with a particular command-line utility, type the command name followed by /?, as in this example:

```
ping /?
```

Now, let's go through some of the TCP/IP diagnostic and command-line utilities provided with Windows.

ipconfig

ipconfig is one of the most useful command-line utilities provided with Windows because it displays the current IP address information for each of your computer's network adapters and active dial-up connections. On networks that assign addresses automatically, ipconfig can tell you what your computer's IP address is, if you ever need to know it.

Within an open Command Prompt window, the command ipconfig prints the following information (of course, the IP,

 note

If you're a Unix devotee, you'll find these utilities familiar, if not identical, to their Unix counterparts. If you're new to TCP/IP networking or debugging, you might find these utilities a little unfriendly. (Welcome to the world of networking!)

subnet, and gateway information ipconfig provides will be different for your computer, and you might see a dial-up connection listed instead of a network adapter):

```
Windows IP Configuration
Ethernet adapter Local Area Connection:
Connection-specific DNS Suffix . . :
Link-local IPv6 Address . . . . . : fe80::8014:cfc7:9a98:cdfe%10
IPv4 Address. . . . . . . . . . . : 192.168.0.106
Subnet Mask . . . . . . . . . . . : 255.255.255.0
Default Gateway . . . . . . . . . : 192.168.0.1
```

(You can ignore the Tunnel Adapter information; this is part of the Version 6 Internet Protocol system, which is used only on large, managed corporate networks.)

If you type the command

```
ipconfig /all
```

Windows displays additional information about your network settings, including the information shown in Table 17.1.

Table 17.1 Information Displayed by `ipconfig/all`

Setting	What It Means
Host Name	The name you gave your computer.
Primary DNS Suffix	The Internet domain to which your computer belongs. (You might temporarily belong to others as well while using a dial-up connection.) This might be blank; it is not a problem.
Node Type	The method that Windows uses to locate other computers on your LAN when you use Windows Networking. This usually is Hybrid or Broadcast.
DNS Suffix Search List	Alternative domain names used if you type just part of a hostname and the default domain does not provide a match.
Connection-specific DNS Suffix	The domain name for this particular connection. This is most applicable to dial-up connections.
DHCP Enabled	If set to Yes, this adapter is set to receive its IP address automatically; if set to No, the address was set manually.
DNS Servers	IP addresses of domain name servers.

`ipconfig` displays most of the information that can be set in the Network and Dial-Up Connection Properties dialog box, but it shows their real-world values. This makes it an invaluable "first stop" when troubleshooting any network problem. If you determine that an Internet connection problem lies in your equipment somewhere (because you cannot access Internet destinations), typing **ipconfig /all** can tell you whether your network setup is correct. You need this information at hand before calling your ISP for assistance.

ping

If you try to browse the Internet or share files with other computers or devices on your LAN and get no response, the reason could be that the other computer isn't receiving your data or isn't responding. After `ipconfig`, `ping` is the most useful tool to determine where your Internet connection or your network has stopped working.

Here's how it works:

1. The `ping` command sends a few packets of data to any computer you specify.

2. The other computer should immediately send these packets back to you.

3. `ping` lets you know whether the packets come back.

Therefore, `ping` tests the low-level communication between two computers. If `ping` works, you know that your network wiring, TCP/IP software, and any routers in between you and the other computer are working. `ping` takes several options that can customize the type and amount of output it reports back to you. Three especially useful variations of these options exist; the first two are

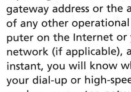
tip

You can type `ping x.x.x.x`, replacing *x.x.x.x* with the default gateway address or the address of any other operational computer on the Internet or your network (if applicable), and in an instant, you will know whether your dial-up or high-speed modem, computer, network hardware, and cabling are operating properly. If echoes come back, the physical part of your network is functioning properly. If they don't, you can use `tracert` and other tools (explained later in this chapter) to see why.

```
ping hostname
```

where *hostname* is the name of one of the computers on your network, and

```
ping nnn.nnn.nnn.nnn
```

where *nnn.nnn.nnn.nnn* is a computer's numeric IP address, as discovered by `ipconfig`. That is, you can ping a computer either by its name or by its IP address. These variations transmit four packets to the host or IP address you specify and tell you whether they return. This command returns the following information:

```
C:\> ping www.mycompany.com
Pinging sumatra.mycompany.com [202.222.132.163] with 32 bytes of data:
Reply from 202.222.132.163: bytes=32 time<10ms TTL=32
Reply from 202.222.132.163: bytes=32 time<10ms TTL=32
Reply from 202.222.132.163: bytes=32 time<10ms TTL=32
Reply from 202.222.132.163: bytes=32 time<10ms TTL=32
```

In this example, the fact that the reply packets came back tells us that the computer can communicate with www.mycompany.com. It also tells us that everything in between my computer and mycompany.com is working.

The third useful variation is to add the `-t` option. This makes `ping` run endlessly once per second until you press Ctrl+C. This capability is especially helpful if you're looking at indicator lights on your network hub, changing cables, and so on. The endless testing lets you just watch the screen to see whether any changes you make cause a difference.

ping is a great quick test of connectivity to any location. If the ping test fails, use tracert to tell you where the problem is. ping is a good, quick tool to use to discover whether an Internet site is alive. (However, some large companies have made their servers not respond to ping tests. For example, ping www.microsoft.com never works, even with a good Internet connection. It's not just that Microsoft got tired of being the first site everyone thought of to test their Internet connections; malicious people also can use ping to suck up all of a company's Internet bandwidth. www.Google.com does return pings, though.)

> **note**
>
> It's not uncommon for one packet of the four to be lost; when the Internet gets congested, sometimes ping packets are discarded as unimportant. If any come back, the intervening networks are working. It's also not unusual for the name that appears after "pinging" to be different from what you typed. Some computers have alternative names.

tracert

The tracert command is similar to ping: It sends packets to a remote host and sees whether packets return. However, tracert adds a wrinkle: it checks the connectivity to each individual router in the path between you and the remote host. (Routers are the devices that connect one network to another. The Internet itself is the conglomeration of a few million networks all connected by routers.) If your computer and Internet connection are working but you still can't reach some or all Internet sites, tracert can help you find the blockage.

In the output of tracert, the address it tests first is your local network's gateway (if you connect to the Internet via a high-speed connection or a LAN) or the modem-answering equipment at your ISP's office (if you're using a dial-up connection). If this first address responds, you know that your modem, LAN, or broadband connection is working. If the connection stops after two or three routers, the problem is in your ISP's network. If the problem occurs farther out, there might be an Internet outage somewhere else in the country.

Here's an example that shows the route between my network and the fictitious web server www.fictitious.net. Typing

```
tracert www.fictitious.net
```

returns the following:

```
Tracing route to www.fictitious.com [204.179.107.3]
over a maximum of 30 hops:
1  <10 ms  <10 ms   <10 ms  190.mycompany.com [202.201.200.190]
2  <10 ms  <10 ms   10 ms   129.mycompany.com [202.201.200.129]
3   20 ms   20 ms   20 ms   w001.z216112073.sjc-ca.dsl.cnc.net [217.112.73.1]
4   10 ms   10 ms   10 ms   206.83.66.153
5   10 ms   10 ms   10 ms   rt001f0801.sjc-ca.concentric.net [206.83.90.161]
6   10 ms   20 ms   20 ms   us-ca-sjc-core2-f5-0.rtr.concentric.net [205.158.11.133]
7   10 ms   20 ms   10 ms   us-ca-sjc-core1-g4-0-0.rtr.concentric.net [205.158.10.2]
8   10 ms   20 ms   20 ms   us-ca-pa-core1-a9-0d1.rtr.concentric.net [205.158.11.14]
```

```
9   10 ms   20 ms   20 ms ATM2-0-0.br2.pao1.ALTER.NET [137.39.23.189]
10  10 ms   20 ms   20 ms 125.ATM3-0.XR1.PAO1.ALTER.NET [152.63.49.170]
11  10 ms   10 ms   20 ms 289.at-1-0-0.XR3.SCL1.ALTER.NET [152.63.49.98]
12  20 ms   20 ms   20 ms 295.ATM8-0-0.GW2.SCL1.ALTER.NET [152.63.48.113]
13  20 ms   20 ms   20 ms 2250-gw.customer.ALTER.NET [157.130.193.14]
14  41 ms   30 ms   20 ms www.fictitious.com [204.179.107.3]
Trace complete.
```

You can see that between my computer and this web server, data passes through 13 intermediate routers owned by two ISPs.

You should be aware of a couple of tracert oddities. First, notice in the example that on the command line I typed www.fictitious.net, but tracert printed www.fictitious.com. That's not unusual. Web servers sometimes have alternative names. tracert starts with a reverse name lookup to find the *canonical* (primary) name for a given IP address.

You might run into another glitch as well. For security reasons, many organizations use firewall software or devices, which block tracert packets at the firewall between their LAN and the Internet. In these instances, tracert will never reach its intended destination, even when regular communications are working correctly. Instead, you'll see an endless list that looks similar to this:

 tip

As mentioned at the start of the chapter, when your Internet connection is working, run tracert to trace the path between your computer and a few Internet hosts. Print and save the listings. Someday when you're having Internet problems, you can use these listings as a baseline reference. It's very helpful to know whether packets are stopping in your LAN, in your ISP's network, or beyond when you pick up the phone to yell about it.

```
14   *   *   * Request timed out.
15   *   *   * Request timed out.
16   *   *   * Request timed out.
```

This continues up to the tracert limit of 30 probes. If this happens, just press Ctrl+C to cancel the test. If tracert could reach routers outside your own LAN or PC, your equipment and Internet connection are fine—and that's all you can directly control.

Third-Party Utilities

In addition to the utilities provided with Windows, you can use some third-party tools to help diagnose your connection and gather Internet information. In the following sections, we describe some web-based utilities.

WhatIsMyIP

If you are using a router, your network uses one "public" IP address to communicate with the Internet, using a mechanism called Network Address Translation (NAT). The public address is different from the private one assigned to your computer. It's not always easy or convenient to find out your public IP address from your router. Solution: Just open www.whatismyip.com in your web browser, and you'll see your public address in a flash.

➡ *To find out how NAT works, **see** "NAT and Internet Connection Sharing," **p. 407.***

Speed Check

Ever wondered how to find the real-world transfer rate of your Internet connection? There are several speed test websites that you can use, but we like www.speedtest.net (click Begin Test, not Start Now or Start Scan) and www.dslreports.com (click Speed Test on the menu bar). You'll get valid results only if you perform the test while your computer and other computers on your network are sitting idle, not downloading, uploading to the cloud, or streaming content.

Reverse tracert

As discussed earlier, the tracert program investigates the path that data you send through the Internet takes to reach another location. Interestingly, data coming back to you can take a different path, depending on the way your ISP has set up its own internal network.

It's handy to know the path data takes coming to you. If you record this information while your Internet connection is working and subsequently run into trouble, you can have a friend perform a tracert to you. (You need to give him your IP address, which you can find using the ipconfig command.) If the results differ, you might be able to tell whether the problem is with your computer, your ISP, or the Internet.

You can visit www.traceroute.org for a list of hundreds of web servers that can perform a traceroute test from their site to you. Don't be surprised if the test results take awhile to appear; these tests can take a minute or longer.

CREATING A WINDOWS NETWORK

Creating or Joining a Network

If you have two or more computers in your home or office, for about the cost of a trip to the movies, you can set up a network that will let everyone trade music, videos, and documents, use the same printer and Internet connection, and back up files, almost effortlessly. It's not as hard or expensive as you might think. After you've done the planning and shopping, you should be able to get a network up and running in an hour or two.

This chapter should give you all the information you need. Then check out Chapter 19, "Connecting Your Network to the Internet," and if you have computers with older versions of Windows or other operating systems, Chapter 20, "Networking with Other Operating Systems."

If you're just adding a computer to an existing Ethernet network, you can skip ahead to the section "Installing Network Adapters." If you're joining an existing wireless network, see "Joining a Wireless Network" in Chapter 36, "Wireless Networking."

 note

If you have high-speed Internet service and your ISP provided you with a router when you started your service, you already have the makings of a network. If you want to share files and printers, perform backups, and so on, you just need to make sure that your router is set up securely, and you might need to change a few settings in Windows. You can skip ahead to "Installing Network Adapters," later in this chapter, to see how to do this.

Also, there's a housekeeping item to mention here. Throughout this chapter we give this instruction for getting to the networking settings panel: Click the network icon in the taskbar, and then select Network & Internet Settings, Status. On small screens, or if you've made the Settings window narrow, you'll need to touch or click the word *Status* to see the settings we discuss. In most cases, though, Windows will show you the Status page automatically, so you won't actually need to click Status (no harm if you do, though). We want the instructions to work for everyone, so we include the step of clicking Status. On mobile phones, where there is no taskbar, you get to Network & Internet Settings from the main Settings screen.

Planning Your Network

You must plan your network around your own particular needs. What do you expect from a network? The following tasks are some you might want your network to perform:

- Share printers, files, optical (Blu-ray, DVD, and CD) drives, music, and videos between your devices

- Share an Internet connection

- Provide wireless Internet access to laptops and mobile devices

- Receive faxes directly on one computer and print or route them to individuals automatically

- Provide access to another network at another location

- Provide remote access so that you can reach your LAN from elsewhere, via the Internet or even a modem

- Host a website

- Operate a database server

- Play multiuser games

You should make a list of your networking goals. You must provide adequate capacity to meet these and future needs, but you also don't need to overbuild.

On the other hand, if you need access to large databases, require the centralized user account control provided by the Windows Server operating system, or require centralized backup of all workstations, you must plan and invest more carefully. We discuss some of the issues you should consider in the next section.

Are You Being Served?

If you're planning a network of more than just a few computers, you need to make a big decision: whether to use Windows Server. The Server versions provide a raft of networking services that Windows 10 doesn't have, but you must learn how to configure and support them.

note

When we talk about Windows Server here, we mean the *business* Server versions. There was at one time a product called Windows Home Server, but it was meant just to let you back up files across the network.

Instant Networking

If your goal is simply to share printers, files, and an Internet connection among just a few computers that are fairly close together, here's a recipe for instant networking. Get the following items at your local computer store or at an online shop such as amazon.com, tigerdirect.com, or newegg.com. Big office supply and consumer electronics stores are also a good bet, especially if a sale or rebate offer is available.

- A network adapter for each computer that doesn't already have a network interface. Any computer capable of running Windows 10 will almost certainly have an Ethernet or wireless adapter built in. For any really old computers that don't, you need to add one. A hard-wired Ethernet adapter costs $5–$45. A wireless network adapter costs $20–$50.

- A Wireless-N router with a built-in four-port switch for $20–$90. We recommend using a wireless router even if you aren't setting up a shared Internet connection, and even if you don't yet have devices that use wireless networking. However, if you're sure you won't ever want to use a wireless connection, you can instead buy a four- or eight-port 10/100 Ethernet Switch. You need one port for every computer you want to hook up. If you have broadband Internet service, it's likely that your ISP already provided you with a router that supports both Wi-Fi and Ethernet connections.

- One CAT-5e Ethernet cable for each computer that doesn't have a wireless adapter. You'll place the switch or router next to one of the computers, so you'll need one 4-foot cable. The other cables must be long enough to reach from the other computers to the switch. These cables can be very inexpensive online and tend to be overpriced in stores.

When you have these parts, skip ahead to the "Installing Network Adapters" section, later in this chapter. If you get a wireless router, be sure to set up WPA2 wireless security, even if you aren't going to use the wireless part right away. We describe how to do that under "Setting Up a New Wireless Network," later in this chapter.

Table 18.1 lists the primary trade-offs between the regular desktop versions of Windows and Windows Server.

Table 18.1 Primary Differences Between Desktop Versions of Windows and Windows Server

Desktop Windows	Windows Server
Allows up to 20 file and printer sharing connections with other computers.	Can provide unlimited connections, but there are client licensing fees.
Cost is low.	Requires an extra computer, a copy of Windows Server, and possibly additional fees for client access licenses. The added costs will easily exceed $1,000. For example, a copy of Windows Server Essentials, which can serve 25 clients, costs $500 (though you can find it for less), and you must buy a computer on which to run it.

Table 18.1 Continued

Desktop Windows	Windows Server
Configuration is simple.	Is complex to configure and administer.
Each computer must be administered separately (setting up user accounts, for example).	Has centralized administration.
Managing file security can be difficult when you have more than one user per computer.	Centralized user management eases the task of managing file security.
Two levels of user security: standard and administrator.	Provides extremely fine-grained control of what each user can and cannot do.
Only one signed-in user can work at a time.	Supports multiple simultaneous users via Remote Desktop or Thin Client devices, subject to client access license fees.
Fax modem can't be shared with other computers.	One fax modem and phone line can be shared by multiple computers.
Rudimentary remote access, connection sharing, and WAN support are provided.	These features are more sophisticated.

For us, manageability is the main issue. As you add more and more users, centralized management becomes more and more important. If you have a network of 10 or more computers, we recommend using at least one copy of Windows Server.

You can certainly use Server with smaller networks, too. The following are reasons for doing so:

- You want to join your network to a Server domain somewhere else. This is often the case in a business's branch office.

- You want to support multiple simultaneous remote desktop or virtual private network (VPN) users. (Alternatively, you could buy inexpensive VPN routers or software to handle this task.)

- You want to exercise strict security controls, support multiple signed-in users on one computer, restrict your users' abilities to change system settings, or use automatic application installation.

- You want to take advantage of advanced networking services such as Group Policy, DHCP, DNS, and so on.

If you decide you need or want Windows Server, you should get a book dedicated to that OS, and a big box of Alka-Seltzer, before you go any further.

When to Hire a Professional

You've probably heard this adage: "If you want something done right, do it yourself!" It is true, to a point. Sometimes, though, the benefit of hiring someone else outweighs the pleasure of doing it yourself.

For a home network, you should definitely try to set it up yourself. Call it a learning experience, get friends to help, and, if you run into problems, a high-school–aged neighbor can probably get them straightened out in 15 minutes. As long as you don't have to run wires through the wall or construct your own cables, you should be able to manage this job even with no prior networking experience. When something is called "Plug and Play" now, it really is.

The balance tips the other way for a business. If you depend on your computers to get your work done, getting them set up should be your first concern, but keeping them working should be your second, third, and fourth. When your business is hanging in the balance, you should consider the cost of computer failure when you're deciding whether it's worth spending money on setup and installation. Hiring a good consultant or contractor will give you the following:

- An established relationship. If something goes wrong, you'll already know whom to call, and that person will already know the details of your system.

- A professional installation job.

- The benefit of full-time experience in network and system design without needing to pay a full-time salary.

- Documentation that describes how your network is set up.

- Time you can spend doing something more productive than installing a network.

If you do hire someone else to build your network, you should check out that person's references and credentials first. You also should stay involved in the process so that you understand the choices and decisions that are made.

Choosing a Network and Cabling System

For a simple home or small office network, you can choose among four types of network connections:

- **10/100BASE-T Ethernet over CAT-5 cables**—These cables look like telephone cables, with a fatter version of a telephone modular connector at each end. This networking scheme is dirt cheap and ultra-reliable and can carry data at up to 100Mbps.

- **1000Mbps (Gigabit) Ethernet over CAT-5E or CAT-6 cables**—These cables look like CAT-5 cables, but they are capable of carrying the higher-speed signals required by Gigabit Ethernet. The higher speed is great but worth the extra cost only if you routinely back up hard disks or copy huge video files over your network, *and* if the devices you're copying to and from can keep up with gigabit speeds. (Many can't.) You'll also want to consider using Gigabit Ethernet if you have Internet service that provides 50 Mbps or more. We talk more about this in the following sections. You'll often see Gigabit Ethernet referred to in computer specs as 10/100/1000Mbps.

- **802.11n, -ac or -g wireless networking**—Wireless (Wi-Fi) networking sends data over a radio signal, so no cabling is necessary. It's easy to set up, but it can't be used over long distances, and in some buildings, the signal might not go as far or as fast as the advertising leads you to believe it will.

- **Powerline networking**—You can purchase network adapters that send data signals between your electrical outlets. In most cases, though, you might be better off using Wi-Fi.

note

The CAT in CAT-5 cable stands for Category, a rating scheme that indicates the maximum speed at which the cable is designed and certified to carry data at distances of up to 100 meters (about 330 feet). The primary categories for twisted pair cabling are

Category	Maximum Speed	Typical Usage
CAT-1	1 Mbps	Telephone service
CAT-2	4 Mbps	Token Ring networking (obsolete)
CAT-3	10 Mbps	Ethernet
CAT-4	16 Mbps	Token Ring (obsolete)
CAT-5	100 Mbps	Fast Ethernet
CAT-5e	1000 Mbps	Gigabit Ethernet
CAT-6	1000 Mbps	Gigabit Ethernet
CAT-6a	10000 Mbps	10 Gigabit Ethernet

(For the record, there are some additional types: CAT-7 and 7a have a questionable future, and CAT-8 is meant for use in data centers.) All of these cable types have four pairs of wires, with the wires in each pair twisted together to minimize the effect of outside electrical interference. The most commonly used CAT-1 through CAT-6 cabling has no metal or foil wrapped around the outside of the wires, just a plastic jacket. This type of cable is called unshielded twisted pair, or UTP. Shielded STP cable adds a braided metal or foil layer around the twisted wires to provide additional protection from electrical interference. CAT-6a and 8 cable is shielded and is used mainly for very high speed (10 Gbps and up) "backbone" network connections. Shielded (and expensive) versions of the lower CAT levels exist for use in electrically noisy environments such as factories.

For any given type of service, you must use cabling of the required CAT level or higher, but never lower. You could use CAT-6 cabling for telephone wiring, but you can't expect reliable service if you try to use CAT-3 cable for gigabit Ethernet. You may notice that CAT-5e and CAT-6 have the same maximum speed. CAT-6 works better for Gigabit Ethernet on long cable runs and can carry 10Gbps Ethernet up to 50 meters.

Each step up on the CAT scale increases the cost of the cable by about 20%, give or take. Still, we recommend at least CAT-5e for all new installations so that if you decide later to upgrade to gigabit Ethernet, you won't have to replace your cabling.

For most homes and offices, a combination of 10/100 Ethernet and wireless is a winning combination, but any of these four options will provide perfectly adequate performance.

In the following sections, we go over each type in a little more detail. Then we discuss additional network features you might want to consider, such as printing and Internet connectivity.

10/100BASE-T Ethernet

10/100BASE-T Ethernet networks use unshielded twisted-pair cabling (commonly called UTP or CAT-5 cable) run from each computer to a device called a switch or router, as shown in Figure 18.1.

Figure 18.1
A 10/100BASE-T network connects each computer to a central device called a switch, router, or hub.

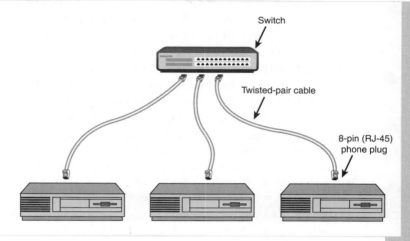

Switch

Twisted-pair cable

8-pin (RJ-45) phone plug

 tip

Most home routers, which are used to share a broadband Internet connection and establish a wireless network, include a switch, and most people can base their network on one of these.

Whether or not you're going to set up a shared broadband Internet connection, we recommend that you buy a wireless router instead of a plain switch, just to get the wireless networking and DHCP services it provides (more on that later in the chapter). On sale, these routers can cost no more than a plain switch. We've even seen ads for $20 routers with a $20 mail-in rebate. See Chapter 19 for advice about hardware-connection-sharing devices.

The 10/100 part of the name means that the equipment can run at 100Mbps, but it can automatically slow down to 10Mbps if it's connected to older 10BASE-T equipment. However, 10BASE-T equipment hasn't been made in more than a decade, so that's unlikely to be an issue.

The cables look like telephone cables, and the connectors look like wider versions of telephone modular plugs, but it's a dangerous comparison because the electrical properties of the cables and connectors are specifically tuned for networking, and ordinary telephone cabling *will not work*.

These networks require you to use cable designated CAT-5 or better. They have labels on the wire that state this clearly. CAT-5, CAT-5e, CAT-6, and CAT-6a are all fine. You can buy premade network cables in lengths of 3–50 feet, or you can buy bulk cable and attach the connectors yourself. We discuss this more in the "Installing Network Wiring" section, later in this chapter. All cable connectors and data wall jacks must be certified at (at least) the same level as the cable.

 tip

If your network is small or temporary, you can run network cables along walls and desks. Otherwise, you probably should keep them out of the way and protect them from accidental damage by installing them within the walls or ceiling of your home or office. If you use in-wall wiring, the work should be done by someone with professional-level skills. You also can get cable covers and sleeves to hide and protect cables where they run across floors, walls, or furniture.

A cable is run from each computer to a switch, which routes the signals between each computer. You must get a switch that has at least as many ports (sockets) as you have computers, plus a spare or two. 10/100BASE-T switches cost roughly $5–$10 per port.

No 10/100 BASE-T cable can be more than 100 meters (328 feet) in length. To extend farther than that, you must add an additional switch in the middle of a longer cable run or use fiber optic cabling.

For the rare computer that doesn't have a built-in Ethernet adapter, 10/100BASE-T network interface cards (NICs) are available for as little as $5 each (if you catch a sale) and are made by dozens of companies. Most generic-brand, cheap-o NICs are based on one of a handful of standard circuit chips, so they'll usually work just fine, even if they're not listed in the Windows Compatibility Center at www.microsoft.com/windows/compatibility.

Overall, 10/100BASE-T networking is as inexpensive as it gets. Hooking up three computers will set you back between $20 and $75. It's easy to set up, and it's very reliable. On the down side, though, you do need to run those wires around.

 tip

Multiple switches can be connected if your network grows beyond the capacity of your first switch. Therefore, you can add on instead of entirely replacing your original equipment.

note

Add-on adapters come in two styles: internal PCI cards for desktop computers and external adapters that you connect to a USB socket. You probably don't need to add one, though, because just about any computer capable of running Windows 10 already has a Wi-Fi adapter or an Ethernet adapter built in.

801.11ac, 802.11n, and 802.11g Wireless (Wi-Fi) Networking

One way to build a network without switches, cables, connectors, drills, swearing, tools, or outside contractors is to go wireless. Prices have fallen to the point that wireless connectivity is competitive with wired networks, even before the installation cost savings are factored in.

There are three common standards for wireless data networking: 802.11g (or Wireless-G), 802.11n (or Wireless-N), and the latest generation of wireless titled 802.11ac (Wireless-AC), named after the industry standard documents on which they're based. (I should say "the latest generation in common use." Faster, more advanced Wi-Fi standards are always in the pipeline). Networking hardware is labeled and marketed using the fastest standard it supports, so for example, you might see a router labeled as an 802.11n router, but the software in the devices can typically also support at least some older, slower standards.

802.11g supports data speeds up to 54Mbps and is compatible with older equipment designed for 802.11b (11Mbps). Some manufacturers offer Wireless-G equipment that operates at up to 108Mbps, but you get this speed boost only if you buy all

 note

Some additional terminology: *Wi-Fi* stands for Wireless Fidelity. It's an industry term that doesn't mean anything in particular, but it's kind of catchy. It's used to refer to any variant of 802.11 wireless networking. Wireless local area networks are often called *WLANs*.

your equipment from the same manufacturer (and even then, you must read the packaging carefully to see whether the double-speed function will work with the particular parts you're buying). Wireless-G can transmit data about 100 feet indoors and up to 300 feet outdoors—at most. And at these longer distances, lower signal strengths will result in data errors, so the equipment will switch down to lower data speeds.

A better level of service is offered by the newer 802.11n (Wireless-N) standard. It comes with higher speeds—150Mbps or more, depending on the number of antennas used—and greater range than Wireless-G. Here's the skinny on Wireless-N:

- Devices designed for Wireless-N, -G, and -B are compatible and can be used together on the same network. That is, a -G network adapter in a computer can talk with an -N router, and vice versa. However, they'll communicate with each other at the lower -G speed. Older -B equipment can be used, too, but again, at the lower -B speed.

- Having -G or -B equipment on the network can drag down the speed as much as 25%, even for -N devices talking to -N, if the older devices are transmitting at the same time.

- Wireless-N signals should travel about twice as far as Wireless-G: about 200 feet indoors and about 600 feet outdoors. However, this applies only when an -N device is talking to another -N device. Getting a Wireless-N router won't improve reception for a distant Wireless-G or -B device.

- Wireless-N can operate in the 2.4GHz frequency band and the 5GHz band. Only "dual-radio" routers can operate at both frequencies at the same time, however. Single-radio routers must switch back and forth, slowing performance if both frequencies are used at the same time. The 5GHz band tends to work better than 2.4GHz at shorter distances. At 5GHz, the signal can't travel as far, but there tends to be less interference from neighboring networks, cordless phones, and so on.

Most Wi-Fi equipment sold today is Wireless-N.

The newest standard in production use is 802.11ac, which offers transfer rates of 500Mbps to well over 1Gbps—staggeringly fast for a wireless connection, at a commensurately high price. To get the top speeds, you need an expensive multiple-antenna router and a multiple-antenna wireless adapter on each computer and home entertainment device. Considering that most home Internet service can feed your network at less than one-tenth of Wireless-AC's speed, unless you have ultra-high-speed Internet service or you're distributing video to multiple ultra-high-def televisions, for most users this level of Wi-Fi service is overkill.

Whichever version you use, Wi-Fi networking products in real-world operating conditions typically provide data throughput at about half the advertised speed. If your computer doesn't have Wi-Fi built in, the cost of adding a USB or internal adapter is about $25–$70. You also must add a device that coordinates the communication between Wi-Fi–enabled computers, the Internet, and any computers that have wired Ethernet connections. There are four types of devices:

- **Router**—These devices transfer data to and from Wi-Fi–connected devices, and typically also have Ethernet jacks for wired computers. In addition, they have one designated Ethernet port that connects to a DSL or cable Internet modem or other external network. The routing function isolates your wireless and Ethernet-wired computers from that Internet connection so that you can safely share files and other content on your network. Many broadband (cable or DSL) modems have a Wi-Fi router built in.

- **Access Point or Wireless/Ethernet Bridge**—These are like routers except they simply pass data back and forth between Wi-Fi devices and a wired, Ethernet network, without the firewall function that a router provides.

- **Wireless Range Extender**—These simply relay data between Wi-Fi–connected devices and another router or access point. If you find that your computer or tablet can't get a good signal when it tries to connect directly to your router or access point, you might be able to get better performance by installing a range extender halfway between them.

- **Mesh router**—This is a fairly new category of device that combines the functions of a router and range extender. The concept is that you distribute several identical devices around your home or office, to provide strong Wi-Fi signals wherever you might have connectivity problems. Only one has to be connected to the Internet. The devices automatically connect to each other and route data between your devices, each other, and the Internet using the best signal available. Google, Linksys, and other manufacturers sell mesh devices. They're somewhat pricey (well over $100 per device), but they tend to require very little effort to set up or expand.

Some manufactures make devices that can perform more than one or even all three of these functions by changing software settings in the device.

Wi-Fi works well in typical home environments where you don't have solid metal sheeting separating rooms or floors, over distances of several rooms. For longer distances, or in office settings, you might need to install multiple Wi-Fi devices (called routers, repeaters, or access points) to get good coverage. We talk more about these shortly. Wi-Fi equipment tends to lose the signal every so often, struggling for a few seconds to regain the connection. For this reason, wired Ethernet is the more reliable, faster option for computers that are within easy wiring distance. You can use both because most Wi-Fi routers have Ethernet jacks that let you plug in wired computers.

Figure 18.2 shows a typical family of wireless products: a wireless access point (Wireless-Ethernet bridge), a wireless router that can also share a DSL or other broadband Internet connection, an internal wireless network adapter for desktop computers, and a PC card adapter for older laptops.

Powerline Networking

HomePlug (HomePlug Powerline Alliance) adapters send network data through your home or office's electrical wiring and are plugged in to a wall socket. These provide 10Mbps to 1Gbps performance, and all you need is an electrical outlet near each of the connected computers. Powerline networking can't cross the utility company's transformers, though, so it usually works only within a single home or office, and it might even have difficulty communicating between some power outlets, if they are on different power line branches.

Also, you can get HomePlug devices called *bridges*, which are specifically designed to link a wired network to the powerline network, for about $80. You can use one of these to connect with a router or wired computers. Figure 18.3 shows how this would look in a typical home network.

Adapters that can piggyback network signals on your home's telephone wiring (called HomePNA or HPNA equipment) also are available, but this technology has fallen out of favor and is not manufactured by the major networking companies anymore.

Figure 18.2
Typical wireless networking equipment. Clockwise from upper left: access point, router, PCI adapter, PC Card adapter. (Photo used by permission of D-Link.)

Figure 18.3
Typical powerline networking setup, showing HomePlug adapters and bridges.

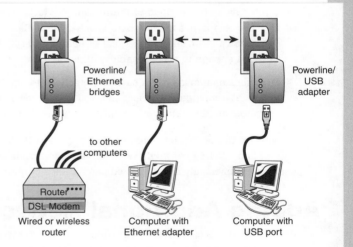

1000Mbps Ethernet (Gigabit Ethernet)

Gigabit Ethernet networking is probably overkill for most home and small office networks, but Gigabit speed can help if you back up your hard disk over your network from one computer to another, routinely copy large video files, or stream high-definition video to multiple televisions. The adapter cost is so low that many new PCs and all Macs come with 10/100/1000Mbps Ethernet adapters built in as standard equipment.

It sounds great at first, but here are some things to consider:

- It won't speed up your Internet connection (unless, perhaps, you have Fiber-to-the-Home service), and it won't improve the streaming of regular HD video within your home. Standard 100Mbps Ethernet will do just fine for these applications.

- Most Internet modems/routers have a built-in Ethernet switch that supports only 100Mbps connections. So, any computers plugged in to them won't get gigabit throughput to each other. We discuss this in the accompanying note.

- You will realize a speed benefit only when a large amount of data is moving between two devices that both have gigabit connections *and* when both can actually feed data to the network at high speed.

---

 note

Most wireless cable/DSL-sharing routers have built-in switches that support at most only 100Mbps, or only 10Mbps in some cases. If you use a combination cable/DSL modem and router, and yours tops out at 100Mbps, plug in your computers to a gigabit (10/100/1000Mbps) switch using CAT-6 or CAT-6a cables and then connect the switch's "cascade" port to your router. Otherwise, your computers will talk only at 100Mbps maximum.

- If you have to buy a gigabit Ethernet adapter for a desktop computer (that is, if the adapter built in to the computer's motherboard is only 10/100Mbps), it makes sense to go gigabit only if you can install a PCI-e adapter. Regular PCI cards and USB adapters can't move data to and from the CPU fast enough to make gigabit worthwhile.

- Most consumer/small office network-attached storage (disk) devices are way too slow internally to benefit from gigabit connections. You *should* see a benefit when backing up to or copying files to or from another Windows computer's shared drive.

If you want to use Gigabit Ethernet, you must use CAT-5E, CAT-6, or CAT-6a certified connectors and cabling; CAT-5 gear *might* work for very short cable lengths, but don't chance it. You should use only commercially manufactured patch cables or professional-quality custom wiring.

Adding Additional Networking Functions

Besides sharing files between computers, you can do several other things with a network. In the next few sections, we outline some additional features you might want to include in your network.

Printing and Faxing

Individual computers can share the local printers attached to them on the local network. Other computers can then access the printer through the network, provided the host computer is running. However, if you need to put a printer farther than about 10 feet away from a networked computer, beyond the reach of a standard USB or parallel cable, you have three choices:

- Use a network-capable printer and connect it directly to your network. Most new printers have Ethernet or wireless networking capability built in. For some printers, you can buy an add-on network printer module.

- Alternatively, you can buy a "print server" module, which connects to the printer on one side and to a network cable on the other, for about $40. Network supply catalogs list myriad such devices. Some newer Internet routers and wireless access points have a print server built in.

- Get a really long cable and take your chances. The electrical signal for a USB or parallel printer connection is not supposed to be extended more than a few feet (10 feet for USB, 12 feet for USB-2). Buy a high-quality shielded cable. You might get data errors (bad printed characters) with this approach.

The first two approaches are very nice because they allow any computer to communicate directly with the printer. They don't require you to leave one computer turned on all the time. With standard printer sharing, the computer that "owns" the printer must be turned on for other computers to use the printer.

If several people on your network need to send or receive faxes, you might want to set up a network-based faxing system. (Faxes, you ask? People still send faxes? Well, yes, some people do.) Unfortunately, Windows 10 does not let you share your fax modem with other users on your network, as Windows Server does. If you want to share a single fax line with several users on your network, you must use a third-party solution. The easiest approach is to use a "network-ready" all-in-one printer/scanner/fax unit. If you shop for one of these, be sure that its faxing features are network compatible.

 note

A network-capable all-in-one laser printer/scanner/fax/copier is a great addition. Anyone on the network can use it to print, send faxes, or scan documents. Read reviews before you buy, though, because some devices are great at advanced networking but not so great at the basics, such as feeding paper through without getting jammed up.

Third-party software products are available that can give network users shared access to a fax modem. The former gold standard product was Symantec's WinFax Pro, but it has been discontinued, and most of the products still on the market seem to be oriented toward large corporations. For a small office network, you might consider products such as Snappy Fax Network Server from www.snappysoftware.com or ActFax from www.actfax.com.

Providing Internet Connectivity

One of the best reasons for having a network is to share high-speed Internet service. It's far less expensive, and far safer security-wise, to have one connection to the Internet for the entire LAN than to let users fend for themselves. In fact, most DSL and cable Internet providers now supply preconfigured routers when you start your service. If that's the case for you, you might only need to configure your computers to use the shared connection, as we discuss later in this chapter under "Configuring a Peer-to-Peer Network."

Windows has a built-in Internet Connection Sharing feature that lets a single computer use a dial-up, cable, or DSL modem and make the connection on behalf of any user on your LAN. You can also use an inexpensive hardware device called a *router* to make the connection. I strongly prefer the hardware devices over Windows Internet Connection Sharing. This topic is important enough that it gets its own chapter. If you want to share an Internet connection on your network, you should read Chapter 19 before you buy any equipment.

You should also study Chapter 33, "Protecting Your Network from Hackers and Snoops," and pay close attention to the section titled "Preparation: Network Security Basics" to build in proper safeguards against hacking and abuse. This is especially important with full-time cable/DSL connections.

Providing Remote Access

You also can provide connectivity to your network from the outside world, either through the Internet or a dial-up modem. This connectivity enables you to access your LAN resources from home or out in the field, with full assurance that your network is safe from outside attacks. Chapter 37, "Networking on the Road," covers Internet VPN network access, and Chapter 39, "Remote Desktop and Remote Access," covers Remote Desktop.

If you want to access your home network while you're away, you might also consider getting a connection-sharing router with built-in VPN support, as mentioned in the next section. These days, most people use a cloud-based file storage system, such as OneDrive or Google Drive, to eliminate the need for this kind of remote access, but you must weigh the convenience they provide against the potential loss of privacy that comes with the cloud services.

Connecting to a Remote Network

Windows supports a Virtual Private Networking (VPN) mechanism that lets you temporarily connect your Windows device to a network in a remote location through the Internet. (We talk about that in Chapter 37.)

You could also permanently tie your entire LAN to a network in another location so that you and the other network's users can share files and printers as if you were all in the same room, without having to establish individual temporary connections. Windows Server has many features to support this capability, but you can also do it with smaller networks without Windows Server. There are two straightforward ways to do this: by getting routers that have built-in virtual private networking (VPN) support and by using a software service. For a hardware approach, Linksys, Asus, Trendnet, and other manufacturers sell inexpensive routers with VPN capability. The router in one office is set up as the VPN "host" or server, and the routers in other offices are set up to connect to that. This ties the separate networks together. For a software solution, check out the Hamachi product from logmein.com. You can tie individual computers into a VPN, or you can set up one computer on each network to act as a "gateway."

Installing Network Adapters

Most computers capable of running Windows 10 already have an Ethernet or Wi-Fi adapter built in. However, if yours doesn't have one, or if you have to add an additional adapter in your computer, follow the manufacturer's instructions for installing its product for Windows 10, 8.1, or 8. If there are instructions for Windows 7 or Vista but not Windows 8, 8.1, or 10, those instructions should work fine. And if there are no instructions at all, just follow these steps:

1. If you have purchased an internal card, shut down Windows, shut off the computer, unplug it, open the case, and install the card in an empty slot. Close the case, plug in the cord, turn back on the computer, and then restart Windows.

    If you are adding an external USB adapter, be sure you're logged on with an administrator account, plug it in while Windows is running, and skip ahead to step 3.

 tip

If you've never worked inside your computer, jump ahead to Chapter 28, "Managing Your Hardware," for advice and handy tips.

2. When you're back at the Windows sign-in screen, sign in using an account with administrator privileges. Windows displays the New Hardware Detected dialog box when you log in.

3. In most cases, Windows should already have the software it needs to run your network adapter. If Windows cannot find a suitable driver for your adapter, it might ask you to insert the driver disc that your network card's manufacturer should have provided. It also might offer to get a driver from Windows Update. If you have an Internet connection up at this time, this online option is very useful.

    If you are asked, insert the requested disc and click OK. In the unlikely event that Windows says that it cannot locate an appropriate device driver, try again, but this time click the Browse button. Locate a folder whose name resembles that of your version of Windows, and click OK. If both 32-bit and 64-bit folders are listed, be sure to choose the version that matches your version of Windows.

 note

The exact names of the folders containing device drivers vary from vendor to vendor. You might have to poke around a little on the disc to find the right folder.

4. After Windows has installed the card's driver software, it automatically configures and uses the card. Check the Device Manager, as described in the next section, to see whether the card is installed and functioning. Then you can proceed to "Installing Network Wiring," later in this chapter.

    ➡ *For more detailed instructions about installing devices and drivers,* **see** *"Installing Devices,"* **p. 629,** *and "Working with Device Drivers,"* **p. 640.**

Checking Existing Adapters

If your adapter was already installed when you set up Windows, it should be ready to go. Follow these steps to see whether the adapter is already set up:

1. Press Windows Logo+X (or right-click the Start button) and select Device Manager. Expand the Network Adapters section by clicking the triangular arrow icon to the left of its name.

2. Look for an entry for your network card. If it appears and does not have a yellow icon with an exclamation point (!) in it to the left of its name, the card is installed and correctly configured. In this case, you can skip ahead to "Installing Network Wiring."

If an entry appears but has a yellow exclamation point icon by its name, the card is not correctly configured.

3. If no entry exists for the card, the adapter is not fully plugged in to its connector, it's damaged, or it is not Plug-and-Play capable. Be sure the card is installed correctly. If you can't get it to appear, replace it.

Installing Multiple Network Adapters

You might want to install multiple network adapters in your computer in the following situations:

 note

If you see an exclamation point icon in the Network Adapters list, skip ahead to Chapter 26, "Troubleshooting and Repairing Problems," for tips on getting the card to work before you proceed. Here's a tip: Network adapters are really inexpensive, so if you're having trouble with an old adapter, just go get a new one.

- You simultaneously connect to two or more different networks with different IP addresses or protocols. You'd use a separate adapter to connect to each network.

- You want to share a broadband cable or DSL Internet connection with other computers on your LAN without using a router. We strongly recommend using a router, as discussed in Chapter 20, but you can also do this using one adapter to connect to your LAN and another to connect to your cable or DSL modem.

- You have two different network types, such as powerline and Ethernet, and you want the computers on both LAN types to be able to communicate. You could use a hardware bridge or access point, but you could also install both types of adapters in one of your computers and use the Bridging feature to connect the networks. We discuss bridging later in this chapter.

We suggest you use the following procedure to install multiple adapters:

1. Install, configure, and test the first adapter. (If you're doing this to share an Internet connection, install and configure the one you'll use for the Internet connection first. Be sure you can successfully browse the Internet before you proceed.)

2. Click the network icon at the right end of the taskbar and select Network & Internet Settings, Status, Change Adapter Options. Select the icon for the network adapter—it will likely be named Ethernet or Local Area Connection—and choose Rename This Connection in the ribbon. (Or right-click the icon and select Rename.) Change the connection's name to something that indicates what it's used for, such as "Connection to Cable Modem" or "Office Ethernet Network."

3. Write the name on a piece of tape or a sticky label and apply it to the back of your computer above the network adapter or on the edge plate of the network card.

4. Install the second adapter. Configure it and repeat steps 2 and 3 with the new connection icon. Rename this connection appropriately—for example, "LAN" or "Wireless Net"—and label the adapter socket.

If you follow these steps, you'll be able to easily distinguish the two connections instead of needing to remember which connection icon is which.

Installing Network Wiring

When your network adapters are installed, the next step is to get your computers connected. Installing the cables can be the most difficult task of setting up a network if you have to run cable through walls. How you proceed depends on the type of networking adapters you have:

- If you're using wireless adapters, of course, you don't need to worry about wiring. Lucky you. You can just skip ahead to "Installing a Wireless Network," later in this chapter.

- If you're using a powerline networking adapter, follow the manufacturer's installation instructions. If you're using a powerline bridge, plug in the bridge to a wall socket and connect it to your computer or other networked device with a CAT-5 (or higher) cable. Follow the manufacturer's instructions for configuring the adapter's security features. You should enable encryption if it's available. Then skip ahead to the "Configuring a Peer-to-Peer Network" section, later in the chapter.

- If you're using wired Ethernet adapters, you must decide how to route your wiring and what type of cables to use.

The remainder of this section discusses Ethernet wiring.

Cabling for Ethernet Networks

If your computers are close together, you can purchase Ethernet cables to connect your computers to a switch or router. (They are often called *patch cables*, a term that originated in the telephone industry. In the old days, switchboard operators used flexible cables to connect, or "patch," one phone circuit to another.) You can run these cables through the habitable area of your home or office by routing them behind furniture, around partitions, and so on. Just don't put them where they'll be crushed, walked on, tripped over, run over by desk chair wheels, or chewed by pets. Office supply and hardware stores sell special cable covers that you can use if you need to run a cable where it's exposed to foot traffic (where it would be a tripping hazard) or to protect it from a pet that likes to chew on things. These covers are also good for wires that need to run up walls or over doorways.

 tip

As you install each network card and plug in the cables, you should see a green light turn on at the switch or router and at the network adapter. These lights indicate that the network wiring is correct.

You can do a web search for the phrase "Cable Management" to get some ideas of what kinds of products are available.

If the cables need to run through walls or stretch long distances, you should consider having them installed inside the walls with plug-in jacks, just like your telephone wiring. We discuss this topic later in this section.

Switch Lights Do Not Come On

If one or more link lights do not come on when the associated computers are connected to your switch, router, or hub, the problem lies in one of the cables between the computer and the switch. Which one is it? To find out, do the following:

1. Move the computer right next to the switch. You can leave the keyboard, mouse, and monitor behind. Just plug in the computer, turn it on, and use a commercially manufactured or known-to-be-working patch cable to connect the computer to the switch. If the light doesn't come on regardless of which switch connection socket you use, you probably have a bad network card.

2. If you were using any patch cables when you first tried to get the computer connected, use a new cable to connect the same computer and switch socket. This trick might identify a bad cable.

3. If the LAN card, switch, and patch cables are all working, the problem is in whatever is left, which would be your in-wall wiring. Check the connectors for proper crimping, and check that the wire pairs are correctly wired end to end. You might need to use a cable analyzer if you can't spot the problem by eye. These devices cost about $75. You connect a "transmitter" box to one end of your cabling and a "receiver" to the other. The receiver has four LEDs that blink in a 1-2-3-4 sequence if your wiring is correct.

General Cabling Tips

You can determine how much cable you need by measuring the distance between computers and your switch location(s). Remember to account for vertical distances, too, where cables run from the floor up to a desktop or go up and over a partition or wall.

 caution

If you need to run cables through the ceiling space of an office building, you should check with your building management to see whether the ceiling is listed as a plenum or air-conditioning air return. You might be required by law to use certified plenum cable and follow all applicable electrical codes. Plenum cable is formulated not to emit toxic smoke in a fire.

Keep in mind the following points:

- We refer to CAT-5 here, but if you're using 1000Mbps Ethernet, you must use CAT-5E, CAT-6, or CAT-6a cable and connectors.

- Existing household telephone wire probably won't work. If the wires inside the cable jacket are red, green, black, and yellow: no way. The jacket must have CAT-5 (or higher) printed on it. It must have color-matched twisted pairs of wires; usually, each pair has one wire in a solid color and the other white with colored stripes. The colors are usually green, orange, blue, and brown.

- You must use at least CAT-5-quality wiring and components throughout, and not just the cables. Any jacks, plugs, connectors, terminal blocks, patch cables, and so on also must be at least CAT-5 certified.

- If you're installing in-wall wiring, follow professional CAT-5 wiring practices throughout. Be sure not to untwist more than half an inch of any pair of wires when attaching cables to connectors. Don't solder or splice the wires.

> **note**
>
> If you really want to get into the nuts and bolts, so to speak, of pulling your own cable, a good starting point is Frank Derfler and Les Freed's *Practical Network Cabling* (Que, ISBN 078972247X).

- When you're installing cables, be gentle. Don't pull, kink, or stretch them. Don't bend them sharply around corners; you should allow at least a 1-inch radius for bends. To attach cables to a wall or baseboard, use only special cable staples or rigid cable clips that don't squeeze the cable, as shown in Figure 18.4. Your local electronics store or hardware store can sell you the right kind of clips.

Figure 18.4
Use rigid cable clips or staples that don't squeeze the cable if you nail it to a wall or baseboard.

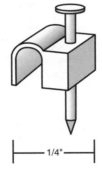
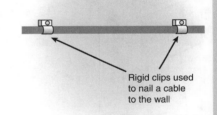

1/4"

Rigid clips used to nail a cable to the wall

- Keep network cables away from AC power wiring and away from electrically noisy devices such as fluorescent lights, arc welders, diathermy machines, and the like. (I've never actually seen a diathermy machine, but I hear they're trouble.)

Wiring with Patch Cables

If your computers are close together and you can simply run cables directly between your computers and switch, you've got it made. Buy CAT-5 (or better) cables of the appropriate length online or at your local computer store. Just plug (click) them in, and you're finished. Figure 18.1 shows how to connect your computers to the switch.

> **note**
>
> The modular plugs used in Ethernet networking are often called *RJ-45 connectors*. To pick a technical nit here, the connector used in networking is really called an *8P8C connector*. The "true telephone RJ-45" connector is slightly different, and not compatible. If you're buying RJ-45 connectors, just make sure that the package says that they're for networking use.

If you have the desire and patience, you can build custom-length cables from crimp-on connectors and bulk cable stock. Making your own cables requires about $75 worth of tools, though, and more detailed instructions than we can give here. Making just a few cables probably doesn't make buying the tools worthwhile. Factory-assembled cables are also more reliable than homemade ones because the connectors are attached by machine. They're worth the extra few dollars.

For the ambitious or parsimonious reader, Figure 18.5 shows the correct way to order the wires in the connector.

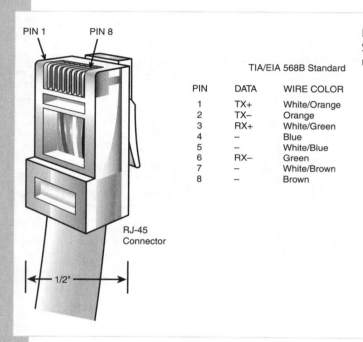

Figure 18.5
Standard wiring order for UTP network cables.

TIA/EIA 568B Standard

PIN	DATA	WIRE COLOR
1	TX+	White/Orange
2	TX–	Orange
3	RX+	White/Green
4	–	Blue
5	–	White/Blue
6	RX–	Green
7	–	White/Brown
8	–	Brown

PIN 1   PIN 8

RJ-45
Connector

1/2"

Installing In-Wall Wiring

In-wall wiring is the most professional and permanent way to go. However, this job often involves climbing around in the attic or under a building, drilling through walls, or working in an office telephone closet. Hiring someone to get the job done might cost $30–$75 per computer or more, but you'll get a professional job.

In-wall wiring is brought out to network-style modular jacks mounted to the baseboard of your wall. These RJ-45 jacks look similar to telephone modular jacks but are wider. You need patch cables to connect the jacks to your computers and switch, as shown in Figure 18.6.

 tip

Search a printed or online directory of local businesses (such as yellowpages.com or maps.yahoo.com) for "Telephone Wiring," and ask the contractors you call whether they have experience with network wiring.

Figure 18.6
Connect your computers and switch to the network jacks using short patch cables.

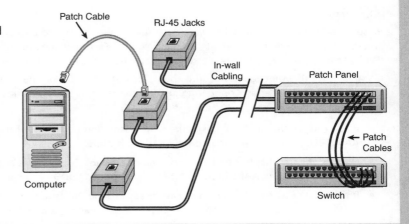

Connecting Just Two Computers

If you're making a network of just two computers (say, to copy files from an old to a new computer), you might be able to take a shortcut and eliminate the need for a network switch or additional special hardware. If you want to add on to your network later, you can always add the extra gear then.

If you are connecting two computers, simply run a special cable called an *Ethernet crossover cable* from one computer's network adapter to the other, and you're finished. This special type of cable reverses the send and receive signals between the two ends and eliminates the need for a switch. You can purchase an Ethernet crossover cable from a computer store or network supply shop, or you can make one, as shown in Figure 18.7.

Figure 18.7
Wiring for a UTP crossover cable. The cable reverses the send and receive wires so that two network cards can be directly connected without a switch. Note that the green pair and orange pair are reversed across the cable.

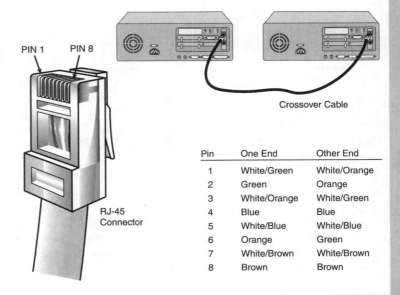

Pin	One End	Other End
1	White/Green	White/Orange
2	Green	Orange
3	White/Orange	White/Green
4	Blue	Blue
5	White/Blue	White/Blue
6	Orange	Green
7	White/Brown	White/Brown
8	Brown	Brown

tip

Be sure that your crossover cable is labeled as such. It won't work to connect a computer to some switches, and you'll go nuts wondering what's wrong if you try. Factory-made models usually have yellow ends. (When I make them myself, I draw three rings around each end of the cable with a permanent-ink marker.)

If you have a cable that you're not sure about, look at the colors on the little wires inside the clear plastic connectors at the two ends. Considering just the colors on the wires, without regard to whether the colors are solid or striped:

- If you can see that each color is in the same position at both ends of the cable, in the arrangement AABCCBDD, you have a standard Ethernet patch cable.

- If a pair of wires that is together at one end of the cable is split apart at the other end (that is, if one end has the pattern AABCCBDD and the other has BBACCADD), you have an Ethernet crossover cable.

- If the pairs of wire are arranged symmetrically around the center of the connector (that is, if the pattern is ABCDDCBA), the cable is a telephone cable and *not* an Ethernet cable. You can't use this type of cable for networking.

Connecting Multiple Switches

You might want to use more than one switch to reduce the number of long network cables you need if you have groups of computers in two or more locations. For example, you can connect the computers on each "end" of the network to the nearest switch and then connect the switch to a main switch. Figure 18.8 shows a typical arrangement using this technique.

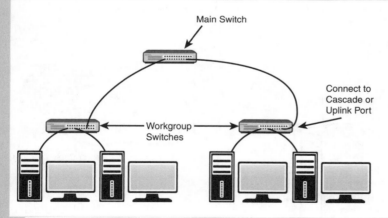

Figure 18.8
You can connect groups of computers with multiple switches to reduce the number of long cables needed. Use the cascade port on the remote switches to connect to the central switch.

 note

A switch's *uplink* or *cascade* port is a connector designed to be connected to another switch. Some switches have a separate connector for this purpose, whereas others make one of their regular ports do double-duty by providing a pushbutton that turns the last switch port into a cascade port. Still others handle this automatically. Refer to your switch's manual to see what to do with your particular hardware.

If you need to add a computer to your LAN and your switch has no unused connectors, you don't need to replace the switch; you can just add a switch. To add a computer to a fully loaded switch, unplug one cable from the original switch to free up a port. Connect this cable and your new computer to the new switch. Finally, connect the new switch's cascade port to the now-free port on the original switch, as shown in Figure 18.9.

Figure 18.9
You can expand your network by cascading switches. The instructions included with your switch describe how to connect two switches using a patch cable. Some switches have a dedicated uplink port, some have a pushbutton that turns a regular port into an uplink port, and some figure it out automatically.

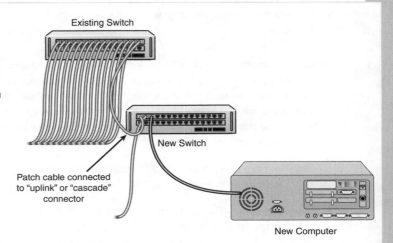

Existing Switch

New Switch

Patch cable connected to "uplink" or "cascade" connector

New Computer

Installing a Wireless Network

If you are using a wireless router, you must configure wireless security and networking options after installing your network adapters. You must do this even if you are just using it for its wired Ethernet connections and don't plan on using its wireless capability.

You really do have to worry about wireless network security. In my home, I can pick up signals from four separate wireless networks: mine, the house next door's, and two others, (I can't tell whose they are.) It's not uncommon to find that you can receive signals from several neighbors. And people do actually drive around with laptops in their car, looking for free Internet access or looking to break in to your computers. To protect against both freeloaders and hackers, you can use one or two protection techniques: *encryption*, which scrambles data, and *authentication*, which certifies that a given computer should be allowed to connect to the network. You can use either encryption alone or both encryption and authentication.

Wireless Network Setup Choices

To be able to distinguish your network's signal from others and to secure your network, you will be asked to make the following choices when you set up a wireless network:

> ## ⚠ caution
>
> If you want to use file and printer sharing on your wireless network, you *must* use wireless security; otherwise, random people will be able to get at your computer.
>
> If you want to set up an "open" wireless hotspot to share your Internet connection with friends, neighbors, or the world, that's great, but you must not use file and printer sharing on the same network. See "Special Notes for Wireless Networking" in Chapter 19 for a safer option.

- **An SSID (Service Set Identifier)**—A short name that you give your network, up to 32 characters in length. This could be your last name, your company name, your pet's name, or whatever makes sense to you. If you are setting up an open wireless network (with no password) and want to ensure that your network can never be shared with others via Microsoft's Wi-Fi Sense feature, put the phrase _optout somewhere in the network name. For example, you might name the network lucynet_optout.

  To learn more about Wi-Fi Sense, **see** "Wi-Fi Sense," **p. 25**, and "Sharing Wi-Fi Network Settings with Friends," **p. 388**.

- **A security type**—The authentication method that your network uses to determine whether a given computer should be allowed to connect, and for ensuring that you really are connecting to the router or access point you intend to use, rather than a malicious device impersonating it. For home and small office use, the choices are as follows, starting with the most secure:

  - **WPA2-Personal**—An improved version of WPA-Personal. This is the best choice for home and small office networks.

  - **WPA-Personal**—A method that uses a passphrase to validate each computer's membership in the network. The passphrase also serves as an encryption key. It has been found to be insecure—a determined hacker can bypass it. Don't use it unless your wireless router can't use WPA2 and its software can't be upgraded.

  - **No Authentication (open)**—No authentication is performed; any computer can connect to the network.

  On corporate networks, other security types are sometimes used: 802.1X, WPA-Enterprise, and WPA2-Enterprise. These systems use a network server, smart card, or software certificate to validate network membership.

- **An encryption type**—The encryption method used to secure network data against eavesdropping. The options available depend on the security (authentication) type selected. The choices, starting with the most secure, are as follows:

  - **AES**—An improved encryption method that can be used with any of the WPA security types. AES is more secure and may offer faster network transmission. This is the best choice for home and small office networks.

  - **TKIP**—An encryption method that can be used with any of the WPA security types. It, too, can be broken by hackers. A better choice is AES.

- **WEP**—Data is encrypted using the WEP protocol using a 40-, 128-, or 256-bit key. WEP encryption can very easily be broken by a hacker using easily available software. Don't use it unless you have no choice (for example, if your network must support an old TiVo unit that can't use a better security option).

- **None**—No data encryption is performed. This option is available only when the security type is set to No Authentication.

Your router might offer an AEK/TKIP option; that is, it can let newer equipment use AEK while older equipment uses TKIP. Don't select this option unless you really do have old equipment that can't use AES. Making TKIP available under any circumstance opens the security hole. Choose just AES.

- **An encryption key**—The key used to encrypt and decrypt data sent over the network. The different encryption methods use keys of different lengths. Longer (more bits) is better.

  - For WPA or WPA2 encryption, enter a passphrase: a word or phrase using any eight or more letters or characters—the more the better, up to 63. The passphrase is case sensitive and can contain spaces but must not begin or end with a space. You might use two random words separated by punctuation symbols (for example, something like topiary#clownlike).

  - For WEP encryption, Windows 10 supports 40-bit and 128-bit security. A 128-bit WEP key must be exactly 26 hexadecimal digits—that is, the numerals 0 through 9 and the letters *A* through *F*. It could look something like this: 5e534e503d4e214d7b6758284c. You can Google "Random WEP Key Generator" if you want help coming up with one.

    A 40-bit key consists of exactly 10 hexadecimal digits. Windows 10 will let you join an existing 40-bit WEP network but not create a new one.

    Some routers and some earlier versions of Windows let you enter a WEP key as a text phrase, but the text method was not standardized and was pretty much guaranteed not to work across brands of wireless routers and access points, so it has been abandoned.

The encryption key should be kept secret because, with it, someone can connect to your network and from there get to your data and your shared files.

Whatever method you use, you might want to write down the passphrase or key on a sticky note and put it on the underside of your wireless router.

- **A channel number**—The channel number selects the frequency used to transmit your network's data. The channels used in North America are usually 1, 6, and 11. The other channels overlap these and can interfere with each other. For double-bandwidth Wireless-N, the choices are 3 and 11. The preferred channel numbers are different in other countries.

  Some wireless routers select a channel automatically. If you must choose one, see the tips under "Getting Maximum Wireless Speed," later in this chapter.

Why are there so many different security methods? Because thieves, like rust, never sleep, and it seems that as soon as a new, safer method is standardized, someone figures out a

> **note**
>
> Windows 10, 8.1, 8, 7, Vista, and XP with Service Pack 3 all have built-in support for WPA2. If your router doesn't support WPA2 or WPA, you might be able to install updated firmware to get it. If that's not possible, a new wireless router shouldn't set you back more than $20 to $90. Just sayin'.

way to break it. WEP stands for Wired-Equivalent Privacy, but that turned out to be overly optimistic: A determined person can break WEP security in as little as a minute. WPA (which stands for Wi-Fi Protected Access) uses an improved encrypting scheme and can deter most attacks, but it, too, turns out to be crackable. WPA2 is a further improvement upon that, and it's the best option we have at present. If you use a complex password, it should deter all but the most determined hackers (and I don't think it wouldn't keep the National Security Agency scratching its collective head for too long, if you know what I mean).

Which encryption method should you use to set up your network? On a home or small office network, you're limited by the least capable of the devices on your network—your weakest link. So, use the strongest encryption method and the longest key that is supported by *all* the devices and computers on your network. This means that if you have even one computer that doesn't support WPA2, you must use WPA or WEP, and if you have even one computer that doesn't support 256-bit keys, you must use a 128-bit key. If you have a router, access point, or network adapter that doesn't support WPA, it's worth checking to see whether you can update its internal software (firmware) or drivers to support this stronger encryption method.

Setting Up a New Wireless Network

If you're setting up a new wireless network using a wireless router or access point, the hardest part of the job is correctly setting up security and Internet access settings in the router itself. There are three ways to configure a new router:

- You can use a setup program provided by the router's manufacturer on a CD or DVD. This is usually the quickest and easiest method because the setup program knows exactly how to configure your router. Using high-speed Internet service, the setup program also might be able to set up the router to connect to your Internet service at the same time. (The next two options don't do that.)

- If your router supports Wi-Fi Protected Setup (WPS), you can use the Set Up a Network Wizard provided with Windows 10. If your router has an eight-digit numeric PIN code printed on the bottom, or if it has a pushbutton labeled WPS, you can use this wizard.

- You can set it up manually by connecting to the router using a web browser.

 tip

Before you get started, you might want to check the router manufacturer's website to see whether a firmware update is available. (*Firmware* is the software built in to the device.) Firmware updates are usually issued when serious bugs have been found and fixed, so it's definitely worth checking. Update the firmware following the manufacturer's instructions *before* you start using the network because the update process sometimes blows out any settings you've made in the router, and you'll have to start over as if it were new.

We give general instructions for these three setup methods in the following sections. The manufacturer's instructions will be more detailed.

Whichever method you use, as mentioned in the previous section, you need to select up to five things to set up a wireless network: an SSID (name), security type, encryption type, encryption key, and possibly a channel number. A setup program or the Set Up a Network Wizard in Windows might help you make these selections automatically.

Using the Manufacturer's Setup Program

The easiest way to set up a wireless router is using a program provided by the manufacturer. Connect one of your computers to the wireless router using an Ethernet cable, and then run the program from the manufacturer's CD or DVD.

The setup program will typically prompt you for the settings required by the Internet access part of the router, which it uses to connect to your Internet service provider. It will also suggest default settings for the Wi-Fi side of the router, which you may change. As mentioned previously, select WPA2/AES security unless your router or one or more of your computers doesn't support it.

You should write down the final settings, especially the security key. The setup program will then install the settings in the router. When your computers detect the new wireless network, you can connect to it and type in the security key.

Using the Set Up a Network Wizard

If your router supports the Wi-Fi Protected Setup (WPS) automatic configuration scheme, Windows 10 can set up the router for you automatically. You'll need the router's eight-digit PIN to use this method. The PIN might be printed on a label on the bottom of the router, or you might be able to find out what the PIN is by connecting to the router using a web browser. We tell how to do this shortly. Also, this method works only on a router that has all of its factory-default settings and hasn't yet been configured. (If you have a used WPS-capable router, you might be able to use its setup web page to restore its factory-default settings.)

To use the Set Up a Network Wizard, follow these steps:

1. Connect your computer to one of the LAN ports on your wireless router using an Ethernet cable, and then power up the router. Wait 60 seconds or so before proceeding. If Windows asks, "Do you want to allow your PC to be discoverable by PCs and other devices on this network?" select Yes. This tells Windows that you are on a trusted, private network.

2. Click or touch and hold the Network icon in the taskbar, and then select Network & Internet Settings, Status.

    Notice that a network name is listed at the top of the window, as shown in Figure 18.10. (In the figure, the name is Ethernet, although if you have previously attached to the same router using a Wi-Fi connection, Windows might display the Wi-Fi network's name.) If under that it says "Private Network," proceed to step 3. If it says "Public Network," click Change Connection Properties and select Private. Then click the window's back arrow (found in the upper-left corner) twice to get back to the Network & Internet Settings Status page.

3. Scroll down and select Network and Sharing Center. Under Change Your Networking Settings, select Set Up a New Connection or Network. Highlight Set Up a New Network and click Next.

4. Wait for your wireless router to appear in the dialog box. When it does, select it and click Next.

    If it doesn't appear within 90 seconds, it might not be WPS capable, or it might already have been configured. If so, skip ahead to the next section, "Configuring Manually."

5. Enter the PIN code printed on your router and click Next. If the PIN is not printed, see whether you can get it out of the router. Follow steps 2 through 5 in the section titled "Configuring

Manually" to get into the router. See whether any of its setup screens display the WPS PIN. (On one router I tested, I found this under Wireless, Wi-Fi Protected Setup.)

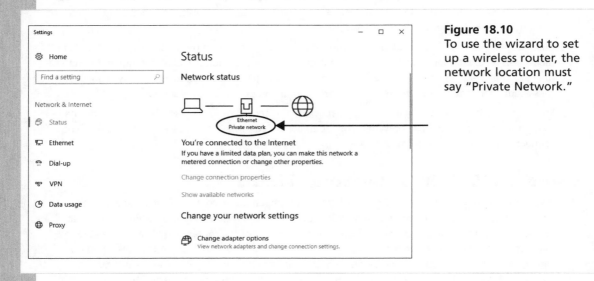

Figure 18.10
To use the wizard to set up a wireless router, the network location must say "Private Network."

6. Click the arrow next to Change Passphrase, Security Level and Encryption Type. Adjust the network name if you like, as shown in Figure 18.11. You may also change the passphrase if you want.

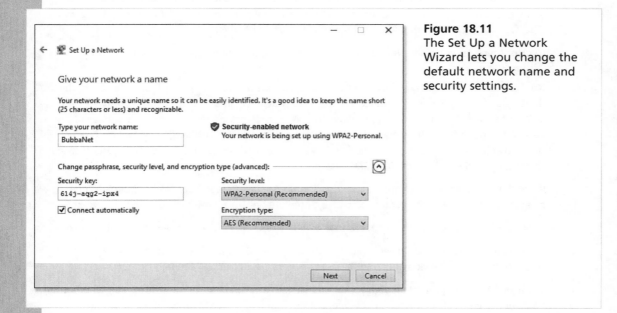

Figure 18.11
The Set Up a Network Wizard lets you change the default network name and security settings.

If not all of your computers support WPA2 security, you can downgrade the security level to WPA or WEP, but we strongly recommend against this. (See the discussion earlier in this chapter under "Wireless Network Setup Choices.")

When the settings are made, click Next.

7. The wizard will configure the router and eventually display the security key. Write this down and keep a copy of it in a safe place. (If your location is secure, you can write it on a sticky note and attach it to the router itself, being sure not to block any ventilation holes.)

We suggest that you also click Print These Network Settings. If you don't have a printer set up, select Print as a PDF and save the resulting file in your Documents library.

After you've followed these steps, all your computers can attach to the wireless network using the network key that you or the wizard selected.

➡ *If you need to set up Internet service as well,* **see** *"Setting Up Internet Service," p. 388.*

Configuring Manually

If you must configure your router manually, your best bet is to follow the manufacturer's instructions. We can't give you specific instructions here, but we can give a general outline of the process:

1. Connect your computer to one of the LAN ports on your wireless router using an Ethernet cable, and then power up the router. Wait 60 seconds or so before proceeding. If you are prompted to turn sharing on or off, turn on sharing.

2. Press Windows Logo+X and select Command Prompt or Windows PowerShell from the pop-up menu, whichever appears. Type the command `ipconfig` and press Enter.

3. Look for the heading that reads something like "Ethernet Adapter Ethernet," and under that, look for the Default Gateway setting. It will look like 192.168.0.1 or 192.168.1.1, or something similar.

4. Open a web browser (Edge or Internet Explorer will do), and in the Address bar, type `http://` followed by the default gateway numbers (for example, `http://192.168.0.1`) and press Enter.

5. Log on to the router using its administrative username and password. You'll have to read the instruction manual or search the Web to find the default password for your router. Often, username `admin` and password `admin` or `password` will work.

   You should change the default password as your first step. If you do change it, be sure to write down the new password and store it in a secure place.

6. Use the router's web page menus to locate the Wireless Configuration page. Enter a network name (SSID), select a security type, and enter a key.

7. Use the appropriate "save settings" button or menu choice, wait 30 seconds, and try to have one of your other computers connect to the router using a wireless adapter, following the instructions under "Joining a Wireless Network" on p. 824.

When other computers can connect successfully, if the computer you used for setup has a wireless adapter, you can disconnect the Ethernet cable. Ethernet connections are faster and more reliable than wireless, though, so use wired connections whenever it's convenient to do so.

When your computer can connect to the wireless router, you can have the router establish an Internet connection for you.

Setting Up Internet Service

When your wireless network is working and your computers can connect to the wireless router, you will probably want to have the router share a high-speed Internet connection.

If you used the manufacturer's setup program to configure your router, it might have set this up for you already. If you have to set up the Internet side of your router manually, try to follow the manufacturer's instructions. We can give you only general instructions here.

Routers are usually factory-set to use automatic address assignment (this is called DHCP configuration), so in many cases you can simply plug in the router's WAN port to your cable or DSL modem, and it will immediately work. It depends on your Internet service, though, and in many instances you must do some setup.

To set up shared Internet service, go to the router's setup web pages by following steps 2 through 5 in the preceding section, "Configuring Manually." Locate the router's wide area network (WAN) or Internet setup web pages. Many routers have a menu option you can select to run an Internet setup wizard; otherwise, you'll have to set up the connection manually.

In general terms, there are three ways to connect:

- If your wireless router's WAN (Internet) port is connected to a network that already has a full-time Internet connection, choose the router's "direct connection" option.

- If you use cable Internet service, most likely you'll select the DHCP option. You might have to enter a specific hostname supplied by your cable company. Other cable ISPs key off your network adapter's MAC address, so you might have to call your ISP to inform it of the router's MAC address. This is usually printed on the bottom of the router.

- If you use DSL service, most likely you'll select the PPPoE option. You'll have to enter a username and password.

Your ISP should help you get the Internet connection working, or at least it should provide you with the information you need to get the connection working.

See Chapter 19 for more detailed instructions on connecting your LAN to the Internet.

Sharing Wi-Fi Network Settings with Friends

Windows 10 has a feature called Wi-Fi Sense that lets you and others connect to Wi-Fi networks automatically. The feature was conceived as a way to let phone and tablet users save money on cellular data transfer fees by automatically using free Wi-Fi services whenever possible.

Microsoft learns about free, unsecured hotspots by monitoring the use of networks to which you and other Windows users successfully connect (which is creepy, but also helpful). When Microsoft sees that several users have made successful high-speed connections to a given network, it disseminates information about that network to other Windows users. If you set up an unsecured Wi-Fi network, Wi-Fi Sense might well assist the general public in using it. (This is, of course, what you're inviting by setting up an unsecured network.)

The original release of Windows 10 included a way to let your friends use your secured (password-protected) Wi-Fi network, without having to provide them with the password. However, this aspect of the Wi-Fi Sense feature was removed from Windows 10 as of the Anniversary Update released in August 2016. Your Wi-Fi password can no longer be automatically shared with others.

 note

If you set up an open, unsecured network, you can prevent Microsoft from adding it to the Wi-Fi Sense database by adding the phrase _optout to the network's name, as discussed earlier in the chapter. But since it's unsecured, people can still use it without any password, if they're in range.

Getting Maximum Wireless Speed

802.11n wireless networking supports speeds of up to 150Mbps, which is a huge improvement over older 801.11g and 802.11b equipment. However, you won't get the maximum possible speed if any of these conditions exist:

- There are other nearby networks using radio channels that overlap your network.

- You have older Wireless-G or -B equipment on the same network as -N (perhaps an old laptop or TiVo). Wi-Fi equipment can't run at full speed when it is also communicating with equipment running older Wi-Fi protocols.

- You are using the insecure WEP or WPA security protocol (perhaps because you have older equipment that doesn't support WPA2) or are using TKIP encryption. The 802.11n specification sets a maximum speed of 54Mbps if WEP, WPA, or TKIP are in use. Higher speeds are permitted by the specification only with WPA2/AES.

- Your router is not using the legal maximum transmitting power.

The following sections tell you how to fix these conditions.

Eliminate Overlapping Channels

The 2.4GHz band used by wireless gear supports 11 to 14 radio frequency channels so that you don't have to share radio bandwidth with your neighbors. The surprising fact is that many of these channels overlap each other to a large extent; a given channel overlaps about two and a half channels on either side. If your neighbor's wireless router is using channel 1 and you set your router to use channel 2, there can still be considerable interference. Plus, both networks will be slowed down if you're using them at the same time.

To avoid this situation, press Windows Logo+X and select Command Prompt or Windows Power-Shell from the pop-up menu, whichever appears. Type **netsh wlan show networks mode=bssid** and press Enter. This lists each neighboring network, its signal strength (as a percentage of something—what, I don't know), and its channel. Examine the list, ignoring your own network. Select a channel for your network that doesn't conflict with at least the strongest of your neighbors' networks.

In the United States, Canada, and Mexico, if you are using Wireless-G, or a standard 20MHz bandwidth Wireless-N router, try to select from channels 1, 6, and 11 only. Try to pick a channel that's five channels away from any strong neighboring signals. Also, some cordless phones use the same 2.4GHz radio band as Wi-Fi. You can help prevent this interference by using 900MHz cordless phones.

If you are using a double-rate 40MHz bandwidth 2.4GHz Wireless-N router, use either channel 3 or channel 11. In Europe and elsewhere, find out what channels are recommended in your region.

Set your router to use this channel. Your other wireless devices will automatically catch on within minutes.

You could also repeat this exercise in the 5GHz band if your router supports it. Many more channels are available, there's much less overlap between them, and not many cordless phones use the 5GHz band. Use a channel several numbers away from any neighboring 5GHz networks.

Tune Up Wireless Security

If you want to get the best Wireless-N performance, use the WPA2/AES security setting on your router. Doing so just requires a setting change on the router. The connecting devices will work it out on their own.

If you have some equipment that doesn't support WPA2, you'll get maximum performance if you set up to use a separate, lower-speed network, as described in the next section.

Separate Your Wireless-AC, -N, -G, and -B Networks

Wireless-AC, -N, -G, and -B equipment can interoperate; however, having lower-speed equipment can slow down the performance of higher-speed equipment when both are transmitting at the same time and even for several seconds afterward. If you have mixed equipment, you can get peak speed on your network in two ways:

- Use a two-radio (simultaneous dual-band) router. Set up different network names (SSIDs) for the two frequency bands. Set any Wireless-N equipment to use the 5GHz network and all of your -B and -G equipment to use the 2.4GHz network. This requires a two-radio router, however, and 5GHz signals don't have the same reach as 2.4GHz. (Wireless-AC always uses 5GHz.)

- Alternatively, use two routers: one for your high-speed devices and an inexpensive second one for your older gear.

To set up two routers, configure the first Wireless-AC or -N router as your primary wireless network. Choose a clear channel, as described previously, and give it a network name (SSID) like "MyWirelessN." Set it up with WPA2/AES security.

Configure the other router as an access point. This turns off its routing features and turns it into a simple "repeater" so that devices on the separate wireless networks can communicate directly. (This way you can use Windows file and printer sharing between computers on the different networks.) Most routers can be set up this way; check the instructions. Select a channel that doesn't conflict with your other router. (For example, in the United States, if your main router is set for channel 1, set this one to channel 6 or 13.) Give it a distinct SSID name, like "MyWirelessG."

Set up WPA2/AES security if the router and your -G and -B devices support it. Position it at least 6 feet away from the other router. Now, just plug in this device's WAN port to one of your first router's LAN ports. Have your slower devices connect to this alternative network name. You won't be able to share files or printers between the two networks.

Bump Up the Power?

Around the world, countries have differing regulations for the allowed frequencies and maximum power that unlicensed transmitters such as wireless routers can use. To play it safe, most routers are shipped with settings that adhere to the lowest common denominator, which means that your router might be operating at a lower power than is legally permissible in your area. It can be worth checking your router's advanced wireless settings to see if there is a setting for the regulatory domain (operating region) or the transmitter power.

The rules for the maximum-allowed power are esoteric, and the allowed wattage depends on the frequency band and the efficiency (gain) of the antenna used. For most antennas, in North America the maximum 2.4GHz power is 100mW. If your router came configured with a power setting lower than 60mW, you might bump up the power to 60mW to see if this improves your data speed. It might not. (And for many routers, much more than 60mW could shorten the life of the router and actually degrade the signal.) If increasing the power doesn't improve your data speed, put it back to the original setting.

Also, while it might seem counterintuitive, in areas where there are a lot of wireless networks, increasing power can actually reduce performance because it makes networks overlap and interfere with each other, and it lets you wander farther from your own base station to areas where you'll pick up more interference. In an urban or congested area, it can be better to use a few more wireless access points with less power than to try to extend one to a larger area.

Configuring a Peer-to-Peer Network

When you're sure that the wired or wireless physical connection between your computers is set up correctly, you're ready to configure Windows 10. With today's Plug-and-Play network adapters, and with all the needed software built in to Windows, this configuration is a snap.

If your computer is part of a Windows Server domain network, which is often the case in a corporate setting, skip ahead to "Joining a Windows Domain Network."

Configuring the TCP/IP Protocol

After all your network adapters are installed—and, if you're using a wired network, cabled together— you must ensure that each computer is assigned an IP address. This is a number that uniquely identifies each computer on the network. These numbers are assigned in one of the following ways:

- If you have a router, or if one of your computers shares its Internet connection using Windows Internet Connection Sharing, or if you are on a corporate LAN running Windows Server, each computer will be assigned an IP address automatically. They're doled out by the Dynamic Host Configuration Protocol (DHCP) service that runs on the router or in the sharing computer. This is why we recommend using a router even if you aren't setting up a shared Internet connection.

By default, Windows sets up new network adapters to receive an address this way. If your network fits into this category, you don't have to change any settings, and you can just skip ahead to the section "If You Have a Shared Internet Connection."

- Each computer can be given an address manually, which is called a *static address* as opposed to a dynamic (automatic) one. If you are not going to use a router or a shared Internet connection, you should set up static addressing. We tell you how shortly.

- If no static settings are made but no DHCP server exists on the network, Windows will automatically assign IP addresses anyway. Although the network will work, this is not an ideal situation and can slow down Windows. The setup steps shown in the following two sections let you avoid having IP addresses be assigned this way.

If you're setting up a new computer on an existing network, use whatever scheme the existing computers use; check their settings and follow suit with your new one. Otherwise, use either of the schemes described in the following two sections.

If You Have No Shared Internet Connection

If you're setting up a new network from scratch, and you do not have a connection-sharing computer, router, or wireless access point, you should use static addressing.

For most home and small office networks, the following static address scheme should work fine:

- **IP Address**—192.168.1.11 for your first computer, 192.168.1.12 for your second computer, 192.168.1.13 for your third, and so on.

  We strongly suggest that you keep a list of your computers and the addresses you assign to them.

- **Subnet Mask**—255.255.255.0

- **Default Gateway**—Leave blank

- **Preferred DNS Server**—Leave blank

- **Alternate DNS Server**—Leave blank

Follow these steps on each computer to ensure that the network is set up correctly:

1. Click the Network icon that appears at the right end of the taskbar and select Network & Internet Settings, Status, Change Adapter Options. Right-click the Ethernet or Wireless Connection icon that corresponds to your LAN connection and select Properties.

2. In the Networking tab, scroll to the bottom of the list box and select Internet Protocol Version 4 (TCP/IPv4). Click Properties.

3. In the General tab, change the settings. Figure 18.12 shows an example, but you must use the address values appropriate for your computer and your network. Click OK.

 tip

If your computer will move back and forth between a network that uses automatic configuration and a network that uses static settings—say, between work and home—select Obtain an IP Address Automatically. A tab named Alternate Configuration appears. Select the Alternate Configuration tab and configure the static settings. Windows will use these static settings only when a DHCP server is not present.

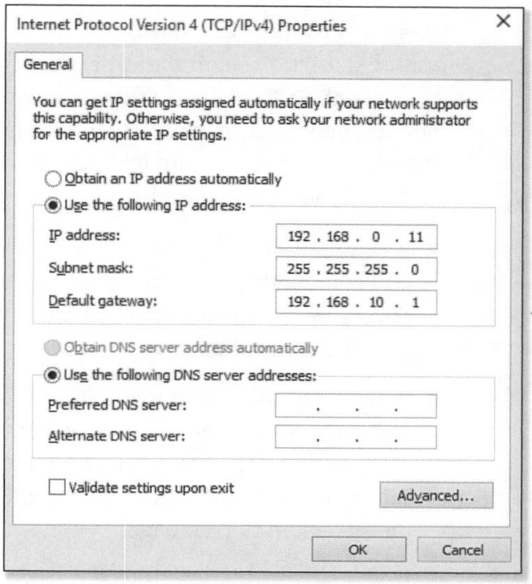

Figure 18.12
Make IP address settings within the Internet Protocol Version 4 (TCP/IPv4) Properties dialog box.

Internet Protocol Version 4 (TCP/IPv4) Properties ✕

General

You can get IP settings assigned automatically if your network supports this capability. Otherwise, you need to ask your network administrator for the appropriate IP settings.

○ Obtain an IP address automatically
● Use the following IP address:

IP address: | 192 . 168 . 0 . 11 |
Subnet mask: | 255 . 255 . 255 . 0 |
Default gateway: | 192 . 168 . 10 . 1 |

○ Obtain DNS server address automatically
● Use the following DNS server addresses:

Preferred DNS server: | . . . |
Alternate DNS server: | . . . |

☐ Validate settings upon exit   [Advanced...]

[OK] [Cancel]

If You Have a Shared Internet Connection

As mentioned previously, if you plan to share an Internet connection with all the computers on your network, you should read Chapter 19 first. Keep the following tips in mind:

- If you will use Windows Internet Connection Sharing, first set up the one computer that will be sharing its connection, as described in Chapter 19, and then set up networking in your other computers.

- All the computers, including the one sharing its Internet connection, should have their Ethernet connections set to Obtain an IP Address Automatically and Obtain DNS Server Address Automatically (refer to Figure 18.12).

- If you will be using a router, configure the router first, following the manufacturer's instructions. Enable its DHCP feature. If you can, set the starting DHCP IP address to 100 so that numbers from 2 to 99 can be used for computers with static settings. Also, if your ISP has provided you with a static IP address for your router, be sure to enter your ISP's DNS server addresses in the router's setup screens so it can pass them to your computers.

Now that your new network connection is set up, be sure to set the correct file sharing option, as described in the next section. This is a critical part of Windows networking security.

 note

If you add a shared Internet connection later, go to every one of your computers, bring up the TCP/IPv4 Properties dialog box shown in Figure 18.12 again, and select Obtain an IP Address Automatically and Obtain DNS Server Address Automatically. Otherwise, the shared connection will not work.

Enabling and Disabling Sharing

When you connect to a new network for the first time, Windows 10 automatically disables file and printer sharing through the connection, to protect you from hackers. It initially assumes that the network is public, thus untrusted, even dangerous. Within a minute it should pop up a notification asking, "Do you want to allow your PC to be discoverable by PCs and other devices on this network?" The question is confusing. It should have been worded this way: "Do you trust the other computers on this network and want to share files with them?" Answer it this way:

- If you have connected to a private network, where you trust *all* the people using other devices and computers on this network, select Yes. File and printer sharing is enabled, as is Network Discovery, which makes your computer visible to other users and makes their computers visible to you. It's also possible to join a homegroup, which we discuss shortly.

- If you have connected to a public network, say, at an airport, hotel, coffee shop, or someone else's home or business, or if you have made a direct Ethernet connection to a cable or DSL modem that does not have a router, select No. You don't want other random computers on the Internet poking into your computer. File and printer sharing and Network Discovery are disabled on this network connection.

If you need to, you can later change this setting manually.

Here's a good rule of thumb: If you don't *need* to use file sharing and printer sharing in a given location, consider the network a public network, and select No. You can always change it later.

To change the sharing (Network Location) setting manually, follow these steps:

1. Touch or click the network icon on the taskbar.

2. Touch or click Properties under the icon labeled with the name of your network connection.

3. Select Public or Private.

To control the file sharing and device discovery functions separately, click the network icon on the taskbar and select Open Network & Internet Settings, Status. Scroll down, and then select Network and Sharing Center, Change Advanced Sharing Settings. Expand the desired profile section (usually Private). You will see individual controls for file and printer sharing and for network discovery there.

> **⚡ caution**
>
> Any connection that leads directly to the Internet without your own firewall or router in between *must* have sharing turned off and be designated a public network, to protect your computer from the hackers and bad software "out there." This holds no matter how you make the connection: plug-in Ethernet, wireless, dial-up, or a direct connection to a cable or DSL modem.

Setting Your Computer Identification

After you've configured your network, the next step is to make sure that each of the computers on your network has a unique name and is a member of the same domain or workgroup.

If you are part of a Windows domain-type network, your system administrator will give you the information you need to set your computer identification.

If you are setting up your own network without Windows Server, on each of your Windows 10 devices and computers, right-click the Start button or press Windows Logo+X, and then select System. Under Device Specifications, look at the Device Name entry. On previous versions of Windows, press Windows Logo+R, type **sysdm.cpl**, press Enter, and check the Full Computer Name entry. Does each device have a different name? If so, you're all set.

If two devices have the same name, you must pick one to change. To rename a Windows 10 PC, click Rename This PC. Enter a new name, click Next, and then click Restart Now and let the computer restart. For earlier versions of Windows, click the Change button. You are asked to select the option that best describes your computer:

- This Computer Is Part of a Business Network; I Use It to Connect to Other Computers at Work.

- This Is a Home Computer; It's Not Part of a Business Network.

Which one you choose makes a significant difference. If you choose the "Home Computer" option, click Next, then Finish, as directed. The wizard sets up your computer for peer-to-peer networking with the workgroup name WORKGROUP and then finishes.

If you are on a business network with Windows Server, the rest of the procedure is described under "Joining a Windows Domain Network" later in this chapter.

 caution

You should be sure that every computer on your network uses the same workgroup name if you want them to be able to easily share files and printers.

Configuring Windows Firewall

It is a good idea to check that Windows Firewall is set up correctly; otherwise, you could end up exposed to Internet hacking, or you could find that your network is so locked down that you can't use file and printer sharing. Windows Firewall is discussed in more detail in Chapter 33.

If your Windows 10 computer is connected to a domain network, your network manager will set up a firewall "profile" that controls security when you are connected to the corporate network. You shouldn't be able to change these settings. Your network manager will also probably configure another "default" profile to protect you when you are disconnected from the corporate network, such as when you are traveling or using your computer at home.

In this section, we assume that you are managing your own computer and that your network is not protected by a professionally installed firewall, nor have you installed third-party firewall software. As a home or small office user, go through this quick checklist of steps to confirm that your network will function safely:

1. Click the taskbar's Network icon, and select Network & Internet Settings, Status. Then scroll down and select Windows Firewall.

2. Click the Private Network or Public Network headings, and it should say Firewall is On. If the entry says Off, click the blue word *Network* and set the Windows Defender Firewall switch to On. Then click the back arrow in the upper-left corner and confirm that the firewall is on for both Private and Public networks.

3. The Private Network profile should be labeled "active" if your network was set up as a private network, as discussed earlier in the chapter.

These are the default settings, but it's best to check them to be sure.

File and Printer Sharing Without a Router: Avoiding the Unidentified Network Problem

If you are setting up a small network of computers that connect with each other through an Ethernet switch or crossover cable, but not a router, you'll run in to a problem with the Windows Network Location feature. This is the mechanism that Windows uses to identify one network from another so that it can then label them as public or private. Windows uniquely identifies each network that your computer joins by the Media Access Control address (MAC address), a physical hardware identification number, of the network adapter at the network's TCP/IP gateway address. On a network without a router, Windows automatically assigns IP addresses; however, there is no gateway address and thus no MAC address to examine, so Windows cannot tell this network from any other network. It will call the network an unidentified network and will not let you enable file or printer sharing on it.

You can solve this problem in either of two ways:

- Use an inexpensive DSL/modem connection-sharing router instead of a switch, and just don't connect its WAN port to a DSL or cable modem. You can get these used on eBay or Craigslist for just a few dollars.

- Assign IP addresses to each of your computers manually, using addresses like 192.168.0.2, 192.168.0.3, and upward. (Skip 192.168.0.1 in case you eventually do add a router.) In each computer, when you assign an IP address using the dialog box shown in Figure 18.12, enter as the gateway address the IP address of one of the *other* computers on your network. This workaround is clunky, but it works. The other computer must be turned on for your computer to be able to identify the network and enable sharing. When you save the address settings, Windows will ask you whether you want your computer to be discoverable by PCs and other devices on your network. To enable sharing, select Yes.

Setting Up a Homegroup

Windows versions 7 and later include a networking feature called HomeGroup that can make sharing files, folders, printers, and music/video media very easy. A homegroup lets each user decide whether to share specific categories of documents, music, video, printers, and so on, or even specific folders and files. Every user on every computer in the homegroup can see the items, once shared, without worrying about passwords or usernames. It's all just there, organized, and easy to get to.

HomeGroup networking works by setting up one password that is used to join each computer to the group. Any user on any of the member computers can see any of the group's shared folders and printers.

> **note**
>
> It's *HomeGroup* here and *homegroup* almost everywhere else in this chapter because the genius lawyers at Microsoft want people to use the trademarked word *HomeGroup* when we talk about the product feature but use *homegroup* when we talk about a group of computers that *use* the feature. Got that?

Is a homegroup right for you? Consider these points to decide whether to use this feature:

- The HomeGroup feature works only with Windows 7 and later. (However, computers running Windows Vista, XP, Mac OS, Linux, and so on can still share with a homegroup and use folders and printers shared by a homegroup, if you take the additional steps discussed under "Using Windows Vista and XP with a Homegroup," in Chapter 20.)

- Within a homegroup, you can't decide individually which other users can see your shared stuff and which users can't. Anybody who can use a computer that's a member of the homegroup can use the content that you decide to share.

What you *can* control is whether to share your stuff and whether the other users can just view and use your stuff or modify, delete, and add to it.

If you don't need to control access on a person-by-person basis, a homegroup is definitely a convenient thing to set up. If a homegroup isn't right for you, skip ahead to the next section, "Alternatives to Using a Homegroup." Changing your mind later on is easy, so don't worry too much about this issue.

To set up a new homegroup, log on to one of your Windows 10 computers and perform the following steps:

1. Click the network icon in the taskbar and select Network & Internet Settings, Status. Then scroll down and click HomeGroup.

2. Click Create a Homegroup, and then click Next.

3. Select which types of your content you want to share with everyone else in the homegroup, as shown in Figure 18.13.

note

If you have a device or computer that is part of a domain network when you connect at work, you can still join it to your homegroup at home. At home, you'll be able to use folders and printers shared by other computers in the homegroup, but you won't be able to share any of your computer's folders with the group.

Figure 18.13
Select the types of files you want to share with everyone else in the homegroup. This selection applies only to your own files; other users get to choose for themselves what they want to share.

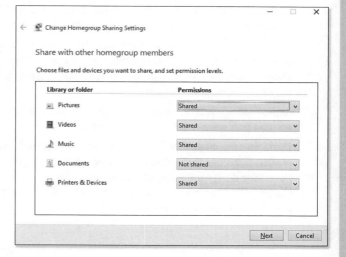

For each category (Pictures, Documents, Music, and/or Videos, documents), select Shared to let other users see your files. For Printers and Devices, select Shared so that other users can use your computer's printer. (You can easily change these selections later, as discussed in Chapter 21, "Using a Windows Network.")

You can select Not Shared for any category of your files that you don't want other users to see. When you're satisfied, click Next.

4. Windows will display the HomeGroup password. Jot this down. You'll need it to join your other Windows 7, 8, 8.1, and 10 computers to the homegroup. Upper- and lowercase matter, by the way. Then click Finish. This will bring you back to the Network & Internet Status page.

If you want to use a different HomeGroup password than the one Windows chose, you can, and now is the time to change it. Click HomeGroup again, and then click Change the Password. Follow the prompts to choose a new password.

 note

If you are signed in to Windows with a Microsoft (online) account when you set up your homegroup, and then you use that same account to sign in to another computer on your network, the HomeGroup password will be automatically filled in for you when you start to enroll the new computer into the group. HomeGroup passwords are one of the things that Windows syncs between the computers you use. (It's an odd thing for Microsoft to have done, because HomeGroup passwords are a "per-computer" rather than a "per-user" attribute.)

5. You or another computer owner can now go to another Windows 10, 8.1, or 8 computer on your network, log on, and repeat this process. This time, instead of Create a Homegroup, you'll be able to click Join Now to join the existing homegroup.

On a Windows 7 computer, go to the Control Panel. Select Homegroup and Sharing Options and then Join Now.

If you have just created a new homegroup or joined a computer to an existing homegroup, wait a few minutes before shutting down the computer so that Windows can set up sharing on the computer's folders.

Repeat step 5 with any other Windows 7 through 10 computers that you want to join to the homegroup.

Users on each computer will have to log on and decide which of their materials they want to share with the homegroup. Until they do, their names won't appear in the HomeGroup listing in File Explorer. We talk about this in the section "Sharing with a Homegroup" in Chapter 21.

 tip

If you forget the password, click the taskbar's Network icon, and then select Network & Internet Settings, Status, HomeGroup, View or Print the Homegroup Password.

 note

If you have computers running Windows XP, Vista, Mac OS, Linux, or other OSs, read Chapter 20 to see how to make it easier to share files and printers with these other OSs.

Alternatives to Using a Homegroup

HomeGroup security gives anyone in the group access to any shared folder or printer. If you need to restrict access to shared folders and printers on a user-by-user basis, or if you have computers that don't run Windows 7 and later, you might instead want to set up the traditional Windows file sharing scheme. There are two ways you can configure traditional sharing:

- If you have OSs other than Windows 7 and later on your network and you don't need per-user security, you can turn off Password Protected Sharing. To do this, click the network icon at the right end of the taskbar and select Network & Internet Settings, Status, Sharing Options. Scroll down to All Networks and click the down arrow to open the list. Scroll down more and select Turn Off Password Protected Sharing.

  This makes any shared folder or printer available to anybody who can connect to your network, with no passwords required at all, so be careful what you share and who you let use your network.

  If you have computers running Windows XP, Vista, Mac OS, Linux, or other OSs, read Chapter 20 for more information on sharing with these OSs.

- If you need to control in detail which users can use which shared files and folders, leave Password Protected Sharing turned on (which is the same as disabling Simple File Sharing on Windows XP). You will have to set up the same user accounts with the same passwords on each of your computers so that people can access shared folders and printers.

  For more information on Password Protected Sharing, including ways it works differently on Windows 8 and 10 than previous versions of Windows, **see** *"Configuring Passwords and File Sharing,"* **p. 762.**

Wrapping Up

This step completes the procedure for setting up Windows networking on one Windows 10 computer. After you have configured, connected, and—if required to—restarted each of your computers, click the File Explorer (folder) icon in the taskbar, or press Windows Logo+X and select File Explorer. Look for the Network and Homegroup items at the left edge of the Window, as shown in Figure 18.14.

Remember that the ribbon's tools are activated when you select items in the *right-hand* pane, not the left. This can be confusing at times.

If your network is up and running and sharing and discovery are enabled, you should see one icon for every computer you've connected. Double-click any icon to see what that computer is sharing with the network.

If you don't see other computers in the Network window, well, we have a whole chapter devoted to network troubleshooting. For suggestions, **see** *"Getting Started,"* **p. 476.**

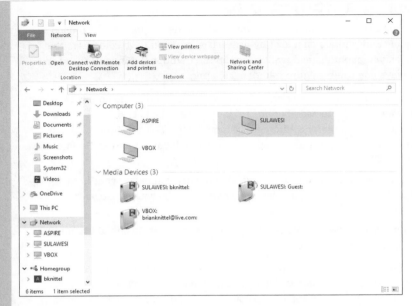

Figure 18.14
Links at the left edge of File Explorer let you explore your network, and your homegroup if you have one.

If you set up a homegroup, the Homegroup list will have an entry for each user who has elected to share files. There might be entries for the other users on your own computer, as well as users on other computers. Shared printers *should* already be listed automatically in your Devices and Printers Control Panel applet, although if you have one or more printers that are not connected via USB cables, you might have to take additional steps to share them.

You're almost finished. You have just a little more reading to do:

- You'll certainly be connecting to the Internet, and when you do, you risk exposing your network to the entire world. Refer to Chapter 33 to find out what risks you'll be exposed to and what you can do to protect your LAN. If you use Internet Connection Sharing or a connection-sharing router, you're in pretty good shape. But in any case, going through Chapter 33 carefully is very important.

- Read Chapter 21 to learn how to get the most out of your Windows network.

- See Chapter 37 for instructions on enabling remote access to your computer and network.

- See Chapter 20 for information about networking with Macs, Unix, Linux, and older versions of Windows, as well as installing advanced networking services.

Joining a Windows Domain Network

If your computer is to be part of a domain network run by a version of Windows Server, it must be "joined" to the domain so that Windows will delegate its security functions to the network. Your network administrator should take care of this task for you. If you must do it yourself, you will need four pieces of information:

- The name to be given to your computer.

- The domain name for your network.

- Your domain logon name and password.

- Any specific configuration information for the Internet Protocol (TCP/IP). In most cases, it is not necessary to make any changes in the default settings.

The location of the Join Domain button was changed in the Fall 2017 Creator's Update. Use the following procedure to make your computer a member of your network domain, while connected to the domain's network:

1. Sign in to Windows with a Computer Administrator account.

2. Click Start, Settings (gear icon), Accounts, Access Work or School, Connect, Join This Device to a Local Active Directory Domain.

3. Enter the Active Directory domain name provided by your administrator (for example, bigcorp. local), and click Next.

4. Enter the network login name and password supplied by your network administrator. Then click Next.

5. The next prompt offers to add an account to the PC. You have two choices:

   - If you want your domain account to be able to manage hardware, software, and files on your own computer, enter your user account name and set the Account Type to Administrator. Then click Next.

   - If you want to manage your computer using the original "local" account that you set up when you started using the computer, click Skip.

6. If the network administrator has not yet prepared the domain to accept your computer, you will be prompted for the credentials for an account that has domain administrator privileges. An administrator might have to assist you here.

7. Click Restart Now.

(Alternatively, if you prefer to use the domain join method from previous versions of Windows, press Windows Logo+R, type `sysdm.cpl` and Enter, and then use the Network ID or Change buttons.)

When your computer has been joined to the domain and restarted, the login process might be slightly changed. If the Welcome screen says, "Press Ctrl+Alt+Del to sign in," type this key combination. (Hold down the Ctrl and Alt keys, press the Del key, and then release all the keys.)

The first time you sign in, the icon for your original nondomain ("local") account might still appear. If an icon for your domain account does not appear, select Other User. Then enter the username and password for your domain account. If the correct domain name doesn't appear, enter your account name in the format *domainname\username*.

To sign in using a local account, select Other Account. Under Sign In Options, select the "key" icon, and then select How Do I Sign On to Another Domain? Enter your local account name in the format *computername\username*, as shown on the screen.

To sign in using a Microsoft account, select the "box-and-cursor" icon and enter your online account name and password.

 note

If your computer is disconnected from the network or you want to install new hardware, you can still sign in using a local account. At the Welcome screen, select Other User.

Disconnecting from a Domain Network

If you have a computer or tablet that you use for both work and personal use and the device is joined to your work domain, you can still use a nondomain (local) account for your personal use. You can set up a local account before you join the device to the domain or, if your network administrator has given your account Local Administrator privileges, you can create a new local account using Settings, Accounts, Family & Other People, Add Someone Else to This PC.

If you want to remove the computer's domain membership entirely and just use the device for personal use, follow these steps to disconnect the device from the domain:

1. Be sure that you know the login name and password of a nondomain Administrator account so that you can manage the computer after it's been disconnected. If you need to create a new Administrator account, click Start, Settings (gear icon), Accounts, Settings, Accounts, Family & Other People, Add Someone Else to This PC.

   If your network administrator has prevented you from adding local accounts, you will need to get her to help do this before you proceed.

   ➡ *For more information on creating accounts,* **see** *"Setting Up User Accounts," **p. 75.***

2. Click Start, Settings (gear icon), Accounts, Access Work or School.

3. Click the icon labeled Connected To (your domain) AD Domain, and then click Disconnect, Yes.

4. Enter the username and password of the Administrator account that you will use to manage the computer after you disconnect, and then click OK, Restart Now.

After your computer restarts, you can log in using a Microsoft or local account. Documents and other content saved by domain users who had previously logged in will be available to any Administrator user who delves into the folders under C:\users using Windows Explorer, so you might want to delete any sensitive information they contain.

Also, if your computer uses BitLocker to encrypt the contents of its disk or flash storage, you should make a copy of your drives' BitLocker recovery keys on removable media, because now that you are disconnected from the domain, the domain administrator will not be able to reset the BitLocker password for you if you forget it. To back up the recovery key, type the word **bitlocker** into the taskbar's search box, and then select Manage BitLocker from the search results. Next to each drive that is listed as having BitLocker turned on, select Back Up Your Recovery Key. (You might need to select the down arrow to the right of the drive name to see this option.) You can save the key to your Microsoft (online) account or to removable media, or you can print it. Alternatively, you can just select Turn BitLocker Off to unencrypt your drive(s).

Bridging Two Network Types

A Windows computer can connect or bridge two different network types through software, letting the devices on both networks communicate with each other. This can eliminate the need to buy a hardware device to connect two disparate networks (although it works only when your Windows computer is turned on). Figure 18.15 shows an example of what bridging can do. In the figure, one computer serves as a bridge between an Ethernet LAN and a powerline LAN. (Previous versions of Windows could do this, too. In this book, we just describe how to set it up using a Windows 10 computer as the bridge.)

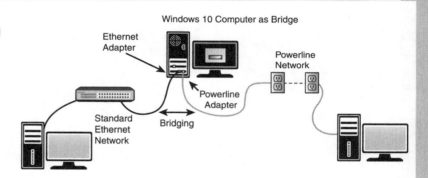

Figure 18.15
Bridging a powerline and Ethernet network with Windows 10. Computers on either network can communicate as if they were directly connected.

Bridging is similar to routing, but it's more appropriate for small LANs because it's easier to configure and doesn't require different sets of IP addresses on each network segment. Technically, bridging occurs at the physical level of the network protocol stack. Windows forwards network traffic, including broadcasts and packets of all protocol types received on either adapter, to the other. In effect, it creates one larger network.

To enable bridging in your Windows 10 computer, install and configure two or more network adapters, as described under "Installing Multiple Network Adapters," earlier in this chapter. However, don't worry about setting up the Internet Protocol (TCP/IP) parameters for either of the adapters yet. Then do the following:

1. At the right end of the taskbar, click the network icon and select Network & Internet Settings, Status. Then scroll down and select Change Adapter Settings.

2. Select the icons for the network adapters you want to bridge by clicking the first, holding down the Ctrl key, and clicking the second.

3. Right-click one of the now-highlighted icons and select Bridge Connections.

4. A new icon named Network Bridge appears. Select this new icon and, if you want, rename it appropriately—for example, "Ethernet to Powerline Bridge."

5. Double-click the new Network Bridge icon. Select Internet Protocol (TCP/IP) and configure your computer's TCP/IP settings. You must do this last because any TCP/IP settings for the original two adapters are lost.

After you've created a bridge, your two network adapters function as one and share one IP address, so Microsoft disables the "network properties" of the individual network adapters. You must configure your computer's network properties with the Network Bridge icon.

Remember that the connection between the two networks depends on the computer with the bridge being powered on.

You can remove the bridge later by right-clicking the Network Bridge icon and clicking Delete.

CONNECTING YOUR NETWORK TO THE INTERNET

Sharing an Internet Connection

The preceding chapter shows how to create an inexpensive local area network (LAN) to tie your computers together. With a network in place, a single high-speed Internet connection can serve all the computers in your home or office, or you can share a modem connection made from one designated Windows computer.

A shared Internet connection can actually provide better protection against hackers than can an individual connection because a shared connection must funnel through a router device or a software service that blocks outside attempts to connect to your computers—except on your terms. In this chapter, we show you how to set this up.

 note

You should also read Chapter 33, "Protecting Your Network from Hackers and Snoops," for more details on protecting your network from hacking.

Before we start, we have a housekeeping item to mention. Throughout this chapter we give this instruction for getting to the networking settings panel: "Click the network icon in the taskbar, and then select Network & Internet Settings, Status." On small screens, or if you've made the Settings window narrow, you'll need to touch or click the word *Status* to see the settings we discuss. In most cases, though, Windows will show you the Status page automatically, so you won't actually need to click Status (no harm if you do, though). We want the instructions to work for everyone, so we include the step of clicking Status. On mobile phones, where there is no taskbar, you get to Network & Internet Settings from the main Settings screen.

Selecting a Way to Make the Connection

When you're using a single computer, you most likely use a broadband cable, DSL, or satellite modem to connect to your ISP as needed. (Cellular data and old-fashioned dial-up services are also possibilities, but they're fairly rare for home and small office computers.) To share your Internet service with other computers, using a network, you can use an inexpensive hardware device called a *router* or *residential gateway* to serve as a bridge between your network and a cable or DSL modem. Your ISP might have provided you with a router, but if it didn't, adding one is easy and inexpensive. The router then automatically manages your Internet connection.

As an overview, Figure 19.1 shows three ways to hook up the computers on your LAN to an Internet service provider (ISP). Throughout this chapter, we refer to these as schemes A, B, and C. They are as follows:

A. Router with a broadband modem—A router enables a single Internet connection to be shared with multiple computers. This method is more secure than directly connecting your computer to the modem because the router shields Windows from the Internet.

A Wi-Fi router, which will provide both wireless (Wi-Fi) and plug-in Ethernet connections, will give you the most flexibility.

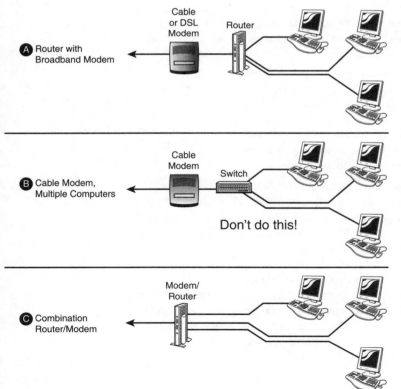

Figure 19.1
Ways to connect your LAN to the Internet.

B. Cable modem, multiple computers—This setup, with just a cable modem and no routing function, is one that some cable ISPs recommend for a home with more than one computer. It is a *bad idea*. You can't use this method and also use file and printer sharing. Use scheme A or C. See "Special Notes for Cable Service," later in this chapter, for more information.

C. Combination Router/Modem—Some ISPs provide a device that combines the functions of a modem and router in the same package. Again, it's best if the device supports both Wi-Fi and Ethernet connections.

Now let's look at the issues involved in having a single ISP connection serve multiple computers.

Managing IP Addresses

Connecting a LAN to the Internet requires you to delve into some issues about how computers are identified on your LAN and on the Internet. Each computer on your LAN uses a unique network identification number called an *IP address* that is used to route data to the correct computer. As long as the data stays on your LAN, it doesn't matter what numbers are used; your LAN is essentially a private affair.

When you connect to the Internet, though, those random numbers can't be used to direct data to you; your ISP must assign a *public* IP address to you so that other computers on the Internet can properly route data to your ISP and then to you.

Now, when you establish a solo connection from your computer to the Internet, this isn't a big problem. When you connect, your ISP assigns your computer a temporary public IP address. Any computer on the Internet can send data to you using this address. When you want to connect a LAN, though, it's not quite as easy. Two approaches are used:

- You can get a valid public IP address for each of your computers.

- You can use one public IP address and share it among all the users of your LAN.

The first approach is called *routed* Internet service because your ISP assigns a set of consecutive IP addresses for your LAN—one for each of your computers—and routes all data for these addresses to your site. This can be done using a specially configured router and usually incurs extra monthly charges for each IP address beyond the first.

The second approach is by far the most common for home and small office use and uses a technique called *Network Address Translation (NAT)*, in which all the computers on your LAN share one public IP address and connection.

NAT and Internet Connection Sharing

The popular routers used in homes and small offices are also called *residential gateways* or, if they have Wi-Fi capability, *wireless routers*. As mentioned in the previous section, in almost all cases they are set up to use NAT to establish all Internet connections using one public IP address. The computer or device running the NAT service mediates all connections between computers on your LAN and the Internet (see Figure 19.2). Most ISPs now provide a NAT router as a standard part of high-speed Internet service.

NAT works a lot like mail delivery to a large commercial office building, where there's one address for many people. Mail is delivered to the mail room, which sorts it and delivers it internally to the correct recipient. With NAT, your router is assigned one public IP address, and all communication between your LAN and the Internet uses this address. The NAT service takes care of changing or translating the IP addresses in data packets from the private, internal IP addresses used on your LAN to the one public address used on the Internet and forwards data from the outside world to your computers.

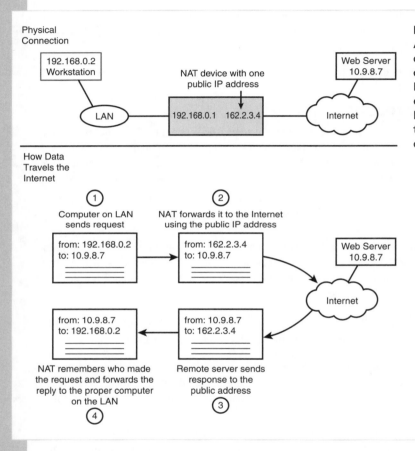

Figure 19.2
A NAT device or program carries out all Internet communications using one IP address. NAT keeps track of outgoing data from your LAN to determine where to send responses from the outside.

Using NAT has several significant consequences:

- You can hook up as many computers on your LAN as you want. Your ISP won't care, or even know, that more than one computer is using the connection. You save money because you pay for only a single connection. (On the other hand, if you have a metered Internet connection, such as satellite data service, everyone is eating away at your quota.)

- You can assign IP addresses inside your LAN however you want. In fact, all the NAT setups we've seen provide DHCP, an automatic IP addressing system, so virtually no manual configuration is needed on the computers you add to your LAN. Just plug in a computer, and it's on the Internet.

- If you want to host a website, VPN, or other service on your LAN and make it available from the Internet, you have some additional setup work to do. When you contact a remote website, NAT knows to send the returned data back to you, but when an unsolicited request comes from outside, NAT must be told where to send the incoming connection. We discuss this scenario later in the chapter.

- NAT serves as an additional firewall to protect your LAN from probing by Internet hackers. Incoming requests, such as those to read your shared folders, are simply ignored if you haven't specifically set up your connection-sharing service to forward requests to a particular computer.

- Some network services can't be made to work with NAT. For example, you might not be able to use some audio and video chat services. These programs expect that the IP address of the computer on which they're running is a public address. Windows ICS and some hardware-sharing routers can sometimes work around this problem using the Universal Plug and Play (UPnP) protocol, which is discussed later in the chapter.

 note

With every version of Windows starting with Windows 98, Microsoft has provided a feature called Internet Connection Sharing (ICS), which lets one designated computer on your network perform the function of a NAT router. Windows 10 includes this capability, but we can't recommend that you use it. To use ICS, you must leave one of your Windows computers turned on so that other computers can reach the Internet. Connection-sharing routers must be left on, too, but they consume very little power compared to what a PC sucks up. Routers are inexpensive, easy to use, and with most offering Wi-Fi service as well, they are much better option for sharing an Internet connection than using ICS.

If your ISP doesn't provide a combination modem/router and you need to get one, look at the products made by Linksys, D-Link, SMC, and Netgear. You can find them at computer stores, office supply stores, and online. On sale, you can pick one up for as little as $20 or less. Wireless versions that include an 802.11n or 802.11g wireless networking base station, as well as a switch for wired Ethernet connections, don't cost that much more. The latest standard for Wi-Fi routers is 802.11ac, and these can transfer data much faster than 802.11n or 802.11g, but they cost somewhat more.

More advanced (and expensive) versions include additional features such as a built-in print server and virtual private networking (VPN) service.

The next section discusses issues that are important to business users. If you're setting up a network for your home, you can skip ahead.

Special Notes for Wireless Networking

If you're setting up a router that provides wireless (Wi-Fi) networking, you must enable wireless data encryption to protect your network from unexpected use by random strangers. People connecting to your wireless network appear to Windows to be part of your own LAN and are trusted accordingly.

➡ *To learn more about setting up a secure wireless network,* **see** *"Installing a Wireless Network,"* **p. 381.**

If you really want to provide free access to your broadband connection as a public service, be sure to use a wireless router that can automatically provide a separate Guest network; computers connecting to the Guest network can't access your or any other computers on the network, just outside Internet servers. Alternatively, provide public access using a second, unsecured wireless router plugged in to your network, as shown in Figure 19.3. Use a different channel number and network name (SSID) from the ones set up for your private wireless LAN. Set up filtering in this router to prevent Windows file-sharing queries from penetrating into your own network. See "Routed Service with Multiple Addresses," later in this chapter, for the list of ports you must block on the private LAN router.

(And remember that someone might use your public connection to send spam or attack other networks. If the FBI knocks on your door someday, don't say we didn't warn you.)

Special Notes for Cable Service

Some cable ISPs can provide you with multiple IP addresses so you can connect multiple computers directly to your cable modem using a simple Ethernet switch and no router. This is scheme B in Figure 19.1. It's a simple setup, but we strongly urge you *not* to use this type of service. Because all of your computers would be directly exposed to the Internet, without the barrier provided by a NAT router, it's not safe to enable and use file and printer sharing on such a network.

> ⚠ **caution**
>
> The scheme B setup requires you to connect your cable modem directly to your LAN, without firewall protection between the Internet and your computers. If you use this scheme, you *must* disable file and printer sharing on each computer. In Windows parlance, you must designate your network a public network. If you don't, you will expose all your computers to a *severe* security risk.

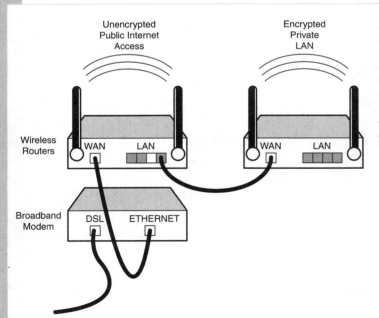

Unencrypted Public Internet Access

Encrypted Private LAN

Wireless Routers

WAN LAN

WAN LAN

Broadband Modem

DSL ETHERNET

Figure 19.3
If you want to provide unsecured, free wireless Internet access to strangers, you can use a second wireless router to protect your own LAN. Windows File Sharing services don't cross the barrier provided by a NAT router.

(Now, many ISPs provide you with a combination modem and router in one box. That would be fine; there's still a router in place, and you have scheme C even through there is just one box. What we're talking about here is a plain cable modem without a routing function.)

If you want to take full advantage of having a LAN in your home or office, use scheme A instead. Simply add an inexpensive connection-sharing router—for as little as $20, as mentioned previously—and you'll get all the benefits of a LAN without the risks of a direct connection.

Configuring Your LAN

In the following sections, we describe how to set up each of the connection schemes diagrammed in Figure 19.1. If you're still in the planning stages for your network, you might want to read all the sections to see what's involved; this information might help you decide what configuration you want to use. If your LAN is already set up and your Internet service is ready to go now, just skip ahead to the appropriate section.

Scheme A—Router with a Broadband Modem

This section shows how to set up the Internet connection method illustrated in Figure 19.1 as scheme A. Your router's manufacturer will provide instructions for installing and configuring it. You might want to first connect the modem directly to one of your computers to make sure your service works. (We discuss how to set up directly connected Internet service in Chapter 14, "Getting Connected.") Then connect the modem and your computer(s) to your router following the manufacturer's instructions, and set up the router.

If you're using cable or DSL Internet service, you'll connect your broadband modem to the router using a short Ethernet patch cable.

Then you'll connect the router to your other computers using one of the two methods shown in Figure 19.4.

You then configure the router, telling it how to contact your ISP and what range of IP addresses to serve up to your LAN. Every device will use a different procedure, so you will have to follow the manufacturer's instructions.

If your ISP uses PPPoE (broadband service that requires a username and password to establish the connection) to establish a connection, you must set up your router to enable PPPoE, and store your logon and password in the router. Some DSL service works this way. If your DSL provider does use PPPoE, you should enable the router's auto-sign-on feature, and you can optionally set up a "keepalive" value that will tell the modem to periodically send network traffic even if you don't, to keep your connection active all the time.

> ### 🔺 caution
> Be sure to change your router's factory-supplied password after you install it. (And write the password somewhere in the router's manual, or put it on a sticky label on the bottom of the router.) Also, be sure to disable outside (Internet) access to the router's management screens.

If you use cable Internet service and your ISP didn't provide you with a special hostname that you had to give to your computer, your ISP probably identifies you by your network adapter's MAC (hardware) address. You might find that your Internet connection won't work when you set up the router. One of your router's setup pages should show you its MAC address. You can either call your ISP's customer service line and tell them that this is your new adapter's MAC address or configure the router to "clone" your computer's MAC address—that is, copy the address from the computer you originally used to set up your cable connection. Your router's setup manual should tell you how to do this.

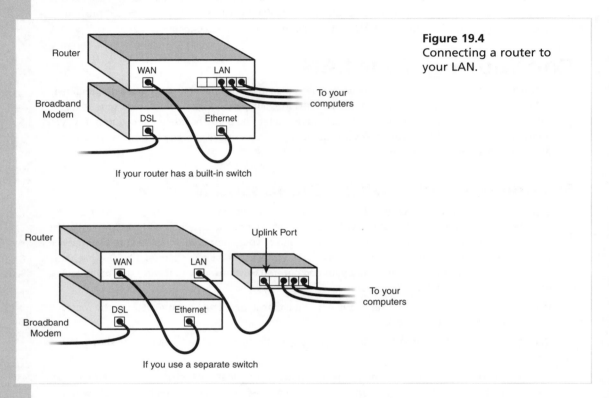

Figure 19.4
Connecting a router to your LAN.

As you are configuring your router, you might want to enable Universal Plug and Play, which is discussed later in this chapter.

 note

If your Internet service has a monthly download limit (as most satellite services do), you might want to tell Windows that you have a metered connection. This will limit the amount of data that Windows Update downloads and will keep some Modern apps from downloading data when you're not actively using them. You might access your metered service through a cellular, Wi-Fi, or Ethernet connection. You'll want to set the network connection that leads to the Internet as metered on all of your Windows 10 devices. To see how to set a connection as metered, **see** "Metered Connections," **p. 820**.

You might also opt for even better hacker protection by having your router filter (block) Microsoft file and printer sharing data. You usually do this on an advanced setup screen labeled Filtering.

See "Routed Service with Multiple Addresses," later in this chapter, for the list of ports that you must block. Figure 19.6 at the end of this chapter shows filtering set up on one common brand of router.

➡ *If your router has wireless networking capability, to learn how to set up that part, see "Installing a Wireless Network," p. 381.*

When the router has been set up, go to each of your computers and follow the instructions under "Configuring the Rest of the Network," later in this chapter.

Scheme B—Cable Modem, Multiple Computers

This section discusses the Internet connection method illustrated in Figure 19.1 as scheme B. This setup is comparable to having all of your computers and devices connected through a public, insecure network in a coffee shop or airport. So, as mentioned earlier in the chapter, you cannot safely use file and printer sharing with this setup. Use this setup only if you don't want file and printer sharing and just want to have several computers with Internet access.

In this configuration, follow your ISP's instructions for setting up each computer separately. The only unusual thing here is that the computers plug into a switch or hub, and the switch or hub plugs into the cable modem; otherwise, each computer is set up exactly as if it were a completely separate, standalone computer with cable Internet service.

To verify whether the network location is set to Public Network on Windows 10, follow these steps:

1. Click the network icon at the right end of the taskbar, and select Network & Internet Settings, Status.

2. Check that the label under your network connection is labeled Public Network. If it is, you can stop here. If it's not, continue with step 3.

3. Click Change Connection Properties, and change the Network Profile setting from Private to Public.

> **⚠ caution**
>
> If you do use this scheme, on each Windows computer (Windows Vista and higher), you must set the network location for the connection that goes to your switch and cable modem to Public Network. Windows XP and earlier versions are no longer supported and are not safe to use with this kind of direct Internet connection no matter how they're set up.

If you later decide that you want to use file and printer sharing, *do not* simply turn Find Devices and Content back on, or enable file and printer sharing, or create a homegroup. Instead, set up a router as in scheme A.

Scheme C—Combination Router/Modem

This section discusses setting up the Internet connection method illustrated in Figure 19.1 as scheme C, using a device that is both a broadband mode and a router. Your ISP should provide instructions for installing and configuring this device.

You can also follow the procedure under "Scheme A—Router with a Broadband Modem," earlier in this chapter, except that you can skip the first two paragraphs because you don't have a separate modem to test, and you don't have to use a cable to connect your modem and router.

When the router has been set up, go to each of your computers and follow the instructions under "Configuring the Rest of the Network," later in this chapter.

Routed Service with Multiple Addresses

If you need to have fixed, *public* IP addresses for multiple computers on your network, you need what is called routed Internet service, where your ISP assigns you more than one fixed IP address. This isn't a common requirement for homes or even small businesses unless you run multiple computers that offer the same services (with the same network port numbers), and they have to be accessible by the public. If you need this type of Internet service, you already know it. Routed service can be obtained with business-class cable or DSL service, Frame Relay, ATM, or other technologies.

The wiring will look like either scheme A or scheme C in Figure 19.1. Routed service requires a more fully featured router than the inexpensive residential gateways we discuss in this chapter. In some cases, though, standard combination modem/router can do the job. Your ISP can help you decide what equipment is needed.

If you get this type of service, you have something that is *functionally* similar to Scheme B, in which your computers and your LAN are directly exposed to the Internet. Unlike scheme B, which has no router, you *can* use file and printer sharing safely, but only if your router is carefully configured to filter and block all incoming network traffic except for that directed at the ports that you need to support for your public services. Setting up this kind of filtering is beyond the scope of this book and is best set up by a networking professional or, if you completely trust them, your ISP's tech support staff.

 caution

If your router is not properly configured to filter out NetBIOS traffic, your network will be exposed to hackers. After setting things up, visit www.grc.com and use the ShieldsUP pages there to be sure your computers are properly protected. For more information about network security, see Chapter 33.

To repeat, it is *absolutely essential* that your router be set up to protect your network. You must ensure that at least these three items are taken care of:

- The router must be set up with filters to prevent Microsoft file-sharing service (NetBIOS and NetBT) packets from entering or leaving your LAN. In technical terms, the router must be set up to block TCP and UDP on port 137, UDP on port 138, and TCP on ports 139 and 445. It should "drop" rather than "reject" packets, if possible. This helps prevent hackers from discovering that these services are present but blocked. Better to let them think they're not there at all.

- Be *absolutely* sure to change your router's administrative password from the factory default value to something hard to guess, with uppercase letters, lowercase letters, numbers, and punctuation. Don't let your ISP talk you out of this. Also, you should let them know what the new password is so they can get into the router from their end if needed.

- Disable SNMP access, or change the SNMP read and read-write "community names" to something other than the default. Again, use something with letters, numbers, and punctuation.

Second, either your ISP will set up your router to automatically assign network addresses to your computers using DHCP, or you will have to set up a fixed IP address for each computer manually, using the IP address, network mask, gateway address, and DNS server addresses supplied by your ISP. Be absolutely sure that Windows Defender Firewall is enabled or a comparable third-party firewall service is installed on each of your computers.

Universal Plug and Play

Your router might have a feature called Universal Plug and Play (UPnP). UPnP provides a way for software running on your computer to communicate with the router. Specifically, UPnP provides a means for the following:

- The router to tell software on your computer that it is separated from the Internet by NAT. This may let some software—the video and audio parts of most messaging programs, in particular— have a better chance of working.

- Software running on the network to tell the router to forward expected incoming connections to the correct computer. Online messaging programs often require this. When the computer on the other end of the connection starts sending data, the router would not know to send it to your computer. UPnP lets UPnP-aware application programs automatically set up forwarding in the router.

- Other types of as-yet-undeveloped hardware devices to announce their presence on the network so that Windows can automatically take advantage of the services they provide.

To use UPnP, you must enable the feature in your router. It's usually disabled by default. If your router doesn't currently support UPnP, you might have to download and install a firmware upgrade from the manufacturer. Most newer routers do support UPnP.

Configuring the Rest of the Network

Whichever scheme you used, configuring the rest of your LAN should be relatively easy after you've set up the connection and router. On each of your Windows 10 computers that use a wired Ethernet connection to the router, follow these steps:

1. Click the network icon in the taskbar and select Network & Internet Settings, Status. Under Change Your Network Settings, select Change Adapter Options. Right-click the computer's Ethernet or Wireless network icon, depending on which you're using, and select Properties.

2. Select Internet Protocol Version 4 (TCP/IPv4), and then select Properties.

3. Check Obtain an IP Address Automatically and Obtain DNS Server Address Automatically. Then click OK.

4. Repeat steps 2 and 3 for Internet Protocol Version 6 (TCP/IPv6), but instead of selecting Internet Protocol Version 4 in step 2, select Internet Protocol Version 6. Click Close to close the dialog box.

5. When finished, you should be able to open a web browser and view a website.

(On versions of Windows other than Windows 10, you will have to use different selections to get to your network adapter's settings. You should be able to get to them from the Control Panel.)

That's all you need to do to share your Internet connection. If your network will host servers that need to be reachable from the outside world, proceed with the next section.

Making Services Available

You might want to make some internal network services available to the outside world through your Internet connection. You would want to do this in these situations:

> **caution**
>
> Make absolutely sure that Windows Defender Firewall is turned on to protect your network from hackers. For more information on network security, see Chapter 33.

- You want to host a web server using Internet Information Services (IIS).

- You want to enable incoming VPN access to your LAN so you can securely connect from home or afield.

- You want to enable incoming Remote Desktop access to your computer.

If you have set up routed Internet service with multiple IP addresses, you don't have to worry about this because your network connection is wide open and doesn't use NAT. As long as the outside users know the IP address of the computer hosting your service—or its DNS name if you have set up DNS service—you're on the air already.

Otherwise, you have either Windows Defender Firewall, NAT, or both in the way of incoming access. To make specific services accessible, configure Windows Defender Firewall on the service hosting computer, and you must configure your router to forward incoming requests to that computer.

> **note**
>
> If you're interested in being able to reach your computer over the Internet using Remote Desktop, see Chapter 39, "Remote Desktop and Remote Access," which is entirely devoted to the subject.

On the computer that is providing the service itself, you must tell Windows Defender Firewall to allow incoming connections to the service by following these steps:

1. Click the Network icon in the taskbar, and select Network & Internet Settings, Status. Then scroll down and select Windows Firewall. Scroll down, select Advanced Settings, and approve the User Account Control Prompt.

2. In the left pane, click Inbound Rules. Locate the service that this computer is providing, and find the line for the Private profile. If the service is listed with Yes in the Enabled column and Allow in the Action column, you can proceed to configure the computer that is sharing its Internet connection.

3. If the service isn't already listed, click New Rule in the right pane. Click Port, click Next, select TCP or UDP, and enter the specific port number or port number range required by the service. Table 19.1 lists common services, port numbers, and protocols. (For the FTP and DNS services, you have to make two entries.) Alternatively, you could add a new rule and select Program, to enable *all* incoming connections to a given application.

4. Click Next and click Allow the Connection.

5. Click Next and leave all three check boxes (Domain, Private, Public) checked.

6. Click Next. For the rule name, enter the name of the service you're enabling, add an optional description, and click Finish.

Table 19.1   Common Services and Port Numbers

Service	Protocol	Port
Domain Name Service (DNS)	TCP and UDP	53
FTP Server	TCP	20 and 21
Internet Mail Server (SMTP)	TCP	25
Post Office Protocol Version 3 (POP3)	TCP	110
Remote Desktop	TCP	3389
Secure Shell (SSH)	TCP	22
Secure Web Server (HTTPS)	TCP	443
Symantec PCAnywhere	TCP	5631
Telnet Server	TCP	23
Web Server (HTTP)	TCP	80

Next, you must tell your router to forward incoming requests for each designated service to the computer that will handle them.

Some home/small office routers let you forward incoming Internet requests to a network computer by specifying the computer's name. If yours permits this, you're in luck because it means you can let the router assign IP addresses to your computer as it pleases. The router's forwarding feature will always find the right service for each computer because it can find them by name.

Other routers require you to forward services by IP address, not by computer name. If, like most networks, yours is set up to have computers obtain their IP addresses automatically, your computers are moving targets because their IP address could change from day to day, and the forwarding feature will likely send requests to the wrong address.

So you must make special arrangements for assigning addresses to the computers on your LAN that you want to use to host services. On your router's setup screens, make a note of the range of IP addresses that it will hand out to computers requesting automatic (DHCP) configuration. Most routers have a place to enter a starting IP address and a maximum number of addresses. For instance, the starting number might be 2, with a limit of 100 addresses. For each computer that will provide an outside service, pick a number between 2 and 254 that is *not* in the range of addresses handed out by the router, and use that as the last number in the computer's IP address. We recommend using address 250 and working downward from there for any other computers that require a static address.

To configure the computer's network address, follow the instructions under "Port Forwarding with a Router" in Chapter 39, with these changes:

- The material in Chapter 39 shows instructions for setting up access to the Remote Desktop service, using protocol TCP and port 3389. You can use the same procedure to set up access to your service, except substitute the protocol and port numbers for the service you're enabling.

- Use a static IP address ending with .250 for the first computer you set up to receive incoming connections. Use .249 for the second computer, and work downward from there. Be sure to keep a list of the computers you assign static addresses to as well as the addresses you assign.

For services that use TCP/UDP in unpredictable ways, you must use another approach to forwarding on your LAN. Some services, such as many text, voice, or video chat programs, communicate their *private*, internal IP address to the computer on the other end of the connection; when the other computer tries to send data to this private address, it fails. To use these services with a hardware router, you must enable UPnP, as described earlier in the chapter.

Other services use network protocols other than TCP and UDP, and most routers can't be set up to forward them. Incoming Microsoft VPN connections fall into this category. Some routers have built-in support for Microsoft's PPTP protocol. If yours has this support, your router's manual will tell you how to forward VPN connections to a host computer.

Otherwise, to support nonstandard services of this sort, you have to tell the router to forward *all* unrecognized incoming data to one designated computer. In effect, this exposes that computer to the Internet, so it's a fairly significant security risk. In fact, most routers call this targeted computer a *DMZ host*, referring to the notorious Korean no-man's-land called the Demilitarized Zone and the peculiar danger one faces standing in it.

To enable a DMZ host, you need to use a fixed IP address on the designated computer, as described in the preceding section. Use your router's configuration screen to specify this selected IP address as the DMZ host. The configuration screen for my particular router is shown in Figure 19.5; yours might differ.

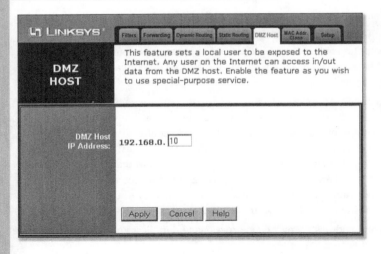

Figure 19.5
Enabling a DMZ host to receive all unrecognized incoming connection requests. This is an option of last resort if you can't forward incoming connections any other way.

Figure 19.6
Configuring filters to block
Microsoft file-sharing services.

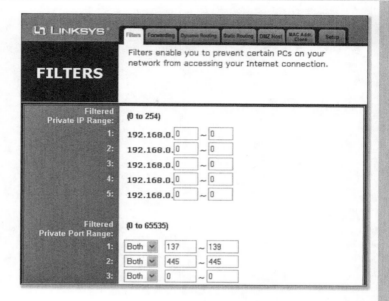

Now, designating a DMZ host means that this computer is fully exposed to the Internet, so you must protect it with a firewall of some sort. On this computer, you *must* set its network location to Public, and it can't participate in file sharing or a homegroup.

You should also set up filtering in your router to block ports 137–139 and 445. Figure 19.6 shows how this is done on my Linksys router; your router might use a different method.

 tip
Enabling filtering for these ports is not a bad idea even if you're not using a DMZ host. Doing this is essential if you set up a DMZ host.

NETWORKING WITH OTHER OPERATING SYSTEMS

Making Windows Play Well with Others

It's easy enough to plug a couple Windows 10 computers together and call it a network, but real-life networks are seldom so simple, even at home. Networks usually have a mix of operating systems, and Windows often has to be coaxed into getting along with them.

On a real-life local area network (LAN) with multiple operating systems (OSes), it's not enough that computers be capable of coexisting on the same network cable at the same time. They need to actually work *with* each other, or *internetwork* so that users of these various systems can share files and printers. At best, this sharing should occur without anyone even knowing that alternative platforms are involved. Achieving this kind of seamlessness can range from effortless to excruciating.

If you're shopping for such a network appliance, be sure that the device supports the SMB2 network file sharing protocol used by Windows, as the older SMB protocol has severe security problems and has been disabled in Windows 10. There is a way to enable Windows 10's use of SMB, but this is dangerous because several computer viruses and worms use SMB's flaws to jump from computer to computer across a network. Instead, buy (or update) a network appliance that supports SMB2.

Also, be very careful to check what format the device uses on its disks and what maximum file size it supports. Some devices support a maximum file size of only 4GB, depending on the disk format and internal software used. Such a device might be okay for storing documents and photos, but it will be incapable of storing complete movies and computer

Save the Heartache—Buy a Network Appliance

One way to avoid most of the hassles of internetworking is to buy a *network appliance*, also called *network-attached storage (NAS)*—a small server computer that "speaks" all the networking languages you need (Windows, Unix, Macintosh, or whatever). These devices can cost less than $200 and can put terabytes of storage on your network for anyone to access. They tend to be very easy to set up, and a few even provide printer sharing, Internet connection sharing, wireless connectivity, an email server, a firewall, and a web server all in the same box. Products for the home and small office are made by Cisco (www.cicso.com), D-Link (http://www.dlink.com), Buffalo Technology (www.buffalotech.com), LG (www.lg.com), QNAP (www.qnap.com), Seagate (www.seagate.com), and several other companies.

backup files, many of which run 6GB in size or more. Other devices use proprietary networking drivers or proprietary disk formats. Personally, I'd use only a NAS device that employs standard file access protocols (SMB2, NFS, and so on) and a disk format that can be read by Windows or Linux (so, FAT or NTFS, or ext3 or ext4 if you use Linux; and FAT only if you can accept the 4GB file size limit. Doing so means that if the hardware box were to die, I could at least put its hard disk into a desktop computer and extract its contents.

If a network appliance isn't in the cards, you must get your computers to interoperate directly. This chapter shows you how to get computers running Windows, Mac OS X, Unix, and Linux to play together nicely.

Windows 10, 8.1, 8, and 7 have some networking features that weren't in older versions, and some features have been removed. With respect to internetworking, this list provides a summary of the most significant changes since Windows Vista and XP:

- Windows 10, 8.1, 8, and 7 behave differently from previous versions of Windows when Password Protected Sharing is turned off. This topic is discussed later in the section "Password Protection and Simple File Sharing."

- The NetBEUI network protocol is no longer available. This could affect you if your network includes computers running Windows XP or—heaven forbid—earlier versions. We discuss this topic in more detail when we talk about networking with older versions of Windows later in this chapter.

- The Link Level Discovery Protocol (LLDP) lets Windows eke out a map of the connections between your computers and the other hardware on your network. The network map feature appears only in Windows 7 and Vista, so you might not care about this. If you do use the map display, or if your organization uses LLDP with third-party network management tools, LLDP support is available for Windows XP via a download and is included in all the more recent versions. It's also in Server 2003 and later Server editions. Connections to computers running older versions of Windows will not be diagrammed on the network map. Computers running Linux and Mac OS X won't appear, either, unless you add a third-party program such as Open LLDP (at http://openlldp.sourceforge.net). Some commercial network-mapping applications (such as Network Topology Mapper at www.solarwinds.com) have a Mac LLDP responder.

However, although some things change, other things stay the same. You probably won't be surprised to learn that the Network Browser service (the relatively obscure software component responsible for collecting the list of names of the computers that show up in File Explorer under Network) is still present—and still works only when it feels like it.

In addition to covering internetworking issues, this chapter discusses some of the advanced and optional networking features provided with Windows 10. These features are not needed for "vanilla" Windows networks, but they are used for the more complex networks found in corporate environments.

Internetworking with Windows 8.1, 8, 7, Vista, and XP

Windows 10's file and printer sharing services work quite well with Windows 8.1, 8, 7, Vista, XP, and the various Windows Server versions. All of these OSs were intended from the start to work well with the TCP/IP network protocol favored by modern versions of Windows.

For all practical purposes, Windows 10, 8.1, 8, and Windows 7 networking are virtually identical. There are no compatibility issues to worry about other than getting the Network Location set correctly (discussed in Chapter 18, "Creating a Windows Network," in the section "Enabling and Disabling Sharing").

If your network has computers running versions of Windows older than Windows 7, the differences in OSs can show up in these areas:

- **Default networking protocols**—You might have configured any *really* old computers to use the NetBIOS or SPX/IPX protocol as the primary networking protocol. Windows 7 through 10 require that you use TCP/IP. And, it's best if you use only TCP/IP.

- **LLDP mapping**—By default, Windows XP computers did not come with support for LLDP, and without it, these computers will appear as "orphans" on the network map display in Windows 7 and Vista. You can download and install an LLDP add-on for XP if you like.

- **Password Protected Sharing (Simple File Sharing)**—Windows can provide username/password security for shared files and folders. Windows 10, 8.1, 8, 7, Vista, and XP also have a "password-less" option.

- **Homegroup networking**—Windows 10, 8.1, 8, and 7 let you join your computers into a homegroup, which simplifies file-sharing security. A homegroup member can still share files and printers with older versions of Windows, but there are some subtleties that we explain in this chapter.

We cover these topics in the following sections.

Setting TCP/IP as the Default Network Protocol

When freshly installed, Windows XP was set up to use the TCP/IP network protocol for file and printer sharing by default. If your network previously included Windows 95, 98, Me, 2000, or NT computers, you might have changed the network protocols to simplify internetworking with the older operating systems.

Because newer versions of Windows support only TCP/IP, you must make sure that TCP/IP is enabled on your Windows XP computers. Also, Windows networking works much more reliably when every computer on the network has the same set of protocols installed. You should ensure that TCP/IP is the only installed network protocol.

Follow these steps on any computers that run Windows XP:

 note

If your computer is connected to a corporate network, your network administrator will make all necessary changes for you.

1. Sign in using a Computer Administrator account.

2. Click Start, Control Panel, Network and Internet Connections; then click the Network Connections icon.

3. Right-click the Local Area Connection icon and select Properties.

4. Look in the list of installed components and make sure that Internet Protocol (TCP/IP) is listed. If not, click Install, select Protocols, click Add, and select Internet Protocol (TCP/IP). If your network uses manually assigned (static) IP addresses, configure the Internet Protocol entry just as you configured your newer computers.

5. Look in the list of installed components for the NWLink IPX/SPX or NetBEUI protocols. Select these entries and click Uninstall.

6. Click OK to close the Local Area Connection Properties dialog box.

7. From the menu in the Network Connections window, select Advanced, Advanced Settings. Select the Adapters and Bindings tab.

8. In the top list, select Local Area Connection. In the lower list, make sure that Internet Protocol (TCP/IP) is checked under both File and Printer Sharing for Microsoft Networks and Client for Microsoft Networks.

9. Click OK to close the dialog box.

After checking all your computers, restart all your computers if you had to make changes on any of them.

Password Protection and Simple File Sharing

On small Windows networks (that is, networks that aren't managed by a Windows Server computer using the Domain security model), each computer is separately responsible for managing usernames and passwords. Before Windows XP, this made it difficult to share files across the network securely. You had to create accounts for each of your users on every one of your computers, using the same password for each user on each computer.

Windows XP introduced a concept called Simple File Sharing that, when enabled, entirely eliminated security for file sharing. All network access was done in the context of the Guest user account, regardless of the remote user's actual account name. Essentially, anyone with physical access to your network could access any shared file. This made it much easier for other people in your home and office to get to each other's files. (And, horrifyingly, everyone on the Internet could also get at your files, until XP Service Pack 2 came out.)

Windows 10, 8.1, 8, 7, and Vista also include Simple File Sharing, although it's now called Password Protected Sharing. And, because the names are different, the effect of disabling and enabling the feature is reversed on the two newer operating systems. Table 20.1 shows the settings and the results.

Table 20.1 File-Sharing Settings

Windows 10, 8.1, 8, 7, Vista Password Protected Sharing	Windows XP Professional Simple File Sharing	Account and Password
On	Off	Required
Off	On	Not required

You cannot always change this setting. In Windows XP Home Edition, Simple File Sharing is always on and cannot be turned off. So, other computers cannot connect to resources shared by XP Home using individual username/password security. In all other versions of Windows, the feature can be turned on or off, except if the computer is a member of a domain network. In this case, passwords are always required.

Finally, Windows 10, 8.1, 8, and 7 have a twist in the way that security works when Password Protected Sharing is turned off. On Vista and XP, when passwords are not required, all incoming network access uses the Guest account. Thus, anyone on the network can access any file in a shared folder if the file can be accessed by the user account Guest or by the user group Everyone.

But the following happens when a remote user attempts to use a folder or file shared by a Windows 10, 8.1, 8, or 7 computer with Password Protected Sharing turned off:

- If the remote user's account name matches an account in the sharing computer *and* that account has a password set, that account is used for file access.

- If the remote user's account matches an account in the sharing computer, but that account has no password set, the Guest account is used.

- If the remote user's account matches no account in the sharing computer, the Guest account is used.

This change might seem convoluted, but it is actually very useful. First, this change was necessary to support the new HomeGroup feature. All homegroup member computers use a special password-protected account named HomeGroupUser$ to access other member computers, and this change lets it work whether Password Protected Sharing is turned on or off. Second, it gives you the option of giving designated users additional access privileges, without requiring you to set up a full-blown security scheme.

We know this discussion has probably given you a headache by now. You probably just want to know how to get at the library of pictures stored on your old computer. In the end, however, deciding how to set things up can be pretty easy, based on how concerned you need to be about security.

To see how to set up your network, decide which of the following three categories best describes your environment:

tip

If you change your password on any computer, it's a good idea to make the same change on every computer where you have an account. This way, you won't be asked to supply your password whenever you use network resources.

- **My computer is part of a corporate domain network.**

  In this case, accounts and passwords are always required. Your network administrator sets these up. Use the Security tab on any folder that you share to select the users and groups to which you want to grant access.

- **Ease of use is my priority, and network security is not a great concern.**

  In this case, turn off Password Protected Sharing on your Windows 10, 8.1, 8, 7, and Vista computers, and enable Simple File Sharing on any Windows XP Professional computers. This way, anyone on the network can access any shared folder.

  You must make sure that a firewall is set up to block file and printer sharing access over your Internet connection. Use a connection-sharing router, Windows Firewall, or a third-party firewall program to do this. If you have a wireless network, you must enable WPA2 security so random strangers can't get in.

- **Security is important to me; I want specific control over which individual users can use specific shared files and folders.**

  In this case, turn on Password Protected Sharing on your Windows 10, 8.1, 8, 7, and Vista computers and disable Simple File Sharing on any XP Professional computers. Do not share sensitive resources from any computer that runs Windows XP Home Edition. (Because security is important to you, you have of course already gotten rid of or updated your Windows XP computers, because it's no longer supported by Microsoft and doesn't get bug and security patches.) Do not create a homegroup.

  On every computer that does share sensitive folders or printers with the network, you must create an account for every user who needs access to the shared folders or printers. For each user, be sure to create an account with the same name and the same password as on that user's own computer.

To change the Password Protect Sharing setting, sign on as an Administrator. Then, on Windows 10, follow these steps:

1. Click the network icon in the taskbar, select Network & Internet Settings, and if only a column of network categories appears, select Status. Scroll down and select Sharing Options.

2. Scroll down, open the All Networks section, and scroll to its bottom. The last item is Password Protected Sharing, and you can turn it on or off there.

On Windows 7 and 8, follow these steps:

1. Right-click the network icon in the desktop's notification area and select Open Network and Sharing Center, and then select Change Advanced Sharing Settings.

2. Scroll down, open the All Networks section, and scroll to its bottom. The last item is Password Protected Sharing, and you can turn it on or off there.

To change the Password Protected Sharing setting on Windows Vista, follow these steps:

1. Click Start, Control Panel, Set Up File Sharing (under Network and Internet).

2. Click the circular icon with the down arrow to the right of Password Protected Sharing, change the Password Protected Sharing setting, and click Apply. You might need to confirm a user account control prompt. (A better alternative: Upgrade the computer to Windows 7 or 10.)

To change the Simple File Sharing setting on Windows XP Professional, follow these steps:

1. Sign in as a Computer Administrator.

2. Click Start, My Computer.

3. Press and release the Alt key to display the menu. Select Tools, Folder Options, and then select the View tab.

4. Scroll to the bottom of the Advanced Settings list. Simple File Sharing is the last entry in the list. Check or uncheck the entry as desired. Remember that Simple File Sharing *on* is the same as Password Protected Sharing *off*.

> **note**
>
> All these rules about whether a password is required are interpreted by the computer that is *sharing* a folder or printer. When any version of Windows *uses* a folder or printer shared by another computer, that other computer sets the rules for requiring a password. For example, XP Home Edition never requires an account or password when someone wants to use its shared folders, but it can still use password-protected shared resources shared by, say, Windows 10 or even a Windows domain server.

For more discussion of file-sharing password arrangements, see Chapter 18, "Creating a Windows Network," and Chapter 33, "Protecting Your Network from Hackers and Snoops."

Using Windows Vista and XP with a Homegroup

If you have two or more Windows 7, 8, 8.1, or Windows 10 computers, you can set up a homegroup (as described in Chapter 18) to simplify sharing libraries, folders, and printers. The HomeGroup system is based on regular Windows file sharing, so computers running other operating systems can also participate in your network.

The easiest way to make XP and Vista fit in with a homegroup is to turn off Password Protected Sharing on all your computers. The instructions for changing this setting were given in the preceding section.

With Password Protected Sharing off, homegroup member computers will connect to each other using the special HomeGroupUser$ account, but all other combinations will use the Guest account.

This means you need to make sure that resources are shared so that Everyone can use them. In particular, the file security settings for the shared folder and its contents must be set so that Everyone has read or read and write permission.

To ensure that this happens, use the following procedures when you're sharing folders on various versions of Windows:

- **Windows 10**—Right-click a folder or library and select Give Access To, Homegroup (View), or Homegroup (View and Edit). Then right-click it again and select Give Access To, Specific People. Type or select Everyone in the drop-down list, and then click Add. If you want other users to be able to change the contents of the folder, next to Everyone, click the word *Read* in the Permissions column and select Read/Write. Click Share to finish.

- **Windows 7, 8, and 8.1**—Follow the preceding instructions for Windows 10, except the right-click menu choice is Share With rather than Give Access To.

- **Windows Vista**—Right-click a folder and select Share. Type or select Everyone in the drop-down list, and then click Add. If you want other users to be able to change the contents of the folder, next to Everyone, click the word *Reader* in the Permissions column and select Contributor. Click Share to finish.

- **Windows XP Professional or Home Edition**—Right-click a folder and select Sharing and Security. Select Sharing This Folder and click Apply. Select the Security tab. Under Group or User Names, if there is an entry for Everyone, select it; otherwise, click Add, type **Everyone**, press Enter, and select the entry for Everyone. In the lower section (in the Allow column), Read & Execute, List Folder Contents, and Read should be checked. If you would like to let other network users modify the contents of the folder, check Modify. Click OK to finish.

▲ caution

If you give Everyone permission to change files, you must be sure that your network is well secured. If you have a wireless network, you must have it set up so that it has WPA2 security enabled (that is, so that a password or key is required to use the network). If you connect to the Internet, you must be sure that Windows Firewall or a third-party firewall product is set up to block Windows file sharing. If you don't secure your network, "Everyone" means "anyone in the world," and that's a recipe for disaster.

But if you want to use passwords to grant or deny access to specific users and specific shared folders, you should leave Password Protected Sharing turned on. In this case, you could deal with your Windows Vista and XP computers in two ways:

- Set up accounts on every computer using the same account name and password for each person, on each computer. This will give you complete control over who has access to which folders shared by Windows 10, 8.1, 8, 7, Vista, and XP Professional. (Per-user security is not available on folders shared by XP Home.)

- Set up a single account that you'll use for file sharing, perhaps named *share*, on every computer, with the same password on every computer. Use this account when you set the permissions on shared folders, and use this account when Windows asks for an account and password when you connect to another computer.

If you share your printer, it's enough just to enable sharing. By default, all versions of Windows enable the Everyone group to print to every installed printer, so anyone on the network should be able to print to any shared printer without needing the security settings to be changed.

Internetworking with Unix and Linux

The Unix operating system, originally developed in the 1970s at AT&T's Bell Laboratories as a platform for internal software development and as a "workbench" for programmers, is still evolving and growing. Today, hundreds of millions of people use Unix or Unix-like OSs such as Linux every day, sometimes without even knowing it, on everything from iMacs to Androids, laptops to mainframes, routers to Raspberry Pi, and...well, the list goes on and on.

The following sections look at ways to network Windows 10 with Unix-type OSs. Although many of the examples involve Linux, most of the examples can be translated to almost any Unix-type OS. And because typing "Unix-like" is already getting tiresome, from here on, we sometimes write just "Unix," but we always mean "Unix and Linux and Mac OS X."

OS X, by the way, has most of the networking command-line tools familiar to Unix users. For file sharing, OS X has specific built-in support for working with Windows, as discussed in the next section.

NFS

Windows 10 Pro, Enterprise, and Education editions come with optional client support for the Network File System (NFS) file sharing system used on many UNIX and Linux systems. These editions can use files and folders shared by NFS file servers, but they cannot share folders to the network using NFS.

To install client support for NFS file resources, follow these steps:

1. Log on as a computer administrator.

2. In the taskbar's search box, type **features** and from the results, select Turn Windows Features On or Off. (Alternatively, press Windows Logo+R, and then type **optionalfeatures** and press Enter.)

3. Expand (click the plus sign) the Services for NFS entry and check both Administrative Tools and Client for NFS. Click OK to complete the installation.

4. In the taskbar's search box, type **NFS**, and then select Services for Network File System from the results. (It's also on the Start menu under Windows Administrative Tools.)

This displays the Services for Network File System management tool. The right pane contains only help information. Click on any of the links to display the Windows Help pages for NFS. The management functions are all in the Properties pages of the items in the left pane. Your NFS administrator should help you with configuration instructions, but here are some tips:

1. To select the method that NFS should use to map Windows logon names to UNIX logon names, right-click Services for NFS in the left pane and select Properties. If your network provides UNIX name-mapping information through Active Directory, check Active Directory and enter the name

of the Windows domain. If a User Name Mapping Service server exists on the network, check Use Name Mapping and enter the hostname of the mapping server. Either way, your network administrator should provide you with this information.

If you select neither Active Directory nor User Name Mapping, the NFS client will access shares anonymously. The NFS server might restrict or reject anonymous access.

2. To select whether to use "hard" or "soft" mounts, right-click Client for NFS in the left pane and select Properties. The Client Settings tab determines how many times the client service will attempt to reconnect to a server that goes offline or becomes unreachable. Microsoft recommends using soft mounts, although your network administrator might advise otherwise.

    This Properties dialog box Client Settings tab also lets you determine whether the client uses TCP, UDP, or TCP and UDP for NFS access. You should be able to use the default TCP+UDP setting.

3. To set the Unix access mask that the client should use when creating new files or folders in an NFS share, right-click Client for NFS in the left pane, select Properties, and view the File Permissions tab. Check the boxes corresponding to the permissions that you want to grant on new files that you might create. (This setting corresponds to the umask setting in a Unix shell; the default Client settings correspond to a umask of **755**.)

To start or stop the client service, right-click Client for NFS and select Start Service or Stop Service. Normally, it should start immediately on installation and whenever you start Windows.

Samba

Samba is an open source (free) software suite available on most Unix-like OSs. The Samba server program makes it possible for Unix computers to share folders and printers that Windows users can access, and the Samba client tools let Unix users access folders and printers shared by Windows computers. The names of the Samba programs start with the letters smb, which stands for Server Message Block. This is the name of the network protocol on which Windows file sharing is based.

note

You can get more information about Samba and download a version for most Unix systems from www.samba.org. Most Linux distributions include a version of Samba and install it by default. For a good Samba introduction and reference, check out *The Official Samba-3 HOWTO and Reference Guide* (Prentice Hall, 2006, ISBN 0131882228), also available online at www.samba.org/samba/docs/man/Samba3-HOWTO.

Samba Client Tools

To access file services shared by Windows computers from Unix, you must know exactly what resources are available from a given host on the network. Samba includes a command-line program called smbclient for just that purpose. This application enables you to list available Windows shares and printers from within Unix. For example, the command smbclient -L //lombok lists all the folders and printers shared by the computer named lombok.

When you know the name of the desired shared folder, the smbmount command enables you to mount the Windows share on the local (Unix) file system. The following command mounts the SharedDocs folder shared by computer lombok to the local directory /mnt/winshare:

```
smbmount //lombok/shareddocs /mnt/winshare -U brian
```

The -U switch tells smbclient what username to use when trying to mount the share. You are prompted for a password.

note

If you are using a Microsoft (online) account on your Windows 10 PC, the username that you need to supply to connect to it for file sharing is not the email address you use when you sign in. To find the real name of your Windows computer account, press Windows Logo+X and select Command Prompt or Windows Power-Shell, whichever appears in the pop-up menu. In the window that opens, you will see something like this: c:\users\brian_000>. The word after *users* is your account name (in this example, it's brian_000). Use this name when you try to connect to a shared Windows folder.

You also can use a Windows printer from a Unix client, but the procedure is complex and beyond the scope of this chapter. Some Linux distributions include a GUI print configuration tool to simplify the process. In any case, we recommend that you read the SMB How-To at http://en.tldp.org/HOWTO/SMB-HOWTO.html.

note

If the Windows computer is running Windows 10, 8.1, 8, or 7 with Password Protected Sharing turned off, you can specify any nonexistent account name to gain access using the Guest account. If you specify a valid account name, you will gain access using this account. Password Protected Sharing is discussed earlier in the section "Password Protection and Simple File Sharing."

Samba Server Tools

Samba also includes tools and servers to make your Unix system look like a Windows-based network server; this capability lets your Windows computers use files and printers shared by Unix systems.

The parameters for configuring Samba in a server capacity are contained in the file /etc/smb.conf on the Unix host. The default file included with Samba has comments for every parameter to explain each one. Configuring the Samba server is beyond the scope of this book; however, we can offer a few pointers:

- Some OSs, such as Mac OS X prior to 10.7 Lion, include a GUI tool to configure Samba file sharing. These tools make the job a lot easier.

- If you must set up file sharing by hand, read the documentation and FAQs for your Samba version before starting the setup procedure. A good place to start is the previously mentioned site, http://en.tldp.org/HOWTO/SMB-HOWTO.html.

- Configure Samba for user-specific passwords with the security option. You must set up Unix user accounts for each of your Windows users. Alternatively, you can set up a single Unix account that all Windows users will share. Windows users would need to supply the selected username and password when they use Unix shares.

  Set encrypt passwords = yes in smb.conf. You also must set up a user and password file for Samba's use, which is usually specified with the smb.conf entry smb passwd file = /etc/smbpasswd. Your Samba documentation explains how to do this.

- Alternatively, you can use share-level security without a password. This makes Samba behave similarly to a Windows host with Password Protected Sharing turned off. However, in this case, you must take care to prevent SMB access to your Unix computer from the Internet. To be precise, you must be sure that TCP port 445 is blocked.

When you have finished editing the smb.conf file, you can test to see that the syntax is correct by using the Samba program testparm. testparm checks smb.conf for internal "correctness" before you actually use it in a production environment.

Printing to Unix Queues from Windows

You can configure Samba to offer standard Windows shared printer service. As an alternative, Windows 10 has built-in support to send output to Unix-based printers using the LPR remote printing protocol. You can install a standard Windows printer whose output is directed to a Unix system and can use this printer just as you would any local or networked Windows printer.

➡ *For instruction on connecting to an LPR-based printer from Windows, **see** "Using Unix and LPR Printers," p. 458.*

Printing to Windows Printers from Unix

You can install software on Windows 10 to let Unix users print to any local printers shared by Windows. This is the receiving end of the LPR protocol, and it's called Line Printer Daemon (LPD) Print Service.

To install this service on a Windows host, sign in as a Computer Administrator and follow these steps:

1. In the taskbar's search box, type **features** and then select Turn Windows Features On or Off. (Alternatively, press Windows Logo+R, and then type **optionalfeatures** and press Enter.)

2. Scroll through the list of features and open Print and Document Services.

3. Check LPD Print Service, and then click OK.

Carriage Returns and Line Feeds Are Mangled

Say you send plain-text files from Unix machines to Windows printers using lpr and Print Services for Unix, and you find that carriage returns and line feeds are mangled (for example, line feeds are inserted where just carriage returns were present in text that should have been overprinted). In this case, you must disable the translation of both newlines and carriage returns, or just carriage returns, by adding a value to the Registry. Follow these steps:

1. Find the key HKEY_LOCAL_MACHINE\System\CurrentControlSet\Control\Print\ Printers*printername*\PrinterDriverData, where *printername* is the name of the shared printer the Unix user is using.

2. Select the key PrinterDriverData and choose Edit, New, DWORD Value. Enter the name **Winprint_TextNoTranslation** and set the value to **1**.

3. To prevent the server from replacing CR with CR+LF but still have it replace LF with CR+LF, add the DWORD value Winprint_TextNoCRTranslation with the value 1.

4. After making either of these additions, go to Computer Management, view Services, right-click TCP/IP Print Server, and select Restart.

➡ *For instructions and warnings about using the Registry Editor, see "Using Regedit,"*
   p. 659.

Some Windows printer drivers do not correctly implement overprinted lines. You might find that these lines are now correctly stacked on top of each other, but only the text from the topmost line is visible. You might need to use the binary mode flag (-o l) in your lpr command and add a form feed to the end of your file.

If you later decide to undo the Registry change, you can remove the value item or set its value to 0 and then restart the LPD service.

Internetworking with Macintosh

The Apple Macintosh is arguably *the* computer of choice in the music, graphics arts, design, and publishing worlds. Although Macs used to live pretty much in a world apart, this is no longer true, and it's common now for both Macs and Windows computers to coexist on the same network.

Microsoft used to provide software to support file sharing for Macs, but it lost interest in providing this support. Fortunately, Apple stepped up and has provided Windows-compatible networking support as a standard part of OS X since OS X 10.7 (Lion). You can also add Windows networking support to older Mac OS computers. We cover these options in the next several sections. First, though, let's talk about other issues that come up when Windows and Macs need to work together.

Compatibility Issues

If you share files between Macs and Windows computers on your network, you need to be aware of some compatibility issues.

Resource Data Issues

The first issue arises because a Mac file can consist of multiple, independent parts: the file's data itself and, optionally, additional data sets called Extended Attributes that contain additional information about the contents of the file. OS X manages the separate streams of data within one file. The parts can be read from and written to completely independently.

Mac OS versions before OS X called these separate data sets *forks*, and each file had two or three:

- The data fork, which contains data, document text, program code, and so on

- The resource fork, which in applications contains language-specific strings and dialog box layouts for programs, and in documents contains the association information that links a document to the application that created it

- Finder info, which for newer applications contains the link to the application that should be used to open the file, the file icon's position, and so on

For compatibility purposes, OS X still supports applications that expect data and resource forks. Resource fork data and finder info are stored as Extended Attribute streams.

The Windows NTFS file format system (used on the C: drive for all Windows installations) also supports the concept of separate data streams within a file, but, unfortunately, the Windows SMB network file sharing system doesn't. There's no way to communicate the separate streams when a file is copied over the network. So, when files are copied over a LAN from a Mac to a Windows (or other SMB-based) shared folder, the Mac stores the Extended Attribute data in a separate, hidden file. For example, if the Mac file is named `special.doc`, the Extended Attribute data is put in the same folder in a file named `._special.doc`. (It's invisible on Windows unless you enable the display of hidden files in File Explorer.) If a Mac opens or copies `special.doc` from a SMB shared folder, it recombines the data from both files.

The problem is that if you move, edit, or rename the main document or application file in Windows, the attributes file might be left behind or end up with the wrong name. Then, on the Mac side, the Mac will no longer know what application to use to open the document—and in the case of an application program, the application might not run. Therefore, it's best not to store Mac applications or documents on Windows shares if they might be renamed or moved.

Mac Files Have Lost Application Associations

After a Windows user edits a shared file and a Mac user tries to open the file, the Mac Finder might say it can't find the application required to open the document. What happened is that the file's Extended Attribute or resource fork was lost when a Windows user edited the file in

Windows, so the file's Type and Creator codes are missing. The Mac user should drag and drop the file onto the application's icon or manually locate the application and then resave the file. This will restore the association for future edits.

The Type and Creator codes can also be set using a Mac resource editor. However, resource editing is tricky and best not done unless it's an emergency.

Type and Creator codes are case sensitive. MSWD is not the same as mswd. Case can often cause confusion if you must restore the codes after they were stripped on a trip through Windows or DOS.

Filename Compatibility Issues

Mac filenames can have up to 255 characters and can contain any character except the colon (:), which is considered a reserved character.

Windows permits filenames up to 256 characters in length but has a longer list of reserved characters: the colon (:), backslash (\), forward slash (/), question mark (?), asterisk (*), quotation mark ("), greater-than symbol (>), less-than symbol (<), and pipe symbol (|). Therefore, for files that will be shared, it's best to avoid all of these characters when you name files on your Mac.

Working with Windows Resources from Mac OS X

Mac OS X comes with Windows-compatible networking support built in. This means that Macs running OS X can connect directly to drives and folders shared by Windows computers. You don't even need to use the command line; the Mac GUI can connect to folders shared by Windows computers as easily as those shared by Macs.

Using Windows Shared Files on the Mac

On OS X 10.5 and later editions, you can easily browse folders shared by Windows computers—or network file storage devices that use Windows file-sharing protocols—from any Finder window. In the left pane, under Shared, you can select a Windows computer or file-sharing device from the list of detected computers and then browse into its shared folders, as shown in Figure 20.1.

 note

This section shows you how to use Windows shared files from your Mac and how to share files from your Mac for use by Windows. To see how to set up file sharing on Windows, see Chapter 21, "Using a Windows Network."

When you select a remote computer, OS X attempts to connect to the computer using your Mac account's username and password so that it can display a list of available shared folders. If this fails, you can use a different account by clicking the Connect As button that appears in the upper-right corner of the Finder window. We discuss accounts in the next section, "Selecting a Windows Account."

If you are using OS X 10.4 or earlier, or if the Windows computer does not appear in the list of local computers that the Finder displays under Shared, there is an alternative way to connect. Select the Finder and choose Go, Connect to Server. The dialog box shown in Figure 20.2 appears.

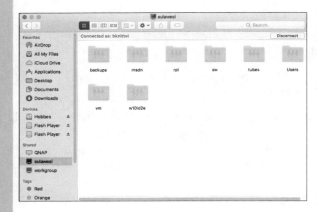

Figure 20.1
The Finder in OS X 10.5 and later lets you easily select and connect to both Mac and Windows computers.

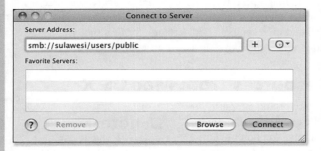

Figure 20.2
The Connect to Server dialog box lets a Mac OS X computer connect directly to a folder shared by Windows. Enter **smb:** followed by the share's UNC path, or click Browse.

 tip

If you cannot make the connection work even though you know that the remote computer or storage device is working, try changing the server address field so that it starts with cifs:// instead of smb://. This tells the Mac to use the older SMB1 network protocol instead of the default SMB2 protocol. Some network storage devices have problems with Apple's implementation of SMB2. This won't be necessary when connecting to a Windows 10 shared folder, and in fact, Windows 10 has SMB1 turned off by default because it has security and performance problems.

You can enter the UNC name of the shared folder directly, in the format smb://*computername*/ *sharename*, where *computername* is the name of the Windows computer or its IP address, and *sharename* is the name of the shared folder. For example, the Public folder on a computer named sulawesi could be entered as smb://sulawesi/users/public, or using the computer's IP address, as something like smb://192.168.0.12/users/public. Click Connect to proceed.

You can click the + button to add the path to the Favorites list. You also can click the Browse button to select from a list of detected Mac and Windows computers.

Selecting a Windows Account

Whichever connection method you use, when you connect, a login dialog box might appear. If you're connecting to a Windows 10 computer on a home or small office network, the following applies:

- If Password Protected Sharing is enabled, or to access files that are shared only to specified user accounts, choose Connect As Registered User. Enter a username and password that is valid on the Windows computer. (On a home or small office workgroup network, you can ignore the Workgroup or Domain entry, if it appears. Fill in just the Name and Password entries.) You will connect with the file and folder access rights associated with this account.

- If you have disabled Password Protected Sharing, select Connect As Guest; alternatively, enter the username Guest with no password. (Actually, you can enter any invalid username, with any password.) This gives you the file and folder access rights granted to Everyone.

In most cases, using Guest access means that you will have access only to the shared folder \Users\Public, but no other shared folders, unless the person who shared the other folders explicitly granted rights to Everyone. You likely won't even be able to view the list of users folders inside \Users so that you can get to the Public folder. If you can't view the contents of the Users folder, use the Finder's Go, Connect To Server menu item to directly connect to folder smb://*computername* /Users/Public, as shown in Figure 20.2.

 note

If you are using a Microsoft (online) account on your Windows 10 PC, the username you need to supply to it for file sharing is not the email address you use when you sign in. To find the real name of your Windows computer account, press Windows Logo+X and select Command Prompt or Windows PowerShell, whichever appears in the pop-up menu. In the window that opens, you will see something like this: c:\users\ brian_000>. The word after users is your account name. (In this example, it's brian_000.) Use this name when you try to connect from your Mac to a shared Windows folder.

If you are connecting to a Windows computer on a Windows domain network, enter a valid domain username and password. When the Mac has made the network connection, the shared folder is displayed in a Finder window like any other folder.

To disconnect from the network share on OS X 10.5 or later, click the Eject button next to the computer's name under Shared in the Finder window. On OS X 10.4, drag the shared folder desktop icon to the trash or locate it in the Finder and click the Eject button.

Now recall the point we made earlier about Mac files having multiple parts, or forks. If you copy a file from a Mac to a shared Windows folder, Windows might create an extra hidden file to contain the Extended Attribute information for the file.

 note

When a Mac user opens a Window share, the Finder creates a file named .DS_ Store and sometimes also one named ._.DS_Store. These hold Mac desktop information. Windows users should ignore these files, just as Mac users should ignore the file desktop.ini.

The attribute file's name will consist of a period and an underscore followed by the name of the main file. Windows users must move and rename these files together; otherwise, Mac users will receive errors when they try to access the files.

Using Windows Printers on the Mac

If you are using a Mac, to use a printer that is shared by a Windows computer, follow these steps:

1. On the Windows computer, when you share the printer, be sure to use a share name that's no more than 12 letters long. If you use a longer name, the printer might not appear in the list of printers on the Mac.

2. On the Mac, open System Preferences and select Printers & Scanners (or, on earlier versions of OS-X, Printers & Fax).

3. If the page is locked, click the lock icon and enter an administrator's credentials. Click the + button to add a printer. On OS X 10.4, at the bottom of the Printer Browser dialog box, click More Printers.

4. At the top of the next Printer Browser dialog box, select Windows (on OS X 10.5 and later) or Windows Printing (on OS X 10.4), and underneath, select the appropriate Windows workgroup name. In the computer list, choose the name of the computer that is sharing the printer you want to use.

> **note**
>
> In our testing we found that there could be delays of up to a couple of minutes between printing a document from the Mac and having the Windows printer start up.

5. In the Connect To dialog box, you might be prompted to enter a username and password that is valid on the Windows computer. (See the preceding section, "Selecting a Windows Account.") If you turned off Password Protected Sharing on the Windows computer, you can select Connect As: Guest (or enter username Guest with no password).

6. Select the desired shared printer in the list. Open the Print Using list (on OS X 10.5 and later) or the Printer Model list (on OS X 10.4), and then select the correct printer manufacturer name and model. Finally, click Add.

This procedure adds the Windows printer to the list of available printers on your Mac.

Using Mac Shared Files on Windows

Mac OS X computers can share folders with Windows computers over the network, thanks to the Windows-compatible software that is installed as part of OS X.

To enable Windows-compatible file sharing on OS X 10.5 (Leopard) or later, follow these steps:

1. Open System Preferences and select Sharing. If the panel is locked, click the lock icon and enter an administrative password.

2. If File Sharing is not checked, check it. Select folders to share, and for each selected folder, choose the user accounts that can access the share. This much is standard for file sharing on the Macs. The next step lets you use these same folders from Windows computers.

tip

To save yourself a world of pain, create user accounts on your Mac and Windows computers using the same account names (short names, in Mac parlance) and passwords on both types of computers. From the Windows side, you cannot use or even see a list of the folders or printers shared by the Mac unless you are using a Windows account that matches up with one on the Mac and that has been enabled on the Sharing page. If you want to use Microsoft (online) accounts on Windows 10, create local Windows accounts first, using the same account names as you use on your Macs, and then turn those Windows accounts into Microsoft accounts. We discuss this in Chapter 3, "Your First Hour with Windows 10," in the section "Setting Up User Accounts."

3. Click Options, and then check Share Files and Folders Using SMB (Windows), as shown in Figure 20.3.

Figure 20.3
Enable Windows-compatible file sharing from the Options button on the System Preferences Sharing page.

4. If your version of OS X includes the section titled Windows File Sharing, check the names of the Mac accounts whose shared files will be accessed from PCs. You will need to reenter the passwords for these accounts so that the Mac can store the passwords in a way that lets the Mac authenticate the users when they connect from a Windows device. (Remember that this list shows the users' full names. When you connect remotely, you must use the users' account names.)

To enable Windows-compatible file sharing on OS X 10.4 (Tiger), follow these steps:

1. Open System Preferences and select Sharing. Check Windows Sharing.

2. Click the Accounts button and check the names of the accounts that you want to permit to be used for Windows Sharing connections.

3. Click Show All and select Accounts.

On Windows, you can use Mac shared folders just as you use folders shared from any Windows computer. Macs appear in the list of available computers in the Network folder, and you can open the shared folders from those icons.

You can also specify a Mac shared folder directly by using its UNC pathname. By default, OS X 10.5 shares users' Public folders, with share names based on each user's full name. For example, the path to my Public folder might be \\computername\brian knittel's public folder. OS X 10.4 shares users' entire home directories by default, using each user's short name. Therefore, on OS 10.4, my home directory's UNC path might be \\computername\bknittel.

note

When you open the Network folder icon for a Mac running OS X 10.4 or use the net view command to view the items shared by a Mac running OS X 10.4, you will see only shared folders and printers that you have permission to use.

Using Mac Shared Printers on Windows

After enabling Windows Sharing in System Preferences, you can share your Mac's printer(s) with Windows users. On newer version of OS X, check Printer Sharing in the list at the left side of the Sharing panel, and then check all of the printers that you want to share with others. On older versions of OS X, select Show All in the Settings panel, click Print & Fax, view the Sharing tab, click Share These Printers with Other Computers, and then check all the printers that you want to make available to others.

Then follow these steps on the Mac:

1. Set up accounts on both the Mac and on Windows, using the same account name and the same password on both computers. Be sure to read the preceding tip that starts with, "To save yourself a world of pain."

2. On the Mac, enable SMB File Sharing on the Mac as described in the preceding section, "Using Mac Shared Files on Windows." Be sure to enable Windows File Sharing for the accounts that you will want to use for printing. Then enable Printer Sharing on the System Preferences Sharing page. Select the printer that you want to use from Windows.

You must now trick Windows into using a PostScript printer driver, no matter what type of printer the Mac is really sharing. The Mac accepts only PostScript printer codes and converts the PostScript to the appropriate codes for its installed printer.

To connect to the shared Mac printer from Windows, follow these steps:

1. Click Start, Settings (gear icon), Devices, Printers & Scanners, Add A Printer Or Scanner. If the Mac's shared printer doesn't appear within 30 seconds, click The Printer That I Want Isn't Listed. Then select Add a Bluetooth, Wireless or Network Discoverable Printer, and click Next.

2. Wait for the desired Mac printer to appear in the list. If it appears, double-click it and go on to step 3.

If requirements 1 and 2 from the previous list aren't met, the printer won't appear. It also won't appear if the Mac is on a different subnet than the Windows computer. In this case, click Cancel. Repeat the process but this time select Select a Shared Printer by Name, and then enter the printer share name as *ipaddress**sharename*, where *ipaddress* is the IP address of the Mac and *sharename* is the name of the Mac printer. On a business network, you might be able to type the Mac's hostname rather than its IP address.

If you followed the previous steps and the printer still does not appear, skip ahead to step 5.

3. When the message "The server for the printer does not have the correct printer driver installed" appears, click OK.

4. In the Manufacturer list, select HP. In the Printers list, if the Mac printer is a color printer, select HP Color LaserJet 2800 Series PS. If the Mac printer is a black-and-white printer, select HP LaserJet 2300 Series PS. Then click OK. Skip ahead to step 6.

5. You might find that the shared printer does not appear in step 2. This could be due to compatibility issues with the OS X printer sharing software. If this happens, cancel out and close the Settings panel. With your web browser, visit support.apple.com and search for **download bonjour windows**. (*Don't* search for or download this software from any site other than support.apple.com!) Follow the link "Download Bonjour Print Services for Windows v2.0.2" or a higher version. Download and install the software. Double-click the Bonjour Printer Wizard that it puts on your desktop. This should let you locate and set up the Mac printer. When you're asked to choose a manufacturer and driver, pick a brand and model close to the printer's actual model but definitely choose a Postscript (sometimes labeled PS) driver.

6. Open the Windows Settings panel if it's not open already (Windows Logo + I), and select Devices, Printers & Scanners. Click the icon for the Mac printer and select Manage, Print a Test Page. If all went well, the printer will print a Windows printer test page. It may take a couple of minutes for the printout to appear.

Installing Optional Network Components

Windows 10 comes with some networking features or services that are not used in most networks but can be essential in others. We don't cover these features in great detail because your network manager will probably install them for you if they're used on your LAN.

Table 20.2 describes the optional features. Not every component is available on every version of Windows 10. To enable any of the components, type the word **features** into the taskbar's search box. Then select Turn Windows Features On or Off from the results. Alternatively, press Windows Logo+R, type **optionalfeatures**, and then press Enter.

Check the box next to each desired feature, and then click OK.

Table 20.2   Windows 10 Optional Networking Features

Category/Component	Description
Web and Application Services	
Windows Communication Foundation HTTP Activation	The HTTP Activation system can be used by .NET application software to run services on demand. This component is enabled by the application program(s) as needed. (This selection is located under Microsoft .NET Framework 3.5 as well as under .NET Framework 4.5 Advanced Services, WCF Services.)
Microsoft Message Queue (MSMQ) Server	MSMQ Server is a tool used primarily in distributed database applications. It is provided primarily for use by software developers who are writing and testing such applications.
Work Folders Client	This tool syncs files between your Windows computer and a shared file repository on managed network servers. The result is a sort of private, corporate version of OneDrive.
Management and Monitoring Tools	
Data Center Bridging	Enables management of special Ethernet adapters used in certain large-scale network environments.
MultiPoint Connector	This tool lets Windows workstations and devices be managed by MultiPoint Server in, for example, classroom settings.
Simple Network Management Protocol (SNMP)	SNMP is a remote monitoring and measurement tool used by some network management systems.
WMI SNMP Provider	This service enables Windows Management Instrumentation (WMI) applications to access SNMP data.
Telnet Client	This application enables you to connect computers and network devices using a command-line interface. It has significant network security risks and should not be enabled unless required by a network administrator.
TFTP Client	This tool can be used to retrieve files from a TFTP server. It is used primarily to test network boot servers or to retrieve network device firmware.
Networking Services	
Active Directory Lightweight Directory Services	This service provides Lightweight Directory Access Protocol (LDAP) support, letting custom applications search Active Directory on a domain network.
Services for NFS	This service lets Windows 10 mount (use) network shared folders using the Network File System (NFS) protocol, commonly used with Unix servers. Available on Windows 10 Pro, Enterprise, and Education.
SMB 1.0/CIFS File Sharing Support	This service provides support for this older version of the Windows file-sharing network protocols. It's installed by default but may be removed on corporate networks for security reasons. Modern versions of Windows and Mac OS X use SMB2 by default.

Table 20.2 Continued

Category/Component	Description
SMB Direct	This service provides support for very high-speed network adapters capable of Remote Direct Memory Access (RDMA) operation.
Internet Printing Client	This client provides support for network- or Internet-hosted printers or printing services using the Internet Printing Protocol (IPP).
LPD Print Service	This service lets Unix computers send print output to your Windows computer's shared printers.
LPR Port Monitor	This tool enables you to send print output to network-connected printers or Unix servers. (IPC, LPD, and LPR are found in the Print and Document Services list.)
RAS Connection Manager Administration Kit (CMAK)	This tool enables network managers to create predefined dial-up and VPN network connections for enterprise users.
RIP Listener	This service is used to listen for network routing information in large networks. Don't install it unless it's required by your network administrator.
Simple TCPIP Services	This suite of services performs simple functions for testing purposes, such as echoing data to a remote computer and generating a stream of data. Don't install these services unless you're instructed to do so by a network administrator. Hackers can use them to tie up your network with pointless traffic.

The Reliable Multicast Protocol is installed using a different procedure from that used to install the other services listed in Table 20.2. If required, it can be installed for a specific network adapter using these steps:

1. Click the Network icon in the taskbar, select Network & Internet Settings, and if only a column of network categories appears, select Status. Then click Change Adapter Options.

2. Right-click a network adapter and select Properties.

3. Click Install. Select Protocol, and then click Add.

4. Select Reliable Multicast Protocol and click OK.

Using the Hosts File

If you have an office LAN, especially one with mixed and matched computers, you probably, like me, have a chart of computer names and IP addresses posted on your wall—not just computers, but routers, firewalls, monitored devices, and all manner of devices. (Who knows? Your next espresso machine might have an Ethernet port on it.)

On a corporate or enterprise LAN, the LAN administrators enter each device into the organization's domain name service (DNS) so that you can type a command such as ping firewall instead of needing to type ping firewall.mycompany.com or, worse, something like ping 192.168.56.102.

On a home or small office LAN, though, you probably don't have your own domain name server. The hosts file is the answer to this annoying situation. You can add entries to the file \windows\system32\drivers\etc\hosts to associate names with IP addresses for devices that have fixed (static) IP addresses. The Windows domain name lookup software looks first in the hosts file before consulting the network, so you can add entries for your own workgroup's computers and devices, as long as they have fixed addresses, regardless of OS.

(You can't use the hosts file for devices that have dynamic addresses assigned by DHCP. Windows, though, can usually figure out the names of other Windows computers, even if they have static addresses.)

The format is simple, but editing it is a bit tricky because it's a protected file. The hosts file has become a target for adware hackers, who put fake entries in it to hijack your web browser.

To edit it, press Windows Logo+X, select Command Prompt (Admin) or Windows PowerShell (Admin), whichever appears in the pop-up menu, and confirm the User Account Control prompt. Then, when the Command Prompt window opens, type **notepad \windows\system32\drivers\ etc\hosts** and press Enter.

At the top of the file, there are a bunch of comment lines starting with #. You can leave them there. At the bottom, add lines to the file, listing IP addresses at the left margin, followed by some whitespace (tabs or spaces), followed by one or more names. You can enter simple names or full domain names. Simple names are assumed to belong to your own domain.

The lines below the comments in my hosts file look like this:

```
192.168.0.1  router
192.168.0.45  macmini
```

I added an entry to give a name to my network's wireless router. I can now configure the router by typing **//router** into my web browser instead of typing a bunch of numbers.

Then I added an entry for my Mac computer, macmini. This way, I can view its web server's home page from a web browser using http://macmini instead of needing to remember its IP address.

This file also serves as a sort of documentation of my network because it records important IP addresses. One thing you must watch out for, though, is that Windows checks this file before using the real DNS system to look up names. If you put a name in your LAN's (or the Internet's) DNS system and the computer's IP address later changes, your hosts file will be incorrect. It's best to use this file only for machines that are in nobody's DNS system.

USING A WINDOWS NETWORK

Windows Was Made to Network

Most homes and offices have more than one computer, and you'll quickly find that as days go by, you end up using most or all of them. You'll download a file, and a few days later, when you want to use that file...where is it? You hardly need to ask: If you're searching for the file on the computer you're using now, 9 times out of 10 it will turn out to be on some other computer. This is not just a fact of life, it's a law of nature. But with a network, you can easily access any file and any printer, on any computer, from your own, thus short-circuiting the law—for a while at least. A network also lets everyone in your home or office share printers and an Internet connection, thus saving you time and money.

In traditional desktop apps at least, using files and printers on the network is the same as using files and printers on your own hard drive. The "look and feel" are identical. The only new tasks you have to learn are how to find resources shared by others and how to make your own computer's resources available to others on the network. In Modern-style apps, you can easily print to networked printers. For files and folders, you might be stuck using local hard disk folders unless the app enables you to browse through arbitrary folders. It depends on how the app was written.

By the way, we use the word *resource* frequently in this chapter. When we say *resource*, we mean a shared folder or printer on someone else's computer, which you can access through the LAN or the Internet. The *American Heritage Dictionary* defines a resource as "an available supply that can be drawn upon when needed." That's actually a perfect description of a network resource: It's there for you to use—provided that you can find it and that you have permission.

Another word that's frequently used is *share*. You might say that you are sharing a printer or folder on your computer with the network, which means you're making it available to other users on other computers. It's also fairly common to use the word *share* as a noun, as in "I saved the document in the network share," meaning, a shared folder somewhere on the network.

Windows networks work pretty much the same way whether they're in your home, in a small office, or in a large corporate setting. "Domain" networks managed by computers running Windows Server software, though, might have some additional features. The following are some notable differences you might see on a domain network:

- The network administrator can set up *roaming profiles* so that your settings, preferences, Documents folder, and so on are centrally stored on the network and are available to you on any computer on your LAN or even at other network sites.

- Active Directory (AD) gives you added search functions to find users and printers on your network. These search functions appear as added icons and menu choices that only AD network computers have.

- The network administrator might use *policy* functions to limit your access to applications, Windows features, and settings. If you are on a domain network and can't find an option mentioned in this chapter, ask your network manager if its use has been restricted.

If you are using a home or small office workgroup network, don't feel left out. Because a workgroup typically has fewer than ten computers, the searching and management functions provided by AD simply aren't necessary.

 note

It's true that cloud services like OneDrive, Google Drive, and Dropbox can also help you access any of your content from any computer you use, but file sharing on your own network can be simpler to set up, doesn't cost any more regardless of how much you store, and can be more secure: If someone gets your password or hacks into one of these cloud services, that person has all of your data, and you might never even know it.

Using Shared Folders in Windows 10

Windows lets you share folders and their contents with other network users. Users within your network can see the folders and, if permission settings allow it, access the files in them just as they would any file on their own hard drives. In the following sections, we show you how to use files and folders shared by other users. Later in the chapter, you learn how to share folders on your own computer.

Browsing Through a Homegroup

Start by clicking the taskbar's File Explorer icon to open File Explorer. If your computer is a member of a homegroup, on the left side of the File Explorer window, you'll see the title "Homegroup." Under this are entries for each user's account, on each of the homegroup computers. Anyone who has elected to share materials with the homegroup—and whose computer is turned on—will be listed here.

➡ *If you can't or don't want to use a homegroup, skip ahead to "Browsing a Network's Computers," p. 447.*

➡ *To see how to set up a homegroup for your Windows 10, 8.1, 8, and 7 computers, see "Setting Up a Homegroup," p. 396.*

The Homegroup list includes accounts for any additional users on your own computer, as well as the users on other computers.

You can open these entries to see what files and folders are being shared, as shown in Figure 21.1. It doesn't matter whether the other users' materials are stored in another account on your computer or are on another computer on your network; it works the same way regardless. You can see only materials that users elected to share.

Figure 21.1
If your computer is a member of a homegroup, you can view the materials shared by other members of your group in File Explorer.

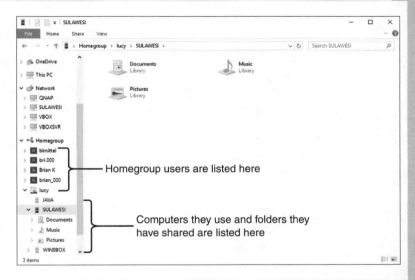

If the other users gave the homegroup permission to make changes to the folder, you'll be able to edit, delete, and rename files and add new files. Otherwise, you'll just be able to view, read, print, and play the files. If you want to make changes in this case, just drag a copy from another user's folder into one of your own folders or onto your desktop.

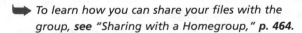 *To learn how you can share your files with the group,* see "Sharing with a Homegroup," p. 464.

Regardless of whether you have a homegroup set up, you can browse through files and folders shared by any networked computer using the Network list, as described next.

Browsing a Network's Computers

In any File Explorer window (for example, in the This PC or Documents window), the left pane contains an item titled Network. If you open this item, you'll see icons for every active

> ## note
> Computers whose workgroup or domain name is different from yours might take longer to appear, but all computers on your computer's same physical network subnet should eventually show up. On a large network, such as you'd find in a large business setting, computers on other subnets and those separated by firewalls and routers will not appear. You can still use their resources by typing their share names directly in UNC format, as described later in the section "Network Power User Topics."

computer on your network. (On an enterprise network, where there may be multiple locations or groups of networked computers, you will see only computers on your local network.) You'll see a screen like the one shown in Figure 21.2.

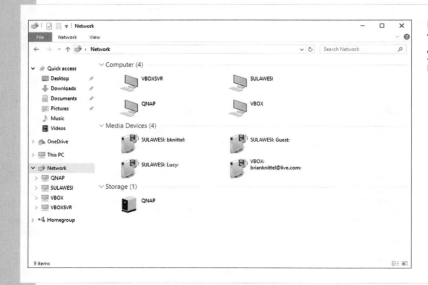

Figure 21.2
The Network display lets you browse through your network's resources.

The Network window shows computers with shared folders, shared Media Center libraries, and network hardware. You can browse into any of the folder icons to locate shared files and folders you want to use.

tip

Digging down to the network can take time and effort, so if you use a particular shared file or folder frequently, use one of these methods to retain quick access to it:

- **Create a shortcut**—Hold down the Alt key while you drag the file or folder into your desktop. You can leave the shortcut there or move it to some other convenient location.

- **Create a bookmark**—Browse to locate a computer or folder. In the File Explorer window's left or right pane, right-click the computer or folder and select Pin to Quick Access; alternatively, select it, and in the Home ribbon, select Pin to Quick Access.

- **Create a Start menu tile**—Right-click a computer, folder, or application icon and select Pin to Start.

When you browse into other Windows 10, 8.1, 8, 7, and Vista computers, you will notice that the entire \users folder structure is shared, with the name Users. This folder contains everyone's user profiles and documents, and it is shared by default. What preserves everyone's privacy and security is that each user must give other users (or other groups, or everyone) permission to read a folder or file in order for them to even see that it exists. This scheme makes it much simpler to control which items you share, simply by changing the security settings on the files and folders themselves. We address this issue more later in the section "Sharing Resources."

 note

Remember, for all folders shared by Windows 10, 8.1, 8, 7, Vista, and Windows Server 2008 and later, to even see that a folder or file exists inside a shared folder, you must have permission to read the file or view the folder's contents. In folders shared by other operating systems, you might be able to see the names of files and folders that you don't have permission to open.

On Windows 10, 8.1, 8, and 7 computers, the Public folder is shared "in place," meaning it's found inside the shared Users folder and is not shared separately under its own name, as it was on Windows Vista and XP. The Public Folder Sharing option in the Advanced Sharing Settings page controls whether remote users can have access to the Public folder.

In contrast, when you browse into Windows Vista and XP computers, the Public user profile is shared separately, under the name Public or Shared Documents. On Windows XP, shared user profiles are shared individually as separate shares.

Viewing a Computer or Shared Folder Directly Using Its UNC Path

If you know the Universal Naming Convention (UNC) pathname of a shared folder on a specific computer, you can instantly view its files by typing the UNC path into the Address box at the top of any File Explorer window. You can type a path that includes just a computer name, a computer name followed by a folder's share name, or a longer path that specifies subfolders or a file within the shared folder.

 tip

If you're using Windows 10 Pro or Enterprise edition, you can make someone else's shared folder's contents available to you even when your computer is disconnected from the network. For instructions, see "Offline Files" on page **839**.

For example, suppose you want to see the folders shared by a computer named "laptop." Open a File Explorer window from the taskbar or by right-clicking the Start button and selecting File Explorer. Click in the Address box, and the "breadcrumb" path will disappear. Then type **laptop** and press Enter. This displays all of the laptop's shared folders, without your having to browse your way there. Likewise, you can see the files shared by a user whose account is named "lucy" on that computer using **laptop\users\lucy**.

We talk more about UNC pathnames later in the chapter, in the section "Understanding the Universal Naming Convention."

Searching the Network

If you'd like to find a particular file but don't know where it is, browsing through the network isn't a particularly easy way to find it. However, you can quickly locate shared folders and files by name and by content using the Search box in the upper right of any File Explorer window.

To begin a search, open any File Explorer window (say, from the taskbar or by right-clicking the Start button and selecting File Explorer). Then follow the instructions in the following sections to find files, computers, or printers.

Searching for Files or Folders

You can search a particular network computer for files and folders, by name and by content, using these steps:

1. Open a File Explorer window and select Network in the left pane.

2. Expand the Network list and click the name of a computer.

   Alternatively, you can just type the computer's UNC name into File Explorer's Address window, for example, \\laptop.

3. Click in the search box in the window's upper-right and type all or part of the desired filename, or a word or phrase to be found in the file.

This search will locate files and folders within the contents of all shared folders on that computer, but only those that you have permission to view. Searching across the network can take quite awhile. If you have an idea where the desired file might be, you can speed things up considerably if you dig down into one or more levels of folders inside the network computer's icon before you start the search.

➡ *To learn more about searching for files,* **see** *"Searching Your PC," p. 172.*

To search all the shared folders and libraries in a homegroup, the steps are similar:

1. Open a File Explorer window and select Homegroup in the left pane.

2. Type all or part of the desired filename—or a word or phrase to be found in the file—in the Search box in the upper right.

This procedure searches all of the libraries you and others have shared, on all computers that are turned on and connected to the network.

On an Active Directory network, the domain administrator can choose to list, or *publish*, some shared folders in the directory; these folders might contain important resources that the company wants to make widely accessible and easy to find. See "Searching Active Directory," later in the chapter, for more information. If you are trying to find a particular shared folder, but it has not been explicitly published in the directory, you're out of luck; there's no other way to find it besides browsing through the network's computers or searching specific computers as described earlier in this section.

Searching for Computers

To search for a computer by name, select the word *Network* in the File Explorer window's left pane and type all or part of a computer name in the Search box. Windows will display an icon for each matching computer.

You can explore any of the listed computers to view its shared folders or printers; if you delve into the shared folders, you can open or copy the available files as you find them.

Searching for Printers

Searching for printers is possible only on an Active Directory network. In a large corporation's network, hundreds or thousands of network printers might be scattered over a large area. Find Printers lets an AD network user find just the right type of printer using a powerful query form. This feature is handy if you're a business traveler using the network in an unfamiliar office, or if you're in such a large office setting that you aren't familiar with all the printing resources on your network.

 tip

On an Active Directory network, view the entire directory the first time you use Find Printers. This will give you an idea of how location and printer names are organized in your company. If too many names are listed, you can click Clear All to clear the search listing and then restrict your search using a location name that makes sense for your network. For example, if your company has put floor and room numbers such as "10-123" in the Location column, you could restrict your search to printers on the tenth floor by searching for "10-" in Location.

To search AD for a printer, open File Explorer and select Network in the left pane. In the ribbon, click Search Active Directory and select Printers from the Find drop-down list. You can leave the scope set to Entire Directory, or you can select a subdomain next to the word *In*.

You can search for printers in three ways: by name and location, by printer capabilities, or by more advanced attributes. To find all the printers in the directory, leave the form blank, as shown in Figure 21.3, and click Find Now. To search for printers with capabilities such as double-sized printing or color, select the Features tab, select the desired features, and then click Find Now. See the accompanying tip to see how to find just the printers in your location.

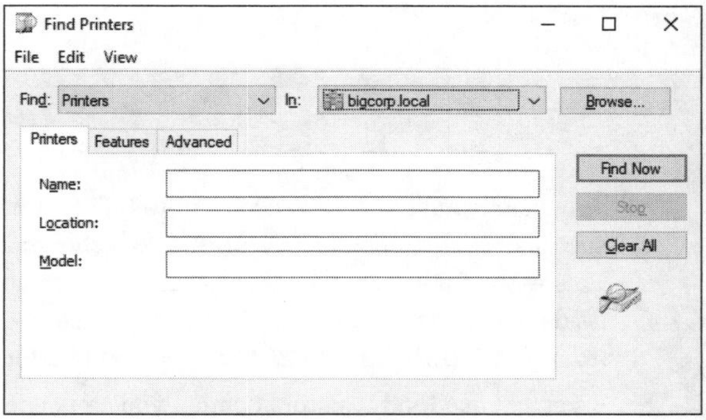

Figure 21.3
You can search Active Directory for a printer based on location or capabilities (features) that you require.

Searching Active Directory

On an enterprise domain-type network, Active Directory contains information on many more objects than just users, computers, and printers. It includes shared folders, organizational units, policy settings, certificate templates, containers (business groupings), foreign security principals, remote storage services, RPC services (used for advanced client/server software applications), and trusted domains. It can also contain information for other objects defined by your own organization. Most of this information is used only by domain administrators to configure Windows networks over vast distances; however, you can search for anything and can specify your qualifications based on more than 100 different criteria.

To make an AD search, select Network in the left pane of File Explorer and select Search Active Directory in the Ribbon. The AD search tool appears, as shown in Figure 21.4. To start, select one of several search categories in the Find drop-down list. You can use a quick form-based search for any of the most useful objects.

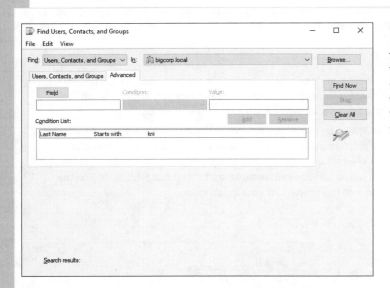

Figure 21.4
Using the Active Directory search tool, you can use a simplified form for any of several categories of directory objects, or you can use the Advanced tab to construct queries using any of the available fields.

You can also use the Advanced tab to build specific queries such as "Last Name Starts with *Kni*," as shown in Figure 21.4. This is the full-blown search system, and here you have 53 fields to choose from when searching for users—everything from *A* to *Z* (*Assistant* to *ZIP Code*) if you need it.

If you choose Find: Custom Search, you can choose from the whole gamut of fields in the entire catalog of AD objects,

 note
For a brief introduction to LDAP queries, you might visit https://technet.microsoft.com and search for "LDAP Query Basics."

and in the Advanced tab, you can enter Lightweight Directory Access Protocol (LDAP) queries directly for submission to the AD service. This is the native query syntax for Active Directory, and it's available here mostly for system debugging.

note

In the following discussion, we refer to "files," but the issues are the same for both the files and the folders inside any shared folder.

Security and File Sharing

Windows 10, 8.1, 8, and 7 computers let network users see only the files and folders that they actually have permission to use, based in most cases on their username and password. It's worth explaining just how that permission is determined. The topic is not that difficult, but it's complicated by the fact that permissions are calculated by Windows networking in several different ways, depending on settings and the versions of Windows you encounter.

Two levels of security are involved when Windows grants a user access to a file over a network:

- Permission settings on the file itself, which would apply if the user logged on at the computer directly.

- Network permissions, which act as additional *restrictions* when a file is accessed over the network but don't grant any additional *permissions* that a user wouldn't have if she tried to access the file while logged in directly to the computer. We explain why this is done shortly. Let's look at file permissions first.

File Permissions and Networking

File permissions determine who can read, modify, write to, or delete a file or folder based on their user account. Files and folders stored on a disk formatted with the NTFS file system (which is always used on the disk that contains Windows 7, 8, 8.1, or 10) can have these permission settings applied on a user-by-user basis as well as by membership in groups such as Administrators and even Everyone. When you log on to a computer, these settings determine which files you can look at and which you can change.

➡ *For more information about file permissions,* **see** *"Setting Security Permissions on Files and Folders," p. 732.*

When you access a file over a network, this permission system still applies. What can get confusing is, how does the remote computer determine who you are? The answer to that question depends on the versions of Windows you and it are running, and on several settings. Here are some scenarios you might encounter. Go down through the list to find the first scenario that describes your situation, and stop there. In the following discussion, "the remote computer" refers to a computer on the network that has a file you want to use, and you are using "your computer" to get to that file.

- If your computer and the remote computer are members of a domain network, and you're logged on using your domain account, your user account is recognized by all computers on the network. You'll get access to the file if its permission settings grant access to your account or to any groups to which you belong.

- If your computer and the remote computer are members of a homegroup, and if you left enabled the Advanced Sharing setting Allow Windows to Manage Homegroup Connections, as it is by default, your computer will connect to all other homegroup computers using the built-in user account HomeGroupUser$, which is a member of group HomeUsers. Whenever users share a library, folder, or file with their homegroup, Windows sets permissions on that library, folder, or file so that the HomeUsers group has Read or Read and Write access. In this way, all users in the homegroup get the same access rights to the shared resources. So, you'll get access if the remote folder was shared with the homegroup.

- If the remote computer runs Windows 10, 8.1, 8, 7, or Vista with Password Protected Sharing turned on, or XP Professional with Simple File Sharing disabled, or Windows Server in a domain that your computer is not a member of, the remote computer will check to see whether it has an account set up with the same name and password as the account you are using on your computer. If so, it will grant you access to files based on rights set for that account name. If the account name or password doesn't match, your computer will prompt you to enter an account name or password that *is* valid on the remote computer.

- If both your computer and the remote computer run Windows 10, 8.1, 8, or 7, and the remote computer has Password Protected Sharing turned off, a rule unique to these versions of Windows applies:

  If the remote computer has an account with the same name as your account, and that account has a password set, and your password is the same on both computers, you will be given access to a file based on privileges set for your account on the remote machine.

- If none of the preceding scenarios apply, the remote computer attempts to access the file using the Guest account. You'll be able to use only files that are readable or writable by Everyone or Guest.

Phew! We know this looks like a big mess, but it actually boils down to just two alternatives: A remote computer either will use a specific account to access files, in which case you can get to the files that this account can see; or it will use the Guest account, in which case you only can get to files that are marked as usable by Everyone or Guest.

Another point to remember is that files stored on removable media typically don't use the NTFS format and don't have any per-user permission settings. Flash media formatted with the FAT or ExFAT file systems are readable and writable by everyone, and CD/DVD-ROMs are readable by everyone who connects to the computer. Network permissions, described next, do apply.

Network Permissions

The preceding permission scheme applies equally to files accessed over the network and files accessed directly by logging in to a computer. When you share a folder or drive with the network, though, you can assign privileges, again based on user and group names, that act like a filter for the file permissions we just discussed. A network user gets only the privileges that are listed in *both* file permissions *and* network permissions. Figure 21.5 shows how this works.

Figure 21.5
You only get access rights that are given to you both through file permissions and through network permissions.

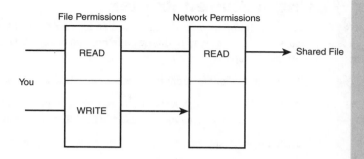

Another way to look at this is that a network user *loses* any permissions that are *omitted* from the network permission list. This scheme can be used in complex ways, but mostly only two situations are used:

- If you share a folder and set its network privilege list to give Read access but not Write access to Everyone, then users get Read access *if* their user account gives them permission, but *nobody* gets to modify its files over the network.

- If you set the network permissions so that Everyone has both Read and Write permissions, users get exactly what they'd get if they tried to use the file while logged on directly—no more, no less. Access will still be governed by the permissions set for each file and folder.

These are the two ways Windows sets up network permissions when you share folders using the techniques we describe later in the chapter.

Using Printers on the Network

Whether you're part of a large corporation or a small workgroup, or even if you're a home user with just two computers, network printing is a great time and money saver. Why connect a printer to each computer when it will spend most of its time idle? By not having to buy a printer for each user, you can spend the money you save more constructively on faster, higher-quality, and more interesting printers. For instance, you might add a color photo-quality printer to give your network users more output choices.

Later in the chapter, we describe how to share a printer attached to your computer; right now, let's look at using a printer that has already been shared elsewhere on the network.

Windows can directly attach to printers shared by any computer that supports Microsoft Networking services, which includes any version of Windows released since 1993, OS/2, Mac OS X, as well as Unix and Unix-like operating systems running the Samba service. Windows can also connect to networked printers that use the LPR protocol or other TCP/IP protocols.

Using a Shared Printer

To use a shared printer, you must add an icon for the printer to your Printers & Scanners settings panel. The easiest way to do this is to browse or search your network for shared printers by following these steps:

1. Open File Explorer from the taskbar, or right-click the Start button and select File Explorer.

2. In the left pane, click Network. Locate the computer that is sharing the printer you want to use. (On a large network, you can use the Search box to help find it.) Double-click the computer icon.

3. Double-click the icon for the printer you want to use.

4. Windows will try to get the printer's driver software from the computer that is sharing the printer. Click Install Driver if you trust the owner of the other computer. You will also need to approve a User Account Control prompt. Windows may automatically locate and install a driver if the driver software is "signed" (that is, certified as having come directly from the stated manufacturer without any modification). However, if you can't trust the other computer, click Cancel. Then use the procedure that immediately follows this one so that you can select your own driver software.

5. When the process finishes, view the new printer in the Printers & Scanners settings panel, using either of these methods:

   ■ Click Start, Settings (gear icon), Devices, Printers & Scanners.

   ■ In the taskbar's search box, type **printers**, and then select Printers & Scanners.

There should be an icon for the printer under the heading Printers & Scanners. If you want to verify that the printer will actually work correctly for you, click the printer icon and select Manage, Print a Test Page.

note

Don't make any changes to the printer's Printer Properties settings without the permission of the printer's owner.

There is another setting you might want to change on the Printers & Scanners panel. Normally, when you select and use a printer from an app, Windows 10 automatically makes that printer the default choice the next time you go to print anything. If you want to keep a specific printer as the default, even if you sometimes choose a different printer, uncheck Let Windows Manage My Default Printer. Then click the icon for the printer you want to use most of the time, and click Manage, Set As Default. You can easily change these settings again later if you want.

That's all there is to it. You can now use this printer just like any other Windows printer, so the printer-management discussion in Chapter 7, "Devices and Printers," applies to network printers, too. The only difference is that the remote computer's administrator might not have given you management privileges for the printer, so you might not be able to change the printer's properties or delete print jobs created by other users.

An alternative way to add a printer is with the Add Printer Wizard, using these steps:

1. Open Printers & Scanners as described in step 5 of the previous procedure, and at the top, select Add a Printer or Scanner.

2. Windows displays a list of networked printers that it knows about, such as ones that it finds shared within the same workgroup. If the printer you want to use is listed, select it, click Next, and then proceed with step 4.

3. If the printer to which you want to connect isn't listed, click (drumroll, please) The Printer That I Want Isn't Listed.

   You're then presented with another dialog box, where you can type the location and name of the printer to which you want to connect. If you know its network name already, click Select a Shared Printer by Name and enter the share name into the Name box in UNC format—for example, `\\kevins\LaserJet`. Click Next to finish installing the printer. If you don't know the name, click Browse, and you'll be able to dig into your network to find the printer.

4. After you've identified and selected the shared printer, click Next. If a suitable printer driver is not found automatically, Windows will prompt for one. Select the printer's manufacturer and model number from the displayed lists. If the printer model isn't listed, click Windows Update to see whether the driver can be downloaded. Otherwise, follow the steps under "What to Do If Your Printer Isn't Listed" in Chapter 7.

5. Follow any additional instructions to finish setting up the printer.

Again, as noted previously, you can now use this printer like any other Windows printer, and if you plan to use it most or all of the time, you might want to make it your default printer.

Using Printers over the Internet with IPP

The Internet Printing Protocol (IPP) sends output to printers over the Internet. Some companies and service bureaus provide this sort of service. If you need to connect to an IPP-based printer, follow these steps:

1. Type the word **features** in the Taskbar's search box, and then select Turn Windows Features On or Off. Scroll down the list and click the + sign next to Print and Document Services. If Internet Printing Client is not already checked, check it. Then click OK. You must perform this step only once.

2. Click Start, Settings (gear icon), Devices, Printers & Scanners, add a Printer or Scanner. When the phrase *The Printer That I Want Isn't Listed* appears, click it.

3. Click Select a Shared Printer by Name, enter the URL supplied by the print service provider, and then click Next.

4. You might be prompted to select the printer manufacturer and model number. The print service provider will tell you which model to select.

5. You might also be prompted to enter a username and password, which will be supplied by the service provider. By default, Windows will use your current logon name, domain, and password.

 tip

If you use a printing service while traveling, remember to delete the printer from your Printers folder when you leave town; you don't want to accidentally send a report to Kathmandu after you've returned to Kalamazoo.

When the new printer icon is installed, you have a fully functional Windows printer. You can view the pending jobs and set your print and page preferences as usual, as long as you're connected to the Internet (or the LAN, in a service establishment).

Using Unix and LPR Printers

In the Unix world, most shared printers use a protocol called LPR/LPD.

 *For more information about Unix printing, **see** "Internetworking with Unix and Linux," p. 429.*

The LPR protocol is also used outside Unix. Manufacturers such as Hewlett-Packard make direct network-connected printers that accept the LPR protocol, and many companies sell small LPR-based print server devices that can attach to your printer. You can connect one of these printers to your LAN, configure its TCP/IP settings to match your LAN, and immediately print without running a cable from a computer to the printer. This way, you can place a printer in a more convenient place than can be reached by a 10-foot printer cable. Better yet, you can use these networked printers without requiring that a Windows computer be left turned on to manage it.

To have Windows send output to an LPR print queue or device, follow these steps:

1. Type the word **features** in the Taskbar's search box, and then select Turn Windows Features On or Off. Scroll down the list and click the + sign next to Print and Document Services. If LPR Port Monitor is not already checked, check it. Then click OK. You must perform this step only once.

2. Click Start, Settings (gear icon), Devices, Printers & Scanners, add a Printer or Scanner. When the phrase *The Printer That I Want Isn't Listed* appears, click it.

3. Select Add a Printer Using a TCP/IP Address or Hostname and click Next.

4. Enter the IP address or hostname of the Unix or print server and the name of the print queue on that server.

5. If Windows fails to determine what type of printer you are connecting to, click Cancel and then repeat the process. This time, set Device Type to TCP/IP Device and uncheck Query the Printer and Automatically Select the Device to Use. After you click Next, manually select the manufacturer and printer model. (If the appropriate driver is not listed, you might be able to get it by clicking Windows Update.) Then click Next to proceed with the printer installation.

Because an LPR printer is considered a local printer, you can share it with others on your network. Your computer will talk directly to the printer, while other computers will connect through yours. Alternatively, they can each connect to it directly, as you did.

note

If you enter the wrong IP address, hostname, or print queue name, click the printer's icon and then select Manage, Printer Properties. Select the Ports tab, highlight the LPR port, and click Delete Port. Click Add Port and then enter the correct information. When the new port has been added, check the box next to its name. Click OK.

Using Other Network-Connected Printers

Windows 10 can use other types of network-connected printers as well. Some printer models come with a built-in network connection (either wired or wireless), and others have a network adapter option. You can also buy network printer servers, which are small boxes with a network connector and one to three printer-connection ports. These devices let you locate printers in a convenient area, which doesn't need to be near a computer.

The installation procedures for various printer and server models vary. Your networked printer or print server has specific installation instructions. You have a choice about how the printer will be shared on your network:

- You can install the network-to-printer connection software on *one* of your Windows computers and then use standard Windows printer sharing to make the printer available to the other computers on your network.

- You can install the printer's connection software on *each* of your computers.

With the first method, you guarantee that print jobs will be run "first come, first served" because one computer will provide a single queue for the printer. Another plus is that you have to do the software setup only once; it's much easier to set up the additional workstations to use the standard Windows shared printer. The one computer must be left on for others to use the printer, however.

With the second method, each computer contacts the printer independently. If more than one user attempts to print at the same time, the "winner" will be chosen by the printer at random while the other users wait. However, no computers need to be left on because each workstation contacts the printer directly.

You can use either method. The first one is simplest and is best suited for a busy office. The second method is probably more convenient for home networks and small offices.

Network Power User Topics

The following sections present some Windows networking techniques that can help you get the most out of your network. You can scan through these sections for any tips that might be helpful in your home or office.

Backing Up Your Computer over the Network

You can back up the contents of your hard disk, or the attached external drives on your computer, to another computer's hard disk over the network. On all Windows 10 versions, you can back up to a shared network folder using the built-in File History and System Image backup mechanisms discussed in Chapter 32, "Protecting Your Data from Loss and Theft."

You can also back up files over the network using command-line tools. We give an example of this at the end of this chapter in the "Managing Network Resources Using the Command Line" section.

Finally, most third-party backup programs let you back up to a network location.

Sharing and Using an Entire Drive

Shared folders don't have to be subfolders. Computer owners can share the *root folder* of a disk drive, making the entire drive available over the network. This capability is especially useful with DVD, CD, and USB disk drives. For example, if an entire DVD-ROM drive is shared, you can access the data disc in it from any computer on the network.

Just so you know, Windows automatically shares your entire hard drive with the special name C$. (Any other hard drives would also be shared as D$, E$, and so on.) These shares don't show up when you browse the network; the dollar sign at the end tells Windows to keep the name hidden. Oddly enough, they don't appear if you view the drive's Sharing properties either. You can see them only if you type **net share** at the Command Prompt. And, you can't use these shares on a home/small office workgroup network; they can be accessed only by network administrators on a domain network.

 tip

You can use the technique of sharing an entire drive to install software on a computer that has no working CD/DVD drive but does have a working network connection. Put the disc into a computer that does have a working optical drive and share that drive. Then use the network share from the computer that has no optical drive.

However, you can get around this by sharing the root (top-level) folder of one of your drives using a share name of your own choosing. For example, you could right-click your DVD drive in the File Explorer window and then share the drive using the name **dvd**, using the instructions for sharing a folder found later in the chapter. Then, on another computer, you can map a drive letter to the shared disc, using the instructions under "Mapping Drive Letters," also found later in this chapter.

Understanding the Universal Naming Convention

You can specify folders and files on your own hard disk using a full pathname and filename in the standard Windows filename syntax that looks like this:

```
c:\folder\subfolder\filename
```

Similarly, you can specify printers, folders, and files on a network using a syntax called the *Universal Naming Convention (UNC)*, which looks like this:

```
\\computername\sharename\subfolder\filename
```

Notice that a UNC name uses backslashes, not forward slashes like an Internet URL. Anywhere a Windows application lets you enter a pathname or filename, you can also enter a UNC name.

A UNC share name is a sort of "shortcut" to a real folder on the remote computer's hard disk. It can be anywhere in the folder structure on the disk; it doesn't have to be a top-level folder. When users on the network access a shared folder, they can't see "up" into the higher-level folders.

For example, I might have a folder on my hard disk named C:\users\brian\documents\plans. If I want to give office mates the use of these business documents, I might share that folder with the share name plans. My computer is named sulawesi, so the UNC name for this folder will be \\sulawesi\plans.

If a spreadsheet file named `to do list.xls` exists in this folder, on my computer its full path and filename would be `C:\users\brian\documents\plans\to do list.xls`. A user on another computer can refer to this same file by its UNC name, `\\sulawesi\plans\to do list.xls`.

If the computer whose files you want to use is on a LAN using Active Directory or is part of a distant company network, you might have to specify the remote computer's fully qualified domain name. Your network administrator will have to tell you what name to use, and it will look something like the following:

`\\sulawesi.mycompany.com\docs\to do list.xls`

If you know only a remote computer's IP network address, you can use it as the computer name, as in this example:

`\\192.168.0.10\docs\to do list.xls`

Shared printers are also given share names and are specified by their UNC path. For example, if I share my HP LaserJet 4V printer, I might give it the share name `HPLaser`, and it will be known on the network as `\\sulawesi\HPLaser`. Here, it's not a folder but rather a printer. You can't tell this from the name, but Windows keeps track of the type of resource.

 note

Elsewhere in this chapter, we use UNC names such as `\\server\ folder` as a sort of generic name. By server, we mean the name of the computer that's sharing the folder. It doesn't have to be a Windows Server; it can be any computer on your network. You must use your network's actual computer names and shared folder names.

Mapping Drive Letters

If you frequently use the same shared network folder, you can make it a "permanent houseguest" of your computer by *mapping* the network folder to an unused drive letter on your computer—one of the letters after your hard drive's usual C: and the DVD-ROM drive's usual D:. Mapping gives you several benefits:

- The mapped drive appears along with your computer's other real, physical drives in the This PC view, enabling you to quickly browse, open, and save files.

- Access to the shared folder is faster because Windows maintains an open connection to the sharing computer.

- MS-DOS applications (some people do still use them!) can use the shared folder through the assigned letter. Most legacy DOS applications can't accept UNC-formatted names such as `\\server\shared\subfolder\file`, but they can use a path such as `k:\subfolder\file`.

- Best of all: You can map a shared folder using an alternative username and password to gain access rights that you might not have with your current Windows login name.

To map a drive, follow these steps:

1. Click the File Explorer icon in the taskbar to open File Explorer. Select This PC in the Navigation pane, at the left. In the File ribbon, select Map Network Drive to open the Map Network Drive dialog box.

Alternatively, in File Explorer's left pane under Network, select the name of the computer that is sharing the folder you want to use. In the right pane, right-click the icon of the folder you want to use and select Map Network Drive.

2. Select an unused drive letter from the drop-down list, as shown in Figure 21.6. You can pick a drive letter that has some association for you with the resource you'll be using: E for Editorial, S for Sales—whatever makes sense to you. I usually start with Z: and work backward from there if I map more than one drive.

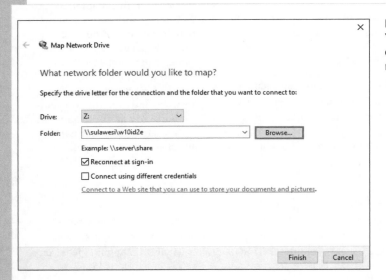

Figure 21.6
You can select any unused drive letter to use for the drive mapping.

3. If you didn't start by using the right-click method, you must select the name of the shared folder you want to assign to the drive letter. You can type the UNC-formatted name, if you know it already—for example, *servername**sharename*.

Alternatively, you can click Browse to poke through your network's resources and select the shared folder, as described earlier in this chapter. Find and select the desired shared folder, and then click OK.

4. There are two additional optional steps:

- If you want this mapping to reappear every time you log on, check Reconnect at Logon. If you don't check this box, the mapping will disappear when you log off.

- If your current Windows username and password don't give you permission to use the shared resource, or if your username isn't recognized at the other computer, select Connect Using a Different Username. (This works only if usernames are actually used on the networked computer. If it always grants access via the Guest account, as discussed under "File Permissions and Networking," earlier in this chapter, it doesn't matter what account information you supply.)

5. Click Finish.

6. If you selected Connect Using a Different Username, Windows prompts you for a username and password. Enter them, and then click OK.

After you map a drive letter, the drive appears in File Explorer under This PC, along with your local disk drives. You might notice a couple of funny things with these drives:

note

You must use the same username for *all* connections to a given computer. If you have other drive letters already mapped to the other computer with your original username, you must unmap those drives before you can make a drive mapping with a different username.

- If you haven't accessed the network drive for 20 minutes or so, it might turn gray, indicating that the network connection to the remote computer has been disconnected. When you use the drive again, Windows will reconnect and the drive entry will turn black.

- If the remote computer (or you) really goes offline, a red X appears through the drive.

Mapping a Drive to a Subfolder

When you're setting up a drive mapping, as described in the previous section, and you use the Browse button to select a shared folder, you might notice that Windows lets you

tip

If you're using Windows 10 Professional or Enterprise edition, you can make the drive's contents available even when you're disconnected from the network. For instructions, see "Offline Files" on page **839**.

delve into the shared folders themselves. If you drill down into a subfolder and select it as the location to use in mapping a drive letter, you'll find that the mapped drive starts at the subfolder. That is, the subfolder becomes the mapped drive's "root directory," and you can't explore upward into the shared folder that contains it. You can map a drive letter to a subfolder using the GUI method described in the preceding section or using the `net use` command-line utility described later.

This feature is most useful for administrators in setting up scripts to map drives based on a user's login name. For example, documents might be stored in subfolders of \\server\home according to username. Mapping drive M: to the folder \\server\home\%username% lets each user get at his documents (directly) via the same folder `M:\`, and discourages users from poking around in other people's folders.

Sharing Resources

In the following sections, we show you how to share folders and printers with other users on your network.

You can elect to share your files with others in several different ways:

- If your computer is part of a homegroup, you can share your libraries with the homegroup. Users on the member computers will be able to see anything you save in a shared library.

- You can move files to a folder under \Users\Public, which is called the Public user profile. Here, anyone can access them automatically, without your having to do anything else but enable sharing on the Public folder, as described shortly.

- You can elect to share any files or folders that reside anywhere within your own profile folder, which is found under \Users on the hard disk. Other network users will be able to find those files by browsing into your computer's Users share name.

- You can create new, separate folders on your hard disk and share them under their own share names.

In the past, it was common to create separate folders and share them independently. To some extent, this makes it easier for other users to locate shared folders because each folder has its own name. On Windows 10, 8.1, 8, and 7, however, Microsoft suggests "sharing in place," using any of the first three methods. These folders are easier to set up, but it's perhaps a bit harder on people who want to find those shared materials because they must dig into the Users folder. Any of the methods are acceptable, though; it really just depends on how you prefer to organize your files.

 note

On a large enterprise LAN, most important network resources, shared folders, and printers are set up and tightly controlled by network managers. You might not be able to share resources from your own computer, although in many companies you can, and it's useful to know how to do this so that you can easily give coworkers access to files that you use in common.

On a home or office workgroup network, any Administrator-level user can set up and manage file and printer sharing.

The following sections describe how to share folders these various ways.

Sharing with a Homegroup

If your computer is a member of a homegroup, you can share the entire contents of any of your folders so that the other members of the homegroup can see and use files in them. Use the following procedure:

1. At the right end of the taskbar, click the network icon, select Network & Internet Settings, and then select HomeGroup.

2. Select Change What You're Sharing with the Homegroup.

3. Set the drop-down list box next to each folder name to Shared or Not Shared, as shown in Figure 21.7. When you're finished, click Next and then Finish.

When you change a library's setting from Not Shared to Shared, the libraries will be shared *read-only*. All other homegroup members can see, view, play, and print any of the files in your shared libraries, but by default, they can't add to, change, delete, or rename them. You can change that, if you want, by using the following instructions.

Figure 21.7
You can change your mind about sharing or not sharing your content and printers with the homegroup at any time.

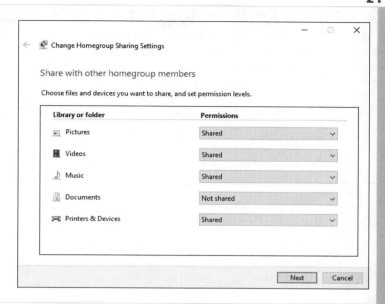

Setting Permissions for Homegroup Sharing

If you want to let other users add to or change the files in any of your libraries, or if you want to enable or prevent access to a specific library, folder, or individual file, use this procedure:

1. Locate the library, folder, or file in File Explorer. In most cases, you'll want to select the Documents, Music, or other folders under This PC, but you can also share any other folder on your computer. Right-click the folder's or file's icon, and select Give Access To.

2. Select one of these choices:

   - **Remove Access**—Keeps everyone else out of the library, file, or folder.

   - **Homegroup (view)**—Lets everyone else in the homegroup read but not add to, change, rename, or delete the file(s).

   - **Homegroup (view and edit)**—Lets all other homegroup users not only view but also make changes to the selected library, folder, or file. This includes adding new files, deleting files, and so on.

   - **Specific people**—Enables you to choose access levels for individual users. This might not work quite as you might guess, as we explain next.

The first time you share a new folder, use one of the two Give Access To Homegroup options. This makes the folder appear in the Homegroup listing on everyone else's computer. *Then*, if you want to customize access for specific people, right-click again and select Give Access To, Specific People to make adjustments.

Editing Permissions for Specific People

The last choice, Specific People, lets you set permissions for yourself, for the homegroup, for Everyone, and for individual user accounts using the permissions list shown in the File Sharing dialog box (see Figure 21.8).

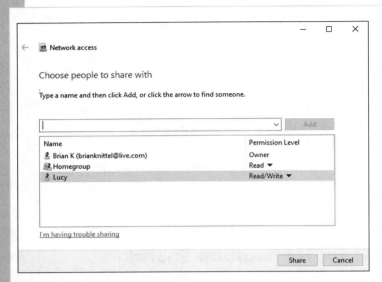

Figure 21.8
You can control the type of access to a shared library, folder, or file that is granted to your homegroup and in some cases to specific user accounts.

Any entries you add for individual users *won't* apply when other users in your homegroup try to use the shared resource over the network because member computers always use a common built-in account. Only the permissions for the Homegroup entry matter. Entries for individual user names affect those users when they log in on your computer, or for network access from computers that aren't members of the homegroup or computers not running Windows 10, 8.1, 8, or 7. And whether a specific account or the Guest account will be used depends on that complex list of situations we provided under "File Permissions and Networking," earlier in this chapter.

If you have computers on your network that run older versions of Windows, and therefore can't be members of the homegroup, you can give their users easy access to your shared files in either of two ways:

- If you turn off Password Protected Sharing on your computer, add the group name Everyone to the permission list. The other computers will get access to the files this way.

- If you want to leave Password Protected Sharing turned on for your computer, create accounts for each of the other computers' users on your computer, using their account names and passwords. Or you can create a single user account named, for example, "sharing" on your computer, assign a password to it, and have all of the other users use this account when they connect over the network. Add this account to the permissions list and then grant it Read or Read/Write access.

note

If you add Everyone to the list, the permissions you give to it will set the minimum access level granted to, well, everyone. Specifically, if you grant Everyone Read/Write access, this trumps any other settings in the list. *Anyone* will be able to change the files.

To change the permissions granted to a user or group listed in the File Sharing dialog box shown in Figure 21.8, change the entry in the Permission Level column to Read, Read/Write, or Remove, which removes the entry from the list. To add a new entry, select a name from the drop-down list next to the Add button and click the Add button. You can then change the new entry's Permission Level.

Your account is listed as the file's or folder's owner, and you can't change this entry.

Sharing the Public Profile Folder

There is a very simple way to share files and folders with other users if your network includes computers running older versions of Windows that can't participate in a homegroup. The trick is to use the folder named \Users\Public on the drive that contains Windows. If you enable Public Folder Sharing, this folder will be readable and writable by everyone on the network.

To enable sharing the Public folder, follow these steps:

1. At the right end of the taskbar, click the network icon and select Network & Internet Settings.

2. Scroll down if necessary and click Sharing Options.

3. Scroll down and click the down-arrow button that opens the All Networks section. Under Public Folder Sharing, select Turn On Sharing. Then click Save Changes.

 tip

In most previous versions of Windows, the Public folder was listed in the [My] Computer display as "Shared Documents." On Windows 8, 8.1, and 10, you can get to its subfolders by using File Explorer to browse into c:\users\Public under This PC. If you've enabled the display of Library folders, you can also browse into the Public folders inside your various libraries.

Following these steps makes the folder available to anyone who can connect to your computer over the network. Next, you must make it possible for people to connect. You can do this in either of two ways:

- Leave Password Protected Sharing turned on. Each of the other users on the network will need an account on your computer. You can create individual accounts, or you can create a single account, set a password on it, and have all the other users use that same name and password when they go to use your computer's shared folder Users\Public. (The folder's full UNC name is *computername*\Users\Public, with the actual name of your computer substituted in place of *computername*.)

- In the Sharing Options screen, turn off Password Protected Sharing. Now anyone who can connect to your network will be able to read and write files in your computer's shared folder Users\Public.

If you use this second option, be careful to let only trustworthy people connect to your network. If you have a wireless network, you *must* have WPA2 security enabled on it.

Once the Public folder has been shared, you must move or copy files or folders that you want to share into the Public folder structure.

Sharing Your Own Folders in Place

To share a folder that's inside your user profile (for example, a folder inside your Documents folder), just right-click the folder in any File Explorer and select Give Access To. You can even share just a single file in the same manner.

The entire \Users directory structure is shared by default on Windows 10, so all that's necessary is to let Windows change your file's or folder's permissions so that network users can see it. This is called "sharing in place." Just follow the steps:

 tip

If you move files from your own private folders into the Public folders using File Explorer, Windows will automatically update the files' permissions settings as it moves or copies them so that network users can work with them. If you use Command Prompt tools to move files, permissions are not modified, and the file likely will not be readable or writable by network users. You might need to manually add the group Everyone to the files' or folders' permissions list.

1. Locate your file or folder in File Explorer. Right-click it and select Give Access To.

2. If your computer is a member of a homegroup, select one of the two Homegroup options, as outlined previously under "Setting Permissions for Homegroup Sharing." This makes the folder appear in everyone else's Homegroup listing. If you want to customize access to the folder, right-click it again, select Give Access To, Specific People, and proceed as described under "Editing Permissions for Specific People."

   Otherwise, if the Homegroup options don't appear, select Specific People and then proceed as described under "Editing Permissions for Specific People."

If you later want to stop sharing this file or folder, right-click and select Give Access To, Remove Access.

Sharing Folders Independently

To share a folder that isn't inside your user profile folder, follow these steps:

1. Locate the folder in File Explorer, or to share an entire drive, select the name of the DVD-ROM, USB, or hard drive from the list in the This PC section.

2. Right-click the folder's or drive's icon and choose Give Access To.

3. If your computer is a member of a homegroup, proceed as outlined previously under "Setting Permissions for Homegroup Sharing." Be sure to select one of the two Homegroup options first, even if you intend to customize access for specific users or change the share name later.

4. If your computer is not a member of a homegroup, or if you want to grant access to non-homegroup computers, select Specific People and proceed as described previously under "Editing Permissions for Specific People."

5. Say you want to customize the share name or select specific users with which to share the folder. After you've finished sharing using the preceding steps, right-click the folder's or drive's icon

again, select Properties, and select the Sharing tab. Click Advanced Sharing and correct the share name as desired. You can also enter a comment that will appear when people browse to this folder over the network.

You can use the Permissions button to limit the access users have to the shared files when they're using them over the network. As we discussed earlier in the chapter, a file's Security settings control each user's access to the file, even if the Sharing Permissions settings give everyone Read/Write permission. Sharing Permissions just let you further restrict access by unchecking boxes in the Allow column.

6. Click OK to close the dialog box.

 tip

You can prevent other users from seeing your shared folder when they browse the network by adding a dollar sign to the end of the share name, as in `mystuff$`. They must know to type this name to use the shared folder. This technique alone does not prevent users from seeing your files if they know the share name.

If you later want to stop sharing the folder or drive, follow these steps:

1. Locate the folder or drive in File Explorer. Right-click it and select Properties.

2. Select the Sharing tab, and then click Advanced Sharing.

3. Uncheck Share This Folder, and then click OK.

 note

If you are canceling sharing of an entire drive, you might notice that the administrative share C$, D$, or other is not listed. You can safely uncheck Share This Folder, and the administrative share will not be canceled.

Alternatively, you can locate the folder, right-click it, and select Give Access To, Remove Access. However, this method not only removes the share but also can change file permissions.

File Is in Use by Another User

If you try to edit a file in a folder you've shared on the network and receive an error message indicating that the file is in use by another user, you can find out which remote user has the file open by using the Shared Folders tool in Computer Management, as described later in the section "Monitoring Use of Your Shared Folders."

You can wait for the remote user to finish using your file, or you can ask that person to quit. Only in a dire emergency should you use the Shared Folders tool to disconnect the remote user or close the file. Possible reasons you might do this are that the remote user's computer has crashed but your computer thinks the connection is still established, or the remote user is an intruder.

Sharing Printers

You can share any of your "local" printers so that other people on the network can use them. A local printer is any printer that is directly cabled to your computer or to which you connected via the network using LPR or other direct network protocols.

To be sure that printer sharing is enabled, do the following. (You should need to do this only once.)

1. Click the network icon in the taskbar and select Network & Internet Settings.

2. Look to see what type of network you're attached to. If your network is labeled Public Network, and you really are connected to a public network (for example, in a cafe, hotel, or school), you should not enable file and printer sharing; this would expose your computer to hackers. If the label says Public Network but you really are on a safe, protected home or office network, change the label to Private as described in "Take Care When you Share" on page **821**.

3. Scroll down if necessary and select Sharing Options.

4. Under the Private or Domain network profile (whichever is labeled Current), make sure that Turn On Network Discovery and Turn On File and Printer Sharing are both selected. If they aren't, correct the settings and click Save Changes; otherwise, click Cancel. This will take you back to the Network & Internet Settings page.

5. If your computer is part of a homegroup, select HomeGroup, just underneath Sharing Options. If Printers & Devices isn't listed as being shared, select Change What You're Sharing with the Homegroup, set Printers & Devices to Shared, and click Next and then Finish.

Now you can share any printer that is directly attached to your computer. To share a printer, follow these steps:

1. Click Start, Settings (gear icon), Devices, Printers & Scanners.

2. Under Printers & Scanners, click the printer's icon and select Manage, Printer Properties.

3. Select the Sharing tab.

4. If Share This Printer isn't already checked, check it. Windows will fill in a share name for the printer. If you like, you can shorten or simplify it.

5. Click OK.

Other people on your network can now use your printer by following the instructions earlier in the section "Using a Shared Printer."

In most cases, that's all you need to do. In some cases, you might want to change some of the advanced settings described in the next few sections, but these are optional.

Setting Printer Permissions

If you have a workgroup network and have disabled Password Protected Sharing, or if you have set up a homegroup, you don't need to worry about setting permissions for printers: Anyone can use your shared printer. If you're on a domain network or have chosen to use detailed user-level permissions on your workgroup network, you can control access to your shared printers with security attributes that can be assigned to users or groups, as shown in Figure 21.9 and described in Table 21.1.

Figure 21.9
The Security tab lets you assign printer-management permissions for users, groups, and the creator of each print job.

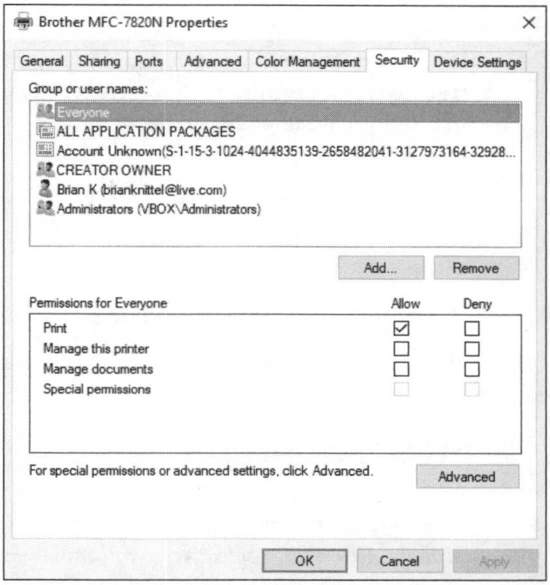

Table 21.1 Printer Permissions

Permission	Lets the User or Group...
Print	Send output to the printer.
Manage this printer	Change printer configuration settings as well as share or unshare a printer.
Manage documents	For the CREATOR OWNER entry, this permission lets a user suspend or delete his own print jobs. For other users and groups, this permission lets the user cancel or suspend other users' print jobs.
Special permissions	Don't bother with this entry; it just controls whether a user can change the permission settings.

You don't have to change any of the default permission settings unless you want to restrict the use of the printer to just specific users on your network. If this is the case, open the Printers & Scanners settings panel. Click the icon for the printer whose settings you want to change, and select Printer Properties. View the Security tab. There, select the group Everyone, and then click Remove. Next, click Add to add specific users or groups, and then give them Print permission. (You could also give someone Manage This Printer or Manage Documents permission if you want to let that person change the printer's settings or delete other users' print jobs.)

Don't change the CREATOR OWNER entry, however. It should have the Manage Documents permission checked so that each user can delete her own print jobs from the queue.

Changing the Location of the Spool Directory

When jobs are queued up to print, Windows stores the data it has prepared for the printer in a folder on the computer that's sharing the printer. Data for your own print jobs and for any network users will end up on your hard drive temporarily. If the drive holding your Windows folder is getting full, and you'd rather house this print data on another drive, you can change the location of the spool directory.

To change the location of the Windows print spooler folder, follow these steps:

1. Open the Printers & Scanners settings panel. Scroll down, and under Related Settings, click Print Server Properties.

2. Select the Advanced tab and click Change Advanced Settings.

3. Enter a new location for the Spool Folder and click OK.

Printer Pooling

If your network involves heavy-duty printing, you might find that your printers are the bottleneck in getting your work done. One solution is to get faster printers, and another is to add multiple printers. However, if you have two printers shared separately, you'll have to choose one or the other when you print, and you'll almost certainly encounter bank-line syndrome: The other line always seems to move faster.

The way around this problem is to use printer pooling. You can set up one printer queue that sends its output to two or more printers. The documents line up single-file, and the printers take jobs from the front of the line, first come, first served.

To set up pooled printers, follow these steps:

1. Buy identical printers—at least, they must be identical from the software point of view.

2. Set up and test one printer, and then configure network sharing for it.

3. Install the extra printer(s) on the same computer as the first. If you use network-connected printers, you must add the necessary additional network ports.

4. View the first printer's Printer Properties dialog box and select the Ports tab. Mark Enable Printer Pooling and check the ports for the additional printers. Then delete the printer icons for the second and subsequent printers. You should be left with one icon for the pool.

That's all there is to it; Windows passes print jobs to as many printers as you select on the Ports tab.

Managing Your Network

When you select Network in the left (Navigation) pane of the File Explorer window, the ribbon lists some tasks that can help you manage your network:

- **Network and Sharing Center**—Opens the Network and Sharing Center window, from which you can change homegroup settings, manage network adapters, and run automatic network troubleshooting wizards.

- **Add Devices and Printers**—Opens a wizard to connect to a locally attached, Bluetooth, wireless, or networked printer.

(These are the "old" Windows Control panel tools for performing these tasks. You can use them if you find them comfortably familiar. Earlier in this chapter, we described how to perform these same tasks using "new" Settings panels.)

If you click a computer or server name in the right pane (not the left), additional computer-specific task options appear in the ribbon:

- **Open**—Lets you browse the computer's shared folders and printers.

- **Connect with Remote Desktop Connection**—Lets you log on to and use the computer remotely.

- **View Printers**—Lets you browse just the computer's or server's shared printers.

Windows provides additional tools with which you can monitor the use of the files you're sharing as well as command-line tools with which you can manage network resources that you use and share.

Monitoring Use of Your Shared Folders

If you've shared folders on your LAN, you might want to know who's using them. For example, you might need to know this information if someone were editing a file in your shared folder. If you tried to edit the same file, you'd be told by your word processor that the file was "in use by another." But by whom?

The Computer Management tool can help you. Right-click the Start button or press Windows Logo+X, select Computer Management, and open the Shared Folders item in the left pane. The Sessions and Open Files sections can show you who is using your shared folders as well as which files they currently have open. In an emergency, you can right-click an entry and disconnect a user or close an open file or choose to disconnect all open files. This is a drastic measure and is sure to mess up the remote user(s), so use it only when absolutely necessary.

Managing Network Resources Using the Command Line

You can perform drive mappings and printer selections with the command line just as easily as from the GUI. If you find yourself repeating certain network and file operations day after day, it makes sense to try to automate these processes by putting commands into batch files.

The net command comes to us virtually unchanged since the original PC network software developed by Microsoft and IBM debuted in 1984. There are so many variations of the net command that I think of them as separate commands: net view, net use, net *whatever*. Each net command contains a word that selects a subcommand or operation type.

Interestingly, the net command not only can manage and explore your network but also can start and stop Windows services and create user accounts and groups. You can get online help listing all the net subcommands by typing **net /?**, and you can get detailed help by typing **net command /?**, where *command* is any one of the net subcommands.

The `net use` command makes and disconnects drive mappings and establishes printer redirection for console (command-line) applications. The basic command is as follows:

```
net use drive: sharename
```

The following example maps drive letter Q to the shared folder `\\abalone\book`:

```
net use q: \\abalone\book
```

You can't replace the shared folder attached to an already mapped drive, so you should try to delete a previous mapping before trying to make a new one:

```
net use q: /delete
net use q: \\abalone\book
```

Here is an example of a batch file that performs a simple computer-to-computer backup of some important files. Let's say I want to back up the folder `C:\book`, and all of its subfolders, from my computer to a shared folder on another computer named `abalone`. I could put the following commands into a file named `backup_book.bat`:

```
@echo off
net use q: /delete 1>nul 2>nul
net use q: \\abalone\book
robocopy c:\book q: /e
net use q: /delete
```

The `net use` commands I just explained. The `robocopy` command copies my book folder to the remote computer. The option `/e` tells it to copy subdirectories, even empty ones. By default, robocopy automatically copies only files that are newer in the source folder(s) than in the destination. So this does the job as efficiently as possible. I just have to type **backup_book** and it's done. Isn't the command line great?!

On 32-bit copies of Windows, the `net use` command also maps network printers to the legacy DOS printer devices LPT1, LPT2, and LPT3. The following command lets MS-DOS applications send output to a network printer, by redirecting the LPT1 device:

```
net use lpt1: \\server\printername
```

The following command cancels redirection:

```
net use lpt1: /delete
```

tip

If the drive mapping didn't exist beforehand, the `/delete` command will print an error message. That's fine if you're typing commands directly in the Command Prompt window. If you perform drive mapping in a batch file, the error message would be disconcerting. You can prevent it from appearing by issuing the command this way:

```
net use q: /delete >nul
2>nul
```

NUL is a special filename to Windows; it's basically a black hole for data. Directing all output to NUL makes sure that the command doesn't display anything.

TROUBLESHOOTING YOUR NETWORK

When Good Networks Go Bad

As part of my software consulting work, I end up doing a fair bit of network support for my clients. And every time I get a call from a client with a network problem, I cringe. I never know whether it's going to take 10 minutes or a week to fix. Sometimes the problem isn't so bad; I've fixed more than one "broken" computer by simply plugging it in. If such an easy fix doesn't present itself immediately, though, a bit of a cold sweat breaks out on my forehead. The problem could be anything. How do you even start to find a nasty problem in the maze of cards, wires, drivers, and hidden, inexplicable system services? And it's difficult enough debugging the stuff that belongs there. What if viruses, adware, or rootkits are messing up the works?

Well, if you work for a corporation with a network support staff, of course, the answer to any of these questions is to call the help desk and then take a refreshing walk around the block while someone else sweats over your network. It's great if you can get that kind of support. If you want to (or have to) go it alone, though, the good news is that some tools provided with Windows can help you find the problem. After discussing troubleshooting in general, this chapter shows you how to use these tools.

In reading this chapter, you probably won't find the solution to any particular network problem you're having. I can't really help you solve any one specific problem here, but I can show you some of the tools available to help you identify the source of a problem you might have.

Getting Started

In years of helping clients and friends with hardware, software, and network problems, what I've noticed is that the most common—and most frustrating—way people report a problem is to say "I can't..." or "The computer won't...." Unfortunately, knowing what *doesn't* happen isn't helpful; after all, at any given time, there are an infinite number of things that aren't happening. I always have to ask, "What *does* happen when you try?" The answer to that question usually gets me well on the way to solving the problem. The original report usually leaves out important error messages and symptoms that can identify the problem. If you can get someone to express a problem in terms of what *is* happening, rather than what isn't, you'll go from "My online banking doesn't work" to something like "The website says my password is invalid" or "Windows says that I don't have any network connections." This leads from the vague toward something you can grapple with.

Extending that principle, as you work on a problem, pay as much attention to what *does* work as to what doesn't. Knowing what isn't broken lets you eliminate whole categories of problems. For example, check to see whether a problem affects just one computer or all the computers on your home or office network. If other computers can manage the task that one computer is having trouble with, you know that the problem is located *in that one computer*, or in its connection to the others.

The following are some other questions I always ask:

- Does the problem occur all the time or just sometimes?

- Can you reproduce the problem consistently? If you can define a step-by-step procedure to reproduce the problem, can you reduce it to the shortest, most direct procedure possible?

- Has the system ever worked, even once? If so, when did it stop working, and what happened just before that? What might have changed?

These questions can help you determine whether the problem is fundamental (for example, due to a nonfunctioning router) or interactive (that is, due to a conflict with other users, with new software, or confined to a particular subsystem of the network). You might be able to spot the problem right off the bat if you look at the scene this way. If you can't, you can use some tools to help narrow down the problem.

Generally, network problems fall into one or more of these categories:

- Application software

- Network clients

- Name-resolving services

- Network protocols

- Addressing and network configuration

- Driver software

- Network cards and hardware configuration

- Wiring/hubs/Wi-Fi connectivity

- Routers

- Internet connectivity

If you can determine which category a problem falls in, you're halfway to finding the culprit. At that point, diagnostic tools and good, old-fashioned deductive reasoning come into play. (That, and random plugging and unplugging of things.)

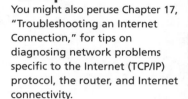

tip

You might also peruse Chapter 17, "Troubleshooting an Internet Connection," for tips on diagnosing network problems specific to the Internet (TCP/IP) protocol, the router, and Internet connectivity.

You might be able to eliminate one or more categories right away. For example, if your computer can communicate with some other computers but not all of them, and your network uses a central switch or hub, you can deduce that at least your computer's network card and the wiring from your computer to the switch are working properly.

Windows comes with some diagnostic tools to help you narrow down further the cause of a network problem. The following sections outline these tools and suggest how to use them.

Using Troubleshooters and Diagnostic Tools

Each diagnostic tool described in this section serves to test the operation of one or more of the categories mentioned in the preceding section. The tools are discussed in roughly the order you should try them.

Some tools can be used to find problems in any of the many networking components. These tools quickly identify many problems.

The Network and Sharing Center

The Network and Sharing Center is the first place to start diagnosing a network problem because it can quickly take you to Windows network troubleshooters, status displays, and network settings. There are several ways to bring up the Network and Sharing Center. Here are two easy ways:

- Click Start, Settings (gear icon), Network & Internet. Scroll down and select Network and Sharing Center.

- Right-click the Start button or press Windows Logo+X. Select Network Connections. Scroll down and select Network and Sharing Center.

Either method brings up the window shown in Figure 22.1.

Under View Your Active Networks, Windows displays information about any active network or direct Internet connections. For example, in Figure 22.1, you can see that I am attached to a LAN through the network adapter named Ethernet. The network location is set to Private, which means that file and printer sharing are allowed. The network can reach the Internet, and the computer is joined to (is a member of) a homegroup.

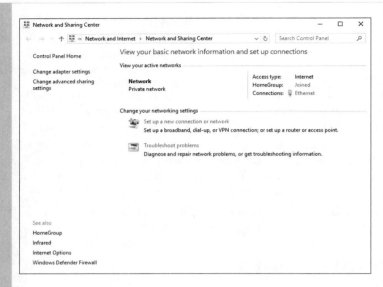

Figure 22.1
The Network and Sharing Center gives you a quick overview of your network and Internet status and leads to other diagnostic and setup tools.

> ➡ *If you want to use file sharing and/or the HomeGroup feature, your network location must be "Private Network." For more information, see "Setting Up a Homegroup," p. 396.*

This window leads to several other useful tools:

- To see whether various networking features are turned on or off, click Change Advanced Sharing Settings.

- To let Windows try to diagnose your network problem, click Troubleshoot Problems. Then select a troubleshooter for the particular problem you're having. (See "Network Troubleshooters," later in the chapter, for a description of these tools.)

- To check or modify the settings for one of your network adapters, click Change Adapter Settings.

- To check or change your homegroup settings, click HomeGroup in the lower-left portion of the window.

- To see whether your computer can find other computers on your network, click Network and Internet in the Windows address bar, at the top of the window, or click the up arrow just to the left of the address bar; then click View Network Computers and Devices. We discuss this next.

If you're having problems with file and printer sharing, the first thing to check is the Network window.

Network

The Network window lets you determine whether your computer can "see" other computers on your network that are sharing files, printers, or media. Use any of these methods to view the Network window:

note

Other computers will appear only if your Network Location setting is Private Network, which is set in the Network and Sharing Center window. Otherwise, file and printer sharing is disabled.

- From the desktop, click the File Explorer icon pinned to the taskbar. Then click Network in the Navigation pane at the left.

- In the taskbar's search box, type **view network**, and then select View Network Computers and Devices from the search results.

- Press Windows Logo+X and select File Explorer. Then click Network in the Navigation pane at the left.

The window that appears should look something like Figure 22.2, except that the names of the computers on your network will be different.

Figure 22.2
The Network view shows other computers your computer knows about.

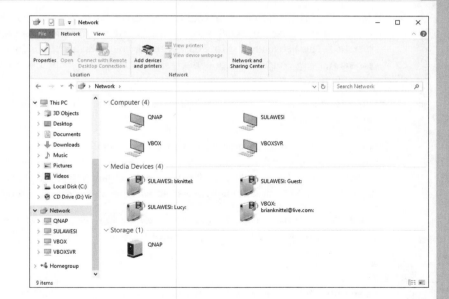

If you see at least one other computer besides your own displayed here, your computer's network cabling, network adapter, and drivers are working correctly. Also, both your computer and the computers shown are running the Network Discovery service and/or file sharing.

If other computers don't appear, check the following:

- If your network is protected from the Internet by a firewall or a router, be sure that the Network Location is shown as Private Network. Check the Network and Sharing Center, as discussed in the preceding section. If it's set to Public, click the Network icon in the taskbar, and select Network & Internet Settings, Change Connection Properties, Private. On the other hand, if Network Location is already set to Private, at the left side of the Network and Sharing Center window, click Change Advanced Sharing Settings, and be sure that Turn On Network Discovery and Turn On File and Printer Sharing are selected.

- If your computer is directly connected to the Internet in a public place such as a school or an Internet cafe, it's not safe to enable file sharing. Your network type must be set to Public, and file sharing should be disabled. Other computers should not appear in the Network list.

➡️ *For more information, see "Take Care When You Share," p. 821.*

If a computer that you want to connect to is powered up, connected to the network, and correctly configured but still doesn't appear in the Network list, try these procedures:

- Wait 10 minutes, and then press the F5 key or right-click the window and select Refresh. Other computers might appear this time.

- Check each of the computers in your workgroup and make sure that each computer is set to use the same workgroup name and that each computer has the same set of network protocols installed. This is usually an issue only with very old versions of Windows. In particular, any computers running Windows XP or earlier versions must be reconfigured to use only TCP/IP and not IPX/SPX or NetBEUI.

- Be sure that other computers' firewall software is set up to permit file and printer sharing on the local subnet.

Frankly, the software that Windows uses to identify other computers on the local network, called the Browser service, is flaky at best, and sometimes no computers appear in this display even when networking is fine. This can happen if you have more than one physical network (both wireless and Ethernet, for example, or multiple wireless access points), or, for no good reason at all.

➡️ *For information about networking with older versions of Windows, see Chapter 20, "Networking with Other Operating Systems."*

 tip

Sometimes add-on software can wreak havoc with networking and especially file sharing. If you install the Cisco VPN Client for work, for example, it might install an unconfigurable firewall component that is turned on *all the time*, even when you're not connected through the VPN, and it blocks your computer from sharing files or printers. Nice, huh? If this happens, uninstall the Cisco VPN and run the installer again using the Command Prompt window. Put DONTINSTALLFIREWALL=1 at the end of the command line.

This is just one example of the kind of thing that can happen. If networking suddenly stops working after you've installed a program or app, google the program name and see if others have had the same problem.

If you are having trouble with file and printer sharing with some or all of your other computers, and this screen didn't identify the problem, go back to the Network and Sharing Center and click Change Advanced Sharing Settings. This displays settings that Windows uses with home/work (private) networks and public networks, respectively. The settings are divided into three or four parts:

- **Private**—Settings used for a network connection that leads to home or office networks. A network can be a home or work network, even if it provides Internet access, as long as a router or firewall is placed between the network and the Internet, and as long as you trust all the computers plugged in to the network.

- **Guest or Public**—Settings used for network connections that lead directly to networks in an insecure environment. A public network could be a direct Internet connection (for example, a connection plugged in directly to a DSL or cable modem) or a network in a public place such as a hotel or cafe, where you do not trust the other computers.

- **Domain**—Settings used for a network connection that leads to a workplace domain network. This section appears only if the computer has been joined to a domain network, and network security policy might prevent you from changing these settings.

- **All Networks**—Settings used on all network connections. These settings control file-sharing and media-sharing security options.

The first three sections are location-dependent settings, and the settings in the All Network section are location independent. The default settings are listed in Tables 22.1 and 22.2.

Table 22.1   Location-Dependent Advanced Sharing Settings

Setting	Private/Domain Default	Public Default	Description
Network Discovery	On	Off	When off, other computers will not appear on the network map, and your computer will not appear on other computers' maps.
File and Printer Sharing	On	Off	When off, your computer will not share its files or printers with other computers. You can still use files and printers shared by other computers.
HomeGroup Connections	Windows	—	By default, Windows manages the user account and password used for HomeGroup sharing. For more information, see "Setting Up a Homegroup" in Chapter 18, "Creating a Windows Network." HomeGroup connections are available on private networks only.

Table 22.2 Location-Independent Advanced Sharing Settings

Setting	Default	Description
Public Folder Sharing	On	When off, the Public user folder will not be shared. When on, it is shared, and anyone can store or change files in it. (This setting applies only when File and Printer Sharing is turned on.)
Media Streaming	On	This setting leads to options that control how music and video are shared with networked media-playing devices and computers.
File Sharing Connections	128-bit	By default, encrypted network connections use a strong key.
Password Protected Sharing	On	When on, other users must have a user account and password to use shared files and printers that are not accessed via a homegroup. When off, other users who don't have an account on your computer, or who have an account with no password, will be granted access to shared files and printers via the Guest account. (For more information, see "Configuring Passwords and File Sharing" in Chapter 33, "Protecting Your Network from Hackers and Snoops.")

Network Troubleshooters

Windows 10 has a set of network repair tools called *troubleshooters* that are said (by Microsoft) to be capable of recognizing and diagnosing more than 100 network problems. We're skeptical of claims like this; but, on the other hand, it takes only a few seconds to let these tools examine your network and offer whatever advice they can, so it's absolutely worth letting them take a crack at whatever problems you're experiencing.

There are several different network troubleshooters, each dealing with different categories of problems. You have two ways of getting to them that look very different but run the same set of tools.

The quickest way to start is to click the network icon at the right end of the taskbar and select Network & Internet Settings. Scroll down and click Network Troubleshooter. This method runs some basic network adapter tests and might prompt you to select the type of problem you're experiencing. It then runs the appropriate troubleshooting programs. We won't describe this further; it's self-explanatory once you've started the process.

You can also access the individual troubleshooters directly. Click Start, Settings (gear icon). Scroll down and select Update & Security, then, in the left column, select Troubleshoot. Then select one of the network troubleshooters from the list in the right-hand side. Your computer might not show all of these and might have additional troubleshooters to offer.

- **Internet Connections**—Select this option if you are having a problem reaching the Internet in general, or even one particular website.

 tip

Whichever troubleshooter(s) you use, if the word *Advanced* appears on the first screen, click on that word to expose a set of options. Be sure that Apply Repairs Automatically is checked, and then click on Run As Administrator.

- **Connection to a Workplace Using DirectAccess**—Select this option if you can't access your corporate network over the Internet via the DirectAccess virtual private networking feature.

- **HomeGroup**—Select this option if you're having problems accessing a homegroup.

- **Incoming Connections**—Select this option if other computers can't connect to your computer's shared files or to other programs or services that you want to make available on your computer (for example, Remote Desktop, a web server, and so on).

- **Network Adapter**—Select this option if you're having general problems accessing the Internet or network resources and suspect a hardware problem.

- **Shared Folders**—Select this option if you can't access a network shared file or folder whose name you know.

Windows displays a box that says "Identifying the problem..." and then displays a results window that explains what was found to be wrong, what Windows did about it (if anything), what the outcome was, and where to go for more assistance.

If the diagnostics tool doesn't solve your network problem, check Windows Defender Firewall to be sure it isn't blocking a desired network service.

 note

The troubleshooters aren't good at determining that nothing is actually wrong with their particular area of concern. If a troubleshooter says that it can't find the problem, it might mean that there *is* no problem with that specific topic. Try another troubleshooter.

Windows Defender Firewall

Another configuration setting that could prevent file and printer sharing from working correctly is Windows Defender Firewall. To ensure that file and printer sharing isn't blocked, open the Windows Defender Firewall window. To get there, click the Network icon in the taskbar and select Network & Internet Settings. Scroll down and select Network and Sharing Center; then at the bottom left, select Windows Defender Firewall. (Or, press Windows Logo+R, type `firewall.cpl`, and press Enter.)

Windows Defender Firewall filters network activity based on the type of network to which you're attached. For both private and public networks, unless you're using a third-party firewall product, the Windows Defender Firewall State should be labeled "On," and Incoming Connections should be set to Block All Connections to Apps That Are Not on the List of Allowed Apps.

On the top left of the screen, click Allow an App or Feature Through Windows Defender Firewall to view the settings. Scroll down the list to find File and Printer Sharing. File and Printer Sharing should be checked in the Private column, and in the Domain column if it exists, but *not* in the Public column. Farther up, Core Networking should be checked in all columns. If any of these is wrong, click Change Settings, make the correction, and then click OK.

 note

At the time this was written, Microsoft appears to be partway through the process of moving Windows Firewall settings from the old Control Panel to new Settings panels. It's not entirely consistent, but it appears that links labeled "Windows Firewall" lead to a new Settings panel, while links labeled "Windows Defender Firewall" lead to the older Control Panel version. We recommend using the latter here. We'll update this section if the older version is ever removed entirely.

(File Sharing over SMB Direct, if it appears, is usually unchecked. That's fine. This feature can be enabled only on Windows Pro for Workstations and is used only with special network adapters and file servers.)

➡ *For more information about configuring the firewall,* **see** *"Configuring Windows Firewall,"* **p. 395.**

If the firewall settings appear to be correct, the next step is to check Windows Event Viewer to see whether Windows has left a record of any network problems there.

Event Viewer

Event Viewer is another important diagnostic tool and one of the first to check because Windows often silently records useful information about problems with hardware and software in an Event Log. To check, open the Event Viewer using one of these two methods:

- Press Windows Logo+X or right-click the Start button, and then select Event Viewer.

- In the taskbar's search box type **event**, and then click Event Viewer.

Start by selecting Custom Views, Administrative Events in the left Navigation pane. It can take awhile for anything to appear. The list shows significant management events from all of the various Windows events logs (and there are a lot of them!). Look for anything that might mention a networking error.

If nothing useful appears there, select Windows Logs and then examine the System, Application, and Security logs in turn. Finally, open Applications and Services Logs, Microsoft, Windows, and under any of the network-related categories, view the Operational and Admin logs.

Event Viewer displays Event Log entries, most recent first, on the right (see Figure 22.3).

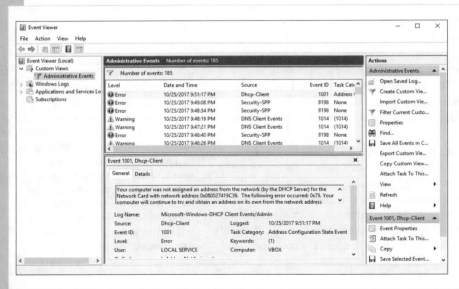

Figure 22.3
Event Viewer might display important diagnostic information when you have network problems.

Log entries for serious errors are displayed with an exclamation mark (!) in a red circle; warnings appear with an exclamation mark in a yellow triangle. Informational entries (marked with a blue *i*) usually don't relate to problems. Double-click any error or warning entries in the log to view the detailed description and any associated data recorded with the entry. The Warning entry in Figure 22.3 indicates that my computer couldn't acquire a network address in a reasonable amount of time. It turns out that my router had come unplugged.

These messages are usually significant and informative to help diagnose network problems; they might indicate that a network card is malfunctioning, that a domain controller for authentication or a DHCP server for configuration can't be found, and so on. The Source column in the Event Log indicates which Windows component or service recorded the event. These names are usually fairly cryptic. Table 22.3 lists a few of the more common nonobvious ones.

Table 22.3   Network Sources of Event Log Entries

Source	Description
Application Popup	Can come from any system utility; these warning messages are usually significant.
Atapi	IDE hard disk/CD-ROM controller.
Browser, bowser	Name resolution system for Client for Microsoft Networks.
Dhcp-Client	Network address assignment service client.
DNS Client Events	Network name lookup client.
Dnsapi	DNS client component.
Dnscache	DNS client component.
MrxSmb	Client for Microsoft Networks.
NetBT	Client for Microsoft Networks.
RasClient, RasMan	Dial-up networking.
Time Service	Computer clock synchronization service.

If you're at a loss to solve the problem, even with the information given, check the configuration of the indicated component, or remove and reinstall it to see whether you can clear up the problem.

Device Manager

Hardware problems with your network card will most likely be recorded in the Event Log. If you suspect that your network card is the culprit, and nothing is recorded in the Event Log, check the Device Manager.

You have two easy ways to open the Device Manager:

- Press Windows Logo+X and select Device Manager.

- In the taskbar's search box, type **manager**, and then select Device Manager from the search results.

 tip

A problem with one network system usually causes other problems. Therefore, the oldest error message in a closely timed sequence of errors is *usually* the most significant, with subsequent errors just a result of the first failure. Because the Event Log is ordered "most-recent first," you might get the most useful information down a bit from the top of the list.

Any unrecognized devices or devices with detectable hardware problems or configuration conflicts appear with a yellow ! icon when you display the Device Manager. If no yellow icons appear, you don't have a *detected* hardware problem. This doesn't mean that you don't have a problem, but the odds are slim that your network card is the problem.

If devices are shown with ! icons, double-click the device name to see the Windows explanation of the device status and any problems. A device that you've told Windows not to use (disabled) will have a circle with a downward-pointing arrow in it; this is generally not a problem.

 tip

The real cause of your problem might reveal itself at system startup time rather than when you observe the problem. Reboot your system and note the time. Then reproduce the problem. Check the Event Log for messages starting at the reboot time.

➡ *For more detailed instructions and tips on device troubleshooting,* **see** *Chapter 26, "Troubleshooting and Repairing Problems."*

Testing Network Cables

If your computer can't communicate with any other computer on your LAN, and the Device Manager doesn't indicate a faulty network card, you *might* have a wiring problem. Wiring problems can be the most difficult to solve because it's difficult to prove that data is leaving one computer but not arriving at another. The ping program, discussed later in this chapter, can help with this problem.

➡ *To learn how you can use the ping command to diagnose Internet-related problems, as opposed to LAN problems,* **see** *"ping," p. 354.*

If your computer is not properly wired into the LAN or is connected through a wireless network, in many cases, Windows will display an offline icon right on the notification area and indicate that your network is disconnected. It might not, though, so you shouldn't take a lack of this kind of message to mean that no wiring problems exist.

If your network uses CAT-5 or higher cabling plugged into a switch or hub, there's usually a green LED indicator on each network card and at each port on the switch. Be sure that the lights are on at each end of your network cable and those for the other computers on your LAN.

You also can use inexpensive (about $50) cable-test devices that check for continuity and correct pin-to-pin wiring order for UTP wiring. They come as a set of two boxes. One gets plugged into each end of a given cable run, and a set of blinking lights tells you whether all four wire pairs are connected and in the correct order. It's nice to have one of these devices if you install your own network cabling or make your own patch cables.

Checking Network Configuration

If hardware isn't at fault, you might have a fundamental network configuration problem. Often the Event Log and Device Manager give these problems away, but if they don't, you can use another batch of tools to check the computer's network configuration.

ipconfig

If your computer can't communicate with others on your LAN, after you check the Event Log and Device Manager, use the `ipconfig` command-line utility to see whether your computer has a valid IP address. Check other computers on the LAN, too, to ensure that they do as well.

To use this tool, open a Command Prompt window: Right-click or touch and hold the Start button and select Command Prompt or Windows PowerShell (whichever appears). Then type the following command:

`ipconfig /all`

Next, press Enter. The results should look something like this; you might have to scroll the window up to see the first part:

```
Windows IP Configuration
      Host Name . . . . . . . . . . . . : java
      Primary Dns Suffix . . . . . . . : mycompany.com
      Node Type . . . . . . . . . . . : Hybrid
      IP Routing Enabled. . . . . . . : Yes
      WINS Proxy Enabled. . . . . . . : No
 Ethernet adapter Local Area Connection:
      Connection-specific DNS Suffix . . :
      Description . . . . . . . . . . : Intel 21140-Based PCI Fast Ethernet Adapter
      Physical Address. . . . . . . . : 00-03-FF-DD-CA-5F
      DHCP Enabled. . . . . . . . . . : Yes
      Autoconfiguration Enabled . . . . : Yes
      Link-local IPv6 Address . . . . . : fe80::ed10:dff9:693c:803d%8(Preferred)
      IPv4 Address. . . . . . . . . . : 192.168.15.108(Preferred)
      Subnet Mask . . . . . . . . . . : 255.255.255.0
      Lease Obtained. . . . . . . . . : Thursday, August 6, 2015 3:13:14 PM
      Lease Expires . . . . . . . . . : Friday, August 7, 2015 3:13:26 PM
      Default Gateway . . . . . . . . : 192.168.15.1
      DHCP Server . . . . . . . . . . : 192.168.15.1
      DHCPv6 IAID . . . . . . . . . . : 201327615
      DNS Servers . . . . . . . . . . : 192.168.15.1
      NetBIOS over Tcpip. . . . . . . : Enabled
```

(Unless you're troubleshooting IPv6 Teredo connections, ignore the parts that mention Tunnel Adapters.)

The most important items to look for are the following:

- **Host Name**—This should be set to the desired name for each computer. If you can correspond with some computers but not others, be sure that the ones that don't work are turned on and correctly named. Make sure you don't have two computers with the same name and that none of the computer names are the same as the workgroup name.

note

To learn more about IP addressing, network masks, and configuration, visit http://support.microsoft.com and search for article number 164015, "Understanding TCP/IP Addressing and Subnetting Basics."

- **IP Address**—This should be set appropriately for your network. If your LAN uses Internet Connection Sharing (ICS), the address will be a number in the range 192.168.0.1 through 192.168.0.254. If your LAN has a connection-sharing router, the IP address will *usually* use numbers starting with 192.168.*x*, where *x* is a number between 0 to 100.

  If your IP address starts with the numbers 169.254, your computer is set for automatic configuration but no DHCP server was found, so Windows has chosen an IP address by itself. This is fine if your LAN uses this automatic configuration system; perhaps you've just connected a few computers so you can share files and printers. However, if you expected to get Internet access through your network—that is, if you use ICS or a hardware Internet connection router, or you have a more complex network with a DHCP server—this is a serious problem. Restart the connecting-sharing computer or the router and then restart your computer and try again.

- **Network Mask**—This is usually 255.255.255.0, but other settings are possible. All computers on the same LAN should have the same network mask.

Each computer on the same LAN should have a similar valid IP address and the same network mask. If they don't, check your network configuration. You also can use the built-in Windows Repair function to help fix problems with DHCP-based (automatic) IP address assignment.

System

You can check a computer's identification and workgroup or domain membership setup from the System window. It's best to use the old style System dialog box rather than the new System Settings panel for this. To view it, open File Explorer using its taskbar icon or the Start menu icon. Select This PC in the left pane, and then select Properties at the top left end of the ribbon menu, or right-click This PC in the left pane and select Properties.

Look at the bottom of the screen for the computer name and domain or workgroup name, as shown in Figure 22.4.

On a home/small office Workgroup network, the workgroup name should be the same on all computers on your workgroup LAN. (It's usually workgroup). All of the computer names *must* be different from each other.

On a corporate Windows domain network, you should see your computer's name displayed as part of a Windows domain name (for example, my computer named bribox might be called bribox.mycompany.com on a domain network) and the domain name displayed separately. Your domain name might

> **note**
>
> None of your computers can use the workgroup or domain name as its computer name. If you find this issue on one of your computers, change that computer's name.

not include .com. It might say .local instead or use a different ending. In any case, be sure that your computer is actually a domain member. If the word *Workgroup* appears instead, your computer is not a domain member and will not be able to use domain logins or some domain resources.

Network Connections

You can manually check all installed network protocols and services and their configuration by viewing Network Connections and viewing the properties for Local Area Connection. To view this screen, open the Network & Internet Settings as discussed at the start of this chapter and click

Change Adapter Options. Right-click your Ethernet icon (or the appropriate wireless connection icon) and select Properties.

Confirm that each required protocol is installed and correctly configured. In general, the settings on each computer on your LAN should match, except that the IP address differs (usually only in the last of its four dot-separated numbers). If your LAN uses automatic IP address configuration, use the `ipconfig` command, described earlier, to check the settings.

Figure 22.4
Your computer's name and workgroup or domain membership are displayed at the bottom of the System window.

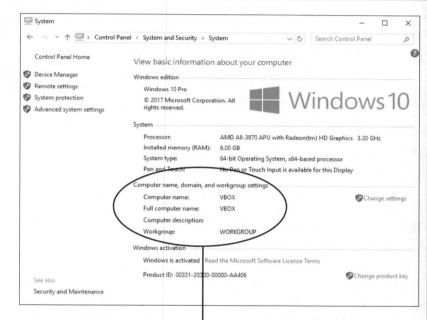

Computer name and workgroup or domain name are shown here

Testing Network Connectivity with `ping`

`ping` is the fundamental tool for testing TCP/IP network connectivity. Because most networks today use the Internet (TCP/IP) protocol for file and printer sharing services, as well as for Internet access, most Windows users can use the `ping` test to confirm that their network cabling, hardware, and the TCP/IP protocol are all functioning correctly. `ping` sends several data packets to a specified computer and waits for the other computer to send the packets back. By default, it sends four packets and prints the results of the four tests.

To see whether the network can carry data between a pair of computers, use the `ipconfig` command (described previously) to find the IP address of the two computers. Then, on one computer, in the open Command Prompt window, type the following command:

```
ping 127.0.0.1
```

This command tests the networking software of the computer by sending packets to the special internal IP address 127.0.0.1. This test has the computer send data to itself. It should print the following:

```
Reply from 127.0.0.1: bytes=32 time<10ms TTL=128
Reply from 127.0.0.1: bytes=32 time<10ms TTL=128
Reply from 127.0.0.1: bytes=32 time<10ms TTL=128
Reply from 127.0.0.1: bytes=32 time<10ms TTL=128
```

If it doesn't, the TCP/IP protocol itself is incorrectly installed or configured. In that case, check the computer's IP address configuration or, if that seems correct, remove and reinstall the Internet Protocol from the Ethernet connection icon in Network Connections. (I have to say, in more than 20 years of working with PC networks, I've never seen this test fail.)

If your computer can send data to itself, go to a second computer on your LAN. Find its IP address by running `ipconfig` on that computer. Go back to the first computer and type the `ping` command again, using the address of the second computer, as in this example:

```
ping 192.168.0.23
```

Of course, you should use the other computer's real IP address in place of 192.168.0.23. You should get four replies, as before:

```
Reply from 192.168.0.23: bytes=32 time<10ms TTL=32
Reply from 192.168.0.23: bytes=32 time<10ms TTL=32
Reply from 192.168.0.23: bytes=32 time<10ms TTL=32
Reply from 192.168.0.23: bytes=32 time<10ms TTL=32
```

These replies indicate that `ping` has successfully sent data to the other machine and received it back.

If, on the other hand, the `ping` command returns "Request timed out," the packets either didn't make it to the other computer or were not returned. In either case, you have a problem with your cabling or wireless connection, network adapter, or the TCP/IP protocol setup. Another problem could be that Windows Defender Firewall or a third-party firewall product is blocking the `ping` data. This will almost certainly happen if the computer you are pinging has its network location set to Public rather than Private.

You can use `ping` to determine which computers can send to which other computers on your LAN or across wide area networks (WANs) or the Internet. `ping` should also work when given a computer's IP address or its network name.

 note

If you enter a computer name, and `ping` can't determine the computer's IP address, the problem isn't necessarily a wiring problem. It could be that the DNS or WINS name lookup system is not working correctly. Try using an IP address with `ping`, in this case, to help determine what the problem really is.

Diagnosing File and Printer Sharing Problems

If the test in the previous section doesn't point to a problem—that is, if basic network connectivity is fine, but you're still having problems with file or printer sharing—the next step depends on whether you have a workgroup or domain-type network.

If you're on a domain network, it's time to call your network administrator for assistance. He or she has more training and experience in network troubleshooting than we can impart in the space allowed here.

If you're on a home or small office workgroup network, there are a few things you might try. Here are some tips:

- Did you make sure that file sharing is enabled on each of your computers?

- Do your Windows 10, 8.1, or 8 computers say Private as their network location? Do your Windows 7 and Vista computers say Home or Work? The Public setting blocks file sharing.

  On Windows XP, there is no network location setting. Instead, open Windows Firewall, view the Exceptions list, and make sure that File and Printer Sharing is checked.

  If you use Internet Connection Sharing, restart the computer that's sharing your Internet connection and wait a minute or two after it's booted up. Then restart your other computers. This may help. The ICS computer needs to be up and running *before* any other computers on your LAN start up. Similarly, if you use a connection-sharing router, wired or wireless, unplug it, wait a few seconds, and then plug it back in. Wait about a minute and see if this has fixed the problem.

- If you can see the folders shared by another computer but can't move any files into them, or edit files in them, then your network is fine. You just have a permissions problem. On the computer that is sharing the folders, be sure that the folders are shared so that remote visitors can change files.

  ➡ For more information on shared folders, **see** "Using Shared Folders in Windows 10," **p. 446.**

If the *sharing* computer has Password Protected Sharing enabled (or has Simple File Sharing turned off if the computer is running XP), the owner of that computer should check to see that your user account has permission to read and modify the files in the shared folder. In the folder or files' Security properties, check to see that your user account is listed or that the group you're in (for example, Users or Everyone) has the necessary permissions.

➡ For more information on file permissions, **see** "Setting Security Permissions on Files and Folders," **p. 732.**

In Windows 10, 8.1, 8, and 7, Password Protected Sharing works differently than it does on Vista and XP. If you can't access a file over the network that you know you could access if you were signed in directly at the sharing computer, that computer might be using the Guest account to access the file instead of yours.

➡ *For more information on Password Protected Sharing,* **see** *"Configuring Passwords and File Sharing," **p. 762.***

One way you can tell whether this feature is causing your problem is to sign in at the sharing computer. Next, in File Explorer, right-click This PC, or in Windows Explorer, click [My] Computer, and then select Manage. In the left Navigation pane, open the Shared Folders item and select Sessions. Try to access the problem file or folder from across the network. You should see an entry for the networked computer. If the username is Guest, you will only be able to read or write files that group Everyone can read or write. See Chapter 33 for a discussion about the way Password Protected Sharing works in various situations.

WINDOWS MANAGEMENT TOOLS

Managing Windows

Our goal in this book is to help you plumb the true depths of Windows 10, and our premise is that this goal can't be met by toeing the line and doing only what the Help system tells you. Rather, we believe you can reach this goal only by taking various off-the-beaten-track routes that go beyond Windows orthodoxy.

The topics in this chapter illustrate this approach quite nicely. The tools we discuss—Group Policy Editor, Microsoft Management Console, and Services—aren't difficult to use, but they put an amazing amount of power and flexibility into your hands. We discuss them in depth because you'll be using these important tools in other chapters of the book. However, you can scour the Windows 10 Help system all day long, and you'll find only a few scant references to these tools. To be sure, Microsoft is being cautious because these are powerful tools, and the average user can wreak all kinds of havoc if these features are used incorrectly. However, your purchase of this book is proof that you are not an average user. So, when you follow the instructions in this chapter, we're sure you'll have no trouble at all using these tools.

We begin with an in-depth look at the Group Policy editor, which gives very fine-grained control over just about every aspect of Windows.

(And just in case you're wondering why the Settings app and Control Panel aren't discussed in this chapter: we cover these tools all throughout this book, in chapters and sections that discuss specific system services and components.)

Policing Windows 10 with Group Policies

In a few places throughout this book, we've shown that you can perform some pretty amazing things by using a tool that's about as hidden as any Windows power tool can be: the Local Group Policy Editor. That Microsoft has buried this program in a mostly untraveled section of the Windows landscape isn't the least bit surprising, because in the wrong hands the Local Group Policy Editor can wreak all kinds of havoc on a system. It's a kind of electronic Pandora's box that, if opened by careless or inexperienced hands, can loose all kinds of evil upon the Windows world.

Of course, none of this doom-and-gloom applies to you, dear reader, because you're a cautious and prudent wielder of all the Windows power tools. This means that you'll use the Local Group Policy Editor in a safe, prudent manner, and you'll create a system restore point if you plan to make any major changes. We knew we could count on you.

As you see in this section, the Local Group Policy Editor isn't even remotely hard to use. However, it's such a powerful tool that it's important for you to know exactly how it works, which will help ensure that nothing goes awry when you're making your changes.

Understanding Group Policies

Put simply, *group policies* are settings that control how Windows works. You can use them to customize the Windows 10 interface, restrict access to certain areas, specify security settings, and much more. Policy settings can force, hide, or reveal thousands of aspects of Windows.

Group policies are mostly used by system administrators who want to make sure that novice users don't have access to dangerous tools (such as the Registry Editor) or who want to ensure a consistent computing experience across multiple machines. Group policies are also ideally suited to situations in which multiple users share a single computer. However, group policies can be useful on single-user standalone machines, as you see in various sections of this book.

Local Group Policy Editor and Windows Versions

The power of the Local Group Policy Editor is aptly illustrated not only by the fact that Microsoft hides the program deep in the bowels of the system, but most tellingly by the fact that Microsoft didn't even offer the Local Group Policy Editor in some Windows versions. For Windows 10, the Local Group Policy Editor is not available in Windows 10 Mobile or Windows 10 Home, but it is available in Windows 10 Pro and Windows 10 Enterprise. In earlier versions of Windows, this tool was also removed from the Home versions. In other words, those Windows versions that Microsoft expects novices to be using are the same Windows versions where Microsoft doesn't even include the Local Group Policy Editor, just to be safe.

Of course, plenty of experienced users use the lesser Windows versions that don't include the Local Group Policy Editor, mostly because they're cheaper than high-end versions such as Windows 10 Pro. So, what's a would-be policy editor to do when faced with having no Local Group Policy Editor?

The short answer is, don't sweat it. That is, although the Local Group Policy Editor does provide an easy-to-use interface for many powerful settings, it's not the only way to put those settings into effect. Most group policies correspond to settings in the Windows Registry, so you can get the identical tweak on any basic Windows system by modifying the appropriate Registry setting instead. In this book, we've tried to augment group policy tweaks with the corresponding Registry tweak, just in case you don't have access to the Local Group Policy Editor.

 tip

Understanding that most group policies have parallel settings in the Registry is all fine and dandy, but how on earth are you supposed to know which of the Registry's thousands upon thousands of settings is the one you want? The old method was to export the Registry to a REG file, make the change in the Local Group Policy Editor, export the Registry again, and then compare the two files. *Way* too much work (and impossible if all you have to work with is a basic Windows version)! You can also try filtering the policies as described later (see "Filtering Policies"). Fortunately, Microsoft has Excel workbooks that list every single group policy value and give the corresponding Registry setting. Links to the different reference workbooks for Vista, Windows 7, and Windows 8.1 and Windows 10 can be found here: www.microsoft.com/en-us/download/details.aspx?id=25250.

 note

The primary purpose of the Group Policy mechanism is to allow administrators on enterprise networks to easily manage whole groups of users and computers (hence the name), enforcing correct settings, and prohibiting too much fooling around by employees (which usually translates to costly support and service calls). Needless to say, if you are using a computer on a corporate network, and you are not a domain administrator, you will almost certainly be prevented from using the Group Policy tool thanks to Group Policy settings your administrators made.

 note

Given a setting that you can tweak using either the Local Group Policy Editor or the Registry Editor (and assuming you're running a version of Windows that comes with the Local Group Policy Editor), which tool should you choose? We highly recommend using the Local Group Policy Editor because (as you'll see next) it offers a simpler and more straightforward user interface, which means it saves time, and you'll be much less likely to make an error.

Launching the Local Group Policy Editor

As we've said, you make changes to group policies using the Local Group Policy Editor, a Microsoft Management Console snap-in. To start the Local Group Policy Editor, you have two choices:

- In the taskbar's Search box, type **gpedit**, and then click Edit Group Policy in the search results.

- Press Windows Logo+R to open the Run dialog box, type **gpedit.msc**, and then press Enter.

Figure 23.1 shows the Local Group Policy Editor window that appears. (The word *Local* refers to the fact that you're editing group policies on your own computer, not on some remote computer.)

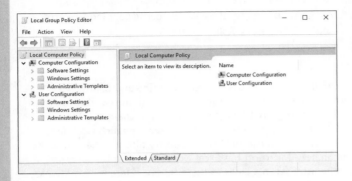

Figure 23.1
You use the Local Group Policy Editor to modify group policies on your PC.

Working with Group Policies

The Local Group Policy Editor window is divided into two sections:

- **Left pane**—This pane contains a tree-like hierarchy of policy categories, which is divided into two main categories: Computer Configuration and User Configuration. The Computer Configuration policies apply to all users and are implemented before the logon. The User Configuration policies apply only to the current user and, therefore, are not applied until that user logs on.

- **Right pane**—This pane contains the policies for whichever category is selected in the left pane.

The idea, then, is to open the tree's branches in the left pane to find the category you want. When you click the category, its policies appear in the right pane. For example, Figure 23.2 shows the Local Group Policy Editor window with the User Configuration, Administrative Templates, Control Panel category selected.

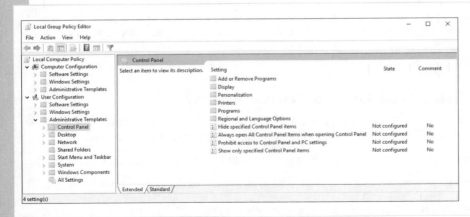

Figure 23.2
When you select a category in the left pane, the category's policies appear in the right pane.

In the right pane, the Setting column tells you the name of the policy, and the State column tells you the current state of the policy. Click a policy to see its description on the left side of the pane, as shown in Figure 23.3. If you don't see the description, click the Extended tab.

Figure 23.3
Click a policy to see its description.

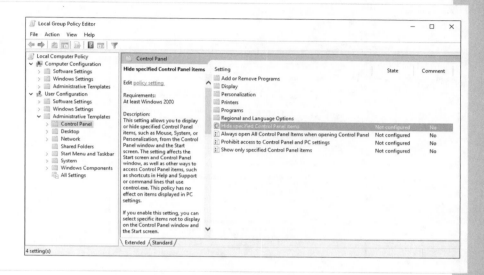

Configuring a Policy

To configure a policy, double-click it. The type of window you see depends on the policy:

 note
Take note of the Requirements value in the policy window. This value tells you which versions of Windows support the policy.

- For simple policies, you see a window similar to the one shown in Figure 23.4. These kinds of policies take one of three states: Not Configured (the policy is not in effect), Enabled (the policy is in effect and its setting is enabled), and Disabled (the policy is in effect and its setting is disabled).

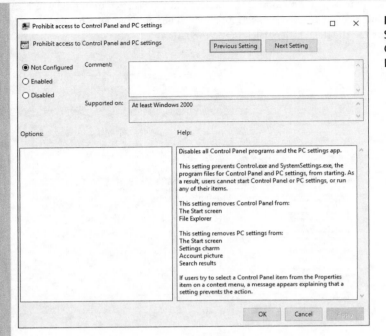

Figure 23.4
Simple policies are Not
Configured, Enabled, or
Disabled.

- Other kinds of policies require extra information when the policy is enabled. For example, Figure 23.5 shows the window for the Hide Specified Control Panel Items policy (described in detail later in the "Removing an Icon from Control Panel" section). When the Enabled option is activated, one or more controls in the Options box become enabled. In this case, the Show button becomes enabled, and you click it to specify which Control Panel items you want to hide.

Filtering Policies

We've been saying for years that the Local Group Policy Editor desperately needs a search feature. There are nearly 3,000 policies, and they're scattered around dozens of folders. Trying to find the policy you need by rooting around in the Local Group Policy Editor is like trying to find a particularly small needle in a particularly large haystack.

Fortunately, although the Windows 10 version of the Local Group Policy Editor still isn't searchable (unless you export it to a text file by selecting Action, Export List), it does come with two features that make it quite a bit easier to track down a wayward policy:

- The two Administrative Templates branches (one in Computer Configuration and the other in User Configuration) each come with a new sub-branch called All Settings. Selecting this branch displays a complete list of all the policies in that Administrative Templates branch. (Almost all non-security-related policies are in the Administrative Templates branches, so that's why they get singled out for special treatment.)

- A beefed-up filtering feature is provided that's useful for cutting the vastness of the policy landscape down to size.

Figure 23.5
More complex policies also require extra information, such as a list of folders to display in the Places bar.

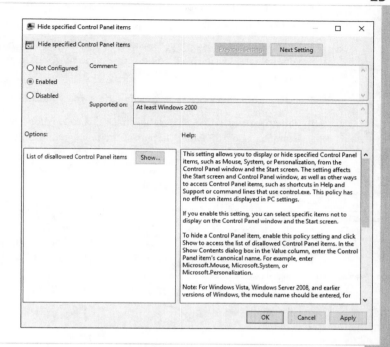

In combination, these two features make it much easier to find what you're looking for. The basic idea is that you select the All Settings branch that you want to work with and then set up a filter that defines what you're looking for. Local Group Policy Editor then displays just those policies that match your filter criteria.

To show you how this works, let's run through an example. Suppose we want to find the Hide Specified Control Panel Items policy shown earlier in Figure 23.5. Here's how we'd use a filter to locate it:

1. Select the User Configuration, Administrative Templates, All Settings branch.

2. Select Action, Filter Options to open the Filter Options dialog box.

3. Make sure the Enable Keyword Filters box is checked.

4. Use the Filter for Word(s) text box to type a word or phrase that should match the policy you're looking for. In our example, we know that "Control Panel" is part of the policy name, so we'll use that as the filter text.

5. Use the associated drop-down list to choose how you want the policy text to match your search text:

   ■ **Any**—Choose this option to match only those policies that include at least one of your search terms. (This option is selected by default.)

- **All**—Choose this option to match only those policies that include all your search terms in any order.

- **Exact**—Choose this option to match only those policies that include text that exactly matches your search phrase. We'll be filtering on the phrase "Control Panel," so we'll use an exact match.

6. Use the Within check boxes to specify where you want the filter to look for matches:

- **Policy Setting Title**—Select this check box to look for matches in the policy name. In our example, "Control Panel" is part of the policy name, and it's a relatively unique term, so it should suffice to only filter on the title, as shown in Figure 23.6.

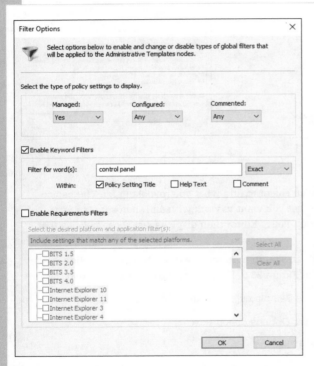

Figure 23.6
In the Windows 10 Local Group Policy Editor, you can use the Filter Options dialog box to find the policy you need.

- **Help Text**—Select this check box to look for matches in the policy description.

- **Comment**—Select this check box to look for matches in the Comments text. (Each policy comes with a Comments box that you can use to add your two cents' worth about any policy.)

7. Click OK.

With your filter in place, select Action, Filter On (or click to activate the Filter button in the toolbar). The Local Group Policy Editor displays just those policies that match your filter settings. For example, Figure 23.7 shows the results when the filter in Figure 23.6 is turned on. As you can see, the Hide Specified Control Panel Items policy is among the results.

Figure 23.7
The results when the filter set up in Figure 23.6 is turned on.

Filter

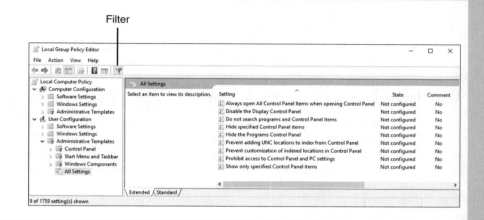

Group Policy Examples

Although you can find plenty of examples of group policies in action throughout this book, I'm a firm believer that you can't get enough of this powerful tool. With that in mind, the next few sections take you through a few of our favorite policies.

Removing an Icon from Control Panel

You can gain a bit more control over the Control Panel by configuring it not to display icons that you don't ever use or that aren't applicable to your system. Here's how it's done:

1. Open the Local Group Policy Editor window, as described earlier in this chapter.

2. Select the User Configuration, Administrative Templates, Control Panel branch.

3. Double-click the Hide Specified Control Panel Items policy.

4. Click the Enabled option.

5. Click the Show button. The Show Contents dialog box appears.

6. For each Control Panel icon you want to hide, type the icon name and press Enter.

7. Click OK to return to the Hide Specified Control Panel Items dialog box.

8. Click OK. Windows 10 puts the policy into effect.

To perform the same tweak in the Registry, open the following key:

```
HKCU\Software\Microsoft\Windows\CurrentVersion\Policies\Explorer
```

Add a DWORD value named `DisallowCpl` and set it equal to 1. Also, create a new key named `DisallowCpl`, and within that key create a new String value for each Control Panel icon you want to disable. Give the settings the names 1, 2, 3, and so on, and for each one set the value to the name of the Control Panel icon you want to disable.

Showing Only Specified Control Panel Icons

Disabling a few Control Panel icons is useful because it reduces a bit of the clutter in the All Control Panel Items window. However, what if you want to set up a computer for a novice user and you'd like that person to have access to just a few relatively harmless icons such as Display and Personalization? In that case, it's *way* too much work to disable most of the icons one at a time. A much easier approach is to specify just those few Control Panel icons you want the user to see. Here's how:

1. Open the Local Group Policy Editor window, as described earlier in this chapter.

2. Select the User Configuration, Administrative Templates, Control Panel branch.

3. Double-click the Show Only Specified Control Panel Items policy.

4. Click the Enabled option.

5. Click the Show button. The Show Contents dialog box appears.

6. For each Control Panel icon you want to show, type the icon name and press Enter.

7. Click OK to return to the Show Only Specified Control Panel Items dialog box.

8. Click OK. Windows 10 puts the policy into effect.

To perform the same tweak in the Registry, open the following key:

```
HKCU\Software\Microsoft\Windows\CurrentVersion\Policies\Explorer
```

Add a DWORD value named `RestrictCpl` and set it equal to 1. Also, create a new key named `RestrictCpl`, and within that key create a new String value for each Control Panel icon you want to show. Give the settings the names 1, 2, 3, and so on, and for each one set the value to the name of the Control Panel icon you want to show.

Other Control Panel Policies

While you have the Local Group Policy Editor up and running, consider the other two Control Panel–related policies that appear in the User Configuration, Administrative Templates, Control Panel branch:

- **Always Open All Control Panel Items When Opening Control Panel**—If you enable this policy, Control Panel is always displayed in the All Control Panel Items window, and the user can't change to the Category view. If you disable this policy, Control Panel is always displayed in the Category view, and the user can't change to the All Control Panel Items window.

- **Prohibit Access to Control Panel and PC Settings**—If you enable this policy, users can't access Control Panel at all.

Customizing the Windows Security Window

When you press Ctrl+Alt+Delete while logged on to Windows 10, you see the Windows Security window, which contains the following items, as shown in Figure 23.8:

- **Lock**—Click this button to hide the desktop and display the Lock screen. To return to the desktop, you must enter your Windows 10 user account password. This feature is useful if you're going to leave Windows 10 unattended and don't want another person accessing the desktop. However, there is a much faster way to lock the computer: just press Windows Logo+L.

Figure 23.8
In Windows 10, press Ctrl+Alt+ Delete to display the Windows Security options.

- **Switch User**—Click this button to switch to a different user account while also leaving your current user account running.

- **Sign Out**—Click this button to display the sign-in screen, which lets you log on using a different user account.

- **Task Manager**—Click this button to open Task Manager.

Of these four commands, all but Switch User are customizable using group policies. So, if you find that you never use one or more of those commands, or (more likely) if you want to prevent a user from accessing one or more of the commands, you can use group policies to remove them from the Windows Security window. Here are the steps to follow:

1. Open the Local Group Policy Editor window, as described earlier in this chapter.

2. Open the User Configuration, Administrative Templates, System, Ctrl+Alt+Del Options branch.

3. Double-click one of the following policies (ignore the Remove Change Password policy, which isn't supported in Windows 10):

   - **Remove Lock Computer**—You can use this policy to disable the Lock item in the Windows Security window.

   - **Remove Task Manager**—You can use this policy to disable the Task Manager item in the Windows Security window.

   - **Remove Logoff**—You can use this policy to disable the Sign Out item in the Windows Security window.

4. In the policy dialog box that appears, click Enabled and then click OK.

5. Repeat steps 3 and 4 to disable all the buttons you don't need.

Figure 23.9 shows the Windows Security window with the three buttons removed.

To perform the same tweak using the Registry, launch the Registry Editor and open the following key:

`HKCU\Software\Microsoft\Windows\CurrentVersion\Policies\System`

Change the value of one or more of the following settings to 1:

`DisableLockWorkstationDisableTaskMgr`

To remove the Log Off button via the Registry, open the following key:

`HKCU\Software\Microsoft\Windows\CurrentVersion\Policies\Explorer`

Change the value of the `NoLogoff` setting to 1.

 note

In most cases, you would probably only want to disable these features on a computer that was going to be accessible to the public, for instance, in a kiosk or public display. In this case, you'd have to disable a lot more than just these; in particular, you must ensure nobody can get to the command prompt.

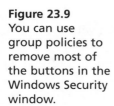

Figure 23.9
You can use group policies to remove most of the buttons in the Windows Security window.

Enabling the Shutdown Event Tracker

When you run the Shut Down command, Windows 10 proceeds to power down without any more input from you (unless any running programs have documents with unsaved changes). That's usually a good thing, but you might want to keep track of why you shut down or restart Windows 10, or why the system itself initiates a shutdown or restart. To do that, you can enable a feature called Shutdown Event Tracker. With this feature, you can document the shutdown event by specifying whether it is planned or unplanned, selecting a reason for the shutdown, and adding a comment that describes the shutdown.

Here are the steps to follow to use a group policy to enable the Shutdown Event Tracker feature:

1. Open the Local Group Policy Editor window, as described earlier in this chapter.

2. Navigate to the Computer Configuration, Administrative Templates, All Settings branch.

3. Double-click the Display Shutdown Event Tracker policy.

4. Click Enabled.

5. In the Shutdown Event Tracker Should Be Displayed list, select Always.

6. Click OK.

Now when you run the Shut Down command, you see the dialog box shown in Figure 23.10. Use the list to select the reason for the shutdown, and then click Continue.

Figure 23.10
The Shut Down Windows dialog box appears with the Shutdown Event Tracker feature enabled.

To enable the Shutdown Event Tracker on systems without the Local Group Policy Editor, open the Registry Editor and dig down to the following key:

`HKLM\Software\Policies\Microsoft\Windows NT\Reliability`

Change the value of the following two settings to 1:

```
ShutdownReasonOn
ShutdownReasonUI
```

Configuring the Microsoft Management Console

The Microsoft Management Console (MMC) is a system administration program that can act as a host application for a variety of tools. The advantage of MMC is that it displays each tool as a *console*, a two-pane view that has a tree-like hierarchy in the left pane (this is called the *tree pane*) and a *taskpad* in the right pane that shows the contents of each branch (this is called the *results pane*). This gives each tool a similar interface, which makes it easier to use the tools. You can also customize the console view in a number of ways, create custom taskpad views, and save a particular set of tools to reuse later. These tools are called *snap-ins* because you can "snap them in" (that is, attach them) as *nodes* to the console root.

This section gives you an overview of the MMC and shows you a few techniques for getting the most out of its often-useful tools.

Reviewing the Windows 10 Snap-Ins

When you work with the MMC interface, you're really editing a Microsoft Common Console Document, an .msc file that stores one or more snap-ins, the console view, and the taskpad view used by each snap-in branch. You learn how to create custom .msc files in this chapter, but you should know that Windows 10 comes with a large number of predefined MSC snap-ins, and we've summarized them in Table 23.1.

Table 23.1 The Default Windows 10 Snap-Ins

Snap-in	File	Description
ActiveX Control	N/A	Launches the Insert ActiveX Control Wizard, which enables you to choose an ActiveX control to display as a node. (We haven't been able to find a good use for this one yet!)
Authorization Manager	azman.msc	Used by developers to set permissions on applications.
Certificates	certmgr.msc	Enables you to browse the security certificates on your system.
Component Services	comexp.msc	Enables you to view and work with Component Object Model (COM) services.
Computer Management	compmgmt.msc	Contains a number of snap-ins for managing various aspects of Windows 10. You can examine hidden and visible shared folders, set group policies, access Device Manager, manage hard disks, and much more.
Device Manager	devmgmt.msc	Enables you to add and manage your system hardware.
Disk Management	diskmgmt.msc	Enables you to view and manage all the disk drives on your system.
Event Viewer	eventvwr.msc	Enables you to view the Windows 10 event logs.
Folder	N/A	Adds a folder to your list of snap-ins so that you can arrange and organize them.
Group Policy Object Editor	gpedit.msc	Enables you to work with group policies.
IP Security Monitor	N/A	Enables you to monitor Internet Protocol (IP) security settings.
IP Security Policy Management	N/A	Enables you to create IP Security (IPsec) policies.
Link to Web Address	N/A	Adds a node that displays the contents of a specified web page.
Local Users and Groups	lusrmgr.msc	Enables you to add, modify, and delete user accounts.
Performance Monitor	perfmon.msc	Enables you to monitor one or more performance counters.
Print Management	printman-agement.msc	Enables you to view and manage either local printers or network print servers.
Resultant Set of Policy	rsop.msc	Shows the applied group policies for the current user.
Security Configuration and Analysis	N/A	Enables you to open an existing security database or build a new security database based on a security template you create using the Security Templates snap-in.

Table 23.1 Continued

Snap-in	File	Description
Security Templates	N/A	Enables you to create a security template where you enable and configure one or more security-related policies.
Services	services.msc	Enables you to start, stop, enable, and disable services.
Shared Folders	fsmgmt.msc	Enables you to monitor activity on your shared folders.
Task Scheduler	taskschd.msc	Enables you to schedule programs, scripts, and other items.
TPM Management	tpm.msc	Enables you to configure and work with Trusted Platform Module (TPM) security devices.
Windows Defender Firewall with Advanced Security	wf.msc	Presents an advanced Windows Defender Firewall interface.
WMI Control	wmimgmt.msc	Enables you to configure properties related to Windows Management Instrumentation.

Launching the MMC

To get the MMC onscreen, you have two choices:

- To start with a blank console, either click in the taskbar's Search box or press Windows Logo+R to open the Run dialog box, type **mmc**, and then press Enter.

- To start with an existing snap-in, either click in the taskbar's Search box or press Windows Logo+R to open the Run dialog box, type the name of the .msc file you want to load (refer to Table 23.1), and then press Enter.

Figure 23.11 shows a blank MMC window. We show you how to add snap-ins to the console in the next section.

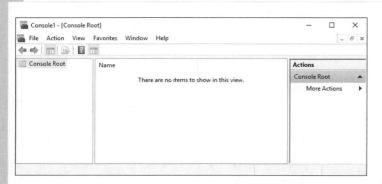

Figure 23.11
The Microsoft Management Console ready for customizing.

Adding a Snap-In

You start building your console file by adding one or more snap-ins to the console root, which is the top-level MMC container. (Even if you loaded the MMC by launching an existing snap-in, you can still add more snap-ins to the console.) Here are the steps to follow:

 tip

You can help organize your snap-ins by adding subfolders to the console root. In the list of snap-ins, select Folder and then click Add. When you return to the MMC, right-click the new subfolder and then click Rename to give the subfolder a useful name. To add a snap-in inside this subfolder, select File, Add/Remove Snap-In (or press Ctrl+M) to open the Add/Remove Snap-in dialog box. Click Advanced, check the Allow Changing the Parent Snap-in box, and then click OK. In the new Parent Snap-in list that appears, choose the subfolder you added. See Figure 23.14, later in this section, for some sample subfolders.

1. Select File, Add/Remove Snap-In (or press Ctrl+M). The MMC displays the Add or Remove Snap-Ins dialog box, shown in Figure 23.12.

Figure 23.12
You use the Add or Remove Snap-Ins dialog box to populate the MMC with snap-in nodes.

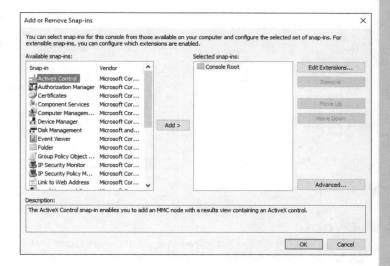

2. In the Available Snap-ins list, select the snap-in you want to use.

3. Click Add.

4. If the snap-in can work with remote computers, you see a dialog box similar to the one shown in Figure 23.13. To have the snap-in manage a remote machine, select Another Computer, type the computer name in the text box, and then click Finish.

5. Repeat steps 2–4 to add other snap-ins to the console.

6. Click OK.

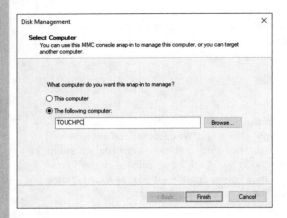

Figure 23.13
Some snap-ins can manage remote computers as well as the local machine.

Figure 23.14 shows the MMC with a custom console consisting of several snap-ins and subfolders.

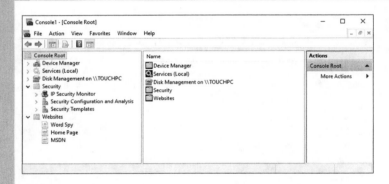

Figure 23.14
The MMC with a custom console.

 note

In Figure 23.14, the items in the Websites subfolder are based on the Link to Web Address snap-in, which is a special snap-in that displays the current version of whatever web page you specify. When you add the snap-in, the MMC runs the Link to Web Address Wizard. Type the web page address (either an Internet URL or a path to a local or network page), click Next, type a name for the snap-in, and then click Finish.

Saving a Console

If you think you want to reuse your custom console later on, you should save it to an .msc file. Here are the steps to follow:

1. Select File, Save (or press Ctrl+S) to open the Save As dialog box.

2. Type a filename for the console.

3. Select a location for the console file.

4. Click Save.

Creating a Custom Taskpad View

A *taskpad view* is a custom configuration of the MMC results (right) pane for a given snap-in. By default, the results pane shows a list of the snap-in's contents—for example, the list of categories and devices in the Device Manager snap-in and the list of installed services in the Services snap-in. However, you can customize this view with one or more tasks that run commands defined by the snap-in, or any program or script that you specify. You can also control the size of the list, whether the list is displayed horizontally or vertically in the results pane, and more.

> ## tip
>
> By default, MMC assumes you want to save your console file in the Administrative Tools folder. However, if you want to be able to launch your console file from the Start menu or the Run dialog box, you should save it in the %SystemRoot%\System32 folder, along with the predefined snap-ins.

Here are the steps to follow to create a custom taskpad view:

1. Select a snap-in in the tree pane, as follows:

   ■ If you want to apply the taskpad view to a specific snap-in, select that snap-in.

   ■ If you want to apply the taskpad view to a group of snap-ins that use the same snap-in type, specify one snap-in from the group. For example, if you want to customize all the folders, select any folder (such as the Console Root folder); similarly, if you want to customize all the Link to Web Address snap-ins, select one of them.

2. Select Action, New Taskpad View to launch the New Taskpad View Wizard.

3. Click Next to open the Taskpad Style dialog box, shown in Figure 23.15.

Figure 23.15
Use the New Taskpad View Wizard to create your custom taskpad view.

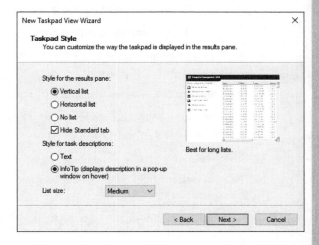

4. Use the following controls to set up the style of taskpad you want:

- **Style for the Results Pane**—Select an option for displaying the snap-in's results: Vertical List (this is best for lists with a large number of items), Horizontal List (this is best for web pages or lists with a large number of columns), or No List (choose this option if you want only tasks to appear in the results pane).

- **Hide Standard Tab**—After you create the new taskpad view, the MMC displays two tabs in the results pane: The Extended tab shows your custom taskpad view, and the Standard tab shows the default view. To keep the option of displaying the default view, deactivate the Hide Standard Tab dialog box.

- **Style for Task Descriptions**—When you add descriptions for your tasks later on, you can have the MMC display each description either as text below the task link or as an Info Tip pop-up box that appears when you hover the mouse over the task link.

- **List Size**—Choose the size of the list: Small (good if you add lots of tasks), Medium (this is the default), or Large (good if you have few or no tasks).

5. Click Next. The Taskpad Reuse dialog box appears.

6. The wizard assumes you want to apply the new taskpad view to all snap-ins of the same type. If you want to apply the taskpad view only to the current snap-in, select the Selected Tree Item option.

7. Click Next. The Name and Description dialog box appears.

8. Type a name and optional description for the taskpad view and then click Next. The final wizard dialog box appears.

9. If you don't want to add tasks to the new view, uncheck the Add New Tasks to This Taskpad After the Wizard Closes box.

10. Click Finish. If you elected to add tasks to the view, the New Task Wizard appears.

11. Click Next. The Command Type dialog box appears.

12. Select one of the following command types:

- **Menu Command**—Select this option to create a task that runs an MMC or snap-in menu command.

- **Shell Command**—Select this option to create a task that runs a program, script, or batch file.

- **Navigation**—Select this option to create a task that takes you to another snap-in that's in your MMC Favorites list.

13. Click Next.

14. How you proceed from here depends on the command type you selected in step 12:

- **Menu Command**—In the Menu Command dialog box, first select an item from the Command Source list.

note

To add a snap-in to the MMC Favorites list, select the snap-in in the tree pane and then select Favorites, Add to Favorites.

Choose Item Listed in the Results Pane to apply the command to whatever item is currently selected in the results pane; choose Node in the Tree to select a command based on an item in the MMC tree pane.

- **Shell Command**—In the Command Line dialog box, use the Command text box to specify the path to the program executable, script, or batch file that you want the task to run. You can also specify startup parameters, the Start In folder, and a Run window type.

- **Navigation**—In the Navigation dialog box, select the items from the MMC Favorites list.

15. Click Next. The Name and Description dialog box appears.

16. Edit the task name and description, and then click Next. The Task Icon dialog box appears, as shown in Figure 23.16.

Figure 23.16
Use the Task Icon dialog box to choose an icon to display with your task.

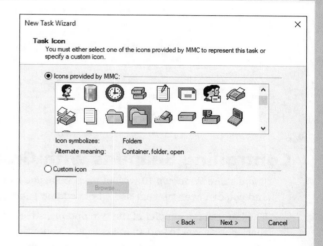

17. Click Next. The final New Task Wizard dialog box appears.

18. If you want to add more tasks, check the When I Click Finish, Run This Wizard Again box.

19. Click Finish.

20. If you elected to add more tasks, repeat steps 11–19, as needed.

> **note**
> To make changes to a custom taskpad view, right-click the snap-in and then click Edit Taskpad View.

Figure 23.17 shows the MMC with a custom taskpad view applied to a Link to Web Address snap-in.

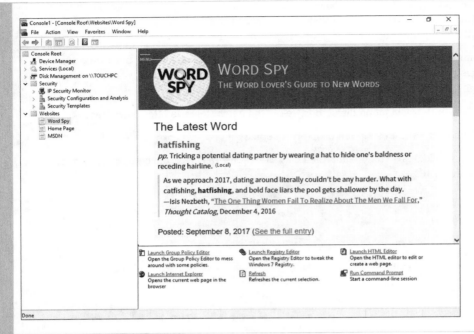

Figure 23.17
A custom
taskpad view.

Controlling Snap-Ins with Group Policies

If you share Windows 10 with other people, you can control which snap-ins they're allowed to use, and you can even prevent users from adding snap-ins to the MMC.

The latter is the simpler of the two options, so let's begin with that. The MMC has an *author mode* that enables you to add snap-ins to it. If you prevent the MMC from entering author mode, you prevent users from adding snap-ins. You can do this using a group policy. Note, too, that this policy also prevents users from entering author mode for those snap-ins that can be opened directly (from the taskbar Search box, from the Run dialog box, from the command line, from Administrative Tools, and so on). Here are the steps to follow:

1. Open the Local Group Policy Editor, as described earlier in this chapter in the section "Launching the Local Group Policy Editor."

2. Navigate to the User Configuration, Administrative Templates, Windows Components, Microsoft Management Console branch.

3. Double-click the Restrict the User from Entering Author Mode policy.

4. Activate the Enabled option.

5. Click OK.

Rather than blocking off the MMC entirely, you might prefer to allow users access only to specific snap-ins. Here are the steps to follow:

1. Open the Local Group Policy Editor.

2. Navigate to the User Configuration, Administrative Templates, Windows Components, Microsoft Management Console branch.

3. Double-click the Restrict Users to the Explicitly Permitted List of Snap-Ins policy.

4. Activate the Enabled option.

5. Click OK.

6. Navigate to the User Configuration, Administrative Templates, Windows Components, Microsoft Management Console, Restricted/Permitted Snap-Ins branch.

7. Double-click a snap-in that you want users to access.

8. Activate the Enabled option.

9. Click OK.

10. Repeat steps 7–9 for each snap-in that you want users to access.

Controlling Services

Windows 10 comes with a long list of programs called *services* that operate behind the scenes and perform essential tasks either on their own or in support of other programs or Windows features. These services are background routines that enable the system to perform tasks such as logging on to the network, managing disks, collecting performance data, and writing event logs. Windows 10 comes with more than 160 installed services.

You won't have to interact with services very often, but when they do come up, you'll be glad to have this section's tools in your Windows 10 toolbox. For example, although services usually operate behind the scenes, you might need to pause, stop, and start services, as well as configure how services load at startup. The following sections show you the various methods you can use to perform these service tasks.

Controlling Services with the Services Snap-in

The standard interface for the Windows 10 services is the Services snap-in, which you can load by using any of the following techniques:

- Click in the taskbar's Search box or press Windows Logo+R to display the Run dialog box, type **services.msc**, and press Enter.

- In Control Panel, select Small Icons or Large Icons in the View list, click Administrative Tools, and then click Services.

- Press Windows Logo+X (or right-click the Start button), click Computer Management, and then select the Services and Applications, Services branch.

➡ *To learn how to add Command Prompt (Admin) to the Start Menu's shortcut menu, see "Adding Command Prompt to the Shortcut Menu," p. 129.*

The Services snap-in that appears displays a list of the installed services. For each service, it displays the name of the service and a brief description, the current status of the service (Running, Paused, or blank for a stopped service), the service's startup type (such as Automatic or Manual), and the name of the system account the service uses to log on at startup. When you select a service, the Extended tab of the taskpad view shows the service name and description and offers links to control the service status (such as Start, Stop, or Restart). Figure 23.18 shows an example.

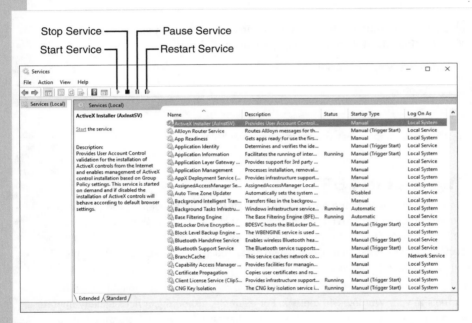

Figure 23.18
You can use the Services snap-in to control the Windows 10 services.

To change the status of a service, select it and then use one of the following techniques:

- To start a stopped service, either click the Start link in the taskpad or click the Start Service toolbar button.

- To stop a running service, either click the Stop link in the taskpad or click the Stop Service toolbar button.

- To pause a running service, either click the Pause link in the taskpad or click the Pause Service toolbar button. (Note that only a few services support the Pause Service task.)

- To resume a paused service, either click the Restart link in the taskpad or click the Restart Service toolbar button.

 note

If a service is started but has no Stop link and the Stop toolbar button is disabled, this means the service is essential to Windows 10 and can't be stopped. Examples of essential services include DCOM Server Process Launcher, Group Policy Client, Plug and Play, Remote Procedure Call (RPC), and Security Accounts Manager.

caution

It's possible that a service might be dependent on one or more other services, and if those services aren't running, the dependent service will not work properly. If you stop a service that has dependent services, Windows 10 also stops the dependents. However, when you restart the main service, Windows 10 might not start the dependent services as well. You need to start those services by hand. To see which services depend on a particular service, double-click that service to open its property sheet, and then display the Dependencies tab. Dependent services are shown in the list titled The Following System Components Depend on This Service.

To change the way a service starts when you boot Windows 10, follow these steps:

1. Double-click the service you want to work with to open its property sheet. Figure 23.19 shows an example.

Figure 23.19
You use a service's property sheet to control its startup type.

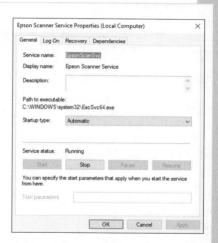

2. In the General tab, use the Startup Type list to select one of the following types:

- **Automatic**—The service starts automatically when Windows 10 boots. The service is started before the logon screen appears.

- **Automatic (Delayed Start)**—The service starts automatically when Windows 10 boots, but not until you log on.

- **Manual**—The service does not start when Windows 10 boots. You must start the service yourself.

- **Disabled**—The service does not start when Windows 10 boots, and you can't start the service manually.

3. Click OK.

 note

If the Startup Type list is disabled, this means the service is essential to Windows 10 and must be started automatically when the system boots.

Controlling Services at the Command Prompt

If you regularly stop and start certain services, loading the Services snap-in and manually stopping and then restarting each service can be time-consuming. A better method is to take advantage of the NET STOP and NET START command-line tools, which enable you to stop and start any service that isn't disabled. If a service can be paused and restarted, you can also use the NET PAUSE and NET CONTINUE commands to control the service. Each of these commands uses the same syntax:

tip

If you make changes to service startup types and you find your system is unstable or causing problems, the best thing to do is return each service to its default startup type.

```
NET STOP Service
NET START Service
NET PAUSE Service
NET CONTINUE Service
```

Service is the name of the service you want to control. Use the same value that appears in the Name column of the Services snap-in. If the name contains a space, surround the name with quotation marks.

Here are some examples:

tip

To see a list of the currently running services, open a command-line session and enter the command net start without the Service parameter.

```
net start Fax
net stop "Disk Defragmenter"
net pause "Windows Audio"
net continue "Windows Time"
```

You can combine multiple commands in a batch file to easily control several services with a single task.

Controlling Services with a Script

If you want to automate service control but also want to control the startup type, you need to go beyond the command line and create scripts that manage your services. Windows Management Instrumentation (WMI) has a class called Win32_Service that represents a Windows service. You can return an instance of this class to work with a specific service on Windows 10. After you have the service object, you can query its current status with the State property, determine whether the service is running with the Started property, and return the service's startup type with the StartMode property. You can also change the service state using the StartService, StopService, PauseService, and ResumeService methods.

Listing 23.1 presents a script that uses most of these properties and methods.

➡ To learn how to run scripts, **see** "Windows Script Host," **p. 685.**

Listing 23.1 A WMI Script That Toggles a Service's State Between Started and Stopped

```
Option Explicit
Dim strComputer, strServiceName, intReturn
Dim objWMI, objServices, objService
'
' Get the WMI service
'
strComputer = "localhost"
Set objWMI = GetObject("winmgmts:{impersonationLevel=impersonate}!\\" & _
  strComputer & "\root\cimv2")
'
' Specify the service name
'
strServiceName = "Remote Registry"
'
' Get the service instance
'
Set objServices = objWMI.ExecQuery("SELECT * FROM Win32_Service " & _
        "WHERE DisplayName = '" & strServiceName & "'")
For Each objService In objServices
  '
  ' Save the service name
  '
  strServiceName = objService.DisplayName
  '
  ' Is the service started?
  '
  If objService.Started Then
    '
    ' Can it be stopped?
    '
    If objService.AcceptStop Then
      '
      ' Attempt to stop the service
      '
      intReturn = objService.StopService
      '
      ' Check the return value
      '
      If intReturn <> 0 Then
        '
        ' Display the error message
        '
        WScript.Echo "ERROR: The " & strServiceName & " service " & _
              "failed to stop. The return code is " & intReturn
      Else
        '
        ' Display the current state
        '
```

```
        WScript.Echo "The " & strServiceName & " service is now " & _
                objService.State
      End If
    Else
      '
      ' Display the error message
      '
      WScript.Echo "ERROR: The " & strServiceName & " service " & _
              "cannot be stopped."
    End If
  Else
    '
    ' Attempt to start the service
    '
    intReturn = objService.StartService

    ' Check the return value
    '
    If intReturn <> 0 Then
      '
      ' Display the error message
      '
      WScript.Echo "ERROR: The " & strServiceName & " service " & _
              "failed to start. The return code is " & intReturn
    Else
      '
      ' Display the current state
      '
      WScript.Echo "The " & strServiceName & " service is now " & _
              objService.State
    End If
  End If
Next
'
' Release the objects
'
Set objWMI = Nothing
Set objServices = Nothing
Set objService = Nothing
```

This script gets the WMI service object and uses its ExecQuery method to return an instance of the Win32_Service class by using the WHERE clause to look for a specific service name. That name was earlier stored in the strServiceName variable. In the For Each...Next loop, the script first checks to see whether the service is currently started by checking its Started property:

- If the Started property returns True, the service is running, so we want to stop it. The script then checks the service's AcceptStop property, which returns False for essential Windows 10 services that can't be stopped. In this case, the script returns an error message. If AcceptStop returns True, the script attempts to stop the service by running the StopService method.

■ If the Started property returns False, the service is stopped, so we want to start it. The script attempts to start the service by running the StartService method.

The StopService and StartService methods generate the return codes shown in Table 23.2.

Table 23.2 Return Codes Generated by the StartService and StopService Methods

Return Code	Description
0	Success
1	Not supported
2	Access denied
3	Dependent services running
4	Invalid service control
5	Service cannot accept control
6	Service not active
7	Service request timeout
8	Unknown failure
9	Path not found
10	Service already stopped
11	Service database locked
12	Service dependency deleted
13	Service dependency failure
14	Service disabled
15	Service logon failed
16	Service marked for deletion
17	Service no thread
18	Status circular dependency
19	Status—duplicate name
20	Status—invalid name
21	Status—invalid parameter
22	Status—invalid service account
23	Status—service exists
24	Service already paused

For both the StopService and StartService methods, the script stores the return code in the intReturn variable and then checks to see whether it's a number other than 0. If so, the script displays an error message that includes the return code; otherwise, the script displays the new state of the service (as given by the State property).

Making Windows Shut Down Services Faster

If it seems to take Windows forever to shut down, the culprit might be all those services that it has running. Windows has to shut down each service one by one before it can shut down the PC. In each case, Windows waits a certain amount of time for the service to close, and if it hasn't closed in that time, Windows kills the service. It's that waiting for services to shut themselves down that can really bring the shutdown process to its knees.

However, most services shut down as soon as they get the command from Windows. So, although it's polite of Windows to give some services a bit of extra time, it's really wasted time because in most cases Windows is just going to have to kill those slow services anyway. In that case, you should configure Windows 10 to tell it to kill services faster. Here's how:

 tip

You can also reduce the amount of time that Windows 10 waits before killing any running applications at shutdown. In the Registry Editor, navigate to the following key:

`HKEY_CURRENT_USER\ControlPanel\Desktop`

Double-click the WaitToKillAppTimeout setting. (If you don't see this setting, select Edit, New, String Value, type **WaitToKillAppTimeout**, and click OK.) Change the value to 5000 and click OK.

1. Select Start, type **regedit**, press Enter, and then enter your User Account Control credentials. The Registry Editor appears.

2. Navigate to the following key:

   `HKEY_LOCAL_MACHINE\SYSTEM\CurrentControlSet\Control`

3. Double-click the WaitToKillServiceTimeout setting.

4. Reduce the value to 1000.

5. Click OK.

(Don't do this, though, if your computer has services that really could need a while to shut down, such as database services that might have a lot of data to save to disk or online backup services.)

Resetting a Broken Service

If Windows 10 is acting erratically (or, we should say, if it's acting more erratically than usual), the problem could be a service that's somehow gotten corrupted. How can you tell? The most obvious clue is an error message that tells you a particular service isn't running or couldn't start. You can also check the Event Viewer for service errors. Finally, if a particular feature of Windows 10 is acting funny and you know that a service is associated with that feature, you might suspect that service is causing the trouble.

To fix the problem (hopefully!), you can reset the broken service. The procedure involves the following four general steps:

1. Determine the name of the service that is (or that you suspect is) broken.

2. Delete the service.

3. Load a backup copy of the system hive into the Registry.

4. Copy the service from the backup hive copy to the service's actual Registry location.

Here is more detail on each of those four steps.

Determine the Name of the Service

To begin, follow these steps to determine the name of the service:

1. Open the Services snap-in, as described earlier in this chapter.

2. Double-click the service you want to reset.

3. In the General tab, locate the Service Name value.

4. Click OK.

Delete the Service

Next, follow these steps to delete the service:

1. Select Start, type **command**, right-click Command Prompt in the results, click Run as Administrator, and then enter your User Account Control credentials. Windows 10 opens an Administrator Command Prompt session.

2. Type the following (where *service* is the service name that you noted in the previous set of steps):

   ```
   sc delete service
   ```

3. Press Enter. Windows 10 attempts to delete the service.

 note

If the deletion isn't successful, double-check the service name. If you're sure you have the name right, try deleting the service using the Registry Editor instead. Open the Registry Editor, navigate to the HKEY_LOCAL_ MACHINE\System\ CurrentControlSet\Services key, and then locate the service. Right-click the service and then click Delete.

If the deletion works properly, you see the following message:

```
[SC] DeleteService SUCCESS
```

Note that you need the Command Prompt again a bit later, so leave the session open for now.

Load a Backup Copy of the System Hive

Now follow these steps to load a fresh copy of the system hive:

1. Select Start, type **regedit**, press Enter, and then enter your User Account Control credentials to open the Registry Editor.

2. Select the HKEY_LOCAL_MACHINE key.

3. Select File, Load Hive to open the Load Hive dialog box.

4. Open the system backup file:

   %SystemRoot%\system32\config\RegBack\SYSTEM.OLD

5. Click Open. The Registry Editor prompts you for a key name.

6. Type **reset** and click OK.

You now have the backup copy of the system hive loaded into the HKLM\reset key.

Copy the Service from the Backup

Now you complete the operation by copying the service from this backup. Here are the steps:

1. Return to the Command Prompt.

2. Type the following (where service is the *service* name you noted in the first set of steps):

```
reg copy hklm\reset\controlset001\services\service
hklm\system\currentcontrolset\services\service /s /f
```

3. Press Enter. Windows 10 copies the backup version of the service to the original Registry location.

4. Reboot your PC to put the change into effect.

Monitoring Performance

Performance optimization is a bit of a black art in that every user has different needs, every configuration has different operating parameters, and every system can react in a unique and unpredictable way to performance tweaks. That means if you want to optimize your system, you have to get to know how it works, what it needs, and how it reacts to changes. You can do this by just using the system and paying attention to how things look and feel, but a more rigorous approach is often called for. To that end, the next few sections take you on a brief tour of Windows 10's performance-monitoring capabilities.

Monitoring Performance with Task Manager

The Task Manager utility is excellent for getting a quick overview of the current state of the system. To get it onscreen, press Ctrl+Alt+Delete to open the Windows Security screen, and then click the Task Manager link. Once Task Manager shows up, click More Details to expand the window if it's not already in the expanded view.

 tip

To bypass the Windows Security screen, either press Ctrl+Shift+Esc or right-click an empty section of the taskbar and click Task Manager.

The Processes tab, shown in Figure 23.20, displays a list of the programs, services, and system components currently running on your system.

Figure 23.20
The Task Manager Processes tab lists your system's running programs and services.

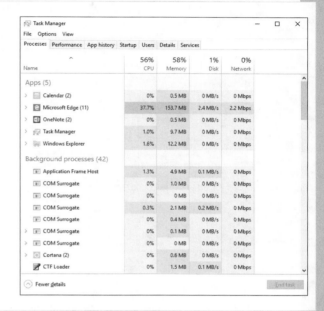

In addition to the name and status of each process, you see four performance measures:

- **CPU**—The values in this column tell you the percentage of CPU resources that each process is using. If your system seems sluggish, look for a process consuming all or nearly all the resources of the CPU. Most programs will monopolize the CPU occasionally for short periods, but a program that is stuck at 100 (percent) for a long time most likely has some kind of problem. In that case, try shutting down the program. If that doesn't work, click the program's process and then click End Task.

- **Memory**—This value tells you approximately how much memory a process is using. This value is less useful because a process might genuinely require a lot of memory to operate. However, if this value is steadily increasing for a process that you're not using, it could indicate a problem, and you should shut down the process.

- **Disk**—This column shows the total hard disk I/O transfer rate (disk reads and writes in megabytes per second).

- **Network**—This column shows the total network data transfer rate (data sent and received in megabits per second).

The Performance tab, shown in Figure 23.21, offers a more substantial collection of performance data.

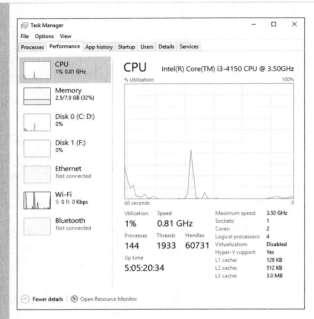

Figure 23.21
The Task Manager Performance tab lists various numbers related to your system's memory components.

Click the items on the left—CPU, Memory, Disk, and various network interfaces—to see one or more graphs that show current activity, as well as several values related to the system component. Here's what they mean:

- **CPU: Utilization**—This is the current value and the graphed values over time for the CPU usage, which is the total percentage of CPU resources that your running processes are using.

- **CPU: Speed**—The current clock speed of the CPU. Compare this to the Maximum Speed value on the right.

- **CPU: Processes**—The number of processes currently running.

- **CPU: Threads**—The number of threads used by all running processes. A *thread* is a single processor task executed by a process, and most processes can use two or more threads at the same time to speed up execution.

- **CPU: Handles**—The number of object handles used by all running processes. A *handle* is a pointer to a resource. For example, if a process wants to use a particular service offered by a particular object, the process asks the object for a handle to that service.

- **CPU: Up Time**—The number of days, hours, minutes, and seconds that you have been logged on to Windows 10 in the current session.

- **Memory: Memory Usage**—A graph of the current amount of memory in use compared to the total amount of memory in the system over time.

- **Memory: Memory Composition**—The current proportion of used to unused memory.

- **Memory: In Use**—The total amount of RAM currently being used by the system.

- **Memory: Available**—The amount of physical RAM that Windows 10 has available for your programs. Note that Windows 10 does not include the system cache (see the Memory: Cached value, later in this list) in this total.

- **Memory: Committed**—The minimum and maximum values of the page file. What is a page file? Your computer can address memory beyond the amount physically installed on the system. This nonphysical memory is *virtual memory* implemented by setting up a piece of your hard disk to emulate physical memory. This hard disk storage is actually a single file called a *page file* (or sometimes a *paging file* or a *swap file*). When physical memory is full, Windows 10 makes room for new data by taking some data that's currently in memory and swapping it out to the page file.

- **Memory: Cached**—The amount of physical RAM that Windows 10 has set aside to store recently used programs and documents. This is called the *system cache.*

- **Memory: Paged Pool**—This value is the amount of virtual memory, in megabytes, that Windows 10 has allocated to the process in the *paged pool*—the system memory area that Windows 10 uses for objects that can be written back to the disk when the system doesn't need them. The most active processes have the largest paged pool values, so it's normal for this value to increase over time. However, it's unusual for any one process to have a significantly large paged pool value. You can improve performance by shutting down and restarting such a process.

 note

A *page fault* occurs when a process requests a page from virtual memory and the system can't find the page. (A *page* is an area of virtual memory used to transfer data between virtual memory and a storage medium, usually the hard disk.) The system then either retrieves the data from another virtual memory location (this is called a *soft page fault*) or from the hard disk (this is called a *hard page fault*). Unfortunately, Task Manager doesn't give you any data on page faults. For this, you need to use Performance Monitor, as described later in the "Using the Performance Monitor" section.

- **Memory: Non-paged Pool**—This value is the amount of virtual memory, in megabytes, that Windows 10 has allocated to the process in the *non-paged pool*—the system memory area that Windows 10 uses for objects that must remain in memory and therefore can't be written back to the disk when the system doesn't need them. Because the non-paged pool takes up physical RAM on the system, if memory is running low, processes that require a lot of non-paged pool memory could generate lots of page faults and slow down the system. Consider closing some programs to reduce memory usage.

- **Disk: Active Time**—The percentage utilization of the hard disk, both over time (the Active Time graph) and current (the Active Time value).

- **Disk: Disk Transfer Rate**—The rate over time at which data is transferred through the hard disk system in kilobytes per second.

- **Disk: Average Response Time**—The average time in milliseconds that the hard disk takes to respond to read and write requests.

- **Disk: Read Speed**—The current speed in kilobytes per second at which the system is reading data from the hard disk.

- **Disk: Write Speed**—The current speed in kilobytes per second at which the system is writing data to the hard disk.

- **Ethernet/Wi-Fi: Throughput**—The speed over time in kilobits per second at which network data is passing through whatever network interface you selected.

- **Ethernet/Wi-Fi: Send**—The current speed in kilobits per second at which the network interface is sending data.

- **Ethernet/Wi-Fi: Receive**—The current speed in kilobits per second at which the network interface is receiving data.

Here are two notes related to the Memory values that will help you monitor memory-related performance issues:

- If the Memory: Available value approaches zero, this means your system is starving for memory. You might have too many programs running or a large program is using lots of memory.

- If the Memory: Cached value is much less than half the total memory installed, this means your system isn't operating as efficiently as it could because Windows 10 can't store enough recently used data in memory. Because Windows 10 gives up some of the system cache when it needs RAM, close down programs you don't need.

In all these situations, the quickest solution is to reduce the system's memory footprint by closing either documents or applications. For the latter, use the Processes tab to determine which applications are using the most memory, and shut down the ones you can live without for now. The better solution is to add more physical RAM to your system. This decreases the likelihood that Windows 10 will need to use the paging file, and it enables Windows 10 to increase the size of the system cache, which greatly improves performance.

Using the Resource Monitor

The Task Manager should serve most of your performance-monitoring needs. However, Windows 10 comes with another tool for monitoring your system yourself: the Resource Monitor. You load this tool by opening Control Panel, opening the Administrative Tools, and then opening Resource Monitor. (You can also find it by typing **resource** in the taskbar's Search box or by clicking the Open Resource Monitor link in Task Manager's Performance tab.) Figure 23.22 shows the window that appears.

The Resource Monitor is divided into five tabs:

Figure 23.22
The Resource Monitor
enables you to
monitor various
aspects of your
system.

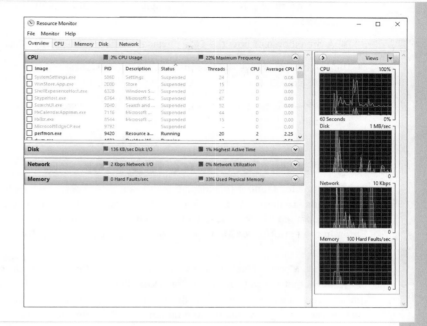

- **Overview**—This tab shows a couple of basic metrics in four categories—CPU, Disk, Network, and Memory—as well as graphs that show current activity in each of these categories. To see more data about a category (as with the CPU category in Figure 23.22 showing Disk, Network, and Memory), click the downward-pointing arrow on the right side of the category header.

- **CPU**—This tab shows the CPU resources your system is using. In two lists, named Processes and Services, you see for each item the current status (such as Running), the CPU percentage currently being used, and the average CPU percentage. In the Processes list, you also see the number of threads used by each process. You get graphs for overall CPU usage, service CPU usage, and CPU usage by processor (or by core).

- **Memory**—This tab displays a list of processes; for each one it shows:

  - The average number of hard memory faults per minute

  - The total memory committed to the process

  - The *working set* (the number of kilobytes resident in memory)

  - The amount of *shareable* memory (memory that other processes can use if needed)

 note

A *memory fault* does not refer to a physical problem; instead, it means that the system could not find the data it needed in the file system cache. If the system finds the data elsewhere in memory, it is a *soft fault*; if the system has to go to the hard disk to retrieve the data, it is a *hard fault*.

- The amount of *private* memory (memory that is dedicated to the process and cannot be shared)

- A breakdown of how the PC's physical memory is currently allocated

- **Disk**—This tab shows the total hard disk I/O transfer rate (disk reads and writes in bytes per minute), as well as separate read and write transfer rates.

- **Network**—This tab shows the total network *data transfer rate* (data sent and received in bytes per minute).

Using the Performance Monitor

The Performance Monitor provides you with real-time reports on how various system settings and components are performing. You load it by opening Control Panel, opening the Administrative Tools, and then opening Performance Monitor, or you can type **perf** in the taskbar's Search box and press Enter. In the Performance Monitor window, open the Monitoring Tools branch and click Performance Monitor.

Performance Monitor displays real-time data using *performance counters*, which are measurements of system activity or the current system state. For each counter, Performance Monitor displays a graph of recent values over a time space (the default time space is 100 seconds) as well as statistics such as the average, maximum, and minimum values over that span.

By default, Performance Monitor doesn't show counters. To add one to the Performance Monitor window, follow these steps:

1. Right-click anywhere inside the Performance Monitor and then click Add Counters. The Add Counters dialog box appears.

2. To use the Available Counters list, click the downward-pointing arrow beside a counter category (such as Memory, Paging File, or Processor). A list of available counters appears.

3. Select the counter you want to use. (If you need more information about the item, check the Show Description box.)

4. If the counter has multiple instances, they appear in the Instances of Selected Object list. Click the instance you want to use.

5. Click Add.

6. Repeat steps 2–5 to add any other counters you want to monitor.

7. Click OK.

The counter appears at the bottom of the window (see Figure 23.23). A different-colored line represents each counter, and that color corresponds to the colored lines shown in the graph. Note, too, that you can get specific numbers for a counter—the most recent value, the average, the minimum, and the maximum—by clicking a counter and reading the boxes just below the graphs. The idea is that you should configure Performance Monitor to show the processes you're interested in (page file size, free memory, and so on) and then keep it running while you perform your normal chores. By examining the Performance Monitor readouts from time to time, you gain an appreciation of what is typical on your system. If you encounter performance problems, you can check Performance Monitor to see whether you've run into any bottlenecks or anomalies.

Performance Monitor has a few new features that make it easier to use and a more powerful diagnostics tool:

Figure 23.23
Use Performance Monitor to keep an eye on various system settings and components.

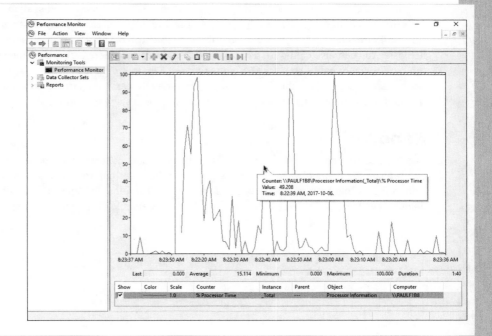

- If you're using a counter with a significantly different scale, you can scale the output so that the counter appears within the graph. For example, the graph's vertical axis runs from 0 to 100; if you're displaying a percentage counter, the Scale value is 1.0, which means the graph numbers correspond directly to the percentages (50 on the graph corresponds to 50%). If you're also showing, say, the Commit Limit counter, which shows values in bytes, the numbers can run in the billions. The Commit Limit counter's Scale value is 0.00000001, so the value 20 on the graph corresponds to 2 billion bytes.

- You can save the current graph as a GIF image file: Right-click the graph and then click Save Image As.

- You can toggle the display of individual counters on and off. You do this by toggling the check boxes in the Show column.

- You can change the duration of the sample (the number of seconds of data that appear on the chart). Right-click the chart, click Properties, click the General tab, and then modify the Duration value. You can specify a value between 2 and 1,000 seconds.

- You can see individual data points by hovering the mouse pointer over a counter. After a second or two, Performance Monitor displays the counter name, the time and date of the sample, and the counter value at that time (refer to Figure 23.23).

Data Collector Sets

A *data collector* is a custom set of performance counters, event traces, and system-configuration data that you define and save so that you can run and view the results any time you need them. You can configure a data collector set to run for a preset length of time or until the set reaches a specified size. You can also configure a data collector to run on a schedule. For example, you could run the data collector every hour for 15 minutes from 9 a.m. to 5 p.m. This enables you to benchmark performance and analyze the results not only intraday (to compare performance at different times of the day) but also interday (to see whether performance is slowing over time).

Reports

The Reports section holds the reports created by each data collector set. These are `.blg` files, and you can see the results by clicking the report and then switching to Sysmon view. (Click the Chart icon in the toolbar.) Alternatively, open the folder that contains the report file in File Explorer (the default save location is `%SystemDrive%\perflogs`) and double-click the report file.

TWEAKING AND CUSTOMIZING WINDOWS

Customizing File Explorer

Although we're sure you have countless more important things to do with your precious time, at least some of your Windows 10 face time will be spent dealing with files, folders, and other Windows "f-words." These file system maintenance chores are the unglamorous side of the digital lifestyle, but they are, regrettably, necessary for the smooth functioning of that lifestyle.

This means that you'll likely be spending a lot of time with File Explorer over the years, so customizing it to your liking will make you more efficient and more productive, and setting up File Explorer to suit your style should serve to remove just a bit of the drudgery of day-to-day file maintenance. This section takes you through a few of our favorite File Explorer customizations.

Customizing the Ribbon

File Explorer's ribbon interface is a great way to expose all the program's functionality, but it can sometimes be hard to locate the command you want to use. Also, some commands take several clicks because you must first click the tab, then drop down a list, and only then click the command.

If you have commands that you use frequently, you can put them within easy reach by adding them to the Quick Access Toolbar. Because the Quick Access Toolbar is always visible, any of its commands can be launched with just a single click.

The easiest way to go about this is to add one or more of the default commands. Click the Customize Quick Access Toolbar arrow (pointed out in Figure 24.1). The commands with check marks beside them are already on the Quick Access Toolbar, so click any of the other commands (such as Redo or Rename) to add it.

To add any command to the Customize Quick Access Toolbar, first, open the tab that contains the command you want to add. Right-click the command and then click Add to Quick Access Toolbar.

Customize Quick Access

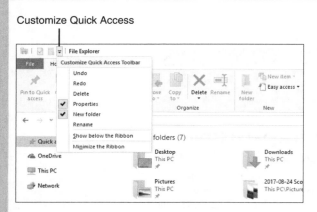

Figure 24.1
Click the Customize Quick Access Toolbar arrow, and then click a command.

Getting More Room for the Quick Access Toolbar

By default, the Quick Access Toolbar appears at the top of the File Explorer window in the title bar. Unfortunately, whenever File Explorer displays a Tools tab, it truncates the Quick Access Toolbar to show only seven icons. To work around this problem, right-click the Customize Quick Access Toolbar and then click Show Below the Ribbon, which moves the toolbar below the ribbon, so you always see all its commands.

Changing the View

The icons in File Explorer's content area can be viewed in no less than *eight* different ways, which seems a tad excessive to us, but Windows has never been about restraint when it comes to interface choices. To see a list of these views, display the View tab and then click the More arrow that appears in the lower-right corner of the Layout gallery. You get four choices for icon sizes:

- Extra Large Icons (shortcut key: Ctrl+Shift+1)

- Large Icons (Ctrl+Shift+2; see also Figure 24.2)

- Medium Icons (Ctrl+Shift+3)

- Small Icons (Ctrl+Shift+4)

Figure 24.2
File Explorer's Content view.

Large Icons

Details

You also get four other choices:

- **List**—This view divides the content area into as many rows as will fit vertically, and it displays the folders and files alphabetically down the rows and across the columns. For each object, File Explorer shows the object's icon and name. The shortcut key for this view is Ctrl+Shift+5.

- **Details**—This view displays a vertical list of icons, where each icon shows the data in all the displayed property columns (such as Name, Date Modified, Type, and Size). See "Viewing More Properties," later in this chapter, to learn how to add to these columns. You can also choose this view by clicking the Details icon in the lower-right corner, as pointed out in Figure 24.2. The shortcut key for this view is Ctrl+Shift+6.

- **Tiles**—This view divides the content area into as many columns as will fit horizontally, and it displays the folders and files alphabetically across the columns and down the rows. For each object, File Explorer shows the object's icon, name, file type, and (for files only) size. The shortcut key for this view is Ctrl+Shift+7.

> **tip**
> The default property columns you see depend on the template that the folder is using. To change the folder template for a folder not already part of a library, right-click the folder, click Properties, and then display the Customize tab. In the Optimize This Folder For list, choose the type you want: General Items, Documents, Pictures, Music, or Videos.

- **Content**—This view displays a vertical list of objects, and for each object, it displays the following:

  - The object's icon

  - The object's name

  - The object's last modified date

  - The object's size (files only)

  - Metadata associated with the object, such as author names and tags

  - The album name, genre, and track length (for music; see Figure 24.2)

  - The dimensions and date taken (for photos)

The shortcut key for this view is Ctrl+Shift+8.

Viewing More Properties

File Explorer's Details view is the preferred choice for power users because it displays a great deal of information in a relatively compact format. (The Content view also provides lots of information, but each object takes up quite a bit of space, and the object properties that you see aren't customizable.) Details view also gives you a great deal of flexibility. For example, here are some techniques you can use when working with the Details view:

 tip

In the Details view, to adjust all the columns so that they're exactly as wide as their widest data, right-click any column header and then click Size All Columns to Fit.

- You can change the order of the property columns by dragging the column headings to the left or right.

- You can sort on a column by clicking the column heading.

- You can adjust the width of a column by pointing the mouse at the right or left edge of the column's heading (the pointer changes to a two-headed arrow) and dragging the pointer left or right.

- You can adjust the width of a column so that it's as wide as its widest data by double-clicking the right edge of the column's heading.

Also, the Details view is informative because it shows you not only the name of each file but also other properties, depending on the folder:

- **Documents**—Name, Date Modified, Type, and Size

- **Pictures**—Name, Date, Tags, Size, and Rating

- **Videos**—Name, Date, Type, Size, and Length

- **Music**—Name (a combination of the track number and track title), Contributing Artists, Album, # (track number), and Title

All these properties are useful, to be sure, but File Explorer can display many more file properties. In fact, there are nearly 300 properties in all, and they include useful information such as the dimensions of a picture file, the bit rate of a music file, and the frame rate of a video file. To see these and other properties, you have two choices:

- To see the most common properties for the current folder type, select View, Add Columns (or right-click any column header), and then click the property you want to add, such as Date modified or Dimensions.

- To see the complete property list, select View, Add Columns, Choose Columns (or right-click any column header and then click More). The Choose Details dialog box that appears (see Figure 24.3) enables you to check the boxes for the properties you want to see, as well as rearrange the column order.

Figure 24.3
Use the Choose Details dialog box to add or remove property columns in File Explorer.

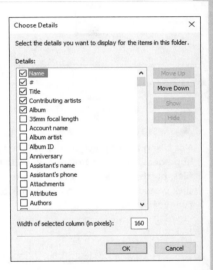

Turning On File Extensions

Microsoft figures that, crucial or not, the file extension concept is just too hard for new users to grasp. Therefore, right out of the box, File Explorer doesn't display file extensions. This might not sound like a big whoop, but not being able to see the extension for each file can be downright confusing. To see why, suppose you have a folder with multiple documents that use the same primary name. This is a pretty common scenario, but it's also a fiendish one because it's often difficult to tell which file is which.

For example, Figure 24.4 shows a folder with 18 different files, all apparently named Project. Windows unrealistically expects users to tell files apart just by examining their icons. To make matters worse, if the file is an image, Windows 10 shows a thumbnail of the image instead of an icon. (This happens in thumbnail views such as Tiles, Medium Icons, and Large Icons.) The result is that in Figure 24.4 it's impossible to tell at a glance which image is a GIF, which is a JPEG, and so on.

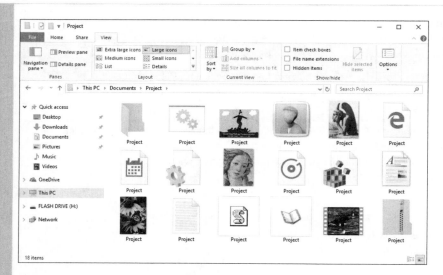

 note

Not being able to recognize a JPEG or a text file isn't a huge deal in the larger scheme of things, but it *is* a huge deal if you can't recognize a file type that could lead to trouble. We're talking here about executable files, batch files, Registry files, and script files that could harbor malicious code that an imprudent double-click would unleash. With extensions turned off, a virus program named `funny.jpg.exe` will appear as `funny.jpg` and look safe to open.

The need to become an expert in Windows iconography is bad enough, but it gets worse. Not being able to see file extensions also leads to two other problems:

- **You can't rename extensions**—For example, suppose you have a text file named `index.txt` and you want to rename it `index.html` to make it a web page file. Nope, sorry, you can't do it with file extensions hidden. If you try—that is, if you click the file, press F2 to choose the Rename command, and then type **index.html**—you just end up with a text file named `index.html.txt`.

- **You can't save a document under an extension of your choice**—Similarly, with file extensions turned off, Windows 10 forces you to save a file using the default extension associated with an application. For example, if you're working in Notepad, every file you save must have a `.txt` extension. If you create your own web pages, for example, you can't rename these text files with typical web page extensions such as `.htm`, `.html`, `.asp`, and so on.

 tip

There is a way to get around the inability to save a file under an extension of your choice in an application. In the Save As dialog box, use the Save as Type list to select the All Files option, if it exists. You can then use the File Name text box to type the filename with the extension you prefer to use.

You can overcome all these problems and risks by turning on file extensions. To do that, display the View tab and then check the File Name Extensions box. Figure 24.5 shows the Project files with extensions in full display.

Figure 24.5
With file extensions turned on, it's much easier to tell the files apart.

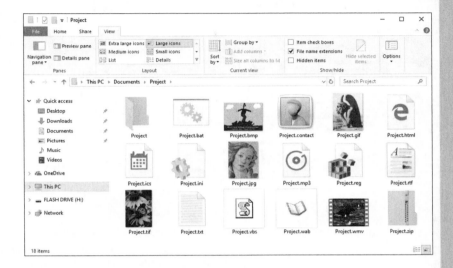

Exploring the View Options

File Explorer's view boasts a large number of customization options that you need to be familiar with. To see these options, you have three choices:

- In File Explorer, select View, Options.

- Open Control Panel's File Explorer Options icon.

- In the taskbar's Search box, type **folder**, and then click File Explorer Options in the search results.

Either way, you can find the view options, appropriately enough, on the View tab of the File Explorer Options (also called Folder Options) dialog box, as shown in Figure 24.6.

Here's a complete list of the various items in the Advanced Settings list:

- **Always Show Icons, Never Thumbnails**—Check this box to prevent File Explorer from displaying file thumbnails. This can speed up the display of some folders that are heavy on pictures and other "thumbnail-able" file types.

- **Always Show Menus**—Checking this item restores the menu bar. Note that this has no effect in folder windows because in those windows the menu bar has been replaced by the ribbon. However, it does display the menu bar in other File Explorer windows, most notably Control Panel.

Figure 24.6
The View tab has quite a few options for customizing File Explorer.

- **Display File Icon on Thumbnails**—When this box is checked, File Explorer superimposes the file type icon on the lower-right corner of each file's thumbnail. This is usually a good idea because the extra icon enables you to figure out the file type at a glance. However, if you find the icon getting in the way of the thumbnail image, uncheck this setting.

- **Display File Size Information in Folder Tips**—When this setting is checked and you hover your mouse pointer over a folder icon, File Explorer calculates the size of the files and subfolders within the folder and displays the size in a pop-up banner. This information is useful, but if you find that your system takes too long to calculate the file size, consider unchecking this setting.

 note

If you check the Display File Size Information in Folder Tips setting, you must also check the Show Pop-Up Description for Folder and Desktop Items setting, described later.

- **Display the Full Path in the Title Bar**—Check this setting to place the full pathname of the current folder in the File Explorer title bar. The full pathname includes the drive, the names of the parent folders, and the name of the current folder.

- **Hidden Files and Folders**—Windows 10 hides certain types of files by default. This makes sense for novice users because they could accidentally delete or rename an important file. However, it's a pain for more advanced users who might require access to these files. You can use these options to tell File Explorer which files to display:

 note

Files are hidden from view by having their Hidden attribute checked. You can work with this attribute directly by right-clicking a visible file, clicking Properties, and then toggling the Hidden setting on and off.

- **Don't Show Hidden Files, Folders, or Drives**—Check this option to avoid displaying objects that have the Hidden attribute set.

- **Show Hidden Files, Folders, and Drives**—Check this option to display the hidden files.

- **Hide Empty Drives**—When this setting is checked, File Explorer does not include empty drives in the This PC folders section. This is potentially confusing (because you might attach a drive and wonder why it doesn't show up) and not all that sensible (because you're just as likely to want to work with an empty drive as a nonempty one), so consider unchecking this option.

- **Hide Extensions for Known File Types**—Unchecking this setting is an alternative way to display file extensions.

- **Hide Folder Merge Conflicts**—When this option is checked, File Explorer doesn't pester you about merging folders when data that you're copying or moving includes a folder that already exists in the destination. If you always want to know when a folder merge is taking place, uncheck this option.

- **Hide Protected Operating System Files**—This setting is checked by default, and it tells Windows 10 to hide files that have the System attribute activated. This is not usually a problem because you rarely have to do anything with the Windows system files. However, if you do need to see one of these files, uncheck this setting. When Windows 10 asks whether you're sure, click Yes.

- **Launch Folder Windows in a Separate Process**—Checking this setting tells Windows 10 to create a new thread in memory for each folder you open. This makes File Explorer more stable because a problem with one thread won't crash the others. However, this also means that File Explorer requires far greater amounts of system resources and memory. Check this option only if your system has plenty of memory (at least 2GB).

- **Restore Previous Folder Windows at Logon**—If you check this setting, Windows 10 notes which folders you have open when you log off. The next time you log on and display the desktop, Windows 10 displays those folders again. This is a very useful option if you normally have one or two particular folder windows open all day long: It saves you having to reopen those folders each time you start Windows 10.

- **Show Drive Letters**—If you uncheck this box, File Explorer hides the drive letters in the Computer folder and in the address bar when you open a drive.

Renaming Drives for Easier Access

If you hide drive letters, File Explorer displays drive names such as Local Disk. This information isn't particularly useful, so consider renaming your drives with monikers that are meaningful (some examples: System Drive, Data Partition, and DVD Drive). Right-click the drive and then click Rename. Note that you must enter administrator credentials to perform this operation.

- **Show Encrypted or Compressed NTFS Files in Color**—When this setting is checked, File Explorer shows the names of encrypted files in a green font and the names of compressed files in a blue font. This is a useful way to distinguish these from regular files, but you can uncheck this setting if you prefer to view all your files in a single color. Note that this applies only to files on NTFS partitions because only NTFS supports file encryption and compression.

- **Show Pop-Up Description for Folder and Desktop Items**—Some icons display a pop-up banner when you point the mouse at them. For example, the default desktop icons display a pop-up banner that describes each icon. Use this setting to turn these pop-ups on and off.

- **Show Preview Handlers in Preview Pane**—When this box is checked, File Explorer includes controls for previewing certain types of files in the Reading pane. For example, when you display a video file in the Reading pane, File Explorer includes playback controls such as Play, Pause, and Stop.

- **Show Status Bar**—This option toggles the status bar on and off.

- **Show Sync Provider Notifications**—Uncheck this box to prevent File Explorer from showing intrusive notifications—that is to say, *ads*—from Microsoft and its partners.

- **Use Check Boxes to Select Items**—Check this box to add check boxes beside each folder and file. You can then select objects by checking their boxes.

- **Use Sharing Wizard**—When this box is checked, Windows 10 uses a simplified file and folder sharing method called the Sharing Wizard. Power users will want to disable the Sharing Wizard.

- **When Typing into List View**—These options determine File Explorer's behavior when you open a folder and begin typing:

  - **Automatically Type into the Search Box**—Check this option to have your typing appear in the Search box.

  - **Select the Typed Item in the View**—Check this option to jump to the first item in the folder with a name that begins with the letter you type.

- **Expand to Open Folder**—Check this box to tell File Explorer to expand the navigation pane hierarchy down to whatever folder is currently open.

- **Show All Folders**—Check this box to add the Desktop folder to the navigation pane, which includes all the Desktop subfolders: One Drive, your user account, This PC, Libraries, Network, Homegroup, Control Panel, and Recycle Bin.

- **Show Libraries**—Check this box to add a Libraries icon to the navigation pane.

Customizing the Taskbar for Easier Program and Document Launching

On the Windows 10 desktop, the taskbar acts somewhat like a mini-application. The purpose of this "application" is to launch other programs, display a button for each running program, and enable you to switch from one program to another. Like most applications these days, the taskbar also has its own toolbars that, in this case, enable you to launch programs and documents.

Improving Productivity by Configuring Taskbar Settings

The taskbar comes with a few options that can help you be more productive either by saving a few mouse clicks or by giving you more screen room to display your applications, so let's start there. Follow these steps to set these taskbar settings:

1. Right-click the taskbar and then click Taskbar Settings. The Taskbar dialog box appears with the Taskbar tab displayed, as shown in Figure 24.7.

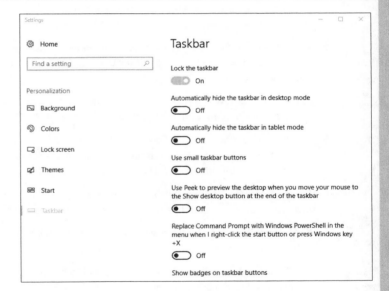

Figure 24.7
Use the Taskbar tab to set up the taskbar for improved productivity.

2. Check or uncheck the following options, as required, to boost your productivity:

- **Lock the Taskbar**—When this switch is On, you can't resize the taskbar, and you can't resize or move any taskbar toolbars. This capability is useful if you share your computer with other users and you don't want to waste time resetting the taskbar if someone else changes it.

- **Automatically Hide the Taskbar in Desktop Mode**— When this switch is On, Windows 10 reduces the taskbar to a thin line at the bottom of the screen when you're not

 tip
You can also toggle taskbar locking on and off by right-clicking an empty section of the taskbar and then clicking Lock the Taskbar.

using it. This capability is useful if you want a bit more screen room for your applications. To redisplay the taskbar, move the mouse pointer to the bottom of the screen. Note, however, that you should consider leaving this option unchecked if you use the taskbar frequently; otherwise, auto-hiding it will slow you down because it takes Windows 10 a second or two to restore the taskbar when you hover the mouse pointer over it.

- **Automatically Hide the Taskbar in Tablet Mode—** This is the same as the above switch, except it controls whether the taskbar is hidden when you use Tablet mode.

- **Use Small Taskbar Buttons—**Turn this switch on to shrink the taskbar's program buttons. This not only reduces the overall height of the taskbar (so you get more room for the desktop and your programs), but enables you to populate the taskbar with more buttons.

3. If you don't want to use Windows 10's Peek feature, for some reason, click the switch to off for Use Peek to Preview the Desktop.

 note

Peek is Windows 10's answer to the perennial question, "Why should I put anything on my desktop if I can't see it?" If you have Peek activated, click the right edge of the taskbar, and Windows 10 temporarily hides your open windows so that you can see the desktop. Click the right edge of the taskbar again, and your windows rematerialize. Nice!

4. To prevent Windows 10 from showing badges on taskbar buttons (such as the number of unread messages in the Mail app), click the Show Badges on Taskbar Buttons switch to Off.

5. Use the Taskbar Location on Screen list to choose where you want to situate the taskbar: Bottom, Left, Right, or Top. For example, if you want to maximize the available screen height, move the taskbar to one side or the other.

6. Use the Combine Taskbar Buttons list to choose how you want Windows 10 to group taskbar buttons when an application has multiple windows or tabs open:

- **Always, Hide Labels—**Choose this option to have Windows 10 always group similar taskbar buttons.

- **When Taskbar Is Full—**Choose this option to have Windows 10 group similar taskbar buttons only when the taskbar has no more open space to display buttons.

- **Never—**Choose this option to have Windows 10 never group similar taskbar buttons.

➡ *To learn how to customize the notification area,* **see** *"Customizing Notifications," **p. 235.***

7. Click X at the top right to close the Taskbar dialog box.

Pinning a Favorite Program to the Taskbar

In Chapter 4, "Using the Windows 10 Interface," you learned that you can pin an icon for your favorite program to the Start menu. That's handy, but that solution still requires two or more clicks to launch a program. We live in a "multiple clicks bad, one click good" world, so what you really need is an even faster way of launching programs.

That way is, of course, the taskbar, which offers (depending on your configuration) at least one example—the File Explorer icon—that is pinned to the taskbar and hence requires but a single click to launch.

If you're coming to Windows 10 from Windows Vista (or even XP), you might think of these icons as being glorified Quick Launch toolbar icons, but there's a big difference: In Windows 10, when you click a pinned taskbar icon, it turns into its own running program icon. In other words, a separate icon doesn't show up on the taskbar; instead, Windows 10 puts a blue bar under the icon to indicate that its program is running.

So how can you get in on this one-click action for your own programs? You can pin those programs to the taskbar. You have four choices:

- In File Explorer, right-click a program's icon or a program's shortcut and then click Pin to Taskbar.

- In the Start menu, display the program you want to pin, right-click that program, and then click Pin to Taskbar.

- If the program is already running, right-click its taskbar icon and then click Pin This Program to Taskbar.

- In File Explorer, drag a program's icon or a program's shortcut to an empty section of the taskbar and then drop it.

If you decide later that you no longer want a program pinned to the taskbar, right-click the program's taskbar icon and then click Unpin This Program from Taskbar.

 tip

After you've pinned a program to the taskbar, you can use that icon to open documents that aren't normally associated with the program. You normally do this by right-clicking the document, clicking Open With, and then selecting the other program. In Windows 10, however, you can hold down Shift, click and drag the document, and drop it on the program's taskbar icon.

Using the Windows Key to Start Taskbar Programs

We're a big fan of the super-duper Windows 10 taskbar because it offers the easiest way to launch our favorite desktop programs: Just click the icon. However, even that easy-as-pie method is ever-so-slightly inconvenient when your hands are busy typing. It would be a tad more efficient if you could launch taskbar icons from the comfort of your keyboard.

But wait, you can! In Windows 10, you can use the Windows Logo key and the numbers across the top of your keyboard (*not* the ones on the numeric keypad) to press taskbar icons into service without having to reach all the way over to the mouse.

The trick here is that Windows 10 numbers the pinned taskbar icons starting at 1 for the leftmost icon (not including the Task View icon), 2 for the icon to its right, and so on. The first nine icons are numbered from 1 to 9 (again, left to right), and if

 note

Bear in mind that when Windows 10 numbers the taskbar icons, it looks only at the pinned icons. For example, suppose you start a program and then decide later to pin some other program to the taskbar. That pinned icon will be the fifth icon on the taskbar, but it will be the fourth *pinned* icon, so you'd launch it by pressing Windows Logo+4.

there's a tenth icon it's numbered as 0. To select a particular pinned taskbar icon from the keyboard, hold down the Windows Logo key and press the corresponding icon number on the top row of the keyboard. For example, on most Windows 10 systems, Microsoft Edge is the first pinned taskbar icon from the left, so you can start it by pressing Windows Logo+1.

Taking Control of the Notification Area

The notification area (sometimes called by its old name, the *system tray*) on the right side of the taskbar has been a fixture on the Windows landscape since Windows 95, and for most people it's either really useful or it's a complete waste of otherwise useful taskbar space. You're more likely to fall into the latter camp if your notification area in earlier versions of Windows was bristling with icons, as shown in Figure 24.8.

Figure 24.8
Remember Windows XP and its out-of-control notification area?

Horror stories of notification areas threatening to take over the taskbar must have inspired Microsoft to rein in the bloat, so it modified the notification area in Windows 7, and the same modifications are used in Windows 8/8.1. Now, no matter how many of your installed programs try to run rough-shod over the notification area, you'll always see *only* the following icons: Network, Volume, Action Center, Power (if you have a portable PC), and Touch Keyboard (if you have a touch PC). Bliss!

That doesn't mean all your other notification area icons are gone for good—they're just hidden, although in two different ways:

- Some icons are visible, but to see them you have to click the upward-pointing arrow on the left side of the notification area (see Figure 24.9).

Figure 24.9
In Windows 10, you must click the arrow to see your other notification area icons.

- Some icons are completely hidden, but you do see any notification messages displayed by those icons.

This setup simplifies things considerably and gives you more taskbar breathing room, but there are times when it's not so convenient. For example, if you frequently control a program by right-clicking its notification area icon, you either have that extra click to get at the icon, or you can't get at it at all. Fortunately, you can customize the notification area to show an icon directly, hide it in the extra menu, or remove it completely and see just its notifications. Here's how:

1. Click Start, Settings, Personalization, Taskbar. Scroll down to the Notification Area section, and click Select Which Icons Appear on the Taskbar, to get to the screen shown in Figure 24.10.

Figure 24.10
You can select which icons appear in the notification area. The ones turned "off" appear only when they have something to say.

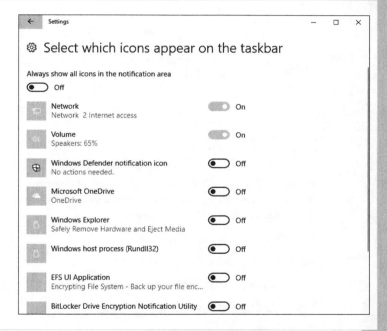

2. If you want to see every available icon full time, click the Always Show All Icons in the Notification Area switch to On. Otherwise, click the switches beside the individual icons to turn each one on or off.

3. Click Back, and then in the notification area, click the Turn System Icons On or Off link. The Turn System Icons On or Off screen appears, as shown in Figure 24.11.

4. Click the switch to Off for each system icon you don't use.

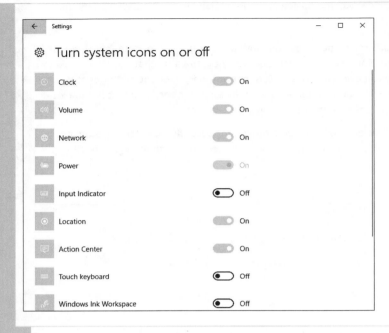

Figure 24.11
Use the Turn System Icons On or Off screen to specify which system icons appear in the notification area.

If you have zero use for the notification area, you can disable it entirely by following these steps:

1. In the taskbar's Search box (or the Run dialog box; press Windows Logo+R), type **gpedit.msc**, and then press Enter. The Local Group Policy Editor appears.

2. Open the User Configuration branch.

3. Open the Administrative Templates branch.

4. Click the Start Menu and Taskbar branch.

5. Double-click the Hide the Notification Area policy, click Enabled, and then click OK.

6. Double-click the Remove Clock from the System Notification Area policy, click Enabled, and then click OK.

7. Log off and then log back on to put the policy into effect.

 note
These steps require the Group Policy Editor, which is available only with Windows 10 Pro and Windows 10 Enterprise. If you're not running one of these versions, we'll show you how to perform the same tweak using the Registry.

If you prefer (or need) to implement this policy via the Registry, first open the Registry Editor (click Start, type **regedit**, press Enter, and enter your UAC credentials). Navigate to the following key:

HKCU\Software\Microsoft\Windows\CurrentVersion\Policies\Explorer

(If you don't see the Explorer key, click the Policies key, select Edit, New, Key, type **Explorer**, and press Enter.)

Now follow these steps:

1. Select Edit, New, DWORD (32-bit) Value.

2. Type **NoTrayItemsDisplay** and press Enter.

3. Press Enter to open the NoTrayItemsDisplay setting, type **1**, and then click OK.

4. Select Edit, New, DWORD (32-bit) Value.

5. Type **HideClock** and press Enter.

6. Press Enter to open the HideClock setting, type **1**, and then click OK.

7. Log off, and then log back on to put the policies into effect.

Displaying the Built-In Taskbar Toolbars

Windows 10 taskbar comes with three default toolbars and three default buttons:

- **Address**—This toolbar contains a text box into which you can type a local address (such as a folder or file path), a network address (a UNC path), or an Internet address. When you press Enter or click the Go button, Windows 10 loads the address into File Explorer (if you entered a local or network folder address), an application (if you entered a file path), or Internet Explorer (if you entered an Internet address). In other words, this toolbar works just like the address bar used by File Explorer and Internet Explorer.

- **Desktop**—This toolbar contains all the desktop icons, as well as an icon for Internet Explorer and submenus for your user folder and the following folders: Public, Computer, Network, Control Panel, and Recycle Bin.

- **Links**—This toolbar contains several buttons that link to predefined Internet sites. This is the same as the links toolbar that appears in Internet Explorer.

- **Task View**—This button activates the Task View feature.

- **People**—This button gives you quick access to your contacts.

- **Windows Ink Workspace**—This button provides quick access to the Windows Ink feature (sticky notes and sketching tools).

- **Touch Keyboard**—This button (displayed by default on a tablet PC) contains just a single icon—the Touch Keyboard icon—which, when clicked, displays the onscreen touch keyboard. (This toolbar is displayed by default on touch PCs and tablets.)

Unlocking the Taskbar

You can adjust the size of a toolbar by clicking and dragging the toolbar's left edge. However, this won't work if the taskbar is locked. To unlock the taskbar, right-click an empty section of the taskbar and then click Lock the Taskbar to deactivate it.

To toggle these toolbars on and off, right-click an empty spot on the taskbar and then use the following techniques:

- Click Toolbars and then click the toolbar you want to work with.

- Click Show Task View Button, Show People Button, Show Windows Ink Workspace Button, or Show Touch Keyboard Button to toggle these buttons on and off.

Setting Some Taskbar Toolbar Options

After you've displayed a toolbar, you can set a number of options to customize the look of the toolbar and to make it easier to work with. (Note that you need to unlock the taskbar to see these options; right-click the taskbar, and then click to deactivate the Lock the Taskbar option.) Right-click an empty section of the toolbar, and then click one of the following commands (although note that not all these commands are available for all toolbars):

- **View**—This command displays a submenu with two options: Large Icons and Small Icons. These commands determine the size of the toolbar's icons. For example, if a toolbar has more icons than can be shown given its current size, switch to the Small Icons view.

- **Show Text**—This command toggles the icon titles on and off. Turning on the titles makes it easier to decipher what each icon does, but you'll see fewer icons in a given space.

- **Show Title**—This command toggles the toolbar title (displayed to the left of the icons) on and off.

Creating New Taskbar Toolbars

In addition to the predefined taskbar toolbars, you can create new toolbars that display the contents of any folder on your system. For example, if you have a folder of programs or documents that you launch regularly, you can get one-click access to those items by displaying that folder as a toolbar. Here are the steps to follow:

1. Right-click an empty spot on the toolbar, and then click Toolbars, New Toolbar. Windows 10 displays the New Toolbar dialog box.

2. Select the folder you want to display as a toolbar. (Alternatively, click New Folder to create a new subfolder within the currently selected folder.)

3. Click Select Folder. Windows 10 creates the new toolbar.

25

MANAGING HARD DISKS AND STORAGE SPACES

Dealing with Hard Disk Errors

Our hard disks store our programs and, most important, our precious data, so they have a special place in the computing firmament. The new solid-state drives have no moving parts, so they're extremely reliable, but that doesn't mean you'll never have problems. Defective drives are rare, but not unicorn-rare, and there's always the chance that Windows—through a programming error, an app or system crash, or a sudden shutdown (such as a power outage)—could mess up your hard disk.

So, what can you do about this? In older versions of Windows, you had basically two choices:

- Wait until Windows recognized a disk error (for example, when you tried to open a corrupted file). In this case, Windows would run a program called Error Checking (actually, its command-line equivalent called chkdsk) that scanned your hard disk for problems and could repair them automatically.

- Run the Error Checking program yourself on a regular schedule (say, once a month or so) or when you suspected a hard disk error.

In both cases, Windows would not be able to run Error Checking right away on the Windows volume (usually drive C) because it had files in use. Instead, Windows would schedule Error Checking to run during the next boot. (Windows would be able to run Error Checking immediately on any other volume.)

The major downside to all this was that Error Checking would have to take the Windows volume offline to scan and repair it. That wasn't a big deal for a small hard disk, but with drive capacities getting into the hundreds and then thousands of gigabytes, these disk scans were taking forever. And the fuller the volume was (technically, the more files it stored), the longer the check would take—sometimes several hours for extremely large disks with tons of files. Windows 7 improved things a bit by making Error Checking itself faster, but Microsoft realized it was facing a losing battle, and that hard disk size would easily outpace any performance improvements that could be squeezed out of Error Checking.

 note

Although most hard disks consist of a single storage area, you'll see later in this chapter that you can split a hard disk into multiple storage areas, and these areas are called *volumes* (see "Dividing Your Hard Drive into Two Volumes"). A volume is also known as a *logical drive*, so we'll often refer to a volume as a hard drive in this chapter and throughout the book.

The solution to this dilemma is a feature of Windows 10's NTFS file system called self-healing, where certain disk errors can be fixed on-the-fly without having to take the entire volume offline. This feature was introduced in Windows Vista, where it applied to only a few relatively rare errors, but since Windows 8, Microsoft has significantly increased the number of problems that can be self-healed. This means that many drive errors will get fixed behind the scenes without your even knowing an error occurred (and, more importantly, without having to take the Windows volume offline).

Hard Drive Health States

From a hard drive point of view, the main innovation introduced in Windows 8 and continued with all versions of Windows 10 is a running assessment of the current health of the drive. Specifically, Windows 8/8.1 and Windows 10 always see your hard drive as being in one of the five following states:

- **Healthy**—This state means that your hard drive is online and currently has no errors or corruption. When you open Control Panel's Security and Maintenance icon and then view the Maintenance section (in the Search box, type **maintenance**, and then select Security and Maintenance), the Drive Status value shows "All drives are working properly," as you can see in Figure 25.1.

Figure 25.1
Security and Maintenance's Drive Status when your hard drives are healthy.

- **Self-healing**—This state means that Windows has detected an error and is in the process of repairing it using NTFS self-healing. This transient state lasts a very short time, and you see no indication either on the desktop or in the Security and Maintenance pane.

- **Error verification**—This state means that Windows has detected a possible hard drive error that it can't self-heal. We say "possible" because some problems that appear to be hard drive corruption are actually intermittent memory errors. Rather than just escalating the health status to the next level, Windows runs a feature called the *spot verification service*, which attempts to verify that the error is a drive-related one. This is also a transient state that lasts a very short time.

- **Scan required**—This state means that the spot verification service has confirmed the hard drive error and the system now needs to scan the hard drive. That scan is scheduled to run during the next automatic maintenance window. However, as you can see in Figure 25.2, Security and Maintenance shows a "Scan drive for errors" message, and you can run the scan immediately by clicking the Run Scan button. The drive remains online, and you can work normally while the scan runs. During the scan, Windows logs the error, determines the precise fix required, and escalates the health status to the next level.

  ➡ *To learn about the automatic maintenance window,* **see** *"Setting the Automatic Maintenance Schedule,"* **p. 614.**

Figure 25.2
Security and
Maintenance shows
"Scan drive for errors"
when Windows detects
a hard drive error.

- **Restart required**—This state occurs after the drive scan has logged the error and determined the repair that's required, which Windows calls a *spot fix*. The notification area displays a "Restart to repair drive errors" message, and the same message appears in Security and Maintenance, as shown in Figure 25.3. You can click Restart to begin the spot fix process. Because the full hard drive has already been scanned and the needed fix has already been determined, repairing the hard drive adds only a few seconds to the restart. Note that the restart is *required* to repair the system volume (which must go offline to effect the repairs) but is actually *optional* for nonsystem volumes. Windows displays the restart message for all volumes so that users don't have to take any direct action to repair the drive. However, for nonsystem volumes, advanced users can initiate the repair manually without a restart, as we describe in the next section.

Figure 25.3
Security and Maintenance shows "Restart to repair drive errors" when Windows is ready to fix a hard drive problem.

Repairing a Drive Manually

On a multivolume system, when Windows 10 is ready to spot fix a drive, and it alerts you that a restart is required, it is unfortunately vague as to which drive requires the repair. If you'd rather not restart now, you can check the drives yourself and, if the repair is required on a nonsystem drive, you can run the repair manually to avoid the restart. Follow these steps:

1. Open File Explorer and then select This PC.

2. Right-click the first hard drive (this is usually drive C, which is almost always the system volume; look for the Windows logo on the drive icon) and then click Properties. The drive's Properties dialog box appears.

3. Display the Tools tab.

4. Click the Check button. One of two things will happen:

   - You see the message "You don't need to scan this drive." This means the drive is in the Healthy state, so no repair is necessary. Repeat steps 2 to 4 to check the next drive.

   - You see the message "Repair this drive," as shown in Figure 25.4. If this is the system volume, you need to restart your computer to repair the drive. Otherwise, continue with step 5.

5. Click Repair Drive. Windows 10 repairs the nonsystem volume and returns its status to Healthy.

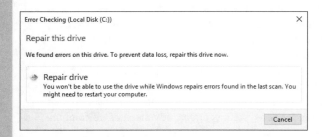

Figure 25.4
Check each hard drive.

Checking Free Disk Space

Hard disks with capacities measured in the hundreds of gigabytes are standard even in low-end systems nowadays, and multi-terabyte hard disks are now commonplace. This means that disk space is much less of a problem than it used to be. Still, you need to keep track of how much free space you have on your disk drives, particularly the %SystemDrive% (usually drive C:), which usually stores the virtual memory page file.

One way to error check free space is to view the This PC folder using either Tiles view or Content view (which include the free space and total disk space with each drive icon), or Details view (which includes columns for Total Size and Free Space).

Alternatively, use Windows 10's Storage Usage feature, which not only shows you a disk's total capacity and its current used and free space, but also how the used space is allocated between system files, apps, media files, documents, and more. In the Search box, type **storage** and then click Storage. This opens the Storage settings, and you then click the drive you want to check out. Windows 10 displays the disk's storage allocation, as you can see in Figure 25.5.

Figure 25.5
In the Settings app's Storage screen, click a drive to see its free space and how its used space is allocated among different file types.

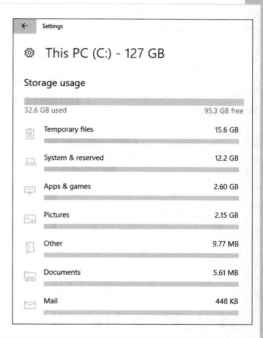

Listing 25.1 presents a VBScript procedure that displays the status and free space for each drive on your system.

➡ *To learn how to run scripts, **see** "Windows Script Host," **p. 685.***

Listing 25.1 A VBScript Example That Displays the Status and Free Space for Your System's Drives

```
Option Explicit
Dim objFSO, colDiskDrives, objDiskDrive, strMessage

' Create the File System Object
Set objFSO = CreateObject("Scripting.FileSystemObject")

' Get the collection of disk drives
Set colDiskDrives = objFSO.Drives

' Run through the collection
strMessage = "Disk Drive Status Report" & vbCrLf & vbCrLf
For Each objDiskDrive in colDiskDrives

  ' Add the drive letter to the message
 strMessage = strMessage & "Drive: " & objDiskDrive.DriveLetter & vbCrLf

  ' Check the drive status
  If objDiskDrive.IsReady = True Then

   ' If it's ready, add the status and the free space to the message
   strMessage = strMessage & "Status: Ready" & vbCrLf
   strMessage = strMessage & "Free space: " & objDiskDrive.FreeSpace
   strMessage = strMessage & vbCrLf & vbCrLf
  Else

   ' Otherwise, just add the status to the message
   strMessage = strMessage & "Status: Not Ready" & vbCrLf & vbCrLf
  End If
Next

' Display the message
Wscript.Echo strMessage
```

This script creates a `FileSystemObject` and then uses its `Drives` property to return the system's collection of disk drives. Then a `For Each...Next` loop runs through the collection, gathering the drive letter, the status, and if the disk is ready, the free space. It then displays the drive data.

Deleting Unnecessary Files

If you find that a hard disk volume is getting low on free space, you should delete any unneeded files and programs. We'll shortly take you through some procedures for deleting disk detritus manually, but you should know that Windows 10 also comes with a handy feature called Storage Sense that can automate the deletion of at least some of your system's unnecessary files. Follow these steps to activate and configure Storage Sense:

1. In the taskbar's Search box, type `storage` and then click Storage to open the Storage settings.

2. Click the Storage Sense switch to On.

3. Click Change How We Free Up Space to display the Storage Sense settings.

4. In the Temporary Files section, click to activate the check box for each type of temporary file you want Storage Sense to delete automatically:

   - **Delete temporary files that my apps aren't using**—Activate this check box to have Storage Sense remove temporary files created by your apps but that are no longer being used by those apps. This one's a no-brainer.

   - **Delete files that have been in the recycle bin for over 30 days**—Activate this check box to have Storage Sense remove files that you deleted more than a month ago. This seems reasonable, but if you think there's even a small chance you might want to restore an older deleted file, then deactivate this check box.

   - **Delete files in the Downloads folder that haven't changed in 30 days**—Activate this check box to have Storage Sense remove downloaded files that have been sitting unchanged in the Downloads folder for over a month. This check box is deactivated by default, which makes sense to us because we like to keep our downloads just in case we have to reinstall an app. An alternative in that case would be to move your downloads to an external hard drive or to your OneDrive.

5. If you're low on disk space, you can click Clean Now to run Storage Sense using the current settings.

Windows 10 also comes with a Disk Cleanup utility that enables you to remove certain types of files quickly and easily. Before discussing this utility, let's look at a few methods you can use to perform a spring cleaning on your hard disk by hand:

- **Uninstall programs you don't use**—It's easy to download new software for a trial run. Unfortunately, that also means it's easy to have unused programs cluttering your hard disk. Uninstall these and other rejected applications.

- **Delete downloaded program archives**—Your hard disk is also probably littered with ZIP files or other downloaded archives. For those programs you use, you should consider moving the archive files to a removable medium for storage. For programs you don't use, you should delete the archive files.

- **Move documents you don't need very often**—Our hard drives are stuffed with ancient documents that we use only rarely, if at all: old projects, business records from days gone by, photos and videos from occasions held long ago, and so on. You probably don't want to delete any of this, but you can free up hard disk space by moving those old documents to removable media such as an external hard drive or a flash drive.

After you've performed these tasks, you should next run the Disk Cleanup utility, which can automatically remove some of the preceding file categories, as well as several other types of files, including downloaded programs, Internet Explorer cache files, the hibernation files, Recycle Bin deletions, temporary files, file system thumbnails, and offline files. Here's how it works:

 tip

Windows 10 also offers a faster route to the Disk Cleanup window. In the Run dialog box (select Windows Logo+R), type `cleanmgr /drive`, where drive is the letter of the *drive* you want to work with (for example, `cleanmgr /dc`), and then press Enter.

1. Open File Explorer and then select This PC.

2. Right-click the drive you want to clean up and then click Properties. The drive's Properties dialog box appears.

3. In the General tab, click Disk Cleanup. Disk Cleanup scans the drive to see which files can be deleted.

4. Click Clean Up System Files. Disk Cleanup displays a more comprehensive list of file types it can delete, as shown in Figure 25.6.

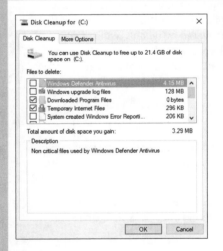

Figure 25.6
Disk Cleanup can automatically and safely remove certain types of files from a disk drive.

5. In the Files to Delete list, check the box beside each category of the files you want to remove. If you're not sure what an item represents, select it and read the text in the Description box. Note, too, that for most of these items you can click View Files to see what you'll be deleting.

6. Click OK. Disk Cleanup asks whether you're sure that you want to delete the files.

7. Click Delete Files. Disk Cleanup deletes the selected files.

Saving Disk Cleanup Settings

You can save your Disk Cleanup settings and run them again at any time. This capability is handy if, for example, you want to delete all your downloaded program files and temporary Internet files at shutdown. Display the Start screen (or open the Run dialog box), type the following command, and then press Enter:

```
cleanmgr /sageset:1
```

Note that the number 1 in the command is arbitrary: you can enter any number between 0 and 65535. This launches Disk Cleanup with an expanded set of file types to delete. Make your choices and click OK. This saves your settings to the Registry; it doesn't delete the files. To delete the files, use the Run dialog box to type the following command, and then press Enter:

```
cleanmgr /sagerun:1
```

You can also create a shortcut for this command, add it to a batch file, or schedule it with the Task Scheduler.

Defragmenting Your Hard Disk

Windows 10 comes with a utility called Optimize Drives that's an essential tool for tuning your hard disk. The job of Optimize Drives is to rid your hard disk of file fragmentation. (Note that this only applies to mechanical hard disks. The solid-state drives used in tablets and some laptops and desktops don't benefit from defragmentation.)

File fragmentation is one of those terms that sounds scarier than it actually is. It simply means that a file is stored on your hard disk in scattered, noncontiguous areas. This is a performance drag because it means that when Windows 10 tries to open such a file, the disk drive's read/write heads must make several stops to collect the various pieces. If a lot of files are fragmented, it can slow even the fastest hard disk to a crawl.

Why doesn't Windows 10 just store files contiguously? Recall that Windows 10 stores files on disk in clusters and that these clusters have a fixed size, depending on the disk's capacity. Recall, too, that Windows 10 uses a file directory to keep track of each file's whereabouts. When you delete a file, Windows 10 doesn't actually clean out the clusters associated with the file. Instead, it just marks the deleted file's clusters as unused.

To see how fragmentation occurs, let's look at an example. Suppose that three files—FIRST.TXT, SECOND.TXT, and THIRD.TXT—are stored on a disk and that they use up four, three, and five clusters, respectively. Figure 25.7 shows how they might look on the disk.

If you now delete SECOND.TXT, clusters 5, 6, and 7 become available. But suppose that the next file you save—call it FOURTH.TXT—takes up five clusters. What happens? Well, Windows 10 looks for the first available clusters. It finds that 5, 6, and 7 are free, so it uses them for the first three clusters of FOURTH.TXT. Windows continues and finds that clusters 13 and 14 are free, so it uses them for the final two clusters of FOURTH.TXT. Figure 25.8 shows how things look now.

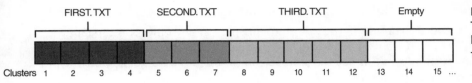

Figure 25.7
Three files before fragmentation.

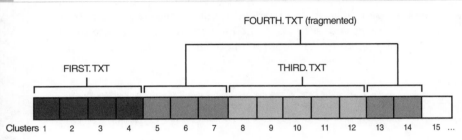

Figure 25.8
A fragmented file.

As you can see, FOURTH.TXT is stored noncontiguously; in other words, it's fragmented. Although a file fragmented in two pieces isn't that bad, it's possible for large files to split into dozens of blocks, dramatically slowing down access to these files. The Optimize Drives tool can help fix this.

Running the Optimize Drives Tool

The good news with Windows 10 is that its defragmenting tool Optimize Drives is set up to run automatically. The default schedule is once a week during the maintenance window. This means you should never need to defragment your system manually. However, you might want to run a defragment before loading a particularly large software program.

Before using Optimize Drives, you should perform a couple of housekeeping chores:

- Delete any files from your hard disk that you don't need, as described in the "Deleting Unnecessary Files" section earlier in this chapter. Defragmenting junk files only slows down the whole process.

- Open Security and Maintenance and check your hard drive's status as described earlier in this chapter (refer to "Dealing with Hard Disk Errors"). Run a scan or repair if the drive status is anything but Healthy.

> ⓦ **tip**
> The built-in Optimize Drives utility does an adequate job of defragmenting, but if you're serious about performance, you might want to check out third-party defragmenting tools like PerfectDisk (raxco.com) that can do a much better job.

Follow these steps to use Optimize Drives:

1. In the taskbar's Search box, type **defrag**, and then click Defragment and Optimize Drives in the search results. Alternatively, in File Explorer, open the This PC folder, right-click the drive you want to defragment, click Properties, display the Tools tab in the dialog box that appears, and then click the Optimize button. Either way, the Optimize Drives window appears, as shown in Figure 25.9.

Figure 25.9
Use Optimize Drives to eliminate file fragmentation and improve hard disk performance.

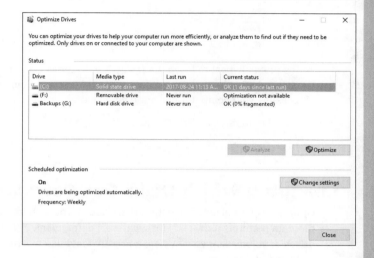

2. Click the disk you want to defragment.

3. Click Optimize. Windows 10 defragments your hard drives.

4. When the defragment is complete, click Close.

 tip
In some cases, you can defragment a drive even further by running Optimize Drives on the drive twice in a row. (That is, optimize a drive once, and when it's done, immediately do it again.)

Changing the Optimization Schedule

If you want to run Optimize Drives on a different day, at a different time, more often or less often, follow these steps to change the default schedule:

1. In the taskbar's Search box, type **defrag**, and then click Defragment and Optimize Your Drives in the search results.

2. Click Change Settings to display the Optimize Drives: Optimization Schedule dialog box, shown in Figure 25.10.

3. Make sure that the Run on a Schedule box is checked.

4. Use the Frequency list to select the defragment frequency: Daily, Weekly, or Monthly.

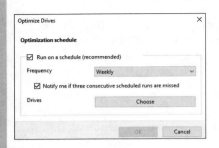

Figure 25.10
Use this dialog box to set up a custom defrag schedule.

5. It's probably best to leave the Notify Me If Three Consecutive Scheduled Runs Are Missed box checked. This lets you know if Windows 10 has not been able to optimize your drives in a while because your computer has not been idle during the maintenance window.

6. Click OK to return to the Optimize Drives window.

7. Click Close.

Changing Which Disks Get Defragmented

Optimize Drives also has a feature that enables you to select which disks get worked on when the program performs its weekly (or whatever) defragment. This feature is useful if you have many hard drives or volumes on your system and you would like to restrict the ones that Optimize Drives works on to speed things up.

Follow these steps to specify which disks get defragmented:

1. In the taskbar's Search box, type **defrag**, and then click Defragment and Optimize Your Drives in the search results.

2. Click Change Settings to display the Optimize Drives: Optimization Schedule dialog box.

3. Click Choose to display the Optimize Drives dialog box, shown in Figure 25.11.

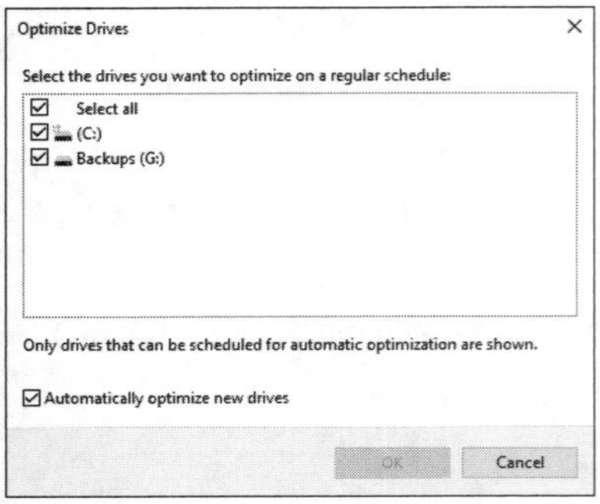

Figure 25.11
Use this dialog box to choose which disks get defragmented.

4. Uncheck the box beside any disk you don't want defragmented.

5. If you want Optimize Drives to stop adding new disks to the defragment list, uncheck the Automatically Optimize New Drives box.

6. Click OK to return to the second Optimize Drives dialog box.

7. Click OK to return to the first Optimize Drives dialog box.

8. Click Close.

Working with Storage Spaces

Multiple-terabyte (TB) hard drives are now routine sights. However, if anything, our data is expanding at an even faster rate as we download and rip music, TV shows, movies, and other massive media files. Nowadays, media collections that take up 10 or 20TB are not at all unusual.

In Windows 7 and earlier versions, the only simple way to store 10TB of data was to purchase five 2TB hard drives and split the data across the drives. This is not a great solution because it's difficult both to allocate storage efficiently and to find the file you need. Unfortunately, higher-end solutions such as Redundant Array of Inexpensive Disks (RAID) are complex to implement.

Windows 8 and later solved this problem by offering a feature called *storage spaces*. This feature enables you to combine two or more USB, SATA, or SAS drives into a single storage pool and then create a storage space—that is, a virtualized hard drive—from that pool. You can then use that space just as you would a regular hard drive.

There are two other key characteristics of storage spaces:

- **Resiliency**—This means that the storage space protects your data should a hard drive in the storage pool fail. *Mirroring* is usually the best choice here, and you can select either two-way (which creates a second copy of each file and requires at least two drives) or three-way (which creates three copies and requires at least three drives). You can also use *parity* resiliency, where Windows stores information about the data within the storage space that enables the lost data to be reconstructed in the event of a failure. Because of the overhead of maintaining this extra information, parity resiliency is best suited for spaces that mostly consist of large files that aren't updated very often (such as digital movies and recorded TV shows).

- **Logical size**—You can specify a logical storage space size that is larger than the current physical capacity. For example, if you have five 2TB drives, you can still create a storage space with a logical size of, say, 20TB. Windows will then alert you when you need to add more drives to the storage space.

Follow these steps to create a storage pool:

1. Connect the USB, SATA, or SAS drives you want to use.

2. In the taskbar's Search box, type **storage**, and then click Manage Storage Spaces in the search results. The Manage Storage Spaces window appears.

3. Click Create a New Pool and Storage Space, and when User Account Control asks you to confirm, click Yes or enter administrative credentials. Windows 10 displays a list of drives you can use to create the storage pool, as shown in Figure 25.12.

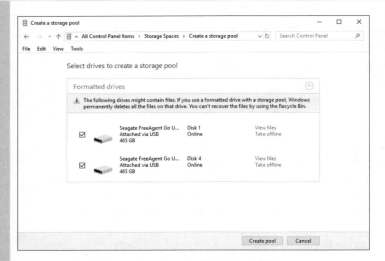

Figure 25.12
Use this dialog box to choose
which disks are included in the
storage pool.

4. Click the check box beside each drive you want to use, and then click Create Pool.

5. Type a name for the storage pool and select a drive letter.

6. Select a resiliency type.

7. Type the logical size you want for the storage pool.

8. Click Create Storage Space. Windows 10 pools the hard drives and creates the storage space.

To add a drive to the storage space, follow steps 1 to 4, click Add Drives, check the new drive's box, and then click Add Drives.

Managing Your Disks

You've seen so far that Windows 10 takes a number of steps to relieve you of the burden of managing your hard disks and other drives:

- Windows 10 monitors your hard disk for errors, automatically repairs corruption that can be self-healed, scans other errors automatically during the maintenance window, and prompts you to restart your PC to conduct spot fix repairs.

- Windows 10 optimizes your drives automatically once a week (or whatever schedule you choose).

- Storage spaces enable you to easily combine multiple drives into a single storage area of any size where data can span the drives and is protected by resiliency.

We all want to use Windows for productive, creative, or playful pursuits, so anything that relieves us of the burden of routine maintenance is welcome in our books. Still, many disk-related chores are not covered by this list and are not automated in any way, so they require you to "lift up the hood" and work on your disks yourself.

Your interface for these tasks is the Disk Management snap-in, which you can get onto the desktop using any of the following techniques:

- In the Run dialog box (Windows Logo+R), type **diskmgmt.msc** and press Enter.

- In the taskbar's Search box, type **disk man**, and then click Create and Format Hard Disk Partitions.

- Press Windows Logo+X or right-click the Start button, and then click Disk Management.

You end up at the Disk Management window, which looks similar to the one shown in Figure 25.13. The top half of the window presents a list of volumes on your system and provides data about each volume, including its name, file system, status, capacity, and free space (actual and percentage). The bottom half of the window offers a graphic display of the volumes.

Figure 25.13
The Disk Management snap-in is your tool of choice for many disk chores.

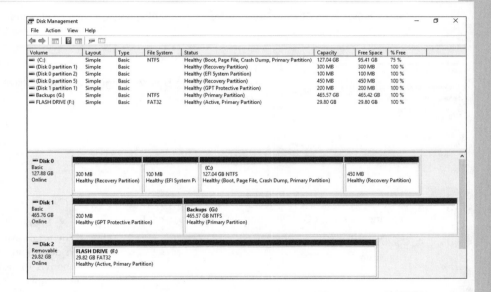

The next few sections take you through some of the more useful tasks you can perform with the Disk Management snap-in.

Assigning a Different Letter to a Disk Drive

Windows 10 assigns letters to all your PC drives. For example, the system volume is usually set up as drive C. If you also have an optical drive, it might be drive D, your PC's memory card slots would be assigned letters beginning with E, and so on.

You won't have to change these drive letters very often, but we've found that it comes up every now and then, so you should know how it's done. For example, some poorly programmed applications are hard-coded to work only if a certain drive letter is present on the system. In most cases, you can fool the program into thinking your system has the necessary drive by assigning the drive letter to a flash drive or memory card slot.

Follow these steps to assign a different letter to a drive:

> ⚑ **caution**
>
> Don't try to change the drive letter assigned to your Windows 10 system volume, which is usually drive C. This drive is vital to the operation of your system, and changing its drive letter would render your PC unusable.

1. In the Disk Management window, right-click the drive you want to work with and then click Change Drive Letter and Paths. (Note that you can right-click the drive either in the Volume list or in the graphical display.) The Change Drive Letter and Paths dialog box appears.

2. Click Change. The Change Drive Letter or Path dialog box appears, as shown in Figure 25.14.

Figure 25.14
Use this dialog box to assign a different drive letter to the drive.

3. Click the down arrow to select the drive letter you want to use, and then click OK. Windows 10 asks you to confirm.

4. Click Yes. Windows 10 assigns the new drive letter to the disk drive.

Dividing Your Hard Drive into Two Volumes

As we mentioned earlier, most hard disks consist of just a single volume that takes up the entire disk, and that volume is almost always drive C. However, it's possible to divide a single hard disk into two (or more) volumes and assign a different drive letter to each—say, C and D.

> **tip**
>
> If the list of available drive letters doesn't include drive A, Windows 10 most likely believes (mistakenly, of course) that your PC has a floppy drive. You solve this problem by disabling this phantom floppy drive. Press Windows Logo+X or right-click the Start button, and then click Device Manager. Open the Floppy Disk Drives branch, click Floppy Disk Drive, select Action, Disable, and then click Yes when Device Manager asks you to confirm.

Why would you want to do such a thing? Lots of reasons, but two are by far the most common:

- You want to install a second operating system on your computer and dual-boot between them. In this case, you need to create a second volume and install the other operating system to that volume.

  ➡ *For information on dual-booting, **see** "Dual- (and Multi-) Booting Windows 10," p. 45.*

- You want to separate your data from Windows. In this case, you need to create a second volume and move your data to that volume. This is a good idea because if you ever have to reinstall Windows from scratch, you can wipe drive C: without having to worry about your data.

Creating multiple volumes on a single hard disk is sometimes called *partitioning*, because a partition is roughly equivalent to (but not quite the same as) a volume.

In Windows versions prior to Vista, partitioning a hard drive required third-party software such as Disk Director (www.acronis.com) or Partition Master (www.partition-tool.com). Windows Vista changed that by offering the welcome ability to manage volumes without extra software, and that Disk Management feature continues in Windows 10. You can reduce the size of a volume, enlarge a volume, create a new volume, and delete an existing volume, all without losing data.

In this section, you learn how to divide a hard drive into two volumes. You do that by first shrinking the existing volume and then creating the new volume in the freed-up disk space. Here are the steps to follow:

1. In the Disk Management window, right-click the drive you want to partition and then click Shrink Volume. Disk Management displays the Shrink *D*: dialog box (where *D* is the drive letter of the volume).

2. Use the Enter the Amount of Space to Shrink in MB text box to type the amount by which you want the volume size reduced, as shown in Figure 25.15. Keep in mind that this will be the approximate size of the new volume that you create a bit later.

Figure 25.15
Enter the amount by which you want the existing volume reduced.

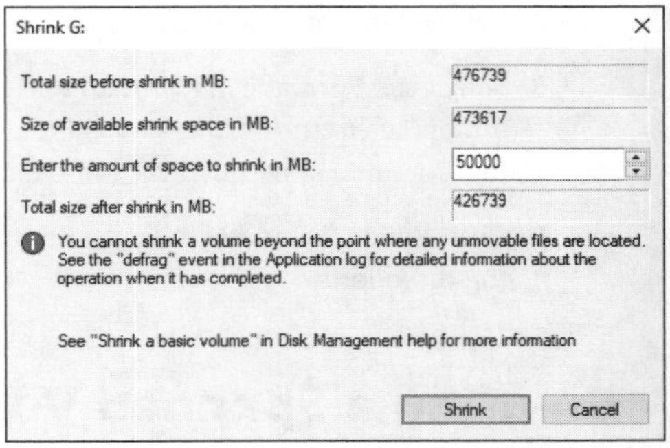

Shrink G: ✕

Total size before shrink in MB:	476739
Size of available shrink space in MB:	473617
Enter the amount of space to shrink in MB:	50000
Total size after shrink in MB:	426739

ⓘ You cannot shrink a volume beyond the point where any unmovable files are located. See the "defrag" event in the Application log for detailed information about the operation when it has completed.

See "Shrink a basic volume" in Disk Management help for more information

[Shrink] [Cancel]

3. Click Shrink. Windows 10 shrinks the volume and displays the freed space as Unallocated, as you can see in Figure 25.16.

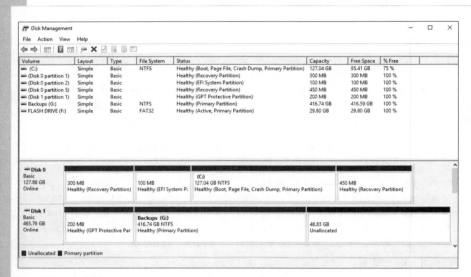

Figure 25.16
The space removed from the existing volume now appears as Unallocated in the Disk Management snap-in.

4. Right-click the Unallocated space and then click New Simple Volume. The New Simple Volume Wizard appears.

5. Click Next. The Specify Volume Size Wizard appears.

6. Make sure that the Simple Volume Size in MB text box is set to the maximum value, and then click Next. The Assign Drive Letter or Path dialog box appears.

7. Select the Assign the Following Drive Letter option, use the list to select the drive letter you want to assign to the new volume, and then click Next.

8. Select the Format This Volume with the Following Settings option, leave the settings as is (you might want to change the Volume Label, however), and click Next.

9. Click Finish. Windows 10 formats the volume and assigns the drive letter.

note

You can't enter a shrink size that's larger than the shrink space you have at your disposal, which is given by the Size of Available Shrink Space value. If you're shrinking drive C, the available shrink space will be quite a bit less than the available free space because Windows reserves quite a bit of space on drive C for the paging file and other system files that may grow over time. Defragmenting first might help.

Creating a Spanned Volume

Earlier you learned about storage spaces, the Windows 10 feature that creates a single storage pool out of multiple hard disks. This is one of the best features in Windows 10, and there's no reason that we can think of not to use it. Still, for the sake of giving you a complete look at Disk Management, the next couple of sections show you the Disk Management tools that mimic storage spaces.

We begin with the *spanned volume*. It is a kind of virtual drive that combines two or more physical hard drives into a single storage area with two main characteristics:

- The new volume is *dynamic* because if you install more drives on the server, you can add those drives to the volume to instantly increase the storage area without losing any existing data.

- The new volume is *spanned* because data is seamlessly stored on all the physical hard drives without your having to worry about where the data is stored. If one of the hard drives fills up, Windows 10 will automatically write new data to one of the other drives in the volume.

Is there a downside to using spanned volumes? Yes, unfortunately, there is a disadvantage, and it's a big one: If one of the hard drives dies, you lose all the data stored in the spanned volume, even data that resides on the remaining functional drives.

In other words, if you go this route, we strongly recommend that you back up the spanned volume to prevent data loss.

Converting Hard Drives to Dynamic Disks

To get started, your first chore is to take the hard drives that you want to use for the spanned volume and convert them to dynamic disks:

1. In the lower half of the Disk Management pane, right-click one of the drives you want to convert to a dynamic volume. Be sure to right-click on the left side of the drive display (where you see the disk designations, such as Disk 0, Disk 1, Disk 2, and so on).

2. Click Convert to Dynamic Disk. Disk Management displays the Convert to Dynamic Disk dialog box.

3. Make sure the box beside the disk is checked, as shown in Figure 25.17, and then click OK. Disk Management displays the Disks to Convert dialog box.

Figure 25.17
Your first task is to convert to dynamic disks those drives you want to include in the spanned volume.

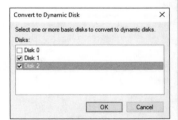

4. Click Convert. Disk Management asks you to confirm.

5. Click Yes. Disk Management converts the drive to a dynamic disk.

6. Repeat steps 1 to 5 to convert any other drives you want to include in the spanned volume.

Combining Dynamic Disks into a Spanned Volume

With your dynamic disks converted, you can now combine them into a spanned volume by following these steps:

1. In the list of hard drives in the lower half of the Disk Management pane, right-click one of the drives you want to include in the spanned volume. Be sure to right-click on the left side of the drive display (where you see the disk designations, such as Disk 0, Disk 1, Disk 2, and so on).

2. Click New Spanned Volume. Disk Management runs the New Spanned Volume Wizard.

3. Click Next. The Select Disks dialog box appears.

4. In the Available list, click a dynamic disk you want to include in the volume and then click Add.

5. Repeat step 4 to add any other drives you want to include in the volume. Figure 25.18 shows a spanned volume with two dynamic disks added.

 note

You don't have to include the entire dynamic disk in the spanned volume. For example, you might want to set aside a portion of the dynamic disk for other storage uses. In that case, click the disk in the Selected list and then use the Select the Amount of Space in MB spin box to set the amount of space you want to assign to the spanned volume.

Figure 25.18
Add the dynamic drives you want to include in the new spanned volume.

6. Click Next. The Assign Drive Letter or Path dialog box appears.

7. Choose a drive letter (the default will probably be D, which is fine) and then click Next. The Format Volume dialog box appears.

8. Assign a Volume Label, if needed, leave the other options as is, and then click Next. The last wizard dialog box appears.

9. Click Finish. Disk Management creates the spanned volume.

Figure 25.19 shows how the new spanned volume (drive F, in this case) appears in Disk Management (the top window) and in the This PC folder (bottom window).

Figure 25.19
The new spanned volume shown in the Disk Management snap-in and the This PC folder.

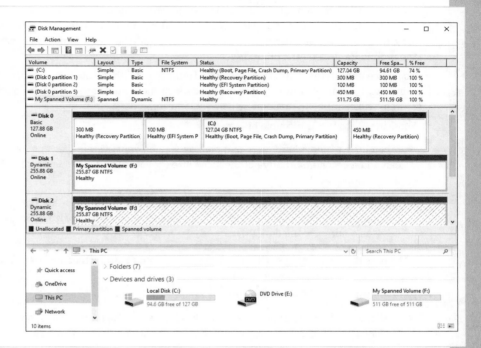

Adding Another Dynamic Disk to the Spanned Volume

If you add a new hard drive to your computer, you can add that drive to the spanned volume. Open the Disk Management snap-in and convert the new drive to a dynamic disk, as we described earlier. Now follow these steps to add the new dynamic disk to the spanned volume:

1. In the list of hard drives in the lower half of the Disk Management pane, right-click one of the disks in your current spanned volume. Be sure to right-click on the right of the drive display (where you see the spanned volume drive letter).

2. Click Extend Volume. Disk Management runs the Extend Volume Wizard.

3. Click Next. The Select Disks dialog box appears.

4. In the Available list, click the new dynamic disk and then click Add.

5. Click Next. The last wizard dialog box appears.

6. Click Finish. Disk Management adds the dynamic disk to the spanned volume.

Creating Mirrored Volumes

A spanned volume provides an easy way to set up a dynamic storage pool using multiple drives, which is great if you don't want your data needs being cramped by a single hard drive. However, what if your concerns are more about data resiliency? That is, if you want to minimize system down-time, then the best way to do that is to have a redundant set of data on another hard drive. That way, if the original hard drive goes down for the count, you can still keep the computer running off the redundant data on the other drives.

You can establish this data redundancy by setting up another volume as a mirror of the original. Windows 10 maintains exact copies of the data on the mirror drive, and if the original drive dies, the system will continue to function by using the mirrored data.

You can go about this a couple of ways:

- If you have a single hard drive and plan on leaving your system files and data on that drive, you can add a second hard drive of the same size (or larger) and use this new hard drive as a mirror for your original data.

- If you've added a second hard drive and are using it to store important data (such as ripped movies or recorded TV shows), you can add a third drive of the same size (or larger) and use this new drive as a mirror of the data drive.

Of course, there's nothing stopping you from combining both techniques, depending on your data needs (and your hard drive budget!).

Here are the steps to follow to mirror a volume:

1. In Disk Management, make sure the disk you want to use for the mirror has no current volumes. If it does have volumes, then for each one, right-click the volume and click Delete Volume.

2. In the list of volumes in the lower half of the Disk Management window, right-click the volume you want to mirror and then click Add Mirror. The Add Mirror dialog box appears.

3. Click the disk you want to use for the mirror and then click Add Mirror. Disk Management warns you that the disk to be mirrored must be converted to a dynamic disk and asks you to confirm this conversion.

4. Click Yes. Disk Management converts the disk to dynamic and then starts mirroring the volume to the other hard drive.

5. Repeat steps 2 to 4 for any other volumes you also want to mirror. Figure 25.20 shows the Disk Management snap-in with Disk 1's drive D being mirrored to the same-sized volume on Disk 2. The original sync might take as little as a few minutes or as much as tens of hours, depending on how much data is to be mirrored.

Figure 25.20
Disk Management
showing a mirror
for drive D.

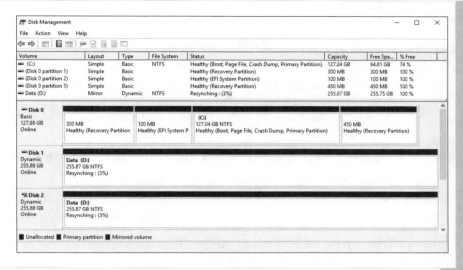

Creating a RAID 5 Volume

So far, you've seen that you can mimic an expandable storage pool by creating a spanned volume that stores data in a single storage area that encompasses two or more hard drives. (See "Creating a Spanned Volume.") Similarly, you saw that you could add resiliency by creating mirrored volumes that store each file and folder on two or more hard drives. (See "Creating Mirrored Volumes.") These easy-to-implement techniques can be really useful, depending on your data and safety needs.

However, we want to show you a third technique that combines spanning and mirroring and includes a bit of load balancing (writing to a second hard drive if one hard drive is busy). This is called *RAID 5* (from the phrase *redundant array of independent disks*), and it has the following characteristics:

- **Three drive minimum**—To implement a RAID 5 volume, you require at least three empty physical drives.

- **Expandable storage pool**—A RAID volume is expandable, so you can add more drives to increase the size of the storage pool. In a three-drive RAID setup, the total available storage space in the volume will be twice the size of the smallest drive; in a four-drive setup, it will be three times the smallest drive; and so on. Therefore, it's best to use drives that are the same size to maximize the available storage area.

- **Data protection**—One of the RAID drives is used as a so-called parity volume, which monitors data integrity to prevent data corruption.

- **Data redundancy**—The other RAID drives are used to store data, with each file and folder being stored multiple times. This means that if one of the data drives fails, you don't lose any data.

- **Load balancing**—RAID monitors drive activity, and if one of the data drives is busy reading or writing data, RAID uses the other drive to perform the current read or write operation.

- **Fault tolerance**—In a RAID setup, if any hard drive goes down, the entire array remains operational, and you don't lose any data. However, it's always best to replace the faulty drive as soon as possible, because if a second drive goes down, you lose everything.

Are there negatives to consider? Yes, as usual:

- **Slow**—The type of RAID we're talking about here is called software RAID because the entire array is maintained and utilized by a software program. Software is inherently slower than hardware, so you might see quite a performance drop when you use a RAID volume, particularly for streaming media files and similar tasks.

- **Expensive**—Because RAID 5 requires a minimum of three hard drives, it can get quite expensive.

---

 tip

What's the solution to slow software RAID? Speedy hardware RAID! This means that you add a RAID-dedicated hardware device to your computer, and that device manages the array. Because the device works directly with the drives (bypassing the CPU), hardware RAID is many times faster than software RAID. Although several types of hardware RAID are available, the most common solution is to insert a RAID controller card inside your computer. These cards usually come with multiple SATA ports (usually two, four, or eight), and you attach your hard drives directly to these controller card ports instead of the motherboard SATA ports. When you start your computer, you see an option to invoke the controller card setup routine, which enables you to choose the disks you want in the array and what type of RAID level you prefer.

With all that in mind, if you want to implement a RAID 5 volume on your computer, follow these steps to set it up:

1. In the list of hard drives in the lower half of the Disk Management pane, right-click one of the drives you want to include in the RAID 5 volume and then click New RAID-5 Volume. Disk Management runs the New RAID-5 Volume Wizard.

2. Click Next. The Select Disks dialog box appears.

3. In the Available list, click a disk you want to include in the volume and then click Add.

4. Repeat step 3 to add any other drives you want to include in the volume. Figure 25.21 shows a RAID 5 volume with three disks added (the minimum).

5. Click Next. The Assign Drive Letter or Path dialog box appears.

6. Choose a drive letter and then click Next. The Format Volume dialog box appears.

7. Assign a volume label, if needed, leave the other options as is, and then click Next. The last wizard dialog box appears.

8. Click Finish. Disk Management warns you that it must convert the disks to dynamic disks and asks you to confirm.

9. Click Yes. Disk Management creates the RAID 5 volume.

Figure 25.21
You must add at least three disks to the RAID 5 volume.

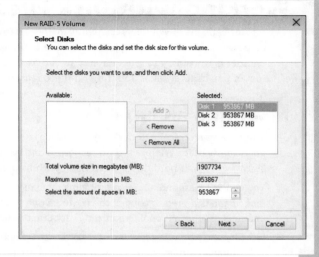

Figure 25.22 shows how the new RAID 5 volume (drive R, in this case, combining Disk 1, Disk 2, and Disk 3) appears in Disk Management.

Figure 25.22
The new RAID 5 volume shown in the Disk Management snap-in.

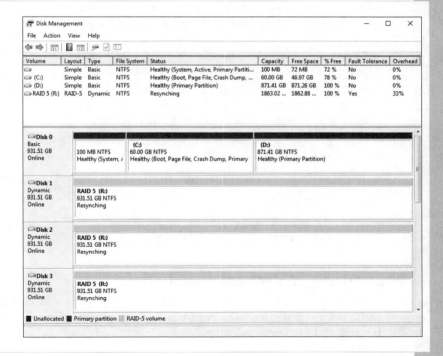

Working with Disk Files

Recent versions of Windows have implemented a few other new storage features that should have all power users leaping with joy. The ability to implement Storage Spaces (described earlier) is one; another is the ability to work directly with disk files such as disc images and virtual hard disks. The rest of this chapter takes you through these features.

Mounting an ISO File

Working with optical (CD or DVD) data discs is a bit of a hassle because you have to insert the disc and then wait for Windows 10 to recognize and mount the disc. An optical disc drive is also much slower than your hard drive, so working with disc files can be time-consuming.

You can work around all these problems by using a *disc image* instead of an actual CD or DVD. A disc image is a precise copy of the contents of an optical disc, including the disc's file system. A disc image is an International Organization for Standardization (ISO) file that uses the .iso file extension.

ISO files are becoming increasingly common. For example, some backup applications use ISO files as their archival format, and plenty of programs are now distributed in the ISO format. When you buy a downloadable application online, you might download it as an ISO file.

In Windows 7 and earlier versions of Windows, you needed a third-party program to view an ISO file or work with its contents. Most of these programs would just burn the ISO file to an optical disc, which just brings us back to the original problems inherent in using discs. Windows 8 changed all that by incorporating support for ISO files right into File Explorer. This means that you no longer need a third-party program to view and work with the contents of an ISO file. Instead, you can use File Explorer to directly mount the ISO as a virtual optical drive.

One consequence of this built-in ISO support is that you don't need to keep copies of your optical discs lying around. Instead, you can convert those discs to ISO files and then store them on your hard drive for easier and faster access.

 note

Unfortunately, File Explorer doesn't come with a feature that enables you to convert optical discs to the ISO format. However, third-party utilities are available to do this. Our favorite example is Free ISO Creator, which you can download from www.freeisocreator.com.

Follow these steps to mount an ISO file:

1. In File Explorer, open the folder that contains the ISO file you want to mount.

2. Select the ISO file.

3. In the Manage tab, click Mount. Windows 10 creates a virtual disc drive for the ISO and displays the contents of the disc image, as shown in Figure 25.23.

Mounting a Virtual Hard Disk

In the same way that an ISO disk image file is an exact replica of an optical disc, a *virtual hard disk* (*VHD*) is a disk image that is an exact replica of a physical hard disk, including the file system and the hard disk's volumes, folders, and files. A virtual hard disk is stored as a VHD file that uses the .vhd or .vhdx file extension.

Figure 25.23
In Windows 10, File Explorer lets you mount and work with ISO files directly.

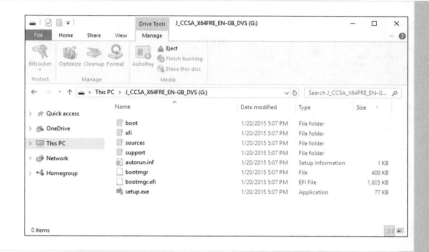

Why would you need such a thing? The most common use by far for VHDs is the hard disk for a virtual machine, especially one created using Microsoft's Hyper-V virtual machine manager.

Windows 10 bakes support for VHD files right into File Explorer, so you can easily view the contents of and copy data from a VHD file without third-party software. File Explorer accomplishes this by enabling you to mount a VHD as a virtual hard disk on your PC.

Follow these steps to mount a virtual hard disk:

1. In File Explorer, open the folder that contains the VHD file you want to mount.

2. Select the .vhd or .vhdx file.

3. Click the Manage tab and then click Mount. Windows 10 creates a virtual hard disk for the VHD and displays the contents of the virtual hard disk, as shown in Figure 25.24.

Creating a Virtual Hard Disk

You might find that you need another hard disk on your PC. For example, you might need a second drive to install another operating system and dual-boot between Windows 10 and the other OS. Or you just might want the drive to store personal files. However, what happens if your PC has no open ports for an external hard disk, and you don't have the expertise or a free drive bay to install an internal hard disk? What if you simply don't want to shell out the bucks for a new hard disk?

In all these cases, you can bypass the need for a physical hard disk by creating a virtual hard disk instead. Windows 10 treats the VHD exactly like a physical hard disk, so whatever operations you can perform on a physical disk, you can do with a virtual one. You can also encrypt a VHD using BitLocker, so a VHD is a great way to store private or sensitive files.

➡️ *To learn about BitLocker, see "Encrypting a Disk with BitLocker," p. 743.*

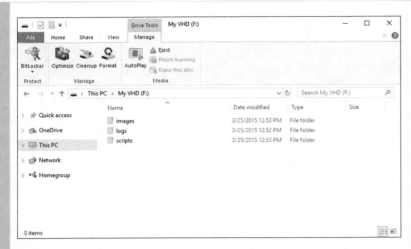

Figure 25.24
You can now use File Explorer to mount and work with virtual hard disk files.

Follow these steps to create a virtual hard disk:

1. In the Disk Management snap-in, select Action, Create VHD. Disk Management displays the Create and Attach Virtual Hard Disk dialog box.

2. Click Browse. The Browse Virtual Disk Files dialog box appears.

3. Choose the folder you want to use to store the VHD, type a name for the VHD, and then click Save.

4. Specify the size of the VHD (in MB, GB, or TB).

5. Select the Virtual Hard Disk Format you want to use:

   - **VHD**—This format is supported by earlier versions of Windows, but it can only create disks up to 2TB.

   - **VHDX**—This format is supported only by Windows 8 and later, but it can create disks up to 16TB and is less prone to file corruption in the event of a power failure.

6. Choose Fixed Size.

7. Click OK. Disk Management creates the virtual hard disk.

Your VHD is now created, but you can't use it yet because it hasn't been configured to store files. This means that you now need to initialize the VHD and add a new simple volume to the disk. To do this, first locate the new VHD in the bottom section of the Disk Management window, right-click the VHD on the left side of the window, and then select Initialize Disk. Check the MBR option and select OK. Now follow the instructions given earlier in this chapter to create a new simple volume on the VHD. (See "Dividing Your Hard Drive into Two Volumes.")

26

TROUBLESHOOTING AND REPAIRING PROBLEMS

A long time ago, somebody proved mathematically that it was impossible to make any reasonably complex software program problem-free. As the number of variables increases, as the interactions of subroutines and objects become more complex, and as the underlying logic of a program grows beyond the ability of a single person to grasp all at once, errors inevitably creep into the code. Given Windows 10's status as possibly the most complex software ever created, the bad news is that there are certainly problems lurking in the weeds. However, the good news is that the overwhelming majority of these problems are extremely obscure and appear only under the rarest circumstances.

This doesn't mean that you're guaranteed a glitch-free computing experience—far from it. Third-party programs and devices cause the majority of computer woes, either because they have inherent problems themselves or because they don't get along well with Windows 10. Using software, devices, and device drivers designed for Windows 10 can help tremendously, as can the maintenance program we outline in the rest of the chapters here in Part VI. But computer problems, like the proverbial death and taxes, are certainties in life, so you need to know how to troubleshoot and resolve the problems that will inevitably come your way. In this chapter, we help you do just that by showing you our favorite techniques for determining problem sources and by taking you through all of Windows 10's recovery tools.

Troubleshooting Strategies: Determining the Source of a Problem

One of the ongoing mysteries that all Windows users experience at one time or another is what might be called the "now you see it, now you don't" problem. This is a glitch that plagues you for a while and then mysteriously vanishes without any intervention on your part. (This also tends to occur when you ask a nearby user or someone from the IT department to look at the problem. Like the automotive problem that goes away when you take the car to a mechanic, computer problems will often resolve themselves as soon as a knowledgeable user sits down at the keyboard.) When this happens, most people just shake their heads and resume working, grateful to no longer have to deal with the problem.

Unfortunately, most computer ills aren't resolved so easily. For these more intractable problems, your first order of business is to hunt down the source of the glitch. This is, at best, a black art, but it can be done if you take a systematic approach. Over the years, we've found that the best approach is to ask a series of questions designed to gather the required information or to narrow down what might be the culprit. The next few sections take you through these questions.

Did You Get an Error Message?

Unfortunately, most computer error messages are obscure and do little to help you resolve a problem directly. However, error codes and error text can help you down the road, either by giving you something to search for in an online database or by providing information to a tech support person. Therefore, you should always write down the full text of any error message that appears.

 tip

If the error message is lengthy and you can still use other programs on your computer, don't bother writing down the full message. Instead, while the message is displayed, press Windows Logo+Print Screen to place an image of the current screen as a PNG file in your Pictures folder.

Does an Error or Warning Appear in the Event Viewer Logs?

Launch the Event Viewer (use the taskbar's Search box to type **event**, and then click View Event Logs), open the Windows Logs branch, and then examine the Application and System logs. In particular, look in the Level column for Error or Warning events. If you see any, double-click each one to read the event description. Figure 26.1 shows an example. Again, although the information here is obscure, the error code and error text give you something to search for in an online database or to give to a tech support person.

 tip

If the error message appears before Windows 10 starts, but you don't have time to write it down, press the Pause Break key to pause the startup. After you record the error, press Ctrl+Pause Break to resume the startup.

Figure 26.1
In the Event Viewer, look for Error and Warning events in the Application and System logs.

Does an Error Appear in System Information?

In the taskbar's Search box, type **msinfo32** and then press Enter to launch the System Information utility. In the Hardware Resources branch, click the Conflicts/Sharing sub-branch for device conflicts. Also, see whether the Components/Problem Devices category lists any devices, as shown in Figure 26.2. Make note of any errors, and then either search for the error online or contact tech support and provide the engineer with the information.

Figure 26.2
You can use the System Information utility to look for device conflicts and problems.

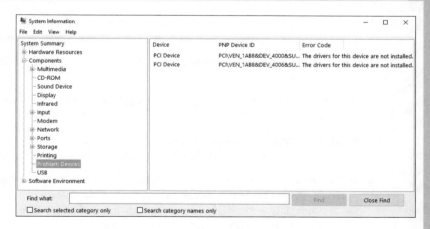

Did You Recently Edit the Registry?

Improper Registry modifications can cause all kinds of mischief. If the problem occurred after editing the Registry, try restoring the changed key or setting. Ideally, if you exported a backup of the offending key, you should import the backup. We show you how to back up the Registry in Chapter 29, "Editing the Windows Registry."

➡ *To learn how to back up a Registry key,* ***see*** *"Backing Up the Registry," **p. 655.***

Did You Recently Change Any Windows Settings?

If the problem started after you changed your Windows configuration, try reversing the change. Even something as seemingly innocent as activating a screensaver can cause problems, so don't rule anything out. If you've made a number of recent changes and you're not sure about everything you did, or if it would take too long to reverse all the changes individually, use System Restore to revert your system to the most recent checkpoint before you made the changes. See "Recovering Using System Restore," later in this chapter.

Did Windows 10 "Spontaneously" Reboot?

When certain errors occur, Windows 10 will reboot itself. This apparently random behavior is actually built in to the system in the event of a system failure—also called a *stop error* or a *blue screen of death (BSOD)*. By default, Windows 10 writes an error event to the system log, dumps the contents of memory into a file, and then reboots the system. So, if your system reboots, check the Event Viewer to see what happened.

You can control how Windows 10 handles system failures by following these steps:

1. In the taskbar's Search box, type **advanced system**, and then click View Advanced System Settings to open the System Properties dialog box with the Advanced tab displayed.

2. In the Startup and Recovery group, click Settings. Figure 26.3 shows the Startup and Recovery dialog box that appears.

3. Configure how Windows 10 handles system failures using the following controls in the System Failure group:

   - **Write an Event to the System Log**—Leave this check box activated to have the system failure recorded in the system log. This enables you to view the event in the Event Viewer.

   - **Automatically Restart**—This is the option that, when activated, causes your system to reboot when a stop error occurs. Deactivate this check box if you want to avoid the reboot. This capability is useful if an error message appears briefly before Windows 10 reboots. By disabling the automatic restart, you give yourself time to read and write down the error message.

Figure 26.3
Use the Startup and Recovery dialog box to configure how Windows 10 handles system failures.

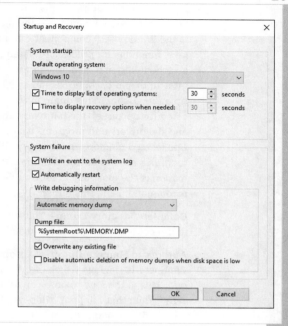

 tip

If the BSOD problem occurs during startup, your computer winds up in an endless loop: you reboot, the problem occurs, the BSOD appears, and then your computer reboots. Unfortunately, the BSOD appears only fleetingly, so you never have enough time to read (much less record) the error message. If this happens, display the Advanced Startup Options menu (see "Navigating the Recovery Environment," later in this chapter), and then select the Disable Automatic Restart on System Failure item. This tells Windows 10 not to reboot after the BSOD appears, so you can then write down the error message and, hopefully, successfully troubleshoot the problem.

- **Write Debugging Information**—This list determines what information Windows 10 saves to disk (in the folder specified in the Dump File text box below the list) when a system failure occurs. This information—it's called a *memory dump*—contains data that can help a tech support employee determine the cause of the problem. You have the following choices:

  - **None**—No debugging information is written.

  - **Small Memory Dump (256 KB)**—This option writes the minimum amount of useful information that could be used to identify what caused the stop error. This 256KB file includes the stop error number and its description, the list of running device drivers, and the processor state.

- **Kernel Memory Dump**—This option writes the contents of the kernel memory to the disk. (The *kernel* is the Windows 10 component that manages low-level functions for processor-related activities such as scheduling and dispatching threads, handling interrupts and exceptions, and synchronizing multiple processors.) This dump includes memory allocated to the kernel, the hardware abstraction layer, and the drivers and programs used by the kernel. Unallocated memory and memory allocated to user programs are not included in the dump. This information is the most useful for troubleshooting, so we recommend using this option.

 note

If a program freezes, you won't be able to shut it down using conventional methods. If you try, you might see a dialog box warning you that the program is not responding. If so, click End Now to force the program to close. If that doesn't work, right-click the taskbar and then click Task Manager. You should see your stuck application listed. Click the program and then click End Task.

- **Complete Memory Dump**—This option writes the entire contents of RAM to the disk.

- **Automatic Memory Dump**—This option is usually the default, and it means that Windows 10 decides which of the other options to use when writing the debugging info. This is the way to go if you're not getting any debugging info written to the disk. Why would that happen? Windows 10 first writes the debugging information to the paging file—`Pagefile.sys` in the root folder of the `%SystemDrive%`. When you restart the computer, Windows 10 then transfers the information to the dump file. Therefore, you must have a large enough paging file to handle the memory dump. If not, you don't see the debugging data. The Automatic Memory Dump option can determine in advance whether there is enough room in the paging file and, if not, it will default to a smaller dump.

- **Active Memory Dump**—This option (which is new to Windows 10) means that Windows 10 writes to the disk only those portions of RAM that were in use when the crash occurred. This is a welcome addition to the debugging options because the active memory is most likely to have information on the crash.

- **Overwrite Any Existing File**—When this option is activated, Windows 10 overwrites any existing dump file with the new dump information. If you deactivate this check box, Windows 10 creates a new dump file with each system failure. Note that this option is enabled only for the Kernel Memory Dump and the Complete Memory Dump (which by default write to the same file: `%SystemRoot%\Memory.dmp`).

- **Disable Automatic Deletion of Memory Dumps When Disk Space Is Low**—Windows 10's Storage Sense technology will automatically delete unneeded files when your PC's hard disk runs low, and this includes memory dumps. If you'd rather not have those files deleted, check this option to have Storage Sense bypass dump files.

➡ *To learn how to configure Storage Sense, see "Deleting Unnecessary Files," p. 556.*

4. Click OK in all the open dialog boxes to put the new settings into effect.

Did You Recently Change Any Application Settings?

If you've recently changed an application setting, try reversing the change to see whether doing so solves the problem. If that doesn't help, here are three other things to try:

- Check the developer's website to see whether an upgrade or patch is available.

- Run the application's Repair option (if it has one), which is often useful for fixing corrupted or missing files. To see whether a program has a Repair option, open Control Panel, click Programs (if you're using Category view), and then Programs and Features. In the Programs and Features window, click the problematic application and then look to see whether a Repair item appears in the taskbar (see Figure 26.4).

Figure 26.4
In the Programs and Features window, click the program and look for a Repair option in the taskbar.

Did You Recently Install a New Program?

If you suspect a new program is causing system instability, restart Windows 10 and try operating the system for a while without using the new program. If the problem doesn't reoccur, the new program is likely the culprit. Try using the program without any other programs running.

You should also examine the program's readme file (if it has one) to look for known problems and possible workarounds. In addition, it's a good idea to check for a Windows 10–compatible version of the program if the program was originally written for an earlier Windows version. Again, you can also try the program's Repair option (if it has one), or you can reinstall the program.

> **tip**
>
> When a program crashes, Windows 10 displays a dialog box asking if you want to see whether a solution to the problem is available. You can control the behavior of this prompt.

Similarly, if you recently upgraded an existing program, try uninstalling the upgrade.

Did You Recently Install a New Device?

If you recently installed a new device or if you recently updated an existing device driver, the new device or driver might be causing the problem. Check Device Manager to see whether there's a problem with the device, as described later in this chapter (see "Troubleshooting Device Problems").

➡️ *For information on using Device Manager for troubleshooting, **see** "Troubleshooting Device Problems," **p. 594**.*

Did You Recently Apply an Update from Windows Update?

It's an unfortunate fact of life that occasionally updates designed to fix one problem end up causing another problem. Fortunately, Windows 10 lets you uninstall an update. Open Control Panel, click Programs (if you're using Category view), click Programs and Features, and then click View Installed Updates. In the Installed Updates window, click the update you want to remove and then click Uninstall.

 tip

If you have Windows 10 set up to perform automatic updating, you can keep tabs on the changes made to your system by selecting Start, Settings, clicking Update & Security to open Windows Update, and then clicking View Installed Update History to see a list of the installed updates, which includes the update's name, status (such as Successfully Installed, Requires a Restart to Finish Installing, or Failed to Install), and date installed.

General Troubleshooting Tips

Figuring out the cause of a problem is often the hardest part of troubleshooting, but by itself, it doesn't do you much good. When you know the source, you need to parlay that information into a fix for the problem. We discussed a few solutions in the previous section, but here are a few other general fixes you need to keep in mind:

- **Close all programs**—You can often fix flaky behavior by shutting down all your open programs and starting them again. This fix is particularly useful for problems caused by low memory or low system resources.

- **Log off Windows 10**—Logging off clears the RAM and thus gives you a slightly cleaner slate than merely closing all your programs.

- **Reboot the computer**—If you're having problems with some system files and devices, logging off won't help because these objects remain loaded. By rebooting, you reload the entire operating system, which is often enough to solve many computer problems.

- **Turn off the computer and restart**—You can often solve a hardware problem by shutting off your machine. Wait for 30 seconds to give all devices time to spin down, and then restart.

- **Check connections, power switches, and so on**—Some of the most common (and some of the most embarrassing) causes of hardware problems are the simple physical things. Therefore, make sure that a device is turned on, check that cable connections are secure, and ensure that insertable devices are properly connected.

More Troubleshooting Tools

Windows 10 comes with diagnostic tools—together, they're called the *Windows Diagnostic Infrastructure (WDI)*—that not only do a better job of finding the source of many common disk, memory, and network problems, but also can detect impending failures and alert you to take corrective or mitigating action (such as backing up your files). The next few sections describe these tools.

Running the Windows 10 Troubleshooters

Windows Vista introduced the idea of the *troubleshooter*, a Help system component that offers a series of solutions that lead you deeper into a problem in an attempt to fix it. In Windows 7, the troubleshooters were beefed up and given their own home within the Control Panel interface, and that home remains in place in Windows 8.x and Windows 10. To see the Windows 10 troubleshooters, use the taskbar's Search box to type **trouble**, and then choose Troubleshoot in the search results.

The Troubleshoot window (see Figure 26.5) is divided into several general categories (Internet Connections, Playing Audio, and so on), as well as more specific problems (Blue Screen, Bluetooth, and so on).

To launch a troubleshooter, click it and then click Run the Troubleshooter.

Figure 26.5
Windows 10's Troubleshoot window offers links to various troubleshooting categories and tasks.

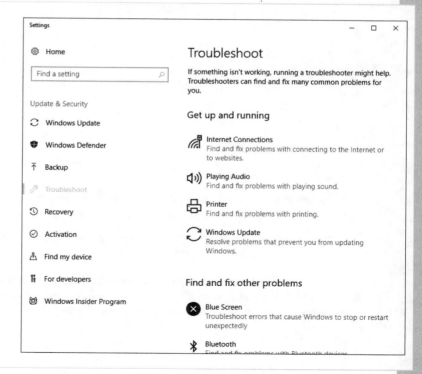

Running the Memory Diagnostics Tool

Few computer problems are as maddening as those related to physical memory defects because they tend to be intermittent and to cause problems in secondary systems, forcing you to waste time on wild goose chases all over your system.

Therefore, it is welcome news indeed that Windows 10 ships with a Windows Memory Diagnostics tool that works with Microsoft Online Crash Analysis to determine whether defective physical memory is the cause of program crashes. If so, Windows Memory Diagnostics lets you know about the problem and schedules a memory test for the next time you start your computer. If it detects actual problems, the system also marks the affected memory area as unusable to avoid future crashes.

Windows 10 also comes with a Memory Leak Diagnosis tool that's part of the Diagnostic Policy Service. If a program is leaking memory (using up increasing amounts of memory over time), Memory Leak Diagnosis will locate the problem and take steps to fix it.

To run the Memory Leak Diagnostics tool, follow these steps:

1. Use the taskbar's Search box to type **memory**, and then click Windows Memory Diagnostic in the search results. The Windows Memory Diagnostic window appears, as shown in Figure 26.6.

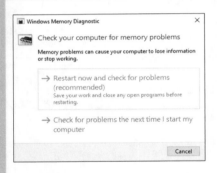

Figure 26.6
Use the Windows Memory Diagnostic tool to check for memory problems.

2. Click one of the following options:

   - **Restart Now and Check for Problems**—Click this option to force an immediate restart and schedule a memory test during startup. Be sure to save your work before clicking this option.

   - **Check for Problems the Next Time I Start My Computer**—Click this option to schedule a memory test to run the next time you boot.

After the test runs (it takes 10 to 15 minutes, depending on how much RAM is in your system), Windows 10 restarts and you see (for a short time) the Windows Memory Diagnostic icon in the taskbar's notification area. This icon displays a notification that shows the results of the memory test.

Checking Your PC's Reliability History

One useful way to troubleshoot an existing problem is to review problems that have occurred in the past and look for a pattern. This might mean looking for similar problems that occurred previously, problems that have occurred at predictable intervals, problems that occurred in conjunction with specific events (such as a software or hardware install), or problems that have escalated over time.

In the past, all this would have required extensive work on your part, but now Windows 10 includes a very useful tool called Reliability Monitor. This tool shows a timeline of hardware and software issues that have affected your PC. These issues are displayed in five categories: application failures, Windows failures, miscellaneous failures, warnings, and information. You can view the issues on a daily or weekly basis.

Based on these issues, Reliability Monitor calculates a *stability index* for your PC, which is a value from 1 to 10, where 10 is the most stable, and 1 is the least.

Follow these steps to use the Reliability Monitor:

1. Use the taskbar's Search box to type `maintenance`, and then click Security and Maintenance in the results. The Security and Maintenance window appears.

2. Open the Maintenance section and click View Reliability History. Control Panel opens the Reliability Monitor window, shown in Figure 26.7.

Figure 26.7 Reliability Monitor calculates a stability index for your PC and shows a timeline of hardware and software problems.

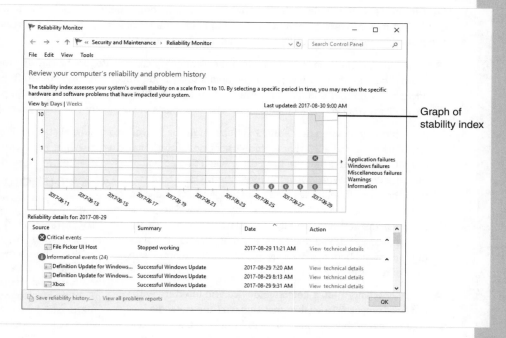

Graph of stability index

3. Click either Days or Weeks to change the timeline view.

4. Click a day or week. Reliability Monitor displays the details of the issues that occurred during that time.

5. To learn more about an issue, click its View Technical Details link to open the Problem Details window.

Troubleshooting Startup

Computers are often frustrating beasts, but few things in computerdom are as maddening as a computer that won't compute or an operating system that won't operate. After all, if your PC won't even start Windows, then Windows can't start any programs, which means *you* can't get any work done.

What you've got on your hands is a rather expensive boat anchor, not to mention a hair-pullingly, teeth-gnashingly frustrating problem that you have to fix *now*. To help save some wear and tear on your hair and teeth, this chapter outlines a few common startup difficulties and their solutions.

 note

For the more critical problems identified by Reliability Monitor, Windows 10 automatically sends a problem report to Microsoft. To see which reports have been sent for your PC, click View All Problem Reports located at the bottom of the screen. If you'd rather not have this diagnostic data sent to Microsoft, open Settings, click Privacy, click the Feedback & Diagnostics tab, and then select the Basic option in the Diagnostic Data section.

Some Things to Try Before Anything Else

Startup problems generally are either trivially easy to fix or are take-it-to-the-repair-shop difficult to solve. Fortunately, startup conundrums often fall into the former camp, and in many cases, one of the following solutions will get your PC back on its electronic feet:

■ Some boot problems mercifully fall into the Temporary Glitch category of startup woes. That is, it could be that your PC has just gone momentarily and temporarily haywire. To find out, shut down the computer and leave it turned off for at least 30 seconds to give everything time to spin down. Turn your PC back on and cross whatever parts of your body you think might help.

■ A setting in your computer's BIOS options might be preventing a normal startup. For example, one of us once had a PC that wouldn't boot no matter what we did. When we decided to check the BIOS, we found that the hard drive wasn't listed as the boot device! When we configured the BIOS to boot from the hard drive, all was well. Restart your PC and then press whatever key or key combination your BIOS requires to access the settings (usually the Delete key or a function key such as F2). If you don't see anything obvious (such as misconfigured boot options), try resetting all the options to the default state.

 caution

Whatever you do, resist the temptation to fiddle with the BIOS settings willy-nilly. If you're not sure what a setting is used for, don't mess with it. If you have Internet access through another computer or device, you might be able to find an online reference for your PC's BIOS, which will let you know what each setting does.

■ Every now and then, a defective device will interfere with the boot process. To ensure that this isn't the case, disconnect every device that can be disconnected, and then try booting your newly naked PC. If you get a successful launch, one of the devices was almost certainly the culprit.

Attach the devices one by one and try rebooting each time until you find out which one is causing the boot failure. You could then reboot without the device, update the device driver (if an
update is available), and try again. If that still doesn't work, the device is probably defective and
should be repaired or replaced.

■ If you get no power when you press your desktop PC's On switch, it's likely you have a defective
power supply on your hands, one or more of the power supply connections have come loose, or
your power cord is not plugged in to a power source or has come loose. Check all the connections and, if they're fine, replace the power supply. If nothing happens when you try to turn on
your notebook or tablet PC, you might be looking at a drained battery. Connect the machine to a
power source and try again.

Disabling Startup Programs

If you're having trouble getting Windows 10 off the ground, a program that launches during the
system startup may be the culprit. How do you know which programs run at startup? You can find
out by launching Windows 10 in Safe mode, running Task Manager (either press Windows Logo+X
or right-click the taskbar, and then click Task Manager), clicking More Details, and selecting the
Startup tab (see Figure 26.8).

Figure 26.8
Task Manager's Startup tab lists the
programs that launch during the
Windows 10 startup.

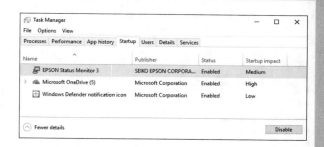

This list comes from the Registry, typically from the following keys:

```
HKEY_CURRENT_USER\SOFTWARE\Microsoft\Windows\CurrentVersion\Run
HKEY_LOCAL_MACHINE\SOFTWARE\Microsoft\Windows\CurrentVersion\Run
```

To find out whether one of the programs is causing Windows 10 to misfire at startup, disable the
startup programs one by one (or use the method shown in the "Troubleshooting by Halves" sidebar
later in this chapter) to see whether that solves the problem. To disable a startup program, click it
and then click Disable.

Disabling Startup Services

If Windows 10 won't start, troubleshooting the problem usually involves trying various advanced startup options. It's almost always a time-consuming and tedious business.

However, what if Windows 10 *will* start, but you encounter problems along the way? Or what if you want to try a few different configurations to see whether you can eliminate startup items or improve Windows 10's overall performance? For these scenarios, don't bother trying out different startup configurations by hand. Instead, take advantage of Windows 10's System Configuration utility, which gives you a graphical front end that offers precise control over how Windows 10 starts.

Launch the System Configuration utility (in the Search box, type `msconfig` and press Enter) and display the General tab, which has three startup options:

- **Normal Startup**—This option loads Windows 10 normally.

- **Diagnostic Startup**—This option loads only those device drivers and system services that are necessary for Windows 10 to boot. This is equivalent to deactivating all the check boxes associated with the Selective Startup option, discussed next.

- **Selective Startup**—When you activate this option (this is the default), the following check boxes become available (see Figure 26.9): Load System Services, Load Startup Items, and Use Original Boot Configuration. From the previous section, you already know how to disable startup items, so here our only concern is system services. The Load System Services category refers to the system services that Windows 10 loads at startup. The specific services loaded by Windows 10 are listed on the Services tab.

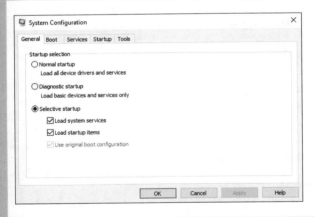

Figure 26.9
Use the System Configuration utility's General tab to troubleshoot the Windows 10 startup.

You use these check boxes to select which portions of the startup should be processed.

To control startup services, the System Configuration utility gives you two choices:

- To prevent Windows 10 from loading nonessential services, activate Selective Startup in the General tab and then deactivate the Load System Services check box. Click OK.

- To prevent Windows 10 from loading specific services, display the Services tab and then deactivate the check box beside the service or services you want to bypass at startup. Click OK.

> ## note
>
> A *service* is a program or process that performs a specific, low-level support function for the operating system or an installed program. For example, Windows 10's Automatic Updates feature is a service.

A Startup Troubleshooting Procedure

Now that you know how to disable startup items and services, here's a basic procedure you can follow to use Task Manager and System Configuration to troubleshoot a startup problem:

1. In System Configuration, activate the Diagnostic Startup option and then reboot the computer. If the problem did not occur during the restart, you know the cause lies in the system services or the startup items.

2. In System Configuration, activate the Selective Startup option.

3. In System Configuration, activate Load System Services; in Task Manager, disable all the startup programs; reboot the computer.

4. In System Configuration, deactivate Load System Services; in Task Manager, enable all the startup programs; reboot the computer.

5. The problem will reoccur either during the step 3 reboot or the step 4 reboot. When this happens, you know that whatever category (services or programs) you enabled before rebooting is the source of the problem:

   - If the problem reoccurred after you activated the Load System Services check box, run System Configuration and select the Services tab.

   - If the problem reoccurred after you enabled the startup programs, run Task Manager and select the Startup tab.

6. If you're in System Configuration on the Services tab, click Disable All to clear all the check boxes; if you're in Task Manager, disable all the programs.

7. Activate one of the services or enable one of the programs and then reboot the computer.

8. Repeat step 7 for each of the other services or programs until the problem reoccurs. When this happens, you know that whatever item you activated or enabled just before rebooting is the source of the problem.

9. In the System Configuration utility's General tab, activate the Normal Startup option.

Troubleshooting by Halves

If you have a large number of items to test (such as in the Services tab), activating one at a time and rebooting can become very tedious very fast. A faster method is to begin by activating the first half of the check boxes in step 7 and reboot. One of two things will happen:

- **The problem doesn't reoccur**—This means that one of the items represented by the deactivated check boxes is the culprit. Clear all the check boxes, activate half of the other check boxes, and then reboot.

- **The problem reoccurs**—This means that one of the activated check boxes is the problem. Activate only half of those check boxes and reboot.

Keep halving the number of activated check boxes until you isolate the offending item.

10. Fix or work around the problem:

- If the problem is a system service, you can disable the service. Use the taskbar's Search box to type **local services**, and then click View Local Services. Double-click the problematic service to open its property sheet. In the Startup Type list, select Disabled and then click OK.

- If the problem is a Startup item, use Task Manager to disable it. If the item is a program, consider repairing, uninstalling, or reinstalling the program.

Troubleshooting Device Problems

Windows 10 has excellent support for most newer devices, and most major hardware vendors have taken steps to update their devices and drivers to run properly with Windows 10. If you use only recent, Plug and Play–compliant devices that qualify for the Designed for Windows 10 logo, you should have a problem-free computing experience (at least from a hardware perspective). Of course, putting *problem-free* and *computing* next to each other is just asking for trouble. Hardware is not foolproof—far from it. Things still can, and will, go wrong, and when they do, you'll need to perform some kind of troubleshooting. (Assuming, of course, that the device doesn't have a physical fault that requires a trip to the repair shop.) Fortunately, Windows 10 also has some handy tools to help you both identify and rectify hardware ills.

Troubleshooting with Device Manager

Device Manager (press Windows Logo+X and then click Device Manager) not only provides you with a comprehensive summary of your system's hardware data, but doubles as a decent troubleshooting tool. To see what I mean, check out the Device Manager window shown in Figure 26.10. See how the Other Devices branch has an Unknown Device item that has an exclamation mark superimposed on its icon? This tells you that there's a problem with the device.

Figure 26.10
The Device Manager uses icons to warn you there's a problem with a device.

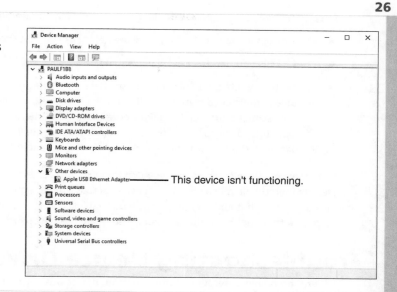

This device isn't functioning.

If you double-click the problem device to open its properties, as shown in Figure 26.11, the Device Status area tells you a bit more about what's wrong. As you can see in Figure 26.11, the problem here is that the device drivers aren't installed. Device Manager usually offers a suggested remedy (such as the Update Driver button shown in Figure 26.11).

Figure 26.11
The Device Status area tells you if the device isn't working properly.

Device Manager uses three different icons to give you an indication of the device's current status:

- A black exclamation mark (!) on a yellow field tells you that there's a problem with the device.

- A red X tells you that the device is disabled or missing.

- A blue i on a white field tells you that the device's Use Automatic Settings check box (on the Resources tab) is deactivated and that at least one of the device's resources was selected manually. Note that the device might be working just fine, so this icon doesn't indicate a problem. If the device isn't working properly, however, the manual setting might be the cause. (For example, the device might have a DIP switch or jumper set to a different resource.)

If your system flags a device, but you don't notice any problems, you can usually get away with just ignoring the flag. I've seen lots of systems that run perfectly well with flagged devices, so this falls under the "If it ain't broke..." school of troubleshooting. The danger here is that tweaking your system to try to get rid of the flag can cause other—usually more serious—problems.

Troubleshooting Device Driver Problems

Other than problems with the hardware itself, device drivers are the cause of most device woes. This is true even if your device doesn't have one of the problem icons mentioned in the previous section. That is, if you open the device's properties sheet, Windows 10 might tell you that the device is "working properly," but all that means is that Windows 10 can establish a simple communications channel with the device. So, if your device isn't working right, but Windows 10 says otherwise, suspect a driver problem. Here are a few tips and pointers for correcting device driver problems:

- **Finish installing the driver**—In some cases, a setup program might not be able to complete its driver installation. This can occur if Windows blocks it from accessing certain areas of the system drive or determines that extra software is required for the driver to work. Rather than aborting the install, Windows only lets it go so far and then displays a notification prompting you to let Windows complete the driver installation. In such cases, Control Panel's Security and Maintenance window shows a Finish Installing Device Software message. Click Install to proceed with the installation.

- **Reinstall the driver**—A driver might be malfunctioning because one or more of its files have become corrupted. You can usually solve this by reinstalling the driver. Just in case a disk fault caused the corruption, you should check the partition where the driver is installed for errors before reinstalling.

- **Upgrade to a signed driver**—Unsigned drivers—that is, device drivers that don't come with a signature from Microsoft that verifies the drivers are safe to install—are accidents waiting for a place to happen in Windows 10, so you should upgrade to a signed driver, if possible. How can you tell whether an installed driver is unsigned? Open the device's properties sheet and then display the Driver tab. Signed driver files display a name beside the Digital Signer label, whereas unsigned drivers display "Not digitally signed" instead.

- **Disable an unsigned driver**—If an unsigned driver is causing system instability and you can't upgrade the driver, try disabling it. In the Driver tab of the device's properties sheet, click Disable.

- **Use the Signature Verification tool**—This program checks your entire system for unsigned drivers. To use it, click inside the taskbar's Search box, type `sigverif`, and press Enter. In the File Signature Verification window, click Start. When the verification is complete, the program displays a list of the unsigned driver files (if any). The results for all the scanned files are written to the log file `Sigverif.txt`, which is copied to the `%SystemRoot%` folder when you close the window that shows the list of unsigned drivers. In the Status column of `Sigverif.txt`, look for files listed as "Not Signed." If you find any, consider upgrading these drivers to signed versions.

- **Try the manufacturer's driver supplied with the device**—If the device came with its own driver, either try updating the driver to the manufacturer's or try running the device's setup program.

- **Download the latest driver from the manufacturer**—Device manufacturers often update drivers to fix bugs, support new operating system versions, add new features, and tweak performance. Go to the manufacturer's website to see whether an updated driver is available.

- **Roll back a driver**—If the device stops working properly after you update the driver, try rolling it back to the old driver. (See the next section.)

Rolling Back a Device Driver

If an updated device driver is giving you problems, you have two ways to fix things:

- If updating the driver was the last action you performed on the system, restore the system to the most recent restore point. (See "Recovering Using System Restore," later in this chapter.)

- If you've updated other things on the system in the meantime, a restore point might restore more than you need. In that case, you need to roll back just the device driver that's causing problems.

Follow these steps to roll back a device driver:

1. Press Windows Logo+X and select Device Manager.

2. Right-click the device and click Properties to open its Properties dialog box.

3. Display the Driver tab.

4. Click Roll Back Driver, and then click OK.

Recovering from a Problem

Ideally, solving a problem will require a specific tweak to the system: a Registry setting change, a driver upgrade, a program uninstall. But sometimes you need to take more of a "big picture" approach to revert your system to some previous state in the hope that you'll leap past the problem and get your system working again. Fortunately, Windows 10 comes with a boatload of tools that can help in both scenarios, and we use the rest of this chapter to tell you about these tools.

Accessing the Recovery Environment

Windows 10 offers a Recovery Environment (RE) that gives you a simple, easily navigated set of screens that offer a number of troubleshooting tools and utilities.

In versions of Windows prior to Windows 8, you could access the advanced startup options by pressing F8 during startup (after your PC completed its Power-On Self Test). That no longer works, but Windows 10 (like Windows 8 and 8.1) offers many other ways to get to the RE and its advanced startup options:

- Use the Settings app from within Windows 10.

- Use the SHUTDOWN command from within Windows 10.

- Use the boot options screen if you dual-boot Windows 10 and another operating system.

- Boot to a recovery drive.

- Boot to a system repair disc.

- Boot to your Windows 10 installation media.

The next few sections discuss each method in more detail.

Accessing the RE via Settings

If you're having trouble with your PC, but you can still start Windows 10, you can use the Settings app to access the RE. Follow these steps to boot to the RE using the Settings app within Windows 10:

1. Click Start, and then click Settings to open the Settings app.

2. Click Update & Security.

3. Click the Recovery tab.

4. In the Advanced Startup section, click Restart Now. The Choose an Option screen appears, as shown in Figure 26.12.

Figure 26.12
When you boot to the Choose an Option screen, click Troubleshoot to see the Recovery Environment tools.

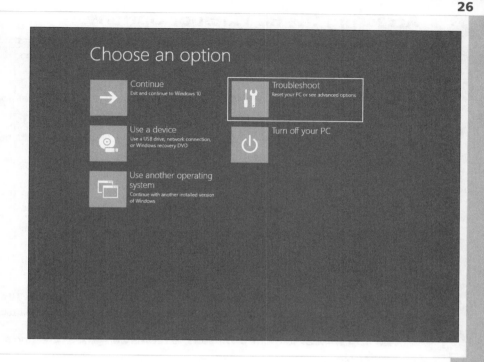

Accessing the RE via the SHUTDOWN Command

Rather than access the RE via the convoluted Settings route, you can create a shortcut that runs the SHUTDOWN command-line utility with the /o switch, which restarts Windows 10 and automatically invokes the RE. Follow these steps to create the shortcut:

1. Right-click the desktop and then select New, Shortcut. The Create Shortcut dialog box appears.

2. Enter the following in the Type the Location of the Item text box and press Enter:

```
shutdown.exe /o /r /t 00
```

3. Type a name for the shortcut and click Finish.

4. Right-click the shortcut and click Properties.

5. Click Change Icon and then click OK when Windows 10 tells you the program contains no icons. Windows 10 displays the icons that come with the shell32.dll file.

6. Select an icon, click OK, and then click OK to close the Properties dialog box.

When you run this shortcut, Windows 10 reboots the system, and you end up at the Choose an Option screen. Click Troubleshoot.

Accessing the RE via Boot Options

If you're having trouble starting Windows 10, but you still have access to your hard drive, you might be able to access the RE if you have already configured your system to dual-boot Windows 10 with another operating system.

➡️ *For information on setting up your system to dual-boot,* **see** *"Dual-Booting Windows 10," p. 45.*

If you dual-boot Windows 10 and other operating systems, follow these steps to boot to the RE:

1. Restart your computer. The Choose an Operating System screen appears.

2. Click Change Defaults or Choose Other Options. The Options screen appears.

3. Click Choose Other Options. The Choose an Option screen appears.

4. Click Troubleshoot.

Accessing the RE via a Recovery Drive

If you're having a problem with your system and are unable to start Windows 10 and can't even access your hard drive, you can still access a version of the RE if you created a recovery drive.

➡️ *To learn how to create a Windows 10 recovery drive,* **see** *"Creating a Recovery Drive," p. 726.*

Follow these steps to boot to the RE using the recovery drive:

1. Insert the recovery drive.

2. Restart your PC and boot to the USB flash drive:

   ■ If you have a newer PC that has a Unified Extensible Firmware Interface (UEFI), Windows 10 will recognize the flash drive automatically and display the Use a Device screen. Click your flash drive in the list that appears.

   ■ If you have an older PC that doesn't support UEFI, you will need to access your PC's BIOS settings and configure them to boot to the flash drive. Right after you turn on the PC, look for a message that says something like "Press Del to access BIOS/Start settings." Press the key, and then use the BIOS interface's boot options to configure your PC to boot to the USB flash drive and disable the Secure Boot feature, if it exists.

3. Click a keyboard layout. The Choose an Option screen appears.

4. Click Troubleshoot.

Accessing the RE via a System Repair Disc

If some problem is preventing you from accessing Windows 10 and your hard drive, but you didn't create a recovery drive, you can still access the RE if you have a Windows 10 system repair disc.

Follow these steps to boot to the RE using a system repair disc:

1. Insert the system repair disc.

2. Restart your PC and boot to the system repair disc. In most cases, wait until you see a message similar to "Press any key to boot from CD or DVD…" and then press a key. If you don't see this message, access the PC's BIOS settings and configure them to boot to the optical drive first and to disable the Secure Boot feature.

3. Click a keyboard layout. The Choose an Option screen appears.

4. Click Troubleshoot.

Accessing the RE via Windows 10 Install Media

If you didn't create a recovery drive or a system repair disc, but you have your Windows 10 installation media, follow these steps to boot to the RE using the install media:

1. Insert your Windows 10 install media.

2. Restart your PC and boot to the install drive.

3. When the Windows Setup dialog box appears, click Next.

4. Click Repair Your Computer. The Choose an Option screen appears.

5. Click Troubleshoot.

 tip

If your system won't boot from the Windows 10 install media (or the system repair disc), you need to adjust the system's BIOS settings to allow this. Restart the computer and look for a startup message that prompts you to press a key or key combination to modify the BIOS settings (which might be called Setup or something similar). Find the boot options and either enable a media drive–based boot or make sure that the option to boot from the media drive comes before the option to boot from the hard disk. If you use a USB keyboard, you may also need to enable an option that lets the BIOS recognize keystrokes after the POST but before the OS starts. You might also need to disable the Secure Boot feature if it exists.

Navigating the Recovery Environment

In the previous few sections, each procedure dropped you off at the Troubleshoot screen, shown in Figure 26.13.

From here, you can reset your PC. (We discuss this option later in this chapter; see "Resetting Your PC.") You can also click Advanced Options to display the Advanced Options screen, shown in Figure 26.14.

From here, you can run System Restore (see "Recovering Using System Restore," later in this chapter), recover a system image (see "Restoring a System Image"), run an automatic repair (see "Automatically Repairing Your PC"), access the Command Prompt to use its command-line tools, or revert to an earlier build of Windows 10.

Figure 26.13
The Troubleshoot screen offers a few troubleshooting tools.

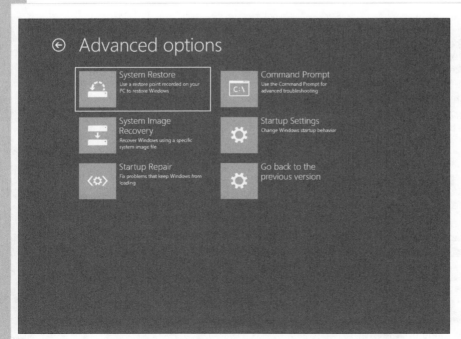

Figure 26.14
The Advanced Options screen offers even more troubleshooting tools.

In most cases, you can also click Startup Settings and then click Restart to access even more startup settings. (Note that you don't see the Startup Settings option if you boot to a recovery drive, a system repair disc, or the Windows 10 install media.) Windows 10 restarts your PC and displays the Startup Settings screen, shown in Figure 26.15.

Figure 26.15
The Startup Settings screen offers several startup options.

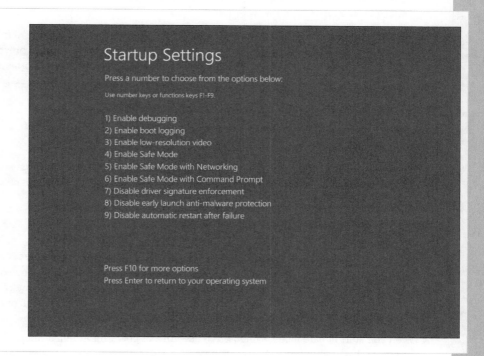

Startup Settings

Press a number to choose from the options below:

Use number keys or functions keys F1-F9.

1) Enable debugging
2) Enable boot logging
3) Enable low-resolution video
4) Enable Safe Mode
5) Enable Safe Mode with Networking
6) Enable Safe Mode with Command Prompt
7) Disable driver signature enforcement
8) Disable early launch anti-malware protection
9) Disable automatic restart after failure

Press F10 for more options
Press Enter to return to your operating system

Press Enter to load Windows 10 in the usual fashion. You can use the other options to control the rest of the startup procedure:

- **Enable Debugging**—This command enables remote debugging of the Windows 10 kernel.

- **Enable Boot Logging**—This option is the same as the Boot Normally option, except that Windows 10 logs the boot process in a text file named ntbtlog.txt that resides in the system root.

- **Enable Low-Resolution Video**—This option loads Windows 10 with the video display set to 640×480 and 256 colors. This is useful if your video output is garbled when you start Windows 10. For example, if your display settings are configured at a resolution that your video card can't handle, boot in the low-resolution mode and then switch to a setting supported by your video card.

- **Enable Safe Mode**—The three Safe Mode options enable you to run a barebones version of Windows 10 for troubleshooting. See "Booting Up in Safe Mode," later in this chapter.

- **Disable Driver Signature Enforcement**—This item prevents Windows 10 from checking whether device drivers have digital signatures. If failing to load that driver is causing system problems, choose this option to ensure that Windows 10 loads an unsigned driver.

- **Disable Early Launch Anti-Malware Driver**—This option prevents Windows 10 from scanning device drivers for malware during startup. If Windows 10 won't start, it's possible that the anti-malware scan is messing with a driver.

- **Disable Automatic Restart After Failure**—This option prevents Windows 10 from restarting automatically when the system crashes. Choose this option if you want to prevent your system from restarting so that you can read an error message or deduce other information that can help you troubleshoot the problem.

You can also press F10 and then press 1 to launch the RE from here.

Booting Up in Safe Mode

You saw in the previous section that Windows 10's Advanced Options menu has tons of startup choices. By far the most useful of these are the various Safe Mode options, which we discuss in more detail in the next few sections.

Safe Mode

If you're having trouble with Windows 10—for example, if a corrupt or incorrect video driver is mangling your display, or if Windows 10 won't start—you can use the Safe Mode option to run a stripped-down version of Windows 10 that includes only the minimal set of device drivers that Windows 10 requires to load. Using this mode you could, for example, reinstall or roll back the offending device driver and then load Windows 10 normally.

When you start in Safe mode, Windows 10 uses the all-powerful Administrator account, which is the account to use when troubleshooting problems. However, caution is required when doing so.

When Windows 10 finally loads, as shown in Figure 26.16, the desktop reminds you that you're in Safe mode by displaying "Safe Mode" in each corner.

You should use the Safe mode option if one of the following conditions occurs:

- Windows 10 doesn't start after the POST ends.

- Windows 10 seems to stall for an extended period.

- You can't print to a local printer.

- Your video display is distorted and possibly unreadable.

- Your computer stalls repeatedly.

- Your computer suddenly slows down and doesn't return to normal without a reboot.

- You need to test an intermittent error condition.

> **note**
>
> If you're curious to know which drivers are loaded during a Safe mode boot, see the subkeys in the following Registry key:
>
> HKEY_LOCAL_MACHINE\SYSTEM\ CurrentControlSet\Control\ SafeBoot\Minimal\

Figure 26.16
Windows 10 in
Safe mode.

Safe Mode with Networking

The Safe Mode with Networking option is identical to plain Safe mode, except that Windows 10's networking drivers are also loaded at startup. This enables you to log on to your network, which is handy if you need to access the network to load a device driver, run a troubleshooting utility, or send a tech support request. This option also gives you Internet access if you connect via a gateway on your network. This is useful if you need to download drivers or contact online tech support.

You should use the Safe Mode with Networking option if one of the following situations occurs:

- Windows 10 fails to start using any of the other Safe mode options.

- The drivers or programs you need to repair a problem exist on a shared network resource.

- You need access to email or other network-based communications for technical support.

- You need to access the Internet via your network to download device drivers or visit an online tech support site.

- Your computer is running a shared Windows 10 installation.

Safe Mode with Command Prompt

The Safe Mode with Command Prompt option is the same as plain Safe mode, except that it doesn't load the Windows 10 GUI. Instead, it runs `cmd.exe` to load a Command Prompt session. You should use the Safe Mode with Command Prompt option if one of the following situations occurs:

- Windows 10 fails to start using any of the other Safe mode options.

- The programs you need to repair a problem must be run from the Command Prompt.

- You can't load the Windows 10 GUI.

Adding Safe Mode to the Boot Options Menu

If you find that you use Safe mode frequently, it can be a real hassle to drill down through the endless startup screens to get to the Advanced Options menu. To work around that problem, you can configure Windows 10 startup to display a boot menu that lets you choose between a regular startup and a Safe mode startup. Here are the steps to follow:

1. Press Windows Logo+X, click Command Prompt (Admin), and then enter your User Account Control credentials.

    ➡ *To learn how to add Command Prompt (Admin) to the Start Menu's shortcut menu,* **see** *"Adding Command Prompt to the Shortcut Menu,"* **p. 129.**

2. At the command line, type the following command and press Enter. (This tells BCDEdit to write your PC's boot info to a file named `boot.txt` on your desktop.)

    `bcdedit /enum /v > %userprofile%\desktop\boot.txt`

3. Leave Command Prompt open and double-click the `boot.txt` file on your desktop to open the file in Notepad.

4. In the Windows Boot Loader section, copy the identifier value (including the opening and closing braces).

5. Return to Command Prompt and type **bcdedit** **/copy** followed by a space.

6. Press Ctrl+V to paste the identifier value you copied in step 4.

7. Type a space followed by **/d "Windows 10 (Safe Mode)"** and then press Enter. BCDEdit copies the boot info to the new entry.

8. In the taskbar's Search box, type **msconfig** and then press Enter to start the System Configuration tool.

9. In the Boot tab, click the Windows 10 (Safe Mode) boot item you just created.

10. Select the Safe Boot check box, as shown in Figure 26.17.

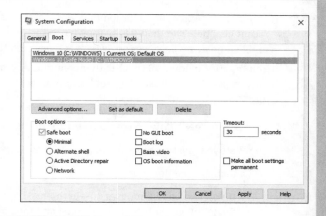

Figure 26.17
In System Configuration's Boot tab, select the new boot info and then choose the Safe Boot option.

11. Click OK. Windows 10 prompts you to restart.

12. Click Exit Without Restart.

Automatically Repairing Your PC

If Windows 10 won't start normally, your first troubleshooting step is almost always to start the system in Safe mode. When you make it to Windows 10, you can investigate the problem and make the necessary changes (such as disabling or rolling back a device driver). But what if your system won't even start in Safe mode?

Your next step should be the RE's Startup Repair option, which attempts various repair strategies that are often useful for getting a PC back on its feet. Here's how to use it:

1. Boot to the RE, as described earlier. (See "Accessing the Recovery Environment.")

2. Click Advanced Options. The Advanced Options screen appears.

3. Click Startup Repair. (If you're running the command from a recovery disk or your install media, you're prompted to select the target operating system, which will be Windows 10.) Windows 10 reboots, and Startup Repair prompts you for your user account.

4. Click your user account. Automatic Repair prompts you for your password.

5. Type your account password and then click Continue. Automatic Repair begins the repair process.

Recovering Using System Restore

If you make a change to your system—such as adding new hardware, updating a device driver, installing a program, or modifying some settings—and then find that the system won't start or acts weirdly, it's a good bet that the change is the culprit. In that case, you can tell Windows 10 to revert to an earlier configuration that worked (that is, a configuration that doesn't include your most recent change). The theory is that by using the previous working configuration, you can make your problem go away because the system is bypassing the change that caused the problem.

You revert Windows 10 to an earlier configuration by using System Restore. We show you how to use System Restore to set restore points in Chapter 32, "Protecting Your Data from Loss and Theft."

➡ *To learn how to create a restore point,* **see** *"Setting System Restore Points,"* **p. 725.**

To revert your system to a restore point, follow these steps:

1. Launch System Restore:

   - **If you can boot Windows 10**—In the taskbar's Search box, type **restore**, click Create a Restore Point in the search results, and then click System Restore.

   - **If you can't boot Windows 10**—Boot to the RE, as described earlier (see "Accessing the Recovery Environment"), click Advanced Options, and then click System Restore.

2. In the initial System Restore dialog box, click Next. System Restore displays a list of restore points.

3. If you don't see the restore point you want to use, click to activate the Show More Restore Points check box, which tells Windows 10 to display all the available restore points.

4. Click the restore point you want to use. There are seven common types of restore points:

   - **System**—A restore point that Windows 10 creates automatically. For example, the System Checkpoint is the restore point that Windows 10 creates each day or when you boot your computer.

   - **Critical Update**—A restore point set prior to installing an important update.

   - **Install**—A restore point set prior to installing a program or optional update.

   - **Uninstall**—A restore point set prior to uninstalling a program or update.

   - **Manual**—A restore point you create yourself.

   - **Undo**—A restore point set prior to a previous use of System Restore to revert the system to an earlier state.

   - **Unknown**—Any restore point that doesn't fit in the preceding categories.

 tip

System Restore is available in Safe mode. Therefore, if Windows 10 won't start properly, perform a Safe mode startup and run System Restore from there.

 note

By default, Windows 10 displays only the restore points from the previous five days. When you activate the Show More Restore Points check box, you tell Windows 10 to also show the restore points that are more than five days old.

5. Click Next. If other hard disks are available in the restore point, Windows 10 displays a list of the disks. Activate the check box beside each disk you want to include in the restore and then click Next.

6. Click Finish. Windows 10 asks you to confirm that you want your system restored.

7. Click Yes. System Restore begins reverting to the restore point. When it's done, it restarts your computer and displays a message telling you the results of the restore.

8. Click Close.

Resetting Your PC

If the Automatic Repair and System Restore features didn't solve your problem, the next recovery step to try is Reset This PC. This tool reinstalls a fresh copy of Windows 10 while optionally keeping your data (but not your settings or your Windows 10 apps). When you reset your PC, the computer boots to the RE, gathers up your personal files, copies them to another part of the hard drive, reinstalls Windows 10, and then restores your data.

> ### caution
>
> Because the reset first makes a copy of your data, you must have enough free space on your hard drive to hold these copies. If you don't have the space, you can't reset your PC.

Here are the steps to follow to reset your PC:

1. Launch Refresh Your PC:

   - **If you can boot Windows 10**—Click Start, then Settings, and then Update & Security. Click the Recovery tab, and then click Get Started under Reset This PC.

   - **If you can't boot Windows 10**—Boot to the RE's Troubleshoot screen, as described earlier (see "Accessing the Recovery Environment") and click Reset This PC. Windows 10 reboots the PC and asks you to choose your user account. Click your user account, type your account password, and then click Continue.

2. Click Keep My Files. Reset This PC displays a list of the desktop programs you'll need to reinstall.

3. Make a note of the programs, and then click Next.

4. Click Reset. Refresh Your PC reboots the computer and runs the refresh.

Restoring a System Image

If you can't reset your PC because you don't have your Windows 10 install media or a recovery drive, you can still get your system back on its feet if you created a backup system image, as we describe in Chapter 32.

➥ *To learn how to create a system image, **see** "Creating a System Image Backup," **p. 728.***

Follow these steps to restore a system image:

1. If you saved the system image to an external hard drive, connect that hard drive. If you used DVDs, insert the last DVD in the set.

2. Boot to the RE, as described earlier (see "Accessing the Recovery Environment").

3. Click Advanced Options. The Advanced Options screen appears.

4. Click System Image Recovery. Windows 10 prompts you to choose a user account.

5. Click your user account, type your password, and then click Continue. System Image Recovery prompts you to select a system image backup and offers two options:

   - **Use the Latest Available System Image**—Activate this option to restore Windows 10 using the most recently created system image. This is almost always the best way to go because it means you'll restore the maximum percentage of your data and programs. If you choose this option, click Next and skip to step 8.

   - **Select a System Image**—Activate this option to select from a list of restore points. This is the way to go if you saved a system image to your network, or if the most recent system image includes some change to your system that you believe is the source of your system problems. Click Next and continue with step 6.

6. Click the location of the system image and then click Next.

7. Click the system image you want to use for the restore and then click Next. If you want to use a system image saved to a network share, click Advanced and then click Search for a System Image on the Network.

8. If you replaced your hard drive, activate the Format and Repartition Disks check box.

9. Click Next. System Image Recovery displays a summary of the restore process.

10. Click Finish. System Image Recovery asks you to confirm.

11. Click Yes. System Image Recovery begins restoring your computer and then reboots to Windows 10 when the restore is complete.

MANAGING YOUR SOFTWARE

Configuring and Managing Windows Update

Microsoft is constantly working to improve Windows 10 with bug fixes, security patches, new program versions, and device driver updates. All these new and improved components are available online, and Windows checks for updates and patches quite often.

Over the past few years, Microsoft has been making the Windows Update mechanism more and more assertive. In many ways, this is good, as history has proven that most users never proactively take any action to update their software, and hundreds of millions of virus-infected computers are the result. So, unless you go to fairly extreme measures (which we describe later in this section), installing updates is no longer optional; you only get some limited control over when they get installed. In the most recent version of Windows 10, you have only two real choices: what time of day updates take place, and how soon to accept updates that merely change Windows features (as opposed to security fixes, which are always installed as soon as possible). We describe these settings in this section.

Configuring Automatic Updates

If you prefer to know what's happening with your computer, it's possible to control the timing of automatic updating. However, as you'll see, the Windows 10 Settings app offers only a limited set of choices, so for maximum control, you'll need to turn to your PC's local group policies.

First, let's see what the Settings app has to offer:

1. Click Start and then click Settings. The Settings app appears.

2. Click Update & Security. If the window is not full screen, you'll need to click Windows Update to display the Windows Update settings.

3. When a full restart is required after installing updates, Windows will notify you via the Notifications panel. You can elect to perform the restart right then if you're not busy. If you postpone the restart, Windows will perform the restart when you're not working. By default, Windows assumes that you don't want restarts between 8 AM and 5 PM daily. You can select Change Active Hours if you have different usual work hours. (Also, see "Setting the Automatic Maintenance Schedule," later in this chapter, which affects when Windows performs other maintenance tasks).

4. When a restart is currently pending, you can click Restart Options to set a time that you'd like the start to occur. This only affects the next restart.

5. Click Advanced Options.

> **note**
>
> To view the updates installed on your computer, click the View Your Update History link.

6. In the Advanced Option Window, select one of the following options to determine how Windows 10 performs the updating:

   - If you have Microsoft Office or other Microsoft products installed, check Give Me Updates for Other Microsoft Products When I Update Windows.

   - Some updates require you to sign in after Windows has restarted for the updating to complete. If you trust Windows to do this for you—and you want to save some time the morning after updates have been delivered—click Sign-In Options to open the Sign-In Options window, and then make sure the Use My Sign In Info to Automatically Finish... switch is On.

> **note**
>
> You might think you can put off updates for longer by simply resetting the Pause Updates switch to On every seven days. Nice try, but Windows is on to you. After you pause updates, you can't pause them again until you've installed any pending updates.

   - If you find that your system's features are changing too often because of frequent Windows 10 updates, click the Pause Upgrades switch to On. This tells Windows 10 to not install any upgrades for seven days. (If, on the other hand, you want to see the latest and greatest changes as soon as possible, see the discussion of the Windows Insider program at the end of this section.)

   - If you have a bandwidth limit on your Internet connection (that is, you have a *metered* connection), then you probably don't want to receive updates (which can be quite large) over that connection. If you do, however, then you can tell Windows Update that it's okay to download updates by checking Enabling This Policy Will Automatically Download Updates, Even Over Metered Data Connections.

➡ *To learn how to configure an Internet connection as a metered connection,* **see "Metered Connections," p. 820.**

- By default, Windows 10 can try to get updates (and apps) faster by using a peer-to-peer system to download them from multiple remote sources, including PCs on your local network and—somewhat alarmingly—PCs on the Internet. This is off, by default, but you can turn it on by clicking Delivery Optimization and then clicking the Allow Downloads from Other PCs switch to On, as shown in Figure 27.1. If you want to get downloads only locally, select the PCs on My Local Network option. If you want to also get downloads from remote PCs, select the PCs on My Local Network, and PCs on the Internet option. To control the bandwidth that Windows 10 uses to download updates and to upload updates to other PCs, click Advanced Options and use the sliders to set your preferred limits. To keep an eye on your PC's update downloading and uploading, click Activity Monitor.

Figure 27.1
Use this screen to control Windows 10's peer-to-peer downloading of apps and updates.

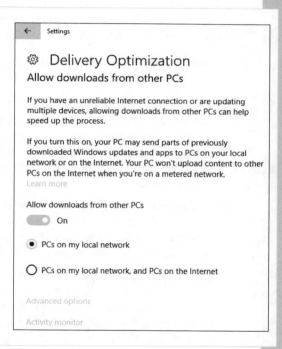

 tip

Unlike in previous versions, Windows 10 offers no built-in mechanism for bypassing individual updates, which means it will sometimes install buggy or unneeded drivers or other updates. To avoid this, download and install a Microsoft troubleshooting tool called Show or Hide Updates. When you run this tool, click Hide Updates and then choose the individual updates that you don't want installed. For details and a download link, see the Microsoft Support page at https://support.microsoft.com/en-us/kb/3073930.

- If you are someone who enjoys change and want to participate in testing new features in Windows 10, you can participate in the voluntary Windows Insider program. You'll receive updates before the general public, and you'll be asked to provide feedback to Microsoft about how well they work. You may receive different versions of some features than other Insiders, as Microsoft often conducts "A/B" tests to compare different ways of doing the same thing, some changes you may never notice, and some changes may be withdrawn and never make it to the mainstream. If this sounds intriguing, go to Settings, Update & Security, Windows Insider Program, and select Get Started.

If you're looking for more fine-grained control over your PC's updating, open the Local Group Policy Editor (press Windows Logo+R, type `gpedit.msc`, and then click OK) and open the Computer Configuration\Administrative Templates\Windows Components\Windows Update branch. Double-click the Configure Automatic Updates policy, click Enabled, and then select one of the following policy options in the Configure Automatic Updating list:

> ➡ *To learn how more about group policies and the Local Group Policy Editor,* **see** *"Policing Windows 10 with Group Policies,"* **p. 494.**

- **Notify for Download and Auto Install**—If you select this option, Windows 10 checks for new updates and then, if any are available, displays a notification to let you know that the updates are ready to download. Click the notification to see the list of updates. Click Download to initiate the download. When the download is complete, Windows 10 displays another notification to let you know that the updates are ready to install. Click the notification, and then click Install to install the updates.

- **Auto Download and Notify for Install**—If you select this option, Windows 10 checks for new updates and then, if any are available, automatically downloads them. When the download is complete, Windows 10 displays a notification to let you know that the updates are ready to install. Click the notification, and then click Install to install the updates.

- **Auto Download and Schedule the Install**—If you select this option, Windows 10 checks for new updates and then automatically downloads any that are available. Windows 10 then schedules the install based on the settings you provide. If you activate the Install During Automatic Maintenance check box, Windows 10 schedules the install to occur during the automatic maintenance window. (See "Setting the Automatic Maintenance Schedule," next.) Otherwise, you can set a day of the week (or Every Day) and a time of day.

- **Allow Local Admin to Choose Setting**—We believe that this option is no longer useful, as the option to choose whether to install updates has been removed.

Setting the Automatic Maintenance Schedule

If you chose the Automatic option (or the Install During Automatic Maintenance Window check box in the Configure Automatic Updates policy), Windows 10 automatically installs updates during the maintenance window, which is defined by default as follows:

- Maintenance is performed each day at 2:00 a.m.

- If you are using your computer, maintenance is postponed until you are no longer using it.

- If your computer is in sleep mode, maintenance is postponed until the computer is awake.

- If the maintenance server is running late, maintenance is postponed until the server is ready, as long as your computer is not being used and is awake.

Windows 10 uses the maintenance window not only to check for updates, but also to run Windows Defender security scans and to perform system diagnostics. If the default 2:00 a.m. window is inconvenient for you, you can configure the maintenance window as follows:

1. In the taskbar's Search box, type `change auto`, and then click Change Automatic Maintenance Settings to display the Automatic Maintenance window (see Figure 27.2). (You can also open Control Panel's Security and Maintenance window, click Maintenance, and then click Change Maintenance Settings.)

Figure 27.2
Use the Automatic Maintenance window to set the automatic maintenance window for your PC.

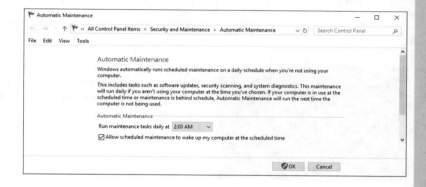

2. Use the Run Maintenance Tasks Daily At list to choose the time you want Windows 10 to attempt to perform its maintenance chores.

3. If you want Windows 10 to wake your sleeping computer (as along as it's plugged in) to perform the maintenance, leave the Allow Scheduled Maintenance to Wake Up My Computer at the Scheduled Time check box activated.

4. Click OK to put the new settings into effect.

Checking for Updates

Previous versions of Windows offered a Never Check for Updates option that meant you had to manually check for updates. However, we live in an age when cybercriminals control massive networks of compromised PCs, and the vast majority of those PCs got compromised because they didn't have the latest updates installed. So, sensibly, Windows 10 doesn't allow PCs to never check for updates. However, you might still want to do a manual check if you're waiting for an important security patch or some other crucial update that you would prefer to install now rather than waiting for the automatic maintenance window.

Whatever your reason, follow these steps to perform a manual check for updates:

1. Click Start, and then click Settings. The Settings app appears.

2. Click Update & Security. This opens the Update & Security settings with the Windows Update tab selected.

3. Click Check for Updates. Windows Update connects to the update server and checks for updates.

If Windows Update determines that one or more updates are available, it goes ahead and installs them. If Windows needs to restart, you see a notification like the one shown in Figure 27.3. (In Settings, the Windows Update tab's Update Status heading also lets you know that a restart has been scheduled.) You can either leave the default restart time as is, or you can take matters into your own hands:

- To schedule your own restart time, click Another Time to open the Restart Options window, and then use the Pick a Time and Pick a Day controls to tell Windows 10 when to restart.

- To restart your PC right away, save your work and click Restart Now.

Figure 27.3
If an update requires a system restart, you see a notification like this one. You can set a custom restart time or restart right away.

Working with Third-Party Software

Outside of hardware woes and user errors (what IT personnel call a PEBCAK—Problem Exists Between Chair and Keyboard), most computer problems are caused by improperly installing a desktop program or installing a desktop program that doesn't mesh correctly with the system. (We're specifically referencing desktop programs here because Modern apps use a standard install routine that is completely controlled by Windows 10 to ensure that each app is installed and configured correctly.) It could be that the installation makes unfortunate changes to the configuration files or that the program replaces a crucial system file with an older version or that the program just wasn't meant to operate on (or wasn't tested with) a machine with this configuration. Whatever the reason, you can minimize these kinds of problems by understanding the desktop installation process as it relates to user accounts and by following a few precautions before installing a new desktop software package.

Running Through a Preinstallation Checklist

The anticipation of a new program often loses its luster when, after a willy-nilly installation, your system starts to behave erratically. The reason is usually that the application's setup program has made adjustments to one or more important configuration files and given your system a case of indigestion in the process. That's the hard way to learn the hazards of a haphazard installation.

*To learn how to install Windows 10 apps, **see** "Installing Apps from the Windows Store," p. 154.*

> ### 🔍 note
>
> To avoid confusion, we'll reiterate that the discussion in this section applies only to desktop programs, not Windows 10 apps, which give you no control over the installation and always mesh properly with your system. We discuss installing Windows 10 apps in Chapter 5, "Windows Apps and the Windows Store."
>
> To avoid such a fate, you should always look before you leap. That is, you should follow a few simple safety measures before double-clicking that setup.exe file. The next few sections take you through a list of things to check before you install any program.

Check for Windows 10 Compatibility

Check to see whether the program is compatible with Windows 10. The easiest and safest setups occur with programs certified to work with Windows 10. In a pinch, if the program says that it's compatible with Windows 7, 8, or 8.1, you should still be okay.

 *You can also configure older programs to operate under Windows 10 using Compatibility Mode; **see** "Understanding Compatibility Mode," p. 623.*

Set a Restore Point

The quickest way to recover from a bad installation is to restore your system to the way it was before you ran the setup program. The only way to do that is to set a system restore point just before you run the program, as we explain in Chapter 32, "Protecting Your Data from Loss and Theft."

 *To learn how to create your own restore points, **see** "Setting System Restore Points," p. 725.*

Read Readme.txt and Other Documentation

Although it's the easiest thing in the world to skip, you really should peruse whatever setup-related documentation the program provides. This includes the appropriate installation material in the manual, Readme text files found on the disc or in the download archive, and whatever else looks promising. By spending a few minutes looking over these resources, you can glean the following information:

- Any advance preparation you need to perform on your system

- What to expect during the installation

- Information you need to have on hand to complete the setup (such as a product's serial number)

- Changes the install program will make to your system or to your data files (if you're upgrading)

- Changes to the program or the documentation that were put into effect after the manual was printed

Virus-Check Downloaded Files

If you downloaded the application, you're installing from the Internet, or if a friend or colleague sent you the installation file as an email attachment, you should scan the file using a good (and up-to-date) virus checker.

Sometimes it pays to be paranoid. You should check for viruses before installing under the following circumstances:

- You ordered the program directly from an unknown developer.

- The package was already open when you purchased it from a dealer. (Buying opened software packages is never a good idea.)

- A friend or colleague gave you the program on a USB flash drive or recordable optical disc or sent it to you over email.

Understand the Effect on Your Data Files

Few software developers want to alienate their installed user base, so they usually emphasize upward compatibility in their upgrades. That is, the new version of the software will almost always be able to read and work with documents created with an older version. However, in the interest of progress, you often find that the data file format used by the latest incarnation of a program is different from its predecessors, and this new format is rarely downward compatible. That is, an older version of the software might gag on a data file that was created by the new version. So, you're faced with two choices:

- Continue to work with your existing documents in the old format, thus possibly forgoing any benefits that come with the new format.

- Update your files and thus risk making them incompatible with the old version of the program, should you decide to uninstall the upgrade.

One possible solution to this dilemma is to make backup copies of all your data files before installing the upgrade. That way, you can always restore the good copies of your documents if the upgrade causes problems or destroys some of your data. If you've already used the upgrade to make changes to some documents, but you want to uninstall the upgrade, most programs have a Save As command that enables you to save the documents in their old format.

Take Control of the Installation

Some setup programs give new meaning to the term brain-dead. You slip in the source disc, run Setup.exe (or whatever), and the program proceeds to impose itself on your hard disk without so much as a how-do-you-do. Thankfully, most installation programs are a bit more thoughtful than that. They usually give you some advance warning about what's to come, and they prompt you for information as they go along. You can use this newfound thoughtfulness to assume a certain level of control over the installation.

In particular, the best programs offer you a choice of installation options, typically Automatic (default) or Custom. Whenever possible, choose the Custom option, if one is available. It gives you maximum control over the components that are installed, including where and how they're installed.

Installing Software

After you've run through this checklist, you're ready to install the program. Here's a summary of the various methods you can use to install a program in Windows 10:

- **AutoPlay install**—If the program comes on a disc or drive that supports AutoPlay, you'll see a notification like the one shown in Figure 27.4. Click the notification to see a list of tasks you can run (see Figure 27.5), and then click Run SETUP.EXE (or whatever Windows has determined is the name of the install executable files).

Figure 27.4
When you insert an install drive or disc, Windows 10 usually displays a notification such as the one shown here.

Figure 27.5
After you click the notification, click the option that runs the application's installation program.

- **Run setup.exe**—For most applications, the installed program is named setup.exe (sometimes it's install.exe). Use File Explorer to find the install program, and then double-click it. Alternatively, press Windows Logo+R to open the Run dialog box, enter the path to the setup.exe file (such as **e:\setup**), and click OK.

- **Decompress downloaded files**—If you downloaded an application from the Internet, the file you receive will be either an .exe file or a .zip file. Either way, you should always store the file in an empty folder just in case it needs to extract files. You then do one of the following:

  - If it's an .exe file, double-click it; in most cases, the install program will launch. In other cases, the program will extract its files and you can then launch setup.exe (or whatever).

  - If it's a .zip file, double-click it, and Windows 10 will open a new compressed folder that shows the contents of the .zip file. If you see an installation program, double-click it. It's more likely, however, that you won't see an install program. Instead, the application is ready to go, and all you have to do is extract the files to a folder and run the application from there.

- **Install from an .inf file**—Some (rare) applications install via an information (.inf) file. To install these programs, right-click the file and then click Install in the shortcut menu that appears.

Managing Your Installed Apps

To manage your installed software, Windows 10 gives you two features: the Apps & Features window, which is part of the Settings app, and the Programs and Features window, which is part of Control Panel.

Opening the Apps & Features Window

To manage all your apps—that is, both Modern apps and desktop programs—use Apps and Features, which you can open by typing **apps** in the taskbar's Search box and then clicking Apps & Features. The window that appears includes a list of all your installed apps, as shown in Figure 27.6. Clicking an app reveals its command buttons, such as Modify and Uninstall (as shown with the EPSON Scan app in Figure 27.6).

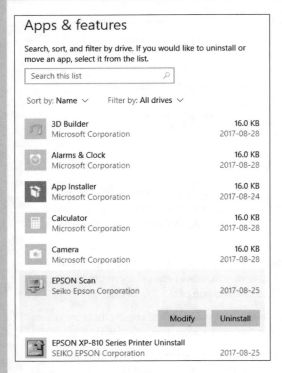

Figure 27.6
You use the Apps & Features window to manage both Modern and desktop apps.

This list of apps can get quite long, so Settings offers three ways to tame it:

- Use the Search This List box to type a search term.

- Use the Sort By list to sort the apps by name, size, or installation date.

- Use the Filter By list to select a drive on which the app you want to manage is installed.

Opening the Programs and Features Window

If you want to manage a desktop program, the Apps and Features window isn't always the best choice because it might take a while to find it among all the Modern apps. A more direct way to deal with desktop apps is to use Control Panel's Programs and Features window. This has the added advantage of giving you more information, and sometimes more actions, for each desktop program.

In the taskbar's Search box, type `control`, click Control Panel in the search results, and then click Uninstall a Program. (If you're running Control Panel in an icon view, click Programs and Features, instead.) This opens the Programs and Features window, shown in Figure 27.7. This operates as a kind of one-stop shop for your installed desktop applications. Note that the view you see in Figure 27.7 is Details view. You can try a different view by clicking the Change Your View icon in the toolbar. (It's to the left of the Get Help question mark icon.)

Figure 27.7
You use the Programs and Features window to change, repair, and uninstall desktop programs.

Items that can be changed or uninstalled via Programs and Features have corresponding Registry entries that come from the following Registry key:

```
HKLM\SOFTWARE\Microsoft\Windows\CurrentVersion\Uninstall
```

Each installed application (as well as many installed Windows components) has a subkey in the Uninstall key. This subkey provides the data you see in the Installed Programs window, including Name (from the DisplayName setting), Publisher (the Publisher setting), Installed On (the InstallDate setting), Size (the EstimatedSize setting), Help Link (from the Help Link at the bottom of screen), and Version (the DisplayVersion setting). Note that not all programs display all this information.

Changing a Software Installation

If you ran a custom version of a program's installation procedure, you might later decide that you'd now like to use some uninstalled components or that you no longer need some installed components. Most applications that allow you to run a custom install also allow you to make changes to the installation after the fact. You have two choices:

- In the Apps & Features window, click the app you want to work with, and then look for a Modify button. (See Figure 27.6 for an example.)

- In the Programs and Features window, click the program you want to work with and then click Change in the taskbar. In some cases, the corresponding command is Uninstall/Change.

When you click Modify or Change (or Uninstall/Change), Windows 10 launches the application's install program (almost always a version that now resides on your hard drive). From there, you follow the instructions to modify the installation.

Repairing a Software Installation

If you find that an application is crashing or behaving erratically, one common cause is that one or more of the application's internal files have become corrupted. You can often resolve such problems by uninstalling and then reinstalling the application. However, some applications come with a repair feature that examines the program's files and replaces any that are corrupted or missing.

In the Programs and Features window (this option isn't available via Apps & Features), click the application you want to fix, and then look for a Repair command in the taskbar. When you click Repair, one of two things happens:

- Windows 10 launches the application's repair program immediately.

- Windows 10 launches the application's install program, and you then select the repair option.

Uninstalling Software

Applications, like the people we meet, fall into three categories: friends for life, acquaintances we deal with occasionally, and those we hope never to speak to again. Avoiding people we dislike is usually just a matter of avoiding contact with them—they'll get the hint after a while. Unlikable applications, however, just don't seem to get it. They keep hanging around like party guests who won't leave. If you have an application that has worn out its welcome, you need to uninstall it so that it's out of your life forever. Again, you have two ways to proceed:

- In the Apps & Features window, click the app you want to remove, and then look for an Uninstall button. (See Figure 27.6 for an example.)

- In the Programs and Features window, click the program you want to remove and then look for an Uninstall command in the taskbar. (Refer to Figure 27.7 for an example.) In some cases, the corresponding command is Uninstall/Change.

When you click Uninstall (or Uninstall/Change), Windows 10 launches the application's install program, and you follow the instructions to uninstall the program.

tip

After you uninstall a program, you might find that it still appears in the Programs and Features list. To fix this, open the Registry Editor (press Windows Logo+R, type **regedit**, and then click OK. Click Yes in the User Account Control dialog box), display the Uninstall key mentioned earlier (see "Opening the Programs and Features Window"), and look for the subkey that represents the program. (If you're not sure, click a subkey and examine the DisplayName setting.) Delete that subkey, and the uninstalled program will disappear from the Programs and Features window.

Understanding Compatibility Mode

Most new software programs are certified as "Windows 10 compatible," meaning they can be installed and run without mishap on any Windows 10 system. But what about older programs that were coded before Windows 10 was released? They can be a bit more problematic. Although Microsoft takes great pains to accommodate older software, it's inevitable that some of those legacy programs will either be unstable while running under Windows 10 or won't run at all.

Why do such incompatibilities arise? One common reason is that the programmers of a legacy application hardwired certain data into the program's code. For example, installation programs often poll the operating system for its version number. If an application is designed for, say, Windows XP, the programmers might have set things up so that the application installs if and only if the operating system returns the Windows XP version number. The program might run perfectly well under any later version of Windows, but this simplistic brain-dead version check prevents it from even installing on anything but Windows XP.

 caution

Although application compatibility can work wonders to give aging programs new life under Windows 10, this doesn't mean that every legacy program will benefit. If history is any guide, some programs simply will not run under Windows 10, no matter which compatibility rabbits you pull out of Windows 10's hat. In some of these cases, you might be able to get a program to run by installing a patch from the manufacturer, so check the program's website to see if updates are available that make the program "Windows 10 friendly."

Another reason incompatibilities arise is that calls to Application Programming Interface (API) functions return unexpected results. For example, the programmers of a very old application might have assumed that the file allocation table (FAT) file system would always be the standard, so when checking for free disk space before installing the program, they'd expect to receive a number that is 2GB or less (the maximum size of a FAT partition). However, FAT32 and NT File System (NTFS) partitions can be considerably larger than 2GB, so a call to the API function that returns the amount of free space on a partition could return a number that blows out a memory buffer and crashes the installation program.

These **types** of problems might make it seem as though getting older programs to run under Windows 10 would be a nightmare. Fortunately, that's not usually the case because the Windows 10 programmers did something very smart: Because many of these application incompatibilities are predictable, the programmers gave Windows 10 the capability to make allowances for them. Therefore, many older programs can run under Windows 10 without modification. In Windows 10, application compatibility refers to a set of concepts and technologies that enables the operating system to adjust its settings or behavior to compensate for the shortcomings of legacy programs. This section shows you how to work with Windows 10's application compatibility tools.

Determining Whether a Program Is Compatible with Windows 10

One way to determine whether an application is compatible with Windows 10 is to go ahead and install it. If the program is not compatible with Windows 10, you might see a dialog box similar to the one shown in Figure 27.8.

This app can't run on your PC

To find a version for your PC, check with the software publisher.

Close

Figure 27.8
You might see a dialog box such as this if you try to install a program that isn't compatible with Windows 10.

A better approach is to find out in advance whether the program is compatible with Windows 10. The most obvious way to do this is to look for the Designed for Windows 10 logo on the box or the product's website. You also can check the manufacturer's website to see whether the company has made an upgrade available.

Running a Program in Compatibility Mode

To help you run programs under Windows 10, especially those programs that worked properly in a previous version of Windows, Windows 10 offers a way to run applications using compatibility layers. This means that Windows 10 runs the program by doing one or more of the following:

- **Running the program in a compatibility mode**—This involves emulating the behavior of a previous version of Windows. Windows 10 can emulate the behavior of Windows 95, Windows 98, Windows Me, Windows XP (with Service Pack 2 or Service Pack 3), Windows Vista (with Service Pack 1 or Service Pack 2), Windows 7, or Windows 8/8.1.

- **Temporarily changing the system's visual display so that it's compatible with the program**—There are five possibilities here:

  - Setting the color depth to 8-bit (256 colors)

  - Setting the color depth to 16-bit (65,536 colors)

  - Changing the screen resolution to 640×480

  - Disabling the display of scaling on high-DPI settings

  - Disabling Windows 10's full-screen mode optimizations

- **Running the program as an administrator**—In some cases, compatibility problems are just permission

> **tip**
> Disabling full-screen optimizations means turning off the Game Bar when running a game full-screen, which often makes older games run faster and with greater stability. You can do this for *all* your games by selecting Settings, Gaming, Game Bar, and then unchecking Show Game Bar When I Play Full Screen Games Microsoft Has Verified.

problems, particularly because Windows 10 locks down certain folders on the system drive to which an older program
(particularly an older installation program) might need to
write files. By running the program as an administrator, you
override these permission problems, and the program should
run normally.

To set up a compatibility layer, right-click the program's executable file or a shortcut to the file, click Properties, and then display the Compatibility tab in the property sheet that appears.
To set the compatibility mode, activate the Run This Program
in Compatibility Mode For check box (see Figure 27.9), and then use the list to choose the Windows
version the program requires. You can also use the check boxes in the Settings group to adjust the
system settings that Windows 10 will switch to when you use the program, including the color
mode, screen resolution, display scaling, and administrator mode.

 note

Windows 10 and Microsoft often
use the terms *compatibility layer*
and *compatibility mode* inter-
changeably, depending on which
compatibility tool you're using. In
some cases, the emulations of previous Windows versions are called
operating system modes.

Figure 27.9
In the property sheet for an executable file,
use the Compatibility tab to set the compatibility layer for the program.

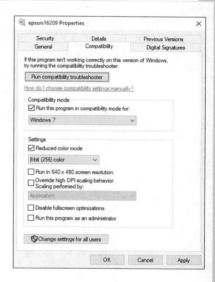

If you don't feel like fiddling with these settings, you can see whether Windows 10 will do the work
for you. In File Explorer, click the program's executable file, click the Manage tab on the ribbon, and
then click Troubleshoot Compatibility. This launches the Program Compatibility Troubleshooter,
shown in Figure 27.10. The easiest route here is to click Try Recommended Settings to see whether

your program runs. If not, click Troubleshoot Program to run through a series of questions that the troubleshooter uses to narrow down the problems you're having and from that suggest one or more compatibility fixes. Note, too, that the Manage tab offers a Run As Administrator command that you can use to easily run the program's executable with administrator permissions.

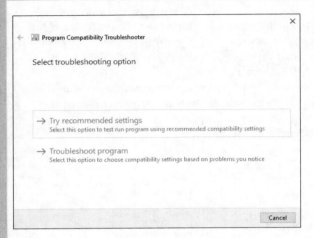

Figure 27.10
The Program Compatibility Troubleshooter might be able to get a recalcitrant legacy program running under Windows 10.

MANAGING YOUR HARDWARE

Windows 10 and Hardware

Man is a shrewd inventor, and is ever taking the hint of a new machine from his own structure, adapting some secret of his own anatomy in iron, wood, and leather, to some required function in the work of the world.

—*Ralph Waldo Emerson*

Emerson's concept of a "machine" was decidedly low tech ("iron, wood, and leather"), but his basic idea is still apt in these high-tech times. Man has taken yet another "secret of his own anatomy" (the brain) and used it as the "hint of a new machine" (the computer). And although even the most advanced computer is still a mere toy compared to the breathtaking complexity of the human brain, some spectacular advancements have been made in the art of hardware in recent years.

One of the hats an operating system must wear is that of an intermediary between you and your hardware. Any OS worth its salt has to translate incomprehensible "devicespeak" into something you can make sense out of, and it must ensure that devices are ready, willing, and able to carry out your commands. Given the sophistication and diversity of today's hardware market, however, that's no easy task.

The good news is that Windows 10 brings to the PC world support for a broad range of hardware, from everyday devices such as keyboards, mice, printers, monitors, video cards, sounds, memory cards, and network cards, to more exotic hardware fare such as multitouch input panels and the latest wireless standards. However, although this hardware support is broad, it's not all that deep, meaning that Windows 10 doesn't have built-in support for many older devices. So, even though lots of hardware vendors have taken at least some steps toward upgrading their devices and drivers, managing hardware is still one of Windows 10's trickier areas. This chapter should help as we take you through lots of practical techniques for installing, updating, and managing devices in Windows 10.

Viewing Your Devices

The simplest device-related task you can perform with Windows 10 is to view a list of the devices installed on your PC. To see this list, click Start, click Settings to open the Settings app, click Devices, and then click Connected Devices. (Alternatively, click the taskbar's Search box, type `other devices`, and then click Bluetooth & Other Devices Settings in the search results.) Figure 28.1 shows the Settings app's Bluetooth & Other Devices window, which is just a simple list of the attached devices and, where applicable, a device's current status. As you see a bit later in this chapter, about the only thing you can do with this list is uninstall a device and install network devices. The Printers & Scanners tab is similar but focuses on just the printing and scanning devices connected to your PC. You can click Add a Printer or Scanner to connect to a networked device.

A desktop feature called Devices and Printers provides a similar list, albeit with much more functionality. To get there, click the taskbar's Search box and type `control`, click Control Panel to open the Control Panel, and click View Devices and Printers (in Category view) or Devices and Printers (in an icon view). Figure 28.2 shows the Devices and Printers window, which divides your devices into several categories, including Printers and a generic Devices category. Clicking a device displays information about it in the Details pane at the bottom of the window. In many cases (particularly printers), you also see several device-related commands in the taskbar, such as Start Scan for a scanner and Eject for an optical drive. You can also double-click a device to see its properties and functions.

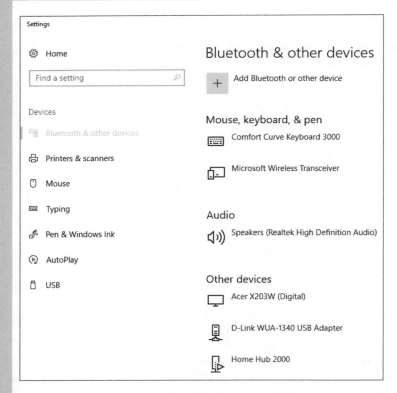

Figure 28.1
In the Settings app, the Bluetooth & Other Devices window presents a basic list of your attached devices.

Figure 28.2
Control Panel's
Devices and Printers
window provides
information and
commands related
to your installed
devices.

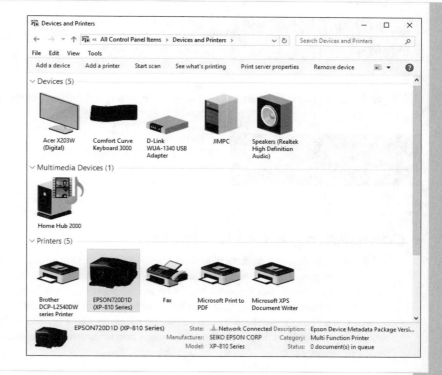

Installing Devices

Before you install a device, it's best to find out in advance whether the device is compatible with Windows 10. The easiest way to do this is to look for the Designed for Windows 10 logo on the box. For older devices, check the manufacturer's website to see whether the company tells you that the device can be run under Windows 10 or if a driver upgrade is available.

Installing Plug and Play Devices

Computing old-timers will remember (none too fondly) the days when installing devices required flipping DIP switches, fiddling with jumpers, or fussing with various IRQ, I/O port, and DMA combinations. If, on the other hand, all the abbreviations in the previous sentence are incomprehensible to you, think yourself lucky that you live in a time when all the devices manufactured in recent years support Plug and Play, which means you simply attach the device and Windows 10 automatically recognizes it and installs the necessary drivers and other software.

How do you know this is happening? You see the Setting Up a Device notification, as shown in Figure 28.3.

Figure 28.3
When you attach a new device, you see the Setting Up a Device notification.

When the install is finished, you see a Device Is Ready notification, as shown in Figure 28.4.

Figure 28.4
When your new device has been installed, you see the Device Is Ready notification.

Completing a Device Install

Plug and Play device installations almost always go off without a hitch. *Almost* always. In some cases, Windows 10 might encounter a problem, or it might not have access to the necessary files to complete the install. You'll see a notification to that effect, but just in case you miss it, the notification also appears in Control Panel's Security and Maintenance window. In the Maintenance section, you'll see a "Finish installing device software" message. Click Install to complete the installation. In most cases, Windows 10 scours the Web for the needed software, downloads it, and then proceeds with the installation.

Installing a Bluetooth Device

You're probably familiar with Wi-Fi, the standard that enables you to perform networking chores without the usual network cables. Bluetooth is a similar technology in that it enables you to exchange data between two devices without any kind of physical connection between them. Bluetooth uses radio frequencies to set up a communications link between the devices. Bluetooth is a short-distance networking technology with a maximum range of about 33 feet (10 meters). If your PC has a built-in Bluetooth receiver (or you insert a USB Bluetooth receiver), you can make connections with a wide variety of devices, including mice, keyboards, headsets, and printers.

In theory, connecting Bluetooth devices should be criminally easy. You turn on each device's Bluetooth feature (in Bluetooth jargon, you make the devices *discoverable*), bring them within 33 feet of each other, and they connect without further ado. In practice, however, there's usually at least a bit of further ado (and sometimes plenty of it). The reason is that, as a security precaution, many Bluetooth devices do not connect automatically to a PC. This makes sense because otherwise it means a stranger with a Bluetooth device could connect to your computer. To prevent an unauthorized user from connecting, most Bluetooth devices require you to enter a password before the connection is made. This is known as *pairing* the two devices.

After you've made your Bluetooth device discoverable, you can follow these steps to pair it with your Windows 10 PC:

1. Click Start and then click Settings. The Settings app appears.

2. Click Devices.

3. In the Bluetooth & Other Devices tab, make sure the Bluetooth switch is On.

4. Click Add Bluetooth or Other Device to open the Add a Device window.

5. Click Bluetooth. Windows 10 begins scouring the nearby airwaves looking for discoverable Bluetooth devices, which it then displays in a list (see Figure 28.5).

Figure 28.5
Click Bluetooth to see a list of discoverable Bluetooth devices.

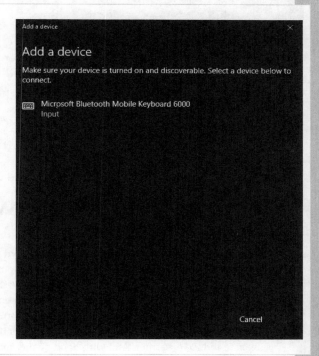

6. Click your Bluetooth device. If the device requires a passcode to complete the pairing, you see a screen similar to the one shown in Figure 28.6.

7. Enter the passcode. Windows 10 pairs with the device.

Figure 28.6
If your Bluetooth device requires a passcode for pairing, you see this screen.

Running Windows 10 with Multiple Monitors

Over the past few years, many studies have shown that you can greatly improve your productivity by doing one thing: adding a second monitor to your system. This enables you to have whatever program you are currently working with displayed on one monitor and your reference materials, email program, or some other secondary program on the second monitor. This setup is more efficient because you no longer have to switch back and forth between the two programs. If you have a notebook PC, a second monitor will almost always be larger than your notebook screen, which helps to reduce eyestrain. And with good-quality monitors now selling for less than $100, running Windows 10 with multiple monitors is pretty much a no-brainer.

To work with two monitors on a single computer, one solution is to install a second video card and attach the second monitor to it. However, most video cards come with multiple output ports, which can be any combination of VGA, DVI, HDMI, and DisplayPort. Also, almost all notebook PCs have at least one video output port that you can use to connect to a second monitor.

After you have installed the new video card (if necessary) and attached the monitors, you then need to tell Windows 10 how you want to use the second monitor. You have three choices:

- Extend the screen across both monitors.

- Duplicate the screen on the second monitor.

- Use only the second monitor as your display.

The next few sections provide you with the details.

Extending the Screen to a Second Monitor

For most people, the extra expense of a second monitor is justified if it increases productivity, and you can do that by extending the Windows 10 interface across a second monitor. In this case, Windows 10 displays the Start button and taskbar on both the original monitor and the second monitor.

After you've connected the second monitor to your Windows PC, the easiest way to extend your desktop to the second monitor is to press Windows Logo+P to open the Project pane, and then click Extend, as shown in Figure 28.7.

Figure 28.7
Use the Project pane to extend your Windows 10 desktop onto your second monitor.

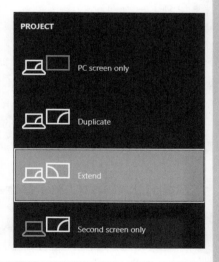

Now you need to choose which monitor is the main display, which is the monitor the system uses to show program windows when you launch them. Follow these steps:

1. Select Start, Settings to run the Settings app, and then click System to open the System window with the Display tab selected, as shown in Figure 28.8.

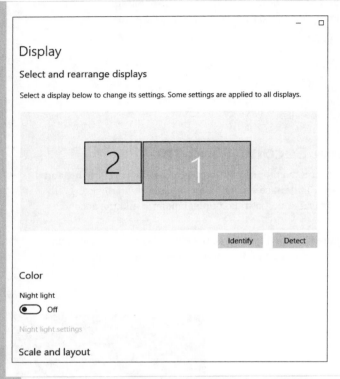

Display

Select and rearrange displays

Select a display below to change its settings. Some settings are applied to all displays.

Identify   Detect

Color

Night light
 Off

Night light settings

Scale and layout

Figure 28.8
Use the Settings app's Display tab to set the main display.

2. Click the monitor you want to set as the main display.

3. Check the Make This My Main Display box.

4. Click Apply.

Duplicating the Screen on a Second Monitor

If you're making a presentation, the ideal setup is to be able to see what's on your main monitor (particularly if you're using a notebook PC) and then duplicate that same screen on the second monitor or projector. Duplicating the screen is also useful if you've connected your PC to a TV and want to control the screen from your PC but see the content on the larger screen.

After you've connected the second monitor to your Windows PC, the easiest way to duplicate the desktop on the second monitor is to press Windows Logo+P to open the Project pane, and then click Duplicate. (Alternatively, you can do this via Settings: Click Start, Settings, System, use the Multiple Displays list to select Duplicate These Displays, and then click Keep Changes.) Windows 10 connects to the second monitor and uses it to display the same content as the main monitor.

note
Ideally, you should be able to move your mouse pointer continuously from the left monitor to the right monitor. If you find that the mouse pointer stops at the right edge of your left monitor, it means you need to exchange the icons of the left and right monitors. To do that, click and drag the left monitor icon to the right of the other monitor icon (or vice versa).

Using Only the Second Monitor

If your second monitor is larger than your main monitor (such as a notebook PC screen and) or has a higher quality image, you might prefer to use only the second monitor as your output screen. This is also a useful scenario if your main monitor is damaged or distorted, so rather than having to dispose of a notebook PC whose monitor is broken or simply not to your liking, use this second monitor option.

After you've connected the second monitor to your Windows PC, the easiest way to switch to using the second monitor is to press Windows Logo+P to open the Project pane, and then click Second Screen Only. (Alternatively, you can do this via Settings: Click Start, Settings, System, use the Multiple Displays list to select Show Only On 2, and then click Keep Changes.) Windows 10 connects to the second monitor and uses it to display the screen output.

Configuring the Taskbar for Multiple Monitors

By default, Windows 10 displays the taskbar on both monitors, and both taskbars display icons for all the running desktop apps, regardless of which monitor the apps appear on. You might want to change these defaults. For example, if you want to maximize the available screen real estate on the secondary display, you can configure Windows 10 to show the taskbar only on the main display. Similarly, you can configure the taskbars to show an icon for a running program only on the display where that program appears.

Here are the steps to follow:

1. Right-click the taskbar, and then click Taskbar Settings. The Taskbar window of the Settings app appears.

2. If you want the taskbar to appear only on the main display, scroll down to the Multiple Displays section, click the Show Taskbar on All Displays switch to Off, and skip the rest of these steps.

3. Use the Show Taskbar Buttons On list to select how you want the buttons displayed:

   - **All Taskbars**—This is the default, and it means that a button for every running desktop program appears on each taskbar.

   - **Main Taskbar and Taskbar Where Window Is Open**—Select this option to display a button for every running desktop program on the main taskbar. If the program's window appears on another display, that display's taskbar also includes a button for the program.

   - **Taskbar Where Window Is Open**—Select this option to display a button for a running program only on the taskbar in the same window.

4. Use the Combine Buttons on Other Taskbars list to choose how you want Windows 10 to group buttons on the secondary taskbars when an application has multiple windows or tabs open:

   - **Always, Hide Labels**—Choose this option to have Windows 10 always group similar taskbar buttons.

   - **When Taskbar Is Full**—Choose this option to have Windows 10 group similar taskbar buttons only when the taskbar has no more open space to display buttons.

   - **Never**—Choose this option to have Windows 10 never group similar taskbar buttons.

Moving Up to Three Monitors

Rocking with two monitors is great, but let's crank things up a notch and go for not two, but *three* monitors! You could have Word on one monitor, reference materials or whatever on a second monitor, and Outlook on the third or use all three monitors together for super wide-screen gaming (on games that support this option). It's almost scary how productive this setup will make you or what fun you can have playing some of your favorite games.

 note

Both AMD and NVIDIA offer *triple*-GPU and *quadruple*-GPU video cards, just in case you feel like running Windows 10 with six or even eight monitors!

How does this setup work? The secret is that you need three output ports on your PC. Many new PCs ship with three or even four output ports—VGA, DVI, HDMI, or DisplayPort—so you just need to match these with your monitor input ports. If your PC has only two output ports, you must install a second video card on your system. However, you can't just plop any old video card in there and hope things will work. Instead, you must use video cards that come with dual-GPU (graphics processing unit) support. Both AMD and NVIDIA offer dual-GPU technologies:

- **AMD CrossFireX**—AMD's dual-GPU technology is called CrossFireX (or CFX). To use it, you need a motherboard with a CrossFireX-compatible chipset and two free PCI Express slots that are designed for CrossFireX, as well as two CrossFireX-capable video cards from the same chipset family. Figure 28.9 shows two video cards connected with a CrossFireX bridge. To learn more about CrossFireX-compatible equipment, see http://www.amd.com/en-us/innovations/software-technologies/technologies-gaming/crossfire.

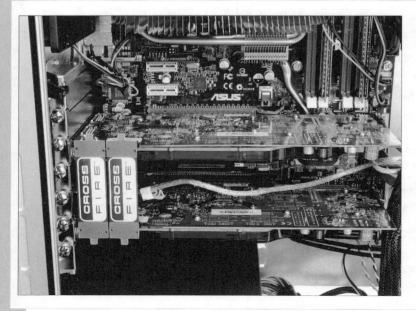

Figure 28.9
Two video cards connected with a CrossFireX bridge.

- **NVIDIA SLI**—NVIDIA's dual-GPU technology is called *scalable link interface (SLI)*. To use it, you need a motherboard with an SLI-compatible chipset and two free PCI Express slots designed for SLI, as well as two SLI-capable video cards that use the same NVIDIA chipset. To learn more about SLI-compatible equipment, see https://www.geforce.com/hardware/technology/sli.

Each of these video cards has two output ports, so you have a total of four ports to use. After you get the cards installed, you run VGA or DVI cables from three of those ports (or four, if you want to go all the way and use four monitors) to the corresponding ports on your monitors. When you next start Windows, install the video card drivers.

Now you're ready to configure Windows to extend the desktop across all your monitors. Here are the steps to follow:

1. Make sure all your monitors are connected and turned on.

2. Select Start, Settings to run the Settings app, and then click System to open the System window with the Display tab selected. You now see icons for four monitors, which represent the four output ports of the video cards.

3. In the Multiple Displays list, select Extend These Displays.

4. Click and drag the monitor icons to the orientation you prefer. For example, you might want your main monitor (the monitor that holds the taskbar) in the middle and the other two monitors on either side.

5. Adjust the resolution for each monitor, as desired.

6. Click Apply.

> **tip**
>
> If you're not sure which three of the four icons represent your actual monitors, select Identify. Windows 10 displays large numbers—1, 2, and 3—on each monitor, and the numbers correspond to the numbered icons in the Screen Resolution window.

Managing Your Hardware with Device Manager

Windows 10 stores all its hardware data in the Registry, but it provides Device Manager to give you a graphical view of the devices on your system. To display Device Manager, you have two choices:

- Click the taskbar's Search box, type **device**, and then click Device Manager in the search results.

- Press Windows Logo+X (or right-click the Start button), and then click Device Manager.

Device Manager's default display is a tree-like outline that lists various hardware types. To see the specific devices, click the plus sign (+) to the left of a device type. For example, opening the Disk Drives branch displays all the hard drives, Flash drives, and memory card slots attached to your computer, as shown in Figure 28.10.

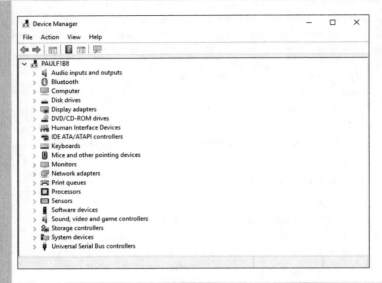

Figure 28.10
Device Manager organizes your computer's hardware in a tree-like hierarchy organized by hardware type.

Controlling the Device Display

Device Manager's default view is by device type, but it also offers several other views, all of which are available on the View menu:

- **Devices by Connection**—This view displays devices according to what they are connected to within your computer. For example, to see which devices connect to the PCI bus, on most systems you'd open the ACPI branch, then the Microsoft ACPI-Compliant System branch, and finally the PCI Bus branch.

- **Devices by Container**—This view displays devices according to the parent device that contains them. For example, a second monitor might contain both a display device and an audio device. Most devices will appear within the computer container (which appears in Device Manager using your PC's name).

- **Resources by Type**—This view displays devices according to the hardware resources they require. Your computer's resources are the communications channels by which devices communicate back and forth with software. There are four types: Direct Memory Access (DMA), Input/Output (IO), Interrupt Request (IRQ), and Memory (a portion of the computer's memory that is allocated to the device and is used to store device data).

- **Resources by Connection**—This view displays the computer's allocated resources according to how they're connected within the computer.

- **Show Hidden Devices**—When you activate this command, Device Manager displays those non–Plug and Play devices that you normally don't need to adjust or troubleshoot. It also displays *nonpresent devices*, which are those that have been installed but aren't currently attached to the computer. (However, refer to "Showing Nonpresent Devices in Device Manager" to be sure you're seeing all devices.)

Viewing Device Properties

Each device listed in Device Manager has its own properties sheet. You can use these properties not only to learn more about the device (such as the resources it's currently using), but also to make adjustments to the device's resources, change the device driver, alter the device's settings (if it has any), and make other changes.

To display the properties sheet for a device, double-click the device to take you to the Properties box or right-click the device and then select Properties. The number of tabs you see depends on the hardware, but most devices have at least the following:

- **General**—This tab gives you general information such as the name of the device, its hardware type, and the manufacturer's name. The Device Status group tells you whether the device is working properly and gives you status information if it's not.

     For information on using Device Manager for troubleshooting, **see** *"Troubleshooting Device Problems," p. 594.*

- **Driver**—This tab gives you information about the device driver and offers several buttons to manage the driver. See "Working with Device Drivers," later in this chapter.

- **Resources**—This tab tells you the hardware resources used by the device.

Showing Nonpresent Devices in Device Manager

We mentioned earlier that if you have any non–Plug and Play devices that you want to work with in Device Manager, you select View, Show Hidden Devices.

That works, but it doesn't mean that Device Manager is now showing all your devices. If you have any devices that you've installed in Windows but that you regularly connect and then disconnect (such as a USB digital camera), Device Manager won't show them. (Windows describes such devices as *ghosted* devices.) That makes a bit of sense because it might be confusing to see nonconnected hardware in Device Manager.

> ## 🔍 note
>
> By setting the DEVMGR_SHOW_ NONPRESENT_DEVICES environment variable in your Command Prompt session, you must launch Device Manager from that session. If you just launch Device Manager in the usual way, you won't see the ghosted devices.

However, what if you're having a problem with a ghosted device? For example, suppose Windows hangs or crashes every time you connect such a device. Ideally, you'd like to use Device Manager to uninstall that device, but you can't because Windows goes belly-up whenever you connect the nasty thing. What do to?

The solution to this kind of problem is to force Device Manager to show ghosted devices. Here's how:

1. Press Windows Logo+X (or right-click the Start button), and then click Command Prompt. Windows 10 launches a new Command Prompt session.

     To learn how to add Command Prompt to the Start Menu's shortcut menu, **see** *"Adding Command Prompt to the Shortcut Menu," p. 129.*

2. Type the following command, and then press Enter:

```
set devmgr_show_nonpresent_devices=1
```

3. Type the following command, and then press Enter to launch Device Manager:

```
devmgmt.msc
```

4. In Device Manager, select View, Show Hidden Devices. Device Manager adds to the device list any ghosted devices installed on your PC.

Working with Device Drivers

For most users, device drivers exist in the nether regions of the PC world, shrouded in obscurity and the mysteries of assembly language programming. As the middlemen brokering the dialogue between Windows 10 and our hardware, however, these complex chunks of code perform a crucial task. After all, it's just not possible to unleash the full potential of your system unless the hardware and the operating system coexist harmoniously and optimally. To that end, you need to ensure that Windows 10 is using appropriate drivers for all your hardware. You do that by updating to the latest drivers and by rolling back drivers that aren't working properly.

Tips for Downloading Device Drivers

Finding device drivers on the World Wide Web is an art in itself. We can't tell you how much of our lives we've wasted rooting around manufacturer websites trying to locate a device driver. Most hardware vendor sites seem to be optimized for sales rather than service, so although you can purchase, say, a new printer with just a mouse click or two, downloading a new driver for that printer can take a frustratingly long time. To help you avoid such frustration, here are some tips from our hard-won experience:

- Download drivers *only* from the device's original manufacturer's website or your PC vendor's website. Never, never, *never* download a driver from any other website, especially one of those "getwindowsdrivers.com" sites. We can almost guarantee that this will bring you a world of grief: virus infections, spyware, ransomware, or worse.

- If the manufacturer offers different sites for different locations (such as different countries), always use the company's "home" site. Most mirror sites aren't true mirrors, and (Murphy's law still being in effect) it's usually the driver you're looking for that a mirror site is missing.

- The temptation when you first enter a site is to use the search feature to find what you want. This works only sporadically for drivers, and the site search engines almost always return marketing or sales material first.

- Instead of the search engine, look for an area of the site dedicated to driver downloads. The good sites will have links to areas called Downloads or Drivers, but it's far more common to have to go through a Support or Customer Service area first.

- Don't try to take any shortcuts to where you *think* the driver might be hiding. Trudge through each step the site provides. For example, it's common to have to select an overall driver category, then a device category, then a line category, and then the specific model you have. This process is tedious, but it almost always gets you where you want to go.

- If the site is particularly ornery, the preceding method might not lead you to your device. In that case, try the search engine. Note that device drivers seem to be particularly poorly indexed, so you might have to try lots of search text variations. One thing that usually works is searching for the exact filename. How can you possibly know that? A method that often works for us is to use Google (www.google.com) or Google Groups (groups.google.com) or some other web search engine to search for the driver. Chances are, someone else has looked for your file and will have the filename (or, if you're really lucky, a direct link to the driver on the manufacturer's site). But again, remember, don't download from any site other than the manufacturer's. Use other sites just to get clues on how to find the correct driver on the manufacturer's site.

 tip

Device driver packages can be quite large, so if you're running Windows 10 on a metered Internet connection, you might not want these big files taking up chunks of your limited download room. To prevent this, click Start, Settings, and then click the Devices icon. In the Bluetooth & Other Devices tab, activate Download Over Metered Connections. Download drivers later when you're on a free Wi-Fi or Ethernet connection.

- When you get to the device's download page, be careful which file you choose. Make sure it's a Windows 10 driver (although in some cases a Windows 8 driver might work), and make sure you're not downloading a utility program or some other nondriver file.

- When you finally get to download the file, be sure to save it to your computer rather than opening it. If you reformat your system or move the device to another computer, you'll be glad you have a local copy of the driver so that you don't have to wrestle with the whole download rigmarole all over again.

Checking Windows Update for Drivers

Before getting to the driver tasks that Windows 10 offers, remember that if Windows 10 can't find drivers when you initially attach a device, it automatically checks Windows Update to see whether any drivers are available. If Windows 10 finds a driver, it installs the software automatically. In most cases, this behavior is desirable because it requires almost no input from you. However, lots of people don't like to use Windows on automatic pilot all the time because doing so can lead to problems. In this case, for example, the Windows Update driver might be older than the driver available at the Windows Update site. If you've downloaded the driver you actually want to use from the manufacturer's website, you don't want whatever is on Windows Update to be installed in its place.

There used to be a fairly simple setting that would let you dictate whether Windows Update drivers would be used always, never, or optionally. Now, you have to go through some complex steps to gain control over Windows Update driver downloads. If you need to exert this sort of control, follow these steps:

1. In the taskbar's Search box, type **gpedit.msc**, and select the result labeled Microsoft Common Console Document.

2. In the left-hand pane, navigate to Computer Configuration, Administrative Templates, System, Device Installation.

3. In the right-hand pane, edit either or both of the following policy settings:

- **Specify Search Order for Device Driver Source Locations**—Open this entry, select Enabled, and then choose one of the following options:

  - **Always Search Windows Update**—This is Windows' normal behavior. Windows will check Windows Update first, and if a driver can't be located, it will look for an installation disc.

  - **Search Windows Update Only If Needed**—Use this setting to prefer locally installed drivers first, and use Windows Update only if one can't be found.

  - **Do Not Search Windows Update**—Use this setting to prevent Windows Update from checking for drivers online. Your selected drivers will always be left alone.

- **Prevent Device Metadata Retrieval from the Internet**—Open this entry and select Enabled to prevent Windows from automatically downloading devices' customized properties pages and icons for the Devices and Printers window.

These settings prevent Windows from overriding your preferred, installed device drivers. Remember, though, that you may need to temporarily change the policies back to Not Configured if you later install new hardware and find that you need Windows Update to get drivers for the new devices.

Updating a Device Driver

Follow these steps to update a device driver:

1. If you have a disc with the updated driver, insert it. If you downloaded the driver from the Internet, decompress the driver file, if necessary.

2. In Device Manager, click the device with which you want to work.

3. Select Action, Update Driver. (You can also click the Update Device Driver button in the toolbar or open the device's properties sheet, display the Driver tab, and click Update Driver.) The Update Driver Software Wizard appears.

> **note**
>
> If your driver download comes packaged in a setup file, it's almost always best just to launch the setup file and let it perform the update for you.

4. Select one of the following two choices:

- **Search Automatically for Updated Driver Software**—Click this option to have Windows 10 check Windows Updates for the driver.

- **Browse My Computer for Driver Software**—Click this option if you have a local device driver, whether on a disc or in a downloaded file. In the dialog box that appears, click Browse, and then select the location of the device driver.

Configuring Windows to Ignore Unsigned Device Drivers

Device drivers that meet the Designed for Windows 10 specifications have been tested for compatibility with Microsoft and are then given a digital signature. This signature tells you that the driver works properly with Windows and that it hasn't been changed since it was tested. (For example, the driver hasn't been infected by a virus or Trojan horse program.) Driver signing also proves the authorship of the driver. All legitimate 64-bit drivers should be signed, and most drivers produced in the last decade should be, too. When you're installing a device, if Windows 10 comes across a driver that has not been digitally signed, it displays a dialog box similar to the one shown in Figure 28.11. Consider this a strong warning that the driver may have come from an illegitimate source or may have been tampered with by a hacker.

Figure 28.11
Windows 10 displays a dialog box similar to this one when it comes across a device driver that does not have a digital signature.

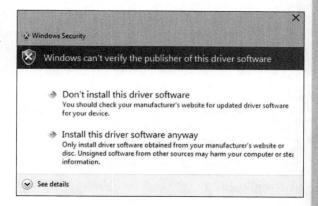

If you click Don't Install This Driver Software, Windows aborts the driver installation, and you won't be able to use the device. This is the most prudent choice in this situation because an unsigned driver can cause all kinds of havoc, including lock-ups, BSODs (blue screens of death), and other system instabilities. You should check the manufacturer's website for an updated driver that's compatible with Windows 10, or you can upgrade to newer hardware that's supported by Windows 10.

> **note**
>
> Test your system thoroughly after installing the driver: use the device, open and use your most common applications, and run some disk utilities. If anything seems awry, roll back the driver, as described in Chapter 26, "Troubleshooting and Repairing Problems." If that doesn't work, use the restore point to roll back the system to its previous configuration.

However, although not installing an unsigned driver is the *prudent* choice, it's not the most *convenient* choice because, in most cases, you probably want to use the device now rather than later. The truth is that *most* of the time these unsigned drivers cause no problems and work as advertised, so as long as you obtained the driver from a source that you're certain is legitimate, it's probably safe to continue with the installation. In any case, Windows always sets a restore point before the installation of an unsigned driver, so you can restore your system to its previous state should anything go wrong.

➡ *To learn how to roll back a driver, **see** "Rolling Back a Device Driver," p. 597.*

By default, Windows gives you the option of either continuing or aborting the installation of the unsigned driver. You can change this behavior to automatically accept or reject all unsigned drivers by following these steps:

1. In the Search box, type **gpedit.msc**, and press Enter to launch the Local Group Policy Editor.

2. Open the User Configuration\Administrative Templates\System\Driver Installation branch.

3. Double-click the Code Signing for Device Drivers policy. Windows displays the Code Signing for Device Drivers dialog box.

4. Click Enabled.

5. From the When Windows Detects a Driver File Without a Digital Signature list, select one of the following items (see Figure 28.12):

   - **Ignore**—Choose this option if you want Windows 10 to install all unsigned drivers.

   - **Warn**—Choose this option if you want Windows 10 to warn you about an unsigned driver by displaying the dialog box shown earlier in Figure 28.11.

   - **Block**—Choose this option if you do not want Windows 10 to install unsigned drivers.

6. Click OK.

> **note**
>
> If you're running a version of Windows 10 that doesn't come with the Group Policy Editor, we'll show you a bit later how to perform this tweak using the Registry.

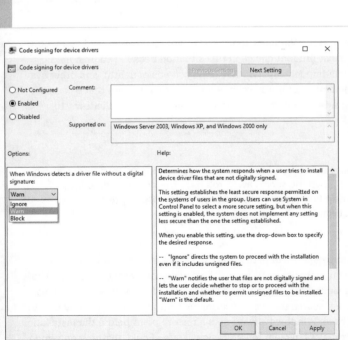

Figure 28.12
Enable the Code Signing for Device Drivers policy, and then choose what you want Windows 10 to do when it comes across an unsigned driver.

If your version of Windows 10 doesn't support the Local Group Policy Editor, follow these steps to set the driver-signing options via the Registry:

1. In the taskbar's Search box, type **regedit**, press Enter, and then enter your User Account Control credentials. Windows 10 launches the Registry Editor.

2. Navigate to the following key:

   HKCU\Software\Policies\Microsoft\

3. If you don't see a Windows NT key, select Edit, New, Key, and then type **Windows NT**.

4. Select Edit, New, Key, and then type **Driver Signing**.

5. Select Edit, New, DWORD, and then type **BehaviorOnFailedVerify**.

6. Double-click the BehaviorOnFailedVerify setting to open it for editing.

7. Type one of the following values:

   - **1**—(Ignore) Use this value if you want Windows 10 to install all unsigned drivers.

   - **2**—(Warn) Use this value if you want Windows 10 to warn you about an unsigned driver by displaying the dialog box shown earlier in Figure 28.11.

   - **3**—(Block) Use this value if you do not want Windows 10 to install any unsigned drivers.

8. Click OK.

 tip

Windows 10 knows that some device drivers will cause system instabilities. It will simply refuse to load these problematic drivers, no matter which action you choose in the Driver Signing Options dialog box. In this case, you'll see a dialog box similar to the one in Figure 28.11, except this one tells you that the driver will not be installed, and your only choice is to cancel the installation.

Write a Complete List of Device Drivers to a Text File

Sometimes you might wish you had a list of all the drivers installed on your PC. For example, if your system crashes, it would be nice to have some kind of record of what drivers are in there. More likely, such a list would come in handy if you have to set up your PC from scratch and you want to know which drivers you have to update.

How do you get such a list? Oddly, Windows doesn't give you any straightforward way to do this. However, you can make your own list by using a script like the one shown in Listing 28.1.

➡ *For information on working with scripts,* **see** *"Windows Script Host," p. 685.*

Listing 28.1   A Script That Writes a Complete List of a PC's Installed Device Drivers to a Text File

```
Option Explicit
On Error Resume Next
Dim strComputer, objWMI, collDrivers, objDriver, intDrivers
```

```
Dim objFSO, strFolder, objFile
' Change YourUserName, below, or use a path of the folder
' where you want to store the text file'
strFolder = "c:\Users\YourUserName\Desktop\"
' Initialize the file system object
Set objFSO = CreateObject("Scripting.FileSystemObject")
' Create the text file
Set objFile = objFSO.CreateTextFile(strFolder & "drivers.txt", True)
 ' Get the WMI object
strComputer = "."
Set objWMI = GetObject("winmgmts:\\" & strComputer)
 ' Return the collection of device drivers on the computer
Set collDrivers = objWMI.ExecQuery _
    ("Select * from Win32_PnPSignedDriver")
' Run through each item in the collection
intDrivers = 0
For Each objDriver in collDrivers
    '
    ' Write the driver data to the text file
    '
    objFile.WriteLine(objDriver.DeviceName)
    objFile.WriteLine("=========================================")
    objFile.WriteLine("Device Class: " & objDriver.DeviceClass)
    objFile.WriteLine("Device Description: " & objDriver.Description)
    objFile.WriteLine("Device ID: " & objDriver.DeviceID)
    objFile.WriteLine("INF Filename: " & objDriver.InfName)
    objFile.WriteLine("Driver Provider: " & objDriver.DriverProviderName)
    objFile.WriteLine("Driver Version: " & objDriver.DriverVersion)
    objFile.WriteLine("")
    intDrivers = intDrivers + 1
Next
' Close the text file
objFile.Close
WScript.Echo "Wrote " & intDrivers & " drivers to the text file."
```

The script uses VBScript's FileSystemObject to connect to the PC's file system. In this case, the script uses FileSystemObject to create a new text file in the folder specified by strFolder. The script then sets up the usual Windows Management Instrumentation (WMI) object and uses WMI to return the collection of installed device drivers. A For Each...Next loop goes through each device and writes various data to the text file, including the device name and description as well as the driver version.

Uninstalling a Device

When you remove a Plug and Play device, the BIOS informs Windows 10 that the device is no longer present. Windows 10, in turn, updates its device list in the Registry, and the peripheral no longer appears in the Device Manager display.

If you're removing a legacy device, however, you need to tell Device Manager that the device no longer exists. To do that, follow these steps:

1. Press Windows Logo+X, click Device Manager, and then click the device in the Device Manager tree.

2. Select Action, Uninstall Device. (Alternatively, click Uninstall Device in the toolbar or open the device's properties sheet, display the Driver tab, and click Uninstall Device.)

3. When Windows 10 warns you that you're about to remove the device, click OK.

Working with Device Security Policies

The Group Policy Editor offers several device-related policies. To see them, open the Group Policy Editor (press Windows Logo+R, type **gpedit.msc**, and press Enter) and select Computer Configuration, Windows Settings, Security Settings, Local Policies, Security Options. Here are the policies in the Devices category:

- **Allow Undock Without Having to Log On**—When this policy is enabled, users can undock a notebook computer without having to log on to Windows 10. (That is, they can undock the computer by pressing the docking station's eject button.) If you want to restrict who can do this, disable this policy.

- **Allowed to Format and Eject Removable Media**—Use this policy to determine the groups allowed to format floppy disks and eject CDs and other removable media.

- **Prevent Users from Installing Printer Drivers**—Enable this policy to prevent users from installing a network printer. Note that this doesn't affect the installation of a local printer.

- **Restrict CD-ROM Access to Locally Logged-On User Only**—Enable this policy to prevent network users from operating the computer's CD-ROM or DVD drive at the same time as a local user. If no local user is accessing the drive, the network user can access it.

 tip

To control who can undock the computer, display Computer Configuration, Windows Settings, Security Settings, Local Policies, User Rights Assignment. Use the Remove Computer from Docking Station policy to assign the users or groups who have this right.

- **Restrict Floppy Access to Locally Logged-On User Only**—Enable this policy to prevent network users from operating the computer's floppy drive at the same time as a local user. If no local user is accessing the drive, the network user can access it.

EDITING THE WINDOWS REGISTRY

What Is the Registry?

The Windows Registry is a database in which Windows and application programs store configuration settings, startup information, hardware settings, user preferences, file locations, license and registration information, last-viewed file lists, and so on. The Registry holds a huge amount of information about installed program components and subcomponents (DLLs, COM objects, and so on). In addition, the Registry stores the associations between file types and the applications that create and use them. For example, the Registry holds the information that tells Windows to use Media Player when you click an MPG movie file. In the early days of DOS and Windows, this kind of information was stored in a random collection of hundreds of files scattered all over your hard disk. Now almost all configuration information for Windows itself is stored in the Registry. While many Modern apps store setup information and preferences online through cloud services, and some desktop applications store information in your user profile folder, under the subfolder AppData, the Registry is still a sort of Grand Central Station for Windows.

Most of the time the Registry does its job behind the scenes. Most Registry information is set and read by Control Panel applets, applications, Windows services, device drivers, and so on. You'll rarely if ever need to touch it directly. However, some settings can be made only by manually changing Registry values, and knowing how the Registry works can help you track down viruses and annoying auto-starting programs. Therefore, it's worth knowing how the Registry is organized and how to make changes when necessary.

tip

If you're already familiar with the Registry, you might want to skip ahead to the section "New Registry Features," where you learn how User Account Control and 64-bit Windows impact the Registry.

How the Registry Is Organized

The Registry is organized a lot like the files and folders on a hard disk. Just as a hard disk can contain partitions, the Registry contains separate sections called *top-level keys*. In each section is a list of named entries, called *keys*, which correspond to the folders on a hard disk. And just as a folder can contain files and more nested folders, a Registry key can contain *values*, which hold information such as numbers or text strings, and more nested keys. Even the way that file folders and Registry keys are described is similar: A folder might be named `\Users\brian\chapter 29`, and a Registry key might be named `\HKEY_CURRENT_USER\Control Panel\Desktop`. You can see this structure in Figure 29.1. `Control Panel` and `Desktop` are the names of keys, and the `Desktop` key contains values, which have names like `ActiveWndTrackTimeout` and `AutoColorization`.

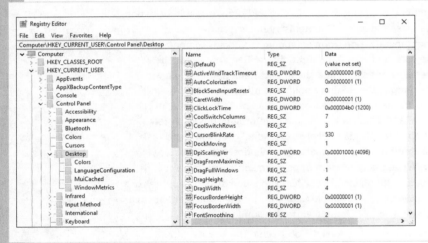

Figure 29.1
The Registry Editor screen shows keys on the left and values on the right.

The two main top-level keys are as follows:

- `HKEY_LOCAL_MACHINE` contains all the hardware and machine-specific setup information for your computer. Most values and keys under `HKEY_LOCAL_MACHINE` can be changed only by Computer Administrator users running with elevated privileges. This helps protect this Registry section from malware.

Some of the primary keys in `HKEY_LOCAL_MACHINE` are as follows:

`BDC00000000` contains system boot information. (The data in this key is actually stored in a separate partition on the boot hard drive.)

`COMPONENTS` contains a list of Windows modules and components. It's not always present in the Registry Editor display.

`HARDWARE` contains information gathered by the Plug and Play system during Windows startup.

`SOFTWARE` contains Windows and application information that applies to all users of the computer. Most software vendors create a subkey under `SOFTWARE` with their company name, with subkeys below that for each of their applications. On 64-bit systems, a subkey named `Wow6432Node` holds information for 32-bit applications and software components. We address this later in the chapter under "Registry Redirection and Reflection."

`SYSTEM` contains information about installed services and device drivers.

- `HKEY_USERS` contains a key for each user account created on the computer, including the accounts used only internally by Windows services.

  The keys under `HKEY_USERS` are mostly named using long numeric strings that are the user account's security identifier (SID) number. Not all accounts' keys are normally visible at the same time. Each account's key is loaded into the Registry when the user logs on and is unloaded a short time after the user logs out. Each user's key contains his or her personal Windows and application settings and preferences. Most entries are secured so that only the owning user can modify them.

The Registry Editor displays three other sections that look as if they are separate top-level keys but are actually views of information inside `HKEY_LOCAL_MACHINE` or `HKEY_USERS`:

- `HKEY_CURRENT_USER` is a shortcut to the subsection of `HKEY_USERS` that corresponds to the currently logged-on user. That is, when *you* run the Registry Editor, `HKEY_CURRENT_USER` shows *your* Windows and application preferences and settings.

  Some of the primary keys in `HKEY_CURRENT_USER` are as follows:

  `Control Panel` holds per-user preferences set by—you guessed it—Control Panel applets.

  `Environment` contains per-user environment variables set in the Advanced Computer Properties dialog box (`sysdm.cpl`).

  `Network` contains information about mapped network drives.

  `Software`, the largest section, contains per-user application preferences and configuration.

- `HKEY_CURRENT_CONFIG` is a shortcut to `HKEY_LOCAL_MACHINE\System\CurrentControlSet\ Hardware Profiles\Current` and contains hardware and device settings specific to the hardware profile used when Windows was started.

- `HKEY_CLASSES_ROOT` stores file associations, the information that Windows uses to link file types to applications, and a huge amount of setup information for Windows software components. It is actually a combined view of the contents of two other Registry sections: `HKEY_LOCAL_MACHINE\Software\Classes`, which holds settings that are made for all users on this computer, and `HKEY_CURRENT_USER\Software\Classes`, which holds personal settings made just by the current user. If the same value is defined in both `HKEY_CURRENT_USER\...` and `HKEY_LOCAL_ MACHINE\...`, the `HKEY_CURRENT_USER` value is used.

 note

`HKEY_LOCAL_MACHINE` is often abbreviated as HKLM, and `HKEY_CURRENT_USER` is often abbreviated as HKCU. We'll use those abbreviations in the rest of this chapter.

Registry keys have the same types of security settings as files and folders. In most cases, you have full control over the keys under your own account's HKCU section, unless an application explicitly removes the Modify or Delete permissions from its keys. And in general, only Computer Administrator users with elevated privileges can edit the contents of HKLM, except keys that were explicitly set to allow other users to edit it. (Some application installers do this.) We talk more about Registry security later in this chapter.

When User Account Control is active, and you are logged on as a Computer Administrator, the Registry Editor requests elevated permissions so that you can edit HKLM keys. This is why you get a User Account Control prompt when you run it. If you are not logged on as a Computer Administrator, the Registry Editor will run with reduced privileges unless you use the Run As Administrator option to start it. We discuss this later in the chapter, too.

New Registry Features

Windows Vista introduced some new features to the Registry: virtualization and 64/32–bit reflection. These features are also present, although somewhat changed, in Windows 7 through 10. The following sections give you a brief tour. The features are called Registry virtualization, redirection, and reflection. This topic is somewhat gnarly and obscure, so on your first read, you might want to skip ahead to the section titled "Backing Up and Restoring the Registry."

Registry Virtualization

In the days before Windows security became a serious concern, many applications stored information in keys under HKLM, typically in a key named along the lines of HKLM\Software\ *ManufacturerName**ApplicationName*, so that the information could be made available to all users on the computer. Imagine a game that keeps track of the highest score achieved by any user. It has to store that high score somewhere accessible to all users, and HKLM is exactly such a place. So, versions of Windows up to and including Windows XP let any application write to this key or its subkeys. But this became an enormous security problem because this also made it very easy for malware to make changes to global Windows settings affecting all users.

User Account Control, introduced in Windows Vista, brought an end to this. Now, by default, only trusted setup programs or programs running with elevated permissions may make changes to keys and values under HKLM\Software. Application developers today are supposed to know this, and if an application really needs to store updatable information under HKLM, its developer needs to create these keys during installation and change their permission settings so that "normal" users can modify them later.

However, tens of thousands of older Windows applications were designed before this change in the rules, and they would stop working if they couldn't make the Registry changes they expect to make. To get around this issue, Microsoft added Registry virtualization. Here's how it works: When User Account Control is enabled, if a standard Windows desktop application or command-line program attempts to store information in HKEY_LOCAL_MACHINE\Software but doesn't have permission to change information there, the information will actually get stored in HKEY_CURRENT_USER\Software\ CLASSES\VirtualStore\MACHINE\Software.

These applications still "see" the information as if it were in the intended location; this alternative key location "overlays" the original location. As a result, old applications that aren't aware of the new, tighter restrictions on HKEY_LOCAL_MACHINE will run without a hitch, although their settings and data will be per-user instead of machinewide.

You must know about this so you can check the alternative locations when you're investigating problems with Registry settings in your system.

If you change a legacy application program's preference setting that should apply to all users of the program, but it affects only you, and the setting isn't changed when other users run the application, most likely the configuration setting is stored in a Registry key under HKEY_LOCAL_MACHINE to which you cannot write. When you make the change, Windows virtualizes the Registry value, and only your account sees the change.

To fix this issue, first try to contact the software manufacturer for an update or workaround. If none exists, try this:

1. Locate the Registry key in which the setting is being saved. Either search the Registry for the setting value or use a Registry change-monitoring tool such as Registrar Registry Manager (or procmon from docs.microsoft.com/sysinternals, under Downloads, Process Utilities, Process Monitor) to see where the application saves your setting.

2. As an Administrator, locate the key in the left pane of the Registry Editor, right-click it, and select Permissions. Select an entry under Group or Users names and check Full Control.

3. Using your account, locate the virtualized copy of the key under HKEY_CLASES_ROOT\ VirtualStore and delete it.

4. Run the application and change the setting again.

After this, everyone should share the same copy of the setting.

Virtualization doesn't occur under some circumstances. In those cases, the application simply is allowed to fail in its attempt to make changes to HKEY_LOCAL_MACHINE. These circumstances are as follows:

- If User Account Control is disabled.

- If virtualization is disabled by your network administrator, using Group Policy on a Windows domain network.

- If the application is a 64-bit or WinRT application.

- If the application program has a *manifest*, a block of data that the developer included inside the application or in a separate file to describe advanced security settings. The logic is that manifests are a relatively new construct. If an application is new enough to have a manifest, its developer should know how to cooperate with User Account Control. Almost all the applications that come with Windows—including Notepad, the Command Prompt interpreter (cmd.exe), and the Registry Editor—have manifests, so almost all Windows utilities do not see virtualized Registry settings.

- If a key is marked with a special flag that indicates that it is not to be redirected. HKEY_LOCAL_ MACHINE\Software\Microsoft\Windows\CurrentVersion\Run is marked this way so that a virus that attempts to set itself up to run at logon via this key won't be capable of doing so. The command-line utility REG can modify the virtualization flag. Type **REG FLAGS /?** at the command-line prompt for more information.

Virtualization is seen as a stopgap measure and may be removed from some future version of Windows, after most applications either store information in HKEY_CURRENT_USER or explicitly set less restrictive permissions on their keys in HKEY_LOCAL_MACHINE when they're installed.

Registry Virtualization for Universal Windows Packages

Apps downloaded and installed from the Windows Store get a slightly different version of Registry virtualization. If the application writes or attempts to change Registry keys in HKLM\Software, a private copy of the added or changed data is stored in the app's folder under C:\Program Files\ WindowsApps*package_name*\registry.dat. This means that Registry changes are made for all users of the app but are not seen by any other apps. Similarly, changes made anywhere in HKCU are stored in a per-app file in your user profile folder, so that changes are visible only to the app.

As a consequence, any data that a Modern app stores in the Registry isn't visible to other any other apps, including the Registry Editor. It's highly unlikely that you'd need to ever edit an app's Registry data, but if you need to, you must manually load the app's registry.dat hive file, as discussed later in the chapter under "Editing Registry Entries for an App or Another User."

Registry Redirection and Reflection

The 64-bit versions of Windows support running 32-bit Windows applications (and, in fact, most software *is* still 32-bit, including the majority of Microsoft Office installations). This presents a problem because many Windows subcomponents (objects and dynamic link libraries) can be present in both 32- and 64-bit versions on the same computer, and information about their file locations and configuration is stored in the Registry under keys whose names were set in stone before Microsoft considered the need to distinguish between the two flavors. To work around this issue, when a 32-bit application attempts to read or write information to a few specific Registry keys, Windows silently uses an alternative location. The application is none the wiser. This is called *Registry redirection*. The result is that 32-bit and 64-bit applications can both use these same, fixed key names, but their information doesn't get intermingled.

Most but not all of the subkeys under HKEY_LOCAL_MACHINE\ Software and HKEY_CURRENT_USER\Software are subject to redirection. Those that are not redirected are considered "shared"; 32-bit and 64-bit applications see the same value. For information about which specific subkeys are redirected and which are shared, go to msdn.microsoft.com and search for the article "Registry Keys Affected By Wow64." (Because the information shown under HKEY_CLASSES_ROOT is actually stored under those two Software keys, many of its keys are redirected, too.)

Redirected information for 32-bit applications is actually stored under HKEY_LOCAL_MACHINE\Software\WOW6432Node (for systemwide settings) and HEY_CURRENT_USER\Software\ WOW6432Node (for per-user settings). When a 32-bit application

tip

This point is *really* important: Most of us use 64-bit versions of Windows now, but if you do end up fiddling with the Registry, most of the time the instructions you'll read online will not take this into account. So if, for example, you're following a suggestion to look for something in HKEY_CURRENT_ USER\Software\SomeSubKey, it's very likely that you'll actually have to look in HKEY_CURRENT_ USER\Software\WOW6432Node\ SomeSubKey. Read on for some more detailed examples.

requests information from a redirected key using the original location, it is fed information from below WOW6432Node.

Here's an example: a software manufacturer might decide to store the locations of its program files under the key HKEY_ LOCAL_MACHINE\Software\PrettyGoodPrograms\MyFiles. A 64-bit application from this vendor will store its information in that actual location. A 32-bit application from this vendor will think it's storing and reading information there, but it will actually be fed the information from HKEY_LOCAL_MACHINE\ Software\WOW6432Node\PrettyGoodPrograms\MyFiles. The 32- and 64-bit programs can thus see entirely different values from the same Registry key.

> **note**
> You must close the 64-bit version of the Registry Editor before you can open the 32-bit version, and vice versa, unless you start the second instance of the Registry Editor with the -m command-line argument. (That is, you would have to start regedit using the command line regedit -m.)

This impacts you, too: when working with the Registry on a 64-bit system, you need to know to look under these two WOW6432Node entries when looking for setup information for 32-bit components. When you're tracking down configuration problems, you should usually check *both* locations.

Alternatively, you can use the 32-bit version of regedit; this presents all information in the standard locations seen by 32-bit applications. When you run regedit from the command line, you get the 64-bit version. However, if you run %systemroot%\syswow64\regedit.exe, you get the 32-bit version and can edit the values seen by 32-bit applications.

Windows Vista had a feature that automatically copied some information set by 32-bit and 64-bit components and applications to *both* the 32- and 64-bit locations. This was called *Registry reflection*. Reflection does not occur in Windows 7 through 10. For more information, visit msdn.microsoft.com and search for the topics "Removal of Windows Registry Reflection." Also, see the Microsoft Knowledge Base article http://support.microsoft.com/kb/305097.

Backing Up and Restoring the Registry

Because the Registry is the *one* place where all the Windows hardware and software settings are stored, it's also the one thing that Windows absolutely needs to run. If you have to use the Registry Editor to manually change Registry settings, we strongly suggest that you back up your Registry *before* you make changes.

Backing Up the Registry

You can back up the Registry in several ways, including (in order of preference) using a third-party Registry-backup program, backing up the entire hard disk using a third-party program or File Recovery, using System Restore, and using the Registry Editor to save a key to a text file. In general, backups that include the *entire* hard disk should include the Registry, because the Registry's data is stored in ordinary files. Some backup applications have a Registry backup as an explicit option. The Windows built-in System Restore feature backs up the HKLM Registry section automatically.

We suggest that before you install a piece of new hardware or a significant software application or update, do a *full* disk backup, including the Registry. Alternatively, use System Restore to manually

create a restore point, in case the application installer does
not do this itself. These methods are discussed later.

Backing Up with Third-Party Registry-Backup Software

Third-party programs are available for you to back up and
restore the Registry. See the section "Other Registry Tools,"
later in this chapter.

If you're adventurous, you can download a free tool called ERUNT from
www.larshederer.homepage.t-online.de/erunt. At the time this was written it was described
as supporting Windows 7, but it should work on Windows 10 as well.

These programs come with instructions on backing up, restoring, repairing, and maintaining the
Registry.

> **note**
>
> Before you manually edit the
> Registry for other purposes, back
> up the Registry by any of the
> means discussed in the next few
> sections.

Backing Up the Hard Disk

You can save the Registry by performing a complete "image" backup of the entire contents of the
hard disk on which Windows resides. To start a backup, in the taskbar's search box, search for
the word *Backup*. Select Backup Settings from the results list, and then choose Go to Backup and
Restore (Windows 7), Create a System Image.

➡ *For more information, **see** "Creating a System Image Backup," **p. 728.***

Alternatively, use a third-party disk backup program and ensure that it's backing up the Registry.
Check your backup software's manual for instructions on saving Registry and system information
when you back up. We suggest that you always include the Registry in your backups.

⚠ caution

Be aware that the backup programs Microsoft provides with Windows 10 do not provide a simple means
of backing up the Registry as insurance against accidents. The System Image backup can take a long time.
Restoring from such a backup, if it's necessary, would take a long time, too. System Restore backs up only
HKEY_LOCAL_MACHINE, not your own HKEY_CURRENT_USER data. System Restore is an effective backup only
if you're modifying just HKEY_LOCAL_MACHINE settings.

Backing Up with System Restore

If you will be changing only entries under HKEY_LOCAL_MACHINE, you can create a restore point to
back up a copy of this part of the Registry. To create a restore point, follow these steps:

1. In the taskbar's search box, type the words **restore point**, and from the results, select Create a
   Restore Point.

2. Be sure that drive C:, the disk volume that contains Windows, is listed in the Protection Settings box with protection On. If it's not on, select Configure, click Turn On System Protection, and then click OK.

3. Click Create, enter a description for the restore point, such as `Before changing Registry`, and then click Create.

Now you can edit the Registry as described later in this chapter.

Backing Up with the Registry Editor

The Registry Editor has a mechanism to export a set of Registry keys and values to a text file. If you can't or won't use a more comprehensive backup system before you manually edit the Registry, at least use this editor to select and back up the key that contains all the subkeys and values you plan to modify. Remember, though, that this method cannot remove entries you add after creating the backup; it can only restore settings you change or delete.

To back up a key and its subkeys and values, follow these steps:

1. In the taskbar's search box, type **regedit**. Then take one of the following actions:

   ■ If you are logged on as a Computer Administrator, click the regedit Windows application icon in the results list and confirm the User Account Control (UAC) prompt.

   ■ If you are not a Computer Administrator and want to back up your own keys in HKCU, follow the same procedure. There will be no UAC prompt.

   ■ If you are not a Computer Administrator and need to back up HKLM keys, right-click the regedit Windows application icon in the search results and select Run As Administrator. Then enter credentials for a Computer Administrator account.

2. Locate and select the key you plan to modify, or a key containing all the keys you plan to modify, in the left pane.

3. Select File, Export.

4. Choose a location and filename to use to store the Registry keys. (I usually use the desktop for temporary files like this, so that I can see them and delete them later.)

5. Select All Files from the Save As Type list and enter a name (possibly with an extension other than `.reg`—for example, `before.sav`).

6. Click Save. The chosen key or keys are then saved as a text file.

 note

The reason for these complicated variations is that malicious programs and email attachments can easily abuse the Registry Editor, so it's subject to UAC restrictions. The Registry Editor must be running in elevated mode to edit, restore, or modify Registry keys that only a Computer Administrator account can change. By the way, the Registry Editor's title bar provides no indication to tell you whether it's running with elevated privileges; you just have to remember.

Restoring the Registry

If you've made Registry changes that cause problems, you can try to remember each and every change you made, reenter the original information, delete any keys you added, and thus undo the changes manually. Good luck! If you were diligent and made a backup before you started, however, you can simply restore the backup and have confidence that the recovery is complete and accurate.

Signs of Registry Problems

Registry corruption can take two forms: either the Registry's database files can be damaged by an errant disk operation, or information can be mangled by a buggy program or an overzealous regedit user. No matter what the cause, the result can be a system that won't run or one that reboots itself over and over.

These could be other signs of Registry corruption or errors:

- Drivers aren't loaded, or they give errors while Windows is booting.
- Software complains about components that aren't registered or cannot be located.
- Undesirable programs attempt to run when you log in.
- Windows does not boot, or it starts up only in Safe mode.

If you made a Registry backup using a disk or Registry backup tool, use the instructions that came with your product to restore the Registry. If you created a restore point or used Regedit, follow the steps described in the following sections.

Restoring the Registry from a Restore Point

If you created a restore point before modifying the Registry, you can back out of the change by following these steps:

1. In the taskbar's search box, type **restore point**, and from the results, select Create a Restore Point. (Alternatively, right-click or touch and hold the Start button, select System, and then at the left, select System Protection.)

2. Click the System Restore button and locate the restore point you created. Select it and click Next; then click Finish. Windows restarts.

If the Registry problem is severe enough that Windows can't boot or get to the System Restore function, you can perform a system restore from the system recovery tools on your Windows setup DVD.

➡ *For instructions on performing a system restore this way, see "Recovering Using System Restore," p. 607.*

Restoring the Registry from Regedit

If a Registry-editing session has gone awry and you need to restore the Registry from a key you saved from within Regedit, follow these steps:

1. In the taskbar's search box, type **regedit**. Then take one of the following actions:

   - If you are logged on as a Computer Administrator, click the regedit Windows application icon in the results list and confirm the User Account Control (UAC) prompt.

   - If you are not a Computer Administrator and want to restore your own keys in HKCU, follow the same procedure. There will be no UAC prompt.

   - If you are not an Administrator and need to restore HKLM keys, right-click the regedit Windows application icon in the search results and select Run As Administrator. Then enter credentials for a Computer Administrator account.

2. In the Registry Editor, select File, Import.

3. Select All Files from the Files of Type list.

4. Locate the file you used to back up the Registry key or keys—for example, before.sav.

5. Select Open.

 tip

If you encounter what you think are Registry problems with add-on software, your best bet is to uninstall the software, if possible, and reinstall it before attempting any Registry restores or repairs.

The saved Registry keys are then imported, replacing any changes or deletions. However, any keys or values you've added to the Registry are not removed. If they are the cause of the problem, this restore will *not* help.

If the Registry problems persist, you can try a rather drastic measure: You can use Regedit to delete the key or keys that were changed and then import the backup file again. This time, any added keys or values are removed. We suggest that you try this approach only with keys related to add-on software, *not* for any of the Microsoft software or hardware keys.

Using Regedit

Most people never need to edit the Registry by hand because most Registry keys are set by the software that uses them. However, you might need to edit the Registry by hand if you're directed by a technical support person who's helping you fix a problem, or when you're following a published procedure to make an adjustment for which there is no Control Panel setting.

In the latter case, before going any further, we need to say this one last time, to make it absolutely clear: Unless you're quite certain that you can't make a mistake, back up the Registry (or at least the section you want to change) before making any changes.

The next few sections cover the basics of the Registry Editor.

Viewing the Registry

The easiest way to run the Registry Editor is to press the Windows Logo key to display the Start menu and type **regedit**. Then take one of the following actions:

- If you are logged on as a Computer Administrator, click the regedit Windows application icon in the results list and confirm the User Account Control (UAC) prompt. The Registry Editor will run with full elevated privileges.

- If you are not a Computer Administrator and want to edit just your own keys in HKEY_CURRENT_ USER, follow the same procedure. There will be no UAC prompt. The Registry Editor will run with reduced privileges, and you will not be able to change systemwide settings.

- If you are not a Computer Administrator and need to edit keys in HKEY_LOCAL_MACHINE, right-click the regedit Windows application icon in the search results and select Run As Administrator. Then enter credentials for a Computer Administrator account.

Regedit offers a two-pane display, as shown earlier in Figure 29.1. The top-level keys, which are listed below Computer, can be expanded just like drives and folders in File Explorer. In the pane on the right are the values for each key. The name of the currently selected key appears in the status bar.

Values have names, just as the files in a folder do, and it's in the values that configuration information is finally stored. Each key has a (Default) value, which is the value of the key itself, and any number of named values. For example, Figure 29.1 shows the key HKEY_CURRENT_USER\Control Panel\Desktop. The value of HKEY_CURRENT_USER\Control Panel\Desktop itself is undefined (blank), and the value HKEY_CURRENT_USER\Control Panel\Desktop\DragFullWindows is 1.

Registry values have a data type, which is usually one of the types shown in Table 29.1. The Registry Editor display lists values by their technical names.

Table 29.1 Data Types Supported by Regedit

Technical Name	"Friendly" Name	Description
REG_SZ	String value	Textual information, a simple string of letters.
REG_BINARY	Binary value	Binary data, displayed as an arbitrary number of hexadecimal digits.
REG_DWORD	DWORD (32-bit) value	A single number displayed in hexadecimal or decimal.
REG_QWORD	QWORD (64-bit) value	A single number displayed in hexadecimal or decimal. QWORD values are used primarily by 64-bit Windows applications.
REG_MULTI_SZ	Multistring value	A string that can contain more than one line of text.
REG_EXPAND_SZ	Expandable string value	Text that can contain environment variables (such as %TEMP%).

Other data types, such as REG_DWORD_BIG_ENDIAN and REG_RESOURCE_LIST, exist, but they are obscure and rare and can't be edited with Regedit.

Searching in the Registry

You can search for a Registry entry by key name, value name, or the contents of a value string. First, select a starting point for the search in the left pane. You can select Computer to select the entire Registry, or you can limit your search to one of the top-level keys or any subordinate key. Next, select Edit, Find from the menu and enter a search string in the Find dialog box. The Find feature is not case sensitive, so it doesn't matter whether you use upper- or lowercase letters. You can check

 note

When I search the Registry, most of the time, I check all the Look At boxes but not Match Whole String Only.

any of the Look At boxes to designate where in the Registry you expect to find the desired text: in the name of a key, in the name of a value, or in the data, the value itself. You can also check Match Whole String Only.

Check Match Whole String Only to search only for items whose whole name or value is the desired string.

Click Find Next to start the search. The Regedit display indicates the first match to your string; by pressing F3, you can repeat the search to look for other instances.

Also remember that Windows might store information in some places you are not familiar with, as discussed previously under "New Registry Features."

 tip

The search function has two limitations:

- You can't enter a backslash (\) in the search string when looking for a key or value name; Regedit won't complain, but it won't find anything, either.
- You can't search for the initial HKEY_xxx part of a key name. That's not actually part of the name; it's just the section of the Registry in which the key resides.

For example, to find a key named HKEY_CLASSES_ROOT\MIDFile\shell\Play\Command, you can't type all that in and have Find jump right to the key. If you already know the full pathname of a key, use the left pane of Regedit to browse for the key directly.

Editing Keys and Values

Regedit has no Save and Undo menu items and no Recycle Bin. Changes to the Registry happen *immediately* and *permanently*. Additions, deletions, and changes are for real. This is the reason for all the warnings to back up before you poke into the Registry.

Adding a Value

To add a value to a key, select the key in the left pane and choose Edit, New. Select the type of value to add; you can select any of the supported Registry data types, which are listed by the "friendly" names shown previously in Table 29.1. The instructions you're following indicate which type of value to add. A new value entry then appears in the right pane.

Type the new value's name and press Enter to edit the value:

- For string values, enter the text of the desired string.

- For DWORD values, choose Decimal or Hexadecimal, and enter the desired value in the chosen format.

- For binary values, enter pairs of hexadecimal characters as instructed. (You'll never be asked to do this, we promise.)

Changing a Value

If you want to change a value, double-click it in the right pane to bring up the Edit Value dialog box. Alternatively, right-click it and select Modify. Then make the desired change and click OK.

That is all you will likely ever need to do with Regedit. However, in the extremely unlikely case that you want to delete a value or add or remove a key, the following sections can help see you through these processes.

Deleting a Value

If you've added a Registry value in the hope of fixing some problem and found that the change wasn't needed, or if you're instructed to delete a value by a Microsoft Knowledge Base article or other special procedure, you can delete the entry by viewing its key and locating the value on the right pane.

Select the value and choose Edit, Delete from the menu, or right-click and select Delete from the context menu. Confirm by clicking Yes.

Adding or Deleting a Key

Keys must be added as subkeys of existing keys; you can't create a new top-level key. To add a key, select an existing key in the left pane and select Edit, New, Key from the menu. Alternatively, right-click the existing key and select New, Key from the context menu. A new key appears in the left pane, where you can edit its name. Press Enter after you enter the name.

You can delete a key by selecting it in the left pane and choosing Edit, Delete from the menu or by right-clicking it and selecting Delete from the context menu. Click Yes to confirm

 note

Many of the keys that control Windows itself have access restrictions and can be modified only by a Computer Administrator, and only when the Registry Editor is running with elevated permissions. For instructions on running with elevated permissions, see "Viewing the Registry," earlier in this chapter.

 caution

There is no Undo command in the Registry Editor. When you delete a value, it's gone for good. Be sure you've made a Registry backup before editing or deleting Registry keys and values.

 caution

Don't attempt to rename keys without a very good reason—for example, because you mistyped the name of the key you were adding. If Windows can't find specific Registry keys it needs, it might not boot or operate correctly.

that you intend to delete the key. Deleting a key deletes its values *and all its subkeys* as well, so without the protection of Undo (or a Registry Recycling Bin), this action is serious.

Renaming a Key

As you have probably guessed, the pattern for renaming a key follows the File Explorer model exactly: Choose the key in the left pane and select Edit, Rename, or right-click the key and select Rename. Finally, enter a new name and press Enter.

Using Copy Key Name

As you have probably noticed by now, the names of Registry keys can be quite long, torturous things. The Registry Editor offers a bit of help to finger-fatigued Registry Editors (and authors): Choosing Edit, Copy Key Name puts the name of the currently selected key into the Clipboard so you can paste it elsewhere if you need to.

Editing Registry Entries for an App or Another User

It's possible that you might need to view and edit Registry data saved by a Modern (Windows Store) app. Registry data for apps is normally seen only by the app itself. To view or change it, you must manually load the app's private hive file.

A *hive* is a file that contains Registry data. The Registry view that you see in the Registry Editor is the sum total of all loaded hive files. The systemwide Registry sections (the keys under HKLM) are loaded when Windows boots. Each user's personal Registry sections (seen as HKCU) are loaded when each user logs on. App hive files are loaded when the app is started, and the data in them is normally visible only to the app itself, overlaid on the rest of the Registry.

As an administrator, you also might find it necessary to edit HKEY_USER entries for some other user. For example, a startup program in HKEY_CURRENT_USER\Software\Windows\CurrentVersion\Run might be causing such trouble that the user can't log on. If you can't log on as that user, you can edit his HKEY_CURRENT_USER Registry keys by loading his Registry data manually. You load the user's Registry *hive* and edit it.

To manually load and edit an app's or user's hive file, follow these steps:

1. Log on as a Computer Administrator and run Regedit with elevated permissions, as discussed in "Viewing the Registry" in this chapter.

2. Select the HKEY_USERS window.

3. Highlight the top-level key HKEY_USERS.

4. Select File, Load Hive.

5. Browse to the desired app folder or user profile folder.

    For an app, locate the app's package folder in C:\Program Files*packagename*. Select file registry.dat, and then click Open.

For a local user account, look in \Users\username. The name of this folder might have the computer name or a domain name attached. For example, on one computer, my profile folder name is bknittel.java. Type the filename **NTUSER.DAT**. (The file will most likely not appear in the Browse dialog box because it's *super hidden*—marked with both the Hidden and System attributes.) Click Open.

6. A dialog box appears, asking you to enter a name for the hive. HKEY_USERS normally loads user hives with a long numeric name, so we suggest that you type the app's name or the user's logon name, or something like users_key. Click OK. The user's Registry data is then loaded and can be edited, as shown in Figure 29.2.

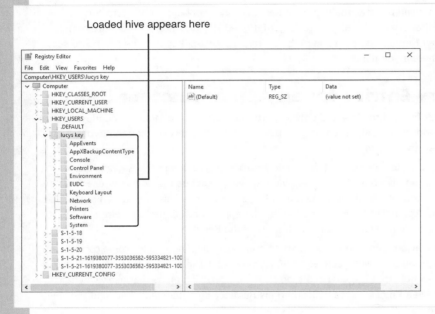

Loaded hive appears here

Figure 29.2
An offline user's Registry hive is now loaded and can be edited.

7. When you're finished editing, unload the hive. Select the key you added under HKEY_USERS (for example, lucys_key in Figure 29.2), and select File, Unload Hive. Confirm by clicking Yes on the warning dialog box.

Editing Registry Entries for Another Windows Installation

If you need to retrieve Registry entries from an installation of Windows on another hard disk or partition, perhaps one that can't boot due to a virus, rootkit, or errant driver, you can load any of that installation's hive files for editing or exporting.

 note
If the other installation is on a different computer, you'll need to move its hard disk into your computer. Then be sure that your computer boots from *your* hard disk, not the one you just added.

To edit the other installation's Registry, you need to locate its hive files. They are usually found in the locations shown in Table 29.2.

Table 29.2   Usual Location of Hive Files

Key	Default Location and Hive File
HKEY_LOCAL_MACHINE\SAM	\windows\system32\config\sam
HKEY_LOCAL_MACHINE\Security	\windows\system32\config\security
HKEY_LOCAL_MACHINE\Software	\windows\system32\config\software
HKEY_LOCAL_MACHINE\System	\windows\system32\config\system
HKEY_LOCAL_MACHINE\Components	\windows\system32\config\components
HKEY_USERS\.Default	\windows\system32\config\default

To edit another Windows installation's Registry, use the technique described in "Editing Registry Entries for an App or Another User," but instead of locating a user's NTUSER.DAT file, locate the desired hive file on the other hard drive or partition. (We omitted the drive letters from Table 29.2. Find the hive file on the drive that corresponds to the other Windows installation.) Unload the hive after you've exported or corrected the desired information.

In some cases, you will find that you cannot view or modify keys loaded from another installation. This occurs if the keys are protected with security attributes that list specific users or groups defined in the other installation. In this case, you need to first take ownership of the keys and then add yourself as a user who is authorized to read or change the keys. The next section describes this process.

 note

You rarely should have to modify Registry security settings, but it does happen. The usual case is that an incorrectly designed program places information in a subkey of HKEY_LOCAL_MACHINE\Software that is intended to be shared and modified by all users running the program. Because Windows does not permit standard users to modify keys in HKEY_LOCAL_MACHINE\Software by default, the program might malfunction. To fix the problem, sometimes you need to modify permissions so that standard users can edit the shared key. Microsoft also sometimes recommends modifying Registry security in emergency security bulletins.

Editing Registry Security

Just as files and folders in an NTFS-formatted disk partition have security attributes to control access based on user and group identity, Registry keys and values also have a complete set of access control attributes that determine who has rights to read, write, and modify each entry.

If you absolutely must change permissions or auditing controls, locate the desired key or value, right-click it, and select Permissions. The Permissions dialog box looks just like the comparable dialog box for files and folders (see Figure 29.3), and it lets you set read, write, and modify rights for specific groups and users. You'll find a corresponding set of audit settings.

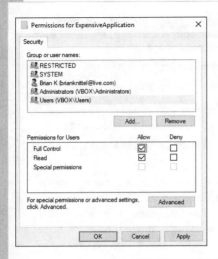

Figure 29.3
Registry key permissions control which users or groups are allowed to see or modify the Registry key and its values.

In most cases, a software vendor supplies precise instructions for making changes necessary to work around an application problem. Here, we describe a general procedure to make a given key that all users can read and write. You might do this to make a key capable of sharing information between users or to repair an alternate Windows installation, as mentioned in the previous section. To set more generous permissions, follow these steps:

1. Locate and select the key in the left pane.

2. Right-click it and select Permissions.

3. Select the Users entry in the top Group or User Names section. If Users is not listed, click Add, type **Users**, and click OK.

4. In the lower section, Permissions for Everyone, check Allow in the Full Control row and then click Apply. If this is successful, click OK.

5. If you are unable to make the changes, even though you're running the Registry Editor as a Computer Administrator user, click Advanced and select the Owner tab.

6. If the Current Owner is listed as unknown, select Administrators in the lower list and click OK.

7. Click OK to close the Advanced Security Settings dialog box, and return to step 3.

This is a risky procedure because it could result in another user or application being unable to access its own Registry keys. Use this as a procedure of last resort.

Other Registry Tools

You can use some third-party tools to edit the Registry and adjust Windows features. Next, we describe three of the more popular utilities.

Registry Toolkit

Registry Toolkit is a shareware Registry Editor made by Funduc software (www.funduc.com) with a nifty search-and-replace system. You can scan the Registry, changing all occurrences of one string to another, which is something most other Windows Registry Editors can't do. Its user interface isn't very comfortable or slick, but if you need to manage a lot of identical changes in the Registry, this is one cool tool. It's free to try, or $25 to register one computer and discounts for multiple computers.

Registrar Registry Manager

Registrar Registry Manager is a powerful Registry-editing tool produced by Resplendence Software Projects (www.resplendence.com), with a drag-and-drop interface. It includes a Registry backup, restore, and defragmentation tool; a Registry-compare tool; an Undo capability; remote Registry editing over the network; and many more features. The full version costs $48, and there is a free "home" version.

Tweak-10

Tweak-10 from Totalidea Software (www.totalidea.com) combines tweaking tools with additional enhancements and plug-ins. The cost is approximately $26 for one computer, with multiple-license discounts available. Check the totalidea.com website for this and other cool Windows tools.

Registry Privileges and Policies

On Windows corporate domain-type networks, Administrators can use the *policy* system to restrict users' ability to change their computer configuration. When you log on using a Domain user account, the policy system downloads and installs Registry settings prepared by system administrators. These Registry settings not only can help automate the setup of networking and other components, but can also restrict your ability to (mis)manage your computer.

Here's how it works: Windows looks at a boatload of Registry entries to determine what features to make available to you. For example, one value determines whether the Start menu is allowed to display the Run item; another makes the Control Panel hide the Power Management settings. Most of these values normally don't appear in the Registry at all, but they can be installed there by the policy system, and Windows security settings prevent users from changing or deleting them.

On a computer that's a member of a Windows Domain network, the policy system is called Group Policy. The settings for each computer and network user are automatically downloaded from master copies kept on the network's domain controllers (servers). On a standalone computer, it's called Local Security Policy. For a more detailed discussion of Local Security Policy, **see** "Tightening Local Security Policy," **p. 773.**

You can't edit these Registry settings using the Registry Editor. Policy settings can only be created, edited, or deleted by the Group Policy or Local Security Policy windows management tools. The policy-based settings overlay keys and values stored in the Registry.

COMMAND-LINE AND AUTOMATION TOOLS

Command-Line Tools

It might seem odd that in a book about the latest and greatest Windows operating system, we would devote an entire chapter encouraging you to use the text-based command-line world, turn your back on 40 years of software advancement, and choose to work in an environment that is proudly stuck in the 1970s. Well, we'll let you in on a little secret: The keyboard can be mightier than the mouse—and a lot faster.

Why is that so? As many power users and experienced administrators already know, it's usually *much* faster to type a few letters to do a job than to take your hands off the keyboard and poke around at endless menus and screens with a mouse or your fingertip. In almost every Windows configuration, you can perform setting and diagnostic tasks from the command line with just a few quick keystrokes (after you've memorized the fairly cryptic things that you have to type, of course). Many important diagnostic tools, such as ping, tracert, and nslookup, are available only from the command line unless you purchase third-party graphical add-ons to perform these functions.

tip

Here's some great news: Microsoft finally, after 15 years without any changes to the command-line environment, is making significant improvements to the Windows 10 version. We tell you about these improvements later in the chapter under "Copying and Pasting in the Command Prompt Window."

And, although the term *batch file* might bring back uncomfortable memories of the old MS-DOS days, batch files and program scripts are still powerful tools that provide a useful way to encapsulate common management functions. Together, command-line utilities, batch files, and scripts based on Windows Script Host and Windows PowerShell provide a complete set of building blocks from which you can develop high-level tools for repetitive or complex tasks.

In this book, we give you a quick introduction to setting up and using the command-line environment. We don't have room for more than that. For much more detail, tutorials, examples, and many helpful tips on using command-line tools, check out Brian's book *Windows 7 and Vista Guide to Scripting, Automation, and Command Line Tools*, published by Que. (The book's title is now dated, but the content remains relevant.)

The Windows 10 Command Prompt Environment

The Command Prompt window lets you type commands and review output, as shown in Figure 30.1. The quickest way to open a Command Prompt window is to use the keyboard: Press Windows Logo+X and then press the shortcut key C or select Command Prompt.

➡ *If Command Prompt is not one of the menu choices but Windows PowerShell is,* **see** *"Command-Line Access from the Power User Menu," p. 673.*

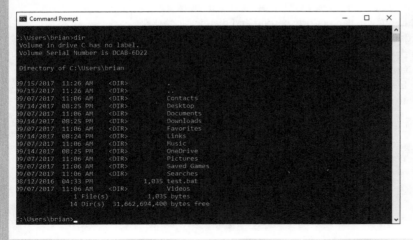

Figure 30.1
The Command Prompt window is the gateway to a world of powerful Windows management tools.

Alternatively, you could perform one of the following actions:

- Right-click or touch and hold the Start button, and then select Command Prompt.

- Press Windows Logo+R; then type **cmd** and press Enter.

- In the taskbar's search box, type **cmd** and wait a moment. On most computers, "Command Prompt" will appear as the only search result. Press Enter to launch it.

- Open File Explorer and select any folder or drive. Then select File, Open Command Prompt, Open Command Prompt.

- On the bottom left of the Start menu, select All Apps and then locate Command Prompt in the Windows System section.

 tip

If you plan on using the Command Prompt window regularly, open a Command Prompt window by one of the means mentioned previously. Locate its icon in the taskbar— it has the tiny characters C:\ in white, against a black background. Right-click it and select Pin to Taskbar. Now you can easily open a Command Prompt window anytime you want, with just a click.

All these methods work equally well.

The main difference between a standard Windows application and a command-line program—which in Windows is technically called a *console program*—is that it doesn't use a graphical display or pull-down menus. Instead, you type commands into the Command Prompt window to tell Windows to do something, and the programs type information back to you. Each command line starts with the name of the program that you want to run, optionally followed by additional information called *arguments*. Arguments tell the program what specifically you want to do. Each program has its own rules about what its arguments signify, which arguments might be required, and which are optional.

Changing Directories

When you are working in the command-line environment, the active location (drive and folder) is known as the *current directory*. The current directory is significant because if you don't specify a location argument with a command that requires one, the current directory is assumed. You can change the current directory by using the cd command like this:

```
cd \windows
```

If you want to change the current drive letter as well as the current directory, put /d on the cd command line, as in **cd /d d:\setup**.

Saving Output

The output of a command-line program usually prints out in the Command Prompt window. You can save output by redirecting it into a file using the > character. For example, the following command lists the files in the current directory and stores the results in the file listing.txt:

```
dir >listing.txt
```

You could then type the command **notepad listing.txt** to view the results. By itself, > creates a new file or replaces an existing file. You can tack output onto the end of (append to) a file using >>, as in this example:

```
dir c:\windows >>listing.txt
```

You can also send the output of one program to another program using ¦ (the pipe character), as in

```
dir c:\windows ¦ findstr /i setup
```

which lists the contents of folder c:\windows and prints out only entries that contain the word *setup* somewhere in the name. One handy use of the pipe mechanism is to send output to the command more, which stops after it displays each screenful, so you can read through a long printout:

```
dir c:\windows ¦ more
```

When it stops printing, you press the spacebar to see the next screen.

There are more ways to redirect program input and output. For more information, visit technet.microsoft.com and search for "Using Command Redirection."

The Search Path

When you type a command, Windows searches first in the current directory, and then in a list of folders called the *search path*, for a file whose name matches the program name you typed and whose name ends with any of several extensions, such as *.exe*, *.bat*, or *.vbs*. The most common program extensions are listed in Table 30.1. Windows examines the file to see what type of program it is and then runs it. It's then the program's job to interpret any arguments you typed after the program name.

 tip

You can pipe a command's output to the program named clip, which puts any text it receives onto the Windows clipboard. From there, you can paste the text anywhere you like. For example, to create a directory listing and put it into Microsoft Word or Notepad, type **dir ¦ clip**.

Then, in Word or Notepad, type Ctrl+V to paste the text that dir generated.

Table 30.1   Typical Executable Program Extensions

Extension	Program Type
.bat, .cmd	Batch file.
.com	Archaic MS-DOS program. (Not available on 64-bit Windows.)
.exe	Windows GUI program, console program, or MS-DOS program. (Windows determines which by examining the contents of the file.)
.js	Script file written in the JavaScript language.
.msc	Microsoft Management Console snap-in.
.vbs	Script file written in the VBScript language.

The search path is defined by a list of folder names in the PATH environment variable, and the complete list of extensions that Windows looks for is defined in the PATHEXT environment variable. The default search path includes the following folders:

```
C:\Windows\system32
C:\Windows
C:\Windows\System32\Wbem
C:\Windows\System32\WindowsPowerShell\v1.0
```

This means that you can run any program file, batch file, or script stored in the current directory or in any of these folders simply by typing its name. You can start both Windows programs and command-line programs in this way. For example, you just have to type **notepad** and press Enter to start the Notepad accessory.

If you create your own batch files, scripts, or programs, it's a good idea to create a separate folder in which to store them and to put that folder in the search path. We show you how to do so later in this chapter, under "Setting the PATH Environment Variable."

Command-Line Access from the Power User Menu

When you press Windows Logo+X or right-click or touch and hold the Start button, Windows displays the Power User pop-up menu. This incredibly useful shortcut gives you instant access to nearly every Windows management tool.

The Power User menu has entries that launch a command-line window, but you must choose which command-line environment appears on the menu: either the traditional Command Prompt window or Windows PowerShell, which we discuss later in the chapter.

You can choose which environment appears on the menu by following these steps:

1. Right-click or touch and hold an unoccupied space on the taskbar; then select Taskbar Settings.

2. To have the menu launch the traditional Command Prompt, turn off Replace Command Prompt with Windows PowerShell. To have it launch Windows PowerShell, turn on Replace Command Prompt with Windows PowerShell. Then you can close the settings box.

The Power User menu actually displays two entries for your chosen command-line environment. The second entry has (Admin) added to the name. That selection launches an elevated version of the program that has full administrative access, as discussed in the next section.

For what it's worth, if all you are doing at the Command Prompt is starting up programs by typing their names, either environment works equally well. As discussed later in the chapter, Windows PowerShell provides advanced processing tools within command lines, but basic commands like dir operate very differently in the two environments.

Running Commands with Elevated Privileges

Some command-line programs require elevated Computer Administrator privileges (via User Account Control) to do their job correctly. To use a Command Prompt window to run a program with elevated privileges, you must run it from a Command Prompt window that is itself elevated.

➡ *To learn more about User Account Control (UAC) and elevation,* **see** *"User Account Control," p. 104.*

When UAC is enabled (and we believe it always should be), you must take deliberate action to open an elevated Command Prompt window. Use one of these methods:

- Press Windows Logo+X, or right-click the Start button or touch and hold the Start button. Then select Command Prompt (Admin).

  ➡ *If Command Prompt (Admin) is not one of the menu choices but Windows PowerShell (Admin) is,* **see** *"Command-Line Access from the Power User Menu," p. 673.*

- If you have pinned Command Prompt to the taskbar, right-click the taskbar icon, right-click Command Prompt in the pop-up menu, and then select Run As Administrator.

- Open File Explorer and select any folder or drive. Then select File, Open Command Prompt, Open Command Prompt As Administrator.

- In the taskbar's search box, type **cmd**. Right-click the Command Prompt result, or on a touch screen, touch and hold until the pop-up menu appears. Select Run As Administrator.

> **caution**
>
> Be *very* careful when using an elevated Command Prompt window. Any commands you start from within this window will run with elevated privileges from the get-go, and you will receive no further UAC prompts when you start them. This includes Windows GUI programs. For example, if you type the command **optionalfeatures**, you will get the Turn Windows Features On or Off dialog box, and you will not have to confirm anything before it starts.

If you want, you can set a Command Prompt shortcut or pinned taskbar icon so that it is elevated by default. Right-click the icon. If you're working with a pinned taskbar icon, right-click Command Prompt. Then select Properties. On the Shortcut tab, click the Advanced button and check Run As Administrator. Be sure to rename the shortcut so that it's clear that it opens an elevated prompt.

To be safe, do not use an elevated Command Prompt window for general-purpose work. Use it only to accomplish a specific task that requires elevated privileges; then close it.

Copying and Pasting in the Command Prompt Window

Although you will usually use output redirection to store the output from command-line programs in files, you can also use cut and paste to move text into or out of a Command Prompt window.

Here's an area where Windows 10 offers real improvements over previous versions of Windows. If you enable the new keyboard shortcut options and QuickEdit mode, you can copy and paste text in console applications just as you would in Windows apps. The mouse cursor selects text in a natural way, and the standard Ctrl+C and Ctrl+V keyboard shortcuts copy and paste, respectively.

To enable the new options, open a Command Prompt window as described previously. Right-click the window's title bar and select Properties. Select the Options tab (shown in Figure 30.2) and make the following settings:

- Under Edit Options, check all four boxes. Quick Edit Mode lets you select text simply by clicking and dragging the mouse cursor. Insert Mode inserts rather than overtypes characters by default when you backspace and type more into a command line. Enable Ctrl Key Shortcuts lets you use Ctrl+C and Ctrl+V to copy and paste and Ctrl+F to search for previous commands. Filter Clipboard Contents on Paste removes tabs from pasted text and turns "fancy" quotes and dash characters into their simple " and - equivalents.

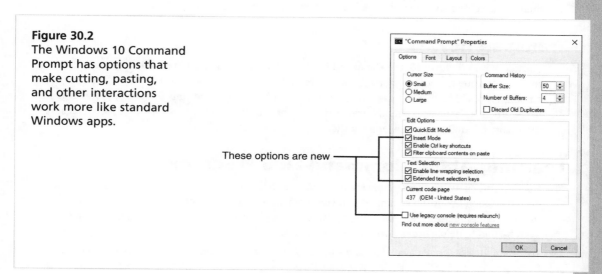

Figure 30.2
The Windows 10 Command Prompt has options that make cutting, pasting, and other interactions work more like standard Windows apps.

These options are new

- Under Text Selection, check both boxes. Enable Line Wrapping Selection makes the cursor select text the way it does in a word processor, wrapping from line to line rather than selecting a rect-angular region. (If you need to use the old rectangular mode, just hold down the Alt key while selecting text.) Extended Text Selection Keys enables a bunch of keyboard shortcuts that you can use to adjust the range of selected text before you copy it to the Clipboard.

- While you're at it, select the Layout tab and check Wrap Text Output on Resize. With this option checked, if text output in the console window wraps onto multiple lines, you can enlarge the window to untangle it.

The Extended Text Selection Keys option enables shortcuts such as Ctrl+A to select all text in the window, Ctrl+M to start "marking" (selecting) text at the cursor position, and Shift+End to extend the selection to the end of the current line. But there are *way* more new keyboard tricks than we can describe in our limited space here. If you're interested, click the Find Out More About New Console Features link at the bottom on the Options tab of the Properties page.

By the way, even with the new options enabled, the old meth-ods of copying and pasting still work. To paste text into the window at the cursor location the old way, you can right-click

> **note**
>
> If you use old console applica-tions or MS-DOS applications and they stop working correctly when you enable these new keyboard and mouse options, try disabling Quick Edit mode. If that doesn't help, check Use Legacy Console on the Options tab of the Prop-erties page. This makes Windows revert to the same console window code that it used in Windows XP through 8.1.

the window's title bar and then select Edit, Paste. Or you can use the keyboard: Press Alt+Spacebar and type **E P**.

To copy text from the window to the Clipboard the old way, right-click the window's title bar and select Edit, Mark. Alternatively, press Alt+Spacebar and type **E M**. Use the mouse to highlight an area of the screen and then press Enter. This copies the text to the Clipboard.

Transparency

Starting with Windows 10, the Command Prompt window can be made partially transparent so that you can see the contents of windows behind it. It's not everyone's cup of tea, but many system administrators have become used to this capability on the Linux and Unix operating systems and like it. To make a console window transparent, right-click its title bar and select Properties. Select the Colors tab and adjust the Opacity slider.

Learning About Command-Line Programs

How do you know what programs are available and how to use them? For that, you must turn to documentation about the command-line environment. For some reason, Microsoft no longer provides this information in the Help and Support system, but you can search online. Some programs can even be told to display their own usage information.

To get an idea of what's available, see Appendix B, "Command-Line Utilities," at the end of this book. And check out Brian's book *Windows 7 and Vista Guide to Scripting, Automation, and Command Line Tools*.

For a general online listing, perform the following Google search:

```
site:microsoft.com command line a-z windows server
```

At the time this was written, the search result titled "Command-Line Reference - TechNet - Microsoft" takes you to the command-line listing that covers several desktop and server versions of Windows. Most of the commands don't change from one version to the next.

Many commands display information about their arguments and syntax if you run them with the /? switch, like so:

```
dir /?
```

Running GUI Programs from the Command Line

Windows will start any program whose name it can find in the search path, whether it's a console application or a GUI program. If you know Windows programs by name, this capability can save you an awful lot of poking around and clicking with the mouse. Just type! Table 30.2 lists just a few GUI programs you can start by typing their name into a Command Prompt window or the Run dialog box (Windows Logo+R).

Table 30.2   Some GUI Program Names

Type	To Launch
explorer	File Explorer. At the Command Prompt, the command explorer opens a File Explorer view of the current directory, which can be especially useful.
lusrmgr.msc	Local Users and Groups
notepad	Windows Notepad
secpol.msc	Local Security Policy
taskschd	Task Scheduler
timedate.cpl	Time and Date (original Control Panel version)
wf	Windows Firewall with Advanced Security

In our books covering previous versions of Windows, I used to list many other program shortcuts, such as eventvwr.msc, to open Event Viewer. However, in Windows 10, the Windows Logo+X shortcut menu provides a much quicker path to most of the useful management tools.

There are also command-line shortcuts to the various Settings screens. Technically, these are Uniform Resource Identifiers (URIs). You can type the word **start** followed by one of these URIs on the command line or in a batch file, or use the URI as the target of a desktop shortcut icon. For example, the command start ms-settings:dateandtime opens the Date and Time settings panel. There are way too many to list here, but a few are listed in Table 30.3. You can find many more in Table 9.2 in Chapter 9, and a complete list by searching online for "ms-settings URI scheme reference."

 note

For those programs whose name ends with the .msc filename extension, you can omit the .msc when you type the name into a Command Prompt window. You must add .msc only when typing into the Run dialog box.

Table 30.3   URIs for Some Settings

URI	Corresponding Settings Page
ms-settings:	Settings home page
ms-settings:dateandtime	Date and time (new Settings version)
ms-settings:tabletmode	Tablet Mode
ms-settings:network-vpn	VPN connections

Setting Environment Variables

Environment variables are short, named text strings that Windows provides to each Windows and console program. Using environment variables is one of the ways in which Windows communicates information such as the location of system files and folders—as set up on your particular computer—to programs. Environment variables indicate where temporary files are stored, what folders contain Windows program files, and other settings that affect program operation and system performance. Also, they can be used in batch files to temporarily hold information about the job at hand.

In Windows 10, the initial environment variables provided to each program and Command Prompt window are configured using the GUI shown in Figure 30.3.

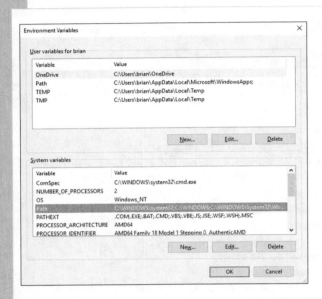

Figure 30.3
Examining the environment variables for the current user (top) and for all users of the system (bottom). The per-user list adds to or overrides the systemwide list.

This dialog box has two sections: System Variables and User Variables. The lower section, System Variables, defines the environment variables that are provided to each user account on the computer. The upper section, User Variables, defines additional default environment variables just for the current user account. They add to or override the variables set up in the systemwide list.

To open this dialog box, if you are signed in with a Computer Administrator account, use one of these methods:

- If you have a Command Prompt window open, type the command **sysdm.cpl** and press Enter. You might need to confirm a UAC prompt. Then select the Advanced tab and click the Environment Variables button.

- Alternatively, in the taskbar's search box, type **envir**, and then select either Edit Environment Variables for Your Account or Edit the System Environment Variables. (Then select the Environment Variables button.)

You can now edit both the upper User Variables (personal settings) and the lower System Variables (systemwide settings) lists.

If you are not signed in with an Computer Administrator account, the process is a bit trickier. Use either of these procedures:

- To edit the systemwide settings, you can use either of the preceding methods, but you'll have to select a Computer Administrator account and supply its password. *Don't* change the upper (personal) part of the dialog box; you will be changing settings for the wrong account.

- To edit your own personal environment variable list, use either of the preceding methods. You can edit just the upper (personal) environment variable list.

After you have the dialog box open, you can create new variables, delete variables, or highlight and edit existing variables using the corresponding buttons. The Environment Variable Edit dialog has been improved over previous versions of windows, and there are buttons that let you select the name of a folder or a file as the value of an environment variable. There is also a new way of editing a list of folder paths, as we will discuss in the following sections.

If you need to alter a variable, you must understand what happens if a conflict exists between environment variables defined in both the System Variables and the User Variables lists. As a rule, Windows examines several locations for definitions, and the last definition seen wins. Windows sets variables from the following sources, in this order:

1. The systemwide variable list.

2. The personal variable list. (At this step, the PATH variable is treated specially. See the next section for details.)

3. Commands set in `autoexec.nt`. (This applies only for MS-DOS or Windows 3.x applications. See "The MS-DOS Environment" later in the chapter for more information.)

4. Subsequent definitions issued by set commands typed in a Command Prompt window or encountered in a batch file. These changes apply only to that particular window instance and will disappear when the window is closed.

Setting the PATH Environment Variable

If you write batch files or scripts, it's useful to put them into one folder and to add this folder name to the PATH variable so that you can run your batch files and scripts simply by typing their names.

Because misediting the PATH variable can prevent Windows from finding applications it needs to run, Windows gives the PATH definition special treatment:

- For the PATH variable, the User Variables definition is appended to (added-on to) the System Variables definition.

- For all other environment variables, a User Variables definition *overrides* a System Variables definition.

In other words, you can enter your own personal folder(s) into the User Variables definition of PATH for your user account, without worrying about copying or messing up the system definitions.

To create a folder for your own scripts and batch files, use one of these two procedures:

- If you want to use the scripts and batch files only for your own use, create a folder and put the full path to the folder into your personal PATH variable. For example, create a folder named c:\scripts.

  Then add a variable named PATH to the upper part of the Environment Variables dialog box (refer to Figure 30.3) with the value c:\scripts. If you need to add more than one folder to your personal PATH, see the following section.

- If you want to create scripts and batch files that can be used by anyone who uses your computer, create a folder and be sure that its permissions are set so that all users can read it.

  For example, create a folder named c:\scripts. Right-click the folder, select Properties, and select the Security tab. If Users does not appear under Group or User Names, click Edit, click Add, and then add Users to the list. Be sure that the Read & Execute permission setting is checked.

  ➡ *To learn more about editing permissions,* **see** *"Setting Security Permissions on Files and Folders," p. 732.*

  Then select the PATH variable in the lower part of the Environment Variables dialog box (shown in Figure 30.3) and select Edit. Add a new entry to the list with the folder name c:\scripts. We tell you how to do this in the next section.

The next time you open a new Command Prompt window, your folder will be part of the PATH, and you will be able to run your batch files and scripts by typing their name.

Editing Path Lists

Some environment variables, such as PATH, may need to list more than one folder name. In this case, Windows expects the folder names to be separated by semicolon (;) characters. When an environment variable value contains what appears to be a list of folder names in this format, the Environment Variable Edit dialog lists the folder paths separately, as shown in Figure 30.4. This is a recent improvement.

In this view, you can select an individual path name in the list and use buttons to move the entry up or down in the list, or delete, replace, or edit it.

Adding a new entry to the list is somewhat tricky due to a bug in this new interface. Here's how to do it: Click New, and then type the letter x. (This is necessary so that the new entry contains at least something.) Then click the Browse button, and locate the actual folder that you wish to add to the path list. Click OK to record the path name. You may now use Move Up or Move Down to change the new item's order in the list if you wish. Finally, click OK to save the change.

By the way, this improved way of editing a path list is only provided when the variable you're editing has at least two folder names in it already. To add a *second* folder name to a variable, you must edit it and type in the semicolon and the second path name yourself. For example, you might set your personal PATH variable to c:\scripts;c:\testing. Once you've saved this, the next time you edit it, you'll get the list view.

And, if you're in the new list editor, you can edit a list the old way, where the full list of paths appears separated by semicolons, by clicking Edit Text.

Figure 30.4
If you edit an environment variable that contains a list of path names, the new editing dialog lets you easily edit and organize the list.

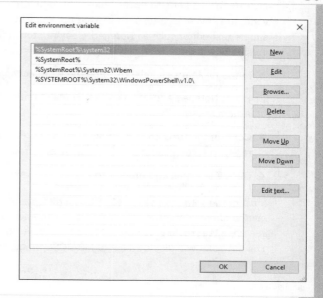

The MS-DOS Environment

If you still use MS-DOS programs, you'll be glad to know that the 32-bit x86 processor versions of Windows 10 still support these programs.

The 32-bit versions of Windows run MS-DOS applications inside a program called ntvdm, which stands for *Windows NT Virtual DOS Machine*. Ntvdm is also used by the Windows 3.x support environment. It simulates the environment that DOS programs expect and makes them work correctly under Windows. Ntvdm runs automatically when you attempt to start an MS-DOS or 16-bit Windows program.

Editing Advanced Settings for a DOS Application

If you're experiencing difficulties while running a specific DOS program, find the program file or a shortcut to it. Right-click it and choose Properties.

Poke through each tab and use the ? (question mark) button for help on the settings. Educational and game programs often require you to adjust the Memory and Compatibility settings.

You can choose to further configure the MS-DOS and Windows 3.x environment by modifying Windows 10's equivalent of the old

 note

The MS-DOS and 16-bit Windows subsystems are not provided with ARM processor or 64-bit versions of Windows. (It's a technical limitation, not a marketing decision.) If you use a 64-bit version of Windows and still need to run MS-DOS or Windows 3.1 applications, you can set up a virtual machine; install a copy of MS-DOS, Windows 3.1, or a 32-bit version of Windows on it; and run your older applications inside the simulated environment. We address this issue in Appendix A, "Virtualization."

CONFIG.SYS and AUTOEXEC.BAT files. These files, called config.nt and autoexec.nt, are used to configure ntvdm each time it's started up. You can edit the config.nt and autoexec.nt files with a simple text editor such as Notepad. They're protected files, however, so you must run an elevated version of Notepad using this procedure:

1. In the taskbar's search box, type the word **notepad**.

2. When Notepad appears as a search result under Apps, right-click it and select Run As Administrator.

3. Confirm the UAC prompt, or enter a Computer Administrator password as requested. (Alternatively, you can just type notepad in an elevated Command Prompt window.)

4. Click File, Open and browse to \windows\system32. Select autoexec.nt or config.nt as desired.

Most of the settings used in MS-DOS 6 still work in config.nt, with some exceptions. For more information about configuring the MS-DOS environment in Windows, go to google.com and enter this search: **site:technet.microsoft.com windows xp devicehigh**. Select the result titled Devicehigh. The left pane will display a list of MS-DOS configuration commands.

---

 note

On 32-bit x86 versions of Windows 10, the first time you try to run a DOS or Windows 3.1 program, Windows will prompt you to install ntvdm, which is a system component that lets you run these 16-bit apps inside Windows. There is also a Control Panel applet that lets you turn the 16-bit support subsystem on or off. Search Control Panel for 16-bit Application Support. The Registry value that controls the subsystem is DisallowedPolicyDefault, in key HKEY_LOCAL_MACHINE\System\CurrentControlSet\Control\WOW. On a corporate network, the network administrator may permanently enable or disable the subsystem through Group Policy.

Issues with ANSI.SYS and DOSKEY

The MS-DOS enhancement ANSI.SYS was used to let programs move the cursor around on the screen. Starting with Windows 10 Build 10540, ANSI support is now available by default for 32-bit and 64-bit Windows console applications in Command Prompt windows, if you're using the default new console and not the legacy console. If your 16-bit MS-DOS applications display unexpected characters on the screen, you might need to install the old MS-DOS driver. Edit config.nt and add the line device=ansi.sys.

On the other hand, DOSKEY—which has been enhanced significantly from the old DOS days—functions only in the 32-bit or 64-bit Windows console environment, and even if you attempt to load it in autoexec.nt, it does not function within the MS-DOS COMMAND.COM shell.

 tip

If you use MS-DOS applications, it's a good idea to edit config.nt and change the line files=40 to files=100. Most of the MS-DOS applications that are still useful today require more than the paltry default allowance of open files, and the memory use to support more is no longer a worry.

Printing from MS-DOS Applications

Most DOS applications can print only to LPT ports. If you want to use a printer that is on a USB port or is out there somewhere on a LAN, you must share the printer (even if it's just attached to your own computer and you're not using a network) and then issue the command

```
net use lpt2: \\localhost\sharename
```

from the Command Prompt window, replacing *sharename* with the name you used when you shared the printer. Direct your DOS program to use LPT2. (You can use LPT1, LPT2, or LPT3, but you must select an LPT port number that does not have an associated physical LPT port in your computer.) Some MS-DOS applications know how to send output directly to networked printers using a UNC share name, so you don't need to use the LPT trick with them.

 note

If you make changes to autoexec.nt or config.nt after having run an MS-DOS program from a Command Prompt window, you must close the Command Prompt window and open a new one for the MS-DOS subsystem to reload and take on the new configuration.

For more information about the net use *command*, **see** *"Managing Network Resources Using the Command Line," **p. 473.***

Batch Files

Although Windows Script Host and Windows PowerShell are more powerful tools for creating your own scripts, it's also useful to know how to use the batch file language. Batch files let you take advantage of the many command-line programs supplied with Windows.

A batch file, at the simplest level, is just a list of Command Prompt commands that have been typed into a file whose extension is .bat or .cmd. When you enter the name of a batch file at the Command Prompt, Windows looks for a file with this name in the current directory and in the folders of the PATH environment variable. Windows treats the lines in the batch file as commands, and runs them one after the other as if you had typed the commands by hand. At this simplest level, a batch file can be a big help if you find yourself typing the same commands over and over.

Beyond this, there are several commands that you can use to write rudimentary programs within a batch file so that it can take different actions depending on what you type on the command line, or depending on the results of the commands it executes. These programming commands have been greatly improved since the MS-DOS days, so writing useful batch files on Windows 10 is much easier now. In particular, the IF and FOR statements have been greatly extended. You can prompt the user for input. It's possible to manipulate strings and filenames and perform arithmetic calculations. You can create subroutines within a single batch file. And there's more.

Unfortunately, we don't have room to provide coverage of batch file programming in this book, but check out *Windows 7 and Vista Guide to Scripting, Automation, and Command Line Tools*, written by yours truly and published by Que.

Some Microsoft documentation is also available online. After reading this chapter, go to www.microsoft.com and search for these phrases:

```
Command Shell Overview
Environment Variables
Using Batch Parameters
Using Batch Files
Using Command Redirection Operators
Cmd
Command-Line Reference
```

Then open a Command Prompt window and type the commands

```
help cmd
help set
help for
help if
```

and so on.

Batch File Tips

Table 30.4 lists several short batch files that I put on every computer that I use. These short command scripts let me edit files, change the path, view a folder with File Explorer, and so on, simply by typing a couple of letters followed by a folder or filename. They don't involve fancy programming, but they save me a significant amount of time when I'm working with the Command Prompt window.

 tip

To learn how to get the most from the batch files and the command line, get Brian's book *Windows 7 and Vista Guide to Scripting, Automation, and Command Line Tools*. The content applies to Windows 10.

Table 30.4   Useful Tiny Batch Files

Filename	Contents and Purpose
ap.bat	`@echo off`
	`for %%p in (%path%) do if /%%p/ == /%1/ goto :EOF`
	`set path=%1;%path%`
	Adds the named folder to the PATH if it is not already listed. (This lasts only as long as the Command Prompt window is open.)
	Example: `ap c:\test`
bye.bat	`@logout`
	Logs off Windows.
	Example: `bye`
e.bat	`@if /%1/ == // (explorer /e,.) else explorer /e,%1`
	Opens File Explorer in Folder mode to view the named directory, or the current directory if no path is entered on the command line.
	Example: `e d:`

Filename	Contents and Purpose
h.bat	`@cd /d %userprofile%` Changes the current directory to your user profile (home) directory. Example: h
n.bat	`@start notepad %1` Edits the named file with Notepad. Example: n test.bat
s.bat	`@cd /d c:\scripts` Makes c:\scripts the current directory, when you want to add or edit batch files and scripts. Example: s

If you create a c:\scripts folder and add it to the PATH, as discussed earlier under "Setting the PATH Environment Variable," you might want to create these same batch files in that folder for your own use.

Windows Script Host

Batch files, which were discussed in the previous section, are great at performing a simple sequence of steps. But it's not always easy to write a batch file for a task that involves decision making, where you have to perform different actions under different circumstances, or when you need to do math or manipulate text and other data. For more complex tasks, there is a more powerful tool called Windows Script Host (WSH).

Scripts written for WSH can massage, digest, and manipulate text files and data, view and change Windows settings, and more. Scripts have an advantage over batch files in that they can perform complex calculations and can manipulate text information in powerful ways because you write them in a full-featured programming language. Also, scripts can send email, manipulate files and folders, and even enlist applications such as Microsoft Word and Excel to present information in tidy, formatted documents and charts.

The "Host" part of the tool's name comes from the fact that it provides a structure for running scripts written in several different programming languages. Windows comes with built-in support for two different scripting languages:

- **VBScript**—Nearly identical to the Visual Basic for Applications (VBA) macro language used in Word and Excel.

- **JScript**—Microsoft's version of the JavaScript language, which is widely used to make web pages interactive. (JavaScript, by the way, is not the same thing as Java. Java is another programming language altogether.)

Also, you can download and install scripting support for other languages. If you have a Unix or Linux background, for example, you might want to use the Perl, Python, or TCL scripting languages. You can get free WSH-compatible versions of these languages at www.activestate.com.

If you are already versed in one of the scripting languages mentioned here, by all means, use it. If you don't already know a scripting language, VBScript is probably the best one to start with because you can also use it to write macros for Microsoft's desktop applications. We use VBScript in the examples in this section.

Some Sample Scripts

We don't have room here to give you even an introductory course in VBScript programming. As mentioned, that topic can fill an entire book. What we can do is give you some examples of how WSH can be used to perform useful tasks and to manage Windows. These sample scripts assume that you have set the default script environment to console mode, as opposed to windowed mode, by typing this command just once in an elevated Command Prompt window:

```
cscript //h:cscript //nologo //s
```

➤ For instructions on opening an elevated Command Prompt window, **see** "Running Commands with Elevated Privileges," p. 673.

Disk and Network Management

WSH comes with tools to examine and modify drives, folders, and files. Here is an example of a VBScript script that performs a reasonably useful task: It displays the amount of free space on each of your computer's drives.

```
set fso = CreateObject("Scripting.FileSystemObject")
set drivelist = fso.Drives
for each drv in drivelist
  if drv.IsReady then
    wscript.echo "Drive", drv.DriveLetter, "has", drv.FreeSpace, "bytes free"
  end if
next
```

Type this script into a file named freespace.vbs in your batch file directory, and then type the command-line command **freespace**. On my computer, this prints the following:

```
Drive C: has 15866540032 bytes free
Drive D: has 27937067008 bytes free
Drive F: has 335872000 bytes free
Drive H: has 460791808 bytes free
```

WSH can also work with networking features. The following VBScript script displays your computer's current network drive mappings:

```
set wshNetwork = CreateObject("WScript.Network") ' create the helper object
set maps = wshNetwork.EnumNetworkDrives          ' collection describes mapped drives
for i = 0 to maps.Length-2 step 2                 ' step through collection by twos
  wscript.echo "Drive", maps.item(i), "is mapped to", maps.item(i+1)
next
```

Windows Management Instrumentation

Windows Management Instrumentation (WMI) is a system service that provides access to virtually every aspect of a Windows computer system, from the hardware components up to the highest-level system services.

The following script lists the status of each system service installed on your computer. This script file can be named showservices.vbs. (The underscores at the end of some of the lines are part of the script.)

```
set services = GetObject("winmgmts:{impersonationlevel=impersonate," & _
    "authenticationlevel=pkt}!" & _
    "/root/CIMV2:Win32_Service")        ' get services WMI info
for each svc in services.Instances_     ' display information for each service
  wscript.echo svc.name, "State:", svc.State, "Startup:", svc.StartMode
next
```

On my computer, the first few lines of output from this script look like this:

```
AJRouter State: Stopped Startup: Manual
ALG State: Stopped Startup: Manual
AppIDSvc State: Stopped Startup: Manual
```

Remember, too, that because these are command-line programs, you can redirect the output of these scripts into a file. The following command puts the service list into the file listing.txt, which you could then view and edit with Notepad:

```
showservices >listing.txt
```

Windows PowerShell

Not satisfied with the programming power provided by Windows Script Host, Microsoft went on to create yet another scripting and management tool called Windows PowerShell (WPS), which debuted in Windows 7. In many ways, WPS looks and acts like the familiar Command Prompt window, but it's actually a very strange animal, and it gives you access to some powerful programming tools. We don't have room in this book to teach you much about it, but we do describe how it differs from batch files and scripts, and we point you to resources that will help you learn more.

We used the word *strange*. Can a computer program be strange? Definitely! For one thing, it's object-oriented. Most Windows PowerShell commands (which are properly called *cmdlets*) generate streams of *objects*, not text. Objects are computer representations of real-world things. They have *properties* that describe attributes of the things they represent and *methods* that let you manipulate the things. For example, an object that represents a specific file on your hard disk might have properties such as Name, Size, and LastWriteTime, as well as methods such as Delete, Edit, and Open. Windows PowerShell works with objects in an unusual, and ultimately very powerful, way.

If you type **dir** in a regular Command Prompt window, the command shell generates a bunch of text listing the current folder's files by name. The dir command is programmed very specifically to print information about files in text form. That's all it can do.

In WPS, typing **dir** also prints out a list of filenames, but something completely different happens behind the scenes. In WPS, dir is a shortcut for the Get-Childitem cmdlet, which in its simplest use generates a stream of File objects; each object represents one of the files in a folder, and each object has properties and methods (for example, name and size). When an object (of any sort) lands in the WPS prompt window, WPS prints out a line of text listing the object's most important properties. For a File object, this includes the file's name, size, and the date it was created. So, when you type dir, WPS produces a stream of File objects, and they end up as a nice, tabular listing of files, as shown in Figure 30.5.

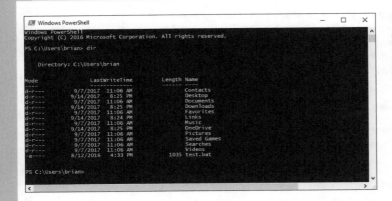

Figure 30.5
As its name suggests, Windows PowerShell provides extremely powerful object-oriented commands and scripting tools.

The result is the same as in the old Command Prompt environment, but it's happening in a general, more abstract way. The cmdlet doesn't know about or care about text or formatting; it simply spits out a bunch of File objects. And the WPS window will turn any list of objects into a nice tabular listing. That includes files, user accounts, hard drives, Windows services—whatever.

Also, WPS includes a full-scale object-oriented programming language and has access to Microsoft's .NET programming platform, which means WPS scripts can perform complex computations and communicate with other computers and networked (cloud) services.

To open WPS and try it yourself, you can use any of the following methods:

- In the taskbar's search box, type **powershell** and then select Windows Powershell from the search results.

- Press Windows Logo+R, type **powershell**, and press Enter.

- In a Command Prompt window, type **powershell** and press Enter. When starting this way, you can type **exit** to return to the normal Command Prompt environment.

The PowerShell window appears as shown in Figure 30.5.

You can also choose to have Windows PowerShell appear on the handy Windows Logo+X pop-up menu.

➡️ *To put Windows PowerShell in the pop-up menu instead of Command Prompt,* **see** *"Command-Line Access from the Power User Menu," p. 673.*

WPS lets you do complex things with objects right in a command line, without writing scripts or programming. You can use the familiar | (pipe) symbol to direct streams of objects from one cmdlet to another, and this lets you do very complex, specific things with tools that are separately very simple and general-purpose in nature. For example, the following command will list all files in the current folder that are more than six months old:

```
dir | where-object { $_.LastWriteTime -lt (get-date).addmonths(-6)}
```

This command looks complex at first, but it's not so bad. This command line strings two cmdlets together:

- `dir`—Spits out a list of all the File objects in the current directory. Here, they don't land in the WPS command window, so they don't make a text listing. Instead, the pipe (|) symbol instructs WPS to pass the objects to the next command.

- `where-object`—Passes just some of the objects through, based on the filtering condition inside the curly brackets. In this example, it passes through only those files that have not been changed for more than six months (that is, whose `LastWriteTime` value is less than the date/time six months back). So only the objects representing old files are passed on.

 caution

The filtered file objects spill out into the WPS window, where they are printed out as a nicely formatted list. If you were, say, cleaning out a temporary or log file folder, you could extend this command to delete all the old files it found:

```
dir | where-object
{ $_.LastWriteTime -lt
(get-date).addmonths(-6)}
| remove-item
```

In this version of the command, `where-object` passes file objects to `remove-item`, which deletes the files. Please don't just type this command to try it out, however, because you might inadvertently delete important Windows files in your profile folder!

As we said earlier, you're not limited to using commands that you type into the WPS window. WPS has a full-scale programming language with variables, loops, subroutines, user-defined objects, and so on. You can use these at the Command Prompt or in script files. You also can create shortcuts (called *aliases*) for commonly used commands and scripts to make typing easier, and a bunch of aliases are predefined for you.

tip

If you write your own script files, you should know that, by default, Windows has a security setting that prevents the running of unsigned PowerShell scripts. (Signing is a way of digitally proving who created the script and requires the purchase of a code-signing certificate). To override this restriction, click Start, Settings, Update & Security, For Developers. Scroll down to the PowerShell section, check Change Execution Policy, and then click Apply.

For more information about WPS, check out Brian's book *Windows 7 and Vista Guide to Scripting, Automation, and Command Line Tools* or the Sams book *Windows PowerShell Unleashed*, Second Edition.

The Windows Subsystem for Linux

In Windows 10 Build 14316 and later, and for 64-bit versions only, yet another command-line environment is available: The Windows Subsystem for Linux (WSL), which includes the bash command-line shell and many associated software development and utility programs. With WSL, Windows can run command-line executable programs that were compiled and linked for the Linux environment (specifically, the Ubuntu, OpenSUSE or SUSE Linux Enterprise Server distributions, with more likely on the way).

In Windows, the term *subsystem* indicates a program execution environment that mimics a "foreign" operating system so completely that programs built (compiled and linked) for the other operating system can run directly, within Windows, without using a virtual machine environment. For example, as we discussed earlier in this chapter, all 32-bit versions of Windows include subsystems to run MS-DOS and 16-bit Windows programs directly. 64-bit versions of Windows use a subsystem to run 32-bit Windows programs. (Some older versions of Windows supported subsystems—no longer available—to run OS/2 and Posix UNIX applications.)

WSL is the newest such tool, and while it's esoteric, if you're a UNIX or Linux fan, its arrival is exciting news. WSL is meant to make life easier for software developers who have to write, test, or deploy programs on multiple platforms, such as Windows, Linux, Microsoft Azure, and so on, by giving you access to the same, best tools from both Windows and Linux, on the same desktop, at the same time. While it's aimed at developers and testers and isn't really intended to be a general-purpose Windows scripting and automation tool, with some effort it can be.

We don't have room to describe it in detail here, but we can give you a brief overview. WSL mimics an almost complete implementation of the Ubuntu or SUSE Linux command-line environment and includes many Linux applications, such as bash, a command-line shell, ssh and scp Secure Shell clients, git, a source code management tool, and apt-get, a Linux package installer. With apt-get, you can download and install any of thousands of common Linux command-line applications, libraries, and development packages, such as the gcc compiler suite.

In addition, the Windows console window environment has been enhanced to better support ANSI cursor control and color coding escape sequences, so Linux applications such as vim work correctly.

At the time this was written, WSL has some limitations that you should be aware of:

- It supports Linux command-line applications only, not X Window graphical applications. (You could conceivably run a Windows-based X Server on your computer and have Linux applications connect to that, but configuration can be difficult.)

- Not all Linux system calls and ioctls are fully (or correctly) implemented. For example, applications that attempt to access low-level network drivers might fail. However, WSL is under active development, and compatibility issues are being addressed.

- Each Windows user who uses WSL gets a private, completely independent copy of the WSL filesystem and all application files the first time they run bash. The Linux environment is installed in a simulated Unix filesystem whose files reside in your user profile under %userprofile%\ AppData\Local\lxss. Linux applications run chrooted in rootfs in that folder and see a fully Linux-compatible file system.

- To Linux applications, the drives on which your computer's Windows files reside appear under /mnt, so Linux applications can reach outside the chroot jail through that path. (This also means: If you try to gzip, copy, or otherwise archive your WSL filesystem, be sure to exclude /mnt, or you'll capture the contents of every drive on your computer.)

- Problems can occur if Linux applications try to work with files in the Windows file system (through the folders they see under /mnt) or if Windows applications try to access Linux files under %userprofile%\AppData\Local\lxss. Besides the difference in text file line endings (CR+LF for Windows, LF-only for Linux), Linux applications expect a file system with full case-sensitivity, where, for example, makefile and Makefile are distinct files. For Windows applications, and for Linux applications working below /mnt, filenames are case-preserving but not case-sensitive, and this can lead to problems when there are files whose names differ only by case. Furthermore, if you write to the Linux file tree from a Windows application, Linux file attributes and permissions might be lost, causing problems within the Linux subsystem.

- In your Linux filesystem, your user account has root permissions inside WSL. This presents a security risk. Windows malware or Linux malware could modify or replace programs in your Linux filesystem, and you could then inadvertently run these modified programs.

At the time this was written, WSL is still a beta-quality product, but it's under vigorous, active development.

To install WSL, follow these steps:

1. The WSL app has to be installed on an internal hard drive, not removable media. If you previously changed the default location for app storage, open the Settings app and search for Change Where New Content Is Saved. Be sure that New Apps Will Save To is set to an internal hard drive such as This PC (C:).

2. Search the taskbar for Settings for Turn Windows Features On or Off, or run optionalfeatures from the command line or Windows Logo+R dialog. Check Windows Subsystem for Linux and select OK. (Prior to the Creator's Update version, it was necessary to enable Developer's Mode to see this option. This is no longer required.)

3. When the feature has been installed and Windows has restarted, open the Store app and search for WSL, or visit https://aka.ms/wslstore in your browser. Select one of the available Linux distributions and click Get to install it. Then, when a notification appears that the app has been installed, click Launch. This creates a copy of the distribution's file system in your user profile.

4. At the end of the installation process, you will need to enter a username and password for your Linux user account. It will have administrator rights (via sudo) *within* the Linux environment. You don't need to use the same username and password that you use for Windows; in fact, you probably shouldn't, because the password will be stored in the Linux file system, and even though it's encrypted, it's an unnecessary security risk to have your windows credentials made available. When you start a Linux process, this account will be signed in automatically. You should need to supply it only if you perform administrative actions with sudo.

Henceforth, if you have only one Linux distribution installed, you can run bash in a Command Prompt window or using Windows Logo+R. (If you install multiple Linux distributions, you should launch the specific distribution using its Start menu tile or command-line name, for example, ubuntu or open.

A large number of programs are installed with WSL distributions. Ubuntu includes utilities like ssh, apt-get, grep, awk, and sed; text editors vim and nano; text formatters tbl, eqn, and groff (with LaTeX just an apt-get away); and much more.

The Linux command-line environment is very similar to the Windows environment, because both trace their roots to the UNIX operating system. You should know that its keyboard shortcuts are quite different from Windows'. Here are a few items that may trip you up:

- Ctrl+C kills the current program.

- Ctrl+D indicates "End of File" and terminates input to command-line programs reading from the standard input (console).

- Ctrl+S halts output to the console window. Type Ctrl+Q to resume. (A better way to manage a flurry of output is to pipe a program's output through more or less.)

- Ctrl+Z "freezes" the current program and returns you to the command prompt. The program is still there, suspended. To resume where you left off, type the command **fg**.

To terminate bash and return to the Windows Command Prompt, press Ctrl+D or type **exit**.

Task Scheduler

Windows Task Scheduler is an automation tool that lets you specify programs to be run automatically at specified dates and times and on certain events, such as system startup, users logging on, and even the occurrence of any event that can be logged in the Event Viewer.

What kinds of tasks would you run with Task Scheduler? As mentioned, the tasks need to run without user interaction. So they are typically maintenance tasks, such as defragmenting the hard disk, cleaning out temporary files, and so on. Windows uses Task Scheduler for this very purpose, and you'll notice that several preinstalled scheduled tasks are set up when Windows is installed to do this very sort of thing.

Task Scheduler is especially useful with batch files and scripts because these scheduled programs can usually be designed to run without any user interaction. It's truly the ultimate automation tool because you don't even have to be there when it's working!

 note

When Task Scheduler runs a task as a different user than the one currently logged on, the logged-on user cannot see or interact with the program. Be sure that scheduled tasks can operate without user input and exit cleanly when they've done their work. And keep in mind that once an application or service is running, even if it was launched through a scheduled task, it will affect system performance just as if you started it manually.

note

Obviously, the computer must be alive to run a task, so if you expect it to do a disk cleanup at 4:00 a.m., be sure to leave the computer on. If a scheduled task is missed because the computer was turned off, Windows will perform the task the next time the computer is started but the task will now be running while you're using the computer, which is probably what you were trying to avoid by scheduling it to run at night.

There are several ways to open the Task Scheduler:

- Click in the taskbar's search box and type **tasks**. Then select Task Scheduler from the search results.

- Press Windows Logo+R, type **taskschd.msc**, and then press Enter.

- At the Command Prompt, type **taskschd** and press Enter.

Then, in the left pane, select Task Scheduler Library.

You can create two types of tasks in Task Scheduler:

- **Basic tasks**—Designed to be run using the current user's account and to support a single triggering event or time.

- **Tasks**—Can be run using any specified user account and can be configured to run whether or not the user is logged in. Tasks can also be run in Windows XP or Windows Server 2003 compatibility mode and can be configured to run with elevated priority if necessary.

To create a Basic task in Task Scheduler, follow these steps:

1. Open Task Scheduler as discussed earlier in this section. In the top-center pane, Task Scheduler displays a summary list of tasks that started or completed during the last 24 hours and displays a list of active tasks below that. (Here, *active* means "defined and enabled to run at the specified time or event." It doesn't necessarily mean "actively running right now.")

2. The Actions pane is located on the right side. Click Create Basic Task. The Create Basic Task Wizard opens.

3. Enter the name of the task and a description. Enter whatever you want, to remind you of what the task does. Click Next to continue.

4. On the Task Trigger screen, select when to run the task. You can choose daily, weekly, monthly, one time, when the computer starts, when you log on, or when a specific event is logged.

   You can use the When a Specific Event Is Logged option to trigger the task when a specific Event Log entry is recorded. For example, you could use this to perform some sort of notification if a disk error event occurs. You'll need to enter the event's numeric ID number. (To find an event's ID number, find an occurrence of the event in the Windows Event Log.)

5. Click Next.

6. If you chose Daily, Weekly, Monthly, or One Time, you are asked when to perform the task. Specify applicable time options, such as time of day, as required. Click Next.

7. Select what action you want the task to do (start a program, send an email, or display a message). Click Next to continue.

8. If you selected Start a Program, use Browse to locate the program, batch file, or script. (For Windows applications, browse in the \Windows or \Windows\system32 folders. For third-party applications, search in the \Program Files folders. For scripts you've written yourself, browse to the folder in which you've stored the script or batch file.) Then provide any necessary command-line switches or settings, as shown in Figure 30.6, and if you want to specify a default drive and folder for the program, enter the path to the desired folder.

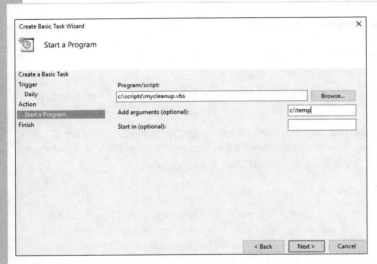

Figure 30.6
Completing the configuration of a basic task.

If you selected Send an Email, enter the information for sender, receiver, SMTP email server, message, and so forth.

If you selected Display a Message, enter the message title and message text. Then click Next.

 tip

If you're scheduling a Windows Script Host script, remember that you will most likely not be present when it runs, so you won't be there to clear any message boxes that it displays. Be sure either to set cscript as the default script processor, rather than wscript, so that wscript.echo statements don't display message boxes, or be careful not to use wscript.echo, MessageBox(), or InputBox(). To change the default script processor, type the command **cscript //h:cscript** in an elevated Command Prompt window. Alternatively, use cscript.exe as the scheduled command, and put the full path and name of the script file, in quotation marks, as the first argument.

9. Review the task on the Summary screen. If you want to set advanced options such as idle time, what to do if the computer is running on batteries, and what to do after the task completes, check Open the Properties Dialog for This Task When I Click Finish. Click Finish to complete the task.

For more advanced scheduling, use the Create Task selection. The Create Task interface uses a multitabbed interface instead of a wizard. The General tab includes security options, whereas the Triggers tab permits you to specify multiple triggers for a task. (The task will be performed whenever *any* of the triggers occurs.) The Actions tab supports multiple actions in a task; the Conditions tab includes options to configure idle time, power, and network connection requirements; and the Settings tab supports conditions for running and stopping a task. Use Create Task, rather than Create Basic Task, when you need these additional settings in your task.

A Task Scheduler Conundrum

If you change the name of your computer, Scheduled Tasks might display this message: "An error has occurred for task *xxxx*. Error message: The specified account name is not valid." However, the problem task won't appear in the list of tasks, so you can't do anything about it. This happens to any scheduled task that was associated with a specific user account as the logon trigger, as the user credential for the task, and so on. The same thing happens if you delete a user account that was named in a Scheduled Task. To fix the problem, follow these steps:

1. Open File Explorer and browse to `c:\windows\system32\tasks`. You must approve a prompt to get permission to access this folder. It contains an XML text file for each scheduled task.

2. Delete the files for any broken tasks that you simply want to delete.

3. To repair a broken task, move the file for the broken task entry from `\windows\system32\tasks` into another folder. You must *move* it, not *copy* it. You can do this by using File Explorer or the move command in a Command Prompt window.

4. Open the task file in its new location using Notepad. Fix the computer name and/or account name wherever it occurs, and save the file. Repeat steps 3 and 4 for any other problem tasks.

5. Open Scheduled Tasks or, if it's already open, select Action, Refresh. There should be no error messages now because the problem tasks were removed.

6. Under the Action menu, use the Import command to locate and import the edited task file. This restores the scheduled task. Repeat this step for any other edited task files.

PROTECTING WINDOWS FROM VIRUSES AND SPYWARE

Avoiding Viruses and Spyware: The Basics

Let's begin with a look at protecting your PC from direct attacks: that is when an unauthorized *cracker* (which we define as a hacker who has succumbed to the Dark Side of the Force) sits down at your keyboard and tries to gain access to your system. Sure, it may be unlikely that a malicious user would gain physical access to the computer in your home or office, but it's not impossible.

Crackers specialize in breaking into systems ("cracking" system security, hence the name), and at any given time, hundreds (perhaps even thousands) of crackers roam cyberspace looking for potential targets. If you're online right now, the restless and far-seeing eyes of the crackers are bound to find you eventually.

Sounds unlikely, you say? You wish. The crackers are armed with programs that automatically search through millions of IP addresses (the addresses that uniquely identify any computer or device connected to the Internet). The crackers are specifically looking for computers that aren't secure, and if they find one, they'll pounce on it and crack their way into the system.

Again, if all this sounds unlikely or that it would take them forever to find you, think again. Tests have shown that new and completely unprotected systems routinely get cracked within 20 minutes of connecting to the Internet!

First, a Few Simple Precautions

So how do you thwart the world's crackers? We often joke that it's easy if you follow a simple five-prong plan:

- Don't connect to the Internet. Ever.

- Don't install programs on your computer. No, not even that one.

- Don't insert any media or connect any hardware to your computer. Definitely no DVDs, CDs, or USB drives. Keyboards and mice are dicey as well.

- Don't let anyone else work with, touch, glance at, talk about, or come within 20 feet of your computer.

- Burglar-proof your home or office.

The point here is that if you use your computer (and live your life) in an even remotely normal way, you open up your machine to security risks. That's a bleak assessment, for sure, but fortunately it doesn't take a lot of effort on your part to turn your computer into a maximum-security area. The security techniques in this chapter (and the next three chapters) will get to that goal, but first make sure you've nailed down the basics:

- **Leave User Account Control (UAC) turned on**—Yes, we know UAC is a hassle, but if you're coming to Windows 10 from Windows Vista, you'll find that it's way better now because it doesn't get in your face nearly as often. UAC is the best thing that's happened to Windows security in a long time, and it's a fact of life that your computer is much more secure when UAC has got your back. See "Making Sure User Account Control Is Turned On," later in this chapter.

- **Be paranoid**—The belief that everyone's out to get you may be a sign of trouble in the real world, but it's just common sense in the computer world. Assume someone will sit down at your desk when you're not around; assume someone will try to log on to your computer when you leave for the night; assume all uninvited email attachments are viruses; assume unknown websites are malicious; assume any offer that sounds too good to be true probably is.

- **Keep to yourself**—We all share lots of personal info online these days, but there's sharing and then there's asking-for-trouble sharing. Don't tell anybody any of your passwords. Don't put your email address online unless it's disguised in some way (for example, by writing it as "*username* at *yourdomain* dot com"). Don't give out sensitive personal data such as your Social Security number, bank account number, or even your address and phone number (unless making a purchase with a reputable vendor). Only give your credit card data to online vendors you trust implicitly; even better, get a secure PayPal account and use that instead.

- **Test the firewall**—A firewall's not much good if it leaves your computer vulnerable to attack, so you should test the

 note

To access the router setup pages, open a web browser, type the router address, and then press Enter. See your device documentation for the correct URL, but for most routers the address is http://192.168.1.1, http://192.168.0.1, or http://192.168.1.254. In most cases, you must log in with a username and password, so, again, see your documentation.

firewall to make sure it's doing its job. We show you several ways to do this in Chapter 33, "Protecting Your Network from Hackers and Snoops."

➡️ *For the details on using Windows Defender Firewall,* **see** *"Configuring Windows Defender Firewall," p. 775.*

- **Take advantage of your router's firewall, too**—Why have one line of defense when in all probability you can have two? If your network has a router and that router connects to the Internet, then it, too, has an IP address that crackers can scan for vulnerabilities, particularly holes that expose your network. To prevent this, most routers come with built-in hardware firewalls that provide robust security. Access your router's setup pages, locate the firewall settings (see Figure 31.1 for an example), and then make sure the firewall is turned on.

Figure 31.1
If your network has a router, make sure its firewall is turned on.

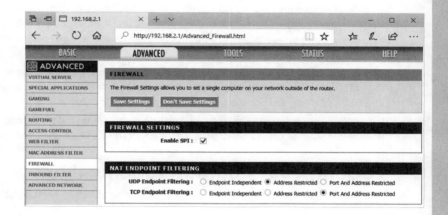

- **Update, update, update**—Many crackers take advantage of known Windows vulnerabilities to compromise a system. To avoid this, keep your PC updated with the latest patches, fixes, and service packs, for Windows and for *every* app you install. Most updates are designed to plug security leaks.

➡️ *To learn more about keeping your PC updated,* **see** *"Configuring and Managing Windows Update," p. 611.*

- **Beware attachments**—Never open an email attachment that comes from someone you don't know. Even if you know the sender, check the message: If it's vague or extremely short (or just doesn't sound like the sender), you should be immediately suspicious about the attachment. Otherwise, if the attachment isn't something you're expecting, assume that the sender's system is infected. Write back and confirm that the sender emailed the message. Be especially suspicious of any email that references money owed by you, money owed to you, or packages shipped to you.

- **Assume the worst**—Back up your data regularly, keep your receipts, keep all email correspondence, and read the fine print.

Locking Your Computer

In Chapter 32, "Protecting Your Data from Loss and Theft," you learn a few more security tweaks, including important measures such as advanced file permissions and encryption. These two features are great, but they each have one small flaw: They rely on the assumption that after you've entered a legitimate username and password to log on to your Windows user account, only *you* will use your computer. This means that after you log on, you become a "trusted" user and you have full access to your files, even if they're protected by permissions and encryption.

This assumption is certainly reasonable on the surface. After all, you wouldn't want to have to enter your account credentials every time you want to open, edit, create, or delete a document. So while you're logged on and at your desk, you get full access to your stuff.

But what happens when you leave your desk? If you remain logged on to Windows, any other person who sits down at your computer can take advantage of your trusted-user status to view and work with secure files (including copying them to a USB flash drive inserted by the snoop). This is what we mean by permissions and encryption having a flaw, and it's a potentially significant security hole in large offices where it wouldn't be hard for someone to pull up your chair while you're stuck in yet another meeting.

One way to prevent this problem would be to turn off your computer every time you leave your desk. That way, any would-be snoop would have to get past your login to get to your files. This, obviously, is wildly impractical and inefficient.

Is there a better solution? You bet: You can lock your system before leaving your desk. Anyone who tries to use your computer must enter your password to access the Windows desktop.

Locking Your Computer Manually

Windows 10 gives you three ways to lock your computer before heading off:

- In the Start menu, click your username and then click Lock.
- Press Windows Logo+L, or right-click the Start button.
- Press Ctrl+Alt+Delete, and then click Lock.

Whichever method you use, you end up at the Windows 10 Lock screen. Press any key to switch to the sign-in screen.

Locking Your Computer Automatically

The locking techniques from the previous section are easy enough to do, but the hard part is *remembering* to do them. If you're late for a meeting or a rendezvous, locking up your machine is probably the last thing on your mind as you dash out the door. The usual course of events in these situations is that just as you arrive at your destination you remember that you forgot to lock your PC, and you then spend the next hour fretting about your defenseless computer.

To avoid the fretting (not to mention the possible intrusion), you can configure your computer to lock automatically after a period of inactivity. Here's how it's done:

1. In the taskbar's Search box, type **screen saver**.

2. Click Change Screen Saver.

3. If you want to have a screen saver kick in after your PC is inactive for a while, select a screen saver from the Screen Saver list.

4. Check the On Resume, Display Logon Screen box.

5. Use the Wait spin box to set the interval (in minutes) of idle time that Windows 10 waits before locking your PC.

6. Click OK.

Requiring Ctrl+Alt+Delete at Startup

Protecting your Windows 10 user account with a password, though an excellent idea, is not fool-proof. Hackers are an endlessly resourceful bunch, and some of the smarter ones figured out a way to defeat the user account password system. The trick is that they install a virus or Trojan horse program—usually via an infected email message or malicious website—that loads itself when you start your computer. This program then displays a *fake* version of the Windows 10 sign-in screen. When you type your username and password into this dialog box, the program records it, and your system security is compromised.

To thwart this clever ruse, Windows 10 enables you to configure your system so that you must press Ctrl+Alt+Delete before you can sign in. This key combination ensures that the authentic sign-in screen appears.

To require that users must press Ctrl+Alt+Delete before they can sign in, follow these steps:

1. Press Windows Logo+R to display the Run dialog box.

2. Type `control userpasswords2`, and then click OK. The User Accounts dialog box appears.

3. Display the Advanced tab.

4. Check the Require Users to Press Ctrl+Alt+Delete box.

5. Click OK.

Checking Your Computer's Security Settings

Windows 10 comes with four security features enabled by default:

- Windows Defender Firewall is turned on.

- Windows Defender protects your computer against spyware in real time and by scanning your PC on a schedule.

- User Account Control is turned on.

- The Administrator account is disabled.

However, even though these are the default settings, they're important enough not to be left to chance. The next four sections show you how to check that these crucial security settings really are enabled on your PC.

Making Sure Windows Defender Firewall Is Turned On

By far the most important thing you need to do to thwart crackers is to have a software firewall running on your computer. A firewall is a security feature that blocks unauthorized attempts to send data to your computer. The best firewalls completely hide your computer from the Internet, so those dastardly crackers don't even know you're there! Windows Defender Firewall is turned on by default, but you should periodically check this, just to be safe:

1. In the taskbar's Search box, type **firewall** and then click Windows Defender Firewall in the search results. The Windows Defender Firewall window appears. Look at the Windows Defender Firewall State value. If it says On, as shown in Figure 31.2, you're fine; otherwise, continue to step 2.

This value should be On.

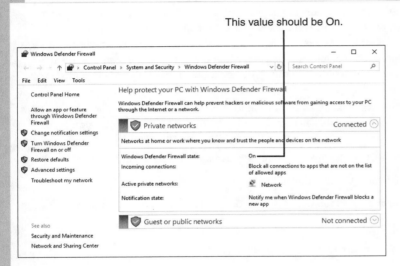

Figure 31.2
In the Windows Defender Firewall window, make sure the firewall state value is On.

2. Click the link Turn Windows Defender Firewall On or Off. The Customize Settings window appears.

3. In the Private Network Settings section, activate the Turn On Windows Defender Firewall option.

4. In the Public Network Settings section, activate the Turn On Windows Defender Firewall option.

5. Click OK.

Making Sure Windows Defender Is Turned On

We've been troubleshooting Windows PCs for many years. It used to be that users accidentally deleting system files or making ill-advised attempts to edit the Registry or some other important configuration file caused most problems. Earlier versions of Windows (particularly XP) could either prevent these kinds of PEBCAK (Problem Exists Between Chair And Keyboard) issues or recover from them without a lot of trouble. However, we're all too well aware of the latest menace to rise in the past few years, and it has taken over as the top cause of desperate troubleshooting calls we receive: *malware*, the generic term for malicious software such as viruses and Trojan horses.

The worst malware offender by far these days is *spyware*, a plague upon the earth that threatens to deprive a significant portion of the online world of its sanity. As often happens with new concepts, the term *spyware* has become encrusted with multiple meanings as people attach similar ideas to a convenient and popular label. However, spyware is generally defined as any program that surreptitiously monitors a user's computer activities—particularly the typing of passwords, PINs, and credit card numbers—or harvests sensitive data on the user's computer and then sends that information to an individual or a company via the user's Internet connection (the so-called *back channel*) without the user's consent.

You might think that having a robust firewall between you and the bad guys would make malware a problem of the past. Unfortunately, that's not true. These programs piggyback on other legitimate programs that users actually *want* to download, such as file-sharing programs, download managers, and screensavers. A *drive-by download* is the download and installation of a program without a user's knowledge or consent. This relates closely to a *pop-up download*—the download and installation of a program after the user clicks an option in a pop-up browser window, particularly when the option's intent is vaguely or misleadingly worded.

To make matters even worse, most spyware embeds itself deep into a system, and removing it is a delicate and time-consuming operation beyond the abilities of even experienced users. Some programs actually come with an Uninstall option, but it's nothing but a ruse, of course. The program appears to remove itself from the system, but what it actually does is a *covert reinstall*—it reinstalls a fresh version of itself when the computer is idle.

Then there is malware that declares itself quite loudly: *ransomware*, which encrypts all of the data on your hard drive *and* all drives accessible over your network, with a secret password, and only promises to restore it if you pay a ransom through an untraceable account. If you pay up, sometimes you actually do get your data back, and sometimes you don't.

All this means that you need to buttress your firewall with an antispyware program that can watch out for these unwanted programs and prevent them from getting their hooks into your system. In versions of Windows prior to Vista, you needed to install a third-party program. However, Windows Vista came with an antispyware program named Windows Defender, and that tool remains part of Windows 10. In Windows 10 Creator's Update, Windows Defender has been beefed up to a full-fledged antimalware program.

Windows Defender protects your computer from malware in two ways. It can scan your system for evidence of installed malware programs (and remove or disable those programs, if necessary), and it can monitor your system in real time to watch for activities that indicate the presence of malware (such as a drive-by download or data being sent via a back channel).

If the real-time protection feature of Windows Defender is turned off, you usually see the notification message shown in Figure 31.3. Click that message to turn on real-time protection.

Figure 31.3
Windows 10 displays this notification if Windows Defender isn't monitoring your system in real time for malware.

Turn on virus protection
Virus protection is turned off. Tap or click to turn on Windows Defender Antivirus.
Security and Maintenance

If you don't see that notification, open the Windows Defender Security Center by typing **defender** in the taskbar's Search box and then clicking Windows Defender Security Center in the search results. Now follow these steps to ensure that Windows Defender is actively monitoring your system for suspicious activity:

1. Click the Virus & Threat Protection tab.

2. Click Virus & Threat Protection Settings.

3. Click the Real-Time Protection switch to On and then enter your User Account Control credentials.

Spyware Scanning

For the scanning portion of its defenses, Windows Defender supports four different scan types:

- **Quick**—This scan checks just those areas of your system where it is likely to find evidence of spyware. This scan usually takes just a couple of minutes. This scan is the default and you can run it from the Virus & Threat Protection tab by clicking Quick Scan.

- **Full**—This scan checks for evidence of spyware in system memory, all running processes, and the system drive (usually drive C), and it performs a deep scan on all folders. This scan might take 30 minutes or more, depending on your system. To run this scan, click Advanced Scan in the Virus & Threat Protection tab to open the Advanced Scans window (see Figure 31.4), activate the Full Scan option, and then click Scan Now.

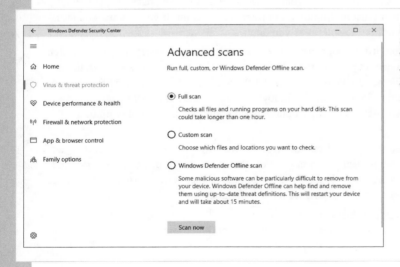

Figure 31.4
Click Advanced Scan in the Virus & Threat Protection tab to open the Advanced Scans window.

- **Custom**—This scan checks just the drive or folder you select. The length of the scan depends on the number of objects in the location. To run this scan, click Advanced Scan in the Virus & Threat Protection tab, activate the Custom option, and then click Scan Now. This displays a dialog box that lets you choose the drive and folder you want scanned, and then click Select Folder to start the scan.

- **Offline**—An offline scan checks your hard disk before Windows completely boots up. This can help Windows Defender find some particularly nasty forms of malware called *rootkits*, which hide below the operating system and can't be detected while it's running. To start an offline scan, save any work in progress. Then click Advanced Scan in the Virus & Threat Protection tab, activate the Windows Defender Offline Scan option, and then Scan Now. Windows will shut down, restart, and scan your computer. It can take a while.

Windows Defender Settings

You can use the Windows Defender Security Center to configure Windows Defender. In the Virus & Threat Protection tab, click Virus & Threat Protection Settings. You can then work with the following options:

- **Real-Time Protection**—This switch toggles real-time protection on and off.

- **Cloud-Delivered Protection**—This switch toggles cloud protection on and off. When cloud protection is on, you authorize Windows 10 to send data on malicious activity to a Microsoft cloud network that analyzes the threat and (at least theoretically) enables Microsoft to respond more quickly to new problems.

- **Automatic Sample Submission**—When this switch is On, you authorize Windows 10 to anonymously send examples of infected files from your PC to Microsoft. You can also send a suspicious file directly to Microsoft by clicking the Submit a Sample Manually link.

- **Controlled Folder Access**—If you click this switch to On, Windows Defender protects your user account folders from unauthorized changes. We talk about this important feature in more detail in the next section.

- **Exclusions**—Click the Add or Remove Exclusions link to specify files, folders, or system processes that you don't want Windows Defender to scan.

- **Notifications**—Click the Change Notification Settings link to control the types of notification the program sends you.

Making Sure Controlled Folder Access Is Turned On

The Controlled Folder Access setting has been called Microsoft's anti-ransomware feature. *Ransomware*, in case you don't know, is a form of malware that encrypts some or all of your data and then asks for a ransom (usually paid in the untraceable Bitcoin digital currency) to decrypt your files. However, when Controlled Folder Access is on the job, Windows 10 monitors your protected folders and prevents ransomware from encrypting them (or any malicious app from messing with them in any way). With ransomware an increasingly prevalent threat these days, we highly recommend setting the Controlled Folder Access switch to On.

Adding a Protected Folder

By default, your user account folders and your PC's Public folders are protected when you activate Controlled Folder Access. If you store sensitive, private, or precious documents elsewhere on your PC, you should protect those folders as well by following these steps:

1. Open the Windows Defender Security Center by typing **defender** in the taskbar's Search box and then clicking Windows Defender Security Center in the search results.

2. Click Virus & Threat Protection.

3. Click Virus & Threat Protection Settings.

4. Click the Controlled Folder Access switch to On, if you haven't done so already.

5. Click Protected Folders to see the list of folders that are already protected.

6. Click Add a Protected Folder.

7. In the Select Folder dialog box, click the folder you want to protect, and then click Select Folder. The User Account Control dialog box appears.

8. Enter your UAC credentials to finish protecting the folder.

9. Repeat steps 6–8 to protect other folders as needed.

To remove a protected folder, follow steps 1–6 to display the list of protected folders, click the folder you no longer want to protect, click Remove, click OK when Windows Defender asks you to confirm, and then enter your UAC credentials.

Giving a Trusted App Access to Your Protected Folders

With Controlled Folder Access turned on, apps that Microsoft has deemed friendly (such as any app obtained through the Microsoft Store) automatically have access to the protected folders. However, you might find that one of your other apps no longer has access to your protected folders. That's not a problem because you can follow these steps to give an app you trust permission to access those folders:

1. Open the Windows Defender Security Center by typing **defender** in the taskbar's Search box and then clicking Windows Defender Security Center in the search results.

2. Click Virus & Threat Protection.

3. Click Virus & Threat Protection Settings.

4. Click Allow an App Through Controlled Folder Access.

5. Click Add an Allowed App.

6. Use the Open dialog box to click the executable (.exe) file for the app, and then click Open. The User Account Control dialog box appears.

7. Enter your UAC credentials to finish allowing the app access to your protected folders.

To revoke an app's access to your protected folders, follow steps 1–4 to display the list of allowed apps, click the app you want to remove, click Remove, and then enter your UAC credentials.

Making Sure User Account Control Is Turned On

We talk about User Account Control in detail later in this chapter. For now, let's just make sure it's enabled on your system:

1. In the taskbar's Search box, type **uac**, and then click Change User Account Control Settings in the search results. The User Account Control Settings dialog box appears.

2. Make sure the slider is set to anything other than Never Notify at the bottom. Again, we explain the different settings a bit later. If you're not sure what to go with, for now choose Default (second from the top).

3. Click OK.

4. Restart your computer to put the new setting into effect.

Making Sure the Administrator Account Is Disabled

One of the confusing aspects about Windows 10 is that the Administrator account seems to disappear after the setup is complete. That's because, for security reasons, Windows 10 doesn't give you access to this all-powerful account. (The initial account you set up has administrator permissions, but it's not the account named Administrator.) However, there are ways to activate this account, so it pays to take a second and make sure it's still in its disabled state.

You can do this in several ways, but here's a quick look at two of them:

- **Using the Local Security Policy Editor**—In the taskbar's Search box, type `secpol.msc`, and then click secpol.msc. In the Local Security Policy window, open the Local Policies, Security Options branch, and then double-click the Accounts: Administrator Account Status policy. Click Disabled, and then click OK.

- **Using the Local Users and Groups snap-in**—In the taskbar's Search box, type `lusrmgr.msc`, and then click lusrmgr.msc. In the Local Users and Groups snap-in, click Users and then double-click Administrator. In the Administrator Properties dialog box, check the Account Is Disabled box and then click OK.

Both these methods suffer from a serious drawback: They work only in Windows 10 Pro or Enterprise. Fortunately, we haven't exhausted all the ways to activate Windows 10's Administrator account. Here's a method that works with *all* versions of Windows 10:

1. Press Windows Logo+X (or right-click the Start button) to display the Advanced Tools menu.

2. Click Command Prompt (Admin). The User Account Control dialog box appears.

    ➡ *To learn how to add Command Prompt (Admin) to the Start Menu's shortcut menu,* *see "Adding Command Prompt to the Shortcut Menu," p. 129.*

3. Enter your UAC credentials to continue.

4. At the command line, enter the following command:

```
net user Administrator /active:no
```

Understanding User Account Control (UAC)

Most of the security-related problems in versions of Windows prior to Vista boiled down to a single root cause: Most users were running Windows with administrator-level permissions. Administrators can do *anything* to a Windows machine, including installing programs, adding devices, updating drivers, installing updates and patches, changing Registry settings, running administrative tools, and creating and modifying user accounts. This is convenient, but it leads to a huge problem: Any malware that insinuates itself onto your system will also be capable of operating with administrative permissions, thus enabling the program to wreak havoc on the computer and just about anything connected to it.

Windows Vista tried to solve this problem, and its solution was called User Account Control (UAC), which used a principle called the *least-privileged user*. The goal is to prevent any program from making system-wide changes such as modifying the Local Machine area of the registry, adding or changing files in the Windows or Program Files folders, and so on, without the user making a conscious decision to let it. Still, some updates are permitted:

- Adding printers

- Changing wireless security options (such as adding a WEP or WPA key)

- Changing other user-specific settings and user-owned files

The User Account Control mechanism works by running most programs with fewer actual permissions than the user's account type would normally grant. For example, even when an administrator runs a program, the program can't change files in the Program Files directory, install device drivers, start or stop system services, and so on. A program that needs to do these things (for example, an installer, the registry editor, and so on) has to be marked as requiring *elevation*, that is, to be run with the maximum privileges that the user is entitled to. When you run a program that is marked for elevation, Windows displays a dialog box that requires you to grant permission for the program to run. Then it gains full administrator privileges.

Privileges are parceled out to three types of account:

- **Administrator account**—This built-in account can do anything to the computer; programs run by this account are always elevated.

- **Administrators group**—Members of this group (except the one "real" Administrator account) run programs with limited permissions but can elevate their privileges when required just by clicking a button in a dialog box. (See the next section.)

- **Standard Users group**—These are the least-privileged users, although they, too, can elevate their privileges when needed by supplying the name and password of an Administrators group account.

If there was a problem with UAC as it was implemented in Vista, it was that it was a tad, well, *enthusiastic* (to put the best face on it). Any minor setting change (even changing the date or time) displayed that elevation prompt, and if you were setting up a new computer, or you were a dedicated settings changer, UAC probably caused you to tear out more than a few clumps of hair in frustration.

The good (some would say great) news in Windows 7 was that Microsoft did two things to rein in UAC:

- It made UAC configurable so that you could tailor the notifications to suit your situation.

- It set up the default configuration of UAC so that it only rarely prompted you for elevation when you changed the settings on your PC. It did this by *automatically* elevating most Microsoft system tools.

Two notable (and excusable) exceptions were when you changed the UAC configuration itself and when you started the Registry Editor. These tools, and any third-party program, bring up the UAC prompt.

Elevating Privileges

The idea of elevating privileges is at the heart of the UAC security model. In Windows XP, you could use the Run As command to run a task as a different user (that is, one with higher privileges). In Windows 10 (as with Windows 8/8.1, Windows 7, and Vista), you usually don't need to do this because Windows 10 prompts you for the elevation automatically.

With your main Windows 10 user account (which, again, is a member of the Administrators group), you run most tasks with the privileges of a standard user, providing extra security. When you attempt a task that requires administrative privileges, Windows 10 prompts for your consent by displaying a User Account Control dialog box similar to the one shown in Figure 31.5. (We're assuming here that you're using the default UAC setting.) Click Yes to permit the task to proceed. If this dialog box appears unexpectedly instead of in response to an action you've just taken, it's possible that a malware program is trying to perform some task that requires administrative privileges; you can thwart that task by clicking No instead.

Figure 31.5
When your main Windows 10 administrative account launches a task that requires elevated privileges, Windows 10 displays this dialog box to ask for consent.

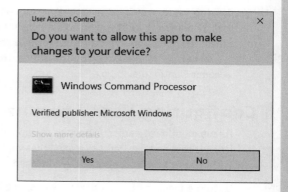

If you're running as a standard user and attempt a task that requires administrative privileges, Windows 10 uses an extra level of protection. That is, instead of just prompting you for consent, it prompts you for the PIN or password of the main administrative account, as shown in Figure 31.6. You can select More choices to choose a different account, or to choose between entering a PIN or password. Type the PIN or password for an administrative account, and then click Yes. Again, if this dialog box shows up unexpectedly, it might be malware, so you should click No to prevent the task from going through.

 note

If you don't want standard users to be presented with this elevation prompt, see "Preventing Elevation for All Standard Users," at the end of this section.

Figure 31.6
When a standard user launches a task that requires administrative privileges, Windows 10 displays this dialog box to ask for administrative credentials.

Note, too, that in both cases Windows 10 switches to secure desktop mode, which means that you can't do anything else with Windows 10 until you give your consent or credentials or cancel the operation. Windows 10 indicates the secure desktop by darkening everything on the screen except the User Account Control dialog box.

Configuring User Account Control

As we mentioned earlier, Windows 10 supports a configurable UAC so that you can set it to a level that you're comfortable with. Here's how to configure UAC in Windows 10:

1. In the taskbar's Search box, type **uac**, and then click Change User Account Control Settings in the search results. The User Account Control Settings window appears, as shown in Figure 31.7.

2. Use the slider to choose one of the following four UAC settings:

   - **Always Notify**—This is the top level, and it works much like UAC in Windows Vista in that you're prompted for elevation when you change Windows settings and when programs try to change settings or install software.

   - **Default**—This is the second highest level, and it prompts you for elevation only when programs try to change settings and install software. This level uses secure desktop mode to display the UAC dialog box.

 note

It's also possible to elevate your privileges for any individual program. In File Explorer, you do this either by right-clicking the program file or shortcut, or by clicking the file and then clicking the Manage tab, and then clicking Run as Administrator.

 tip

You can elevate your privileges for commands you run through the taskbar's Search box: type the command, hold down Ctrl+Shift, and then press Enter.

Figure 31.7
In Windows 10, you can use the User Account Control Settings window to set up UAC as you see fit.

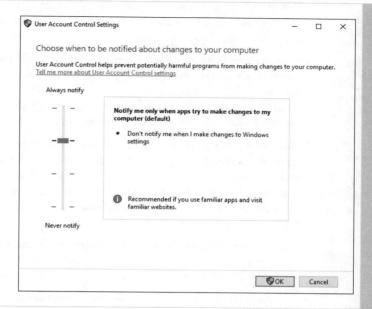

- **No Secure Desktop**—This is the second lowest level, and it's the same as the Default level (that is, it prompts you for elevation only when programs try to change settings and install software), but this level doesn't use secure desktop mode when displaying the UAC dialog box. (However, in this mode, malware could interact with and accept the UAC prompt for you.)

- **Never Notify**—This is the bottom level, and it turns off UAC. Of course you, as a responsible PC user, would never select this setting, right? We figured as much.

3. Click OK. The User Account Control dialog box appears.

4. Enter your UAC credentials to put the new setting into effect.

> **tip**
>
> If you have a specific application that doesn't work correctly when UAC is turned on, right-click its shortcut, select Properties, and on the Compatibility tab select Run As Administrator. Leave UAC turned on. This way, your system will still be protected from malware arriving from other sources.

Setting User Account Control Policies

You can customize User Account Control to a certain extent by using local group policies. In the Local Security Policy snap-in (in the taskbar's Search box, type `secpol.msc` and then click secpol.msc), open the Local Policies, Security Options branch. Here, you'll find 10 policies related to User Account Control:

- **User Account Control: Admin Approval Mode for the Built-In Administrator Account**—This policy controls whether the Administrator account falls under User Account Control. If you enable this policy, the Administrator account is treated like any other account in the Administrators group and the user must click Continue in the consent dialog box when Windows 10 requires approval for an action.

- **User Account Control: Allow UIAccess Applications to Prompt for Elevation Without Using the Secure Desktop**—Use this policy to enable or disable whether Windows 10 allows elevation for accessibility applications that require access to the user interface of another window without using the secure desktop mode. Choose this only if your particular applications have severe compatibility problems with the normal secure desktop prompt.

- **User Account Control: Behavior of the Elevation Prompt for Administrators in Admin Approval Mode**—This policy controls the prompt that appears when the main administrative account requires elevated privileges. The default setting is Prompt for Consent for Non-Windows Binaries, where the user clicks either Yes or No. You can also choose Prompt for Credentials to force the user to type her password. If you choose No Prompt, the main administrative account can't elevate its privileges.

- **User Account Control: Behavior of the Elevation Prompt for Standard Users**—This policy controls the prompt that appears when a standard user requires elevated privileges. For a more detailed look at this policy, see "Preventing Elevation for All Standard Users," next.

- **User Account Control: Detect Application Installations and Prompt for Elevation**—Use this policy to enable or disable automatic privilege elevation while installing programs.

- **User Account Control: Only Elevate Executables That Are Signed and Validated**—Use this policy to enable or disable whether Windows 10 checks the security signature of any program that asks for elevated privileges.

- **User Account Control: Only Elevate UIAccess Applications That Are Installed in Secure Locations**—Use this policy to enable or disable whether Windows 10 allows elevation for accessibility applications that require access to the user interface of another window only if they are installed in a secure location (such as the %ProgramFiles% folder).

- **User Account Control: Run All Administrators in Admin Approval Mode**—Use this policy to enable or disable running the main administrative account (excluding the Administrator account) as a standard user.

- **User Account Control: Switch to the Secure Desktop When Prompting for Elevation**—Use this policy to enable or disable whether Windows 10 switches to the secure desktop when the elevation prompts appear.

- **User Account Control: Virtualize File and Registry Write Failures to Per-User Locations**—Use this policy to enable or disable file and Registry virtualization for standard users.

 note

File and Registry virtualization creates virtual %SystemRoot% and %ProgramFiles% folders as well as a virtual HKEY_LOCAL_MACHINE Registry key, all of which are stored with the user's files. This enables a program installer to proceed without jeopardizing actual system files.

Preventing Elevation for All Standard Users

You saw earlier (in "Elevating Privileges") that when a standard user attempts a task that requires elevation, he sees a UAC dialog box that requires an administrator password, and the screen switches to secure desktop mode.

There are two problems with this:

- Standard users almost never have the proper credentials to elevate an action.

- The combination of the sudden appearance of the User Account Control dialog box and the change into secure desktop mode is confusing for many users, particularly the inexperienced.

These two problems mean that in most cases it would be better if standard users didn't get prompted to elevate their privileges. Instead, it would be better to display an Access Denied message and let the users move on from there.

You can use the Local Security Policy snap-in to set this up. Here are the steps to follow:

1. From the Start screen, type **secpol.msc**, and then click secpol.msc. The Local Security Policy snap-in appears.

2. Open the Local Policies branch.

3. Click the Security Options branch.

4. Double-click the User Account Control: Behavior of the Elevation Prompt for Standard Users policy.

5. In the drop-down list, choose Automatically Deny Elevation Requests, as shown in Figure 31.8.

6. Click OK to put the new setting into effect.

> **note**
>
> These steps require the Local Security Policy snap-in, which is available only with Windows 10 Pro. If you're not running this version, normally we'd show you how to modify the Registry to get the same effect. Unfortunately, the policy value we tweak here doesn't have a Registry equivalent for security reasons.

Figure 31.8
Open the User Account Control: Behavior of the Elevation Prompt for Standard Users policy and choose Automatically Deny Elevation Requests.

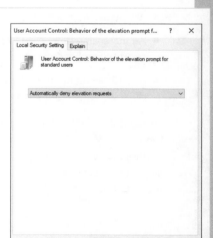

Now when a standard user attempts something that requires elevated privileges, he just sees a simple dialog box like the one shown in Figure 31.9. The user has to click the Close button to continue.

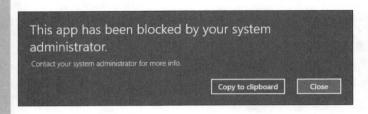

Figure 31.9
When standard users are denied elevation requests, they see a simple dialog box when they attempt an administrator-level task.

Enhancing Your Browsing Security

As more people, businesses, and organizations have established a presence online, the world has become an increasingly connected place. And the more connected the world becomes, the more opportunities arise for communicating with others, doing research, sharing information, and collaborating on projects. The flip side to this new connectedness is the increased risk of connecting with a remote user whose intentions are less than honorable. The person at the other end of the connection could be a fraud artist who sets up a legitimate-looking website to steal your password or credit card number or a cracker who breaks into your Internet account. It could be a virus programmer who sends a Trojan horse attached to an email or a website operator who uses web browser security holes to run malicious code on your machine.

While all this was happening, Microsoft's operating systems seemed to become less secure. It's difficult to say whether overall operating system security got worse with each new release, but it's not hard to see that a perfect security storm was brewing:

- Thanks to the Internet, news of vulnerabilities spread quickly and efficiently.

- An increasing number of malicious users online worked to exploit those vulnerabilities.

- An increasing number of Windows users got online, most of whom didn't keep up with the latest security patches from Microsoft. Actually, most users didn't install security patches *ever*.

- An increasing number of online users had always-on broadband connections, which gave malicious users more time to locate and break into poorly patched machines.

So, even though it might have been the case that each new version of Windows was no less secure than its predecessors, it *appeared* that Windows was becoming increasingly vulnerable to attack.

Surfing the Web may be inherently insecure, but fortunately, Microsoft Edge comes with several defensive weapons that you can deploy. The next few sections take a look at the most important ones.

Blocking Pop-Up Windows

Among the most annoying things on the Web are those ubiquitous pop-up windows that infest your screen with advertisements when you visit certain sites. (A variation on the theme is the *pop-under*, a window that opens under your current browser window, so you don't know it's there until you close the window.) Pop-up windows can also be dangerous because some unscrupulous software makers have figured out ways to use them to install software on your computer without your permission. They're nasty things, any way you look at them.

Fortunately, Microsoft has given us a way to stop most pop-ups before they start. Microsoft Edge comes with a feature called the *Pop-Up Blocker* that looks for pop-ups and prevents them from opening. It's not perfect (the occasional pop-under still breaks through the defenses), but it makes surfing sites much more pleasant.

Microsoft Edge comes with the Pop-Up Blocker already activated, but you can follow these steps to make sure:

1. In Microsoft Edge, click the More button (the ellipsis) in the upper-right corner of the window.

2. Click Settings to open the Settings pane.

3. Click View Advanced Settings to open the Advanced Settings pane.

4. Make sure the Block Pop-Ups switch is On.

Pop-Up Blocker monitors your surfing and steps in front of any pop-up window that tries to disturb your peace. In Microsoft Edge, a Notification bar appears at the bottom of the window to let you know that Pop-Up Blocker thwarted a pop-up (see Figure 31.10). The Notification bar offers the following choices:

- **Allow Once**—Click this command to enable pop-ups on the site just this one time.

- **Always Allow**—Click this command to allow future pop-ups for the current domain.

Figure 31.10
When the Pop-Up Blocker has your back, it displays the Notification bar each time it thwarts a pop-up.

Microsoft Edge blocked a pop-up from *.popuptest.com.   Allow once ∨   Always allow   ✕

Making Sure SmartScreen Is On

Windows Defender offers a technology called SmartScreen that acts as a kind of anti-malware filter for websites, downloads, and website apps. If you use Microsoft Edge to surf to a website or try to download a file that SmartScreen recognizes as containing malicious code, Edge displays a warning. If a website tries to run an app or use a file that SmartScreen doesn't recognize, Edge displays a warning.

These warnings are turned on by default, but it's worth it to follow these steps to make sure:

1. Type **defender** in the taskbar's Search box and then click Windows Defender Security Center in the search results.

2. Click the App & Browser Control tab.

3. Under the Check Apps and Files heading, make sure the Warn option is activated. (If you want to ensure unrecognized apps or files don't get loaded, you can activate the Block option, instead.)

4. Under the SmartScreen for Microsoft Edge heading, make sure the Warn option is activated. (If you want to ensure malicious website scripts or downloads don't run, you can activate the Block option, instead.)

PROTECTING YOUR DATA FROM LOSS AND THEFT

Preparing for Trouble

Computer problems, like the proverbial death and taxes, seem to be one of those constants in life. Whether it's a hard disk giving up the ghost, a power failure that trashes your files, or a virus that invades your system, the issue isn't *whether* something will go wrong, but rather *when* it will happen. Instead of waiting to deal with these difficulties after they've occurred (what we call *pound-of-cure mode*), you need to become proactive and perform maintenance on your system in advance (*ounce-of-prevention mode*). This not only reduces the chances that something will go wrong but also sets up your system to recover more easily from any problems that do occur.

A big part of ounce-of-prevention mode is the unwavering belief that someday something *will* go wrong with your computer. That might sound unduly pessimistic, but hey, this is a PC we're talking about here, and it's never a question of *if* the thing will go belly up one day, but rather *when* that day will come.

With that gloomy mindset, the only sensible thing to do is prepare for that dire day so that you're ready to get your system back on its feet. So, part of your Windows 10 maintenance chores should be getting a few things ready that will serve you well on the day your PC decides to go haywire on you. Besides performing a system image backup (which we describe a bit later), you should be setting system restore points and creating a system recovery disc. The next two sections cover these last two techniques.

Backing Up File Versions with File History

High-end databases have long supported the idea of the *transaction*, a collection of data modifications—inserts, deletions, updates, and so on—treated as a unit, meaning that either all the modifications occur or not one of them does. For example, consider a finance database system that needs to perform a single chore: transfer a specified amount of money from one account to another. This involves two discrete steps (I'm simplifying here): debit one account by the specified amount and credit the other account for the same amount. If the database system did not treat these two steps as a single transaction, you could run into problems. For example, if the system successfully debited the first account but for some reason was unable to credit the second account, the system would be left in an unbalanced state. By treating the two steps as a single transaction, the system does not commit any changes unless both steps occur successfully. If the credit to the second account fails, the transaction is rolled back to the beginning, meaning that the debit to the first account is reversed and the system reverts to a stable state.

What does all this have to do with the Windows 10 file system? It's actually directly related because Windows 10 includes an interesting technology called *Transactional NTFS*, or TxF, for short. (New Technology File System [NTFS] is the default Windows 10 file system.) TxF applies the same transactional database ideas to the file system. Put simply, with TxF, if some mishap occurs to your data—it could be a system crash, a program crash, an overwrite of an important file, or even just imprudent edits to a file—Windows 10 enables you to roll back the file to a previous version. It's kind of like System Restore, except that it works not for the entire system, but for individual files and folders.

Windows 10's capability to restore previous versions of files and folders comes from two processes:

- Once an hour, Windows 10 creates a shadow copy of your user account files. A shadow copy is essentially a snapshot of the disk's contents at a particular point in time. It doesn't necessarily take up a lot of extra disk space: Windows only has to allocate space to hold data changes made after the snapshot is taken.

- After creating the shadow copy, Windows 10 uses transactional NTFS to intercept all calls to the file system. Windows 10 maintains a meticulous log of those calls so that it knows exactly which files and folders in your user account have changed.

These processes enable Windows 10 to store previous versions of files and folders, where a "previous" version is defined as a version of the object that changed after a shadow copy was created. For example, suppose that you make changes to a particular document on two successive days. This means that you'll end up with three previous versions of the document: today's, yesterday's, and the day before yesterday's.

Taken together, these previous versions represent the document's *file history*, and you can access and work with previous versions by activating the File History feature. When you turn on File History and specify an external drive to store the data, Windows 10 begins monitoring your libraries, your desktop, your contacts, and your Internet Explorer favorites. Once an hour, Windows 10 checks to see if any of this data has changed since the last check. If it has, Windows 10 saves copies of the changed files to the external drive.

Once you have some data saved, you can then use it to restore a previous version of a file, as described later in this chapter.

Selecting the File History Drive

To get started, connect an external drive to your PC. The drive should have enough capacity to hold your user account files, so an external hard drive is probably best. Now you need to set up the external drive for use with File History.

The easiest way to do this is to look for the notification that appears a few moments after you connect the drive. Click the notification, and then click Configure This Drive for Backup.

If you miss the notification, follow these steps instead. There are (of course) several ways to do the same thing. This is the way we do it:

1. Click Start, Settings, Update & Security, Backup. The Backup settings window appears.

2. If you see the Automatically Back Up My Files switch and that switch is set to On, you can skip the rest of these steps. Otherwise, click Add a Drive. Settings displays a list of disk drives connected to your PC.

3. Examine the list of available drives, which will be similar to the one shown in Figure 32.1, Click the name of the drive you wish to use.

Figure 32.1
Windows 10 should recognize your external drive and add it to the Select a Drive panel.

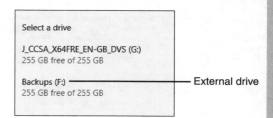

Select a drive

J_CCSA_X64FRE_EN-GB_DVS (G:)
255 GB free of 255 GB

Backups (F:) ——————————————— External drive
255 GB free of 255 GB

4. The Backup window adds the Automatically Back Up My Files switch and sets it to On.

Using a Network Share as the File History Drive

If you want to back up to a drive shared on your network, where the share requires a username and password (that's not the same as the username and password for your Windows account), or if you want to use a folder *within* a network share, you will have to use the Control Panel version of the File History settings panel.

1. From the Backup settings panel, select More Options. Scroll down and select See Advanced Settings.

2. Click Select Drive.

3. Click Add Network Location. Windows opens the Select Folder dialog box and displays the Network folder, but you can browse around to other locations or drives.

4. Locate the shared folder you want to use, digging down into subfolders if desired. If the share requires a password, you may need to type the UNC path into the Folder box. You will then be prompted to enter the required credentials. Be sure to check Remember My Credentials so that Windows can connect to the shared folder every time it saves files to the backup set. Make sure the network share is selected, and then click Select Folder. The shared folder now appears in the list of available backup drives and locations under Select a File History Drive.

5. Select the shared file location, and then click OK. This location will be used for future File History backups, as shown in Figure 32.2.

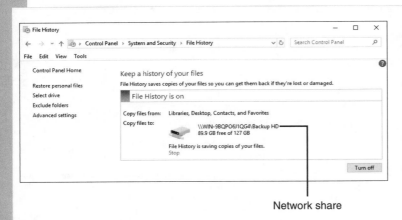

Figure 32.2
The Control Panel version of File History settings lets you manually enter a network shared folder path, and password, if needed.

Network share

Including and Excluding Folders in Your File History

By default, File History stores copies of everything in your Windows 10 libraries—including Documents, Music, Photos, and Videos—as well as your desktop items, contacts, and Internet Explorer favorites. While the profile folders are the "correct" place for you to have stored all of your data, you might create folders in other parts of the hard drive, perhaps even in the root folder. You may well want these files to be backed up by File History. If you do, you have to manually add them to the backup list.

Likewise, in some situations, you might not want every file to be included in your history. For example, if your external drive has a limited capacity, you might want to exclude extremely large files, such as recorded TV shows or ripped movies in your Videos library. Or, you might have sensitive or private files in your Documents library that you do not want copied to the external drive because that drive can easily be stolen or lost. (A similar caveat applies to storing sensitive files on a shared network folder that other people might also be able to access.)

Whatever the reason, you can configure File History to include and exclude particulars folder from being copied to the external drive by following these steps:

1. Click Start, Settings, Update & Security, Backup to display the Backup settings window; then select More Options. The Backup Options window appears.

2. To add additional folders to the backup set, scroll down to Back Up These Folders, and click Add a Folder. Browse to the desired folder (it might even be on a different internal drive), and select Choose This Folder. Repeat for any additional folders that you want to protect. All subfolders within the selected folder will also be backed up, unless you manually exclude them.

3. To exclude folders from being backed up, scroll down to Exclude These Folders. Click Add a Folder. Browse to the desired folder (it might even be on a different internal drive), and select Choose This Folder. Repeat for any additional folders that you want to exclude. All subfolders within the selected folder will also be excluded.

The listed folders will be added to or excluded from future backups.

To later remove a folder you've added or excluded, open the Backup Options window, click on the folder in the Back Up These Folders section, and click Remove.

Configuring File History

File History uses the following default settings:

- **File History looks for changed files every hour**—If you are particularly busy, you might prefer a more frequent save interval to ensure you don't lose any data. On the other hand, if you are running out of space on the external drive, you might prefer a less frequent save interval to preserve space.

- **File History does not delete any of the file versions it saves**—To free up space on the external drive, you can configure File History to delete versions after a specified time or when space is needed on the drive.

 tip
You don't have to wait until the next scheduled backup. If File History is turned on and you have important changes you'd prefer to save right away, open Backup Settings, select More Options, and then click Back Up Now.

Follow these steps to configure these settings:

1. Click Start, Settings, Update & Security, Backup to display the Backup settings window, and then select More Options. The Backup Options window appears, as shown in Figure 32.3.

2. To change the backup frequency, scroll down to Back Up My Files, and select a frequency from Every 10 Minutes to Daily.

3. Under Keep My Backups, you can change the retention for backup copies to Forever, Until Space Is Needed, or one of the listed durations ranging from months to years.

4. If you're using an external drive (or a second internal drive) and your computer is part of a home-group, you can allow other homegroup users the chance to use the same drive for their backups. To do this, scroll the settings page *way* down and select See Advanced Settings. Then, at the left, select Advanced Settings. As shown in Figure 32.3, under HomeGroup, check Recommend This Drive.

5. If you want to keep an eye on what File History is doing, in this same Advanced Settings page click Open File History Event Logs to View Recent Events or Errors. This launches the Event Viewer and displays the File History Backup Log.

6. Click Save Changes to put the new settings into effect.

Figure 32.3
Use the Backup Options window to configure the backups for your PC.

Cleaning Up File History to Save Disk Space

If your external drive is running low on free space, you can delete some older versions right away. Open the File History backup settings page, select More Options, scroll *way* down to See Advanced Settings, and then, at the left, click Advanced Settings. Click Clean Up Versions to open the File History Cleanup dialog box, select a time frame for the files you want to remove (from Older Than 1 Month to Older Than 2 Years, or All But the Latest One), and then click Clean Up. (Note that you only see the Clean Up Versions link if File History has at least one set of file versions stored on your PC.)

 note

If you need to remove the external drive temporarily (for example, if you need to use the port for another device), you should turn off File History before disconnecting the external drive. In the taskbar's Search box, type **history** and then click Backup Settings. Turn the Automatically Back Up My Files switch to Off.

Restoring a Previous Version of a File

When you enable File History on your PC, as described earlier in this chapter, Windows 10 periodically—by default, once an hour—looks for files that have changed since the last check. If it finds a changed file, it takes a "snapshot" of that file and saves that version of the file to the external drive that you specified when you set up File History. This gives Windows 10 the capability to reverse the changes you have made to a file by reverting to an earlier state of the file. An earlier state of a file is called a *previous version*.

Why would you want to revert to a previous version of a file? One reason is that you might improperly edit the file by deleting or changing important data. In some cases, you might be able to restore that data by going back to a previous version of the file. Another reason is that the file might become corrupted if the program or Windows 10 crashes. You can get back a working version of the file by restoring a previous version.

> **note**
>
> Windows 10 also keeps track of previous versions of folders, which is useful if an entire folder becomes corrupted because of a system crash.

There are two ways to restore a previous version of a file.

If you can locate the file that you want to restore in File Explorer, follow these steps:

1. In File Explorer, right-click the file and select Restore Previous Versions.

2. From the list of saved versions, select the version you want to get back.

3. At the bottom of the dialog, make one of the following selections:

   - **Open**—Click Open to view the file as it was at the time it was backed up. Once opened, you can copy needed information out of file and simply close it, or, if you wish, use Save As to save it with a new name or location. (The saved file will have today's date.)

   - **Open in File History**—Click the arrow on the Open button and select Open in File History. You can preview the file and if desired click the "Restore" button to recover it.

   - **Restore**—Click the Restore button to recover the file as it was when it was backed up. The present version of the file will be lost.

   - **Restore To**—Click the arrow on the Restore button and select Restore To. Select a new location to store the recovered file. The present version will stay as and where it is.

Another way to recover files—and the easiest way if the file you want to recover has been deleted—is to follow these steps:

1. Click Start, Settings, Update & Security, Backup to display the Backup settings window, and then select More Options. The Backup Options window appears.

2. Scroll *way* down, and then select Restore Files from a Current Backup

3. The Home – File History window appears, as shown in Figure 32.4. The most recent backup is selected, but you can scroll through different backups by clicking the previous and next backup buttons at the bottom of the window, on either side of the round green Restore button. (You can use these buttons at any time, even after you've delved into subfolders.)

4. Delve into the folders to find the file(s) or folder(s) you wish to return to their previous state. You can select more than one object. Note that if you select a folder, all of the files and subfolders in it will be restored to their previous state at the time of the backup.

5. Click the green Restore to Original Location (pointed out in Figure 32.4). If the original folder has a file with the same name, File History asks what you want to do. Select an option:

   - **Replace the File in the Destination Folder**—Click this option to overwrite the existing file with the previous version.

   - **Skip This File**—Click this option to skip the restore and do nothing.

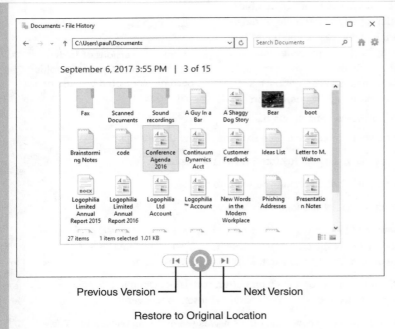

Figure 32.4
Use the Home – File History window to choose which previous version you want to restore.

- **Compare Info for Both Files**—Click this option to display the File Conflict dialog box (see Figure 32.5), which shows the original and the previous version side by side, along with the last modification date and time and the file size. Check the box beside the version you want to keep, and then click Continue. To keep both versions, check both boxes. File History restores the previous version with (2) appended to its filename.

Figure 32.5
If the original folder has a file with the same name and you're not sure which one to keep, use the File Conflict dialog box to decide.

Setting System Restore Points

One of the biggest causes of Windows instability in the past was the tendency of some newly installed programs simply to not get along with Windows. The problem could be an executable file that didn't mesh with the Windows system or a Registry change that caused havoc on other programs or on Windows. Similarly, hardware installs often caused problems by adding faulty device drivers to the system or by corrupting the Registry.

To help guard against software or hardware installations that bring down the system, Windows 10 offers the System Restore feature. Its job is straightforward yet clever: to take periodic snapshots—called *restore points* or *protection points*—of your system, each of which includes the currently installed program files, Registry settings, and other crucial system data. The idea is that if a program or device installation causes problems on your system, you use System Restore to revert your system to the most recent restore point before the installation.

System Restore automatically creates restore points under the following conditions:

- **Every week**—This is called a *system checkpoint*, and it's set once a week during the automatic maintenance window as long as your computer is running. If your computer isn't running, the system checkpoint is created the next time you start your computer, assuming that it has been at least a week since that previous system checkpoint was set.

- **Before installing certain applications**—Some applications (notably Windows Live Essentials and Microsoft Office) are aware of System Restore and will ask it to create a restore point prior to installation.

- **Before installing a Windows Update patch**—System Restore creates a restore point before you install a patch either by hand via the Windows Update site or via the Automatic Updates feature.

- **Before installing an unsigned device driver**—Windows 10 warns you about installing unsigned drivers. If you choose to go ahead, the system creates a restore point before installing the driver.

- **Before reverting to a previous configuration using System Restore**—Sometimes, reverting to an earlier configuration doesn't fix the current problem, or it creates its own set of problems. In these cases, System Restore creates a restore point before reverting so that you can undo the restoration.

It's also possible to create a restore point manually using the System Protection feature. Here are the steps to follow:

1. In the taskbar's Search box, type **restore**, and then click Create a Restore Point in the search results. This opens the System Properties dialog box with the System Protection tab displayed, as shown in Figure 32.6.

2. Sometimes Windows does not enable System Protection when it is installed. In the Protection Settings list, locate your System drive, usually drive C. If Protection is shown as Off, click this line to highlight it, and then click Configure. Adjust the Max Usage slider to 10 to 15 percent, or at least 20GB of space, and then click OK. The Protection Settings list should show drive C as On now.

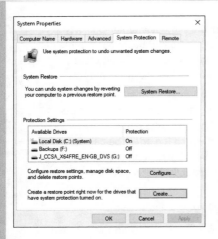

Figure 32.6
Use the System Protection tab to set a restore point.

3. To create automatic restore points for other drives (especially drives on which you install apps), click the drive in the Protection Settings list, click Configure, click the Turn On System Protection option, and then click OK.

4. Click Create to display the Create a Restore Point dialog box.

5. Type a description for the new restore point, and then click Create. System Protection creates the restore point and displays a dialog box to let you know the restore point was created successfully.

6. Click Close to return to the System Properties dialog box.

7. Click OK.

➡ *To learn how to revert your PC to an earlier restore point,* **see** *"Recovering Using System Restore," p. 607.*

Creating More Room for Restore Points

Windows sets aside a certain amount of your hard disk space for restore points. (The percentage depends on the size of the disk.) When that space is used up, Windows 10 deletes the oldest restore points as new ones are added. If you use restore points frequently and you have lots of free space on your hard drive, consider increasing the amount of space allotted to restore points. Click the drive in the Protection Settings list, click Configure, and use the Max Usage slider to set the amount of disk space you want. If the hard disk is getting low on free space, you can also click the Delete button to remove all the restore points from the hard disk.

Creating a Recovery Drive

We all hope our computers operate trouble-free over their lifetimes, but we know from bitter experience that this is rarely the case. Computers are incredibly complex systems, so it is almost inevitable that a PC will develop glitches. If your hard drive is still accessible, you can boot to Windows 10 and access the recovery tools, as we described in Chapter 26, "Troubleshooting and Repairing Problems."

> ➡ *To learn how to boot to the Windows 10 recovery tools,* **see** *"Accessing the Recovery Environment," p. 598.*

If you can't boot your PC, however, you must boot using some other drive. If you have your Windows 10 installation media, you can boot using that drive. If you don't have the installation media, you can still recover if you've created a USB recovery drive. This is a USB flash drive that contains the Windows 10 recovery environment, which enables you to refresh or reset your PC, use System Restore, recover a system image, and more.

Before you can boot to a recovery drive, such as a USB flash drive, you need to create the drive. Follow these steps:

1. Insert the USB flash drive you want to use. Note that the drive must have a capacity of at least 512MB. (See the accompanying Caution.) Also, Windows 10 will erase all data on the drive, so make sure it doesn't contain any files you want to keep.

> ## 📶 caution
>
> The 512MB capacity applies only if you don't also want to include your PC's Recovery partition on the recovery drive. If you do want to include this partition (it's a good idea), you'll need a flash drive with enough capacity to hold the system recover partition, which might be 5 to 15GB, or more. (To check, use the taskbar's Search box to type `diskmgmt.msc`, press Enter, and then use the Disk Management snap-in to view the size of the Recovery partition.)

2. In the taskbar's Search box, type **recovery** and then click Recovery Drive. User Account Control appears.

3. Click Yes or enter administrator credentials in the User Account Control dialog box to continue. The Recovery Drive Wizard appears.

4. If you don't want to add your PC's Recovery partition to the recovery drive, uncheck Back Up System Files to the Recovery Drive. Click Next. The Recovery Drive Wizard prompts you to choose the USB flash drive, as shown in Figure 32.7.

5. Click the drive, if it isn't selected already, and then click Next. The Recovery Drive Wizard warns you that all the data on the drive will be deleted.

6. Click Create. The wizard formats the drive and copies the recovery tools and data.

7. Click Finish.

Remove the drive, label it, and then put it someplace where you'll be able to find it later, just in case.

 tip

To make sure your recovery drive works properly, you should test it by booting your PC to the drive. Insert the recovery drive and then restart your PC. How you boot to the drive depends on your system. Some PCs display a menu of boot devices, and you select the USB drive from that menu. In other cases, you see a message telling you to press a key.

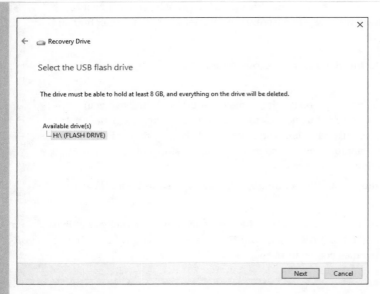

Figure 32.7
Select the flash drive that you inserted in step 1.

Creating a System Image Backup

The worst-case scenario for PC problems is a system crash that renders your hard disk or system files unusable. Your only recourse in such a case is to start from scratch with either a reformatted hard disk or a new hard disk. This usually means that you have to reinstall Windows 10 and then reinstall and reconfigure all your applications. In other words, you're looking at the better part of a day or, more likely, a few days, to recover your system. However, Windows 10 has a feature that takes most of the pain out of recovering your system. It's called a *system image* backup, and it's part of the system recovery options that we discussed in Chapter 26.

➡️ *To learn how to restore your PC from an image, **see** "Restoring a System Image," **p. 609.***

The system image backup is actually a complete backup of your Windows 10 installation, virtually every byte on your hard drive. It takes a long time to create a system image (at least several hours, depending on how much stuff you have), but it's worthwhile for the peace of mind. Here are the steps to follow to create the system image:

1. Click Start, Settings, Update & Security, Backup to display the Backup settings window; then select More Options. The Backup Options window appears.

2. Click Go to Backup and Restore (Windows 7).

3. At the left, select Create a System Image. The Create a System Image Wizard appears.

4. The wizard asks you to specify a backup destination. You have three choices, as shown in Figure 32.8. (Click Next when you're ready to continue.)

Figure 32.8
You can create the system image on a hard drive, on DVDs, or on a network share.

■ **On a Hard Disk**—Select this option if you want to use a disk drive on your computer. If you have multiple drives, use the list to select the one you want to use.

■ **On One or More DVDs**—Select this option if you want to use DVDs to hold the backup. Depending on how much data your PC holds, you could be talking about using dozens of discs for this (at least!), so we don't recommend this option.

■ **On a Network Location**—Select this option if you want to use a shared network folder. Either type the address of the share or click Select and then click Browse to use the Browse for Folder dialog box to choose the shared network folder. Make sure it's a share for which you have permission to add data. Type a username and password for accessing the share, and then click OK.

> **⚠ caution**
> Many people make the mistake of creating the system image once and then ignoring it, forgetting that their systems aren't set in stone. Over the coming days and weeks, you'll be installing apps, tweaking settings, and of course creating lots of new documents and other data. This means that you should periodically create a fresh system image. Should disaster strike, you'll be able to recover most of your system.

5. The system image backup automatically includes your internal hard disk in the system image, and you can't change that. However, if you also have external hard drives, you can add them to the backup by clicking their check boxes. Click Next. Windows Backup asks you to confirm your backup settings.

6. Click Start Backup. Windows Backup creates the system image.

7. Click OK.

If you used a hard drive and you have multiple external drives lying around, be sure to label the one that contains the system image so you'll be able to find it later.

We strongly recommend that if you have a recording CD or DVD drive, you also get a blank, recordable CD or DVD and use the Create a System Repair disc option on the same Windows 7 Backup screen. You can boot from this disc if you ever need to restore your hard disk from the system image backup. It can be *very* difficult to get Windows to restore an image backup if your computer's hardware configuration changes. It's all the more difficult if you don't have this System Repair disc.

Protecting a File

Much day-to-day work in Windows 10 is required but not terribly important. Most memos, letters, and notes are run-of-the-mill and don't require extra protection. Occasionally, however, you may create or work with a file that *is* important. It could be a carefully crafted letter, a memo detailing important company strategy, or a collection of hard-won brainstorming notes. Whatever the content, such a file requires extra protection to ensure that you don't lose your work.

Making a File Read-Only

You can set advanced file permissions that can prevent a document from being changed or even deleted. (See "Setting Security Permissions on Files and Folders," later in the chapter.) If your only concern is preventing other people from making changes to a document, a simpler technique you can use is making the document *read-only*. This means that although other people can make changes to a document, they cannot save those changes (except to a new file). The following steps show you how to make a file read-only:

1. Use File Explorer to open the folder that contains the file you want to protect.

2. Click the file.

3. In the Home tab, click the top half of the Properties button. The file's Properties dialog box appears.

4. Click the General tab.

5. Check the Read-Only box, as shown in Figure 32.9.

6. Click OK. The file is now read-only.

To confirm that the file is protected, open it, make changes to the file, and then save it. The program displays the Save As dialog box. Click Save, and then when the programs asks if you want to overwrite the file, click Yes. Instead of overwriting the file, the program just tells you that the file is read-only.

Figure 32.9
Click the Read-Only check box to prevent a file from being changed.

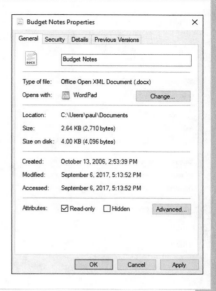

Hiding a File

If you have a file that contains sensitive or secret data, making it read-only isn't good enough because you probably don't want unauthorized users to even *see* the contents of the file much less change them. To prevent other people from viewing a file, you can hide it so that it doesn't appear during a cursory examination of the folder's contents. Here are the steps to follow:

1. Use File Explorer to open the folder that contains the file you want to hide.

2. Click the file.

3. In the Home tab, click the top half of the Properties button. The file's Properties dialog box appears.

4. Click the General tab.

5. Click the Hidden check box, as shown in Figure 32.10.

6. Click Advanced to open the Advanced Attributes dialog box.

7. Uncheck the Allow This File to Have Contents Indexed in Addition to File Properties box. This is optional, but it does prevent the file's data from being found during a file search.

8. Click OK to return to the Properties dialog box.

9. Click OK. The file is now hidden.

To see a hidden file, first use File Explorer to open the folder containing the file. In the ribbon, click the View tab and then check the Hidden Items box. (Don't expect this to hide a file from someone strongly determined to find it, however.)

In the next section, we show you how to apply user-specific file protection settings.

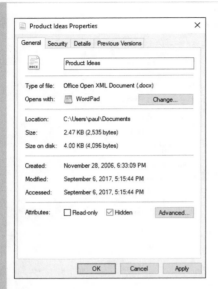

Figure 32.10
Check the Hidden box to prevent a file from being seen.

Setting Security Permissions on Files and Folders

At the file system level, security for Windows 10 is most often handled by assigning *permissions* to a file or folder. Permissions specify whether a local user or group is allowed to access a file or folder and, if access is allowed, they also specify what the user or group is allowed to do with the file or folder. For example, a user may be allowed only to read the contents of a file or folder, whereas another may be allowed to make changes to the file or folder.

Windows 10 offers a basic set of six permissions for folders and five permissions for files:

- **Full Control**—A user or group can perform any of the actions listed. A user or group can also change permissions.

- **Modify**—A user or group can view the file or folder contents, open files, edit files, create new files and subfolders, delete files, and run programs.

- **Read and Execute**—A user or group can view the file or folder contents, open files, and run programs.

- **List Folder Contents (folders only)**—A user or group can view the folder contents.

- **Read**—A user or group can open files but cannot edit them.

- **Write**—A user or group can create new files and subfolders as well as open and edit existing files.

There is also a long list of so-called *special permissions* that offer more fine-grained control over file and folder security. (We'll run through these special permissions a bit later; see "Assigning Special Permissions.")

Permissions are often handled most easily by using the built-in security groups. Each security group is defined with a specific set of permissions and rights, and any user added to a group is automatically granted that group's permissions and rights. There are two main security groups:

- **Administrators**—Members of this group have complete control over the computer, meaning they can access all folders and files; install and uninstall programs (including legacy programs) and devices; create, modify, and remove user accounts; install Windows updates, service packs, and fixes; use Safe mode; repair Windows; take ownership of objects; and more.

- **Users**—Members of this group (also known as *standard users*) can access files only in their own folders and in the computer's shared folders, change their account's password and picture, and run programs and install programs that don't require administrative-level rights.

In addition to those groups, Windows 10 defines up to a dozen others that you'll use less often. (Actually, most of these extra groups are of interest only to corporate IT personnel.) Note that the permissions assigned to these groups are automatically assigned to members of the Administrators group. This means that if you have an Administrator account, you don't also have to be a member of any other group to perform the tasks specific to that group. Here's the list of groups:

- **Access Control Assistance Operators**—Members of this group can perform remote queries to determine the permissions assigned to a computer's resources.

- **Backup Operators**—Members of this group can access the Backup program and use it to back up and restore folders and files, no matter what permissions are set on those objects.

- **Cryptographic Operators**—Members of this group can perform cryptographic tasks.

- **Distributed COM Users**—Members of this group can start, activate, and use Distributed COM (DCOM) objects.

- **Event Log Readers**—Members of this group can access and read Windows 10's event logs.

- **Guests**—Members of this group have the same privileges as those of the Users group. The exception is the default Guest account, which is not allowed to change its account password.

- **HomeUsers**—Members of this group can access Homegroup resources. You see this group only if a Homegroup is set up on your network.

- **Hyper-V Administrators**—Members of this group have complete access to all the features of the Hyper-V virtualization software.

- **IIS_IUSRS**—Members of this group can access an Internet Information Server website installed on the Windows 10 computer.

- **Network Configuration Operators**—Members of this group have a subset of the administrator-level rights that enables them to install and configure networking features.

- **Performance Log Users**—Members of this group can use the Windows Performance Diagnostic Console snap-in to monitor performance counters, logs, and alerts, both locally and remotely.

- **Performance Monitor Users**—Members of this group can use the Windows Performance Diagnostic Console snap-in to monitor performance counters only, both locally and remotely.

- **Power Users**—Members of this group have a subset of the Administrators group privileges. Power users can't back up or restore files, replace system files, take ownership of files, or install or remove device drivers. Also, power users can't install applications that explicitly require the user to be a member of the Administrators group.

- **Remote Desktop Users**—Members of this group can log on to the computer from a remote location using the Remote Desktop feature.

- **Remote Management Users**—Members of this group have access to Windows Management Instrumentation (WMI) resources using Windows management protocols such as the WS-Management service.

- **Replicator**—Members of this group can replicate files across a domain.

- **System Managed Accounts Group**—This group is used only for those accounts that are automatically created, modified, and deleted by Windows itself.

- **WinRMRemoteWMIUsers**—Members of this group have access to Windows Management Instrumentation (WMI) resources via the Windows Remote Management service.

Assigning a User to a Security Group

The advantage of using security groups to assign permissions is that once you set the group's permissions on a file or folder, you never have to change the security again on that object. Instead, any new users you create, you assign to the appropriate security group, and they automatically inherit that group's permissions.

Here are the steps to follow to assign a user to a Windows 10 security group:

1. Press Windows Logo+R to display the Run dialog box.

2. In the Open text box, type `control userpasswords2`.

3. Click OK. Windows 10 displays the User Accounts dialog box.

4. Click the user you want to work with, and then click Properties. The user's property sheet appears.

5. Display the Group Membership tab.

6. Click the Other option.

7. Use the Other list to select the security group. Notice that Windows provides a short description of the selected group, as shown in Figure 32.11.

8. Click OK. Windows 10 assigns the user to the security group.

Assigning a User to Multiple Security Groups

If you want to assign a user to more than one security group, the User Account dialog box method that we ran through in the preceding section won't work. If you have Windows 10 Pro or Enterprise, you can use the Local Users and Groups snap-in to assign a user to multiple groups. Here's how:

Figure 32.11
In the Group Membership tab, click Other and then select a security group.

1. In the taskbar's Search box, type `lusrmgr.msc` and then press Enter. The Local Users and Groups snap-in appears.

2. Select the Users branch, and then double-click the user you want to work with. The user's property sheet appears.

3. Display the Member Of tab, which shows the groups assigned to the user (see Figure 32.12).

Figure 32.12
Use the Local User and Groups snap-in to assign a user to multiple security groups.

4. Click Add. Windows 10 displays the Select Groups dialog box.

5. If you know the name of the group, type it in the large text box. Otherwise, click Advanced, Find Now, and then double-click the group in the list that appears.

6. Repeat step 5 to assign the user to other groups, as needed.

7. Click OK. Windows 10 adds the groups to the Member Of tab.

8. Click OK. Windows 10 assigns the user to the security groups the next time the user logs on.

Assigning Standard Permissions

When you're ready to assign any of the standard permissions that we discussed earlier to a user or group, follow these steps:

1. In File Explorer, click the file or folder you want to secure.

2. Display the Home tab, and then click the top half of the Properties button to display the Properties dialog box.

3. Display the Security tab.

4. Click Edit. The Permissions for *Object* dialog box appears, where *Object* is the name of the file or folder.

5. Click Add to open the Select Users or Groups dialog box.

6. If you know the name of the user or group you want to add, type it in the large text box. Otherwise, click Advanced, Find Now, and then double-click the user or group in the list that appears.

7. Click OK. Windows 10 returns you to the Permissions for *Object* dialog box with the new user or group added.

8. Use the check boxes in the Allow and Deny columns to assign the permissions you want for this user or group, as shown in Figure 32.13.

9. Click OK in all the open dialog boxes.

Assigning Special Permissions

In some situations, you might want more fine-tuned control over a user's or group's permissions. For example, you may want to allow a user to add new files to a folder, but not new subfolders. Similarly, you might want to give a user full control over a file or folder but deny that user the ability to change permissions or take ownership of the object.

For these more specific situations, Windows 10 offers a set of 14 special permissions for folders and 13 special permissions for files:

- **Full Control**—A user or group can perform any of the actions listed here.

- **Traverse Folder/Execute File**—A user or group can open the folder to get to another folder or can execute a program file.

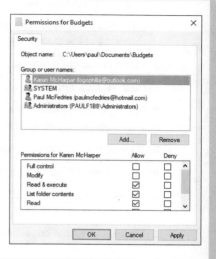

Figure 32.13
Use a file or folder's Permissions dialog box to assign standard permissions for a user or security group.

- **List Folder/Read Data**—A user or group can view the folder contents or can read the contents of a file.

- **Read Attributes**—A user or group can read the folder's or file's attributes, such as Read-Only or Hidden.

- **Read Extended Attributes**—A user or group can read the folder's or file's extended attributes. (These are extra attributes assigned by certain programs.)

- **Create Files/Write Data**—A user or group can create new files within a folder or can make changes to a file.

- **Create Folders/Append Data**—A user or group can create new subfolders within a folder or can add new data to the end of a file (but can't change any existing file data).

- **Write Attributes**—A user or group can change the folder's or file's attributes.

- **Write Extended Attributes**—A user or group can change the folder's or file's extended attributes.

- **Delete Subfolders and Files**—A user or group can delete subfolders and files within the folder.

- **Delete**—A user or group can delete the folders or file.

- **Read Permissions**—A user or group can read the folder's or file's permissions.

- **Change Permissions**—A user or group can edit the folder's or file's permissions.

- **Take Ownership**—A user or group can take ownership of the folder or file.

> **note**
> To see a file's or folder's attributes, right-click the item, click Properties, and then display the General tab.

Here are the steps to follow to assign special permissions to a file or folder:

1. In File Explorer, click the file or folder you want to secure.

2. Display the Home tab, and then click the top half of the Properties button.

3. Display the Security tab.

4. Click Advanced. The Advanced Security Settings for *Object* dialog box appears, where *Object* is the name of the file or folder.

5. In the Permissions tab, click Add. The Permission Entry for *Object* dialog box appears.

6. Click Select a Principal.

7. If you know the name of the user or group you want to work with, type it in the large text box. Otherwise, click Advanced, Find Now, and then double-click the user or group in the list that appears.

8. Click Show Advanced Permissions.

9. In the Type list, select either Allow or Deny.

10. Use the check boxes to assign the permissions you want for this user or group, as shown in Figure 32.14.

11. Click OK in all the open dialog boxes.

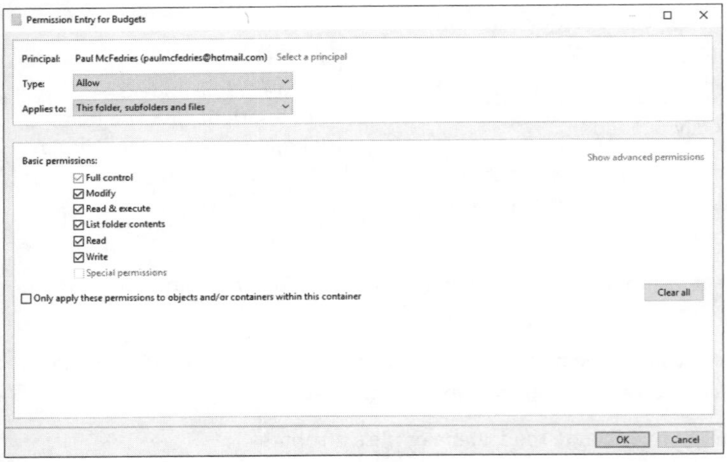

Figure 32.14
Use a file or folder's Permission Entry dialog box to assign special permissions for a user or security group.

Fixing Permission Problems by Taking Ownership of Your Files

When you're working in Windows 10, you might have trouble with a folder (or a file) because Windows tells you that you don't have permission to edit (add to, delete, whatever) the folder. The result is often a series of annoying User Account Control dialog boxes.

You might think the solution is to give your user account Full Control permissions on the folder, but it's not as easy as that. Why not? Because you're not the owner of the folder. (If you were, you'd have the permissions you need automatically.) So the solution is first to take ownership of the folder and then assign your user account full control permissions over the folder.

Here are the steps to follow:

1. Use File Explorer to locate the folder you want to take ownership of.

2. Display the Home tab, and then click the top half of the Properties button.

3. Display the Security tab.

4. Click Advanced to open the Advanced Security Settings dialog box.

5. Display the Permissions tab.

6. Click the Change link that appears beside Owner. The Select User or Group dialog box appears.

7. Type your username, and then click OK.

8. Check the Replace Owner on Subcontainers and Objects box, as shown in Figure 32.15.

Figure 32.15
Use a folder's Advanced Security Settings dialog box to take ownership of the folder.

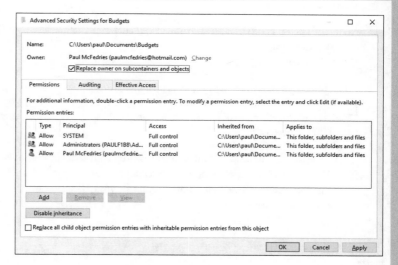

9. Click OK to return to the Security tab of the folder's Properties dialog box.

10. If you don't see your user account in the Group or User Names list, click Edit, click Add, type your username, and click OK.

11. Click your username.

12. Click the Full Control check box in the Allow column.

13. Click OK.

Note that, obviously, this is quite a bit of work. If you have to do it only every once in a while, it's no big thing, but if you find you have to take ownership regularly, you'll probably want an

 note
You can download this REG file from www.mcfedries.com/book.php?title=windows-10-in-depth.

easier way to go about it. You've got it! Listing 32.1 shows a Registry Editor file that modifies the Registry in such a way that you end up with a Take Ownership command in the shortcut menu that appears if you right-click any folder and any file.

Listing 32.1   A Registry Editor File That Creates a Take Ownership Command

```
Windows Registry Editor Version 5.00

[HKEY_CLASSES_ROOT\*\shell\runas]
@="Take Ownership"
"NoWorkingDirectory"=""

[HKEY_CLASSES_ROOT\*\shell\runas\command]
@="cmd.exe /c takeown /f \"%1\" && icacls \"%1\" /grant administrators:F"
"IsolatedCommand"="cmd.exe /c takeown /f \"%1\" && icacls \"%1\" /grant
administrators:F"

[HKEY_CLASSES_ROOT\Directory\shell\runas]
@="Take Ownership"
"NoWorkingDirectory"=""

[HKEY_CLASSES_ROOT\Directory\shell\runas\command]
@="cmd.exe /c takeown /f \"%1\" /r /d y && icacls \"%1\" /grant administrators:F /t"
"IsolatedCommand"="cmd.exe /c takeown /f \"%1\" /r /d y && icacls \"%1\" /grant
administrators:F /t"
```

To use the file, double-click it and then enter your UAC credentials when prompted. As you can see in Figure 32.16, right-clicking (in this case) a folder displays a shortcut menu with a new Take Ownership command. Click that command, enter your UAC credentials, and sit back as Windows does all the hard work for you!

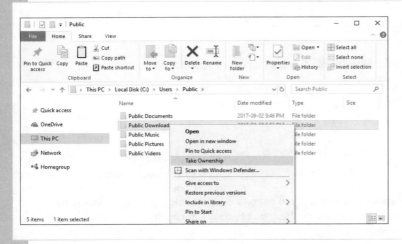

Figure 32.16
When you install the Registry modification, you see the Take Ownership command when you right-click a file.

Encrypting Files and Folders

If a snoop can't log on to your Windows PC, does that mean your data is safe? No, unfortunately, it most certainly does not. If a cracker has physical access to your PC—either by sneaking into your office or by stealing your computer—the cracker can use advanced utilities to view the contents of your hard drive. This means that if your PC contains extremely sensitive or confidential information—personal financial files, medical histories, corporate salary data, trade secrets, business plans, journals, or diaries—it wouldn't be hard for the interloper to read and even copy that data.

 note

To use file encryption, the drive must use NTFS. To check the current file system, open File Explorer, click This PC, click the drive, select Computer and then Properties, and in the General tab, examine the file system information in the Properties dialog box. If you need to convert a drive to NTFS, press Windows Logo+X, click Command Prompt (Admin), and then click Yes when User Account Control asks you to confirm. At the command prompt, type **convert d: /fs:ntfs**, where d is the letter of the hard drive you want to convert, and press Enter. If Windows asks to "dismount the volume," press Y and then Enter.

➡️ *To learn how to add Command Prompt (Admin) to the Start Menu's shortcut menu,* **see** *"Adding Command Prompt to the Shortcut Menu,"* **p. 129.**

If you're worried about anyone viewing these or other "for your eyes only" files, Windows 10 Pro enables you to *encrypt* the file information. Encryption encodes the file to make it completely unreadable by anyone unless the person logs on to your Windows 10 account. After you encrypt your files, you work with them exactly as you did before, with no noticeable loss of performance.

Encrypting a Folder

Follow these steps to encrypt important data:

1. Use File Explorer to display the icon of the folder containing the data that you want to encrypt.

2. In the Home tab, click the top half of the Properties button to open the folder's property sheet.

3. Click the General tab.

4. Click Advanced. The Advanced Attributes dialog box appears.

5. Click to activate the Encrypt Contents to Secure Data check box.

6. Click OK in each open dialog box. The Confirm Attribute Changes dialog box appears.

 tip

Although it's possible to encrypt individual files, encrypting an entire folder is easier because Windows 10 then automatically encrypts new files that you add to the folder.

7. Click the Apply Changes to This Folder, Subfolders and Files option.

8. Click OK. Windows encrypts the folder's contents.

Backing Up Your Encryption Key

When you sign in to Windows 10, it uses your credentials to access the encryption key that decrypts the folder so you can access it. This encryption key is stored on your hard disk for easy and fast access. However, like any file or folder on your hard disk, the encryption key can become corrupted. If that happens, you lose access to the encrypted data, so key corruption is a disaster waiting to happen. To avoid that disaster, you should back up the encryption key to a removable drive for safekeeping.

When you encrypt a folder for the first time, Windows 10 displays a notification suggesting you back up the encryption key, as shown in Figure 32.17. Click that notification to get started. If you miss the notification, click the Show Hidden Icons arrow in the taskbar's notification area, and then click the Encrypting File System icon.

> **⊙ tip**
>
> By default, Windows displays the names of encrypted files and folders in a green font, which helps you to differentiate these items from unencrypted files and folders. If you'd rather see encrypted filenames and folder names in the regular font, open any folder window and select View, Options. Click the View tab, click to uncheck the Show Encrypted or Compressed NTFS Files in Color box, and then click OK.

Figure 32.17
When you first use the encrypting file system, you see this notification prompting you to back up your encryption key.

Follow these steps to back up your encryption key to a removable drive:

1. In the initial Encrypting File System dialog box, click Back Up Now. The Certificate Export Wizard appears.

2. Click Next. The Export File Format dialog box appears.

3. The default format is fine, so click Next. The Security dialog box appears and prompts you for a password to protect the encryption key.

4. Check the Password text box, type the password in both the Password text box and then the Confirm Password text box, and then click Next. The File to Export dialog box appears.

5. Insert a removable drive, such as a USB flash drive.

6. Click Browse, click This PC, double-click the removable drive, type a filename, and then click Save.

7. Click Next.

8. Click Finish, and then click OK when the wizard tells you the export was successful.

Encrypting a Disk with BitLocker

Take Windows 10 security technologies such as the bidirectional Windows Firewall, Windows Defender, and Windows Service Hardening; throw in good patch-management policies (that is, applying security patches as soon as they're available); and add a dash of common sense. If you do so, your computer should never be compromised by malware while Windows 10 is running.

Windows Service Hardening

Windows Service Hardening is an under-the-hood Windows 10 security feature designed to limit the damage that a compromised service can wreak upon a system by implementing the following security techniques:

- All services run in a lower privilege level.
- All services have been stripped of permissions that they don't require.
- All services are assigned a security identifier (SID) that uniquely identifies each service. This enables a system resource to create its own access control list (ACL) that specifies exactly which SIDs can access the resource. If a service that's not on the ACL tries to access the resource, Windows 10 blocks the service.
- A system resource can restrict which services are allowed write permission to the resource.
- All services come with network restrictions that prevent services from accessing the network in ways not defined by the service's normal operating parameters.

However, what about when Windows 10 is not running? If your computer is stolen or if an attacker breaks into your home or office, your machine can be compromised in a couple of different ways:

- By booting to a removable drive and using command-line utilities to reset the administrator password
- By using a removable drive–based operating system to access your hard disk and reset folder and file permissions

Either exploit gives the attacker access to the contents of your computer. If you have sensitive data on your machine—financial data, company secrets, and so on—the results could be disastrous.

To help you prevent a malicious user from accessing your sensitive data, Windows 10 Pro (as well as the Enterprise and Education editions and possibly Windows 10 Home, depending on whether your PC setup can handle encryption) comes with a technology called BitLocker that encrypts an entire hard drive. That way, even if a malicious user gains physical access to your computer, he won't be able to read the drive contents. BitLocker works by storing the keys that encrypt and decrypt the sectors on a system drive in a Trusted Platform Module (TPM) 1.2 chip, which is a hardware component available on many newer machines.

Enabling BitLocker on a System with a TPM

To enable BitLocker on a system that comes with a TPM, use the taskbar's Search box to type **bit**, and then click Manage BitLocker. In the BitLocker Drive Encryption window, shown in Figure 32.18, click the Turn On BitLocker link associated with your hard drive.

 note
To find out whether your computer has a TPM chip installed, restart the machine and then access the computer's BIOS settings (usually by pressing Delete or some other key; watch for a startup message that tells you how to access the BIOS). In most cases, look for a Security section and see if it lists a TPM entry.

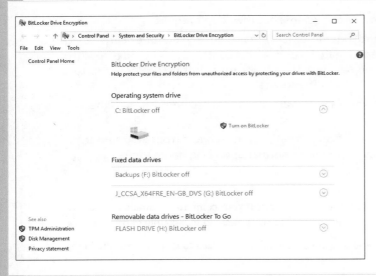

Figure 32.18
Use the BitLocker Drive Encryption window to turn BitLocker on and off.

 note
You can also use the Trusted Platform Module (TPM) Management snap-in to work with the TPM chip on your computer. If you're in the BitLocker Drive Encryption window, click TPM Administration. Otherwise, use the taskbar's Search box to type **tpm.msc** and then press Enter. This snap-in enables you to view the current status of the TPM chip, view information about the chip manufacturer, and perform chip-management functions.

Enabling BitLocker on a System Without a TPM

If your PC doesn't have a TPM chip, you can still use BitLocker. In this case, however, you'll be forced to jump an extra hurdle when you start your computer. This hurdle will either be an extra password that you must enter or a USB flash drive that you must insert. Only by doing this will Windows 10 decrypt the drive and enable you to work with your computer in the normal way.

First, you must configure Windows 10 to allow BitLocker on a system without a TPM. Here's how it's done:

1. In the taskbar's Search box, type **gpedit.msc** and then press Enter to open the Local Group Policy Editor.

2. Open the Computer Configuration, Administrative Templates, Windows Components, BitLocker Drive Encryption, Operating System Drives branch.

3. Double-click the Require Additional Authentication at Startup policy.

4. Select Enabled.

5. Click to check the Allow BitLocker Without a Compatible TPM box, as shown in Figure 32.19.

Figure 32.19
Use the Require Additional Authentication at Startup policy to configure Windows 10 to use BitLocker without a TPM.

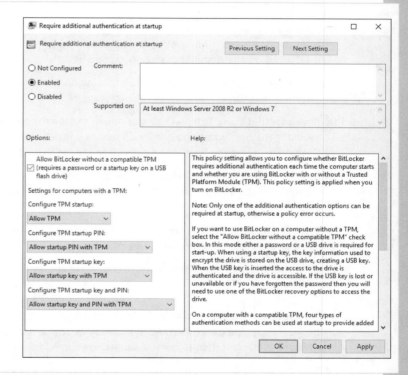

6. Click OK.

7. To ensure that Windows 10 recognizes the new policy right away, press Windows Logo+R to open the Run dialog box, type **gpupdate /force**, and click OK.

You can now enable BitLocker:

1. In the taskbar's Search box, type **bit**, and then click Manage BitLocker to open the BitLocker Drive Encryption window.

2. Click the Turn On BitLocker link beside your hard drive. The BitLocker Drive Encryption Wizard appears and asks how you want to unlock your drive when you start the system.

3. Make your choice:

   ▪ **Insert a USB Flash Drive**—Click this option to require a flash drive to be inserted at startup. Insert the flash drive, wait until the wizard recognizes it, and then click Save.

   ▪ **Enter a Password**—Click this option to require a password at startup. Type your password in the two text boxes, and then click Next.

4. The wizard now asks how you want to store your recovery key, which you'll need if you ever have trouble unlocking your PC. Click one (or more) of the following options:

   ▪ **Save to your Microsoft account**—Click this option to save the recovery key as part of your Microsoft account.

   ▪ **Save to a USB Flash Drive**—Click this option to save the recovery key to a flash drive. This is probably the best way to go because it means you can recover your files just by inserting the flash drive. Insert the flash drive, select it in the list that appears, and then click Save.

   ▪ **Save to a File**—Click this option to save the recovery key to a separate hard drive on your system. Use the Save BitLocker Recovery Key As dialog box to choose a location, and then click Save.

   ▪ **Print the Recovery Key**—Click this option to print out the recovery key. Choose your printer in the dialog box that appears, and then click Print.

5. Click Next. The wizard asks how much of your drive you want to encrypt.

6. Select an option:

   ▪ **Encrypt Used Disk Space Only**—This option encrypts only the current data on the drive; any new data you add gets encrypted automatically. This is a much faster option, but it might not give you total protection if you've been using your PC for a while.

   ▪ **Encrypt Entire Drive**—This option encrypts both the current data on the drive and the drive's empty space. This takes quite a bit longer, but it offers total security because it also encrypts deleted data that remains on the hard drive and could otherwise be read by a snoop with low-level file utilities.

7. Click Next. The wizard prompts you to choose an encryption mode.

 note

If your version of Windows 10 doesn't offer the Local Group Policy Editor, you can still configure BitLocker to work on non-TPM systems by editing the Registry. However, this requires creating and configuring a new Registry key and a half dozen settings. To make this easier, we created a REG file that does everything automatically. You can download this file from www.mcfedries.com/ book.php?title=windows-10-in-depth.

8. Select an option:

   - **New Encryption Mode**—Choose this option if you're only encrypting fixed drives, or if you're encrypting removable drives that will never be used with editions of Windows prior to Windows 10 Version 1511 (Windows 10's first major update, which was released in November 2015).

   - **Compatible Mode**—Choose this option if you're encrypting removable drives that will be used with editions of Windows prior to Windows 10 Version 1511.

9. Click Next.

10. The wizard lets you know that BitLocker now needs to be activated.

11. Make sure the Run BitLocker System Check setting is activated, and then click Continue. BitLocker tells you your system won't be encrypted until you restart.

12. Restart your PC.

13. If you chose to enter a password at startup, you see the BitLocker screen shown in Figure 32.20. Type your BitLocker password and press Enter. If you chose a flash drive startup, make sure the flash drive is inserted.

Figure 32.20
If you chose to enter a password at startup, use this screen to type the password, and then press Enter.

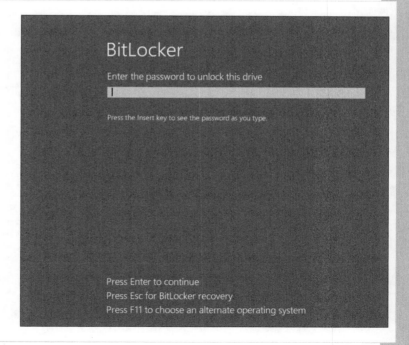

14. Sign in to Windows 10. BitLocker begins encrypting your hard drive.

33

PROTECTING YOUR NETWORK FROM HACKERS AND SNOOPS

It's a Cold, Cruel World

I have relatives, friends, and neighbors who say that they never locked the front door to their house when they were growing up. What a charming thought! It's nearly inconceivable today to do this. I don't think it's because people have gotten any worse or that there's a higher percentage of bad people; it's that there are just more people. A lot more. The odds have gotten greater that an unlocked door would lead to theft simply because there are more people walking down the street, past your door, and eventually one of them will give it a push.

And here's the thing: With an Internet connection in your home or business, there are about three billion people and three billion computers able to reach your (virtual) door. The percentage of them who would commit theft or other mayhem may be small, but... do the math. The inescapable truth is that every minute of every day, some hacker, spammer, information bandit, prankster, thief, bottom-feeder, otherwise bad guy, or, more likely, one of the hundreds of millions of virus-infected computers the bad guys control will probe, prod, and test your defenses. Is your network up to the task?

It can be. Effective network design is foremost a task of planning. It's especially true in this case: *Before* you connect to the Internet, you must plan for security, whether you have a single computer or a large local area network (LAN).

Explaining everything that you can and should do would be impossible. In this chapter, we give you an

 note

You should know this: Even if you don't have a network but have just one computer that is only occasionally connected to the Internet, you're still at risk. The material in this chapter applies to almost everyone!

idea of what network security entails. We talk about the types of risks you'll be exposed to and the means people use to minimize this exposure; then we end with some tips and to-do lists. If you want to have a network or security consultant take care of implementation for you, that's great. This chapter gives you the background to understand what the consultant is doing. If you want to go it on your own, consider this chapter to be a survey course, with your assignment to continue to research, write, and implement a security plan.

---

tip

This chapter gives you a good background on the ways that the "bad guys" can get into your computer and cause damage. If you don't want to read about this, skip ahead to "Specific Configuration Steps for Windows 10," later in the chapter. If even that's too much, we can give you the short version in one paragraph:

Windows 10 has far better security than, say, Windows XP, right out of the box. *Don't* turn off User Account Control (UAC), Windows Defender Firewall, Windows Defender, or delay Windows Updates, no matter what anyone else tells you. *Do* back up your hard disk frequently. If you do that and make no changes to Microsoft's default security settings, you'll be better off than 95 percent of the people out there.

Who Would Be Interested in My Computer?

Most of us don't give security risks a second thought. After all, who is a data thief going to target: me or the Pentagon? Who'd be interested in my computer? Well, the sad truth is that thousands of people out there would be delighted to find that they could connect to *your* computer. They might be looking for ways to get your credit card information, passwords for computers and websites, or a way to get to other computers on your LAN. Even more, they would love to find that they could install software on your computer that they could then use to send spam and probe other people's computers. They might even use your computer to launch attacks against corporate or governmental networks. *Don't doubt that this could happen to you.* Much of the spam you receive is sent from home computers that have been taken over by criminals thanks to software bugs and through the conduit of an unsecured Internet connection. An estimated 5 to 33 percent of computers worldwide are infected with malware. (That's tens of millions to hundreds of millions of infected computers.)

For a decade, Microsoft shrugged off any responsibility for preventing this, but starting with Windows XP Service Pack 2, it started enabling the strictest network security settings by default instead of requiring you to take explicit steps to enable them. And with the advent of high-speed, always-on Internet connections, the risks were increasing because computers stayed connected and exposed for longer periods of time.

🔍 note

If your computer is connected to a Windows domain-type network, your network administrators probably have taken care of all this for you. In fact, you might not even be able to make any changes in your computer's network or security settings. If this is the case, even if you're not too interested in this topic and don't read any other part of this chapter, you should read and carry out the steps in the section "Specific Configuration Steps for Windows 10."

Windows Vista introduced User Account Control (UAC), which requires the user to respond to a prompt before the system will change sensitive system settings or install software, thereby making sure the user is aware of and approves the action. UAC also provides a mechanism to run some programs (especially network- and Internet-connected programs) with lower than normal privileges, so that if the program gets compromised, it can do less damage to files and other software on the computer. Other steps were taken to help block the methods that viruses use to gain control of the operating system. These technical defenses have been improved upon with each successive version of Windows.

Starting with Windows 7, Microsoft improved things further by having Windows automatically batten down the hatches again anytime it detects that it has been connected to a new network (for example, at a Wi-Fi hotspot or a friend's home). You must explicitly open things up by telling Windows that the new network is safe. This feature is called Network Location, and we discuss it later in the chapter.

In this chapter, we explain a bit about how network attacks and defenses work. We tell you ways to prevent and prepare for recovery from a hacker attack. And most importantly, we show you what to do to make your system secure.

If outside attacks weren't enough, in a business environment, security risks can come from *inside* a network environment as well as from outside. Inside, you might be subject to highly sophisticated eavesdropping techniques or even simple theft. I know of a company whose entire customer list and confidential pricing database walked out the door one night with the receptionist, whose significant other worked for the competition. The theft was easy; at the time, any employee could read and print any file on the company's network. Computer security is a real and serious issue. And it only helps to think about it *before* things go wrong.

Types of Attack

Before we talk about how to defend your computer against attack, let's briefly go through the types of attacks you're facing. Hackers can work their way into your computer and network using several methods. Here are some of them:

- **Password cracking**—Given a user account name, so-called cracking software can tirelessly try dictionary words, proper names, and random combinations in the hope of guessing a correct password. If your passwords aren't complex (that is, if they're not composed of a combination of upper- and lowercase letters, numbers, and punctuation characters), this doesn't take long to accomplish. If you make your computer(s) directly accessible over the Internet via Remote Desktop or if you run a public FTP, web, or email server, I can *promise* you that you will be the target of this sort of automated attack.

- **Address spoofing**—If you've seen the caller ID service used on telephones, you know that it can be used to screen calls: You answer the phone only if you recognize the caller. But what if telemarketers could make the device say, "Mom's calling"? There's an analogy to this in networking. Hackers can send "spoofed" network commands into a network with a trusted IP address.

- **Impersonation**—By tricking Internet routers and the domain name registry system, hackers can have Internet or network data traffic routed to their own computers instead of the legitimate website server. With a fake website in operation, they can collect credit card numbers and other valuable data. This type of attack is on the rise due to vulnerabilities in the Internet's basic infrastructure.

- **Eavesdropping**—Wiretaps on your telephone or network cable, or monitoring of the radio emissions from your computer and monitor, can let the more sophisticated hackers and spies see what you're seeing and record what you're typing. This may sound like KGB/CIA-type stuff, but it's done. And wireless networks, which are everywhere these days, are extremely vulnerable to eavesdropping.

- **Exploits**—It's a given that complex software has bugs. Some bugs make programs fail in such a way that part of the program itself gets replaced by data from the user. Exploiting this sort of bug, hackers can run their own software on your computer, without your knowledge or permission. It sounds farfetched, but new exploits against Microsoft's products alone are reported about once a week. Add-on products such as Adobe Acrobat Viewer, Adobe Flash Player, and Oracle's Java have also been responsible for a huge number of exploits because virtually every computer in the world has these programs, and their earlier versions didn't automatically seek and install updates. Even computer hardware can have exploitable bugs, as demonstrated by the so-called Meltdown and Spectre attacks that emerged as this book was being published.

  Security researchers try to stay ahead of the hackers by finding exploits and reporting them to the responsible manufacturer before they get used "in the wild," but you'll often see reports of bugs that are detected only after criminals have started to use them. These are called "zero-day" exploits, meaning, zero days elapsed between their detection and their exploitation. You can be sure that even the most up-to-date copy of Windows has exploits just waiting to be used.

- **Backdoors**—Some software developers put special features into programs intended for their use only, usually to help in debugging. These backdoors sometimes circumvent security features. Hackers discover and trade information on these and are only too happy to use the Internet to see if they work on your computer. It is also widely believed that some government agencies insist that encryption and security software have backdoors for use by said government agencies. How would you know?

- **Open doors**—All the attack methods described previously involve direct and malicious actions to try to break into your system. But this isn't always necessary: Sometimes a computer can be left open in such a way that it just offers itself to the public. Just as leaving your front door wide open might invite burglary, leaving a computer unsecured by passwords and without proper controls on network access allows hackers to read and write your files by the simplest means. Password Protected Sharing, which we discuss later in the chapter, mitigates this risk somewhat.

- **Viruses and Trojan horses**—The ancient Greeks came up with the idea 3,200 years ago, and the Trojan horse trick is still alive and well today. Shareware programs used to be the favored way to distribute disguised attack software, but today email attachments and websites are the favored method. Most email providers automatically strip out obviously executable email attachments, so the current trend is for viruses to send their payloads in ZIP and PDF file attachments. File- and music-sharing programs, Registry cleanup tools, and other "free" software utilities are another great source of unwanted add-ons commonly called *spyware*, *adware*, *ransomware*, and *malware.* You may also hear the term *rootkit*, which refers to a virus that burrows so deeply into the operating system that it can prevent you from detecting its presence when you list files or active running programs. Other sources of viruses are hacked or malicious websites that use web browser or media player exploits to install malware just by viewing the site. Sometimes legitimate, high-volume websites get hacked to do this (so-called *drive-by* attacks, where you get infected just doing innocent web browsing), or links to these sites are sent in spam and phishing email.

- **Phishing and social engineering**—A more subtle approach than brute-force hacking is to simply call or email someone who has useful information and ask for it. One variation on this approach is called *phishing*, in which the criminals send email that purports to come from a bank or other service provider, saying there was some sort of account glitch and asking the user to reply with her password and Social Security number so the glitch can be fixed. P. T. Barnum said there's a sucker born every minute. Sadly, this works out to 1,440 suckers per day or more than half a million per year, and it's not too hard to reach a lot of them with one bulk email. For more information about phishing, see Chapter 34, "Protecting Yourself from Fraud and Spam."

- **Denial of service (DoS)**—Every hacker is interested in your credit cards or business secrets. Some are just plain vandals, however, and it's enough for them to know that you can't get your work done. They might erase your hard drive or, more subtly, crash your server or tie up your Internet connection with a torrent of meaningless data. In any case, you're inconvenienced.

- **Identity theft**—Hackers often attempt to steal personal information, such as your name, date of birth, address, credit card, and Social Security number. Armed with this information, they can proceed to open credit card and bank accounts; redirect your mail; take over your email, online (cloud) services, and social networking accounts; obtain services; purchase goods; claim your tax refund; and so on, all without your knowledge. This is one of the most vicious attacks and can have a profound and lasting effect on victims. Computers can expose you to identity theft in several ways: You might provide personal information to a phishing scheme or to an unscrupulous online seller yourself. Hackers can break into your computer or that of an online seller and steal your information stored there. Criminals can tap into your home or business network, a wireless network in a public space, or even the wiring at an Internet service provider and capture unencrypted information flowing through the network there.

If all this makes you nervous about connecting to the Internet, we've done our job well. Before you pull the plug, though, read on.

Your Lines of Defense

Making your computer and network completely impervious to all these forms of attacks is quite impossible, if for no other reason than that there is always a human element that you cannot control, and there are always bugs and exploits not yet anticipated.

You *can* do a great deal, however, if you plan ahead. Furthermore, as new software introduces new features and risks, and as existing flaws are identified and repaired, you have to keep on top of things to maintain your defenses. The most important part of the process is that you spend some time thinking about security.

The following sections delve into the four main lines of computer defense:

- Preparation

- Active defense

- Testing, logging, and monitoring

- Disaster planning

You can omit any of these measures, of course, if you weigh what you have at risk against what these efforts will cost you and decide that the benefit isn't worth the effort.

What we're describing sounds like a lot of work, and it can be if you take full-fledged measures in a business environment. Nevertheless, even if you're a home user, we encourage you to consider each of the following steps and to put them into effect with as much diligence as you can muster.

Preparation: Network Security Basics

Preparation involves eliminating unnecessary sources of risk before they can be attacked. You should take the following steps:

- Invest time in planning and policies. If you want to be really diligent about security, for each of the strategies we describe in this chapter, outline how you plan to implement each one.

- Structure your network to restrict unauthorized access. Do you really need to allow users to remotely gain access to your network via a virtual private network (VPN) or Remote Desktop, or can you forego this? Eliminating points of access reduces risk but also convenience. You have to decide where to strike the balance.

- If you're concerned about unauthorized in-house access to your computers, be sure that every user account is set up with a good password—one with a combination of uppercase and lower-case letters and numbers and punctuation. Don't use the same password across different types of computer accounts or online services. (As painful as this is, you really do have to use different passwords everywhere. For ways to help reduce the pain, see "Identity-Management Software" on page **794**.

- Ensure that an effective firewall is in place between your LAN and the Internet. We show you how to use Windows Defender Firewall later in this chapter.

- Install only needed services. The less network software you have installed, the less you'll have to maintain through updates, and the fewer potential openings you'll offer to attackers. For example, don't install SNMP or Internet Information Services (IIS) unless you really need them. Don't install the optional Simple TCP Services network service; it provides no useful function, only archaic services that make great DoS attack targets. And whenever you buy a new computer, use the Add or Remove Programs control panel to go through the list of programs that came prein-stalled, and uninstall any that you don't want.

- You might subscribe to the free @RISK security bulletin mailing list at www.sans.org/newsletters. I personally also check my computer with http://browsercheck.qualys.com every few weeks. This web-based tool examines your web browser and plug-ins for web-based applications and lets you know if you're not up to date.

  If you use Microsoft IIS to host a website, pay particular attention to announcements regarding Internet Explorer and IIS. Internet Explorer and IIS together account for the lion's share of Windows security problems.

- Use software known to be secure and (relatively) bug-free. Uninstall any application programs pre-installed by your computer manufacturer that you know you don't want. The fewer programs on your computer, the fewer as-yet-undiscovered bugs there are waiting to bite you later.

- Use the Windows Automatic Updates feature. For every software application you use, proactively check the manufacturers' websites for updates, and install updates promptly when they become available. Enable the automatic-updating feature for any program that has one. Be *very* wary of shareware and freeware, unless you can be sure of its pedigree and safety.

- Download software, such as printer and other device drivers, only from the original manufacturer's own website, *never* from a third-party website.

- Use an antivirus program, and keep it updated. You can buy a third-party product, get a free third-party product, or use Microsoft's Windows Defender, which comes preinstalled on Windows 10. Whichever program you select, be sure to keep it up to date. (And you can now enable Windows Defender to perform scans in addition to any third-party antivirus program you install.)

- Properly configure your computers, file systems, software, and user accounts to maintain appropriate access control. We discuss this in detail later in the chapter.

- Hide from the outside world as much information about your systems as possible. Don't give hackers any assistance by revealing user account or computer names, if you can help it. For example, if you set up your own Internet domain, put as little information into DNS as you can get away with. Don't install SNMP unless you need it, and be sure to block it at your Internet firewall.

 tip

The most important program to keep up to date is Windows itself. We suggest that you keep up to date on Windows bugs and fixes through the Automatic Updates feature *and* through independent watchdogs. On Windows 10 Home, this isn't optional. Windows will download and install all updates. On Windows 10 Pro and Enterprise, we recommend that you do not defer updates unless you have very good reason to and have excellent perimeter defenses. (And no pesky users, who tend to mess things up no matter what you do.)

Security is partly a technical issue and partly a matter of organizational policy. No matter how you've configured your computers and network, one user with a modem and a lack of responsibility can open a door into the best-protected network.

If you manage computers for other people, you should decide which security-related issues you want to leave to your users' discretion and which you want to mandate as a matter of policy. On a Windows domain network, the operating system enforces some of these points, but if you don't have a domain server, you might need to rely on communication and trust alone. The following are some issues to ponder:

- Do you trust users to create and protect their own shared folders, or should this be done by management only?

- Do you want to let users run a web server, an FTP server, or other network services, each of which provides benefits but also increases risk?

- Are your users allowed to create simple alphabetic passwords without numbers or punctuation? (You can enforce more complex passwords using a Windows security policy setting.)

- Are users allowed to send and receive personal email from the network?

- Are users allowed to install software they obtain themselves?

- Are users allowed to share access to their desktops with Remote Desktop, Remote Assistance, Quick Assist, TeamViewer, GoToMyPC, LogMeIn, VNC, PCAnywhere, or other remote-control software?

Make public your management and personnel policies regarding network security and appropriate use of computer resources.

If your own users don't respect the integrity of your network, you don't stand a chance against the outside world. A crucial part of any effective security strategy is making up the rules in advance and ensuring that everyone knows and adheres to them.

Active Defenses

Active defense means actively resisting known methods of attack. Active defenses include these:

- Firewalls and gateways to block dangerous or inappropriate Internet traffic as it passes between your network and the Internet at large

- Encryption and authentication to limit access based on some sort of credentials (such as a password)

- Efforts to keep up to date on security and risks, especially with respect to Windows but also all installed applications

- Antivirus programs to detect and delete malware that makes it through your other defenses

When your network is in place, your next job is to configure it to restrict access as much as possible. This task involves blocking network traffic that is known to be dangerous and configuring network protocols to use the most secure communications protocols possible.

Firewalls and NAT (Connection-Sharing) Devices

Using a firewall is an effective way to secure your network. From the viewpoint of design and maintenance, it is also the most efficient tool because you can focus your efforts on one critical place: the interface between your internal network and the Internet.

A *firewall* is a program or piece of hardware that intercepts all data that passes between two networks—for example, between your computer or LAN and the Internet. The firewall inspects each incoming and outgoing data packet and permits only certain packets to pass. Generally, a firewall is set up to permit traffic for safe protocols such as those used for email and web browsing. It blocks packets that carry file-sharing or computer administration commands.

Network Address Translation (NAT), the technology behind Internet Connection Sharing and connection-sharing routers, insulates your network from the Internet by funneling all of your LAN's network traffic through one IP address—the Internet analog of a telephone number. Like an office's switchboard operator, NAT lets all your computers place outgoing connections at will, but it intercepts all incoming connection attempts. If an incoming data request was anticipated, it's forwarded to one of your computers, but all other incoming network requests are rejected or ignored. Microsoft's Internet Connection Sharing and hardware Internet Connection Sharing routers use a NAT scheme.

➡️ *To learn more about this topic, **see** "NAT and Internet Connection Sharing," **p. 407.***

The use of either NAT or a firewall, or both, can protect your network by letting you specify exactly how much of your network's resources you expose to the Internet. Luckily, almost every Internet service provider now provides NAT routers as standard equipment and direct, unprotected Internet connections are becoming rare.

Windows Defender Firewall

One of Windows 10's most important security features is the built-in Windows Defender Firewall software. (In previous versions of Windows it was called just Windows Firewall.)

Windows Defender Firewall is enabled on every hard-wired, wireless, or dial-up network connection. On those connections that lead directly to the Internet, it blocks virtually all attempts by outside computers to reach your computer, so it prevents computers on the Internet from accessing your shared files, Remote Desktop, Remote Administration, and other "sensitive" functions.

On an Internet-facing connection, Windows Defender Firewall by default blocks all attempts by other computers to reach your computer, except in response to communications that you initiate yourself. For example, if you try to view a web page, your computer starts the process by connecting to a web server out on the Internet. Windows Defender Firewall knows that the returning data is in response to your request, so it allows the reply to return to your computer. However, someone "out there" who tries to view your shared files will be rebuffed. Any unsolicited, incoming connection will simply be ignored.

This type of network haughtiness is generally a good thing, except that it would also prevent you from sharing your computer with the people you do want to share with. For example, it would block file and printer sharing on your home network, Remote Assistance and Quick Assist, and other desirable services. So Windows Defender Firewall can make *exceptions* that permit incoming connections from other computers on a case-by-case basis. By that, we mean that it can differentiate connections based on the software involved (which is discerned by the connection's *port number*) by the remote computer's *network address*, which lets Windows know whether the request comes from a computer on your own network or from a computer "out there" on the Internet. Windows Defender Firewall uses a third criterion for judging incoming requests: the "public" or "private" label attached to the particular network adapter through which a request comes.

This is a *huge* improvement over Windows XP and Vista, and here's why: When you're at home, the other computers on your network share a common network address scheme (just as most telephone numbers in a neighborhood start with the same area code and possibly prefix digits). Those computers can be trusted to share your files and printers. However, if you take your computer to a hotel or coffee shop, the other computers on that local network should *not* be trusted, even though they will share the same network addressing scheme. With Windows Vista and earlier versions, you had to manually reconfigure the firewall every time you moved your computer from one network to another so that you didn't inadvertently expose your shared files to unknown people.

On Windows 7 through 10, this reconfiguring is automatic. When you connect your computer to a network for the first time, Windows asks you whether the network is private or public, though the question is phrased in a different way on each version of Windows. Windows 10 asks, "Do you want to allow your PC to be discoverable by other PCs and devices on this network?" (On Windows 8.1, the question was, unfortunately, "Do you want to find PCs, devices, and content on this network?" which seems backward, in my opinion.)

If you say no, Windows labels the network as public, one where you don't trust the other connected computers. This would be an appropriate choice in a coffee shop or hotel or for a connection from your computer directly to a DSL or cable modem. If you say yes, Windows assumes you're using a private network, where you trust the other computers that are directly attached. This network might connect to the Internet through a router, but you can still consider it private because your local trusted computers can be distinguished by sharing a common network address.

 note

Windows Defender Firewall has the advantage that it can permit incoming connections for programs such as Remote Assistance and Quick Assist. On the other hand, it's part of the very operating system it's trying to protect, and if either Windows *or* Windows Defender Firewall gets compromised, your computer's a goner.

Windows Defender Firewall is enabled by default when you install Windows. You can also enable or disable it manually by selecting the Change Settings task on the Windows Defender Firewall window. (We tell you how to do this later in the chapter, under "Specific Configuration Steps for Windows 10.") You also can tell Windows Defender Firewall whether you want it to permit incoming requests for specific services. If you have a web server installed on your computer, for example, you need to tell Windows Defender Firewall to permit incoming HTTP data.

If you have an external firewall device—such as a commercial firewall server or a connection-sharing router with filter rules—this device will perform firewall duties for you. But, even with this, there is no good reason to disable Windows Defender Firewall. You're better off using *both*.

Packet Filtering

If you use a hardware Internet Connection Sharing router (also called a *residential gateway*) or a full-fledged network router for your Internet service, you can instruct it to block data that carries services you don't want exposed to the Internet. This is called *packet filtering*. You can set up this filtering in addition to NAT to provide an additional layer of protection.

Filtering works like this: Each Internet data packet contains identifying numbers that indicate the protocol type (such as TCP or UDP) and the IP address for the source and destination computers. Some protocols also have an additional number called a *port*, which identifies the program that is to receive the packet. The WWW service, for example, expects TCP protocol packets addressed to port 80. A domain name server listens for UDP packets on port 53.

A packet that arrives at the firewall from either side is examined; then it is either passed on or discarded, according to a set of rules that list the protocols and ports permitted or prohibited for each direction. A prohibited packet can be dropped silently, or the router can reject the packet with an error message returned to the sender indicating that the requested network service is unavailable. If possible, specify the silent treatment. (Why tell hackers that a desired service is present, even if it's unavailable to them? In security, silence is golden.) Some routers can also make a log entry or send an alert indicating that an unwanted connection was attempted.

Configuring routers for filtering is beyond the scope of this book, but Table 33.1 lists some relevant protocols and ports. If your router lets you block incoming requests separately from outgoing requests, you should block incoming requests for all the services listed, unless you are *sure* you want to enable access to them. If you have a basic gateway router that doesn't provide separate incoming and outgoing filters, you probably want to filter only those services that are marked with an asterisk (*).

Table 33.1 Services That You Might Want to Block

Protocol	Port(s)	Associated Service
TCP	20–21	FTP—File Transfer Protocol.
TCP	22	SSH—Secure Shell protocol, an encrypted version of Telnet.
TCP*	23	Telnet—Passwords are sent with encryption by this remote terminal service, which also is used to configure some routers.
TCP	53	DNS—Domain name service. Block only TCP mode "zone" transfers, which reveal machine names.
TCP+UDP	67	BOOTP—Bootstrap protocol (similar to DHCP). Unnecessary.
TCP+UDP*	69	TFTP—Trivial File Transfer Protocol. No security.
TCP	110	POP3—Post Office Protocol.
TCP+UDP*	137–139	NetBIOS—These ports are used by Microsoft File Sharing.
UDP*	161–162	SNMP—Simple Network Monitoring Protocol. Reveals too much information and can be used to reconfigure the router.
TCP*	445	SMB—Windows File Sharing can use port 445 as well as ports 137–139.
TCP	515	LPD—Unix printer-sharing protocol supported by Windows.
UDP, TCP	1900, 5000	Universal Plug and Play—Can be used to reconfigure routers.

As stated earlier, if you use a hardware router to connect to the Internet, we can't show you the specifics for your device. We can give you an example, though. My Linksys cable/DSL–sharing router uses a web browser for configuration, and there's a page for setting up filters, as shown in Figure 33.1. In this figure, I've blocked the ports for Microsoft file-sharing services.

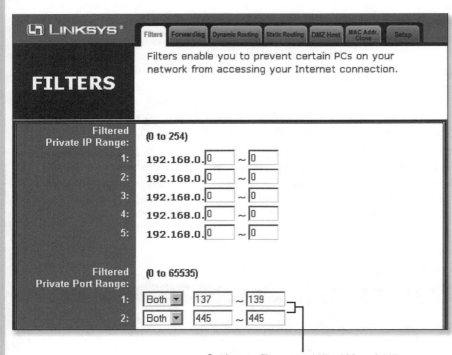

Figure 33.1
Configuring packet filters in a typical Internet Connection Sharing router.

Settings to filter ports 137—139 and 445

In a business setting, your ISP might have provided a router manufactured by FlowPoint, Cisco, Motorola, or another manufacturer. These are complex devices, and your ISP will help you set up yours. Insist that your ISP install filters for ports 137, 138, 139, and 445, at the very least.

Using NAT or Internet Connection Sharing

By either name, Network Address Translation (NAT) has two big security benefits. First, it can be used to hide an entire network behind one IP address. Then, while it transparently passes connections from you out to the Internet, it rejects all incoming connection attempts except those that you explicitly

 caution

Microsoft's Internet Connection Sharing (ICS) blocks incoming access to other computers on the LAN, but unless Windows Defender Firewall is also enabled, it does *not* protect the computer that is sharing the Internet connection. If you use ICS, you *must* enable Windows Defender Firewall on the same connection, or you must use a third-party software firewall application.

direct to waiting servers inside your LAN. Packet filtering isn't absolutely necessary with NAT, although adding it can't hurt.

➡️ *To learn more about NAT, see "NAT and Internet Connection Sharing," **p. 407.***

You learned how to configure Windows Internet Connection Sharing in Chapter 19, "Connecting Your Network to the Internet," so we won't repeat that information here.

If you have built a network with another type of router or connection-sharing device, you must follow the manufacturer's instructions or get help from your ISP to set it up.

Using Add-On Firewall Products for Windows

Commercial products called *personal firewalls* are designed for use on PCs. These types of products—Norton Internet Security (www.symantec.com), for instance—range in price from free to about $80. Now that Windows includes an integral firewall, and Microsoft offers a free antivirus program, add-on products might no longer be necessary, and I personally don't think that it's worth paying for a software firewall program alone. Windows Defender Firewall is good enough, it's free, and it's built in. It's *far* more important that you keep Windows and all of your add-on applications up to date and use Windows Security Essentials or a third-party antivirus/antispyware program. On the other hand, some of the third-party firewalls do monitor *outgoing* Internet connections, and this can let them detect a virus that slipped by an antivirus program, due to the virus's activity. That's pretty cool.

Securing Your Router

If you use a router for your Internet connection and rely on it to provide network protection, you *must* make it require a secure password. If your router doesn't require a password, *anyone* can connect to it across the Internet and delete the filters you've set up. (As configured by the manufacturers and ISPs, connection-sharing routers are set up with the same password. Usually, it's password. On the plus side, they typically won't accept configuration commands from the Internet, but only from your own network.)

To lock down your router, you have to follow procedures for your specific router. You'll want to do the following:

- Change the router's administrative password to a combination of uppercase and lowercase letters, numbers, and punctuation. Be sure to write it down somewhere, and keep it in a secure place. (I usually write the password on a sticky label and attach it to the bottom of the router.)

- If the router supports the SNMP protocol, change the read-only and read-write community names (which are, in effect, passwords) to a secret word or a very long random string of random characters. Better yet, prohibit write access via SNMP, or disable SNMP entirely.

- If the router supports management via the Telnet protocol, change all Telnet login passwords, whether administrative or informational, or disable Telnet access.

Configuring Passwords and File Sharing

Windows 10 supports password-protected and passwordless file sharing. Before we explain this, we need to give you some background. In the original Windows NT workgroup network security model, when you attempted to use a network resource shared by another computer, Windows would see if your username and password matched an account on that remote computer. One of four things would happen:

- If the username and password exactly matched an account defined on the remote computer, you got that user's privileges on the remote machine for reading and writing files.

- If the username matched but the password didn't, you were prompted to enter the correct password.

- If the username didn't match any predefined account, or if you failed to supply the correct password, you got the privileges accorded to the Guest account *if* the Guest account was enabled.

- If the Guest account was disabled—and it usually was—you were denied access.

The problem with this system is that it required you to create user accounts on each computer you wanted to reach over the network. Multiply, say, five users by five computers, and you had 25 user accounts to configure. What a pain! (People pay big bucks for a Windows Server–based domain network to eliminate this very hassle.) Because it was so much trouble, people usually enabled the Guest account.

 note

When you disabled Password Protected Sharing in the past, you got what was called Simple File Sharing on Windows XP, but with a twist: On XP, when Simple File Sharing was in effect, every network accessed shared resources using the Guest account, no matter what username and password were supplied. On Windows 7 through 10, if the remote user's username matches a user account and the account has a password set, he'll be able to access the shared resources using that account's privileges. The Guest account is used only when the remote user's account doesn't match one on the Windows computer, or if the matching account has no password.

If your computer is a member of a Windows domain network, you cannot disable Password Protected Sharing.

Windows 7, 8, 8.1, and 10 have a feature called the HomeGroup that provides a way around the headaches of managing lots of user accounts and passwords. When you make a computer a member of a homegroup, it uses a built-in user account named HomeGroupUser$ when it accesses shared resources on other computers in the group. All the member computers have this same account name set up, with the same password (which is derived from the homegroup's password in some way), so all member computers can use any shared resource. When you share a library, folder, or printer with the homegroup, Windows gives the user account HomeGroupUser$ permission to read or to read/write the files in that folder. It's a simple, convenient scheme, but only computers with these newer versions of Windows computers can take advantage of it.

Another way to avoid password headaches is to disable the use of passwords for network resources entirely. If you disable Password Protected Sharing, the contents of the Public folder and all other shared folders are accessible to everyone on the network, even if they don't have a user account and password on your computer, and regardless of the operating system they're using. This is ideal if you want to share everything in your Public folder and do not need to set sharing permissions for individuals.

From a security perspective, only a few folders are accessible when Password Protected Sharing is disabled, and although anybody with access to the network can access them, the damage an intruder can do is limited to stealing or modifying just the files in a few folders that are known to be public.

If you do disable Password Protected Sharing, it's *crucial* that you have a firewall in place. Otherwise, everyone on the Internet will have the same rights in your shared folders as you.

By default, Windows 10 has Password Protected Sharing enabled, which limits access to the Public folder and all other shared folders to users with a user account and password on your computer, or to member computers in a homegroup.

If you want to make the Public folder accessible to everyone on your network without having to create for each person an account on every computer, you have four choices:

- If you are on a home or small office network and you have only (or mostly) Windows 7, 8, 8.1, and 10 computers, you can enable the HomeGroup networking feature, as discussed in Chapter 18, "Creating a Windows Network."

- You can set up accounts for every user on your computer so that all will access the shared folder using their own account. You'll need to be sure that all users use the same password for their account on every computer.

- You can create a special user account, for example, named "share," and give people you trust the password to this account. Everyone can use this same username and password to access the shared folder on your computer.

- You can disable Password Protected Sharing. To do this, right-click the network icon at the right end of the taskbar and select Open Network & Internet Settings, and then select Status, Sharing options. (Alternatively, open File Explorer, select Network at the left, click Properties in the ribbon, and then select Change Advanced Sharing Settings.)

  Scroll down, and under All Networks, locate Password Protected Sharing. Click Turn Off Password Protected Sharing, and then click Save Changes.

Setting Up Restrictive Access Controls

Possibly the most important and difficult step you can take is to limit access to shared files, folders, and printers. You can use the guidelines shown in Table 33.2 to help organize a security review of every machine on your network.

Table 33.2 Restricting Access Controls

Access Point	Controls
File Sharing	Share only folders that need to be shared. Use Password Protected Sharing.
Passwords	Set up *all* accounts to require passwords. You can configure your computers to require long passwords if you want to enforce good internal security. We show you how to do this later in the chapter.
Partitions	If you install IIS and want to make a website or FTP site available to the Internet, set up a separate NTFS partition on your hard drive *just* for website files.
Access Control	Don't disable User Account Control. In fact, even with UAC in place, it's a good idea not to use a Computer Administrator account for your day-to-day work. Instead, create a Standard user account for yourself and type in an Administrator password when you're prompted to.
FTP	If you install a public FTP server, do not let FTP share a FAT-formatted drive or partition. Also, you must prevent anonymous FTP users from writing to your hard drive.
SMTP	Configuring an email system is beyond the scope of this book. But if you operate an email server, consider storing incoming mail in a separate partition, to avoid getting overrun with too much mail. Also, you must prohibit "relaying" from outside SMTP servers to outside domains, lest your server be used as a spam relay site.
HTTP (Web)	Don't enable both Script/Execute permission and Write permission on the same folder. Enabling both permissions would permit outside users to install and run arbitrary programs on your computer. You should manually install any needed scripts or CGI programs. (The WebDAV/FrontPage extensions can publish scripts to protected directories, but they perform strong user authentication before doing so.)
SNMP	This network-monitoring option is a useful tool for large networks, but it also poses a security risk. Don't install SNMP unless you need it, and if you do, change the "community name" from public to something confidential and difficult to guess. Block SNMP traffic through your Internet connection with filtering.

Testing, Logging, and Monitoring

Testing, logging, and monitoring involve testing your defense strategies and detecting breaches. It's tedious, but who would you rather have be the first to find out that your system is hackable: you or "them"? Your testing steps should include these:

- Testing your defenses before you connect to the Internet

- Detecting and recording suspicious activity on the network and in application software

You can't second-guess what 100 million potential "visitors" might do to your computer or network, but you should at least be sure that all your roadblocks stop the traffic you were expecting them to stop.

Testing Your Defenses

Some companies hire expert hackers to attempt to break into their networks. You can do this, too, or you can try to be your own hacker. Before you connect to the Internet, and periodically thereafter, try to break into your own system. Find its weaknesses.

 note

If you're on a corporate network, contact your network manager before trying this. If your company uses intrusion monitoring, this probe might set off alarms and get you in hot water.

Go through each of your defenses and each of the security policy changes you made, and try each of the things you thought they should prevent.

First, connect to the Internet, visit www.grc.com, and view the ShieldsUP page. (Its author, Steve Gibson, is a very bright guy and has lots of interesting things to say, but be forewarned that some of it is a bit hyperbolic.) This website attempts to connect to Microsoft Networking and TCP/IP services on your computer to see whether any are accessible from the outside world. This is a great tool! Click Proceed, and then click the File Sharing and Common Ports buttons to see whether this testing system exposes any vulnerabilities. Don't worry if the only test your computer fails is the ping test. If you have an Internet router or use Internet Connecting Sharing, try the UPnP test.

As a second test, find out what your public IP address is. An easy way to find out is to open www. whatismyip.com in Internet Explorer. Then enlist the help of a friend or go to a computer that is *not* on your site but connected to the Internet some other way. Open File Explorer (*not* Internet Explorer) and, in the Address box, type \\ *1.2.3.4*, but in place of *1.2.3.4*, type the IP address that you recorded earlier. This attempts to connect to your computer for file sharing. You should not be able to see any shared folders, and you shouldn't even be prompted for a username or password. If you have more than one public IP address, test all of them.

 ## Shared Folders Are Visible to the Internet

First, be sure Windows Defender Firewall is enabled on all of your network's computers. You should also enable filtering on your Internet connection. At the very least, you must block TCP/UDP ports 137–139 and 445. Don't leave this unfixed.

If you have several computers connected to a cable modem with just a hub and no connection-sharing router, you should read Chapter 19 for alternative ways to share your cable Internet connection.

If you have installed a web or FTP server, attempt to view any protected pages *without* using the correct username or password. With FTP, try using the login name *anonymous* and the password *guest*. Try to copy files to the FTP site while connected as *anonymous*—you shouldn't be able to.

Sensitive Web Pages or FTP Folders Are Visible to the Internet

When you access your self-hosted website from the Internet using a web browser or anonymous FTP and can view folders that you thought were private and protected, be sure that the shared folders are not on a FAT-formatted disk partition. FAT disks don't support user-level file protection. Share only folders from NTFS-formatted disks.

Then check the folder's NTFS permissions to be sure that anonymous access is not permitted. Locate the folders in File Explorer on the computer running IIS. View the folders' Properties page and view the Security tab. Be sure that none of the following users or groups are granted access to the folder: Everyone, IUSR_*XXXX* (where *XXXX* is your computer name), IUSR, or IIS_IUSRS. On the folders you wish to protect, grant read and write privileges only to authorized users. In the IIS management console, you can also explicitly disable anonymous access to the website's folder or a specific folder.

Use network-testing utilities to attempt to connect to any other of the network services you think you have blocked, such as SNMP.

Network Services Are Not Being Blocked

If you can connect to your computer across the Internet with remote administration tools such as the Registry Editor, with SNMP viewers, or with other tools that use network services, network services are not being blocked.

Look up the protocol type (for example, UDP or TCP) and port numbers of the unblocked services, and configure filters in your router to block these services. Your ISP might be able to help you with this problem. You also might have disabled Windows Defender Firewall by mistake.

Attempt to use Telnet to connect to your router, if you have one. If you are prompted for a login, try the factory default login name and password listed in the router's manual. If you've blocked Telnet with a packet filter setting, you should not be prompted for a password. If you are prompted, be sure the factory default password does not work, because you should have changed it.

More advanced port-scanning tools are available to perform many of these tests automatically. We caution you to use these sorts of tools in addition to, not instead of, the other tests listed here.

Monitoring Suspicious Activity

If you use Windows Defender Firewall, you can configure it to keep a record of rejected connection attempts. Here's how:

1. Sign in using an Administrator account, and in the taskbar's search box type **firewall**.

2. In the search results, select Windows Defender Firewall with Advanced Security.

3. Under Action, select Properties. Select one of the available profile tabs (Private Profile, in most cases) and click the Customize button within the Logging area. Set Log Dropped Packets to Yes; then click OK.

4. Take note of the location of the log file, and then click OK. By default, the log file is `\windows\ system32\LogFiles\Firewall\pfirewall.log`.

You can enable this setting for all profiles if you wish. Inspect the log file periodically by viewing it with Notepad.

Disaster Planning: Preparing for Recovery After an Attack

Disaster planning should be a key part of your security strategy. The old saying "Hope for the best and prepare for the worst" certainly applies to network security. Murphy's Law predicts that if you don't have a way to recover from a network or security disaster, you'll soon need one. If you're prepared, you can recover quickly and may even be able to learn something useful from the experience. Here are some suggestions to help you prepare for the worst:

- Make permanent, archived "baseline" full-image backups of exposed computers *before* they're connected to the Internet and anytime system software is changed.

- Make frequent backups once online.

- Prepare written, thorough, and *tested* computer restore procedures.

- Write and maintain documentation of your software and network configuration.

- Prepare an incident plan. Think through what you'd have to do to cut off Internet access, and then restore your computers and servers, and write it all down step by step.

A little planning now will go a long way toward helping you through this situation. The key is having a good backup of all critical software. Each of the points discussed in the preceding list is covered in more detail in the following sections.

Making a Baseline Backup Before You Go Online

You should make a permanent "baseline" full-image backup of your computer before you connect with the Internet for the first time so that you know it doesn't have any virus infections. Make this backup onto a removable disk or tape that can be kept separate from your computer, and keep this backup permanently. You can use it as a starting point for recovery if your system is compromised. To restore your backup, you will also need a System Recovery Drive.

➡️ *To learn more about making these recovery tools, see "Creating a Recovery Drive," p. 726, and "Creating a System Image Backup," p. 728.*

Making Frequent Backups When You're Online

We hate to sound like a broken record on this point, but you should have a backup plan and stick to it. Make backups at some sensible interval and always after a session of extensive or significant changes (for example, after installing new software or adding users). In a business setting, you might want to have your backup program schedule a backup every day automatically. (You *do* have to remember to change the backup media, even if the backups are automatic.) In a business setting, backup media should be rotated offsite to prevent against loss from theft or fire. You may want to do this even for home backups: Take an external hard drive or DVD backup to a friend's house for safekeeping.

Online backup services such as Carbonite and SOS Online Backup are fantastic tools. They usually don't back up Windows and applications, but they do frequently back up your personal files. But although cloud-based backup is an incredibly useful and valuable tool, don't count on it alone. It can protect you from data loss due to fire or equipment failure; however, a thief who cracks your password may well delete all your backed-up data. Keep a physical backup somewhere, too.

Writing and Testing Server Restore Procedures

We can tell you from personal experience that the only feeling more sickening than losing your system is finding out that the backups you've been diligently making are incomplete or unreadable. Whatever your backup scheme is, be sure it works!

This step is difficult to take, but we urge you to try to completely rebuild a system after an imaginary break-in or disk failure. Use a sacrificial computer, of course, not your main computer, and allow yourself a whole day for this exercise. Go through all the steps: reformat hard disks, reinstall Windows or use the image feature, reinstall backup software (if you use a third-party product), and restore the most recent backups. You will find this a very enlightening experience, well worth the cost in time and effort. Finding the problem with your system *before* you need the backup is much better than finding it afterward.

Also be sure to document the whole restoration process so that you can repeat it later. After a disaster, you'll be under considerable stress, so you might forget a step or make a mistake. Having a clear, written, tested procedure goes a long way toward making the recovery process easier and more likely to succeed.

Writing and Maintaining Documentation

It's in your own best interest to maintain a log of all software installed on your computers, along with software settings, hardware types and settings, configuration choices, network address information, and so on. (Do you vaguely remember some sort of ordeal after AT&T replaced your wireless router last year? How *did* you resolve that problem, anyway?)

In businesses, this information is often part of the "oral tradition," but a written record is an important insurance

 tip

Windows has no utilities to print the configuration settings for software and network systems. You can use Alt+PrntScrn to record the configurations for each program and network component and then paste the images into WordPad or Microsoft Word.

policy against loss due to memory lapses or personnel changes. Record all installation and configuration details.

Then *print a copy* of this documentation so you'll be able to refer to it if your computer crashes.

Make a library of software DVDs and CD-ROMs, repair disks, startup disks, utility disks, backup disks, tapes, manuals, and notebooks that record your configurations and observations. Keep them together in one place and locked up, if possible.

Preparing an Incident Plan

A system crash, virus infection, or network intrusion is a highly stressful event. A written plan of action made now will help you keep a clear head when things go wrong. The actual event probably won't go as you imagined, but at least you'll have some good first steps to follow while you get your wits about you.

If you know a break-in has been successful, you must take immediate action. First, immediately disconnect your network from the Internet. Then find out what happened.

Unless you have an exact understanding of what happened and can fix the problem, you should clean out your system entirely. This means that you should reformat your hard drive, install Windows and all applications from CDs/DVDs or pristine disks, and make a clean start. Then you can look at recent backups to see whether you have any you know aren't compromised, restore them, and then go on.

But most of all, have a plan. The following are some steps to include in your incident plan:

- Write down exactly how to properly shut down computers and servers.

- Make a list of people to notify, including company officials, your computer support staff, your ISP, an incident response team, your therapist, and anyone else who will be involved in dealing with the aftermath.

- If you had a hacker break-in at your business, check www.first.org to see whether you are eligible for assistance from one of the many Forum for Incident Response and Security Teams (FIRST) response teams around the world.

  Alternatively, the Computer Emergency Response Team Coordination Center (CERT-CC) might be able to help you or at least can get information from your break-in to help protect others. Check www.cert.org.

- You can find a great deal of general information on effective incident response planning at www.cert.org. CERT offers training seminars, libraries, security (bug) advisories, and technical tips as well.

Specific Configuration Steps for Windows 10

Many of the points mentioned in this chapter so far are general, conceptual ideas that should be helpful in planning a security strategy, but perhaps not specific enough to directly implement. The following sections provide some specific instructions to tighten security on your Windows 10 computer or LAN. These instructions are for a single Windows 10 computer or a workgroup without a Windows Server. Windows Server offers more powerful and integrated security tools than are available with Windows alone (and happily for you, it's the domain administrator's job to set up everything).

Windows 10's Security Features

Right out of the box, Windows 10 has better security tools built in than previous versions of Windows. If you do nothing else but let these tools do their job, you'll be better off than most people, and certainly far better off than anyone still running Windows XP. These are the built-in security features:

- **User Account Control**—UAC makes sure that programs don't have the ability to change important Windows settings without you giving your approval. This helps prevent virus programs from taking over your computer and disabling your computer's other security features.

    ➡ *For more details, see "User Account Control," p. 104.*

- **Protected Mode Web Browsers**—Web browsers are the primary gateway for bad software to get into your computer. You don't even have to deliberately install the bad stuff or go to shady websites to get it; hackers take over well-known, legitimate websites and modify the sites' pages so that just viewing them pulls virus and Trojan horse software into your computer. This risk is so great most current web browsers have been designed to run with limited privileges and can't, for example, store files outside a restricted set of folders, and can't change system settings or services. The idea is that if malware does get in by exploiting a browser flaw, it shouldn't, in theory, be able to do much damage. (It *can* impair your web browsing, though, and if you inadvertently grant malware permission to modify your system by accepting an unexpected User Account Control prompt, well, it's pretty much all over.)

    The term for this type of defense is called "sandboxing" or "protected mode browsing." Microsoft's Edge and Internet Explorer browsers use this strategy, and some third-party browsers, such as Google Chrome, do as well.

- **Microsoft Edge**—Microsoft Edge improves upon Internet Explorer's defenses by using an internal viewer for Flash media files (on the presumption that Microsoft can write a safer Flash player than Adobe Corporation can), and restricting the types of external plug-in software that can be added to Edge. But, it's a big, brand-new program, so we are sure that at least some security flaws will emerge.

- **Windows Defender Firewall**—Windows Defender Firewall blocks other computers on the Internet from connecting to your computer.

    ➡ *For more information, see "Windows Defender Firewall," p. 757.*

- **Windows Defender**—Defender is an antimalware program that scans your hard disk and monitors your Internet downloads for certain categories of malicious software. It's preinstalled on

Windows 10 in most cases. The version that comes with Windows 10 has both antivirus and anti-spyware capabilities, and it takes the place of the Microsoft Security Essentials program that you could download for previous versions of Windows.

Starting with the Windows 10 Anniversary update, Windows Defender can now work in tandem with any third-party alternative antivirus program you install, giving you a "second opinion" on the health of your computer. We show you how to enable this "Limited Periodic Scanning" feature in Chapter 31.

➡ *For more information,* **see** *"Making Sure Windows Defender Is Turned On,"* **p. 702.**

All these features are good at their jobs. Together, they're even better. The best bit of security advice we can give you is this: *Do not disable any of them.* In particular, don't disable UAC. If you find that any of the security features cause some problems with one of your applications, fix the problem *just for that application* instead of disabling the security feature outright. For example, if you have a program that doesn't work well under UAC, use the Run As Administrator setting on that application's shortcut to let *just that program* bypass UAC.

If you just follow that advice, you'll be in pretty good shape. If you want to ratchet up your defenses another notch or two, read on.

If You Don't Have a LAN

If you have a Windows 10 computer that connects directly to the Internet but doesn't connect to a home or office LAN, it's still part of a network (a really big one). You need to take only a few steps to be sure you're safe when browsing the Internet:

- If you use Microsoft Office or other Microsoft applications, click or touch Start, Settings, Update & Security, Windows Update, Advanced Options. Be sure that Give Me Updates for Other Microsoft Products When I Update Windows is checked. This will let Windows automatically download updates and security fixes for Office as well as Windows. Many third-party applications now have an "automatically check for updates" feature, and you should take advantage of that when possible.

- Enable Macro Virus Protection in your Microsoft Office applications.

- Be sure that Windows Defender is turned on, even if you have another antivirus program installed. If your computer came with a commercial antivirus program preinstalled, when it expires, you should immediately either pay for continued service or uninstall it and then immediately install another product, such as the free Windows Defender.

- When you connect to the Internet, be sure to stay connected long enough for Windows Update to download needed updates.

- Be very wary of viruses and Trojan horses in email attachments and downloaded software. Install a virus scan program, and discard unsolicited email with attachments without opening it. If you use Outlook or Windows Mail, you can disable the preview pane that automatically displays email. Several viruses have exploited this open-without-asking feature.

- Keep all of your computers and devices up to date with Windows Update, service packs, app updates, virus scanner updates, and so on, regardless of operating system. Check for updates every couple weeks, at the very least. View http://browsercheck.qualys.com every few weeks. Enable automatic updating in any application that permits it, such as Adobe Reader and Flash viewer, Java Runtime, and so on.

- On Windows 10 Pro and Enterprise, make the Security Policy changes suggested later in this chapter under "Tightening Local Security Policy." Local Security Policy can't be changed on Windows 10 Home.

- Use strong passwords on each of your accounts, including the Administrator account. For all passwords, use a combination of uppercase letters *and* lowercase letters *and* numbers *and* punctuation; don't use your name or other simple words. Don't use the same password that you also use on an email account or website.

- Be absolutely certain that Windows Defender Firewall is enabled on a network adapter that connects to a Broadband modem and on any dial-up connection icons.

If You Do Have a LAN

If your computer is connected to others through a LAN, follow the suggestions from the list in the preceding section, on each computer.

Also, if you use a wireless network, you must use encryption to protect your network. Otherwise, thanks to passwordless file sharing, random people passing by could have the same access to your shared files as you do. Use WPA2 encryption if all of your computers and routers support it; otherwise, use WPA or WEP only if you have devices that don't support WPA2 and can't be upgraded or replaced.

Keep Up to Date

New bugs in major operating systems and applications software are found every week, and patches and updates are issued almost as frequently. Even Microsoft's own public servers have been taken out by virus software.

Software manufacturers, including Microsoft, have become quite forthcoming with information about security risks, bugs, and the like. It wasn't always the case; they mostly figured that if they kept the problems a secret, fewer bad guys would find out about them, so their customers would be better off (and it saved them the embarrassment of admitting the seriousness of their bugs). Information is shared so quickly among the bad guys now that it has become essential for companies to inform users of security problems as soon as a defensive strategy can be devised.

I personally like to visit http://browsercheck.qualys.com every few weeks. This web page checks Internet Explorer and its plug-ins for software that is known to have security bugs.

You might also check out the following:

- www.sans.org

- www.cert.org

- www.first.org

- www.cerias.purdue.edu/coast

- www.greatcircle.com

- Usenet newsgroups: comp.security.*, comp.risks

Some of these sites point you toward security-related mailing lists. Forewarned is forearmed.

Tightening Local Security Policy

You should set your machine's own (local) security policy whether you have a standalone computer or are on a LAN. The Local Security Policy lets Windows enforce some commonsense security rules, such as requiring a password of a certain minimum length or requiring users to change their passwords after a certain number of days. This tool is available only on Windows 10 Pro and Enterprise, however. The more basic Windows 10 Home and Mobile versions have to settle for default security policies.

If your computer is part of a Windows domain-type network, your Local Security Policy settings will almost certainly be superseded by policies set by your domain administrator, but you should set them anyway so that you're protected if your domain administrator doesn't specify a so-called global policy. To configure Local Security Policy, log in as a computer administrator. Press Windows Logo+R, type **secpol.msc**, and press Enter. (Alternatively, search for secpol.msc from the taskbar.) This opens the Local Security Policy editor, as shown in Figure 33.2.

Figure 33.2
The Local Security Policy Editor lets you tighten security by restricting unsafe configuration options.

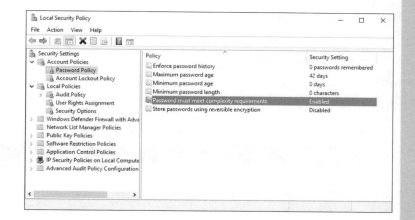

To change the settings, select the policy categories from the left pane and double-click one of the policy names listed in the right pane. A Properties dialog box will appear in which you can change the setting.

You don't need to change all the policies; we list the important ones in the following sections.

Account Policies

Account policies can be used to enforce long, difficult, frequently changed passwords and make it hard for users to recycle the same passwords when forced to change. You should lock out accounts that fail several login attempts, locally or over the LAN. In the Local Security Policy window's left pane, open the list under Account Policies and select Password Policy or Account Lockout Policy to see the available settings. Table 33.3 shows the Password Policy changes we suggest you make, and Table 33.4 shows the options at your disposal for locking out an account if someone is attempting to guess passwords.

Table 33.3 Password Policy Settings

Password Policy	Local Setting
Enforce password history	Ten passwords remembered
Minimum password length	Eight characters
Passwords must meet complexity requirements	Enabled
Store password using reversible encryption	Disabled

Table 33.4 Account Lockout Policy Settings

Account Lockout Policy	Local Setting
Account lockout duration	30 minutes
Account lockout threshold	Five invalid logon attempts
Reset account lockout counter after	30 minutes

Local Policies

You should have Windows make an entry in the Event Log whenever someone oversteps her bounds. Table 33.5 shows the recommended audit policy changes.

Table 33.5 Audit Policy Settings

Audit Policy	Local Setting
Audit account logon events	Failure
Audit account management	Failure
Audit directory service access	Failure
Audit logon events	Failure
Audit policy change	Success, Failure
Audit system events	Failure

No changes are necessary in the User Rights Assignment section, but you might want to view these entries to see what sorts of permission restrictions Windows uses.

 note

If you're interested in how Windows regulates the operation of your computer, look at the settings under User Rights Assignment and Security Options. You'll probably never need to change any of these settings, but these two sections are the heart of Windows' security controls.

Finally, go through the security options, as listed in Table 33.6. Security options are used to restrict what users can do with system options.

Table 33.6 Security Options Settings

Security Option	Local Setting
Interactive logon: Message text	You can display a sort of "Posted: No Trespassing" warning for users attempting to log on with this entry.
Devices: Prevent users from installing printer drivers	Disabled by default. If you want to prevent users from installing printer drivers or installing potentially untested printer and hardware drivers, check out the options for these settings.
Audit: Shut down system	A common hacker trick is to fill up audit logs with junk immediately if unable to log messages and then break in. If you want, you can have security audits shut down Windows when the Security Event Log fills. The downside is that it makes your security system a denial-of-service risk.

When you log out and back in, the new restrictive security policies will take effect.

Configuring Windows Defender Firewall

The purpose of Windows Defender Firewall is to examine all incoming network data, looking for attempts to connect to your computer. The firewall maintains a list of networking services for which incoming connections should be permitted, within a given range of network addresses. For example, by default, on a private network, Windows Defender Firewall permits file-sharing connections only from computers on the same "subnet" or LAN as your computer. Attempts by users outside your immediate network to contact your computer are rebuffed. This prevents Internet users from examining your shared files. (Outgoing requests, attempts by your computer to connect to others, are not restricted.)

 note

You might ask, why don't spyware and virus programs disable or create exceptions in Windows Firewall so that their data can get through? They will certainly try. However, UAC ensures that unless you give them permission, they won't have the privileges necessary to open up the firewall. Most application setup programs are run with elevated privileges, so they do have the opportunity to configure Windows Defender Firewall as part of the setup process. You will be shown a UAC prompt before such a setup program runs.

Windows Defender Firewall also monitors application programs and system services that announce their willingness to receive connections through the network. These are compared against a list of authorized programs. If an unexpected program sets itself up to receive incoming network connections, the firewall displays a pop-up message similar to the one shown in Figure 33.3, giving you the opportunity to either prevent the program from receiving any network traffic (Cancel) or add the program to the authorized list (Allow Access). This gives you a chance to prevent "spyware" and Trojan horses from doing their dirty work. (The installers for some applications such as Windows Messenger instruct Windows Defender Firewall to unblock their data connections at the time they're installed, so you might not always get this prompt with a new networked application.)

Figure 33.3
Windows Defender Firewall displays a pop-up message if a previously unauthorized program asks to receive network connections.

If you don't recognize the program listed in a Windows Defender Firewall pop-up, click Cancel. This is a break from the way Windows programs usually work: Cancel here doesn't mean "don't do anything now." In this case, it actually does make an entry in the firewall's program list, and the entry is set up to block the program.

As mentioned previously in this chapter, Windows Defender Firewall has separate settings for each application based on whether your computer is connected to a public or a private network. In most cases, it's best to allow a program to receive connections on private networks, but not public. This is certainly the case for file and printer sharing and Windows management functions. The exceptions to this principle would be programs that are meant to work with other Internet users, such as chat and telephony programs.

The remainder of this section discusses the various setup options for Windows Defender Firewall.

> ### 🔍 note
> On a corporate network, your network manager might enforce or prevent the use of Windows Defender Firewall and may restrict your capability to change its settings while your computer is connected to the network.

Enable and Disable Windows Defender Firewall

To configure Windows Defender Firewall, click Start, Settings. In the Settings search box, type `firewall`. From the results, select Windows Defender Firewall. This is an old-style Control Panel. The firewall's current settings are listed in the right pane, as shown in Figure 33.4.

Figure 33.4
Windows Defender Firewall displays its current settings in the right pane. To configure it, click a task in the left pane.

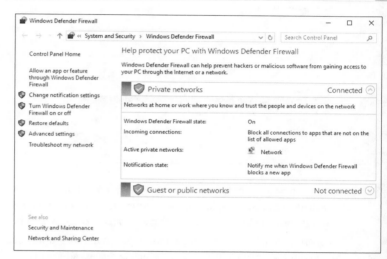

Typically, you should not need to change the firewall's default settings. However, if you do have to make a change, click one of the left pane tasks, which are described in turn in the following sections.

Allow an App or Feature Through Windows Defender Firewall

If you use a program that has to receive incoming network connections, its setup program should configure Windows Defender Firewall to permit incoming connections; failing that, the first time you run it, you should see a pop-up notification like that shown in Figure 33.3. If you handle that pop-up incorrectly or want to change the setting, select the Allow an App or Feature Through Windows Defender Firewall task to bring up the dialog box shown in Figure 33.5. Then click Change Settings.

To entirely prevent a program from connecting through the network and to the Internet, find it in the list and uncheck the box to the *left* of its name.

To enable a program's connections, find it in the list, and check the box to the left of its name. Then check either or both of the boxes to the right, to permit it to receive connections through a private network or a public network.

Figure 33.5
The Allowed Apps and Features list lets you list programs and network features (ports) that should be able to receive incoming connections. Connections can be accepted or blocked based on whether they are received through a private or a public network connection.

To make a new entry for a specific program so that it can receive connections, click Allow Another App. Then click Browse, locate the program file (.exe file), and click Open. Click Add. In the new list entry, review the Private and Public check boxes to make sure that they are set correctly. Click OK.

To open the firewall for specific network port numbers, rather than whole applications, you'll have to use the Advanced Settings task, which is discussed shortly.

Change Notification Settings, Turn Windows Defender Firewall On or Off

The Change Notification Settings and Turn Windows Defender Firewall On or Off tasks bring up the same screen, shown in Figure 33.6. From there, you can turn Windows Defender Firewall on or off. You can also check a box that blocks *all* incoming connections regardless of any entries in the Allowed Apps list. (This corresponds to the Block All Incoming Connections and Don't Allow Exceptions check boxes in Windows Vista and XP, respectively.) Finally, you can enable or disable the pop-up that occurs when a new application wants to receive incoming connections. If you disable notification, newly discovered applications will be blocked silently.

In Windows Vista and earlier versions, you needed to disable all firewall exceptions when you brought your computer to a public location, but on Windows 7 through 10, as mentioned previously, this is not necessary.

Restore Defaults

The Restore Defaults task restores Windows Defender Firewall to its default settings and clears out any additions you've made to the Allowed Apps list. This might cause networking applications such as instant messaging programs and remote control programs like VNC to stop working until you reinstall them, but it will resecure your computer and restore the functioning of standard services such as file and print sharing.

Figure 33.6
Figure 33.6
The Change Notification
Settings and Turn Windows
Defender Firewall on or off
tasks let you turn Windows
Defender Firewall on or off
and configure its pop-up
notification.

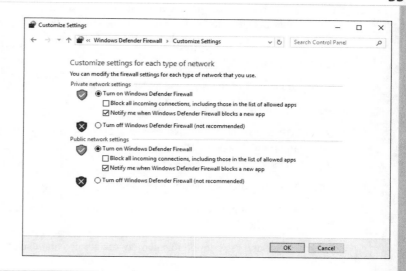

Advanced Settings

The Advanced Settings task brings up the Windows Defender Firewall with Advanced Security administrative program, shown in Figure 33.7. (You can also get there by searching the taskbar's search box for *firewall*. The search result is Windows Defender Firewall with Advanced Security.)

Figure 33.7
The Windows
Defender Firewall
with Advanced
Security app
lets you open
exceptions for a
network service
based on a port
number.

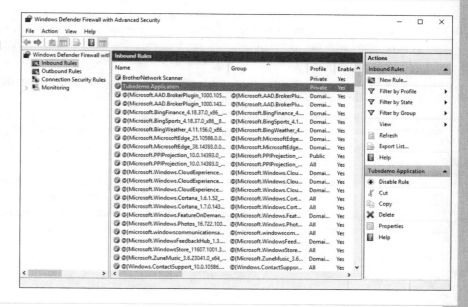

You will need to use this program if you want to open the firewall for a network service based on its port number because the basic firewall Allowed Apps list does not let you do this. To open an exception for a TCP or UDP network port, follow these steps:

1. In the left pane, click Inbound Rules.

2. In the Actions list to the right, select New Rule.

3. Select Port and click Next.

4. Select TCP or UDP, and then select Specific Local Ports. Enter the port number or a port number range, and then click Next. (To open an exception for both TCP and UDP, you must enter two separate rules.)

5. Select Allow the Connection and click Next.

6. Select the types of networks from which the connection should be accepted: Domain (corporate), Private, or Public. Click Next.

7. Enter a name and description for the network service and click Next.

---

 tip

Are you curious to know what programs and services on your computer are actively listening for incoming network connections? Just follow these convoluted steps:

1. Press Windows Logo+X or touch and hold the Start button, and then select Command Prompt (Admin) or Windows PowerShell (Admin), whichever appears. When the User Account Control window appears, click Yes.

2. When the window opens, type the command **netstat -ab > x** and press Enter. This might take quite a long time to run. When the prompt reappears, type **notepad x** and press Enter. This displays a list of ports along with the names of the programs that are using them. (Be aware that this list shows listening ports even if the port is being blocked by Windows Defender Firewall.)

An even better way to view this information is to download and run the program at http://live.sysinternals.com/tcpview.exe.

If you don't recognize a listening program's name, use Google to see if it's discussed on any web pages; this might help you determine whether it's a legitimate Windows program or some sort of malware.

You can also use the Advanced firewall tool to open an exception for a protocol other than TCP or UDP, and you can filter based on the remote IP address and port number; we won't describe this other than to suggest that at step 3, select Custom. It can also provide outbound connection filtering, but that is outside the scope of this book and is rarely necessary.

More About Security

This chapter just barely scratched the surface of what there is to know and do about network security. Lots of great books have been published on the topic. You can get lots more information on the Web. First, as we mentioned earlier, www.sans.org and www.cert.org are great places to start looking into the security community. Steve Gibson has plenty to say about security at www.grc.com; it's educational and entertaining.

Finally, you might look into additional measures you can take to protect your computer and your network. You can configure networks in many ways. For example, it's common to keep public web or email servers separate from the rest of your LAN.

In any case, we're glad you're interested enough in security to have read to the end of the chapter.

34

PROTECTING YOURSELF FROM FRAUD AND SPAM

Phishing for Information

In just a short few decades, the Internet has revolutionized communication, commerce, entertainment, and...crime. It's sad, but the reality is that every pond has its bottom feeders. And the Internet is a very large pond indeed.

Some years ago, before the Internet was commonly available to home users, America Online (AOL) was an innovative service accessed by dial-up modems. It was appealing but not cheap. Some people figured out that obtaining free access was as simple as using a program to generate a fake credit card number and using that to open an AOL account. It took AOL a few weeks to figure out that the credit card number was no good, after which another fake number got the ball rolling again.

AOL eventually put a stop to this, so, naturally, even more reprehensible practices ensued. A program called AOHell emerged. It could send a barrage of instant messages to subscribers, posing as an AOL representative, luring them into providing personal account information. Voilà, free credit card numbers. The program's creator referred to this practice as *phishing*, a play on the earlier term *phone phreaking*, in which people tricked the telephone system into connecting free long-distance calls.

AOHell has been retired, but the basic concept is still used by thieves around the world: the use of diffuse targets (a broad swath of victims), social engineering (a plausible story), and technology to gather the information volunteered. This is the essence of phishing.

By all accounts, phishing is prevalent and highly successful. Studies done on human susceptibility to specific, concocted phishing scams have varied greatly in results, with anywhere from 3 to 70 percent of the message recipients being susceptible. But even if just one person in a hundred falls prey, with the number of people online today, the number of potential victims is astounding.

Common Types of Fraud

You are certain to run into many categories of online fraud, of which classic phishing is just one. We list a few of them here. Regardless of the con, the criminals are after one of the following things:

- **Your personal and financial information**—You'll give it to them, and they'll use it to go on a spending spree or sell it to other criminals.

- **Your money**—You'll send them money and get nothing in return.

- **Your computer**—You'll follow a link to a bogus website or even a legitimate website that's been hacked. Your computer will get infected with a virus just by viewing the web page, in what's called a *drive-by attack*. The criminals will record your keystrokes to get your password and banking information, or they'll use your computer to commit any number of online crimes: sending spam, collecting information stolen by phishing, launching denial-of-service attacks, breaking codes and passwords, committing "click fraud".... The list goes on and on.

It's pretty ugly stuff. The following sections detail a few of the techniques criminals use to lure you in.

Classic Phishing

An email arrives seemingly from an organization or business that you're actually affiliated with. The email says something significant has happened. There is endless variety to the messages used, but the goal is always to arouse your curiosity, your concern, or both. Here are some examples:

- Your account was suspended due to suspicious activity. You need to respond immediately to restore your account.

- A sum of money was posted to your account; can you confirm it?

- An expensive online purchase you made is on its way to you.

- Someone tried to change the password on your account. Click the link if it wasn't you. (This is a clever one. It seems as though it might be safe to confirm that you *didn't* do anything.)

You receive instructions to log on to a website to confirm or deny the activity. It's a phony website, decked out to look just like the real one, and you'll be asked to provide personal information to log on. Of course, this scam works only if you actually have an account with the purported sender. They don't know if *you* do or not. But that doesn't matter. They send hundreds of millions of these emails, so they'll hit plenty of actual customers just due to the numbers.

The Stranded Friend

You get an email, Facebook message, or other online message from a friend or relative who's traveling or is in jail and has lost his wallet and passport. He is apologetic but desperate and needs you to wire some money urgently. The message really is coming from your friend's account, which has been taken over by a criminal who bought the username and password online from other criminals who use software to guess passwords.

 tip

If you don't want your email or social networking account used to try to con you and your friends, *don't use the same password on multiple websites*. If hackers break into one poorly protected website and steal the username and password list, they'll use it to break into your accounts on other websites. Most people use the same password everywhere, so this pays off in a big way. Hackers get your password by hacking into poorly protected, little online business sites (such as Yahoo!, LinkedIn, Myspace, and Adobe Corporation, from which hackers lifted, collectively, over 2 *billion* email addresses, passwords, and security questions), and then they use that same password to get into your Facebook account, email account, bank account, and so on. To learn about some tools that can help you cope with the many passwords you'll need, see "Identity-Management Software," later in this chapter.

Advance Fee Fraud

You are invited into an exchange in which someone will send you money, and you're to send them less money back. For example, you post something for sale on Craigslist, usually something for which you're asking at least several hundred dollars. Someone wants you to ship the item to them, and it's quite a distance. They offer to pay with a cashier's check or money order made out for the amount of the item plus *plenty* more to cover whatever shipping will cost, and you're supposed to send the leftover money back to them. The money order or cashier's check will turn out to be phony, but you won't find out until after you've sent them the change.

"Nigerian Letter" Scam

There is a large sum of money in an account in a distant foreign country (not necessarily Nigeria—it could be any country). A very respectable, high-ranking person is looking for help getting it out of that country into yours, and he found *you*. He will split the sum with you in return for your help. If you respond, it will turn out that you will have to wire him money to help cover his expenses in getting the process started.

Lottery and Giveaway Scams

It's your lucky day: you won the lottery, airplane tickets, a chance to be on a TV show, a $100 coupon at Starbucks, a magazine subscription, a mail-order bride.... Well, whatever it is, it's free, valuable, rare, and exciting. You'll just have to provide a credit card number to cover shipping and handling.

Trojan Horses

An email arrives from a plausible source: the post office, a shipping company, or an online reseller such as Amazon. The email makes it sound as if you're about to miss something important, and it has an attachment that contains an important invoice, a past-due notice, instructions for picking up a package, a confirmation of a tax refund, or some such. It's just interesting enough and plausible enough that you open the attachment to see what it is. A virus then takes over your computer.

There really is no end to the inventive means that criminals come up with to part you from your money. Most seem laughably obvious—the bad grammar and spelling, the incorrect information, the implausible scenario.... However, I promise you that one day, one will slip by your internal BS detector. It has happened to me, and it will happen to you. You won't even think about it. You'll just click and....

You can just hope that before you type in your banking password or your credit card number, you'll have a second thought and want to find out if the thing is real or not. That can take a bit of investigation, as we discuss in the next section.

Live Phish: A Real-World Example

A typical phishing email tends to report that some activity has taken place in your account with a specific organization: a password was changed, a deposit or withdrawal was made, money was transferred, a shipment was made, or an important message is waiting. The email requires that you click a web link to attend to the matter immediately, to confirm the activity, or to deny that you initiated it. Now, you'll know right away it's phony if you aren't actually affiliated with the bank or company in question. But if you are affiliated, you might not know whether it's a fraud, at least not right away. You have to look deeper.

Figure 34.1 shows an example of a rather sad attempt I found in my inbox.

Figure 34.1
Phishing email from...well, it's not really from Bank of America.

On the surface, it appears that I'll lose access to my bank account if I don't sign in soon to confirm my password and banking information. I don't think so! The writing in this particular email isn't as bad as most, but the "From" line mentions a different bank entirely and has a very strange email address!

So, this one is pretty clearly a fake, but some phishing letters are actually pretty good. Let's see what other clues there might be to tell us this letter isn't legitimate.

> ### ⚠ caution
>
> The phishing lure's aim is to trick you first into opening the email and then clicking a web link and divulging your banking password. In other cases, criminals exploit bugs in web browsers, PDF viewers, and media players to create websites that put viruses and spyware onto visitors' computers just by opening the site. These are technically called *drive-bys* because you get hit just for being to the wrong place, without even typing anything. We talk about these more in Chapter 31, "Protecting Windows from Viruses and Spyware." The takeaway message is, it's best never to even view an email if you have the slightest suspicion about it, let alone click on any links it contains.

The main clue that this email is not the real deal lies in the web link. The linked phrase Update Account Here seems innocuous, and in most phishing emails the links do look absolutely legitimate. It doesn't matter either way; the displayed text is not the actual "active" address inside the link. It doesn't matter what *any* blue underlined text says, because the text you see is just an arbitrary description of the underlying actual URL. Before you click a link in any email that seems even the least bit suspicious, look to see where any link it contains would take you.

Here's how to check if you're using Microsoft Edge (the default, Modern-style browser supplied with Windows 10):

1. Hover the mouse over the link, and then look toward the lower-left part of the browser window. A URL should be displayed in a small pop-up box. If the URL looks bogus, it *is* bogus. Stop! But this text can be easily forged. If the URL looks reasonable, don't trust it yet. Instead, proceed to step 2.

2. Right-click the link and select Copy Link. Then, in the taskbar's search box, type **notepad**. From the search results, select Notepad. Type Ctrl+V, or, on the menu, select Edit, Paste. Now look at the link.

If you are using Internet Explorer, follow these steps instead:

1. Hover the mouse over the link, and then look in the status bar in the lower-left part of the browser. A URL should be displayed there. If the URL looks bogus, it *is* bogus. Stop! But this text can be easily forged. If the URL looks reasonable, don't trust it yet. Instead, proceed to step 2.

2. Right-click the link and select Properties. If the link is too long to fit in two lines, you might not see it entirely, but if you click and drag over the link, it will scroll to display the entire link. Alternatively, follow step 2 in the preceding procedure for Edge, and examine the link in Notepad.

If the URL display says something like `onclick();` rather than a recognizable URL, the link's target is determined by script programming inside the email or web page, and you can't easily or reliably determine where it leads. If you see this, treat the email as very suspicious. (Scripting of clicks isn't evil by itself, but because you can't see what the script will do if you click the link, you have to assume the worst.)

If the actual URL doesn't look like it leads to the organization you expected, stop! And even if it looks reasonable, you should examine it carefully, as we will explain.

In my sample phishing email, I found that the real link was this:

```
http://highendrecruiting.com/wp-content/USbank/
```

The USbank part might have seemed plausible if the letter hadn't said it was from Bank of America, but look at the domain name, the part between // and the first /. highendrecruiting.com is not what you'd expect for a bank website.

Other URLs aren't so obviously bogus. Another phishing email I received had a link to `http://bofamerica.online.tc/sitekey/`. Doesn't look so bad, does it? But start at the *end* of the domain name and work backward. The .tc at the end is a dead giveaway. Tc is the country code for the Turks and Caicos Islands. It's a lovely place, but Bank of America isn't based there!

A domain name that is clearly invalid is a dead giveaway that this email is bogus. An all-numeric addresses like http://64.101.32.1012/bankofamerica.com would also have been a sign of an invalid site location. Corporate websites *never* use numeric addresses.

Finally, notice that the link starts with http: instead of https:, so it's not a secure web page. *No* truly secure login page starts with http:.

So this phishing email gave itself away as a fraud; however, some are not so easy to spot. Sometimes the email's language and formatting are perfect, and only by looking at the URL do you see a clue.

---

 tip

The commonly recognized site names that end with suffixes such as .com, .org, and .gov should be immediately preceded by the core organization name and immediately followed by a slash (if anything). Some examples of normal URLs include the following:

https://www.mybank.com

https://accounts.mybank.com/mainpage.asp

Here are some URLs that are likely malicious:

http://www.myba.nk.com

http://www.mybánk.com

http://www.mybank.info

http://www.mybank.com.elsewhere.com

http://www.elsewhere.com/mybank

http://www.mybank.com.*xx*, where *xx* is not your country code

http://202.12.29.20/mybank.com

Don't enter account, password, or personal information into a web page that uses the http: prefix. If it doesn't start with https:, consider it suspicious. And a legitimate corporate domain name is owned by the corresponding company. See "Whois Database" at the end of this chapter for a way to find out who actually owns a domain name.

Although the astute observer might not fall for the particular phishing email I got, it's highly possible that a bleary-eyed, unsuspecting computer user who has not yet had morning coffee might miss its warning signs. This is where Microsoft's SmartScreen Filter comes in. Figure 34.2 shows an example of what is presented when a suspicious link is clicked.

Figure 34.2
The SmartScreen Filter at work.

When the SmartScreen Filter is enabled, Edge and Internet Explorer send every URL you click to Microsoft for screening against a list of known fraudulent or virus-infested websites. In the case of this phishing email, the browser has communicated in no uncertain terms that it is a known dangerous site. Under the More Information item, there is an option to continue to the web page, if desired, but the link states that clicking to proceed is not recommended.

 note
If a website doesn't get flagged by the SmartScreen filter, it doesn't prove that it is legitimate; it just might not have been detected yet. But, a website that *is* flagged is very probably bad.

To be sure that the SmartScreen Filter is enabled, open Internet Explorer, click the gear (Settings) icon in the IE toolbar, and then select Safety. If the pop-up menu contains the choice Turn Off SmartScreen Filter, it's currently on, and you don't need to do anything. Just press Esc or click outside the IE window. Otherwise, select Turn On SmartScreen Filter.

Then open the Microsoft Edge browser. Click the ... item at the right end of the navigation bar, select Settings, and then scroll down and select View Advanced Settings. Scroll down and be sure that Help Protect Me from Malicious Sites... is turned on.

As stated earlier, when the filter is enabled, every URL you view is sent to Microsoft for checking against a list of known bad sites. This list is built up by feedback from users, information gathered from spam and presumably verified by Microsoft staff. When a site is under investigation, Internet Explorer might prompt you to "vote" on your feeling about the site's safety.

note

Does SmartScreen slow down your web surfing? Not by much, if at all. When you browse to a website, your browser starts downloading the site's content, and it sends the URL to Microsoft's SmartScreen servers at the same time. The amount of information exchanged is very small, and the browser continues to download content while SmartScreen is checking. If the response from SmartScreen is delayed, the software will still decide—based on its analysis of the web page content itself—whether or not to go ahead and display the page, so you don't have to worry that if Microsoft's servers go down, you'll be stuck.

Regardless of whether SmartScreen flags a web page or not, our recommendation is to *never* click on any link in any threatening, worrisome, confusing, or unexpected email notification. Instead, if you think the notice *might* be real, and if the host name in the URL listed in the notification matches a website you actually use, open the real website by typing in the URL by hand.

For notices about unexpected charges to your credit cards or other accounts, check the credit card's or account's website directly, to see if there is actually a pending or finalized charge or order you didn't expect, by typing in the site's URL by hand.

Otherwise, our suggestion is just to ignore the email, and in the very unlikely event that a bogus charge does appear, contact your credit card company to dispute it.

Viewing a Site That Was Flagged Incorrectly

If the SmartScreen Filter flags a site that you *know* is safe, click the down arrow next to More Information in the warning screen. You can tell Microsoft that you think the site is legitimate by clicking Report That This Site Does Not Contain Threats. You can continue past the warning to view the site by clicking Disregard and Continue.

Flagging a Fraudulent Site

If you find that the SmartScreen Filter fails to flag a site that you feel is fraudulent, follow these steps:

- If you're using the new Modern-style Microsoft Edge browser, click the ... symbol at the top of the browser, and select Send Feedback. Then Report Unsafe Site.

- In Internet Explorer, click the gear (Settings) icon in the IE toolbar; then select Safety, Report Unsafe Website.

Follow the prompts to complete the report.

Sacrificing Privacy for Security

If you feel that the SmartScreen Filter feature sounds good but also a little bit creepy, I agree with you. On the one hand, it's nice to have this sort of protection available, because a lot of people just don't have the time to sort out where every email link leads. On the other hand, the filter doesn't just monitor links from fraudulent emails: It communicates data about every web page you visit and every web search you perform. Microsoft states that the information is transmitted in encrypted form and that it has "taken steps to help ensure that no personally identifiable information is retained or used for purposes other than improving online safety"—that is, neither your IP address nor the URLs you visit are archived.

However, it's still very likely that your data could be captured and scanned by, oh, say, a large government agency with a huge secret budget, and it would be illegal for Microsoft to tell you that this was occurring, if they even knew. Personally, I leave SmartScreen Filter turned on. I'm just suggesting that you treat corporate privacy policies as skeptically as you do emails from random banks.

 caution

Microsoft's SmartScreen Filter tries to make educated guesses about the validity of URLs, but in reality, it's only as good as Microsoft's list of known phishing sites. *Don't rely on it entirely!* Be very skeptical. If you suspect that an email allegedly from one of your financial institutions or organizations is not legitimate, *don't click any links in the email*. Instead, visit the organization's website directly by typing its URL yourself, or call your bank and ask if the email is legitimate.

More Help from the Browser

In addition to the SmartScreen Filter, all web browsers should display a lock icon when you are viewing a site whose data is encrypted in transit and whose identity is at least reasonably assured. The lock icon is displayed right next to the URL it describes, as shown in Figure 34.3.

You can view the site's certificate information by clicking the lock icon, and it will show up against a red background if there is anything odd about the site's certificate.

The lock section of the address bar is shaded green if the site's identity is (reasonably) assured with Extended Validation (previously High Assurance SSL) certificates. This indicates that the site has submitted to a rigorous identification process and has paid for the new certificate type.

 caution

A new trend on the Web will make bad URLs harder to spot: Internationalized Domain Names (IDNs). Until recently, you had to worry about only your native alphabet or character set in the URL bar, but now you can get international character sets that could look similar to something in your native language yet be a different site entirely. Would you think it was safe to paypál.com or eßay.com? Use a keen eye to watch for accent marks and oddly shaped characters!

Microsoft Edge   Lock icon

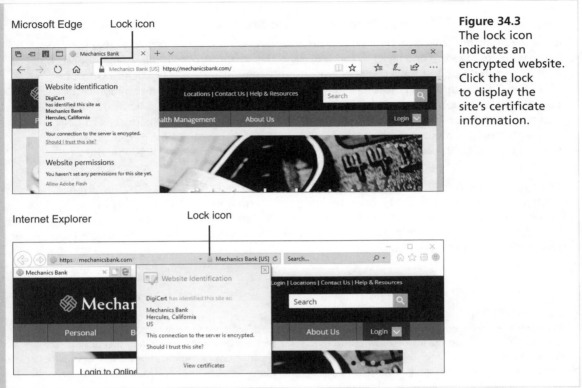

Figure 34.3
The lock icon indicates an encrypted website. Click the lock to display the site's certificate information.

Internet Explorer   Lock icon

How to Protect Yourself on a Public Computer

If you use a public computer, for example, a computer in a library, an Internet cafe, or even a friend's house for that matter, you should be concerned that the computer might be infected with viruses that may monitor your activity and steal your information. *Never* use a public computer to conduct banking or work with sensitive information. Think twice even about checking your email or social networking account; your logon name and password might be recorded and collected by criminals before you even sign out.

If you *do* use a public computer to conduct personal business, consider using private browsing, where the browser deletes all information about your browsing activity when you close it. Most browsers have this capability. In Microsoft's browsers, the feature is called InPrivate Browsing. To use it in Edge, click the ... icon at the right side of the window, and then select New InPrivate Window. In Internet Explorer, press and release the Alt key to display the menu, and then select Tools, InPrivate Browsing. Be sure to close all browser windows when you're finished working.

If InPrivate Browsing doesn't work with the site you're using and you have to use a browser in its normal mode, be absolutely *sure* to sign out of any website you logged on to. And when you're finished, before you walk away, clean up the browser's cache of retained information using these steps. Here are instructions for Windows 10:

- If you're using the Microsoft Edge web browser, select the ... item at the right end of the navigation bar, select Settings, scroll down to Clear Browsing Data, click Choose What to Clear, check all the items, and then click Clear.

- If you're using Internet Explorer, click the gear (Settings) icon on the toolbar, and then select Safety, Delete Browsing History. By default, Temporary Internet Files and Website Files, Cookies and Website Data and History are checked. Check Form Data and Passwords as well; then click Delete.

Previous versions of Windows and other web browsers have similar tools, but you might have to hunt for them.

If you're out and about, it's much safer to use your own computer, tablet, or smart phone to reach the Internet. Even public WiFi has its risks, though. Always be sure to type **https:** rather than **http:** for URLs when you browse or conduct business over a WiFi connection outside your home or office.

➡ *For more information about using public WiFi securely,* **see** *"At a Public Hot Spot," p. 828.*

Two-Way Authentication

Authentication is the process of proving that you are who you claim to be. The frequent use of bogus websites demonstrates the need not only for users to prove their identity to a site, but also for a site to prove its identity to the users. One way to accomplish this type of two-way authentication is for a user to choose a secret symbol, such as a small picture of a tropical sunset, which is known only between the user and the site. Henceforth, whenever that user visits the site, that tropical sunset picture is displayed alongside the rest of the site information. A malicious site replica will not know which symbol to produce, so even if a user is tricked into visiting one, it will be clear that the site is not authentic. Many financial institutions are using this system now, and you may already have seen it in action.

The system works by placing a unique signature on your computer. When you visit the site and provide a valid account name, the site checks this to see whether your computer has been used successfully before. If it has, the picture of the sunset (for example) is displayed along with the password prompt. You will recognize the picture, know it's the right site, and type in the password. Nice plan. But what if you are at a computer that you don't usually use? In that case, you will be asked to answer some additional security questions before the site will display the secret symbol and ask for your password.

Two-Factor Authentication

Two-factor authentication involves two forms of identification: something you know and something you have. A password or PIN is something you know. Something you have can come in many different forms but is usually either an electronic token (device) of some sort, which displays a frequently changing code number or a biological property, such as your fingerprint or retina, that can be used to identify you. Another two-factor technique that's become common is a one-time code that's sent to you by text message, or less often, by email. (In this case, the thing you have is your phone or a separate logon on a different web service.)

Using two factors to prove who you are is much better than using a password alone: Whereas a password can be electronically stolen, obtaining both a password and a unique physical device—or a finger, for that matter—is substantially more difficult.

One challenge with two-factor authentication is that the computer must be capable of validating the "something you have." For example, to scan your finger for authentication, the computer must be equipped with a fingerprint reader. To use a special electronic token, you need a piece of equipment that can validate the token. When you consider that some institutions have millions of customers, the cost of extra hardware adds up.

 tip

If your bank, email provider, social media site, or any other website you use offers text message or emailed two-factor authentication on its website, be sure to sign up for and take advantage of it. It greatly reduces the chances that a security breach somewhere else will compromise your information and money.

Windows includes built-in support for new and better two-factor security devices such as biometric readers, so hopefully, the use of this sort of equipment will increase. (On the other hand, with all the large-scale data thefts we see these days, I doubt that even these security measures will be useful in the long term. Once "XXX Corp." accidentally leaks a few hundred million electronic fingerprint records, the scheme won't be worth using anymore.)

Identity-Management Software

Because no centralized or standard system exists for managing usernames and passwords across different websites, users are forced to improvise solutions for managing their various electronic identities. The solution most people employ is just to use the same password on every site. Unfortunately, doing so is extremely risky. Just one data theft from one of the sites or vendors you use will expose your "favorite" username, email address, and password (and more) to the world.

A different, complex password for every site is the right way to go, but it's impossible to remember them all. You might end up cutting and pasting the information from a Word document every time you log on, but this is incredibly unwieldy, and most people end up going back to the one-password-everywhere-who-would-care-about-my-data-anyway method.

You can take up your web browsers' offers to memorize passwords for you, and that's a partial help, but, you're still stuck keeping manual records of your many passwords for when you travel and as a backup.

There's another way, though, using third-party tools. Password-management programs keep track of all your various usernames and passwords and store them in a safe, encrypted format. They often have browser-integrated features that, with your permission, automatically fill in your credentials by site. Programs such as Roboform, LastPass, and 1Password provide one-click logons and enable you to use diverse and more complex usernames and passwords because you don't have to remember them. However, you can still get them out of the program when you want to. It's nice to know that with so many people focused on making life difficult with malware, innovative and pragmatic software developers are making life on the Web easier.

Fighting Spam

Email users of the world are no doubt nostalgic for a time when Spam was just tasty pork product. Now it is the scourge of email systems throughout the world, as unsolicited email messages from an ever-increasing number of junk-mail senders congest mail systems and take up space on our computers. Spam is such a problem because, on the scale of subversive electronic activities, it is fairly easy to do, fairly difficult to be caught, and very inexpensive for the sender. Despite ridiculously low response rates, spammers continue to dupe shady advertisers into paying for it.

Although the most important cost involved with spam is in human time—time spent reading, deleting, and devising ways to fight it—there's actually a huge environmental cost as well: To filter out the estimated 95 trillion junk emails sent in 2010, computers burned through enough electricity to generate more than 28 million metric tons of CO_2 emissions. In 2016, the volume of spam appears to have dropped to about half the volume in 2010, due to better spam filtering by online email providers and the takedown of some criminal enterprises, but the numbers are still staggering.

Thankfully, antispam technology continues to get better, and you can take several practical steps to both make spam less of a nuisance and reduce the risk that it will lead to even more serious problems, such as email-borne viruses and information theft.

If you want to avoid spam, it helps to understand a bit about how you get targeted in the first place. Spammers generally find email addresses by harvesting them from public sources, such as message boards or web pages. They buy them from website operators who aren't above selling email addresses they've collected from visitors, registration pages, or guest books. They may distribute virus software that steals email address books from victims' computers. They also use special programs called *spambots* to methodically crawl the Web for email addresses wherever they might be. Then, because they're not above scamming their own customers, they pad their lists with a huge percentage of email addresses they just make up using common names and domain suffixes. Because little cost or penalty is associated with sending spam to the wrong email

 tip

To make it more challenging for spam tools to guess an email address, use uncommon combinations instead of common naming conventions. Although it's less intuitive than john_doe@myemail.com, using initials and meaningful (to you) combinations of numbers, such as jhd0213@myemail.com, makes you a more difficult spam target.

address, spammers trade and compile enormous email lists, with many incorrect and probably some legitimate addresses as well. If your email address ends up on one of these lists, it will probably stay there, so the best defense is to keep your email address off the list in the first place.

And it should go without saying: never purchase anything, hire anyone, or respond in any way to any offer you receive in a spam solicitation, no matter how appealing it might be. That only validates spam as an effective marketing tool.

Protecting Your Email Address

The best way to avoid getting on spammers' lists is to share your email address only when necessary and only with the trusted few. One of the simplest ways that information is inadvertently shared is bad email etiquette. When you send a single email to multiple people, it's best to use the Bcc field and keep the names out of the To and Cc lines. The exception to this rule is when you are on a private network, such as a corporate email system, where the email will not generally travel over the Internet unprotected.

Another way to reduce spam is to use multiple email addresses for different purposes. One email address could be a primary address for trusted friends or merchants, and another could be for sites that are less familiar or for times you need to register with a site for a one-time use. Keeping one address for important communications and another for "junk email" not only is effective at reducing spam, but also can help protect you in other ways. In the phishing example earlier in this chapter, an email arrived from PayPal at my junk email address, yet I knew I had provided PayPal with my trusted email address, so it was a clear red flag. This approach works even better if you have yet more-specific email addresses for important lines of communication. Free email address services abound. Many of them have good spam-filtering capabilities, so they make good choices for a junk email address. (I'm very impressed with Gmail.)

 note

Here's an unsolicited plug: In my experience, the spam filtering provided by Google's Gmail and the related Google Apps for Business is absolutely amazing, filtering out about 99.98% of the 1,000 or so spams targeted at my email address each day. About 900 of these are refused outright; that is, the Gmail email server recognizes that the email sender is a virus or known spam program and won't even allow it into their system. Of the remainder, maybe one per week makes it into my Inbox; the rest are automatically categorized as spam and filed accordingly.

In the past year, only a few legitimate emails were incorrectly categorized as spam, and only one was a personal email; the rest were bulk mailings from companies that I've done business with. That's an incredible success rate, and it's far better than any of the other online email services I use—some of which are abysmal.

Better yet, some email systems let you add a suffix to your email address. For example, if my address is brian@myisp.com, I can also use brian+paypal@myisp.com and brian+amazon@myisp.com; in fact, I can use brian+*anything*@myisp.com. If you have such a service, make up a distinct email address every time you register your email address on a website. Then, if one of these appears in a spam list, you can block just that address and never be bothered by it again. (And send a nastygram to the website owner while you're at it.)

Using Spam Filtering

Despite good faith and antispam tactics, an email address *will* eventually receive some spam. Spammers might be innovative, but equally innovative people are at work preventing spam from taking valuable time away from your life. Spam filters analyze email and relegate spam to a junk mail folder or the like. They use various methods, including some similar to other antimalware programs, to detect and get rid of spam before it hits your inbox. All online email service providers, such as Yahoo! Mail, Gmail, and so on, provide free spam filtering as a matter of their own survival as much as for good customer service. Filtering spam at the server level is actually more effective than filtering it in your own computer, because servers will typically receive the same spam email for thousands of customers at once, giving it a higher profile.

Besides filtering by email service providers, some email programs can perform filtering as well. Microsoft Outlook, which is part of the Office productivity suite, includes spam filtering. Most third-party email programs offer spam filtering as well.

You may also install an aftermarket spam filter as an add-on. It will insert itself between your email program and the Internet. There are even some plug-in hardware devices that protect from spam at the network level.

If you still get large quantities of spam, you might consider changing email providers. Or you might keep your current account and have it forward all of your email to an account on a service with better filtering. Then read your email on the second service.

Avoiding Spammers' Tricks

Spammers have hundreds or maybe thousands of tricks up their grimy sleeves to bypass filters. Still, you can do plenty of simple things to limit exposure and reduce junk email in its various forms.

Some spammers appear repentantly courteous. That is, they have violated your inbox by being there uninvited, but now that they have your attention, please don't be offended, because you can simply click this link to opt out of receiving any more spam from them. Honest.

Do not reply to spam that claims to provide an "opt out" or "unsubscribe" link. By clicking the link in an attempt to stop receiving spam, you are confirming that your email address is good. You are just increasing your value as a spam target, and your spam level likely will increase. In fact, it's a good idea to never respond to spam, especially to buy anything. Although it is possible some well-intentioned but ill-advised vendors are using spam to sell legitimate products, all purveyors of spam are suspect simply because of the insidious nature of the communication: unsolicited, unauthorized, unwelcome, and often illegal. Avoid spam like the plague it is. If you suspect an email message is spam, you're probably right. Don't opt out. Don't even open it; just delete it or click your email program's "This is spam" button.

Read the terms of use and privacy policies when you register with a website to make sure the site will not sell or share your information. Often at the end of the form are preselected check boxes indicating that you'd love to receive email from them, their sponsors, their affiliates, and so on. Clicking those boxes is considered opting in and permits them to legally bombard you with spam. Many spammers disregard the law anyway, but it's never a good idea to give them carte blanche with your inbox.

The right way for an upstanding website to manage an email list is called *confirmed opt-in*, and you've probably used it before. Good citizens of the Internet will not start sending email to you until they have confirmed, by receiving email from your email address, that you actually want it. Without such confirmation, anyone could type your email address into a hundred different Send Me Mail forms, some of which are perhaps distasteful, and every day you'd have an inbox full of junk. This is such an important premise that, in general, if it's not a confirmed opt-in, it might as well be spam.

Junk email can come from the most unlikely sources. Well-intentioned relatives bent on protecting their loved ones from syringes on movie seats, international kidney thieves, or cancer-causing agents in shampoo are responsible for a type of spam that's hard to avoid because, although it might be tempting, you don't want to filter *everything* that comes from them. And if you feel the urge to forward a tantalizing or tender tidbit, before asking others to spend time reading the message, take a moment to search and make sure it's true.

 note

Several Internet sites have evolved to fight electronic chain letters, spam, and especially urban legends that compel so many people to send massive amounts of ultimately groundless email and Facebook posts. Snopes.com has emerged as an excellent source to determine whether an email is fact or fiction. Use it often. Your friends, relatives, and the collective IQ of humanity will thank you.

Taking Action Against Email Abuse

So far, this chapter has taken the Aikido route to spam and fraud defense: avoidance and being "like water." Among our many techniques, we sidestep dangerous links, make email addresses slippery to spambots, and use identity management software to leave would-be keyloggers with nothing. These are useful defensive techniques, but sometimes an offensive approach to vanquishing online foes is more effective and satisfying. Some spammers can be identified and extinguished. Once discovered, phishing sites can be quickly put out of business.

Many commercial Internet sites provide readily available tools to report suspicious activity. For example, eBay and PayPal request that you forward suspected fake emails to spoof@ebay.com or spoof@paypal.com, respectively. They will quickly take appropriate action. Responsible sites display security or fraud-related links on the front page, so you can easily find their preferred mode of communication. If you suspect a phishing scam, consider taking a moment to find the right email address and report it. You may save someone else a lot of heartache and will validate your own "sleuthiness." If you stumble upon a suspected phishing site with Internet Explorer, report the site using the SmartScreen Filter tool discussed under "Flagging a Fraudulent Site," earlier in this chapter.

Reporting spam can be easy, too. Free email services used with a web browser often provide a "report spam" button that can automatically notify the provider to take action. This removes the message from your inbox and, more importantly, could help eliminate hundreds of thousands of other copies in other people's inboxes.

If you prefer to use a separate email program, such as Windows Mail, a plethora of add-ons can help you report and eliminate most spam. Some of the most interesting and effective ones use collaborative networks. Like the free email services that have potentially millions of users, these add-ons are based on the premise that humans can filter spam better than any algorithm alone. When a number of users identify a particular message as spam, the other members of the network can be spared the trouble. It's a successful strategy used by companies such as Cloudmark, and there are other successful strategies as the field continues to evolve to provide convenient, active ways to fight spam.

On the other hand, there are not-quite-so-convenient yet more active ways for those who desire to "get medieval" on spammers. With a little practice, it's not difficult to track down email headers using publicly available Internet resources. You can often identify the service provider whose network was used to send spam, and they can opt to shut down the spammer's Internet access if enough complaints are received. Additionally, the Federal Trade Commission encourages you to forward spam to the appropriate governmental agencies for analysis. Consider forwarding particularly obnoxious spam to one of the following addresses:

Type of Spam	Forward to
Asking you to send money through the U.S. mail	fraud@usps.gov
Prescription drugs, medical devices, dietary supplements	webcomplaints@ora.fda.gov
Nonprescription drugs	otcfraud@cder.fda.gov
Stocks or bonds	enforcement@sec.gov
"Nigerian"-type scams	419.fcd@usss.treas.gov
Any sort of spam	spam@uce.gov

The government will likely not respond to individual complaints, but it will go after the worst spammers. Every so often you hear of an arrest, followed by a distinct downturn in the daily worldwide volume of spam.

Whois Database

Anyone registering an Internet domain name is required to file contact information with a domain registry. This is supposed to be public information, and you can use it to find out whether a domain is owned by the company it purports to be and how to contact the owners of a domain whose customers have sent spam mail or with whom you have other concerns.

Finding the registrar for a given domain name can be cumbersome. You can find the registrar information for any .aero, .arpa, .biz, .com, .coop, .edu, .info, .int, .museum, .net, or .org domain via the following web page: www.internic.net/whois.html.

The search results from this page indicate the URL of the whois lookup page for the associated domain registrar. Enter the domain name again on that page, and you should see the contact information.

It's a bit harder to find the registrar associated with two-letter country code domains ending in, for example, .au, .de, .it, and so on. The InterNIC site recommends searching through www.uwhois.com.

You can find the owner of an IP address (for example, the address from which an email arrived) through a similar lookup at www.arin.net/whois. Enter an IP address to find the owner of the block of IP addresses from which the specific address was allocated. This is usually an ISP or, in some cases, an organization that has had IP addresses assigned to it directly. You might have to visit www.apnic.net or another registry.

35

WINDOWS ON MOBILE DEVICES

Windows 10 on Tablets and Mobile Devices

The Apple iPad was not the first tablet-format computer. Between the tablet's debut on TV in *Star Trek* in 1966 (well, yes, it was only a prop, but in concept it was precisely what we have now) and the release of the iPad in 2010, there were many attempts to produce a usable computer in the tablet format, with the power of a PC in a digital version of the venerable yellow steno pad.

There were small versions, notably the pioneering Apple Newton and the incredibly successful Palm Pilot, followed by a host of similar devices called personal digital assistants (PDAs). This name captured the essence of these devices: They were personal, they were digital, and they did assist you. But they weren't close in power to a personal computer. They never really grew up.

There were also many attempts to make PCs "grow down," with early tablet or "slate" formats appearing in the late 1980s, and convertibles, which are laptops whose display cover can hinge back or turn around so that it lies flat but open on the case. This got us something close to today's tablet. However, several limitations conspired to keep them either slow, or thick and heavy, and in either case, rare and expensive. Every few years starting in the 1980s someone gave a keynote speech at the huge Comdex consumer electronics show saying that tablet computers with pen input devices would soon be taking off, but they never did.

Most of the limitations were technological: With the available micro-processor CPUs, you could have either fast performance or low power usage, but not both. With the available battery technologies, it took pounds of batteries to power a fast CPU long enough to get any reasonable amount of work done. Early liquid crystal display (LCD) screens were thick, usually monochrome, and expensive. (My first color LCD monitor was 15" diagonal and cost nearly $1,000!)

Over time, the technologies improved dramatically. Screamingly fast low-power CPUs emerged. Lithium polymer technology gave us batteries the size of a matchbook that deliver power like little nuclear reactors (and meltdowns that are nearly as spectacular!). LCD display costs fell so much that CRT monitors aren't even manufactured anymore. And advances in touchscreen technology have made the finger a viable and fairly precise input device; odd little styli, which are easily lost, are no longer necessary.

The final missing ingredient was imagination, and that was something that Steve Jobs and the team at Apple had in breathtaking abundance. What they brought to the tablet was an insistence on simplicity, performance, and perfect smoothness, both literally and figuratively. Many companies could have produced the iPad before Apple did, but nobody did, mostly because nobody but Steve Jobs believed that something could be that good. And it turns out that people really did want things that are that good. For the last several years, Apple's revenues from iPhones and iPads have exceeded Microsoft's revenues from *everything* it does and sells. (However, Android-based phones and tablets are taking an ever-increasing bite out of Apple's sales.)

The software on most tablets was, until recently, essentially repurposed smartphone software: Apple's iOS and Google's Android were phone operating systems first and were later copied onto larger devices. These tiny operating systems grew up in a very power-, CPU-, and memory-constrained environment, and they grew to be very good while still sticking to a very lean diet. Now mobile devices can support an operating system as complex as Windows 10. For this to happen, Windows had to learn how to run lean, and processors and batteries and Flash memory had to advance enough to meet Windows in the middle.

As we are writing this book, Microsoft is manufacturing and selling tablet computers of its own, the latest called Microsoft Surface 4 and Surface Pro 4, which have Intel processors that execute the same instruction set that's used on desktop PCs. They run Windows 10 in its entirety, with every capability that the desktop version has. Other vendors also sell Intel-compatible tablets that can run Windows 10 Home or Pro. The price and performance of these tablets vary widely, from $1800 for the highest-end Surface 4 Pro tablets, to (*really* quite decent) entry-level tablets such as the RCA Cambio 11.6, which can be had for $150, including a detachable keyboard.

An earlier generation of lower-end Microsoft Surface tablets used an ARM microprocessor, and they were sold with an operating system called Windows RT. Technically, Windows RT was almost 100% identical to Windows 8, except that its programs were turned into instructions for the ARM processor instead of the usual Intel x86 or x64 processors used in desktops and notebooks. While Microsoft claimed that it was a "new" operating system and couldn't run traditional Windows Desktop applications, it did: It came preinstalled with Microsoft Office applications (compiled for the ARM processor), and the Desktop and the Command Prompt windows were there for everyone to see. It turned out to be confusing to consumers, and expensive for Microsoft to support, so the RT product line was terminated.

Windows Phone was another operating system product entirely; its program "source code" was developed entirely separately from the mainstream Windows, and it had its own features, bugs, quirks, and development team.

Starting with Windows 10, Microsoft made a fairly bold decision to use just one Windows program source code for all devices. The main capabilities are now broken into categories defined by the amount of available screen space rather than by arbitrary marketing decisions:

> **note**
>
> Just to be complete, a third product category called Windows 10 IoT Core runs on small devices with perhaps no screen at all. IoT stands for Internet of Things, and this version of Windows is meant to be built into hobby projects, robots, and smart appliances such as refrigerators, vending machines, and the like. We don't discuss it in this book at all, other than to say it's pretty cool, you can tinker with it for free, and you can read about it at dev.windows.com/iot.

- Phones and tablets with screens smaller than 7 inches diagonal can be manufactured with ARM or Intel-compatible microprocessors. They must run Windows 10 Mobile, which supports Modern-style and Universal Windows Platform apps but not traditional desktop apps (thus, no Microsoft Office).

- Desktops and devices with screens 9 inches diagonal or larger and with an Intel-compatible processor (only) must run the full version of Windows 10 Home, Pro, Enterprise, or Education. Applications can be Modern or traditional desktop apps. The device must also have at least 2GB of RAM, 16GB of storage, networking capability, and for newly manufactured devices, a Trusted Platform Module (TPM) chip that can securely store encrypted password data.

- Devices with touch screens between 7 and 9 inches diagonal can run Windows Mobile, but if they have an Intel processor and meet the memory and other requirements, they can run full Windows desktop versions.

  (If you're interested in seeing the full specification, visit msdn.microsoft.com and search for "Minimum hardware requirements.")

This book was written with the second, more capable category of devices that run Windows 10 Home, Pro, or Enterprise in mind. But, for the most part, tablets and phones running Window 10 Mobile can be used and managed in the same way. The underlying operating systems are the same, and almost all of its settings screens are the same.

In this chapter, we show you how Windows 10 helps you get the most out of a portable device's hardware, whether it's a tablet or laptop or a convertible that lands somewhere in between. In subsequent chapters, we focus on networking and tools that you can use with both portable or desktop computers for working while away from home or the office.

Managing Mobile Computers

Portable computers come in an ever-increasing variety and go by many names: laptops, notebooks, netbooks, slates, pads, and tablets. (Not to mention "phablets," the tongue-in-cheek name for smartphones so big they barely fit in a pocket.) These are no longer an expensive perk provided only to jet-setting executives: Consumers now buy more portable computers than desktops for home and personal use. Consequently, portable devices have become powerful and inexpensive, and support for their special needs by Windows has grown considerably. The following sections describe some of the Windows 10 features that apply to these computers-on-the-go.

Airplane Mode

Whether you're in an airplane or not, when you're not using your device's Wi-Fi, Bluetooth, GPS, and cellular data connection, and, on a phone, the cellular voice line, you can extend the device's battery life (and avoid a confrontation with a flight attendant) by turning on Airplane mode, which disables all of the device's various data radios. To turn Airplane mode on or off, click or touch the taskbar's Network icon. Then click or touch the Airplane Mode button, shown in Figure 35.1, to turn it on or off. The button is a dull gray when Airplane mode is off (that is, when radios are turned on) and appears lit up when Airplane mode is on (that is, when radios are turned off).

Network icon   Action Center

Figure 35.1
Click or touch the network icon to control Airplane mode. You can also use the Action Center.

By default, there is also an Airplane Mode button in the Action Center. If you have a touchscreen, simply swipe your finger from just outside the right edge of the screen in toward the middle to open the Action Center.

Even when Airplane mode is active, you can separately turn Wi-Fi networking on or off using the Wi-Fi button, which is also located on the Network panel shown in Figure 35.1. This lets you, for example, take advantage of in-flight Wi-Fi while still leaving cellular voice and data radios turned off.

 tip
I also use Airplane mode when I'm using my phone to stream music and don't want the phone to ring or text message notifications to play over the stereo.

Computer Puts Itself into Airplane Mode

If you find that your device keeps turning Airplane mode on by itself, it could be that the device has a physical switch that turns the Wi-Fi networking adapter on and off. When this switch is turned off, Windows might assume that you want to be in Airplane mode. If you really do want to be in Airplane mode, then this is fine. If not, turn on the Wi-Fi switch, and then use the Wi-Fi button in the Action Center to turn Wi-Fi off via software. This will leave other features like GPS and Bluetooth turned on.

Getting the Most Out of Your Battery

The central processing unit (CPU) chip and graphics processor unit (GPU) chip can be the two biggest energy guzzlers in a computer, but in most cases, they spend little of their time actually working. For example, as I type this chapter, my computer's CPU takes less than a millisecond to react to each keystroke and update the display. The CPU and display processor might be occupied with useful work much less than 0.1% of the time. Modern processors can take advantage of the relatively long lulls by slowing their processing speed or clock speed way down between bursts of activity to significantly reduce power consumption. This extends battery life on mobile devices (and makes desktop PCs quieter because their CPU runs cooler and their fans can be slowed down).

Additionally, devices can conserve energy by dimming the backlight lamp that illuminates the display and by turning off hardware devices such as the disk drive, DVD or CD drive, network adapter, GPS, modem, and so on when they are not actively being used.

Of course, when you're watching a movie (which requires a lot of processor effort to decode the DVD's data into millions of pixels per second) or performing heavy-duty calculations, power consumption can go way up.

You can adjust how Windows manages hardware power consumption and how fast the processor is allowed to run by creating *power profiles*. These are collections of settings that can be applied in different situations. We discuss them shortly. Also, Windows 10 has a new feature called Battery Saver that kicks in when your battery runs low to take additional power-saving measures.

Battery Saver

In Windows 10, the feature called Battery Saver helps extend the time your device can run on battery power by suspending the operation of apps that are in the background (that is, which are open but which aren't open on your screen at present). Normally, apps can do work such as checking for email or fetching the latest weather data, even when they're not displayed. When your device's battery is getting low, Battery Saver kicks in and stops this sort of background activity until your device is plugged in or is recharged. This feature helps reduce energy-consuming processing and network data transfers.

 note

When you're working on battery power, you can hover your mouse over the battery icon in the taskbar, and Windows will pop up a balloon notification that shows roughly how much time remains on your battery before it will need to shut down.

By default, Battery Saver kicks in when your device is running on battery power and the battery falls below 20 percent charged. When Battery Saver is active, a leaf appears in the battery icon in this panel and in the taskbar. When your device is unplugged and on battery power, you can also manually turn Battery Saver on or off. You can use the Battery Saver button in the Action Center, but this tool is better: Click or touch the battery icon in the taskbar to bring up the battery panel shown in Figure 35.2. Drag the Power Mode slider all the way to the left to turn on Battery Saver, or somewhere to the right to make a trade-off between battery life and performance.

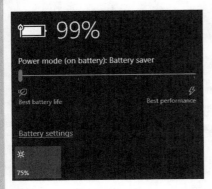

Figure 35.2
Touch the taskbar's Battery icon to adjust your power consumption.

If Battery Saver ends up annoying you, you change these settings using either of these methods:

- Click the battery icon in the taskbar to display the battery panel. Then select Battery Settings.
- In the taskbar's Search box, type **battery**. Then, in the results, select Battery Saver.

Then you can make any of the following changes:

- Uncheck Turn Battery Saver On Automatically.... You can then control Battery Saver manually by clicking the Battery icon in the taskbar and using the Battery Saver button.
- Change the threshold at which Battery Saver kicks in.
- Uncheck Lower Screen Brightness... to stop Battery Saver from dimming the screen.
- Click Battery Usage By App to see how power usage is divvied up by app when you're running on batteries. Touch an app's name that you want to allow to run in the background even when the battery is low. (You will probably want to do this only after you find yourself annoyed when a given app doesn't run.)
  You can elect to let Windows decide whether to run the app in the background, or you can uncheck Let Windows Decide and then choose whether to let the app run in the background.

You can get more fine-grained control of how power is consumed when running on batteries by working with power profiles.

Power Profiles

As we mentioned previously, power profiles are collections of power management settings that are applied automatically in different situations. Out of the box, Windows 10 enables you to choose from three profiles:

- **Balanced**—Select this profile to strike a fair balance between power savings and performance. You'll still get full processing power when it's needed. When a portable device is unplugged, display brightness is automatically reduced and the device goes to sleep sooner than when it's plugged in.

- **Power Saver**—Select this profile when you want to extend the battery life as long as possible, even if it noticeably slows the processor. Windows may also eliminate some graphical effects.

- **High Performance**—Select this profile when you want maximum speed even when your computer is running on battery power. (You might need to click the arrow next to Show Additional Plans to see this option.)

To view, choose, or modify power profiles, right-click (or touch and hold) the Start button, or press Windows Logo+X, and then select Power Options. Scroll down, if necessary, and select Additional Power Settings, Change Plan Settings to bring up the window shown in Figure 35.3. Here, you can select how long Windows should wait before darkening the screen and putting the computer to sleep under AC power and battery power.

Figure 35.3
On the Edit Plan Settings page, you can adjust various power-saving timers.

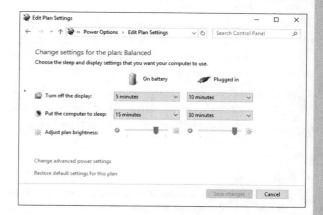

If you rarely stop while you are actually working, but tend to leave for a while when you do stop, you might gain additional battery life by reducing the time before turning off the display or shutting down when on battery power. Dimming the display can help, too, if you're not working outdoors.

To really change the speed-versus-power compromise, click Change Advanced Power Settings to get the dialog box shown in Figure 35.4. Here, you can change quite a number of power-related delays and rates. Each setting has two values: one to use when on AC power and another to use when on battery power.

 note
If you have a scenario that's begging for its own profile, you can add a new one to this list. To do so, on the Power Options page, click Create a Power Plan in the left pane.

If you really do love tweaking, you can click the + next to the item to expand it and look at some of the more interesting advanced settings:

- **Hard Disk**—Set the time that the disk is allowed to spin after being used. The default time on battery is 10 minutes. If your usage pattern usually spins the disk right back up just after it shuts down, you might increase this time. If your device has a solid state disk (SSD), this setting is not relevant.

- **Wireless Adapter Settings**—You can choose any of four settings, from Maximum Performance to Maximum Power Saving (and presumably slower and less reliable data transfer). If your wireless

Figure 35.4
The Power Options Advanced Settings dialog box lets you adjust power management settings for a large number of specific devices.

access point is nearby, Maximum Power Saving might help extend battery life. (And as mentioned earlier in the chapter, you can use the Airplane Mode switch on the Networks panel to completely turn off your device's data radio.)

- **Sleep**—Hybrid Sleep is a mode in which Windows will wake up the computer after a certain time in Sleep mode (the Hibernate After time) and perform a full hibernate. You can extend battery life by reducing the Hibernate After time. The trade-off is that Windows takes longer to start up after hibernating.

 note

When Hybrid Sleep is enabled (the default setting), the shutdown options on the Start menu and in the Change What the Power Buttons Do Control Panel applet list Sleep as a choice but not Hibernate because hibernating is automatic in this case. If you want to manually control when Windows sleeps and when it hibernates, you must disable Hybrid Sleep. Then the Start menu's shutdown button and the power button setup applet will offer Hibernate as an option. If you disable Hybrid Sleep, you must remember to manually shut down or hibernate your computer if you're not going to be using it for an extended time; otherwise, you risk losing data if the device loses power.

- **Processor Power Management**—You can set the lowest and highest processor states (speeds) in terms of percentage of maximum speed. Setting a low minimum speed increases battery life without costing much in performance. Reducing the maximum speed helps battery life but also takes a bite out of performance.

- **Multimedia Settings**—If you use Windows Media Sharing, this setting can prevent Windows from going to sleep while it's sharing media. Sleep cuts off your remote players.

- **Battery**—You can select the battery percentage levels at which Windows takes action to warn you about power loss or shutdown and what actions to take at low and critically low power levels. You should not select Sleep as the Critical Battery Action because Windows might not be able to keep system RAM alive when the battery level falls even further. If the battery dies in Sleep mode, you might lose unsaved data.

Using Windows Mobility Center

If you have a laptop or tablet running Windows 10 Home or Pro, you have a nifty little app called Windows Mobility Center that desktop computers don't have. To open the Windows Mobility Center, shown in Figure 35.5, use any one of these methods:

- Right-click the battery icon in the taskbar and select Windows Mobility Center.

- Right-click the Start button or press Windows Logo+X, and then select Mobility Center.

- In the taskbar's Search box, type `mobil`. From the search results, select Windows Mobility Center.

Figure 35.5
Windows Mobility Center has tools for quickly changing settings on mobile computers.

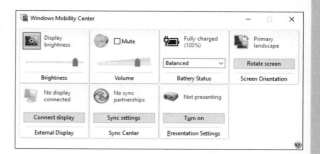

The Windows Mobility Center is normally available only on mobile devices and laptops. To trick Windows into letting you use it on a desktop computer, **see** the note on Chapter 38

The Windows Mobility Center is designed to bring together in one window most of the settings you'll want to change while using your portable computer remotely. The settings pertain mostly to power management (so you can make your device's battery last as long as possible) and display management because many people use laptops to make business and school presentations. Your computer's Windows Mobility Center may display some or all of the following controls:

- **Brightness**—The slider lets you increase or decrease your screen's backlight brightness. A lower setting should make your computer run longer on a battery charge. Windows remembers separate brightness settings for battery- and AC-powered operation, stores them as part of a power profile, and selects the chosen brightness level when the power status changes. (Alternatively, you can click or touch the battery icon in the taskbar and then click or touch the Brightness button to change brightness in 25-percent steps.)

- **Volume**—The slider controls your computer's speaker volume, and the Mute check box lets you instantly shut off the sound. This capability may be useful, for example, if you're in a meeting and someone keeps sending you noisy IM pop-ups. (And again, there is also a volume control in the taskbar that you control by clicking the Speakers/Headphones icon.)

- **Battery Status**—The icon shows you whether you are running on AC or battery-only power. (The power plug in the icon shown in Figure 35.1 indicates that the computer is on AC power.) We discussed power profiles in the previous section, "Getting the Most Out of Your Battery."

- **Screen Orientation**—On tablet PCs, this control lets you switch the display between portrait (taller than wide) and landscape (wider than tall) orientation. Generally, in portrait orientation, it's easier to read documents, and in landscape, it's easier to watch movies.

- **External Display**—When an external display monitor or projector has been connected to your computer's external display connector, this control lets you select what appears on the external display. We discuss External Display in detail in Chapter 38, "Meetings, Conferencing, and Collaboration." (By the way, you can also control internal and external display by pressing Windows Logo+P.)

- **Sync Center**—The Sync Center is used to copy files to or from an external device such as a smartphone or to update copies of network server files that you've obtained using the Offline Files feature. We discuss Sync Center in the section "Offline Files" in Chapter 37, "Networking on the Road."

- **Presentation Settings**—When you turn on Presentation Settings, Windows suppresses some behaviors that could disrupt your presentation

> ⊗ **tip**
>
> In Windows 7 and Windows Vista, the Logo+X keyboard shortcut opened the Mobility Center. In Windows 10, this shortcut is equivalent to right-clicking the Start button; it brings up a menu of administrative tools (handy, but not quite what you were after). Mobility Center is on this menu. Just click it.
>
> If you want to pin the Mobility Center to the desktop's taskbar, bring it up, right-click its icon in the taskbar, and select Pin to Taskbar.

We discuss Presentation Settings in Chapter 38.

Your device's manufacturer might have added additional controls not listed here.

One thing to remember, which isn't obvious from looking, is that for most of the tiles in the Mobility Center, you can click on the graphical icons at the upper-left corner of each tile to change the associated settings. For example, under Presentation Settings, the button just says Turn On. You can click the little projector icon to change what Presentation Mode actually does.

Using Tablet Input Methods

Although some tablets include a keyboard that either clips on or is built in to the cover, not all tablets include a keyboard, and you'll find that you can actually do reasonably well without one. In the following sections, we discuss how to enter text and graphics using alternative input methods. Later, we discuss how to use touch or a stylus or pen for input.

Even with a keyboard, sometimes you might want to use some of the following five methods:

- Use the touch keyboard

- Use the On-Screen Keyboard

- Use your fingers on a multitouch screen (a screen that can track multiple touch points at the same time so that it can distinguish gestures that involve one, two, three fingers, or more)

- Use a stylus or pen to draw

- Use your fingers or a pen with handwriting recognition

Each technique receives some special assists from Windows, as you'll see.

Touch Keyboard

Windows 10 has a nifty onscreen keyboard called the touch keyboard. It was designed specifically for use with your fingers on a tablet or other mobile device's touchscreen. Whenever text input is possible (that is, when the vertical bar cursor is displayed in a window or in an entry field that can accept text), you can use the touch keyboard.

You can also use a mouse or stylus with the touch keyboard. Several physical layouts are available for the touch keyboard. You can change layouts by touching or clicking the keyboard settings icon at the top left of the touch keyboard, as shown in Figure 35.6. The layout options are as follows:

 note

If the touch keyboard doesn't appear when the cursor is in an input field, right-click or touch and hold a blank spot on the taskbar; then select Show Touch Keyboard Button. Click or touch the touch keyboard icon in the taskbar.

- **Default Layout**—This layout has large, widely spaced keys. It's nice on a tablet-sized screen. You can press and hold, or touch and flick, keys to get digits from the top row of keys or accented letters from many of the letter keys. You can press &123 to display a set of symbols and a numeric keypad with the numbers arranged as on a telephone (1 at top), and there is an Emoji (smiley face) keyboard as well.

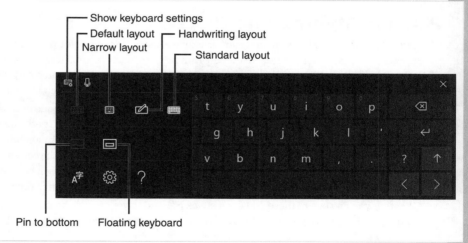

Figure 35.6
The keyboard icon on the touch keyboard lets you select a keyboard layout or the Handwriting Input panel.

Show keyboard settings
Default layout — Handwriting layout
Narrow layout
Standard layout

Pin to bottom   Floating keyboard

- **Narrow Layout**—This is the default layout shrunk to half the screen in width.

- **Handwriting Input**—This isn't a keyboard as such; instead, it lets you enter and edit text using a stylus or pen (or mouse or finger, in a pinch). Handwriting input is discussed under "Using Handwriting Recognition," later in this chapter.

- **Standard Layout**—This layout uses the familiar standard IBM PC keyboard layout. It's the only touch keyboard layout that lets you use the Windows Logo key, which is part of many Windows keyboard shortcuts.

Also, you can select the Floating Keyboard button to let you move the keyboard around the screen. The default Pin to Bottom setting ties the keyboard to the bottom of the screen.

The On-Screen Keyboard

Besides the touch keyboard, you can use the On-Screen Keyboard (OSK) that has been brought forward through several previous Windows versions. It's one of the Accessibility Tools discussed in Chapter 8, "Accessories and Accessibility."

You can't have both the touch keyboard and the OSK on the screen at the same time. Opening one closes the other. However, you can use either one with both desktop and Modern-style apps.

Touch Input and Gestures

A touch interface is adequate for text entry, but where it really shines is in interacting with software: selecting and moving things around, turning and resizing them, and so on. Windows 10 recognizes a number of specific fingertip movements, and you need to know them to get the most out of any Windows 10 computer that has touch input, whether it's a tablet, a notebook, or a desktop computer with a touchscreen. The visual response to your physical gestures is quite pleasing somehow, and this is one of the reasons that people are so enthusiastic about tablet computers.

 We give you a quick run-through of the most important touch gestures in "The Touch Tour," p. 67, and we cover touch input and gestures under "Navigating Windows 10 with a Touch Interface," p. 112.

Pen and Stylus Input

Most devices with a touch screen can recognize a touch from a fingertip or from a stylus, a soft-tipped stick that's more or less just a pen with no ink. Touch screens tend to have fairly low resolution; that is, they don't usually measure the location of the touch very precisely because they're designed primarily to sense a touch interaction that's the width of the tip of your finger.

For more precise work, you can purchase specialized electronic drawing pads or tablets that have a much finer measurement resolution, often a hundredth of an inch or less. These come with an electronic stylus or pen that has one or more buttons on it, which can signal the computer when you squeeze the buttons or press the stylus against the pad. They are especially useful with professional drafting and drawing applications and can be more comfortable to use than a touchscreen because they lie flat on your desk. The Wacom Bamboo product line is a good example of this type of drawing pad.

Whether you use one of these pads or a stylus pressed to your touchscreen, Windows 10 has special entry modes for pens and styli. These have evolved as part of Microsoft's long-term interest in "pen computing," which was demonstrated by its first pen-input software release in 1991 and continues to this day. (Remember earlier in the chapter when we referred to those recurrent "The Tablet Is Coming" keynote speeches at Comdex? Bill Gates was giving them as far back as 1994.) Windows interacts with pens in two ways: through Pen Flicks, where Windows recognizes some specific pen gestures, and handwriting recognition, where handwritten letters are turned into typewritten characters. We discuss these in the following sections. Windows Ink Workspace is a new tool that's especially useful with a pen or stylus. Pen Flicks will be available only if your computer has an input device that Windows recognizes as a pen or stylus device.

> **⚓ caution**
>
> You can use a pen or stylus with most touchscreen devices, although you must take care to use one designed specifically for your screen. The wrong kind of tip either might not work at all or might scratch or damage the screen's transparent electronic layers.

Windows Ink Workspace

With the Windows 10 Anniversary Update, Microsoft added a new pen- and touch-centric tool called Windows Ink Workspace, which puts an icon for a quick pop-up panel of pen and touch tools right in the notification area of your taskbar. The icon and the pop-up tool panel are shown in Figure 35.7.

Figure 35.7
Windows Ink Workspace gives you instant access to a pen or touch toolkit from an icon in your taskbar.

Windows Ink Workspace icon

When you open Windows Ink Workspace, you see three tools in large tiles on the panel: Sticky Notes, Sketch Pad, and Screen Sketch. Below them are recently used pen-enabled apps, and then some advertising (which you can disable, as discussed at the end of this section). Touch, click, or tap with your stylus any of these apps to open them.

 note

The Windows Ink Workspace icon is enabled automatically if your device has a touchscreen or pen input device. You can enable it even if you don't have one of these; it works fine with just a mouse. If it doesn't appear, right-click an empty spot on the taskbar and check Show Windows Ink Workspace Button.

We discuss Sticky Notes in Chapter 5, under "The Windows Apps."

Sketch Pad

The Sketch Pad app is a simple full-screen drawing tool that lets you draw on the screen using your finger or stylus. A toolbar (see Figure 35.8) appears across the top. You can select various types, colors, and widths of pen. The Ruler icon adds a straightedge that you can draw against. Move it by dragging with one finger, and rotate it using two fingers. If you don't have a pen or stylus, or you just want to finger paint, touch the Touch Writing button to let you draw with your finger. If you don't enable Touch Writing, the screen will not respond to touch. This can be confusing if you don't have a pen or stylus, but if you do, it can be useful because it prevents your hand from making marks if you rest it on the screen. The icons on the right let you clear (erase), save, or share your creation or copy it to the clipboard for pasting into some other document.

Figure 35.8
The Sketch Pad app toolbar lets you choose drawing tools or save or share your creation.

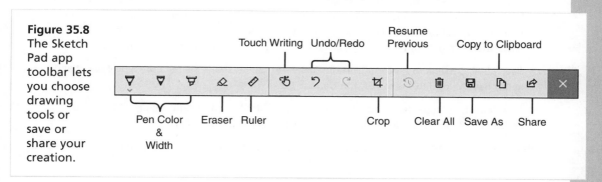

Screen Sketch

Screen Sketch is almost exactly the same tool as Sketch Pad, except that it starts by taking a picture of your device's screen at the moment you launch it. You can then draw over the image. Unlike Sketch Pad, your work won't be retained if you close the app without using the Save As icon. Next time you launch the app, you start with a fresh screen capture, but you can step back to a sketch by clicking Resume Previous. The Clear All icon erases your additions but leaves the underlying image intact.

Pen & Windows Ink Settings

Some settings affect how Windows Ink Workspace works. To view them, click Start, Settings (gear icon), Devices, Pen & Windows Ink. Or, just type Pen into the search box on the taskbar, and select Pen Settings from the results.

The settings fall into several categories:

- **Pen**—This lets you indicate your right- or left-handedness and disable touchscreen input when you are using a pen or stylus. (As mentioned earlier, this can be helpful if you tend to brush or rest your hand on the screen as you draw.) The Visual Effects switch enables visual pressure feedback, used by some pen or stylus devices. You can turn off Show Cursor to remove the Windows cursor from the screen.

- **Windows Ink Workspace**—You can disable the app advertising section that appears at the bottom of the Windows Ink Workspace panel.

- **Pen Shortcuts**—If your pen or stylus has a pressable button at its top (not tip), you can configure the actions that Windows performs when you click, double-click, or hold down the button.

Configuring Touch and Pen Input

Several settings affect touch and pen input. We describe them briefly here:

- **To tell Windows whether you're left or right handed**—Click Start, Settings (gear icon), Devices, Pen & Windows Ink. At the top, set your handedness preference. This tells Windows to display balloon notifications where you can see them, not underneath your pen or hand.

- **If your pen or finger can't move the cursor to the full extremes of your screen**—(This problem can occur with optical or resistive touch screens. If it occurs with a capacitive touch screen, there might be a driver issue.) In the taskbar's Search box, type `calibrate` and select Calibrate the Screen for Pen or Touch Input from the search results. Then click or touch Calibrate. Select Pen Input or Touch Input, and click Yes if you see a User Account Control prompt. Tap the crosshair each time it appears on the screen, as directed. Click Yes to save the calibration data.

- **Set Tablet Buttons to Perform Certain Tasks**—In the taskbar's Search box, type `tablet` and select Set Tablet Buttons to Perform Certain Tasks.

- **To select the pen gestures that equate to single-, double-, and right-clicks**—Click Start, Settings (gear icon), Devices, Pen & Windows Ink. Scroll down to Pen Shortcuts.

We discuss other settings, such as Pen Flicks, in subsequent sections of this chapter.

Configuring Pen Flicks

If your computer has a touch-sensitive screen or pad that identifies itself to Windows as a pen input device, Windows should enable the recognition of a set of gestures called *Pen Flicks* that can control Windows and edit your input. Some tablet computers include a stylus, and their screens are identified by the manufacturer as pen devices. You can also purchase external pen and stylus input devices, such as the Wacom Bamboo series of pen devices; they can be very handy on desktop computers if you like to draw or create artwork. These devices should come with Windows 10-, 8.1-, 8-, or 7-compatible drivers that are recognized as pen devices.

Earlier in this chapter, under Windows Ink Workspace, we covered a touch and pen drawing toolkit that is new to Windows 10. That section, and the previous section Configuring Pen and Touch Input, covers some pen settings. In this section, we discuss the Pen Flicks system, which has been around since Window XP and is designed to let you communicate editing commands using a stylus.

> **note**
>
> If your pen can't move the cursor to the full extremes of your screen, your input device needs to be recalibrated. We discuss how to calibrate touch or pen inputs in the preceding section.

To enable and configure Pen Flicks, in the taskbar's Search box, type **flicks**. From the search results, select Turn Flicks On and Off. There you can entirely enable or disable Pen Flicks, and you can elect to have the pen perform navigation only or both navigation and editing. Figure 35.9a shows Flicks set to perform both functions.

To perform a Flick, press the pen to your screen or input tablet and quickly snap it a short distance up, down, left, or right, with the pen rising off the surface at the end of the gesture. Flick

Figure 35.9
You can have the pen perform navigation or both navigation and editing using the Pen and Touch dialog box (left). You can also customize what the Flicks do (right).

(a) Pen and Touch dialog box

(b) Customize Flicks dialog box

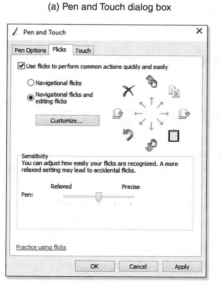

as if you were trying to brush away a spot of dirt on the screen. If you've enabled Navigational and Editing Flicks, you can flick diagonally as well, giving you eight possible flick gestures. In the Pen and Touch dialog box, you can select Practice Using Flicks to bring up a tutorial window that teaches you how to reliably perform a Flick gesture.

In the Pen and Touch dialog box, you can also click Customize to change the interpretation of the four or eight Flicks. The Customize Flicks dialog box is shown in Figure 35.9b.

The default functions are listed in Table 35.1.

Table 35.1   Pen and Touch Flick Actions

Direction	Action
Up	Drag (slide) the active window up
Down	Drag (slide) the active window down
Left	Scroll the active window down (forward)
Right	Scroll the active window up (back)
Up Left	Delete the last character or the selected text or object
Down Left	Undo
Up Right	Copy
Down Right	Paste

You can change the meaning of these Flicks to any of the 20 predefined actions, such as Cut, Open, or Save, or you can map a flick to a keystroke, such as Alt+M or Ctrl+Ins.

The manufacturer of your stylus screen or pen device may have added additional functions not described here. Check its documentation, or you can open the Control Panel, select View By: Small Icons, and look for a nonstandard Control Panel item added by the device's manufacturer. For example, the Wacom device mentioned earlier adds a Control Panel applet named Bamboo Preferences.

Using Handwriting Recognition

If you have a tablet computer that includes a stylus input device, or if you have an add-on writing or drawing tablet or pen, you may want to use these devices to handwrite text input rather than typing or using the touch keyboard. (You can also write with the mouse or your finger, although it's not quite as convenient as with a pen.)

To write, open the touch keyboard, touch or click the keyboard icon, and select the Handwriting Input icon shown previously. The Handwriting Input panel initially appears as shown in Figure 35.10. There are buttons for emoji, the spacebar, Delete and Enter keys, and the button that brings up a number and symbol keypad. To enter text, simply write on the line in the input box using either separate (block) letters or cursive, which, amazingly, Windows does a very good job of recognizing. It does this by looking up likely words in an internal dictionary of your local language, so if you write a word that isn't in the dictionary, it is much less likely to get the word right. You can train it to recognize new words, though, as described shortly.

Figure 35.10
The Handwriting Input panel lets you write text by hand and easily edit it if necessary. The panel changes when you start writing.

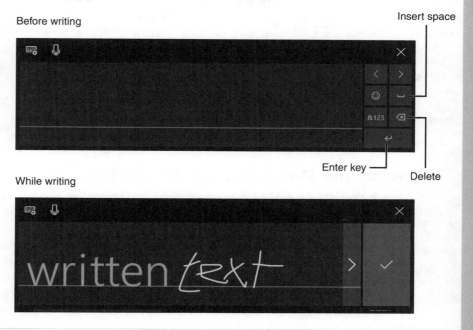

Before writing

Insert space

Enter key

Delete

While writing

As you write, the panel changes to the lower version in Figure 35.10. Windows replaces each word you wrote with its best guess and puts additional guesses above the text area. You can tap a word to correct the text that appeared. As you write, Windows transfers the words it's recognized into the application that is taking input, but you can scroll forward and back using the large left and right arrows to make corrections or press the check mark to accept all text and clear the input panel. Sometimes Windows corrects its own mistakes as it sees more of what you are writing, so it might help to just continue writing and go back a few words later to change an incorrect word.

Handwriting Gestures

You can edit recognized text displayed in the Handwriting Input panel using simple pen gestures:

- **Deleting**—To delete a written letter, draw a line backward through it. Be sure to draw across the full width of the characters you want to delete.

- **Joining**—To join two separate words, draw a line backward underneath the horizontal line in the text input box, from the beginning of the second word back to the end of the first word, curving a little down and back up. In other words, make a little smile linking the two words.

- **Inserting**—To insert a space between letters, draw a line straight up from below the text.

The editing gestures are illustrated in Figure 35.11. More often than not, you won't need to use them; Windows often guesses the correct word or words by itself, and you can simply choose them from the list displayed above the input region.

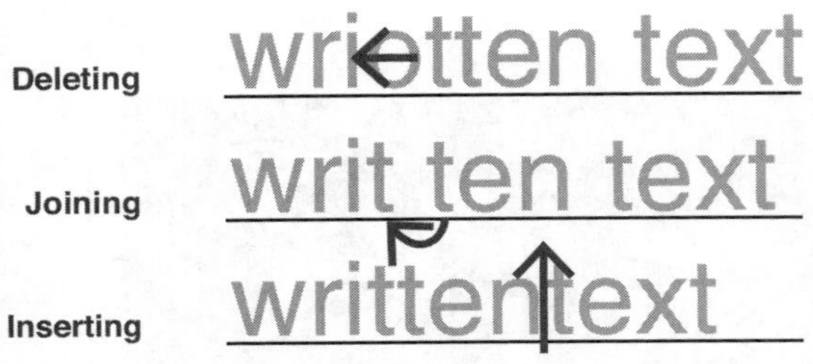

Deleting

Joining

Inserting

Figure 35.11
You can edit handwritten text using these pen gestures.

Training the Handwriting Recognizer

Windows does a pretty good job of recognizing standard English written in generic block or cursive form. If you start to use handwriting input a lot, though, you'll find that it has trouble with some of the details and quirks of your own handwriting.

Windows will slowly learn to accommodate those quirks on its own if you use the Correcting mode described in the previous section to choose the alternate spellings that Windows suggests or to add new words to the dictionary. You can speed up the learning process considerably by doing a little one-on-one training (which Microsoft calls *personalization*) with the handwriting system.

To start the Handwriting Personalization Wizard, click or touch Start, Settings, Devices, Pen & Windows Ink. Scroll down to Handwriting Input Panel and select Get to Know My Handwriting. The Handwriting Personalization Wizard appears. You can perform any or all the following training exercises:

- **To run through a standardized training session**—Click Teach the Recognizer Your Handwriting Style, Sentences. Write the requested sentences and symbols in your own, most comfortable writing style. This takes awhile. There are 50 sentences to write!

  After the arduous Sentences session, if you want Windows to learn to recognize your handwritten numbers and other symbols, click Teach the Recognizer Your Handwriting Style, Numbers, Symbols, and Letters.

- **To teach Windows to recognize a specific word that it has trouble with**—Click Target Specific Recognition Errors, Character or Word You Specify.

- **To help Windows distinguish between similar letter forms**—Select Target Specific Recognition Errors, Characters with Similar Shapes.

WIRELESS NETWORKING

Wireless Networking in Windows 10

Wireless (Wi-Fi) and cellular data networks are everywhere. From home to work to just about everywhere on the road, it seems as though you can fire up a wireless-capable device and get connected no matter where you are. Wireless networks are popular for several reasons, including low costs to get started and, more important, ease of configuration and use.

With the rapid growth of wireless networking has come evolving standards. The 802.11 series of standards was created by the networking industry to ensure hardware and software interoperability among wireless networking vendors. The current state-of-the-art standards 802.11n and 802.11ac are important steps forward for wireless performance and reliability, and we're sure that network industry gurus are hard at work at whatever's coming next.

And while people have been using cellular telephone networks to get data service for mobile devices for some time, the software for making and managing these connections

 note

Windows 10 has a useful new feature called Mobile Hotspot that lets your device share its Internet connection to other nearby devices over Wi-Fi. You can use this to give other computers Internet access from one Windows 10 device that has a cellular or paid Wi-Fi plan. You also can use this feature to instantly create a private Wi-Fi network for file and printer sharing. We talk more about this feature later in this chapter under "Mobile Hotspot."

was vendor specific and could be cumbersome to use. Today (thanks largely to Apple's iPhones and iPads), consumers have come to expect seamless, effortless, and ubiquitous data service, so Microsoft has integrated cellular data into the built-in, native networking stack in Windows 10. If you use cellular (for example, 3G, 4G, or LTE) data service on your Windows 10 device, you'll be able to manage it using the same control panels we describe in this chapter. Configuration might still be vendor specific, but your vendor will help with this, and it's not something you'll have to do on a day-to-day basis.

Before we get going, we have a housekeeping item to mention. Throughout this chapter we give this instruction for getting to the networking settings panel: "Click the network icon in the taskbar, and then select Network & Internet Settings, Status." On small screens, or if you've made the Settings window narrow, you'll need to touch or click the word *Status* to see the settings discussed. In most cases, though, Windows will show you the Status page automatically, so you won't actually need to click Status (no harm if you do, though). We want the instructions to work for everyone, so we include the step of clicking Status. On mobile phones, where there is no taskbar, you get to Network & Internet Settings from the main Settings screen.

Metered Connections

Cellular and satellite Internet connections often come with usage restrictions, extra charges, or speed reductions if you exceed a certain amount of data transfer per billing cycle. Windows lets you designate such connections as Metered so that Windows knows to minimize the amount of data transferred over them. For instance, when the only available Internet connection is metered, Windows Update will download only critical security patches but not feature updates.

To indicate that your Internet connection is metered, connect to the Internet solely through the metered connection. (So, for example, if you have both cellular and Wi-Fi service at present, turn off Wi-Fi for a moment using the Action Center.) Then click the Network icon in the taskbar and select Network & Internet Settings, Change Connection Properties. Scroll down to Metered Connection, and turn Set As Metered Connection On.

If you connect to your metered service through Wi-Fi (for example, if your home Wi-Fi network is connected to a satellite service), do this while connected through Wi-Fi. Or change the specific Wi-Fi connection setting to Metered as discussed near the end of this chapter under "Changing and Deleting Wireless Settings."

When you have a metered connection, Windows will track your data usage, though you must manually reset the counters if you want to zero the usage statistics at the beginning of each billing cycle. To view or reset the usage info, click the Network icon in the taskbar, select Network & Internet Settings, and then select Data Usage in the left column. Click View Usage Details to see how much data each app has transferred, and click Reset Usage Stats to zero the counters.

note

If you exclusively use metered Internet service, you won't get all of the Windows Update content that you should get; or you will eventually get it but it may put you over your data plan's transfer limits. So you should periodically connect to an unlimited Wi-Fi service and run Windows Update. To do this, click Start, Settings (gear icon), Update & Security, Check for Updates. Do this, say, once a month.

If you can't do this, and you definitely want all updates, you can tell Windows Update to download non-critical updates even over a metered connection. In the Update & Security settings page we just mentioned, select Advanced Options, and then check Enabling This Policy. Click the back arrow at the upper-left corner of the window, and then select Check for Updates again. Be aware that this could download up to several gigabytes if a full update of Windows 10 is available. You might want to turn the update-over-metered-connections setting back off after you perform an update, and turn it on only when you are confident it's okay to do so.

Wi-Fi Networks

Most Wi-Fi networks use a wireless router, base station, or access point. These are called *infrastructure networks*; all communications on the network are between the computers and the access point. You can also tie a group of computers together without an access point; this is called an *ad hoc network*. In this type of network, the computers talk directly to each other. The intended scenario for an ad hoc network is a group of students or business people connecting at a conference table to share files and information.

The first part of this chapter shows you how to use infrastructure networks that have already been set up. Later in the chapter, we also briefly discuss the Mobile Hotspot feature that you can use to share an Internet connection and to create a private ad hoc network for quick file sharing between a group of computers at, for example, a meeting.

➡ *For information on setting up a new wireless network for your home or office,* ***see*** *"Installing a Wireless Network," **p. 381**.*

Take Care When You Share

Wireless networking is just another network connection type as far as Windows is concerned, so file and printer sharing is also available. Other wireless users can work with your shared folders, files, and printers, just as if you and they were connected to a wired network. This capability might be just what you want in your home or office. However, when you're at a public location or are using an unsecured, unencrypted wireless network, everyone else who connects to the network, whether or not you know and trust them, might also be able to get to your same shared folders, files, and printers.

To prevent random, unknown people from seeing your shared resources, the Network Location feature keeps track of the identities of various networks to which you attach, and it lets you designate whether each one is safe for file sharing. There are actually three location "types": Public network, Private network, and Domain (corporate) network. In more detail, the standard types are as follows:

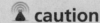
caution

Be sure to select the appropriate network location when Windows prompts you after you've connected to a new network. If in doubt, select Public. You can always change it to a less restrictive setting later if you find that you need to use network services that require the Private network setting.

- **Public network**—A network where other computers and users can't be trusted. The Public network location should be selected for any network link that is directly connected to the Internet without an intervening router or hardware firewall; a network in a cafe, airport, university, or other public location; or a home or office that you are visiting. When you designate a network as a Public network, Windows file and printer sharing is blocked to protect your computer.

- **Private network**—A network at home or work that is trusted to be secure. Either it has no Internet connection, or its Internet connection is protected by an external firewall or a connection-sharing router. Also, you trust all the users and the other computers on the network to access files and printers shared by your computer. Examples of Private networks are home and business networks managed by you or someone you trust.

note

Windows determines each network's identity by examining the physical network adapter (MAC) address of the network's gateway IP address. If you are on a network with no gateway address set (that is, no router and no shared Internet connection), Windows will permanently label the network an "Unknown Network," will not prompt you to select a location, and will not let you manually change the network location. It will be stuck as Public.

➡ *For information about dealing with the Unknown Network problem,* **see** *"File and Printer Sharing Without a Router: Avoiding the Unidentified Network Problem,"* **p. 396.**

- **Domain network**—A network that is managed by one or more computers running a Windows Server OS. This is a trusted network, and the security of the network and its member computers is managed by network administrators.

The first time you connect to a given network, Windows should prompt you to select the appropriate network location. Windows can take up to a couple of minutes to prompt you after you've connected to a new network for the first time. For whatever reason, you can't hurry the process along. During this time, it will treat the network as a public network, and file sharing will be disabled. Wait a minute or so for Windows to prompt you.

You can view the current setting through the Network and Sharing Center. On Domain networks, this location is not changeable, but it can be changed for the other types of networks.

If you need to change a network's location type, click or touch the Network icon in the taskbar, select Network & Internet Settings, and then select Change Connection Properties.

After connecting, you can change these default settings, but you really should *not* enable file and printer sharing when you're connected to a network that might contain computers that are unknown to you or are not under your control.

Connecting with Wi-Fi Sense

Windows 10 (on all devices) has a feature that lets your computer or device connect automatically to some Wi-Fi networks as you travel around. Microsoft sends your computer the information required to connect to networks it knows about in your area so that your computer can automatically get to the Internet using Wi-Fi even if you don't know the names and passwords of these networks. It's especially useful if you also use a cellular data service because using Wi-Fi whenever possible reduces your data plan usage. The feature was originally called Wi-Fi Sense, and although this name has disappeared from Windows 10's setup screens, the function is still present.

Wi-Fi Sense can connect you to two categories of Wi-Fi networks:

- Open (passwordless, unsecured) networks to which other Windows users' computers have successfully connected. When you connect to an unsecured network, Windows sends the network name and location to Microsoft, which can then pass this information along to other users via Wi-Fi Sense.

- Networks run by organizations that have made arrangements with Microsoft to provide public access.

(In the original release of Windows 10, you could also choose to let Microsoft automatically connect your Skype and phone book contacts to secured Wi-Fi networks whose password you knew, but this disturbing aspect of Wi-Fi Sense was removed in the summer of 2016.)

Wi-Fi Sense works only if your device has Locations Services turned on, so it can tell where you are. Automatic connection to networks shared by contacts is available only if you are signed in using a Microsoft (online) account.

Windows 10 also supports HotSpot 2.0, which is a networking protocol that makes it possible to automatically connect to and transition between some Wi-Fi hot spots as you travel, after just one sign-on, without always having to reselect and log on to the networks every time you come in range to a different network router.

To enable these Wi-Fi functions, follow these steps:

1. Click or touch the network icon in the taskbar and select Network & Internet Settings. Then, in the left column, select Wi-Fi and, if necessary, scroll down to Wi-Fi Services.

2. To connect automatically to free or public networks that Microsoft knows about, turn on the switch under Connect to Suggested Open Hotspots.

3. To be notified about available fee-based Wi-Fi networks, turn on the switch under Find Paid Plans for Suggested Open Hotspots Near Me. This might be useful when you're traveling.

4. To be notified about available Hotspot 2.0 networks, turn on the switch under Let Me Use Online Sign-Up to Get Connected.

5. Be sure that Location services are turned on. To do this, open the Action Center (click the icon in the far-right end of the taskbar or press Windows Logo +A), and be sure that the Location button is enabled.

Now your computer will be able to connect to public and shared Wi-Fi networks as you travel around.

Joining a Wireless Network

The Windows Networks panel makes connecting to a wireless network easier than ever. This section shows you how to connect to wireless networks in some common—but distinctly different—scenarios.

The basic steps are the same in each case:

1. Click the network icon at the right end of the taskbar.

2. The Networks panel opens, as shown in Figure 36.1. Windows displays a list of the names (SSIDs) of the wireless networks that it "hears." Networks that require a passphrase or key are labeled Secured. Your current network, if any, is marked Connected.

Figure 36.1
Open the Networks panel, and then select the wireless network you want to use.

Click or touch a network name. If you want to use this network whenever you're in its range, check Connect Automatically. If you are connecting to the network only temporarily, and you're in range of another network that you would normally prefer to use, uncheck Connect Automatically. Then select Connect.

3. Windows determines what type of security the network is using. If the network is encrypted, it prompts you to enter the network key. Enter the passphrase or the 10- or 26-digit hexadecimal key that was used when the network was set up. The network's owner will have to tell you what this is. A passphrase is case-sensitive. A WEP hexadecimal key consists of the digits 0 through 9 and the letters A through F and is exactly 10 or exactly 26 characters long. This type of key is not case sensitive.

If you are signed in using a Microsoft [online] account, and you have previously connected to this wireless network using a different computer or device, you might not need to enter the password; the network information is part of your user profile and is synced from device to device, unless you disabled this in your account's privacy settings.

4. When you have connected to a new network for the first time, after some 10 to 30 seconds Windows should ask whether the network is public or private. It is very important that you make the right selection, so we discuss this setting in detail in the following sections.

Windows will save the password you enter, so the next time you return to this location, you can reconnect without having to re-enter it. You can change other connections as described later in this chapter under "Managing Wireless Network Connections."

The following sections tell you how to proceed to protect your privacy, depending on the type of network you've chosen: corporate, your home/small office, someone else's home or office, or a public place.

Windows Is Unable to Find Any Networks

If you are using a laptop and the list of available wireless networks is empty, check to see whether your laptop has an on/off switch for the wireless adapter (this is put there to let you save battery power when you're not using the network). Be sure the switch is turned on.

Then be sure Wi-Fi networking is enabled in software. If you have a touchscreen, swipe your finger from outside the right edge of the screen in toward the middle to open the Action Center. Alternatively, press Windows Logo+A, or click the icon at the far right end of the taskbar, past the time of day. Check the Quick Action buttons to be sure Airplane Mode is turned off and Wi-Fi is turned on.

Also, be sure the wireless network adapter itself is enabled in software. Click the network icon in the taskbar, select Network & Internet Settings, Change Adapter Options, and see whether the wireless network connection icon is labeled "Disabled." If so, right-click it and select Enable.

If that's not it, there is a chance that your computer isn't within range of any wireless access point. I've been in hotels where the wireless signal is almost nonexistent in one room but excellent in a nearby room. Radio interference is just one of the causes of weak and nonexistent signals when connecting to a wireless network. Unfortunately, little can be done about this problem aside from moving closer to the access point—or in the case of interference, removing the source of the interference.

Unable to Connect to Wireless Network

Sometimes when you attempt to connect to a wireless network, you are not asked to enter a key, or the connection never completes.

For several reasons, you might not be able to connect to a wireless network, even though Windows says that the network is otherwise in range and available. With anything from poor signal strength, an incorrectly typed encryption key, to problems with the wireless access point or DHCP server, the range of problems that can arise when connecting to a wireless network seems limitless.

The Networks panel that appears when you click the taskbar's network icon indicates signal strength next to each wireless network as a series of white bars arranged as a quarter of a circle. If all or most of the bars are gray, the signal might be too weak to use. You might get a better signal if you move somewhere closer to the network router.

If the network appears to connect you but Windows displays "Limited Access" next to the connection name in the Networks panel, the router to which you've connected might have lost its Internet connection.

It's also possible that Windows was unable to actually complete the connection and has gotten stuck in negotiating the connection. Go to the wireless router or router/modem, power it off, wait a few seconds, and then power it back up. (If it's someone else's device, get permission before doing this!) Wait awhile and try again. I've seen this solve the problem on many occasions.

If nothing else works, your best bet is to make Windows delete what it knows about the wireless network using the procedure under "Deleting Wireless Profiles," later in this chapter, and then try again to make the connection.

In the Corporate Environment

Wireless networks in a business setting are frequently configured using automated means. For large enterprises, your computer will be preloaded with a certificate, a sort of digital fingerprint that identifies your computer as being authorized to use the corporate network, and the wireless network will be configured for you. Wireless network clients can now be configured via Group Policy (in other words, *by other people*—and there's nothing you can do about it) as well as through the command line using netsh commands for wireless adapters, as shown later in this chapter.

At Your Home or Small Office

A wireless network at your home or small office usually doesn't have the same configuration needs as in a large enterprise setting. Wireless networks are configured manually in these environments, using an inexpensive access point or router. Some Internet service providers offer a preconfigured wireless router as standard equipment.

Within a minute of connecting for the first time, Windows should ask you if the network is public or private. If the network is under your control, and you trust the other users and computers on the network, you can select Private. This enables file and printer sharing over the network. If the network is a place where you can't trust every other computer and user, select Private. *If in doubt, click Private. You can always change the settings later.*

 tip

Always be sure to change the default management password on any access points or routers that you own. Even if you have to write the password on a piece of paper and tape it to the bottom of the device, this is still more secure than leaving the default password in place.

In Someone Else's Home or Office

When you're away from home or the home office, you might find yourself connecting to another person's wireless network. A common scenario is when you visit an office and need to access files on this office network, or people on that network need to access files on your computer.

Make the connection as described in the previous section, but be sure you're not inadvertently making the contents of your computer available to other people on the network. Follow these precautionary steps:

1. When you make the connection, if you're asked if the network is public or private, select Private, and you're finished.

2. If you aren't prompted shortly after you make the connection, click or touch the Network icon in the taskbar, select Network & Internet Settings, and check in the diagram at the top of the Status page to see whether the connection is labeled Private or Public. If it says Private, select Change Connection Properties, Public.

Even with the location set to Public, you can still use network resources shared by others on the network. They just won't be able to get into *your* computer.

If for some reason you *do* want to temporarily let someone there use files or printers shared by your computer, here's the safest way to do it:

1. Click or touch the Network icon in the taskbar, select Network & Internet Settings, Change Connection Properties, Private. Then click the Back arrow at the upper-left corner of the page.

2. In the left column, select Status. Then scroll down and select Sharing Options. Scroll down, open the All Networks section, and be sure that Turn On Password Protected Sharing is selected, as shown in Figure 36.2. Click Save Changes.

3. Create a user account just for the person who needs access to your computer (see Chapter 3), and create a password for it.

4. Right-click a folder you want the other user to access, select Give Access To, and then click Specific People to open the File Sharing dialog box. Enter the account name, click Add, and then Share.

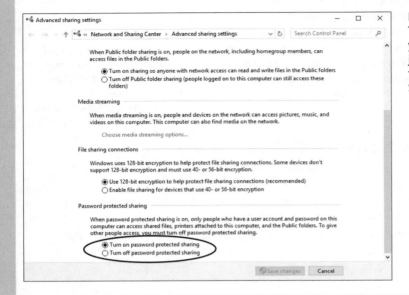

Figure 36.2
To safely share files on your computer with just one individual, use the Password Protected Sharing option.

You can later remove the user account or change its password.

➡ *For information on creating a new user account,* ***see*** *"Setting Up User Accounts,"* ***p. 75.***

➡ *For additional information on sharing files safely,* ***see*** *Chapter 21, "Using a Windows Network."*

At a Public Hot Spot

Public wireless network hot spots (also called *Wi-Fi hot spots*) are quite helpful when you're on the road and need to check email, get travel information, or just surf the Web. But public hot spots can also be places for would-be attackers to find easy victims.

One path for attack at a public hot spot is through files that client computers accidentally share. When you connect, follow these steps:

1. When you make the connection, if you're asked whether the connection is public or private, select public.

2. If you aren't prompted within a minute after you connect, click or touch the Network icon in the taskbar, select Network & Internet Settings, and make sure that the network is labeled Private under the diagram at the top of the window. If it says Private, select Change Connection Properties, and select Public.

> ⚠ **caution**
> On a public wireless network, always use an encrypted connection to any service to which you supply a username or password, such as email, file transfers, or social media. If you use a website for email or social media, make sure the URL starts with https: rather than http:. If you use a standalone email or file transfer program, be sure it is set up to use only encrypted connections.

On open unsecured public hotspots, it's possible for eavesdroppers to listen in on other people's wireless traffic. Even if the network is secured with encryption, it's possible for eavesdroppers to listen to traffic if they can break the encryption scheme. It can take them mere seconds to break WEP encryption, for example.

Therefore, at a public location, you should be *very* careful when you use websites that display sensitive information or that require you to enter a password. If the URL of the website starts with *https:*, your data will be protected. If the URL starts with just *http:*, think twice about signing in.

Mobile Hotspot

Earlier in the chapter, we discussed joining a wireless infrastructure network where devices rely on a base station called an access point or a wireless router. Windows 10 has a feature that turns your Wi-Fi–equipped Windows device into a wireless router, creates its own Wi-Fi network, and shares your device's Internet connection through this network. Up to eight other devices (computers, laptops, tablets, and smartphones) can connect to your device to access the Internet, and the connected devices can share files and printers with each other as well (with some limitations that we'll discuss shortly). You can share any type of Internet connection: cellular, free, paid Wi-Fi, or Ethernet. The Wi-Fi network that Mobile Hotspot creates is secure, so other devices can treat it as a Private network, safe for file sharing even if you're in a public place like a coffee shop or school.

To create a Wi-Fi network so that other users can connect through your device to the Internet, and, if desired, share files and printers, follow these steps:

1. Connect to the Internet with your own device (unless your only objective is file and printer sharing).

2. Click the network icon in the taskbar and select Network & Internet Settings. Alternatively, click Start, Settings (gear icon), Network & Internet. Then, in the left column, select Mobile Hotspot.

3. The screen will show the Wi-Fi network name and password that other devices will use to connect to your computer. By default, the network name will be the name of your computer plus some digits, and the password will be a string of random characters. To change the name or password to something easier to remember (but not easy to guess), click Edit. Make the changes, and then click Save. Make a note of the network name and password. You'll need to provide this to other users.

4. If your computer has multiple network adapters, set Share My Internet Connection From to the name of the network that leads to the Internet. (If your goal is only to set up a secure network for file sharing, and you don't care about Internet sharing, you can leave this setting alone.)

5. If you have Windows Mobile (phone) devices that have Bluetooth, and you'd like them to be able to turn the Mobile Hotspot feature on and off remotely, set Turn On Remotely on.

6. At the top of the page, set Mobile Hotspot to on. After a few seconds, other devices should be able to connect. You can see which devices are connected on this settings page.

To connect to your Mobile Hotspot, users of other devices (whether Windows or not) should open their Wi-Fi settings menu, select the network name that you noted in step 2, and enter the password you gave them. If they are running Windows and want to use file or printer sharing on the Wi-Fi connection, when Windows prompts them to select a network type, they should select Private (or Home Network, for earlier versions of Windows).

---

 note

If you don't care about file sharing with Mobile Hotspot users, you can skip this note. If you want to use file sharing, there is a glitch that you must work around: it's easy to tell other computers to treat the Mobile Hotspot network as Private, but your computer, which has created the network, sees it Public, so it won't let the other devices get to folders and printers you've shared. There is a way to fix this, although it's cumbersome: Right-click the Start button or press Windows Logo+X, and then select Windows PowerShell (Admin). If this choice isn't available, select Command Prompt (Admin), type the command **powershell**, and then press Enter. Then type **get-netconnectionprofile** and press Enter. This will list several network names. Locate the one that has the name of the Mobile Hotspot you created.

Two lines under that name, look for the word *InterfaceIndex*, followed by a number. Take note of the number. Then type the command

```
set-netconnectionprofile -interfaceindex ## -networkcategory private
```

replacing ## with the number you saw after InterfaceIndex, and press Enter. Close the PowerShell window. Now your computer sees the hot spot network as private, and it will share files with other devices. You only have to do this once, even if you turn Mobile Hotspot off and back on later.

If your device has cellular or satellite Internet service with a download limit, be sure that it's set up as a metered connection. Be sure that other Windows 10 devices that are now connected to your computer also treat their Internet link as metered, so that they don't, for example, try to download a large Windows Update. And, ask the other users to be careful with their Internet usage.

To set a network connection as metered on any Windows 10 device, click the network icon in the taskbar, select Network & Internet Setting (or, go through the main Settings page to get there), select Change Connection Properties, scroll down to Metered Connection, and set the switch to On.

When the other devices no longer need your Internet service, it's best to turn the feature off. Repeat step 1 in the preceding procedure, and turn Mobile Hotspot off. Even quicker, click the Action Center icon in the taskbar or press Windows Logo+A, and use the Mobile Hotspot pushbutton.

Managing Wireless Network Connections

If you travel and connect to different networks, Windows will collect a list of several known networks.

When Windows is not currently connected to any wireless network, it scans through its list of known networks, in order. If any are in range, and you have enabled automatic connection, Windows selects the one it thinks you're most likely to want to use and then connects.

In most cases, this system works without adjustments, but there are ways to change the preferences if necessary, as we discuss in the next few sections.

Changing and Deleting Wireless Settings

If you have to change the security information for an existing wireless connection, for example, to change the security key, click the taskbar's Network icon, and select Network & Internet Settings, Change Adapter Options. Right-click the wireless adapter, and select Status, Wireless Properties. Select the Security tab. You can now use the Security tab to change the security type and security key. Click OK when you are finished. Alternatively, you can tell Windows to "forget" the known network, as described next, and then reconnect to it.

To delete the record of a previously used Wi-Fi network from your computer, click the Network icon in the taskbar and select Network & Internet Settings. In the left column, select Wi-Fi and then select Manage Known Networks. Click on the name of the network you wish to remove, and select Forget.

You can also use the preceding steps to change the Metered setting for a known connection.

You might notice that Manage Known Networks lists known networks in order of preference, but there is no simple way to change the order of preference from here. You must indicate your preference using the steps in the next section.

Setting Up Preferred Wireless Networks

Once you successfully connect to any new network, Windows remembers the network's details as a *profile*, which is a collection of settings for a given network. By default, Windows keeps profiles for all networks to which you've previously attached, and—unless you've disabled automatic connection—reconnects when one becomes available. This lets you move from place to place, while Windows automatically connects to whatever network is appropriate.

If you are in an area where your computer can receive signals from two or more known networks—that is, networks to which you've previously connected—at the same time, you might want to tell Windows which one to use in preference to the others. One might have faster download speeds. Or you might want to connect to your neighbor's network when yours is out of reach, but if both are available, you want to use yours.

How does Windows know which to use? In Windows 7 and earlier versions, you could sort the list of known networks into your own preferred order. Windows would use whatever available network was topmost in the list.

Windows 10 doesn't let you manually sort the list of networks, but it does let you switch between available networks, and it keeps track of which network you end up actually using, if more than one is available. To train Windows, you must manually switch networks, using these steps:

1. View the list of available networks by clicking the network icon in the taskbar.

   If you are currently connected to a network, it will be labeled Connected.

2. If you want to connect to a different network, click or touch its name and then select Connect.

Windows should remember your preference for this connection over the other one for future connections.

You can also give hints to Windows by changing a network's connection properties. You can put each network into one of three priority categories. To set these categories, click the taskbar's Network icon, and select Network & Internet Settings, Change Adapter Options. Right-click the wireless adapter, and then select Status, Wireless Properties. Designate how you want Windows to treat the network. Here's the list of options (see Figure 36.3):

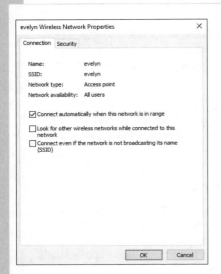

Figure 36.3
In the wireless network's Properties dialog box, use the Connection tab to specify how you want Windows to treat the wireless network.

- **This is a top-choice network. I'm happy to use this one anytime. Stick with this network until the signal is lost.** Check Connect Automatically When This Network Is in Range, and uncheck Look for Other Wireless Networks While Connected to This Network.

- **This is a backup network.** Use it if necessary, but if a top-choice network becomes available, switch over to the better one—check Connect Automatically, and then also check Look for Other Wireless Networks.

- **This is a special-purpose network or a last resort.** Connect to it only when I tell you to—uncheck Connect Automatically.

Adding a Network Manually

Some people instruct their wireless routers not to advertise their network name (SSID), as a sort of security measure. The thinking is, if the network is invisible, people won't try to use it.

This approach doesn't really make them secure, just difficult for you to connect to. A network that does not broadcast its network name (SSID) usually will not appear in the list of available networks (although it might if Windows overhears network traffic that includes the name). To connect to such a hidden network, you must enter its connection information manually. Follow these steps:

1. Click the network icon at the right end of the taskbar; then select Network & Internet Settings.

2. In the left column, select Wi-Fi, and then select Manage Known Networks, Add a New Network.

3. Enter the network's name (SSID), set the security type, and enter the key if required.

4. Check Connect Even If This Network Is Not Broadcasting. You should *not* check Start This Connection Automatically. If you do, your computer will frequently broadcast the name of the network it's looking for, advertising its name to everyone nearby.

5. Click Save, and then click Close to save the new profile.

 note

Just so you know, a hacker can find such "invisible" networks without any problem using easily available software that lets them eavesdrop on the wirelessly transmitted data. Even data encrypted by the WEP or WPA methods can be read. For your own networks, if you really want to secure them, encrypt them with WPA2. (And even then, a highly motivated hacker might still be able to break in.)

To later connect to a network with a hidden SSID when you're in range, open the list of available networks, click the name of the network, and click Connect. Be aware that this network name will always appear in the list of available networks, even when it's not in range.

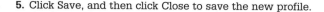

NETWORKING ON THE ROAD

Windows Unplugged: Mobile and Remote Networking

Some people predict that one day a global Internet will cover every inch of the earth's surface, giving us an always-on, always-available stream of data they call the "Evernet." We're not quite there yet, but today the Internet is available in pretty much any city you might visit, and it has become easy to stay in touch with home while you're traveling. It really is starting to matter less and less where you are because your data, services, and online life are now present just about everywhere you go.

Windows 10 supports you when you're away from home or the office with some pretty spiffy portability and networking features, including these features that are covered in other chapters:

- OneDrive, Microsoft ("online") accounts, and other cloud services ensure that your account preferences, passwords, data, and apps are available no matter where you are and what device you're using. This topic is mentioned in Chapter 5, "Windows Apps and the Windows Store," but we talk here about how to use it more effectively when you're on the road.

- The Battery Saver and Windows Mobility Center tools let you easily manage your computer's display, power consumption, and networking features. These tools are covered in Chapter 35, "Windows on Mobile Devices."

- Wireless networking support lets Windows stay connected when you're on the go. For information, see Chapter 36, "Wireless Networking."

- If you don't always have access to a Wi-Fi hot spot, some Windows devices have a built-in cellular modem so you can get Internet data wherever there is cell service. If it's not built in, you can purchase and add an external cellular modem and data plan to most devices. In addition, Windows 10 will let your device share this data service with other nearby devices through Wi-Fi, using the new Mobile Hotspot feature. (For more information, see "Mobile Hotspot," **p. 829**.)

  Working the other way, if your Windows device doesn't have a cellular connection, your smartphone might be able to share its data service with your computer via Wi-Fi. This phone feature might be called something like Data Tethering or Personal Hotspot.

- Windows 10 Pro makes it easier to use a portable or laptop computer to make business or school presentations. Presentations are covered in Chapter 38, "Meetings, Conferencing, and Collaboration."

- Windows has a nifty Remote Desktop feature that lets you connect to and use your own home-based computer from somewhere else, over the Internet. This and numerous similar third-party tools are covered in Chapter 39, "Remote Desktop and Remote Access."

This chapter shows how to use several Windows 10 mobile networking features that help you get the most out of mobile (laptop, notebook, netbook, or tablet) computers while you're working away from home or the office:

- Dial-up and virtual private network (VPN) networking let you access a remote network when you're traveling, and you can even set up remote access to your own home or office network.

- The download-on-demand feature of OneDrive lets you limit how much data your device has to store and download, but it also lets you access any file you need over an Internet connection.

- The Offline Files feature lets you automatically keep up-to-date personal copies of the files stored in your network's folders. This is a private version of what OneDrive does for cloud storage.

> **note**
>
> Some tablets and other small devices run a version of Windows called Windows 10 Mobile. Although many of the features and settings we discuss in this chapter apply to Windows 10 Mobile, this chapter primarily addresses portable devices with an Intel-compatible processor running Windows 10 Home, Pro, or Enterprise.

We'll start with OneDrive features that help you when you're on the road.

OneDrive

Microsoft's OneDrive cloud file storage product is built into Windows 10 and has features that can really help when you're on the road. When you are signed in to Windows 10 using a Microsoft account, OneDrive is automatically connected. If you're using a local account, you can open the OneDrive app and add a OneDrive account on its settings page. Files and folders you store in

OneDrive automatically appear on all devices that you use with the same Microsoft or OneDrive account. However, this might not be exactly what you want, as we'll discuss next.

By the way, as with most cloud storage services, OneDrive works on a "freemium" business model: You can use up to a certain amount of storage space for free, but if you need more, you must pay for a premium subscription. At the time this was written, each Microsoft account is granted 5GB of free storage space. If you need more, there are various paid plans, ranging from $2/month for 50GB of storage to $100/year for a group subscription that includes Office 365 (the online version of Microsoft Word, Excel, and so on) and 1TB of storage for each of five users.

On-Demand Downloading

If you (or your organization) have a lot of data stored on OneDrive, you might find it problematic keeping that much data synced up on your computer or portable device—either it takes up too much of your local storage, or too many items get changed frequently, and your Internet bandwidth is taken up constantly syncing large files. (For example, I have a cloud storage folder that's shared with someone who does construction work, and I keep finding that several gigabytes of architectural drawings that I don't need have been copied onto my computer, effectively choking my Internet connection. *That's* why I couldn't watch Netflix the night before!)

To help with this problem, OneDrive has a feature that lets you specify that the contents of some or all files and folders are to be kept online, but not on your local hard drive. They'll still appear in the OneDrive folder on your device as if they were really there, so you can always see what's available. Then the file's contents are transferred to your device only if you actually try to open, view, or change a particular file. This has some pros and cons:

- It can save a lot of storage space on your device and a lot of Internet bandwidth copying files that you might not even need or use.

- You need a working Internet connection to download a file that wasn't already there before, and, if it's a large file, it could take a while for its contents to be delivered when you need it.

You'll have to weigh these pros and cons yourself, but you can choose whether to have files always downloaded, or downloaded-on-demand, on a folder by folder basis, depending on what works best for you.

To use this feature, right-click the OneDrive icon in the Notification area of the taskbar (it looks like two overlapping clouds, and if your taskbar is full you might need to press the ∧ symbol to see it) and select Settings. Select the Settings tab, check Files On Demand, and then click OK.

With this initial setting, all files and folders will be downloaded on demand. Any files already downloaded might stay there, although Windows might decide to release their contents in order to save local storage (disk) space—it decides on its own.

When you look in your OneDrive folder, a blue cloud symbol will appear over the icon for a file that is available but not downloaded. It will be downloaded automatically if you open the file. A green circle with a checkmark indicates that the file contents are already present on your device and are ready to use.

You can manually manage which files and folders are kept locally and which are downloaded only as needed by right-clicking a file or folder and making one of the following selections:

- **Always Available Online**—Select this (a checkmark appears) to have the file or folder and its contents always downloaded and ready to use, even when you have no Internet service.

  If already checked, selecting this item unchecks it. The file or the folder and its contents will now be downloaded on demand. If it's already downloaded, Windows might choose to release the file's contents to free up disk space at some point in the future.

- **Free Up Space**—Select this to tell Windows to release the file's contents immediately. If the file was marked Always Available Online, this will be unchecked. The contents will be downloaded again when needed (or if you check Always Available Online).

Next, we discuss another feature of OneDrive that helps you get to files that you *haven't* stored in the cloud.

Fetching Files from Your PC

OneDrive has another feature that might seem pretty surprising: you can give OneDrive access to all of the files on your PC or other device, and it will let you reach into your device from anywhere in the world to retrieve any file you need, as long as your device is turned on. This makes it a possible alternative to setting up the remote access options that we discuss in Chapter 39; if all you need is to pick up a file now and then, and not to run programs on your home computer, maybe OneDrive is all you need. Your home device has to be turned on for this to work, connected to the Internet, and OneDrive has to be running. But if you can ensure this, you can get to your files from anywhere.

note

This feature might not be available if your computer is part of an organization's domain network. It can be disabled by network managers.

To enable this feature, follow these steps:

1. To use this feature, right-click the OneDrive icon in the Notification area of the taskbar (it looks like two overlapping clouds, and if your taskbar is full you might need to press the ∧ symbol to see it) and select Settings.

2. Select the Settings tab, check Let Me Use OneDrive to Fetch Any of My Files on This PC, and then click OK.

3. Right-click the OneDrive icon in the notification area again, and then select Exit, Close OneDrive.

4. Restart the OneDrive app. The easiest way is to type **onedrive** into the taskbar's search box, and then select OneDrive from the results.

5. If you want to ensure that your PC is always on when you need to connect to it from somewhere else, right-click the Start button or press Windows Logo+X, and then select Power Options. Under Sleep, set all entries to Never, and then close the Settings window.

Now you should be able to view the files on your PC from somewhere else. To do this, follow these steps:

1. Open a web browser and view onedrive.microsoft.com. Sign in with the same Windows account you use with OneDrive on the PC that has your files.

2. In the left column, select PCs, and then select the name of the computer that has the files you want to see.

3. The first time you connect, you might be asked to verify whether you are the actual user of the PC. You can choose to receive a text message or email. Click the method that you'd like to use, and follow the prompts.

4. When you've verified your identity, you can browse through the PC's files, as shown in Figure 37.1. The first set of files are the folders in your user profile. Below those are tiles for the full contents of the drives in your PC and any network drives that are mapped.

Figure 37.1
When File Fetching is enabled, you can use a web browser anywhere to get to the files on your home PC.

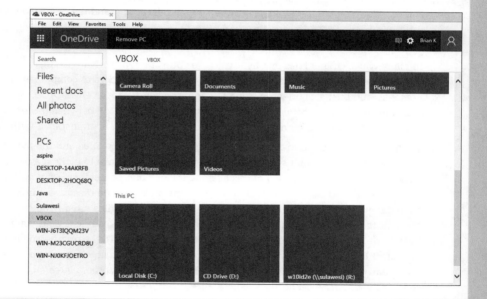

Browsing through and fetching files from your home PC can be slow if the home PC has a slow Internet upload speed, which is often the case, but it's usually faster to wait a bit for a forgotten file to be transferred than to fly home to get it!

Offline Files

You might recognize the "Offline" problem: If you have a portable computer that you sometimes use with your office network and sometimes use out in the field, you probably make copies of important "online" documents—documents stored on the network server—on your laptop. But if you make changes to one of your "offline" copies, the network's copy will be out of date. Likewise, if someone updates the original on the network, your copy will be out of date. And trying to remember where the originals came from and who has the most recent version of a given file is a painful job. I admit that more than once I've accidentally overwritten a file I'd worked on with an older copy—or worse, overwritten somebody else's work—because I wasn't paying attention to the files' date and time stamps.

 note

The Offline Files feature is available only on Windows 10 Pro and Enterprise editions. The Sync Center is present on all versions, though, because it can also work with handheld devices such as PDAs and smartphones. If your version of Windows doesn't support Offline Files (or even if it does), you should know about Microsoft's SyncToy tool, which is a free program you can download from Microsoft.com. (Search for **Synctoy**; you want version 2.0 or later.) SyncToy can do a pretty good job of copying new and updated files back and forth between a network location and a folder on your portable computer. It's not quite as seamless as Offline Files, but it can do just as good a job. If you're a command-line junkie, the robocopy command can also sync files and folders between any two locations, and it works across a network.

In many ways, Offline Files and SyncToy give you your own "private cloud," networked file storage that you manage yourself. If you don't want to bother, a plethora of companies provide both personal- and business-oriented cloud storage, such as Microsoft's OneDrive, Google Drive, Dropbox, and so on. These services have applications that do the job of syncing the network's and your personal copies of files automatically. OneDrive, in particular, is preinstalled with Windows.

Windows has a solution to this housekeeping problem: Offline Files and the Sync Center. Here's how it works: When you use a network folder and tell Windows to make it available for offline use, Windows stashes away a copy of (*caches*) the folder's files somewhere on your hard drive, but all you see is the original network folder on your screen. When you disconnect from the network, the shared file folder appears to remain on your screen, with its files intact. You can still add, delete, and edit the files. For all intents and purposes, Windows makes it look as if you're still connected to the network. Meanwhile, network users continue to work with the original, online copies. When you reconnect later, Windows will set everything right again thanks to a program called the Sync Center. Files you've modified will be copied to the network, and files others have modified will refresh old copies in your offline cache.

You'll find that the Offline Files system works really well and is more powerful than it seems at first glance. The following are some of the potential applications:

- Maintaining an up-to-date copy of a set of shared files on both a server (or desktop computer) and a remote or portable computer. If you keep a project's files in a file folder marked for offline use, Windows keeps the copies up to date on all your computers.

- "Pushing" application software or data from a network to a portable computer. If software or data is kept in an offline file, your portable computer can update itself whenever you connect or dock to the LAN.

- Automatically backing up important files from your computer to an alternative location. Your computer can connect to a dial-up or network computer on a timer and refresh your offline files and folders automatically.

It's easy to make folders available offline, as you'll see in the next section.

Identifying Files and Folders for Offline Use

note

The server we're talking about might be in the next room, which isn't very "remote" at all, but that's what we'll call it for simplicity's sake. In this section, a "remote" server refers to some other computer that you access via networking.

You can mark specific files, subfolders, or even entire shared folders from a "remote" server for offline use.

While you're connected to the remote network, view the desired items in File Explorer. If you've mapped a drive letter to the shared folder, you can select the mapped drive in the This PC section; otherwise, you can see it in the Network section.

When you find the mapped drive, file, folder, or folders you want to use while offline, select it (or them), right-click, and select Always Available Offline.

You can also select a file or folder in File Explorer's right pane—that is, the right-hand contents window rather than the left pane tree listing—and use the ribbon's Easy Access button to select Always Available Offline. The ribbon works only on items you select in the right pane, not the left pane. (If the File Explorer window isn't wide enough, Easy Access can be hard to find. It's in the section labeled New.)

Be cautious about marking entire shared drives or folders available offline, though, unless you're sure how much data they contain and you're sure you want it all. You could end up with gigabytes of stuff you don't need. (Remember, all of this stuff will be copied to your own hard drive.)

note

Before you mark a folder for offline use, check to make sure you don't have any of its files open in Word, Excel, or so on. Open files can't be copied.

Can't Make File Available Offline

If Always Available Offline isn't displayed as an option when you right-click a file or folder, several things could be wrong. You must be using Windows 10 Pro or Enterprise; Windows 10 Home and Mobile don't have this feature. Also, you can't enable offline access by right-clicking an entry in the Favorites list in File Explorer. It's not available there. To make an entire shared folder available offline, open a remote computer's entry under Network and right-click the folder there, or map a drive letter to the shared folder and right-click the drive letter.

The feature might also be disabled. To check, click in the taskbar's search box and type **sync center**. Select Sync Center from the results; then select Manage Offline Files. On the General tab, if you see a button labeled Enable Offline Files, click it. Another cause could be that your network manager might have disabled Offline Files via group policy, in which case you're out of luck.

Files of This Type Cannot Be Made Available Offline

If you mark files or folders for offline use, you might receive the error "Files of this type cannot be made available offline." Some file types (for example, Microsoft Access MDB database files) usually should not be available offline because such files are generally used by multiple LAN users simultaneously, and there's no way to reconcile changes made by offline and online users. Your network manager might have designated one or more files as being unavailable for offline use for this reason. Ask your network manager to check Group Policy entry Computer Configuration\Administrative Templates\Network\Offline Files\Files not cached.

The first time you mark a file or folder for offline use, Windows copies it (and all its contents) from the network location to a hidden folder on your hard drive. This process can take awhile if there is a lot to copy or if your network connection is slow. If any files cannot be copied, you can click the Sync Center link to see their names and the reasons for the problem.

When the file, folder, or folders have been copied, you will be able to use the network folders whether you're connected to the network or not. When you're offline, the items will still appear to be in their original network folder locations even though you're actually using copies hidden away somewhere on your hard drive. Windows takes care of that part.

 note

The most common reason a file can't be copied is that it is open and in use by an application. If this is the case for any of your files, close the application and perform another sync, as discussed later in this section. Another common problem is that thumbs.db, a hidden file Windows creates in folders that contain pictures, is sometimes in use by File Explorer and can't be copied. You can ignore problems with thumbs.db. Just right-click the file's name in the Sync Results window and select Ignore.

Using Files While Offline

When you've marked a file, folder, or mapped network drive as Always Available Offline, a small green Sync Center icon appears on the topmost folder or file marked for offline use, as shown in Figure 37.2. If you select any item inside an offline folder, the text at the bottom of the File Explorer window shows the item's status.

When files and folders are marked for offline use, the marked files and folders will remain in the File Explorer display even when the network copies are unavailable.

 caution

If the files that you're copying from your network contain sensitive information, you might want to ask Windows to encrypt the copies stored on your computer. To see how to do this, skip ahead to "Managing and Encrypting Offline Files," later in this chapter.

Figure 37.2
When a folder or network drive is Always Available Offline, a green Sync Center icon is displayed on the top-level folder, and the status bar shows the sync status of any item inside.

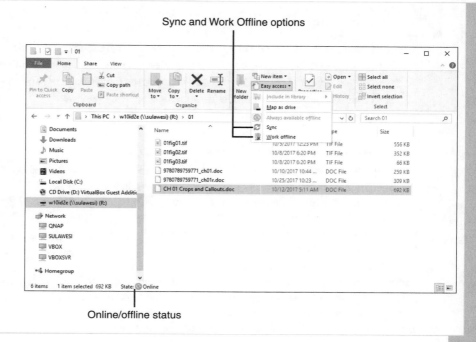

Sync and Work Offline options

Online/offline status

 tip

If your network or VPN connection is unreliable, you might find that your applications sometimes hang when you're trying to save your work to a network folder. If this happens to you frequently, the Work Offline feature is your new best friend. With it, you can force Windows to use a local, cached copy of a document while you edit it and then sync it back up after you've saved your changes. Here's how to do it: Locate a network folder in File Explorer. Mark it Always Available Offline. Open the folder in File Explorer. In the Home tab, select Easy Access (it can be hard to find; it's in the New section, as shown in Figure 37.2) and then select Work Offline. This tells Windows to use the folder's local copies, not the network copies, even if the network is available. Edit the file(s) you need to edit and then, back in File Explorer, select Home, Easy Access and unselect Work Offline. This should run the Sync Center and copy your changes back to the network.

When you are offline, you can add new files and delete, view, and edit files in any folder that you marked Always Available Offline. If you had mapped a drive letter to the network folder, the drive letter still functions. Folders or files that were not marked Always Available Offline will disappear from the display when you disconnect from the network.

Offline Files Are Missing

If you can't find files or folders you know you clearly marked for offline use, you might not have synchronized after marking the file, its folder, or a containing folder for offline use. The solution is to go back online and synchronize. Then check the Sync Conflicts page to see if Windows says that it couldn't copy your file for some reason.

You can also rename files, and the network copy of the file will be renamed the next time you connect and sync up.

However, in most cases, you cannot rename a folder while it is offline. On some corporate networks, you may be able to rename "redirected" folders if your network administrator has enabled this feature. In general, though, it's best not to try to rename an offline folder while you're offline.

Overall, the Offline Files system works very well. You can happily work away as if you were really still connected to the network. All network files and folders stay right where you're used to them being. The only difference is that your changes won't be visible to others on the network until you reconnect.

> **⚠ caution**
>
> If you delete a file from a network folder, while you are either offline or online, it will be deleted from your computer immediately and permanently. Files stored on a network are not saved in the Recycle Bin when you delete them!

When you do reconnect, you should promptly synchronize your offline files and folders with the network folders so that both sets will be up to date.

Using Sync Center

You can synchronize files anytime you are connected to the network that contains the original shared folder, whether you connect by LAN, modem, or VPN. You can start a synchronization in any of several ways:

- In the taskbar's search box, type **sync center**. From the results, select Sync Center and then click Sync All.

- In File Explorer, right-click a specific shared file or folder and select Sync, Sync Selected Offline Files.

- If you have a portable device, right-click the Start button or press Windows Logo+X, select Mobility Center, click the Sync Settings button, and then click Sync All.

Synchronization can also occur automatically:

- When you reconnect to the network and Windows is idle.

- When you log on and off.

- At specified times and days of the week. For a scheduled synchronization, Windows can even automatically make a dial-up connection.

The Sync Center has the job of reconciling changes made to the online and offline copies of the files.

The Sync Center will automatically copy new or changed files from your computer to the network, and vice versa. However, three situations exist in which it will need some help:

- If both you and another user have changed the same file, you'll have to pick which version to keep.

- If you deleted a file while you were disconnected, you'll have to decide whether you want to also delete the network's copy.

- If a network user deleted a file from the real network folder while you were disconnected, you'll have to confirm that you want to delete your copy.

If any problems occur while syncing files, the Sync Center icon in the notification area on your task-bar will display an exclamation mark in a yellow triangle as a warning. Double-click the Sync Center icon to display the Sync Center, and then click View Sync Conflicts in the tasks list. This displays the Conflicts page, as shown in Figure 37.3.

Figure 37.3
The Conflicts page lists files that cannot be reconciled without help.

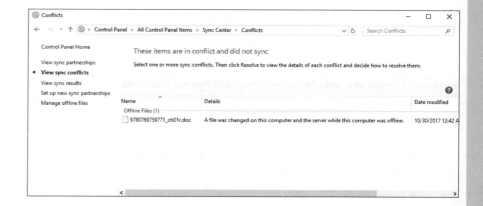

Double-click the first listed file. This displays an explanation of why Sync Center can't update the file, and you see a selection of choices to resolve the issue. For example, if both you and a network user modified the same file while you were disconnected, the dialog box will look like the one shown in Figure 37.4.

Continue through the conflict list to resolve each problem.

 caution
If the sync process fails because a file is in use, you should repeat the synchronization when no one is editing files in the shared folder; otherwise, you might lose changes to some files.

Figure 37.4
When two users have modified the same file, you can choose to keep one or both versions. The selected version(s) will be copied to your computer and the network.

Managing and Encrypting Offline Files

To manage the Offline Files feature, in the taskbar's search box, type *sync center*, and then select Sync Center from the results. (Or, as we mentioned previously, use the Mobility Center button.) In the left pane, click Manage Offline Files. The Offline Files dialog box has four tabs:

- **General**—Here, you can enable or disable the Offline Files feature entirely. You can also see a list of all files that have been copied to your hard disk for offline use.

- **Disk Usage**—This tab lets you monitor or limit the amount of disk space used by offline file copies.

- **Encryption**—Here, you can select to encrypt the network files that are stored on your hard disk. This makes them safe from theft should your computer fall into the wrong hands.

  ➡️ *If you enable encryption and your computer is not joined to a corporate network, see "Backing Up Your Encryption Key," p. 742.*

- **Network**—If Windows detects that you have a slow network connection (dial-up, for instance), Windows can automatically elect to work with offline copies and will sync them up periodically while you continue to work. You can set the frequency with which Windows checks for a slow connection. The default is every five minutes.

Finally, remember that you can uncheck Always Available Offline on a file or folder anytime to remove it from the cached file list. This will delete the cached copies of the files in that folder.

Making Your Shared Folders Available for Offline Use by Others

When you've marked a network file for offline use, Windows makes a copy of the file on your hard disk. Windows can use your local copy of the file even while you're still connected to the network; this could really save time, for example, if you are running an application from a network folder. On the other hand, this would not be appropriate for files that change frequently or for database files that are used by multiple users concurrently.

Therefore, Windows must know whether it's appropriate to serve up cached copies for online use, and it leaves the choice up to the person who *shares*, not uses, a given network folder. So, when you share a folder on your computer, you can specify the way Windows will make this folder available for offline use by others.

Normally, Windows will not give users its cached copy of a file if the network copy is available. It's useful to change this default setting if you are sharing a folder that has "read-only" documents that don't change often, or a folder that contains application programs. In this case, you may be able to give users faster access by following these steps:

1. Use File Explorer or This PC to locate the folder you're sharing. Right-click it and select Properties.

2. View the Sharing tab. Click the Advanced Sharing button. If Share This Folder is not checked, check it now.

3. Click the Caching button.

4. Select one of the following caching options:

   - **Only the Files and Programs That Users Specify Are Available Offline**—Lets users make the choice of whether to make the folder contents available offline. This is the default setting.

   - **No Files or Programs from the Shared Folder Are Available Offline**—Prevents users from making the folder's contents available offline.

   - **All Files and Programs That Users Open from the Shared Folder Are Automatically Available Offline**—Causes other computers to automatically make the contents of any file opened from the folder available for use offline. Furthermore, even while connected, if users run an application program from the network folder, their computer will use their cached copy for speedier performance. This is automatic for Windows 10, 8.1, 8, 7, and Vista computers. Check Optimize for Performance to let Windows XP computers do this as well.

5. Click OK to close the Offline Settings dialog box, and then click OK to close the Advanced Sharing dialog box.

The amount of disk space allocated to "automatically" available offline files is limited to an amount set on the Disk Usage tab (click Change Limits) in the Sync Center's Manage Offline Files dialog box.

VPN and Dial-Up Networking

Windows can connect to a remote Windows network via a dial-up modem or via an encrypted connection called a virtual private network (VPN) that's routed through the Internet. Using these services, all file sharing, printing, and directory services are available just as if you were directly connected to the remote network (albeit through a slower connection.) You can open shared folders, transfer files, and use email as if you were "there," and then disconnect when you're finished.

A VPN connection can also let you securely connect to a remote network at work, home, or overseas, in such a way that your data can't be read by hackers, criminals, or governments that are monitoring local Internet traffic. Your communications reach the Internet from the remote, safer location and appear to originate from there.

The receiving end of a VPN or a dial-up networking connection is usually handled by the Remote Access Services (RAS) provided by Windows Server or third-party remote connection devices manufactured by networking companies such as Cisco and Alcatel-Lucent. Interestingly, Windows comes with a stripped-down version of RAS so you can set up your own Windows computer to receive a single incoming modem or VPN connection. You can use this, for example, to get access to your office computer and LAN from home, provided that your company's security policies permit this.

In this chapter, you learn how to use a VPN to access a remote network over the Internet. We don't address dial-up (modem) networking because its use has all but disappeared due to its low speed and limited bandwidth. You learn how to allow incoming connections later in the chapter.

Virtual Private Networking

A virtual private network lets you connect to a remote network in a secure way. A VPN creates what is effectively a tunnel between your computer and a remote network, a tunnel that can pass data freely and securely through potentially hostile intermediate territory like the Internet. Authorized data is encapsulated in special packets that are passed through your computer's firewall and the remote network's firewall. These are inspected by a VPN server before being released to the protected network.

---

 note

Several companies manufacture VPN software and hardware solutions, some of which are faster and provide better management tools than Microsoft's VPN system. If your organization uses a VPN product purchased from a company such as Juniper Networks, Check Point Software Technologies, or Cisco Systems, you'll have to follow their instructions for installing and using their VPN software.

Smaller-scale alternatives include a series of Internet Connection Sharing routers made by Linksys that have VPN capabilities built in, and software products like Hamachi (from logmein.com) or Radmin VPN (from radmin-vpn.com). If you're interested in setting up a permanent VPN between locations you use, you might want to check out these solutions.

Figure 37.5 illustrates the concept, showing a VPN connection between a computer out on the Internet and a server on a protected network. The computer sends your data (1) through a VPN connection that encapsulates it (2) and transmits it over the Internet (3). A firewall (4) passes VPN packets but blocks all others. The VPN server verifies the authenticity of the data, extracts it (5), and transmits the original packet (6) on to the desired remote server. The encapsulation process allows for encryption of your data as it transits the Internet and allows "private" IP addresses to be used as the endpoints of the network connection.

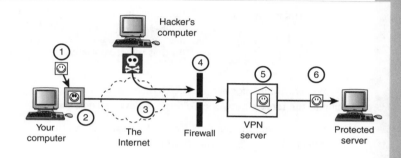

Figure 37.5
A virtual private network encapsulates and encrypts data that is passed over the Internet.

After you have a regular Internet connection established, Windows establishes the link between your computer and a VPN server on the remote network. After it's connected, in effect, you are a part of the distant LAN. The connection won't be as fast as a direct LAN connection, but a VPN can be very useful for copying files and securely accessing Remote Desktop connections.

Both desktop and server versions of Windows come with VPN software built in. In the next section, we describe how to use Microsoft's VPN system.

Setting Up a VPN Connection

To create a VPN connection to a remote network or computer, you need a working Internet connection. You also must obtain or confirm the information shown in Table 37.1 from the remote network's or computer's manager.

Table 37.1 Information Needed for a VPN or RAS Dial-Up Connection

Information	Reason
VPN server	You need either the hostname or the IP address of the remote VPN server computer.
Type of VPN	Windows 10 has built-in support for the Windows VPN service only. You must install separate software to connect to VPNs from other vendors.
Protocols in use	The remote network must support TCP/IP. Windows 10 does not support networking with the IPX/SPX or NetBEUI protocol.
TCP/IP configuration	You should confirm that the Remote Access Server assigns TCP/IP information automatically (dynamically) via DHCP. Usually, the answer is yes.

Table 37.1 Continued

Information	Reason
Mail servers	You might need to obtain the IP addresses or names of SMTP, POP, Exchange, Lotus Notes, or Microsoft Mail servers if you want to use these applications while connected to the remote network.
User ID and password	You must be ready to supply a username and password to the remote server. If you're calling into a Windows workstation or server, use the same Windows username and password you use on that remote network.

Armed with this information, you're ready to create a connection to the remote network. To do so, follow these steps:

1. Click or touch the network icon in the taskbar, and then select Network & Internet Settings.

2. Click VPN in the navigation pane at the left, and then click Add a VPN Connection to bring up the panel shown in Figure 37.6.

 note

If you use your device on an Enterprise (business) network, your network manager might set up DirectAccess for you, which is an automatic VPN connection system. If so, you can skip the steps in this chapter because your VPN connection is always on.

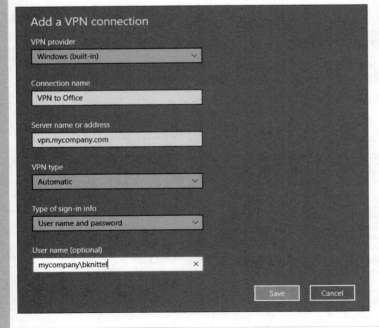

Figure 37.6
The Add a VPN Connection panel lets you select a supported VPN provider and enter the required connection information.

3. Under VPN provider, select the type of VPN to which you're connecting. If your VPN type is not listed, you must add third-party software from the VPN vendor. Your IT department can provide this software.

4. Under Connection Name, type a name for the connection that makes sense to you.

5. Under Server Name or Address, enter the public hostname or IP address of the VPN server.

6. Fill in other connection information as provided by the manager of the remote network. You might need to scroll down to see all the input fields. Click the box if you want your sign-in information to be remembered. Finally, click Save to save the new connection.

Before you connect for the first time, you might want to check the new connection's settings, as described in the next section.

Editing a VPN Connection's Properties

To edit the properties of a VPN, follow these steps:

1. If you are not already viewing the VPN settings page, click or touch the network icon in the taskbar, and select Network & Internet Settings, VPN.

2. In the VPN Settings window, click or touch the icon for the desired VPN connection, and then select Advanced Options.

3. Click the Edit button to change any of the information you initially entered, or change proxy settings by scrolling down. Clear Sign-In Info erases any memorized password.

If you are connecting to a small network that has only one subnet (one range of network addresses), and if you want to browse the Internet while you're also using the dial-up or VPN connection, you might be able to change the connection's gateway setting so that Windows won't route connections to Internet-based hosts through the VPN or dial-up connection. This will work for Microsoft VPN connections but might not work with third-party VPN products that prevent "go-around" routing for security reasons. If it does work, it will speed up web browsing considerably. To change the gateway setting, follow these steps:

1. Click the network icon in the taskbar and select Network & Internet Settings, Change Adapter Options. Right-click the icon for your VPN connection, and then select Properties.

2. Select the Networking tab, select Internet Protocol Version 4, and choose Properties. Then click the Advanced button.

3. Uncheck Use Default Gateway on Remote Network. Then click OK to close each open dialog.

On more complex networks that have several disjointed ranges of network addresses, routing around the VPN requires complex setup steps that are beyond the scope of this book.

After you've finished making any needed changes to the connection's options, click OK.

Establishing a VPN Connection

To make a VPN connection to a remote network, be sure you first have a working Internet connection. Then follow these steps:

1. Click or touch the network icon in the taskbar.

2. At the top of the Network pop-up panel, click or touch the name of the VPN connection you want to start, and then click Connect.

3. If credentials are not already stored for the connection, Windows opens a dialog box or a panel to let you enter your login name, password, and (if appropriate) your account's Windows domain name.

   Enter the login name, password, and Windows domain name (if appropriate) for your account on the remote computer or network. If you do have a domain login name, you can enter it in the form *username@domainname* or *domainname\username*.

   However, if you are connecting to a Windows 10, 8.1, or 8 computer and you have a Microsoft account, you can't enter your account in *username@domain.com* format. You must use the local account name, which the remote computer owner can tell you. (She saw it when she set up incoming VPN access.) This is described later in the chapter.

4. Click OK. Windows shows you the progress of your connection as it contacts the remote server, verifies your username and password, and registers your computer on the remote network.

   If the connection fails, you'll most likely get a reasonable explanation: The password or account name was invalid, the remote system is not accepting connections, and the like. If you entered an incorrect username or password, you are usually given two more chances to reenter the information before the other end hangs up on you.

   If the connection completes successfully, and you hover your mouse pointer over the taskbar's network icon, a small balloon will appear showing the active network connections. If you click the network icon, you'll see the active dial-up or VPN connection in the list of active connections with the word *Connected* under it.

In most cases, the remote network will be a corporate network or a network you control, so if Windows asks you whether the network is public or private, you should select private.

> ➡️ *If Windows doesn't ask you if the network is public or private the first time you connect, or to change the resulting network location from Public to Private or vice versa, **see** "Take Care When You Share," **p. 821**. If you are connecting to a Windows domain network, you might not be prompted because this setting might be under control of the remote network.*

You can now use the remote network's resources, as discussed next.

VPN Connection Fails with Error Number 720 or 629

If you are trying to make a VPN connection to a computer you set up yourself to receive incoming connections, and the connection fails with error 720 or 629, most likely the computer you are using to establish the connection has an active LAN connection in the same network address range as the computer to which you're connecting—even though the networks aren't physically attached. It's just an unfortunate coincidence. You must fix this at the VPN host computer. In its Network Connections window, right-click the Incoming Connections icon and select Properties. Select the Networking tab, highlight Internet Protocol Version 4, and select Properties. Uncheck Allow Callers to Access My Local Area Network and then check Select IP Addresses. Set the From value to 192.168.111.2 and the To value to 192.168.111.20.

VPN Connection Fails Without Certificate

If you receive the message "Unable to negotiate the encryption you requested without a certificate" when you attempt to make a VPN connection, you are trying to connect to a VPN server with a higher level of encryption than your computer or the other computer is configured to carry out. Contact your network administrator to get the appropriate certificate installed.

Using Remote Network Resources

When you're connected through a VPN, you can use network resources exactly as if you were physically on the remote network. The Network folder, shared folders, and network printers all function as if you were directly connected.

The following are some tips for effective remote networking:

- Don't try to run application software that is installed on the remote network itself. Starting it could take quite a long time! (However, if you have previously connected directly to the network, and the Offline Files system is in use, you might have a cached copy of the application on your hard disk. Your network manager will set this up for you if it's a reasonable thing to use.)

- If you get disconnected while you are editing a document that was originally stored on the remote network, immediately use Save As to save it on your local hard disk the moment you notice that the connection has been disrupted. Then, when the connection is reestablished, save it back to its original location. This will help you avoid losing your work.

- You can place shortcuts to network folders on your desktop or in other folders for quick access.

- If the remote LAN has Internet access, you should be able to browse the Internet while you're connected to the LAN, although it can be slower to do so because data from Internet sites goes first to the remote network and then through the VPN connection to you. See "Editing a VPN

Connection's Properties" in this chapter for information about an option that can speed up Internet browsing. Some VPN products will not respect this setting, however, and might filter or block access to Internet sites while you're connected over the VPN.

- If you use a standalone email program, you might have trouble sending mail while you're connected through the VPN. Your ISP might not accept outgoing mail because your connection appears to be coming from the "wrong" network. We discuss this in the next section.

Using Email and Network Connections

If you use your computer with remote LANs as well as the Internet, or if you use different ISPs in different situations, you might need to be careful with the email programs you use. Most email programs don't make it easy for you to associate different mail servers with different connections.

Although most email servers enable you to *retrieve* your mail from anywhere on the Internet, most are very picky about whom they let *send* email. Generally, to use an SMTP server to send out mail, you must be using a computer whose IP address is known by the server as belonging to its own network, or you must provide a username and password to the outgoing mail server (that is, you must *authenticate*).

If your ISP lets you (or requires you) to use authenticated SMTP (that is, if you set your email program to supply a username and password to the outgoing mail server), you should have no problem sending mail from anywhere.

If you can't use authenticated SMTP, see if your favorite email program can configure separate "identities," each with associated incoming and outgoing servers. Set up a separate identity for each network you use, and configure each identity to use the correct outgoing SMTP server for its associated network. When you make a dial-up or VPN network connection, set your email program to use the corresponding identity.

Monitoring and Ending a VPN Connection

To check the status of a VPN connection, click the network icon in the taskbar. The VPN connection icon will be labeled "Connected" if the VPN connection is active. To get more detailed information, select Network & Internet Settings, Change Adapter Options. Right-click the icon for the VPN connection and select Status. This displays a dialog box showing the number of bytes sent and received.

To end a VPN connection, click the network icon in the taskbar, click the VPN connection's icon, and then click Disconnect.

Incoming VPN Access

All editions of Windows have a stripped-down Remote Access Server (RAS) built in, and you can use it to connect to your computer by modem or through the Internet, from another location using any computer running Windows. (In this book, we just talk about VPN connectivity, although a modem connection could be set up using a similar procedure.) After you're connected, you can access your computer's shared files and printers just as you can on your home or office network. At most, one remote user can connect at a time. And OneDrive's Fetch Files feature, which we discussed at the beginning of this chapter, might provide a much easier way to get at your files from afar. However, the choice is up to you.

 note

Setting up your computer to receive Microsoft VPN connections is fairly complex, as you can see from the following instructions, and might not even be possible if you share an Internet connection using a router. If you want to make VPN connections to your own computer or home network, you might want to check out Hamachi, an alternative "zero configuration" VPN system, available at logmeinhamachi.com, or the free Radmin VPN product from www.radmin-vpn.com.

Setting up an incoming Internet (VPN) connection requires an always-on Internet connection, whose external IP address you know and can reach from the Internet at large. Your computer must also always be left on and must not put itself to sleep when not in use. We talk about ways to establish an Internet hostname using static addressing or dynamic DNS providers in Chapter 39, so we won't repeat that discussion here. Besides a discoverable IP address, you will have to configure your Internet router or Windows Internet Connection Sharing (ICS) service to forward VPN data through the firewall to the computer you're going to set up to receive VPN connections. We discuss this in more detail shortly, under "Enabling Incoming VPN Connections with NAT." We will tell you right up front that very few hardware connection-sharing routers can be set up to forward VPN connections.

 note

Windows Firewall doesn't have to be told to permit incoming VPN connections because it knows to let them in.

Setting Up VPN Access

To enable VPN access, follow these steps:

1. Click the network icon in the taskbar, and select Network & Internet Settings. Then click Change Adapter Options.

2. If the standard menu bar (File, Edit, and so on) isn't displayed, press and release the Alt key. Then click File, New Incoming Connection.

 caution

Permitting remote access opens up security risks. Before you try to enable incoming access on a computer at work, be sure that your company permits it. In some companies, you could be fired for violating the security policies.

3. Select the user accounts that will be permitted to access your computer remotely. This step is very important: Check only the names of those users to whom you really want and need to give access. The fewer accounts you enable, the less likely that someone might accidentally break into your computer.

   Note that if you have any users who have Microsoft accounts, they (or you) will appear in this list with usernames along the lines of brian_000. You might want to write down the names. Users will need to use these "local" names, and their Microsoft password, when they connect to your computer.

Under no circumstances should you check Guest, HomeGroupUser$, or a name that looks like IUSR_*xxx* or IWAM_*xxx*.

4. After selecting users, click Next. Then select the means that you will use for remote access. Check Through the Internet and then click Next. (If your computer has an analog modem attached to it, you can select it, too, in this step, to provide dial-up networking access.)

5. Windows displays a list of network protocols and services that will be made available to the connection. Select the Internet Protocol Version 4 (TCP/IP) entry and then click Properties. Select Specify IP Addresses and then set the From value to 192.168.111.2 and the To value to 192.168.111.20. Click OK.

6. Make sure that Internet Protocol Version 4 (TCP/IP) is checked and that Internet Protocol Version 6 (TCP/IP) is unchecked. Then click Allow Access. When the final window appears, click Close.

---

 note

The Add Someone button lets you create a username and password that someone can use to connect remotely but not log on directly at the computer. A user added this way will only be able to use the network resources available to Everyone unless you explicitly grant this account access rights to the resources. You can delete such an account only by using the Computer Management Local Users and Groups tool.

When the incoming connection information has been entered, a new Incoming Connection icon appears in your Network Connections window. To view this, click the Network icon in the taskbar and then select Network & Internet Settings, Change Adapter Options.

 note

If you enable dial-up access, the selected modem will answer all incoming calls on its telephone line.

When someone connects to your computer, a new icon appears in the Network Connections folder showing that person's username. If necessary, you can right-click this to disconnect this user.

Enabling Incoming VPN Connections with NAT

Windows Internet Connection Sharing (ICS) and routers that share Internet connectivity use an IP-addressing trick called Network Address Translation (NAT) to serve an entire LAN with only one public IP address. Thus, incoming connections, such as from a VPN client to a VPN host, have to be directed to a single host computer on the internal network.

If you use a shared Internet connection, only one computer can be designated as the recipient of incoming VPN connections. If you use Microsoft's ICS, that one computer must be the one sharing its connection. It will receive and properly handle VPN requests.

If you use a router, the VPN server can be any computer you want to designate. Your router must be set up to forward the following packet types to the designated computer:

- TCP port 1723

- GRE (protocol 47—not the same as port 47!)

Unfortunately, some of the cheaper routers designed for home use don't have a way to explicitly forward GRE packets. There are several ways around this problem:

- Some routers know about Microsoft's Point-to-Point Tunneling Protocol (PPTP), and you can specify the computer that is to receive incoming VPN connections.

- If the option doesn't work, someone might suggest that you designate the VPN computer as a DMZ host so that it receives *all* unrecognized incoming packets. This is a bad idea because that computer becomes vulnerable to hacker attacks. You would have to designate the computer's network location as Public to protect it, and this means it could not participate in sharing files or printers, which is what you wanted to do with the VPN to start with. Therefore, we don't recommend that you do this. If you do, you must at least configure your router to block Microsoft File Sharing packets on TCP and UDP ports 137 through 139 and port 445. A better idea follows.

- As an alternative to using Microsoft's VPN software, you can use a router that has the capability to receive incoming VPN connections; Linksys makes some. You have to use their routers at all of your locations, however. You might also investigate a software VPN solution such as the ones we mentioned at the beginning of this section.

Disabling Incoming Connections

To disable incoming VPN connections, follow these steps:

1. Click the network icon in the taskbar, and then select Network & Internet Settings, Change Adapter Options.

2. To temporarily disable incoming connections, right-click the Incoming Connections icon and select Properties. Uncheck the modem entry and the Virtual Private Networking check box, and then click OK.

3. To completely disable incoming connections, right-click the Incoming Connections icon and select Delete.

Multiple LAN Connections

Most desktop computers sit where they are installed, gathering dust until they're obsolete. But portable computer users often carry their computers from office to office, docking, or plugging in to several LANs. Although Windows makes it very easy for you to manage different dial-up and VPN connections, it's difficult to manage connections to different LANs if the network configuration settings are manually set.

IP settings are the difficult ones. If all of your networks are set up to use DHCP for automatic TCP/IP configuration, you won't encounter any problems; your computer will absorb the local information each time you connect.

If your TCP/IP settings are set manually, things aren't so simple. Microsoft has come up with a partial solution called Alternate Configuration. You can configure your computer for automatic IP address assignment on most networks and manual assignment on one. The way this works is that

Windows looks for a DHCP server when it boots up, and if it doesn't find one, it uses the Alternate Configuration. This can be a static IP address, or the default setting Automatic Private IP Address, whereby Windows chooses a random address in the 169.254 subnet.

This means that your computer can automatically adjust itself to multiple networks, at most one of which requires manual IP address settings.

To set up Alternate Configuration, click the Network icon in the taskbar and select Network & Internet Settings, Change Adapter Options. Right-click your LAN connection icon (usually named Ethernet or Wi-Fi), and select Properties. On the Networking tab, double-click Internet Protocol Version 4 (TCP/IP). Be sure in the General tab, the Obtain an IP Address Automatically setting is enabled; if not, this discussion doesn't apply to your computer. View the Alternate Configuration tab and choose User Configured to enter the static LAN's information. Finally, click OK.

If you need to commute between multiple networks that require manual configuration, you'll have to change the General settings each time you connect to a different network. We suggest that you stick a 3-by-5-inch card with the settings for each network in your laptop carrying case for handy reference.

MEETINGS, CONFERENCING, AND COLLABORATION

Windows 10 Plays Well with Others

Today's computers are not tools used in isolation. They're portals through which people communicate and work just as easily from across the globe as from across the room. Business users and students are increasingly relying on computers to make presentations and give reports (making them at least more colorful, if not more interesting).

In this chapter, we cover several Windows features that make it easier for you to work with others:

- When you use your laptop or tablet computer to display a business or class presentation, the Presentation Settings feature lets you tell Windows not to disrupt your presentation with messages, noises, or the screen saver.

- If you use a laptop computer, the Project panel makes it easy to control an external monitor or a projector.

- If you want to work on a document or project with someone else, you need help with your computer, or you want to demonstrate some computer task or application to others using their computer, Remote Assistance or Quick Assist may be just what you need.

We start by looking at Windows 10's support for making presentations.

Making Presentations with a Mobile Computer

If you use a mobile (laptop or tablet) computer, Windows 10 has features that make giving presentations smoother and easier. The Project settings panel lets you manage an external monitor or a projector. Presentation Settings, which is part of the Windows Mobility Center discussed in Chapter 37, "Networking on the Road," keeps Windows from interrupting your presentation. We discuss Presentation Settings first.

Adjusting Presentation Settings

One of the more thoughtful features of Windows 10 Pro and Enterprise is the Presentation Settings section in Windows Mobility Center. When you indicate that you are making a presentation, Windows takes steps to keep itself out of your way. (This feature is part of Windows 10 Pro, Enterprise, and the corresponding Education editions, but not Windows 10 Home.) Presentation Settings can make the following accommodations:

- Display a screen background chosen to minimize distraction or promote your company logo.

- Disable the screen saver so that if you leave the computer alone for a few minutes, it doesn't treat the audience to an animated aquarium or a slideshow that includes pictures of you dressed for a Halloween party in really bad drag.

- Disable pop-up notifications and reminders from Windows services.

- Set the speaker volume so that you aren't bothered by sounds associated with events such as mouse clicks, Window resizing, and the like.

- Disable automatic shutdown so that your computer won't go to sleep while you're talking. (There is, unfortunately, no corresponding setting for the audience.)

> **tip**
>
> It's not obvious from looking that you can click on them, but the little icon in the upper-left corner of each Mobility Center tile leads to a settings page for the corresponding feature.

 note

Presentation Settings and the Windows Mobility Center are available only if you are using a mobile (laptop or tablet) computer. However, there is a Registry hack you can use to enable it on a desktop computer: using the Registry Editor (covered in Chapter 29, "Editing the Windows Registry"), select the key HKEY_CURRENT_USER\Software\Microsoft and create the key MobilePC. Select this new key, create the key AdaptableSettings, and within that, create a DWORD value named SkipBatteryCheck with a value of 1. Then select the key MobilePC again. Create another new key named MobilityCenter, and within it a DWORD value named RunOnDesktop with a value of 1. Once that's done, to open the Mobility Center, press Windows Logo+R, type **mblctr**, and press Enter. This can get tiresome, so you might want to pin it to your taskbar.

To tell Windows how to behave when you're making a presentation, bring up the Windows Mobility Center using these steps:

1. If you have a keyboard, press Windows Logo+X and then press b or select Mobility Center.

   If you don't have a keyboard, touch and hold the Start button, and then release it when the touch indicator turns to a square. Select Windows Mobility Center.

2. At the upper-left corner of the Presentation Settings tile, click the small icon that looks like a video projector. The Presentation Settings dialog box appears, as shown in Figure 38.1.

Figure 38.1
Presentation Settings lets you tell Windows how you want it to appear during a presentation.

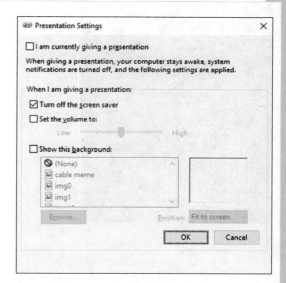

3. Check the check boxes next to the desired accommodations, preselect the sound volume, and set a desktop background if desired. Save your presentation Settings Preferences by clicking OK.

Whenever you are making a presentation, bring up the Windows Mobility Center by following step 1 again. Then, in the Presentation Settings tile, click Turn On. You can use the other tiles to adjust the volume and display.

You can later change the presentation options, if necessary, by clicking the small icon in the Presentation Settings tile again.

Controlling an External Display

The Project settings panel lets you control what appears on any connected external display or monitor attached to your laptop or tablet computer.

 tip
If you used the Windows Logo+X keyboard shortcut in Windows 7 or Vista, you'll find that this shortcut now brings up a list of administrative tools. Mobility Center is in there; just click it. If you make a lot of presentations, you can pin the Mobility Center to the taskbar. Bring it up, right-click its icon in the taskbar, and select Pin to Taskbar.

To start, attach your external monitor or projector, or connect to a network-attached projector as described in the next section. Then take any one of the following equivalent actions:

- Press Windows Logo+P to bring up the Project settings panel, shown in Figure 38.2.

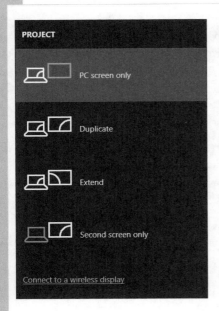

Figure 38.2
Select whether to extend or duplicate your desktop on the new display.

- If you have a touchscreen, open the Action Center using a swipe in from the right edge of the screen, and then touch the Project quick action button.

- In the taskbar's search box type **project**, and then select Project to a Second Screen.

- If you have the Windows Mobility Center open, as discussed in the previous section, click the Connect Display or Disconnect Display button in the External Display tile.

The Project panel lets you choose how to use the added screen real estate.

Then select one of the four display options:

- **PC Screen Only**—The external display will be blacked out.

- **Duplicate**—The same display will appear on both monitors. Use this setting if you need to see your own presentation and can't see the external display.

- **Extend**—The Windows desktop will be spread across both displays. You could put your notes on one display and something for the audience to see on the other. I tried this once for a presentation and found it awkward; it was like trying to pat my head and rub my belly at the same time. Maybe that was just me.

- **Second Screen Only**—The computer's internal display will be shut off, and only the attached display will be used.

note

If you select the Duplicate option, your screen's resolution might be reduced. Windows will use the highest reasonable screen resolution supported by both monitors. If both displays don't have the same shape, the external display might look pinched or stretched. If this happens, right-click the desktop, select Screen Resolution, click in the Resolution box, and adjust the resolution slider that appears to find a more acceptable setting. Click Apply after making each adjustment. You'll have to find a compromise because you can't select different resolutions for the two monitors when the Duplicate setting is in effect.

Later, when you disconnect the external display, Windows should automatically reset your laptop's screen resolution to its original setting. If it doesn't, follow the preceding instructions and move the resolution slider to the laptop display's native resolution—usually the topmost position.

Click one of the icons or press Enter to save the setting. You can press Windows Logo+P to change it back later.

➡ *To learn about Windows 10's other accessories for mobile computers, **see** "Using Windows Mobility Center," **p. 809.***

➡ *For more information about managing external displays, **see** "Running Windows 10 with Multiple Monitors," **p. 632.***

Connecting to Wireless Displays

Windows 10 includes support for connecting to video projectors that are reached over a wireless network, rather than requiring them to be attached directly to your computer. You might find a wireless projector in a corporate conference room. You can also project your Windows display via a wireless network to a computer monitor or television screen, through a small, inexpensive receiver that hooks up to the monitor or television through an HDMI cable. These are called Miracast devices, and they're made by several manufacturers.

To use such a network-attached projector, press Windows Logo+A, or swipe in from the right edge of the screen to open the Action Center, and then click or touch Connect. Alternatively, press Windows Logo+P to view the Project panel shown in Figure 38.2, and select Connect to a Wireless Display.

Next, follow any additional prompts to direct your presentation output to the connected projector. You can press Windows Logo+P to change the way your laptop and the external display are configured, as discussed in the previous section.

To stop projecting, open the Connect panel again using the Project button in the Action Center or by pressing Windows Logo+P and selecting Connect to a Wireless Display. Then, under the name of your display, click or touch Disconnect.

Remote Assistance and Quick Assist

Windows 10 comes with a built-in tool called Remote Assistance that lets two people work together on one Windows computer—with one person at the computer and one working remotely, over the Internet. It's designed mainly to let a person get technical assistance from someone who's not nearby. But it can work just as well as a "let's do this together" tool as a "let me help you with this" tool. At the end of this chapter, we discuss some programs that you can use to connect three or more people.

Windows 10 comes with an alternative version of Remote Assistance called Quick Assist. Quick Assist is essentially the same tool, except that it makes starting up a remote connection a lot easier, as we will see shortly.

> **note**
>
> You can also collaborate using the third-party remote access tools that we describe in Chapter 39 under "Third-Party Remote Control Tools." You might want to give these tools a try yourself.

Remote Assistance and Quick Assist are, in turn, based on the same technology as the Remote Desktop feature we discuss in Chapter 39, although there are significant differences between them:

- Quick Assist works only if both computers are running Windows 10 with the Anniversary (or later) Update installed. At this point, this means virtually all copies of Windows 10.

- With Quick Assist and Remote Assistance, both the local and the remote users see the same screen at the same time, and both can move the mouse, type on the keyboard, and so forth. It's meant for collaboration. With Remote Desktop, when a remote user is working, the computer's monitor can only display the Welcome screen. It's assumed nobody is at the other end.

- Quick Assist and Remote Assistance don't make the local computer's hard drives available, nor do they transmit sound, as Remote Desktop does.

- Quick Assist and Remote Assistance connections can't be made *ad lib*. One Windows user must invite another through email, a Microsoft online account, or Windows Live Messenger. Alternatively, one user can offer assistance to another using Messenger. In any case, the procedure requires the simultaneous cooperation of users at both ends of the connection.

- Quick Assist and Remote Assistance enable you to use a text chat window or voice chat while the desktop session is active.

Establishing a connection with Quick Assist is easy, and, well… quick. Establishing a connection with Remote Assistance can be a challenge. You can use Remote Assistance on Windows 10, 8.1, 8, 7, and Vista even if you are using a shared Internet connection (that is, if you have a router between your local network and the Internet). This is a big improvement over Remote Assistance on Windows XP, which rarely worked over a shared connection.

Enabling Remote Assistance and Quick Assist

Remote Assistance and Quick Assist are usually enabled by default when you install Windows, but before you try to use it to get help the first time, you should confirm that it is correctly set up by following these steps. And if you want to connect to someone else's computer, talk them through these same steps before you start.

1. In the taskbar's search box, type **remote**. In the search results, you may need to click the Settings heading to show the Settings results section. Select Allow Remote Assistance Invitations to Be Sent from This Computer.

2. If a UAC prompt appears, enter an Administrator account and password, as requested. This brings up the System Properties dialog box.

3. In the Remote tab, be sure that Allow Remote Assistance Connections to This Computer is checked. If it isn't, check it.

4. Click the Advanced button.

5. Check Create Invitations That Can Only Be Used from Computers Running Windows Vista or Later.

   If you intend to use Quick Assist to demonstrate something to someone you invite, and have them just watch without being able to interact with the screen, uncheck Allow This Computer to Be Controlled Remotely. Otherwise, you can leave this checked. With Remote Assistance, you have to explicitly give them permission to interact after you connect.

6. Click OK to save your changes.

You only need to perform these steps once.

Requesting Assistance with Quick Assist

To invite a friend or colleague to work with you on your computer, you both must have a working Internet connection. First, contact your friend and confirm that she is ready to work with you.

If either one of you has an earlier version of Windows, skip ahead to the next section titled "Requesting Remote Assistance the Old Way," where we describe the procedure for using Windows Vista through 8.1. But if you both have Windows 10 (Anniversary update or later), use the following steps:

1. On her computer, your friend will need to sign in to Windows using a Microsoft account.

2. Click in your taskbar's search box. (If a search box doesn't appear, click or touch the circle icon in the taskbar.) Type the word **quick**. Have your friend do the same. Both of you should select Quick Assist.

3. On your computer, select Get Assistance. Have your friend select give Give Assistance. (We describe the process of giving assistance later in this section, under "Responding to an Assistance Request.")

4. Your friend will be shown a six-digit code, like 123456. She can email it to you, read it to you over the phone, text it, or send it to you by some other means. On your computer, Quick Assist will ask you to type in this code. Type it in, and then click Submit. (You might need to scroll the window down to see the Submit button.)

5. You will be asked to give permission to share your screen. Click Allow.

Quick Assist will start up. A small tab will appear at the top of your screen. There are just two controls: an X to end Quick Assist, and a Pause icon (| |) to suspend Quick Assist. You can use the Pause button to temporarily hide your screen from your friend, for instance, while you look up a password or read email.

Requesting Remote Assistance the Old Way

If you want to get assistance from a friend whose computer runs Windows 8.1, 8, 7, or Vista, follow these steps:

1. In your taskbar's search box, type the word **invite**. In the search results, select Invite Someone to Connect to Your PC and Help You, or Offer to Help Someone Else. (The icon you want says all that.) Then click Invite Someone You Trust to Help You.

2. Windows needs to send an "invitation" to your friend. Use one of these methods:

   - If you have previously worked with this friend, her name might be listed and you can click the name to repeat the previous invitation.

   - If the other person is using Windows 10, 8.1, 8, or 7, click Use Easy Connect. (If Easy Connect is grayed out, go back to the previous section, "Enabling Remote Assistance and Quick Assist," and check the box discussed in step 5.)

   - If you have an email application installed on your computer, select Use Email to Send an Invitation.

   - Otherwise, if you use a web-based email program, select Save This Invitation as a File. Choose a location to save the invitation file and make note of it. You'll have to send this file as an email attachment later or get the file to your friend some other way.

 note

If your friend uses Windows Vista or XP, tell her to be sure to type the password in uppercase.

3. Windows will display a password composed of 12 letters and digits. The password is shown with three groups of letters shaded in different colors to make it easier to read; the shading isn't important. Give this password to the person you are inviting to help, by phone text message, email, or whatever means you have available.

4. If you selected Use Easy Connect, just wait for your friend to start up Remote Assistance (using the steps in the next section) and type in the password you gave to her. (If your friend's computer initially says that Easy Connect is not available, have her click Cancel and try again. I've seen it take two tries.)

If you selected Use Email to Send an Invitation, your default email program will pop up with an email ready to address and send. Enter your friend's email address and send the email. The important part is the attachment, which is a file named something along the lines of Invitation.MsRcIncident. Don't delete the attachment!

If you selected Save This Invitation as a File, use your web-based email system to send the invitation file you created in step 4 to your friend as an attachment. The file has a name along the lines of Invitation.MsRcIncident. Alternatively, get the invitation file to your friend by other means, such as a flash drive or a network folder.

 note

If you use a dial-up Internet connection or a DSL service that requires you to sign on, your Internet IP address changes every time you connect. The Remote Assistance invitation uses this address to tell the other person's computer how to contact you, so it will work only if you stay connected from the time you send the invitation to the time your friend responds.

5. Windows will display a window that says "Waiting for an Incoming Connection." Leave this window alone until your friend receives the invitation and responds.

When your friend responds to your request for assistance, a dialog box will appear on your screen, asking whether it's okay for her to connect. Click Yes, and after a short while—perhaps a minute or so—a window will appear with which you can control the Remote Assistance session. If you're not also on the phone with each other, click Chat to expand the window so that you can type messages back and forth as you work, as shown in Figure 38.3.

Figure 38.3
When your "remote assistant" has connected, use this window to chat and control the connection.

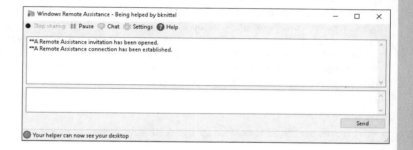

At this point, your friend can see your screen and can watch what you do with it, but she can't actually do anything with your computer. She first has to ask to take control, and you have to consent. Then either of you can type, move the mouse, and otherwise poke around and use your computer.

When a friend asks to take control of your computer, a request will pop up on your screen. If she's just going to work with normal Windows applications such as Word, just click Yes to let her take control. However, if she needs to manage Windows itself, for example, to install or remove software, you must decide who is going to handle the User Account Control (UAC) prompts that might appear. By default, your friend won't be able to see or respond to them. You have two options:

- If you want to respond to all UAC prompts yourself, just click Yes to let her connect. If she performs an action that requires security confirmation, her screen will go black for a moment, and you'll have to respond to the UAC prompt.

- If you want to let her change Windows settings without your intervention, check Allow *Username* to Respond to User Account Control Prompts, and then click Yes. You will be asked to confirm a UAC prompt yourself at this point.

 note
If you don't completely trust the person who's helping you, make this setting change right away: Click Settings, check Use ESC Key to Stop Sharing Control, and then click OK. This way, after you've given the person control, if you don't like what she's doing, you can press the Esc key, and she'll immediately be locked out. Unfortunately, if the person presses Esc for any reason while working, the same thing will happen, and she'll be locked out, so you'll have to grant access again. This can get irritating, but it does let you control what someone else is doing.

note

If you don't have Administrator privileges on your own computer, you won't be able to give your friend permission to perform administrative actions that require a UAC confirmation either. There are two ways to work around this situation.

If your friend knows an Administrator password and will tell you what it is, check Allow *Username* to Respond to User Account Control Prompts and click Yes. When the prompt appears, select the account and enter the password she gave you.

A second possible workaround doesn't work on Windows 10 Home and requires some advance setup before you use Remote Assistance, and an administrator has to do it. Here are the steps: In the taskbar's search box type **policy**. Select Edit Group Policy from the search results. Under Local Computer Policy, browse into Computer Configuration, Windows Settings, Security Settings, Local Policies, Security Options. In the right pane, open User Account Control: Allow UIAccess Applications to Prompt for Elevation Without Using the Secure Desktop and select Enabled. Click OK and then restart Windows. With this option enabled, the remote user will be able to respond to UAC prompts even if the logged-on user doesn't know an Administrator password. (On a domain network, this setting can be enabled or disabled through Group Policy.)

Now your friend should be able to work your keyboard and mouse and help you.

The Windows Remote Assistance toolbar has a few other features that you will find useful:

- If you want a moment of privacy, perhaps to read email or look at a sensitive file, click Pause. This will black out the other person's view of your screen without disconnecting that person. Click Continue to restore the view.

- To communicate with your friend via text messaging, click Chat. The Remote Assistance toolbar will enlarge. Type your comments into the lower box on the window and press Enter (or click Send), and your friend will see what you type. You'll see your friend's responses in the upper part of the window. Click the Chat button again to shrink the toolbar back to its original size.

- To take control away from your friend, click Stop Sharing. Your friend will still be able to see your screen but can only watch. She must request control again to do anything.

When you're finished, click Disconnect to end the Remote Assistance session.

Responding to an Assistance Request

A friend, colleague, or customer can invite you to provide Remote Assistance using Quick Assist, Easy Connect, or an invitation email or file. Use one of the following procedures to respond to such a request.

Responding to Quick Assist

If you want to assist someone and both of you have Windows 10 (Anniversary update or later), use the following procedure:

1. In your taskbar's search box, type the word **quick**. Have your friend do the same. Both of you should select Quick Assist.

2. On your computer, select Give Assistance. Have your friend select give Get Assistance.

3. Sign in to the Quick Assist app using a Microsoft account.

4. You will be shown a six-digit code, like 123456. Give this code to your friend by email, phone, text message, or some other means. On your friend's computer, Quick Assist will ask her for this code. She has to type it; then click Submit. (She might need to scroll the window down to see the Submit button.) She will be asked to give permission to share her screen and should click Allow.

After about 10 to 30 seconds, you will see her screen within the Quick Assist window, as shown in Figure 38.4.

Figure 38.4
The Quick Assist window shows your friend's screen. You can interact with it as if you were there.

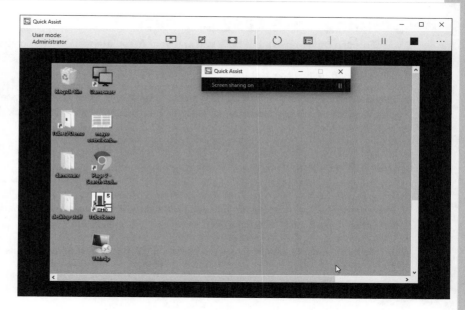

In this window, you can use your mouse, touchscreen, and keyboard to interact with her computer as if you were there. There is a menu at the top of the Quick Assist window with the following icons. You can click the . . . icon at the far right to show the icons' names.

■ **Select Monitor**—If the remote computer has multiple monitors, this option lets you choose to view the combined view of all monitors or to view one individual monitor.

■ **Annotate**—Displays a menu of drawing tools, which you can use, for example, to circle an icon that you want her to learn about. Close the Annotate toolbar to remove whatever you've drawn.

■ **Actual Size**—Makes the pixels in the Quick Assist window exactly match the other person's screen. You might have to scroll around to see all of your friend's desktop. This choice alternates with Fit Screen.

- **Fit Screen**—Scales the contents of your friend's screen to fit your Quick Assist window.

- **Restart**—Reboots your friend's computer. Use this with caution!

- **Task Manager**—Displays the Task Manager on your friend's computer, which you might use to help identify problems or locate a runaway program.

- **Pause**—Pauses the Quick Assist session. You will not see your friend's screen while the session is paused. You can use this to give her privacy, if necessary.

- **End**—Closes the Quick Assist session.

When you are finished helping your friend, close the Quick Assist window or click End.

Responding with Easy Connect

If you can't use Quick Assist, but both you and your friend are using some combination of Windows 10, 8.1, 8, or 7, you can use Easy Connect. Your friend will use Easy Connect to invite you. To respond, follow these steps:

1. In the taskbar's search box, type the word **invite**. In the results, select Invite Someone to Connect to Your PC and Help You, or Offer to Help Someone Else. Then click Help Someone Who Has Invited You.

   If you have helped this person previously, his name might be listed, and you can simply click it to accept the new invitation.

2. Select Use Easy Connect.

3. Type the password your friend gave you. It consists of 12 letters and numbers and is not case sensitive. (Upper- and lowercase don't matter.) Then press Enter.

When the connection is established, skip ahead to "Working with Remote Assistance."

Responding to an Invitation Email or File

Your friend might send you an email with an attachment containing an invitation file named something like `Invitation.MsRcIncident`. Alternatively, he might send you the file through a network or a portable drive.

To accept an email invitation, open the message's attachment. (How you do that depends on your email program. If you use web-based email, you might have to download the attachment separately.) Opening the attachment should activate the Remote Assistance connection. If you receive the invitation as a file, just double-click the file's icon.

You will be asked to enter the password associated with the invitation. The person who invited you will have to tell you what it is. If your friend is using Windows Vista or XP, you must type the password exactly as he did—that is, upper- and

 note

If Windows is unable to establish a connection to the person who invited you, ask him to be sure that the box labeled Create Invitations That Can Only Be Used from Computers Running Windows 7 or Later is checked, as described in the "Enabling Remote Assistance and Quick Assist" section, earlier in this chapter. Then have him send you a new invitation.

lowercase matter. If he is using Windows 10, 8.1, 8, or 7, the password consists of 12 letters and numbers. Upper- and lowercase don't matter.

Working with Remote Assistance

After you've responded to the assistance invitation, it can take more than a minute for the required software to load and for the other user's desktop to finally appear on your screen, as shown in Figure 38.5.

Figure 38.5
The Remote Assistance screen has a control panel at the top and a view of the remote user's screen underneath.

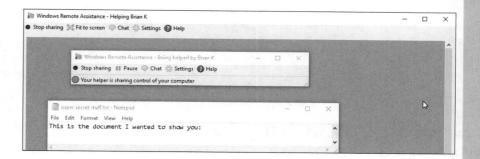

Across the top is a menu of controls. The choices are as follows:

- **Request Control**—Click to begin using the other computer's mouse and keyboard. The remote user will have to grant permission (You'll see the request dialog appear on the screen, but you can't click Yes; your friend has to.) After you have control of the other computer, both of you can use your mouse and keyboard. This menu choice alternates with Stop Sharing.

- **Stop Sharing**—Disconnects your keyboard and mouse from the remote computer.

- **Actual Size**—Click to make the size of the Remote Assistance window exactly match the other person's screen. You might have to scroll around to see all of his desktop. This choice alternates with Fit to Screen.

- **Fit to Screen**—Click to shrink the view of the other computer's screen so that it fits perfectly in your Remote Assistance window. You won't have to use the scrollbars to see the far corners anymore, but the text might be tiny. Maximize your Remote Assistance window to improve the display.

- **Chat**—Click to open a text chat panel in the left side of the Remote Assistance window. Type your messages into the small box at the bottom of the Chat area.

- **Settings**—Click to turn off the recording of the remote session that Windows makes by default.

- **Help**—Click to display online help for Remote Assistance.

If your friend clicks the Stop Sharing button, shown in Figure 38.5, you'll lose control of the remote screen. Just click Request Control again to ask for permission to resume working. You will also lose control if the other person enabled the setting that makes the Esc key stop sharing, and *you* press the Esc key for any reason while you're working. You'll have to request control again.

Using Third-Party Tools

If you want to help someone remotely, Remote Assistance can be a great tool, and it does come pre-installed with Windows, but it sometimes refuses to work. Luckily, several third-party tools are as good as or better than Remote Assistance (and Remote Desktop), and most of them work even when Remote Assistance and Remote Desktop won't. We talk more about these tools in Chapter 39 in the section "Third-Party Remote Control Tools," and at the end of this chapter, so we won't repeat those discussions here.

You might also try one of the online meeting tools described in the next section. They're typically designed to let a group of people work together on a common project, but most of them could also let two people work together to solve a problem with Windows.

Online Meeting Tools

A shared, common computer screen can be a great tool for groups of people working together on a common project in diverse locations. One person makes a change, say, in a Word document or a PowerPoint presentation, and everyone sees the results in real time.

Remote Assistance, described in the previous section, is a fine tool for this task when just two people want to collaborate—if it works. And Google Docs and Microsoft's Office 365 cloud document tools do let multiple people edit the same document at the same time, and everyone sees everyone's changes in real time. However, these tools are limited to just a few types of documents, and the applications themselves are rudimentary. Therefore, for true online collaboration tools, you'll need to look to other vendors.

In the section "Third-Party Remote Control Tools" of Chapter 39, we discuss alternative remote control programs that can let two people work together. Table 38.1 lists additional tools that you can use when you want to connect three or more people. Several of them offer a free trial, good discounts for annual subscriptions, and meeting access on Surface tablets, Macs, iOS, and Android devices.

Table 38.1   Third-Party Collaboration Tools

Program and URL	Comments
Adobe Connect www.adobe.com/products/ adobeconnect	$50/month for up to 25 participants. Can include videoconferencing. Free trial available.
Cisco WebEx www.webex.com	Free for up to three participants, $24/month for up to eight, and up from there. Optional voice conferencing by telephone.

Program and URL	Comments
GoToMeeting free.gotomeeting.com	From the LogMeIn people. Free for up to three participants, $19/month for up to ten participants, and up from there.
Join.me join.me	Free for one "presenter." Paid subscription required to share control, $24/month.
Mikogo www.mikogo.com	Free for one "viewer," $16/month for up to 25 participants, and up from there.
TeamViewer www.teamviewer.com	Free for personal use. One-time purchase for business licenses.
Yugma www.yugma.com	Free version "broadcasts" your desktop to one person; $10/month and up for versions that share keyboard and mouse control.

More such tools are appearing all the time, so you might want to supplement this list with some Google searching. You might search the Store app, too.

 note

One point to keep in mind is that with these services, the contents of your conference pass through the companies' servers. You don't know what country they're in. You don't have any way of knowing if they or some random country's government agencies are listening in. Personally, if I was discussing a sensitive business or personal topic, I'd be wary of using a third-party service. At the very least, I'd select one that advertises *end-to-end encryption*, which means that data is encrypted from the time it leaves your computer until it arrives at your collaborator's computer and is not unencrypted anywhere in between, even within the service provider's network. But there is a difference between "is not unencrypted" and "cannot be unencrypted," and no one can absolutely guarantee that your data is not being captured.

REMOTE DESKTOP AND REMOTE ACCESS

Using Your Computer Remotely

With today's global availability of the Internet, you expect to be able to access the websites that hold your email and data from anywhere, anytime. You can store documents in the cloud for global access. But what about stuff that you didn't remember to—or don't want to—store "out there"? Why can't you have the same global access to your own private data on your computer at home? Well, as it turns out, you can, through features that are built in to Windows, and also through some third-party products. We describe these in this chapter.

If your computer runs Windows 10 Pro, Enterprise, Education, or Pro Eduction edition, your computer has a spiffy feature called Remote Desktop that lets it accept connections from another computer. When you travel, you can see your home computer's screen, move its mouse and type on its keyboard, open files, and even print, just as if you were really sitting in front of it. The neat part is that you can do this from any computer that runs just about any version of Windows or Mac OS X, and even iOS and Android devices.

If you have the Home version of Windows 10, the hosting side of Remote Desktop isn't included, but you can still get remote access to your computer using a third-party program such as TeamViewer, which we discuss at the end of the chapter.

Whatever program you use, Figure 39.1 shows how it works. Your keystrokes, mouse, and touch movements get sent from one computer to your own computer, wherever it is. The remote computer's display, sound, and print output travel back to you and appear on the local computer.

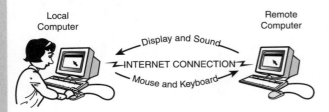

Figure 39.1
You can use any computer running Windows, iOS, or OS X to connect to and control your computer.

This is just what you need when you're out of town and need to read a file you left on the computer back home, or if you want to read your office email from home.

As we mentioned, the *client* part of Remote Desktop, which lets you connect *to* other computers, runs on any version of Windows, and there are official Microsoft Remote Desktop clients for OS X, iOS, and Android. The Remote Desktop *service*, which lets a computer be controlled *by* a remote connection, is available only on some Windows versions:

- Windows 10 Pro, Education Pro, Enterprise, and Education (including S editions)

- Windows 8 and 8.1 Pro and Enterprise

- Windows 7 Professional, Ultimate, and Enterprise

- Windows Vista Professional, Ultimate, and Enterprise

- Windows XP Professional

- All versions of Windows Server since Windows 2000 Server

Even if your computer does have Remote Desktop capability, you might want to check out the third-party tools. We recommend reading about both options before you decide to use one or the other. Here are the trade-offs:

 note
You don't have to be miles away to take advantage of Remote Desktop either. You can also use it to access other computers in your home or office, using your local area network (LAN). For example, you can use it to start a lengthy computing or printing job on someone else's computer without leaving your own desk.

- Remote Desktop can be considerably harder to set up than the third-party programs if you want access through the Internet.

- Better support is available for the third-party client programs on Android devices than for Remote Desktop.

- Remote Desktop won't let you collaborate with or assist someone who's sitting at the remote computer because it blanks out the remote computer's screen while you're connected from afar. The third-party tools that we discuss at the end of this chapter will let you work with someone who's at the remote computer.

➡ *And Windows has a separate, built-in tool for screen-sharing. If collaboration is what you're after, **see** "Remote Assistance," p. 863.*

- Remote Desktop might offer better security. The third-party options that provide access over the Internet open a data connection between your computer and the host company's servers. They keep a "pipeline" open into your computer from their facilities at all times. You must trust that they'll never get hacked themselves; otherwise, criminals or governmental agencies could conceivably snoop into your computer from their facilities. (On the other hand, third-party vendors will block access to someone who's trying to guess passwords. Remote Desktop will happily let someone test passwords all day.)

- Remote Desktop works well between computers on a home or office LAN, and on a LAN that isn't connected to the Internet. Most of the third-party products require Internet access, so they won't work on a disconnected LAN.

- Remote Desktop automatically transmits sound and lets you print from the home (host) computer to your current location. Not all third-party programs do this.

You'll have to decide for yourself whether you're more concerned about convenience or privacy. Over the past few years, I've switched from Remote Desktop to a third-party program for remote access to my own personal computer, but I still use only Remote Desktop for business networks.

The remainder of this chapter consists of three major sections. The first part shows you how to set up your computer so that you can access it remotely. The second part shows you how to connect to another computer using the Remote Desktop Client. The third part discusses third-party alternatives.

By the way, Remote Desktop is a scaled-down version of Windows Terminal Services, a component of the Windows Server versions that lets multiple users run programs on one central server. By "scaled down," we mean that only one person is allowed to connect to a computer running a desktop version of Windows at a time, either remotely or with the regular monitor and keyboard. So if you connect remotely, a local user is temporarily kicked out to the Welcome screen. And if a user signs in at the home computer while you're connected remotely, you'll be disconnected. You won't lose your work—you can reconnect later and pick up where you left off—but the bottom line is that only one person at a time is allowed to use a given Windows 10 computer.

Setting Up Access to Your Own Computer

This section tells you how to set up remote access to your own computer. If you want to use the Remote Desktop Connection client to access another computer, skip ahead to "Connecting to Other Computers with Remote Desktop," later in this chapter.

As mentioned previously, incoming Remote Desktop connections are available only on Windows Pro, Enterprise (corporate), and their corresponding Education versions. If you don't have one of these versions, see the last section in this chapter, which discusses third-party options.

Across a LAN (that is, between computers in your home or office), Remote Desktop works right "out of the box"; you just have to enable the feature. However, if you want to use Remote Desktop to reach your computer over the Internet, you must set up several other things in advance. The procedure might

> ⚠ **caution**
>
> If your computer is part of a corporate network, check with your network administrators before attempting to make any changes to the Remote Desktop settings. (In all likelihood, these settings will be locked anyway; you probably won't be able to change them.)

sound complex as you read it, but it really isn't that bad. Just go through the process step by step. You can go about this in other ways, of course, but what we give you here is a procedure that's suitable for a home or small office user with Windows 10 Pro.

Again, some web-based programs do much the same thing as Remote Desktop. Several of them are free, and most of them require very little setup work; in particular, they completely bypass the networking issues we discuss shortly. If the instructions in this section sound too difficult, or if the setup doesn't work for you, check out the section "Third-Party Remote Control Tools" at the end of the chapter.

 note

A password *must* be set on a user's account before that user can connect to the computer using Remote Desktop. Users without passwords will not be allowed to sign in remotely, even if they appear in the list of permitted users.

Enabling Remote Desktop Access to Your Computer

To enable incoming Remote Desktop connections on your computer, it's easiest to use a tool that Microsoft provides, using these steps:

1. Open your web browser and go to www.microsoft.com. Search for *download microsoft remote access assistant*. Select the result.

2. Scroll down past the advertising and click Download, and then open (run) the file. Confirm the security prompt, if there is one, and select Install.

3. Accept the license, and then select Get Started. Accept the User account Control prompt, and the tool will make the necessary adjustments. The assistant enables Remote Access, sets your computer to never go to sleep, and makes sure that Windows Firewall will allow the connection.

When the process is complete, note what it says next to PC Name. You can use this name or IP address to try connecting to your PC using Remote Desktop from another PC on your own network (though you're not yet ready to gain access over the Internet). Click Close when you're finished.

 note

After running the assistant, your PC will not put itself to sleep when unattended, so it will always be ready to receive incoming connections. You can use its power menu to shut it down or put it to sleep. In the future, if you are sure that you don't need to receive Remote Desktop connections and you want the automatic sleep function to come back, right-click the Start button, select Power Options, and reenable Sleep after some amount of time (say, 30 minutes).

By default, all Administrator-level accounts will be allowed to connect to the computer. If you want to grant Remote Desktop access to any Standard users, follow only steps 1, 3, and 4 in the next procedure; otherwise, if you used the assistant, you can skip ahead to "Establishing 24/7 Access."

If you can't or don't want to use the assistant, you can set up Remote Access manually. Follow these steps:

1. Click Start, Settings (gear icon), System, and in the left column, select Remote Desktop.

2. Turn on the Enable Remote Desktop switch, and then click Confirm.

3. If you want to grant Remote Desktop access to any Standard users, scroll down, and click Select Users That can Remotely Access This PC. Click Add, Advanced, Find Now, and then locate the desired name in the Search Results section. Double-click the name. To add another name, click Advanced and Find Now again.

4. Click OK to close all the dialog boxes, and then close Settings. If you used the assistant to set up Remote Access, skip ahead to "Establishing 24/7 Access."

If your computer is set to go to sleep when it sits unused for a while, and you want the computer to be available for incoming connections at all times, you'll have to disable automatic sleep. To do this, right-click the Start button and select Power Options. (Or click Start, Settings, System, Power & Sleep.) Under Sleep, change the setting(s) to Never. On a device with a battery, there might be two Sleep settings. Now you can close Settings.

Now confirm that Remote Desktop connections are correctly set up to be allowed through the Windows Firewall. In the taskbar's search box, type **firewall**, and then select Allow an App Through Windows Firewall. Scroll down the list of Allowed Apps and Features and locate Remote Desktop. Be sure it's checked under both Private and Public. If it isn't, click Change Settings, and then check the boxes. Click OK.

If you just want to use Remote Desktop within your home or office network, you're finished, and you can skip ahead to the "Connecting to Other Computers with Remote Desktop" section. However, if you want to reach your computer through the Internet, you have more work to do.

> ### ⚠ caution
>
> Be sure that every user account that can be reached via Remote Desktop (that is, every Administrator account and any Standard accounts that you select in step 4) has a strong password. This means a password with uppercase letters and lowercase letters and one or more numbers or punctuation, and it is at least eight characters in length. I like to use two-word passwords like this: Autumn/Robot5.

> ### note
>
> If you are using an add-on third-party firewall product, configure it to permit incoming Remote Desktop connections on TCP port 3389.

Establishing 24/7 Access

Because you won't be there at your home or office to turn on your computer and establish an Internet connection, you must set up things so that your computer and connection are always working.

First, if you are setting up access to a desktop PC, you must be sure that your computer will turn itself back on if the power goes out while you're not there. You do this from the computer's BIOS or

UEFI setup screen. To get there, click Start, Power. Hold the Shift key down while you click Restart. In the Choose an Option screen, select Troubleshoot, Advanced Options. If there is a selection titled UEFI Firmware Settings, select that and see whether there is an option for recovering from an AC power failure.

If there is no UEFI Firmware Settings tile, click the back arrow twice and select Continue. Wait for the screen to go black, and then press the Setup hotkey. The screen should tell you what to press; it's usually the Delete, F10, or F2 key, depending on your PC's manufacturer. Then look for the Power Management settings. Find an entry titled AC Power Recovery or something similar. Some computers have an option labeled Last Setting, which turns on the computer only if it was already on when the power failed. If it's available, you can select that. Otherwise, select the setting that turns on your computer whenever the AC power comes on. Then save the BIOS settings and restart Windows.

Besides a 24/7 computer, you need a 24/7 Internet connection. If you have cable Internet service or a type of DSL service that does not require you to enter a username or password, you already have an always-on Internet connection and can skip ahead to the next section. Otherwise, if you have Internet service that is connection-based, you need to take one of the following actions:

- See whether your DSL provider can upgrade your service to provide a static IP address and always-on service. This option might be inexpensive enough to make it worthwhile.

- Use a router. If you don't have a router already, buying one is a worthwhile investment. They cost roughly $20 to $100 and can provide wireless networking capability and Internet connection sharing for your home or office. Chapter 19, "Connecting Your Network to the Internet," tells how to set up a router for DSL service. Be sure to enable the router's "keepalive" feature so that your connection is kept going all the time.

- If you use the Internet Connection Sharing utility that comes with Windows, you can add a third-party program to force Windows to keep the connection open all the time. The DynDNS Updater program (which we discuss later) can do this for you.

Next, you must make sure you can locate your computer from out on the Internet.

Setting Up Dynamic DNS

All Internet connections are established on the basis of a number called an *IP address*, which is to your Internet connection what your telephone number is to your phone. When you're somewhere else, you'll need a way to let Windows find your home computer's IP address so that Remote Desktop can establish a connection back to it. The problem is that, for most Internet service, your home IP address can change from day to day.

The solution to this problem is to use a dynamic domain name service (DDNS). You'll use the service to give your computer a name, such as *brian.likes-pie.com*. (Seriously.) Your router, or add-on software in your computer, will keep the service updated whenever your computer's address changes.

note

Many DDNS providers exist, and some of them, such as no-ip.com, offer free services. You can find them easily enough by doing a Google search for *free DDNS service*. Here, we give you step-by-step instructions for setting up DynDNS Pro service at Dyn.com because it's directly supported by many hardware connection-sharing routers. If your router doesn't support it, you can install the company's IP address updating program on your computer. The company name has changed from DynDNS.com to Dyn.com, and the price has unfortunately gone from free to $40 per year, but that covers up to 30 device names, and it's still a great product. You can try it out free with the 7-day free trial offer.

To be clear, if you have a static IP address, you can use any DNS service to map your IP address to a hostname+domain name. If you have a dynamic address or a connection-based Internet service, you can use any Dynamic DNS service; however, the process for installing and configuring it will be different from what we describe here.

To set up dynamic domain name service at Dyn.com, follow these steps:

1. Open your preferred web browser and go to Dyn.com. Select Products, Dynamic DNS. Scroll down to the 7-day Free Trial section and select Start trial. Follow the instructions to create an account.

2. If your network uses a Linksys router, Dyn.com has an easy-setup wizard you can download after you've created your account that automates the setup process. Otherwise, proceed with the following steps.

3. After you have created your account and are logged in to the Dyn.com site using your new account, navigate to DynDNS Pro and then select Add New Hostname.

4. Enter a hostname that you can easily remember, and select a domain name from the pull-down list. (I entered hostname `brian` and selected the domain `likes-pie.com`. This gives my computer the Internet name `brian.likes-pie.com`.) If someone else has claimed the name you chose, change the name or domain and try again until you succeed. Be sure to write down the host-name and domain name that you eventually select.

5. Leave Wildcard unchecked and Service Type set to Host with IP Address. Click the link Your Current Location's IP Address Is... to record that address.

Next, set up a DNS client program so that changes to your IP address are sent to Dyn.com. There are two ways to do this. If you have a hardware Internet router, it might be able to update your IP address automatically. You can find support information on Dyn.com to help you do this.

Alternatively, install a Dynamic DNS updating tool on the computer you're enabling for Remote Desktop access. This is a software service that will periodically determine your network's public IP address and will update your name-to-address mapping in Dyn.com's server.

Here's how to do this on the computer you're enabling for Remote Desktop access:

1. Sign in as a computer administrator. Open your web browser and go to help.dyn.com. Click Dyn Update Clients. Under Windows, select the most recent Installation Guide. On the guide page, select Download the Dyn Update Client for Windows. When prompted, select Run, and then approve the User Account Control prompt.

2. Step through the installation screens, using the default settings (except uncheck Enable Dyn Internet Guide on This PC).

3. When the program starts, enter the Dyn.com account username and password that you created previously. In the list of hosts, click the check box for the hostname you created for this computer, and then click OK.

The Dyn Updater service will now keep your hostname updated with your public IP address whenever it changes. (This Windows service runs whenever your computer is turned on, whether or not you are signed in.)

To be sure that the service is working, right-click the Start button and select Command Prompt or Windows PowerShell, whichever appears. Type the command `ping` followed by the hostname and domain name you chose for your computer; for example, `ping brian.likes-pie.com`. Press Enter and be sure that the command finds your IP address and doesn't print "Could not find host."

Now your registered hostname will always point to your computer, even when your IP address changes. After a change, it might take up to an hour for the update to occur, but changes should be infrequent.

Configuring Port Forwarding

The last setup step is to make sure that incoming Remote Desktop connections from the Internet make it to the right computer. If your computer connects directly to your cable or DSL modem, you can skip this step. Otherwise, you must instruct your sharing computer or router to forward Remote Desktop data through to your computer. To be precise, you must set up your sharing computer or router to forward incoming requests on TCP port 3389 to the computer you want to reach by Remote Desktop.

The procedure depends on whether you are using the ICS service built in to Windows or a hardware-sharing router. Use one of the procedures described in the next two sections.

Port Forwarding with a Router

If you are using a hardware connection-sharing router, setup is somewhat difficult but is worthwhile. We give you an overview of the process here. To learn more about forwarding network requests on a shared Internet connection, see "Making Services Available" in Chapter 19.

First, because your router doesn't know your computers by their names, you must set up a fixed IP address on the computer that you will be using via Remote Desktop, using these steps:

1. Press Windows Logo+X and select Command Prompt or Windows PowerShell, whichever appears in the list. Type the command `ipconfig /all` and press Enter. Locate the Local Area Connection part of the printout, which will look something like this. (I omitted a few entries.) You might need to scroll the window to see it all.

```
Ethernet adapter Local Area Connection:
  Connection-specific DNS Suffix . : somewhere.com
  Description . . . . . . . . . . . : NVIDIA nForce Networking Controller
```

```
Physical Address. . . . . . . . . : 00-53-8F-D2-CA-5F
DHCP Enabled. . . . . . . . . . . : Yes
Autoconfiguration Enabled . . . . : Yes
IPv4 Address. . . . . . . . . . . : 192.168.0.102
Subnet Mask . . . . . . . . . . . : 255.255.255.0
Default Gateway . . . . . . . . . : 192.168.0.1
DHCP Server . . . . . . . . . . . : 192.168.0.1
DNS Servers . . . . . . . . . . . : 200.123.45.6
                                    200.123.67.8
```

The important information is bold. (On your computer, the numbers will be different. Use your numbers, not these!)

If the entry DHCP Enabled says No, you don't have to change anything here. Just note the IPv4 Address entry, skip steps 2 through 8, and configure your router.

2. Click the network icon at the right end of the taskbar and select Network & Internet Settings, Status (if the Status page isn't already shown), Change Adapter Options.

3. Right-click the icon that represents your LAN connection (most likely Ethernet or Wireless) and select Properties.

4. In the Networking tab, select the Internet Protocol Version 4 (TCP/IPv4) entry and click Properties.

5. In the General tab, check Use the Following IP Address. Enter the first three parts of your original IP address exactly as you see it in your Command Prompt window, but replace the last part with 250 (for example, 192.168.0.250). The first three sets of digits might be different on your network.

6. For the subnet mask and default gateway, enter the same numbers that were displayed in the Command Prompt window.

7. Check Use the Following DNS Server Addresses. Enter the one or two DNS Server addresses that were displayed in the Command Prompt window.

8. Click OK.

(If you need to set up any other computers to have fixed IP addresses, use the same procedure but use addresses ending in .249, .248, .247, and so on, counting backward from .250.)

Now you must instruct your router to forward Remote Desktop connections to this computer. Open Internet Explorer and enter **http://** followed by the Default Gateway address you noted in step 1 (for example, http://192.168.0.1). Then press Enter. Every router uses a slightly different scheme, but Figure 39.2 shows a typical router. You need to find the router's setup screen and enable its Port Forwarding feature, which some routers call Virtual Server or Applications and Gaming.

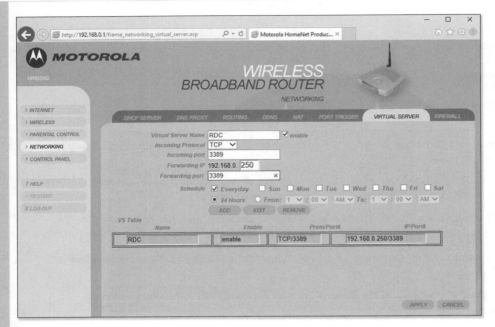

Figure 39.2
Use your router's setup system to forward TCP port 3389 to your computer.

On the router, you must enter the fixed IP address that you assigned to your computer and tell the router to forward connections on TCP port 3389 to this address. If a range of port numbers is required, or if external and internal numbers are entered separately, enter **3389** in all fields.

Now you should be able to reach your computer from anywhere on the Internet using the hostname you set up on Dyn.com. (To try it, you'll have to use an Internet connection somewhere else, not on your own network!)

Port Forwarding with Internet Connection Sharing

If you use the built-in Windows ICS service to share an Internet connection on one computer with the rest of your LAN, the forwarding procedure is pretty straightforward using these steps:

1. Go to the computer that is sharing its connection (whether or not it's the one you want to reach via Remote Desktop) and sign in as a computer administrator.

2. View the Properties dialog box for the local area connection that corresponds to the Internet connection itself. On a Windows 10 version, click the network icon in the taskbar, and select Network & Internet Settings, Status (if the Status page isn't already shown), Change Adapter Options.

3. Locate the connection icon that goes to your Internet service. It will have the word *Shared* under or next to it. Right-click the icon, select Properties, and view the Sharing tab.

4. Click Settings and, under Services, check Remote Desktop. In the Service Settings dialog box, enter the name of the computer that you want to make available via Remote Desktop, and click

OK. (To find the name of the computer, view its System or System Properties screen by going to the Start menu and typing **system**, and then select System Information or select System.)

5. When you're finished, click OK to close all the dialog boxes.

Now you should be able to reach your computer from anywhere on the Internet using the hostname you set up on Dyn.com and the Remote Desktop Connection client program described in the next section.

Connecting to Other Computers with Remote Desktop

To establish a connection to another computer using the Remote Desktop system, you need a Remote Desktop client program, which is sometimes called Remote Desktop Connection or Terminal Services Client. You can get this program in several ways:

- On Windows 10 and Windows 8.1, you can choose from two Remote Desktop clients. There is a Modern-style version named Remote Desktop that you can download at no cost from the Store app. There is also the traditional desktop client, which is always preinstalled.

  To get the Modern version, open the Store app and search for Microsoft Remote Desktop. Several results might come up. You want the one named just Microsoft Remote Desktop, without *Preview* or any other words. Click Get to download and install it.

  To use either the modern or the traditional client, in the taskbar's search box, type **remote**. To use the Modern app, under Apps, select Remote Desktop. To use the desktop version, select Remote Desktop Connection. We describe both clients later in this chapter. You can also run the desktop version by typing **mstsc** at the Command Prompt.

- On Windows 7 and Vista, click Start, All Programs, Accessories, Remote Desktop Connection. This is the Desktop version.

  On Windows XP, click Start, All Programs, Accessories, Communications, Remote Desktop Connection.

  The version that came with XP lacks support for multiple monitors and plug-and-play devices. You can upgrade the version on XP by downloading and installing the latest version, as described in the next paragraph.

- You can download a client from www.microsoft.com/download. Search for Remote Desktop Connection and get the latest version available for your operating system. You can find versions there for Windows and Mac OS X.

- If you have an iOS or Android device, such as an iPad, search your device's app store (Apple Store or Google Play) for a Remote Desktop client published by Microsoft. Other vendors have published Remote Desktop–compatible apps, but be wary of using one from an unfamiliar company. Because you will be letting the app have your Windows password, you should only get a Remote Desktop app published by Microsoft.

  The Remote Desktop app on iOS and Android devices is similar to the Modern-style Windows app described in this chapter, so you should be able to use it following the instructions provided here.

In the next two sections, we discuss the Modern-style and traditional desktop client programs. The traditional Remote Desktop client has more keyboard, display, sound, and printing options than the Modern version. Try them both and see which you prefer.

Using the Modern-Style Remote Desktop App

To start a connection to a remote computer from a Windows 10 computer using the Modern client, go to the Start menu and type **remote**. If Remote Desktop appears, select it. If it does not appear under Apps, go to the Store app and download it.

The Modern app that gets installed on Windows 10 is a new "Universal" app, and at the time this was written (with version #1010), it lacks support for some features available on the desktop client such as the use of local printers. It is being revised frequently, though, and you can expect improvements in the future. If you need any of the missing features, use the desktop app instead.

When the Remote Desktop app opens, you can do any of the following things:

- At the top of the app, click + and then select Desktop Computer to enter the name or address of a remote computer, such as the name you set up in the first part of this chapter (in my case, `brian.likes-pie.com`). You can leave User Account set to Ask Me Every Time, or, to simplify future logons, select Add Account and enter a user account name and password. Click Show More, and if you would like to give this connection a more informative name, type a new name under Display Name. Then click Save.

- To connect to a computer you've added previously, just click its icon.

- You can select the ... symbol on a connection icon and remove or edit it. The Edit option lets you customize its connection settings or delete a saved credential (password) stored for the connection. Click Show More to see the large number of options for connections, including Update the Remote Session Resolution on Resize. This is on by default, and resizing the App window changes the remote computer's resolution. If you turn this off, the App's view just scales what the remote computer is showing.

- Select the Settings (gear) icon to set a default user account for new connections and a few other things. The default settings work well, but you can examine the settings to see what you can change.

- Click + and then Add Remote Resources to connect to a corporate app server. (Instructions for using this feature would be provided by a network administrator.) Once connected, you can use the Modern-style client as discussed in the rest of this section.

The first time you connect to a remote computer, if that computer is not on a secured network, you will be warned that the computer to which you're connecting might not be the one you expect. If you trust that the hostname you entered really

 tip

If you are signing in to a Windows 8, 8.1, or Windows 10 computer with a Microsoft (online) account, your username is an email address of the form *myname@something.com*. Try connecting with that first. If Windows rejects your sign-in and gives you a bad username or password message, try typing `MicrosoftAccount\` before your username. For example, I might type `MicrosoftAccount\ brianknittel@live.com`.

does lead to the computer you want to use, check Don't Ask About This Certificate Again, and then click Connect.

After the connection is made, you can use the remote computer as if you were sitting there.

The keyboard and mouse control the *remote* computer. The Windows Logo keyboard shortcuts, in particular, by default are sent to the remote computer and act there. Only the Ctrl+Alt+Del key combination acts locally; you can type Ctrl+Alt+End to send Ctrl+Alt+Del to the remote computer.

➡ *For more useful keyboard shortcuts that you can use while working with the remote computer, see Table 39.2, p. 893.*

If you want the standard Windows shortcut keys like Windows Logo+Tab and Shift+PrtScr to apply to the local computer instead, you must change a connection setting. Select the ... icon at the top of the screen, select Home, Settings, and scroll down to Use Keyboard Commands With. The choices are

- **My local PC only**—Special shortcut keys are not sent to the remote computer. Windows Logo+Tab, for example, will switch between the apps on your local computer.

- **My remote session when it's in full screen**—Shortcut keys are local when you've sized the Remote Desktop window down or when you're using the app's menus.

- **My remote session when it's in use**—Shortcut keys are always sent to the remote computer when Remote Desktop is your active app.

This setting applies to all connections, so you may eventually wish to change it back to the default setting, My Remote Session When It's in Full Screen.

On a touchscreen, multitouch gestures always act on the local computer. If you have no keyboard on your device, you'll need to use the Remote Desktop app's app commands to transmit these actions to a remote Windows 10, 8.1, or 8 computer.

To manage your remote connection, click or touch the . . . menu icon at the top center of the screen. The connection menu has three selections:

- **Home**—Returns to the initial screen with tiles for each remembered connection. You can use this to start additional connections to other PCs.

- **Disconnect**—Disconnects from the remote session, leaving it signed in. We discuss this in more detail shortly.

- **Full Screen**—Switches between a full-screen and a resizable window display of the remote computer's screen.

Click or touch the magnifying glass icon at the top center of the screen to zoom in on the remote screen. This can be helpful if you are connecting from a device with a screen that's much smaller than the remote computer's and text is too small to read. While you're zoomed in, you might need to pan (scroll) the screen view. If you have a touchscreen, a circle with arrows appears in the upper-left corner, as shown in Figure 39.3. Touch your finger to this circle and drag your finger around to pan the zoomed screen. (The circle doesn't move but the screen contents do.) If you don't have a touchscreen, move the mouse cursor to the right or bottom edge of the screen. Scrollbars will appear, and you can use those to pan. Click or touch the magnifying glass again to zoom back out.

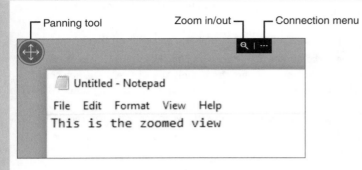

Panning tool — Zoom in/out — Connection menu

Untitled - Notepad

File   Edit   Format   View   Help

This is the zoomed view

Figure 39.3
If you have a touchscreen, the zoomed view lets you pan the screen by touching the circle icon in the upper left corner.

When you're finished working remotely, to disconnect from the remote computer and leave it signed in, running your apps, touch or click the . . . box at the top of the screen, and then select Disconnect. (The Power button in the remote computer's Start menu or Windows 8 or 8.1 Settings charm also disconnects, leaving you signed in.)

To sign out entirely, open to the *remote computer's* Start menu or screen and sign out in the normal way. For Windows 10, select your picture icon on the Start menu, and then select Sign Out. This signs you out and then closes the connection.

Using the Standard Remote Desktop Client

To run the desktop Remote Desktop client, in the taskbar's search box, type **remote**, and then select Remote Desktop Connection. (We list the ways to run it from earlier versions of Windows in the section "Connecting to Other Computers with Remote Desktop," earlier in this chapter.) If you're using the Remote Desktop client on any earlier version of Windows, or on a Mac, this is the type of client you'll be using.

Two Monitors Are Better Than One

If the computer you're using to establish the remote connection has two or more monitors, you might be able to use them all for the remote connection.

If you're connecting from a computer that is running Windows 10, 8.1, 8, or 7, when you start the traditional Remote Desktop Client, click the Options button, select the Display tab, and select Use All of My Monitors for the Remote Session. When you connect to the remote computer, set the Display size to Full Screen. (This works only with the Remote Desktop Connection client version 7.0 or higher, as provided with Windows 10, 8.1, 8, and 7, or downloaded from microsoft.com.)

When you run the Remote Desktop Client, you'll see the Remote Desktop Connection dialog box (see Figure 39.4).

Figure 39.4
The Remote Desktop Connection dialog box enables you to configure the connection and select the remote computer to use.

Enter the IP address or registered DNS name of the computer you want to use. If you have set up a DDNS hostname, as described in the first part of this chapter, the name might look something like brian.likes-pie.com. If you're connecting to a computer on your own home or office network, it's enough just to type its computer name.

At this point, you can select options that control how the remote connection is made, how large a window to use, and so on.

Selecting Connection Options

In the Remote Desktop Connection dialog box, you can set several connection options. In most cases, you can use the default settings and simply click Connect to start the connection, but several of the options can be quite useful.

To view the option categories, click the Show Options button. The dialog box expands to show five tabs, which you can select by clicking the tab names across the top. You will rarely need to adjust any of these settings. However, some situations might require you to change settings before making a Remote Desktop connection. Table 39.1 lists these situations.

Table 39.1 Some Reasons to Change Remote Desktop Settings

Situation	Setting Change
You always connect across the Internet or your remote computer is not on a secure corporate LAN.	On the Advanced tab, set Server Authentication to Connect and Don't Warn Me.
You are using a dial-up Internet connection.	On the Experience tab, change the Connection Speed to Modem (56kbps). On the Local Resources tab, click Settings and set Remote audio playback to Do Not Play.
The remote computer has a slow Internet upload speed.	Most home Internet service has a fast download connection but a slow upload speed, often less than 500Kbps. If you're connecting to a computer that has a slow upload speed and the screen updates sluggishly, disconnect, and on the Experience tab, set the Performance setting to Low-Speed Broadband. Then try again.
You must work with the local and remote screens simultaneously.	On the Display tab, change the resolution to a size smaller than your local screen, perhaps 800×600.
You must see as much of the remote computer's screen as possible.	On the Display tab, change the resolution to Full Screen. If the remote computer runs Windows 7 or later and you have multiple monitors on your local computer, check Use All My Monitors for the Remote Session.
You must be able to print from the applications on the remote computer and get the printouts where you are working.	On the Local Resources tab, check Printers.
You don't need to print while connected.	On the Local Resources tab, uncheck Printers.
You want remote applications to be able to access files on the computer where you are working.	On the Local Resources tab, click More, expand the Drives list, and then click the boxes next to the drive letter(s) you want to be made available to the remote computer.
You must use an application that uses a device attached to a COM port (for example, a Palm Pilot).	On the Local Resources tab, click More and then check Ports.
You want the Windows key to be sent to the remote computer even when your remote connection isn't in Full-Screen mode.	On the Local Resources tab, set Apply Windows Key Combinations to On the Remote Computer.

The Full-Screen setting is very useful if you have serious work to do on the remote computer because it gives you the maximum amount of desktop space on which to work. (It also helps because the Windows Logo key will be sent to the remote computer rather than acting on the local computer.) Although the resulting connection will fill your local computer's screen, you can still switch back and forth between remote and local work, as described in the next section.

When you have made the necessary settings, you might want to save them as the default settings for future connections. To do this, select the General tab and click Save under Connection settings.

Finally, after you have made any necessary option settings, click Connect to begin the connection. Windows prompts you to enter your username and password before it establishes the connection.

 tip

If you routinely make connections to different computers using different settings, you can set up Remote Desktop Connection files with the computer name and all options preset. To do this, after you have made the necessary settings, under Connection Settings, click Save As and then select a filename. You can create shortcuts to the saved files and put them on your desktop, put them in your Start page, or pin them to your taskbar.

 note

If you are connecting to a Windows Server Domain computer, you usually will enter your domain sign-in in the form *domainname\username*. If you need to specify a local machine account, enter `machinename\username`, as in `mycomputer\Administrator`.

The program prompts you to enter a username and password. Type the username and password you use on the remote computer, the one to which you're connecting. Entering the password is optional and, in most cases, not entering it here is safer. Let the remote system prompt you for your password.

If you want the sign-in name and password to be stored (relatively securely) in the local computer so that future connections can be automatic, enter the password and check Remember My Credentials.

Finally, click OK to begin the connection.

 caution

Do *not* check Remember My Credentials if you are using a computer in a public place, or one that is not your own or is not secure, because otherwise, anyone who has access to the account you're using will be able to connect to the remote computer using your sign-in.

 Sign-In Is Denied

If the remote computer connects but will not let you sign in, the account you tried to use might have a blank password or might be a Standard account that was not entered as an account authorized to connect remotely. See "Enabling Remote Desktop Access to Your Computer," earlier in the chapter, for instructions on authorizing accounts. An account must have a password set before you can use it remotely.

If Network Level Authentication is being used and the connection to the remote computer does not use the IPsec network security protocol, you might get a warning that the remote computer's identity cannot be validated. (Thus, you *could* end up giving your password to a counterfeit computer.) In most cases, this is not a problem, so you can click Yes. You also can check Don't Prompt Me Again for Connections to This Computer, or you can use the Advanced tab in the connection options, as described earlier, to prevent this warning from reoccurring.

Using the Remote Connection

When you're signed in, you'll see the remote computer's desktop, and you can use it as if you were actually sitting in front of it. In a full-screen connection, the title bar at the top of the screen tells you that you're viewing the remote computer's screen. The title bar might slide up out of view, but you can hover the mouse pointer near the top of the screen to bring it back. You can also click the Minimize button to hide the remote screen, or you can click the Maximize button to switch between a windowed or full-screen view.

The keyboard, mouse, display, and sound (unless you disabled it) should be fully functional. It all works quite well—and it can even be difficult to remember which computer you're actually using!

If you elected to make the local computer's disk drives available in the Connection Options dialog box, the local computer's drives appear when you open File Explorer on the remote computer. Access to these drives is fairly slow and annoying. Still, you can take advantage of this to copy files between the local and remote computers.

Also, any printers attached to your local computer will appear as choices if you print from applications on the remote computer, as long as a compatible printer driver is available on the *remote* computer. Printers might not work if you are connecting from a Mac or a computer that is running an older version of Windows.

Using Keyboard Shortcuts

While you're connected, you might want to use keyboard shortcuts such as Alt+Tab to switch between applications and Windows Logo+R to run a command. These shortcuts can confuse Windows, which won't know whether to switch applications on the local computer or the remote computer. There are three ways to make the Alt and Windows special functions act on the remote computer:

- Put the remote connection window into Full-Screen mode. Then all Windows keys will be sent to the remote computer, except Ctrl+Alt+Del. To send Ctrl+Alt+Del, press Ctrl+Alt+End.

- Before you make the connection, view the Local Resources options page and set "Apply Windows Key Combinations" to "On the Remote Computer." (And, as before, this fixes all but Ctrl+Alt+Del.)

 tip

If the computer to which you're connecting has more than one monitor or a larger monitor than the one you're currently using, when you start an application, its window might not be visible. The problem is that when the application was last used, its window was placed on a secondary monitor and its position is now completely off the Remote Desktop screen. To make it visible, hover the mouse pointer over the program's icon in the taskbar. When the preview window appears, right-click it and select Move (or Restore and then Move). Then press and hold the arrow keys to slide the window into view. Press Enter when it's visible; then finish positioning it with your mouse.

- Memorize and use the alternative key combinations listed in Table 39.2. These replacement keystrokes don't work, by the way, if you are using either of the preceding two alternatives.

Table 39.2 Some Remote Desktop Keyboard Shortcuts

Use These Keys	To Transmit This to the Remote Computer
Alt+PgUp, Alt+PgDn	Alt+Tab (to switch programs)
Alt+End	Ctrl+Alt+Del (to open Task Monitor)
Alt+Home	Ctrl+Esc (to display the Start Screen on Windows 8 or 8.1, and the Start menu on all other versions)
Alt+Del	Alt+Space (to display a window's System menu)
Ctrl+Alt+Break	Alt+Enter (to toggle Full Screen)
Ctrl+Alt+Plus on numeric pad	Alt+PrtScr (to print the screen to the Clipboard)
Ctrl+Alt+End	Ctrl+Alt+Del (to display Task Manager)

Table 39.2 shows the alternative keyboard shortcuts that you can use if the window isn't in Full-Screen mode and you haven't selected to send all Windows key combinations to the remote computer.

When you've finished using the remote computer, sign out using the normal means for the remote version of Windows. (For example, for Windows 10, click your picture icon in the Start menu, and then select Sign Out.) If you want to leave yourself signed in with applications running, use the remote computer's normal power or shutdown menu, which will say Disconnect instead. (For Windows 10, click the Power icon in the lower-left part of the remote computer's Start menu, and then select Disconnect, or just close the Remote Desktop connection window.) You can later reconnect via Remote Desktop or by signing in at the remote computer itself.

I use Remote Desktop to use my work computer from home, and I've found that I save a lot of time by never signing out entirely. When I finish at work, I just press Windows Logo+L ("Lock") to switch out to the Welcome screen. Then I can reconnect from home and pick up where I left off. Likewise, at home, when I'm finished, I simply disconnect, so I never actually sign out.

If you're using Remote Desktop to use your own computer, this probably won't matter to you because you'll probably never see what happens on the other screen. However, if you use Remote Desktop to work on someone else's computer, let that person know what will happen before starting; otherwise, the two of you could get into a tussle, repeatedly kicking the other person off the computer, with neither of you knowing that the other person is there trying to get something done. (I've had this happen.)

 tip

If you're a command-line fanatic like I am, you might want to launch Remote Desktop connections from the command prompt. The command mstsc /v:*hostname* opens a connection to the named computer. The command mstsc filename.rdp uses connection settings you previously saved in a file using the GUI. Type **mstsc /?** for more useful options.

> ### One User at a Time
>
> Desktop versions of Windows permit only one person to use each computer. If you attempt to connect to a computer with Remote Desktop while another user is signed in, you will have the choice of disconnecting yourself or forcing that user to the Welcome (sign-in) screen. And, if Fast User Switching is not enabled on the remote computer, that user is summarily signed out and loses any work in process.
>
> If you sign in using the same username as the local user, though, you simply take over the desktop without forcing a sign-out.
>
> If someone else signs in to the remote computer while you're connected from afar, your session is disconnected. Again, if Fast User Switching is enabled on the remote computer, you can simply reconnect later and pick up where you left off. Otherwise, the same deal applies: If it is a different user, your applications are shut down.

Third-Party Remote Control Tools

If you don't want to set up Remote Desktop, you might want to consider using one of several third-party remote control tools. A bunch of web-based products have emerged that work very well. Many of them have free versions, or at least a free trial period, and most have some advantages over Remote Desktop: They let you connect to any version of Windows (even Home versions) and Apple's OS X, and they require almost no setup, even if you have a router on your Internet connection. Here are some products to check out:

- **LogMeIn**—For $249 per year for two host computers, you get remote control, file transfer, sound, and printing. Mac and Windows versions are available. A free trial is available. No network setup is necessary. Find information at logmein.com. The free iOS and Android client app is called LogMeIn Ignition. It's superb.

- **TeamViewer**—Available free for personal, noncommercial use, TeamViewer requires no network setup and can even make your LAN available to the remote client computer through a built-in VPN service. Both Windows and Mac clients and hosts are available. Check out teamviewer.com.

- **I'm InTouch**—Another no-network-setup remote access product. The remote client is Java based, so you could access your PC from your BlackBerry. There are iOS and Android clients, too. Check out www.01com.com. A free 30-day trial is available. Pricing is from $100/year.

- **LapLink Everywhere (formerly Carbon Copy)**—Requires no network setup. Clients are available for iOS and PocketPCs as well as PCs. Information can be found at www.laplink.com. $50/yr or $100/yr for three computers.

- **GoToMyPC**—A fairly expensive commercial subscription-based product that offers remote access through any web browser, from the company that pioneered the zero-setup remote access category. Information can be found at get.gotomypc.com. You can access your computer from Windows, OS X, Android, and iOS. A free 7-day trial is available. $20/mo.

- **Radmin**—A low-cost remote control program. Information can be found at www.radmin.com. Requires network setup (either port forwarding or the free radmin VPN program installed on both the local and remote computers), but there is no annual fee (free 30-day trial). $49.

- **VNC**—A free, open source program initially developed by AT&T. A big plus for VNC is that both host and client programs are available for virtually every OS. (It's used for remote access to Mac OS X, in fact.) Several VNC versions are available, with TightVNC and RealVNC being the most popular. For information, check out www.tightvnc.com and www.realvnc.com. VNC products require network setup and do not encrypt their data, so they are *not safe* for connecting directly over the Internet. They are fine to use on a home or business LAN or over a VPN connection.

 note

The products that require network setup can also access a computer across a LAN or corporate network. If you want to access a remote computer via a dial-up modem, though, you must use one of the old-school programs, such as Symantec PCAnywhere, which is no longer sold but which you can find on sites such as eBay. Alternatively, you can set up an incoming dial-up networking connection for your computer and use Remote Desktop or a network-based remote control program such as VNC.

VIRTUALIZATION

A virtual machine (VM) program simulates the hardware functions of a computer within an application running on another computer. It lets you run an entire operating system as an application program so that you can work in various operating systems without rebooting. Virtualization has been used on big mainframe computers since the 1960s, and it is now also used on PCs and PC-type server computers. You could conceivably have Windows XP, Windows Vista, Windows 7, Windows 8, Windows 8.1, Windows 10, various versions of Windows Server and Linux, and other operating systems all running at once on your desktop. You can also run a copy of Windows inside a virtual computer on a machine running Linux, Mac OS X, or other versions of Windows.

Virtualization is a handy way for individuals and organizations to run multiple operating systems without having to set up dual- or multiboot environments or purchase additional hardware. IT departments use virtualization to consolidate multiple server computers into a smaller number of machines and to test software updates and patches before rolling them out to end users; and developers use virtualization when creating, testing, and documenting software programs. End users most commonly use virtualization to run applications that require an older version of Windows on a computer that has a newer version of Windows.

In virtualization vocabulary, the *host* operating system is the one that runs the physical computer. A *guest* operating system runs inside the virtual machine system provided by the host. In this appendix, we talk about Windows 10 as both host and guest.

Windows 10 now supports a "thin" virtualization environment called Windows Containers, which is compatible with the Docker application virtualization management system. A Container is a virtual machine file that encapsulates just a single web- or network-based service application rather than an entire interactive operating system. The containerized application can't interact with or modify the copy of Windows that hosts it; all of the application's data and what it "thinks" are its changes to the host's file system and Registry are stored separately in the container's virtual hard disk file. Containers can thus be moved or copied from one host to another at will, simplifying maintenance, deployment, and scaling of the hosted service. We talk more about Windows Containers at the end of this appendix.

Windows 10 as a Host: Running Other Operating Systems Inside Windows 10

You can install a virtualization host program so that you can run other operating systems inside Windows 10. Microsoft's Hyper-V product is included with the 64-bit versions of Windows 10 Professional, Enterprise, and Education editions. Hyper-V is Microsoft's industrial-strength VM system used across the Windows Server product line. In this section, we show you how to activate Hyper-V (which by default is not enabled), how to create new virtual machines (VMs), and how to convert an existing physical installation of Windows into a VM that you can then run inside Windows 10.

If you want to run virtual machines inside Windows 10 Mobile or Home, or in any 32-bit version of Windows 10, you'll have to use a different virtual machine manager, such as Oracle's VirtualBox (free, from www.virtualbox.org) or VMware's VMware Workstation Pro ($249, from www.vmware.com). I used VirtualBox extensively while writing this book and found it completely adequate. There are some screen-refreshing issues at times (which were annoying but not deal-killers), but there are also frequent bug-fix updates to the program.

Microsoft's previous virtualization offerings, Microsoft Virtual PC and Windows Virtual PC, do not work on Windows 8 through 10. The Windows XP Mode system—a preconfigured, virtualized copy of Windows XP that Microsoft offered to Windows 7 Professional, Ultimate, and Enterprise users—is also not available on Windows 8 through 10. We talk about converting existing Virtual PC and XP Mode virtual machines for Hyper-V in the following sections.

The version of Hyper-V provided with Windows 10 is called Client Hyper-V, and it's almost identical to VM manager used on the industrial-strength Windows Server operating systems. When Hyper-V is installed and you start your computer, Hyper-V actually loads first, and Windows 10 loads on top of it as a sort of half-client/half-partner. Your copy of Windows 10 won't be running on the "bare metal" exactly, but it's also not as restricted as a regular virtual machine would be—and there's almost no performance hit. Windows 10 runs as what's called Hyper-V's Management Operating System, and it has direct access to the computer's hardware. You can see this in the Device Manager, which shows that Windows 10 still "sees" your computer's real hardware devices, not the simulated Intel network adapter and video adapter that a regular Hyper-V VM sees.

> **note**
>
> In Windows 10 Builds 10565 and later, Hyper supports Nested Virtualization, which lets you install and run Hyper-V inside a virtual machine, and that guest Hyper-V can run its own virtual machines. The practical use of this is to test and demonstrate server configurations. To use this feature, you need an Intel processor with VT-x hardware support. For more information, visit msdn.microsoft.com and search for "Nested Virtualization."

Installing and Configuring Hyper-V

To install Hyper-V on Windows 10, type `control` in the taskbar's Search box, and then click Control Panel in the search results. Select Programs and then select Turn Windows Features On or Off.

Check the Hyper-V box (so that you install both Hyper-V Management Tools and Hyper-V Platform), and then click OK. Windows will need to restart once or twice.

When you sign back in, at the Start menu, select Hyper-V Manager. When this opens on the desktop, you might want to right-click its icon in the taskbar and select Pin This Program to Taskbar.

The next step is to create a virtual network switch (network hub) that your virtual computer will use to connect to your LAN and to the Internet. To do this, in the Actions panel, select Virtual Switch Manager. Select New Virtual Switch. In the list of switch types, select External and click Next, which will let your virtual machines connect to your LAN through your computer's network adapter. Click Create Virtual Switch. Change the name to Shared Network Switch. If your computer has more than one network adapter, under External Network, select the adapter that leads to your LAN and to the Internet. Be sure to keep Allow Management Operating System to Share This Network Adapter checked. The Management Operating System is your copy of Windows 10, and you don't want to disconnect it from the network adapter.

Finally, click OK to close the Virtual Switch Manager.

(You can also use the Virtual Switch Manager to create private networks that connect only virtual machines, or a network that contains only VMs and your own computer, but that's beyond the scope of this book.)

Creating Virtual Machines

To create a new virtual computer, follow these steps:

1. At the Start menu, select Hyper-V Manager, shown in Figure A.1.

Figure A.1
The Hyper-V Manager lets you create and manage virtual machines.

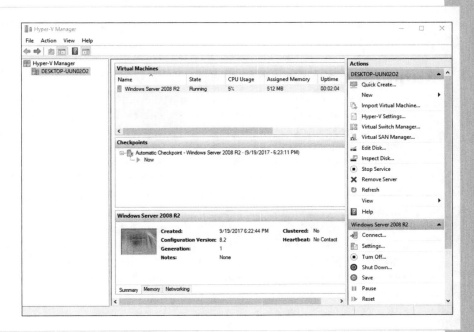

2. In the right pane, select New, Virtual Machine and then click Next.

3. Enter a name for the new VM and click Next.

4. Enter the amount of RAM the VM should see, according to the needs of the guest operating system. If your computer has 8GB of RAM or more, you can probably be somewhat generous, offering 2GB to 4GB, or more, but be aware that most 32-bit operating systems won't be able to use any more than 3GB. Check Use Dynamic Memory to let Windows automatically manage the partitioning of your computer's physical RAM between the VMs and your applications. Then click Next.

5. To give the VM access to your network, select the Shared Network Switch that you created when you installed Hyper-V. Click Next.

6. Unless you have an existing virtual hard disk you want to use, select Create a Virtual Hard Disk, type in a name for it that ends with .vhdx, and set a *maximum* size limit for its contents. Windows won't preallocate a file of this size, but the disk file could grow to this size.

   If, instead, you want to use the .vhd format so that the file will be compatible with other virtualization programs, in the Action pane, select New, Hard Disk and use the wizard to create a new .vhd hard disk. Then, back in the Connect Virtual Hard Disk dialog box, select Use an Existing Virtual Hard Disk and browse to the file you created.

   Then click Next.

7. If you want to attach a physical or virtual (*.iso* file) CD or DVD to the virtual machine when it boots for the first time so that you can install an operating system, make this selection on the Installation Options screen. Click Next and then Finish.

The virtual machine is now ready to start. The first time you boot it up, install the Integration Services, as described in the next section.

Running and Connecting to a VM

Hyper-V virtual machines run entirely outside Windows 10. The Virtual machines it manages are not desktop applications on your own computer. They have distinct, separate operating systems that are running on what might as well be some other computer; it just so happens that the other computer occupies the same physical space as yours. To "see" a virtual machine's screen, you use the Hyper-V Virtual Machine Connection program, which is a version of the Remote Desktop connection program that knows how to find VMs on your own computer or other computers.

It's easiest to start from the Hyper-V Manager, which you can run from the Start menu (or if you pinned it to the taskbar, from the desktop). You might find that you need to right-click its icon and select Run As Administrator for it to see your virtual machines, but try it without doing this first.

In the Virtual Machines list, select the VM that you want to start, and from the Actions menu or in the section below the left Actions panel, select Connect. This will display a Remote Desktop–like window that shows that the computer is turned off. Now, from the Actions menu or from the Actions panel, select Start.

From this point, you can start, stop, pause, and take "snapshots" of the virtual machine's current configuration using the Hyper-V manager window, and you interact with the VM through the Virtual Machine Connection window, which is shown in Figure A.2. (A snapshot is a backup that you can use to restore the virtual machine's hard disk to the exact contents it had when the snapshot was taken.)

Figure A.2
The Virtual Machine Connection program lets you view and interact with a virtual machine.

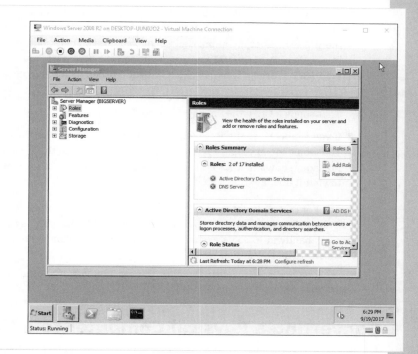

Here are some tips for interacting with the VM:

- Once you have an operating system installed and running, try to install the Hyper-V Integration Services (IS) inside the VM. There are versions for Windows and Linux. This installs modified disk, network, and mouse drivers inside the VM that "know" about the Hyper-V environment and communicate directly with your real disk, network, and mouse without going through the overhead of working with simulated hardware. For Windows operating systems, IS lets you cut and paste between the host and guest operating systems, and it makes the mouse smoothly cross in and out of the Virtual Machine Connection window.

  To install Integration Services, in the Virtual Machine Connection window, select Action, Insert Integration Services Setup Disk. This attaches a CD image file to the VM, and from there, Auto-run should run the IS installer. If the installer doesn't start automatically, locate the CD drive inside the VM and run the setup program manually.

- Until you install the Integration Services, you have to click the mouse inside the Virtual Machine Connection window for the guest OS to see it, and once you do, the guest "captures" the mouse. It won't leave the connection window. Press Ctrl+Alt+Left arrow to release it back to Windows 10.

- Use the Media menu item to select CD, DVD, and floppy disk images to mount inside the VM.

- When you're finished working with the VM, you have several choices: You can shut it down using the guest OS's own internal menus; you can click Action, Shut Down to send the signal the VM would get if you pressed a real computer's Power button; or you can click Action, Save to store a copy of the VM's current state to your hard disk. You can resume it later. (This is like hibernation, except it happens outside rather than inside the guest OS.)

- If the guest operating system requires you to press Ctrl+Alt+Del to sign in, press Ctrl+Alt+End. That sends a Ctrl+Alt+Del keystroke to the guest.

- If you simply close the Virtual Machine Connection window, the guest OS *does not stop running*. You won't see anything saying that it's running even in the Task Manager. Only the Hyper-V Manager shows that it's still active. You must reconnect to the VM or use the Hyper-V Manager to shut it down.

Remember that a virtual machine can tie up a considerable amount of your computer's RAM. If it's cranking away at something, it will keep your CPU busy on its tasks and can up use your network bandwidth. So be aware that having virtual machines running takes resources away from Windows 10 and your own work.

There is plenty more to using Hyper-V. You can find lots of information online at https://technet.microsoft.com.

Converting a Physical Computer to a VM

If you're like me, you probably have one or two old computers that you rarely use anymore but you keep around because of one application you use once or twice a year, and some files you *might* want to get to someday. If so, you may be able to vacuum up the contents of its hard disk into a virtual machine so that you can run the old computer anytime you want, right from within Windows 10. Older computers often have hard disks that are fairly small by today's standards—under 300GB in most cases, with most of that unused—so copying their contents into a single file on your new hard disk, which might be 2 TB or more, isn't that unreasonable.

We'll give you the procedure for Hyper-V. Other products such as VMware have their own physical-to-virtual disk tools. This procedure isn't guaranteed to work, but it's worth a shot.

First, prepare the old machine for imaging. Clean up anything you can think of cleaning up: Run the Disk Cleanup Wizard, delete temporary Internet files, and so on. If you feel daring, run Device Manager to delete the installed network and display adapters, but this step is optional. Remove any huge files you're certain you don't want. Remove any unwanted startup programs. (The free tool live.sysinternals.com/autoruns.exe is great for finding these.) Then empty the Recycle Bin.

The next step is to capture an image of the hard disk in the old computer. You can temporarily install the old disk in your new computer, or you can perform the imaging step on the old computer and then either save the image file on a detachable USB hard drive or save it across the network to your Windows 10 computer. To create the image, download and run Disk2VHD from sysinternals.com. (This site is owned by Microsoft, by the way, and it's safe.) Follow Disk2VHD's instructions to create an image of the old disk. Leave Create Vhdx checked to create the newer *.vhdx* file format, unless you also want to use the disk image with other virtualization programs such as VirtualBox. Save the .vhdx or *.vhd* file directly to your Windows 10 computer, or transport it on a removable drive and then copy it to your Windows 10 computer. Put the file on your Windows 10 system in c:\users\Public\Documents\Hyper-V\Virtual Hard Disks.

Now, on Windows 10, run the Hyper-V Manager and create a new VM using the steps described earlier in this appendix, but with these changes:

- At the Connect Virtual Hard Disk Step, select Use an Existing Virtual Hard Disk and then browse to the .vhdx or .vhd file you created in the previous step.

- Under Installation Options, select Install an Operating System Later.

- When you boot the machine for the first time, install the Integration Options.

Windows XP Mode Virtual Machines

If you used Windows XP Mode under Windows 7, you have a fully bootable VHD file containing Windows XP that has your old Windows applications and data already set up, and you might want to continue to use it under Windows 10. Unfortunately, this copy of Windows XP is not licensed to be used on Windows 10, and if you try to do so, Windows product activation enforces the license restriction. You technically can move a Windows XP Mode virtual machine to Hyper-V, but once you start it up, Windows XP detects the new environment and initiates a product activation cycle that you can't complete.

You can, however, keep the XP Mode virtual hard disk and the files it contains. Open the Windows XP Mode application, and from within it, use the DISK2VHD application described in the previous section to create a snapshot of the disk as seen from *inside* the copy of XP. (Windows XP Mode overlays many separate VHD files, and only from within XP Mode do you see the correct, composite disk image.) Copy the created image file to your Windows 10 computer. On Windows 10, you can double-click this file's icon to mount and view the contents of the virtual hard disk file. Then you can copy files out of the disk image.

Windows 10 as a Guest: Running Windows 10 Inside Other Operating Systems

You can run Windows 10 as a guest operating system in some virtual machine host systems. It runs well in Hyper-V, so you can run a Windows 10 guest inside a Windows 10 host. (Why would someone do that? Here are a couple of reasons: for sandboxing; that is, testing software in an environment where it can't do any damage, and for testing software on all the various editions in both 32-bit and 64-bit versions.) You also might want to work with Windows 10 on a computer that happens to run Mac OS X, Linux, or an older version of Windows as its primary OS.

If the host OS runs a 64-bit operating system, you should be able to install and run both the 32-bit and the 64-bit versions of Windows 10. If the host runs as a 32-bit operating system, you will only be able to run the 32-bit versions of Windows 10.

At the time this was written, and as we mentioned earlier, Microsoft's Hyper-V, Oracle's VirtualBox, and VMware's VMware Workstation can run Windows 10 as a guest. By the time you read this, other VM software vendors might have made their products able to run Windows 10. These products are available for Windows XP through Windows 10, Mac OS X, and Linux, so you can run Windows 10 within any of these host operating systems.

Unfortunately, neither Microsoft Virtual PC nor Windows Virtual PC can run Windows 10 as a guest OS. These programs were available as free downloads for Windows 7, Vista, and XP. You can run Windows 10 on these older versions of Windows using one of the aforementioned third-party VM applications. Windows 10 runs well in VirtualBox, but it works only if the CPU in the host computer has hardware virtualization support.

 note

Be sure to check the licensing terms for your copy of Windows 10 to see whether you can install it in a virtual machine. Generally, the OEM licenses for a copy of Windows 10 that comes preinstalled on a new computer are tied to the computer itself. You might be able to run your copy of Windows 10 in a VM on the same computer. (This capability can be useful, as we mentioned earlier, for testing and sandboxing.) To run Windows 10 on a different computer, you would need an additional license.

Booting a VHD File on Hardware

If you have Windows 7 Ultimate or Enterprise, Windows 8.1 Professional or Enterprise, Windows 8.1 Professional or Enterprise, Windows 10 Professional, Enterprise or Education, or Windows Server versions from Server 2008R2 and up, your computer can physically boot and run these operating systems from installations stored in a VHD virtual disk file. You can take advantage of this to physically boot and run the operating system stored within the VHD file directly, with your computer's real display and other hardware, rather than in a virtual machine. We recommend making a backup copy of the VHD file before you try this.

To set up a new boot option, you can use an inexpensive third-party GUI boot manager tool such as EasyBCD (www.neosmart.net), or you can use the BCDEDIT command-line tool provided with Windows. Follow these steps:

1. Open an elevated Command Prompt window. To do this on Windows 10, press Windows Logo+X and then select Command Prompt (Admin) on the pop-up menu.

2. Type the following command:

   ```
   bcdedit /copy {default} /d "New Name"
   ```

   Replace *New Name* with the name you'd like to give the new boot option—something like Windows 7 Ultimate 32bit VHD. This will print a new globally unique identifier (GUID), something like {e88fb488-e1a9-11dd-8a96-a967342a44b3}.

3. Press Alt+Space and type **E K** to prepare to copy text to the clipboard. Then use the mouse to select the new GUID, including its curly brackets, and press Enter. (On Windows 10, you might be able to just highlight the text and press Ctrl+C, but the preceding method always works.)

4. Type the following three commands, replacing {*guid*} with the identifier you just copied. Press Ctrl+V or Alt+Space **E P** to paste it in. Type the actual path to your bootable VHD file in place of [*C:*]*path**filename*. In these commands, the square brackets don't mean that the drive letter is optional; you really must type them in literally, as shown.

```
bcdedit /set {guid} device vhd="[C:]\path\filename.vhd"
bcdedit /set {guid} osdevice vhd="[C:]\path\filename.vhd"
bcdedit /set {guid} detecthal on
```

Now you should be able to restart and select the new OS entry from the boot menu.

When the VHD copy of Windows starts, it will see your computer's physical hardware for the first time and *should* install the appropriate devices. You should be able to switch back and forth between booting it on real hardware and booting it inside Hyper-V or another VM manager. There could conceivably be some complaining by Windows Product Activation; however, a license that covers a VM installation should cover the bare-metal execution of the same OS installation as well, because it's all installed on the same hardware and CPU. The OS may *see* different hardware due to virtualization, but it's running on the same system in both cases.

---

 note

My experience has been that the boot manager installed on your real hard disk has come from the same or a more recent version than the version of Windows you're trying to boot from VHD. This means that if your computer has, say, only Windows 7 installed on its hard disk, it won't be able to boot Windows 10 from a VHD file successfully. A Windows 10 computer, though, can boot and run Windows 7 through 10 from a VHD file.

Also, be aware that Windows will not be able to perform a full-version update to a copy of Windows 10 booted from a VHD file. Windows Update will be able to install patches, but it will not perform an update that requires a full Windows installation. To do that, you would have to boot the VHD file within a virtual machine program such as VirtualBox or Hyper-V.

B

COMMAND-LINE UTILITIES

Working with Disk Management Tools

Windows 10 comes with a large collection of command-line disk management tools that enable you to check disks or partitions for errors, as well as defragment, format, partition, and convert disks. Table B.1 lists the disk management tools you can use with Windows 10.

 If you need a refresher on accessing and using the command line, see Chapter 30, "Command-Line and Automation Tools."

🔍 note

In this section, we use the word *volume* to refer to any disk, partition, or mount point.

The next three sections give you more detailed coverage of the CHKDSK, CHKNTFS, and DEFRAG tools.

Table B.1 Windows 10's Command-Line Disk Management Tools

Tool	Description
CHKDSK	Checks a specified volume for errors.
CHKNTFS	Configures automatic disk checking.
CONVERT	Converts a specified volume to a different file system.
DEFRAG	Defragments a specified volume.
DISKCOMP	Compares the contents of two floppy disks. (This tool does not compare hard disks or other types of removable media, such as memory cards.)
DISKCOPY	Copies the contents of one floppy disk to another. (This tool does not copy hard disks or other types of removable media, such as memory cards.)
DISKPART	Enables you to list, create, select, delete, and extend disk partitions.
EXPAND	Extracts one or more files from a compressed file, such as a.cab file found on some installation discs.
FORMAT	Formats the specified volume.
FSUTIL	Performs a number of file system tasks.
LABEL	Changes or deletes the name of a specified volume.
MOUNTVOL	Creates, displays, or deletes a mount point.
VOL	Displays the name and serial number of a specified volume.

CHKDSK: Checking for Hard Disk Errors

In Chapter 25, "Managing Hard Disks and Storage Spaces," you learned how to use the Check Disk utility to check a hard disk for errors. Check Disk also comes with a command-line version called CHKDSK that you can run in a Command Prompt window.

Here's the syntax for CHKDSK:

```
CHKDSK [volume [filename]] [/F] [/V] [/R] [/B] [/X] [/I] [/C] [/L:[size]] [/scan]
[/forceofflinefix] [/perf] [/spotfix] [/freeorphanedchains] [/markclean]
[/offlinescanandfix] [/sdcleanup]
```

volume	The drive letter (followed by a colon) or mount point.
filename	On FAT16 and FAT32 disks, the name of the file to check. Include the path if the file isn't in the current folder.
/F	Tells CHKDSK to fix errors automatically and then mark the *volume* as clean (that is, error-free). This is the same as running the Check Disk GUI with the Automatically Fix File System Errors option activated.
/V	Runs CHKDSK in verbose mode. On FAT16 and FAT32 drives, CHKDSK displays the path and name of every file on the disk; on NTFS drives, CHKDSK displays cleanup messages, if any.

/R	Tells CHKDSK to scan the disk surface for bad sectors and recover data from the bad sectors, if possible. (The /F switch is implied.) This is the same as running the Check Disk GUI with the Scan For and Attempt Recovery of Bad Sectors option activated.
/B	Tells CHKDSK to clear the list of bad sectors on the disk and then recheck the entire disk. Including this parameter is the same as including the /R parameter.
/X	On NTFS nonsystem disks that have open files, forces the volume to dismount, invalidates the open file handles, and then runs the scan. (The /F switch is implied.)
/I	On NTFS disks, tells CHKDSK to check only the file system's index entries.
/C	On NTFS disks, tells CHKDSK to skip the checking of cycles within the folder structure. This is a rare error, so using /C to skip the cycle check can speed up the disk check.
/L:[*size*]	On NTFS disks, tells CHKDSK to set the size of its log file to the specified number of kilobytes. The default size is 65,536, which is plenty big enough for most systems, so you should never need to change the size. Note that if you include this switch without the *size* parameter, CHKDSK tells you the current size of the log file.
/scan	On NTFS disks, scans the volume for errors while leaving the volume online.
/forceofflinefix	On NTFS disks, forces CHKDSK to queue all volume errors for offline repair, even errors that can be fixed while the volume is online. The /scan parameter must also be included.
/perf	On NTFS disks, requests more system resources to increase scan performance. The /scan parameter must also be included.
/spotfix	On NTFS disks, spot fixes the volume.
/freeorphanedchains	On FAT/FAT32 disks, tells CHKDSK to free any chains of orphaned clusters for other files to use. If you don't include this switch, CHKDSK tries to recover the data from orphaned clusters.
/markclean	On FAT/FAT32 disks, marks the volume as clean if CHKDSK doesn't find errors. This works even if you don't include the /F switch.
/offlinescanandfix	On NTFS disks, takes the volume offline and runs a scan and repair on the volume.
/sdcleanup	On NTFS disks, removes security descriptor data that is no longer needed. (The /F switch is implied.)

For example, to run a read-only check—that is, a check that doesn't repair errors—on drive C, you enter the following command:

```
chkdsk c:
```

Note that when you use the /F switch to fix errors, CHKDSK must lock the volume to prevent running processes from using the volume during the check. If you use the /F switch on the %SystemDrive%, which is the drive where Windows 10 is installed (usually drive C:), CHKDSK can't lock the drive, and you see the following message:

note

To run the CHKDSK utility on the system drive, you must use an administrator Command Prompt session. Press Windows Logo+X (or right-click the Start button), click Command Prompt (Admin), and then enter your User Account Control credentials.

```
Cannot lock current drive.
Chkdsk cannot run because the volume is in use by another
process. Would you like to schedule this volume to be
checked the next time the system restarts? (Y/N)
```

If you press Y and Enter, CHKDSK schedules a check for drive C: to run the next time you reboot Windows 10.

CHKNTFS: Scheduling Automatic Disk Checks

You saw in the preceding section that CHKDSK prompts you to schedule an automatic disk check during the next reboot if you run CHKDSK /F on the system drive (usually drive C: in Windows 10).

If you press Y and Enter at these prompts, CHKDSK adds the AUTOCHK utility to the following Registry setting:

```
HKLM\SYSTEM\CurrentControlSet\Control\Session Manager\BootExecute
```

This setting specifies the programs that Windows 10 should run at boot time when the Session Manager is loading. AUTOCHK is the automatic version of CHKDSK that runs at system startup.

Windows 10 also comes with a command-line tool named CHKNTFS that enables you to cancel pending automatic disk checks, schedule boot-time disk checks without using CHKDSK, and set the time that AUTOCHK counts down before running the automatic disk checks.

Here's the syntax for CHKNTFS:

```
CHKNTFS [volume ][/C volume:] [/X volume:] [/D] [/T:[time]]
```

volume	Specifies a drive letter (followed by a colon) or mount point.
/C *volume*	Tells CHKNTFS to schedule an automatic startup disk check for the specified volume. You can specify multiple volumes (separated by spaces).
/X *volume*	Tells CHKNTFS to exclude the specified *volume* from an automatic startup disk check. You can specify multiple volumes (separated by spaces).
/D	Tells CHKNTFS to exclude all volumes from an automatic startup disk check.
/T:[*time*]	Specifies the time that AUTOCHK counts down before starting the automatic disk checks.

When you run CHKNTFS with just a volume name, you see one of the following:

- If the volume is not scheduled for a startup disk check, you see the volume's file system:

  `The type of the file system is NTFS.`

- If the volume is scheduled for a startup disk check, you see the following message:

  `Chkdsk has been scheduled manually to run on next reboot.`

- If Windows 10's Storage Manager has detected an error on the volume, it marks the volume as *dirty*, so in this case, you see the following message (using drive C: as an example):

  `C: is dirty. You may use the /C option to schedule chkdsk for this drive.`

This last message is confusing because Windows 10 *always* performs an automatic startup disk check of any volume that's marked as dirty. What you can do with CHKNTFS is bypass the automatic startup disk check of any volume that is marked as dirty. To do that, run CHKNTFS with the /X switch, as in this example:

`chkntfs /x c:`

If a volume isn't already marked as dirty, you can force CHKDSK to check a volume at startup by running CHKNTFS with the /C switch. For example, the following command sets up an automatic start check for the D: drive:

`chkntfs /c d:`

Note that the /C switch is cumulative, meaning that if you run it multiple times and specify a different volume each time, CHKNTFS adds each new volume to the list of volumes to check at startup. Instead of running multiple commands, however, you can specify multiple volumes in a single command, like so:

`chkntfs /c c: d:`

 To learn how to add Command Prompt (Admin) to the Start Menu's shortcut menu, **see** *"Adding Command Prompt to the Shortcut Menu," p. 129.*

If you know a volume has been scheduled for a startup check but you want to cancel that check, run CHKNTFS with the /X switch, as in this example:

`chkntfs /x d:`

 note

To manually mark a volume as dirty, use the FSUTIL DIRTY SET *volume* command, where *volume* is the drive you want to work with. For example, the following command marks drive C: as dirty:

`fsutil dirty set c:`

If you're not sure whether a drive is dirty, either run CHKNTFS *volume* or run FSUTIL DIRTY QUERY *volume*, as in this example:

`fsutil dirty query c:`

Note, however, that FSUTIL doesn't give you any way to unmark a drive as dirty.

note

To run the CHKNTFS utility on the system drive, you must use an administrator Command Prompt session. Press Windows Logo+X (or right-click the Start button), click Command Prompt (Admin), and then enter your User Account Control credentials.

You can also specify multiple volumes if needed:

```
chkntfs /x c: d:
```

If you know that multiple volumes are scheduled for automatic startup checks, you can cancel all the checks by running CHKNTFS with the /D switch:

```
chkntfs /d
```

If you've scheduled a startup check for one or more volumes, or if a volume is marked as dirty, the next time you reboot Windows 10, you see a message similar to the following (which uses drive C: as an example):

```
Checking file system on C:
The type of the file system is NTFS.
Volume label is SYS.

One of your disks needs to be checked for consistency. You
may cancel the disk check, but it is strongly recommended
that you continue.
To skip disk checking, press any key within 10 second(s).
```

The number of seconds in the last line counts down to 0. If you press a key before the countdown ends, Windows 10 skips the disk check; otherwise, it continues with CHKDSK.

You can change the initial countdown value by running CHKNTFS with the /T switch, followed by the number of seconds you want to use for the countdown. For example, the following command sets the countdown to 30 seconds:

⚠ caution

Pressing any key to skip the disk check usually works only with wired keyboards. On most wireless keyboards, pressing a key has no effect.

```
chkntfs /t:30
```

Note that if you run the command CHKNTFS /T (that is, you don't specify a countdown value), CHKNTFS returns the current countdown value.

DEFRAG: Defragmenting the System Drive

In Chapter 25, you learned how to defragment a volume using Windows 10's Optimize Drives program. If you want to schedule a defragment or perform this chore from a batch file, you have to use the DEFRAG command-line tool. Here's the syntax:

```
DEFRAG disks [task(s)] [/A] [/C] [/D] [/E] [/G] [/H] [/I n] [/K] [/L] [/M] [/O] [/T] [/U]
[/V] [/X]
```

disks	Specifies the drive letter (followed by a colon) of each disk you want to defragment. (Separate multiple drives with a space.)
task(s)	As this book went to press, Microsoft had not provided information on this new parameter.
/A	Tells DEFRAG only to analyze the disk.

Switch	Description
/C	Tells DEFRAG to defragment all the system's drives.
/D	Tells DEFRAG to run a traditional optimization (that is, one that does not include the *task(s)* parameter; this is the default switch, meaning that this is the type of optimization that DEFRAG runs if you don't specify switches).
/E	Tells DEFRAG to defragment all the system's drives except those specified with the disks parameter.
/G	Optimize the drive's storage tiers.
/H	Runs DEFRAG with a higher program priority for better performance.
/I *n*	Tells DEFRAG to run tier optimization for at most *n* seconds.
/K	Runs DEFRAG as a slab consolidation, which, if you use a storage pool on a thinly provisioned volume, moves data from lightly used allocation units—called slabs—to more heavily used slabs, thus enabling the lightly used (and now empty) slabs to be returned to the storage pool.
/L	Runs DEFRAG as a retrim operation on a solid-state drive (SSD), which marks all sectors formerly used by deleted files as not being currently in use.
/M	Tells DEFRAG to defragment all the specified drives at the same time (in parallel).
/O	Tells DEFRAG to analyze each type of media being used during the operation and to modify the type of optimization based on each media type.
/T	Tells DEFRAG to show the progress of an already running defrag.
/U	Tells DEFRAG to show the progress of the defrag.
/V	Runs DEFRAG in verbose mode, which displays both the analysis report and the defragmentation report.
/X	Consolidates the free space on the volume.

 note

To run the DEFRAG utility, you must use an administrator Command Prompt session. Press Windows Logo+X (or right-click the Start button), click Command Prompt (Admin), and then enter your User Account Control credentials.

For example, to get an analysis report of the fragmentation of drive C:, enter the following command:

```
defrag c: /a
```

If the volume isn't too fragmented, you see a report similar to this:

```
Post Defragmentation Report:
        Volume Information:
            Volume size            = 116.49 GB
            Free space             = 106.89 GB
            Total fragmented space = 1%
            Largest free space size = 56.49 GB
```

```
        Note: File fragments larger than 64MB are not
        included in the fragmentation statistics.
        You do not need to defragment this volume.
```

However, if the drive is quite fragmented, you see a report similar to the following:

```
Post Defragmentation Report:
        Volume Information:
            Volume size              = 397.12 GB
            Free space               = 198.32 GB
            Total fragmented space   = 9%
            Largest free space size  = 158.43 GB
        Note: File fragments larger than 64MB are not
        included in the fragmentation statistics.
```

It is recommended that you defragment this volume.

If you try to defragment a volume that is running low on disk space, DEFRAG displays the following message:

```
Volume DATA has only 9% free space available for use by Disk Defragmenter.
To run effectively, Disk Defragmenter requires at least 15% usable free space.
There is not enough disk space to properly complete the operation.
Delete some unneeded files on your hard disk, and then try again.
```

Working with File and Folder Management Tools

File Explorer is the GUI tool of choice for most file and folder operations. However, Windows 10 comes with an impressive collection of command-line file and folder tools that let you perform all the standard operations, such as renaming, copying, moving, and deleting, as well as more interesting chores, such as changing file attributes and comparing the contents of two files. Table B.2 lists the file and folder management tools you can use with Windows 10.

Table B.2 Windows 10's Command-Line File and Folder Management Tools

Tool	Description
ATTRIB	Displays, applies, or removes attributes for the specified file or folder.
CD	Changes to the specified folder.
COMP	Compares the contents of two specified files, byte by byte.
COMPACT	Displays or modifies the compression settings for the specified file or folder (which must be located on an NTFS partition).
COPY	Creates a copy of the specified file or folder in another location.
DEL	Deletes the specified file or folder.
DIR	Displays a directory listing for the current folder or for the specified file or folder.

Tool	Description
FC	Compares the content of two specified files.
FIND	Searches for and displays all the instances of a specified string in a file.
FINDSTR	Uses a regular expression to search for and display all the instances of a specified string in a file.
MKDIR	Creates the specified folder.
MOVE	Moves the specified file or folder to another location.
REN	Changes the name of the specified file or folder.
REPLACE	Replaces files in the destination folder with files in the source folder that have the same name.
RMDIR	Deletes the specified folder.
SORT	Sorts the specified file and then displays the results.
SFC	Runs the System File Checker, which scans and verifies the protected Windows 10 files.
TAKEOWN	Enables an administrator to take ownership of the specified file.
TREE	Displays a graphical tree diagram showing the subfolder hierarchy of the current folder or the specified folder.
WHERE	Searches for and displays all the files that match a specified pattern in the current folder and in the PATH folders.
XCOPY	Creates a copy of the specified file or folder in another location. This tool offers many more options than the COPY command.

The next few sections take a closer look at a half dozen of these tools: ATTRIB, FIND, REN, REPLACE, SORT, and XCOPY.

Before getting to the tools, we should mention that most of the file and folder management tools work with the standard wildcard characters: ? and *. In a file or folder specification, you use ? to substitute for a single character, and you use * to substitute for multiple characters. Here are some examples:

File Specification	Matches
Budget201?.xlsx	Budget2017.xlsx, Budget2018.xlsx, and so on
Memo.doc?	Memo.doc, Memo.docx, Memo.docm, and so on
*.txt	ReadMe.txt, log.txt, to-do.txt, and so on
*201?.pptx	Report2016.pptx, Budget2017.pptx, Conference2018.pptx, and so on
.	Every file

ATTRIB: **Modifying File and Folder Attributes**

A file's *attributes* are special codes that indicate the status of the file. There are nine attributes you can work with:

- **Archive**—When this attribute is turned on, it means the file has been modified since it was last backed up.

- **Hidden**—When this attribute is turned on, it means the file doesn't show up in a DIR listing and isn't included when you run most command-line tools. For example, if you run DEL *.* in a folder, Windows 10 deletes all the files in that folder, except the hidden files.

- **Integrity**—When this attribute is set, it means the volume is configured with *integrity*, where data is stored in such a way that it is protected from certain types of file errors. Although technically available in Windows 10, this attribute works only with Windows 10 Server volumes formatted with the Resilient File System (ReFS) file system.

- **Offline**—When this attribute is turned on, it indicates that the file is not currently available because its data has been moved to offline storage.

- **No scrub**—When this attribute is set, the file is skipped by the scrubber, which is a background service that identifies and (if possible) fixes certain types of file errors. Again, this attribute works only with Windows 10 Server volumes formatted with the ReFS file system.

- **Not content indexed**—When this attribute is set, the file's contents will not be indexed for searching.

- **Read-only**—When this attribute is turned on, it means the file can't be modified or erased.

- **Pinned**—When this attribute is set, it indicates the file is an NTFS *sparse* file. This tells Windows to allocate on disk only the file's nonzero (meaningful) data.

- **System**—When this attribute is turned on, it means the file is an operating system file (that is, a file that was installed with Windows 10).

The ATTRIB command lets you turn these attributes on or off. Here's the syntax:

```
ATTRIB [+A ¦ -A] [+H ¦ -H] [+I ¦ -I] [+O ¦ -O] [+P ¦ -P] [+R ¦ -R] [+S ¦ -S] [+U ¦ -U]
[+V ¦ -V] [+X ¦ -X]
filename [/S [/D] [/L]]
```

+A	Sets the archive attribute.
-A	Clears the archive attribute.
+H	Sets the hidden attribute.
-H	Clears the hidden attribute.
+I	Sets the content not indexed attribute.
-I	Clears the content not indexed attribute.
+O	Sets the offline attribute.

-O	Clears the offline attribute.
+P	Sets the pinned attribute.
-P	Clears the pinned attribute.
+R	Sets the read-only attribute.
-R	Clears the read-only attribute.
+S	Sets the system attribute.
-S	Clears the system attribute.
+U	Sets the integrity attribute.
-U	Clears the integrity attribute.
+V	Sets the integrity attribute.
-V	Clears the integrity attribute.
+X	Sets the no scrub attribute.
-X	Clears the no scrub attribute.
filename	Specifies the file or files you want to work with.
/S	Applies the attribute change to the matching files in the current folder and all of its subfolders.
/D	Applies the attribute change only to the current folder's subfolders. You must use this switch with /S.
/L	Applies the command to a symbolic link (that is, an NTFS file system object that points to another file system object, which is called the target) rather than to the target of the symbolic link.

For example, if you want to hide all the .docx files in the current directory, use the following command:

```
attrib +h *.docx
```

As another example, if you've ever tried to delete or edit a file and received the message "Access denied," the file is likely read-only. You can turn off the read-only attribute by running ATTRIB with the -R switch, as in this example:

```
attrib -r readonly.txt
```

You can also use ATTRIB for protecting important or sensitive files. When you hide a file, it doesn't show up in a listing produced by the DIR command. Out of sight is out of mind, so someone taking a casual glance at your files won't see the hidden ones and, therefore, won't be tempted to display or erase them.

Although a hidden file is invisible, it's not totally safe. Someone who knows the name of the file can attempt to modify the file by opening it with the appropriate program. As an added

 note

If you want to check out a file's attributes, use the DIR command's /A switch. Use /AA to see files with their archive attribute set; /AH for hidden files; /AI for not content indexed files; /AR for read-only files; /AS for system files; and /AX for integrity files.

measure of safety, you can set the file's read-only attribute. When you do this, the file can't be modified. You can set both attributes by using a single command:

```
attrib +h +r payroll.xlsx
```

FIND: Locating a Text String in a File

You use the FIND command to search for a string inside a file. Here's the syntax:

```
FIND [/C] [/I] [/N] [/V] [/OFF[LINE]] "string" filename
```

/C	Displays the number of times that *string* appears in filename.
/I	Performs a search that is not case sensitive.
/N	Displays each match of *string* in *filename* with the line number in *filename* where each match occurs.
/V	Displays the lines in *filename* that don't contain *string*.
/OFF[LINE]	Tells FIND to not skip files that have their offline attribute set.
string	Specifies the string you want to search for.
filename	Specifies the file you want to search in. (Note that you can't use wildcards with the FIND command.) If the filename contains one or more spaces, surround it with double quotation marks.

For example, to find the string *Xbox* in a file named WishList.txt, you use the following command:

```
find "Xbox" WishList.txt
```

If the string you want to find contains double quotation marks, you need to place two quotation marks in the search string. For example, to find the phrase *Dave "The Hammer" Schultz* in the file players.doc, use the following command:

```
find "Dave ""The Hammer"" Schultz" players.doc
```

 note

The FIND command doesn't work with the XML-based file formats used in Microsoft Office 2007 and later. However, it works fine with most documents created in earlier versions of Office.

 tip

The FIND command doesn't accept wildcard characters in the filename parameter. That's too bad because it's often useful to search multiple files for a string. Fortunately, you can work around this limitation by using a FOR loop where the command you run on each file is FIND. Here's the general syntax to use:

```
FOR %f IN (filespec) DO FIND "string" %f
```

Replace filespec with the file specification you want to use and *string* with the string you want to search for. For example, the following command runs through all the .doc files in the current folder and searches each file for the string *Thanksgiving*:

```
FOR %f IN (*.doc) DO FIND "Thanksgiving" %f
```

If the file specification will match files with spaces in their names, you need to surround the last %f parameter with quotation marks, like so:

```
FOR %f IN (*.doc) DO FIND "Thanksgiving" "%f"
```

One of the most common uses of the FIND command is as a filter in pipe operations. In this case, instead of a filename, you pipe the output of another command through FIND. In this case, FIND searches this input for a specified string and, if it finds a match, displays the line that contains the string.

For example, the last line of a DIR listing tells you the number of bytes free on the current drive. Rather than wade through the entire DIR output just to get this information, use this command instead:

```
dir ¦ find "free"
```

You'll see something like the following:

```
2 Dir(s) 28,903,331,184 bytes free
```

FIND scours the DIR listing piped to it and looks for the word *free*. You can use this technique to display specific lines from, say, a CHKDSK report. For example, searching for *bad* finds the number of bad sectors on the disk.

REN: Renaming a File or Folder

You use the REN (or RENAME) command to change the name of one or more files and folders. Here's the syntax:

```
REN old_filename new_filename
```

old_filename	The original filename
new_filename	The new filename

For example, the following command renames Budget 2017.xlsx to Budget 20187.xlsx:

```
ren "Budget 2017.xlsx" "Budget 2018.xlsx"
```

A simple file or folder rename such as this probably isn't something you'll ever fire up a command-line session to do because renaming a single object is faster and easier in File Explorer. However, the real power of the REN command is that it accepts wildcards in the file specifications. This enables you to rename several files at once—something you can't do in File Explorer.

For example, suppose you have a folder full of files, many of which contain 2017 somewhere in the filename. To rename all those files by changing 2017 to 2018, you would use the following command:

```
ren *2017* *2018*
```

Similarly, if you have a folder full of files that use the .htm extension and you want to change each extension to .asp, you use the following command:

```
ren *.htm *.asp
```

Note that for these multiple-file renames to work, in most cases the original filename text and the new filename text must be the same length. For example, digital cameras often supply photos with names such as `img_1234.jpg` and `img_5678.jpg`. If you have a number of related photos in a folder, you might want to give them more meaningful names. If the photos are from a vacation in Rome, you might prefer names such as `Rome_Vacation_1234.jpg` and `Rome_Vacation_5678.jpg`. Unfortunately, the REN command can't handle this type of change. However, it can rename the files to `Rome_1234.jpg` and `Rome_5678.jpg`:

```
ren img_* Rome*
```

The exception to the same-length rule is if the replacement occurs at the end of the filenames. For example, the following command renames all files with the `.jpeg` extension to `.jpg`:

```
ren *.jpeg *.jpg
```

REPLACE: Smarter File Copying

If there was such a thing as a Most Underrated Command award, REPLACE would win it hands down. This command, which you almost never hear about, can do three very useful (and very different) things:

- It copies files, but only if their names match those in the target directory.
- It copies files, but only if their names don't exist in the target directory.
- It copies files, but only if their names match those in the target directory and the matching files in the target directory are older than the files being copied.

Here's the syntax:

```
REPLACE source_files target /A /U /P /R /S /W
```

source_files	Indicates the path and file specification of the files you want to copy.
target	Specifies the folder to which you want to copy the files.
/A	Copies only new files to the *target* folder. You can't use this switch with /S or /U.
/U	Copies files that have the same name in the *target* folder and that are newer than the matching files in the *target* folder. You can't use this switch with /A.
/P	Prompts you for confirmation before replacing files.
/R	Replaces read-only files.
/S	Replaces files in the *target* folder's subfolders. You can't use this switch with /A.
/W	Waits for you to insert a disk before starting.

If you don't specify switches, REPLACE copies a file from the source folder to the target folder if and only if it finds a file with a matching name in the target.

More useful is the REPLACE command's updating mode, where it copies a file from the source folder to the target folder if and only if it finds a file with a matching name in the target and that target file is older than the source file. A good example where updating comes in handy is copying some files to a disk or memory card so that you can use them on another machine (such as taking files from your computer at work to use them at home). When you need to copy the files back to the first machine, the following REPLACE command does the job. (This assumes the disk or memory card is in the G: drive.)

```
replace g:*.* %UserProfile% /s /u
```

For each file on the G: drive, REPLACE looks for matching filenames anywhere in the %UserProfile% folder and its subfolders (thanks to the /S switch) and replaces only the ones that are newer (the /U switch).

What if you created some new files on the other computer? To copy those to the first machine, use the /A switch, as follows:

```
replace g:*.* %UserProfile%\Documents /a
```

In this case, REPLACE copies a file from the G: drive only if it doesn't exist in the %UserProfile%\ Documents folder. (You must specify a target folder because you can't use the /S switch with /A.)

SORT: **Sorting the Contents of a File**

When you obtain a file from the Internet or some other source, the data in the file may not appear in the order you want. What we usually do in such cases is import the file into Word or Excel and then use the program's Sort feature. This process sometimes involves extra steps (such as converting text to a table in Word), so it's not always an efficient way to work.

If the file is text, it's often easier and faster to run the SORT command-line tool. By default, SORT takes the content of the file, sorts it in ascending alphanumeric order (0 to 9, then *a* to *z*, and then A to Z) starting at the beginning of each line in the file, and then displays the sorted results. You can also run descending order sorts, write the results to the same file or another file, and more. Here's the syntax:

```
SORT [input_file] [/+n] [/R] [/L locale] [/M kilobytes] [/REC characters]
[/T temp_folder] [/O output_file]
```

input_file	Names the file you want to sort.
/+n	Specifies the starting character position (n) of the sort. The default is 1 (that is, the first character on each line in the file).
/R	Sorts the file in descending order (Z to A, then z to a, and then 9 to 0).
/L *locale*	Specifies a locale for sorting other than the default system locale. Your only choice here is to use "C" to sort the file using the binary values for each character.
/M *kilobytes*	Specifies the amount of memory, in kilobytes, that SORT uses during the operation. If you don't specify this value, SORT uses a minimum of 160KB and a maximum of 90% of available memory.

/REC *characters*	Specifies the maximum length, in characters, of each line in the file. The default value is 4,096 characters, and the maximum value is 65,535 characters.
/T *temp_folder*	Specifies the folder that SORT should use to hold the temporary files it uses during the sort.
/O *output_file*	Specifies the file that SORT should create to store the results of the sort. You can specify a different file or the input file.

For example, the following SORT command sorts the data in records.txt and stores the results in sorted_records.txt:

```
sort records.txt sorted_records.txt
```

XCOPY: Advanced File Copying

The XCOPY command is one of the most powerful of the file management command-line tools, and you can use it for some fairly sophisticated file copying operations. Here's the syntax for XCOPY:

```
XCOPY source destination [/A ¦ /M] [/B] [/C] [/D[:mm-dd--yyyy]]
[/EXCLUDE:file1[+file2[+file3]]] [/F] [/G] [/H] [/I] [/J] [/K] [/L] [/N]
[/O] [/P] [/Q] [/R] [/S [/E]] [/T] [/U] [/V] [/W] [/X] [/Y ¦ -Y] [/Z]
```

source	Specifies the path and names of the files you want to copy.
destination	Indicates the location where you want the source files copied.
[/A]	Tells XCOPY to copy only those *source* files that have their archive attribute turned on. The archive attribute is not changed. If you use /A, you can't also use /M.
[/M]	Tells XCOPY to copy only those *source* files that have their archive attribute turned on. The archive attribute is turned off. If you use /M, you can't also use /A.
[/B]	Tells XCOPY to copy the file's symbolic link instead of the file itself.
[/C]	Tells XCOPY to ignore any errors that occur during the copy operation; otherwise, XCOPY aborts the operation if an error occurs.
[/D[:mm-dd-yyyy]]	Copies only those *source* files that changed on or after the date specified by mm-dd-yyyy. If you don't specify a date, using /D tells XCOPY to copy those *source* files that are newer than *destination* files that have the same name.
[/EXCLUDE: *file1* [+file2[+file3]]]	Tells XCOPY to not copy the files or file specification given by *file1*, *file2*, *file3*, and so on.
[/F]	Displays the *source* and *destination* filename during the copy operation.
[/G]	Creates decrypted copies of encrypted *source* files.
[/H]	Tells XCOPY to include in the copy operation any hidden and system files in the *source* folder.

[/I]	Tells XCOPY to create the *destination* folder. For this to work, the *source* value must be a folder or a file specification with wildcards.
[/J]	Tells XCOPY to use unbuffered input/output during the copy operation, which improves performance for very large files.
[/K]	For each *source* file that has its read-only attribute set, tells XCOPY to maintain the read-only attribute on the corresponding *destination* file.
[/L]	Displays a list of the files that XCOPY will copy. (No files are copied if you use /L.)
[/N]	Tells XCOPY to use 8.3 filenames in the *destination* folder. Use this switch if the *destination* folder is a FAT partition that doesn't support long filenames.
[/O]	Tells XCOPY to also copy ownership and discretionary access control list data to the *destination*.
[/P]	Prompts you to confirm each file copy.
[/Q]	Tells XCOPY not to display messages during the copy.
[/R]	Includes read-only files in the copy.
[/S]	Tells XCOPY to also include the *source* folder's subfolders in the copy.
[/E]	Tells XCOPY to include empty subfolders in the copy if you specify the /S or /T switch.
[/T]	Tells XCOPY to copy the *source* folder subfolder structure. (No files are copied, just the subfolders.)
[/U]	Copies only those source files that exist in the *destination* folder.
[/V]	Tells XCOPY to verify that each *destination* copy is identical to the original *source* file.
[/W]	Displays the message "Press any key to begin copying file(s)" before copying. You must press a key to launch the copy (or press Ctrl+C to cancel).
[/X]	Tells XCOPY to also copy file audit settings and system access control list data to the *destination*. (This switch implies /O.)
[/Y]	Tells XCOPY not to ask you whether you want to overwrite existing files in the *destination*.
[/-Y]	Tells XCOPY to ask you whether you want to overwrite existing files in the *destination*. Use this switch if you've set the %COPYCMD% environment variable to /Y, which suppresses overwrite prompts for XCOPY, COPY, and MOVE.
[/Z]	If you're copying to a network *destination*, this switch tells XCOPY to restart to the copy if the network connection goes down during the operation.

In its basic form, XCOPY works just like COPY. So, for example, to copy all the .doc files in the current folder to a folder called Documents in the G: drive, use the following command:

```
xcopy *.doc g:\documents
```

Besides being faster, XCOPY also contains a number of features not found in the puny COPY command. Think of it as COPY on steroids. (The X in XCOPY means that it's an extended COPY command.) For example, suppose you want to copy all the .doc files in the current folder and all the .doc files in any attached subfolders to G:\Documents. With COPY, you first have to create the appropriate folders on the destination partition and then perform separate COPY commands for each folder, which is not very efficient, to say the least. With XCOPY, all you do is add a single switch:

```
xcopy *.doc g:\documents /s
xcopy *.bat d:\batch /s
```

The /S switch tells XCOPY to copy the current folder and all nonempty subfolders, and to create the appropriate folders in the destination, as needed. (If you want XCOPY to copy empty subfolders, include the /E switch as well.)

Another useful feature of XCOPY is the ability to copy files by date. This is handy for performing incremental backups of files that you modified on or after a specific date. For example, suppose you keep your word processing documents in %UserProfile%\Documents and you want to make backup copies in your Windows 10 user share of all the .doc files that have changed since August 23, 2016. You can do this by using the following command:

```
xcopy %userprofile%\documents\*.doc \\server\users\%Username%\ /d:08-23-2016
```

It's common to use XCOPY in batch files, but take care to handle errors. For example, what if a batch file tries to use XCOPY but there's not enough memory? Or what if the user presses Ctrl+C during the copy? It might seem impossible to check for these kinds of errors; yet doing it is not only possible but also really quite straightforward.

When certain commands finish, they always file a report on the progress of the operation. This report, or exit code, is a number that specifies how the operation went. For example, Table B.3 lists the exit codes that the XCOPY command uses.

Table B.3   XCOPY Exit Codes

Exit Code	What It Means
0	Everything's okay; the files were copied.
1	Nothing happened because no files were found to copy.
2	The user pressed Ctrl+C to abort the copy.
4	The command failed because there wasn't enough memory or disk space, something was wrong with the command's syntax, or an invalid drive name was entered.
5	The command failed because of a disk error.

What does all this mean for your batch files? You can use a variation of the IF command—IF ERRORLEVEL—to test for these exit codes. For example, here's a batch file that uses some of the XCOPY exit codes to check for errors:

```
@ECHO OFF
XCOPY %1 %2
IF ERRORLEVEL 4 GOTO ERROR
IF ERRORLEVEL 2 GOTO CTRL+C
IF ERRORLEVEL 1 GOTO NO_FILES
GOTO DONE
:ERROR
ECHO Bad news! The copy failed because there wasn't
ECHO enough memory or disk space or because there was
ECHO something wrong with your file specs . . .
GOTO DONE
:CTRL+C
ECHO Hey, what gives? You pressed Ctrl+C to abort . . .
GOTO DONE
:NO_FILES
ECHO Bad news! No files were found to copy . . .
:DONE
```

As you can see, the ERRORLEVEL conditions check for the individual exit codes and then use GOTO to jump to the appropriate label.

One of the most important things to know about the IF ERRORLEVEL test is how Windows 10 interprets it. For example, consider the following IF command:

```
IF ERRORLEVEL 2 GOTO CTRL+C
```

Windows 10 interprets this command as "If the exit code from the last command is equal to or greater than 2, jump to the Ctrl+C label." This has two important consequences for your batch files:

note

How does a batch file know what a command's exit code was? When Windows 10 gets an exit code from a command, it stores that code in a special data area set aside for exit code information. When Windows 10 sees the IF ERRORLEVEL command in a batch file, it retrieves the exit code from the data area so that it can be compared to whatever is in the IF condition.

- The test IF ERRORLEVEL 0 doesn't tell you much because it's always true. If you just want to find out whether the command failed, use the test IF NOT ERRORLEVEL 0.

- To get the correct results, always test the *highest* ERRORLEVEL first and then work your way down.

Working with System Management Tools

System management is one of those catchall terms that encompasses a wide range of tasks, from simple adjustments such as changing the system date and time to more complex tweaks such as modifying the Registry. Windows 10's command-line system management tools also enable you to monitor system performance, shut down or restart the computer, and even modify the huge Windows Management Instrumentation (WMI) interface. Table B.4 lists the system management command-line tools that apply to Windows 10.

Table B.4 Windows 10's Command-Line System Management Tools

Tool	Description
BCDEDIT	Displays or modifies the Boot Manager startup parameters
CHCP	Displays or changes the number of active console code pages
DATE	Displays or sets the system date
EVENTCREATE	Creates a custom event in an event log
REG	Adds, modifies, displays, and deletes Registry keys and settings
REGSVR32	Registers dynamic link library (DLL) files as command components in the Registry
SHUTDOWN	Shuts down or restarts Windows 10 or a remote computer
SYSTEMINFO	Displays a wide range of detailed configuration information about the computer
TIME	Displays or sets the system time
TYPEPERF	Monitors a performance counter
WHOAMI	Displays information about the current user, including the domain name (not applicable to Windows 10), computer name, username, security group membership, and security privileges
WMIC	Operates the Windows Management Instrumentation command-line tool that provides command-line access to the WMI interface

The next few sections take more detailed looks at five of these command-line tools: REG, SHUTDOWN, SYSTEMINFO, TYPEPERF, and WHOAMI.

REG: Working with Registry Keys and Settings

In Chapter 29, "Editing the Windows Registry," you learned how to view, add, and modify Registry keys and settings using the Registry Editor. That's the easiest and safest way to make Registry changes. However, there may be some settings that you change quite often. In such cases, it can become burdensome to be frequently launching the Registry Editor and changing the settings. A better idea is to create a shortcut or batch file that uses the REG command-line tool to make your Registry changes for you.

REG actually consists of 11 subcommands, each of which enables you to perform different Registry tasks:

REG ADD	Adds new keys or settings to the Registry. You can also use this command to modify existing settings.
REG QUERY	Displays the current values of one or more settings in one or more keys.
REG COMPARE	Compares the values of two Registry keys or settings.
REG COPY	Copies Registry keys or settings to another part of the Registry.
REG DELETE	Deletes a key or setting.
REG EXPORT	Exports a key to a .reg file.

REG IMPORT	Imports the contents of a `.reg` file.
REG SAVE	Copies Registry keys or settings to a hive (.hiv) file.
REG RESTORE	Writes a hive file into an existing Registry key. The hive file must be created using `REG SAVE`.
REG LOAD	Loads a hive file into a new Registry key. The hive file must be created using `REG SAVE`.
REG UNLOAD	Unloads a hive file that was loaded using `REG LOAD`.

We won't go through all these commands. Instead, we'll focus on the three most common Registry tasks: viewing, adding, and changing Registry data.

To view the current value of the Registry setting, you use the REG QUERY command:

```
REG QUERY KeyName [/V ValueName ¦ /VE] [/C] [/D] [/E] [/F data] [/K ¦ [/S]
   [/SE separator] [/T type] [/Z] [/reg:32 ¦ /reg:64]
```

KeyName	Specifies the Registry key that contains the setting or settings you want to view. The *KeyName* must include a root key value: HKCR, HKCU, HKLM, HKU, or HKCC. Place quotation marks around key names that include spaces.
/V ValueName	Specifies the Registry setting in *KeyName* that you want to view.
/VE	Tells REG to look for empty settings (that is, settings with a null value).
/C	Runs a case-sensitive query.
/E	Returns only exact matches.
/F data	Specifies the data that REG should match in the *KeyName* settings.
/K	Queries only key names, not settings.
/S	Tells REG to query the subkeys of *KeyName*.
/SE separator	Defines the separator to search for in REG_MULTI_SZ settings.
/T type	Specifies the setting type or types to search: REG_SZ, REG_MULTI_SZ, REG_EXPAND_SZ, REG_DWORD, REG_BINARY, or REG_NONE.
/Z	Tells REG to include the numeric equivalent of the setting type in the query results.
/reg:32	Tells REG to access *KeyName* using the 32-bit Registry view.
/reg:64	Tells REG to access *KeyName* using the 64-bit Registry view.

For example, if you want to know the current value of the RegisteredOwner setting in HKLM\ Software\Microsoft\Windows NT\CurrentVersion, run the following command:

```
reg query "hklm\software\microsoft\windows nt\currentversion" registeredowner
```

The Registry Editor has a Find command that enables you to look for text within the Registry. However, it would occasionally be useful to see a list of the Registry keys and settings that contains a particular bit of text. You can do this by using the /F switch. For example, suppose you want to see a list of all the HKLM keys and settings that contain the text *Windows Defender*. Here's a command that will do this:

```
reg query hklm /f "Windows Defender" /s
```

To add a key or setting to the Registry, use the `REG ADD` command:

```
REG ADD KeyName [/V ValueName ¦ /VE] [/D data] [/F ¦ [/S separator] [/T type]
[/reg:32 ¦ /reg:64]
```

KeyName	Specifies the Registry key that you want to add or to which you want to add a setting. The *KeyName* must include a root key value: HKCR, HKCU, HKLM, HKU, or HKCC. Place quotation marks around key names that include spaces.
/V *ValueName*	Specifies the setting you want to add to *KeyName*.
/VE	Tells REG to add an empty setting.
/D *data*	Specifies the data that REG should use as the value for the new setting.
/F	Modifies an existing key or setting without prompting to confirm the change.
/S *separator*	Defines the separator to use between multiple instances of data in a new REG_MULTI_SZ setting.
/T *type*	Specifies the setting type: REG_SZ, REG_MULTI_SZ, REG_EXPAND_SZ, REG_DWORD, REG_DWORD_BIG_ENDIAN, REG_DWORD_LITTLE_ENDIAN, REG_BINARY, or REG_LINK.
/reg:32	Tells REG to access *KeyName* using the 32-bit Registry view.
/reg:64	Tells REG to access *KeyName* using the 64-bit Registry view.

For example, the following command adds a key named `MySettings` to the HKCU root key:

```
reg add hkcu\MySettings
```

Here's another example that adds a setting named `CurrentProject` to the new `MySettings` key and sets the value of the new setting to `Win 8 In Depth`:

```
reg add hkcu\MySettings /v CurrentProject /d "Win 8 In Depth"
```

If you want to make changes to an existing setting, run REG ADD on the setting. For example, to change the `HKCU\MySettings\CurrentProject` setting to `Windows 10 In Depth`, you run the following command:

```
reg add hkcu\MySettings /v CurrentProject /d
"Windows 10 In Depth"
```

Windows 10 responds with the following prompt:

```
Value CurrentProject exists, overwrite (Yes/No)?
```

To change the existing value, press **Y** and press Enter.

 tip

To avoid being prompted when changing existing settings, add the /F switch to the REG ADD command.

SHUTDOWN: **Shutting Down or Restarting the System**

You can use the SHUTDOWN command to restart or shut down your computer (or a remote computer on your network). Here's the full syntax:

```
SHUTDOWN [[/R] ¦ [/G] ¦ [/S] ¦ [/SG] ¦ [/L] ¦ [/H] ¦ [/I] ¦ [/P] ¦ [/E] ¦ [/A] ¦
[/O]] [/F ¦
    [/HYBRID] [/SOFT] [FW] [/D [P¦U:]major:minor] [/M \\ComputerName] [/T seconds]
    [/C "comment"]
```

/R	Restarts the computer.
/G	Restarts the computer and, after you log on, restarts any applications that were running.
/S	Shuts down the computer.
/SG	Shuts down the computer and then restarts any registered applications on the next boot.
/L	Logs off the current user immediately.
/H	Puts the computer into hibernation, if the computer supports hibernation mode.
/I	Displays the Remote Shutdown dialog box, which enables you to specify many of the options provided by these switches.
/P	Turns off the local computer immediately (that is, without the usual warning interval).
/E	Enables you to document the reason for an unexpected shutdown.
/A	Cancels the pending restart or shutdown.
/O	Restarts the PC into the Recovery Environment. You must also include the /R switch.
/F	Forces all running programs on the target computer to shut down without warning. This, obviously, is dangerous and should be used only as a last resort.
/HYBRID	Shuts down the PC and prepares it for a fast restart. You must also include the /S switch.
/SOFT	Skips hardware initialization during the next reboot. You must also include the /S switch.
/FW	During the next restart, automatically boots the PC into its firmware setup utility. You must also include the /S switch.
/D [P¦U:] major:minor]	Specifies the reason for the shutdown. Include P: to indicate the shutdown is planned; include U: to indicate the shutdown is unplanned. Use values between 0 and 255 for major and between 0 and 65535 for minor. Windows also defines a number of predefined values for the major and minor parameters:

major	minor	Reason
0	0	Other
0	5	Other Failure: System Unresponsive

1	1	Hardware: Maintenance
1	2	Hardware: Installation
2	2	Operating System: Recovery
2	3	Operating System: Upgrade
2	4	Operating System: Reconfiguration
2	16	Operating System: Service Pack
2	17	Operating System: Hot Fix
2	18	Operating System: Security Fix
4	1	Application: Maintenance
4	2	Application: Installation
4	5	Application: Unresponsive
4	6	Application: Unstable
5	15	System Failure: Stop Error
5	19	Security Issue
5	20	Loss of Network Connectivity
6	11	Power Failure: Cord Unplugged
6	12	Power Failure: Environment
7	0	Legacy API Shutdown
/M \\ ComputerName	Specifies the remote computer you want to shut down.	
/T seconds	Specifies the number of seconds after which the computer is shut down. The default is 30 seconds, and you can specify any number up to 600.	
/C "comment"	The comment text (which can be a maximum of 127 characters) appears in the dialog box and warns the user of the pending shutdown. This comment text also appears in the shutdown event that is added to the System log in Event Viewer. (Look for an Event ID of 1074.)	

For example, to restart your computer immediately, use the following command:

```
shutdown /r /t 0
```

If you've launched a restart or shutdown using some nonzero value for /T, and you need to cancel the pending shutdown, run SHUTDOWN with the /A switch before the timeout interval is over:

```
shutdown /a
```

SYSTEMINFO: Returning System Configuration Data

If you want to get information about various aspects of your computer, a good place to start is the SYSTEMINFO command-line tool, which displays data about the following aspects of your system:

- The operating system name, version, manufacturer, and configuration type

- The registered owner and organization

- The original install date

- The system boot time

- The computer manufacturer, model, and system type

- The system processors

- The BIOS version

- The total and available physical memory

- The paging file's maximum size, available size, in-use value, and location

- The installed hotfixes

- The network interface card data, such as the name, connection, DHCP status, and IP address (or addresses)

You can see all this data (and more), as well as control the output, by running SYSTEMINFO with the following syntax:

```
SYSTEMINFO [/S computer] [/U [domain]\username] [/P password]
    [/FO format] [/NH]
```

/S computer	Specifies the name of the remote computer for which you want to view the system configuration.
/U [domain]\ username	Indicates the username and, optionally, the domain of the account under which you want to run the SYSTEMINFO command.
/P password	Specifies the password of the account you specified with /U.
/FO format	Indicates the output format, where format is one of the following values:
	table—The output is displayed in a row-and-column format, with headers in the first row and values in subsequent rows.
	list—The output is displayed in a two-column list, with the headers in the first column and values in the second column.
	csv—The output is displayed with headers and values separated by commas. The headers appear on the first line.
/NH	Tells SYSTEMINFO not to include column headers when you use the /FO switch with either table or csv.

The output of SYSTEMINFO is quite long, so pipe it through the MORE command to see the output one screen at a time:

```
systeminfo ¦ more
```

If you want to examine the output in another program or import the results into Excel or Access, redirect the output to a file and use the appropriate format. For example, Excel can read .csv files, so you can redirect the SYSTEMINFO output to a .csv file while using csv as the output format:

```
systeminfo /fo csv > systeminfo.csv
```

TYPEPERF: **Monitoring Performance**

In Chapter 23, "Windows Management Tools," you learned how to use the Performance Monitor utility to track the real-time performance of counters in various categories such as processor and memory.

➡️ For the details on the Performance Monitor utility, **see** "Using the Performance Monitor," **p. 530.**

You can get the same benefit without the Performance Monitor GUI by using the powerful TYPEPERF command-line tool. Here's the syntax:

```
TYPEPERF [counter1 [counter2 ...]] [-CF file] [-O file] [-F format]
  [-SI interval] [-SC samples] [-Q [object]] [-QX [object]]
  [-CONFIG file] [-S computer] [-Y]
```

[counter1 counter2...]	Specifies the path of the performance counter to monitor. If you want to track multiple counters, separate each counter path with a space. If any path includes spaces, surround the path with quotation marks.
-CF file	Loads the counters from file, where file is a text file that lists the counter paths on separate lines.
-O file	Specifies the path and the name of the file that will store the performance data.
-F format	Specifies the format for the output file format given by the /O switch, where format is one of the following values:
	csv—The output is displayed with each counter separated by a comma and each sample on its own line. This is the default output format.
	tsv—The output is displayed with each counter separated by a tab and each sample on its own line.
	bin—The output is displayed in binary format.
-SI interval	Specifies the time interval between samples. The interval parameter uses the form [mm:] ss. The default interval is 1 second.

-SC *samples*	Specifies the number of samples to collect. If you omit this switch, TYPEPERF samples continuously until you press Ctrl+C to cancel.
-Q [*object*]	Lists the available counters for *object* without instances.
-QX [*object*]	Lists the available counters for *object* with instances.
-CONFIG *file*	Specifies the pathname of the settings file that contains the TYPEPERF parameters you want to run.
-S *computer*	Specifies that the performance counters should be monitored on the PC named computer if no *computer* name is specified in the counter path.
-Y	Answers yes to any prompts generated by TYPEPERF.

The official syntax of a counter path looks like this:

[*Computer*]*Object*([*Parent*/][*Instance*][#*Index*])*Counter*

Computer	The computer on which the counter is to be monitored. If you omit a computer name, TYPEPERF monitors the counter on the local computer.
Object	The performance object—such as Processor, Memory, or PhysicalDisk—that contains the counter.
Parent	The container instance of the specified *Instance*.
Instance	The instance of the *Object*, if it has multiple instances. For example, in a two- (or dual-core) processor system, the instances are 0 (for the first processor), 1 (for the second processor), and Total (for both processors combined). You can also use an asterisk (*) to represent all the instances in *Object*.
Index	The index number of the specified *Instance*.
Counter	The name of the performance counter. You can also use an asterisk (*) to represent all the counters in Object(Instance).

In practice, however, you rarely use the *Computer*, *Parent*, and *Index* parts of the path, so most counter paths use one of the following two formats:

*Object**Counter*
Object(*Instance*)*Counter*

For example, here's the path for the Memory object's Available MBytes counter:

\Memory\Available MBytes

Here's a TYPEPERF command that displays five samples of this counter:

typeperf "\Memory\Available Mbytes" -sc 5

Similarly, here's the path for the `Processor object's % Processor Time` counter, using the first processor instance:

```
\Processor(0)\% Processor Time
```

Here's a `TYPEPERF` command that displays 10 samples of this counter every 3 seconds and saves the results to a file named `ProcessorTime.txt`:

```
typeperf "\Processor(0)\% Processor Time" -sc 10 -si 3 -o ProcessorTime.txt
```

To use the `-CONFIG` parameter with `TYPEPERF`, you must create a text file that stores the command-line parameters you want to use. This configuration file consists of a series of parameter/value pairs that use the following general format:

```
[Parameter]
Value
```

Here, *Parameter* is text that specifies a `TYPEPERF` parameter—such as F for the `-F` parameter and S for the `-S` parameter. Use C to specify one or more counter paths, and *Value* is the value you want to assign to the parameter.

For example, consider the following command:

```
typeperf "\PhysicalDisk(_Total)\% Idle Time" -si 5 -sc 10 -o idletime.txt
```

To run the same command using the `-CONFIG` parameter, you first need to create a file with the following text:

```
[c]
\PhysicalDisk(_Total)\% Idle Time
[si]
5
[sc]
10
[o]
idletime.txt
```

If this file is named `IdleTimeCounter.txt`, you can run it at any time with the following command (assuming `IdleTimeCounter.txt` resides in the current folder):

```
typeperf -config IdleTimeCounter.txt
```

WHOAMI: Getting Information About the Current User

The `WHOAMI` command gives you information about the user who is currently logged on to the computer:

```
WHOAMI [/UPN ¦ /FQDN ¦ LOGONID] [/USER ¦ /GROUPS ¦ /CLAIMS ¦ /PRIV] [/ALL]
[/FO format] [/NH]
```

/UPN	(Domains only) Returns the current user's name using the user principal name (UPN) format.
/FQDN	(Domains only) Returns the current user's name using the fully qualified domain name (FQDN) format.
/LOGONID	Returns the current user's security identifier (SID).
/USER	Returns the current username using the *computer\user* format.
/GROUPS	Returns the groups of which the current user is a member.
/CLAIMS	(Domains only) Returns the current user's claims.
/PRIV	Returns the current user's privileges.
/ALL	Returns the current user's SID, username, groups, and privileges.
/FO *format*	Specifies the output *format*, where *format* is one of the following values:
	table—The output is displayed in a row-and-column format, with headers in the first row and values in subsequent rows.
	list—The output is displayed in a two-column list, with headers in the first column and values in the second column.
	csv—The output is displayed with headers and values separated by commas. The headers appear on the first line.
/NH	Tells WHOAMI not to display column headers in the output.

You probably won't use this command often on the Windows 10 computer because you'll almost always be logged on as administrator. However, WHOAMI is useful when you're working on a client computer and you're not sure who is currently logged on.

For example, the following command redirects the current user's SID, username, groups, and privileges to a file named whoami.txt using the list format:

```
whoami /all /fo list > whoami.txt
```

Working with Users, Groups, and Shares

You can script your user and group chores by taking advantage of the NET USER and NET LOCALGROUP commands. These commands enable you to add users, change passwords, modify accounts, add users to groups, and remove users from groups. Note that you must run these commands under the Administrator account, so press Windows Logo+X, click Command Prompt (Admin), and then enter your User Account Control credentials.

NET USER: Working with Users

You use the NET USER command to add users, set account passwords, disable accounts, set account options (such as the times of day the user is allowed to log on), and remove accounts. For local users, the NET USER command has the following syntax:

```
NET USER [username [password ¦ * ¦ /RANDOM] [/ADD] [/DELETE] [options]]
```

username	Specifies the name of the user you want to add or work with. If you run NET USER with only the name of an existing user, the command displays the user's account data.
password	Indicates the password you want to assign to the user. If you use *, Windows 10 prompts you for the password; if you use the /RANDOM switch, Windows 10 assigns a random password (containing eight characters, consisting of a random mix of letters, numbers, and symbols), and then displays the password on the console.
/ADD	Creates a new user account.
/DELETE	Deletes the specified user account.
options	These are optional switches you can append to the command:
	/ACTIVE:{YES ¦ NO}—Specifies whether the account is active or disabled.
	/EXPIRES:{*date* ¦ NEVER}—The date (expressed in the system's Short Date format) on which the account expires.
	/HOMEDIR:*path*—The home folder for the user, which should be a subfolder within %SystemDrive%\Users (make sure that the folder exists).
	/PASSWORDCHG:{YES ¦ NO}—Specifies whether the user is allowed to change his password.
	/PASSWORDREQ:{YES ¦ NO}—Specifies whether the user is required to have a password.
	/PROFILEPATH:*path*—The folder that contains the user's profile.
	/SCRIPTPATH:*path*—The folder that contains the user's logon script.
	/TIMES:{*times* ¦ ALL}—Specifies the times that the user is allowed to log on to the system. Use single days or day ranges (for example, Sa or M-F). For times, use 24-hour notation or 12-hour notation with am or pm. Separate the day and time with a comma, and separate day/time combinations with semicolons. Here are some examples: M-F,9am-5pm M,W,F,08:00-13:00 Sa,12pm-6pm;Su,1pm-5pm

Note, too, that if you execute NET USER without parameters, it displays a list of the local user accounts.

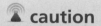 **caution**

If you use the /RANDOM switch to create a random password, be sure to make a note of the new password so that you can communicate it to the new user.

tip

If you want to force a user to log off when his logon hours expire, open the Local Group Policy Editor and select Computer Configuration, Windows Settings, Security Settings, Local Policies, Security Options. In the Network Security category, enable the Force Logoff When Logon Hours Expire policy.

NET LOCALGROUP: Working with Groups

You use the NET LOCALGROUP command to add users to and remove users from a specified security group. NET LOCALGROUP has the following syntax:

```
NET LOCALGROUP [group name1 [name2 ...] {/ADD ¦ /DELETE}
```

group	Specifies the name of the security group with which you want to work.
name1 [*name2* ...]	Specifies one or more usernames you want to add or delete, separated by spaces.
/ADD	Adds the user or users to the group.
/DELETE	Removes the user or users from the group.

NET USE: Mapping Folders

You can also map a network folder to a local drive letter by using a Command Prompt session and the NET USE command. Although you probably won't use this method very often, it's handy to know how it works, just in case. Here's the basic syntax:

```
NET USE [drive] [share] [password] [/USER:user]
  [/PERSISTENT:[YES ¦ NO]] ¦ /DELETE]
```

drive	Specifies the drive letter (following by a colon) of the local drive to which you want the network folder mapped.
share	Indicates the network address of the folder.
password	Specifies the password required to connect to the shared folder (that is, the password associated with the username, specified next).
/USER:*user*	Specifies the username you want to use to connect to the shared folder.
/PERSISTENT:	Enables you to reconnect the mapped network drive the next time you log on when you add YES.
/DELETE	Deletes the existing mapping that's associated with *drive*.

For example, the following command maps the shared folder \\PAULSPC\Paul\Writing\Books to the Z: drive:

```
net use z: \\paulspc\paul\writing\books /persistent:yes
```

Working with Network Troubleshooting Tools

Windows 10 TCP/IP comes with a few command-line utilities you can use to review your TCP/IP settings and troubleshoot problems. Here's a list of the available utilities:

- **ARP**—This utility displays (or modifies) the IP-to-Ethernet or IP-to-Token Ring address translation tables used by the Address Resolution Protocol (ARP) in TCP/IP. Enter the command **arp -?** for the syntax.

- **NBTSTAT**—This utility displays the protocol statistics and the current TCP/IP connections using NBT (NetBIOS over TCP/IP). Enter **nbtstat -?** for the syntax.

- **NETSTAT**—This utility displays the protocol statistics and current TCP/IP connections. Enter the command **netstat -?** to display the syntax.

- **NSLOOKUP**—This utility queries the Domain Name System (DNS) that associates host and domain names with IP addresses, DNS servers, mail servers, and so on. Enter commands **nslookup** then **help** to display the syntax. (It's a complex tool; if we had room, we could devote an entire chapter to it.)

- **PING**—This utility can check a network connection to a remote computer. This is one of the most commonly used TCP/IP diagnostic tools, so we describe it in more detail in Chapter 17, "Troubleshooting an Internet Connection."

- **ROUTE**—This utility can be used to manipulate a network routing table (LMHOSTS). Enter **route -?** for the syntax.

- **TRACERT**—This utility can check the route taken to a remote host. We also explain this valuable diagnostic command in Chapter 17.

- **IPCONFIG**—This utility displays the current TCP/IP network configuration. If you run the command ipconfig without switches, the utility returns your system's current IP address, subnet mask, and default gateway. If you run the command ipconfig /all, the utility returns more detailed information.

INDEX

B

E

I

O

T

U

V